MAINE
HANDBOOK

MAINE
HANDBOOK

MAINE
HANDBOOK
FIRST EDITION

KATHLEEN M. BRANDES

MOON
TRAVEL
HANDBOOKS

MAINE HANDBOOK
FIRST EDITION

Published by
Moon Publications, Inc.
P.O. Box 3040
Chico, California 95927-3040, USA

Printed by
Colorcraft Ltd.

© Text and photographs copyright Kathleen M. Brandes, 1998.
All rights reserved.

© Illustrations and maps copyright Moon Publications, Inc., 1998.
All rights reserved.

Some photos and illustrations are used by permission
and are the property of the original copyright owners.

ISBN: 1-56691-094-3
ISSN: 1096-9551

Editor: Gregor Krause
Map Editor: Gina Wilson Birtcil
Copy Editors: Emily Kendrick, Asha Johnson
Production & Design: David Hurst
Cartography: Chris Folks, Mike Morgenfeld, and Rob Warner
Index: Emily Kendrick

Front cover photo: Muscongus Bay, Round Pond, Maine.
Photo courtesy of David Ransaw Photographics.

All photos by Kathleen M. Brandes unless otherwise noted.

Distributed in the United States and Canada by Publishers Group West

Printed in China

Please send all comments,
corrections, additions,
amendments, and critiques to:

**MAINE HANDBOOK
MOON TRAVEL HANDBOOKS
P.O. BOX 3040
CHICO, CA 95927-3040, USA
e-mail: travel@moon.com
www.moon.com**

Printing History
1st edition—May 1998

To Michael Drons,
with love and appreciation

CONTENTS

SPECIAL TOPICS
_____

Joshua L. Chamberlain—
   Maine's Civil War Hero . . . . _175_
Rules for Monhegan Visitors . . . . _248_

ABBREVIATIONS

AP—American Plan
AT—Appalachian Trail
BYOL—Bring Your Own Liquor
CPCOG—Greater Portland Council
   of Governments

d—double occupancy
FOA—Friends of Acadia
FR—fire road
MAP—Modified American Plan
s—single occupancy

MAPS

MAP SYMBOLS

- ◉ State Capital
- ○ City
- ○ Town
- ⬭ U.S. Interstate
- ⬭ U.S. Highway
- ◯ State Highway
- ⤬ Customs Station

- ★ Point of Interest
- • Accommodation
- ▼ Restaurant/Bar
- ▪ Other Location
- ▲ Mountain
- ⚑ State Park
- 🎿 Ski Area
- 🅦 Waterfall

- ═══ Superhighway
- ── Primary Road
- ── Secondary Road
- ┈┈┈ Unpaved Road
- ─ ─ ─ Footpath
- ┈┈┈┈ Ferry
- ▬▬ Water

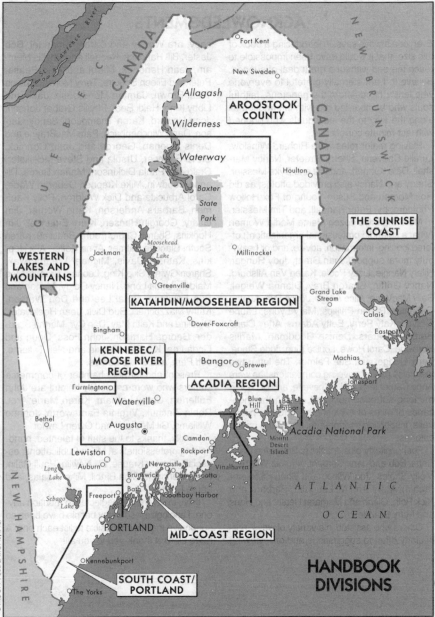

CANADA

St. Lawrence River

QUEBEC

CANADA

NEW BRUNSWICK

Fort Kent

New Sweden

Allagash

AROOSTOOK COUNTY

Wilderness

Waterway

Houlton

Baxter State Park

THE SUNRISE COAST

WESTERN LAKES AND MOUNTAINS

Jackman

Moosehead Lake

Millinocket

Grand Lake Stream

Greenville

Calais

KATAHDIN/MOOSEHEAD REGION

Eastport

Dover-Foxcroft

Machias

Bingham

KENNEBEC/ MOOSE RIVER REGION

Bangor   Brewer

Jonesport

Farmington

ACADIA REGION

Waterville

Blue Hill   Bar Harbor

Bethel

Augusta

Camden

Acadia National Park

Lewiston

Rockport

Mount Desert Island

NEW HAMPSHIRE

Auburn

Newcastle

Vinalhaven

Long Lake

Brunswick   Damariscotta

Sebago Lake

Bath   Boothbay Harbor

ATLANTIC OCEAN

Freeport

PORTLAND

MID-COAST REGION

Kennebunkport

The Yorks

SOUTH COAST/ PORTLAND

HANDBOOK DIVISIONS

© MOON PUBLICATIONS, INC.

ACKNOWLEDGMENTS

Everyone always says, in introducing a book of this size, that it would have been impossible to reach the end without a great deal of support. Believe it. I am eternally grateful to everyone who lent a hand—from the generous, faithful souls who bombarded me with information all along the way to the individuals who phoned with last-minute corrections.

Playing major roles were Richard Winslow, Lurelle Cheverie, Sherry Streeter, Nancy Marshall, Dale Kuhnert, and Pat and Dyke Messler. Sherry and Nancy also provided photos, as did Ros Morgan and Susan Young of Fox Hollow Photography, Peter Randall, and Tim Messler.

More than two dozen Maine Media Women (what a splendid professional organization!) offered lodging, information, advice, and/or heavy-duty moral support: Joan Grant, Judy Hunger, Hilary Nangle, Lizzy Poole, Karen Van Allsburg, Nancy Griffin, Sharon Bray, Dianna Weigel, Sally MacVane, Alice Arlens, Joyce Pye, Agatha Cabaniss, Perian Phillips, Mary Lyons, Laurie Graves, Katy Perry, Betty Adams, Arley Clark, Barbara Waters, Denise Goodman, Marilis Hornidge, Carol Howe, Louise King, Jude Stone, Terry Dodge, and Sue Palmer. The latter two were also patient traveling companions, as were Anne Carpenter, Lurelle Cheverie, and of course my long-suffering husband, during the thousands of miles of exploring back roads, hiking trails, inspecting bedspreads, and toting up the calories.

For hospitality-plus, thanks to Betsy and Chris Betts, Bob and Jane Sargent, Virginia Whitney, Molly Sholes, Jon Wilson and Sherry Streeter (again), Mary Ann McLaughlin, Barbara and Nick Roth, Glenn and Margaret Heath, and Hans and Mary Brandes.

Others who assisted in a variety of ways, particularly offering suggestions and/or reviewing copy, are Woody and Carole Emanuel, Bob Jaster, Bill Hancock, Kendall and Phyllis Merriam, Jean Hendrick, Marni and Alan Pease, Peter and Eileen Spectre, Terry Morris, Jim and Trudi Brown, Jamien Morehouse, Jack and Libby King, Heidi Beal, Phyllis Graber Jensen, Joan Howard, Karen Thompson, Sandy Garson, Dana Winchenbach, Pam MacBrayne and Denis Moonan, George and Joan Connick, Steve Spencer, Ursula and Steve McAllister, Craig and Paula Dickinson, Marian Burns, Dianne Goodwin, Mike Krepner, Deborah Wade, Carol Arbuckle and Dick Waldron, Polly Kaufman, Barbara Anderson, Karin Womer, Jim Geary, Georgia Hansen, Kerry Emanuel, Jim Hopkins, Sharon Church, John Beaulieu, Karen South, Blanche Palmer, Anne Kofler, Alix Hopkins, Kathryn Davis, Michael Weatherwax, Sharon Gwinn, Skip King, Leonard Brooks, Meg Maiden, Linda Long, Nancy Goldy, Marion and Ben Bowman, Coral Lee and Don Watson, Kathy Mazzuchelli, Bud Dick, Jean Hoekwater, Caroline and Keith May, Don Cyr, Martha Scudder, George Harrison, John Foss, Doug and Linda Lee, Kip Files, Vickie and Neil Taliento, Jeff Perk, and Steve Lantos.

Present and former chamber of commerce staffers who were especially helpful are John Fullerton, Cathy Latham, Karen Marie Arel, Robin Zinchuk, Virginia Farnsworth, Joanne Williams, Gil Merriam, and Owen Lawlor.

Finally, thanks to the staff of talented, hand-holding professionals at Moon Publications, especially Gregor Krause, Bill Newlin, Pauli Galin, Emily Kendrick, Gina Birtcil, Mike Sigalas, and Laura Foulke.

If I've inadvertently neglected to mention anyone, I apologize—so many people have been so supportive that it's impossible to list each one. A huge blanket thank-you to you all!

WE WELCOME YOUR COMMENTS

Compiling a guidebook of this size is a lot like shoveling out the mythical Augean stables—the job is never done. After seriously depreciating two Toyotas, expanding our waistlines, subsidizing Ma Bell, and making herculean efforts to check and double-check everything included here, we're resigned to the fact that Maine is not a static place; given the pace of contemporary life, prices rise, opening hours change, businesses fail or change hands, and new places await discovery. We welcome your comments, corrections, and suggestions about any and all of the above, so we can consider them for inclusion in the second edition of the *Maine Handbook*. Send it all to:

Maine Handbook
P.O. Box 3040
Chico, CA 95927-3040
e-mail: travel@moon.com

BOB RACE

INTRODUCTION

One of Maine-born author and Smith College professor Mary Ellen Chase's young students once mused, "Maine is different from all other states, isn't it? I suppose that's because God never quite finished it."

Maine may indeed be a work in progress, but it's a masterwork. Tucked into the northeasternmost corner of the United States and comprising 33,215 square miles, Maine boldly promotes itself as "The Way Life Should Be." Not to say that everything's perfect, mind you, but it is an extraordinarily special place.

There's a reason—no, lots of reasons—why more than eight million people visit every year, why longtime summer folk finally just pick up stakes and *settle* here, why Maine lobsters are the best, why Maine politicians become national household names. The traditional Maine traits of honesty, thrift, frankness, and ruggedness remain refreshingly appealing.

Also appealing is the state's natural wealth, which draws raves not only from all the "people from away" but also from the state's 1.2 million residents. Acadia National Park, 28 state parks, and tax-funded public preserves cover more than half a million acres—and residents and nonresidents alike have full access to all this real estate.

Maine's wrinkled, 5,500-mile coastline, if pulled taut from Eastport southward, would stretch past Florida! Along that coast are 64 lighthouses, more than 4,600 islands, 90% of the *nation's* lobsters, and the eastern seaboard's highest peak.

And if you get enough of the natural highs, you can poke into museums, galleries, boutiques, microbreweries, antiques shops, and playgrounds—and attend any number of concerts, plays, festivals, and county and country fairs.

Maine's a national natural treasure—a fact observed by 19th-century author Harriet Beecher Stowe from her Brunswick home: "It seems to us quite wonderful that in all the ecstasies that have been lavished on American scenery, this beautiful state of Maine should have been so much neglected [by visitors]; for nothing is or can be so wildly and peculiarly beautiful." Within two decades, tourism had begun in earnest, Maine could no longer claim neglect, and Stowe's words proved just slightly premature.

THE LAND

"Man is born to die, his works are short-lived/ Buildings crumble, monuments decay, wealth vanishes." With those words, Governor Percival P. Baxter in 1931 deeded to the people of Maine the first parcel of thousands of wilderness acres to remain "forever wild." Today, we know this natural treasure as Baxter State Park. Mile-high Katahdin, centerpiece of the park and the northern terminus of the Appalachian Trail, remains, as the governor stipulated, "the mountain of the people of Maine." Governor Baxter's incredible foresight preserved what surely could and likely would have been denuded, developed, and ultimately destroyed. And Baxter State Park is only the beginning of Maine's natural treasures.

The Pine Tree State boasts more than 17 million acres of forest—covering 89% of the state; 5,900 lakes and ponds; 4,617 saltwater islands; 10 mountains over 4,000 feet and nearly a hundred mountains higher than 3,000 feet. The highest peak in the state is Katahdin, at 5,267 feet. (Katahdin is an Indian word meaning "greatest mountain," making Mt. Katahdin redundant.)

Maine's largest lake is Moosehead, in Greenville, 30 miles long and 20 miles across at its widest point, with a maximum depth of 246 feet. Remote enough to have remained unspoiled, the area is fantastic for camping, fishing, boating, swimming, hiking, and moosespotting.

Bounded by the Gulf of Maine (Atlantic Ocean), the St. Croix River, New Brunswick Province, the St. John River, Quebec Province, and the state of New Hampshire (and the only state in the Union bordered by only one other state), Maine is the largest of the six New England states, roughly equivalent in size to the five others combined—offering plenty of space to hike, bike, camp, sail, ski, swim, or just hang out. The state extends from 43° 05' to 47° 28' north latitude, and 66° 56' to 80° 50' west longitude. (Technically, Maine dips even farther southeast to take in five islands in the offshore Isles of Shoals.) It's all stitched together by 22,574 miles of highways and 3,561 bridges.

Rivers to the Gulf

Maine's 5,000-plus rivers and streams provide nearly half of the watershed for the Gulf of Maine. The major rivers are the Penobscot (350 miles), the St. John (211 miles), the Androscoggin (175 miles), the Kennebec (150 miles), the Saco (104 miles), and the St. Croix (75 miles). The St. John and its tributaries flow northeast; all the others flow more or less south or southeast.

The Penobscot and the Kennebec are navigable upstream—to Bangor and Richmond (just below Augusta);

STATE SYMBOLS

State Animal	Moose *(Alces alces americana)*
State Bird	Chickadee *(Parus atricapillus)*
State Cat	Maine Coon
State Fish	Landlocked Salmon *(Salmo salar)*
State Flower	White Pine Cone and Tassel *(Pinus strobus)*
State Fossil	*Pertica quadrifaria,* a six-foot-high plant that lived in Maine nearly 400 million years ago
State Insect	Honeybee *(Apis mellifera)*
State Mineral	Tourmaline
State Motto	*Dirigo* (Meaning "I lead" or "I direct"—in line with the late-19th-century political maxim, "As Maine goes, so goes the nation"—*dirigo* is emblazoned on the state flag.)
State Nickname	Pine Tree State (Pine is the most prominent tree species in Maine, the source of wood for durable masts throughout the Great Age of Sail. A pine tree appears in the center of Maine's state seal.)

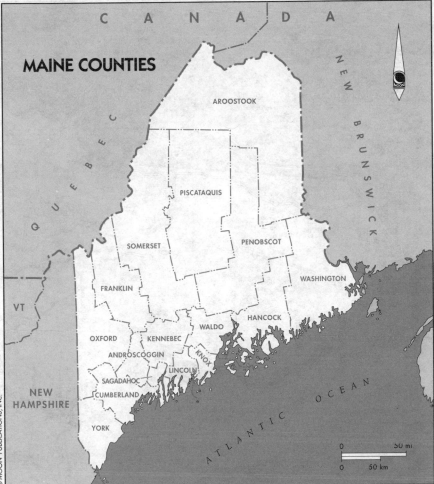

MAINE COUNTIES

on their upper reaches, dam-controlled flows make for splendid whitewater rafting.

In the Beginning . . .

Maine is an outdoor classroom for Geology 101, a living lesson in what the glaciers did and how they did it. Geologically, Maine is something of a youngster; the oldest rocks, found in the Chain of Ponds area, not far from Sugarloaf/USA, are only 1.6 billion years old—more than two billion years younger than the world's oldest rocks.

But most significant is the great ice sheet that began to spread over Maine about 25,000 years ago, during the late Wisconsin Ice Age. As it moved southward from Canada, this continental glacier scraped, gouged, pulverized, and depressed the bedrock in its path. On it continued, charging up the north faces of mountains, clipping off their tops and moving southward, leaving behind jagged cliffs on the mountains' southern faces and odd deposits of stone and clay. By about 21,000 years ago, glacial

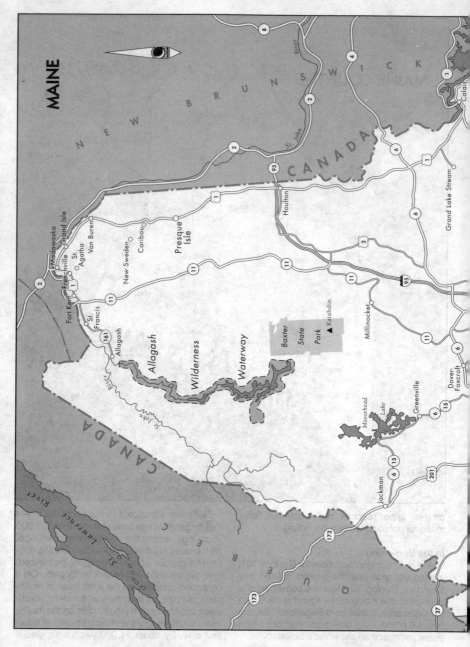

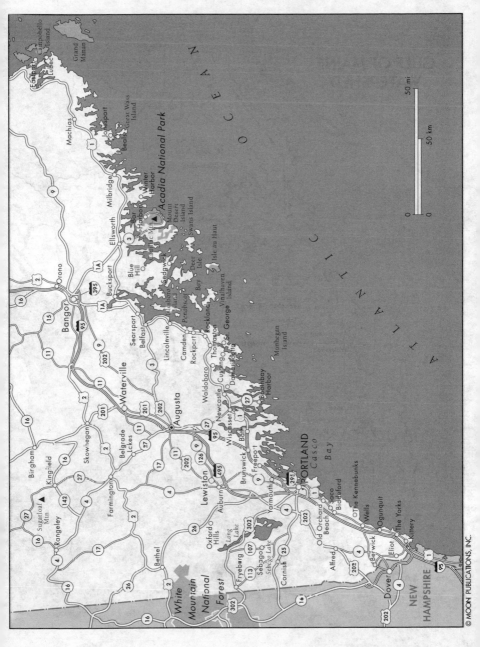

© MOON PUBLICATIONS, INC.

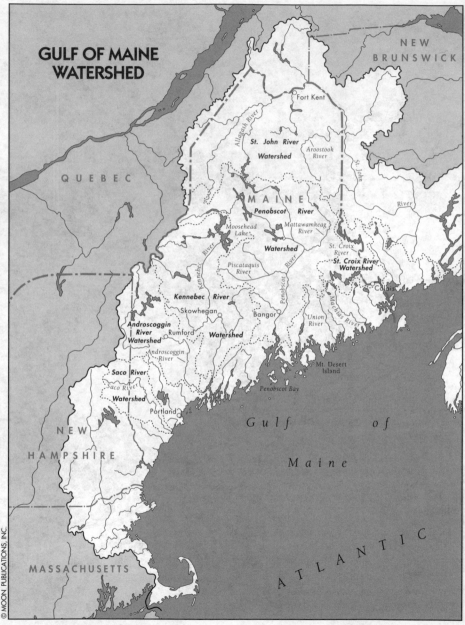

GULF OF MAINE
WATERSHED

NEW
BRUNSWICK

QUEBEC

Fort Kent

St. John River
Watershed

Aroostook
River

MAINE

St. John
River

Penobscot River

Moosehead
Lake

Mattawamkeag
River

Watershed

St. Croix
River

Piscataquis
River

St. Croix River
Watershed

Kennebec River

Calais

Kennebec River

Skowhegan

Penobscot River

Bangor

Union
River

Androscoggin
River
Watershed

Rumford

Watershed

Machias River

Androscoggin
River

Mt. Desert
Island

Saco River

Penobscot Bay

Watershed

Portland

Gulf   of

NEW

Maine

HAMPSHIRE

ATLANTIC

MASSACHUSETTS

ice extended well out over the Gulf of Maine, perhaps as far as the Georges Bank fishing grounds.

But all that began to change with meltdown, beginning about 18,000 years ago. As the glacier melted and receded, ocean water moved in, covering much of the coastal plain and working its way inland up the rivers. By 11,000 years ago, glaciation had pulled back completely from Maine, revealing the South Coast's beaches and the unusual geologic traits—eskers and erratics, kettleholes and moraines, even a fjord—that make the rest of the state such a fascinating natural laboratory.

Today's Landscape

Seven distinct looks make up the contemporary Maine landscape. Along the southwest coast, from Kittery to Portland, are fine-sand beaches, marshlands, and only the occasional rocky headland. The Mid-Coast, from Portland to the Penobscot River, features one finger of rocky land after another, all jutting out into the Gulf of Maine and all incredibly scenic. The Down East coast, from the Penobscot River to Eastport and including fantastic Acadia National Park, has many similarities to the Mid-Coast (gorgeous rocky peninsulas, offshore islands, granite everywhere), but, except on Mount Desert Island, takes on a different look and feel by virtue of its slower pace, higher tides, and quieter villages.

The Down East mountains, roughly straddling "the Airline" (Rt. 9 from Bangor to Calais), are marked by open blueberry fields, serious woodlands, and mountains that seem to appear out of nowhere. The central upland—essentially a huge S-shape extending from the Portland area through Augusta, Waterville, and Skowhegan, then on up into Aroostook County, at the top of the state—is characterized by lakes, ponds, rolling fields, and occasional woodlands, interspersed with river valleys. Aroostook County is the state's agricultural jackpot. The northern region, essentially the valleys of the north-flowing St. John and Allagash Rivers, was the last part of Maine to lose the glacier and is today dense forest, crisscrossed with logging roads (you can count the settlements on two hands). The mountain upland, taking in all the state's major elevations and extending from inland York

County to Baxter State Park, is rugged, beautiful, and the premier region for skiing, hiking, camping, and whitewater rafting.

CLIMATE

Whoever said, "If you don't like the weather, wait a minute" must have spent several minutes in Maine. The good news is that if the weather is lousy, it's bound to change before long. And when it does, it's intoxicating. Brilliant, cloud-free Maine weather has lured many a visitor to put down roots, buy a retirement home, or at least invest in a summer retreat here.

The serendipity of it all necessitates two caveats: *Always pack warmer clothing than you think you'll need.* And *never arrive without a sweater or jacket—even at the height of summer.*

The National Weather Service separates Maine into three distinct climatological divisions —coastal, southern interior, and northern interior (several subdivisions also appear regularly in forecasts).

The **coastal** division, which includes Portland, runs from Kittery northeast to Eastport and about 20 miles inland. Here, the ocean moderates the climate, making coastal winters warmer and summers cooler than in the interior (relatively speaking, of course). From early June through August, the Portland area—fairly typical of coastal weather—may have 3-8 days of temperatures over 90° F, 25-40 days over 80°, 14-24 days of fog, and 5-10 inches of rain. Normal annual precipitation for the Portland area is 44 inches of rain and 71 inches of snow (the snow total is misleading, though, since intermittent thaws clear away much of the base).

The **southern interior** division, covering the bottom one-third of the state, sees the warmest weather in summer, the most clear days each year, and an average snowfall of 60-90 inches. The **northern interior** part of the state, with the highest mountains, covers the upper two-thirds of Maine and boasts a mixed bag of snowy winters, warm summers, and the state's lowest rainfall.

The Seasons

Maine has four distinct seasons: summer, fall, winter, and mud. Lovers of spring need to look elsewhere in March, the lowest month on the popularity scale with its mud-caked vehicles, soggy everything, irritable temperaments, tank-trap roads, and often the worst snowstorm of the year.

Summer can be idyllic—with moderate temperatures, clear air, and wispy breezes—but it can also close in with fog, rain, and chills. Prevailing winds are from the southwest. Officially, summer runs from June 20 or 21 to September 20 or 21, but June, July, and August is

cruising Penobscot Bay

SHERRY STREETER

FALL FOLIAGE

The timing of Maine's fall foliage owes a great deal to the summer weather that precedes it, and so does the quality (although the annual spectacle never disappoints). In early September, as deciduous trees ready themselves for winter, they stop producing chlorophyll, and the green begins to disappear from their leaves. Taking its place are the spectacular pigments—brilliant reds, yellows, and oranges—that paint the leaves and, consequently, warm the hearts of every "leaf-peeper," shopkeeper, innkeeper, and restaurateur in the region.

The colorful display begins slowly, reaches a peak, then fades—starting in the north in early September and working down to the southwest corner by mid-October. Peak foliage in **Aroostook County** usually occurs in late September or early October, about three weeks after the colors have begun to appear. Along the **South Coast, Mid-Coast,** and **sunrise coast,** the peak can occur as late as the middle of October, with the last bits of color hanging on even beyond that.

Trees put on their most magnificent show after a summer of moderate heat and rainfall—a summer of excessive heat and scant rainfall means colors will be less brilliant and disappear more quickly. Throw a September or October northeaster or hurricane into the mix and estimates are up for grabs.

So predictions are imprecise, and you'll need to allow some schedule flexibility to take advantage of the changes in different parts of the state. From late August to mid-October, check the Maine Department of Conservation's Web site (www.state.me. us/doc/foliage/foliage.htm) for frequently updated maps and reports on the foliage status (this is gauged by the percentage of leaf drop in every region of the state). For up-to-date fall-foliage information beginning around mid-September, contact the Maine Office of Tourism's fall-foliage hotline: (800) 533-9595 or, in Maine, (207) 623-0363.

A reminder: Fall-foliage trips are extremely popular and increasing annually, so lodging can be scarce. Plan ahead and make reservations, especially in the Kennebunks, Boothbay Harbor, Camden, Bar Harbor, Greenville, and Bethel.

more like it, with temperatures in the Portland area averaging 70° F during the day and in the 50s at night. The normal growing season is 148 days.

A poll of Mainers might well show autumn as the favorite season—days are still warmish, nights are cool, winds are optimum for sailors, and the foliage is brilliant. Fall colors usually begin appearing far to the north, in Fort Kent, about mid-September, reaching their peak in that region by the end of the month. The last of the color begins in late September in the southernmost part of the state and fades by mid-October. Early autumn, however, is also the height of hurricane season, the only potential flaw this time of year.

Winter, officially December 20 or 21 to March 20 or 21, means deep snow in the western mountains, deep cold in the North Woods, and an unpredictable potpourri along the coast. It also means great alpine skiing at Sugarloaf/USA, Sunday River, Shawnee Peak, Mt. Abram, and Saddleback; splendid snowmobiling on a huge network of trails; and such other pursuits as cross-country skiing, ice fishing, snowshoe-ing, ice-skating, dogsledding, ice-climbing, and winter trekking and camping.

Spring, officially March 20 or 21 to June 20 or 21, is the frequent butt of jokes. It's an ill-defined season that arrives much too late and departs all too quickly. Ice floes dot inland lakes and ponds until "ice-out," in early to mid-May; spring planting can't occur until well into May; lilacs explode in late May and disappear by mid-June. And just when you finally can enjoy being outside, blackflies stretch their wings and satisfy their hunger pangs. Even the moose head for open spaces when the blackflies show up.

Northeasters and Hurricanes

A northeaster is a counterclockwise, swirling storm that brings wild winds out of—you guessed it—the northeast. One can occur any time of year, whenever the conditions brew it up. Depending on the season, the winds are accompanied by rain, sleet, snow, or all of them together.

Hurricane season officially runs June-Nov. but is most prevalent late Aug.-September. Some years, the Maine coast remains out of harm's way; other years, head-on hurricanes and even glancing blows have eroded beaches, flooded roads, splintered boats, downed trees, knocked out power, and inflicted major residential and commercial damage. Winds—the greatest culprit—average 74-90 mph. A **hurricane watch** is announced on radio and TV about 36 hours beforehand, followed by a **hurricane warning,** indicating that the storm is imminent. Find shelter, away from plate-glass windows, and wait it out. If especially high winds are predicted, make every effort to secure yourself, your vehicle, and your possessions. Resist the urge to head for the shore to watch the show; rogue waves, combined with ultra-high tides, have been known to sweep away unwary onlookers.

Sea Smoke and Fog

Fog and sea smoke, two atmospheric phenomena resulting from opposing conditions, are only distantly related. But both can radically affect visibility and therefore be hazardous. In winter, when the ocean is at least 40° F warmer than the air, billowy sea smoke rises from the water, creating great photo ops for camera buffs but especially dangerous conditions for mariners.

In any season, when the ocean (or lake or land) is colder than the air, fog sets in, creating perilous conditions for drivers, mariners, and pilots. Romantics, however, see it otherwise, reveling in the womblike ambience and the muffled moans of foghorns. Between April and October, Portland averages about 31 days with heavy fog, when visibility may be a quarter-mile or less.

Storm Warnings

The National Weather Service's official daytime signal system for wind velocity consists of a series of flags representing specific wind speeds and sea conditions. Beachgoers and anyone planning to venture out in a kayak, canoe, sailboat, or powerboat should heed these signals. The flags are posted on all public beaches, and warnings are announced on TV and radio weather broadcasts, as well as on cable TV's Weather Channel and the NOAA broadcast network.

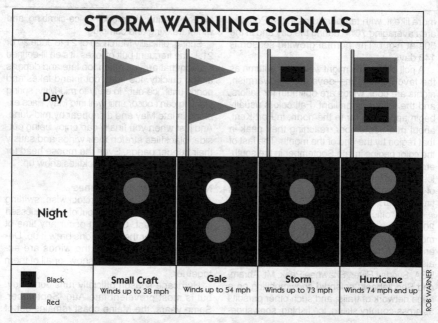

STORM WARNING SIGNALS

	Small Craft	Gale	Storm	Hurricane
Day				
Night				
	Winds up to 38 mph	Winds up to 54 mph	Winds up to 73 mph	Winds 74 mph and up

Black
Red

ROB WARNER

FLORA AND FAUNA

From this elevation, just on the skirts of the clouds, we could overlook the country, west and south, for a hundred miles. There it was, the State of Maine, which we had seen on the map, but not much like that. Immeasurable forest for the sun to shine on. . . . No clearing, no house. It did not look as if a solitary traveler had cut so much as a walking stick there. Countless lakes . . . and mountains. The forest looked like a firm grass sward, and the effect of these lakes in its midst has been well compared . . . to that of a mirror broken into a thousand fragments, and widely scattered over the grass, reflecting the full blaze of the sun.

—Henry David Thoreau,
The Maine Woods

Looking out over Maine from Mt. Katahdin today, as Thoreau did in 1857, you get a view that is still a mass of green stretching to the sea, broken by blue lakes and rivers. Although the forest has been cut several times since Thoreau saw it, Maine is proportionately still the most forested state in the nation.

It also is clearly one of the best watered. Receiving an average of more than 40 inches of precipitation a year, Maine is abundantly endowed with swamps, bogs, ponds, lakes, streams, and rivers. These, in turn, drain from a coast deeply indented by coves, estuaries, and bays.

In this state of trees and water, nature dominates more than most—Maine is the least densely populated state east of the Mississippi River. Here, where boreal and temperate ecosystems meet and mix, lives a rich diversity of plants and animals.

The Alpine Tundra

Three continental storm tracks converge on Maine, and the state's western mountains bear the brunt of the weather they bring. Stretching from Katahdin in the north along most of Maine's border with Quebec and New Hampshire, these mountains have a far colder climate than their temperate latitude might suggest.

Timberline here occurs at only about 4,000 feet, and where the mountaintops reach above that, the environment is truly arctic—an alpine-tundra habitat where only the hardiest species can live. Beautiful, pale-green "map" lichens cover many of the exposed rocks like shapes cut from an atlas, and sedges and rushes take root in the patches of thin topsoil. As many as 30 alpine plant species—typically found hundreds of miles to the north—grow in crevices or hollows in the lee of the blasting winds. Small and low-growing to conserve energy in this harsh climate, such plants as **bearberry willow, Lapland rosebay, alpine azalea, diapensia, mountain cranberry,** and **black crowberry** reward the observant hiker with white, yellow, pink, and magenta flowers in late June and July.

Areas above treeline are generally inhospitable to most animals other than secretive **voles, mice,** and **lemmings.** Even so, summer or winter, a hiker is likely to be aware of at least one other species—the **northern raven.** More than any of the 300 or so other bird species that regularly occur in Maine, the raven is the bird of the state's wild places, its mountain ridges, rocky coasts, and remote forests. Solid black, like a crow, but larger and stockier and with a wedge-shaped tail and broad wings, the northern raven is a magnificent flyer—soaring, hovering, diving, and often turning loops and rolls as though playing in the wind. Known to be among the most intelligent of all animals, ravens are quite social, actively communicating with one another in throaty croaks as they range over the landscape in search of carrion and other available plant and animal foods.

At treeline and below, where conditions are moderate enough to allow black spruce and balsam fir to take hold, fauna becomes far more diverse. Among the wind- and ice-stunted trees, called *krummholz* (crooked wood), forage **northern juncos** and **white-throated sparrows.** The latter's plaintive whistle (often mnemonically rendered as "Old Sam Peabody, Peabody, Peabody") is one of the most evocative sounds of the Maine woods.

The Boreal or Northern Forest

Mention the Maine woods and the image that is likely to come to mind is the boreal forests of **spruce** and **fir.** In 1857, Thoreau captured the character of these woods when he wrote, "It is all mossy and moosey. In some of those dense fir and spruce woods there is hardly room for the smoke to go up. The trees are a standing night, and every fir and spruce which you fell is a plume plucked from night's raven wing. Then at night the general stillness is more impressive than any sound, but occasionally you hear the note of an owl farther or nearer in the woods, and if near a lake, the semi-human cry of the loons at their unearthly revels."

Well adapted to a short growing season, low temperatures, and rocky, nutrient-poor soils, spruce and fir do dominate the woods on mountainsides, in low-lying areas beside watercourses, and along the coast. By not having to produce new foliage every year, these evergreens conserve scarce nutrients and also retain their needles, which capture sunlight for photosynthesis during all but the coldest months. The needles also wick moisture from the low clouds and fog that frequently bathe their preferred habitat, bringing annual precipitation to more than 80 inches a year in some areas.

In the lush boreal forest environment grows a diverse ground cover of herbaceous plants, including **bearberry, bunchberry, clintonia, starflower,** and **wood sorrel.** In older spruce-fir stands, mosses and lichens often carpet much of the forest floor in a soft tapestry of greens and gray-blues. Maine is extraordinarily rich in **lichens,** with more than 700 species identified so far—20% of the total found in all of North America. **Usnea** is a familiar one; its common name, old man's beard, comes from its wispy strands, which drip from the branches of spruce trees. The **northern parula,** a small blue, green, and yellow bird of the wood warbler family, weaves its ball-shaped pendulum nest from usnea.

The spruce-fir forest is prime habitat for many other species that are among the most sought-after by birders: **black-backed** and **three-toed woodpeckers,** the audaciously bold **gray jay** (or camp robber), **boreal chickadee, yellow-throated flycatcher, white-winged crossbill, Swainson's thrush,** and a half-dozen other gemlike wood warblers.

Among the more unusual birds of this forest type is the **spruce grouse.** Sometimes hard to spot because it does not flush, a spruce grouse is so tame that a careful person can actually touch one. Not surprisingly, the spruce grouse earned the nickname "fool hen" early in the 19th century, and no doubt it would have become extinct long ago but for its menu preference of spruce and fir needles, which render its meat bitter and inedible (you can get an idea by tasting a few needles yourself).

Few of Maine's 56 mammal species are restricted to the boreal forest, but several are very characteristic of it. Most obvious from its trilling, far-carrying chatter, is the **red squirrel.** Piles of cone remnants on the forest floor mark a red squirrel's recent banquet. The red squirrel itself is the favored prey of another coniferous forest inhabitant, the **pine marten.** An arboreal member of the mustelid family—which in Maine also includes **skunk, weasel, fisher,** and **otter**—the pine marten is a sleek, low-slung predator with blond to brown fur, an orange throat patch, and a long, bushy tail. Its beautiful pelt nearly led to the animal's obliteration from Maine through overtrapping, but with protection, the marten population has rebounded.

Nearly half a century of protection also allowed the population recovery of Maine's most prominent mammal, the **moose.** Standing 6-7 feet tall at the shoulder and weighing as much as 1,200 pounds, the moose is the largest member of the Cervidae or deer family. A bull's massive antlers, which it sheds and regrows each year, may span five or more feet and weigh 75 pounds. The animal's long legs and bulbous nose give it an ungainly appearance, but the moose is ideally adapted to a life spent wading through deep snow, dense thickets, and swamps.

Usually the best place to observe a moose is at the edge of a body of water on a summer afternoon or evening. Wading out into the water, the animal may submerge its entire head to browse on the succulent aquatic plants below the surface. The water also offers a respite from the swarms of biting insects that plague moose (and people who venture into these woods without bug repellent). Except for a limited hunting season, moose have little to fear from humans and often will allow close approach. Be careful,

RACHEL TAYLOR

however, and give them the respect their imposing size suggests; cows can be very protective of their calves, and bulls can be unpredictable, particularly during the fall rutting (mating) season.

Another word of caution about moose: When driving, especially in spring and early summer, be alert for moose wandering out of the woods and onto roadways to escape the flies. Moose are dark brown, their eyes do not reflect headlights like most other animals' do, and they do not get out of the way—of cars or anything else. Colliding with a half-ton animal can be a tragedy for all involved. Pay particular attention while driving in Oxford, Franklin, Somerset (especially Rt. 201), Piscataquis, and Aroostook Counties, but with an estimated 25,000-30,000 moose statewide, they can and do turn up anywhere and everywhere—even in downtown Portland and on offshore islands.

Protection from unlimited hunting was not the only reason for the dramatic increase in Maine's moose population; the invention of the chain saw and the skidder have played parts, too. In a few days, one or two men can now cut and yard a tract of forest that a whole crew of lumbermen with saws and horses formerly took weeks to harvest. With the increase in logging, particularly the clearcutting of spruce and fir (whose long fibers are favored for papermaking), vast areas have been opened up for regeneration by fast-growing, sun-loving hardwoods. The leaves of these young **white birch, poplar, pin cherry,** and **striped maple** are a veritable moose salad bar.

The Transition Zone: Northern Hardwood Forest

Although hardwoods have replaced spruce and fir in many areas, mixed woods of **sugar maple, American beech, yellow birch, red oak, red spruce, eastern hemlock,** and **white pine** have always been a major part of Maine's natural and social histories. This northern hard-

wood forest, as it is termed by ecologists, is a transitional zone between northern and southern ecosystems and rich in species diversity.

Dominated by deciduous trees, this forest community is highly seasonal. Spring snowmelt brings a pulse of life to the newly exposed forest floor as herbaceous plants race to develop and flower before the trees overhead leaf out and limit the available sunlight. (Blink and you can practically miss a Maine spring.) **Trout lily, goldthread, trillium, violets, gaywing,** and **pink lady's slipper** are among the many woodland wildflowers whose blooms make a walk in the forest so rewarding at this time of year. Deciduous trees, shrubs, and a dozen species of ferns also must make the most of their short (four-month) growing season. In the Maine woods, the buds of mid-May unfurl into a full canopy of leaves by the first week of June.

Late spring and early summer in the northern hardwood forest is also a time of intense animal activity. Runoff from the melting snowpack has filled countless low-lying depressions throughout the woods. These ephemeral swamps and vernal pools are a haven for an enormous variety of aquatic invertebrates, insects, amphibians, and reptiles. Choruses of spring **peepers,** Maine's smallest—but seemingly loudest—frog, alert everyone with their high-pitched calls that the ice is going out and breeding season is at hand. Measuring only about an inch in length, these tiny frogs with X-shaped patterns on their backs can be surprisingly difficult to see without some determined effort. Look on the branches of shrubs overhanging the water—males often use them as perches from which to call prospective mates. But then why stop with peepers? There are eight other frog and toad species in Maine to search for, too.

Spring is also the best time to look for **salamanders.** Driving a country road on a rainy night in mid-April provides an opportunity to witness one of nature's great mass migrations, as salamanders and frogs of several species emerge from their wintering sites and make their way across roads to breeding pools and streams. Once breeding is completed, most salamanders return to the terrestrial environment, where they burrow into crevices or the moist litter of the forest floor. The movement of amphibians from wetlands to uplands has an important ecological function, providing a mechanism for the return of nutrients that runoff washes into low-lying areas. This may seem hard to believe until one considers the numbers of individuals involved in this movement. To illustrate, the total biomass of Maine's **redback salamander** population—just one of the eight salamander species found here—is heavier than the combined weight of all the state's moose!

The many bird species characteristic of the northern hardwood forest are also most in evidence during the late spring and early summer, when the males are engaged in holding breeding territory and attracting mates. For most passerines—perching birds—this means singing. Especially during the early-morning and evening hours, the woods are alive with choruses of song from such birds as the **purple finch, white-throated sparrow, solitary vireo, black-throated blue warbler, Canada warbler, mourning warbler, northern waterthrush,** and the most beautiful singer of them all, the **hermit thrush.**

Providing abundant browse as well as tubers, berries, and nuts, the northern hardwood forest supports many of Maine's mammal species. The **red-backed vole, snowshoe hare, porcupine,** and **white-tailed deer** are relatively abundant and in turn are prey for **fox, bobcat, fisher,** and **eastern coyote.** Now well established since its expansion into Maine in the 1950s and 1960s, the eastern coyote has filled the niche at the top of the food chain once held by wolves and mountain lions before their extermination from the state in the late 19th century. **Black bears,** of which Maine has an estimated 25,000, are technically classified as carnivores and will take a moose calf or deer on occasion, but most of their diet consists of vegetation, insects, and fish. In the fall, bears feast on beechnuts and acorns, putting on extra fat for the coming winter, which they spend sleeping (not hibernating, as is often presumed) in a sheltered spot dug out beneath a rock or log.

Autumn is a time of spectacular beauty in Maine's northern hardwood forest. With the shortening days and cooler temperatures of September, the dominant green chlorophyll molecules in deciduous leaves start breaking down. As they do, the yellow, orange, and red pigments (which are always present in the leaves—and serve to capture light in parts of the spectrum not captured by the chlorophyll) are revealed. Sugar maples put on the most dazzling display, but beech, birches, red maple, and poplar add their colors to make up an autumn landscape famous the world over.

Ecologically, one of the most significant mammals in the Maine woods is the **beaver.** After being trapped almost to extinction in the 1800s, this large swimming rodent has recolonized streams, rivers, and ponds throughout the state. Well known for its ability as a dam builder, the beaver can change low-lying woodland into a complex aquatic ecosystem. The impounded water behind the dam often kills the trees it inundates, but these provide ideal nest cavities for **mergansers, wood ducks, owls, woodpeckers,** and **swallows.** The still water is also a nursery for a rich diversity of invertebrates, fish, amphibians, and Maine's seven aquatic turtle species, most common of which is the beautiful but very shy **eastern painted turtle.**

The Aquatic Environment

Small woodland pools and streams are, of course, only a part of Maine's aquatic environment. The state's nearly 6,000 lakes and ponds provide open-water and deep-water habitats for many additional species. A favorite among them is the **common loon,** symbol of north country lakes across the continent. Loons impart a sense of wildness and mystery with their haunting calls and yodels resonating off the surrounding pines on still summer nights. Adding to their popular appeal are their striking black-and-white plumage, accented with red eyes, and their ability to vanish below the surface and seem to reappear in another part of the lake moments later. The annual census of Maine's common loons since the 1970s indicates a relatively stable population of about 3,200 breeding pairs.

Below the surface of Maine's lakes, ponds, rivers, and streams, 69 freshwater fish species live in the state, of which 17 were introduced. Among these exotic transplants are some of the most sought-after game fish, including **smallmouth** and **largemouth bass, rainbow trout,** and **northern pike.** These introductions may have benefited anglers, but they have displaced native species in many watersheds.

Several of Maine's native fish have interesting histories in that they became landlocked during the retreat of the glacier. At that time, Maine was climatically much like northern Canada is today, and **arctic charr** ran up its rivers to spawn at the edges of the ice. As the ice continued to recede, some of these fish became trapped but nevertheless managed to survive and establish themselves in their new landlocked environments. Two remnant subspecies now exist: the **blueback charr**, which lives in the cold, deep water of 10 northern Maine lakes, and the **Sunapee charr**, now found only in three lakes in Maine and two in Idaho. A similar history belongs to the **landlocked salmon**, a form of Atlantic salmon that many regard as the state's premier game fish and is now widely stocked throughout the state and around the country.

Atlantic salmon still run up some Maine rivers every year to spawn, but dams and heavy commercial fishing at sea have depleted their numbers and distribution to a fraction of what they once were. Unlike salmon species on the Pacific coast, adult Atlantic salmon survive the fall spawning period and make their way back out to sea again. The young, or parr, hatch the following spring and live in streams and rivers for the next two or three years before migrating to the waters off Greenland. Active efforts are now underway to restore this species, including capturing and trucking the fish around dams. Salmon is just one of the species whose life cycle starts in fresh water and requires migrations to and from the sea. Called anadromous fish, others include **striped bass, sturgeon, shad, alewives, smelt,** and **eels**. All were once far more numerous in Maine, but fortunately pollution control and management efforts in the past three decades have helped their populations rebound slightly from their historic low numbers.

Estuaries and Mudflats

Maine's estuaries, where fresh and salt water meet, are ecosystems of outstanding biological importance. South of Cape Elizabeth, where the Maine coast is low and sandy, estuaries harbor large salt marshes of **spartina** grasses that can tolerate the frequent variations in salinity as runoff and tides fluctuate. Producing an estimated four times more plant material than an equivalent area of wheat, these spartina marshes provide abundant nutrients and shelter for a

host of marine organisms that ultimately account for as much as 60% of the value of the state's commercial fisheries.

The tidal range along the Maine coast varies 9-26 vertical feet, southwest to northeast. Where the tide inundates sheltered estuaries for more than a few hours at a time, spartina grasses cannot take hold, and mudflats dominate. Although it may look like a barren wasteland at low tide, a mudflat is also a highly productive environment and home to abundant marine life. Several species of tiny primitive worms called **nematodes** can inhabit the mud in densities of 2,000 or more per square inch. Larger worm species are also very common. One, the **bloodworm**, grows up to a foot in length and is harvested in quantity for use as sportfishing bait.

More highly savored among the mudflat residents is the **soft-shelled clam**, famous for its outstanding flavor and an essential ingredient of an authentic Maine lobsterbake. But because clams are suspension feeders—filtering phytoplankton through their long siphon, or "neck"—they can accumulate pollutants that cause illness, including hepatitis. Many Maine mudflats are closed to clam harvesting because of leaking septic systems, so it's best to check with the state's Department of Marine Resources or the local municipal office before digging a mess of clams yourself.

For birds—and birders—salt marshes and mudflats are an unparalleled attraction. Long-legged wading birds such as **glossy ibis, snowy egret, little blue heron, great blue heron, tricolored heron, green heron,** and **blackcrowned night heron** frequent the marshes in great numbers throughout the summer months, hunting the shallow waters for mummichogs and other small salt-marsh fish, crustaceans, and invertebrates. From mid-May to early June, and then again from mid-July until mid-September, migrating shorebirds pass through Maine to and from their subarctic breeding grounds. On a good day, a discerning birder can find 17 or more species of shorebirds probing the mudflats and marshes with pointed bills in search of their preferred foods. In turn, the large flocks of shorebirds don't escape the notice of their own predators—**merlins** and **peregrine falcons** dash in to catch a meal.

The Rocky Shoreline and the Marine Environment

On the more exposed rocky shores—the dominant shoreline from Cape Elizabeth all the way Down East to Lubec—where currents and waves keep mud and sand from accumulating, the plant and animal communities are entirely different from those in the inland aquatic areas. The most important requirement for life in this impenetrable, rockbound environment is probably the ability to hang on tight. **Barnacles,** the calcium-armored crustaceans that attach themselves to the rocks immediately below the high-tide line, have developed a fascinating battery of adaptations to survive not only pounding waves but also prolonged exposure to air, solar heat, and extreme winter cold. Glued in place, however, they cannot escape being eaten by **dog whelks,** the predatory snails that also inhabit this intertidal zone. Whelks are larger and more elongate than the more numerous and ubiquitous **periwinkle,** accidentally transplanted from Europe in the mid-19th century.

Also hanging onto these rocks, but at a lower level, are the brown algae—seaweeds. Like a marine forest, the four species of **rockweed** provide shelter for a wide variety of life beneath their fronds. A world of discovery awaits those who make the effort to go out onto the rocks at low tide and look under the clumps of seaweed and into the tidepools they shelter. Venture into these chilly waters with mask, fins, and wetsuit and still another world opens for natural history exploration. Beds of **blue mussels, sea urchins, sea stars,** and **sea cucumbers** dot the bottom close to shore. In crevices between and beneath the rocks lurk **rock crabs** and **lobsters.** Now a symbol of the Maine coast and the delicious seafoods it provides, the lobster was once considered "poor man's food"—so plentiful that it was spread on fields as fertilizer. Although lobsters are fa less common than they once were, they are one of Maine's most closely monitored species, and their population continues to support a large and thriving commercial fishing industry.

Sadly, the same cannot be said fo. most of Maine's other commercially harvested marine fish. When Euro-

peans first came to these shores four centuries ago, **cod, haddock, halibut, hake, flounder, herring,** and **tuna** were abundant. No longer. Overharvested, their seabed habitat torn up by relentless dragging, these groundfish have all but disappeared. It will be decades before these species can recover—and then only if effective regulations can be put in place soon.

The familiar doglike face of the **harbor seal,** often seen peering alertly from the surface just offshore, provides a reminder that wildlife populations are resilient—if given a chance. A century ago, there was a bounty on harbor seals because it was thought they ate too many lobsters and fish. Needless to say, neither fish nor lobsters increased when the seals all but disappeared. With the bounty's repeal and the advent of legal protection, Maine's harbor seal population has bounced back to an estimated 15,000-20,000. Scores of them can regularly be seen basking on offshore ledges, drying their tan, brown, black, silver, or reddish coats in the sun. Though it's tempting to approach for a closer look, avoid bringing a boat too near these haulout ledges, as it causes the seals to flush into the water and imposes an unnecessary stress on the pups, which already face a first-year mortality rate of 30%.

Positive changes in our relationships with wildlife are even more apparent with the return of birds to the Maine coast. Watching the numerous **herring gulls** and **great black-backed gulls** soaring on a fresh ocean breeze today, it's hard to imagine that a century ago, egg collecting had so reduced their numbers that they were a rare sight. In 1903, there were just three pairs of **common eiders** left in Maine; today, 25,000 pairs nest along the coast. With creative help from dedicated researchers using sound recordings, decoys, and prepared burrows, **Atlantic puffins** are recolonizing historic offshore nesting islands. **Osprey** and **bald eagles,** almost free of the lingering vestiges of DDT and other pesticides, now range the length of the coast and up Maine's major rivers.

BOB RACE

Looking into the Future
Many Maine plants and animals, however, remain subjects of concern. Listed or proposed for listing as endangered or threatened species in the state are 178 vascular plants and 54 vertebrates. Too little is known about most of the lesser plants and animals to determine what their status is, but as natural habitats continue to decline in size or become degraded, it is likely that many of these species will disappear from the state. It is impossible to say exactly what will be lost when any of these species cease to exist here, but, to quote conservationist Aldo Leopold, "To keep every cog and wheel is the first precaution of intelligent tinkering."

It is clear, however, that life in Maine has been enriched by the recovery of populations of pine marten, moose, harbor seal, eider, and others. The natural persistence and tenacity of wildlife suggests that such species as the Atlantic salmon, wolf, and mountain lion will someday return to Maine—provided we give them the chance and the space to survive.

"Flora and Fauna" was written by William P. Hancock, director of the Environmental Centers Department and the Maine Audubon Society, and former editor of *Habitat* magazine. For more information and flora and fauna field guides, see the Booklist.

HISTORY

Prehistoric Mainers: the Paleoindians
As the great continental glacier receded northwestward from Maine some 12,000 years ago, some prehistoric grapevine must have alerted small bands of hunter-gatherers—fur-clad Paleoindians—to scrub sprouting in the tundra, burgeoning mammal populations, and the ocean's bountiful food supply. Because come they did, at first seasonally, then year-round. Anyone who thinks tourism is a recent Maine phenomenon need only explore the shoreline in Damariscotta, Boothbay Harbor, and Bar Harbor, where heaps of cast-off oyster shells and clamshells document the migration of early Native Americans from woodlands to waterfront. Yes, "the shore" has been a summertime magnet for millennia.

Archaeological evidence from the Archaic period in Maine—roughly 8000-1000 B.C.—is fairly scant, but paleontologists have unearthed stone tools and weapons and small campsites attesting to a nomadic lifestyle supported by fishing and hunting (with fishing becoming more extensive as time went on). Toward the end of the tradition, during the late Archaic period, emerged a rather anomalous Indian culture known officially as the Moorehead phase but informally called the Red Paint People, due to their curious trait of using a distinctive red ocher (pulverized hematite) in burials. Dark red puddles and stone artifacts have led excavators to burial pits as far north as the St. John River.

Just as mysteriously as they had arrived, the Red Paint People disappeared abruptly and inexplicably around 1800 B.C.

Following them almost immediately—and almost as suddenly—hunter-gatherers of the Susquehanna Tradition arrived from well to the south, moved across Maine's interior as far as the St. John River, and remained until about 1600 B.C., when they, too, enigmatically vanished. Excavations have turned up relatively sophisticated stone tools and evidence that they cremated their dead. It was nearly 1,000 years before a major new cultural phase appeared.

The next great leap forward was marked by the advent of potterymaking, introduced around 700 B.C. The Ceramic period stretched to the 16th century, and cone-shaped pots (initially stamped, later incised with coiled-rope motifs) survived until the introduction of metals from Europe. Houses of sorts—seasonal wigwam-style dwellings for fishermen and their families—appeared along the coast and on offshore islands.

The Europeans Arrive
The identity of the first Europeans to set foot in Maine is a matter of debate. Historians dispute the romantically popular notion that Norse explorers checked out this part of the New World as early as A.D. 1000. Even an 11th-century Norse coin found in 1961 in Brooklin (on the Blue Hill Peninsula) probably was carried there from farther north.

Not until the late 15th century, the onset of the great Age of Discovery, did credible reports of the New World (including what's now Maine) filter back to Europe's courts and universities. Thanks to innovations in naval architecture, shipbuilding, and navigation, astonishingly courageous fellows crossed the Atlantic in search of rumored treasure and new routes for reaching it.

John Cabot, sailing from England aboard the ship *Mathew*, may have been the first European to reach Maine, in 1498, but historians have never confirmed a landing site. No question remains, however, about the account of Giovanni da Verrazzano, an Italian explorer commanding *La Dauphine* under the French flag, who reached the Maine coast in May 1524, probably at the tip of the Phippsburg Peninsula. Encountering less-than-friendly Indians, Verrazzano did a minimum of business and continued onward. His brother's map of the site labels it "The Land of Bad People." Esteban Gomez and John Rut followed in Verrazzano's wake, but nothing came of their exploits.

Nearly half a century passed before the Maine coast turned up again on European explorers' agendas. This time, interest was fueled by reports of a Brigadoon-like area called Norumbega (or Oranbega, as one map had it), a myth that arose, gathered steam, and took on a life of its own in the decades following Verrazzano's voyage.

By the early 17th century, when Europeans began arriving in more than twos and threes and getting serious about colonization, Native American agriculture was already underway at the mouths of the Saco and Kennebec Rivers, the cod fishery was thriving on offshore islands, Indians far to the north were hot to trade furs for European goodies, and the birch-bark canoe was the transport of choice on inland waterways.

In mid-May 1602, Bartholomew Gosnold, en route to a settlement off Cape Cod aboard the *Concord*, landed along Maine's southern coast. The following year, merchant trader Martin Pring and his boats *Speedwell* and *Discoverer* explored farther Down East, backtracked to Cape Cod, and returned to England with tales that inflamed curiosity and enough sassafras to satisfy royal appetites. Pring produced a detailed survey of the Maine coast from Kittery to Bucksport, including offshore islands.

On May 18, 1605, George Waymouth, skippering the *Archangel*, reached Monhegan Island, 11 miles off the Maine coast, and moored for the night in Monhegan Harbor (still treacherous even today, exposed to the weather from the southwest and northeast and subject to meteorological beatings and heaving swells. Yachting guides urge sailors not to expect to anchor, moor, or tie up there). The next day, Waymouth crossed the bay and scouted the mainland. He took five Indians hostage and sailed up the St. George River, near present-day Thomaston. As maritime historian Roger Duncan puts it, "The Plimoth Pilgrims were little boys in short pants when George Waymouth was exploring this coastline."

Waymouth returned to England and awarded his hostages to officials Sir John Popham and Sir Ferdinando Gorges, who, their curiosity piqued, quickly agreed to subsidize the colonization effort. In 1607, the *Gift of God* and the *Mary and John* sailed for the New World carrying two of Waymouth's captives. After returning them to their native Pemaquid area, Captains George Popham and Raleigh Gilbert continued westward, establishing a colony (St. George or Ft. George) at the tip of the Phippsburg Peninsula in mid-August 1607 and exploring the shoreline between Portland and Pemaquid. Frigid weather, untimely deaths (including Popham's), and a storehouse fire doomed what's called the Popham Colony, but not before the hundred or so settlers built the 30-ton pinnace *Virginia*, the New World's first such vessel. When Gilbert received word of an inheritance waiting in England, he and the remaining colonists returned to the Old World.

In 1614, swashbuckling Capt. John Smith, exploring from the Penobscot River westward to Cape Cod, reached Monhegan Island nine years after Waymouth's visit. Smith's meticulous map of the region was the first to use the "New England" appellation, and the 1616 publication of his *Description of New-England* became the catalyst for permanent settlements.

The French and the English Square Off

English dominance of exploration west of the Penobscot River in the early 17th century coincided roughly with French activity east of the river.

In 1604, French nobleman Pierre du Gua, Sieur de Monts, set out with cartographer Samuel de Champlain to map the coastline, first reaching Nova Scotia's Bay of Fundy and then sailing up the St. Croix River. In midriver, just west of present-day Calais, a crew planted gardens and erected buildings on today's St. Croix Island while de Monts and Champlain went off exploring. The two men reached the island Champlain named *l'Isle des Monts Deserts* and present-day Bangor before returning to face the winter with their ill-fated compatriots. Scurvy, lack of fuel and water, and a ferocious winter wiped out nearly half of the 79 men. In spring 1605, de Monts, Champlain, and other survivors headed southwest, exploring the coastline all the way to Cape Cod before heading northeast again and settling permanently at Nova Scotia's Port Royal (now Annapolis Royal).

Eight years later, French Jesuit missionaries en route to the Kennebec River ended up on Mount Desert Island and, with a band of French laymen, set about establishing the St. Sauveur settlement. But leadership squabbles led to building delays, and English marauder Samuel Argall—assigned to reclaim English territory—arrived to find them easy prey. The colony was leveled, the settlers were set adrift in small boats, the priests were carted off to Virginia, and Argall moved on to destroy Port Royal.

By the 1620s, more than four dozen English fishing vessels were combing New England waters in search of cod, and year-round fishing depots had sprung up along the coast between Pemaquid and Portland. At the same time, English trappers and dealers began usurping the Indians' fur trade—a valuable income source.

The Massachusetts Bay Colony was established in 1630 and England's Council of New England, headed by Sir Fordinando Gorges, began making vast land grants throughout Maine, giving rise to permanent settlements, many dependent on agriculture. Among the earliest communities were Kittery, York, Wells, Saco, Scarborough, Falmouth, and Pemaquid—places where they tilled the acidic soil, fished the waters, eked out a barely-above-subsistence living, coped with predators and endless winters, bartered goods and services, and set up local governments and courts.

By the late 17th century, as these communities expanded, so did their requirements and responsibilities. Roads and bridges were built, preachers and teachers were hired, and militias were organized to deal with internecine and Indian skirmishes.

Even though England yearned to control the entire Maine coastline, her turf, realistically, was primarily south and west of the Penobscot River. The French had expanded out from their Canadian colony of Acadia, for the most part north and east of the Penobscot. Unlike the absentee bosses who controlled the English territory, French merchants actually showed up, forming good relationships with the Indians and cornering the market in fishing, lumbering, and fur trading. And French Jesuit priests converted many a Native American to Catholicism. Intermittently, overlapping Anglo-French land claims sparked locally messy conflicts.

In the mid-17th century, the strategic heart of French administration and activity in Maine was Ft. Pentagoet, a sturdy stone outpost built in 1635 in what is now Castine. From here, the French controlled coastal trade between the St. George River and Mount Desert Island and well up the Penobscot River. In 1654, England captured and occupied the fort and much of French Acadia, but, thanks to the 1667 Treaty of Breda, title returned to the French in 1670, and Pentagoet briefly became Acadia's capital.

A short but nasty Dutch foray against Acadia in 1674 resulted in Pentagoet's destruction ("levell'd with ye ground," by one account) and the raising of a third national flag over Castine.

The Indian Wars (1675-1760)

Caught in the middle of 17th- and 18th-century Anglo-French disputes throughout Maine were the Wabanaki (People of the Dawn), the collective name for the state's major Native American tribal groups, all of whom spoke Algonquian languages. Modern ethnographers label these groups the Micmacs, Maliseets, Passamaquoddies, and Penobscots.

In the early 17th century, exposure to European diseases took its toll, wiping out three-quarters of the Wabanaki in the years 1616-19. Opportunistic English and French traders quickly moved into the breach, and the Indians struggled to survive and regroup.

But regroup they did—less than three generations later, a series of six Indian wars began, lasting nearly a century and pitting the Wabanaki most often against the English but occasionally against other Wabanaki. The conflicts, largely provoked by Anglo-French tensions in Europe, were King Philip's War (1675-78), King William's War (1688-99), Queen Anne's War (1703-13), Dummer's War (1721-26), King George's War (1744-48), and the French and Indian War (1754-60). Not until a get-together in 1762 at Ft. Pownall (now Stockton Springs) did peace effectively return to the region—just in time for the heating up of the revolutionary movement.

Comes the Revolution

Near the end of the last Indian War, just beyond Maine's eastern border, a watershed event led to more than a century of cultural and political fallout. During the so-called Acadian Dispersal, in 1755, the English expelled from Nova Scotia some 10,000 French-speaking Acadians who refused to pledge allegiance to the British Crown. Scattered as far south as Louisi-

1810 headstone in Richmond

ana and west toward New Brunswick and Quebec, the Acadians lost farms, homes, and possessions in this *grand dérangement*. Not until 1785 was land allocated for resettlement of Acadians along both sides of the Upper St. John River, where thousands of their descendants remain today. Henry Wadsworth Longfellow's epic poem *Evangeline* dramatically relates the sorry Acadian saga.

In the District of Maine, on the other hand, with relative peace following a century of intermittent warfare, settlement again exploded, particularly in the southernmost counties. The 1764 census tallied Maine's population at just under 25,000; a decade later, the number had doubled. New towns emerged almost overnight, often heavily subsidized by wealthy investors from the parent Massachusetts Bay Colony. With almost 4,000 residents, the largest town in the district was Falmouth (later renamed Portland).

In 1770, 27 Maine towns became eligible, based on population, to send representatives to the Massachusetts General Court, the colony's legislative body. But only six coastal towns could actually afford to send anyone, sowing seeds of resentment among settlers who were thus saddled with taxes without representation. Sporadic mob action accompanied unrest in southern Maine, but the flashpoint occurred in the Boston area.

On April 18, 1775, Paul Revere set out on America's most famous horseback ride—from Lexington to Concord, Massachusetts—to announce the onset of what became the American Revolution. Most of the Revolution's action occurred south of Maine, but not all of it.

In June, the Down East outpost of Machias was the site of the war's first naval engagement. The well-armed but unsuspecting British vessel HMS *Margaretta* sailed into the bay and was besieged by local residents angry about a Machias merchant's sweetheart deal with the British. Before celebrating their David-and-Goliath victory, the rebels captured the *Margaretta*, killed her captain, then captured two more British ships sent to the rescue.

In the fall of 1775, Col. Benedict Arnold—better known to history as a notorious turncoat—assembled 1,100 sturdy men for a flawed and futile "March on Quebec" to dislodge the English.

From Newburyport, Massachusetts, they sailed to the mouth of the Kennebec River, near Bath, then headed inland with the tide. In Pittston, six miles south of Augusta and close to the head of navigation, they transferred to a fleet of 220 locally made bateaux and laid over three nights at Ft. Western in Augusta. Then they set off, poling, paddling, and portaging their way upriver. Skowhegan, Norridgewock, and Chain of Ponds were among the landmarks along the grueling route. The men endured cold, hunger, swamps, disease, dense underbrush, and the loss of nearly 600 of their comrades before reaching Quebec in late 1775. In the Kennebec River Valley, Arnold Trail historical signposts today mark highlights (or, more aptly, lowlights) of the expedition.

Four years later, another futile attempt to dislodge the British, this time in the District of Maine, resulted in America's worst naval defeat until World War II—a little-publicized debacle called the Penobscot Expedition. On August 14, 1779, as more than 40 American warships and transports carrying more than 2,000 Massachusetts men blockaded Castine to flush out a relatively small enclave of leftover Brits, a seven-vessel Royal Navy fleet appeared. Despite their own greater numbers, about 30 of the American ships turned tail up the Penobscot River. The captains torched their vessels, exploding the ammunition and leaving the survivors to walk in disgrace to Augusta or even Boston. Each side took close to a hundred casualties, three commanders —including Paul Revere— were court-martialed, and Massachusetts was about $7 million poorer.

The American Revolution officially came to a close on September 3, 1783, with the signing of the Treaty of Paris between the United States and Great Britain. The U.S.-Canada border was set at the St. Croix River, but, in a massive oversight, boundary lines were left unresolved for thousands of square miles in the northern District of Maine.

Trade Troubles and the War of 1812

In 1807, President Thomas Jefferson imposed the Embargo Act, banning trade with foreign entities—specifically France and Britain. With thousands of miles of coastline and harbor villages dependent on trade for revenue and basic necessities, Maine reeled. By the time the act was repealed, under President James Madison in 1809, France and Britain were almost unscathed, but the bottom had dropped out of New England's economy.

An active smuggling operation based in Eastport kept Mainers from utter despair, but the economy still had continued its downslide. In 1812, the fledgling United States declared war on Great Britain, again disrupting coastal trade. In the fall of 1814, the situation reached its nadir when the British invaded the Maine coast and occupied all the shoreline between the St. Croix and Penobscot Rivers. Later that same year, the Treaty of Ghent finally halted the squabble, forced the British to withdraw from Maine, and allowed the locals to get on with economic recovery.

Statehood

In October 1819, Mainers held a constitutional convention at the First Parish Church on Congress St. in Portland. (Known affectionately as "Old Jerusalem," the church was later replaced by the present-day structure.) The convention crafted a constitution modeled on that of Massachusetts, with two notable differences: Maine would have no official church (Massachusetts had the Puritans' Congregational Church), and Maine would place no religious requirements or restrictions on its gubernatorial candidates. When votes came in from 241 Maine towns, only nine voted against ratification.

For Maine, March 15, 1820, was one of those good news/bad news days: after 35 years of separatist agitation, the District of Maine broke from Massachusetts (signing the separation allegedly, and disputedly, at the Jameson Tavern in Freeport) and became the 23rd state in the Union. However, the Missouri Compromise, enacted by Congress only 12 days earlier to balance admission of slave and free states, mandated that the slave state of Missouri be admitted on the same day. Maine had abolished slavery in 1788, and there was deep resentment over the linkage.

Portland became the new state's capital (albeit only briefly; it switched to Augusta in 1832), and William King, one of statehood's most outspoken advocates, became the first governor.

Trouble in the North Country

Without an official boundary established on Maine's far northern frontier, turf battles were always simmering just under the surface. Timber was the sticking point—everyone wanted the vast wooded acreage. Finally, in early 1839, militia reinforcements descended on the disputed area, heating up what has come to be known as the Aroostook War, a border confrontation with no battles and no casualties (except a farmer who was shot by friendly militia). It's a blip in the historical timeline, but remnants of fortifications in Houlton, Ft. Fairfield, and Ft. Kent keep the story alive today. By March 1839, a truce was negotiated, and the 1842 Webster-Ashburton Treaty established the border once and for all.

Maine in the Civil War

In the 1860s, with the state's population slightly more than 600,000, more than 70,000 Mainers suited up and went off to fight in the Civil War—the greatest per capita show of force of any northern state. Some 18,000 of them died in the conflict. Thirty-one Mainers were Union Army generals, the best-known being Joshua L. Chamberlain, a Bowdoin College professor, who commanded the Twentieth Maine regiment and later became president of the college and governor of Maine.

During the war, young battlefield artist Winslow Homer, who later settled in Prouts Neck, south of Portland, created wartime sketches regularly for such publications as *Harper's Weekly*. In Washington, Maine Sen. Hannibal Hamlin was elected vice president under Abraham Lincoln in 1860 (he was removed from the ticket in favor of Andrew Johnson when Lincoln came up for reelection in 1864).

Maine Comes into Its Own

After the Civil War, Maine's influence in Republican-dominated Washington far outweighed the size of its population. In the late 1880s, Mainers held the federal offices of acting vice president, Speaker of the House, secretary of state, Senate majority leader, Supreme Court justice, and several important committee chairmanships. Best known of the notables were James G. Blaine (journalist, presidential aspirant, and secretary of state) and Portland native Thomas Brackett Reed, presidential aspirant and Speaker of the House.

In Maine itself, traditional industries fell into decline after the Civil War, dealing the economy a body blow. Steel ships began replacing Maine's wooden clippers, refrigeration techniques made the block-ice industry obsolete, concrete threatened the granite-quarrying trade, and the output from Southern textile mills began to supplant that from Maine's mills.

Despite Maine's economic difficulties, however, wealthy urbanites began turning their sights toward the state, accumulating land (including islands) and building enormous summer "cottages" for their families, servants, and hangers-on. Bar Harbor was a prime example of the elegant summer colonies that sprung up, but others include Grindstone Neck (Winter Harbor), Prouts Neck (Scarborough), and Islesboro (in Penobscot Bay). Vacationers who preferred fancy hotel-type digs reserved rooms for the summer at such sprawling complexes as Kineo House (on Moosehead Lake), Poland Spring House (west of Portland), or the Samoset Hotel (in Rockland). Built of wood and catering to long-term visitors, these and many others all eventually succumbed to altered vacation patterns and the ravages of fire.

As the 19th century spilled into the 20th, the state broadened its appeal beyond the well-to-do who had snared prime turf in the Victorian era. It launched an active promotion of Maine as "The Nation's Playground," successfully spurring an influx of visitors from all economic levels. By steamboat, train, and soon by car, people came to enjoy the ocean beaches, the woods, the mountains, the lakes, and the quaintness of it all. (Not that these features didn't really exist, but the state's aggressive public relations campaign at the turn of the century stacks up against anything Madison Avenue puts out today.) The only major hiatus in the tourism explosion in the

MAINE WOMEN IN HISTORY

Throughout Maine's history—as everywhere else—attention inevitably focuses on the role of men who have significantly affected the course of progress. In Maine, thanks to eager researchers (notably at the University of Southern Maine) and the annual celebration of Women's History Month, many key women have been identified, highlighted, and saluted. Portland and Brunswick have women's-history walking routes, and the **Maine Women Writers Collection** (open by appointment), at Westbrook College, includes an impressive and expanding inventory of female authors' books, articles, and memorabilia. Here are a few of the standouts—a colorful lot:

Dorothea L. Dix (1802-87), of Hampden, crusaded tirelessly in America and Europe for humane treatment of prisoners and proper care of the retarded and mentally ill. During the Civil War, she was superintendent of Army nurses.

Cornelia T. "Fly Rod" Crosby (1854-1946), of Phillips, was a skilled markswoman and angler who penned articles on hunting and fishing for her local paper, soon gaining a nationwide audience for her writings. Fly Rod Crosby also drew national attention in 1896 at a Madison Square Garden sportsmen's expo for modeling a then-risqué outfit that revealed seven or eight inches of her lower legs.

Lillian Norton (1857-1914), of Farmington, better known as the elegant diva Madame Nordica, won international acclaim in opera circles (and gossipy headlines in tabloid circles) at the turn of the 20th century.

Chansonetta Stanley Emmons (1858-1937), of Kingfield, lugged around a hefty camera to document life in western Maine. Always overshadowed by her famed automaker brothers, she received artistic notice only after her death.

Josephine D. Peary (1863-1955), who summered on Casco Bay's Eagle Island and died in Portland, endured the arctic rigors of Greenland in the late 19th century with her husband, Adm. Robert E. Peary. She gave birth to their first child, Marie (called "Snow Baby" by the Inuit), in a primitive tar-paper dwelling on the second of their expeditions. In the 1950s, the National Geographic Society awarded Mrs. Peary its coveted Medal of Achievement.

Margaret Chase Smith (1897-1995), of Skowhegan, was the first woman elected to the US Senate (1948) and the first woman nominated for the presidency by a major party (1964). In 1950, her "Declaration of Conscience" speech catapulted her to national prominence as an intrepid opponent of McCarthyism.

Mollie Spotted Elk (Mary Alice Nelson) (1903-77), a Penobscot from Indian Island near Bangor, gained renown as an accomplished exotic dancer in 1920s New York and 1930s Paris, then returned to Indian Island in 1940 married to a French journalist (who died in 1941) and mother of a daughter, Jean.

It's important also to acknowledge the debt due thousands of now-anonymous pioneering women who made their mark managing households during colonial times, maintaining communications links during the Civil War, slaving away in textile mills and shoe factories during and after the Industrial Revolution, and propping up the shipbuilding efforts at Bath Iron Works during World War II, while the men were off at the front.

century's first two decades was 1914-18, when 35,062 Mainers joined many thousands of other Americans in going off bravely to the European front to fight in World War I. Two years after the cessation of hostilities, in 1920 (the centennial of its statehood), Maine women were the first in the nation to troop to the polls after ratification of the Nineteenth Amendment granted universal suffrage.

Maine was slow to feel the repercussions of the Great Depression, but eventually they came, with bank failures all over the state. Federally subsidized programs, such as the Civilian Conservation Corps (CCC) and the Works Progress Administration (WPA), left lasting legacies in Maine.

Politically, the state has contributed notables on both sides of the aisle. In 1954, Maine elected as its governor Edmund S. Muskie, only the fifth Democrat in the job since 1854. In 1958, Muskie ran for and won a seat in the Senate, and in 1980 he became secretary of state under President Jimmy Carter. Muskie died in 1996.

Elected in 1980, Waterville's George J. Mitchell made a respected name for himself as a Democratic senator and Senate majority leader before retiring in 1996, when Maine became only the second state in the union to have two women senators (Olympia Snowe and Susan Collins, both Republicans). Following his re-election, President Bill Clinton appointed Mitchell's distinguished congressional colleague and three-term senator, Republican William Cohen of Bangor, secretary of defense.

ECONOMY AND GOVERNMENT

ECONOMY

Maine's sprawling, relatively uninhabited, mostly rural or coastal acreage lends the state its famous scenic beauty, but the lack of large urban centers also makes for something of a patchwork economy. That patchwork extends to individuals, who frequently hold down two or even three jobs to meet their families' needs. In summer, teachers become lobstermen or coaches, and ski instructors become lifeguards and waiters. And factory workers supplement their incomes by cutting firewood on the side.

The Two Mainstays: Forest Products and Tourism

Forests cover a larger percentage of Maine than they do any other state (89%). While the trees are stately and sweet smelling and keep the landscape largely evergreen through the long, snowy winters, the forests also provide diverse employment—everything from tree-felling to working in paper and pulp mills—for nearly 14,000 of Maine's 1.2 million residents.

Paper mills have long been a mainstay of the state's economy, although labor problems, foreign competition, and environmental restrictions have caused several to curtail or cease operation in recent decades. Out in the woods, workers fell trees to provide raw material not only for paper but also for lumber, shingles, plywood, veneers, and even toothpicks. The woods are also harvested for the firewood burned as primary or supplemental heat in about 75% of Maine's homes.

Woods work is exhausting and dangerous but nowhere near as hazardous as in the past, when massive logs were dumped into Maine's rivers and sent downstream to riverside or coastal mills for processing. Worst jobs of all were those of the river drivers, who "rode" the logs, prodded them onward in heavy current and wild water, and broke up log jams en route. Environmental regulations halted the casualty-prone log drives in the 1970s.

Despite the traditional, colorful, natural-resource-based businesses for which Maine is noted, the second-biggest contributors to the state's economy now are in the area of tourism—particularly meals, lodging, and outdoor pursuits. Mid-1990s figures indicate that tourism's annual contribution to Maine coffers fluctuates between $1.2 billion and $3 billion. Most tourism dollars are earned in July and August, so the weather gods, gasoline prices, and the general state of the national economy can cause major jolts. If there's sometimes not enough summer for fair-weather visitors, there's sometimes not enough winter for others. Maine's skiing and snowmobiling industries are dependent on the legendary long, cold, snowy winters in inland Maine, and Mother Nature usually cooperates.

Fishing

Along Maine's 5,500 miles of convoluted shore, many communities have depended for generations on fishing—now primarily for lobster but also for groundfish, scallops, shrimp, and, since the early 1990s, sea urchins. Each fishery is strictly regulated; some are seasonal, some are year-round.

More than 8,000 Maine residents hold commercial lobstering licenses, but you don't need to check licenses to recognize a lobstering community: dotting the shore are docks piled high with green, yellow, and white wire-mesh lobster traps (a colorful recent change from the era of traps made of unpainted wooden laths), and lobsterboats bob at their moorings, cruise up to the dock for fuel, or sit in their owners' yards awaiting the next season. In recent years, Maine's catch has totaled around 30 million pounds of lobster.

Complicated by the everyday risks of drowning, hypothermia, and wind-whipped storms, fishing isn't for wimps. Well aware of the perils, the fishermen pride themselves on their ruggedness.

Potatoes and Broccoli

The state's principal cultivated agricultural crop is potatoes. Raising some two billion pounds annually, Maine ranks fifth or sixth in the nation in potato production—and in the space devoted to potato farming (a total of 78,000 acres). The tubers are grown mostly in the northernmost county of Aroostook, known simply as "the County."

Since 1980, broccoli has moved up quickly as the County's second-biggest crop—notwithstanding George Bush's disdain for the vegetable. During the fall broccoli harvest, one Aroostook County truckstop even gives you a free head of broccoli with a fuel fill-up.

Blueberries

Maine's primary wild-grown food product is the native, low-growing, wild blueberry—smaller and sweeter than the cultivated variety. The state harvests 98% of the country's low-bush wild blueberries. While these are found in many Maine counties and commercially harvested in several, Washington County holds the lead in the state's blueberry production. In restaurants and lodgings, chefs and innkeepers have invented incredibly creative ways for using blueberries: in muffins, ice cream, chutney, jam, pies, vinegar, cakes, wine, doughnuts, and even gourmet entrées.

Aquaculture

If fishing, harvesting blueberries and potatoes, and cutting timber are old, traditional industries, Maine's fish-farming industry is new—and growing. In Cobscook Bay, just off Lubec and Eastport, pens from several Atlantic salmon "farms" lie near the shore. Shellfish farmers successfully grow oysters in the Mid-Coast area, and growers raise mussels all along the coast. Wild seaweed is harvested by several companies for use as food (including the specialized Japanese food market), food additives, pet-food supplements, and lawn fertilizer.

Major Corporations

Because of its large area and small population spread unevenly around the state, economic planners sometimes refer to "three Maines." The north is sparsely populated with little industry. The central area has a few more population centers and more industry. The south—more populous, more prosperous, and closer to Boston—has more industry, is subject to more development pressure, and attracts more tourists to the state's few sandy beaches.

The same geographic constraints mean Maine has only a few major employers. Bath Iron Works, the state's biggest single employer, builds and repairs large ships, primarily for the US Navy. In recent years, BIW has won contracts for a series of Aegis missile cruisers. L.L. Bean, the internationally famous sportswear outfitter, still keeps its Freeport store open 24 hours a day, seven days a week, even though hunters en route to the woods are no longer their primary clients. Late-night customers nowadays tend to be people on a lark—just proving to themselves that they really *can* do their shopping at 3 a.m. MBNA, the United States' largest affinity credit-card company (and second-largest credit-card firm), arrived in Maine in 1993 and has expanded exponentially since then, primarily in the Mid-Coast region.

GOVERNMENT

Politics in Maine isn't quite as variable and unpredictable as the weather, but pundits are almost as wary as weather forecasters about making predictions. Despite a long tradition of Republicanism—dating especially from the late 19th century—Maine's voters and politicians have a national reputation for being independent-minded, electing Democrats, Republicans, or independents more for their character than their political persuasions.

Four of the most notable recent examples are Margaret Chase Smith, Edmund S. Muskie, George J. Mitchell, and William Cohen—two Republicans and two Democrats, all Maine natives. Republican Sen. Margaret Chase Smith proved her flintiness when she spoke out against McCarthyism in the 1950s. Ed Muskie, the first prominent Democrat to come out of Maine, won every race he entered except an aborted bid for the presidency in 1972. George Mitchell, who became Senate majority leader in 1989, retired from elective office in 1996 with a stellar reputation. William Cohen, Republican congressman and then senator, became secretary of defense in the Democratic Clinton administration in 1997. In a manifestation of Maine's strong tradition of bipartisanship, Mitchell and Cohen worked together closely on many issues to benefit the state and the nation (they even wrote a book together).

In the 1970s, Maine elected an independent governor, James Longley, whose memory is still respected (Longley's son was later elected to Congress as a Republican, and his daughter to the state senate as a Democrat). In 1994, Maine voted in another independent, Angus King, a relatively young veteran of careers in business, broadcasting, and law. The governor serves a term of four years, limited to two terms. (In October 1997, the popular, photogenic King, to no one's surprise, announced his intention to seek a second term.)

Like many states, Maine has a hardworking, overburdened judiciary. It boasts the smallest number of general-jurisdiction judges of any state judiciary (and ranks fifth from the bottom in money spent on judicial and legal services), but it's the fifth-most-productive in resolving civil cases and 12th in resolving criminal cases. The state's Supreme Judicial Court has a chief justice and six associate justices.

Maine is ruled by a bicameral, biennial citizen legislature comprising 151 members in the House of Representatives and 35 members in the State Senate, including a relatively high percentage of women and a fairly high proportion of retirees. Members of both houses serve two-year terms. Along with the governor, they meet at the State House in Augusta to pass legislation and administer an annual state budget of around $2 billion. In 1993, voters passed a statewide term-limits referendum restricting legislators to four terms.

Whereas nearly two dozen Maine cities are ruled by city councils, some 450 smaller towns and plantations retain the traditional form of rule: annual town meetings. Town meetings generally are held in March, when newspaper pages bulge with reports containing classic quotes from citizens exercising their rights to vote and vent. A few examples: "I believe in the pursuit of happiness until that pursuit infringes on the happiness of others"; "I don't know of anyone's dog running loose except my own, and I've arrested her several times"; and "Don't listen to him; he's from New Jersey."

Nonresidents are welcome to attend town meetings. Although, of course, you can't vote, a town meeting is a great way to experience actual local government. Refreshments are usually available—typically, proceeds benefit some local cause—and sometimes there's even a potluck lunch or supper. The meeting provides the live entertainment.

"Economy and Government" was written by Nancy Griffin, who formerly covered state government for UPI.

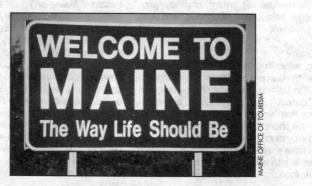

WELCOME TO MAINE
The Way Life Should Be

MAINE OFFICE OF TOURISM

THE PEOPLE

Maine's population didn't top the one-million mark until 1970. Twenty years later, according to the 1990 census, 1,227,928 residents lived in the state. And the official 1994 estimate shows a steady increase, to 1,240,000. Cumberland County, comprising the Portland area, has the highest head count; far-inland Piscataquis County, whose largest town is Dover-Foxcroft, is the least populous.

Despite the longstanding presence of several substantial ethnic groups, plus four Native American tribes, diversity is a relatively recent phenomenon in Maine, and the population is more than 90% Caucasian. A steady influx of refugees, beginning after the Vietnam War, forced the state to address diversity issues, and that continues today.

Natives vs. "People from Away"

People who weren't born in Maine aren't natives. Even people who *were* may experience close scrutiny of their credentials (there's an old saying: "If a cat has kittens in the oven, that don't make them muffins.") In Maine, there are natives and *natives*. Every day, the obituary pages describe Mainers who have barely left the houses in which they were born—even in which their grandparents were born. We're talking roots!

Along with this kind of heritage comes a whole vocabulary all its own—lingo distinctive to Maine or at least New England. For help in translation, see the glossary.

Part of the "native" picture is the matter of "native" produce. Hand-lettered signs sprout everywhere during the summer advertising Native corn, Native peas, even—believe it or not—Native ice. In Maine, homegrown is well grown.

"People from away," on the other hand, are those whose families haven't lived here a generation or more. But people from away (also called flatlanders) exist all over Maine, and they have come to stay, putting down roots of their own and altering the way the state is run, looks, and *will* look. Senators Snowe and Collins are natives, but Governor King is from away, as are

most of his cabinet members. You'll find other flatlanders as teachers, corporate executives, artists, retirees, writers, town selectmen, and even lobstermen.

In the 19th century, arriving flatlanders were mostly "rusticators" or "summer complaints"—summer residents who lived well, often in enclaves, and never set foot in the state off season. They did, however, pay property taxes, contribute to causes, and provide employment for local residents. Another 19th-century wave of people from away came from the bottom of the economic ladder: Irish escaping the potato famine and French-Canadians fleeing poverty in Quebec. Both groups experienced subtle and overt anti-Catholicism but rather quickly assimilated into the mainstream, taking jobs in mills and factories and becoming staunch American patriots.

The late 1960s and early 1970s brought bunches of "back-to-the-landers," who scorned plumbing and electricity and adopted retrograde ways of life. Although a few pockets of diehards still exist, most have changed with the times and adopted contemporary mores (and conveniences).

Today, technocrats arrive from away with computers, faxes, cell phones, and other high-tech gear and "commute" via the Internet and modern electronics. Maine has played a national leadership role in telecommunications reform —thanks to the university system's early push for installation of state-of-the-art fiber optics.

Native Americans

In Maine, the *real* natives are the Wabanaki (People of the Dawn)—the Micmac, Maliseet, Penobscot, and Passamaquoddy tribes of the eastern woodlands. Many live in or near three reservations, near the headquarters for their tribal governors. The Penobscots are based on Indian Island, in Old Town, near Bangor; Passamaquoddies are at Pleasant Point, in Perry, near Eastport, and at Indian Township, in Princeton, near Calais. Other Native American population clusters—known as "off-reservation Indians"—are the

Aroostook Band of Micmacs, based in Presque Isle, and the Houlton Band of Maliseets, in Littleton, near Houlton.

In 1965, Maine became the first state to establish a Department of Indian Affairs, but just five years later the Passamaquoddy and Penobscot tribes initiated a 10-year-long land-claims case involving 12.5 million Maine acres (about two-thirds of the state) weaseled from the Indians by Massachusetts in 1794. In late 1980, a landmark agreement, signed by President Jimmy Carter, awarded the tribes $80.6 million in reparations. Controversy has surrounded the settlement—including complaints about its inadequacy—but the pluses seem to have outweighed the minuses, as investments and capital distributions have allowed the Indians to find jobs, upgrade their homes, improve their medical care, and seek higher educational opportunities. One can only hope that the funds will also spur the tribes to revive and maintain their splendid cultural traditions.

Several well-attended annual summer festivals—in Bar Harbor, Grand Lake Stream, and Perry—highlight Indian traditions and heighten awareness of Native American culture. Basketmaking, canoebuilding, and traditional dancing are all parts of the scene. Museums in Orono, Old Town, Perry, Augusta, Bar Harbor, Hinckley, and New Portland feature Indian artifacts, interactive displays, historic photographs, and special programs.

Acadians and Franco-Americans

Within about three decades of their 1755 expulsion from Nova Scotia in *le grand dérangement,* Acadians had established new communities and new lives in northern Maine's St. John Valley. Gradually, they explored farther into central and southern Maine and west into New Hampshire. The Acadian diaspora has profoundly influenced Maine and its culture, and it continues to do so today. Biddeford, Lewiston, Augusta, and Madawaska hold annual Acadian or Franco-American festivals; French is spoken on the streets of Bangor and Fort Kent; and Lewiston, Biddeford, and Fort Kent boast extensive Franco-American and Acadian research collections.

African-Americans

Although Maine's African-American population is small, the state has had an African-American community since the 17th century; by the 1764 census, there were 322 slaves and free blacks in the District of Maine. Segregation remained the rule, however, so in the 19th century, blacks established their own parish, the Abyssinian Church, in Portland. Efforts are now underway to restore the long-closed church as an African-American cultural center and gathering place for Greater Portland's black community. For researchers delving into "Maine's black experience," the University of Southern Maine, in Portland, houses the African-American Archive of Maine, a significant collection of historic books, letters, and artifacts donated by Gerald Talbot, the first African-American to serve in the Maine Legislature.

Finns, Swedes, and Lebanese

Finns came to Maine in several 19th-century waves, primarily to work the granite quarries on the coast and on offshore islands and the slate quarries in Monson, near Greenville. Finnish families clustered near the quarries in St. George and on Vinalhaven and Hurricane Islands—all with landscapes similar to those of their homeland. Today, names such as Laukka, Lehtinen, Hamalainen, and Harjula are interspersed among the Yankee names in the Mid-Coast region.

In 1870, an idealistic American diplomat named William Widgery Thomas established a model agricultural community with 50 brave Swedes in the heart of Aroostook County. Their enclave, New Sweden, remains today, as does the town of Stockholm, and descendants of the pioneers have spread throughout Maine.

At the turn of the 20th century, Lebanese (and some Syrians) began descending on Waterville, where they found work in the textile mills and eventually established St. Joseph's Maronite Church in 1927. One of these immigrants was the mother of former senator George Mitchell.

Russians, Ukrainians, and Byelorussians

Arriving after World War II, Slavic immigrants established a unique community in Richmond, near Augusta. Only a tiny nucleus remains today, along with an onion-domed church, but a stroll through the local cemetery hints at the extent of the original colony.

The Newest Arrivals: Refugees from War
War has been the impetus for the more recent arrival of Asians, Africans, Central Americans, and Eastern Europeans. Most have settled in the Portland area, making that city the state's center of diversity. Vietnamese and Cambodians began settling in Maine in the mid-1970s. A handful of Afghanis who fled the Soviet-Afghan conflict also ended up in Portland. Somalis, Ethiopians, and Sudanese fled their war-torn countries in the early to mid-1990s, and Bosnians began arriving in the mid-1990s. With every new conflict comes a new stream of immigrants—world citizens are becoming Mainers, and Mainers are becoming world citizens.

THE ARTS IN MAINE

Every creative soul longs for inspiration and motivation to jump-start a painting or a poem, a statue or a novel. Maine has exerted a powerful lunar-like gravitational pull on creative types. The craggy shoreline, dense forests, and visually rich beauty—infused with hidebound Yankee traditions and an often harsh existence—have served well inspiring artists and writers to create work of national and international repute.

Beginning around the mid-19th century, when people from away descended on Maine for their summer getaways, little pockets of creative energy flourished (largely but not exclusively along the coast), and art and literature reaped the benefits. These weren't Maine's first artists or earliest writers, but they represented a turning point, a stepped-up pace of artistic and literary activity.

FINE ART

In 1850, in a watershed moment for Maine landscape painting, Hudson River School artist par-excellence Frederic Edwin Church (1826-1900) vacationed on Mount Desert Island. Influenced by the luminist tradition of such contemporaries as Fitz Hugh Lane (1804-65), who summered in Castine, Church accurately but romantically depicted the dramatic tableaux of Maine's coast and woodlands that even today attract slews of admirers.

By the 1880s, however, impressionism had become the style du jour and was being practiced by a coterie of artists who collected around Charles Herbert Woodbury (1864-1940) in Ogunquit. His program made Ogunquit the best-known summer art school in New England. After Hamilton Easter Field established another art school in town, modernism soon asserted itself.

Among the artists who took up summertime Ogunquit residence was Walt Kuhn (1877-1949), a key organizer of New York's 1913 landmark Armory Show of modern art.

Meanwhile, in the south, impressionist Childe Hassam (1859-1935), part of writer Celia Thaxter's circle, produced several hundred works on Maine's remote Appledore Island, in the Isles of Shoals off Kittery, and illustrated Thaxter's *An Island Garden*.

Another artistic summer colony found its niche in 1903, when Robert Henri (born Robert Henry Cozad; 1865-1929), charismatic leader of the Ashcan School of realist/modernists, visited Monhegan Island, about 11 miles offshore. Artists who followed him there included Rockwell Kent (1882-1971), Edward Hopper (1882-1967), George Bellows (1882-1925), and Randall Davey (1887-1964). Among the many other artists associated with Monhegan images are William Kienbusch (1914-80), Reuben Tam (1916-91), and printmakers Leo Meissner (1895-1977) and Stow Wengenroth (1906-78).

But colonies were of scant interest to other notables, who chose to derive their inspiration from Maine's stark natural beauty and work mostly in their own orbits. Among these are genre painter Eastman Johnson (1824-1906); romantic realist Winslow Homer (1836-1910), who lived in Maine for 27 years and whose studio in Prouts Neck (Scarborough) still overlooks the surf-tossed scenery he so often depicted; pointillist watercolorist Maurice Prendergast (1858-1924); John Marin (1870-1953), a cubist who painted Down East subjects, mostly around Deer Isle and Addison (Cape Split); Lewiston native Marsden Hartley (1877-1943), who first showed his abstractionist work in New York in 1909 and later worked in Berlin; Fairfield Porter

(1907-75), whose family summered on Great Spruce Head Island, in East Penobscot Bay; Andrew Wyeth (b. 1917), whose reputation as a romantic realist in the late 20th century surpassed that of his illustrator father, N.C. Wyeth (1882-1945).

On a parallel track was sculptor Louise Nevelson (1899-1988), raised in a poor Russian-immigrant family in Rockland and far better known outside her home state for her monumental wood sculptures slathered in black or gold. Two other noted sculptors with Maine connections were William Zorach and Gaston Lachaise, both of whom lived in Georgetown, near Bath.

Today, Maine has no major community known exclusively for its summer art colony. Sure, there are artistic clusters here and there, united by the urge for creative networking and moral support—especially when threatened with reduced government subsidy. Among these artistic pockets, all close to the ocean, are the Kennebunks, Portland, Monhegan Island, Rockland, Deer Isle, and Eastport.

Year-round or seasonal Maine residents with national (and international) reputations include Lincolnville's Neil Welliver and Alex Katz, North Haven's Eric Hopkins, Deer Isle's Karl Schrag, Eustis's Marguerite Robichaux, Tenants Harbor's Jamie Wyeth (third generation of the famous family), Kennebunk's Edward Betts, Port Clyde's William Thon, and Cushing's Lois Dodd and Alan Magee.

The state's most prestigious summer art program—better known in Manhattan than in Maine—is the highly selective Skowhegan School of Painting and Sculpture, Box 449, Skowhegan 04976, tel. (207) 474-9345; off-season 200 Park Ave. So., New York, NY 10003, tel. (212) 529-0505, founded in 1946. From nearly 1,000 applicants, 65 young artists are chosen each year to spend nine weeks (mid-June-mid-Aug.) on the school's 300-acre lakeside campus in East Madison. An evening lecture series is open to the public.

The two best collections of Maine art are at the **Portland Museum of Art,** 7 Congress Sq., Portland 04101, tel. (207) 775-6148, and the **Farnsworth Art Museum,** 352 Main St., Rockland 04841, tel. (207) 596-6457. The Farnsworth, in fact, focuses only on Maine art, primarily in the 20th century. In 1996, both museums saw their already-impressive holdings greatly en-

hanced when philanthropic collector Elizabeth Noyce bequeathed her comprehensive Maine collection to them.

The **Ogunquit Museum of American Art,** appropriately, also has a respectable Maine collection. Other Maine paintings, not always on exhibit, are at the Bowdoin College Museum of Art, in Brunswick; Bates College Museum of Art, in Lewiston; and Colby College Museum of Art, in Waterville. Colby has a huge collection of works by painter Alex Katz.

CRAFTS

Any survey of Maine art, however brief, must include the significant role of crafts in the state's artistic tradition. As with painters, sculptors, and writers, craftspeople have gravitated to Maine—most notably since the establishment in 1950 of the **Haystack Mountain School of Crafts.** Started in the Belfast area, the school put down roots on Deer Isle in 1960. Each summer, internationally famed artisans—sculptors, glassmakers, weavers, jewelers, potters, papermakers, and printmakers—become the faculty for the unique school, which has weekday classes and 24-hour studio access for adult students on its handsome 40-acre campus. For information, write to Haystack Mountain School of Crafts, Sunshine Rd., P.O. Box 518, Deer Isle 04627, tel. (207) 348-2306, fax 348-2307. Not surprisingly, Deer Isle is also the headquarters for the Maine Crafts Association, P.O. Box 228, Deer Isle 04627, tel. (207) 348-9943, which has about 200 members around the state.

DOWN EAST LITERATURE

Maine's first big-name writer was probably the early 17th-century French explorer Samuel de Champlain (1570-1635), who scouted the Maine coast, established a colony in 1604 near present-day Calais, and lived to describe in detail his experiences. Several decades after Champlain's forays, English naturalist John Josselyn visited Scarborough and in the 1670s published the first two books accurately describing Maine's flora and fauna (aptly describing, for example, blackflies as "not only a pesterment but a plague to the country").

Now, at the cusp of the 21st century, Maine's best-known author is Bangor resident Stephen King (b. 1947), wizard of the weird. Many of his dozens of horror novels and stories are set in Maine, and several have been filmed for the big screen here. King and his author-wife, Tabitha, are avid fans of both education and team sports and have generously distributed their largesse among schools and teams in the Bangor area.

Other best-selling contemporary authors writing in or about Maine include Carolyn Chute (b. 1948), resident of Parsonsfield and author of the raw novels *The Beans of Egypt, Maine* and *Letourneau's Used Auto Parts,* and Cathie Pelletier (b. 1953), raised in tiny Allagash and author of such humor-filled novels as *The Funeral Makers* and *The Bubble Reputation.*

Chroniclers of the Great Outdoors

John Josselyn was perhaps the first practitioner of Maine's strong naturalist tradition in American letters, but the Pine Tree State's rugged scenic beauty and largely unspoiled environment have given rise to many ecologically and environmentally concerned writers. Henry David Thoreau (1817-62), well known for poking around Walden Pond and other points south, undertook three Maine treks—in 1846, 1853, and 1857—and chronicled his trails, climbs, and canoe routes in *The Maine Woods,* published two years after his death.

The 20th century saw the arrival in Maine of crusader Rachel Carson (1907-64), whose 1962 wake-up call, *Silent Spring,* was based partly on Maine observations and research. The Rachel Carson National Wildlife Refuge, headquartered in Wells and comprising 10 chunks of environmentally sensitive coastal real estate, covers nearly 3,500 acres between Kittery Point and the Mid-Coast region.

The tiny town of Nobleboro, near Damariscotta, drew nature writer Henry Beston (1888-1968), author of, among other things, *The Outermost House* (about Cape Cod); his *Northern Farm* lyrically chronicles a year in Maine. Beston's wife, Elizabeth Coatsworth (1893-1986), wrote more than 90 books—including *Chimney Farm,* about their life in Nobleboro.

Fannie Hardy Eckstorm (1865-1946), born in Brewer to Maine's most prosperous fur trader, graduated from Smith College and became a noted expert on Maine (and specifically Native

American) folklore. Among her extensive writings, *Indian Place-Names of the Penobscot Valley and the Maine Coast,* published in 1941, remains a sine qua non for researchers.

The out-of-doors and inner spirits shaped Cape Rosier adoptees Helen and Scott Nearing, whose 1954 *Living the Good Life* became the bible of Maine's back-to-the-landers.

Classic Writings on the State

Historical novels, such as *Arundel,* were the specialty of Kennebunk native Kenneth Roberts (1885-1957), but Roberts also wrote *Trending into Maine,* a potpourri of Maine observations and experiences (the original edition was illustrated by N.C. Wyeth). Kennebunkport's Booth Tarkington (1869-1946), author of the *Penrod* novels and *The Magnificent Ambersons,* described 1920s Kennebunkport in *Mary's Neck,* published in 1932.

A little subgenre of sociological literary classics comprises astute observations (mostly by women) of daily life in various parts of the state. Some are fiction, some nonfiction, some barely disguised *romans à clef.* Probably the best known chronicler of such observations is Sarah Orne Jewett (1849-1909), author of *The Country of the Pointed Firs,* a fictionalized 1896 account of "Dunnet's Landing" (actually Tenants Harbor); her ties, however, are in the South Berwick area, where she spent most of her life. Also in South Berwick, Gladys Hasty Carroll (b. 1904) scrutinized everyday life in her hamlet, Dunnybrook, in *As the Earth Turns* (a title later "borrowed" and tweaked by a soap-opera producer). Lura Beam (1887-1978) focused on her childhood in the Washington County village of Marshfield in *A Maine Hamlet,* published in 1957, while Louise Dickinson Rich (1903-72) entertainingly described her experiences in the North Woods in *We Took to the Woods* and Down East in *The Peninsula.* Ruth Moore (1903-89), born on Gott's Island, near Acadia National Park, published her first book at the age of 40. Her tales, recently brought back into print, have earned her a whole new, appreciative audience. A native of northern Maine, from a mixed French and American family, Helen Hamlin (b. 1917) wrote *Nine Mile Bridge,* a gritty narrative of her three years at Churchill Lake, near the Allagash headwaters, where she taught school and her husband was a game warden. Elisabeth Ogilvie

(b. 1917) came to Maine in 1944 and lived for many years on remote Ragged Island, transformed into "Bennett's Island" in her fascinating "tide trilogy": *High Tide at Noon, Storm Tide,* and *The Ebbing Tide.* Ben Ames Williams (1887-1953), the token male in this roundup of perceptive observers, in 1940 produced *Come Spring,* an epic tale of hardy pioneers founding the town of Union.

Seldom recognized for her Maine connection, antislavery crusader Harriet Beecher Stowe (1811-96) lived in Brunswick in the mid-19th century, where she wrote *The Pearl of Orr's Island,* a folkloric novel about a tiny nearby fishing community.

Mary Ellen Chase was a Maine native, born in Blue Hill in 1887. She became an English professor at Smith College in 1926 and wrote about 30 books, including some about the Bible as literature. She died in 1973.

Two books do a creditable job of excerpting Maine literature—something of a daunting task. The most comprehensive is *Maine Speaks: An Anthology of Maine Literature,* published in 1989 by the Maine Writers and Publishers Alliance. *The Quotable Moose: A Contemporary Maine Reader,* edited by Wesley McNair and published in 1994 by the University Press of New England, focuses on 20th-century authors.

A World of Her Own
For Marguerite Yourcenar (1903-87), Maine provided solitude and inspiration for subjects ranging far beyond the state's borders. Yourcenar was a longtime Northeast Harbor resident and the first woman elected to the prestigious Académie Française. Her house, now a shrine to her work, is open to the public in summer.

Essayists, Critics, and Humorists Native and Transplanted
Maine's best-known essayist is and was E.B. White (1899-1985), who bought a farm in tiny Brooklin in 1933 and continued writing for *The New Yorker. One Man's Meat,* published in 1944, is one of the best collections of his wry, perceptive writings. His legions of admirers also include two generations raised on his classic children's stories *Stuart Little, Charlotte's Web,* and *The Trumpet of the Swan.*

Now settled in Sargentville, not far from Brooklin but far from her New York ties, writer and critic Doris Grumbach (b. 1918) has written two particularly wise works from the perspective of a Maine transplant: *Fifty Days of Solitude* and *Coming into the End Zone.*

Maine's best exemplars of humorous writing are Artemus Ward (born Charles Farrar Browne; 1834-67) and John Gould (b. 1909), whose life in rural Friendship has provided grist for many a tale. Gould's hilarious columns in the *Christian Science Monitor* and his steady book output have made him the icon of Maine humor.

Pine Tree Poets
Born in Portland, Henry Wadsworth Longfellow (1807-82) is Maine's most famous poet; his marine themes clearly stem from his seashore childhood (in "My Lost Youth," he rhapsodized, "Often I think of the beautiful town/That is seated by the sea . . .").

Widely recognized in her own era, poet Celia Thaxter (1835-94) held court on Appledore Island in the Isles of Shoals, welcoming artists, authors, and musicians to her summer salon. Today, she's best known for *An Island Garden,* published in 1894 and detailing her attempts at horticultural TLC in a hostile environment.

Self-effacing Edwin Arlington Robinson (1865-1935) would probably be the first to squirm if he knew his hometown of Gardiner now organizes an annual Edwin Arlington Robinson Poetry Festival. Edna St. Vincent Millay (1892-1950) has connections to Camden, Rockland, and Union and described a stunning Camden panorama in "Renascence."

Whitehead Island, near Rockland, was the birthplace of Wilbert Snow (1883-1977). Snow went on to become president of Connecticut's Wesleyan University (his 1968 memoir, *Codline's Child,* makes fascinating reading).

A longtime resident of York, May Sarton (1912-95) approached cult status as a guru of feminist poetry and prose—as well as an articulate analyst of death and dying during her terminal illness.

Among respected Maine poets today are Philip Booth (b. 1925), a resident of Castine; William Carpenter (b. 1940), of Stockton Springs; and

Appleton's Kate Barnes (b. 1932), named Maine's Poet Laureate in 1996. Although she comes by her acclaim legitimately, Barnes is also genetically disposed, being the daughter of writers Henry Beston and Elizabeth Coatsworth.

Maine Lit. for Little Ones

Besides E.B. White's children's classics, *Stuart Little, Charlotte's Web,* and *The Trumpet of the Swan,* America's kids were also weaned on books written and illustrated by Maine island summer resident Robert McCloskey (b. 1914), notably *Time of Wonder, One Morning in Maine,* and *Blueberries for Sal.* Neck-and-neck in popularity is prolific Walpole illustrator-writer Barbara Cooney (b. 1917), whose award-winning titles include *Miss Rumphius, Island Boy,* and *Hattie and the Wild Waves.* Cooney has produced more than 100 books, and it seems as if everyone has a different favorite.

C.A. (Charles Asbury) Stephens (1844-1931) for 60 years wrote for the magazine *Youth's Companion.* In 1995, a collection of his vivid children's stories was reissued as *Stories from the Old Squire's Farm.*

Maine can also lay partial claim to Kate Douglas Wiggin (1856-1923), author of the eternally popular *Rebecca of Sunnybrook Farm;* she spent summers at Quillcote, in Hollis, west of Portland.

The Mother Lode of Maine Writing

Anyone interested in reading writing about and out of Maine should contact **Maine Writers & Publishers Alliance,** 12 Pleasant St., Brunswick 04011, tel. (207) 729-6333, fax 725-1014, an energetic networking organization founded in 1975. The membership association maintains an office/bookshop (open to the public), offers workshops for members and nonmembers, produces a monthly newsletter, and markets the work of hundreds of past and present Maine writers. Members ($30 a year) receive book and workshop discounts.

BOB RACE

ON THE ROAD
SIGHTSEEING HIGHLIGHTS

Cities, Towns, Villages
Even the dinkiest Maine hamlet has its own special character, but a handful of communities make good destinations in themselves as well as base camps for day-trips. Except for Portland—which has its own cachet—most still have a unique small-town flavor, although summer traffic sometimes stretches the space limits. Most scenic are Camden/Rockport, Blue Hill/Castine, the Kennebunks, Bar Harbor, and Rangeley. Most historic? Belfast/Searsport, Damariscotta/Newcastle, and Wiscasset, Bethel, Machias, and Greenville. For a little and a lot of everything, head for Portland.

Parks for Picnics and Easy Hikes
Best parks for kids of all ages are Bradbury Mountain State Park in Pownal, Camden Hills State Park in Camden, Lily Bay State Park on Moosehead Lake near Greenville, Cobscook Bay State Park near Eastport, Grafton Notch State Park near Bethel, Holbrook Island Sanctuary State Park in Brooksville, and Mount Blue State Park in Weld.

Mountains to Climb
For climbing challenges that range from easy to moderate to rigorous, best choices are Blue Hill Mountain in Blue Hill, Cadillac Mountain on Mount Desert Island, Mount Agamenticus in York, Mount Battie in Camden, Katahdin in Baxter State Park, Borestone Mountain Sanctuary near Monson, Table Rock near Bethel, and Tumbledown Mountain in Weld. Easiest of these is Blue Hill Mountain; toughest is Katahdin.

Beaches
Warmest water is along lakefronts—such as Sebago Lake State Park—and in southern Maine, such as Ferry Beach State Park, in Saco, and Ogunquit Beach. Scenic standouts, with chillier water, are Popham Beach State Park in Phippsburg (near Bath) and Sand Beach in Acadia National Park. On hot midsummer days (fairly infrequent in Maine), plan to arrive early at any beach—parking is at a premium.

Lighthouses Close Up
All of Maine's 64 working lighthouses have now been automated by the US Coast Guard, and none are open to the public, but their settings inevitably are spectacular, so seek 'em out. Among the easiest to approach are Cape Neddick Light (known as Nubble Light), in York; Portland Head Light, in Cape Elizabeth; Pemaquid Point Light, near Damariscotta; Mar-

shall Point Light, near Port Clyde; Owls Head Light, near Rockland; Rockland Breakwater Light; Bass Harbor Head Light, on Mount Desert Island; Hockamock Head Light, on Swans Island; and West Quoddy Head Light, near Lubec. In 1997, more than half of the working lighthouses were deeded to the Rockland-based Island Institute, whose Maine Lights Program is gradually turning over individual lights to nonprofit organizations.

Museums/Historic Sites

Maine is a mecca for fans of museums and history. See "Museums and Historic Sites" under "Arts and Entertainment," below, for a list of highlights.

BOAT TRIPS

Getting on the water is no problem in Maine. You can play mail carrier aboard the Great Pond mailboat in Belgrade Lakes or the Casco Bay mailboat in Portland; watch for whales out of Bar Harbor, Eastport, or Ogunquit; join the regular commuters on the car ferries to Islesboro, Vinalhaven, and Swans Island; or take a nostalgia trip aboard the paddlewheeler *Songo River Queen II* in Naples, the SS *Katahdin* on Moosehead Lake, or one of the antique and replica windjammer schooners sailing for 3-6 days out of Camden, Rockport, and Rockland.

A MAINE VISITOR'S TOP TEN LIST

It's a tough, thankless job to single out sightseeing highlights in Maine. But, unless you have years to spend, such a big chunk of real estate needs some whittling down to be made explorable. So the following is offered as a list of sites you can't really claim to have "done" Maine without sampling.

1. Acadia National Park. Maine's only national park, 40,000-plus acres, open all year. Drive, bike, hike, cross-country ski, or even snowshoe the park's roads and trails; canoe or kayak the lakes and ponds; swim in its chilly ocean waters; or sail the surrounding bays and harbors.

2. Monhegan Island. A car-free, carefree gem a dozen miles off the coast, reachable by boat from Port Clyde, New Harbor, and Boothbay Harbor. Pack a picnic and spend a day hiking the wooded, surf-bashed island, which has inspired artists and photographers for more than a century.

3. Portland Museum of Art. Maine's premier art museum, smack in the heart of the state's largest city. While you're at it, explore the boutiques, bistros, and bars in the surrounding Downtown Arts District and a few blocks away in the retrofitted Old Port.

4. L.L. Bean, Inc. The giant, world-famous sportswear retailer and hub of the hubbub in Freeport—Maine's outlet bonanza (second-largest outlet cluster is in Kittery, on the Maine-New Hampshire bor-

der). Bean's also has a factory outlet store in downtown Portland.

5. Kennebunkport, Camden, and Blue Hill. Okay, we're cheating a little. These are neck-and-neck on any must-see list; all have historic homes, upscale shops, and waterfront vistas to die for.

6. Portland Head Light. Cape Elizabeth landmark and Maine's oldest lighthouse (1791), at the edge of 94-acre Fort Williams Park. Great spot for an all-day family outing (don't forget your kite).

7. Kennebec River whitewater rafting. Headquartered in the area around The Forks. Licensed firms take advantage of controlled dam releases on the state's most popular rafting river.

8. Maine Maritime Museum. Ten acres of indoor and outdoor exhibits celebrating the state's nautical heritage. River cruises operate regularly throughout the summer.

9. Baxter State Park. Camping, hiking, canoeing in 200,000-plus acres of pristine wilderness owned by the people of Maine, near Millinocket. Best avoided in June, when blackflies exert ownership, annoying both man and beast.

10. Sunday River Ski Resort. The state's biggest ski and snowboard area, near Bethel, with 126 well-groomed trails.

TRAIN RIDES

The long hiatus in passenger-train service in Maine has drummed up lots of business for excursion trips. The Belfast and Moosehead Lake Railroad, headquartered in Unity, operates trips out of Unity and Belfast; the Maine Coast Railroad does roundtrips out of Wiscasset; and the Maine Narrow Gauge Railroad is "the little train that could," running very popular short trips on harborfront track in downtown Portland.

OUTDOOR RECREATION

You'll never have enough vacation to take advantage of all the outdoor recreational possibilities Maine offers in summer, fall, and winter. Below is a roundup of sites and activities; details appear in the specific regional chapters (see the Booklist for specialized recreational guides). For a uniquely Maine resource, staff members at L.L. Bean pride themselves on their knowledge of the outdoors and are, even at the height of summer, incredibly helpful. Depending on your recreational interest, stop in at the appropriate department and pick their brains.

ACADIA NATIONAL PARK

Three million visitors show up each year at Maine's only national park, and officials fret about overcrowding, but there's still plenty of room in these 40,000 or so acres for a fantastic, all-round recreational experience: camping (530 sites), hiking, rock climbing, bicycling, canoeing/kayaking, cross-country skiing, and snow-shoeing. Included within park jurisdiction are several less-crowded spaces on parts of three offshore islands and the Schoodic Peninsula, just north of the main chunk of the park. During the summer, there's an ambitious schedule of nature walks, hikes, cruises, and lecture programs (some wheelchair accessible). Canoe, kayak, and bike rentals are available in Bar Harbor. For park information call or write Acadia National Park, P.O. Box 177, Bar Harbor 04609, tel. (207) 288-3338. From May through October, the visitor center in Hulls Cove provides orientation and information; November through April, the park headquarters office (Rt. 233, same phone) serves as a scaled-down info center.

STATE PARKS

Despite midsummer overcrowding at some locations and recurring budget constraints, Maine's 28 state parks are spectacularly situated and fairly well maintained for fishing, swim-

canoeing in Baxter State Park

ming, hiking, canoeing, picnicking, birding, and camping. The state also supervises some undeveloped parks, more than a dozen state historic sites, and about half a million acres of Public Reserved Lands. For more information contact Bureau of Parks and Lands, 22 State House Station, Augusta 04333, tel. (207) 287-3821.

In 1930, Maine Governor Percival P. Baxter, determined to preserve a chunk of Maine real estate for Maine residents and posterity, began accumulating acreage—including Katahdin, Maine's highest mountain—to create Baxter State Park. Under separate jurisdiction from the state park system, this recreational wilderness covers 204,733 acres containing 46 mountain peaks and 175 miles of trails. One unpaved road (20 mph limit) traverses the park; no pets or radios are allowed; no gasoline or drinking water is available; and camping (the only way to stay in Baxter—at tentsites, lean-tos, or rustic log cabins) is carry-in, carry-out. Competition is fierce on midsummer weekends; it's pure luck to find space. The reward? Rare alpine flowers, unique rock formations, wildlife sightings, and incomparable hiking, canoeing, and photography. Day use is free for Maine residents; $8 per vehicle for nonresidents. Information: Baxter State Park Authority, 64 Balsam Dr., Millinocket 04462, tel. (207) 723-5140.

SAILING

With 5,500 miles of in-and-out coastline, several thousand offshore islands, and countless nooks and crannies for dropping anchor, Maine is a sailor's paradise. If you've brought your own yacht or chartered one here, you'll quickly discover some scenic standouts and never run out of places to go. The most popular cruising centers are Boothbay Harbor, Rockland, North Haven, Camden, Castine, Blue Hill, Northeast Harbor, and Southwest Harbor.

Start off on the right tack with the Maine sailors' bible, *A Cruising Guide to the Maine Coast, 3rd ed.,* by Hank and Jan Taft and Curtis Rindlaub, available in hardcover and paperback. Don't try to cover the whole coast; choose beginning and ending points and take the circuit in small doses.

Fog is the biggest enemy of overambitious

itineraries; the farther Down East you go (toward Canada), the sparser the facilities and the greater the likelihood of fog. One of the best cruising months is September, with crisp air, fine breezes, minimal fog, and uncrowded harbors. If you belong to a yacht club elsewhere, bring your membership card; Maine clubs offer reciprocal privileges.

If you're not lucky enough to have your own boat or enough spare change to charter one, see "Getting Afloat," below, for other ways to escape to sea.

CANOEING AND KAYAKING

Thanks to the inspiration and creativity of Native Americans, we're able to explore Maine's streams, lakes, rivers, estuaries, and coastline in canoes and kayaks. If you wish to do it on your own, you'll want to rely on three excellent resources: the *AMC River Guide: Maine, AMC Quiet Water Canoe Guide: Maine,* by Alex Wilson and John Hayes, and *Canoeing* (three regional booklets) from DeLorme Mapping. See the Booklist for details. For information on a handful of first-rate canoeing tours, see "Special-Interest Tours" under "Getting Around," below.

Best places to rent canoes are Andover, Belgrade Lakes, Bethel, Blue Hill, Brownfield, Fryeburg, Gouldsboro, Jackman, Medway and Millinocket (near Baxter State Park), Mount Desert Island, Oquossoc (near Rangeley), Portland, Rangeley, Rockport, and Rockwood (on Moosehead Lake). Kayak rentals are available in Bar Harbor, Bethel, Blue Hill, Boothbay Harbor, Corea, Damariscotta, Fryeburg, Gouldsboro, Kennebunkport, Medway, Orrs Island, Peaks Island, Portland, Rockport, and Rockwood.

Native Trails, Inc., a nonprofit organization spearheaded by Mike Krepner and based in Waldoboro, is working to trace, map, and recreate ancient Native American canoe routes throughout Maine, primarily in the northeastern corner. Long overgrown and nearly lost to history, the routes are still rudimentary. Some maps already are available; contact Box 240, Waldoboro 04572, tel. (207) 832-5255.

Each summer, L.L. Bean sponsors two weekend-long paddling schools for all skill levels;

neither program is cheap, but you're certain to increase your dexterity and meet lots of like-minded enthusiasts. Canoe Camp is held on Moose Pond in Bridgton in mid-June. The Atlantic Coast Sea Kayak Symposium occurs in mid-July at Maine Maritime Academy in Castine. For information on both, contact the L.L. Bean Outdoor Discovery Program, tel. (800) 341-4341, ext. 6666 (weekdays only).

Maine Sport Outfitters, Rt. 1, Rockport, tel. (800) 722-0826 or (207) 236-8797, operates a sea-kayaking program that includes six-day island camping trips, three-day family trips, five-day teen adventures, and shorter instructional trips. Beginners are welcome, and you can even rent camping gear at the store.

Maine is also, of course, the home of the Old Town Canoe Company, builders of classic canoes since the turn of the century. Even if a canoe isn't on your shopping list, you can still enjoy a visit to the Old Town Canoe Factory Outlet, 130 N. Main St., Old Town 04468, tel. (207) 827-5513, just north of Bangor.

WHITEWATER RAFTING

From late April to mid-October, fleets of multi-person self-bailing rafts operated by more than two dozen outfitters bump and grind down the Kennebec, Dead, and Penobscot Rivers in western Maine's mountains. Begun in the mid-1970s, whitewater rafting has become a multimillion-dollar industry—much of it headquartered in and around The Forks, a nondescript hamlet at the junction of the Kennebec and the Dead. All outfitters are state-licensed and state-monitored, and all three rivers are dam-controlled; two have scheduled daily water releases during the season. Trips require busing to put-in sites. Since The Forks is about a three hours' drive north of Portland, and rafting trips get going early, consider spending pre- and post-rafting nights nearby.

Trip options range from half-day runs (most popular) to multi-day, three-river experiences. All offer real upper-arm workouts, hearty riverside cookouts, and post-trip video reruns. Best prices are midweek. On spring and fall trips (also cheaper), wetsuits may be mandatory (rentals are available). Spring brings wildest (and iciest) water, fall (late September and early October) the best scenery. Several outfitters offer adventure packages, combining rafting with mountain biking, hiking, or rock climbing; a few also have year-round sports facilities.

Rank beginners and family groups (although no kids under 12) should opt for the 12-mile Kennebec River trip, starting just below Harris Station (a hydroelectric dam) and ending at The Forks. Four miles of Class IV rapids through the Kennebec Gorge—including the quaintly named Magic Falls—precede a rather leisurely coast downstream to the takeout.

The thrills multiply on the 14-mile Penobscot River trip (no kids under 15), starting below McKay Station (another hydro dam), heading into Ripogenus Gorge, and negotiating Class IV and V rapids named Exterminator, Bone Cruncher, and Cribwork. Beyond are Class III and IV rapids, with some quiet spots in between, en route to the takeout, at Pockwockamus Falls. To avoid long bus rides, several outfitters based in The Forks have established secondary operations (including lodgings, dining facilities, and hot tubs) in the Pockwockamus neighborhood.

Even more challenging, especially in May, is the 16-mile Dead River trip, with plenty of Class IV and V whitewater. Dam releases are less frequent on the Dead—only two or three times a month—so not all outfitters offer Dead River trips.

Companies with top reputations are **Northern Outdoors,** oldest in Maine, Rt. 201, P.O. Box 100, The Forks 04985, tel. (207) 663-4466 or (800) 765-7238, fax (207) 663-2244; **New England Outdoor Center,** Rice Farm Rd., Millinocket 04462, tel. (207) 723-5438 or (800) 766-7238; **Unicorn Expeditions,** Rt. 201, Lake Parlin, Jackman 04945, tel. (207) 668-7629 or (800) 864-2676, fax (207) 668-7627; and **Wilderness Expeditions,** based at The Birches on Moosehead Lake, P.O. Box 41, Rockwood 04478, tel. (800) 825-9453, fax (207) 534-8835. **Raft Maine,** an industry association comprising 10 or so rafting companies, maintains a reservations clearinghouse at (800) 723-8633. Cost ranges are $65-114 per person on the Kennebec, $80-114 on the Dead, and $75-114 on the Penobscot.

SWIMMING

Southern Maine's beaches, stretching from York to South Portland, provide the state's best saltwater swimming and sunning spots. Some beaches are municipal, some are parts of state parks. Remember that the Atlantic water is chilly but warms up (relatively speaking) as the tide comes in. Water temperatures are highest in August, but the closer you get to Canada, the colder you'll find the water. Sand Beach, in Acadia National Park, gets several stars for its setting—but none for water temperature.

Warmer water is a better bet in the state's countless freshwater lakes and ponds. Several of the best swimming spots are within state parks. Outdoor municipal swimming pools and indoor YMCA and health-club pools draw crowds year-round.

FISHING AND HUNTING

The best general reference on hunting and fishing is the *Maine Guide to Hunting and Fishing,* a 50-plus-page booklet published annually by the Maine Publicity Bureau, P.O. Box 2300, Hallowell 04347, tel. (207) 623-0363, and containing articles, regulations, and ads for lodgings, restaurants, and gear. For copies of official regulations, contact the **Maine Department of Inland Fisheries and Wildlife,** 284 State St., 41 State House Station, Augusta 04333, tel. (207) 287-8000; recorded seasonal information: tel. (207) 287-8003.

In Maine, recreational fishing can involve anything from dangling a baited line off a creaky wharf to fly-fishing remote inland streams to heading offshore aboard a sportfishing "party boat." No license is needed for saltwater fishing. Adult (16 and over) freshwater fishing licenses for nonresidents of Maine cost $9 for one day, $21 for three days, $34 for seven days, and $50 for a season pass. Fees for noncitizens of the United States ("aliens" in the regulations) are higher—a season pass, for example, runs $70.

Unless you know someone who can show you the ropes, the best way to experience Maine's fishing and/or hunting possibilities is to book in at one of Maine's several dozen sporting camps, where you can get information, swap stories with kindred spirits, and perhaps sign on with a Registered Maine Guide—a licensed specialist who'll provide a boat, gear, and expertise. Some guides operate independently, some work with sporting-camp owners or outfitters. For a list of available guides, and the services they offer, contact the **Maine Professional Guides Association,** P.O. Box 847, Augusta 04332, tel. (207) 785-2061.

A small-game hunting license (permitting hunting of all species except deer, bear, turkey, moose, raccoon, and bobcat) costs $55 for any nonresident 16 and older, $70 for noncitizens.

BICYCLING

As elsewhere, mountain biking and bicycle touring in Maine mushroomed in the 1990s. While Maine's Department of Transportation struggles to keep pace with the demand for roadway bike lanes and multiuse offroad trails, commercial operators have scrambled to carve out mountain-bike parks—particularly at Sunday River and Sugarloaf/USA, western Maine's major ski resorts. Despite the heightened interest in touring, there are still no safe roadside routes connecting southern and northern Maine —or, for that matter, coastal and western Maine. Certain areas, such as Mount Desert Island, have extensive bike-lane networks, but most of the state's roads are narrow, with average-to-awful shoulders. Increasingly popular for easy, mostly level cycling are the ferry-connected offshore islands: Vinalhaven, Chebeague, Cliff, Islesboro, North Haven, Swans, and Peaks. Island roads are narrow and sometimes unpaved, but at least traffic is far lighter than on mainland byways.

Leading the charge for user-friendly cycling, and acting as Maine's bicycling clearinghouses, are the **Bicycle Coalition of Maine,** P.O. Box 5275, Augusta 04332, tel. (207) 865-3636, and **Bicycle Transportation Alliance of Portland,** P.O. Box 4506, Portland 04112. Both organizations have produced several carefully researched, inexpensive bike-route maps for Mid-Coast and southern Maine. To contact Maine members of the **League of American Bicyclists,** call (207) 772-1616.

Bike shops and bike clubs around the state sponsor group rides, usually on summer evenings and weekends. Some are scheduled, some impromptu; some require shuttling to starting points; and some combine cycling and socializing. Best source of information for rides and races north of Portland is the flyer produced by the Maine Freewheelers Bicycle Club, P.O. Box 2037, Bangor 04402. Most bike shops have copies. Club membership is only $10 a year, but nonmembers are welcome to participate in the many activities.

Best places for bike rentals are Bar Harbor, Bath, Bethel, Brewer, Camden, Kennebunkport, Lewiston, Ogunquit, Orono, Portland, Rockport, Searsport, and Southwest Harbor.

An annual ride of passage for cyclists is the 180-mile **Trek Across Maine: Sunday River to the Sea,** a three-day, pedal-at-your-own-pace marathon from Bethel to Rockland, benefiting the American Lung Association of Maine (ALAM). Drawing nearly 2,000 cyclists of all ages, the scenic trek, in early June, wins high praises for its top-notch organization. Registration ($40) begins early in the year, and participants have to guarantee minimum pledges of $350 (higher pledges earn incentive prizes). For information contact ALAM, 122 State St., Augusta 04330, tel. (800) 458-6472, fax (207) 626-2919.

HIKING

Maine's pioneer eco-tourist, Henry David Thoreau, was a big believer in "going afoot," and who's to disagree when thousands of miles of hiking trails await? You can stroll the shorelines, wander the woods, bushwhack in the boonies, and conquer Katahdin. There's no central clearinghouse for hiking information, but a couple of contacts and a couple of specialized publications can provide more than enough dope.

Best hiking contact for **Acadia National Park** is the park's visitor center, P.O. Box 177, Bar Harbor 04609, tel. (207) 288-3338. For state parks and public lands, contact the **Maine Bureau of Parks and Lands,** 22 State House Station, Augusta 04333, tel. (207) 287-3821 (it has hiking maps for state parks). Dozens of spectacular hiking sites come under the jurisdiction of

The Nature Conservancy, 14 Maine St., Fort Andross, Brunswick 04011, tel. (207) 729-5181, fax 729-4118, and the **Maine Audubon Society,** 118 US1, P.O. Box 6009, Falmouth 04105, tel. (207) 781-2330, fax 781-6185. Both are membership organizations, but their properties are open to nonmembers. Ask Maine Audubon for its schedule of moderately priced, always excellent in-state field trips. They're very popular, so well-in-advance reservations are necessary.

Best hiking reference books are *50 Hikes in the Maine Mountains,* by Cloe Chunn, *50 Hikes in Southern and Coastal Maine,* by John Gibson, and two Appalachian Mountain Club (AMC) publications: *Maine Mountain Guide* and *Nature Walks in Southern Maine,* by Jan Collins and Joe McCarthy. Other good resources include *Hikes in and around Maine's Lake Region,* by Marita Wiser; *Hiking* (three regional booklets), from DeLorme Mapping; *A Walk in the Park: Acadia's Hiking Guide,* by Tom St. Germain; and *Katahdin: A Guide to Baxter State Park & Katahdin,* by Stephen Clark.

GOLF

You can tee off at more than 125 golf courses in Maine—along the shore, on islands, and deep in the mountains. There's lots of variety here. An informal poll lists the most scenic courses as Kebo Valley (in Bar Harbor, the nation's eighth oldest), Sugarloaf/USA (Carrabassett Valley), Mingo Springs (Rangeley), Point Sebago (Casco), and Samoset Resort (Rockport). The same poll lists the toughest as The Woodlands (private, in Falmouth), Samoset Resort, Kebo Valley, Sable Oaks (South Portland), Martindale (also private, in Auburn), and Sugarloaf/USA. Best information sources are *Maine's Golf Newspaper,* a free tabloid published monthly during the season, and *Maine Golf Inc.* magazine, published 10 times a year. Both are available in sporting-goods stores, pro shops, and some bookstores. The official **Maine State Golf Association** is at P.O. Box 419, Auburn 04212, tel. (207) 795-6742, fax 784-8803.

If lousy weather sets in and you're in the Portland area, head for Fore Season Golf, 1037 Forest Ave., Portland 04103, tel. (207) 797-

8835, an indoor facility with computerized golf simulators where you can play virtual golf at any of 17 North American PGA-tour courses. A good shot earns you applause from a sound-effects machine. It's open daily 6 a.m.-1 a.m., year-round.

OTHER SUMMER ACTIVITIES

The mountains of western Maine's Oxford County are pockmarked with disused quarries just waiting for enthusiastic rockhounds. The best source of maps, information, tools, and gear is area landmark **Perham's of West Paris,** Rts. 26 and 219, P.O. Box 280, West Paris 04289, tel. (800) 371-4367, open every day but Thanksgiving and Christmas. They'll give you free quarry maps, sell you equipment, and point you in the right direction. (Skip quarry areas during hunting season; hunting is allowed there.) You can also buy gold-panning gear and head for the Swift River in Byron—best locale for sifting out bits of the precious metal. Don't get overeager, though; the prize nuggets have long since been retrieved. A helpful guide is *A Collector's Guide to Maine Mineral Localities,* by W.B. Thompson et al.

SPECTATOR SPORTS

Portland is the best spot for professional sports, since it's home to the **Portland Sea Dogs,** farm team of the Florida Marlins baseball club, and the **Portland Pirates,** farm team of the Washington Capitols ice-hockey club. The Sea Dogs play early April-early Sept. at Hadlock Field, 271 Park Ave., Portland 04102. For a home-game schedule and ticket info, call (207) 874-9300. Home ice for the Pirates, who play throughout the winter, is the 8,700-seat Cumberland County Civic Center, 1 Civic Center Sq., Portland 04101. Schedule and ticket info: tel. (207) 828-4665.

During the winter, basketball is the game of choice, played by high school and college athletes in every corner of the state. University of Maine ice-hockey and basketball teams have garnered tons of awards and tons of loyal fans. The UMaine women's basketball team has an even bigger following than the men's team.

Check sports pages in the *Portland Press Herald* and the *Bangor Daily News* for full schedules of games.

SKIING AND SNOWBOARDING

In the winter of 1870-71, a handful of Swedish immigrants in Aroostook County's New Sweden introduced the sport of skiing, and it's been downhill ever since. Maine now has two major ski resorts—**Sunday River Ski Resort,** in Bethel, and **Sugarloaf/USA,** in Carrabassett Valley (both operate under the umbrella of the giant American Skiing Company). You can check them out on-line at www.sundayriver.com or www.sugarloaf.com, respectively; you'll find trail maps, skiing advice, and information on weather and snow conditions, accommodations, and Internet browser discounts. Both resorts are full-service, year-round destinations, with lots of lodgings, restaurants, ski and gift shops, instruction, and entertainment.

A dozen good medium-size and small ski areas specialize in child-friendliness and reasonable lift prices in Auburn, Bridgton, Camden, Farmington, Greenville, Island Falls, Locke Mills, Mars Hill, Presque Isle, Rangeley, and Skowhegan. Ski areas with **night skiing** are Camden Snow Bowl (Camden), Eaton Mountain (Skowhegan), Lost Valley (Auburn), and Shawnee Peak (Bridgton).

Cross-country skiing has taken on a life of its own in Maine, especially in years when the weather gods cooperate. Sugarloaf has its own Ski Touring Center, and the privately owned Sunday River Inn Ski Touring Center supplements the downhill and snowboarding facilities at Sunday River Ski Resort. Both centers rent skis, offer lessons, and have miles of mapped and groomed trails of varying difficulty. In the winters when snow piles up along the coast (not every year), there's no more splendid cross-country spot than Acadia National Park, where trails follow more than 50 miles of carriage roads through woods, across stone bridges, and along seaview ledges. For information about Acadia snow conditions, call (207) 288-3338.

The **Maine Nordic Ski Council,** P.O. Box 645, Bethel 04217, tel. (207) 824-3976, an industry association, produces an annual brochure with info on nearly 20 ski centers in the southern and western parts of the state. For snow conditions Nov.-April, call (800) 754-9263.

L.L. Bean annually holds a two-day **cross-country ski festival** at Gould Academy in Bethel the first weekend in February. Included in the minimal registration fee (kids 14 and under are free) are workshops, lectures, and demos by Olympians, authors, and other noted experts. Beginners and experts, kids and adults—there's fun and help for everyone. Bring your own skis or rent when you get there. Preregistration is required. Call (800) 341-4341, ext. 6666 weekdays.

Sugarloaf, Sunday River, Ski Mt. Abram, and Saddleback (in Rangeley) have developed **snowboard** parks with daunting challenges. Sunday River has a leftover Detroit city bus for younger (and the growing number of older) snowboarders to bonk off; Sugarloaf has buried a bunch of old Saabs for the same purpose. The phenomenal growth in snowboarding since the late 1980s means dramatic changes lie ahead at all of the ski areas, with new gimmicks continually being added to attract neophytes and satisfy daredevils. Stay tuned.

SNOWMOBILING

Once considered a rough-and-ready, exclusive pursuit for hard-driving, hard-drinking good ol' boys, snowmobiling (or snowsledding) is, after snowboarding, one of Maine's fastest-growing winter sports. Development of ultraprotective sportswear, establishment of the Maine Snowmobile Association, and maintenance of an astonishing, 10,000-mile trail network have opened the pastime to a far broader clientele. Park rangers, preachers, schoolkids, and eight-to-fivers have long commuted by snowmobile in the North Woods, but weekends used to bring out a different species. Now everyone's at it seven days a week. As the snow gets deeper, motels fill up, their parking lots overrun with the machines. All snowmobiles must be registered by the state; in 1996, registrations reached an all-time high of 73,000.

Best and most scenic locales for snowmobiling are Rockwood and Greenville (both on Moosehead Lake), Millinocket (next to Baxter State Park), Jackman, Bethel, and Rangeley, where snowmobile rentals, restaurants, and accommodations are all available. Aroostook County, at the top of Maine, is prime snowmobiling country—often with the best snow in the state—but you'll spend a long time going and coming.

Serving as the clearinghouse and advocacy group for nearly 300 local clubs is the **Maine Snowmobile Association (MSA),** 3 Sewall St., P.O. Box 77, Augusta 04330, tel. (207) 622-6983. For up-to-date snow-condition info Dec.-March, call the MSA hotline: (800) 880-7669.

OTHER WINTER SPORTS

Most every corner of Maine has a popular spot for **ice-skating,** and some communities make a real effort to keep the ice clear and maintain smooth skating surfaces. There's no central information source; see the regional chapters for recommendations.

Snowshoes—awkward-looking, functional footwear originally made of wood and hides—have been around at least since the Stone Age, allowing access through the deepest snowdrifts; in northern Maine's pre-snowmobile days, snowshoes were essential to survival. Nowadays, however, **snowshoeing** has gained new popularity as a low-impact, low-cost winter sport. No lift tickets needed, no fancy gear required (recreational snowshoes—metal or wood—cost $100-150). L.L. Bean's Outdoor Discovery Program, tel. (800) 341-4341, ext. 6666, runs snowshoeing courses, as does the Sugarloaf/USA Ski Touring Center, tel. (207) 237-6830. Both rent snowshoes, and so does Norumbega Outfitters, 58 Fore St., Portland 04101, tel. (207) 773-0910.

The Camden Snow Bowl ski area has Maine's only **toboggan chute.** Because of unpredictable snow and ice in this coastal town, be sure to call ahead for conditions—the 400-foot speedway ends on Hosmer Pond, and if it isn't frozen, there's no go. You'll need to have your own toboggan (preferably a wooden one). Best time to come is the first weekend in February, when the **National Toboggan Championships** are held here. For details, call (207) 236-3438 or 236-4404.

Once dubbed "a cold version of shuffleboard," the Scottish national sport of curling has dozens of enthusiastic supporters at Maine's only curling rink, the **Belfast Curling Club,** operating from early November to early April. Leagues play regularly on weeknights, and the club holds tournaments (called bonspiels) and open houses several times during the season. Info: Belfast Curling Club, Belmont Ave., Rt. 3, Belfast 04915, tel. (207) 338-9851 (rink) or 338-5900 (chamber of commerce).

ARTS AND ENTERTAINMENT

Next to ecotourism, cultural tourism (for lack of a better term) has become Maine's focus in the 1990s. And why not? The state boasts enough arts-related sites and activities to keep residents and visitors on the move from New Year's Day to Christmas. The flavor varies a bit from summer to winter and back again—due partly to demand, partly to weather—but unless you'd rather be navel-gazing in the North Woods, shunning the outside world, you can tap into a mix of activities and have no problem staying busy.

MUSEUMS AND HISTORIC SITES

If museums and history intrigue you, you'll have no dearth of options in Maine. The best museums and sites for **kids** are the Children's Museum of Maine, in Portland; the Maine State Museum, in Augusta; and Fort Knox State Historic Site, near Bucksport.

Best **art** museums are the Portland Museum of Art, the Farnsworth Art Museum in Rockland, and the art museums at Bowdoin College in Brunswick and Colby College in Waterville.

Best **marine** museums are the Maine Maritime Museum, in Bath, and the Penobscot Marine Museum (Maine's oldest), in Searsport. The Owls Head Transportation Museum in Owls Head, near Rockland, focuses on wheeled and winged vehicles—it's the best such collection in the state and even beyond.

Maine's most **eclectic** and **one-of-a-kind** museums—where every display case holds a surprise—include the Nylander Museum, in Caribou; the Wilson Museum, in Castine; and the L.C. Bates Museum, in Hinckley.

Unique **history** museums include the 1770 Burnham Tavern, in Machias; the 1754 Old Fort Western, in Augusta; the 1870s Norlands Living History Center, in Livermore; and the 1885 Franklin D. Roosevelt Cottage, on Campobello Island, near Lubec. The Old York Historical Society has a sprawling collection of historic museum buildings.

Self-explanatory are the **collections** in the Jones Museum of Glass and Ceramics, near Sebago Lake; the Webb Museum of Vintage Fashion, in Island Falls; the Lumberman's Museum, in Patten; the Seashore Trolley Museum, in Kennebunkport; the Wendell Gilley Museum of Bird Carving, in Southwest Harbor; and the Peary-MacMillan Arctic Museum, at Bowdoin College, in Brunswick. Music boxes fill the Musical Wonder House in Wiscasset, and operatic costumes fill the Nordica Homestead Museum, in Farmington (birthplace of early-20th-century opera diva Madame Lillian Nordica). The Shaker Museum, in New Gloucester, represents the life and work of the nation's only remaining Shaker colony.

The state publishes the useful free annual booklet *Museums and Historic Homes;* for a copy, contact the Maine Publicity Bureau, P.O. Box 2300, Hallowell 04347, tel. (207) 623-0363.

ART AND CRAFTS

Ask an artist why she or he creates in Maine and you'll hear, "It's the light," "It's the setting," or "It's the support network" (you *won't* often hear, "It's the money"). Whatever the reason, the creative juices generate superb work that fills galleries large and small from Kittery to Fort Kent. The best statewide resource for finding nearly 200 studios, shops, and galleries is the free annual *Maine Cultural Guide,* published by the Maine Crafts Association, P.O. Box 228, Deer Isle 04627, tel. (207) 348-9943. Included in the 80-page booklet is a month-by-month calendar of shows, workshops, and related events.

Two educational institutions that draw recognized craftspeople from around the country and beyond are the **Haystack Mountain School of Crafts,** P.O. Box 518, Deer Isle 04627, tel. (207) 348-2306, which offers courses for talented artisans in a huge variety of media, and the **Watershed Center for the Ceramic Arts,** 19 Brick Hill Rd., Newcastle 04553, tel. (207) 882-6075, which has residencies, lectures, and studio space for professionals as well as community pottery courses for adults, children, and families.

THEATER

Professional and semiprofessional companies and community troupes command stages throughout the year, but summer brings out most of the thespians and their audiences. Among the best and longest-running summer theaters (with emphases on musicals) are Ogunquit Playhouse, in Ogunquit; Maine State Music Theater, in Brunswick; and Lakewood Theater, in Madison (near Skowhegan). Shakespeare and other literary lights take center stage at the Theater at Monmouth (between Lewiston and Augusta), where Italianate Cumston Hall provides the perfect setting for Shakespeare productions. Each summer, Acadia Repertory Company presents a range of contemporary and classic plays in the idyllic village of Somesville (near Bar Harbor). Recently restored after decades of decline is the historic Deertrees Theater, in Harrison, a comfortably rustic performance space for plays and concerts.

Maine is home, too, to many community theater groups using nonprofessional yet extremely capable talent. Among the best are Cold Comfort Productions, in Castine; Camden Civic Theatre, in Camden; Belfast Maskers, in Belfast; Gaslight Theater, in Hallowell; and the Sanford Maine Stage Company, in Sanford.

During the winter, Bangor's Penobscot Theatre enters its real season, and in Portland, the options include Portland Stage Company, Mad Horse Theatre, Oak Street Theatre, Portland Players, and the Lyric Theater (the latter two perform on weekends in South Portland). The Children's Theatre of Maine also performs weekends in Portland.

Also during the winter, the drama departments of Maine's universities and colleges mount theatrical performances. Check newspaper listings for schedules at the University of Maine campuses (especially Orono, Portland, and Machias) and at Bowdoin, Bates, and Colby Colleges.

DANCE

Although performance dance groups have sprung up in spots, and Bates College puts on a nationally acclaimed dance festival each summer in Lewiston, Portland is the state's center of dance, boasting the contemporary Ram Island Dance Company and classical companies such as the Maine State Ballet and the Portland Ballet. Check listings for their performance schedules.

If you're more interested in participating than spectating, Maine Ballroom Dance, 614A Congress St., tel. (207) 773-0002, holds weekly dances in Portland—and a renewed interest in ballroom dancing has spurred classes and dances in other parts of the state.

Check newspapers, bulletin boards, and telephone poles for notices of contradances—once described as "brief whirling encounters of the safest kind." Vaguely comparable to square or line dancing, old-fashioned/new-fashioned contradances involve a chunk of exercise, a bit of potluck, and a chance to schmooze with likeminded souls. Held in town, American Legion, and grange halls, most are "chem-free." Dress up or down and get into the spirit. The best statewide information source is Down East Friends of the Folk Arts (DEFFA), RR 2, Box 192, Ellsworth 04605, which publishes the monthly *DEFFA Newsletter,* listing dozens of contradances, Scottish dances, and folk music events.

MUSIC

Scheduled and impromptu concerts—jazz, bluegrass, classical, rock, folk, funk, zydeco, and difficult to categorize—occur statewide throughout the summer. (The pace slows slightly in winter but definitely doesn't stop.) Best summertime options for classical music are the chamber-music series in Rockport (Bay Chamber Concerts), Machias (Machias Bay Chamber Concerts), and Harrison (Sebago/Long Lake Chamber Music Festival); and the concert series in Bar Harbor (Arcady Music Festival, Bar Harbor Music Festival), Blue Hill (Kneisel Hall), and Hancock (Le Domaine School). In the Portland area, the Portland String Quartet and the Portland Symphony Orchestra perform year-round, sometimes alfresco in summer. The Portland Concert Association and Rockport Bay Chamber Concerts present regular winter series; tickets are by subscription, but individual tickets usually are available.

For a unique musical immersion, plan well ahead and book a week at **Quisisana,** on the shores of western Maine's spectacular Kezar Lake. Aspiring (and ultra-talented) musicians earn their keep by day and perform opera, piano concerts, and more each night in the lakeside music hall—much to the delight of enthusiastic guests at the decades-old summer resort. Even the rustic cabins have musical names. One newspaper described Quisisana as "Where Mozart Goes on Vacation." Quisisana, Center Lovell 04016, tel. (207) 925-3500 or, off-season, P.O. Box 142, Larchmont, NY 10538, tel. (914) 833-0293.

NIGHTLIFE

For a year-round concentration of live entertainment and nightlife, Portland is the place to be. On any given night (and especially on weekends), you can find jazz, blues, folk, hip-hop, oldies, rock, country, grunge, and all the latest buzzword music styles—plus comedy improv, karaoke, poetry slams, and "exotic dance" spots. Best sources for entertainment ads and listings are *Casco Bay Weekly* and *Face Magazine,* free tabloids available in shops and restaurants throughout the Portland area. (*Face* appears every other week.) The tabloid *Go,* a supplement in Thursday's *Portland Press Herald,* also carries a listing of club and disco schedules.

To find the best-known club outside Portland, you'll have to go all the way to Blue Hill, about 135 miles northeast, where the Left Bank Bakery & Cafe, tel. (207) 374-2201, showcases top talent in folk, jazz, and blues.

FESTIVALS, FAIRS, AND OTHER EVENTS

While there is a great concentration of activity in summer, hundreds of special events occur all year long in Maine. In addition to an endless round of concerts, plays, art shows, and other cultural offerings, here's a sampling of the most intriguing, enduring, and enjoyable festivals and fairs that turn up on Maine's annual calendar. These and lots more are described in the regional sections. Also check calendars of events in free tabloids and on local bulletin boards for other goings-on. A good way to sample local flavor is to attend commemorations—especially centennials—of town foundings, town separations, and other noteworthy events. Everyone turns out, enthusiasm is contagious, and the eats are always homemade. If you're basing your itinerary on specific events, be sure to call ahead to confirm dates and times.

January
Down East Sled Dog Race, Greenville, tel. (207) 695-2702; **Torchlight Parade,** Saddleback Mountain (Rangeley), tel. (207) 864-5671; **White White World Week,** Sugarloaf/USA, tel. (207) 237-2000.

February
Heritage Day, Dr. Moses Mason House, Bethel, tel. (207) 824-2908; **National Toboggan Championships,** Camden, tel. (207) 236-4404; **Winter Carnival,** Caribou, tel. (207) 498-6156.

March
Norlands Maple Days (maple syrup festivities), Livermore, tel. (207) 897-4366; **Sno-Fest,** Jackman, tel. (207) 668-4171.

April
Aucocisco (ecosensitive 10-day festival celebrating Casco Bay), Portland, tel. (207) 772-6828; **Fishermen's Festival,** Boothbay Harbor, tel. (207) 633-2353; **Piscataquis River Canoe Race,** Guilford to Dover-Foxcroft, tel. (207) 564-7533.

May
Fiddlehead Festival (celebration of the fiddlehead-fern harvest), Unity, tel. (207) 948-3131;

Memorial Day celebrations—parades, dinners, craft fairs—statewide; **Moosemainea** (a month-long tribute to the favorite local beast, including a census of sightings), Greenville, tel. (207) 695-2702.

June

Acadian Festival, Madawaska, tel. (207) 728-7000; **La Kermesse** (Franco-American festival), Biddeford, tel. (207) 282-1567; **Lupine Festival,** Eastport, tel. (207) 853-4644; **Midsummer Festival,** New Sweden, tel. (207) 896-3370, (commemorating the town's Old World heritage); **National Trails Day,** statewide; **Old Port Festival,** Portland, tel. (207) 772-6828; **Salmon Falls Day,** South Berwick, tel. (207) 384-5030; **Taste of the Port,** Kennebunkport, tel. (207) 967-0857; **Windjammer Days,** Boothbay Harbor, tel. (207) 633-2353.

July

Central Maine Egg Festival, Pittsfield, tel. (207) 487-5102; **Crown of Maine Hot Air Balloon Festival,** Caribou, tel. (207) 498-6156; **Downeast Dulcimer and Folk Harp Festival,** Bar Harbor, tel. (207) 288-5653; **Fourth of July celebrations,** statewide, but best locations include Bar Harbor, Bath, Bethel, Boothbay Harbor, Eastport, Greenville, Jonesport, Rangeley, Thomaston, and York; **Full Circle Summer Fair** (organic, ecosensitive, artsy, New Age-ish festival of crafts, music, and food sponsored by

Radio Station WERU, sometimes known as Radio Free Spirit), Union, tel. (207) 374-2313; **Maine Potato Blossom Festival,** Fort Fairfield, tel. (207) 472-3802; **Mollyockett Day** (town-wide festivities commemorating a Native American maiden), Bethel, tel. (207) 824-2282; **Moxie Festival** (highlighting the Depression-era soft drink Moxie), Lisbon Falls, tel. (207) 783-2249; **Schooner Days** (celebrating traditional sailing vessels), Rockland, tel. (207) 596-0376; **World's Fair** (a tongue-in-cheek country fair), North Waterford, tel. (207) 287-3221; **Yarmouth Clam Festival,** Yarmouth, tel. (207) 846-3984.

August

Bangor State Fair, Bangor, tel. (207) 942-9000; **Great Falls Balloon Festival,** Lewiston, tel. (207) 783-2249; **International Festival,** Calais (cooperative activities with St. Stephen, New Brunswick), tel. (207) 454-2308; **Maine Antiques Festival,** Union, tel. (207) 563-1013; **Maine Festival of the Arts** (showcasing the best of Maine's visual and performing arts), Brunswick, tel. (207) 772-9012; **Maine Highland Games** (Scottish festival), Brunswick, tel. (207) 549-7451 or 725-8797; **Maine Lobster Festival,** Rockland, tel. (207) 596-0376; **Olde Bristol Days** (great small-town celebration), Pemaquid Peninsula, tel. (207) 563-8340; **Rangeley Lakes Blueberry Festival,** Rangeley, tel. (207) 864-5571; **Riverfest,** Kennebunkport, tel. (207) 967-0857; **Sankofa Festival** (multicultural arts and crafts), Belfast, tel.

Fourth of July parades, like Rockport's, are folksy, small-town affairs.

(207) 338-5900; **Skowhegan Log Days** (commemorating the lumbering tradition), Skowhegan, tel. (207) 474-3621; **Wild Blueberry Festival,** Machias, tel. (207) 255-4402.

September
Blue Hill Fair, Blue Hill, tel. (207) 374-9976; **Common Ground Country Fair** (Maine's best country fair, focusing on environmental consciousness and 100% organic everything), Unity, tel. (207) 622-3118; **Eastport Salmon Festival,** Eastport, tel. (207) 853-4644; **International Seaplane Fly-In,** Greenville, tel. (207) 695-2702; **Laudholm Trust Nature Crafts Festival** (high-quality juried craft fair), Wells, tel. (207) 646-1555.

October
Fall Festival, Camden, tel. (207) 236-4404; **Fryeburg Fair** (the state's biggest, best, and most popular agricultural fair), Fryeburg, tel. (207) 935-3268.

November
Christmas craft fairs, statewide, in locations such as Augusta, Bangor, Bath, Boothbay Harbor, Farmington, Fort Kent, Lewiston, Machias, Portland, and Waterville; **Maine Brewers' Festival,** Portland; **Thanksgiving Dinner at Sunday River** (free with lift ticket), Bethel, tel. (207) 824-3000, ext. 374.

December
Chester Greenwood Day (commemorating the inventor of earmuffs), Farmington, tel. (207) 778-4215; **Christmas by the Sea,** Camden/Rockport/Lincolnville, tel. (207) 236-4404; **Christmas Prelude,** Kennebunk/Kennebunkport, tel. (207) 967-0857; **New Year's Eve in Portland** (the best place in the state to ring in the New Year), tel. (207) 772-9012.

ACCOMMODATIONS

Depending on your lifestyle, your wallet, and the condition of your back, getting a night's rest in Maine can entail anything from luxurious resorts to the remotest of campsites.

B&BS AND COUNTRY INNS

Nearly 500 licensed bed and breakfasts—from cozy mom-and-pop enterprises to antiques-filled mansions—welcome visitors to Maine. If you don't mind sacrificing a bit of privacy in your comings and goings, B&Bs are prime venues for swapping tips on sightseeing, restaurants, and lodging; bumping into former colleagues; or launching lasting friendships or even new careers.

Although American B&Bs are European in inspiration, there are differences: prices are relatively higher here than in Europe; here, you're more likely to find a private bath; here, too, many hosts are not area natives, though they compensate with congeniality and enthusiasm for their adopted turf. Most hosts pride themselves on their breakfasts, which can be continental, buffet-style, or sumptuous (and anything-with-

blueberries ranks as the preferred specialty du jour).

The round-the-clock demands of operating a B&B lead to burnout for hosts who overdo it, so don't be surprised if an establishment has changed hands by the time you arrive. A sign posted at one B&B sums it up well: Open 24 hours year-round. Additional services: caterer, chauffeur, moneylender, tutor, nurse, seamstress, psychologist, laundress, etc. Consider "etc." the operative word. The longest-lived B&Bs hire inn-sitters, night managers, or at least enough staff to share the chores. Few allow pets or smoking indoors, many are not equipped for small children, and few have in-room TVs or telephones. When planning overnight stays, be considerate; if your schedule demands a very early departure, for instance, look for more anonymous lodgings where you won't disturb hosts or other guests.

Throughout Maine, you'll also find superb specimens of country inns—and not just in rural areas. In general, while you're likely to run into the same congeniality in the inns that exists at B&Bs, and while prices tend to be in the same range, country inns often have more rooms and staff, and most rooms have private baths. Most inns also have dining rooms open to the public for dinner and sometimes lunch.

Prices for a high-season double occupancy room at a Maine B&B or inn range from about $40 to more than $200. About half of Maine's B&Bs are closed Nov.-May; except in the ski areas around Bethel and Kingfield, the year-round operations usually have reduced rates in winter. For a free copy of the *Maine Guide to Inns & Bed & Breakfasts,* an annual booklet covering nearly 300 establishments, contact the Maine Publicity Bureau, P.O. Box 2300, Hallowell 04347, tel. (207) 623-0363. In southern Maine, Donna Little operates the state's largest B&B reservations service: **Bed & Breakfast of Maine,** 377 Gray Rd., Falmouth 04105, tel. (207) 797-5540, fax 797-7599.

FARM B&BS

For a moderate price, these rural slice-of-life digs offer guests a chance to hobnob with honest-to-goodness farmers and resident menageries of sheep, cows, goats, ducks, llamas, chickens, geese, deer, turkeys, or potbellied pigs. Price for a high-season double ranges from $35 with shared bath to $110 with private bath and other amenities. Most of the farms welcome children but prohibit pets and smoking. For a free brochure describing nearly 20 farm B&Bs, contact the **Maine Farm Vacation B&B Association,** 377 Gray Rd., Rt. 26, Falmouth 04105, tel. (207) 797-5540, fax 797-7599.

SPORTING CAMPS

These traditional log-cabin colonies—ranging from rustic to semi-elegant—cater to fans of fishing, hiking, rafting, swimming, canoeing, rock-climbing, birdwatching, nature photography, cross-country skiing, snowmobiling, and hunting. Deer, moose, and bear are frequent visitors. Most sporting camps are located "up back"—above Bangor in the remote northern two-thirds of the state. Some camps are accessible by state roads, some by logging roads, some only by boat or floatplane (or, in winter, snowmobile or skiplane). Some serve legendary meals on the American Plan, others have do-it-

yourself cooking facilities; some boast modern conveniences, others have outhouses and gas lights.

Facilities at sporting camps include canoe and boat rentals, guide service, and nonresident freshwater fishing licenses. Cabins accommodating 2-12 people are arranged in complexes of as few as five or as many as 20 buildings. During the summer, most sporting camps stipulate a one-week minimum stay, and early reservations are essential. Many guests return year after year, generation after generation—although most don't go to the extreme of the man who bequeathed mantelpiece ornaments to the cabin he'd enjoyed every summer for 50 years.

For a free directory of its 50-plus members, contact **Maine Sporting Camp Association,** P.O. Box 89, Jay 04239, tel. (800) 305-3057. An entertaining survey of several dozen Maine sporting camps and their owners appears in Alice Arlen's *In the Maine Woods,* an illustrated paperback (see the Booklist).

HOTELS, MOTELS, RESORTS, CONDOMINIUMS

Just as in every other state, hotels and motels abound in Maine. The state's resort complexes can be counted on two hands. Condominium rentals are clustered primarily in York County, the Camden/Rockport area, and the Sunday River and Sugarloaf/USA areas. Hint: Although best known as ski resorts, Sunday River and Sugarloaf/USA are year-round destinations, and off-season rates are in effect for their condos in summer—a great time to be in Maine's western mountains. Names and telephone numbers (including many toll-free numbers) of nearly 500 members of the **Maine Innkeepers Association** are listed in the organization's annual directory. For a free copy, contact the association at 305 Commercial St., Portland 04101, tel. (207) 773-7670.

CAMPGROUNDS AND CAMPSITES

Maine is a camper's nirvana, with countless camping facilities ranging from wilderness outposts to state-of-the-art RV resorts.

Federal Campgrounds and Campsites
Straddling the Maine-New Hampshire border, the **White Mountain National Forest** covers 49,800 acres in Maine, encompassing five Forest Service campgrounds boasting well water, trash pickup, and toilets in addition to tentsites and fireplaces. Four of the campgrounds are open year-round, but access and facilities are limited mid-Oct.-mid-May. Five backcountry lean-tos are open year-round. For information about camping, hiking, or the National Forest itself, contact the Evans Notch Ranger District, White Mountain National Forest, RR 2, Box 2270, Bethel 04217, tel. (207) 824-2134.

Three National Park Service campgrounds lie within **Acadia National Park,** including lean-tos on Isle au Haut. Blackwoods, on Mount Desert Island, and Duck Harbor, on Isle au Haut, require reservations during the high season; Seawall, on Mount Desert Island, operates on a first-come, first-served basis. Specifics about camping and the park itself are available by writing or calling the Superintendent, Acadia National Park, Bar Harbor 04609, tel. (207) 288-3338.

Along the 276-mile Maine segment of the **Appalachian Trail,** some 40 campsites—each about a day's hike apart—have tenting areas or lean-tos. The Maine Appalachian Trail Club, P.O. Box 283, Augusta 04330, which maintains the Maine section, produces the essential *Guide to the Appalachian Trail in Maine,* which includes seven strip maps.

State Campgrounds and Campsites
Various branches of the state government supervise and/or maintain campsites and campgrounds all over Maine. Unfortunately, even though their territories overlap, there is no single source for information on campsites owned and operated by the state.

Details on camping along the **Allagash Wilderness Waterway** and in Maine's 12 **state parks** are available from the Bureau of Parks and Lands, 22 State House Station, Augusta 04333, tel. (207) 287-3821. A reservation system is in effect for 11 of the 12 state parks that offer camping, and, even though there's an extra charge, reservations are definitely advisable between mid-June and Labor Day. Only a small number of sites in each park are allocated on a first-come, first-served basis; the rest are by

reservation. Some state parks, such as Sebago Lake and Camden Hills, fill up quickly.

For reservations, at least seven days ahead of the first night you want to stay (minimum stay is two nights, maximum 14 nights), call (207) 287-3824 or (800) 332-1501 (in Maine) 9 a.m.-4 p.m. weekdays between January and late August. Have your Visa or MasterCard ready; nonresident camping fees range from $14-16 per site per night, plus the state's seven percent lodging tax. Camping fees for Maine residents are 25% cheaper. Reservation fee is $2 per site per night. Round-the-clock reservations are available by fax at (207) 287-6170. Sebago Lake and Lily Bay State Parks open for camping on May 1; the others open May 15; all close either September 30 or October 15.

For information on primitive campsites on nearly half a million acres of public lands, contact the Bureau of Parks and Lands, 22 State House Station, Augusta 04333, tel. (207) 287-3821.

The **Maine Forest Service** supervises 88 northern Maine campsites equipped with pit toilets and fireplaces. Call the regional Maine Forest Service headquarters in Island Falls, tel. (207) 463-2214, or the office in Old Town, tel. (207) 827-6191, or Greenville, tel. (207) 695-3721.

Owned by Maine residents but administered separately from the state park system, **Baxter State Park** contains 10 campgrounds offering a variety of accommodations—wilderness sites, campground tentsites, bunkhouses, lean-tos, and 23 log cabins. Depending on their location, some campgrounds open as early as May 15; all close by October 15. Winter camping is allowed at specified sites Dec. 1-April 1, but rigid safety rules are strictly enforced, and no park roads are plowed. Pets, radios, and cell phones are prohibited in the park. The Baxter State Park Authority, 64 Balsam Dr., Millinocket 04462, tel. (207) 723-5140, begins accepting summer reservations by mail or in person on the first workday in January. Guaranteeing a spot, particularly one of the 23 log cabins, means reserving in January (fees are nonrefundable but reasonable). Plan ahead and be flexible; choice dates and locations fill up quickly.

County Campsites
The only county-operated camping facilities (campsites and lean-tos, plus hot showers and

bathrooms) are located at **Mattawamkeag Wilderness Park,** managed by Penobscot County (east of Baxter State Park). For information, contact the Mattawamkeag Wilderness Park, Rt. 2, Box 5, Mattawamkeag 04459, tel. (207) 736-4881.

Wilderness Commercial Campsites

Responsible for recreation management on three million acres of paper-company land, **North Maine Woods, Inc.,** publishes maps of and information on its authorized campsites (equipped with toilets and fire rings) and designated fire-permit campsites (primitive sites requiring Maine Forest Service fire permits). Camping permits are issued at checkpoints when you enter the paper companies' roads, but quotas are in effect, so it's best to call or write **North Maine Woods, Inc.,** P.O. Box 421, Ashland 04732, tel. (207) 435-6213, for reservations.

Commercial Campgrounds

The annual *Maine Camping Guide* lists locations and facilities for more than 200 commercial campgrounds throughout the state. For a free copy of the booklet, contact the **Maine Campground Owners Association,** 655 Main St., Lewiston 04240, tel. (207) 782-5874.

HOSTELS

For the young at heart, Maine has three summertime hostels affiliated with Hostelling International—one in Portland, tel. (207) 874-3281; one in South Hiram, on the New Hampshire border, tel. (207) 625-7509; and one in Bar Har-

bor, near Acadia National Park, tel. (207) 288-5587. If you're not already a Hostelling International member, sign up by calling (202) 783-6161. A year's membership is $25 for adults (over 17), $10 for youths, $35 for families, $15 for senior citizens (over 54), $250 for a life membership. Once you're enrolled, you contact hostels directly, or call (800) 444-6111.

Several unofficial hostels—inns with dorm-style rooms—are located in the ski areas of western Maine.

SEASONAL RENTALS

You'll find advertisements for cabins, cottages, condos, RV sites, and campsites—for rent by the week, month, or season—in every corner of the state (realtors who handle seasonal rentals are listed in the appropriate regional chapters of this book). Remember that highest prices will prevail in July and August. A good source of independent rentals is the classified section of the monthly *Down East* magazine, P.O. Box 679, Camden 04843, tel. (800) 727-7422. The March, April, and May issues usually contain the most comprehensive listings. Also helpful is the *Maine Guide to Camp & Cottage Rentals,* a free booklet published annually by the Maine Publicity Bureau, P.O. Box 2300, Hallowell 04347, tel. (207) 623-0363. Short- and long-term winter condo rentals are available in the ski areas around Bethel (near Sunday River), Sugarloaf/USA, and Rangeley (home of Saddleback); inexpensive dormitory accommodations also rent by the week around Sunday River, Shawnee Peak, Mt. Abram, Saddleback, and Sugarloaf/USA.

FOOD AND DRINK

Say the word Maine and what comes to mind, gustatorily speaking? Lobsters, potatoes, and blueberries? Of course, but don't overlook mussels, farm-raised venison and lamb, maple syrup, fiddlehead ferns, Atlantic salmon, and baked beans. And if you're in Maine on the Fourth of July, the traditional dinner is salmon and peas—Atlantic salmon, that is, and peas fresh from the garden. Throughout the summer, food-oriented festivals celebrate the state's comestible bounty; they highlight salmon (Eastport), strawberries (South Berwick and lots of small communities), blueberries (Machias and Union), potatoes (Houlton and Fort Fairfield), eggs (Pittsfield), clams (Yarmouth), and lobsters (Rockland, Winter Harbor, Bar Harbor).

LOBSTER GALORE

What looks rather like a squished spider on Maine's license plate is actually, of course, the state's favorite menu item—a lobster. Whether you eat it indoors in a fancy restaurant or alfresco at one of the dozens of coastal lobster "pounds" or wharves (where you can dress down and make a mess), lobster wins high honors for low fat, calories, and cholesterol. You'll have plenty of choices as to how it's prepared—steamed, boiled, or broiled in the shell; in a lobster roll (chopped up with a bit of mayo in a hamburger or hot dog roll); or dressed up in designer sauces. Mainers dispute the advantages of hard-shell versus soft-shell, but July-Sept., most newcomers prefer the ease of eating (and the lower price) of the soft-shelled variety—called shedders, since they've recently shed their carapaces and grown new ones.

If you're camping or renting or cringe at cooking lobsters, contact a nearby lobster pound (look under "Lobsters" in the Yellow Pages telephone directory) and ask them to steam or boil the crustaceans for you (some will even deliver, along with all the fixin's).

For the ultimate lobster feeding frenzy, plan to be in Rockland the first weekend in August,

when volunteers at the annual Maine Lobster Festival stoke up world's largest lobster cooker and serve nonstop dinners to more than 50,000 enthusiastic diners.

BLUEBERRIES

What's black and blue and red all over? Maine's wild-blueberry barrens (fields), depending on what time of year you find them. They're black in fall and spring, when most growers torch their fields to jump-start the next year's crop. By August, after a summer full of a million rented bees pollinating the blossoms, a blue haze forms over the knee-high shrubs—interspersed with bent-over bodies carrying old-fashioned rakes to harvest the ripe berries. And they're red after harvest, when they turn brilliant red, then maroon.

Although most of the Down East barren barons harvest their crops for the lucrative wholesale market—averaging 65 million pounds annually—a few growers let you pick your own blueberries in mid-August. Contact the Maine Blueberry Commission (tel. 207-581-1475) or the Department of Agriculture (tel. 207-287-3491) for locations, recipes, and other wild-blueberry information.

The best place to simply *appreciate* blueberries is Machias, site of the renowned annual Wild Blueberry Festival, held the third weekend in August. While harvesting is underway in the surrounding fields, you can stuff your face with blueberry-everything—muffins, jam, pancakes, ice cream, pies. Plus you can collect blueberry-logo napkins, T-shirts, fridge magnets, pottery, and jewelry; then top it off with a tour of the town's Maine Wild Blueberry processing plant.

POTATOES

Native to South America, the potato is king in northern Maine—more specifically, in Aroostook County, where 92% of the state's spuds are grown. Potatoes grow in nearly 80,000

THE LOBSTER EXPERIENCE

No Maine visit can be considered complete without the "real Maine" experience of a "lobsta dinnah" at a lobster wharf/pound/shack. Keep an eye on the weather, pick a sunny day, and head out.

If you spot a lobster place with Restaurant in its name and no outside dining, keep going. What you're looking for is the genuine article; you want to eat outdoors, at a wooden picnic table, with a knockout view of boats and the sea. Whatever place you choose, the drill is much the same, and the "dinners" are served anytime from noon on (some places close as early as 7 p.m.). First of all, dress very casually so you can manhandle the lobster without messing up your good clothes. If you want beer or wine, call ahead; you may need to bring your own, since most such operations don't have liquor licenses. In the evening, carry some insect repellent, in case mosquitoes crash the party (many places light citronella candles or dispense Skin-So-Soft to keep the bugs at bay).

A basic one-pound lobster and go-withs (cole slaw, potato chips, and butter or fake butter for dipping) should run $12 or less. Depending on your hunger, though, you may want to indulge in a shore dinner (lobster, steamed clams, potato chips, and maybe cole slaw or corn), for which you may have to part with $15-20. Don't skip dessert in either case; many lobster pounds are known for their homemade pies.

Typically, you'll need to survey a chalkboard or whiteboard menu and step up to a window to order. You'll either give the person your name or get a number. A few places have staff to deliver your meal, but usually you head back for the window when your name or number is called. Don your plastic lobster bib and begin the attack. If you're a neophyte, watch a pro at a nearby table. Some pounds have "how-to" info on printed paper placemats. If you're really worried, write ahead to the Maine Lobster Promotion Council, 382 Harlow St., Bangor 04401—they publish a brochure with detailed instructions. Don't worry about doing it "wrong"; you'll eventually get what you came for, and it'll be an experience to remember.

Here are 20 of the best places to experience lobster. All are described in detail in the regional chapters.

Barnacle Billy's Lobster Pound, Perkins Cove, Ogunquit, tel. (207) 646-5575

Beal's Lobster Pier, Southwest Harbor (Mount Desert Island), tel. (207) 244-3202

Boothbay Region Lobstermen's Co-op, Boothbay Harbor, tel. (207) 633-4900

Chauncey Creek Lobster Pier, Kittery Point, tel. (207) 439-1030

Cod End, Tenants Harbor (near Thomaston), tel. (207) 372-6782

Dennett's Wharf, Castine, tel. (207) 326-9045

Eaton's Lobster Pool, Little Deer Isle, tel. (207) 348-2383

Holbrook's Lobster Wharf, Cundy's Harbor (near Brunswick), tel. (207) 725-0708

The Lobster House, Small Point (near Bath), tel. (207) 389-1596

The Lobster Pound, Lincolnville Beach, tel. (207) 789-5550

The Lobster Shack, Two Lights Rd., Cape Elizabeth (near Portland), tel. (207) 799-1677

Pemaquid Fishermen's Co-op, Pemaquid Harbor (near Damariscotta), tel. (207) 677-2801

Robinson's Wharf, Southport (near Boothbay Harbor), tel. (207) 633-3830

Shaw's Fish & Lobster Wharf, New Harbor (near Damariscotta), tel. (207) 677-2200

South Bristol Fishermen's Coop, South Bristol (near Damariscotta), tel. (207) 644-8224

Thurston's Lobster Pound, Steamboat Wharf, Bernard (Mount Desert Island), tel. (207) 244-7600

Tidal Falls Lobster Pound, Hancock (near Mount Desert Island), tel. (207) 422-6818

Trenton Bridge Lobster Pound, Trenton (near Bar Harbor), tel. (207) 667-2977

Waterman's Beach Lobsters, South Thomaston (near Rockland), tel. (207) 594-2489

Young's Lobster Pound, East Belfast, tel. (207) 338-1160

acres, appear on every restaurant menu and family table, are peddled by the bagful in countless roadside stands, and are stored in huge, half-buried barns. Annual festivals celebrate the arrival on the plants of delicate pink and white summer blossoms and, later in the year, the annual potato harvest. In September, schools in the County even close down for a week or two while students and teachers help with the harvest. The annual result is more than two billion pounds of potatoes—making Maine the nation's fifth- or sixth-largest potato producer. The most unusual dish you'll find in potato country is *poutine,* a mound of French fries smothered with brown gravy and melted cheese. Who knows what it does to your arteries, but it's a traditional favorite of northern Maine's French-speaking Acadians. For a free cookbook of prizewinning potato recipes, contact the **Maine Potato Board,** 744 Main St., P.O. Box 669, Presque Isle 04769, tel. (207) 769-5061, fax 764-4148.

OTHER MAINE SPECIALTIES

For a few weeks in May, right around Mother's Day (the second Sunday in May), a wonderful delicacy starts sprouting along Maine woodland streams: **fiddleheads,** the still-furled tops of the ostrich fern *(Matteuccia struthiopteris).* Tasting vaguely like asparagus, fiddleheads have been on May menus ever since Native Americans taught the colonists to forage for the tasty vegetable. Don't go fiddleheading unless you're with a pro, though; the look-alikes are best left to the woods critters. Cookbook writers have dreamed up a zillion ways to prepare these treats, but nothing beats steaming them for 5-7 minutes and serving them with lemon butter. If you find them on a restaurant menu, indulge.

As with fiddleheads, we owe thanks to Native Americans for introducing us to **maple syrup,** one of Maine's major agricultural exports. The

---

SUGARING OFF ~ MAINE'S MAPLE SYRUP

March in Maine brings warmer days and cold nights—the ideal climate for maple-syrup production. Maple trees all over Maine sprout faucet-like taps (inserted into half-inch holes drilled into the trees), from which hang metal buckets. The taps release the tree sap drop by drop into the buckets. The best syrup comes from the sugar or rock maple —*Acer saccharum.* On Maine Maple Sunday (fourth Sunday in March), several dozen syrup producers open their rustic sugarhouses to the public for "sugaring-off" parties—to celebrate the sap harvest and share the final phase in the production process. Woodsmoke billows from the sugarhouse chimney while everyone inside gathers around huge kettles used to boil down the watery sap. (A single gallon of syrup starts with 30-40 gallons of sap.) Finally, it's time to sample the syrup every which way—on pancakes and waffles, in tea, on ice cream, in puddings, in muffins, even just drizzled over snow. Most producers also have containers of syrup for sale.

The state annually publishes a list of Maine Maple Sunday sites. For a copy, contact the Maine Department of Agriculture, 28 State House Station, Augusta 04333; tel. (207) 287-3491.

If you can't be in Maine during March, the syrup is available in supermarkets, convenience stores, and specialty shops around the state. Look for organic syrup certified by the Maine Organic Farmers and

Gardeners Association (MOFGA)—a guarantee that the tapped trees are free of fertilizers and pesticides and the processing is chemical-free.

Maine maple syrup has a life beyond blueberry pancakes or sourdough waffles; here's a traditional Franco-American recipe for a scrumptious dessert.

Maple Walnut Pie
9-inch pie shell
2 tbsp. unsalted butter
4 whole eggs
2 c. maple syrup
2 tsp. apple cider vinegar
1/4 c. chopped walnuts

Preheat the oven to 400°. Bake the pie shell according to directions. Allow to cool. Melt butter and set aside to cool. In a medium-size bowl, beat eggs with an electric beater until thick, about three minutes. Continuing to beat the eggs, add maple syrup slowly but steadily. Add melted butter and vinegar and blend thoroughly. Pour maple mixture into the pie shell and bake about 40 minutes, until the top is light brown. (Watch for signs of burning.) Remove pie from oven and place on a rack to cool. Before serving, decorate the edges of the pie with the chopped walnuts. Bon appetit!

syrup comes in four different color/flavors (from light amber to extra dark amber), and inspectors monitor syrup quality strictly.

FARMERS' MARKETS

After a tentative beginning in the 1970s and 1980s, farmers' markets have become ritual stops for locals and visitors in more than three dozen Maine communities from Kittery to Fort Kent. Their biggest asset is serendipity—you never know what you'll find. Everything is locally grown and often organic, and it's hard to resist walking away with far more than you need. Herbs, unusual vegetables, seedlings, baked goods, meat, free-range chicken, goat cheese, herb vinegars, berries, honey, and jams are just a few of the possibilities. Some markets also offer live entertainment, crafts booths, even petting zoos. Maine has a short growing season, but green-thumbers make the most of it. Although each market has its own schedule, most are set up (usually outdoors) one or two days a week. The season varies, depending on location. July and August are the big months, but some open as early as April and others run as late as November. For a brochure listing all the markets, call the Maine Department of Agriculture, (207) 287-3941.

RESTAURANTS FOR EVERY TASTE AND BUDGET

Naturally, the golden arches and their clones have saturated Maine, so expect to bump into all the eat-and-run household words: Burger King, McDonald's, KFC, Dunkin' Donuts, Pizza Hut, Taco Bell. Depending on your interests and budget, however, you'll also find old-fashioned diners (Moody's in Waldoboro, A-1 Diner in Gardiner, Farmington Diner in Farmington), the state's best-known 24-hour truck stop (Dysart's, near Bangor), and four branches of the quirkily hilarious Road Kill Cafe (Greenville, Rangeley, York Beach, and Windham). In out-of-the-way spots, you can eat in country stores or family-oriented restaurants (usually labeled as such), or sporting camps with public dining rooms (in the Rangeley and Greenville areas).

Don't overlook roadside take-out stands. Most are Maine institutions with long-standing (literally) clienteles. If you spot a waiting line and have the time, join the crowd. Some of the best are Flo's Steamed Dogs in York (the sauce is legendary), Wasses Wagon in Rockland (which now has "branch wagons"), and Scott's Place in Camden. Superb take-out ice cream comes from The Viking in Ogunquit, Ben and Jerry's in Freeport, Round Top in Damariscotta, Miss Plum's in Rockport, and Spencer's in Bradley (north of Bangor).

You'll find gourmet take-out fare (and shorter waiting lines) at such emporia as the Market Basket in Rockport, Penobscot Provisions in Stonington, Clayton's in Yarmouth, and the Pine Cone Public House in Waldoboro.

Ethnic cuisine is easiest to find in Portland, which allegedly has the nation's highest number of restaurant seats per capita. Here you can dine around the world from menus Afghan, Indian, Japanese, Chinese, French, Italian (both north and south), Russian, Vietnamese, Greek, Thai, and Mexican. Beyond Portland, there are German restaurants in Kittery and Oakland (near Waterville); Indian restaurants in Camden and Bangor; a Pakistani restaurant (Bahaar) in Bangor; Thai restaurants in Rockland, Northport, and Ellsworth; and Chinese restaurants of varying quality all over the state.

At the upper end of the food-and-money chain are inn/hotel dining rooms catering to the credit-card and/or trust-fund set: Black Point Inn in Scarborough, Spruce Point Inn in Boothbay, The Colony in Kennebunkport, Samoset Resort in Rockport, Asticou Inn in Northeast Harbor, Inn by the Sea in Cape Elizabeth.

Maine won't win any national prizes for its number of haute-cuisine restaurants, but what's here is outstanding. Some of the best are the White Barn Inn (Kennebunkport); Arrows and Hurricane (both in Ogunquit); Le Domaine (Hancock); George's (Bar Harbor); Robinhood Free Meetinghouse (Georgetown, near Bath); The Firepond and Jonathan's (both in Blue Hill); One Stanley Avenue (Kingfield); Le Bistro (Seal Harbor, near Bar Harbor); and Aubergine, Back Bay Grill, Cafe Always, and Zephyr Grill (all in Portland).

BEANHOLE BEANS

"To be happy in New England," wrote one Joseph P. MacCarthy at the turn of the 20th century, "you must select the Puritans for your ancestors . . . [and] eat beans on Saturday night." There is no better way to check this out than to attend a "beanhole" bean supper—a real-live legacy of colonial times, with dinner baked in a hole in the ground.

Generally scheduled, appropriately, for a Saturday night (check local newspapers), a beanhole bean supper demands plenty of advance preparation from its hosts—as well as a secret ingredient or two (don't even think about trying to pry the recipe out of the cooks). The supper always includes hot dogs, cole slaw, relishes, home-baked breads, and homemade desserts, but the beans are the star attraction. (Typically, the suppers are also alcohol-free.) Not only are they feasts; they're also bargains, never setting you back more than about $6.

As one example, at **Cushing**, a mid-coast community where artist Andrew Wyeth summers, the beans at the Broad Cove Church's annual mid-July beanhole bean supper, served family style at long picnic tables, are legendary—attracting nearly 200 eager diners. Minus the secrets, here's what happens:

Early Friday morning: church volunteers load 10 pounds of dry pea and soldier (yelloweye) beans into each of four large kettles and add water to cover. The beans are left to soak and soften for six or seven hours. Two or three volunteers uncover the churchyard's four rock-lined beanholes (each about

three feet deep), fill the holes with hardwood kindling, ignite the wood, and keep the fires burning until late afternoon, when the wood is reduced to red-hot coals.

Early Friday afternoon: The veteran chefs parboil the beans and stir in the seasonings. Typical additions are brown sugar, molasses, mustard, salt, pepper, and salt pork (the secret is in the exact proportions). When the beans are precooked to the cooks' satisfaction, the kettle lids are secured with wire and the pots are lugged outdoors.

Friday midafternoon: With the beans ready to go underground, some of the hot coals are quickly shoveled out of the pits. The kettles are lowered into the pits and the coals replaced around the sides of the kettles and atop their lids. The pits are covered with heavy sheet metal, topped with a thick layer of sand and a tarpaulin. The round-the-clock baking begins, and no one peeks before it's finished.

Saturday midafternoon: Even the veterans start getting nervous just before the pits are uncovered. Was the seasoning right? Did too much water cook away? Did the beans dry out? Not to worry, though—failures just don't happen here.

Saturday night: When a pot is excavated for the first of three seatings (about 5 p.m.), the line is already long. The chefs check their handiwork and the supper begins. No one minds waiting for the second and third seatings—while others eat, a sing-along gets underway in the church, keeping everyone entertained.

PUBLIC SUPPERS

These are a guaranteed way to sample an array of Down East home cooking, meet "real Mainers" (and maybe other adventurous fellow travelers), and be finished before the sun sets. Check calendars in local newspapers for listings of public suppers (or their variations—chowder suppers, potluck suppers, beanhole bean dinners). These events are designed to help swell the coffers of the various volunteer organizations who sponsor them—fire department auxiliaries, historical societies, church groups, festival committees. Count on a minimal charge, but feel free to add a little extra. Reservations are seldom required, but you may have to call for directions. Also, be sure to arrive on time—the regulars know who makes the best pie, and it disappears fast

ALCOHOLIC BEVERAGES

As is customary in the United States, Maine's minimum drinking age is 21 years—and bar owners, bartenders, and serving staff can be held accountable for serving underage imbibers. Owners and employees also may be held liable for accidents caused by *legal* drinkers. Stiff anti-drunk-driving efforts in Maine (including random roadblocks, license revocation or suspension, hefty fines, and jail terms) have reduced but by no means halted the fatalities. If your blood alcohol level is .08% or higher, you are legally considered to be operating under the influence (generally speaking, a 160-pound person could be legally intoxicated after consuming four drinks within an hour; a 120-pound person could be intoxicated after three drinks). Minimum fine for a first offense is $300.

Liquor sales in Maine are controlled by the state. Cities and larger towns have state-operated liquor stores, while outlying areas have "agency stores"—typically, convenience stores licensed to sell liquor. Amid a huge strip of factory outlets on Rt. 1 in Kittery is the state's only discount liquor store—designed to compete with neighboring New Hampshire's statewide cut-rate liquor emporia. Prices are dramatically lower at the Kittery store, but some Mainers drive to New Hampshire rather than support a discriminatory policy that favors residents of southernmost Maine.

Beer and wine (including fortified wines, such as vermouth and sherry) are available in agency stores as well as food markets large and small.

The policy in restaurants varies. Many lobster pounds encourage patrons to bring their own. Restaurants that do not serve alcohol themselves but are helpful to alcohol-toting guests—supplying corkscrews and maybe even setups—are noted in the listings in this book with a designation of BYOL. When an establishment doesn't allow liquor (rare), that, too, is noted.

MICROBREWS OF MAINE

Fads and fashions reach Maine in slow motion from the West Coast or New York, but once they catch on, watch out! Take the microbrewery phenomenon. Maine now has one of the nation's highest numbers of microbreweries per capita, and microbrewing is the state's fastest-growing industry. The pioneer of all this micro-entrepreneurship is Portland's D.L. Geary Brewing Company, which began producing Geary's Pale Ale in 1986. Some two dozen other breweries now create more than 100 different ales, stouts, lagers, and porters—along with the occasional seasonal oddities. Brewpubs and even "brewtiques" are sprouting up everywhere, and microbrewery tours attract both aficionados and neophytes. Best place to graze through all of the state's award-winning brews is the annual Maine Brewers' Festival, held in Portland the first weekend in November (sort of a belated Oktoberfest). If a November visit doesn't suit, dozens of restaurants feature Maine beers on tap year-round. Drop in at one of these brewpubs, all affiliated with microbreweries:

Bray's Brewpub, Rts. 302 and 35, Naples
Federal Jack's Brewpub, 8 Western Ave., Kennebunk
Gritty McDuff's, Lower Main St., Freeport, and 396 Fore St., Portland
Lompoc Café and Brewpub, 36 Rodick St., Bar Harbor
Sea Dog Tavern, 26 Front St., Bangor, and 43 Mechanic St., Camden
Sunday River Brewing Company, 1 Sunday River Rd., Bethel
Theo's, Sugarloaf Access Rd., Carrabassett Valley

GETTING THERE

Maine has two major airports, two major bus networks, a toll highway, and some ad hoc local transportation systems that fill in the gaps.

BY AIR

Maine's airline gateways are **Portland International Jetport** (PWM), tel. (207) 774-7301, and **Bangor International Airport** (BGR), tel. (207) 947-0384. The "international" in their names is a bit misleading; neither has direct scheduled service to any international destination. Charter flights from Europe often stop at Bangor for refueling and customs clearance, and sometimes bad weather diverts flights there, but Boston's Logan Airport is the nearest facility with direct flights to Europe and other international destinations.

You'll want to fly into Bangor if you're headed for the North Woods, Bar Harbor and Acadia National Park, or the Down East counties of Washington and Hancock. But Portland is the more logical choice if you're visiting southern Maine—the beaches, Portland, or the coastal towns up to Damariscotta—or the Bethel area of western Maine. If your destination is the Camden-Rockport area, which is equidistant between the two, your choice is a toss-up (you may want to make your decision based on flight schedules). Being on the coast, the Portland airport is more subject to fog shutdowns than Bangor, but fog delays can afflict Boston's Logan Airport even more, and many Bangor flights originate (or stop) in Boston.

Airlines serving both Portland and Bangor are **Continental,** tel. (800) 525-0280, **Delta,** tel. (800) 638-7333, **United,** tel. (800) 241-6522, and **US Airways,** tel. (800) 428-4322.

Augusta State Airport, tel. (207) 287-3185, the base for state government flights, has commercial service to and from Boston via **Continental Connection** (formerly Colgan Air), tel. (800) 525-0280, a commuter line with a commendable safety record. Other airports accessible via Continental Connection from Boston are **Hancock County Airport,** near Bar Harbor, and **Knox County Regional Airport,** near Rockland and Camden. All the airlines increase their flight frequency during the summer to accommodate increased demand. (See "Getting Around" for information on Pine State Airlines' intrastate service to Portland, Augusta, Presque Isle, and Frenchville.)

Airport Facilities

Portland's three-story terminal received a $10 million facelift in 1996, and amenities now include a newsstand/gift shop, coffee shop, restaurant/lounge, restrooms, large waiting area with comfortable seats, and plenty of coin- and card-operated telephones. The Thomas Cook travel agency has an office here, as do Avis, Budget, Hertz, and National car-rental agencies. Visitor information is dispensed from a desk (not always staffed, unfortunately) located between the gates and the baggage-claim area. No need to rush out to grab your luggage—Portland has one of the slowest baggage-claim operations in the country. After you arrive, plan to stop at the restrooms, browse through the gift shop, and pick up tourism information—and even then you may still have to wait for your luggage. Complaints to management elicit the response that Portland is the terminus of many airline routes, and the airline companies (who provide the baggage handlers) give low priority to locations that don't require fast turnaround. As a result, carry-on luggage is a plus here. Baggage-handling offices surround the luggage carousels, but if you have an emergency, contact Jetport Manager Jeff Schultes at (207) 773-8462.

Bangor's airport has scaled-down versions of Portland's facilities but all the necessary amenities: Avis, Budget, and Hertz rental cars (with Enterprise, Thrifty, and Rent-a-Wreck nearby); newsstand/gift shop; and waiting area with restrooms and phones. Baggage claim is more efficient than Portland's, but if you need help, contact Airport Manager Bob Ziegelaar at (207) 947-0384.

Ground Transportation

Portland's Metro Bus Line, tel. (207) 774-0351,

provides scheduled service throughout the city. Taxis are always available at the airport. In addition to the car-rental agencies inside the terminal itself, Alamo and Thrifty have offices within the airport complex, and both companies are reliable, generally less expensive than the bigger names, and provide shuttle service between the terminal and their offices and parking lots.

If you're planning to arrive in Portland and head directly up the coast anywere between the airport and Camden, call ahead to Mid-Coast Limousine, tel. (800) 937-2424 or (207) 236-2424, and schedule a pickup. You might be lucky and find one of their limos at the airport, but they operate by reservation, so don't take the chance.

If you're going from Portland to Sunday River Ski Resort in Bethel, contact Bethel Express, tel. (207) 824-4646, 24 hours in advance, for van service from the Portland Jetport or the Concord Trailways bus terminal in Portland. Cost is about $70 per person, but a full van will lower the rate.

Mermaid Transportation, in Portland, tel. (800) 696-2463, operates the best van service between Boston and Portland. Cost is $36 one-way. Pickup and dropoff, by reservation only, are at Portland Jetport and Logan Airport but can be arranged for Falmouth Shopping Center, just north of Portland, for a small extra charge.

BY CAR

The major highway access to Maine is the **Maine Turnpike,** which links up with I-95 at the New Hampshire border. Other busy access points are **Rt. 302,** from North Conway, NH, entering Maine at Fryeburg; **Rt. 2,** from Vermont and New Hampshire, entering at Bethel; **Rt. 201,** from Quebec, entering north of Jackman; and a handful of crossing points from New Brunswick into Aroostook and Washington Counties in northern Maine.

BY BUS

Concord Trailways, tel. (800) 639-3317, departs downtown Boston (South Station Transportation Center) and Logan Airport for Portland eight times daily, making pickups at all Logan airline terminals (lower level). The Portland bus terminal is the Trailways Transportation Center, 100 Sewall St., on a side road behind the Doubletree Inn, just off Rt. 22 (Congress St. W) and close to I-295 Exit 5. Three daily express buses continue on from Portland to Bangor; two nonexpress buses go along the coast as far as Searsport, then head inland to the Trailways terminal in Bangor.

BY RAIL

After nearly 30 years of off-and-on wrangling and pleading with Amtrak to restore Boston-to-Portland passenger rail service, in 1994 the agency announced that it would resume service. Since then, however, it's been dragging its feet. Call Amtrak, tel. (800) 872-7245, for an update and stay tuned.

GETTING AROUND

By Air
State, county, and municipal airports are sprinkled all over Maine—from Presque Isle to Eastport to Bar Harbor, Augusta, and Lewiston. (Each is described in the relevant regional chapter of this book.) Unfortunately, except for special charters, the only intrastate air link is via **Pine State Airlines,** tel. (800) 353-6334, which flies nine-seat Cessnas twice each weekday between Portland and Frenchville, with stops in Augusta and Presque Isle. Roundtrip fare is under $400.

Penobscot Air Service, based at Knox County Municipal Airport in Owls Head, near Rockland, flies on demand to several airstrip-equipped islands in Penobscot Bay. Several firms in the Katahdin/Moosehead Lake region and in Rangeley operate summer floatplanes and winter skiplanes to provide access to wilderness sporting camps. For a sightseeing treat during fall foliage season (late September and early October in that area), reserve a seat on one of the **fire-warden flights,** where you'll spend more than an hour flying low over sparkling lakes, mul-

Floatplanes (and, in winter, skiplanes) are vital elements of life in the North Woods.

ticolored forests, and, unfortunately, the clearcuts, too. Keep an eye out for moose and don't forget your camera!

By Bus

Ground transportation exists in Maine, but it's far from adequate. For instance, there's no bus service to western Maine from Portland (only private van service), and only two long-distance companies cover the state. No smoking on buses.

Concord Trailways, tel. (800) 639-3317, has the best intrastate bus network, with routes designed to assist students, island ferry passengers, and day-trippers. Buses from Boston's Logan Airport stop in downtown Portland and follow a mostly coastal route through Brunswick, Bath, Wiscasset, Damariscotta, Waldoboro, Rockland, Camden, Belfast, and Searsport, ending in Bangor, then following the same route in reverse. (During the school year, the route also includes Bowdoin College in Brunswick and the University of Maine campus in Orono.)

Vermont Transit, tel. (800) 537-3330, a division of Greyhound Bus Lines, follows an inland route, linking Lewiston, Augusta, and Waterville with Bangor, Calais, and Caribou. Vermont and Concord compete only on the Portland-Bangor run, where Vermont's fares tend to be somewhat lower than Concord's. Several express buses operate daily between Portland and Bangor.

Once-a-day buses to and from Caribou and Calais coordinate with the Bangor bus schedules. The Caribou line, stopping in Medway (near Millinocket), Houlton, and Presque Isle, is operated by **Cyr Bus Lines,** in Bangor, tel. (207) 942-3354. The Calais line, stopping in Ellsworth, Gouldsboro, Machias, and Perry, is operated by **West's Coastal Connection,** in Milbridge, tel. (800) 596-2823 or (207) 546-2823.

Major cities such as Portland, South Portland, Lewiston/Auburn, and Bangor have **city bus service,** with some wheelchair-accessible vehicles. Some smaller communities have established **local shuttle vans** or **trolley buses,** but most of these are seasonal. Trolleybuses operate (for a fee) in the Yorks, Ogunquit, Wells, the Kennebunks, and Boothbay. A free shuttle service operates in Camden.

By Car

No matter how much time and resourcefulness you summon up, you'll never really appreciate Maine without a car. The state has more than 22,000 miles of paved (mostly two-lane) roads and countless miles of unpaved country roads and logging routes (used by giant timber trucks). Down every little peninsula jutting into the Atlantic lies a picturesque village or park or ocean view. Inland, roads wind over the hills and through the woods. Even I-95, the state's major artery, boasts scenic vistas that bring photographers to a screeching halt. (Of course, a radar-equipped cop or antlers-equipped moose can deliver the same result for any driver.)

Note that the interstate can be a bit confusing to motorists; it's important to consult a map and pay close attention to the green directional signs to avoid heading off in the wrong direction. Between York and Falmouth, I-95 is the same as the Maine Turnpike. At Falmouth, the turnpike becomes I-495 and veers inland, while I-95 continues along the coast for 20 miles before heading inland, joining up again with the turnpike in Gardiner. The 100-mile turnpike begins in York and ends in Augusta. Service areas are infrequent on the 'pike, and aren't on both sides of the highway, so stop when you see one (even if you might not need it); don't wait for the next one.

Maximum speed on I-95 and the Maine Turnpike is 65 mph—55 mph on some stretches. In snow, sleet, or dense fog, the limit drops to 45 mph (only rarely does the highway close). On other roads, the speed limit is usually 55 mph in rural areas and posted in built-up areas.

Two lanes wide from Kittery to Fort Kent, US1 is the state's most congested road, particularly in July and August. Mileage distances can be extremely deceptive, since it will take you much longer than anticipated to get from point A to point B. If you ask about distances, chances are good that you'll receive an answer in hours rather than miles. Plan accordingly. If you're trying to make time, it's best to take the turnpike or I-95; if you want to see Maine, take Rt. 1 and lots of little offshoots. (Acadia National Park Visitors often can make better time from the New Hampshire border by taking I-95 to the Bangor area, then heading southeast on Rt. 1A.) That said, bear in mind that the turnpike itself becomes mega-congested on summer weekends, and especially summer *holiday* weekends. More than 300,000 vehicles use the turnpike on Memorial Day and Labor Day weekends. Worst times on the turnpike are Friday 4-8 p.m. (northbound), Saturday 11 a.m.-2 p.m. (southbound; weekly cottage rentals run from Saturday noon to Saturday noon), and Sunday 3-7 p.m. (southbound). On three-day holiday weekends, avoid it Monday 3-7 p.m. (southbound).

Rental cars are available at the Portland, Bangor, and most smaller airports. All the major chains are represented—Alamo, Avis, Budget, Hertz, National, Thrifty, even Rent-A-Wreck. If you're planning to arrive on a July or August weekend, or on Memorial Day or Labor Day weekend, call well ahead for a reservation or you may be out of luck.

Almost all **gas stations** in Maine are self-serve (pumps are marked Self; at those marked Full, an attendant will pump the gas for you).

Important Driving Regulations: Seat belts are mandatory in Maine. You cannot be stopped for not wearing one, but if you're stopped for any other reason, you can be fined if you're not buckled in. Maine allows **right turns at red lights,** after you stop and check for oncoming traffic. In rare cases, you'll see a No Turn on Red sign—in which case, heed it. *Never* pass a **stopped school bus** in either direction. Wait until the bus's red lights have stopped flashing and all children are well off the road. A new law took effect in August 1997 requiring drivers to turn on their car's **headlights** any time the windshield wipers are operating.

Roadside Assistance: Since Maine is enslaved to the automobile, it's not a bad idea for vacationers to carry membership in AAA or some other similar program in the event of breakdowns, flat tires, and other car crises. Contact your nearest AAA office or AAA Northern New England, 425 Marginal Way, Portland 04101, tel. (207) 780-6800 or (800) 482-7497.

By Rail
Except for the erratic wintertime **Ski Express,** connecting the Portland area and Sunday River Ski Resort, riding the rails within Maine means hopping aboard one of four excursion lines or visiting the Boothbay Railway Museum or Kennebunkport's Seacoast Trolley Museum. Best known of the excursions are those operated by the **Belfast and Moosehead Lake Railroad,** departing from the Belfast waterfront as well as from the town of Unity, inland from Belfast. In downtown Portland, the **Maine Narrow Gauge Railway Museum** offers short rides in spiffed-up antique railway cars. Wiscasset's **Maine Coast Railroad** departs from the riverfront and follows an especially scenic route through woods and fields. Financial difficulties have plagued the **Sandy River Railway,** in the mountains of western Maine, but the train still operates out of Phillips on the third Sunday of each month in the summer. See the destination chapters for details on each of these.

Hitchhiking

Even though Maine's public transportation network is woefully inadequate, and the crime rate is fourth-lowest in the nation, it's still risky to hitchhike or pick up hitchhikers. Sure, pick up a schoolchild in an out-of-the-way village, or kids headed home from the beach; just use common sense.

SPECIAL-INTEREST TOURS

In addition to the one-size-fits-all bus tours described below, Maine has become a hot ticket on the ecotourism circuit, with organized trips specializing in bicycling, walking and hiking, canoeing and kayaking, birding, llama trekking, dogsledding, and winter camping.

Bus Tours

Major national bus-tour companies include Maine on their New England itineraries, but most offer only summer coastal trips (usually Kennebunkport to Bar Harbor) or fall-foliage tours (inland, then across to New Hampshire and Vermont). Neither itinerary offers much chance to see what Maine has to offer. **Tauck Tours,** P.O. Box 5027, Westport, CT 06881, tel. (203) 226-6911, one of the oldest, best, and priciest domestic tour companies, spends only a day or two in Maine on its well-managed New England swings. **Maine Line Tours,** 184 Main St., South Portland 04106, tel. (207) 799-8527 or (800) 341-0322, offers mostly out-of-state tours from Maine, but it's worth checking out their one-day options, especially the Rangeley Lakes fall-foliage junket, which includes lunch, for about $40.

Walking Tours

Each fall, **Walking the World (WTW),** featuring outdoor adventures for the 50-and-over set, offers two well-planned, eight-day walks along the Maine coast with local guides. Participants carry only daypacks but need to be in reasonably good condition (WTW sends out pre-trip training advice). Lodging is at B&Bs. Cost, excluding airfare, runs about $1,500. Contact WTW at P.O. Box 1186, Fort Collins, CO 80522, tel. (970) 225-0500 or (800) 340-9255. Acadia National Park is the primary focus for the half-dozen five-day, easy-to-moderate walks orga-nized by **Country Walkers,** P.O. Box 180, Waterbury, VT 05676, tel. (802) 244-1387, fax 244-5661, a well-managed firm started in 1980. Lodgings are at country inns. Cost, excluding airfare, is about $1,000.

Bicycle Tours

Vermont Bicycle Touring, a longtime tour operator, schedules 20 five-day pedals each summer in the Mid-Coast and Blue Hill areas, with lodging at inns and B&Bs. Cost (excluding airfare) is $900-1,000, plus $100 bike and helmet rental.

Canoeing Tours

Approaching legend status as Maine wilderness guides are Alexandra and Garrett Conover, highly skilled traditionalists who lead five- to seven-day trips in wood-and-canvas canoes on the St. John, Allagash, and Penobscot (West Branch) Rivers, plus paddles on Loon Lake, Caucomgomoc Stream, and the area around isolated Chesuncook Village. Costs range from $550 to under $800 (excluding airfare). The Conovers also do some winter snowshoeing trips. Their company is **North Woods Ways,** Willimantic, mailing address RR 2, Box 159A, Guilford 04443, tel. (207) 997-3723.

Marty Brown organizes canoe trips everywhere from the Arctic to the Zambezi; you can join him in Maine on a six-day St. Croix River run, not far from his Washington County base camp. St. Croix trips operate between Memorial Day (still too chilly) and mid-October (spectacular foliage); cost is under $700 (not counting travel; discount if you bring your own canoe). **Sunrise County Canoe Expeditions,** Cathance Lake, Grove Post Office 04638, tel. (800) 748-3730 or (207) 454-7708, fax (207) 454-3315.

Although Mike Patterson is a Registered Maine Guide who can handle most any kind of outdoor pursuit, his specialty is canoe trips, late May to late September, on all Maine's major rivers: the Allagash, St. John, Machias, St. Croix, Penobscot (east and west branches), and Moose. Costs average $100 per person per day. Neophytes should consider the Moose River Bow Trip, a classic, easy, four-day loop providing a fine wilderness canoeing experience for just under $400. In addition to running his own company, he also freelances with other canoe-trip organizers and teaches clinics in the art of canoe poling. **Wilds of Maine Guide Service Inc.,** 2 Abby Ln., Yarmouth 04096, tel. (207) 846-9735.

Fran Doonan and "Trapper Dave" Mussey lead four or five multiday trips each summer in wood-and-canvas canoes they've built. They concentrate on the Allagash River and the West Branch of the Penobscot. Cost is $500-600. They also make and sell traditional ash pack baskets, leather mukluks, and maple toboggans. Want to make your own? Sign up for one of their workshops. **Maine Journeys,** RR 1, Box 130, Charleston 04422, tel. (207) 285-3332.

Other Specialty Tours

Year-round outdoor experiences and women-only trips are the stock-in-trade of Kevin Slater and Polly Mahoney's **Mahoosuc Guide Service,** based in western Maine's mountains. Five- or six-day wilderness canoe trips ($395-750) tackle the Penobscot River (east and west branches), the St. John, the Allagash (including a fall foliage trip), and the Moose. During their superb two- to-five-day dogsledding trips ($325-725), accommodations are in woodstove-heated tents. Some of their huskies are Iditarod veterans. Polly also leads women-only dogsledding and canoe trips ($200-375). Between late December and mid-March, become a dilettante musher on a one-day midweek Umbagog trip

($115; it's very popular), including a hearty campfire lunch. Mahoosuc Guide Service, Box 245, Bear River Rd., Newry 04261, tel. (207) 824-2073.

Also in western Maine is **The Telemark Inn Wilderness Lodge,** site of the state's original llama treks. Owner Steve Crone organizes treks lasting one day ($85, including lunch; $65 for kids), two days (spring and fall weekends only; $229 adults, $149 kids), three days ($450 and $325), and four days ($550 and $400). The inn has six basic guest rooms as well as mountain-bike trails, cross-country-skiing packages, meals, sleigh rides, sauna, and gear rental (snowshoes, skates, skis)—lots of options for a real getaway. The Telemark Inn, King's Highway, RFD 2, Box 800, Bethel 04217, tel. (207) 836-2703.

An expert Maine-based guide accompanies the annual four-day, late-September Monhegan Island birding tour run by **Field Guides Incorporated,** a first-rate international firm. Known by birders as a migrant trap for vagrant species, car-free Monhegan is a haven for migrating birds, many of whom have lost their bearings—giving birders a chance to see specimens that aren't typical here. The trip is limited to 12 persons; cost is under $500 (excluding transportation). Contact Field Guides at P.O. Box 160723, Austin, TX 78716, tel. (800) 728-4953 or (512) 327-4953, fax (512) 327-9231.

GETTING AFLOAT

MAINE STATE FERRY SYSTEM

Unless you're lucky enough to have your own boat, the only way to reach Vinalhaven, North Haven, Matinicus, Islesboro, Swans Island, and Frenchboro is via the state ferry system. All of the system's vessels carry cars, trucks, bicycles, strollers, pets (leashed or caged), groceries, lumber, and whatever else. Ferry captains are real pros, accustomed to battling the elements, including fog and choppy seas. The biggest bottleneck tends to be periodic reconstruction of dock and terminal facilities, but the service continues nonetheless, with only minor delays.

For various reasons, the ferry service has been known to increase fares without much

warning, so consider the following rates ballpark figures. (Reservations, bicycles, and cars all cost extra.) Roundtrip fares for **Vinalhaven, North Haven,** and **Frenchboro** in 1997 were $9 adult, $4 children, $8 for an adult bicycle (without rider), $4 for a child's bicycle, and $26 for a car (including driver). **Islesboro** fares were $4.50, $2, $4, $2, and $13. **Swans Island** fares were $6, $3, $5, $2, and $18. Payment is cash only, unless you are reserving by mail (see below); no credit cards. To keep the ferry-dependent islanders happy, roundtrip tickets purchased on the islands are less expensive than on the mainland, but unless you have a friend "over there" who can get tickets to you, no logistical wizardry can help you take advantage of this discount.

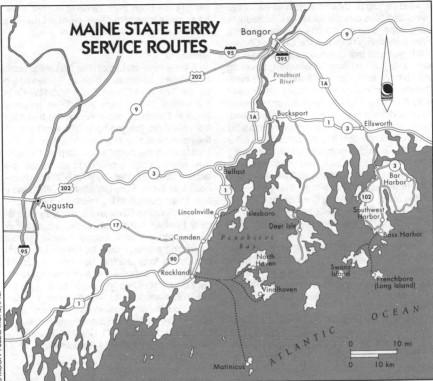

MAINE STATE FERRY SERVICE ROUTES

Vehicle reservations ($5 or $6, depending on destination, nonrefundable) are strongly recommended for July and August weekends but cannot be made more than 30 days in advance. Send your request, along with a money order or check for the full fare plus the reservation fee, to the terminal from which you will be departing (see addresses below). Or, if you're in the area, you can reserve by stopping in at the terminal a few days or a week ahead. Reservations are held until 15 minutes before departure.

A different schedule prevails on each of the state ferry routes, but keep in mind that except for one Vinalhaven boat, the final ferry from the mainland each day *remains on the island,* so don't miss the last departure or you'll have an unexpected island stay (and beds can be scarce).

Ferries depart from Rockland for **Matinicus**

only 24 times a year, making the 23-mile crossing in 135 minutes. The schedule is dependent on tides, weather, and vessel availability, and fares are subject to change, so check with the Rockland terminal, tel. (207) 596-2202.

For general recorded **schedule information,** call (207) 624-7777; for a daily update, call (800) 491-4883. For a copy of the printed schedule, contact Maine State Ferry Service, 517A Main St., P.O. Box 645, Rockland 04841, tel. (207) 596-2202.

Vinalhaven and North Haven

(For details on visiting North Haven and Vinalhaven, see "Rockland's Ferry-Linked Islands" in the Mid-Coast Region chapter.)

Vinalhaven and North Haven boats—as well as Matinicus ones—depart from Rockland's North End, across US1 from the Navigator Motor

Inn and the Old Granite Inn (watch for distinctive five-sided blue directional signs). Schedules vary, depending on the day and the season. From April through October, the *Captain Charles Philbrook* and the *Governor Curtis* make six trips a day to and from Vinalhaven, covering the 15 miles in 75 minutes. Earliest boats in either direction depart at 7 a.m., latest ones at 4:30 p.m. The *Captain Neal Burgess* makes two roundtrips a day to North Haven year-round, beginning at 8 a.m. in North Haven and 9:30 a.m. in Rockland. July through October, an extra roundtrip is added around midday. Crossing time for the 12.5 miles is one hour. Last boat from North Haven departs at 3:45 p.m., last boat from Rockland at 5 p.m. You can reach offices of the Maine State Ferry Service at P.O. Box 191, Vinalhaven 04863, tel. (207) 863-4421, or P.O. Box 225, North Haven 04853, tel. (207) 867-4441.

The Vinalhaven and North Haven routes see heavy vehicle traffic, so it is essential to arrive at the ferry terminal well in advance if you plan to take a car to either island and you don't have a reservation. (The same goes for the return trip.) Don't push your luck.

Lodgings are limited on both islands, so call ahead to reserve beds, especially during late July and early August. Local innkeepers are extremely accommodating and can help with alternative arrangements when fog or heavy seas cancel a trip, but the islands reach saturation that time of year.

The roads on Vinalhaven and North Haven are narrow and shoulderless—as in so much of Maine—but the islands are still manageable for **cycling.** Remember to obey the rules of the road and use common sense, though. Park your car at the Rockland ferry terminal and take your bicycle on the ferry—that's far cheaper than taking a car. Nearest bike rentals are at Maine Sport Outfitters, Rt. 1, P.O. Box 956, Rockport 04856, tel. (800) 722-0826 or (207) 236-8797, fax (207) 236-7123. The $15 daily rate includes helmet and lock; a car rack is another $5 daily.

Another option is to go along just for the ride, without car or bike, and make a simple day of it —the Penobscot Bay scenery alone is worth the trip. Between boats on Vinalhaven, you can explore the downtown Carvers Harbor area, hike Lane's Island Preserve, swim at Lawson's Quarry, and picnic in Grimes Park.

Islesboro

Just three miles off Lincolnville (five miles north of Camden), Islesboro is a quick, 20-minute trip via the *Margaret Chase Smith.* Mid-May-Oct., the vessel makes nine roundtrips Monday through Saturday, departing on the half-hour from Islesboro (beginning at 7:30 a.m.) and on the hour (beginning at 8 a.m.) from Lincolnville. Last boat off the island is at 4:30 p.m. On Sunday, when there are only eight roundtrips, the captain sleeps in: boats begin at 8:30 from Islesboro and 9 a.m. from Lincolnville. Off-season, fewer trips operate in the middle of the day.

To explore this 10-mile-long, relatively level island best known as an exclusive summer colony, you *will* want a car or bicycle; except for visiting a small museum, there's little to do around the ferry landing. However, roads are narrow and winding—and some islanders resent the influx of two-wheelers—so be particularly conscientious and sensible here. You can leave your car on the mainland, at a parking lot across from the ferry landing. Information: Maine State Ferry Service, P.O. Box 214, Lincolnville 04849, tel. (207) 789-5611 (Lincolnville) or (207) 734-6935 (Islesboro).

Swans Island and Frenchboro

The Bass Harbor ferry terminal, tucked into the southwestern corner of Mount Desert Island, serves as the base for boats to Swans Island and Frenchboro. The terminal building is minuscule, but the ferry system's distinctive five-sided blue signs appear all over Mount Desert, so you'll have no trouble finding it. Allow some time to check out Bass Harbor, maybe even spend the night. (See "Southwest Harbor and Vicinity," under "Mount Desert Island" in the Acadia Region chapter.)

Getting to Swans Island, six miles offshore, takes 40 minutes aboard the *Captain Henry Lee,* which makes six roundtrips Mon.-Sat. and four on Sunday late May to mid-October. Here, too, you'll want a car or bicycle—preferably a mountain bike—to negotiate unpaved side roads.

Frenchboro, the only hamlet on sparsely populated Long Island, lies eight and a quarter miles off Bass Harbor, 50 minutes and 50 years away. The *Captain Henry Lee* serves the island with twice-weekly trips, but there are no lodgings and no campgrounds. Wednesday, the boat leaves Bass Harbor at 9 a.m., returning from Frenchboro at 10 a.m. Thursday, it departs Bass Harbor at 12:30 p.m., then returns from Frenchboro via Swans Island at 1:30 p.m. You should go for the ride and a glimpse of a remote island harbor, but you're on your own if you decide not to return on the boat.

Parking opposite the Bass Harbor ferry terminal is $4 per day. Information: Maine State Ferry Service, P.O. Box 114, Bass Harbor 04653, tel. (207) 244-3254; Maine State Ferry Service, P.O. Box 158, Swans Island 04685, tel. (207) 526-4273.

CASCO BAY LINES

Residents of the Casco Bay islands—Portland's bedroom communities—cheerfully commute to work and school on the bright yellow ferries of **Casco Bay Lines,** Commercial and Franklin Sts., Old Port, Portland 04101, tel. (207) 774-7871, the nation's oldest continuously operating ferry system. Boats serve **Cliff, Great Chebeague, Little and Great Diamond, Long,** and **Peaks Islands.** No smoking is allowed aboard the vessels; dogs (leashed) and bicycles require their own tickets. An interesting quirk and potential bargain: all tickets are roundtrip, and they're collected when you board in Portland. If you manage to get to one of the islands by some other means—such as via the Chebeague Transportation Company (see below)—there's no charge for going from island to island or returning to Portland on a Casco Bay Lines vessel.

Most frequent boats are on the Peaks Island run, a 20-minute trip. Roundtrip fare is $5.25 in summer, less in winter. Bikes are $3.40 extra (you can also rent one on Peaks, at Brad's Bike Rental & Repair, tel. 207-766-5631, for $4 an hour).

The most interesting Casco Bay Lines trip is the year-round **mailboat run,** which makes a three-hour loop, stopping at five islands, twice

daily. Cost is $9.50 for adults, $8 for seniors, $4.25 for children ages 5-9.

OTHER OFFSHORE SERVICES

Small municipal and private ferry services provide transportation to islands up and down the coast. **Chebeague Transportation Company,** tel. (207) 846-3700, runs its passenger ferry year-round between Cousins Island in Yarmouth and Great Chebeague Island, a 15-minute hop. Roundtrip tickets are $9 for adults. From Boothbay Harbor, New Harbor, and Port Clyde, boats depart for Monhegan Island. The only year-round service to Monhegan, and the shortest route, used for passengers and freight, is via Port Clyde, 12 miles down the St. George Peninsula from Thomaston. Roundtrip tickets are $25 for adults, $12 for children 12 and under, $2 for pets. Don't take a bicycle; the island is too rocky. Reservations are essential in summer; contact the **Monhegan-Thomaston Boat Line,** P.O. Box 238, Port Clyde 04855, tel. (207) 372-8848, fax 372-8547.

Passenger ferries for the 45-minute run to Isle au Haut depart year-round from Stonington, on Deer Isle. Early April through mid-October, roundtrip adult tickets are $24 weekdays, $28 Sunday ($10 weekdays for kids under 12). Winter fares are dramatically lower. (There's only one Sunday boat in summer, none in winter.) From late June to Labor Day, Mon.-Sat. the ferry makes two runs to and from Duck Harbor, the Isle au Haut section of Acadia National Park. No bikes, canoes, kayaks, or pets on this run. Contact the **Isle-au-Haut Company,** Sea Breeze Ave., Stonington 04681, tel. (207) 367-5193 days, or (207) 367-2355 evenings. The passenger ferry *Island Queen* departs year-round from the Upper Town Dock (Clark Point Rd.), in Southwest Harbor, for Islesford (Little Cranberry Island) and Cranberry Isles (Great Cranberry Island), off Mount Desert Island. From mid-June to mid-September, there are four trips daily. Roundtrip fare is $10 adults, $5 kids 3-12. Bikes are $2 extra. Contact the **Cranberry Cove Boating Co.,** Upper Town Dock, Southwest Harbor 04679, tel. (207) 244-5882.

MAINE–NOVA SCOTIA CRUISE FERRIES

Two oceangoing car-and-passenger cruise ferries link Bar Harbor and Portland, Maine, with Yarmouth, in western Nova Scotia, making daily trips throughout the summer. Your choice depends on your interest and itinerary, but consider cruising one way and driving the other. Taking your car aboard is expensive, but you're saving the expense of a long drive from Bar Harbor or an even longer one from Portland. When making plans, remember that Yarmouth is on Atlantic Time—an hour later than Maine's Eastern Standard Time. Pets are not allowed on the ferries' passenger decks, but kennels or crates are available. Be sure to make arrangements in advance.

From **Portland,** the *Scotia Prince* makes a 23-hour overnight roundtrip, with a one-hour stopover in Yarmouth, between early May and late October. One-way tickets are $78 for adults in peak season, $39 for children 5-14, lower in shoulder seasons. Vehicles are additional. Contact **Prince of Fundy Cruises,** International Marine Terminal, 468 Commercial St., P.O. Box 4216, Portland 04101, tel. (800) 341-7540 outside Maine, (800) 482-0955 or (207) 775-5616 in Maine. From **Bar Harbor,** the car-and-passenger ferry departs in early morning on the six-hour cruise to Yarmouth, stops for an hour or so, and returns. Tickets are $42 for adults in peak season, $38 for seniors, $21 for kids 5-12, lower off-season. For more information contact **Bay Ferries,** tel. (888) 249-7245.

WINDJAMMER CRUISES

Taking a windjammer cruise means swinging aboard an antique or replica wooden sailing vessel, stowing your duffel bag, and letting the wind carry you away—overnight or for three or six days.

Named for their ability to "jam" into the wind when they carried freight up and down the New England coast, windjammers conjure images of the Great Age of Sail. Most are rigged as schooners, with two or three soaring wooden masts; one is rigged as a ketch, with two masts

in a slightly different configuration. Another member of the cruise flotilla, though far from a windjammer, is the handsomely restored sardine carrier *Pauline.* Windjammers are 64-132 feet long and carry 20-44 passengers.

You're aboard for the experience, not for luxury, so expect basic accommodations with few frills. Most boats have shared showers and toilets; some have in-cabin sinks. Quarters are fairly tight, but you'll want to spend as much time as possible on deck anyway. Deck tarps provide shelter from rain or sun.

Highlights of a windjammer cruise include stupendous scenery, hearty food, sing-alongs, sunsets to die for, and a grand finale lobster-bake on a deserted shore. Most popular cruising time is the Fourth of July week, when the annual Great Schooner Race in Penobscot Bay lures these majestic vessels for a giant celebration.

Home base for all Maine's cruising windjammer schooners is the Mid-Coast region—nearly two dozen vessels sail out of Camden, Rockport, and Rockland.

When you book a cruise, you receive all the details and directions, but for a typical six-day trip you arrive at the boat by 7 p.m. for the captain's call to meet your fellow passengers. You sleep aboard at the dock that night, then depart mid-morning Monday and spend five nights and days cruising Penobscot Bay, following the wind, the weather, and the whims of the captain. (Many of the windjammers have no engines, only a motorized yawlboat used as a pusher and a water taxi.) You might anchor in a deserted cove and explore the shore, or you might pull into a harbor and hike, shop, and bar-hop. Food aboard is always excellent. When the cruise ends on Saturday morning, most passengers find it hard to leave.

Costs for most of the three- to six-day cruises range from $335-725, with all meals. Windjammer cruising is *not* designed for infants or small children. Best source of information about 10 windjammers is **The Maine Windjammer Association,** P.O. Box 1144, Blue Hill 04614, tel. (800) 807-9463, fax (207) 374-2952. Contact three other first-rate windjammers—*American Eagle, Heritage,* and *Isaac H. Evans*—at **North End Shipyard Schooners,** P.O. Box 482, Rockland 04841, tel. (800) 648-4544, fax (207) 594-8015.

looking over the bowsprit at the waters of Penobscot Bay

SAILING EXCURSIONS

All along the coast, from York to Mount Desert Island, small sailing vessels offer daytime excursions lasting anywhere from two hours to an entire day. Depending on the type of sailing, the size of crew, and the amenities you prefer, you can choose a small sloop, a classic yacht, or a windjammer schooner. Best places for sailing excursions are York Harbor, Kennebunkport, Portland, Boothbay Harbor, East Boothbay, Camden, Rockport, Bar Harbor, Northeast Harbor, and Southwest Harbor.

POWERBOAT EXCURSIONS

Maine's coast, lakes, and rivers are all sites for an incredible variety of excursions in motorized boats. In Naples, you can cruise Long Lake and transit the historic Songo River Lock aboard the restored sternwheeler *Songo River Queen II.* On Great Pond (inspiration for the film *On Golden Pond*), in Belgrade Lakes, you can board a pontoon boat and ride along as the mail carrier delivers mail to dockside boxes. Greenville is the home of the SS *Katahdin* (better known as the *Kate*), a onetime workhorse of the lumber industry that now cruises stunning Moosehead Lake. Jonesport and Cutler, way Down East,

are the departure points for day-long boat trips to the famed puffin colony on Machias Seal Island. You can learn about the lobster industry aboard lobsterboats based in Ogunquit, Kennebunkport, Boothbay Harbor, Camden, Northeast Harbor, and Bar Harbor. From Portland and South Freeport, you can cruise out to Eagle Island, former home of arctic explorer Adm. Robert Peary. (The island is now a State Historic Site, with trails and picnic spots.) Or you can just go along for scenic rides aboard boats leaving Ogunquit, Kennebunk, Bath, Boothbay Harbor, New Harbor, Rockland, Camden, Belfast, Stonington (on Deer Isle), Northeast Harbor and Bass Harbor (both on Mount Desert Island), Rockwood (on Moosehead Lake), and Cutler. See regional chapters for details.

WHALEWATCHING

Your best venues for whalewatching trips are Bar Harbor, Eastport, Kennebunkport, Northeast Harbor, and Portland. Greatest selection is in Bar Harbor, where the College of the Atlantic sponsors the Allied Whale conservation program ("Adopt a Whale"). Since whalewatching sometimes involves riding the swells while waiting for the behemoths to surface, be sure to arm yourself against seasickness.

INFORMATION AND SERVICES

TOURISM INFORMATION AND MAPS

Maine On-Line
In 1995, the Office of Tourism established a Maine home page on the World Wide Web (www.state.me.us). You'll find chamber of commerce addresses, articles, photos, information on lodgings, and access to a variety of Maine tourism businesses. But hundreds of other Maine pages are also up and running or in the works, so surf away.

Local Chambers of Commerce and Tourism Offices
Tourism is Maine's second-largest source of revenue, so almost every community of any size has some kind of information office, ranging from York's mansion-like quarters to tiny log cabins. Some are staffed by volunteers and open only in summer. Most of these communities also produce annual booklets, brochures, or maps loaded with tourism info. In remote areas, local shopkeepers, lodging hosts, and town-office employees are the best alternative information sources. If you haven't planned ahead, ask for suggestions for places to sleep, eat, shop, and play. No question is too foolish—and you can bet they've heard it before. Addresses and phone numbers of local tourism offices are listed in Publicity Bureau's *Maine Invites You* magazine and in the regional chapters of this book.

Maps
Maine is the home of the DeLorme Mapping Company, publisher of *The Maine Atlas and Gazetteer*. Despite an oversize format inconvenient for hiking and kayaking, this 90-page paperbound book just about guarantees that you won't get lost. Scaled at 1/2 inch to the mile, it's meticulously compiled from aerial photographs, satellite images, U.S. Geological Survey maps, and paper-company maps and is revised annually. DeLorme publications are available nationwide in book and map stores, but you can also order with a credit card by calling (800) 227-1656, ext. 5000 outside Maine, (800) 734-5780, ext. 5000 in Maine. The atlas is $16.95 and shipping is $4 (Maine residents need to add six percent sales tax).

DeLorme also publishes an annual edition of *The Maine Map and Guide*, a standard folding map with detailed insets of major cities and towns, and helpful information on the reverse. It's available in supermarkets, convenience stores, gift shops, bookstores, sporting-goods stores, and some tourist offices. If

---

MAINE VISITOR INFORMATION CENTERS

The Maine Publicity Bureau, a private, nonprofit corporation contracted by the state to promote Maine tourism, operates the seven information centers listed below, all at high-traffic locations. All have knowledgeable staff members, free restrooms, extensive racks of free brochures, and maps and booklets for sale. All are open daily 9 a.m.-5 p.m., but 8 a.m.-6 p.m. between July 1 and Columbus Day (early October, same weekend as Canadian Thanksgiving). All but one (Fryeburg) are open year-round.

To receive a free copy of the bureau's annual foldout map and its 300-page *Maine Invites You* magazine—filled with articles, photos, and ads, as well as addresses of all of the state's chambers of commerce/tourism offices—contact: **Maine Publicity Bureau, Inc.,** 325B Water St., P.O. Box 2300, Hallowell 04347-2300; tel. (800) 533-9595 outside Maine, or (207) 623-0363.

Kittery: Accessible from both I-95 and Rt. 1

Yarmouth: I-95 Exit 17 (near Freeport)

Fryeburg: Rt. 302 (near New Hampshire border; seasonal)

Hampden: I-95 northbound at mile 169; I-95 southbound at mile 172 (both near Bangor)

Calais: 7 Union St. (near St. Stephen, New Brunswick, border)

Houlton: Ludlow Rd. (near New Brunswick border)

Bethel: 18 Mayville Rd., Rt. 2 (near New Hampshire border)

you're headed for L.L. Bean and share my addiction to geography, stop in Yarmouth (across from the visitor information center) at the DeLorme Map Store, Rt. 1, tel. (207) 846-7100. Its 42-foot rotating globe alone is worth a visit.

Guidebooks

The Booklist in the back of this book will steer you toward special-focus guides that will supplement (but of course not replace) the *Maine Handbook.* Now out of print but still fascinating as background reading is *Maine: A Guide "Downeast,"* the 1970 edition of the original 1937 Federal Writers' Project volume. It's even more fun if you can pick up a copy of the first edition, an encyclopedic 500-page compendium produced by a talented team of underemployed researchers/writers. Read the history and architecture sections, and check out the old photos. The first edition can be hard to find in Maine's used-book stores, which of course is where everyone looks for it, so start by checking with out-of-state used-book dealers. A copy spotted in Maine in 1996 was going for $15— well worth it.

Where Is It?

Billboards are banned in Maine, but there's no lack of signage. State-sanctioned directional signs, restricted to a standard horizontal format, are posted along roadsides everywhere. Searching for a B&B in the boonies? Watch for a sign with the name and mileage as you get closer. In the more populated areas, the signs approach overkill, and it can be hard to pick out what you're looking for, but in remote terrain the placards are a blessing for the uninitiated. Some businesses have creatively adopted variant colors, but blue generally indicates businesses, brown signifies museums, state parks, and historic sites. State town-to-town mileage signs are green, as are the Maine Turnpike and interstate signs.

CUSTOMS PROCEDURES

Canadian citizens need no visa—just a valid passport—to enter the United States through Maine or any other crossover point. Duty-free limits for Canadians returning home are C$20 after a 24-hour stay, C$100 after 48 hours, and C$300 after seven days (not counting departure day). The first two exemptions can be claimed any number of times; the $300 exemption is valid only once a year.

Canadians visiting the United States for at least 72 hours may bring back gifts valued as high as US$100, but no more than twice a year. Here's an odd regulation, obviously easy to circumvent: Canadians can carry one liter of beer, wine, or liquor as a personal effect but not as a gift.

Visitors are also allowed to bring in 200 cigarettes, 50 cigars (though not Cuban ones), or 4.4 pounds of tobacco. Duty assessed on items over and above the personal exemptions is three and a half percent.

There is no limit on the amount of money or traveler's checks a nonresident may bring into the U.S. If the amount exceeds $10,000, however, it's necessary to fill out an official report form.

No fruit, vegetables, or plant materials can be taken across the border in either direction. A strict customs official once confiscated a flourishing 20-year-old jade plant a friend was carting across the border, and we suspect it's still adorning his living room.

TIME AND MONEY

Time Zone

All of Maine is in the eastern time zone, same as New York, Washington, D.C., Philadelphia, and Orlando, Florida. Eastern standard time (EST) runs from the last Sunday in October to the last Sunday in April; eastern daylight time (EDT), one hour later, prevails otherwise. If your itinerary also includes Canada, remember that the provinces of New Brunswick and Nova Scotia are on Atlantic time—one hour later than eastern.

Every day during the summer, cruise ferries travel between Yarmouth, Nova Scotia, and Portland and Bar Harbor, losing and gaining an hour en route. Their schedules are printed in local time at either terminus—EST in Maine, Atlantic time in Nova Scotia. And Campobello Island, site of the Roosevelt Campobello International Park, operates exclusively on Atlantic time.

Currency
Since much of Maine borders Canada, don't be surprised to see a few Canadian coins mixed in with American ones when you receive change from a purchase. In such cases, Canadian and US quarters are equivalent, although the exchange rate is in fact drastically different. In 1997, C$1 is worth only US 72 cents. Most ser-

vices (including banks) will accept a handful of Canadian coins at par, but you'll occasionally spot No Canadian Currency signs. Until the early 1980s, the two currencies were exchangeable one-for-one, but they've been drawing apart ever since (the mid-1990s disparity led to a tourism vacuum afflicting such southern Maine communities as Ogunquit and Old Or-

USEFUL CONTACTS

Acadia National Park, P.O. Box 177, Bar Harbor 04609, tel. (207) 288-3338 (general information) or (800) 365-2267 (camping reservations).

Allagash Wilderness Waterway, tel. (207) 941-4014 (general information) or 435-7963 (dispatch center).

Allied Whale (Adopt-a-Whale program), College of the Atlantic, 105 Eden St., Bar Harbor 04609, tel. (207) 288-5644.

American Automobile Association, tel. (800) 482-7497 (general road info) or (800) 222-4357, mid-Nov.-March (winter road conditions).

Appalachian Mountain Club, Maine Chapter, tel. (207) 799-5312.

Bangor International Airport, tel. (207) 947-0384.

Baxter State Park Headquarters, 64 Balsam Dr., Millinocket 04462, tel. (207) 723-5140 (general information by phone; reservations by mail or in person).

Bicycle Coalition of Maine, P.O. Box 5275, Augusta 04332 (statewide advocacy group).

Bicycle Transportation Alliance of Portland, P.O. Box 4506, Portland 04112, tel. (207) 773-3053.

Casco Bay Lines, Commercial and Franklin Sts., Portland 04101, tel. (207) 774-7871 (ferries to Casco Bay islands).

Concord Trailways, tel. (800) 699-3317 (bus service to and from Boston's Logan Airport).

Greater Portland Landmarks, 165 State St., Portland 04101, tel. (207) 774-5561 (Portland-area historic preservation and site information; weekly guided tours).

Greater Portland Visitor Information Center, 305 Commercial St., Portland 04101, tel. (207) 772-5800.

Hurricane Island Outward Bound School, P.O. Box 429, Rockland 04841, tel. (207) 594-5548 (sailing and wilderness courses).

Island Institute, 410 Main St., Rockland 04841, tel. (207) 594-9209, fax 594-9314 (clearinghouse/advocate for Maine's islands).

Kennebec River water-flow information, tel. (800) 287-0999.

L.L. Bean, 95 Main St. (Rt. 1), Freeport 04032, tel. (800) 341-4341, ext. 6666.

Maine Appalachian Trail Club, P.O. Box 283, Augusta 04332.

Maine Audubon Society, 118 U.S. Rt. 1, P.O. Box 6009, Falmouth 04105, tel. (207) 781-2330, fax 781-6185.

Maine Bureau of Parks and Lands, 22 State House Station, Augusta 04333, tel. (207) 287-3821 (general information); tel. (800) 332-1501 in Maine, or (207) 287-3824 or fax 287-6170 (state park camping reservations).

Maine Campground Owners Association, 655 Main St., Lewiston 04240, tel. (207) 782-5874, fax 782-4497 (commercial campground information clearinghouse).

Maine Coast Heritage Trust, 169 Park Row, Brunswick 04011, tel. (207) 729-7366 (conservation land-trust clearinghouse).

chard Beach—longtime destinations of French-Canadian vacationers).

It's not absolutely necessary to exchange currency when traveling between the two countries, but Canadian dollars are worth far less (and US dollars far more) in the United States. Also, the farther south of Canada you roam, the more likely it is you'll find resistance to Canadian currency in restaurants and shops. It's easier to convert it than to try to spend it in Maine.

Banks and Automated Teller Machines
Typical Maine banking hours are 9 a.m.-3 p.m. weekdays, occasionally with later hours on Friday. Drive-up windows at many banks tend to open as much as an hour earlier and stay open

---

Maine Crafts Association, 6 Dow Rd., P.O. Box 228, Deer Isle 04627, tel. (207) 348-9943.

Maine Department of Inland Fisheries and Wildlife, 284 State St., 41 State House Station, Augusta 04333, tel. (207) 287-8000 (fishing license information) or 287-5230 (boating regulations).

Maine Forest Service, tel. (207) 287-2791 (campfire permit information).

Maine Historical Society, 485 Congress St., Portland 04101, tel. (207) 774-1822 (museum; research).

Maine Island Trail Association, 328 Main St., Rockland 04841, tel. (207) 596-6456 or 41A Union Wharf, Portland 04101, tel. (207) 761-8225 (conservation-oriented coastal waterway route for sea kayakers and other boaters).

Maine Outdoor Adventure Club (Portland area), tel. (207) 828-0918.

Maine Publicity Bureau, 325B Water St., P.O. Box 2300, Hallowell 04347, tel. (800) 533-9595 or (207) 623-0363 (state tourism information clearinghouse).

Maine Snowmobile Association, 7 Noyes Pl., P.O. Box 77, Augusta 04330, tel. (207) 622-6983 (general information) or (800) 880-7669 (hotline).

Maine Sporting Camp Association, P.O. Box 89, Jay 04239.

Maine State Ferry Service, 16 State House Station, Augusta 04333, tel. (207) 624-7777 for general schedule information, or (800) 491-4883 for a daily recorded update (ferries to six offshore islands).

Maine State Police, tel. (800) 482-0730.

Maine Turnpike Authority, tel. (800) 675-7453 (road conditions) or (207) 871-7740 (general business).

Maine Windjammer Association, P.O. Box 1144, Blue Hill 04614, tel. (800) 807-9463.

National Weather Service, tel. (207) 688-3210 (recorded local and marine weather).

Nature Conservancy, Maine Chapter, 14 Maine St., Fort Andross, Brunswick 04011, tel. (207) 729-5181, fax 729-4118.

North Maine Woods, Inc., P.O. Box 421, Ashland 04732, tel. (207) 435-6213, fax 435-8479 (timberlands recreational management; campsite reservations).

Poison Control Center, tel. (800) 442-6305.

Portland International Jetport, tel. (207) 774-7301.

Portland Sea Dogs (AA baseball), Hadlock Field, Portland, tel. (207) 879-9500 or (800) 936-3647 (tickets), or (207) 874-0945 (parking hotline).

Raft Maine, P.O. Box 3, Bethel 04217, tel. (207) 824-3694 or (800) 723-8633 (whitewater-rafting clearinghouse).

Sierra Club, Maine Chapter (Portland area), tel. (207) 761-5616.

Ski conditions, tel. (800) 533-9595 (alpine) or (800) 754-9263 (nordic).

U.S. Customs, tel. (207) 780-3328.

White Mountain National Forest, Evans Notch Ranger District, Rt. 2, Mayville Rd., Box 2270, Bethel 04217, tel. (207) 824-2134 (general information).

an hour or so after lobbies close. Some banks also maintain Saturday morning hours, a phenomenon on the increase. But as long as you have an automated teller machine (ATM) or debit card or a credit card, you can go almost anywhere in Maine (offshore islands don't have ATMs) at any time and withdraw money from your personal checking, savings, or credit-card account. Remember that some banks charge a fee for ATM transactions. You can call the electronic banking network connected with your ATM card to find out the closest banking option: Cirrus, tel. (800) 424-7787; PLUS, tel. (800) 843-7587. A recorded message will ask you to enter the area code and first three digits of any local phone number. You'll then hear a listing of nearby ATM machines.

Maine's major banks are Coastal Bank, Key Bank, Fleet Bank, and Peoples Heritage Bank.

If you need to exchange foreign currency—other than Canadian dollars—do it at or near border crossings or in Portland. In small communities, such transactions are more complicated; you may end up spending more time and money than necessary.

Credit Cards/Traveler's Checks
Bank credit cards have become so preferred and so prevalent that it's nearly impossible to rent a car or check into a hotel without one (the alternative is payment in advance or a hefty cash deposit). MasterCard and Visa are most widely accepted in Maine, Discover and American Express are next most popular, but Carte Blanche, Diners Club, and EnRoute (Canadian) lag far behind. The Japan Credit Bureau card is gaining acceptance, particularly in Freeport—a magnet for Japanese travelers. Be aware, however, that small restaurants, shops, and B&Bs off the beaten track often don't accept credit cards; you may need to settle your account with a personal check, cash, or traveler's check.

With the popularity of credit cards, traveler's checks have lost favor, but if you decide to carry them, be sure they are in U.S. dollar amounts.

Most major petroleum firms—Exxon, Texaco, Mobil, Citgo, Getty, Chevron, Sunoco, and Gulf—have filling stations in Maine. Most accept their own credit cards as well as Master-Card, Visa, and Discover. The Irving Corpora-

tion, a Canadian firm with many stations in Maine, doesn't have its own gasoline card but accepts MasterCard, Visa, American Express, and Discover.

Taxes
Maine charges a six percent sales tax on items such as gifts, snacks, books, clothing, and video rentals, and a seven percent tax on all bar, restaurant, and lodging bills. Bear in mind, especially when making reservations by phone, that restaurants and lodgings usually do *not* include the seven percent tax when quoting their prices over the phone. A whopping 10% tax is added to car rental rates.

Tipping
The longtime restaurant tipping standard—15% of the total bill—still prevails in most of Maine. One exception is Portland, where a big-city 20% rate isn't unusual in the upscale restaurants. However, the restaurant tip should depend on the quality of the service (if you've ever worked in a restaurant, you know how much tips are appreciated—but they need to be earned). Don't penalize a waitperson for the kitchen's mistakes, but do reduce the tip if the service is sloppy.

Taxi drivers expect a 15% tip; airport porters expect at least $1 per bag, depending on the difficulty of the job. If a porter simply unloads a suitcase from a car for curbside check-in, 50 cents is plenty; if he has to escort you to a ticket counter—and especially if he arranges for speedier service—a dollar per bag is appropriate.

Tipping in lodgings is another matter. I find inappropriate the increasingly popular envelope-in-the-room strategy. Expense-account travelers can be cavalierly generous, but independent travelers should not have to support low wage scales. I know that's what happens in restaurants, but it probably started the same way and gradually became the rule; I support halting the envelope practice now.

Special Discounts
The automobile association AAA is the largest discounter for tourism, arranging special rates for its members at lodgings, restaurants, museums, ski resorts, and amusement parks. Sometimes there are unadvertised discounts as well.

Contact the AAA office nearest your home or AAA Northern New England, 425 Marginal Way, Portland 04101, tel. (207) 780-6800 or (800) 482-7497.

Anyone planning to spend time in the state parks—especially families—should consider buying a **state park day-use season pass**, issued by the Bureau of Parks and Lands, 22 State House Station, Augusta 04333, tel. (207) 287-3821, but also available at the gates of all major state parks. A $40 vehicle pass allows everyone in the car (or van or camper) free daytime use; a $20 individual pass applies only to the pass-holder. Senior citizens (over 65) get in free, as do children under age five.

Another bargain is the **Children's Fun Pass,** issued by the American Lung Association of Maine (ALAM). For $15, a child 12 and under receives free admission (when accompanied by an adult) to more than 50 Maine attractions (as well as a few dozen more in other New England states), primarily museums, amusement parks, and boat rides, but a few ski areas are also included. A big plus: The pass proceeds benefit smoking-prevention projects for Maine kids. ALAM also markets the **Golf Privilege Card,** providing 70 rounds of golf for $70—a real deal. About 75 courses in Maine, New Brunswick, and Nova Scotia participate in the program. Both passes are available through the American Lung Association of Maine (ALAM), 122 State St., Augusta 04330, tel. (207) 622-6394 or (800) 458-6472, fax (207) 626-2919, beginning early in the year or at all Key Bank branches in Maine beginning in April.

If you're planning to spend any time sampling restaurants in the Greater Portland area, consider joining the **Portland Dine-Around Club,** 477 Congress St., Portland 04101, tel. (207) 775-4711, which gets you two-for-the-price-of-one meals (usually dinner entrées) at 70 or so restaurants with a wide variety of menus, decor, and price ranges. Two or three nights out and you've covered the cost of the $30 membership. Some limitations apply, but it's still a bargain.

Each of Maine's telephone directories contains a special section of discount coupons—more than 300 in Portland, for instance. If you can put your hands on a directory, browse the bargains, clip coupons, and take advantage of deals on pizzas, bagels, balloons, bike tune-ups, photo processing, and lots more.

Bear in mind, when looking for bargains, that the cost of off-season lodging is inevitably lower—sometimes dramatically lower—than during the busiest months of June, July, and August. Some lodgings extend their high-season rates to mid-October (to take in the foliage season), and lodgings in western Maine, near the ski areas, turn the tables—winter is the high season.

COMMUNICATIONS AND MEDIA

Postal and Shipping Services

Post offices in Maine cities and towns are open six days a week, Mon.-Sat., usually 8 a.m.-5 p.m., although Saturday service in smaller communities typically is 8 a.m.-noon. (In the phone book, post offices are listed under US Government.) If you only need stamps for postcards or letters, ask for them at gift shops or look for vending machines at supermarkets (most of these machines only carry domestic postage).

Portland is the home of Maine's first **postal store**—a glitzy, 6,500-square-foot emporium where you can select your own stamps, buy collectors' packets and books, make photocopies, and send faxes. Waiting lines are short, and self-service machines speed things along. The store, 400 Congress St., tel. (207) 871-8464, is open Mon.-Fri. 8 a.m.-7 p.m. and Saturday 9 a.m.-1 p.m., closed Sunday.

Sending an airmail letter overseas costs 60 cents for the first half-ounce, 40 cents for each additional half-ounce. An airmail postcard stamp or a self-contained aerogramme costs 50 cents. A regular letter to Canada is 52 cents for the first ounce, a postcard is 35 cents.

Cities and large towns have strategically placed Express Mail, UPS, and Federal Express boxes. To contact Federal Express, call (800) 238-5355; to contact UPS, call (800) 742-5877. Other national/international delivery services available in Maine are Airborne Express, tel. (800) 247-2676, and DHL, tel. (800) 225-5345.

With more than a dozen franchise offices in various parts of the state, Mail Boxes Etc. offers every imaginable type of packing and shipping assistance, as well as Western Union, photocopy, and fax services. You can even rent a short-term mailbox if you plan to stay in one area several days or longer. If you want to arrange for an address and/or phone/fax number in advance, call Mail Boxes Etc. in Portland, tel. (207) 871-9355, for locations of their other Maine offices.

If you expect to receive mail while in Maine, have your correspondents address it to you c/o General Delivery in the town or city where you expect to be and mark it "Hold for arrival on [your estimated arrival date]." Be sure to give them that post office's correct zip code (every post office has a national zip code directory; overseas residents can check with the nearest U.S. embassy or consulate).

Area Code
Maine has only one telephone area code—207—and in-state phone rates are relatively high. Calling out-of-state (dial 1 plus the area code before the number) often is cheaper! Within Maine, directory assistance is 411; anywhere beyond Maine, it's 1 plus the area code plus 555-1212. From outside Maine, regular and directory-assistance calls require use of the number 1 plus the 207 area code. Any number with an area code of 800 or 888 is toll-free.

Cellular Phones
When you're on vacation, a ringing telephone should be the absolute last thing you want to think about, but needs do arise. Transmission towers are now sprinkled everywhere; only a few pockets—mostly in remote valleys and hollows—are out of cellular-phone range. (Keep in mind, however, that if you're planning to camp in Baxter State Park, you won't be allowed to use your phone or any other kind of electronic equipment. Baxter authorities work hard—and effectively—to maintain the park's "forever wild" philosophy.)

If you're bringing your own phone from out of state, you know the drill for roaming calls. If you need to rent a phone, the major cellular firms are Cellular One, tel. (800) 999-2369; Maine Wireless, tel. (800) 839-5454; UNICEL, tel. (800) 244-9979; United States Cellular, tel. (800) 234-8722; and Western Maine Cellular, tel. (800) 649-7303. Call ahead and make arrangements a few days in advance to be sure they have a phone package on hand. You'll

need to leave a hefty security deposit (typically $200, payable with a credit card and refundable upon return of the phone). A month-long rental, with minimal use, will run at least $50. (Shorter-term rentals are available.) Voice mail and other features will jack up the cost. Assess your needs realistically.

Newspapers, TV, and Radio
Maine's daily newspapers are the *Portland Press Herald,* Augusta's *Kennebec Journal,* the *Bangor Daily News, Lewiston Sun Journal, Biddeford Journal Tribune, Brunswick Times Record,* and Waterville's *Central Maine Morning Sentinel.* Some other papers publish twice or three times a week, and weekly newspapers number in the dozens.

Every major community in the more populous areas of the state has a weekly "shopper," supplemented in summer by special weekly tourist tabloids. You'll see these free publications everywhere: restaurants, convenience stores, gift shops, bookstores, supermarkets, art galleries, and more. Check these for ads and listings of such local activities as concerts, lectures, public suppers, films, hikes, art and museum exhibits, and festivals.

Along the coast, most newspapers publish a daily or weekly tide calendar, essential information for anyone planning to fish, dive, sail, or kayak. The daily papers have a particularly informative weather half-page. The 6 p.m. and 11 p.m. TV newscasts always include tide, sunrise, and sunset details in their weather segments.

Portland and Bangor are Maine's TV centers; each has affiliates of ABC, CBS, and NBC networks. Maine Public Broadcasting Network airs its TV programs on channels 10, 12, 13, or 26, depending on your location. MPBN radio transmits over five different frequencies around the state.

In 1995, Maine licensed its 100th radio station, virtually saturating the airwaves and creating stiff commercial competition. Most now have grabbed programming niches—country, classical, news, sports, big band, talk, oldies, rock. Many pride themselves on being community-oriented, broadcasting information about sports and cultural activities, lost animals, community schedule changes, and more. The most intriguing operation is WERU (89.9 FM), a community radio station headquartered on US1/ME3 in East Orland. A few paid staffers, countless volunteer DJs and hosts, and thousands of supportive listeners keep programming on the air round-the-clock. Affectionately dubbed Radio Free Spirit, the station broadcasts in-depth interviews, extensive calendar information, and an eclectic blend of music.

Down East

Available for $3.50 a copy at newsstands, supermarkets, bookstores, and gift shops everywhere in Maine, *Down East* magazine has been the state's chief booster since 1954. The monthly publication carries a potpourri of articles about places, people, trends, gardens, and history, plus glossy photos, travel tips, boatyard news, calendar items, pages of real estate ads, and dozens of classifieds for seasonal house and cottage rentals. During the year, special supplements focus on Maine travel, gardens, and boating. The *Down East Vacationtime Guide*, a separate, magazine-style publication with thorough coverage of summer activities, appears on newsstands every May. Cost is $3.95.

Down East is the oldest sibling of a publishing family that also includes Down East Books and several fishing and hunting magazines. A mailorder catalog offers Maine books, gifts, and crafts. Headquarters for all this output is a rambling, Shingle-style estate on the east side of Rt. 1 in Rockport, midway between Rockland and Camden. Weekdays 8:30 a.m.-4:30 p.m., you can stop in and browse for magazines, books, and gifts. *Down East* subscriptions officially are $29.90 a year, but rates as low as $22 are available from P.O. Box 679, Camden 04843, or tel. (800) 727-7422.

PUBLIC RESTROOMS

Unfortunately, public restrooms are in shorter supply in Maine than they ought to be, although some of the most visitor-oriented communities (such as Camden, Kennebunkport, Bar Harbor) have recognized the need and built facilities. Sad to say, some businesses post No Public Restrooms on their doors—and mean it. If you're traveling with kids, you're may be accustomed to being resourceful, but here are some general tips. Irving gas stations and McDonald's and Burger King fast-food joints would prefer that you patronize their establishments, but, even if you don't, you can use their restrooms. Some but not all other gas stations also have restrooms; you may need to ask at the office for a key. Restaurants are required to have restrooms, but it may be less awkward to buy a cup of coffee before using the facilities. Public buildings, such as hospitals, courthouses, police stations, libraries, and ferry terminals, have public restrooms, usually wheelchair-accessible. Most municipal parks and state-maintained roadside rest areas have seasonal pit or vault toilets—but no running water.

WHAT TO PACK

Clothing and Gear

In Maine, no matter what your itinerary, you won't be able to make do with a couple of bathing suits, shorts, sandals, and cover-ups; the weather is just too unpredictable. Of course, Maine *is* the home of L.L. Bean, so you could just stop in Freeport as soon as you arrive and buy your vacation wardrobe there. Seriously, though, in summer you'll need to pack shorts, swimwear, raingear, jeans and other long pants, cotton and wool sweaters, warm nightwear, and a warm jacket. For hiking, you'll want sturdy shoes, a brimmed hat, and a waterproof daypack. If you have a yen for freshwater swimming, throw in a pair of Reefrunners for navigating wet grass and slippery rocks. In spring and fall, skip the shorts, swimwear, and Reefrunners, double up on all the rest, and add a pair of gloves or mittens, a wool hat, and rubber-bottomed shoes or boots. In winter, double up even more, but always make sure to pack clothing you can don or doff in layers.

The dress code in summer is relaxed and informal. Unless you plan to plug into the cocktail-party circuit, or you feel more comfortable dressing up for dinner, you don't need to pack fancy clothes (a handful of restaurants require jackets, but most of those keep a few extras on hand). On the other hand, evenings are cool, so shorts won't do. Footwear is required in all restaurants. Unless you're canoeing the Allagash Wilderness Waterway or hiking the 100-Mile Wilderness on the Appalachian Trail, you'll rarely be far from a laundromat, so you shouldn't need to pack masses of underwear.

If you're planning to camp, get out your camping checklist and load up all those items. If you'll be doing any wilderness camping, keep in mind that even though most lean-tos are built facing away from the prevailing wind, it doesn't hurt to pack an extra tarp for wind protection on cold nights.

Other **important gear:** flashlight, compass, Swiss Army knife, small first-aid kit, binoculars, sunglasses, lip balm, camera (with an extra battery), whistle, small waterproof carryall, plastic water bottle with a belt hook or strap, health-insurance card, hiking maps and guides, and, perhaps most important of all, bug dope! If you

plan to spend any time outdoors in Maine between early May and late September, insect repellent is critical for keeping the state's abundant winged annoyances—especially blackflies, mosquitoes, and midges—at bay. Ben's and Cutter's work well, and Avon Skin-So-Soft lotion has become an inadvertent favorite recently (supermarkets and convenience stores seldom carry Avon products, but all carry the clone Skintastic, produced by the manufacturer of Off!). Home-remedy options include rubbing cider vinegar on your skin, drinking alcohol, and eating garlic.

Not much daunts blackflies, but you can lower your appeal by not using perfume, aftershave lotion, or scented shampoo and by wearing light-colored clothing.

HEALTH AND SAFETY

There's too much to do in Maine, and too much to see, to spend even a few hours laid low by illness or mishap. Be sensible—get enough sleep, wear sunscreen and appropriate clothing, know your limits and don't take foolhardy risks, heed weather and warning signs, carry water and snacks while hiking, don't overindulge in food or alcohol, always tell someone where you're going, and watch your step. If you're traveling with children, quadruple your caution.

Hospitals

All the hospitals in Maine's major population centers—primarily in southern Maine—feature round-the-clock emergency-room services with doctors and dentists on duty or on call. In these areas, dial 911 to get help. In sparsely populated corners of the state, regional acute-care hospitals serve large areas, but even small communities have volunteer ambulance corps with certified emergency medical technicians (EMTs) and sometimes paramedics. Coastal hospitals have helipads for emergency evacuations from offshore islands, but Maine has no commercial helicopter ambulance. The state's only helicopter ambulances fly out of the Naval Air Station in Brunswick and the National Guard base in Bangor. For emergencies on the islands, ferries and lobsterboats are commandeered. Float-

planes (skiplanes in the winter) provide evacuation services in the remote North Woods; Forest Service and park rangers and game wardens are essential parts of the response network.

Walk-in, quick-care clinics have sprung up in such areas as Portland, Scarborough, Bethel, Rockland, Camden, Orono, and Bangor. No appointments are necessary, but you should rely on these facilities only for minor cuts and bruises, earaches, allergy shots, low-grade fevers, and other ailments that would relegate you to the bottom of an emergency-room triage list.

Pharmacies

The major pharmacy chains are Rite-Aid and CVS; many Shop 'n Save supermarkets also have pharmacy departments. All carry prescription and nonprescription (over-the-counter) medications. The chains and Shop 'n Save pharmacies are open seven days a week, but not around the clock. Some independent pharmacists post emergency numbers on their doors and will go out of their way to help, but your best bet for a middle-of-the-night medication crisis is the nearest hospital emergency room.

If you take regular medications, be sure to pack an adequate supply, as well as a copy of your prescription in case you lose your medicine or need an unexpected refill.

Alternative Health Care

Nontraditional health-care options are available throughout the state, with concentrations around Portland, Camden/Rockport, and the Blue Hill Peninsula. Holistic practitioners, as well as certified massage therapists and acupuncturists, are listed in the Yellow Pages of local phone books. Also, check the bulletin boards and talk to the managers at food co-ops and health-food stores. They always know where to find homeopathic doctors.

Special Considerations During Hunting Season

During Maine's fall hunting season (late October and all of November)—and especially during deer season—walk or hike only in wooded areas marked No Hunting, No Trespassing, or Posted. And even if an area *is* closed to hunters, don't decide to explore the woods during deer season without wearing a blaze-orange (or "hunter orange") jacket or vest. If you have a dog along, be sure it, too, has an orange vest. Hunters are required to wear two items of orange clothing and typically select a vest and a hat. Orange gear is available in sporting-goods stores, hardware stores, and some supermarkets and convenience stores, especially in traditional hunting areas. To be completely safe, stick to one of the state parks or get your exercise on Sunday—when hunting is illegal.

During hunting season, moose and deer are on the move and made understandably skittish by the hunters invading their turf. At night, particularly in remote wooded areas, they often end up alongside or in the roads, so ratchet up your defensive-driving skills. Reduce your normal speed, use high beams when there's no oncoming traffic, and remain extra-alert. In a moose-vs.-car encounter, no one wins, and human fatalities are common. An encounter between a deer and a car may be less dangerous to humans (although the deer usually dies), but some damage is inevitable.

BLACK FLY
HEADNETS

SEASON'S GREETINGS

MAINE SPORT
Rt. 1, Rockport – 236-7120

AFFLICTIONS

Lyme Disease

A bacterial infection that causes severe arthritis-like symptoms, Lyme disease (named after the Connecticut town where it was first identified, in 1975) has been documented in Maine since 1986. (In Europe, the disease is known as borreliosis.) Although just over 100 cases had been reported in the state by 1996, only a *single* case was reported in 1990, and no reliable statistics exist on visitors who have left the state and experienced delayed onset of the disease—a frequent occurrence. Health officials monitor the situation carefully and issue cautionary warnings during prime tick season—mid-May into August. Lyme disease is spread by bites from tiny deer ticks (not the larger dog ticks, which don't carry it), which feed on the blood of deer, mice, songbirds, and humans. Symptoms include joint pain, extreme fatigue, chills, a stiff neck, headache, and a distinctive ring-like rash. Treatment is a fairly expensive round of antibiotics. Except for the rash, which occurs only in about 60% of victims, the symptoms mimic those of other ailments, such as the flu, so the disease is hard to diagnose. Preventive measures are essential. The rash, which expands gradually and usually is not painful, may appear from three days to a month after a bite. If left untreated, Lyme disease eventually can cause heart and neurological problems and debilitating arthritis.

Highest-risk sites are the wooded, marshy areas of south coastal Maine, between the New Hampshire border and Portland. Another high-risk pocket is Monhegan Island, about 11 miles off the coast. Visitors to Acadia National Park have also reported incidents of Lyme disease.

Two vaccines are in the testing stage, but there is currently no proven inoculation, so take precautions: Wear a long-sleeved shirt and long pants, and tuck the pant legs into your socks. Buy tick repellent at a supermarket or convenience store and use it liberally on your legs. Spray it around your cuffs and beltline. After any hike, check for ticks—especially behind the knees, and in the armpits, navel, and groin. Monitor children carefully. If you find a tick or suspect you have been bitten, head for the nearest hospital emergency room. If you spot a tick on you (or anyone else), remove it with tweezers and save it for analysis. Not all deer ticks are infected with the disease. For a brochure on avoiding and reporting Lyme disease, contact the Arthritis Foundation's Maine Chapter, tel. (800) 639-6650.

Rabies

Incidents of rabies—a life-threatening, nerve-attacking disease for which there is no cure unless treated immediately—have increased dramatically in Maine since 1994. No human has ever survived a case of rabies, and the disease is horrible, so *do not* approach, or let any child approach, any of the animals known to transmit it: raccoons, skunks, squirrels, bats, and foxes. Domestic dogs are required to have biennial rabies inoculations, which provides a front line of defense for humans. If you're bitten by any animal, especially one acting suspiciously, head for the nearest hospital emergency room. The virus travels along nerve roots to the brain, so a facial bite is far more critical, relatively speaking, than a leg bite. Treatment (a series of injections) is not as painful as it once was, but it's very expensive—and much better than the alternative. For statewide information about rabies, contact the Maine Disease Control Administration in Augusta, tel. (207) 287-3591.

Allergies (in the Land of Lobster and Bees)

If your medical history includes extreme allergies to shellfish or bee sting, you know the risks of eating a lobster or wandering around a wildflower meadow. However, if you live in a landlocked area and are new to crustaceans, you might not be aware of the potential hazard. Statistics indicate that less than two percent of adults have a severe shellfish allergy, but for those victims, the reaction sets in quickly. Immediate treatment is needed to keep the airways open. If you have a history of severe allergic reactions to *anything,* be prepared when you come to Maine dreaming of lobster feasts—ask your doctor for a prescription for EpiPen (epinephrine), a preloaded, single-use syringe

containing .3 mg of the drug—enough to tide you over until you can get to a hospital.

Seasickness

Samuel Butler, the 19th-century author of *Erewhon,* wrote, "How holy people look when they are sea-sick." He wasn't kidding. Seasickness conjures visions of the pearly gates and an overwhelming urge for instant salvation. Fortunately, even though the ailment seems to last forever, it's only temporary—depending on where you are, what remedies you have, and how your system responds. If you're planning to do any boating in Maine—particularly sailing—you'll want to be prepared. (Being prepared may keep you from succumbing, since fear of seasickness just about guarantees you'll get it.)

Seasickness allegedly stems from an inner-ear imbalance caused by boat motion, but researchers have had difficulty explaining why some people on a vessel become violently ill and others have no problem at all.

To prevent seasickness, try to stay in good shape. Get enough sleep and food, and keep your clothing warm and dry (not easy on a heeling sailboat). Some veteran sailors swear by salted crackers, sips of water, and bites of fresh ginger. If you start feeling queasy, keep your eyes on the horizon and stay as far away as possible from odors from the engine, the galley, the head, and other seasick passengers. If you become seasick, keep sipping water to prevent dehydration.

Dramamine, Marezine, and Bonine, taken several hours before a boat trip, have long been the preventives of choice. They do cause drowsiness, but anyone who's been seasick will tell you they'd rather be drowsy. Gaining popularity is the scopolamine patch (available by prescription under the trademark Transderm Scop), which gradually releases medication into the bloodstream for up to three days. Behind an ear or a knee is the best location for the little adhesive disc. Wash your hands after you touch it—the medication can cause temporary blurred vision if it comes in contact with your eyes. Children, pregnant women, and the elderly should not use scopolamine. Discuss the minor side effects with the physician who gives you the prescription.

And some people swear by the pressure bracelet, which operates somewhat on the principle of acupressure, telling your brain to ignore the fact that you're not on terra firma. Great success has been reported with these prophylactics in the last decade. Before embarking, especially if the weather is at all iffy, go ahead and put on a patch or a bracelet. Any such preventive measure also improves your mental attitude, relieving anxiety.

Sunstroke

Since Maine lies between 43 and 48° north latitude, sunstroke is not a major problem, but don't push your luck by spending an entire day frying on the beach in south coastal Maine. Not only do you risk sunstroke and dehydration, but you're also asking for skin cancer down the road. Early in the season, slather yourself, and especially children, with plenty of PABA-free sunblock. (PABA can cause skin rashes and eruptions, even on people not abnormally sensitive.) Depending on your skin tone, use sun protection factor (SPF) 15 or higher. If you're in the water a long time, slather on some more. Start with a half hour of solar exposure and increase gradually each day. If you don't get it right, watch for symptoms of sunstroke: fever, profuse sweating, headache, nausea or vomiting, extreme thirst, and sometimes hallucinations. To treat someone with sunstroke, find a breezy spot and place a cold, wet cloth on the victim's forehead. Change it frequently so it stays cold. Offer lots of liquids—strong tea or coffee, fruit juice, water, soft drinks (no alcohol).

Hypothermia and Frostbite

Wind and weather can shift dramatically in Maine, especially at higher elevations, creating prime conditions for contracting hypothermia and frostbite. At risk are hikers, swimmers, canoeists, kayakers, sailors, skiers, even cyclists.

When body temperature plummets below the normal 97-98.6°, hypothermia is likely to set in. Symptoms include disorientation, a flagging pulse rate, prolonged shivering, swelling of the face, and cool skin. Quick action is essential to prevent shock and keep body temperature from dropping into the 80s, where cardiac arrest can occur. Emergency treatment begins with removal of as much wet clothing as possible without causing further exposure. Wrap the victim in anything dry—blankets, sleeping bag, clothing, towels, even large plastic trash bags—to keep body heat from escaping. Be sure the neck and head are covered. Or practice the buddy system—climb into a sleeping bag with the victim and provide skin contact. Do not rub the skin, apply hot water, or elevate the legs. If he or she is conscious, offer high-sugar snacks and non-alcoholic hot drinks (but, again, no alcohol; it dilates blood vessels and disrupts the warming process). As quickly as possible, transport the victim to a hospital emergency room.

When extremities begin turning blue or gray, with red blotches, frostbite may be setting in. As with hypothermia, add warmth slowly but do not rub frostbitten skin. Offer snacks and warm, nonalcoholic liquids.

To prevent hypothermia and frostbite, dress in layers and remove or add them as needed. Wool, waterproof nylon (such as Gore-Tex), and synthetic fleece (such as Polartec) are the best fabrics for repelling dampness. Polyester fleece lining wicks excess moisture away from your body. If you plan to buy a down jacket, be sure it has a waterproof shell; down will just suck up the moisture from snow and rain. Especially in winter, always cover your head, since body heat escapes fastest through the head; a ski mask will protect ears and nose. Wear wool- or fleece-lined gloves and wool socks.

Even during the height of summer, be on the alert for mild hypothermia when children stay in the ocean too long. Bouncing in and out of the water, kids become preoccupied, refuse to admit they are cold, and fall prey to wind chill.

BOB RACE

SOUTH COAST/PORTLAND

Whip over the I-95 bridge from New Hampshire into Maine's South Coast region on a bright summer day and you'll swear the air is cleaner, the sky bluer, the trees greener, the roadside signs more upbeat: Welcome to Maine: The Way Life Should Be. (*Is* it? Or is it instead the way life *used* to be?)

Whether you enter southern Maine via I-95 or the parallel US1, stop first at the Maine Information Center, tel. (207) 439-1319, in Kittery, for maps, brochures, amazingly cheerful staffers, pay phones, clean restrooms, and an outdoor pet-recreation area.

Southernmost York County, part of the Province of Maine, was incorporated in 1636—only 16 years after the Mayflower pilgrims reached Plymouth, Massachusetts—and reeks of history: ancient cemeteries, musty archives, and architecturally stunning homes and public buildings. Probably the best place to dive into that history is Old York, a fascinating six-building museum complex in York Harbor.

Most visitors come to this region for the spectacular attractions of the justly world-famous Maine coast. But there's much more here than inlets, islands, and beaches. Any itinerary is enriched by a visit to inland York County—a trove of "best-kept secrets" and historic sites (it's home to, among other things, the state's first sawmill and the nation's oldest courthouse records). In-

land from the Yorks, the county stretches west and north through farmland and historic towns such as the Berwicks, Waterboro, Newfield, and Alfred, the county seat. When Old Kittery was incorporated, in 1647, Old Berwick was part of it. In 1714, the two areas severed their ties and Berwick incorporated on its own—making it the ninth-oldest incorporated town in Maine. Gradually, it spun off the separate communities of South Berwick in 1814 and North Berwick in 1831. For the history, the architecture, the New England scenery, and the literary past—and a setting made more enjoyable by the dearth of crowds—the region is well worth visiting.

But you can't *not* hit the coast, either. Following US1 northeast from the Yorks, you'll drive (slowly in midsummer) through Ogunquit, Wells, the Kennebunks, Biddeford, Saco, Old Orchard Beach, and on into Greater Portland. Geological fortune smiled on this 50-mile ribbon, endowing it with a string of sandy beaches—nirvana for sun worshipers, less enchanting to swimmers, who need to gird themselves to spend much time in the ocean (especially in early summer, before the water temperature has reached a tolerable level).

After Labor Day (the first Monday in September), the character of these communities changes markedly. Life goes on, but at a different (and still interesting) pace. Crowds and traffic thin, seasonal attractions go into hibernation, and many lodgings in southern Maine drop their rates dramatically, even though daytime weather and even the ocean can still be comfortably warm.

The pace actually increases after summer in Portland, seat of Cumberland County and Maine's premier population center. Greater Portland takes in a sprawling area from Scarborough on the south through Westbrook and Gorham to the west and on northward to Falmouth, Cumberland, Yarmouth, and Freeport.

KITTERY AND ELIOT

As well as being a natural point of entry into the state, Kittery also competes with Freeport, farther up the coast, as an outlet-shopping mecca —Kittery boasts 120 factory outlets, lining both sides of US 1. But before or after you overdose on shoes, china, toys, and underwear, take time to explore the back roads of Maine's oldest town—settled in 1623 and chartered in 1647. Maine is home to a lot of best-kept secrets, and Kittery is certainly one of them. Parks, a small nautical museum, historic architecture, and three lobster restaurants are only a few of the attractions in Kittery and its suburb, Kittery Point.

To reach Kittery's shops and services, as well as Eliot's lodgings, from I-95 northbound, take the Exit 3 cloverleaf, designated Kittery, Coastal Route 1, to Rt. 1. From I-95 southbound, take Exit 2. Follow signs; the twists and turns can be confusing.

Eliot, once a fishing, farming, and shipbuilding center on the Piscataqua River, now boasts well-preserved homes, wide-open spaces, and a sedate personality.

SIGHTS AND RECREATION

Kittery Historical and Naval Museum

Maritime history buffs shouldn't miss the small but well-stocked Kittery Historical and Naval Museum, Rogers Rd., near junction of Rts. 1 and 236, Kittery 03904, tel. (207) 439-3080. A large exhibit hall and a small back room contain ship models, fishing gear, old photos and paintings, and an astonishing collection of scrimshaw (carved whale ivory). Open weekdays June-Oct., 10 a.m.-4 p.m. Admission is $3 adults, $1.50 children (7-15), kids under seven free, family maximum $6.

Portsmouth Naval Shipyard Museum and Visitor Center

The Portsmouth Naval Shipyard has been here since 1800, and even though it has a New Hampshire name, it's actually located in Kittery —a continual source of political wrangling. Security is tight here, so plan ahead if you'd like to see the shipyard's museum. It's open every Thursday 10 a.m.-3 p.m., only by advance appointment; special arrangements can be made for other days, but that's even more complicated. Call museum director Jim Dolph at (207) 438-3550.

Lady Pepperrell House

Formerly open to the public, the 1760 Georgian Lady Pepperrell House, Pepperrell Rd., Rt. 103, shortly before the Fort McClary turnoff, is now privately owned. Nearby, across from the First Congregational Church, is the area's most-visited burying ground. Old-cemetery buffs should bring rubbing gear here for some interesting grave markers. The tomb of Levi Thaxter (husband of poet Celia Thaxter) bears an epitaph written for him by Robert Browning.

Fort McClary Historic Site

Since the early 18th century, fortifications have stood on this 27-acre headland, protecting Portsmouth Harbor from seaborne foes. Contemporary remnants at Fort McClary, Rt. 103, Kittery Point 03905, tel. (207) 439-2845, are several outbuildings, an 1846 blockhouse, granite walls, and earthworks—all with a dynamite view of Portsmouth Harbor. Opposite are the sprawling buildings of the Portsmouth Naval Shipyard. Bring a picnic (covered tables and a lily pond are across the street) and turn the kids loose to run and play. Officially open May 30-Oct. 1, but the site is accessible off season. Admission is $1 adults, 50 cents children (5-11), free for seniors

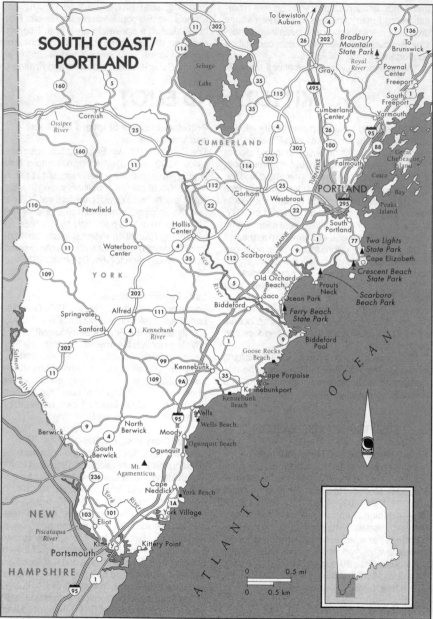

SOUTH COAST/
PORTLAND

© MOON PUBLICATIONS, INC.

(over 65) and kids under five. The fort is two and a half miles east of Rt. 1.

Fort Foster

The only problem with Fort Foster, Pocahontas Rd., off Rt. 103, Gerrish Island, Kittery Point 03905, tel. (207) 439-3800, is that it's no secret, so parking can be scarce at this 90-acre municipal park at the entrance to Portsmouth Harbor; on a hot day, arrive early. Then you can swim, hike the nature trails, fish off the pier (no license needed), picnic, and investigate the tide pools. Bring your sailboard and a kite—there's almost always a breeze. From nearby **Seapoint Beach** on a clear day, there's a wide-open view of the offshore Isles of Shoals, owned jointly by Maine and New Hampshire. The park is open Memorial Day to Labor Day, 10 a.m.-8 p.m., also May and September weekends. Admission is $1 adults, 50 cents children, and $2 for your car; no charge for bicycles.

Brave Boat Harbor

One of the Rachel Carson National Wildlife Refuge's 10 Maine coastal segments is Brave Boat Harbor, a beautifully unspoiled, 560-acre wetlands preserve in Kittery Point with a four-mile (roundtrip) trail. Carry binoculars, wear rubberized boots to maneuver the squishy areas, and slather on the insect repellent. The habitat is particularly sensitive here, so be kind to the environment. Take Rt. 103 to Chauncey Creek Road, continue past the Gerrish Island bridge to Cutts Island Lane. Turn left and park on the left near the small bridge. The trail's left fork leads to an abandoned trolley trestle, overlooking marshlands.

Route 103

The best way to appreciate this part of Maine is to drive or cycle along squiggly Rt. 103 from the Rt. 1 rotary in Kittery through Kittery Point (administratively part of Kittery) and on to Rt. 1A in York. If you're on a bike, the road's narrow in places, but forge ahead. You can even make a day of it, stopping at all the sites mentioned above.

Isles of Shoals

During turf battles in the 17th century, these nine offshore islands were split into two jurisdictions (now the two states of Maine and New Hampshire). Maine received five islands, New Hampshire four. Access to most of these windswept islands is restricted, but several excursion boats cruise the area. New Hampshire's **Star Island**—now a summer center for religious, artistic, and foreign-affairs conferences—allows 100 visitors a day to spend three hours on the island. Book well ahead for this popular trip, which departs daily at 11 a.m., mid-June-Labor Day, from the Portsmouth waterfront. Cost is $17 adults, $9 children (3-11), $16 seniors (65-79); under three and over 79 are free. A shorter, slightly cheaper, and less crowded Star Island trip—including a one-hour guided island walk—departs Sun.-Fri. at 7:30 a.m. Both tours are run by **Isles of Shoals Steamship Co.,** 315 Market St., P.O. Box 311, Portsmouth, NH 03802, tel. (800) 441-4620 or (603) 431-5500.

PRACTICALITIES

Kittery Accommodations

Next door to Cap'n Simeon's Galley and Frisbee's Supermarket, the **Whaleback Inn,** Box 162, Pepperrell Rd., Rt. 103, Kittery Point 03905, tel. (207) 439-9570, is an extremely casual, laissez-faire waterfront spot. Three rooms with shared bath go for $55-65 d. Breakfast is hearty continental. No smoking, no kids under 12, but small pets are welcome. Open May-October.

Just one-half mile mile west of "outlet central" on Rt. 1 is tranquil **Melfair Farm Bed & Breakfast,** 11 Wilson Rd., Rt. 101, Kittery 03904, tel. (207) 439-0320, where hospitable Claire Cane has four guest rooms on her nine-acre farm. One room has a private bath; others share two baths. No smoking, no pets (two well-behaved Dobermans in residence), no credit cards. Children are welcome; there's a two-night minimum on summer and fall holiday weekends. Rates are $60-75 d, lower in shoulder seasons. Open May-December.

Eliot Accommodations

Climb a steep, secluded driveway off Rt. 101, four and a half miles west of Rt. 1, and suddenly you're at **High Meadows Bed & Breakfast,** Goodwin Rd., Rt. 101, Eliot 03903, tel. (207) 439-0590, fax (207) 439-6343, the antiques-filled 1736 home of Elaine and Ray Michaud. Four rooms have private baths, some have canopied four-poster beds. Lots of comfortable corners for relaxing, including the renovated barn. No pets, no children under 12, and smoking only on the terrace. Complimentary afternoon refreshments. If the atmosphere sways you and a loved one, Elaine's a justice of the peace. Open April-Oct., rates run $80-90 d.

The handsomely restored, 18th-century **Moses Paul Inn,** 270 Goodwin Rd., Rt. 101, Eliot 03903, tel. (207) 439-1861 or (800) 552-6058 in Maine, is an oasis of calm—made even more so by congenial innkeepers Joanne Weiss and Larry James. (Joanne's an interpreter for the deaf, Larry's a merchant mariner.) Ten minutes (five and a half miles) from bustling Kittery and you're ensconced on their patio overlooking fields, woods, and gardens. Walking and cross-country-skiing trails adjoin the five-acre spread. User-friendly antiques and an exposed-beam parlor add to the comfort level. There's two first-floor rooms with private baths; three second-floor rooms (up steep stairways) share a bath. Rooms go for $65-75 d, lower rates off season. No pets, no smoking, no children under 12. Open all year.

Family-friendly **Farmstead Bed & Breakfast,** 379 Goodwin Rd., Rt. 101, Eliot 03903, tel. (207) 439-5033, even provides coloring placemats to entertain kids during the sumptuous breakfast. Innkeeper John Lippincott, an Air Force retiree, specializes in cheese strata and seven kinds of pancakes. Six guest rooms, $65-75 d, have private baths. Outside are horseshoes, badminton, a play area, a hammock, a gas grill, and a butterfly garden. The B&B is six miles west of I-95, near the junction of Rt. 236. Open all year.

Best camping spot in the area is **Indian Rivers Campground,** Rt. 101, Eliot 03903, tel. (207) 748-0844, with wooded sites, heated indoor pool, saltwater swimming, boat and canoe rentals, playground, free hookups (no RVs over 30 feet), and noise control. Flaunt the rules and you're out. A tentsite for a family of four is $15 daily, river sites are $1 more. Add $1 for more children, $2 more adults; pets (leashed) are 50 cents. Indian Rivers is seven miles west of Rt. 1, close to the South Berwick town line. Open May-October.

Kittery Food

Fancy dining isn't a Kittery specialty—there's plenty of that within walking distance at Portsmouth (New Hampshire) or driving distance in York. If you came to Maine to eat lobster, though, Kittery has three good spots for a quick fix. **Chauncey Creek Lobster Pier,** Chauncey Creek Rd., off Rt. 103, Kittery Point 03905, tel. (207) 439-1030, has the least pretense and the most character. Step up to the window, place your order, take a number, and grab a table (you may need to share) overlooking tidal Chauncey Creek and the woods on the opposite bank. A lobster roll goes for $7.50 and a packet of Skin-So-Soft for 60 cents. Open mid-May to mid-October 11 a.m.-7 p.m. BYOL. Also in Kittery Point is **Cap'n Simeon's Galley,** 90 Pepperrell Rd., Rt. 103, Kittery Point 03905, tel. (207) 439-3655, serving lunch, dinner, and Sunday brunch. Fresh seafood (mostly fried, albeit in vegetable oil) and a spectacular view are the draws here. Nothing particularly unusual—just decent cooking at reasonable prices, and a casual atmosphere conducive to bringing the kids. Fried clams are particularly tasty (a quart of 'em goes for $19.50), and young ones go for the burgers, dogs, subs, and fries. Open daily for lunch and dinner; closed Tuesday off season. Built on pilings at the edge of the Piscataqua River, **Warren's Lobster House,** 11 Water St., Rt. 1, Kittery 03904, tel. (207) 439-1630, began life as a diner in 1940 and has been packing 'em in ever since. The salad bar is the proverbial meal in itself—load up on the marinated mushrooms. Basic food, moderate prices, ample portions, river view, so-so service. Open daily for lunch and dinner, plus a huge, all-you-can-eat Sunday brunch (11 a.m.-2 p.m.) for $10.95.

Best **breakfast** spot is the **Sunrise Grill,** 182 State Rd., Rt. 1, Kittery Traffic Circle, Kittery 03904, tel. (207) 439-5748, where you can order waffles, granola, omelettes, or Diana's benedict 6:30 a.m.-2 p.m. Lots of salads, sandwiches, and burgers on the lunch menu, from 11 a.m. Thurs.-Sat.; dinner is available 4-8 p.m. BYOL. How about a German eye-opener? **Hänsel & Gretel,** 517 Rt. 1, Kittery 03904, tel. (207) 439-6132, serves up a Wood Cutter breakfast with scrambled eggs, bratwurst, apple slices, potato pancakes, and a pretzel for under $7. The alpine theme is a bit overdone, but the food is reliable and service is quick. Beer and wine only. Open daily for breakfast, lunch, and dinner.

For **picnic fare,** pick up a sandwich or salad at the Sunrise Grill or head down Rt. 103 to **Frisbee's Supermarket,** tel. (207) 439-0014, in Kittery Point, an experience in itself. Established in 1828, the store has marginally modernized but still earns its label as North America's oldest family store—run by the fifth generation of Frisbees. It's open Mon.-Sat. 8 a.m.-6 p.m., Sunday 8:30 a.m.-noon.

Eliot Food
Best kid-friendly place in Eliot for a homemade, reasonably priced meal is **Winnie's Restaurant,** in the Eliot Commons Mall, Rt. 236, two miles west of I-95, Eliot 03903, tel. (207) 439-5527. Breakfast is served all day, and burgers, PB&J, and hot dogs are always on the lunch menu. Open 6:30 a.m.-2 p.m., year-round.

SHOPPING

No question, you'll find bargains at Kittery's 120 (or so) factory outlets—actually a bunch of mini-malls clustered along both sides of Rt. 1. All the household names are here: Bass, Calvin Klein, Eddie Bauer, Izod, Mikasa, Esprit, Lenox, Timberland, Villeroy & Boch, and a hundred more. All shops are open daily; hours tend to vary. There's even the local version of famous Freeport outfitter L.L. Bean: the three-story **Kittery Trading Post,** Rt. 1, Kittery 03904, tel. (207) 439-2700, a 1930s-era sporting-goods emporium with 45,000 square feet of old-fashioned flavor and up-to-date wares. Open Mon.-Sat. 9 a.m.-9 p.m., Sunday 10 a.m.-6 p.m. Try to avoid the outlets on weekends, when you might need to take a number for the try-on rooms. Most of the mini-malls have restrooms and telephones; several have ATM machines.

INFORMATION

The **Kittery-Eliot Chamber of Commerce,** 191 State Rd., Rt. 1, P.O. Box 526, Kittery 03904, tel. (800) 639-9645 or (207) 439-7545, is the best source for information by mail. (Located across from the naval museum, it's open weekdays 10 a.m.-5 p.m.) If you're in the Rt. 1 outlet area, head for the **Kittery-Eliot Welcome Center,** behind McDonald's in the Maine Outlet Mall on Rt. 1, roughly midway along the factory-outlet strip, tel. (207) 439-9478. Hours are Mon.-Sat. 9 a.m.-9 p.m., Sunday 10 a.m.-6 p.m. The center has a touch-pad interactive computer system for local attractions and services.

INLAND YORK COUNTY

Several inland pockets in Maine's southwesternmost county too often go overlooked. The Wabanaki once summered here, sustaining themselves with salmon fishing and flourishing crops of corn and beans. The first Europeans who moved in revved up the agricultural output, established year-round trading centers, and built thriving sawmills (including the state's first) and shipbuilding wharves. The area once known as Old Berwick or Barwick incorporated in 1714 and gave birth to South Berwick in 1814 and North Berwick in 1831.

SOUTH BERWICK

Probably the best-known of the area's present-day communities is the riverside town of South Berwick—thanks to a historical and literary tradition dating back to the 17th century, and antique cemeteries to prove it. The 19th- and 20th-century novels of Sarah Orne Jewett and Gladys Hasty Carroll have lured many a contemporary visitor to explore their rural settings—an area aptly described by Carroll as "a small patch of earth continually occupied but never crowded for more than three hundred years."

Also here is the 150-acre hilltop campus of **Berwick Academy,** Maine's oldest prep school, chartered in 1791 with John Hancock's signature. The coed school's handsome gray-stone William H. Fogg Memorial Library ("The Fogg") is named for the same family connected with Harvard's Fogg Art Museum. Highlight of the library is an incredible collection of 100 19th-century stained-glass windows, many designed by Victorian artist Sarah Wyman Whitman. Thanks to a diligent fundraising effort, the windows recently have been restored to their former glory.

Sights and Recreation

Don't blink or you might miss the tiny sign outside the 19th-century **Sarah Orne Jewett House,** 5 Portland St., Rts. 4 and 236, South Berwick 03908, tel. (207) 384-2454, smack in the center of town. Park on the street and join

Hamilton House

one of the 45-minute tours—you'll learn details of the Jewett family and its star, Sarah (1849-1909), author of *The Country of the Pointed Firs,* a New England classic. Books by and about Sarah are available in the gift shop. Open Wed.-Sun. 11 a.m.-5 p.m., June 1-Oct. 15. Tours begin on the hour—last one at 4 p.m. Admission is $4 adults, $3.50 seniors, and $2 children 12 and under. The house is owned by the Boston-based Society for the Preservation of New England Antiquities (SPNEA), tel. (603) 436-3205.

Dramatically crowning a bluff overlooking the Salmon Falls River and flanked by handsome colonial gardens, 18th-century **Hamilton House,** 18 Vaughan's Ln., South Berwick 03908, tel. (207) 384-5269, evokes history and tradition. Like the Jewett House, the 35-acre site is owned by SPNEA. Knowledgeable guides relate the house's fascinating history in 45-minute tours. Open Wed.-Sun. 11 a.m.-5 p.m., June 1-Oct. 15. Tours begin only on the hour—last one at 4 p.m. Admission is $4 adults, $3.50 seniors, and $2 children 12 and under. Each Sunday at 4 p.m., early July to mid-August, SPNEA hosts **Sunday in the Garden,** a concert-cum-house tour ($5 admission for both; $2.50 for kids). Pray for sun; the concert is moved indoors on rainy days. From Rt. 236 at the southern edge of South Berwick (watch for a signpost), turn left onto Brattle St. and take the second right onto Vaughan's Lane.

A path connects Hamilton House to adjoining **Vaughan Woods State Park,** Old Fields Rd., South Berwick 03908, tel. (207) 384-5160, but it's not easy to find, and there's much more parking space at the main entrance to the 250-acre river's-edge preserve. Three miles of maintained trails wind through this underutilized park, and benches are scattered here and there. There's even a bench looking out over the river and Hamilton House. Picnic tables are located near the parking area, as are outhouses. Open Memorial Day weekend to Labor Day 9 a.m.-8 p.m., but accessible all year. Admission is $1 adults, free for kids 12 and under. As with directions for Hamilton House, take Brattle St. from Rt. 236. (Vine St. and Old South Rd., both off Rt. 236, also will get you there.) Turn left at Old Fields Rd. and continue to the park entrance. Both Hamilton House and Vaughan

Woods are easy bike rides from downtown South Berwick along wide, flat Rt. 236.

Based in a onetime cotton-mill building known as the Counting House, the **Old Berwick Historical Society,** Liberty and Main Sts., Rt. 4, P.O. Box 296, South Berwick 03908, tel. (207) 384-8041, sees a steady stream of genealogists looking for their roots in one of Maine's oldest settlements. Books and documents are only part of the museum's collection, which includes old photos and tools, boat models and nautical instruments, plus special annual exhibits. The **Counting House** is open every Saturday 1-4 p.m., July-Labor Day. Admission is free, but donations are welcomed. Also free is the society's monthly lecture series, Sept.-May; call for schedule.

Festivals and Events
The last weekend of June, the **Annual Strawberry Festival** is a longtime South Berwick tradition and the summer highlight, a huge festival including a pancake breakfast, a craft fair, live entertainment, pony rides, a barbecue, a public supper, races, family games, fireworks, and, of course, all the strawberries you can manage to consume. If you're there Friday morning, pitch in and help hull the berries at the Central School on Main Street.

Accommodations
Once the headmaster's residence for nearby Berwick Academy, the elegant, turn-of-the-20th-century **Academy Street Inn Bed & Breakfast,** 15 Academy St., South Berwick 03908, tel. (207) 384-5633, boasts crystal chandeliers, leaded-glass windows, working fireplaces, flowers everywhere, high-ceilinged rooms full of user-friendly antiques, and bikes for guests. Breakfast is served in the dining room or on the 60-foot screened porch—the only place smoking is permitted. In summer, two rooms have private baths, two share a bath; three have a/c. Rates run $55-70 d. Off season, only three rooms are rented, all with private baths. No pets, no children under 10. Open all year.

Food
A local institution since 1960, **Fogarty's,** 471 Lower Main St., South Berwick 03908, tel. (207) 384-8361, looks like your typical takeout place,

but its claim to fame is the freshest of fish, lightly fried and not dripping with grease. Open all year for lunch, brunch, and dinner.

Information and Services
Best source of local information is the South Berwick Town Office, 180 Main St., South Berwick 03908, tel. (207) 384-2263, open all year: Monday, Tuesday, and Friday 8:30 a.m.-5 p.m., Thursday 8:30 a.m.-6 p.m.; closed Wednesday.

NORTH BERWICK AND BERWICK

As with South Berwick, these historic communities are prime exploration territory for architecture and history buffs—as well as anyone interested in Maine's less crowded corners.

North Berwick
From South Berwick northward along Rt. 4, rolling fields line the roads, and the distinctive summit of Mt. Agamenticus punctures the horizon off to the east. The road is wide and flat—a good cycling route.

The only local lodging is the **Old Morrell Farm Bed & Breakfast,** Morrell's Mill Rd., North Berwick 03906, tel. (207) 676-7600, a real oasis several miles north of town. Patty and Lee Kendrick's beautifully restored 1763 farmhouse is listed on the National Historic Register. The 13-acre farm borders Bauneg Beg Pond, where you can canoe or swim. Or go meet the farm menagerie—cats, dogs, and a flock of Lincoln Longwool sheep. One guest room has a private bath, one shares a bath with the owners ($75 and $55 d, mid-May through October, $65 and $45 d other months). No smoking, no pets; two-night minimum July and August weekends, three-night minimum holiday weekends. By prior arrangement, the Kendricks will prepare an open-hearth dinner—an adventure in itself. The meal costs $25 pp, minimum four people; BYOL. No credit cards. Open all year.

In downtown North Berwick, **Lumpy's Pizza & Subs,** Elm St., Rt. 4, North Berwick 03906, tel. (207) 676-9020, has picnic tables alongside the unpronounceable Nequtaquet River—right around the corner from the thundering falls on the Great Works River. After your pizza, try one of the 32 Shain's ice cream flavors. Open daily 11 a.m.-9 p.m., Memorial Day to Columbus Day; closed Monday other months.

Berwick

Theatergoers head to the Berwick area for the long-running (since 1972) **Hackmatack Playhouse,** 538 Rt. 9, Berwick 03901, tel. (207) 698-1807, midway between North Berwick and Berwick. The popular summer theater, based in a renovated barn reminiscent of a past era, has 8 p.m. performances (comedies and musical comedies) Tues.-Sun. and a 2 p.m. matinee Thursday. The ambience is relaxed and casual but quality is high, though it's a non-Equity house. From mid-July to mid-August, professional-level children's plays go on at 10 a.m. Friday and Saturday. The Hackmatack season runs late June through August. Ticket range is $13-16; discounts for seniors and students except Saturday.

ALFRED

The shire town, or county seat, of York County, Alfred (named for Alfred the Great), also has a long history, having broken away from Sanford, five miles to its south, in 1794. The courthouse here (Kennebunk and Main Sts.) claims the nation's oldest court records, dating from 1636.

The **Blue Door Inn,** Waterboro Rd., Rt. 4/202, Alfred 04002, tel. (207) 490-2353, is best known for its restaurant, in five charming first-floor rooms, with air-conditioning and a reasonably priced menu. The restaurant is open year-round: Wed.-Sat. 6 a.m.-2 p.m. and 4:30-8 p.m.; Tuesday and Sunday 6 a.m.-2 p.m. Upstairs, three comfortable double rooms with a/c share a bath. Lodging costs $50 d, including breakfast off the menu.

Leedy's, Alfred Square, Alfred 04002, tel. (207) 324-5856, is your basic family-and-senior-citizen restaurant, with burgers, seafood, steaks, and sandwiches—even Jell-O for dessert. Prices are basic, too—$2.05 for a cheeseburger. Open all year, except Tuesday, for breakfast, lunch, and dinner.

For antiques and collectibles, start with **Shiretown Antiques Center,** Rt. 4/202, Alfred 04002, tel. (207) 324-3755, where more than 40 dealers show their wares. Joan Sylvester's shop is open

daily 10 a.m.-5 p.m., June-Sept.; closed Tuesday Oct.-May.

Two miles north of Alfred, **Notre Dame Institute,** Shaker Hill Rd., Rt. 4/202, Alfred 04002, tel. (207) 324-6612, a spiritual center overlooking Shaker Pond, was once a Shaker community, but a dwindling congregation forced its sale in the 1930s to the Roman Catholic Brothers of Christian Instruction. Come winter, ice-skaters flock on weekends to the institute's **Brother Gatien Trudeau Arena,** a 128-foot-long public ice rink in a handsome old Shaker barn. It's all done with hoses, cold air, and nonmechanical grooming—nothing artificial here. Rink time is $1 for three hours; skate rental is 25 cents. Call ahead for schedule information.

Festivals and Events

July's **Alfred Festival Day,** an annual community extravaganza, starts with a pancake breakfast and ends with a band concert. In between are a parade, entertainment, bean supper, book sale, food booths, and a craft sale.

Information

Alfred has no chamber of commerce, so the best source of tourism information is the **Town Office,** Saco Rd., Rt. 111, opposite the green, Alfred 04002, tel. (207) 324-5872, open weekdays. For quickie questions on weekends, try the **Alfred Country Store,** across the street, tel. (207) 324-7719.

OTHER AREA ATTRACTIONS

Waterboro Barrens Preserve

Four miles north of Alfred, Waterboro town was incorporated in 1797. In the far northwestern corner of the town limits is one of The Nature Conservancy's newest and least-visited holdings. Central feature of the Waterboro Barrens Preserve is a rare forest of northeastern pitch pine. Three easy-to-moderate loop trails provide access to the 2,173-acre pine barrens— where you're apt to spot deer, moose, ruffed grouse, and rare moths and butterflies. The preserve is open year-round for day use only, closing at sunset. Admission is free. No pets or smoking. From downtown Waterboro (Rt. 4/202), take West Rd. six miles west/northwest to Newfield Rd.; turn right and go one mile to Lake Sherburne Road. Turn right, go one mile to Buff Brook Road. Turn left, go to the parking lot on the left at end of road. For additional information, contact the Maine chapter of The Nature Conservancy, 14 Maine St., Fort Andross, Brunswick 04011, tel. (207) 729-5181.

Willowbrook at Newfield
About six miles northwest of the Waterboro Barrens Preserve (via Newfield Rd.) is tiny Newfield, probably best known for the fascinating 19th-century museum/village known as Willowbrook at Newfield, Main St., just north of Rt. 11, Newfield 04056, tel. (207) 793-2784. Plan to spend several hours here, exploring the 37 buildings listed on the National Register of Historic Places. What's to see? A carriage house, firehouse, country store, schoolhouse, a magnificently restored carousel, and incredible collections of farm tools, toys, sewing machines, and musical instruments. Bring a picnic and camera and soak up the history. Open May 15 through September, daily 10 a.m.-5 p.m. Admission is $7 adults, $3.50 children 6-17, free for kids under six.

Also on Main Street just before Willowbrook, is **Barnswallow Pottery & Antiques,** Newfield 04056, tel. (207) 793-8044, Barbara O'Brien and Dave Crowley's barn-based shop. In addition to antiques and Barbara's superb pottery, they carry unusual garden art. The shop is open daily in summer 9 a.m.-5 p.m., then weekends through Christmas. This is a small operation, so if you're making a special trip, call ahead to be sure someone will be home.

Maine-lly Llamas
Northeast of Waterboro is Maine-lly Llamas Farm Bed & Breakfast, 482 Clark's Mills Rd., Rt. 35, Hollis 04042, tel. (207) 929-3057, fax 929-4057, Gale and John Yohe's working farm with llamas, angora rabbits, turkeys, and great patches of organic gardens. Bring the family here: Two connected guest rooms (shared bath) occupy the upper floor (accessed by steep stairs) of the carriage house. If only one room is occupied, it's $65 d. The whole suite is $95 for up to five people (children under two are free); for $15 more, you can have kitchen facilities and a private den (two-night minimum at the

$110 rate). A full breakfast is included in every arrangement. No pets, no smoking. Kids love the llamas, and Gale leads llama treks (weather and bugs permitting). Cost is $20 an hour for two llamas, $10 for each extra llama. Open May-October.

Back Country Excursions of Maine
Here's major fun for the fat-tire set. Located northwest of Waterboro, Back Country Excursions, RFD 2, Box 365, Limerick 04048, tel./fax (207) 625-8189, has been the state's premier mountain-biking center since 1992. Close-to-Renaissance-man Cliff Krolick takes small groups—from neophytes to pros—pedaling over more than 70 miles of logging roads. He can keep you going three days without retracing your route. Best of all, he contributes part of his proceeds to environmental causes. Everything's ultra-casual at his rustic, hostel-style lodge, set on a knoll amid 12 acres—adjoining 10,000 acres of public lands. Everyone pitches in here, and the camaraderie is contagious. Accommodations range from three lodge rooms (sharing two baths) to a 20-foot-diameter yurt (with thick mattresses) to tentsites. Packages—two nights plus breakfast, lunch, and biking—range $115-165. A half-day biking tour, guided by Cliff, is $20; a full day is $35, including lunch. Bike rentals are extra; you can bring your own.

CORNISH

At York County's northernmost inland boundary, Cornish is a charming little town incorporated as Francisborough in 1791. Local historians boast that in the 1850s many of the splendid homes on the main drag were moved by oxen from other parts of town to be close to the stagecoach route.

A great time to visit Cornish is the last Saturday in September, when the annual **Apple Festival,** held in Thompson Park on Main Street, celebrates the area's major crop with music, a craft fair, and even an apple-pie contest. You can overdose all day on apples and stock up for winter, and do it just as fall foliage is starting to appear. For a spectacular panorama of fall colors along the Ossipee and Saco River Valleys, drive up Towles Hill Rd. (left turn, just west of town). While you're there, stop in at **Highland Farms,** tel. (207) 625-3329, a nationally known breeder of Jersey cows.

If you're a classical music fan, you'll want to be here earlier in the season. From mid-July to mid-August, the **Saco River Festival Association,** P.O. Box 610, Kezar Falls 04047, tel. (207) 625-7116, presents five professional chamber-music concerts (most at 8 p.m., weekends) at the Cornish Elementary School on School Street. Tickets are $10 adults, $5 students.

In the genuinely quaint downtown, shops worth a stop include the **Cornish Trading Company,** Main St., Rt. 25, Cornish 04020, tel. (207) 625-8387 or 625-8477, a terrific group antiques shop in the handsome Masonic building. Variety and price range are broad. Open Wed.-Mon. 10 a.m.-5 p.m. Also on Main Street are **Downtown Delights,** open in summer and dishing out great ice cream, and, around the corner, **Cornish Hardware,** Maine's oldest continuously operating hardware store. Nearby is **The Bag Lady,** Maple St., Rt. 25, Cornish

04020, tel. (207) 625-8421, a local firm that's gone big-time, marketing Cornish-made handbags and luggage nationally in elegant shops and catalogs. The shop is open daily in summer 10 a.m.-5:30 p.m., shorter hours off season. Branches are located in Kennebunkport and Camden.

At the western end of town, near the Towles Hill Road turnoff, is the **Stone Ridge Restaurant,** Rt. 25, Cornish, tel. (207) 625-3250, an informal, inexpensive spot in a gray-shingled house. Prime rib is available every night, and an all-you-can-eat salad bar is under $5. No smoking. Open daily 11:30 a.m.-8 p.m., except Monday, May-Oct.; open Thurs.-Sun. Nov.-April.

Best source of local information is the Cornish **Town Office,** Maple St., Rt. 25, Cornish 04020, tel./fax (207) 625-4324, open weekdays all year. On weekends, stop in at any of the local shops and restaurants.

For information on canoeing the Saco River, see the Western Lakes and Mountains chapter.

THE YORKS

Four villages with distinct personalities—upscale York Harbor, historic York Village, casual York Beach, and semirural Cape Neddick—make up the Town of York. First inhabited by Native Americans, who named it Agamenticus, the area was settled as early as 1624—so history is serious business here. Town high points were the founding, by Sir Ferdinando Gorges, and the arrival of well-to-do vacationers in the 19th century. In between were Indian massacres, economic woes, and population shuffles. Today the town has a winter population of about 10,000 Yorkies; in summer, though, that explodes to 40,000 (a fact made vivid in July and August, when you're searching for a free patch of York Beach sand).

History and genealogy buffs can study the headstones in the Old Burying Ground or comb the archives of the Old York Historical Society. For lighthouse fans, there's Cape Neddick Light Station ("Nubble Light") and, six miles offshore, Boon Island. You can rent horses or mountain bikes on Mt. Agamenticus, board a deep-sea fishing boat in York Harbor, or spend an hour

hiking the Cliff Path in York Harbor. For the kids, there's a zoo, a lobsterboat cruise, a taffymaker, or, of course, back to the beach.

SIGHTS

Nubble Light/Sohier Park

The best-known photo op in York is the distinctive 1879 lighthouse known formally as Cape Neddick Light Station and familiarly as **"The Nubble."** Although there's no access to the lighthouse's island, Sohier Park Welcome Center (with restrooms and volunteer-staffed gift shop, but few tourism publications) provides the perfect viewpoint. Parking, however, is limited. Not a bad idea to walk from the Long Sands parking area or come by bike, even though the road is narrow. Weekdays, this is also a popular spot for scuba divers. The center is open daily 10 a.m.-8 p.m., Memorial Day weekend to mid-Octobter. It's on Nubble Rd., off Rt. 1A, between Long and Short Sands Beaches, York Beach, tel. (207) 363-7608.

THE YORKS

To Portland
To Mt. Agamenticus
To Ogunquit
To Ogunquit

AGAMENTICUS RD.

Cape Neddick

Cape Neddick Beach

Short Sands Beach

YORK'S WILD KINGDOM ★

Long Beach

York Beach

Long Beach

VISITOR CENTER ■

To New Hampshire

York Village

OLD YORK HISTORICAL SOCIETY ★

BARRELL LANE

Steedman Woods

WIGGLY BRIDGE ★

SAYWARD-WHEELER HOUSE ★

CLIFF PATH ★

York Harbor

Harbor Beach

Lobster Cove

Bragdon Island

Stage Neck

Harris Island

To New Hampshire

HARRIS ISLAND RD.

York Harbor

ATLANTIC OCEAN

SOHIER PARK ★
NUBBLE LIGHT ★

© MOON PUBLICATIONS, INC.

0   0.5 mi
0   0.5 km

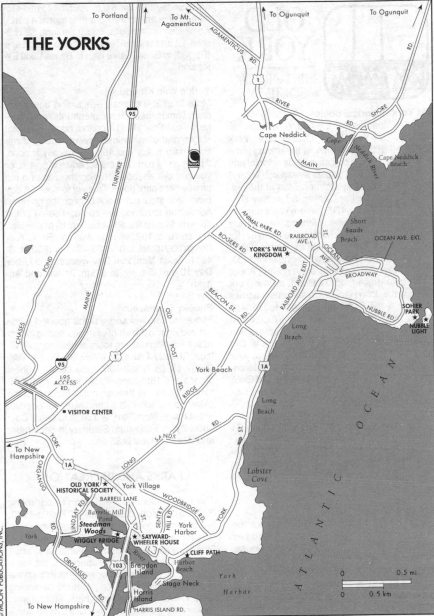

OLD
YORK
HISTORICAL
SOCIETY

Old York Historical Society

Based in York Village, the Old York Historical Society, 207 York St., P.O. Box 312, York 03909, tel. (207) 363-4974, is the driving force behind **Old York**, a collection of six colonial and post-colonial buildings (plus a research library) open throughout the summer. Start at the Jefferds' Tavern Visitor Center, 5 Lindsay Rd., York, tel. (207) 363-4703, where you'll need to pick up tickets. Parking is limited. Nearby are the Old Gaol and the School House (both fun for kids), and the Emerson-Wilcox House. Don't miss the Old Burying Ground, dating from 1735, across the street (rubbings are a no-no.) About a half-mile down Lindsay Road, on the York River, is the John Hancock Warehouse; across the river is the Elizabeth Perkins House. Antiques buffs shouldn't miss the Wilcox and Perkins Houses. Costumed interpreters are based in both houses, as well as in the Old Gaol. Visit some or all of the buildings, at your own pace—no one leads you from one to another. At 196 York St., across from the Old Gaol, is The Museum Shop. The shop and the museum buildings are open Tues.-Sat. 10 a.m.-5 p.m., Sunday 1-5 p.m., mid-June through September. Admission per building is $2 adults, $1 children (6-16); kids under six are free. A six-building combo ticket is $6 adults, $2.50 children. The family combo rate (four persons) is $16. During July and August, admission is free on Wednesday.

Sayward-Wheeler House

Owned by the Boston-based Society for the Preservation of New England Antiquities (SPNEA), the 1718 Sayward-Wheeler House, 79 Barrell Lane Extension, York Harbor, tel. (603) 436-3205 (no local phone number), occupies a prime site at the edge of York Harbor. In the house are lots of period furnishings—all in pristine condition. The house is open Saturday and Sunday 11 a.m.-5 p.m., June 1 to mid-October. Tours are on the hour (last tour at 4 p.m.). Admission is $4 adults, $3.50 seniors, $2 children 12 and under. Take Rt. 1A to Lilac Lane (Rt. 103) to Barrell Lane, then to Barrell Lane Extension.

York's Wild Kingdom

More than 250 animals—including tigers, zebras, llamas, deer, lions, elephants, and monkeys—call York's Wild Kingdom home. Elephant shows and other animal "events" occur three times daily in July and August—usually at noon, 2 p.m., and 4 p.m., but the schedule is posted, or you can call ahead. Between the zoo and the amusement-park rides, it's easy to spend a day here—and there are snack bars on the grounds. Admission (covering the zoo and some of the rides) is $13 adults, $11 children 10 and under. The zoo is at 102 Railroad Ave., off Rt. 1, York Beach 03910, tel. (207) 363-4911 or (800) 456-4911. Open Memorial Day weekend to Labor Day 10 a.m.-5 p.m. (to 6 p.m. in July and August).

Spooky Sightseeing

Flickering candles and a black-hooded guide get you right in the spirit of things during imaginative evening walking tours of historic York village. **Ghostly Tours,** 241 York St., Rt. 1A, York 03909, tel. (207) 363-0000, specializes in ghost stories and 18th-century folklore during its 45-minute meanders through burial grounds in the oldest part of town. The candlelight tour begins about 8 p.m. Mon.-Sat., late June to Labor Day; about 7 p.m. Friday and Saturday in September and October. Cost is $5 pp.

PARKS AND RECREATION

The York Parks and Recreation Department, P.O. Box 9, York 03909, tel. (207) 363-1040, is a dynamic operation that organizes and sponsors races, tournaments, day camps, trail rides, fitness sessions, children's events, and adult craft workshops. Plus it supervises the local beaches. Registration for activities must be done in person (Church St., York Beach) beginning June 1, and York residents have first priority, so some things fill up quickly, but it's worth sending for a copy of the annual Summer Program Guide (available mid-April) to consider the many possibilities.

Walk the Walks

Next to Harbor Beach, near the Stage Neck Inn, a sign marks the beginning of the **Cliff Path,** an ill-maintained walkway worth taking for its dramatic harbor views in the shadow of elegant summer cottages. On the one-hour roundtrip, you'll pass the York Harbor Reading Room (an exclusive club). The path is on private property, traditionally open to the public courtesy of the owners, but controversy surfaces periodically about vandalism and the condition of some sections of the walk, so you'll need to check locally when you arrive. The path is closed during snow, ice, or extra-heavy seas.

A less strenuous route is known variously as the **Shore Path, Harbor Walk,** or **Fisherman's Walk,** running west along the harbor and river from Stage Neck Road (next to Edwards' Harborside Inn) and passes the Sayward-Wheeler House before crossing the tiny, green-painted Wiggly Bridge leading into the **Steedman Woods** preserve. Carry binoculars for good boatwatching and birding in the 16-acre preserve, owned by the Old York Historical Society. A one-mile double-loop trail takes less than an hour of easy strolling.

Swimming

Sunbathing and swimming are big draws in York, with four beaches of varying sizes and accessibility. Bear in mind that traffic can be gridlocked along the beachfront (Rt. 1A) in midsummer, so it may take longer than you expect to get anywhere. **Lifeguards** are on duty mid-June to Labor Day 9:30 a.m.-4 p.m. at Short Sands Beach, Long Beach, and Harbor Beach. Bathhouses at Long Sands and Short Sands are open daily 9 a.m.-7 p.m. in midsummer. Biggest parking space (metered) is at Long Sands, but that one-and-a-half-mile beach also draws the most customers. Scarcest parking is at Harbor Beach, near the Stage Neck Inn, and at Cape Neddick Beach, near the Ogunquit town line.

Mount Agamenticus

Drive to the summit of Mt. Agamenticus and you're at York County's highest point. It's only 692 feet, but it offers panoramic views of ocean, lakes, woods, and sometimes the White Mountains. At the top are the **Summit Cycle Shop,** tel. (207) 363-0470, for mountain-bike rentals (daily, mid-June through September, weekends in May and early June), **Agamenticus Riding Stables,** tel. (207) 361-2840, for lessons and trail rides (open daily 8 a.m.-8 p.m., Memorial Day weekend to Columbus Day), a billboard map of the hiking-trail network, and a curious memorial to St. Aspinquid, a 17th-century Algonquian Indian leader. Take a picnic, a kite, and binoculars. In the fall, if the wind's from the northwest, watch for migrating hawks; in winter, bring a sled for the best downhill run in southern Maine. Contact the **York Parks and Recreation Department,** tel. (207) 363-1040, for info about other activities at the 1,171-acre mountain park. From Rt. 1 in Cape Neddick, take Mountain Rd. (also called Agamenticus Rd.) 4.2 miles west to the access road.

Bicycling

Rent a bike from **Berger's Bike Shop,** 241 York St., York 03909, tel. (207) 363-4070, and you'll probably get around faster in July and August than you would by car. An especially scenic bike route runs eight or nine miles along Rt. 103—very winding, not always well shouldered, but mostly level—from York Village to Kittery Point and Kittery. It's wiser to return the same way, rather than make a loop via Rt. 1, unless zooming traffic and shoulder dropoffs don't intimidate you.

Getting Afloat

If overdosing on lobsters makes you want to see how they're caught, contact **Captain Tom Farnon,** 10 Organug Rd., York 03909, tel. (207) 363-3234, who'll take you out in his 22-foot traditional wooden lobsterboat and load you up on lobster lore. Reservations are necessary, since *The Boat,* as she's called, carries only six people ($6.50 pp). Visit the restroom before you board. Departures are on the hour Mon.-Fri. 10 a.m.-2 p.m., mid-June to mid-Sept., from Town Dock #2, Harris Island Rd., off Rt. 103 in York Harbor.

For **deep-sea fishing,** also out of Town Dock #2, contact Capt. Herb Poole at **Seabury Charters,** tel. (207) 363-5675, for a half-day trip in his 38-foot *Blackback.* During July and August, he runs two trips Tuesday, Wednesday, Friday, Saturday, and Sunday, departing at 7:30 a.m. and 12:30 p.m. Four-passenger minimum, six maximum. Reservations are necessary; call before 9 p.m. Another option is Capt. Bill Coite's 32-foot *Shearwater,* tel. (207) 363-5324, departing Mon.-Thurs. at 8 a.m. and 1 p.m. in July and August. Both operations provide all gear and bait; be sure to pack warm clothes, wear sunblock, and don rubber-soled shoes.

York Beach Scuba, 19 Railroad Ave., P.O. Box 850, York Beach 03910, tel. (207) 363-3330, fax 363-5040, a source for rentals, air, and trips, is conveniently located not far from Sohier Park, a popular dive site.

ENTERTAINMENT

Besides the cinema and theater, many York restaurants have dinner music or evening entertainment in summer.

York Beach Cinema, 6 Beach St., York Beach 03910, tel. (207) 363-2074, screens first-run flicks at 8 p.m. nightly, June through September. On rainy days, there's a 2 p.m. matinee.

For first-rate professional theater, you can't do better than the famed Ogunquit Playhouse, next town north on Rt. 1.

FESTIVALS AND EVENTS

Each year, York produces a poster-size *Summer Social Calendar,* listing activities galore for summer and beyond. For a copy (after May 1), contact the Yorks Chamber of Commerce, Rt. 1, P.O. Box 417, York 03909, tel. (207) 363-4422, or Verna Rundlett, tel. (207) 363-3078. Listed are concerts, church suppers, walking tours, road races, berry festivals, art shows, library schedule, and museum events. Scarcely a day goes by without something on the calendar. Here's a sampling. York Village's Fourth of July celebration is called **Four on the Wharf** and includes colonial food, games, and entertainment. Free. It runs 4-6 p.m. at John Hancock Wharf. Mid-July brings the town's **Annual Summerfest,** with a crafts fair, food booths, and a bean supper. From late July into early August, **York Days** enlivens the town for 10 days with

concerts, dances, walking tours, sandcastle contests, antiques and art shows, a dog show, fireworks, a parade, and public suppers.

Santa Claus comes early to York Beach—the first Sunday in September, to be exact. The **Santa Claus Parade** is Santa's opportunity to bid farewell to summer visitors as he parades through town. It's a big hit; local stores even get in the act with "Christmas sales."

York Village's **Annual Harvestfest** takes place 10 a.m.-4 p.m. the weekend after Columbus Day in October and combines colonial crafts and cooking demonstrations, hayrides, museum tours, entertainment, and an ox roast. This is one of the town's most popular events; most activities are free.

SHOPPING

If you're looking for factory outlets, you'll have to head south on Rt. 1 to Kittery, where there are more than 100 of them. But York has some unique shopping options of its own.

Gifts and Antiques
York Village Crafts, Antiques, and Gifts, 211 York St., Rt. 1A, York 03909, tel. (207) 363-4830, is a three-level emporium based in a restored 1834 church. **York Handcrafters,** a 15-member cooperative, occupies a large room on the first floor. Lots of tasteful stuff; bet you won't leave empty-handed. It's open daily 9 a.m.-5 p.m. April-December. Everything in **Woods to Goods,** 891 Rt. 1, York 03909, tel. (207) 363-6001, comes from inmate woodworkers in Maine and beyond, plus the shop carries Oregon's Prison Blues jeans. Quality and price vary widely, with some genuine bargains and some near-kitsch. Open Mon.-Sat. 9 a.m.-9 p.m., Sunday 10 a.m.-6 p.m. during July and August; open 10 a.m.-5 p.m. other times.

Columbary Antiques, Rt. 1, Cape Neddick 03902, tel. (207) 363-5496, is a high-quality group shop with lots of fragile wares and reasonable prices. Open daily 10 a.m.-5 p.m., April-October; Thurs.-Mon. other months.

Farmers' Market
The Old York Historical Society, tel. (207) 363-4974, sponsors a weekly farmers' market in the

Jefferds' Tavern parking lot (Lindsay Rd. and York St., York Village) each Saturday 9 a.m.-noon, Memorial Day weekend through September. Besides fresh produce, mostly organic, you'll find craft supplies and weekly surprises.

ACCOMMODATIONS

York Harbor

All of the York Harbor lodgings described below are within easy walking distance of Harbor Beach.

Set back from the street on nearly an acre, Wes and Kathie Cook's Victorian **Bell Buoy Bed & Breakfast,** 570 York St., P.O. Box 445, York Harbor 03911, tel. (207) 363-7264, has four second- and third-floor guest rooms (one with private bath; $70-80 d), plus an efficiency suite ($85) with a separate entrance that's ideal for families. There's lots of books for guests and an elegant parlor with giant-screen cable TV. No credit cards; pets allowed only in the suite. Open all year.

Since 1984, hospitable Sue Antal has operated the **Inn at Harmon Park,** 415 York St., P.O. Box 495, York Harbor 03911, tel. (207) 363-2031, a 14-room "cottage" just a block from the water. Having run the chamber of commerce and devoted many hours to community organizations, Sue's a great touring resource. (She's also a justice of the peace, with a price that's right and a long string of weddings under her belt.) Four comfortable guest rooms and a suite have private baths. Rates are $79-109 d, Memorial Day to mid-October, $59-99 d other months. Breakfast is a creative treat, often served on the porch. No credit cards, no pets (Taj the cat rules the roost), no smoking, no children under 12. Open all year.

You can't miss the **Stage Neck Inn,** Stage Neck Rd., P.O. Box 70, York Harbor 03911, tel. (207) 363-3850 or (800) 222-3238, fax (207) 363-2221, occupying its own private peninsula overlooking York Harbor. Modern, resort-style facilities include two pools, tennis courts, fitness center, and spectacular views from balconies and terraces. The formal restaurant (no jeans) and casual grill are open to the public. Three-night minimum July, August, and holiday weekends, two-night minimum off season weekends.

Rates are $150-220 d in midsummer, $100-215 d other months (special packages available). No smoking, no pets. Open all year.

Though not in York Harbor's postal zone, **Dockside Guest Quarters,** Box 205, York 03909, tel. (207) 363-2868, fax 363-1977, faces Stage Neck from Harris Island in the harbor. The Lusty family's inn has five guest rooms in its 1885 Maine House and 16 rooms in four modern buildings with unbeatable views. Everything's open and airy, with a tinge of yachtiness and less formality than the Stage Neck. Bikes and canoes available for guests; marina facilities for boatowners. Rates are $110-155 d in midsummer, depending on room type, $45-100 d other months. Kids under 12 are free in suites and studios. Two-night minimum July, August, and Labor Day weekends. Smoking limited to cottage decks; no pets. Dockside is open early May to late October; eight rooms are available on winter weekends ($60 d). The **Restaurant at Dockside,** tel. (207) 363-2722, is open to the public for lunch and dinner Tues.-Sun., Memorial Day weekend to mid-Oct., specializing in seafood.

York Harbor Inn, Rt. 1A, P.O. Box 573, York Harbor 03911, tel. (207) 363-5119 or (800) 343-3869, fax (207) 363-3545, is an accommodating in-town spot with a country-inn flavor and a variety of room and package-plan options. The oldest section dates from the 17th century. All 35 rooms have phones and a/c; some have four-poster beds, fireplaces, and whirlpools ($99-129 d, slightly lower Nov.-March). The glassed-in dining room gets high marks for creative cuisine, so reservations are essential. The lower-level pub, **The Wine Cellar,** is a favorite local watering hole, often with entertainment weekends. Open all year.

York

The well-maintained, family-run **MicMac Motel,** 317 Rt. 1, York 03909, tel. (207) 363-4944, has an outdoor pool and 10 basic rooms, all with phones. Rates $80-85 d in summer, $65-75 d in spring and fall. No pets. Smoking is allowed in two rooms. Open early April to early December.

York Beach

The Anchorage Inn, 265 Long Beach Ave., P.O. Box 1329, York Beach 03910, tel. (207)

363-5112, fax 363-6753, is close to York Beach's ground zero, so be prepared for plenty of action. Its 178 modern, motel-style rooms are across the street from Long Sands Beach, but it's set back a bit for relief from traffic sounds. (The Atrium building, in back, has less street noise but more noise from the interior pool.) Rates are $95-144 d in season, $50-104 d other months. Facilities include indoor and outdoor pools, fitness center, and restaurant (open Mon.-Thurs. in season, weekends off season). Spa suites, $175-225 d, have private whirlpools. No pets. Open all year.

Everything's casual and flowers are everywhere at the bright-yellow **Katahdin Inn,** 11 Ocean Ave. Ext., P.O. Box 193, York Beach 03910, tel. (207) 363-1824 or (617) 938-0335 off season, overlooking the breakers of Short Sands Beach. Eleven first-, second-, and third-floor rooms (eight with water views) have lots of four-poster beds. Shared baths for most rooms. Breakfast is not included, but several eateries are nearby. Rooms cost $70-90 d, lower rates before June 30 and after Labor Day. Kids under 12 stay free. No smoking. Open Memorial Day weekend through Columbus Day.

Cape Neddick

Innkeeper Dianne Goodwin is far too young to be anyone's grandmother, but you'll feel like a privileged grandchild at the **Cape Neddick House Bed and Breakfast,** 1300 Rt. 1, P.O. Box 70, Cape Neddick 03902, tel. (207) 363-2500, fax 363-4499. No need for lunch after a breakfast here—and Dianne even shares her recipes. The inn is right on busy Rt. 1, but out back are 10 acres of gardens and woods for walkers and birdwatchers. Family antiques fill this homey place, which has been in John Goodwin's family since it was built in 1885. Five air-conditioned guest rooms (with private baths) are named after New England states; the oak headboard on the bed in the Vermont room is amazing. Rates are $85-95 d, lower off season. No pets, no children under six. Open all year.

Campground

Family-owned **Dixon's Campground,** 1740 Rt. 1, Cape Neddick 03902, tel. (207) 363-2131, fax 363-5592, is an especially well-run operation catering to tent campers and small-RV owners

(30-foot RV limit). Two miles south of Ogunquit, Dixon's has 100 open and wooded sites in four clusters on its 40 acres; each cluster has its own showerhouse/restroom. Rates are $24-26 a night (for two), late June through Labor Day, with a three-night minimum. Early and late in the season, it's $21-23 a night. Overnight guests pay a hefty $7.50 pp in midsummer. Facilities include coin-operated showers, free Ogunquit Beach shuttle bus (late June to Labor Day), playground, and camp store. No pets. Dixon's is open Memorial Day weekend to mid-September.

Seasonal Rentals

Several companies manage week- or month-long rental properties, usually houses or condos. Weekly rentals begin and end on Saturday. Best operation is **Sentry Hill Rental,** 43 York St., P.O. Box 593, York Harbor 03911, tel. (207) 363-0904, fax 363-0834. Median price range is $600-1,200 a week.

FOOD

York Harbor

The **Road Kill Cafe,** 756 York St., Long Sands Beach, York Harbor 03911, tel. (207) 351-2928, bills itself as "not your normal restaurant" and means it. The welcome sign reads, Come In, Sit Down, Shut Up. Be prepared for waitstaff hijinks, a hilarious menu, moderate prices, and so-so food. Sure, it's a gimmick (and part of an expanding chain in northern New England), but it's fun. Tastiest item is the Pail o' Nightcrawlers (french fries), for $1.95. Open June-Oct. for breakfast, lunch, and dinner. Although technically in York Harbor, it's almost within spitting distance of York Beach.

Three pricier York Harbor dining options are in the Dockside Guest Quarters, Stage Neck Inn, and York Harbor Inn.

York Village and York

The **Deli Downeast,** 241 York St., York Village, tel. (207) 363-6733, opens at 6 a.m. (and closes at 5 p.m.), with fresh-baked goodies and designer coffees, plus salad bar, sandwiches, soups. At the **Bagel Basket,** 273 York St., York Village, tel. (207) 363-1244, you can choose a traditional or gourmet spread on your bagel (more than a dozen flavors). A bagel with lox spread runs about $3. Open weekdays 7 a.m.-4 p.m., weekends 7 a.m.-2 p.m.

You'll have to look carefully to spot the sign for the **Lunch Break Sandwich Shop,** 264 Rt. 1 South, York 03909, tel. (207) 363-6039, in a small house set back a bit from the highway. Kathy Cole started in 1986 catering to businesses; her satisfied clients urged her to go public, and she has. Sandwiches (average $4), homemade soups, and salads are superb. Get it to go or try for one of the eight tables. In summer, there's more room on the side deck and the garden. Breakfast goodies are ready at 7 a.m. Mon.-Sat.; the shop closes at 3:30 p.m. No credit cards. Open all year. The Lunch Break is across Rt. 1 from the MicMac Motel.

Ruby's, 433 Rt. 1, a mile south of the I-95 exit, York 03909, tel. (207) 363-7980, is the latest incarnation at this hillside location across from Starkey Ford. The wood-fired grill does a great job with some intriguing pizza combos (pulled pork and barbecue sauce, for instance), and grill of my dreams entrées include St. Louis ribs. The El Natural ($4.75) is a tasty veggie burger. Lots of variety and flair here. In nice weather, opt for the enclosed deck. Ruby's is open Mon.-Thurs. 11:30 a.m.-10 p.m., Friday and Saturday 11:30 a.m.-11 p.m., and Sunday 11:30 a.m.-9 p.m.

Homemade pasta, an informal atmosphere, and early-bird specials (before 5:30 p.m.) make **Fazio's Italian Restaurant,** 38 Woodbridge Rd., York, tel. (207) 363-7019, a favorite family dinner spot—so reserve ahead in July and August. Kids under 12 or patrons over 60 can order a light meal for $4.95. And it's no secret that next-door **La Stalla Pizzeria,** tel. (207) 363-1718 (same number for Fazio's take-out fare), under the same ownership, dishes out York's most creative pizza for lunch, dinner, and take-out anytime. Try the 12-inch veggie special. Fazio's opens at 4 p.m. daily, year-round; La Stalla opens at 11 a.m. daily.

The **Brickyard Restaurant,** Rt. 1, a mile south of the I-95 exit, York 03909, tel. (207) 363-1907, is a casual, mom-and-pop sort of place with homestyle cooking dubbed "traditional New England fare." It's open all year Mon.-Sat. 11:30 a.m.-10 p.m., Sunday 11 a.m.-9 p.m.

Since 1972, **The Lobster Barn,** Rt. 1, York 03909, tel. (207) 363-4721 or (800) 341-4849, has been drawing a devoted local clientele to its roadside site. All the usual suspects are here—fried clams, baked haddock, etc.—plus good steaks. A well-stuffed lobster roll runs about $8.95. Open daily, mid-May-Oct., for lunch and dinner; open weekends off season. From Memorial Day weekend to Labor Day, their super-casual outdoor area, **Lobster in the Rough,** is a good option, and there's a playground for the kids.

Higher up the price scale and the ambience level is **Clay Hill Farm,** Agamenticus Rd., on the York-Ogunquit town line, tel. (207) 361-2272, an attractive country-inn type of place two miles west of Rt. 1. It's convenient from both Ogunquit and York. Predictably good regional American entrées are in the $15-22 range; daily specials tend to be more imaginative. Allow time to wander the beautifully landscaped grounds, popular for weddings. Open all year, daily 5:30-9 p.m.; closed Mon.-Wed. in winter. Reservations are essential in July and August.

York Beach

Just follow your nose to **Mimmo's Ristorante,** 243 Long Sands Rd., York Beach 03910, tel. (207) 363-3807—the scent of garlic'll meet you halfway down the beach. Moderately priced, well-prepared Italian menu. BYOL. No smoking. It's wildly popular, so reservations are essential in midsummer (try for the patio). Open all year for dinner, and for breakfast in summer.

See those people with their faces pressed to the glass? They're all watching the taffymakers inside **The Goldenrod,** 2 Railroad Ave., York Beach 03910, tel. (207) 363-2621, where machines spew out 180 Goldenrod Kisses a minute, 65 tons a year—and have been since 1896. (They also accept mail orders.) The Goldenrod is an old-fashioned place, with a tearoom, gift shop, soda fountain, and casual dining room. Open for breakfast (8 a.m.), lunch, and dinner late May to Columbus Day.

The wide-open ocean view couldn't be better than at the **Sun 'n Surf,** Long Beach Ave., Rt. 1A, opposite the Anchorage Inn, York Beach 03910, tel. (207) 363-2961, a cut above most fast-food places. Full liquor license, too. Resist the urge to sit outside, or you'll be sharing your lobster roll ($9 with fries) with kamikaze gulls. Open all year for lunch and dinner.

Café Shelton, 1 Ocean Ave., York Beach 03910, tel. (207) 363-0708, brings a yuppified touch to York Beach, with reasonably priced lunch and dinner menus, plus a kids' menu. Seafood, steaks, and pasta are specialties. Weekend evenings, there's a piano-bar sing-along. Open Mon.-Sat. at noon, Sunday at 9 a.m., May to late October.

Cape Neddick

Sometimes the line runs right out the door of the low-ceilinged, six-stool, chocolate-brown roadside shack housing local institution **Flo's Steamed Dogs,** Rt. 1, opposite the Mountain Rd. turnoff, Cape Neddick 03902. The secret? The spicy, sweet-sour hot-dog sauce (allegedly sought by the H.J. Heinz corporation, but the proprietary Stacy family isn't telling or selling). No menu here—just steamed wieners, chips, and beverages. Open all year, Thurs.-Tues. 11 a.m.-3 p.m.

Before heading for the **Cape Neddick Lobster Pound,** Shore Rd., Cape Neddick 03902, tel. (207) 363-5471, check the tide calendar. The rustic shingled building dripping with lobster-pot buoys has a spectacular harbor view (especially from the deck) at high tide, a rather drab one at low tide, so plan accordingly. Open for dinner Memorial Day weekend to Columbus Day, also for lunch Saturday and Sunday in July and August. Entertainment Friday and Saturday in summer, beginning at 10 p.m.

The views are all indoors at the **Cape Neddick Inn Restaurant,** 1233 Rt. 1, at Rt. 1A, Cape Neddick 03902, tel. (207) 363-2899, where the walls are covered with the work (all for sale) of local talent. Splurge a bit and eat here—it's York's most imaginative menu. If you like duck, you'll love this version ($21); entrées are $13-27. Reservations are essential on summer weekends. No smoking. Open daily 6-9 p.m. (Saturday and Sunday to 9:30 p.m.). Closed Mon.-Tues. mid-October to mid-June, plus all of March.

Serving "food that loves you back," **Frankie & Johnny's Natural Foods,** 1594 Rt. 1 North, Cape Neddick 03902, tel. (207) 363-1909, has a heavy Mediterranean accent—if you don't count the German spaetzle, the Tex-Mex items, and the Maine crab cakes. Best vegetarian menu

in York—in a funky, roadside place where you're served by a "waitron" and you'll need a reservation on summer weekends. No smoking, no credit cards; BYOL. Open daily for dinner in July and August, Thurs.-Sun. in spring and fall.

INFORMATION AND SERVICES

For local info, head for the Shingle-style palace of the **Yorks Chamber of Commerce,** Rt. 1, P.O. Box 417, York 03909, tel. (207) 363-4422, at I-95's York exit. Inside the elegant hillside building, you'll find racks of brochures, restrooms, and a cheerful staff. Open daily in summer. The local weekly (Wednesday) newspapers are the *York County Coast Star,* based in Kennebunk but covering the entire county, and *The York Weekly.* Both produce summer supplements carrying features, ads, calendar listings, and other helpful information.

Emergencies

For emergencies, contact **York Hospital,** 15 Hospital Dr., York 03909; emergency room tel. (207) 351-2157, a respected local institution. The hospital's **Tel-a-Nurse** service, tel. (800) 283-7234, provides free over-the-phone advice for minor medical problems, Mon.-Fri. 5:30-9:30 p.m. and weekends 9 a.m.-9 p.m. For **police, fire, or ambulance services,** dial 911.

Photo Services

Photo:59, Meadowbrook Plaza, Rt. 1, York 03909, tel. (207) 363-1454, is open weekdays 8:30 a.m.-5:30 p.m., Saturday 8:30 a.m.-2:30 p.m., and provides one-hour photo service. Off-season closings are 5 p.m. during the week and 2 p.m. on Saturday.

Kennels

York Country Kennels, Rt. 1, York 03909, tel. (207) 363-7950, is a Hyatt Regency for pets, with wallpaper, heated floors, noontime snacks, and more. Dog fees are based on weight; cat fees are based on lodging amenities. Immunizations must be current. Open Mon.-Sat. 8 a.m.-6 p.m. and Sunday 9-10 a.m. and 3-5 p.m.

Getting Around

The New England Trolley Company operates

a **trolleybus service** daily 10 a.m.-8 p.m., late June to Labor Day. The hour-long counter-clockwise loop begins on the hour at the York Village Shopping Center on Long Sands Rd., stopping at Old York, York Harbor, the Long Sands Bath House, and Nubble Light before returning to the shopping center. Tickets are $3 pp for a narrated tour on the entire loop, valid for the whole day; single-trip partial-loop tickets are $1.50 pp. Take the $3 tour for some fun histori-cal footnotes. Copies of the trolley schedule, listing the 18 or so stops on the route, are wide-ly available around town, as well as at the cham-ber of commerce information center.

York Taxi, tel. (207) 363-7007, operates round-the-clock, ready to transport people, pack-ages, and whatever. Seniors receive a 10% dis-count.

OGUNQUIT AND WELLS

Ogunquit has been a holiday destination since the indigenous residents named it "beautiful place by the sea." What's the appeal? An un-paralleled, unspoiled beach, several top-flight (albeit pricey) restaurants, a dozen art galleries, and a respected art museum with a view second to none. The town has been home to an art colony attracting the glitterati of the painting world starting with Charles Woodbury in the 1920s. The summertime crowds continue, mul-tiplying the minuscule year-round population of about 930. Besides the beach, the most pow-erful magnet is Perkins Cove, a working fish-ing enclave that looks more like a movie set. Best way to approach the cove is via trolleybus or on foot, along the shoreline Marginal Way from downtown Ogunquit—midsummer park-ing in the cove is madness.

Wells, once the parent of Ogunquit and since 1980 its immediate neighbor to the north, was settled in 1640. Nowadays, it's best known as a long, skinny, family-oriented community with about 7,700 year-round residents, seven miles of splendid beachfront, and heavy-duty com-mercial activity: lots of antiques and used-book shops, and a handful of factory outlets. It also claims two spectacular nature preserves worth a drive from anywhere. At the southern end of Wells, abutting Ogunquit, is **Moody,** an enclave named after 18th-century settler Samuel Moody and even rating its own post office.

If swimming isn't your top priority, plan to visit Ogunquit and Wells after Labor Day, when crowds let up, lodging rates drop, weather is still good, and you can find restaurant seats and parking spots.

SIGHTS AND RECREATION

Museums
Not many museums can boast a view as stun-ning as the one at the **Ogunquit Museum of American Art,** 183 Shore Rd., P.O. Box 815, Ogunquit 03907, tel. (207) 646-4909, nor can many communities boast such renown as a summer art colony. Overlooking Narrow Cove, 1.4 miles south of downtown Ogunquit, the mu-seum prides itself on its distinguished permanent collection—works of Marsden Hartley, Rock-well Kent, Walt Kuhn, and Thomas Hart Benton, among others. Newest feature (since July 1996) is the 1,400-square-foot Barn Gallery Associ-ates Wing. Special exhibits are mounted each summer. The museum has a gift shop, wheel-chair access, and landscaped grounds with sculptures, a pond, and manicured lawns. Ad-mission is $3 adults, $2 seniors and students, free for kids under 12. Open July-Sept., Mon.-Sat. 10:30 a.m.-5 p.m., Sunday 2-5 p.m.

Right on the historic Post Road that once linked Boston with points north stands the **His-toric Meetinghouse Museum,** Buzzell Rd. and Rt. 1, opposite Wells Plaza, P.O. Box 801, Wells 04090, tel. (207) 646-4775, a handsome steepled structure on the site of the town's first church (1643). Preserved and maintained by the Historical Society of Wells and Ogunquit, its displays include old photos, ship models, needle-craft, and local memorabilia. On the second floor is a genealogical library where volunteers will help you research your roots (photocopier avail-able). Admission is $2 adults, $1 children 6-15. Open June-mid-Oct. Tuesday and Thursday 1-4 p.m., Wednesday 10 a.m.-4 p.m.

Dozens of vintage vehicles, plus a collection of old-fashioned nickelodeons, fill the **Wells Auto Museum,** Rt. 1, Wells 04090, tel. (207) 646-9064. From the outside, it just looks like a big warehouse, right on the highway. For $1 pp, you can ride in a Model-T. The gift shop has car-oriented items. Admission is $4 adults, $2 children 6-12. Open daily 10 a.m.-5 p.m., mid-June to mid-September, plus Memorial Day and Columbus Day weekends.

Marginal Way

The best times to appreciate this mile-long, shrub-lined, shorefront walkway in Ogunquit are early morning or when everyone's at the beach. En route are tidepools, intriguing rock formations, crashing surf, pocket beaches, benches (though the walking's a cinch, even partially wheelchair-accessible), and a marker listing the day's high and low tides. When the surf's up, keep a close eye on the kids—the sea has no mercy. One end of the paved footpath crosses through the Sparhawk Resort (Shore Rd., one block east of Rt. 1) and the other end crosses next to the Oarweed Cove Restaurant (Shore Rd.) in Perkins Cove. There's also a midpoint access at Israel's Head (behind a sewage plant in lighthouse disguise), but getting a parking space is pure luck. Best advice is to stroll the Marginal Way to Perkins Cove for lunch, shopping, and maybe a boat trip, then return to downtown Ogunquit via trolleybus.

Perkins Cove

Turn-of-the-century photos show Ogunquit's Perkins Cove lined with gray-shingled shacks used by a hardy colony of local fishermen—fellows who headed offshore to make a tough living in little boats. They'd hardly recognize it today. Though the cove remains a working lobster-fishing harbor, several old shacks have been reincarnated as boutiques and restaurants, and photographers go crazy shooting the quaint inlet spanned by a little pedestrian drawbridge. In midsummer, you'll waste precious time looking for one of the three or four dozen parking places, so take advantage of the trolleybus service. In the cove are galleries, gift shops, a range of eateries (fast food to lobster to the superb Hurricane—see "Food in Ogunquit" under "Practicalities," below), boat excursions, and public restrooms.

Beaches

One of Maine's most scenic and unspoiled sandy beachfronts, the three-and-a-half-mile stretch of strand fringed with seagrass is a major magnet for hordes of sunbathers, spectators, swimmers, surfers, and sandcastle-builders. Getting there means crossing the Ogunquit River via one of three access points. For the **Main Beach**—with a spanking new bathhouse and high crowd content—take Beach Street. To reach **Footbridge Beach,** marginally less crowded, either take Ocean St. and the foot-

boat-busy Perkins Cove, Ogunquit

bridge or take Bourne Ave. to Ocean Ave. in adjacent Wells and walk back toward Ogunquit. (**Moody Beach,** at Wells's southern end, technically is private property—a subject of considerable legal dispute; don't risk a squabble.) Lifeguards are on duty all summer at the public beaches, and there are restrooms in all three areas. The beach is free, but parking is not; parking lots charge by the hour ($2 an hour at the Main Beach) or the day ($6 a day at Footbridge Beach), and they fill up early on warm midsummer days. After 3 p.m., some are free. It's far more sensible to opt for the frequent trolleybuses.

Wells beaches continue where Ogunquit's leave off. **Crescent Beach,** Webhannet Dr., between Eldredge and Mile Rds., is the tiniest, with tidepools, no facilities, and limited parking. **Wells Beach,** Mile Rd. to Atlantic Ave., is the major (and most crowded) beach, with lifeguards, restrooms, and parking. Around the other side of Wells Harbor is **Drakes Island Beach** (take Drakes Island Rd., across from the post office), a less crowded spot with restrooms and lifeguards. Walk northeast from Drakes Island Beach and you'll eventually reach Laudholm Beach (see below), with great birding along the way. Summer beach-parking fees in Wells are $7 a day for nonresidents; if you're staying longer, a $25 weekly permit is a better bargain.

Walks and Hikes
Wells National Estuarine Research Reserve: Known locally as Laudholm Farm (the name of the restored 19th-century visitor center), Wells National Estuarine Research Reserve, 342 Laudholm Farm Rd., RR 2, Box 806, Wells 04090, tel. (207) 646-1555, fax 646-2930, occupies 1,600 acres of woods, beach, and coastal saltmarsh on the southern boundary of the Rachel Carson National Wildlife Refuge, just one half-mile east of Rt. 1. Seven miles of trails wind through the property; roam on your own or take one of the daily naturalist-guided tours (call for schedule). Best trail is the Barrier Beach Walk, a 1.4-mile roundtrip that goes through multiple habitats all the way to beautiful Laudholm Beach. Allow one and a half hours. Lyme disease ticks have been found here, so tuck pant legs into socks and stick to the trails (some

of which are wheelchair-accessible). The informative exhibits in the visitors center (open daily May-Oct., weekdays the rest of the year) make a valuable prelude for enjoying the reserve. Trails are accessible 8 a.m.-5 p.m. daily, all year. There's a $2.50 per person fee (family rate $5) for guided tours; $5 parking charge in July and August includes a tour.

Rachel Carson National Wildlife Refuge: Ten chunks of coastal Maine real estate—currently more than 3,000 acres, eventually 7,500 acres, between Kittery Point and Cape Elizabeth—make up this refuge, Rt. 9, RR 2, Box 751, Wells 04090, tel. (207) 646-9226, headquartered at the northern edge of Wells, near the Kennebunkport town line. Pick up a *Carson Trail Guide* at the refuge office (parking space is very limited) and follow the mile-long walkway (wheelchair-accessible) past tidal creeks, salt pans, and saltmarshes. It's a birder's paradise during migration seasons. As with the Laudholm Farm reserve, the Lyme disease tick has been found here, so tuck pant legs into socks and stick to the trail. Office hours are weekdays 8 a.m.-4:30 p.m., year-round; trail access: sunrise to sunset, year-round.

Municipal Recreation Areas
On Rt. 9A, west of I-95 (take Burnt Mill Rd.), the 70-acre **Wells Recreation Area,** tel. (207) 646-5826, has four tennis courts, a fitness trail, basketball courts, baseball field, picnic tables, a jogging track, a large playground, and restrooms. Three-acre **Wells Harbor Community Park,** Lower Landing Rd. (turn off Rt. 1 at the fire station), tel. (207) 646-5113 or 646-2451, has a playground, restrooms, and a concert bandstand (Hope Fenderson Hobbs Memorial Gazebo). **Ogunquit Recreational Area,** Agamenticus Rd., west of I-95, Ogunquit, tel. (207) 646-3032, has three tennis courts.

Bike Rentals
Bikes by the Sea, 315 Main St., Rt. 1, Footbridge Plaza, Ogunquit 03907, tel. (207) 646-5898, is a full-service shop with touring- and mountain-bike rentals, sales, and repairs. Brian Simpson, a former bike rep, really knows his stuff. Open year-round, daily in summer. **Wheels & Waves,** 579 Post Rd., Rt. 1, Wells 04090, tel. (207) 646-5774, rents and services mountain

bikes and sells any kind of board that'll ride the surf. Open all year.

Getting Afloat

Depending on your interest, you can go sailing, deep-sea fishing, or just gawking out of Perkins Cove, Ogunquit. The classic 42-foot wooden sloop *Silverlining,* tel. (207) 361-9800 or 646-1229, takes two-hour sails from the cove at 10 a.m. and 12:30 p.m., 3 p.m., and 5:30 p.m., Memorial Day weekend to Columbus Day. Six-person maximum; reservations advisable. Cost is $28 pp from late June to Labor Day, $25 other times. Between late March and early November, Capt. Tim Tower runs half-day (departing 4 p.m.; $25 pp) and full-day (departing 7:30 a.m.; $45 pp) **deep-sea-fishing trips** aboard the 40-foot *Bunny Clark,* P.O. Box 837, Ogunquit 03907, tel. (207) 646-2214. Reservations are necessary. Tim has a science degree, so he's a wealth of marine-biology information. All gear is provided, and they'll fillet your catch for you; dress warmly and wear sunblock.

Perkins Cove (Barnacle Billy's Dock) is also home port for the Hubbard family's **Finestkind Cruises,** tel. (207) 646-5227, offering one-and-a-half-hour, 14-mile scenic cruises (daily, 10 a.m., noon, 2 p.m., 4 p.m.; $12 adults, $10 kids, under age four free) and one-hour cocktail cruises (daily, 4 p.m., 5:15 p.m., 6:30 p.m., and 7:45 p.m.; $8 adults, $5.50 kids, free for children under age four) in a sheltered powerboat, as well as 50-minute lobstering trips (on the hour, Mon.-Sat. 9 a.m.-3 p.m.; look and listen—no helping; $8 adults, $5.50 kids, under age four free) in a real lobsterboat (no toilets). High season runs July 1 through Labor Day; limited schedule May, June, September, October. Reservations are advisable but usually unnecessary midweek.

Whalewatching is the specialty of Capt. Mark Young's 40-foot *Deborah Ann,* tel. (207) 361-9501, departing 8 a.m. and 1:30 p.m. daily from Perkins Cove, mid-June to Labor Day. Trips last four and a half hours; reservations are essential. Dress warmly and don't forget binoculars. If you're especially motion-sensitive, plan ahead with appropriate medication. Cost (no credit cards) is $28 adults, $23 children 12 and under.

ENTERTAINMENT

Having showcased topnotch professional theater since the 1930s, the 750-seat **Ogunquit Playhouse,** Rt. 1, P.O. Box 915, Ogunquit 03907, tel. (207) 646-5511, knows how to do it right: five comedies and musicals each summer, with big-name stars. The air-conditioned building is wheelchair accessible. The box office is open daily in season, beginning in mid-June. Performances are late June-Aug., Mon.-Sat. at 8:30 p.m.; Wednesday and Thursday matinees at 2:30 p.m. Tickets are $24, and performances often sell out. Parking can be a hassle; consider walking the short distance from the Bourne Lane trolleybus stop. An even older local institution is the 640-seat **Leavitt Fine Arts Theatre,** 40 Main St., Ogunquit 03907, tel. (207) 646-3123, a handsome landmark since 1923. Nightly first-run show at 8 p.m.; matinees on rainy days.

Ogunquit has several nightspots with good reputations for food and live entertainment. Best known is **Jonathan's,** 2 Bourne Lane, P.O. Box 1879, Ogunquit 03907, tel. (207) 646-4777 or (800) 464-9934 in Maine, where national headliners often are on the weekend schedule upstairs. Advance tickets are cheaper than at the door, and dinner guests get preference for seats. Reservations are essential at this popular spot. The informal downstairs restaurant has creative entrées for $14-20 and special dinner-and-show combos. Focus of the dining room is a 600-gallon aquarium. Open April-October. Also respected for its contemporary American menu, plus nightly live entertainment, is **Compass Rose,** 125 Shore Rd., near Perkins Cove, tel. (207) 646-1200, open daily for breakfast (8 a.m.-noon), and dinner and late-night fare (5 p.m.-1 a.m.).

FESTIVALS AND EVENTS

Harbor Weekend, a concert, craft fair, parade, barbecue, and children's activities, takes place the last weekend of June in Harbor Park and other sites in Wells. The **Fourth of July** celebration on Ogunquit Beach includes fireworks and live music. Free from 9:15 p.m. The last

Sunday of the month, Ogunquit Beach also hosts a **Sandcastle-Building Contest.**

The **Sidewalk Art Show** on the second or third Thursday of August brings about 80 artists who display and sell their work along Ogunquit's streets 9 a.m.-5 p.m.

Capriccio is a performing-arts festival, with daytime and evening events held throughout Ogunquit the first week of September. Then, the second weekend that month, Wells National Estuarine Research Reserve (Laudholm Farm) hosts the **Laudholm Nature Crafts Festival,** a two-day juried crafts fair with children's activities and guided nature walks. This is an especially fine event. And the *third* weekend of September, the **Annual Ogunquit Antiques Show** benefits the Historical Society of Ogunquit and Wells. At the Dunaway Center, School St., Ogunquit.

Christmas by the Sea, the second weekend of December, features caroling, tree lighting, shopping specials, Santa Claus, a chowderfest, and a beach bonfire in Ogunquit.

SHOPPING

Antiques and Antiquarian Books

Antiques are a Wells specialty, so there are plenty of choices, with a huge range of prices. **R. Jorgensen Antiques,** 502 Post Rd., Rt. 1, RR 1, Box 1125, Wells 04090, tel. (207) 646-9444, is a phenomenon in itself, filling 10 showrooms in two buildings with European and American 18th- and 19th-century furniture and accessories. Open Jan.-Nov. daily except Wednesday 10 a.m.-5 p.m. **MacDougall-Gionet Antiques,** 2104 Post Rd., Rt. 1, Wells 04090, tel. (207) 646-3531, has been here since the mid-1960s, and its reputation is stellar. The 60-dealer shop —in an 18th-century barn—carries American and European country and formal furniture and accessories. Open Tues.-Sun. 9 a.m.-5 p.m., year-round. In the hamlet of Wells Branch is **The Farm,** 294 Mildram Rd., Wells 04090, tel. (207) 985-2656, with room-format displays of English and French antiques and early Chinese porcelain in a splendidly renovated barn. Owned by the Crouthamels and Hacketts since 1967. From Rt. 1, take Coles Hill Rd. to Mildram Rd., two and a half miles west. Open Thurs.-Tues. 10

a.m.-4 p.m., May 1 to Labor Day; open weekends or by appointment off season.

If you've been scouring antiquarian bookshops for a long-wanted title, chances are you'll find it at **Douglas N. Harding Rare Books,** 2152 Post Rd., Rt. 1, P.O. Box 184, Wells 04090, tel. (207) 646-8785 or (800) 228-1398, fax (207) 646-8862. Or they'll find it for you (for a fee). Well-cataloged and user-friendly, the sprawling bookshop at any given time stocks upwards of 100,000 books, prints, and maps. Hefty selection of Maine and New England histories. Don't count on leaving empty-handed—there're too many temptations. If you miss this one, there's a branch shop in Portland. Open daily 9 a.m.-5 p.m., Jan.-Aug. (to 9 p.m. July and August); daily 9 a.m.-6 p.m., Sept.-December. Other Wells antiquarian bookshops are **The Arringtons,** 1908 Post Rd., Rt. 1, P.O. Box 160, Wells 04090, tel. (207) 646-4124, specializing in military books (open daily 10 a.m.-5 p.m. June-Oct., weekends Nov.-May, other times by appointment), and **East Coast Books, Art, Autographs,** Depot St., P.O. Box 849, Wells 04090, tel./fax (207) 646-3584, open daily 10 a.m.-6 p.m. April to mid-Oct., by appointment other times.

Art Galleries

There's no scarcity of the spectacular scenery that drew artists to Ogunquit in the early 20th century, but it's not the artistic magnet it once was. Yet galleries have popped up here and there, primarily on Shore Road and in Perkins Cove, and several have longstanding reputations. **June Weare Fine Arts,** 111 Shore Rd., Ogunquit 03907, tel. (207) 646-8200, has been here since the mid-1970s, specializing in watercolors. Open daily 10 a.m.-4 p.m. **Ogunquit Art Association,** Bourne Ln. and Shore Rd., P.O. Box 529, Ogunquit 03907, tel. (207) 646-8400, was established in 1928 by Charles Woodbury, who was inspired to open an art school in Perkins Cove. Exhibits, gallery talks, workshops, and other activities are on the seasonal schedule. Open Memorial Day weekend to mid-October. The **Scully Gallery,** with paintings by Fran Scully, has two Ogunquit locations: 330 Rt. 1, tel. (207) 646-7489, and Perkins Cove, tel. (207) 646-2850. **Shore Road Gallery,** 112 Shore Rd., tel. (207) 646-5046, features the work of several dozen artists, jewelers, and craftspeople. Open Memorial Day weekend to Columbus Day, Thurs.-Mon. 11 a.m.-5 p.m.

Clothing and Gifts

Littlefield House Crafts Gallery, Rt. 1, just south of Rt. 109, Wells 04090, tel. (207) 646-1257, occupies a handsome brick building that's been around since the early 19th century. The brick allegedly came from ships' ballasts. Coffee is free while you shop for gifts, crafts, and hobby supplies.

Several mini-lighthouses stand watch over the **Lighthouse Depot,** Post Rd., Rt. 1, P.O. Box 1690, Wells 04090, tel. (207) 646-0608 or (800) 758-1444, fax (207) 646-0516—a truly amazing mecca for lighthouse aficionados. Imagine this: two floors of lighthouse books, sculptures, videos, banners, Christmas ornaments, lawn ornaments, paintings, and replicas running the gamut from pure kitsch to attractive collectibles. Owners Tim Harrison and Kathy Finnegan also publish the *Lighthouse Digest,* a monthly magazine ($24 a year) focusing on North American lighthouses, and produce a large mail-order catalog. Hours are Mon.-Sat. 9 a.m.-8 p.m., Sunday 10 a.m.-5 p.m., July to Columbus Day. It's open Mon.-Sat. 9 a.m.-6 p.m., Sunday 10 a.m.-5 p.m. November, December, and June. January to Memorial Day weekend, it's open Mon.-Sat. 10 a.m.-4 p.m. The shop is about one and a half miles north of the junction of Rts. 1 and 109.

PRACTICALITIES

Accommodations in Ogunquit

Motel-style accommodations are everywhere in Ogunquit, most along Rt. 1, yet finding last-minute rooms in July and August can be a challenge, so book well ahead if you'll be here then.

Hotels and Motels: The Seafarer Motel, Rt. 1, P.O. Box 2099, Ogunquit 03907, tel. (207) 646-4040 or (800) 646-1233, is a great place to take kids: there are indoor and outdoor pools, a coin-operated laundry, a/c, cable TV, phones, and no charge for children under 10. Half of the 80 rooms have kitchenettes and most have two double beds. The Ogunquit Playhouse is across the street; motel staff can arrange for tickets.

The clean, well-managed motel is set back a bit from the highway, but if you're noise-sensitive or prefer a woodsy view, ask for a back-facing room. Prices run $80-112 d in peak season, as low as $55 other times. No pets. Open mid-May to mid-October.

You're within spitting distance of Perkins Cove at the 37-room **Riverside Motel,** Shore Rd., P.O. Box 2244, Ogunquit 03907, tel. (207) 646-2741, where you can perch on your balcony and watch the action—or, for that matter—join it. Rooms with refrigerators and cable TV are $120-130 d in July and August, $80-110 d early and late in the season. No pets; three-night minimum July to mid-August. Open May to late October.

Juniper Hill Inn, 196 Main St., Rt. 1, P.O. Box 2190, Ogunquit 03907, tel. (207) 646-4501 or (800) 646-4544, fax (207) 646-4595, is a particularly well-run motel-style lodging on five acres close to downtown Ogunquit. Amenities include refrigerators, cable TV, coin-operated laundry, fitness center, and indoor and outdoor pools. No pets. Rooms are $124-149 d mid-July to mid-August; $52-129 d January to mid-June and mid-October through December. Open all year.

Owned by Maine's former director of tourism, the deluxe **Grand Hotel,** 102 Shore Rd., P.O. Box 1526, Ogunquit 03907, tel. (207) 646-1231, benefits from her savvy and so do the guests. Twenty-eight bright, modern suites with refrigerators, phones, and cable TV/VCR; indoor heated pool, wheelchair access, and continental breakfast. Suites are $140-190 d mid-July to mid-August, $65-170 other months; two-night minimum July and August weekends. Open April through October.

It's not easy to describe the **Sparhawk Oceanfront Resort,** 41 Shore Rd., P.O. Box 936, Ogunquit 03907, tel. (207) 646-5562, a sprawling, one-of-a-kind place popular with honeymooners, sedate families, and seniors. Lots of tradition in this thriving, six-acre complex—it's had various incarnations since the turn of the 20th century—and the Happily Filled sign regularly hangs out front. Out back is the Atlantic, with forever views, and the Marginal Way starts right here. Tennis courts, gardens, heated pool. No restaurant, but Ogunquit has plenty of options, and breakfast is included with your room. The 82 rooms vary in the different buildings—

Edged by grass and homes, Ogunquit Beach makes a long, sweeping arc.

from motel-type rooms (best views) and suites to inn-type suites; rates run $140-165 d late June to late August (seven-night minimum late June to mid-Aug.), $75-135 d other months. No pets. Open May to late October.

B&Bs: Tucked away on a quiet street, yet close to Perkins Cove, the Victorian **Pine Hill Inn,** 14 Pine Hill Rd., P.O. Box 2336, Ogunquit 03907, tel. (207) 361-1004, has five beautifully decorated rooms (four with private bath) plus a two-bedroom efficiency cottage; prices are $85-95 d, $600 weekly for the cottage. Innkeepers Charles and Diana (Schmidt) promise the royal treatment, and Diana's homemade granola gets raves. No pets, no smoking, no children under 12 except in cottage. MasterCard and Visa accepted, but checks or cash preferred. Open mid-May to mid-October.

Jane and Fred Garland have created a very welcoming ambience at the **Morning Dove,** 30 Bourne Ln., P.O. Box 1940, Ogunquit 03907, tel. (207) 646-3891, a restored 1860s farmhouse within walking distance of many Ogunquit attractions. Seven first-, second-, and third-floor rooms have a/c; most have private baths. A hearty breakfast is served in the huge living/dining room (with a fireplace in winter) or on the porch. No smoking, no pets, no kids under 16. Rates run $75-110 d in summer, $55-75 d in winter. Open all year.

At the **Puffin Inn,** 233 Rt. 1, P.O. Box 2232, Ogunquit 03907, tel. (207) 646-5496, 10 guest rooms have private baths, small fridges, and a/c, and breakfast is expanded continental, served on the enclosed porch. (Two of the rooms —with two double beds each—are in the carriage house out back.) Innkeepers Maurice and Lee Williams particularly enjoy helping with day-trip planning. Children are welcome, but no pets; smoking only on front porch. Cost is $80-95 d late June-Labor Day (two-day minimum), $60-70 other times. Open March-November.

Built in 1899 for a prominent Maine lumbering family, **Rockmere Lodge,** 40 Stearns Rd., P.O. Box 278, Ogunquit 03907, tel. (207) 646-2985, underwent a meticulous six-month restoration, thanks to preservationists Andy Antoniuk and Bob Brown. Near the Marginal Way on a peaceful street, the handsome home has eight very comfortable Victorian guest rooms, all with private baths and cable TV and most with ocean views. Rooms go for $100-150 d in summer, $60-100 d other months, including a generous continental breakfast. A wraparound veranda and "The Lookout," a third-floor windowed nook with wicker chairs, are both available for guests. The woodwork throughout is gorgeous. Every room has a basket of magazines, and beach towels and umbrellas are provided for guests. At Christmas, the house sparkles with the lights of more than a dozen decorated trees. No pets, no smoking, no children under 14. Open all year.

Floors glisten, brass gleams, and breakfast is served on the garden-view porch at the **Hartwell House,** 118 Shore Rd., P.O. Box 393, Ogunquit

03907, tel. (207) 646-7210 or (800) 235-8883, fax (207) 646-6032, where the 11 rooms and three suites (all with private bath and a/c) are divided between two buildings straddling Shore Road. Rooms are beautifully decorated with antiques and reproductions; request a back-facing room in the main house. No pets, no children under 14; smoking only on balconies and patios. Prices run $120-185 d in July and August (two-night minimum), $90-125 d in winter. Off-season packages are available. Open all year.

Resorts: Founded in 1872, **The Cliff House,** Shore Rd., P.O. Box 2274, Ogunquit 03907, tel. (207) 361-1000, fax 361-2122, a self-contained Victorian-era complex, sprawls over 70 acres at the edge of Bald Head Cliff, midway between the centers of York and Ogunquit. The 150 room and suite styles and prices vary widely; all have cable TV and phones and most have a spectacular ocean view ($145-210 d July and August, three-night minimum; $85-180 d other months). Special packages and off-season rates (two-night minimum) are available. Facilities include a fitness center, two pools, and tennis courts. No pets. Open late March through December.

Accommodations in Wells

Like Ogunquit, Wells has a long list of motel-type lodgings, mostly on Rt. 1, and everything fills up in late July and early August. If you're arriving then, don't count on finding last-minute space.

Once part of a giant 19th-century dairy farm, Gayle and David Spofford's **Beach Farm Inn,** Eldredge Rd., RR 1, Box 2125, Wells 04090, tel. (207) 646-7970, is a two-and-a-half-acre oasis in a rather congested area .2 mile off Rt. 1. Guests can borrow bikes, swim in the pool, relax in the library, or walk a quarter of a mile down the road to the beach. Nine rooms (three with private baths) and two cottages go for $70-150 d, including a full breakfast in summer, continental off season. No pets, no smoking, no children under 12 except in cottages. Off season, special weekend packages include dinner. Open mid-March to mid-December.

Food in Ogunquit

Picnic Fare: Enrico's Deli & Market, 311 Rt. 1, Footbridge Plaza, Ogunquit 03907, tel. (207) 646-9238, makes delicious sandwiches and subs big enough for two. Plus they have salads, designer coffees, breakfast goodies, and beer and wine. Collect your picnic fixings and walk from here to Footbridge Beach. Open 7 a.m.-10 p.m. daily in summer, shorter hours off season.

Lobster: In Ogunquit's Perkins Cove is the landmark **Lobster Shack,** tel. (207) 646-2941, a converted fishing shanty where they've been turning out first-rate lobster rolls (and chowder) since the 1950s. Beer, wine, and a few picnic tables. Open only in summer.

Creative marketing, a knockout view, and efficient service help explain why more than a thousand pounds of lobster bite the dust every summer day at **Barnacle Billy's,** Perkins Cove, Ogunquit, tel. (207) 646-5575 or (800) 866-5575. Try for the deck, with a front-row seat on Perkins Cove. For ambience, stick with the original operation; Barnacle Billy's Etc., next door (formerly the Whistling Oyster), is an upmarket version of the same thing. No smoking in either restaurant. Open mid-April to mid-October for lunch and dinner.

Second-generation Hancocks now operate the **Ogunquit Lobster Pound,** Rt. 1, a quarter of a mile north of downtown, Ogunquit 03907, tel. (207) 646-2516, the town's oldest lobster place (since 1944). Choose your own lobster from the tank outside; it's cooked in a numbered mesh bag, in sea water, so what you see is what you get. Steak and chicken are also available. Eat indoors (in a rustic log cabin) or outdoors (shaded by pines); beer and wine only. No reservations, so be prepared to wait on midsummer weekends. Open May to mid-October, daily in midsummer, 11:30 a.m.-9:30 p.m.

Candy and Ice Cream: Harbor Candy Shop, 26 Main St., Ogunquit 03907, tel. (207) 646-8078 or (800) 331-5856, is packed with the most outrageous chocolate imaginable. Fudge, truffles, and turtles are all made here in the shop, and the manager upgrades her candy-making skills in Europe each year. Fortunately or unfortunately, they also accept mail orders. Open all year.

Kids (and lots of adults) will know they've reached ice-cream nirvana at **The Viking,** Rt. 1, opposite the Juniper Hill Inn, Ogunquit 03907, tel. (207) 646-3982, where you can build your own skyscraper sundae from 35 flavors of home-made ice cream and two dozen toppings on the ice-cream smorgasbord. If you must, there's also nonfat frozen yogurt. Open March-Sept., until midnight in summer.

Moderate to Expensive Restaurants: In addition to the restaurants listed here, there's easy access from Ogunquit to the attractive **Clay Hill Farm** restaurant, in a rural setting west of Rt. 1 on Agamenticus Rd., on the York-Ogunquit town line, tel. (207) 361-2272. It serves good regional American fare for $15-22 with daily specials. You'll want to roam the beautiful, landscaped grounds, popular for weddings. Open all year, daily 5:30-9 p.m.; closed Mon.-Wed. in winter. Reservations essential in July and August.

Right in downtown Ogunquit, **Gypsy Sweethearts,** 10 Shore Rd., P.O. Box 593, Ogunquit 03907, tel. (207) 646-7021, occupies four rooms on the ground floor of a restored house. The creative menu includes heart-healthy and vegetarian entrées, plus there's a real-deal create-a-dinner: choose an appetizer (excellent options) and pay $4 extra for potato, vegetable, and bread. Entrée range is $13-22. No smoking. Reservations advised in midsummer. Open mid-May to late October for breakfast (7:30 a.m.-noon) and dinner (5:30-10 p.m.)—daily in midsummer, weekends in spring and fall.

A welcome new kid on the block (since 1995), **Ida Reds,** Rt. 1, next to Ogunquit Playhouse, P.O. Box 1498, Ogunquit 03907, tel. (207) 646-0289, rates right near the top in quality. Under the same ownership as Portland's stellar Back Bay Grill, it whips up outstandingly creative entrées (olive-crusted pork chops, lobster risotto, grilled trout tagliatelle; $15-24) to accompany a selective wine list. No smoking. Reservations are essential in midsummer at this elegantly casual place. Open mid-February through December for dinner, after-theater suppers (in summer), and Sunday brunch. Closed Monday and Tuesday off season.

Diners (and lodgers) have been stopping at **The Old Village Inn,** 30 Main St., Ogunquit 03907, tel. (207) 646-7088, since 1833; the food, service, and warm ambience continue to draw crowds. One of the dining rooms in the historic house has only a single table and a fireplace. Off-season "winter warmer specials" and

summertime early-bird specials (5:30-6:15 p.m.) are bargains. Midsummer reservations are essential. Open daily for dinner Apr.-Nov.; closed Monday in November and December; closed Monday and Tuesday Jan.-March. On summer weekends, breakfast is available to the public as well as guests staying in the inn's six good-size second- and third-floor guest rooms (private baths and a/c). Open all year.

There's not much between you and Spain when you get a window seat at **Hurricane,** Oarweed Ln., Perkins Cove, Ogunquit, tel. (207) 646-6348 or (800) 649-6348 in Maine, one of Ogunquit's best (and most reasonable) restaurants in a town noted for topnotch cuisine. You can't go wrong here, especially with seafood. Small-plate selections—such as Napoleon of smoked salmon and deviled lobster cakes, both under $8—might be appetizers for some, but they're real deals and plenty filling. Dinner entrées are in the $14-21 range. Reservations are essential in July and August, for Sunday jazz brunch (1:30-4:30 p.m.), and on weekends all year. Open daily for lunch and dinner—until 10:30 p.m. late May-mid-Oct., to 9:30 p.m. the rest of the year.

A self-contained Victorian-era resort complex, **The Cliff House,** Shore Rd., P.O. Box 2274, Ogunquit 03907, tel. (207) 361-1000, fax 361-2122, sprawls over 70 acres at the edge of Bald Head Cliff, midway between the centers of York and Ogunquit. The fourth generation now runs the Cliff House, founded in 1872. The dining room, with fantastic ocean views, is open to the public for breakfast and dinner, plus lunch in July and August. Try for the Sunday brunch buffet, 7:30 a.m.-1 p.m. Reservations are required for dinner (no jeans allowed, no smoking); entrée range is $15-23. Before or after dining, wander the grounds. Open late March through December.

Worthwhile Wallet-Cruncher: Restrain yourself for a couple of days and then splurge on an elegant dinner at **Arrows,** Berwick Rd., about one and a half miles west of Rt. 1, Ogunquit 03907, tel. (207) 361-1100, definitely one of the state's finest restaurants. Located in a beautifully restored 18th-century farmhouse overlooking well-tended gardens, Arrows does absolutely everything right. Prices are stratospheric by Maine standards (with wine, you can count on paying well over $100 a couple), but worth it. "Innovative" is too tame to describe the menu. Reservations are essential in midsummer. No smoking. Men should wear jackets. Open for dinner late April to Thanksgiving on the following schedule: weekends only in May, Wed.-Sun. in June, Tues.-Sun. July and August, shorter weeks after Labor Day.

Food in Wells

Breakfasts: Best homemade doughnuts in Wells (and beyond), hands down, are at **Congdon's Doughnuts,** Rt. 1, Wells 04090, tel. (207) 646-4219. Also try the $3.50 Popeye bagel—scrambled eggs, spinach, bacon, and cheese on a spinach bagel. Open daily 6 a.m.-2 p.m. for breakfast and lunch year-round. **Egg in the Nest,** Rt. 1, across from Wells Junior High School, tel. (207) 646-7507, earns points for its creative breakfasts and attractive, homey setting. Open year-round at 7 a.m. daily except Wednesday.

Pizza and Inexpensive Fare: No eatery in this category qualifies as heart-healthy, so don't say you weren't forewarned. **La Stalla Pizzeria,** Rt. 1, opposite the fire station, tel. (207) 646-1718, has the same first-rate reputation for creative toppings as its York parent. On Thursday night, there's an all-you-can-eat buffet for $5.95.

Long-time favorite **Billy's Chowder House,** 216 Mile Rd., just off Rt. 1, tel. (207) 646-7558, has a prime marsh-view location—with wall-to-wall cars in the parking lot. Open mid-January to mid-December for lunch and dinner. **The Hayloft,** Rt. 1, in Moody 04054, tel. (207) 646-4400, gets gold stars for hearty seafood chowder (clams, shrimp, and chunks of lobster) and good burgers. It's a casual, popular place, great for families, so go early. No smoking. Open all year for lunch and dinner. Fried-clam aficionados swear by **Jake's Seafood,** Rt. 1 and Bourne Ave., Moody 04054, tel. (207) 646-6771, but you'll also like their clam chowder and onion rings. Open all year for breakfast, lunch, and dinner.

Your basic family-oriented place, **Maine Diner,** Rt. 1, Wells 04090, tel. (207) 646-4441, has a reputation built on lobster pie and award-winning seafood chowder. Beer and wine only. No smoking. Open 7 a.m.-9:30 p.m. for breakfast, lunch, and dinner (breakfast available anytime).

Moderate to Expensive Restaurants: A loyal local clientele patronizes **Litchfield's,** Rt. 1, Wells 04090, tel. (207) 646-5711, so reservations are a good idea on summer weekends, especially for the Friday-night seafood extravaganza ($6.95), served 5-7:30 p.m. Blackened rib eye, vegetable alfredo, and fried oysters are house specialties, along with a superb fried fisherman's platter. Open daily, all year, for lunch 11:30 a.m.-3 p.m., dinner 5-9:30 p.m. weekdays, 5-10 p.m. weekends, and Sunday brunch 11 a.m.-3 p.m. Piano music accompanies brunch and weekend dinners.

English pub is the theme at **Sir Francis Drake,** Rt. 1, Moody 04054, tel. (207) 646-1800—starting with the pseudo-Tudor exterior. Good selection of British beers on tap, continental and pub cuisine (including fish and chips, bangers and mash), live jazz Friday and Saturday nights. No children under 12. Open all year for dinner from 5 p.m., except Tuesday.

Seals and surf are just beyond the windows at **The Grey Gull,** 321 Webhannet Dr., a mile west of Rt. 1, in Wells 04090, tel. (207) 646-7501, the best restaurant in town. Seafood is a specialty (lobster's always on the menu), but so are Yankee pot roast, creative chicken dishes, pasta entrées, and diet-conscious items; prices range $11-19. Service is superb, wine list is selective, and there's a kids' menu. Reservations are essential in July and August (request a window table). Open for breakfast, 8-10:30 a.m., in summer, brunch and dinner year-round. Closed Mon.-Wed. mid-November to mid-March. Upstairs, the Grey Gull Inn has five reasonably priced rooms with shared baths. Under the same ownership are Clay Hill Farm in the Yorks and the Sea Chambers resort complex in Ogunquit.

INFORMATION AND SERVICES

At the southern edge of the downtown area, the Ogunquit Chamber of Commerce's **Visitor Information Center,** Rt. 1 at Obed's Ln., Box 2289, Ogunquit 03907, tel. (207) 646-5533 or 646-2939, provides all the usual visitor information, including restaurant menus. Ask for the *Touring and Trolley Route Map,* showing the Marginal Way, beach locations, and public restrooms. The chamber of commerce's annual visitor booklet thoughtfully carries a high-tide calendar for the summer months. The info center, which also has restrooms, is open 9 a.m.-5 p.m. weekdays all year, plus weekends in May and evenings during the summer.

Just over the Ogunquit border in Wells (actually in Moody) is the **Wells Information Center,** Rt. 1 at Bourne Ave., P.O. Box 356, Wells 04090, tel. (207) 646-2451. Summer hours are 9 a.m.-5 p.m. daily; off season, it's open Mon.-Fri. 10 a.m.-4 p.m.

The handsome fieldstone **Ogunquit Memorial Library,** 72 Shore Rd., Ogunquit 03907, tel. (207) 646-9024, is the downtown's only National Historic Register building. Open Mon.-Sat. 9 a.m.-noon and 2-5 p.m., June-Oct.; same hours other months, but closed Sunday and Monday.

The local weekly (Wednesday) newspaper is the *York County Coast Star,* based in Kennebunk but covering the entire county. Each Thursday in summer, the paper produces the *Coast Pilot,* a free tabloid supplement covering restaurants, shopping, entertainment, and a tide calendar for York and Kennebunkport.

Emergencies
Nearest hospital to Ogunquit is **York Hospital,** 15 Hospital Dr., York, tel. (207) 363-4321; nearest to Wells are, to the north, the 150-bed **Southern Maine Medical Center,** 1 Medical Center Dr., Biddeford 04005, emergency room tel. (207) 283-7100, and, to the west, **Goodall Hospital,** 25 June St., Sanford 04073, tel. (207) 324-4310. All three have round-the-clock emergency rooms. York Hospital's **Tel-a-Nurse** service, tel. (800) 283-7234, provides free over-the-phone advice for minor medical problems. For **Ogunquit** ambulance, police, and fire emergencies, call (207) 646-5111. For **Wells** ambulance, police, and fire emergencies, call (207) 646-9911.

Photo Services
Ogunquit Camera Shop, 17 Shore Rd., at Wharf Lane, P.O. Box 2092, Ogunquit 03907, tel. (207) 646-2261, provides one-hour print service. Also part of the shop is Cricket's Corner,

with all kinds of last-minute beach-type items. Open all year, daily in summer.

Laundromats
Soaps Laundromat, Rt. 1, Ogunquit Plaza, Ogunquit 03907, tel. (207) 646-1101, has coin-operated machines (and cable TV while you wait), or they'll do your laundry (and dry cleaning) for you. Open 5 a.m.-9 p.m. year-round, to 10 p.m. in midsummer.

Getting Around
From mid-May through Columbus Day, a fleet of **trolley buses**—named Polly, Holly, Dolly, Molly, Jolly, and Wally—makes the rounds of Ogunquit, with 32 stops (signposted). Each time you board, it'll cost you 50 cents, but for the same price you can go the whole route—a great way to get your bearings—in about 40 minutes. Wells, too, has regular trolleybus service, operating daily 9 a.m.-10 p.m., late June to early September. Fare is $1 per trip or $3 for a day pass; a family day pass is $8. The schedule is coordinated with Ogunquit's trolleybus service.

The Coastal Connection, a bus service linking Kittery with Kennebunk, via York, Ogunquit, and Wells, makes four daily roundtrip runs between late June and Labor Day, 8:50 a.m.-5:30 p.m. Fares ($1-3) depend on how far you go. Printed schedules are available at lodgings, information centers, and many other local sites.

Even if guided tours aren't your thing, sign up for one of the two-and-a-half-hour van trips operated four times daily, early May to late October, by **Seacoast Tours,** P.O. Box 1405, Ogunquit 03907, tel. (207) 646-6326 or (800) 328-8687. The vans leave Perkins Cove (or any lodging in Ogunquit) and head south to York or north to the Kennebunks. An umpteenth-generation Mainer—either Faith York or her husband, Larry Ducharme—provides historical tidbits and entertains you as well. Reservations are essential. Tickets are $12.50 adults, $11.50 seniors, $8.50 kids under 12, free for kids five and under. Off season, they'll do private tours on the same routes for $30, two-person minimum.

THE KENNEBUNKS

The world may have first learned of Kenne-bunkport when George Herbert Walker Bush was president and would retreat here periodically, but Walkers and Bushes have owned their summer estate here for three generations. Visitors continue to come to the Kennebunks (the collective name for Kennebunk, Kennebunk-port, Cape Porpoise, and Goose Rocks Beach—combined population about 12,400) hoping to catch a glimpse of the former first family, but they also come for the terrific ambience, the B&Bs, boutiques, boats, biking, and beaches.

The Kennebunks' earliest European settlers arrived in the mid-1600s. By the mid-1700s, shipbuilding had become big business in the area. Two ancient local cemeteries—North Street and Evergreen—provide glimpses of the area's heritage. Its Historic District reveals Kennebunk's moneyed past—the homes where wealthy shipowners and shipbuilders once lived, sending their vessels to the Caribbean and around the globe. Today, unusual shrubs and a dozen varieties of rare maples still line Summer Street—the legacy of ship captains in the global trade. Another legacy is the shiplap construction in many houses—throwbacks to a time when labor was cheap and lumber plentiful. Closer to the beach, in Lower Village, stood the workshops of sailmakers, carpenters, and mast-makers whose output drove the booming trade to success.

While Kennebunkport draws most of the sightseers and summer traffic, Kennebunk feels more like a year-round community. It boasts an interesting, old-fashioned downtown and a mix of shops, restaurants, and attractions. Yes, its beaches, too, are well known, but many visitors drive right through the middle of Kennebunk without stopping to enjoy its assets.

The Kennebunks are communities with conscience—loaded with conservationists working to preserve hikeable, bikeable green space for residents and visitors. Be sure not to miss these trails, bikeways, and offshore islets. Gravestone rubbers will want to check out Evergreen Cemetery, and history buffs should pick up a copy of *Walking in the Port,* ($3) the Kennebunkport His-

torical Society's well-researched booklet of three self-guided historic walking tours. To appreciate the area another way, climb aboard the In-town Trolley, with regular summertime service and lots of entertaining tidbits from the driver.

SIGHTS

Museums
Occupying four restored 19th-century buildings (including the 1825 William Lord store) in downtown Kennebunk, **The Brick Store Museum,** 117 Main St., P.O. Box 177, Kennebunk 04043, tel. (207) 985-4802, fax 985-6887, has garnered a reputation for unusual exhibits: a century of wedding dresses, a two-century history of volunteer firefighting, life in southern Maine during the Civil War. Open Tues.-Sat. 10 a.m.-4:30 p.m., year-round. Admission is $3 adults, free for children 12 and under. For an extra $2, you can tour the nearby **Taylor-Barry House,** 24 Summer St., Kennebunk 04043, an early-19th-century sea captain's house also owned by the museum. Open Tues.-Fri. 1-4 p.m., July-September. Admission to the Taylor-Barry House alone is $3 pp. The museum encourages appreciation for the surrounding Kennebunk Historic District with hour-long **architectural walking tours,** Wednesday 10 a.m. and Friday 1 p.m., June to mid-October. Cost is $3. If this schedule doesn't suit, the museum's well-stocked gift shop sells a walk-it-yourself booklet for $5.

Owned and maintained by the Kennebunkport Historical Society, **The Nott House,** 8 Maine St., Kennebunkport 04046, tel. (207) 967-2751, is a mid-19th-century Greek Revival mansion filled with Victorian furnishings. Open Tues.-Fri. 1-4 p.m., mid-June to Columbus Day. Admission is $3 adults, $2 children. Hour-long architectural walking tours of the Kennebunkport Historic District depart from the Nott House at 10:30 a.m. Wednesday and 1 p.m. Friday during the same months. Cost is $3.

There's nothing quite like an antique electric trolley to dredge up nostalgia for bygone days. With a collection of more than 225 trolleys, the

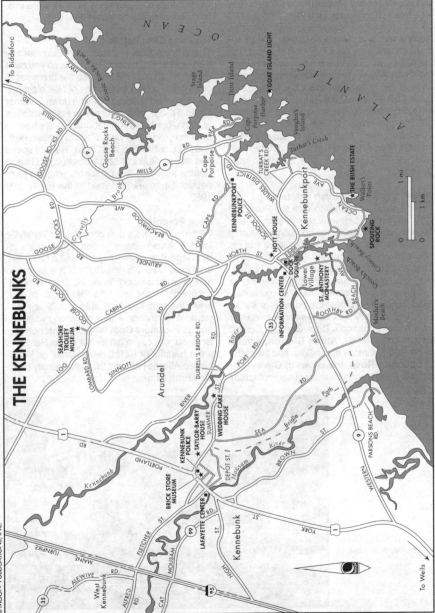

THE KENNEBUNKS

Seashore Trolley Museum, Log Cabin Rd., P.O. Box A, Kennebunkport 04046, tel./fax (207) 967-2800, verges on trolley-mania. Whistles blowing and bells clanging, restored trolleys operate continuously on a four-mile loop through the nearby woods. After a ride, you can check out the activity in the streetcar workshop, grab lunch at the Trolley Fare snack bar, and go wild in the trolley-oriented gift shop. Special events are held throughout the summer; call for schedule. The museum is 1.7 miles southeast of Rt. 1. Open daily, early May to late October; limited hours in May. Also open during Christmas Prelude (see "Festivals and Events," below) in early December.

Walker's Point: The Bush Estate

There's no public access to Walker's Point, but you can join the sidewalk gawkers on Ocean Avenue overlooking George and Barbara Bush's summer compound. The 41st president and his wife lead a low-key, laid-back life when they're here, so if you don't spot them through binoculars, you may well run into them at a shop or restaurant in town. Intown Trolley's regular narrated tours go right past the house—or it's an easy, scenic family walk via Henry Parsons Park from Kennebunkport's Dock Square. On the way, you'll pass **St. Ann's Church,** whose stones came from the ocean floor, and the paths to **Spouting Rock** and **Blowing Cave**—two natural phenomena that create spectacular

water fountains if you manage to be there midway between high and low tides.

Wedding Cake House

The Wedding Cake House, 104 Summer St., Kennebunk, is a private residence, so you can't go inside (a small gift shop on the premises is open to the public), but it's one of Maine's most-photographed buildings. Driving down Summer Street (Rt. 35), midway between the downtowns of Kennebunk and Kennebunkport, it's hard to miss the yellow and white Federal mansion with gobs of gingerbread and Gothic Revival spires and arches. Built in 1826 by shipbuilder George Bourne as a wedding gift for his wife, the Kennebunk landmark remained in the family until 1983.

Cape Porpoise

When your mind's eye conjures up an idyllic lobster-fishing village, it probably looks a lot like Cape Porpoise—only two and a half miles from busy Dock Square. Follow Rt. 9 eastward from Kennebunkport; when Rt. 9 turns north, continue straight, and take Pier Rd. to its end. From the small parking area, you'll see lobsterboats at anchor, a slew of working wharves, and 19th-century **Goat Island Light,** now automated, directly offshore. In Cape Porpoise are a handful of B&Bs, restaurants, galleries, historic Atlantic Hall, and the extra-friendly Bradbury Bros. Market.

Wedding Cake House, Kennebunk

PARKS, PRESERVES, AND RECREATION

Thanks to a dedicated coterie of year-round and summer residents, the foresighted **Kennebunkport Conservation Trust** (KCT), founded in the 1970s, has become a nationwide model for land-trust organizations. The KCT has managed to preserve from development nearly 600 acres of town land (including nearly a dozen small islands off Cape Porpoise Harbor), and most of this acreage is accessible to the public, especially with a sea kayak. Contact the KCT, P.O. Box 7028, Cape Porpoise 04014, for info on its holdings or to volunteer for trail maintenance. Better yet, become a member ($25 a year) and support their efforts.

In addition to all the recreational options listed below, don't miss the Wells National Estuarine Research Reserve or the Rachel Carson National Wildlife Refuge, on Kennebunk's southwestern boundary, or the East Point Sanctuary in Biddeford Pool, northeast of the Kennebunks.

Beaches

Ah, the beaches. The Kennebunks are well endowed with sand but not with parking spaces. Between mid-June and mid-September, you'll need to buy a **parking pass** ($5 a day, $15 a week, $30 a season) from the Kennebunk Town Hall, 1 Summer St., tel. (207)985-3675, or the Kennebunkport Town Hall, Elm St., just off Ocean Ave., tel. (207) 967-4243, or the police stations or the chamber of commerce. *You need a separate pass for each town.* Many lodgings provide free passes for their guests—be sure to ask when making room reservations. Or you can avoid the parking dilemma altogether by hopping aboard the Intown Trolley, which goes right by the major beaches.

The main beaches in **Kennebunk** (east to west, stretching about two miles) are Gooch's (most popular), Kennebunk (locally called Middle or Rocks Beach), and Mother's (a smallish beach next to Lords Point, where there's also a playground). Lifeguards are on duty at Gooch's and Mother's Beaches July-Labor Day. Mother's Beach is the home of the Kennebunk Beach Improvement Association (see below). Ask locally about a couple of other beach options.

Kennebunkport's claim to beach fame is three-mile-long Goose Rocks Beach, one of the loveliest in the area. Parking spaces are scarce and biking on Rt. 9 can be dicey, so the best solution is to book a room nearby. You'll be about five miles east of all the downtown action, but if sun and sand are your primary goals, this is the place. To reach the beach, take Rt. 9 from Dock Square east and north to Dyke Rd. (Clock Farm Corner). Turn right and continue to the end (King's Highway).

The prize for tiniest beach goes to Colony (officially Arundel) Beach, located near The Colony resort complex. It's close to many Kennebunkport lodgings and an easy walk from Dock Square.

Vaughn's Island Preserve

Thanks to the Kennebunkport Conservation Trust, 96-acre Vaughn's Island has been saved for posterity. You'll need to do a little planning, tide-wise, since the island is some 600 feet offshore. Consult a tide calendar and aim for low tide close to new moon or full moon (when the most water drains away). Allow yourself an hour or so before and after low tide, but no longer, or you may need a boat rescue. Wear treaded rubber boots, since the crossing is muddy and slippery with rockweed. Keep an eye on your watch and explore the ocean (east) side of the island, along the beach. It's all worth the effort, and there's a great view of Goat Island Light off to the east. From downtown Kennebunkport, take Maine St. to Wildes District Road. Continue to Shore Rd. (also called Turbat's Creek Rd.), go .6 mile, jog left .2 mile more, and park in the tiny lot at the end, opposite the Shawmut Ocean Resort. The Intown Trolley stops at the Shawmut, so you can also do this without a car.

Emmons Preserve

Also under the stewardship of the Kennebunkport Conservation Trust, the Emmons Preserve has two trails (blazed yellow and pink) meandering through 148 acres of woods and fields on the edge of the Batson River (also called Gravelly Brook). Fall colors here are brilliant, birdlife is abundant, and you can do a loop in half an hour. But why rush? This is a wonderful oasis in the heart of Kennebunkport. From Dock Square, take North St. to Beachwood Ave. (right turn) to unpaved Gravelly Brook Rd. (left turn). The trailhead is on the left, about .2 mile past the brown-shingled Emmons home.

Picnic Rock

About one and a half miles up the Kennebunk River from the ocean, Picnic Rock is the centerpiece of the **Butler Preserve,** a 14-acre enclave managed by The Nature Conservancy. Well named, the rock is a great place for a picnic and a swim, but don't count on being alone. A short trail loops through the preserve. Consider bringing a canoe or kayak (or renting one) and paddle with the tide past beautiful homes and the Cape Arundel Golf Course. From Lower Village Kennebunk, take Rt. 35 west and hang a right onto Old Port Road. When the road gets close to the Kennebunk River, watch for a Nature Conservancy oak-leaf sign on the right. Parking is along Old Port Road; walk down through the preserve to Picnic Rock, right on the river.

Kennebunk Plains Preserve

Also linked to The Nature Conservancy is the 1,164-acre Kennebunk Plains Preserve, nesting site for the endangered grasshopper sparrow and home to dozens of other bird species. Best time to come is August, when hundreds of acres of blueberries are ripe for the picking and the rare northern blazing star carpets parts of the preserve with purple blossoms. You may even see wild turkeys. Most of the preserve—1,041 acres—was purchased by the Land for Maine's Future Board, created by a $35 million state bond issue in 1987. To reach Kennebunk Plains, head northwest on Rt. 99 from Rt. 9A in Kennebunk. About two miles west of I-95, watch for a small, signposted parking area.

St. Anthony's Monastery

Long ago, 35,000 Native Americans used this part of town for a summer camp. They knew a good thing. So did a group of Lithuanian Franciscan monks who in 1947 fled war-ravaged Europe and acquired the 200-acre St. Anthony's Franciscan Monastery, Beach St., Kennebunk (mailing address: P.O. Box 980, Kennebunkport 04046), tel. (207) 967-2011. From 1956 to 1969, they ran a high school here. The monks occupy the handsome Tudor great house, but the well-tended grounds (sprinkled with shrines) are open to the public 6 a.m.-8:30 p.m. in summer, to 6 p.m. in winter. A short path leads from the monastery area to a peaceful gazebo overlooking the Kennebunk River. No pets or bikes. Public restrooms are available., The monastery also has a 60-room **guesthouse** operation, mid-June to mid-September, in the former dorm buildings—clean, basic—where doubles with private bath, TV, and a/c go for $55-65. There's even an outdoor pool. No credit cards.

Cycling

A mandatory stop for anyone interested in biking is Peter Sargent's **Cape-Able Bike Shop,** 83 Arundel Rd., Town House Corners, Kennebunkport 04046, tel. (207) 967-4382 or (800) 220-0907, a local institution since 1974. The shop has all kinds of rentals and accessories, repairs your wounded gear, sponsors Saturday morning group rides, and provides a free area bike map and the best insider info. (The bike map is also available at the chamber of commerce.) One-day mountain-bike rental is $20-25; kids' bikes are $8 a day. Open Mon.-Sat. 9 a.m.-6 p.m., early March to mid-December; also open on Sunday 9 a.m.-1 p.m., early May to mid-October.

Cape-Able has info on a 10-mile Goose Rocks pedal, an eight-mile Cape Porpoise ride, and, if you don't mind a bit of congestion, an eight-mile route through downtown Kennebunkport and over to Kennebunk Beach.

At the height of midsummer traffic, the safest cycling excursion in the area follows an old trolley-line route (called the "bridle path") along the Mousam River in Kennebunk. Easiest places to park are on Railroad Avenue, next to Tom's of Maine, or at the Sea Road School (when school's not in session), both just south of Rt. 35. The three-mile path is also a wonderfully easy walk for the whole family, ending up near Kennebunk Beach.

Golf and Tennis

Three 18-hole golf courses make the sport a big deal in the area. **Cape Arundel Golf Club,** River Rd., Kennebunkport, tel. (207) 967-3494, established in 1897, and **Webhannet Golf Club,** Beach Ave., Kennebunk, tel. (207) 967-2061, established in 1902, are semiprivate, open to nonmembers; call for tee times at least 24 hours ahead. At Cape Arundel, where George Bush plays, greens fees are $30, and no jeans or sweatpants are allowed. In nearby Arundel, **Dutch Elm Golf Course,** Brimstone Rd., Arundel, tel. (207) 282-9850, is a public course with rentals, pro shop, and putting greens.

Tennis courts are scattered around town: **Kennebunk High School,** Fletcher St., Rt. 35, Kennebunk; **Parsons Field,** Park St., Kennebunk; **West Kennebunk Recreation Area,** Holland Rd., West Kennebunk; and **Beachwood Ave.,** Kennebunkport. The chamber of commerce can provide additional details.

GETTING AFLOAT

You don't have to swim to enjoy the water in the Kennebunks. Kayaking, whalewatching, sailing, and an excursion on a lobsterboat are all other options. Wear a hat and rubber-soled shoes, dress in layers, use sunblock, and remember that freaky weather can put the kibosh on your plans at the last minute. Reservations are advisable, sometimes required, for all cruises.

Adventures Incorporated, P.O. Box 943, Kennebunkport 04046, tel. (207) 967-5243, fax 967-4128, operates three-hour, six-mile kayak tours along the coast past Walker's Point and out to Bumpkin Island. Cost is $40 pp. Other possibilities are a one-and-a-half-hour sunset paddle ($25 pp) and a six-hour, 10-mile trip to Cape Porpoise and Goat Island Light ($80). Each trip is rated for difficulty, with a maximum of 10 paddlers per excursion; all trips are weather-dependent. Kayaks are the sit-on, open-cockpit variety; wetsuit shorts and boots are supplied. Tours begin in late May and continue into the fall. The company also runs scuba expeditions with certified diving instructors.

Whale sightings offshore include finbacks, minkes, and humpbacks, and the local cruise boats have had remarkable success. *Indian Whale Watch,* Arundel Wharf, Ocean Ave., Kennebunkport 04046, tel. (207) 967-5912, berthed on the east side of the Kennebunk River, departs daily at 10 a.m., July-Sept. (weekends only in May, June, October). *Nautilus Whale Watch,* P.O. Box 2775, Kennebunkport, tel. (207) 967-0707, tied up on the west side of

the river, next to the bridge, also departs at 10 a.m. Both boats have full galleys, but don't overeat and be sorry later. *First Chance,* 4A Western Ave., Lower Village, Kennebunk 04043, tel. (207) 967-5507 or (800) 767-2628, does two four-hour whalewatch trips daily, weather permitting.

For daysailing, Rich Woodman's 42-foot traditional wooden schooner *Lazyjack,* Schooners Wharf, Ocean Ave., P.O. Box 572, Kennebunkport 04046, tel. (207) 967-8809, departs from behind the Schooners Inn three times daily, weather permitting. Two-hour sails are $30 pp (two-person minimum). The 37-foot yacht *Bellatrix,* Sail-aboard-Bellatrix, Ocean Ave., P.O. Box 2762, Kennebunkport 04046, tel. (207) 967-8685, based at the Nonantum Resort, charges $15 pp for an hour of sailing.

Second Chance, 4A Western Ave., Lower Village, Kennebunk 04043, tel. (207) 967-5507 or (800) 767-2628, under the same ownership as *First Chance,* and docked on the Kennebunk side of the river, next to the Shipyard Shops, heads out five times daily in summer for 90-minute lobstering cruises—watching, not eating. Cost is $12.50 adults, $6 kids 6-12.

KIDS' STUFF

Besides all the parks and recreational activities described above, most of which are great for children, there's **Kennebunk Beach Improvement Association** (KBIA), 19 Beach Ave., Kennebunk 04043, tel. (207) 967-2180—a child-oriented membership organization ideal for families spending extended time here. KBIA sponsors a huge array of week-long programs, early July to late August, for children 3-18. The KBIA complex at Lords Point, next to Mother's Beach, has a swimming pool, playground, social center, and a fleet of boats. Among the three dozen options are arts and crafts, photography, sailing, tennis, swimming, and golf. Every Wednesday night, a family beach party is followed by a supervised film screening (parents can sneak away for a few hours). Family membership is $175, and there's a fee for each activity, but reliable child care would be lots more expensive. Besides, the kids have so much fun.

Kennebunk Parks and Recreation, 1 Summer St., 3rd floor, Kennebunk 04043, tel. (207) 985-6890, also sponsors several dozen summer activities, with activity fees but no membership fee. Registration must be done in person (weekdays 9 a.m.-5 p.m.) or by mail, beginning early June. Programs for tiny tots, kids (golf, track, wrestling, soccer, swimming, chess, tennis), families (rafting, baseball games), adults (tennis, volleyball), and senior citizens (field trips). Send for the annual catalog.

Kennebunkport Parks and Recreation, P.O. Box 566, Kennebunkport 04046, tel. (207) 967-4304, also has a children's summer program. Call or write for the schedule.

Out in the country, two miles west of I-95, is **Russell Acres Farm,** 1797 Alewive Rd., Rt. 35, Kennebunk 04043, tel. (207) 985-2435, fax 985-9089, a 185-acre deer farm where kids can fish in a stocked bass pond and buy some of the best ice cream in the area.

All-day play is the rule at **Parsons Park,** Park St., Kennebunk, a municipal park with tennis courts, creative playground, volleyball court, picnic tables, and a baseball field.

ENTERTAINMENT

Live entertainment is featured, mostly weekends, at Federal Jack's Brewpub and Windows on the Water, as well as the Kennebunkport Inn, The Colony, and The Shawmut Ocean Resort.

River Tree Arts
The area's cultural spearhead is **River Tree Arts** (RTA), P.O. Box 1056, Kennebunkport 04046, tel. (207) 985-4343, an energetic, volunteer-driven organization that sponsors concerts, classes, workshops, exhibits, and educational programs throughout the year. Check newspaper listings for RTA events or call the office.

FESTIVALS AND EVENTS

The **Annual Winter Carnival,** the first weekend in February, occupies the Kennebunks with sleigh rides, spaghetti supper, kids' games, ice-skating, and a snowball-throwing championship. On the first or second Sunday of June, the **B&B, Inn, and Garden Tour** typically takes in more than a dozen stops noon-5 p.m. in the Kennebunks.

In Kennebunkport, the **Craft Fair on the Green** brings a juried craft show, food booths, and live entertainment to Kennebunkport one Saturday near the Fourth of July. Mid-July's weekend **Pondboat Races** in Cape Porpoise are a recently revived local tradition dating from 1939 in which competition is among scale-model schooners under 50 inches long. Models are on display in restored Atlantic Hall all day Saturday, races begin at 1 p.m. Sunday at Cape Porpoise Pier. Thursday evenings from mid-July to mid-August, the **River Tree Arts Summer Concert Series** brings music to Kennebunkport.

Take the kids to the **Kennebearport Teddy Bear Show and Sale,** first or second Saturday in August, but watch the reactions of all the grown-ups. It happens 10 a.m.-4 p.m. at Kennebunk High School.

The first two weekends of December mark the **Christmas Prelude,** during which spectacular decorations adorn historic homes, candle-toting carolers stroll through the Kennebunks, stores have special sales, and Santa Claus shows up in a lobsterboat.

SHOPPING

Lots of small, attractive boutiques surround **Dock Square,** the hub of Kennebunkport, so gridlock often develops in midsummer. Avoid driving through here at the height of the season. Take your time and walk, bike, or ride the local trolleybus.

Art Galleries
Jean Briggs-Novikov represents nearly 100 artists at her topflight **Mast Cove Galleries,** Maine St. and Mast Cove Ln., P.O. Box 2718, Kennebunkport 04046, tel. (207) 967-3453, in a handsome Greek Revival house near the Graves Memorial Library. Prices vary widely, so don't be surprised if you spot something affordable. One of the area's newest galleries, and already earning its own reputation, is **The Gallery on Chase Hill,** 10 Chase Hill Rd., Kennebunk, tel. (207) 967-0049, mailing address

P.O. Box 2786, Kennebunkport 04046. Located in the stunningly restored Captain Chase House, next to the Windows on the Water restaurant, the gallery mounts rotating exhibits and represents a wide variety of Maine and New England artists.

Books

To appreciate the friendly, funky **Kennebunk Book Port,** Dock Square, Kennebunkport 04046, tel. (207) 967-3815 or (800) 382-2710, climb to the second floor of the antique rum warehouse and read the shop slogan: "Ice cream, candy, children, barefeet, short hair, long hair, no hair, cats, dogs and small dragons are welcome here anytime." A timeworn couch—often occupied by a languid cat—looks out over the square. The inventory is especially well chosen by owners Jack and Shirley Fenner, and the loft even has a small section of used books. Open daily, year-round.

Gifts, Crafts, and Clothing

It's tough to describe the inventory at **Marlows,** 39 Main St., Kennebunk 04043, tel. (207) 985-2931—there's lots of it, and everything's so interesting. Cards, candles, toys, books, baskets, jewelry, funky clothing, and on and on. Open all year.

Looking for bargains in women's clothing? Try **Return to Cinda,** Harbor Village Professional Center, Christensen Ln., off Rt. 35, Kennebunk 04043, tel. (207) 967-3800, for good-quality pre-owned stuff. Open Mon.-Wed. 9:30 a.m.-4 p.m., Thurs.-Sat. 9:30 a.m.-6 p.m.

A particularly attractive gift shop is based at the 18th-century **Emma Rose Saltwater Farm,** 190 Mills Rd., Rt. 9, Kennebunkport 04046, tel. (207) 967-5978, where a flock of rare Cotswold sheep roams an 18th-century riverfront farm. Take Rt. 9 about two miles beyond the Cape Porpoise turnoff. Theoretically open daily 10 a.m.-5 p.m., May through Christmas, the shop often has reduced hours after mid-October. A branch shop in Portland's Old Port (195 Commercial St., tel. 207-871-1427) is open all year.

Earth-Friendly Stuff/Natural Foods

Lafayette Center, a handsomely restored mill building housing boutiques and eateries, is also home to the **Tom's of Maine Natural Living Store,** Storer St., just off Main St., Kennebunk 04043, tel. (207) 985-3874, an ecosensitive local firm that makes soaps, toothpaste, oils, and other products. The shop also has herbs, recycled paper, and organic cotton clothing. Open Mon.-Sat. 9:30 a.m.-5 p.m.

If all that intrigues you, head for the Tom's of Maine factory and take a one-hour tour, Mon.-Thurs. at 11 a.m. and 1 p.m. in summer. During the winter, tours are only Wednesdays at 11 a.m. Reservations are essential; maximum 12 people, no minimum. You'll receive a free sample. From the Natural Living Store, take Rt. 35 (Summer St.) to the railroad overpass, then take the first right (Railroad Ave., an unpaved driveway) after the overpass. Parking is ample. After the tour, get some exercise by walking or cycling on the bridle path that starts here.

New Morning Natural Foods, 1 York St., Rts. 1 and 9, Kennebunk 04043, tel. (207) 985-6774, is a relatively new branch of Paul and Sheila Ouellette's Biddeford market by the same name. Super selection of produce and baked goods. **Sunshine Grainery,** 164 Port Rd., Rt. 35, Lower Village, Kennebunk 04043, tel. (207) 967-5758, has a huge inventory of pastas, herbs, coffees, and bulk foods, plus organic beef. Open Mon.-Sat. 10 a.m.-6 p.m.

ACCOMMODATIONS

With about 1,300 beds for rent in the Kennebunks, there's plenty of choice and variety (also see "St. Anthony's Monastery" under "Parks, Preserves, and Recreation," above). However, don't arrive without a reservation in early August or during the Christmas Prelude, or you may find yourself facing a sea of No Vacancy signs. If that happens, the best fallback is the Kennebunk Kennebunkport Chamber of Commerce—the staff has a knack for miracle-working.

The Colony Resort Hotel

Graciously dominating its 11-acre spread at the mouth of the Kennebunk River, The Colony Hotel, Ocean Ave. at King's Hwy., P.O. Box 511, Kennebunkport 04046, tel. (207) 967-3331 or (800) 552-2363, fax (207) 967-8738, comes right out of a bygone era, yet it's racing ahead as the state's foremost "green" resort—the 135-room hotel has made a major recycling commitment. But green doesn't come cheap; this is a splurge choice. Peak-season doubles go for $199-299, MAP (subtract $20 pp for rooms without meals), $140-175 in shoulder season. No smoking, two-night minimum on weekends, pets allowed ($22 extra per day). There's a special feeling here, with cozy corners for reading, lawns and gardens for strolling, a beachfront swimming pool, room service, book delivery from the local bookstore, tennis privileges at the exclusive River Club, bike rentals, massage therapy, badminton, and croquet. Not to mention the legendary Blue Flames—the hotel staff's water-ballet troupe, which performs every Wednesday at 9:30 p.m. in July and August. The hotel dining room is open to the public for breakfast, lunch, and $23 fixed-price dinners; reservations are advisable. The hotel is open mid-May to late October.

B&Bs
By Kennebunks standards, **Cove House Bed & Breakfast,** 11 So. Maine St., RR 3, Box 1615, Kennebunkport 04046, tel. (207) 967-3704, is a moderate option. On a quiet side street, it's still close to shops and restaurants. Former English teacher Kathy Jones has filled the house with antiques—notably a fine collection of flow blue china—and the comfortable, book-lined library proves a magnet for guests. Bring a bike and leave your car here. Or bring a kayak and launch it into Chick's Cove from the backyard. Or walk to nearby Colony Beach. Three rooms (private and shared baths) are $70-90 d in summer; two-night minimum July and August. No smoking, no pets. Open all year.

Ex-Peace Corps volunteer Carolyn McAdams considers it her mission to help guests appreciate the Kennebunks. And, post-sightseeing, she encourages guests at **Lake Brook Bed & Breakfast Guest House,** 57 Western Ave., Rt. 9, Kennebunk 04043, tel. (207) 967-4069, to

KENNEBUNKS ACCOMMODATIONS

Rates listed here are for doubles; all are open year-round unless indicated otherwise. B&Bs provide full breakfast except as indicated. Inquire about free beach parking passes. A two-night minimum may be required on midsummer weekends. Postal codes are as follows: Kennebunk 04043, Kennebunkport 04046

Kennebunk

The Alewife House, 1917 Alewive Rd., Rt. 35, tel. (207) 985-2118. 18th-century farmhouse B&B on six country acres; $85-90; three rooms, two with private baths; expanded continental breakfast; antiques shop; no smoking, no pets, no children under 12; four miles north of Maine Turnpike Exit 3.

Bufflehead Cove Bed & Breakfast Inn, Gomitz Ln., off Rt. 35, tel. (207) 967-3879, mailing address: P.O. Box 499, Kennebunkport 04046. Exquisite Victorian home on quiet tidal cove; $95-250; six rooms (four with water views and private balconies), private baths; no smoking, no pets, no children under 12; midway between downtown Kennebunk and Kennebunkport's Dock Square.

English Robin Guest House, 99 Western Ave., Rt. 9, tel. (207) 967-3505. Small, modern, multi-unit

complex opening onto swimming-pool area; $65-95; two one-room units, one two-story efficiency unit, private baths; cable TV; continental breakfast; children and pets welcome; easy walk to Lower Village and Dock Square.

The Ocean View, 72 Beach Ave., tel. (207) 967-2750. Contemporary oceanfront B&B inn; two buildings; $95-225; five rooms, four suites, private baths; TV; no smoking, no pets, no children under 12; open April-mid-Dec.; across the street from Kennebunk (Middle) Beach, a few steps from Gooch's Beach.

Tiger Lily Farm, 86 Summer St., tel. (207) 985-1985. Farmhouse B&B in Kennebunk Historic District; $90-125; three suites, private baths; phones; TV; no smoking, no pets, children welcome.

William Lord Mansion, 20 Summer St., tel. (207) 985-6213. Exquisitely restored colonial mansion in Kennebunk Historic District; $175; two rooms (one with fireplace), private whirlpool baths; gourmet breakfast; gardens; no smoking, no pets, and no credit cards.

Kennebunkport

Cape Arundel Inn, Ocean Ave., P.O. Box 530A, tel. (207) 967-2125. Fourteen old-fashioned inn and

relax on the veranda of her comfortable marsh-view farmhouse. The three rooms and one suite all have private baths. No pets, smoking only on the veranda. Rates run $80-100 d in summer, lower rates off season. Two-night minimum Memorial Day-Columbus Day. In winter, nearby Lake Brook is dammed for ice skating. Across the street is the Salt Marsh Tavern. The B&B is open all year, but call ahead off season.

The homey, low-key, turn-of-the-20th-century **Green Heron Inn,** 126 Ocean Ave., Kennebunkport 04046, tel. (207) 967-3315, has been in the same family since the 1950s, and many guests are repeats. Ten rooms and a two-story cottage have TV, phones, a/c, private baths. Prices range $85-135 d in summer, lower rates off season (cottage is higher). No credit cards. Also included is breakfast—one of the best and most reasonable in town—served in the coveside breakfast room. Even if you're not staying here, stop in for the $4.95 eggs Benedict or $2.95 homemade granola and yogurt. The

breakfast room is closed Tuesday and Wednesday Nov.-May. The inn is open all year.

Breakfast is also a highlight at **The Captain Fairfield Inn Bed & Breakfast,** Pleasant and Green Sts., P.O. Box 1308, Kennebunkport 04046, tel. (207) 967-4454 or (800) 322-1928, an 1813 National Historic Register home where hospitable innkeepers Dennis and Bonnie Tallagnon do everything right. Nine rooms, filled with antiques (some with fireplaces, some with a/c), have private baths; there's a garden with comfortable lawn chairs; and afternoon tea is served. Close to Colony Beach and Dock Square, but on a quiet side street. No pets, no smoking, no children under six. Rates are $125-195 d mid-June through December, lower off season. Two-night minimum July and August weekends. Open all year.

Nonstop chocolate-chip cookies are a specialty at Ron and Carol Perry's **1802 House Bed and Breakfast Inn,** 15 Locke St., Box 646-A, Kennebunkport 04046, tel. (207) 967-5632 or

---

contemporary motel rooms and efficiencies with ocean views, private baths; $140-160 July and August, lower rates other months; continental breakfast; children welcome, no pets, no smoking; popular restaurant open Mon.-Sat. for dinner; the inn is open late April to late November; closest lodging to Walker's Point.

The Captain Lord Mansion, River Green (Pleasant and Green Sts.), P.O. Box 800, tel. (207) 967-3141 or (800) 522-3141, fax (207) 967-3172. Meticulously restored National Historic Register mansion and carriage house; $149-349 high season, lower rates and packages off season; 16 rooms, private baths; full breakfast; no smoking, no pets, no children under six; close to Dock Square.

The Chetwynd House Inn, Chestnut St., P.O. Box 130M, tel. (207) 967-2235. Kennebunkport's first B&B, in an 1840 sea captain's home; $90-160, special packages off season; four rooms, private baths; a/c; gourmet breakfast; no smoking, no pets; close to Dock Square.

The Inn on South Street, 5 South St., P.O. Box 478A, tel. (207) 967-5151 or (800) 963-5151. National Historic Register B&B; $85-190, special packages off season; three rooms, one suite, private baths; outstanding gardens; Chinese antiques; no smoking, no pets; closed January, March, and November; on a side street near Dock Square.

The Kennebunkport Inn, 1 Dock Square, P.O. Box 111, tel. (207) 967-2621. Attractive traditional inn (19th-century main building and newer River House) in the heart of town (request a back room); $90-229; 34 rooms, private baths; TV; a/c; some room phones; full breakfast; outdoor swimming pool; dining rooms and cozy piano bar open to public.

Kilburn House, 6 Chestnut St., P.O. Box 1309, tel. (207) 967-4762. Three-story Victorian home; $50-140; six rooms (two with private bath), one suite (entire third floor); no smoking, no pets; open May-Oct.; one block to Dock Square.

Kylemere House, 6 South St., P.O. Box 1333, tel. (207) 967-2780. National Historic Register B&B; $90-145; four rooms, private baths; garden; no smoking, no pets, no children under 12; on side street near Dock Square.

Old Fort Inn, Old Fort Ave., P.O. Box M, tel. (207) 967-5353 or (800) 828-3678, fax (207) 967-4547. Full-service inn, historic building, great location; $130-275; 16 rooms, private baths; phones;, a/c; cable TV; outdoor pool; tennis court; bicycles; antiques shop; buffet breakfast; no smoking, no pets; open mid-April to mid-December; on quiet side street near Colony Beach.

(800) 932-5632, a lovely oasis on a back lane within walking distance (10 minutes) of Dock Square. The breakfast room overlooks the Cape Arundel Golf Club, and the Kennebunk River runs by the property. Five rooms and a suite have private baths; some rooms have fireplaces and a/c, TV; $89-249 d, two-night minimum June to October. No pets, no smoking, no children under 12. Open all year.

Personable innkeepers Lindsay and Carol Copeland and their warm staff have made **The Maine Stay Inn & Cottages,** 34 Maine St., Box 500A, Kennebunkport 04046, tel. (207) 967-2117 or (800) 950-2117, a steady draw for repeat visitors. In the architecturally eclectic inn (Italianate Victorian) are four rooms and two suites, all with private baths, plus a flying staircase, elegant furnishings, huge veranda, and third-floor cupola with great views. Across the lawn are 11 modern efficiency cottages—ideal for families—where you can even have a breakfast basket delivered to your door. Rates are $85-210 d. No pets, no smoking. Open all year.

Immediately east of the Wedding Cake House, **The Waldo Emerson Inn,** 108 Summer St., Rt. 35, Kennebunk 04043, tel. (207) 985-4250, has a charming colonial feel—as it should, since the main portion was built in 1784. Maggie and Wayne Carver love to share interesting historical details over tea in the kitchen. For instance, poet Ralph Waldo Emerson spent many a summer in this, his great-uncle's home. Four attractive rooms with private baths; $95-105 d, lower off season. No smoking, no pets, no children under six. Quilters, take note: In the barn is **Mainely Quilts,** Maggie's well-stocked quilt shop, open daily 9 a.m.-5 p.m. in summer.

You'll awake to the sound of lobsterboat engines at **The Inn at Harbor Head,** 41 Pier Rd., Cape Porpoise, RR 2, Box 1180, Kennebunkport 04046, tel. (207) 967-5564, fax 967-1294, an idyllic spot on Cape Porpoise Harbor, two and a half miles from Dock Square. Hand-painted murals, monogrammed bathrobes, flower bouquets, a superb library, hammocks in the yard, and outstanding views are just a few of the pluses here. They'll even send a tide calendar if you're arriving by boat. Five first- and second-floor rooms with private baths; rates are $135-250 d. No pets, no smoking, no children under 12; two-night minimum on weekends.

Closed November, January, and February.

If nonstop beaching is your vacation goal, book a room at **Tides Inn by-the-Sea,** 252 Goose Rocks Beach, Kennebunkport 04046, tel. (207) 967-3757, directly across the street from superb Goose Rocks Beach. Decor at the John Calvin Stevens-designed Victorian inn is funky, whimsical (faux painting, costumed dummies, a resident ghost named Emma), and altogether fun. Next door is **Tides Too,** a modern, condo-type building with efficiencies by the week ($1,700-2,000 for four persons). Inn rooms, with private or shared bath, go for $99-225 d in peak season, lower off season; three-night minimum in season. Limited smoking, no pets. Open mid-May to mid-October. The dining room of Tides Inn by-the-Sea is open to the public for breakfast and creative dinners; the **Sandy Bottom Pub** is a popular local watering hole open from 5 p.m.

Motels and Cottages

With indoor and outdoor heated pools and a good-size fitness center, the **Rhumb Line Motor Lodge,** Ocean Ave., P.O. Box 3067, Kennebunkport 04046, tel. (207) 967-5457 or (800) 337-4862, fax (207) 967-4418, is a magnet for families. This well-managed two-story establishment in a quiet residential area three miles from Dock Square has easy access to the trolleybus service. Fifty-five large rooms (and four suites) have private balcony or patio, phones, a/c, cable TV, and small refrigerators. From late May to mid-September, weather permitting, there are nightly poolside lobsterbakes. Rates are $118-145 d in summer, $68-105 d other months; kids under 12 stay free. Two-night minimum on major holiday weekends. Special packages off season. No pets. Open Feb.-December.

Fifteen trim one- and two-bedroom cottages rim the tidal cove at **Cabot Cove Cottages,** 7 So. Maine St., P.O. Box 1082, Kennebunkport 04046, tel. (207) 967-5424 or (800) 962-5424. Pine-paneled, wicker-furnished efficiencies ($80-145, depending on season) within easy walking distance of Dock Square and Colony Beach are just the ticket for families. Leashed pets are allowed (deposit required), as is smoking. Cottages have TV but no phones. There's also rowboats, picnic tables, a grill, and laundry facilities. Open mid-May to mid-October.

Seasonal Rentals

Weekly and monthly rentals, like nightly room rates, are fairly steep in the Kennebunks. Several real-estate firms handle seasonal rentals. Start with **Kennebunk Beach Realty,** Rts. 9 and 35, P.O. Box 31, Kennebunkport 04046, tel. (207) 967-5481, fax 967-2940, or **Port Properties, Ltd.,** Cooper's Corner, Lower Village, P.O. Box 799, Kennebunkport 04046, tel. (207) 967-4400 or (800) 443-7678.

FOOD

Breakfast

All Day Breakfast, 55 Western Ave., Rt. 9, Lower Village, Kennebunk 04043, tel. (207) 967-5132, is a favorite meeting spot, offering such specialties as invent-your-own omelettes and crepes, Texas French toast, and the ADB sandwich. No smoking. ADB is open daily 7 a.m.-2 p.m. in summer. Off season, it's open Wed.-Sun. 7 a.m.-1 p.m. Closed mid-December to mid-January. Other good eye-opener locales are the Green Heron Inn and The Tides Inn (see above, under "B&Bs"), and, for a splurge, The Colony Hotel.

Picnic Fare/Sweets

Conveniently located next door to the Kennebunk Kennebunkport Chamber of Commerce, **Meserve's Market,** Rt. 35, Lower Village, Kennebunk 04043, tel. (207) 967-5762, has the best wine inventory in town, along with plenty of picnic supplies, newspapers, and all the typical general-store inventory. Open daily, all year.

The monthly newsletter is only one of the unusual features of **Bradbury Bros. Market,** P.O. Box 267, Cape Porpoise 04014, tel. (207) 967-3939, the heart and soul of Cape Porpoise. Here you can collect some gourmet picnic goodies (even house-brand items), hang around for local gossip, even send a fax or mail a letter. Open 7 a.m.-9 p.m. in summer, slightly shorter hours in winter. Owner Tom Bradbury is the guiding light of the Kennebunkport Conservation Trust.

To satisfy your sweet tooth, head out to **Fudge by George,** 1975 Lombard Rd., Arundel 04046, tel. (207) 967-2965, where George Parandelis produces fudge and chocolate candy to die for—and it's available only in his tiny shop.

From Dock Square, take North St. to Log Cabin Rd.; turn left onto Lombard just after the Seashore Trolley Museum. Call ahead to make sure he's open, or stop by when you're visiting the museum.

Lobster-in-the-Rough

Bush-watchers often head to **Mabel's Lobster Claw,** Ocean Ave., Kennebunkport 04046, tel. (207) 967-2562, hoping to spot the former president (the little place is just around the corner from Walker's Point). Try Mabel Hanson's chowder or a lobster roll and see why the restaurant's a favorite.

Moderate and Informal

Nearest thing to being afloat is sitting at a riverfront table at **Arundel Wharf,** 43 Ocean Ave., Kennebunkport 04046, tel. (207) 967-3444, where passing tour and lobsterboats provide plenty of lunchtime entertainment. Captain's chairs and chart-topped tables complete the nautical picture. Service is efficient and friendly. On nasty days, a fireplace warms the indoor dining area. Burgers and fries are always on the menu for kids; adults can enjoy lobster with a touch of class. Open mid-May to mid-December.

On tap at **Federal Jack's Restaurant and Brewpub,** 8 Western Ave., Lower Village, Kennebunk 04043, tel. (207) 967-4322, are the specialty beers of Kennebunkport Brewing Company (part of Shipyard Brewing Company, owned by Miller Brewing Company)—Goat Island Light, Blue Fin Stout, and several seasonal ales. An eclectic regional American lunch and dinner menu keeps kids and adults happy at Federal Jack's, and the brewery also makes nonalcoholic root beer and birch beer. Times vary for the 20-minute brewery tours; inquire. The brewpub is open for lunch and dinner all year; there's live acoustic music on weekends.

Conveniently close to the chamber of commerce and right on the Kennebunk River, **The Boatyard,** 15 Christensen Lane, Lower Village, Kennebunk 04043, tel. (207) 967-8525, has another of the area's prime viewing spots. (Try for an outdoor table.) Chunky lobster stew is a specialty, as is prime rib (Friday and Saturday only, $15.95), and the children's menu has a half-dozen options. Open all year for lunch and dinner.

Moderate to Expensive

Just west of the junction of Rts. 9 and 35, casually elegant **Grissini Trattoria and Panificio,** 27 Western Ave., Kennebunk 04043, tel. (207) 967-2211, has drawn nothing but bravos since it opened. Attentive service, an inspired menu, moderate prices (entrées $9-15), and a bright space make it a winner. In nice weather, try for the sunken patio. Reservations only for six or more, so you may have to wait. Open daily 11:30 a.m.-2:30 p.m. and 5:30-9:30 p.m. April-Dec., shorter hours Jan.-March.

Veteran local restaurateur Jack Nahil has made all the right moves with the **Salt Marsh Tavern,** Rt. 9, Lower Village, Kennebunk 04043, tel. (207) 967-4500, a restored barn overlooking marshlands leading to Kennebunk Beach. The creative regional American menu (grilled salmon with cilantro beurre blanc, for example) often has Mediterranean accents, such as stuffed grape leaves or grilled lamb (entrées $16-26). Quiet piano music adds to the elegant but unstuffy ambience. No smoking. Reservations essential in midsummer. Open for dinner mid-March through December: daily June-Oct.; closed Monday and Tuesday other months.

Winner of a raft of culinary awards, **Windows on the Water,** 12 Chase Hill Rd., Kennebunk 04043, tel. (207) 967-3313, has been packing them in since 1985. Great views from the screened porch, patio, or dining rooms. Among the prizewinning specialties are lobster-stuffed potato, available as a lunch entrée or dinner starter. Significant entrées are $14-24. Sunday brunch (noon-2:30 p.m.) is a bargain—$13.95 for adults, $7.95 for kids under 12. No smoking, reservations advisable. Open daily for lunch and dinner, all year (except Thanksgiving and Christmas).

The biggest pluses (in any order you choose) at **Seascapes,** Pier Rd., Cape Porpoise 04014, tel. (207) 967-8500, are the view, the menu, and the owners. Arthur and Angela LeBlanc, congenial former owners of the Kennebunk Inn, have a gem of a place here. Not only is the view outstanding—with lobsterboats hustling to and fro—but the menu is unendingly creative, with smoked venison, unusual pasta dishes, superb grilled fish, even lobster tortillas (entrées $18-26). There's also a children's menu. The Mediterranean flavor extends to the colorful Vietri pottery on which everything's served. (It's also for sale at the restaurant.) No smoking. Reservations advisable. Open May-Oct. for lunch and dinner.

Worthwhile Wallet-Cruncher

Southern Maine's biggest and best splurge is **The White Barn Inn,** 37 Beach St., Kennebunk, tel. (207) 967-2321, fax 967-1100, mailing address P.O. Box 560C, Kennebunkport 04046—haute cuisine, haute prices, haute-rustic barn. In summer, don't be surprised to run into members of George Bush's clan (probably at the back window table). Soft piano music accompanies impeccable service and an outstanding five-course prix-fixe menu ($58 pp). Reservations are essential—well ahead during July and August. No jeans or sneakers—jackets are required. Smoking only in the bar area. Maine's only AAA five-diamond restaurant, it's part of the Relais et Chateaux network. The adjoining inn has 24 beautifully decorated and inevitably pricey rooms and suites ($150-375 d May to mid-Oct., $140-320 d other months). Open daily for dinner mid-Feb.-Dec.; closed Tuesday in February and March.

INFORMATION AND SERVICES

The **Kennebunk Kennebunkport Chamber of Commerce,** 17 Western Ave., Rt. 9, Lower Village, P.O. Box 740, Kennebunk 04043, tel. (207) 967-0857, fax 967-2867, has an especially helpful staff; inquire about accommodations, restaurant menus, area maps, bike maps, tide calendars, recreation, and beach parking passes. Be sure to request a copy of the handsome annual chamber booklet, available each January and loaded with ads and enough useful information to plan any kind of vacation in the Kennebunks. The office is located in a yellow building next to Meserve's Market, about midway between Rt. 35 and the Kennebunk River. Office hours are Mon.-Fri. 9 a.m.-6 p.m., Saturday 10 a.m.-6 p.m., and Sunday 11 a.m.-4 p.m., June through Columbus Day. Off-season hours are Mon.-Fri. 9 a.m.-5 p.m., plus some Saturdays during winter special events.

The **Kennebunkport Hospitality Center,** Union St. and Ocean Ave., next to Ben & Jerry's,

Kennebunkport 04046, tel. (207) 967-8600, assists with local info and has brochures and public restrooms. Open daily, May-Dec., weekends in April.

The handsome **Louis T. Graves Memorial Library,** Maine St., Kennebunkport 04046, tel. (207) 967-2778, once a bank and customs house, has a story hour for children Fridays. In downtown Kennebunk is the **Kennebunk Free Library,** 112 Main St., Kennebunk 04043, tel. (207) 985-2173.

Newspapers

The local weekly newspaper, the *York County Coast Star,* based in Kennebunk, comes out every Wednesday. Each Thursday in summer, the paper produces the *Coast Pilot,* a free tabloid supplement covering restaurants, shopping, entertainment, and a tide calendar for York and the Kennebunks.

Daily newspapers covering this area are the *Portland Press Herald* and the Biddeford *Journal-Tribune.*

Emergencies

In **Kennebunkport,** contact the police, fire department, and ambulance at (207) 967-3323; in **Kennebunk,** call (207) 985-7113 for fire department and ambulance, (207) 985-6121 for police. The nearest hospital is **Southern Maine Medical Center,** 1 Medical Center Dr., Biddeford, tel. (207) 283-7000. For minor medical problems, head for the **Kennebunk Walk-In Clinic,** 24 Portland Rd., Rt. 1, Kennebunk, tel. (207) 985-6027. York Hospital's **Tel-a-Nurse** service, tel. (800) 283-7234, provides free over-the-phone advice for minor medical problems.

Public Restrooms

Public toilets are located at the information center in Dock Square and at Gooch's and Mother's Beaches, as well as at St. Anthony's Monastery. If you're at Goose Rocks Beach, the Tides Inn allows emergency restroom use for $2.

Laundromat

Maytag Laundromat & Dry Cleaners, 169 Port Rd., Village Marketplace, Lower Village, Kennebunk 04043, tel. (207) 967-5066, is open daily, all year, except Thanksgiving, Christmas, and New Year's Day.

Photo Services

Ocean Exposure, Western Ave., Rt. 9, Lower Village, Kennebunk 04043, tel. (207) 967-0500, does one-hour processing and five-minute enlargements.

Getting Around

The **Intown Trolley,** tel. (207) 967-3686, operates trolleybuses throughout Kennebunk and Kennebunkport, originating on Ocean Avenue and making regular stops at beaches and other attractions. The entire route takes about 45 minutes, with the driver providing a hefty dose of local history and gossip. (If you're lucky, your driver will be Richard Hogue.) Seats are park-bench-style. An all-day ticket (unlimited rides) is $6 for adults, $3 for children.

Another **touring** option is to contact Barbara Cook, tel. (207) 985-7946 or (800) 416-7946, or ask about her at your lodging. A genuine history buff, Barbara operates one-and-a-half-hour bus tours daily in summer 9 a.m.-6 p.m., giving tons of historical background and recounting lots of "Bush stories." Reservations are required; cost is $13 pp. Barbara also owns another bus that makes twice-daily, four-hour excursions to Freeport. Roundtrip cost is $22 pp.

BIDDEFORD AND SACO

Saco and Biddeford have long been upstairs/downstairs sister cities, with wealthy mill owners living in Saco and their workers (and workplaces) located in Biddeford. But even those personalities have always been split—congested, commercial Rt. 1 is part of Saco, and exclusive Biddeford Pool is, of course, in below-stairs Biddeford. Saco still has an attractive downtown, with boutiques and stunning homes on Main Street and beyond. The city's focus nowadays is Saco Island (also called Factory Island), in the middle of the Saco River. Once a massive millworks, the sprawling brick buildings are gradually being retrofitted as shops and offices—an eco-conscious model proven successful in other American cities.

Biddeford boasts a preponderance of secondhand shops downtown—and the state's first discount-coffin store—but is also home to magnificent Biddeford City Theater and the University of New England. And as plans proceed for a riverfront park and other ambitious projects, Biddeford is moving quickly to change its blue-collar milltown image. Another Biddeford hallmark is its Franco-American tradition—thanks to the French-speaking workers who sustained the textile and shoemaking industries in the 19th century. Never is the heritage more evident than during Biddeford's annual La Kermesse festival in late June.

SIGHTS AND RECREATION

York Institute Museum

Founded in 1866, the York Institute Museum, 371 Main St., Saco 04072, tel. (207) 283-3861 or 282-3031, might also be one of the state's best-kept secrets. It shouldn't be. The outstanding collection, some of it rotated annually, includes 18th- and 19th-century paintings, furniture, and other household treasures. Lectures, workshops, and concerts are also part of the museum's annual schedule. Open Tues.-Fri. noon-4 p.m. (Thursday to 8 p.m.), Sept.-May; also open weekends noon-4 p.m., June-August.

The Heath

Owned by The Nature Conservancy, 800-acre Saco Heath Preserve is the nation's southern-most "raised coalesced bog"—where peat accumulated over eons into two above-water dome shapes that eventually merged into a single natural feature. Pick up a map at the parking area and follow the mile-long, self-guided trail through the woods and then into the heath via boardwalk. Best time to come is early to mid-October, when the heath and woodland colors are positively brilliant and insects are on the wane. You're likely to see deer, and perhaps even spot a moose. The preserve entrance is on Rt. 112, Buxton Rd., two miles west of I-95. Open all year, sunrise to sunset, it's also popular with snowshoers and cross-country skiers in winter. For information, contact the **The Nature Conservancy**, 14 Maine St., Fort Andross, Brunswick 04011, tel. (207) 729-5181, fax 729-4118.

Ferry Beach State Park

When the weather's hot, arrive early at **Ferry Beach State Park**, Bay View Rd., off Rt. 9, Saco, tel. (207) 283-0067, a pristine beach backed by dune grass on Saco Bay. In the 117-acre park are changing rooms, restrooms, lifeguard, picnic tables, and five easy interconnected nature trails winding through woodlands, marshlands, and dunes. (Later in the day, keep the insect repellent handy.) Admission is $2 adults, 50 cents children 5-11, free for seniors and kids under five. Open daily, Memorial Day weekend to September 30, but accessible all year. (Trail markers are removed in winter.)

Camp Ellis

Begun as a small fishing village named after early settler Thomas Ellis, Camp Ellis is crowded with longtime summer homes—some precariously close to the shore, courtesy of storm-tossed waves. A nearly mile-long granite jetty—designed to keep silt from clogging the Saco River—has taken the blame for massive beach erosion in the last 20 years. But the jetty is a favorite spot for wetting a line (no fishing license needed) and for panoramic views off toward

Wood Island Light (built in 1808) and Biddeford Pool. Camp Ellis Beach is open to the public, with lifeguards on duty in midsummer. Parking —scarce on hot days—is $5 a day.

East Point Sanctuary

Owned by the Maine Audubon Society, the 30-acre East Point Sanctuary is a splendid preserve at the eastern end of Biddeford Pool. Crashing surf, beach roses, bayberry bushes, and offshore Wood Island Light are all features of the two-part perimeter trail here—skirting the golf course of the exclusive Abenakee Club. Allow at least an hour; even in fog, the setting is dramatic. During spring and fall migrations, it's one of southern Maine's prime birding locales, so you'll have plenty of company if you show up then, and the usual streetside parking may be scarce. Open sunrise to sundown, all year. From Rt. 9 (Main St.) in downtown Biddeford, take Rt. 9/208 (Pool Rd.) southeast about five miles to the Rt. 208 turnoff to Biddeford Pool. Go .6 mile on Rt. 208 (Bridge Rd.), then left onto Mile Stretch Road. Continue to Lester B. Orcutt Blvd., turn left, and go to the end. For further information, contact Maine Audubon Society, 118 Rt. 1, P.O. Box 6009, Falmouth 04105, tel. (207) 781-2330, fax 781-6005.

Golf

Opened in 1922 as a nine-hole course, the **Biddeford & Saco Country Club,** 101 Old Orchard Rd., P.O. Box 448, Saco 04072, tel. (207) 282-9892, added a back nine in 1987 (toughest hole is the 11th). Tee times not usually needed. Open to the public early April to mid-November.

KIDS' STUFF

Along a three-mile stretch of Rt. 1 in Saco sometimes dubbed "Kids' Alley," Funtown/Splashtown USA is just south of the Vacationland Bowling Center and the Saco/Portland South KOA campground. The second big attraction, Aquaboggan Water Park, is about three miles farther north.

Funtown/Splashtown USA

Two adjoining amusement parks merged in 1996, creating Funtown/Splashtown USA, 774 Portland Rd., Saco, tel. (207) 284-5139, 75 acres of nonstop merriment and all the incredible hubbub that goes with it. The Funtown section has food tents, rides for kids, adults, and all ages, and on and on. The Splashtown section has water slides, bumper boats, and more. Funtown opens in early May, Splashtown in mid-June; everything's up and running daily from late June to Labor Day, when Funtown is open 10:30 a.m.-10:30 p.m. and Splashtown 10 a.m.-6 p.m. (Schedules depend on the hundreds of teenage park workers.) Combo passes for all rides in both parks are $24 adults, $20 children; otherwise, it's pay-as-you-go.

Aquaboggan Water Park

Three miles north of Funtown/Splashtown USA, Aquaboggan Water Park, Rt. 1, Saco, tel. (207) 282-3112, is wet and wild, with such stomach-turners as the Yankee Ripper and the Suislide. Wear a bathing suit that won't abandon you in the rough-and-tumble. Also, if you wear glasses, safety straps and plastic lenses are required. Besides all the water stuff, there are shuffle-board courts, mini-golf, an arcade, picnic tables, and snack bars. Lots of ticket options cover varying numbers of attractions: super ticket (for anyone 52 inches or taller) is $24.95; general ticket is $16.95; pool ticket is $11.95. You can pay-as-you-go, one attraction at a time, but it adds up quickly. Open 10 a.m.-6 p.m., late June through Labor Day.

Whistling Wings Farm

Pickles the potbellied pig and lots of other barnyard animals are the star attractions at Whistling Wings Farm, 427 West St., Biddeford 04005, tel. (207) 282-1146. While you're at it, though, you can pick up homemade baked goods and sample their ice cream. Open daily 7 a.m.-6 p.m. in summer.

ENTERTAINMENT AND EVENTS

Biddeford City Theater

Designed by noted architect John Calvin Stevens in 1896, the 500-seat National Historic Register Biddeford City Theater, 205 Main St., P.O. Box 993, Biddeford 04005, tel. (207) 282-0849, has been superbly restored, and acoustics are excellent even when Eva Gray, the resident ghost, mixes it up backstage. A respected community theater group mounts a winter drama season and showcases other talent throughout the year. Check local papers or call for schedule.

La Kermesse
La Kermesse (the fair or the festival) is Biddeford's summer highlight, when nearly 50,000 visitors pour into town on the last full weekend in June (Thurs.-Sun.) to celebrate the town's Franco-American heritage. Local volunteers go all out to plan block parties, a parade, games, carnival, live entertainment, and traditional dancing —most of it centered on Biddeford's St. Louis Field. Then there's *la cuisine franco-américaine;* you can fill up on *boudin, creton, poutine, tourtière, tarte au saumon,* and crêpes (although your arteries may rebel). The camaraderie is contagious, much of it in a French you never learned in language class. As with revelers on St. Patrick's Day who adopt Irish heritage, everyone instantly becomes Franco-American during La Kermesse, but festival organizers have reached out in recent years to other ethnic groups to make this a multicultural event. For more information, call (207) 283-2826.

Generally scheduled for the Saturday of the same weekend, the **Saco Sidewalk Arts Festival** involves more than 150 artists exhibiting their work all along Saco's Main Street. Strolling musicians, kids' activities, and food booths are all part of the well-organized, day-long event.

SHOPPING

Gifts and Clothing
Stone Soup Artisans, 228 Main St., Saco 04072, tel. (207) 283-4715, is a cooperative shop carrying top-quality work from more than 60 artisans affiliated with the **Society of Southern Maine Craftsmen.** Open daily 10 a.m.-5:30 p.m., Memorial Day weekend to Christmas, Mon.-Sat. other months.

Just down the street is **Saco Bay Classics,** 260 Main St., Saco 04072, tel. (207) 283-1400, with a fine selection of high-end, high-quality men's and women's clothing.

Discount Shopping
Bargain-hunting is encouraged at the **West Point Stevens Bed & Bath Mill Store,** 170 Main St., Biddeford 04005, tel. (207) 286-8255, a factory outlet where you can find real deals on mostly irregular towels, comforters, blankets, bedspreads, and sheets, plus remnants for quilters. Be sure to look over the merchandise carefully. Open Mon.-Sat. 9 a.m.-4:30 p.m., all year.

Way-Way General Store
A mile west of I-95, the Way-Way General Store, 93 Buxton Rd., Rt. 112, Saco, tel. (207) 283-1362, is a classic that's been around since Depression days, when the late Eugene Cousens built it; family members still run the place. Penny candy is a specialty, but you never know what you'll find. Open daily all year, the store is in a unique stone-and-tile building down the road from the giant Saco Defense Company.

Farmers' Market
Every Wednesday and Saturday, 7 a.m.-noon, May-Oct., the **Saco Farmers' and Artisans' Market** sets up shop at the Saco Valley Shopping Center, Rt. 1 and Scammon St., Saco. A great combination of seasonal produce and good-quality crafts.

ACCOMMODATIONS AND FOOD

The best address in Saco is the **Crown 'n' Anchor Inn,** 121 North St., P.O. Box 228, Saco 04072, tel. (207) 282-3829. Innkeeper John Barclay will show you around the extraordinary 19-room Thacher-Goodale House, a masterfully restored Greek Revival National Historic Register manse on three in-town acres. Six antiques-filled Victorian guest rooms with private baths are $65-95 d, mid-June to mid-October, $60-90 other months. (The Normandy suite even has two fireplaces.) Breakfast is to die for—served by candlelight on bone china to four guests at a time (seatings at 7, 8:30, and 10 a.m.); plan to skip lunch. No smoking, no children under 12; pets are welcome. The inn will also arrange for Portland and Boston airport pickups. Open all year.

Just east of Rt. 1, the two-story **Classic Motel,** 21 Ocean Park Rd., Saco 04072, tel. (207) 282-5569, has 17 rooms (most are efficiencies) with cable TV plus an indoor pool. Doubles are $85 mid-June to mid-September, $55-65 other months. No pets. Open all year.

Owned by the Pagano family since the 1960s, the basic, well-maintained **Saco Motel,** 473 Main St., Rt. 1, Saco 04072, tel. (207) 284-6952, three miles from the beach, has 26 rooms (some efficiencies) with a/c and cable TV. Doubles are $50-60 July to Labor Day, $35-38 early and late in the season. Giselle Pagano is a great booster of the area and very helpful with touring suggestions. Open early May to mid-November.

A convenient, well-maintained **campground** is the Saco/Portland South KOA, 814A Portland Rd., Rt. 1, Saco 04072, tel./fax (207) 282-0502 or (800) 562-1886, with 120 tent and RV sites, even five tiny cabins ($40 a night), on 30 acres alongside Rt. 1. It's not remote; request a wooded site back from the highway. Among the facilities are a swimming pool, laundry, playground, rec room, and shuttle to the beach (three miles away). Reservations advisable July and August. Sites run $22-24 a night for two persons. No pets. The campground is about one and a half miles from I-95 Exit 5. Open mid-May to mid-October.

Saco Food

It's all too easy to be zipping along Saco's Rt. 1 strip and miss **Cornforth House,** 893 Portland Rd., Rt. 1, Saco 04072, tel. (207) 284-2006. Don't pass it up, even though it's a bit of a splurge. It's a real treat—six dining rooms on the ground floor of a handsome brick Federal-style house. (In December, nine trees, decorated with ribbons and artificial candles, add even more to the charm of the place.) Creative beef, veal, chicken, and seafood entrées range from $14-18. Reservations are essential weekend evenings and Sunday morning. Open Tues.-Sun. 5-9:30 p.m. and Sunday 8 a.m.-noon, mid-March to late December. Also open Monday 5-9:30 p.m., June to mid-October.

Well seasoned after more than half a century, family-oriented **Wormwood's Restaurant,** 16 Bay Ave., Camp Ellis Beach, Saco 04072, tel. (207) 282-9679, next to the stone jetty, still draws the crowds and keeps its clientele happy with ample portions and $4-16 entrées. Seafood is a specialty. Open daily 11:30 a.m.-9 p.m.

Also at Camp Ellis is **Huot's Seafood Restaurant,** Camp Ellis Beach, Saco 04072, tel. (207) 282-1642, a local institution since 1935. Portions are large, prices are not. Open for lunch and dinner.

Biddeford Food

P.M. Inniss Lobster Co., 18 Yates St., Biddeford Pool 04006, tel. (207) 284-5000, claims seniority in the local lobster business, and it's a fine spot for a lobster-roll picnic. Or order a cooked lobster and take it to the beach. Open daily 8 a.m.-8 p.m., to 5 p.m. off season.

Produce is super-fresh and all organic at Paul and Sheila Ouellette's **New Morning Natural Foods,** 230 Main St., Biddeford 04005, tel. (207) 282-1434, a local institution since 1976. The Ouellettes have now added a very popular 24-seat café, open Mon.-Sat. 11 a.m.-2 p.m., serving hefty sourdough-bread sandwiches ($3 and up), a featured entrée (vegetarian or vegan), and homemade vegetarian soups. The food shop is open all year, Mon.-Sat. 9 a.m.-5 p.m. (to 7 p.m. Thursday).

INFORMATION AND SERVICES

The **Biddeford-Saco Chamber of Commerce and Industry,** 110 Main St., Ste. 1202, Saco 04072, tel. (207) 282-1567, fax 282-3149, oversees development and tourism in the two-town area. The office, on Saco Island, is open all year, Mon.-Thurs. 8:30 a.m.-4:30 p.m. and Friday 8:30 a.m.-4 p.m.

The **Dyer Library,** 371 Main St., Saco 04072, tel. (207) 282-3031, next door to the York Institute Museum, attracts scads of genealogists to its vast Maine history collection. Open Tuesday and Thursday 10 a.m.-8 p.m., Wednesday and Friday 10 a.m.-5 p.m., Saturday 9 a.m.-noon.

A huge children's section (the Junior Room) is only one of the pluses at the **McArthur Public Library,** 270 Main St., Biddeford 04005, tel. (207) 284-4181, the oldest public library in the state.

Emergencies
Southern Maine Medical Center, 1 Medical Center Dr., Biddeford 04005, tel. (207) 283-7000, is an up-to-date hospital with a fine reputation and round-the-clock emergency-room care. For **police, fire, or ambulance,** dial 911.

Media
The *Journal Tribune,* tel. (207) 282-1535, published daily in Biddeford, is the primary local information source.

Photo Services
Best Photo, 65 Main St., Biddeford 04005, tel. (207) 282-0181, provides one-hour film-developing service.

Getting Around
Operated by the Biddeford-Saco-Old Orchard Beach Transit Committee, **ShuttleBus** provides weekday and Saturday service (except national holidays) between Biddeford and the Casco Bay Ferry terminal in downtown Portland. In-between stops are Saco, Old Orchard Beach, Scarborough, Maine Mall, Greyhound terminal, and Portland's Monument Square. One-way fare on the entire one-hour route is $3; kids under five are free. (The Saco amusement parks are not on the route.) A separate route connects Biddeford, Saco, and Old Orchard Beach with frequent weekday and weekend service except national holidays. One-way fare on the 30-minute route is $1. Another route, known as Zoom, began operations in 1997 for Biddeford-to-Portland commuters, via the Maine Turnpike. Travel time is 35 minutes. ShuttleBus stops have green-and-white signs.

OLD ORCHARD BEACH

Old Orchard has been vacation-oriented for generations—from the earliest Native Americans through wealthy, turn-of-the-20th-century summer folk (including Rose Fitzgerald and Joe Kennedy, who met on these sands in the days when men strolled around in dress suits and women toted parasols) to the T-shirted pleasure-seekers of today.

But the tourist profile has begun to change a bit since French-Canadian tourism slumped in the late 1980s and early 1990s. (For one thing, shopowners began to diversify their inventory to cater to the year-round clientele.) You'll still hear French on the streets in summer, but families are the target now, giving rise to amusements of every stripe—arcades, concerts, festivals, shopping, and more. There's not a kid on earth who wouldn't have fun in Old Orchard—even if parents find it all a bit overwhelming.

Town fathers have built brick sidewalks, installed Victorian streetlights, and landscaped the downtown. But the miles-long crescent of white sand is what draws crowds to Old Orchard Beach—and you'd better like people if you stop here, because this town welcomes tourists (the population expands from about 7,800 in winter to 100,000 in midsummer).

ENTERTAINMENT AND EVENTS

The biggest beachfront amusement park, **Palace Playland,** 1 Old Orchard St., Old Orchard, tel. (207) 934-2001, has the works: giant water slide, fun house, bumper cars, Ferris wheel, roller coaster, and arcade. Rides are free 6-7 p.m. on Thursday, before the fireworks.

The Pier, jutting 475 feet into the ocean, is a mini-mall of shops, arcades, and fast-food outlets. Far longer when it was built in 1898, it's been lopped off gradually by fires and storms. The current incarnation has been here since the late 1970s.

The Ball Park, 1 Park Ln., Old Orchard Beach 04064, tel. (207) 934-1124, is a 12,500-seat stadium built in the 1980s for a long-forgotten baseball team. Now it's the site of rock concerts, festivals, and sports events—April to October; call for schedule or check with the chamber of commerce.

More sedate entertainment is the rule at the southwestern end of town, in the **Ocean Park** section. Established in 1881 as a religious summer-cottage community, Ocean Park still offers interdenominational services and vacation bible school, but it also has an active cultural associ-

Old Orchard Beach

ation that sponsors concerts, Chautauqua-type lectures, films, and other events throughout the summer. All are open to the public. The Temple is the venue for Sunday-night concerts (7:30 p.m., $4 adults) and films three nights a week ($3). For a schedule, contact the Ocean Park Association, P.O. Box 7296, Ocean Park 04063, tel. (207) 934-9068, fax 934-2823. The association issues an annual 100-page program and business directory containing details on all the events and on the association itself. Cost is $3.

Festivals and Events
Old Orchard's organized fun is about as extensive as anywhere in southern Maine. Here are just a few of the regular events.

Frisbee, bikini, and sand-sculpture contests are highlights of **Beachfest,** which also features music and dancing the last weekend of June.

July brings **Greek Night,** with Greek music, dancing, costumes, and food. Everything's free but the food. You can see fireworks every Thursday night in July (9 or 9:30 p.m.) at the beach. And live bands play at 7 p.m. every Tuesday night July-Labor Day in the town square.

One weekend in mid-August, the **Beach**

Olympics is a family festival of games, exhibitions, and music.

PRACTICALITIES

Accommodations
Old Orchard has hundreds of beds—mostly in motel-style lodgings. The chamber of commerce is the best resource for motels, cottages, and the area's 4,000 campsites. Only recently have a few B&Bs popped up.

On a quiet side street, **The Atlantic Birches Inn,** 20 Portland Ave., Rt. 98, P.O. Box 334, Old Orchard Beach 04064, tel. (207) 934-5295 or (800) 486-1681, has 10 guest rooms with private baths in a Victorian house and separate cottage. Breakfast is hearty continental, and there's a swimming pool; smoking only on the veranda. The beach is an easy walk. No pets. Rates run $65-89 d, July-Labor Day; $45-79 d other months. Open all year, but call ahead off season.

Food
Old Orchard is synonymous with fast food, most of it the order-at-the-counter, carry-it-away variety. For a once-a-year cholesterol pig-out, try **Lisa's Pizza** or **Pier French Fries.** To compound your sins, you can always have "dessert" at **Rick's Famous Fried Foods.** All are on Old Orchard Street, and that's only the beginning.

Joseph's By the Sea, 55 W. Grand Ave., Old Orchard Beach 04064, tel. (207) 934-5044, should be named Joseph's Oasis—a quiet, dignified shorefront restaurant amid all the hoopla. Request a table on the screened patio. The menu—French with a dash of Maine—has entrées in the $13-18 range. Try the specialty Saco Bay soup, Maine-accented bouillabaisse. No smoking. Reservations advisable in midsummer. Open daily for breakfast (7-11 a.m.) and dinner (5-9 p.m. off season, to 10 p.m. in summer), April-October.

Information
The staff at the **Old Orchard Beach Chamber of Commerce,** First St., P.O. Box 600, Old Orchard Beach 04064, tel. (207) 934-2500 or (800) 365-9386, fax (207) 934-4994, is especially helpful.

GREATER PORTLAND

Maine visitors often come hungry only for lobsters, lighthouses, and the great outdoors. As a result, the state's cities tend not to show up on the itinerary. Big mistake. Portland is a must-see—a human-level place offering—among other features—lobsters, lighthouses, and the great outdoors (this is, after all, "Forest City").

With about 64,000 souls (and its bedroom satellites, which triple that head count), Portland is as big as Maine cities get. This makes for a stimulating, cosmopolitan blend in a most manageable environment—a year-round destination, not just a summer place.

Portland's assets merely start with a striking art museum with a world-class permanent collection; a thriving, handsomely restored downtown crammed with shops, galleries, and restaurants of every persuasion and flavor; a cultural agenda that can keep you going all day and out all night; a brand-new, 28-store public market modeled on Seattle's Pike Place; several professional sports teams; and countless miles of hikeable, bikeable urban and suburban turf. Meanwhile, down along the working waterfront, there's serious business—commercial fishing vessels, long-distance passenger boats, and ferries lugging passengers and freight to the islands of Casco Bay.

Greater Portland includes the communities of Westbrook and Gorham to the west; South Portland, Cape Elizabeth, and Scarborough to the south; Falmouth and Cumberland to the north, and the Casco Bay Islands, offshore to the east.

HISTORY

Portland's downtown, a crooked-finger peninsula projecting into Casco Bay and today defined vaguely by I-295 at its "knuckle," was named Machigonne (Great Neck) by the Wabanaki Indians, who held sway when English settlers first arrived in 1632. Characteristically, the Brits renamed the region Falmouth (it included present-day Falmouth, Portland, South Portland, Westbrook, and Cape Elizabeth) and the peninsula Falmouth Neck, but it was some 130 years before they secured real control of

the area. Anglo-French squabbles, spurred by the governments' conflicts in Europe, drew in the Wabanaki from Massachusetts to Nova Scotia. Falmouth was only one of the battlegrounds, and a fairly minor one. Relative calm resumed in the 1760s, only to be broken by the stirrings of rebellion centered in Boston. When Falmouth's citizens expressed support for the incipient revolution, the punishment was a 1775 naval onslaught that wiped out 75% of the houses—a debacle that created a decade-long setback. In 1786, Falmouth Neck became Portland, a thriving trading community where shipping flourished until the 1807 imposition of the Embargo Act. Severing trade and effectively shutting down Portland harbor for a year and a half, the legislation did more harm to America's fledgling colonies than to the French and British it was designed to punish.

In 1820, when Maine became a state, Portland was named its capital. The city became a crucial transportation hub with the arrival of the railroad. The Civil War was barely a blip in Portland's history, but the year after it ended the city suffered a devastating blow: exuberant July 4, 1866 festivities sparked a conflagration that virtually leveled the city. The Great Fire spared only the now-crumbling Portland Observatory and a chunk of the West End. Evidence of the city's Victorian rebirth remains today in many downtown neighborhoods.

Following World War II, Portland slipped into decline for several years, but that is over. The city's waterfront revival began in the 1970s and continues today, despite commercial competition from South Portland's Maine Mall; Congress Street has blossomed as an arts and retail district; public green space is increasing; and an influx of immigrants is changing the city's cultural makeup. Late '90s Portland is on a roll.

PORTLAND NEIGHBORHOODS

The best way to appreciate the character of Portland's neighborhoods is on foot. Like any city, Portland also has a few problem spots (particularly the larger parks), places you need to

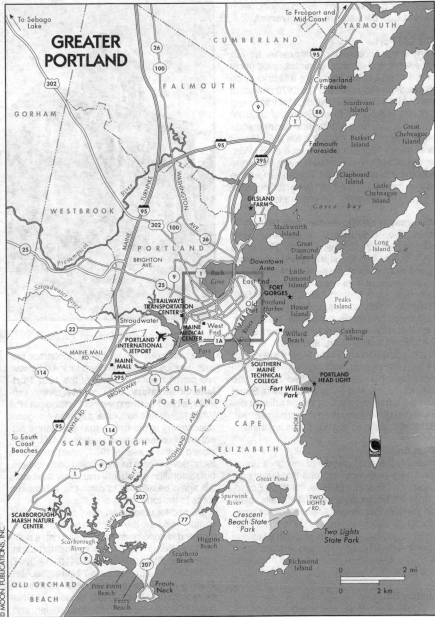

GREATER PORTLAND

To Sebago Lake

To Freeport and Mid-Coast

YARMOUTH

CUMBERLAND

FALMOUTH

GORHAM

Cumberland Foreside

Sturdivant Island

Basket Island

Great Chebeague Island

Falmouth Foreside

Clapboard Island

Little Chebeague Island

WESTBROOK

Casco Bay

GILSLAND FARM

Mackworth Island

Long Island

Presumpscot River

PORTLAND

Great Diamond Island

Downtown Area

Little Diamond Island

Stroudwater River

BRIGHTON AVE.

Back Cove

East End

FORT GORGES

House Island

Peaks Island

TRAILWAYS TRANSPORTATION CENTER

Stroudwater

Portland Harbor

Old Port

Cushings Island

MAINE MEDICAL CENTER

West End

Willard Beach

PORTLAND INTERNATIONAL JETPORT

Fore River

SOUTHERN MAINE TECHNICAL COLLEGE

PORTLAND HEAD LIGHT

MAINE MALL RD.

MAINE MALL

SOUTH PORTLAND

Fort Williams Park

BROADWAY

CAPE ELIZABETH

PAYNE RD.

To South Coast Beaches

SCARBOROUGH

Great Pond

Nonesuch River

HIGHLAND AVE.

SHORE RD.

TWO LIGHTS RD.

SCARBOROUGH MARSH NATURE CENTER

Spurwink River

Crescent Beach State Park

Scarborough River

Two Lights State Park

Higgins Beach

Scarboro Beach

Richmond Island

0   2 mi

0   2 km

OLD ORCHARD BEACH

Pine Point Beach

Prouts Neck

Ferry Beach

avoid after dark, but, compared to major cities in other states, dangers are relatively small.

The Old Port

Tony shops, cobblestone sidewalks, replica streetlights, and a casual, upmarket crowd (most of the time) set the scene for a district once filled with derelict buildings. The 1970s revival of the Old Port has infused funds, foot traffic, and flair into this part of town. Scores of unusual shops, ethnic restaurants, and spontaneous street-corner music make it a fun area to visit year-round. Nightlife centers on the Old Port, where about two dozen bars keep everyone hopping until after midnight. Police keep a close eye on the district, but it can get a bit dicey after 11 p.m. on weekends. Caveat emptor.

Congress Street/Downtown Arts District

Bit by bit, once-declining Congress Street is becoming revitalized, showcasing the best of the city's culture. Artists, starving and otherwise, spend much of their time here, thanks largely to encouragement from the energetic grassroots Downtown Arts District Association (DADA). Galleries, artists' studios, coffeehouses, cafés, craft shops, two libraries, the State Theatre, the Merrill Auditorium, the Portland Museum of Art, the Maine College of Art, and even L.L. Bean and the new Portland Public Market are all part of the renaissance, with no end in sight. On weekdays, between 11 a.m. and 2 p.m., you can hop on any Metro bus on Congress Street and get a free ride through the arts district between Longfellow Square and Exchange Street. Better still, walk, so you don't miss anything.

West End

Probably the most diverse of the city's downtown neighborhoods, and one that largely escaped the Great Fire of 1866, the West End includes the historically and architecturally splendid Western Promenade, Maine Medical Center (the state's largest hospital), the city's best B&Bs, a gay-friendly community with a laissez-faire attitude, a host of cafes and restaurants, as well as a few niches harboring the homeless and forlorn.

Munjoy Hill

A slightly down-at-the-heels neighborhood en-

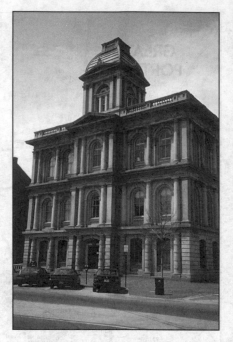

Custom House, Old Port, Portland

clave with a pull-'em-up-by-the-bootstraps attitude, Munjoy Hill is best known for the distinctive red-painted wooden tower of the 1807 **Portland Observatory,** 138 Congress Street. Providing a head-swiveling view of Portland (and the White Mountains on a clear day), the octagonal observatory is the only remaining marine signal tower on the eastern seaboard. Alas, it was closed to the public in 1994, when inspectors found powder-post beetles dining on its timbers, but restoration efforts are underway so visitors will again be allowed to climb the 105 interior steps to the top.

Named for George Munjoy, a wealthy 17th-century resident, the hill has a host of architectural and historic landmarks—well worth a walking tour. Fortunately, Greater Portland Landmarks, 165 State St., Portland 04101, tel. (207) 774-5561, has produced a 24-page booklet, ***Munjoy Hill Historic Guide,*** which documents more than 60 notable sites, including the National Historic Register Eastern Cemetery and, with spectacular harbor views, the Eastern Promenade and Fort Allen Park.

West Bayside/Parkside

A Babel of languages reverberates in these pockets just east of Portland's city hall. West Bayside and Parkside have experienced the arrival of refugees—Cambodian, Laotian, Vietnamese, Central European, and Afghan families —from war-torn lands during the 1980s and 1990s. Nowadays, you'll hear references to Somali Town, an area named for all the resettled refugees from that shattered country. Others have come from Sudan and Ethiopia. All have been assisted by Portland's active **Refugee Resettlement Program.** Many have found employment with **Barber Foods,** a fantastically conscientious firm that hires many new immigrants in its processing plant and provides opportunities for employees to learn English and obtain social services.

Beyond the Peninsula

At the western edge of Portland, close to the Portland Jetport, is the historic area known as **Stroudwater,** once an essential link in Maine water transport. The 20-mile-long **Cumberland and Oxford Canal,** hand-dug in 1828, ran through here as part of the timber-shipping route linking Portland Harbor, the Fore and Presumpscot Rivers, and Sebago Lake. Twenty-eight wooden locks allowed vessels to rise the 265 feet between sea level and the lake. By 1870, trains took over the route, condemning the canal to oblivion. Centerpiece of the Stroudwater area today is the historic 18th-century Tate House.

MUSEUMS, HISTORIC SITES, ATTRACTIONS

Portland Museum of Art

Maine's oldest and finest art museum, the Portland Museum of Art, 7 Congress Sq., Portland 04101, tel. (207) 775-6148, fax 773-7324, recorded hotlines: tel. (207) 773-2787 or (800) 639-4067, earns its renown thanks to a topflight collection of American and impressionist masters and an award-winning I.M. Pei building. Free gallery tours occur at 2 p.m. daily plus Thursday

and Friday at 6 p.m.; galleries are wheelchair-accessible. The museum also has a pleasant café, a well-stocked gift shop, and special activities for children. The café is open for lunch Tues.-Sun. (also Monday in summer) and for dinner Thursday and Friday. From July to Columbus Day, the PMA is open Mon.-Sat. 10 a.m.-5 p.m. (to 9 p.m. Thursday and Friday) and Sunday noon-5 p.m. From Columbus Day to July, it's closed Monday. Admission is $6 adults, $5 seniors and students, $1 children 6-12. Children under six are free. Free admission 5-9 p.m. every Friday. A family festival, with music, activities, films, and tours, occurs the first Friday of each month, 5-7 p.m. Next door, conveniently, is the Children's Museum of Maine.

The Longfellow Connection

A few blocks down Congress Street, you'll step back in time to the era of Portland-born poet Henry Wadsworth Longfellow, who lived in the **Wadsworth-Longfellow House,** 485 Congress St., Portland 04101, tel. (207) 879-0427, as a child in the early 1800s—long before the brick mansion was dwarfed by surrounding high-rises. Wadsworth and Longfellow family furnishings fill the three-story house (owned by the Maine Historical Society), and savvy guides provide insight into Portland's 19th-century life. Even little kids respond to the guides' enthusiasm during the hour-long tours. Purchase tickets next door (489 Congress St.) at the Maine History Gallery, tel. (207) 879-0427, where you can take in the historical society's current exhibits and patronize the gift shop. The Wadsworth-Longfellow House is open Tues.-Sun. 10 a.m.-4 p.m., early June to mid-October. Admission is $4 adults, $2 children under 12. Don't miss the urban oasis—a wonderfully peaceful garden—behind the house. The Maine History Gallery is open all year Tues.-Sun. 10 a.m.-4 p.m., June-Oct.; Wed.-Sat. noon-4 p.m., Nov.-May.

Victoria Mansion

The Italianate Victoria Mansion (also called the Morse-Libby Mansion), 109 Danforth St., Portland 04101, tel. (207) 772-4841, is rife with Victoriana—carved marble fireplaces, elaborate porcelain and paneling, and plenty of trompe l'oeil touches. It's even more spectacular at Christmas, with yards of roping, festooned trees, and carolers. (This is the best time to bring kids, as they may not particularly intrigued by the house itself.) The mansion was built in the late 1850s by Ruggles Sylvester Morse, a Maine-born entrepreneur whose New Orleans–based fortune enabled him to hire 93 craftsmen to complete the house. Today the house is maintained by the nonprofit Victoria Society (originally the Victoria Society of Women). Guided, 45-minute tours begin every half hour (on the quarter-hour). Open Tues.-Sat. 10 a.m.-4 p.m. and Sunday 1-5 p.m., May-October. Also open pre-Christmas weekends for tours and holiday events. Admission is $5 adults, $2 children 6-17.

Riding the Narrow-Gauge Rails

A three-mile ride along Portland's waterfront comes with admission to **The Maine Narrow Gauge Railroad Company and Museum,** 58 Fore St., Portland 04101, tel. (207) 828-0814. The museum owns more than three dozen train cars and has others on long-term loan. A two-car train takes riders along the two-foot-wide track from the museum's building in the Portland Company complex to Fish Point, below the Eastern Promenade—a short but enjoyable excursion. Years ago, hundreds of steam engines were built here. Trains operate mid-May to mid-October, daily 11 a.m.-4 p.m. on the hour. The museum opens at 10 a.m. Off season, trains run on weekends and during school vacations. Tickets are $5 adults, $3 children 4-18; children under four are free. At the eastern end of Fore St., turn at the railroad-crossing sign on the water side; the museum is at the back of the complex.

BEYOND THE PENINSULA

Seeing Stars

Under a 30-foot dome with comfy theater seats and a state-of-the-art laser system, the **South-worth Planetarium,** 96 Falmouth St., Science Building, lower level, University of Southern Maine, Portland 04103, tel. (207) 780-4249, fax 780-4051, presents a changing schedule of astronomy shows (Friday and Saturday 7 p.m.), laser-light shows (Friday and Saturday 8:30 p.m.), and family matinees (Saturday, Sunday, and during school vacations 3 p.m.). If your kids are squirmy, take them to a matinee. No reser-vations are needed. Computer-savvy kids will head for the interactive computers in the exhibit area; the gift shop stocks astronaut ice cream and other science-type stuff. Adult admission is $4 or $5 for one show and $8 for a double feature. Kids, students, and seniors pay $3 or $4 for one, $6 for a double feature. Matinees are $3 pp. For recorded information on moon and planet positions, eclipses, and other astronomical happenings, call the **Skywatch Hotline:** (207) 780-4719. Take Exit 6B off I-295 and go west on Forest Ave. to Falmouth St. (left turn). The Science Building is on the left, after the parking lot.

Tate House

Just down the street from the Portland International Jetport, in the Stroudwater district, is the 1755 **Tate House,** 1270 Westbrook St., P.O. Box 8800, tel. (207) 774-9781, a National Historic Landmark owned by the Colonial Dames of America. Built by Capt. George Tate, prominent in shipbuilding, the house has superb period furnishings and a lovely 18th-century herb garden overlooking the Stroudwater River. Open for 40-minute guided tours June 15-Sept. 15, Tues.-Sat. 10 a.m.-4 p.m., Sunday 1-4 p.m.; open weekends Sept. 15-October. Admission is $4 adults, $1 children under 12. Wednesdays in July and August are "summer garden days," when tea and goodies follow tours of the garden. On Saturday afternoons during the same months, one-hour architectural tours (at 1, 2, and 3 p.m.) cover the entire house "from cellar to clerestory." No extra charge for these special tours. From downtown Portland, it's 3.2 miles; take Congress St. West (Rt. 22) to a left turn at Westbrook Street. If you have spare time at the Portland Jetport, Tate House is an easy walk. Ask for directions at the airport information desk.

Spring Point Museum

The maritime history of Casco Bay and Maine is the focus at the small Spring Point Museum, Fort Rd., South Portland 04106, tel. (207) 799-6337, on the waterfront campus of **Southern Maine Technical College** To reach the college, head over the brand-new Casco Bay Bridge from downtown Portland (Rt. 77), and take a left on Broadway. A permanent exhibit features a section of the 19th-century clipper *Snow Squall,* retrieved from its graveyard in the

Falkland Islands and returned to its Maine birth-place. The museum is open Wed.-Sun. 10 a.m.-4 p.m., Memorial Day weekend to late October. Admission is $2 adults, free for kids under 12.

Micro Pioneer
Kids and adults seem to get into the science of brewing at **D.L. Geary Brewing Company,** 38 Evergreen Dr., Portland 04103, tel. (207) 878-2337, Maine's first microbrewery—oldest east of the Mississippi. Microbrew veterans will recognize Geary's Pale Ale (with a lobster label); newer offerings are Hampshire Special Ale and London Porter. No brewpub here, no tasting, just a chance to find out about the process. Reservations are required for the free, 15- to 45-minute tours Mon.-Fri. at 2 p.m. From downtown, take Forest Ave. (Rt. 100/302) west, just beyond I-95, and turn right onto Riverside Street. Continue to Industrial Way (right), connecting to Riverside Drive.

Prouts Neck
About 12 miles south of downtown Portland, at the junction of Rts. 77 and 207 is Black Point Rd., leading to the exclusive community of Prouts Neck—and the year-round and summer residents want to keep it that way. No Parking and Private Way signs are posted everywhere. Respect private property, but you can visit the **Winslow Homer Studio,** the famed 19th-century artist's haunt for the last 27 years of his life.

The lack of parking thwarts many visitors;

unless you get lucky, or you're staying at the Black Point Inn, it's best to walk or bike to the studio from Scarboro Beach Park.

After you pass the sprawling, gray-shingled Black Point Inn Resort, stop at the seasonal **Prouts Neck Post Office,** tel. (207) 883-4058, where Postmaster Roger Snelling cheerfully greets everyone under a ceiling strung with colorful, toy-size aluminum airplanes—all made from soda cans. (They cost $25 each.) Next door is the **White Pepper Gift Shop,** loaded with high-end trinkets. Continue along the Marginal Way, past the yacht club, to Winslow Homer Rd., marked by a Positively No Passing sign. There's no parking here, either, but you can walk to Homer's small studio, just beyond the gate on the right. It's generally open in July and August, 10 a.m.-4 p.m., but you may want to call (207) 883-2249 to be sure. To the right of the Positively No Passing sign is the beginning of the one-and-a-half-mile **Cliff Walk,** a pathway with spectacular views along the southern and eastern edges of the neck.

WALKING AND HIKING GUIDES AND INFORMATION

So much of Portland can (and should) be covered on foot that it would take a book to list all the possibilities, but several dedicated volunteer groups have produced guides to facilitate the process.

Portland Head Light

Greater Portland Landmarks, 165 State St., Portland 04101, tel. (207) 774-5561, is the doyenne, founded in 1964 to preserve Portland's historic architecture and promote responsible construction. The organization has published more than a dozen books and booklets, including *Discover Historic Portland on Foot,* a packet of four well-researched walking-tour guides to architecturally historic sections of Portland's peninsula: Old Port, Western Promenade, State Street, and Congress Street. It's available at local bookstores, some gift shops, and the visitor information center, 305 Commercial St., Portland 04101, tel. (207) 772-5800, fax 874-9043.

Greater Portland Landmarks also sponsors an annual **summer tour program,** featuring four or five walking trips and excursions to offshore islands, historic churches, revamped buildings, and gardens. Many of the destinations are private or otherwise inaccessible, so these are special opportunities. Registration is limited, and there's only one trip to each site, so call for a schedule no later than May. Tours run mid-July to mid-October, primarily on weekends.

Every Friday and Saturday at 10 a.m., knowledgable volunteer Landmarks guides lead fascinating **walking tours** of Portland's downtown. Reservations aren't needed. Meet at the Victory monument in Monument Square on Congress St.; buy your tickets ($7 pp) at the Victory Deli, facing the square.

Portland Trails, 1 India St., Portland 04101, tel. (207) 775-2411, fax 772-7673, a dynamic, 750-member conservation organization incorporated in 1991, continuously adds to the mileage it has mapped out for hiking and biking around Portland. The group's most recent ambitious undertaking has been the 2.1-mile **Eastern Promenade Trail,** a landscaped bayfront dual pathway circling the base of Munjoy Hill and linking East End Beach to the Old Port. Its goal for the turn of the 21st century? A 30-mile network of Greater Portland multiuse recreational trails. Count on it.

A handy (and free) map/brochure published in 1997 is a great way to start exploring Portland's parks and pathways. The *Trail Guide to Portland, Maine,* a joint project of Portland Trails and the Kids and Transportation Program of the Greater Portland Council of Governments (GPCOG), describes nine parks and nearly a dozen trails for biking, walking/hiking, and cross-country skiing. An insert flyer lists the bus routes for getting to the trailheads. Copies of the map are available at the visitor information center; from Portland Trails, tel. (207) 775-2411; or from David Willauer at the GPCOG, tel. (207) 774-9891.

Newest walking-tour project, in downtown Portland, is the **Portland Women's History Trail,** sponsored by the Women's Studies Program at the University of Southern Maine and the Maine Humanities Council and spearheaded by history professor Polly Kaufman. Four loops cover Congress Street, Munjoy Hill, State Street, and the West End, with nearly two dozen stops on each loop. Among the sites: a long-gone chewing-gum factory where teenage girls worked 10-hour days, a girls' orphan asylum, and City Hall, site of Portland's first women's suffrage meeting in 1870. The trail guide is available in selected bookstores and at the **Maine History Gallery** gift shop, 489 Congress St., Portland 04101, tel. (207) 879-0427.

The **Southern Maine Volkssport Association,** based in Portland and affiliated with the International Volkssport Federation, has several hundred members and annually sponsors a half-dozen *Volksmarsch* events (people's walks) each year, 10K or so, that you can do at your own pace. Most last 2-4 hours. For information, call (207) 774-8306 or 774-8524.

A summertime walking regime rather like the *Volksmarsches* is the **Portland Pacers,** started by the city's Division of Public Health in 1995. Several local organizations are involved, under the umbrella of the Maine Arts Congress Square summer program. Here's the drill: Arrive at Congress Square, downtown Portland, any weekday between 11:30 a.m. and 1:30 p.m., late May through September. (Wear walking shoes appropriate for pavement.) Pick up a tally sheet and maps at the information kiosk, select a route from the nine or so choices, and head out. Routes range from a mile to 2.6 miles, or combine them. When you finish, have your registration sheet validated at the kiosk. (You're on your honor if you return after kiosk hours.) All this is free, noncompetitive, and healthful, and it's a fantastic way to size up the city. There are even incentive prizes as you tote up the miles. For info about additional special walks (such as Peaks Island), contact Barbara Michaels at Public Health, tel. (207) 874-8784 or 874-8618, fax 874-8913.

PARKS, PRESERVES, AND BEACHES

Greater Portland is blessed with green space, thanks largely to the efforts of 19th-century mayor James Phinney Baxter, who foresightedly hired the famed Olmsted Brothers' firm to develop an ambitious plan to ring the city with public parks and promenades. Not all the elements fell into place, but the result is what makes Portland such a livable city. When heading for the beaches, keep in mind that even on a hot day, Atlantic water is not bathtub-warm; you'll need to adjust—make sure you don't go hypothermic by staying in too long. And don't forget the sunblock.

Portland Peninsula
Probably the most visible of the city's parks, 51-acre **Deering Oaks,** Park and Forest Aves. and Deering St., may be best known for the quaint little duck condo in the middle of the pond. Other facilities here are tennis courts, playground, rental paddleboats, the Barking Squirrel Café, lovely gardens, a Saturday farmers' market (7 a.m.-noon), and, in winter, ice skating. (Winter scenes in the film *The Preacher's Wife,* starring Denzel Washington and Whitney Houston and a slew of Portland extras, were shot here.) After dark, steer clear of the park.

At one end of the Eastern Promenade, where it meets Fore Street, **Fort Allen Park** overlooks offshore Fort Gorges (coin-operated telescopes bring it closer). A central gazebo is flanked by an assortment of military souvenirs dating as far back as the War of 1812. All along the "Eastern Prom" are walking paths, benches, play areas, even an ill-maintained fitness trail—all with that terrific view. Down by the water is **East End Beach,** with parking, token sand, and the area's best launching ramp for sea kayaks or power-boats.

West of Downtown
Just beyond I-295, along Baxter Blvd. (Rt. 1) and tidal **Back Cove,** is a skinny green strip

with a three-and-a-half-mile paved trail for walking, jogging, or just watching the sailboards and the skyline. Along the way, you can cross Baxter and spend time picnicking, playing tennis, or flying a kite in 48-acre **Payson Park.**

Talk about an urban oasis. The 85-acre **Fore River Sanctuary,** owned by the Maine Audubon Society, has two and a half miles of blue-blazed trails that wind through a saltmarsh, link up with the historic Cumberland and Oxford Canal towpath, and pass near **Jewell Falls,** Portland's only waterfall, protected by Portland Trails. From downtown Portland, take Congress St. West (Rt. 22), past I-295. From here there are two access routes: either turn right onto Stevens Ave. (Rt. 9), continue to Brighton Ave. (Rt. 25), turn left and go approx. one and a quarter miles to Rowe Ave., turn left and park at the end of the road; or continue past Stevens Ave., about one-half mile to Frost Avenue, take a hard right, then left into the Maine Orthopaedic Center parking lot. Portland Trails raised the funds for the handsome, 90-foot pedestrian bridge at this entrance to the sanctuary. Open daily, sunup to sundown. No pets, free admission.

South of Portland
The Maine Lighthouse Bicycle Tour, a well-planned bike route, takes in several of the following sites; for a handy map guide to the route ($1), stop at the visitor information center.

Just over the brand-new Casco Bay Bridge (formerly the "Million-Dollar Bridge") from downtown Portland (Rt. 77), take Broadway (left) and continue to the end at **Southern Maine Technical College** (SMTC), overlooking the bay. Best time to come here is evenings and weekends, when there's ample parking. Unless it's foggy (when the signal is deafening) or thundering (when you'll expose yourself to lightning), walk out along the 1,000-foot granite breakwater to the **Spring Point Light,** with fabulous views in every direction. Also here are picnic benches, the remains of Fort Preble, and the Peter A. McKernan Hospitality Center. At the southern edge of the SMTC campus is the **Spring Point Shoreway,** a scenic three-mile pathway with views off to House, Peaks, and Cushings Islands. At the end of the shoreway, you'll reach crescent-shaped **Willard Beach,** a neighborhoody sort of place with lifeguards, a changing building, a snack bar, and those same marvelous views. If you're headed directly to Willard Beach from downtown Portland, follow the same directions as above, but instead of entering the SMTC campus, turn right onto Preble Street. Continue to Willow St. (near Willard Square), then go left to the beach. Park in the designated lot, not on the street.

Built in 1791—during George Washington's administration—the stunningly sited **Portland Head Light,** 1000 Shore Rd., Fort Williams Park, Cape Elizabeth 04107, tel. (207) 799-2661, has been immortalized in poetry, photography, and philately. The surf here is awesome. There's no access to the 58-foot automated light tower, but the superbly restored keeper's house has become **The Museum at Portland Head Light,** filled with local history and lighthouse memorabilia. Museum admission is $2 adults, $1 children 6-18. It's open daily 10 a.m.-4 p.m., June-Oct. and weekends 10 a.m.-4 p.m., in April, May, November, and December.

In the 94-acre municipally owned **Fort Williams Park,** surrounding the lighthouse, there's lots of manicured space for kids to run and play. Bring a picnic, binoculars, and some kites. The park has tennis courts and a beach and is open sunup to sundown all year. Kids can climb through the window and door openings of the 1858 Goddard Mansion, a crumbling brick hulk that's the site of wedding photos and serendipitous Shakespearean performances. Serious rock climbers head for the cliff wall next to the beach; climbing is forbidden in the lighthouse area. Three times a summer, the **Portland Symphony Orchestra,** tel. (207) 773-8191, performs pops concerts in the park bandshell. From downtown Portland, take Rt. 77, then Broadway, Cottage Rd., and Shore Rd.— a total of four miles to the south and east.

Almost a vest-pocket park, 40-acre **Two Lights State Park,** Two Lights Rd., off Rt. 77, Cape Elizabeth 04107, tel. (207) 799-5871, has picnicking and restroom facilities, plus a bike rack in the parking area; its biggest asset is the panoramic ocean view from atop a onetime gun battery. Open all year. Summer admission is $2 adults, 50 cents kids 5-11; children under five are free. Before or after visiting the park, take a left just before the park entrance (con-

tinuation of Two Lights Rd.; the sign says Lighthouses). Continue to the parking lot at the end, where you'll see the signal towers for which Two Lights is named. (There's no access to either one; only one still works.) If you haven't brought a picnic for the state park, enjoy the fare and the view at **The Lobster Shack,** 222 Two Lights Rd ,next to the parking area, Cape Elizabeth, tel. (207) 799-1677; it's open daily 11 a.m.-8 p.m., mid-April to mid-October (to 8:30 in July and August).

If you don't mind company, **Crescent Beach State Park,** Rt. 77, Cape Elizabeth 04107, tel. (207) 767-3625, has Greater Portland's largest, most attractive beach—a 243-acre park with changing rooms, lifeguard, restrooms, picnic tables, and a snack bar. It's officially open Memorial Day weekend to September 30, but the beach is accessible all year (off season, expect to meet plenty of dog walkers). Admission is $2.50 adults, 50 cents children 5-11, free for kids under five. Directly offshore is Saco Bay's **Richmond Island**—a 200-acre private preserve with a checkered past dating to the 17th century.

Scarborough's major neighborhood beach is **Higgins Beach,** at the mouth of the Spurwink River. There's plenty of access via local roads to the huge beach—with dunes and tidepools— but parking is nonexistent. Best option is to book a room or rent a cottage nearby. Second-best option is to park at **Baer's Place,** 44 Ocean Ave., two blocks northwest of the beach, Scarborough, tel. (207) 883-6662, a convenience store that charges $4 for the privilege. Turn onto Ocean Ave. from Rt. 77 (Spurwink Road).

Formerly a state park, five-acre **Scarboro Beach Park,** Black Point Rd., Rt. 207, Scarborough 04074, tel. (207) 883-2416, now belongs to the town of Scarborough. Between the parking area and the lovely stretch of beach, you'll pass Massacre Pond, named for a 1703 skirmish between resident Indians and resident wannabes. (Score: Indians 19, wannabes 0.) Parking is limited, but you might want to leave your car here and walk down Black Point Road to visit Prouts Neck. The park is open all year for swimming, surfing, beachcombing, and ice skating. Hours are 9 a.m.-8 p.m. daily, May-Sept.; admission is $3 adults, $2 seniors, $1 kids 5-11.

At 3,100 acres, **Scarborough Marsh,** Pine Point Rd., Rt. 9, Scarborough 04074, tel. (207)

883-5100, Maine's largest saltmarsh, is prime territory for canoeing. Join one of the one-and-a-half-hour daily tours (10 a.m.) or rent a canoe ($10 an hour) at the minuscule Nature Center, operated by Maine Audubon Society, and explore on your own. Guided canoe tours also operate at 3:30 p.m. Tuesday and 6 p.m. Thursday. Cost is $9 adults, $7 children; deduct $1.50 pp if you have your own canoe. July and August full-moon tours ($10 per adult, $8 per child) are particularly exciting; dress warmly and bring a flashlight. Other special programs, some geared primarily for children, include wildflower walks, art classes, and dawn birding trips. All require reservations and fees. Call or write for a schedule: **Maine Audubon Society,** P.O. Box 6009, Falmouth 04105, tel. (207) 781-2330. Located .8 mile east of Rt. 1, the center is open daily 9:30 a.m.-5:30 p.m., mid-June to Labor Day.

Falmouth (North of Portland)
Nearly a dozen of Falmouth's parks, trails, and preserves, official and unofficial, are described and mapped in the *Falmouth Trail Guide,* a handy little booklet published by the Falmouth Conservation Commission. Copies are available at Gilsland Farm, Falmouth Town Hall, and local bookstores. Two of the best options are described below.

A 60-acre wildlife sanctuary/environmental center on the banks of the Presumpscot River, **Gilsland Farm** is state headquarters for the Maine Audubon Society (not affiliated with National Audubon). More than two miles of easy, well-marked trails wind through the grounds, taking in saltmarshes, early-20th-century woodlands, and even contemporary organic gardens. Observation blinds allow inconspicuous spying during bird-migration season. In the new, ecosensitive education center are hands-on exhibits, a treasure-filled gift shop, and classrooms and offices. Open daily, all year (except major holidays). Closed Sunday in January and February. A fee is charged for special events, but otherwise it's all free. The visitor center is a quarter of a mile off Rt. 1. For more info contact the Maine Audubon Society, P.O. Box 6009, Falmouth 04105, tel. (207) 781-2330, fax 781-6185.

Once the summer compound of the prominent Baxter family, Falmouth's 100-acre **Mackworth Island,** reached via a causeway, is now the site of the Governor Baxter School for the Deaf. Limited parking just beyond the security booth on the island. On the one-and-a-half-mile, vehicle-free perimeter path, you'll meet bikers, hikers, and dog walkers. Just off the trail on the north side of the island is the late Governor Percival Baxter's stone-circled pet cemetery, maintained by the state at the behest of Baxter, who donated this island as well as Baxter State Park to the people of Maine. From downtown Portland, take Rt. 1 across the Presumpscot River to Falmouth Foreside. Andrews Ave. (third street on the right) leads to the island. Open sunup to sundown, all year.

If you have a sea kayak (even a rented one), consider a little picnicking excursion to **Basket Island,** a nine-acre island best reached from the Falmouth town landing (Town Landing Rd., just off Rt. 88 in Falmouth Foreside; or take Johnson Rd., southeasterly from Rt. 1 in Falmouth, to connect with Town Landing Road). Owned by The Nature Conservancy, the island has gravel beaches, a saltmarsh, rugosa roses, and the foundation of an old lighthouse. Be forewarned: It also has poison ivy. Pull your kayak onto the beach at the northwestern corner of the island (facing the mainland). No camping or fires allowed. The island is popular with boaters on weekends, so plan to arrive on a weekday. For further information, contact The Nature Conservancy, 14 Maine St., Fort Andross, Brunswick 04011, tel. (207) 729-5181, fax 729-4118.

RECREATION

Cycling
A mandatory stop for anyone planning to get around on two wheels in Greater Portland is **Back Bay Bicycle,** 333 Forest Ave., Portland 04101, tel. (207) 773-6906, where you can get a tune-up, rent a bike, or just talk bikes. Also helpful with rentals (hybrids are $15 a day) and repairs is **Cycle Mania,** 59 Federal St., Portland 04101, tel. (207) 774-2933. **Allspeed Bicycle & Ski,** 1041 Washington Ave., Portland 04103, tel. (207) 878-8741, sells a huge variety of bikes (and skis) and does repairs. All three shops sponsor group rides.

Three excellent **bike-route maps** of historic Portland, the islands, and the lighthouse trail just south of Portland have been produced by the Bicycle Transportation Alliance of Portland (BTAP), a group firmly dedicated to alternative transportation and recreational biking. *Historical Bicycle Tour of Portland* (seven miles), *Two Casco Bay Island Bicycle Tours* (variable mileage), and *Maine Lighthouse Bicycle Tour* (21 miles) are $1 each from the visitor information center or BTAP, P.O. Box 4506, Portland 04112. Or contact local bike enthusiast Sandy Vogels, tel. (207) 879-7440; he'll send you the maps and offer advice, too.

The best locales for island bicycling—fun for families and beginners but not especially challenging for diehards—are Peaks and Great Chebeague Islands.

Golf

You'll have no problem finding a place to tee off in Greater Portland. Some of the best courses are private, so if you have an "in," so much the better, but there are still plenty of public and semiprivate courses for every skill level. If you're planning to play a lot of golf, consider buying an American Lung Association **Golf Privilege Card,** covering greens fees for 70 rounds of golf (at over 50 courses) for $70. Besides, it's a great cause. Many courses on the list require reservations 24 or 48 hours in advance, and some require player's fees. Write or call American Lung Association of Maine, 122 State St., Augusta 04330, tel. (800) 458-6472, fax (207) 626-2919.

Let's just take the 18-hole courses. **Sable Oaks Golf Club,** 505 Country Club Dr., South Portland, tel. (207) 775-6257, is considered one of the toughest and best of Maine's public courses. Tee times are always required. **Gorham Country Club,** McLellan Rd., Gorham, tel. (207) 839-3490, has a par-71 course with plenty of challenging terrain. Call for tee times weekends and holidays. At **Val Halla Golf and Recreation Center,** Greely Rd., off Rt. 9, Cumberland Center, tel. (207) 829-2225, tee times are always required. **Willowdale Golf Club,** 52 Willowdale Rd., Scarborough, tel. (207) 883-9351 or 883-6504, is opposite Scarborough Downs race track. The City of Portland's **Riverside Municipal Golf Course,** 1158 Riverside St., Portland, tel. (207)

797-3524, has an 18-hole par-72 course (Riverside North) and a nine-hole par-35 course (Riverside South). Opt for the 18-hole course. The clubhouse is just west of I-95, between Exits 8 and 9. Call for tee times on weekends.

Out on Great Chebeague Island (just call it Chebeague) is a challenging nine-hole course. The semiprivate **Great Chebeague Golf Club,** founded in 1923, allows nonmembers to play—except Monday and Thursday mornings. Check the Casco Bay Lines and Chebeague Transportation Company's ferry schedules, then call the club, (207) 846-9478, for a tee time. Hazards at holes five and seven include parked cars and a corner of Casco Bay. Clubs ($10 a day) and pull-carts ($2 a day) are available for rent (no motorized carts), and a dress code is enforced.

When lousy weather sets in, the local alternative is **Fore Season Golf,** 1037 Forest Ave., Portland 04104, tel. (207) 797-8835, where you can play virtual golf at more than a dozen famous courses with regulation clubs and balls, thanks to computerized simulators. Cost is $24 an hour. A snack bar keeps you going, and beer and wine are available.

Tennis

Portland's 31 free municipal tennis courts, open dawn to dusk, first-come, first-served, are scattered all over the city. Best ones are in Deering Oaks, Payson Park, and on the Eastern Promenade. The **City of Portland Recreation Division,** 389 Congress St., Portland 04101, tel. (207) 874-8793, manages them all; call for other locations.

Just north of Portland, in Falmouth, indoor courts at the upmarket **Portland Athletic Club,** 196 Rt. 1, Falmouth 04105, tel. (207) 781-2671, are open to the public for $26 an hour weekdays 9 a.m.-4 p.m., as well as weekends. Weekday early birds (before 9 a.m.) can play for $22 an hour. After 4 p.m. weekdays, you'll pay $30. The club also has racquetball, squash, volleyball, aerobics classes, a restaurant, and a kids' center. Open daily 7:30 a.m.-8 p.m. except summer weekends, when the club closes at 3 p.m.

Swimming

Besides the saltwater beaches listed above under "Parks, Preserves, and Beaches," Portland has two municipal pools open to the public:

Reiche Pool, 166 Brackett St., in West End, tel. (207) 874-8874, and **Riverton Pool,** 1600 Forest Ave., Rt. 302, west of I-295, tel. (207) 874-8456. Both are part of community center/school complexes. **South Portland's municipal pool** is at 21 Nelson Rd., tel. (207) 767-7655. Hours for open swimming vary, so call for schedules.

Climbing the Walls

With 24-foot-high walls and 20 major sections covering 5,000 square feet of surface, the **Maine Rock Gym,** 127 Marginal Way, Portland 04101, tel. (207) 780-6370, has become hugely popular since it opened in 1994. Angled walls and molded handholds simulate the real thing, and the gym management rearranges the handholds regularly to maintain variety. During the summer, you can also scale a 40-foot monster outdoor climbing wall. Cost for four hours—including mandatory instructions and gear—is $20. If you've climbed elsewhere, you'll still need to pass a belay test ($5) before being allowed to climb. Rules are enforced and you'll have to sign a liability release. Parents or guardians have to sign for anyone under 18. Vending machines have good-for-you snacks, such as Gatorade and granola bars. Open Tues.-Fri. 2-10 p.m., Sat.-Sun. 11 a.m.-8 p.m. (in summer, opening is at noon Saturday and Sunday).

Spectator Sports

A pseudo-fierce mascot named Slugger stirs up the crowds at baseball games played by the **Portland Sea Dogs,** Hadlock Field, 271 Park Ave., Portland 04102, tel. (207) 879-9500 or (800) 936-3647, fax (207) 780-0310, a AA farm team for the Florida Marlins. Ever since the team arrived, in 1994, loyal local fans have made tickets scarce, so it's essential to reserve well ahead (you'll pay a minimal reservation surcharge) with a major credit card. The season schedule (early April to early September) is available after January 1. General-admission tickets are $4 adults, $2 seniors (62 and over) and kids 16 and under. Reserved seats are $5 adults, $4 all others. Box seats are $6 adults, $5 all others. For hassle-free parking, leave your car at the Doubletree Inn, next to I-295 Exit 5B (southbound)/5A (northbound), and take the continuous Metro Shuttle service ($1 pp) to the ballpark.

For ice hockey action, the **Portland Pirates,** a farm team for the American Hockey League Washington Capitals, plays winter and spring home games at the 8,726-seat Cumberland County Civic Center, 1 Civic Center Sq., Portland 04101, tel. (207) 775-3458, hotline (207) 775-3481, ext. 2.

The civic center is also the locale for year-round special sporting events and exhibition games, as well as ice shows, concerts, and college hockey games. Check the *Portland Press Herald* for schedules or call the center.

Sea Kayaking and Canoeing

Two local businesses have introduced countless new enthusiasts to sea kayaking. In downtown Portland, **Norumbega Outfitters,** 58 Fore St., Portland 04101, tel. (207) 773-0910 or (800) 529-2548, rents kayaks, organizes day-long and longer group paddles, gives instruction (including off season in indoor pools), and provides all kinds of good advice on navigating Casco Bay. (There's a dock behind the shop, so you can start right there.) Open Mon.-Fri. 10 a.m.-7 p.m., Saturday 9 a.m.-5 p.m., Sunday noon-5 p.m.

Out on Peaks Island, 15 minutes offshore via Casco Bay Lines ferry, is **Maine Island Kayak Company,** 70 Luther St., Peaks Island 04108, tel. (207) 766-2373 or (800) 796-2373, a successful tour operation that organizes half-day and day-long local kayaking trips as well as national and international adventures. Maine Island's owner, Tom Bergh, has a flawless reputation for safety and skill. Send for their extensive trip schedule.

To tap into sea-kayaking happenings in the area, call the round-the-clock info line of the **Southern Maine Sea Kayaking Network,** tel. (207) 874-2640.

Based in Scarborough, just south of Portland, **Stephen Randall,** 16 Thomas Dr., Scarborough 04074, tel. (207) 883-2148, is a Registered Maine Guide with more than two decades of Outward Bound and Coast Guard experience. For $12 pp ($6 for kids under 12; $25 minimum), he'll take you in his 20-foot *Grand Laker* canoe for a two-hour tour of Scarborough Marsh and nearby rivers. Steve is skilled in navigation, water safety, fly-fishing, and photography, and he can provide a host of other canoeing options. (He's also invented a terrific car seatback pack for carrying your *Maine Atlas and Gazetteer,* the sine-qua-non volume for touring Maine.)

KIDS' STUFF

The best resource for entertaining children (especially the middle-school set) in Portland is *A Kid's Guide to Getting Around Greater Portland,* a way-cool annotated map published by the Greater Portland Council of Governments, tel. (207) 774-9891, fax 774-7149. It pinpoints parks, rec programs, museums, bike shops, pizza and ice cream places, hospitals, and tons more. Eco-friendly and oriented to alternative transportation, it helps you navigate by bus, bike, boat, and ankle express. No schedule info, but scads of handy phone numbers. Even adults will find it useful. Pick up a free copy at libraries and information centers or call David Willauer at the Kids and Transportation Program of the GPCOG.

The **City of Portland Recreation Division,** 389 Congress St., Portland 04101, tel. (207) 874-8793 or 874-8300, supervises playgrounds and parks throughout the city and sponsors a huge list of summer activities for youngsters, including a "Summer in the Parks" teen program. Call in spring to get the summer schedule.

Children's Museum of Maine

Here's the answer to parents' prayers—a whole museum in downtown Portland catering to kids. At the Children's Museum of Maine, 142 Free St., next to the Portland Museum of Art, Portland 04101, tel. (207) 828-1234, lots of hands-on displays encourage interaction and guarantee involvement for a couple of hours. What's here? A lobsterboat, scaled-down space shuttle, media center, bank, computer lab, and more. First level is for kids up to eight, second level for ages 6-14. Call to check on the special-events schedule. Open daily, Memorial Day weekend to Labor Day, when admission is $5 for everyone over one year old; children under one free. During the school year, the museum is open Wed.-Sun.; admission is $4. Free admission the first Friday of the month during the school year.

Smiling Hill Farm

Six miles west of downtown Portland, 400-acre Smiling Hill Farm, 781 County Rd., Rt. 22, Westbrook 04092, tel. (207) 775-4818, has year-round activities for kids as well as their parents. The **Smiling Hill Barnyard,** open May-Sept., features a petting zoo, pony rides, and a gift shop. Also here is the **Ice Cream Barn,** tel. (207) 775-2408, with a make-your-own sundae bar offering 30 homemade flavors and two dozen or so topping choices. It's open daily 11 a.m.-8 p.m. mid-April through September. In winter, about 20 miles of trails on the farm are beautifully groomed for **cross-country skiing**—weather permitting, of course. Full-day weekend rate is $10 adults ($8 weekdays), $7.50 children 8-17 ($5 weekdays), and free for kids eight and under. Ski or snowshoe rental runs about $10 pp.

GETTING AFLOAT

Casco Bay Lines Cruises

Casco Bay Lines, Commercial and Franklin Sts., Old Port, Portland 04101, tel. (207) 774-7871, the nation's oldest continuously operating ferry system (since the 1920s), is the lifeline between Portland and six inhabited Casco Bay islands. Some 650,000 people patronize the service annually. What better way to sample the islands than to go along for the three-hour ride with mail, groceries, and island residents? The Casco Bay Lines mailboat stops—briefly—at **Long Island, Chebeague, Cliff,** and **Little and Great Diamond Islands.** Departures are 10 a.m. and 2:15 p.m. Memorial Day weekend to mid-October, 10 a.m. and 2:45 p.m. other months. Trips operate every day but Sunday and federal holidays. Fares are $9.50 adults, $8 seniors, and $4.25 children 5-9. Children under five are free. Longest cruise on the Casco Bay Lines schedule is the five-hour, 45-minute summertime trip (late June to Labor Day) to **Bailey Island,** with a two-hour stopover, departing from Portland at 10 a.m. Sun.-Fri. ($13.75 adults, $12.25 seniors, $6.25 children). Bargain alert: For no extra charge, you can stay onboard in Bailey Island and go along for a one-and-a-half-hour nature cruise. The regular adult fare for the nature cruise is $8. No smoking; dogs (on leashes) and bicycles need separate tickets.

Sailboat and Powerboat Excursions

If boats make you queasy, take the easy way out with lunch or dinner at **DiMillo's Floating Restaurant,** a converted car ferry on Portland's waterfront where you can't beat the view.

Down on the Old Port wharves are several excursion-boat businesses. Each has carved out a niche, so choose according to your interest and your schedule. Dress warmly and wear rubber-soled shoes. Remember that all cruises are weather-dependent.

Bay View Cruises operates the *Bay View Lady,* 184 Commercial St., Fisherman's Wharf, Old Port, tel. (207) 761-0496, every day June through September, plus weekends in May and June. Six different cruises range from 40 minutes (lunchtime) to one and a half hours (morning and afternoon) to two hours (sunset). You can feast on lobster during the longer cruises. Cost (cruise only) is $8 adults, $7 seniors, $5 children. The main deck is enclosed and heated; the upper deck has the best views.

The **Olde Port Mariner Fleet,** with four vessels, is based at the head of Long Wharf on Commercial St., tel. (207) 775-0727 or 642-3270 or (800) 437-3270 outside Maine, mailing address 634 Cape Rd., Standish 04084. Six-hour whalewatches are a specialty, departing aboard the *Odyssey* at 10 a.m. daily from late June to Labor Day, plus weekends in early June and after Labor Day. Tickets are $25-35 pp. (Don't overload on breakfast that day.) In July and August, shorter sunset whalewatching trips depart at 5 p.m., returning at sundown. Contact Olde Port also for hour-long harbor cruises, half-day and full-day sportfishing excursions, and dinner cruises.

Also based at Long Wharf is **Eagle Tours,** 1 Long Wharf, Old Port, tel. (207) 774-6498, offering several excursion options, but the best is the four-hour trip (departing 10 a.m.) to 17-acre **Eagle Island,** where arctic explorer Adm. Robert Peary built his summer home. Now owned by the state, the house is open daily, late June to Labor Day, plus September and October weekends. The cruise allows time to visit the house and wander the grounds. Pack a picnic. Cost is $15.

Prince of Fundy Cruises

If Nova Scotia beckons, you can save about

Wharf Street, Old Port, Portland

850 miles of driving (along the coasts of Maine and New Brunswick, then back) by boarding the 475-foot cruise liner MS **Scotia Prince** and sailing. Departures are at 9 p.m., early May to late October, arriving Yarmouth, Nova Scotia at 8 a.m. (9 a.m. Atlantic time). After an hour's layover, the ship returns to Portland, arriving at 8 p.m., only 23 hours after you left. You won't lack for entertainment: the *Scotia Prince* has all the hyperactivity of typical cruise ships, including a casino, floor show, and duty-free shopping. Fares vary, depending on the season and whether you're taking a car or want an overnight cabin. Special packages are available, including roundtrip supersavers with cabin and meals. Normal one-way adult rate without cabin is $78 mid-June to mid-September, $58 earlier and later in the season. Children 5-14 are $39 and $29, free for those under five. Cabin rates are $20-95 (two classes). Cars cost $98 in mid-summer, $80 before and after. Best deal if you're taking a car to Nova Scotia is to aim for **half-**

price car days: any Tuesday or Wednesday late June to late August. No pets in cabins or public areas, no coolers allowed in cabins. Prince of Fundy Cruises, International Marine Terminal, 468 Commercial St., P.O. Box 4216, Portland 04101, tel. (207) 775-5616 or (800) 341-7540, fax (207) 773-7403.

ENTERTAINMENT AND NIGHTLIFE

The best place to find out what's playing at area theaters, cinemas, concert halls, and nightclubs are the *Go* supplement in the Thursday edition of the *Portland Press Herald* and the *Casco Bay Weekly*. Both are available at bookstores and supermarkets; the latter is free.

Also free are the Summer Performance Series presentations, every summer weekday, late June to Labor Day weekend, in one of the downtown pocket parks. Sponsored by Portland's Downtown District (PDD), tel. (207) 772-6828, the action rotates among Monument Square, Congress Square, Tommy's Park, and Post Office Park. Check the *Go* supplement in Thursday's *Portland Press Herald* or call the PDD office.

A unique nonprofit institution, Maine Arts, Inc., 582 Congress St., Portland 04101, tel. (207) 772-9012, is best known for sponsoring two major festivals—New Year's/Portland and early August's Maine Festival. But this dynamic organization also is responsible for concerts, plays, impromptu shows, and other special events throughout the year. Call Maine Arts for schedule details .

Portland Performing Arts
Since the mid-1980s, Portland Performing Arts, 25A Forest Ave., Portland 04101, tel. (207) 761-0591, based in the downtown Portland Performing Arts Center, has been exposing Portlanders to multicultural arts—music and dance performers from Mongolia, Africa, and Kazakhstan, as well as Portland's own ethnic community—under the headlines of Big Sounds from All Over and the House Island Project. Check newspapers for their programs or call the office for a schedule.

State Theatre
After an astonishing renovation that produced a stunning gilded, painted performance space, the 1929 State Theatre, 609 Congress St., Portland 04101, tel. (207) 879-1112 or 879-1111, has had financial ups and downs. Nonetheless, it's the focal point of Congress Street's Downtown Arts District, and the city has worked hard to keep it afloat. Plays, big-name rock concerts, and classical performances have all contributed to the theater's renown. Call for current schedule.

Pops and Classical Music
The Portland Symphony Orchestra and the Portland Concert Association share use of the stage at the magnificently restored Merrill Auditorium, 389 Congress St., Portland 04101, tel. (207) 842-0800, a 1,900-seat theater inside Portland City Hall with two balconies and one of the country's only municipally owned pipe organs. Both the PSO and PCA have extensive, well-patronized fall and winter schedules; the PSO, under longtime conductor Toshiyuki Shimada, presents summer pops concerts in Cape Elizabeth and other locales around the state.

The Portland String Quartet, one of the nation's most enduring chamber-music ensembles, performs in various locations around the state on a schedule arranged by the Lark Society. Call (207) 761-1522 for information.

Drama
Innovative staging and controversial contemporary dramas are typical of the Portland Stage Company, Portland Performing Arts Center, 25A Forest Ave., P.O. Box 1458, Portland 04101, tel. (207) 774-0465, established in 1974 and going strong ever since. Equity pros present a half-dozen plays each winter season in a 290-seat performance space. The Mad Horse Theatre, 955 Forest Ave., Portland 04103, tel. (207) 797-3338, nearly went under in 1995 but has managed to keep afloat with successful winter dramas. Going strong is the Oak Street Theater, 92 Oak St., Portland 04101, tel. (207) 775-5103, performing in a minuscule, audience-capturing space.

Cinemas
Downtown Portland's three movie theaters, with a total of 10 screens, aren't quite highest-tech,

but they'll do just fine, especially since ticket prices are reasonable. At six-screen **Hoyt's Nickelodeon,** Temple and Middle Sts., tel. (207) 772-9751, tickets are always $2.99 and the seats are comfy. The place is casual enough to permit you to bring your own popcorn (don't make a huge deal of it; just carry it in); buy it there and you'll pay through the nose. **The Movies,** 10 Exchange St., tel. (207) 772-9600, screens esoterica such as *The Sexual Life of the Belgians,* and its seats are guaranteed to keep you awake, but tickets ($2.50 Wednesday, $4 otherwise) and popcorn are cheap and there are weekend matinees. Newest on the scene is the three-screen **Keystone Theatre Café,** 504 Congress St., tel. (207) 871-5500, in the Downtown Arts District, near L.L. Bean. Arrive half an hour early to order drinks and dinner, then settle in for the show; films are first-runs, classics, and art flicks. Tickets are $5 evenings, $3.50 matinees.

Beyond downtown are the garden-variety multiplexes: **Hoyts Clark's Pond 8,** behind Maine Mall, South Portland, tel. (207) 879-1511; **Flagship Cinema 10,** Rt. 1, Falmouth, tel. (207) 781-5616; and **Maine Mall Cinema 7,** near I-95 Exit 7, South Portland, tel. (207) 774-1022. Most of the biggies have daily matinees, cheaper than evening screenings.

Brewpubs and Bars
By the time you read this, several more brewpubs will have surfaced; the phenomenon has mushroomed since the early 1990s.

Not only is **Gritty McDuff's** ("Gritty's"), 396 Fore St., Old Port, Portland, tel. (207) 772-2739, one of Maine's most popular breweries, its brewpub was the state's first—opened in 1988. The pub is heavy into burgers and pizza, but British pub fans will appreciate the steak-and-kidney pie and ploughman's lunch. Among the six or seven Gritty's beers and ales on tap are Sebago Light and Black Fly Stout. Gritty's also books live entertainment fairly regularly. Open daily 11:30 a.m.-1 a.m. On Friday and Saturday between Memorial Day and Labor Day, usually at 1 p.m., there's a free 20-minute tour of the brewery. Reservations are required, no free samples. Gritty's has opened a branch in Freeport.

In 1995, a longtime favorite pub, **Three Dollar Dewey's,** 241 Commercial St., Old Port, tel.

(207) 772-3310, moved into its current bigger location, not missing a beat with a loyal crew of regulars. Visiting Brits, Kiwis, and Aussies head here to assuage their homesickness. The menu changes nightly, and it's predictably good. Friday and Saturday nights, it's SRO. With darts, an eclectic jukebox, and something of a behavior code, the **Fifties Pub,** 225 Congress St., Portland, tel. (207) 772-6398, keeps its ferociously loyal clientele coming back for more.

Of all Portland's neighborhood hangouts, **Ruski's,** 212 Danforth St., tel. (207) 774-7604, is the one most authentic—a small, usually crowded onetime speakeasy that rates just as high for breakfast as for nighttime schmoozing. Basic, homemade fare for well under $10. Darts and big-screen TV, too. Dress down or you'll feel out of place. No credit cards. Open Mon.-Sat. 7 a.m.-12:45 a.m., Sunday 9 a.m.-12:45 a.m.

West of I-295, **The Great Lost Bear,** 540 Forest Ave., tel. (207) 772-0300, has no brewery, but it has Portland's hugest inventory of designer beers, more than four dozen. The bear motif and the punny menus are a bit much, but the 15-or-so varieties of burgers are not bad; the "Bear" has been here since 1979. Open Mon.-Sat. 11:30 a.m.-11:30 p.m., Sunday noon-11:30 p.m.

For more upscale tippling, head for **Top of the East,** the lounge at the Radisson-Eastland Hotel, 157 High St., near Congress Sq., Portland 04101, tel. (207) 775-5411, where all of Portland's at your feet and the Sunday jazz brunch is terrific (reservations necessary). A few blocks away, down toward the Old Port, is the elegant, English-library-style lounge at the **Portland Regency Hotel,** 20 Milk St., Portland 04101, tel. (207) 774-4200.

Comedy
Portland's forum for stand-up comedy is the **Comedy Connection,** 6 Custom House Wharf, next to Boone's, in the Old Port, Portland 04101, tel. (207) 774-5554, a crowded, smoky space that draws nationally known pros. Avoid the front tables unless you're inclined to be the fall guy/guinea pig, and don't bring anyone squeamish about the F-word. Bring your sense of humor, enjoy the show, and patronize the waitstaff; they have a tough job. Tickets are $8;

reservations advisable on weekends. Open Wed.-Sun., all year.

Jazz, Blues, Rock, Country, Reggae, Zydeco, Etc.

So many possibilities in this category, but not a lot of veterans. The Portland club scene is a volatile one, tough on investors and reporters. You'll need to scope out the scene when you arrive; the free weekly *Face magazine* has the best listings. A sampling follows. **Granny Killam's Industrial Drink House,** 55 Market St., Portland, tel. (207) 761-5865, draws crowds in the Old Port. **Raoul's Roadside Attraction,** 865 Forest Ave., west of I-295, Portland, tel. (207) 773-6886, hotline (207) 775-2494, is one of the longest-running, still maintaining its funky decor and image. It has lunch weekdays, happy hour 4-7 p.m., and open mike Tuesday evenings. **Zootz,** 31 Forest Ave., Portland, tel. (207) 773-8187, has state-of-the-art, cutting-edge music and DJs to get you out on the dance floor.

Other places that book acts, in or close to the Old Port, are the **Stone Coast Brewing Company,** 14 York St., Portland, tel. (207) 773-2337, **The Basement,** 379 Fore St., Portland, tel. (207) 828-1111, and the **Free Street Taverna,** 128 Free St., Portland, tel. (207) 774-1114.

FESTIVALS AND EVENTS

Each month, the City of Portland publishes a foldout calendar, *Arts! Alive in Portland,* listing concerts, art exhibits, lectures, children's events, theater and dance performances, art classes, and any other cultural events occurring in the city. Pick up a copy at the visitor information center or at City Hall, 389 Congress St., Room 401, tel. (207) 874-8721.

Born in Portland on February 27, 1807, Henry Wadsworth Longfellow merits his own public event, **Longfellow's Birthday Party,** at the Maine Historical Society, 489 Congress St., Portland.

The third and fourth weeks of April, the 10-day **Aucocisco** (a Native American name for Casco Bay) festival celebrates Casco Bay with bay cruises, exhibits, ecology lectures, films, concerts, and the Maine Boatbuilders Show. It all takes place in downtown Portland.

June brings a host of events: the **Old Port Festival,** (one of Portland's largest festivals), with entertainment, food and craft booths, and impromptu fun in Portland's Old Port; **Back Cove Family Day,** with live music, food and crafts, a cardboard canoe race, and games at Payson Park; the **Greek Heritage Festival,** featuring Greek food, dancing, and crafts at Holy Trinity Church, 133 Pleasant St., Portland; and the advent of the **Summer Performance Series,** sponsored by Portland's Downtown District, which runs through early September offering free weekday noon concerts, dramas, and mime, rotating among several downtown parks.

In August, the **Italian Street Festival** showcases music, Italian food, and games at St. Peter's Catholic Church, 72 Federal St., Portland.

The **Maine Brewers' Festival,** the first weekend in November at the Portland Exposition Building, is a big event—which expands every year thanks to the explosion of Maine microbreweries. Samples galore. And from Thanksgiving weekend to Christmas Eve, **Victorian Holiday Portland,** in downtown Portland, harks back with caroling, special sales, concerts, tree lighting, horse-drawn wagons, and Victoria Mansion tours and festivities.

On December 31, **New Year's/Portland** is an annual day- and night-long extravaganza featuring a zillion entertainment events topped off by midnight fireworks. Free shuttle buses, bargain parking rates, food galore, and free international phone calls at City Hall. Sponsored by Maine Arts.

SHOPPING

The Portland peninsula—primarily Congress Street and the Old Port waterfront district—is thick with non-cookie-cutter shops and galleries. This is just a taste to spur your explorations.

Antiquarian Bookstores

Carlson-Turner Books, 241 Congress St., Portland 04101, tel. (207) 773-4200 or (800) 540-7323, based on Munjoy Hill, seems to have Portland's largest used-book inventory. Look for unusual titles and travel narratives. Open Mon.-Sat. 10 a.m.-5 p.m., Sunday noon-5 p.m.,

May-December. Open Fri.-Sun. only Jan.-April, other days by appointment.

Antique maps and atlases are the specialty at the Old Port's **Emerson Booksellers,** 420 Fore St., Portland 04101, tel. (207) 874-2665, but there's an excellent used-book selection as well. Open year-round, longer hours in summer. Also in the Old Port is **Allen Scott Books**, 89 Exchange St., Portland 04101, tel. (207) 774-2190, where antique children's books have now been added to the shelves.

In the heart of the Downtown Arts District, **Douglas Harding Rare Books**, 594 Congress St., Portland 04101, tel. (207) 761-2150, is the well-stocked Portland branch of Harding's long-running Wells operation. Town histories are a specialty. Open Mon.-Sat. 10 a.m.-5:30 p.m., year-round, but call ahead in January and February.

Antiques

Dating back to the early 19th century, **F.O. Bailey Antiquarians,** 141 Middle St., Portland 04101, tel. (207) 774-1479, fax 774-7914, has a solid reputation for its inventory of fine antiques. Most fun is to attend one of their auctions, watch the action, and maybe pick up a bauble or two. Open Mon.-Sat. year-round.

Polly Peters Antiques, 26 Brackett St., Portland 04101, tel. (207) 774-6981, is Polly Blake's funky, fusty shop specializing in eccentric furniture, architectural fragments, and other exotica. Theoretically open Mon.-Thurs. 10 a.m.-5 p.m., but call ahead to be sure.

Art Galleries

The longest-running and most-respected of Portland's galleries is the **Frost Gully Gallery,** 411 Congress St., Portland 04101, tel. (207) 773-2555, established by Tom Crotty in 1966. Representing some of the best of the state's painters and sculptors, the gallery is open weekdays noon-5 p.m., other times by appointment.

Wonderful papier-mâché figures swaying on mobiles, unique jewelry, and dramatic glass pieces are just some of the stunning objets at the **Nancy Margolis Gallery,** 367 Fore St., Old Port, Portland 04101, tel. (207) 775-3822, which exhibits (and sells) the work of dozens of prominent artists. Open Mon.-Sat. 10 a.m.-9 p.m., Sunday 10 a.m.-6 p.m. in summer; shorter hours off season.

Carrying reasonably priced prints as well as original art, the **Pine Tree Shop and Bayview Gallery,** 75 Market St., Old Port, Portland 04101, tel. (207) 773-3007, is eminently affordable. Prints by three generations of Wyeths are a specialty.

Other downtown Portland galleries worth a visit are **The Danforth Gallery,** 34 Danforth St., tel. (207) 775-6245, **Davidson and Daughters Contemporary Art,** 148 High St., tel. (207) 780-0766, **Gallery Seven,** 49 Exchange St., tel. (207) 761-7007, **Greenhut Galleries,** 146 Middle St., tel. (207) 772-2693, and **June Fitzpatrick Gallery,** 112 High St., tel. (207) 772-1961. Call for hours or stop in when you're exploring the area.

Crafts

More than 15 Maine potters—with a wide variety of styles and items—market their wares at the **Maine Potters Market,** 376 Fore St., Portland 04101, tel. (207) 774-1633, an attractive shop in the heart of the Old Port. Established in 1980, the cooperative remains a consistently reliable outlet for some of Maine's best ceramic artisans. Open daily 10 a.m.-6 p.m., to 9 p.m. in midsummer and December.

For the kid in all of us, there's **Northern Sky Toyz,** 388 Fore St., Portland 04101, tel. (207) 828-0911, probably the best kite shop you've ever seen. Price range is vast—$10 to several hundreds—and owners Bob and Nancy Ray can recommend the best places to try out your purchase(s). Open all year.

Gourmet Gadgets

Maine's hands-down best all-round gourmet-cooking resource shop is **The Whip and Spoon,** 161 Commercial St., Old Port, Portland 04101, tel. (207) 774-4020 or (800) 937-9447, fax (207) 774-6261—a grownup toy store. (There's also a branch store near the Maine Mall in South Portland.) Food processors, whisks, tea strainers, and esoteric single-purpose whatsits—you'll find them all here, plus specialty foods, beer-making supplies, cookbooks, exotic coffees, wines, and a very attentive staff willing to demonstrate any gadget that confounds you. Cooking classes are held in spring and fall. Whip and Spoon is open Mon.-Sat. 10 a.m.-8 p.m., Sunday noon-5 p.m., Memorial Day to Christmas. Other months, they're open daily but shorter hours.

Offbeat Shopping

Trustmi, you have to see **Suitsmi,** 35 Pleasant St., Portland 04101, tel. (207) 772-8285, which carries wearables (including jewelry) perfect for rock concerts, funky cafés, and, if you're dying to make a statement, your class reunion.

Shipwreck and Cargo, 207 Commercial St., Old Port, Portland 04101, tel. (207) 775-3057, stocks a wide assortment of marine-related items.

L.L. Bean

In late 1996, the giant Freeport-based sports outfitter established a major presence with a factory store in a vacant building in the Downtown Arts District. Other shops raced to cash in on the clientele. Stay tuned for many more changes in this area. Bean's, 542 Congress St., Portland 04101, tel. (207) 772-5100, is open Mon.-Sat. 8 a.m.-8 p.m., Sunday 10 a.m.-6 p.m.

South Portland/Maine Mall

With more than 120 stores, the Maine Mall, 364 Maine Mall Rd., South Portland 04106, tel. (207) 774-0303 or 828-2060, is the state's largest shopping complex, and several offshoot mini-malls have moved into the neighborhood to take advantage of the traffic. The mall is just off I-95 Exit 7. Major stores in or near the Maine Mall are **Macy's, The Gap, Sears, Brookstone, Eastern Mountain Sports, Talbots, Ecology House, Radio Shack, Bookland, Borders Books, Eddie Bauer,** and a huge **food court** serving up juices, gyros, Mrs. Field's cookies, chocolates, pretzels, ice cream, and cheeses. **Services** available at the mall include ATMs, restrooms, phones, ear piercing, engraving, shoe dying, film developing, car repair, and stroller and wheelchair rental. Mall management has made a major commitment to recycling, so bins are placed throughout the com-

GREATER PORTLAND ACCOMMODATIONS

Lowest rates quoted here tend to be available only off season (typically, Nov.-April, excluding holidays); highest rates are effective in midsummer. Always inquire about special discounts and packages.

DOWNTOWN

Hotels

The three major downtown hotels all have on-site restaurants, of which the best is The Armory at the Portland Regency.

Holiday Inn by the Bay, 88 Spring St., Portland 04101, tel. (207) 775-2311 or (800) 345-5050, fax (207) 761-8224. Across from Civic Center, midway between Old Port and Downtown Arts District; $99-139 d; 239 rooms, many with harbor view; no pets; indoor pool; fitness center; open all year.

Portland Regency Hotel, 20 Milk St., Portland 04101, tel. (207) 774-4200 or (800) 727-3436, fax (207) 775-2150. Elegantly refurbished former armory in Old Port; $139-229 d; 95 rooms; no pets; fitness center; open all year.

Radisson Eastland Hotel, 157 High St., Portland 04101, tel. (207) 775-5411 or (800) 333-3333, fax (207) 775-2872. Historic intown hostelry (built 1929)

near Portland Museum of Art; $85-150 d; 204 rooms; pets allowed (hefty deposit required); harbor-view rooftop lounge; fitness facilities; open all year.

NEAR I-295

Hotels and Inns

The Inn at Portland, 1150 Brighton Ave., Portland 04102, tel. (207) 775-3711 or (800) 289-6469, fax (207) 774-5409. Near Maine Turnpike Exit 8; $60-110 d; 120 rooms; basic, comfortable motel-style accommodations; pets allowed ($10); outdoor pool; kids stay free; open all year.

DoubleTree Hotel, 1230 Congress St., Rt. 22, Portland 04102, tel. (207) 774-5611 or (800) 989-3856, fax (207) 761-1560. Upgraded in 1997 from a Ramada Inn, close to Trailways Transportation Center; $125 d and up; 149 rooms; no pets; indoor pool; fitness facilities; open all year.

Susse Chalet Inn, 340 Park Ave., Portland 04102, tel. (207) 871-0611 or (800) 524-2538, fax (207) 871-8243. Fanciest version of this low-budget chain; near I-295 Exit 5A; $53-92 (max four persons); 105 rooms; no pets; outdoor pool; open all year.

plex. The shops are open daily, with extended Friday and preholiday hours. Many national fast-food chains have eateries within the mall and in walking distance outside.

ACCOMMODATIONS

Downtown Portland

Portland's peninsula isn't overwhelmed with sleeping space. Three major hotels account for most of it; a handful of B&Bs take care of the rest. All are open year-round. Another option, the Portland Summer Hostel, is, as its name indicates, open seasonally.

B&Bs: The biggest plus of Portland's downtown B&Bs is that they're all in West End buildings loaded with history. Each has a fascinating story to tell; all are open year-round.

Sue and Phil Cox are especially hospitable hosts at **The Inn on Carleton,** 46 Carleton St., Portland 04102, tel. (207) 775-1910 or (800) 639-1779, fax (207) 761-2160, a 17-room National Historic Register mansion. Breakfast is a feast. Seven attractively decorated second- and third-floor guest rooms have private and shared baths. No smoking, no pets. $95-140 d June-mid-Oct., $85-125 d other months.

Newest of Portland's B&Bs is **The Danforth,** 163 Danforth St. at Winter St., Portland 04102, tel. (207) 879-8755 or (800) 991-6557, fax (207) 879-8754, a beautifully restored, 21-room Federal-style mansion. Nine guest rooms have such state-of-the-art amenities as fax service and dataports, as well as cable TV, a/c, phones, and working fireplaces. Climb to the cupola for a great view of the Portland Harbor sunrise, and don't miss the gardens. $115-185 d late May through October, $95-165 d other months.

Built in 1877, **The West End Inn,** 146 Pine St.

SOUTH PORTLAND, JETPORT AREA, SCARBOROUGH

Besides the lodgings listed below, other national hotel and motel chains represented in the Jetport/Maine Mall area are Best Western, Days Inn, Econo Lodge, Holiday Inn, Howard Johnson, Motel 6, Sheraton Tara, and Susse Chalet. Most provide airport shuttle service; inquire when making reservations.

Hotels and Motels

Coastline Inn, 80 John Roberts Rd., So. Portland 04106, tel. (207) 772-3838, fax 772-4238. Behind Maine Mall; $50-95 d; 53 rooms; no pets; open all year.

Comfort Inn, 90 Maine Mall Rd., So. Portland 04106, tel. (207) 775-0409 or (800) 228-5150, fax (207) 775-1755. Convenient location for shopping and Jetport; $90-130 d; comfortable rooms; park-and-fly option (surcharge); 128 rooms; no pets; open all year.

Embassy Suites, 1050 Westbrook St., Portland 04102, tel. (207) 775-2200 or (800) 753-8767, fax (207) 775-4052. Closest lodging to Jetport, special windows reduce noise; $119-189 per suite. 119 suites; excellent on-site restaurant; no pets; indoor pool; fitness center; open all year.

Hampton Inn, 171 Philbrook Ave., So. Portland 04106, tel. (207) 773-4400 or (800) 426-7866, fax (207) 773-6786. Close to Maine Mall; $79-125 d; attentive staff; park-and-fly option (surcharge); 118 rooms; no pets; open all year.

Portland Marriott at Sable Oaks, 200 Sable Oaks Dr., So. Portland 04106, tel. (207) 871-8000 or (800) 228-9290, fax (207) 871-7971. Glitzy modern hotel near Maine Mall; $99-159 d; 227 rooms; small pets allowed ($20); indoor pool; fitness center; adjacent golf course; open all year.

Fairfield Inn, 66 Spring St., Scarborough 04074, tel./fax (207) 883-0300 or (800) 228-2800. Part of the Marriott chain, near the junction of I-95 and I-295; $60-109 d; 120 rooms; park-and-fly option; no pets; outdoor pool; open all year.

Peter A. McKernan Hospitality Center

On the campus of Southern Maine Technical College, the Peter A. McKernan Hospitality Center, Fort Rd., So. Portland 04106, tel./fax (207) 767-9672, is the proving ground for culinary and hospitality students, and they aim to please. Eight lovely bayview rooms; turn-of-the-20th-century brick building; $150 d. The dining room serves imaginative, inexpensive-to-moderate meals. Shorefront walking/biking trails nearby. The center keeps a low profile, yet rooms are booked far ahead. Call for brochure and details.

at Neal St., Portland 04102, tel. (207) 772-1377 or (800) 338-1377, has five second- and third-floor guest rooms with private baths and TV. No pets, no a/c. $99-169 d midsummer weekends, $79-149 d other times.

Staying at **The Pomegranate Inn,** 49 Neal St. at Carroll St., Portland 04102, tel. (207) 772-1006 or (800) 356-0408, fax (207) 773-4426, is an adventure in itself, with faux painting, classical statuary, and whimsical touches everywhere. The elegant 1884 Italianate mansion has seven guest rooms and a suite, all with private baths and phones. Two-night minimum summer weekends and holidays. No pets, no smoking, no children under 16. $125-165 d late May through October, $95-135 other months.

Portland Summer Hostel: Affiliated with Hostelling International, the 48-bed Portland Summer Hostel, 645 Congress St., in Portland Hall, Portland 04101, tel. (207) 874-3281, is located in a Best Western motel-turned-university dorm. Doubles with private bath go for $15 a night, including linens, free parking, and a bagel-and-coffee breakfast. There are laundry facilities and a luggage storage area. Reservations are essential—this place is popular, and the congenial international atmosphere is contagious. Open June 1 to the third week in August. Off-season address: Portland Summer Hostel, c/o HI-AYH, Boston, MA 02215, tel. (617) 731-8096.

Beyond Downtown

The B&Bs listed here are open all year, as is one of the country inns. The other inn, and the campgrounds, are seasonal. Island accommodations are included under "Casco Bay Islands," below.

B&Bs: Here's a sleeper, west of I-295 but an easy drive into town. Elizabeth and Doug Andrews have carefully restored the 18th-century **Andrews Lodging Bed & Breakfast,** 417 Auburn St., Rt. 26, Portland 04103, tel. (207) 797-9157, fax 797-9040, which has welcomed guests since the 1920s. Five guest rooms share two baths, a suite has its own bath. Rates run $68-150 d. Big pluses are a lovely solarium, a fully equipped second-floor guest kitchen, and Elizabeth's exquisite gardens. Three kinds of berries grow on the one-and-a-half-acre grounds. In winter, there's ice-skating out back, with skates available for guests. No smoking,

no small children. Pets are $10 extra on first visit, free thereafter.

Slightly farther out from downtown Portland, Sally Merrill's **Sunrise Acres Farm,** 42 Winn Rd., Cumberland 04021, tel. (207) 829-5594, is a 200-acre operation with resident sheep, cattle, and chickens. The decor is elegant, and you can play the grand piano, hang out in the library, or visit the livestock. Three second-floor rooms, one with private bath; one ground-floor room with private bath. Rates are $75 d with private bath, lower for shared bath and off season. No smoking, some pets, no credit cards.

In nearby **Gorham,** an interesting college community 10 miles west of Portland, the Carlozzi family's **PineCrest Bed & Breakfast,** 91 South St., Rt. 114, just off Rt. 25, Gorham 04038, tel. (207) 839-5843, is an updated 19th-century home with three second-floor guest rooms and another room and a suite on the first floor. All have private baths. Prices range $75-90 d mid-June to mid-October, $55-80 d other months. Breakfast is continental. No children under 10, no pets.

Inns: If your wallet and your wardrobe are up to it, you can splurge at a couple of upper-level inns south of Portland. Or you can opt for the third one in the less-stratospheric category. Seven miles south of downtown Portland, **Inn by the Sea,** 40 Bowery Beach Rd., Rt. 77, Cape Elizabeth 04107, tel. (207) 799-3134 or (800) 888-4287, fax (207) 799-4779, is a well-managed modern complex with the stylishly casual feel of an upscale summer house. Forty-three one- and two-bedroom suites and cottages have kitchen facilities and spectacular water views. Best of all, a boardwalk winds down through the saltmarsh to the southern end of Crescent Beach State Park. Facilities at the inn, built in 1986, include a tennis court, outdoor pool, croquet lawn, and bicycles. Rooms go for $180-410 d, not counting breakfast, July and August; $95-270 d other months. Priceless Audubon prints cover the walls in the appropriately named **Audubon Room,** tel. (207) 767-0888, where moderate-to-expensive breakfasts and dinners are served daily to guests—and to the public by reservation. (Try the crab cakes.) Open all year.

You'll get a sense of the **Black Point Inn Resort,** 510 Black Point Rd., Prouts Neck, Scarborough 04074, tel. (207) 883-4126 or (800) 258-0003, fax (207) 883-9976, as soon as you observe the honeymooners, yuppies, dowagers, and sedate film stars rubbing shoulders here. Many guests are repeats. Many also never leave Prouts Neck during their stay—everything's here for a real getaway, including tennis courts, 18-hole golf course, indoor and outdoor pools, bicycles, fitness room, wicker chairs on the glassed-in veranda, sand beach, local library, gift shop, and walking paths. The inn's superb dining room is open to the public by reservation only; don't show up without a jacket. Seventy-four rooms and six suites in the inn and cottages, most with water views; three-night minimum in midsummer. No pets; no children under eight mid-July to mid-August. Rates are $280-370 d, MAP, July to Labor Day; $140-280 d, other times (B&B May and November). Open May-Nov., the inn is 12 miles south of downtown Portland.

Another longtime favorite, across the street from neighborhoody Higgins Beach, is the informal **Higgins Beach Inn,** 34 Ocean Ave., Scarborough 04074, tel. (207) 883-6684, fax 885-9570, just what your mind's eye might conjure up as a traditional, turn-of-the-century summer waterfront hotel. Under new ownership since 1997, the inn has almost the same rates— $55-80 d for the 24 clean, no-frills rooms (14 with private bath). Two-night minimum for major holiday weekends. MAP arrangements are also available, and are a good idea, since the inn's Garofalo's Restaurant has a creative Italian slant, emphasizing seafood. The restaurant is open to the public 5-8:30 p.m. nightly; reservations are advisable, especially on weekends. Children are welcome. No pets, no smoking in guest rooms. Open mid-May to mid-November.

Campgrounds

If camping is more in your budget and interest, two spots are within relatively easy access to downtown Portland. Closest is **Wassamki Springs,** 855 Saco St., Westbrook 04092, tel. (207) 839-4276, a family-run Good Sampark campground on a private lake with a mile of sandy beachfront; it features 160 wooded and shorefront sites on 35 acres. Peak-season tentsites are $15-26 a night (two adults and two kids); discounts for seniors. Recreational facilities include canoe and paddleboat rentals, playground, lots of games—also open to noncampers. Noise rules are strictly enforced. Five miles west of I-95, via Exit 7 or Exit 8. Open May to mid-October.

Bayley's Camping Resort, 27 Ross Rd., Box T-5, Scarborough 04074, tel. (207) 883-6043, is the Disney World of campgrounds, with 470 well-kept sites, well-organized day and night entertainment, and a free double-decker shuttle bus for trips to area attractions. You certainly won't be lonely; facilities include three swimming pools, a rec hall, laundry, horseback-riding ring, playground, horseshoe pits, jacuzzis, general store, restaurant, and mini-golf. From Memorial Day weekend to Labor Day, sites are $29.50 (two persons); kids under two are free. Reservations are advisable mid-June through August; full prepayment is required for one- to four-night reservations. Open May to Columbus Day, with reduced rates early and late in the season.

FOOD

In addition to the many eating choices listed here and in the accompanying chart, check the *Go* supplement in each Thursday's *Portland Press Herald.* Under "Potluck," you'll find listings of **public meals,** usually benefiting nonprofit organizations. Prices are always quite low ($4-6 for adults, $2-4 for children), mealtimes quite early (5 or 6 p.m.), and the flavor quite local.

Downtown Portland

Breakfast: Portland is a breakfast kind of place. Best known for earliest and most filling breakfast, **Becky's Diner,** 390 Commercial St., Old Port, tel. (207) 773-7070, now serves dinner Tuesday through Saturday. How can you beat a haddock dinner for $5.95? Becky's is famous; don't miss it. Open Monday 4 a.m.-2 p.m., Tues.-Fri. 4 a.m.-9 p.m., Saturday 12:01 a.m.-9 p.m., Sunday 12:01 a.m.-1 p.m.

Ethnic Fare: If you like sushi, beat a path to the sushi bar of **Sapporo,** 230 Commercial St., Union Wharf, Old Port, tel. (207) 772-1233, Maine's best—and longest-lasting—Japanese restaurant. Presided over by owner Yoshi

Hayashi, the sushi bar uses fish from Boston, New York, and even Japan. Kids gravitate to the tempura and teriyaki—and of course they're entranced by the in-your-face, table-side preparation. Reservations advisable on weekends. Open for lunch weekdays 11:45 a.m.-2 p.m. and dinner daily at 5 p.m.; no lunch Saturday or Sunday.

If you want Italian cuisine, you'll find several good representatives in town. Best is **The Roma,** 769 Congress St., near Maine Medical Center, tel. (207) 773-9873, in the historic, 19th-century Rines Mansion. Superb Italian and seafood menu at moderate-to-expensive prices in a romantic setting. A Roma specialty is twin lobsters, but diving into a lobster in such elegant surroundings is a lot less fun than enjoying it where you don't have to worry about making a mess, squirting lobster juice in your eyes (or someone else's), dropping shells on the rug, or sending your clothes to the dry cleaner's. Reservations are advisable on weekends. Open weekdays 11:30 a.m.-9 p.m., Saturday 5-9:30 p.m. Also open Sunday 5-8 p.m., June through October. A more family-oriented restaurant, and one that's endured since 1936, is the Reali family's **Village Café,** 112 Newbury St., east of Franklin St., tel. (207) 772-5320. The huge place has an inexpensive menu of respectable Italian food, healthful specials, and free crayons for the kids. Open Mon.-Thurs. 11 a.m.-10 p.m., Fri.-Sat. 11 a.m.-11 p.m., Sunday 11:30 a.m.-8 p.m. (to 9:30 p.m. July and August).

Determinedly Eclectic: Be prepared for surprises, menu-wise, at **Café Always,** 47 Middle St., east of Franklin St., tel. (207) 774-9399—one of Portland's most creative restaurants. Abiding by "no food rules," its nightly rundown might include grilled lobster with Jamaican rum sauce, an unusual Thai dish, and a new twist on northern Italian. But that's only the beginning. Decor is whimsical in this smallish place; reservations are essential. Open Tues.-Sun. for dinner and Sunday for brunch.

Whimsy is also the hallmark at **Katahdin,** 106 High St., corner of Spring St., near the civic center, tel. (207) 774-1740, named after Maine's highest mountain. Murals cover the walls—even in the restrooms, which are outfitted with statuary, plants, and lounge chairs. Regional American specialties are crab cakes (two huge ones)

and pan-fried oysters, but pot roast and London broil have their devotees, too. A secret vegetable concoction, dubbed "red stuff" by regulars, comes with meals. Generous portions and friendly, efficient service. No reservations, so expect to wait on Saturday night. Open Mon.-Thurs. 5-10 p.m., Fri.-Sat. 5-11 p.m.

Bistros: Newest trendy place is **Aubergine,** 555 Congress St., tel. (207) 874-0680, the current home of chef David Grant, who earned his stripes (and stars) at two long-gone Camden restaurants. Occupying the former Raffles Bookstore Café digs, this one's a winner, with attentive service, a carefully crafted French menu, and an adventuresome list of French and American wines. Entrée range is $14-16. No smoking. Nearby is the new L.L. Bean Factory Store. No reservations, so you'll probably need to wait. Open 5:30-10 p.m. Tues.-Sat. and 11 a.m.-2 p.m. Sunday for brunch.

Ever since it opened in 1994, **Bella Bella,** 606 Congress St., tel. (207) 780-1260, has been a runaway hit. At this "rustic Italian" bistro a few steps from the art museum, you can order pasta with no sauce, sauce with no pasta, whatever—everything's made to order. No reservations; the wait is typically 15 or 20 minutes. Beer and wine (large list) only; no smoking. Open daily for dinner, plus breakfast Friday and Saturday.

Seafood: Ask around (even on the Internet) and everyone will tell you the best seafood in town is at **Street & Company,** 33 Wharf St., Old Port, tel. (207) 775-0887. Fresh, beautifully prepared fish is what you get—in an informal, brick-walled environment that's been here since 1989. A local newspaper called this "the best place for dinner if money's no object—or even if it is." Prices are moderate to expensive. Don't show up without a reservation. Beer and wine only; no smoking. Owner Dana Street is also behind the Fore Street Restaurant. Open for dinner at 5:30 p.m. daily.

Pasta, Vegetarian Fare: You never know what'll be on the menu (Indonesian chicken, North African stuffed peppers, Caribbean shrimp cakes?) at funky **Pepperclub,** 78 Middle St., east of Franklin St., tel. (207) 772-0531, but take the risk. Vegetarian specials are always available, and organic meats. If your kids are even vaguely adventuresome, they'll find food to

FOOD IN GREATER PORTLAND

Several years ago, word went around that Portland had more restaurant seats per capita than any other American city. Who counts such things, anyway? But the rumor rings true when you consider the incredible array of choices—from Anthony's Italian Kitchen to the Zuñi Bar and Grill—at least a hundred in downtown Portland alone.

ETHNIC FARE

Afghan
Afghan Restaurant, 419 Congress St., tel. (207) 773-3431. Portland's first and only Afghan eatery. Lots of veggie options, interesting fruit-based entrées, lamb galore. BYOL. Lunch and dinner daily.

Caribbean, Etc.
Cotton St. Cantina, 10 Cotton St., Old Port, tel. (207) 775-3222. Mexican, Cuban, Hawaiian, and Caribbean cuisine, with a dash of Brazil. Homemade tortillas. No smoking. Lunch weekdays, dinner Mon.-Saturday.

Federal Spice, 225 Federal St., east of Franklin St., tel. (207) 774-6404. Order at the counter; everything under $6. Be sure to try yam fries and Southwestern specialties. No credit cards; beer and wine only. Lunch and dinner Mon.-Saturday.

Mediterranean
Free Street Taverna, 128 Free St., near Portland Museum of Art, tel. (207) 774-1114. The city's only Greek restaurant. Incredible wall art. Live music weekends, impromptu entertainment other nights in the downstairs bar. Happy hour 4-7 p.m. weekdays. Dinner daily.

Ribollita, 41 Middle St., Old Port, tel. (207) 774-2972. Small, casual, very popular spot with primo rustic-Italian fare. Reservations advisable. No smoking; beer and wine only. Dinner Mon.-Saturday.

Tex-Mex and Variations
Margarita's Mexican Restaurant and Watering Hole, 242 St. John St., near Union Station Plaza, tel. (207) 874-6444. Part of a New England mini-chain. Moderate (or lower) prices, ultragenerous portions, and close-to-authentic cuisine. Dinner daily; happy hour 4-7 p.m. weekdays. Another branch is at 11 Brown St., tel. (207) 774-9398, across from the civic center.

Zuñi Bar & Grill, 21 Pleasant St., tel. (207) 774-5260. High ceilings, Southwestern colors, amazing tequilas, and determinedly creative entrées. No smoking. Dinner Tues.-Sunday.

Thai, Vietnamese
Bangkok City Center Thai and Seafood Restaurant, 1 City Center, Temple and Free Sts., tel. (207) 772-1118. In an Old Port office complex. Thai-style floor seating in one section. Dinner reservations advisable on weekends. Lunch Mon.-Sat. (excellent buffet), dinner daily.

Saigon Thinh Thanh Vietnamese Restaurant, 608 Congress St., near Portland Museum of Art, tel. (207) 773-2932. Best place to dive into Vietnamese cuisine. Check out the incredible fish tank. Lunch Mon.-Sat., dinner daily.

DOWNTOWN PORTLAND

Expensive
The Back Bay Grill, 65 Portland St., near the main post office, tel. (207) 772-8833. Superbly creative menu; art-deco bistro ambience; first-rate wine list. Reservations advisable, no smoking. Dinner Mon.-Saturday.

David's Restaurant, 164 Middle St., Old Port, tel. (207) 774-4340. Elegant lower-level room with continental menu. Casual first-floor dining, with raw bar. Lunch, dinner, and Saturday and Sunday brunch.

Fore Street, 288 Fore St., Old Port, tel. (207) 775-2717. Noted Maine chef Sam Hayward switched from fussy haute cuisine to chic, brick-oven country fare. No smoking; reservations advisable. Dinner daily.

Moderate
The Barking Squirrel Café, Deering Oaks Park, near I-295, tel. (207) 774-5514. Charming castle-in-the-park with indoor and outdoor tables. Creditable eclectic menu; summer clambakes. Croquet and badminton rentals; skate rentals. Open all year. Lunch and dinner Wed.-Sat., Sunday brunch.

Café Uffa!, 190 State St., at Longfellow Sq., tel. (207) 775-3380. Brunch is the highlight at this ultra-casual, trendy spot at the edge of the Downtown Arts District. No reservations, so expect to wait. Beer and wine only; no smoking. Breakfast and dinner Wed.-Sat., Sunday brunch. *(continues)*

FOOD IN GREATER PORTLAND

(continued)

Hugo's Portland Bistro, 88 Middle St., corner of Franklin St., Old Port, tel. (207) 774-8538. Eclectic place with creative continental menu. Reservations needed, no smoking. Dinner Tues.-Saturday.

Madd Apple Cafe, 23 Forest Ave., next to Portland Performing Arts Center, tel. (207) 774-9698. Veteran café with up-to-the-minute menu and artistic flair. No smoking; beer and wine only. Reservations advisable, especially before PPAC performances. Dinner Tues.-Saturday.

Seamen's Club Restaurant, 375 Fore St., Old Port, tel. (207) 772-7311. Longtime Old Port favorite for chowder and sandwiches; harbor glimpses through upstairs Palladian window. Lunch and dinner daily.

Tabitha Jean's Restaurant, 94 Free St., next to Civic Center, tel. (207) 780-8966. Named for Stephen King's wife and owned by their daughter; regional American menu, including tasty vegetarian and Cajun entrées; gaining popularity fast. No smoking. Breakfast, lunch, and dinner Tues.-Sun., Sunday brunch.

Walter's Café, 15 Exchange St., Old Port, tel. (207) 871-9258. Casual, ultra-popular spot, especially at lunchtime, when noise levels sometimes elevate. Interesting specials, excellent service. No smoking, no reservations. Lunch Mon.-Sat., dinner daily.

West Side Restaurant, 58 Pine St., near Maine Medical Center, tel. (207) 773-8223. Small neighborhood place with creative menu (excellent venison) and summertime patio tables; service a tad slow. No smoking. Lunch and dinner Tues.-Sun., Sunday brunch.

Funky, Inexpensive

Kinicky's, 538 Congress St., next to L.L. Bean, tel. (207) 773-5514. The back room is a '50s throwback guaranteed to make any boomer grin. Try the Donna Reed or Popeye stone-baked pizza at a Formica table, watch old TV reruns, and don't skip the soda fountain. No smoking. Lunch and dinner Mon.-Saturday.

Silly's, 40 Washington Ave., near Cumberland Ave., tel. (207) 772-0360. Eminently eclectic spot with adventuresome take-out or eat-in menu. Jerk chicken and unusual wraps (called Abdullahs) are specialties; great pizza, fries, and milkshakes. No credit cards, no smoking; beer and wine only. Lunch and dinner daily; live music some evenings.

Breakfast and Beyond

Friendship Cafe, 703 Congress St., tel. (207) 871-5005. A relative newcomer, with pumpkin pancakes and great service. Open for breakfast and lunch Mon.-Sat. at 6 a.m., Sunday 6:30 a.m.

Marcy's Breakfast and Lunch, 47 Oak St., corner of Free St., tel. (207) 774-9713. Small, creative operation near art museum. Bring cards: booths have built-in cribbage tables. No credit cards. Open 5 a.m. daily.

Cybercafé

JavaNet, 37 Exchange St., Old Port, tel. (800) 528-2638. Dataport central for cyberjunkies. Hourly Internet rates, your computer or theirs. Tin ceiling, brick walls, decent lighting, plus coffees, sandwiches, and pastries. No smoking. Opens 7 a.m. week-

like here—and prices to match. No reservations, but you can hang out in the lounge with a microbrew or chardonnay. No smoking, no credit cards. Open daily at 5 p.m.

An Old Port fixture since 1989, **Fresh Market Pasta,** 43 Exchange St., Old Port, tel. (207) 773-7146, seems to be everyone's source for the best of what we used to call noodles and macaroni. Besides the fresh pasta (even lobster ravioli), the restaurant offers salads (some sans pasta), super bread, designer coffees, and, if you need more, beer and Italian desserts and wines. Open daily for eat-in or take-out lunch and dinner.

On the Waterfront: It's tough to top **DiMillo's Floating Restaurant,** 25 Long Wharf, Commercial St., Old Port, tel. (207) 772-2216, for its prime waterfront location. The 206-foot converted ferryboat has been tied up here since 1982. Best spots for lunch or a light meal are the outdoor decks. The menu isn't extraordinary, but the view is—Portland Harbor is everywhere you look. Best time to be here is 9 p.m., May-Oct., when the cruise ship *Scotia Prince* passes by, lights ablaze, en route to Nova Scotia. No reservations, but you shouldn't have to wait long for one of the 600 seats. Free parking. Open daily 11 a.m.-11 p.m.

days, 8 a.m. weekends; closes between 10 p.m. and midnight.

Carry-Out and Delis
Aurora Provisions, 64 Pine St., near Maine Medical Center, tel. (207) 871-0201. Nirvana for gourmets and gourmands; choosing is agonizing. Boston's North End transported to Portland's West End. Owned by the founders of anything-goes Café Always. Open 7 a.m.-6 p.m. daily.
    The Spirited Gourmet, 142 St. John St., near Union Station Plaza, tel. (207) 773-2919. Condiments, gourmet goodies, fabulous cold and hot sandwiches (even no-fat ones), daily specials. Wine for off-premises picnics. No smoking, no credit cards. Open weekdays 10 a.m.-6 p.m., Saturday 10 a.m.-2 p.m.

SOUTH PORTLAND/SCARBOROUGH

Inexpensive to Moderate
The Olive Garden Italian Restaurant, 200 Gorham Rd., near Maine Mall, South Portland, tel. (207) 874-9005. Same as others in this national chain: great place to fill up hungry teenagers. Efficient service. Lunch and dinner daily.
    Spurwink Country Kitchen, 150 Spurwink Rd., Rt. 77, Scarborough, tel. (207) 799-1177. Family-oriented, informal eatery noted for its comfort-food menu (boiled dinner, shepherd's pie, homemade soups). Crayon baskets keep the kids busy. No smoking. Beer and wine only. Lunch and dinner Tues.-Sun. mid-April to mid-October.

Moderate to Expensive
Bay Harbor, 231 Front St., South Portland, tel. (207) 799-5552. Fantastic view of Portland and the harbor. Steak and seafood specialties. Reservations advisable, no smoking. Call for directions. Lunch and dinner daily.
    Fuji, 50 Maine Mall Rd., near Western Ave., South Portland, tel. (207) 772-0006. Huge Japanese menu with Thai, Korean, and Chinese additions. Great sushi bar. Comfortable, tasteful ambience. Lunch and dinner daily.
    Snow Squall, 18 Ocean St., South Portland, tel. (207) 799-2232. Just over the new Casco Bay Bridge from downtown Portland. Cheery decor in a rehabbed trolley barn. Superb Sunday brunch; plan to skip dinner. Lunch and dinner daily.

FALMOUTH

Casa Napoli Ristorante, 204 Rt. 1, Falmouth, tel. (207) 781-3342. Well beyond Naples, with lots of Tuscan specialties, fantastic veal dishes, homemade pasta, excellent Italian wine list. Bistro ambience. No smoking, reservations advisable. Lunch weekdays, dinner daily.
    European Bakery and Tea Room, 395 Rt. 1, Falmouth, tel. (207) 781-3541. Genuine Old World, high-cal goodies created from scratch by a Swiss-Greek pastry chef with Maine links. Fabulous tortes and cheesecakes. Open daily.
    Iguana Bay, 196 Rt. 1, 2nd floor of Portland Athletic Club, Falmouth, tel. (207) 781-5308. Unlikely location for an always-interesting Tex-Mex menu. Tropical ambience, nonstop free chips and salsa. No smoking. Lunch, dinner, and Sunday brunch; happy hour Mon.-Sat. 4-6 p.m.

The color's a lot more local just down the street at **The Porthole,** 20 Custom House Wharf, Commercial St., Old Port, tel. (207) 774-6652, a bit of a dive where the all-you-can-eat Friday fish fry ($3.95) pulls in *real* fishermen, in-the-know locals, and fearless tourists. Under second-generation ownership since 1995, the Porthole is still the Porthole. Open daily 6 a.m.-9 p.m.
    Street Food: Portland has maybe a dozen street vendors on a regular basis, but the prize for longevity goes to Mark Gatti, of **Mark's Hot Dogs,** usually set up at the corner of Exchange and Middle Sts., in the Old Port, since 1983.

He gets going about 8:30 a.m. weekdays (plus Saturday in summer) and by noontime looks up at a long line of faithful regulars. Hot dogs, sausages, sauerkraut, condiments—he's got the works.
    Coffee and Tea: You'll never run out of places to overload on caffeine in downtown Portland; coffeehouses seem to have sprung up everywhere you look. **Coffee by Design,** 620 Congress St., Portland 04101, tel. (207) 772-5533, is almost more art gallery than coffeehouse, and it's one of the "hippest" hangouts. The wall art is a big deal here, and you're welcome to buy it. Open from 7 a.m. weekdays,

8 a.m. weekends. A branch coffeehouse/espresso bar, **Coffee by Design Monument Square,** tel. (207) 761-2424, is at 24 Monument Square. **Java Joe's,** 13 Exchange St., Portland 04101, tel. (207) 761-5637, conscientiously buys coffee from Equal Exchange, supporting fair prices and labor practices. Across from The Movies, it's a locale for everything from checkers matches to jazz concerts. **Green Mountain Coffee Roasters,** 15 Temple St., Portland 04101, tel. (207) 773-4475, is high on the list of places to see and be seen. And the coffee is too good.

Ex-professor Jo Anna Spruill runs **Sweet Annie's Tea Shop,** 642 Congress St., Portland 04101, tel. (207) 773-3353. Everything's sedate, even ritualistic in this tiny tearoom: china cups and teapots; little tables and dried flowers; delicious scones. It's a feminine kind of place, but tea lovers of any gender shouldn't pass up this chance for the best cuppa in town. Homemade soups, huge sandwiches, and light suppers are also available. No smoking. Open Tues.-Fri. 9 a.m.-7 p.m., Saturday and Sunday 11 a.m.-5 p.m.

South Portland

Ricetta's Pizzeria, 29 Western Ave., Rt. 9, between Maine Mall and Portland Jetport, South Portland, tel. (207) 775-7400, is regularly voted Greater Portland's best pizza palace. Not surprising when you see the lunchtime-only pizza smorgasbord—all the pizza you can eat, plus salad and soup, for $7.95 ($4.25 for kids under 12). Specialty pizzas are outstanding, or you can invent your own combo. Also on the menu are antipasti, calzones, giant salads, soups, pasta dishes, and high-calorie desserts. Open for lunch and dinner Sun.-Thurs. to 10 p.m., Friday and Saturday to 11 p.m.

One of Greater Portlands best **Chinese** restaurants is tucked away in a mini-mall near the Maine Mall. **Imperial Garden,** 220 Maine Mall Rd., South Portland, tel. (207) 774-4292, produces high-quality Hunan and Szechuan cuisine in an attractive setting. Prices are very reasonable. Open daily for lunch and dinner.

How about a five-course lunch, with a matchless view, for under $10? The students in the hospitality program at Southern Maine Technical College need practice for their cooking and service skills, so their "lab" is the 75-seat restaurant at the **Peter McKernan Hospitality Center** on the college's Spring Point campus, Fort Rd., South Portland, tel. (207) 767-9612. The well-prepared lunch is served attentively Wed.-Fri., promptly at noon, mid-September to early May (except during school vacations). The menu changes daily, with choices for every course. Depending on your entrée, it'll cost $5-7, plus the price of coffee if you request it. No liquor (don't bring any; this is a public school), no credit cards. Reservations required. After lunch, you can stroll the grounds and follow the Spring Point Shoreway down to Willard Beach.

Cape Elizabeth

The Good Table, Rt. 77, Cape Elizabeth, tel. (207) 799-4663, a small, casual place near the entrance to Two Lights State Park, has Mediterranean touches, courtesy of the Greek-American owners, and a real-deal two-for-one special Tues.-Thurs.: two meals for $10.95. The same family owns downtown Portland's Free Street Taverna. Funky old photos cover the walls (even in the restrooms), and each table has a jar of crayons. Sunday brunch is jammed. Open Tues.-Fri. 11 a.m.-9 p.m., Saturday 8 a.m.-9 p.m., Sunday 8 a.m.-3 p.m.

Every Mainer has a favorite lobster eatery (besides home), but **The Lobster Shack,** 222 Two Lights Rd., Cape Elizabeth, tel. (207) 799-1677, tops an awful lot of lists. Seniority helps—it's been here since the 1920s. Scenery, too—a panoramic vista in the shadow of Cape Elizabeth Light. Plus the menu—seafood galore (and hot dogs for those who'd rather). Choose a lobster from the tank; indulge in the lobster stew; grab a table on the rocks and watch the world go by. Opt for a sunny day; the lighthouse's foghorn can kill your conversation when the fog rolls in. Open daily 11 a.m.-8 p.m., mid-April to mid-October (to 8:30 in July and August).

Worthwhile Wallet-Cruncher

Here's a pièce de résistance—at, of all places, the Embassy Suites, next to the Portland International Jetport. **The Chef's Table at Café Stroudwater,** 1050 Westbrook St., Portland 04102, tel. (207) 775-0032, offers Portland's first taste of an intriguing European tradition. For $60 pp (including five wines), a group of four (maximum eight) can reserve the Café

Stroudwater's kitchen table, complete with table-cloth and flowers, any night. (Bring your own CDs if you prefer classical music.) You'll meet the chef and kitchen staff, receive an auto-graphed menu, and enjoy a superb six-course meal. The kitchen's air-conditioned, so it's all very comfortable. Count on a three-hour expe-rience, and, needless to say, book far ahead (credit card required). A slightly fancier menu, with pricier wines, is available for $75 pp. Of course, you can also eat in the **Café Stroud-water** itself, a moderate-to-expensive restau-rant with one of Portland's best brunches.

INFORMATION AND SERVICES

The **Visitor Information Center of the Con-vention and Visitors Bureau of Greater Port-land,** 305 Commercial St., Portland 04101, tel. (207) 772-5800, fax 874-9043, is open all year. Hours are Mon.-Fri. 8 a.m.-6 p.m., weekends and holidays 10 a.m.-6 p.m., mid-May to mid-Oc-tober. This changes to Mon.-Fri. 8 a.m.-5 p.m., weekends and holidays 10 a.m.-3 p.m., mid-October to mid-May. The office has public re-strooms.

The Portland Downtown District, an inde-pendent merchants' association, instituted a very successful **Downtown Guides** program in the summer of 1996. Between early June and Labor Day, a handful of young, enthusiastic guides, dressed in purple shirts (monogrammed Visitor Information), khaki shorts, and bush hats, patrol a 65-acre rectangular downtown area bounded by Congress, Franklin, Commercial, and State Streets. The Old Port District and Congress St. are their busiest locations. Car-rying maps, brochures, and cell phones, they're on the streets Mon.-Sat. 11:30 a.m.-8 p.m., Sun-day 9:30 a.m.-5 p.m. Ask them anything; they love the challenge, and, as one visitor noted, they're "relentlessly friendly."

The **Portland Public Library,** 5 Monument Sq., Portland 04101, tel. (207) 871-1700, has an extremely helpful staff, a bright reading room, and a fine children's room (tel. 207-871-1707). You can even check your e-mail on their com-puters. Open Monday, Wednesday, and Friday 9 a.m.-6 p.m.; Tuesday and Thursday noon-9 p.m.; Friday 9 a.m.-5 p.m. Smaller branch li-

braries include **Munjoy Hill,** 44 Moody St., tel. (207) 772-4581; **Reiche,** 166 Brackett St., in the West End, tel. (207) 774-6871; and **River-ton,** 1600 Forest Ave., west of I-295, tel. (207) 797-2915. Reiche and Riverton are part of school/community center complexes.

For **time and temperature information,** call (207) 775-4321; for the current **weather report,** call (207) 775-7741. For **winter parking infor-mation,** call (207) 879-0300.

Emergencies
In Portland, call 911 for **fire, police, or ambu-lance.**

The state's largest hospital, **Maine Medical Center,** 22 Bramhall St., Portland 04101, emer-gency tel. (207) 871-2381, offers round-the-clock emergency-room care and a cafeteria that can turn out cheap and tasty made-to-order omelettes any hour of the day or night. Also in downtown Portland is Catholic **Mercy Hospi-tal,** 144 State St., Portland 04101, emergency tel. (207) 879-3265.

Media
Portland's (and Maine's) major daily newspa-per is the *Portland Press Herald,* published six mornings a week. The *Maine Sunday Telegram* is under the same ownership. The *Press Herald's* Thursday edition carries a special entertainment supplement—*Go*—listing the week's cultural and recreational activities throughout Greater Portland.

A crusading bent and an irreverent attitude mark the free *Casco Bay Weekly,* with thought-ful articles and comprehensive activities list-ings.

Special Discounts
The **Portland Dine-Around Club** gets you two-for-the-price-of-one meals (usually dinner en-trées) at 70 or so restaurants with a wide variety of menus, decor, and price ranges. Member-ship, good for a year, is $30. Some limitations apply, but it's still a bargain. Portland Dine-Around Club, 477 Congress St., Portland 04101, tel. (207) 775-4711.

Those intent on spending a lot of time on the links should consider purchasing an American Lung Association **Golf Privilege Card,** covering greens fees for 70 rounds of golf (at over 50 courses) for $70. It's a great cause. Many courses on the list require reservations 24 or 48 hours in advance, and some require player's fees. Write or call American Lung Association of Maine, 122 State St., Augusta 04330, tel. (800) 458-6472, fax (207) 626-2919.

Postal Service

Portland is the home of Maine's first **postal store,** 400 Congress St., Portland 04101, tel. (207) 871-8464—a glitzy, 6,500-square-foot emporium where you can select your own stamps, buy collectors' packets and books, make photocopies, and send faxes. Waiting lines are short, and self-service machines speed things along. Open Mon.-Fri. 8 a.m.-7 p.m., Saturday 9 a.m.-1 p.m.

Public Restrooms

In the **Old Port** area, you'll find restrooms at the Convention and Visitors Bureau Visitor Information Center (305 Commercial St.), the Spring Street parking garage (45 Spring St.), and the Casco Bay Lines ferry terminal (Commercial and Franklin Sts.).

In **Congress Street,** you can use the facilities at Portland City Hall (389 Congress St.) and the Portland Public Library (5 Monument Sq.).

In **Midtown,** head for the Cumberland County Civic Center (1 Civic Center Sq.). In the **West End,** use Maine Medical Center.

Of course, if you're in a big hurry, be creative and look for restrooms in hotel lobbies, department stores, and police stations.

Photo Services

Portland Photographics, 85 York St., near the new Casco Bay Bridge, Portland 04101, tel. (207) 774-6210, fax 761-4227, is the choice of many professional photographers, but they'll also process your slides in two or three hours and provide free photo mailers (plus free parking).

GETTING THERE

By Air

Delta, tel. (800) 638-7333, Continental, tel. (800) 525-0280, Northwest, tel. (800) 225-2525, USAir, tel. (800) 428-4322, and United, tel. (800) 241-6522, all serve Portland at the **Portland Inter-**

national Jetport, tel. (207) 774-7301. The three-story terminal underwent a multimillion-dollar facelift in 1996 and contains all the amenities—including offices of Thomas Cook travel and Avis, Budget, Hertz, and National car-rental agencies (Alamo and Thrifty have offices at the edge of the airport complex). Visitor information is available at a desk (not always staffed) between the gates and the baggage-claim area. Baggage-handling offices surround the luggage carousels, but if you have an emergency, contact Jetport Manager Jeff Schultes at (207) 773-8462.

By Bus

Concord Trailways, tel. (800) 639-3317, departs downtown Boston (South Station Transportation Center) and Logan Airport for the hundred-mile trip to Portland eight times daily, making pickups at all Logan airline terminals (lower level). Rates are very reasonable. The bright, modern Concord Trailways bus terminal is at 100 Sewall St., about two blocks off I-295, behind the Doubletree Inn (formerly the Ramada Inn). It's not particularly convenient to downtown for pedestrians, but if you need to leave a car, there's a large parking lot, with unlimited free parking. Two daily nonexpress buses continue from Portland along the coast, ending at the Trailways terminal in Bangor.

Vermont Transit Lines, 950 Congress St., Portland, tel. (207) 772-6587 or (800) 537-3330, a division of Greyhound Bus Lines, serves Maine, the rest of New England, and beyond, connecting with Greyhound routes. The schedule is slightly less convenient than that of Concord Trailways, but rates are lower.

Van Service

Mermaid Transportation in Portland, tel. (207) 772-2509 or (800) 696-2463, fax (207) 772-3919, operates the best van service between Boston and Portland (and vice versa). Pickup and dropoff, five times daily, are at Portland Jetport and Logan Airport, by reservation only. Cost is $36 one-way; kids under two are free, bicycles and caged pets are $10 extra. For a small surcharge, pickup and dropoff can be arranged for Falmouth Shopping Center, just north of Portland. Mermaid also will pick up and drop off customers at three Maine Turnpike exits south of Portland.

Highway Access

The major highway access to Portland is the **Maine Turnpike,** which links up with the I-95 interstate highway system at the New Hampshire border.

GETTING AROUND

Parking garages and lots are strategically located all over downtown Portland, particularly in the Old Port and near the civic center. Unless you're lucky, you'll probably waste a lot of time looking for on-street parking (meters start at 25 cents a half-hour), so a garage or lot is the best option. If you land in a garage or lot with a Park & Shop sticker, you can collect free-parking stamps, each good for an hour, from participating shops and restaurants. You could even end up parking for free.

Portland's bus network, **Metro,** 114 Valley St., P.O. Box 1097, Portland 04104, tel. (207) 774-0351, is well planned and often underutilized. Metro produces a colorful, easy-to-read route map and schedule that facilitates getting around—including a loop (Mon.-Sat. only) linking the Portland International Jetport and the Maine Mall (both in South Portland) with downtown Portland. Buses have wheelchair lifts and bike racks (room for two of each). Free transfers are available between routes. Cost per ride is $1 adults, 75 cents students (with ID), free for kids under five. Sunday bus service is very limited, and there's no service on major national holidays.

For a one-and-a-half-hour **narrated sightseeing tour** of Portland in an air-conditioned 25-passenger van, check with your hotel or contact **Mainely Tours,** 5 1/2 Moulton St., Old Port, Portland 04101, tel. (207) 774-0808. Tours start at their office and include Portland Head Light. Since 1995, Kathy and John Jenkins have been heading out four or five times daily, beginning at 9:30 a.m., mid-May to mid-October. Cost is $11 adults, $10 seniors, $6 children 5-11; kids under five are free. Hotel pickups can be arranged, for a fee; reservations are not usually necessary unless you need a pickup.

Portland and South Portland have a dozen **taxi** fleets, most radio-operated. You won't have much luck trying to flag one down on the street. Reliables in Portland are **ABC Taxi,** tel. (207) 772-8685, **Airport Limo & Taxi,** tel. (207) 773-3433, and **Town Taxi,** tel. (207) 773-1711. In South Portland, call **South Portland Taxi,** tel. (207) 767-5200.

For details on **Casco Bay Lines ferry service** to local islands, see "Getting Afloat," above. **Great Chebeague Island** is on the Casco Bay Lines route, but you can also get there via Chebeague Transportation Company (CTC) from nearby Cousins Island, in Yarmouth. All Casco Bay Lines tickets are roundtrip, and they're collected when you board in Portland, so if you manage to get to one of the islands by some other means, such as via the CTC, there's no charge for going from island to island or returning to Portland on a Casco Bay Lines vessel.

CASCO BAY ISLANDS

Of the six year-round islands, Peaks, Great Diamond, Little Diamond, and Cliff fall within Portland's jurisdiction. Long Island seceded from Portland in 1993 to become a separate municipality; Chebeague belongs to the town of Cumberland. Access to the islands described here is via Casco Bay Lines and, in the case of Chebeague, Chebeague Transportation Company.

If you're planning to do any island bicycling (and you should), be sure to send for a copy of *Two Casco Bay Island Bicycle Tours,* published by the Bicycle Transportation Alliance of Portland (P.O. Box 4506, Portland 04112). Cost is $1. The very helpful brochure/map covers bike routes on Peaks, Chebeague, and Long Islands.

Peaks Island

With frequent ferry service to and from downtown Portland, at $5.25 pp (less in winter), Peaks Island is eminently convenient for commuters and visitors alike. The best way to see it is to take a bike ($3.40 extra on the ferry) and pedal around clockwise to the back (east) side, where there are great views and no hint that the island's within spitting distance of downtown Portland. It'll take maybe an hour to do the four-mile island circuit, which has its hilly moments, but don't rush. Bring a picnic and stay the day. (You can walk the circuit in three or four hours.) On

A Chebeague Transportation ferry plies the waters of Casco Bay.

summer afternoons, you can stop in at the **Fifth Maine Regiment Community Center,** Seashore Ave., P.O. Box 41, Peaks Island 04108, tel. (207) 766-2634 or 766-2308, a Victorian Civil War memorial on the southern side of the island. Inside are historical displays and a small gift shop. If the center is closed, sit on the veranda and enjoy the view. Rental bikes are available on the island from Brad Burkholder at **Brad's Bike Rental & Repair,** 115 Island Ave., Peaks Island 04108, tel. (207) 766-5631. Cost is $4 an hour. In winter, there's cross-country skiing and ice-skating.

Facing the Portland skyline just south of the ferry wharf is **Keller's Bed & Breakfast,** 20 Island Ave., Box 8, Peaks Island 04108, tel. (207) 766-2441, where innkeeper Carolyn Parker has four bayview rooms with private baths and separate entrances. The rate of $90 d includes access to a small sand beach and an all-you-can-eat breakfast in the adjoining **Keller's Restaurant.** The friendly 30-seat restaurant, tel. (207) 766-2149, is open daily 8 a.m.-9 p.m., serving homestyle meals; everything's also available for takeout. No credit cards, two-night B&B minimum on weekends.

Great Diamond Island

Here's a totally different scene. In 1891, the U.S. Government began building an Army post on Great Diamond Island, a 15-minute powerboat ride from the Portland harborfront. Completed in 1907, **Fort McKinley** (named after

President William McKinley) became part of Portland Harbor's five-fort defense system during World Wars I and II. When peace descended, the fort's red-brick structures were left to crumble for nearly five decades. In 1984, developers stepped in, purchased the derelicts, and began restoration—albeit not without financial setbacks and opposition from environmental organizations.

Today, the 193-acre **Diamond Cove** enclave boasts stunning barracks-turned-townhomes, single-family houses, a general store (open daily, mid-June-Labor Day), outdoor theater, a beach bar (open mid-June to mid-September), an art gallery, outdoor pool, health club, no cars (only bikes and golf carts), a supervised children's program, and the first-rate **Diamond's Edge Restaurant,** tel. (207) 766-5850, serving lunch and dinner daily, mid-May to early October. The restaurant's Sunday jazz brunches are incredibly popular, as is the Wednesday-night lobster clambake on the beach. The 42-passenger ferry *Quickwater,* operated by Casco Bay Lines, tel. (207) 774-7871, makes express trips year-round, more often in summer. Cost is $6.35. Staying overnight on the island is a big splurge, but a worthwhile one; buying property is another matter altogether. A two-night townhome booking, July-Labor Day, begins at $400 d, plus $70 for each additional person; rates are 15% lower May-June and Sept.-mid-October. No pets. Diamond Cove, P.O. Box 3572, Portland 04104, tel. (207) 766-5804.

Great Chebeague Island

Everyone calls Great Chebeague just "Chebeague" (pronounced shuh-BIG). Yes, there's a Little Chebeague, but it's a state-owned park, and no one lives there. The fourth regular stop on the Casco Bay Lines ferry route, Chebeague is also accessible via Cousins Island in Yarmouth. It's an hour from Portland (docking at **Chandler's Cove,** on the island's west end) and 15 minutes if you go via Yarmouth (arriving at the **Stone Pier,** closer to the east end).

Settled in the mid-18th century by Europeans (and eons earlier by Native Americans), Chebeague is perhaps best known as the source of wooden "stone sloops" that carried granite from Maine quarries to markets all along the eastern seaboard. Ambrose Hamilton, the Scotsman who started the stone-sloop business, still has many descendants on the island.

Chebeague is the largest of the bay's islands —four and a half miles long, one and a half miles wide, and home to 325 or so year-rounders (swelling to around 2,500 in summer) —and the relatively level terrain makes it easy to get around. Don't plan to bring a car; it's too complicated to arrange. If you need a lift on the island, just call **Veterans' Taxi,** tel. (207) 846-4876.

The best way to get a sense of the place is to bring a bike, requiring a small fee on the ferry. There's no bike-rental place near Chebeague's Casco Bay Lines dock, but **Great Island Bike Rentals,** tel. (207) 846-6568, is based at Sunset House Bed & Breakfast, just up the road from the Chebeague Transportation Company dock. Also, a generous island fellow makes a few bikes available free in his yard, but you can't be choosy. You just borrow one and return it before you leave. From the Stone Pier, his house is on the left side of South Road, just before you reach the Nellie G. Café. You can do a leisurely 10-mile circuit of the island in a couple of hours, but don't rush. The terrain is almost entirely level; no challenge here for big-time cyclists. Pick up an island map at the Portland terminal or on the ferry; all the high points are listed, including two beach-access points off North Road. Along the way is the **Cobbler Shop,** 408 North Rd., tel. (207) 846-7992, where island jill-of-all-trades (including master plumber) Beverly Johnson sells Maine crafts and collectibles.

The shop is open daily in summer and Saturday, Sunday, and Wednesday in winter.

If the tide is right, you can pack a picnic lunch, cross the sandspit from The Hook, and explore **Little Chebeague.** Start out about two hours before low tide (preferably around new moon or full moon, when the most water drains away) and plan to be back on Chebeague no later than two hours after low tide.

Just east of Little Chebeague is state-owned **Crow Island,** beginning of the **Maine Island Trail,** an island-to-island boating route. If you have a sea kayak, it's a lovely little island to explore.

Back on Great Chebeague, when you're ready for a swim, head for **Hamilton Beach,** a beautiful small stretch of sand lined with dune grass, not far from the Chebeague Island Inn. (There's a potty in the little beach shack, known locally as "Phil's Camp.") For a fee, golfers can do nine holes at the **Great Chebeague Golf Club** (207) 846-9478, founded in 1923. Non-members can play anytime except Monday and Thursday mornings. It's possible to rent clubs for $10 a day and pull-carts for $2; a dress code is enforced. Also on this part of the island is **East End Point,** with a spectacular panoramic view of Halfway Rock and the bay. In winter, you can cross-country ski on island trails and the beach, or ice-skate on Sanford Doughty's well-maintained pond.

About three-quarters of a mile from the Stone Pier is the **Chebeague Orchard Inn,** Box 453, Chebeague Island 04017, tel./fax (207) 846-9488, Vickie and Neil Taliento's comfortable, antiques-filled home. Five rooms—all with handmade quilts, some with water views—share one and a half baths. Rates are $80-100 d Memorial Day to mid-October, $64-80 d other months. The congenial Talientos are big supporters of the Maine Island Trail Association, which begins near Chebeague, so you'll get a five percent discount if you arrive by kayak. Coffee's ready at 7 a.m.; breakfast is a feast—overlooking the backyard's bird feeders and apple orchard. There are bikes for guests, a fireplace in the common room, and tons of helpful advice about the island. No smoking, no pets. Open all year.

Beverly Johnson and Becca Rich operate **Cobbler's Place Bed & Breakfast,** 408 North Rd., Chebeague Island 04017, tel. (207) 846-

1237 or 846-4850, fax (207) 846-3587, next to the Cobbler Shop. An informal spot, the B&B has two guest rooms for $60 each—or both for $99, including continental breakfast and use of the kitchen and laundry. Open all year.

Overlooking the Stone Pier and the golf course, the **Chebeague Island Inn,** Chebeague Island 04017, tel. (207) 846-5155, is an imposing three-story hotel with a spectacular sunset-view veranda. Innkeepers Jan and Dick Bowden have been running the operation since 1989, but the inn's been here for decades. Twenty-one comfortable, second- and third-floor guest rooms (15 with private bath) go for $85-125 d, including breakfast, during July and August, $65-110 d May, June, and September. Higher-priced rooms have water views. The dining room, with moderate-to-expensive continental fare and great homemade desserts, serves 1-3 meals daily, depending on the season. Dress is informal. In the basement is the Bounty Pub, a fun

place to gather—as is the massive Great Room, with a huge stone fireplace, on the first floor. No smoking in the rooms or dining room, no pets, no minimum stay. The inn is open mid-May to late September.

Year-round, stop in for lunch or dinner at the **Nellie G. Café,** South Rd., about three-quarters of a mile from the Stone Pier, Chebeague Island 04017, tel. (207) 846-3882, named after a ferry that once served the island. Established in 1995, the café resides in a renovated Cape with about two dozen seats. Everyone's friendly and service is speedy at this very popular spot. A specialty is island crabmeat pie ($13.95), and salad dressings are creative, but the biggest asset is a superb wine list, allegedly recommended by an eminent wine columnist. The take-out menu has pizza, burgers ($3.25 and up), and dollar hot dogs. Open daily 11 a.m.-8 p.m., in summer, closed Monday after Columbus Day.

FREEPORT

Freeport has a special claim to historic fame—it's the place where Maine parted company from Massachusetts in 1820. The documents were signed on March 15, probably in the Jameson Tavern (now a restaurant), making Maine its own separate state.

At the height of the local mackerel-packing industry here, countless tons of the bony fish were shipped out of South Freeport, often in ships built on the shores of the Harraseeket River. Splendid relics of the shipbuilders' era still line the streets of South Freeport—and no architecture buff should miss a walk, cycle, or drive through the village. Even downtown Freeport still reflects the shipbuilder's craft, with contemporary shops tucked in and around handsome historic houses. Some have been converted to B&Bs, others are boutiques, and one even disguises the local McDonald's franchise.

Today, Freeport is best known as the mecca for the shop-till-you-drop set. Ground zero, of course, is sportswear giant L.L. Bean, which has been here since 1912, when founder Leon Leonwood Bean began making his trademark hunting boots (and also unselfishly handed out hot tips on where the fish were biting). More

than 120 retail operations now fan out from that epicenter, and you can find almost anything in Freeport (pop. about 6,900)—except maybe a parking spot in midsummer.

When (or if) you tire of shopping, you can always find quiet refuge in the town's preserves and parks—Mast Landing Sanctuary, Wolf Neck Woods State Park, and Winslow Memorial Park —as well as plenty of local color at the Town Wharf in the still honest-to-goodness fishing village of South Freeport.

An orientation note: Don't be surprised to receive directions (particularly for South Freeport) relative to "the Big Indian." This is a 40-foot-tall landmark at the junction of Rt. 1 and South Freeport Road. If you stop at the Maine Information Center in Yarmouth and continue on Rt. 1 toward Freeport, you can't miss it, just north of the Freeport Inn and the Casco Bay Motel.

SHOPPING

Logically, this category must come first in any discussion of Freeport, since shopping's the biggest game in town. It's pretty much a given that anyone who visits Freeport intends to darken the door of at least one shop. If it's *only* one, it's likely to be "Bean's."

The whole world beats a path to **L.L. Bean,** 95 Main St., Rt. 1, Freeport 04033, tel. (207) 865-4761 or (800) 341-4341—or so it seems in July, August, and December. Established as a hunting/fishing supply shop, this giant sports outfitter now draws nearly four million shoppers and takes in close to $1 billion annually. The last addition to the main store cost some $10 million, increased floor space to nearly 170,000 square feet, and contained a fly-fishing pond and a pseudo-mountain for trying out hiking boots. After that came **L.L.Kids,** 8 Nathan Nye St., a separate building with high-tech features that appeal to younger shoppers and their parents.

Until the 1970s, Bean's remained a rustic store with a creaky staircase and a closet-size women's department. Then a few other merchants began arriving, Bean's expanded, and a feeding frenzy followed. The Bean reputation rests on a savvy staff, high quality, an admirable environmental consciousness, and a no-questions-asked return policy. Bring the kids—for the indoor trout pond, the clean restrooms, and the "real deal" bargain department. The store's open-round-the-clock policy has become its signature, and if you show up at 2 a.m., you'll have much of the store to yourself!

A block south of L.L. Bean, the **Freeport Historical Society** operates an unusual boutique in the restored 1830 Enoch Harrington House. Among the Maine-made items in the six-room **Harrington House Museum Store,** 45 Main St., Rt. 1, Freeport 04032, tel. (207) 865-0477, are furniture, accessories, jewelry, and crafts, all beautifully displayed. While you're at it, you can check out the society's local-history displays. Open 10 a.m.-6 p.m. daily (except major winter holidays), with extended hours in December.

After this, it's up to your whims and your wallet. The stores stretch for several miles up and down Main Street and along many side streets. Pick up a copy of the *Official Map & Visitor Guide* at any of the shops and restaurants, at one of the visitor kiosks, or at the Hose Tower Information Center, Depot St., two blocks east of L.L. Bean. Among the **big-name outlets** are Banana Republic, Benetton, Brooks Brothers, Coach, Cole-Haan, Crabtree & Evelyn, Dansk, Donna Karan, Gap, J. Crew, Levi's, Nieman Marcus, NordicTrack, North Face, Patagonia, Ralph Lauren, and Reebok.

About three miles south of the downtown area, and not a factory outlet, **Blueberries and Granite,** 313 Rt. 1, next to the Big Indian, Freeport 04032, tel. (207) 865-1681 or (800) 462-4268, fax (207) 865-1839, specializes in Maine Exile Products, T-shirts and other stuff for homesick Mainers living elsewhere ("Born in Maine, Living in Exile"). The shop is open all year, Mon.-Sat. 10 a.m.-6 p.m., Sunday noon-5 p.m.

PARKS, PRESERVES, AND OTHER ATTRACTIONS

Winslow Memorial Park

Owned by the town of Freeport, Winslow Memorial Park, Staples Pt., South Freeport, tel. (207) 865-4198, is a spectacular 90-plus-acre seaside park, overlooking the islands of upper Casco Bay. Swim off the beach (changing house, restrooms, but no lifeguards), picnic on the shore, walk the three-quarter-mile nature trail and perch on the point, launch a canoe or kayak, or reserve one of the 100 campsites. The boat landing and beach area are tidal, so boaters and swimmers should plan to be here two hours before and two hours after high tide; otherwise, you're dealing with mudflats. The park opens Memorial Day weekend and closes the last Sunday in September; admission is $1.50 pp, payable at the gatehouse. (Off season, there's no fee.) Inland and waterfront campsites are $16-18 for nonresidents ($5 for each extra tent); no hookups, but some sites can take RVs. From the Big Indian on Rt. 1, take South Freeport Rd. one mile to Staples Point Rd. and continue to the end.

Mast Landing Sanctuary

More than two miles of easy, yellow-blazed trails wind through the 140-acre Mast Landing Sanctuary—an area that once witnessed the trade in mammoth masts for the shipping industry. Pick up a trail map at the parking area and start watching for birds. Best (and longest) route is the 1.6-mile Loop Trail, which passes fruit trees, hardwoods, and an old milldam. (Keep the kids off the dam.) The sanctuary is owned by Maine Audubon Society, Gilsland Farm, P.O. Box 6009, Falmouth 04105, tel. (207) 781-2330, fax 781-6185. Each summer, the society operates a very popular nature day camp here; call for schedule. The sanctuary is open sunrise to sunset, year-round, and is popular in winter with cross-country skiers. Admission is free. From downtown Freeport (Rt. 1), take Bow St. (opposite L.L. Bean) one mile east to Upper Mast Landing Road. Turn left (north) and go 500 feet to the parking area.

Wolf Neck Woods State Park

Five miles of easy to moderate trails meander through 233-acre Wolf Neck Woods State Park, Wolf Neck Rd., Freeport 04032, tel. (207) 865-4465, just a few minutes' cycle or drive from downtown Freeport. You'll need a trail map, available near the parking area. Easiest route (partially wheelchair-accessible) is the Shoreline Walk, about three quarters of a mile, starting near the saltmarsh and skirting Casco Bay. Sprinkled along the trails are helpful interpretive panels explaining various points of natural history—bog life, osprey nesting, glaciation, erosion, and tree decay. Leashed pets are allowed. Adjacent **Googins Island,** an osprey sanctuary, is off-limits. The park sponsors year-round educational programs and guided hikes. Admission is $2 adults, 50 cents children 5-11; kids under five and seniors are free. The park is open Memorial Day weekend to Labor Day, but it's accessible in winter for cross-country skiing. From downtown Freeport, follow Bow St. (across from L.L. Bean) for 2.25 miles; turn right onto Wolf Neck Rd. and go another 2.25 miles.

Wolfe's Neck Farm

The best time to visit Wolfe's Neck Farm, 10 Burnett Rd., Freeport 04032, tel. (207) 865-4469, fax 865-6927, is March and April, for the annual **Calf Watch,** when more than a hundred calves join the herd on the 620-acre farm. During calving season, the farm is open daily 9 a.m.-5 p.m., and kids can see the latest newborns as well as chickens, turkeys, pigs, and other creatures. On December weekends, a **winter open house** includes storytelling, singing, hay rides, and farm tours. Sustainable agriculture and environmental sensitivity are the overriding philosophies at this working farm owned and operated by the nonprofit Wolfe's Neck Farm Foundation. A small retail shop in the farmhouse (open weekdays 9 a.m.-4:30 p.m.) sells high-quality crafts and organic Angus beef.

Also part of the farm is **Recompence Shore Campsites,** 10 Burnett Rd., Freeport 04032, tel. (207) 865-9307, fax 865-0367—an ecosensitive campground with 100 wooded tentsites (a few hookups are available), many on the farm's three-mile-long Casco Bay shorefront. For anyone seeking peace, quiet, and low-tech camping (outhouses and hot showers) in a spectacular setting, this is it. Ice, firewood, and snacks are available at the camp store. As with Winslow Memorial Park, swimming depends on the tides; check the tide calendar in a local newspaper. Rates are $14-20 per night, depending on location, mid-May to mid-October. Take Bow St. (across from L.L. Bean) to Wolf Neck Rd., turn right and go 1.6 miles to Burnett Rd., a left turn.

L.L. Bean Outdoor Discovery Schools

Since the early 1980s, the sports outfitter's Outdoor Discovery Schools have trained thousands of outdoors enthusiasts to improve their skills in fly-fishing, archery, hiking, canoeing, sea kayaking, winter camping, cross-country skiing, orienteering, and cycling. Many of the lectures, seminars, and demonstrations held in Freeport are free, and a regular newsletter lists the schedule. All of the fee programs, plus canoeing and camping trips, require preregistration, well in advance because of their popularity. Some are held in the mountains of western Maine. For information, or to get on the mailing list, contact the program at (800) 341-4341, ext. 6666. Or stop in at the Outdoor Discovery Room on the store's third floor.

Pownal and Gray

Inland, in the two adjoining communities of Pownal and Gray, you'll find an underutilized state park, a hot-air-balloon company, and the state's home for orphaned wildlife.

Bradbury Mountain State Park

Six miles from the hubbub of Freeport and you're in tranquil, wooded, 590-acre Bradbury Mountain State Park, Rt. 9, Pownal 04069, tel. (207) 688-4712, with facilities for picnicking, hiking, and rustic camping, but no swimming. (Sleep here and save your funds for shopping.) Pick up a trail map at the gate and take the easy, .4-mile (roundtrip) Mountain Trail to the 485-foot summit, with superb views east to the ocean and southeast to Portland. In fall, it's gorgeous. Or take the Tote Road Trail, on the western side of the park, where the ghost of Samuel Bradbury occasionally brings a chill to hikers in a hemlock grove. A playground keeps the littlest tykes happy. Admission is $1 adults, 50 cents children 5-11; kids under five and seniors are free. Nonresident camping fee is $10 per site per night. (Bradbury Mountain is one of only two state parks where the camping fee *includes* Maine's seven percent lodging tax.) The park season is May 15-Oct. 15, but there's winter access for cross-country skiing. From Rt. 1, cross over I-95 at Exit 20 and continue west on Pownal Road to Rt. 9.

Flying High

Based three miles west of Freeport, Bob Scheurer's **Freeport Balloon Company,** 41 Tuttle Rd., Pownal 04069, tel. (207) 865-1712, has been taking passengers aloft in a colorfully striped hot-air balloon since 1989. The one-hour flights usually begin about 6 a.m. and a few hours before sunset—when the winds kick up no more than eight mph. Allow about two and a half hours, so you'll have ample time for the traditional post-flight champagne. Reservations are required, along with a $50 deposit—refundable if the weather sours. Maximum is three passengers, no minimum. Cost is $150 pp, $75 for a child under 70 pounds (with two adults). The company operates all year.

Where the Wild Things Are

The **Game Farm and Visitors Center,** Shaker Rd., Rt. 26, Gray 04039, tel. (207) 657-4977, is home for Maine's wild animals when they've been injured, orphaned, or otherwise traumatized. State staffers rehabilitate them and, when possible, release them. You'll see moose, pheasants, owls, turtles, bear, deer, bobcats, and whatever other creatures the wardens happen to have rescued. Other features here are a wildlife garden, interactive displays in the visitors center, an attractive picnic area, and nature trails winding through the farm. Wildlife experts present programs each Sunday at 1 and 3 p.m., mid-June to mid-September. In summer, there are full-moon wildlife walks, 8-10 p.m. Bring a flashlight covered with red cellophane, or buy one when you arrive. No alcohol allowed on the premises; no pets beyond the parking area. Admission is $3.50 adults, $2.50 seniors, $2 children (4-12), free for kids three and under. Open daily 9:30 a.m.-5:30 p.m., April 15 to Veterans' Day; no entry after 4 p.m. The park is three and a half miles north of downtown Gray and I-495 Exit 11. The easiest route is to take Rt. 115 from Main St. in downtown Yarmouth, continuing through North Yarmouth (with stunning old houses) to Gray.

If you're in downtown **Gray** around lunchtime or dinnertime (or, for that matter, for breakfast), stop for super pizza (35 varieties!) at **The Pizza Paddle,** Gray Plaza, Rt. 100, Gray 04039, tel. (207) 657-3161. Prices are downright inexpensive, and there are daily non-pizza specials. Once a month, the $5.50 teriyaki stir-fry special draws a loyal crowd. Open all year, daily 6 a.m.-10 p.m.

ACCOMMODATIONS

If you'd prefer to drop where you shop, Freeport has a large inn, several motels, and more than two dozen B&Bs, so finding a pillow is seldom a problem, but it's still wise to have reservations. A dozen of Freeport's best B&B operators have banded together and established a lodging association; request a brochure from the **Freeport Area Bed & Breakfast Association,** P.O. Box 267, Freeport 04032, tel. (207) 865-1500 or (800) 853-2727.

For camping, see Winslow Memorial Park, Wolfe's Neck Farm, and Bradbury Mountain State Park, above.

Downtown

After a tough day of shopping, you can head for the outdoor pool at **181 Main Street Bed & Breakfast,** 181 Main St., Freeport 04032, tel.

(207) 865-1226 or (800) 235-9750, close to shops and restaurants yet away from much of the traffic. Innkeepers Ed Hassett and David Cates have filled the restored Cape with antiques, books, and handmade quilts. Breakfast is a feast, with corn casserole a specialty. May Elizabeth, a Lab foundling, rules the roost. Seven rooms with private baths; doubles go for $100 late May through October, $85 other months. No smoking, no pets, no small children. Open all year.

One of Freeport's pioneering B&Bs is just across the street, in a restored house where arctic explorer Adm. Donald MacMillan once lived. The **White Cedar Inn,** 178 Main St., Freeport 04032, tel. (207) 865-9099 or (800) 853-1269, Carla and Phil Kerber's 19th-century establishment, has six attractive guest rooms with a/c and private baths. Doubles are $100 July-Oct., $80 other months. No smoking, no pets, no children under 12. Open all year.

In the same neighborhood and slightly less pricey is the **Bayberry Inn,** 8 Maple Ave., Freeport 04032, tel. (207) 865-1868 or (800) 217-2477, a homey Federal-style B&B with five comfortable first- and second-floor guest rooms. Doubles with a/c and private baths are $76-96 July-Oct., $66-86 other months. German-born owner Mara Frank, who opened this place in 1994, welcomes kids. No smoking, no pets. Open all year.

Beyond Downtown

In the historic hamlet known as Porter's Landing—where massive sailing vessels once were launched and loaded—stands **Porter's Landing Bed & Breakfast,** 70 South St., Freeport 04032, tel. (207) 865-4488, Barbara and Peter Guffin's 1830 Greek Revival home. Established as a B&B in 1989, the former Anderson-Chase House underwent a masterful, three-year renovation. In the attached 1870s carriage house are three second-floor rooms with private baths, plus a nifty, skylighted loft for guests' use. Doubles are $100 late May through October, $85 other months. The Guffins are avid hikers, so they're a great resource for outdoors info; after their generous breakfast, you'll need a walk. No smoking, no pets, no children under 12. Open all year. Across from L.L. Bean, take Bow St., then right onto South St., continuing to Porter's Landing.

Slightly farther from downtown, in South Freeport, is the **Atlantic Seal Bed & Breakfast,** 25 Main St., P.O. Box 146, South Freeport 04078, tel. (207) 865-6112, a mid-19th-century Cape-style house with stupendous harbor views and lots of marine collectibles. The suite and one room have private baths; another room has a shared bath. Doubles are $85-135 in season, $65-115 off season. No smoking, no pets, no children under six, no credit cards. Open all year. From late May to late October, owner Thomas Ring operates **Atlantic Seal Cruises** (same phone)—two or three two-and-a-half-hour cruises daily from the nearby Freeport Town Wharf (located in South Freeport) to 17-acre **Eagle Island,** a State Historic Site once owned by Adm. Robert Peary of North Pole fame. The trip includes a lobstering demonstration (except Sunday, when lobstering is banned). Tickets are $20 adults, $15 kids under 12. To get there, take Bow St., then right onto South St. continuing to Porter's Landing; travel along South Freeport Rd. to Main St. (left turn).

Six miles north of I-95 Exit 20, in Durham, is the National Historic Register **Bagley House,** 1290 Royalsborough Rd., Rt. 136, Durham 04222, tel. (207) 865-6566 or (800) 765-1772, fax (207) 353-5878, filled with antiques and superbly run by Sue Backhouse and Sue O'Connor—both ex-nurses—since 1993. Only a 10-minute drive from downtown Freeport, the 1772 house, the oldest in Durham, sits amid six acres of woods and fields. No smoking, no pets; children are welcome. Five guest rooms go for $100-125 d in summer, $85-100 d in winter. Open all year.

Two blocks north of L.L. Bean, near I-95 Exit 20, the **Harraseeket Inn,** 162 Main St., Freeport 04032, tel. (207) 865-9377 or (800) 342-6423, fax (207) 865-1684, is a high-end, 54-room country inn with cable TV, a/c, phones, and dataports; some rooms have fireplaces and jacuzzis. Decor is colonial reproduction. Rooms are $150-235 d, mid-May through October, including buffet breakfast and afternoon tea; they're $100-215 d other months. Special packages and MAP rates are available. The cloth-and-candles **Maine Dining Room,** tel. (207) 865-1085, justifiably famed for its unbelievable Sunday brunch, is open to the public daily 6-9 p.m. (to 9:30 p.m. Friday and Saturday). Dinner entrées are $15-27. No smoking. Reservations are advisable for brunch and dinner. The informal **Broad Arrow Tavern** serves microbrews and moderately priced brick-oven specialties 11:30 a.m.-10:30 or 11 p.m. No smoking.

One of the town's most enduring hostelries, the **Freeport Inn**, 335 Rt. 1, Freeport 04032, tel. (207) 865-3106 or (800) 998-2583, fax (207) 865-6364, overlooks the Cousins River estuary, the Freeport-Yarmouth boundary, three miles south of downtown Freeport. The 86 motel-style rooms go for $70-110 d late May to mid-October, $50-70 d other months. Escape traffic noise by requesting a rear-facing room. Cable TV, a/c, phones, canoe rentals. There's an outdoor pool and a playground, which helps keep kids happy; pets are allowed. The inn's café, open 6 a.m.-8 p.m., has good, reasonably priced meals. A short walk away, along Rt. 1 and actually in Yarmouth, is the inn's bright, modern **Muddy Rudder Restaurant,** tel. (207) 846-3082, an extremely popular spot for lunch, dinner, and weekend entertainment (open until midnight). The inn, café, and restaurant are open all year.

FOOD

Lunch Fare

Two blocks south of L.L. Bean is the **Lobster Cooker,** 39 Main St., Freeport 04032, tel. (207) 865-4349. Lobster rolls are predictably good and not overpriced for the neighborhood. It's a popular place where you order at the counter, so expect to stand in line. Beer and wine available; no credit cards.

Don't laugh. **McDonald's,** 155 Main St., at Mallett Drive, Freeport 04032, tel. (207) 865-9566, is almost incognito—in a historic downtown home two blocks north of L.L. Bean and across from the Harraseeket Inn. No giant golden arches here—only discreet ones at the entrances and exits. Residents allowed capitalism to run rampant in their town, but the idea of a fast-food chain terrified them. Hence this compromise. Lobster sandwiches are available. No smoking. Open all year.

Freeport's original brewpub, **Gritty McDuff's,** Lower Main St., Freeport 04032, tel. (207) 865-4321, is open daily 11:30 a.m.-1 a.m., year-round. Good pub grub, fine pizza, designer brews (try Black Fly Stout or McDuff's Best Bitter), and short, on-demand brewery tours.

When you head toward South Freeport (which you must), stop in at **The Village Store,** 97 South Freeport Rd., next to the post office, South Freeport 04078, tel. (207) 865-4230, for breakfast, lunch, dinner, or a snack—grab one of the few tables or do takeout. This upscale convenience store produces homemade soups, giant muffins, great pizza, hearty sandwiches, even cappuccino—all at ultra-reasonable prices. No smoking, no credit cards. Open daily 6:30 a.m.-8 p.m., year-round.

Once you get to South Freeport, do lobster-in-the-rough at **Harraseeket Lunch & Lobster Company,** Main St., Town Wharf, South Freeport 04078, tel. (207) 865-4888. Grab a waterfront picnic table, place your order, and go at it. (There's also inside dining.) Be prepared for a wait on midsummer weekends. Fried clams are particularly good here. Another option: If you're camping nearby, call ahead, tel. (207) 865-3535, and order boiled lobsters to go. BYOL; no credit cards. Open 11 a.m.-7:45 p.m., May 1 to mid-June; 11 a.m.-8:45 p.m., mid-June to mid-October.

Moderate to Expensive Restaurants

Consider springing for the buffet brunch at the Harraseeket Inn's **Maine Dining Room,** 162 Main St., tel. (207) 865-1085—how can you resist sampling cured Pacific flying-fish roe? or chilled poached salmon? or Maine Coast bouillabaisse? Plus chocolate marble cashew tart for dessert. Be sure to make a reservation, and check your arteries at the door.

Believe it or not, one of Maine's best Chinese restaurants is right around the corner from L.L. Bean. Aficionados beat a path to **China Rose,** 10 School St., Freeport, tel. (207) 865-6886, for Hunan, Mandarin, Sichuan, and Cantonese dishes. The ambience is elegant, the service first-rate. Open for lunch and dinner daily.

Maine was born at the 18th-century **Jameson Tavern,** 115 Main St., just north of L.L. Bean, Freeport 04032, tel. (207) 865-4196, where statehood documents were signed in 1820. Now you can steep yourself in history over lunch or dinner every day, year-round.

The creative, bistro-type dinner menu (entrées $12-18) is huge. In good weather, try for the outside patio. Dining rooms are small and casually elegant; the informal Tap Room has lighter fare. No smoking. Dinner reservations are advisable on weekends. Open 11:30 a.m.-2:30 p.m. and 5-10 p.m.

INFORMATION AND SERVICES

With shopping being Freeport's occupation and preoccupation, the best source of information is the **Freeport Merchants Association,** P.O. Box 452, Freeport 04032, tel. (207) 865-1212 or (800) 865-1994. Its **Hose Tower Information Center** (including restrooms and ATM), on Depot St., two blocks east of L.L. Bean, is open all year. Summer hours are Mon.-Sat. 9 a.m.-9 p.m., Sunday 10 a.m.-6 p.m. Winter hours are 10 a.m.-6 p.m. daily. The association annually produces the invaluable *Official Map & Visitor Guide,* showing locations of all the shops, plus sites of lodgings, restaurants, visitor kiosks, pay phones, restrooms, and car and bike parking. If you're serious about "doing" Freeport, send for a guide before you arrive so you can plan your attack and hit the ground running.

Emergencies
Freeport has no hospital or first-aid center; **Maine Medical Center** is a 20-minute drive to the south, in Portland, tel. (207) 871-0111. The local **ambulance** can be reached at (207) 865-4211; contact the **fire department** at the same number and the **police department** at (207) 865-4212.

Getting There and Getting Around
See "Getting There" under "Greater Portland," for information on flying to the Portland area.

Between May and Christmas, **Mermaid Transportation,** tel. (800) 696-2463, which provides scheduled van service between Boston and Portland airports, also operates **van service** three times daily to Freeport from nearly a dozen hotels and motels in Portland and South Portland. Cost is $15 roundtrip; reservations are required.

If you're driving, park downtown and walk to the shops; then drive to the outlying shopping areas. If you need a ride to outlying shopping areas, or even beyond Freeport, contact **Freeport Taxi,** tel. (207) 865-9494. They take credit cards and have wheelchair-accessible vehicles. Also in Freeport is **Classy Taxi,** tel. (207) 865-0663, with van service to Portland and Boston.

YARMOUTH

Between Freeport to the north and Greater Portland to the south, Yarmouth seldom gets the respect it deserves for its classic architecture, unusual shops, and splendidly scenic Royal River winding through town.

Settled in 1680 and named Old North Yarmouth, the town was twice leveled by Indians (who'd recognized its attractions far earlier) before a third settlement took root in 1727. Yarmouth separated from North Yarmouth in 1849. During the 1800s, more than 300 sailing vessels were built along the Cousins and Royal Rivers. Two energetic volunteer organizations, the **Yarmouth Historical Society** and the **Village Improvement Society,** have managed to encourage historic preservation and stir up curiosity and enthusiasm about the ghosts of Yarmouth's past.

RECREATION

Canoeing Here and There
Locally, the best-known canoeing (and kayaking) route is along the meandering Royal River. For a leisurely day's outing, you can first canoe the river before stopping for a picnic and walk in **Royal River Park.**

To reach the put-in from Main St. (Rt. 88) in Yarmouth, head west on West Main St. (Rt. 115) to Rt. 9. Turn right onto Rt. 9 and go about three miles, crossing railroad tracks and the river; park in the grassy clearing on your right, next to the Gillespie Farms market.

The six-mile downstream paddle is no big challenge—all quiet water, with little current—and you won't be alone, but it's totally relaxing.

KAREN McKINLEY

SHOPPING

A 42-foot rotating globe, exactly one-millionth the size of the earth, dominates the glass-walled lobby of the **DeLorme Mapping Company,** Rt. 1, Yarmouth 04096, tel. (207) 846-7100, the new headquarters opened in mid-1997. DeLorme, internationally known as the source of charts, maps, software, CD-ROMs, and the essential *Maine Atlas and Gazetteer,* also has a new Map Store with a bank of try-out computers and almost every map you could possibly want. The shop is open all year, Mon.-Sat. 8:30 a.m.-6 p.m., Sunday 9:30 a.m.-5 p.m.

Allow 2-4 hours. Toward the end, after you've paddled under a railroad trestle, continue about another 20 minutes, under another trestle, and take out at municipal Royal River Park—just before the river plunges over a dam.

The park has a lovely half-mile walkway bordering the southern shore of the river, roughly between East Elm and Bridge Streets. Near the parking lot and downstream are two fish ladders (to assist fish upstream for spawning), plus you'll see remnants of old mills. To skip the paddling and just visit the park, go west on Main St. (Rt. 88) in downtown Yarmouth, then turn right onto East Elm, cross the railroad tracks, and park in the small lot on your right.

Based here in Yarmouth but covering the entire state, Mike Patterson is a Professional Maine Guide, who organizes canoe trips, late May to late September, on all Maine's major rivers: the Allagash, St. John, Machias, St. Croix, Penobscot (east and west branches), and Moose. Costs average $100-120 pp per day. He also freelances with other canoe-trip organizers and teaches clinics in the art of canoe poling. Contact him at **Wilds of Maine Guide Service Inc.,** 2 Abby Ln., Yarmouth 04096, tel. (207) 846-9735.

FESTIVALS AND EVENTS

The **Yarmouth Clam Festival,** the third weekend in July, is an enormous town-wide extravaganza and the highlight of Yarmouth's summer, with events everywhere you look: a parade, balloon rides, an art show, live music, food booths, pancake breakfasts, a carnival, a clam-shucking contest, and more clams than anyone can eat. If you want to join in, be sure to make lodging reservations well in advance.

One of Maine's best independent bookstores, and definitely the best for marine titles, is **Harbour Books,** 40A Lafayette St., Rt. 88, Lower Falls Landing, Yarmouth 04096, tel. (207) 846-6306. Hardcover best-sellers are always discounted 20%, and you'll get a cloth tote bag if you spend $100 (not hard to do here). Open Mon.-Sat. 9 a.m.-6 p.m. (to 8 p.m. Friday), Sunday noon-5 p.m.

The third generation now runs the show at **A.E. Runge, Jr.,** 139 Main St., Yarmouth 04096, tel. (207) 846-9000, purveyors of Oriental rugs. Tad Runge's selection is particularly interesting, and if high-quality Turkish, Persian, and Caucasian carpets intrigue you, it's well worth a visit. Open all year, Mon.-Fri. 10 a.m.-5 p.m., Saturday 10 a.m.-3 p.m. If you're making a special detour, be sure to call ahead in case he's out hunting down new carpets.

Handworks, 49 Main St., Yarmouth 04096, tel. (207) 846-5513, a cooperative, has an extremely fine selection of Maine crafts. The shop is open Mon.-Fri. 10:30 a.m.-5:30 p.m., Saturday 10 a.m.-5 p.m., April-December. It's open Tues.-Fri. 10:30 a.m.-3 p.m., Saturday 10 a.m.-5 p.m., Jan.-March.

For antiques, don't miss **W.M. Schwind, Jr., Antiques,** 17 E. Main St., Yarmouth 04096, tel. (207) 846-9458, in a splendid 1810 house. Look for country and formal furniture and accessories, including antique glass. Open weekdays 10 a.m.-5 p.m., year-round, other times by appointment.

On the music front, **Play It Again,** 24 Rt. 1, Yarmouth 04096, tel. (207) 846-4711, has a huge selection of tapes, CDs, and videos, but the best part is the free popcorn. Open daily 10 a.m.-10 p.m.

FOOD

Freeport, very nearby, offers many other convenient choices.

Pat's Pizza, 43 Rt. 1, Yarmouth 04096, tel. (207) 846-3701, part of a statewide chain, is predictably good, open for lunch and dinner daily, all year. Best times to go are Sunday and Monday 5-9 p.m., to graze the all-you-can-eat pizza buffet ($3.95 adults, $2.50 kids under 12). Open until midnight Friday and Saturday.

Housed in a retrofitted theater, **Clayton's,** 106 Main St., Yarmouth 04096, tel. (207) 846-1117, creates imaginative sandwiches, salads, and soups that'll keep you going all day. Commandeer one of the half-dozen tables, pick up picnic fare, or just browse the gourmet shop and stock up on exotic condiments, cheeses, and other goodies. You can't go wrong here. Open weekdays 11 a.m.-2:30 p.m. for lunch; the shop is open Mon.-Sat. 9 a.m.-6:30 p.m.

Nor can you go wrong at **Royal River Provisioners,** 38 Lafayette St., Lower Falls Landing, Yarmouth 04096, tel. (207) 846-1332 or (800) 474-4592, fax (207) 846-7989, a cheerful, well-designed place specializing in boat provisioning. But the baked goods and take-out meals are just as terrific on terra firma. Open all year, Tues.-Sat. 10 a.m.-6 p.m. (Lower Falls Landing is the yuppified reincarnation of the old Royal River Packing Company, which packed a million cans of sardines weekly before shutting down in 1980.)

Also in the Lower Falls Landing complex is **The Cannery,** tel. (207) 846-1226, a bright, modern, airy spot overlooking the Royal River and the local marina. The best vantage points are on the deck. Open daily for moderate-to-expensive brunches, lunches, and dinners; seafood is a specialty. Reservations are advisable on weekends, even off season. The Cannery is under the same ownership as Camden's Waterfront Restaurant.

INFORMATION AND SERVICES

The **Maine Information Center,** Rt. 1, at I-95 Exit 17, Yarmouth 04096, tel. (207) 846-0833, is part of the state's tourism-information network. Staffers are particularly attuned to Freeport and Yarmouth, but the center has brochures and maps for the entire state. Also here are restrooms, phones, picnic tables, vending machines, and a dog-walking area.

The **Yarmouth Chamber of Commerce,** 16 Rt. 1, Yarmouth Marketplace, P.O. Box 419, Yarmouth 04096, tel. (207) 846-3984, is a small office open weekdays only.

Photo Services
Photo 59, Rt. 1, Yarmouth Marketplace, Yarmouth 04096, tel. (207) 846-1556, does enlargements while you wait and one-hour photo processing. It's open Mon.-Fri. 9 a.m.-6 p.m., Saturday 9 a.m.-5 p.m.

Getting Around
Yarmouth is the closest jumping-off point for getting to Casco Bay's Great Chebeague Island via the **Chebeague Transportation Company (CTC);** you can also take a longer boat ride from downtown Portland via Casco Bay Lines. The logistics of the CTC operation make it sound complicated, but it really isn't; chalk it up as an adventure. Plans are afoot to simplify the procedure, but don't hold your breath.

Year-round, the CTC operates a 15-minute passenger ferry to the island, carrying more than 100,000 people annually, and also makes special arrangements for car and freight transport. The *Islander* makes the summer runs; the smaller *Big Squaw* does the winter trips.

From early May to late October, as well as during winter holidays, if you're staying overnight on Chebeague, you'll need to drive to the Cumberland Municipal Building in downtown Cumberland (on Drowne Rd., off Tuttle Rd., three quarters of a mile east of Rt. 9), where you'll park your car ($6.50 a day) and board a creaky blue school bus for the 20-minute ride to the Cousins Island dock at the southeastern edge of Yarmouth. The bus, which has bike and baggage racks, departs Cumberland *precisely* 30 minutes before boat time. The boat makes 8-10 roundtrips daily, beginning at 6:40 a.m. on Chebeague and 7 a.m. in Yarmouth. Tickets are available on the boat—$4.50 adults one-way, 75 cents kids under 12; bikes are $3. Reservations are not required.

From November to April, or if you're only going to Chebeague for a weekday, you can drive straight to Cousins Island and hope to find a parking space. From Main St., Yarmouth, take Lafayette St. under I-95, then left onto Princes Point Rd., then left to Gilman Road. Cross the causeway onto the island and continue to Wharf Road. Go left and look for the Blanchard Parking Lot on the left. Parking is $9 a day, but space is not always available.

Best solution of all is to cycle to Cousins Island from downtown Yarmouth (the back roads have bike lanes) and take your bike on the boat to Chebeague.

For a boat schedule and a copy of *A User's Guide to the Chebeague Transportation Company,* call (207) 846-3700 or write the CTC, Chebeague Island 04017.

BOB RACE

MID-COAST REGION

In contrast to the South Coast's gorgeous sandy beaches, the Mid-Coast region features a deeply indented shoreline with snug harbors and long, gnarled fingers of land. Even though these fingers are inconvenient for driving (but wonderful for sailing), this is where you'll find picture-book Maine—drive to the tips of the peninsulas and find lighthouses, fishing villages, B&Bs, and lobster wharves.

Admittedly, I'm biased about this area, where I put down roots in the early 1970s, but at times I almost wish it weren't quite so popular. Problem is, what's not to like? Above all, it's hard to resist championing the scenery.

The Mid-Coast stretches roughly (you'll find disagreement on the boundaries) from Brunswick (in the northeastern corner of Cumberland County) on the Androscoggin River to Stockton Springs on the Penobscot—roughly 95 miles by road, traversing Sagadahoc, Lincoln, Knox, and Waldo Counties.

After York County, the Mid-Coast sees midsummer's greatest population explosion. (Ob-

viously, I'm not the only one promoting the area.) On or near Rt. 1, visitors come for Brunswick's Bowdoin College, Wiscasset's antique shops, Rockland's art galleries, Camden's picturesque mountainside harbor, Lincolnville's pocket beach, and Searsport's sea captains' homes.

From Port Clyde, Rockland, and Lincolnville Beach, car and passenger ferries head offshore to the islands of Monhegan, Vinalhaven, North Haven, Matinicus, and Islesboro—occupied year-round by hardy souls and joined in summer by less-hardy ones. Except for Matinicus, they're great day-trip destinations. If what appeals to you about a ferry trip is traveling on the water, you can get a taste of the great age of sail by booking a three- or six-day cruise on one of the classic windjammer schooners berthed in Rockland, Rockport, and Camden.

In July and August, try to avoid arriving without a reservation. Helpful chamber of commerce staffers in prime locations often can work last-minute miracles, but special events and festivals can fill up all the beds for miles around.

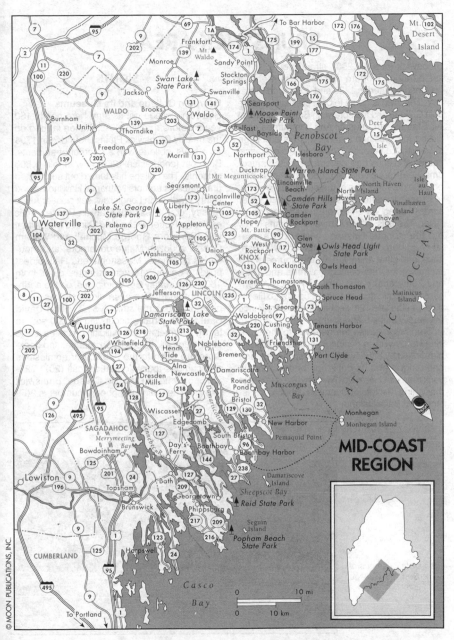

MID-COAST
REGION

BRUNSWICK AREA

Brunswick (pop. 20,250), straddling Rt. 1, relies partly on modern defense dollars—but it was incorporated in 1738 and is steeped in history. The town is home to both prestigious Bowdoin College and the sprawling Brunswick Naval Air Station—an unusual and sometimes conflicting juxtaposition that makes this a college town with a difference. You'll find lots of classic homes and churches, several respected museums, year-round cultural attractions—plus aerobatic extravaganzas at the naval base.

Brunswick and Topsham face each other across roiling waterfalls on the Androscoggin River. The falls, which Native Americans knew by the tongue-twisting name of Ahmelahcogneturcook ("place abundant with fish, birds, and other animals"), were a source of hydropower for 18th-century sawmills and 19th- and 20th-century textile mills. Franco-Americans arrived in droves to beef up the textile industry in the late 19th century (but lost their jobs eventually in the Depression).

Brunswick is also the gateway to the stunning Harpswells, a peninsula/archipelago complex linked by causeways, several bridges, and one unique granite cribstone bridge. Scenic back roads on Harpswell Neck inspire detours to the fishing hamlets of Cundy's Harbor, Orr's Island, and Bailey Island.

SIGHTS

Bowdoin College and Its Museums

Bowdoin College got its start here nearly 150 years before the Naval Air Station landed on the nearby Brunswick Plains. Founded in 1794 as a boys' college with a handful of students, Bowdoin (coed since 1969) now enrolls 1,500 students. The college has turned out such noted graduates as authors Nathaniel Hawthorne and Henry Wadsworth Longfellow, sex pioneer Alfred Kinsey, U.S. President Franklin Pierce, Arctic explorers Robert Peary and Donald MacMillan, U.S. Senators George Mitchell and William Cohen, a dozen Maine governors, and thousands of others. Massachusetts Hall, oldest building on the 110-acre campus, dates from 1802. The stately Bowdoin pines, on the northeast boundary, are even older. Newest campus addition is the striking $4.7 million **David Saul Smith Union,** occupying 40,000 square feet in a former athletic building on the east side of the campus. Its café, pub, lounge, and bookstore are open to the public. For admissions and campus-tour information, call (207) 725-3375, or write to Bowdoin College, Brunswick 04011. (The main switchboard number is 207-725-3000.)

the stately campus of Bowdoin College

MAINE OFFICE OF TOURISM

JOSHUA L. CHAMBERLAIN ~ MAINE'S CIVIL WAR HERO

When the American Civil War began in 1861, Joshua Chamberlain was a 33-year-old logic instructor at Bowdoin College; when it ended, in 1865, Chamberlain had distinguished himself in the Battle of Gettysburg at Little Round Top, earned the Congressional Medal of Honor for the Battle of Petersburg, and had been the man to formally accept the official surrender of Robert E. Lee at Appomattox Court House. He later became governor of Maine and president of Bowdoin College, but Chamberlain's greatest renown, ironically, came more than a century later—when 1990s PBS filmmakers focused on the Civil War and highlighted his strategic military role.

Joshua Lawrence Chamberlain was born in 1828 in Brewer, Maine, son and grandson of soldiers. After graduating from Bowdoin in 1852, he studied for the ministry at Bangor Theological Seminary, then returned to his alma mater as an instructor.

With the nation in turmoil in the early 1860s, Chamberlain signed on to help, receiving a commission as a lieutenant colonel in the Twentieth Maine Volunteers in 1862. After surviving 24 encounters and six battle wounds and having been promoted to general (brigadier, then major), Chamberlain was elected Republican governor of Maine in

1866—by the largest margin in the state's history—only to suffer through four one-year terms of partisan politics. In 1871, Chamberlain became president of Bowdoin College, where he remained until 1883. He then dove into speechmaking and writing, his best-known work being *The Passing of the Armies,* a memoir of the Civil War's final campaigns. From 1900 to 1914, Chamberlain was surveyor of the Port of Portland, a presidential appointment that ended only when complications from a wartime abdominal wound finally did him in. He died at the grand old age of 86.

Brunswick's Joshua L. Chamberlain Museum, located in his onetime home at 226 Maine St., commemorates this illustrious Mainer, and thousands of Civil War buffs annually stream through the door in search of Chamberlain "stuff." To make it easier, the Pejepscot Historical Society has produced a helpful map entitled *Joshua Chamberlain's Brunswick,* highlighting town and college ties to the man—his dorm rooms, his presidential office, his portraits, even his church pew (number 64 at First Parish Church). Chamberlain's gravesite, marked by a reddish granite stone, is in Brunswick's Pine Grove Cemetery, just east of the Bowdoin campus.

Photos and artifacts bring Arctic expeditions to life at the **Peary-MacMillan Arctic Museum,** Hubbard Hall, Bowdoin College, Brunswick 04011, tel. (207) 725-3416. Among the specimens are stuffed animals, a skin kayak, fur clothing, snow goggles, and Inuit carvings—most collected by Arctic pioneers Robert E. Peary and Donald B. Macmillan. The small gift shop specializes in Inuit books and artifacts. Admission is free, but donations are welcome. Open Tues.-Sat. 10 a.m.-5 p.m., Sunday 2-5 p.m.

An astonishing array of Greek and Roman artifacts is only one of the high points at the **Bowdoin College Museum of Art,** Walker Art Building, Bowdoin College, Brunswick 04011, tel. (207) 725-3275. The building alone is worth a look. Designed in the 1890s by Charles McKim of the famed McKim, Mead & White firm, it's a stunning neoclassical edifice with an interior rotunda and stone lions flanking the entry. Also here is an impressive permanent collection of

19th- and 20th-century American art. Admission is free, but donations are welcomed. Open Tues.-Sat. 10 a.m.-5 p.m., Sunday 2-5 p.m.

Pejepscot Historical Society Museums
Side by side in an unusual, cupola-topped duplex facing Brunswick's Mall (village green), the **Pejepscot Museum,** 159 Park Row, and the **Skolfield-Whittier House,** 161 Park Row, are both operated by the Pejepscot Historical Society, tel. (207) 729-6606, founded in 1888 and headquartered at the museum. Focusing on local history, the museum, in the left-hand section, has a collection of more than 50,000 artifacts and mounts an always-interesting special exhibit each year. Admission is free; there's a small gift shop. Open year-round Mon.-Fri. 9 a.m.-5 p.m. (also Saturday 1-4 p.m. in summer). The 17-room Skolfield-Whittier House, on the right-hand side of the building, looks as though the owners just stepped out for the af-

ternoon. Unused from 1925 to 1982, the onetime sea captain's house has elegant Victorian furnishings and lots of exotic artifacts collected on global seafaring stints. Garden restoration is ongoing. Hour-long guided tours (on demand) are $3 adults, $1 children 6-12. Open Memorial Day weekend to Labor Day, Tues.-Fri. 10 a.m.-3 p.m., Saturday 1-4 p.m.

Also operated by the Pejepscot Historical Society, the **Joshua L. Chamberlain Museum,** 226 Maine St., Brunswick, across from First Parish Church, tel. (207) 729-6606, commemorates the Union Army hero of the Civil War's Battle of Gettysburg, who's now gaining long-overdue respect. The partly restored house where Chamberlain lived in the late 19th century (and Henry Wadsworth Longfellow lived 30 years earlier) is a peculiar architectural hodgepodge with six rooms of exhibits of Chamberlain memorabilia, much of it Civil War-related. A gift shop stocks lots of Civil War publications, especially ones covering the Twentieth Maine Volunteers. Guided tours (45 minutes) are $3 adults, $1 children 6-12. Open Memorial Day weekend through September, Tues.-Sat. 10 a.m.-4 p.m. A combo ticket for all three society holdings is $5 adults, $2 children.

Uncle Tom's Church

Across the street from the Chamberlain museum is the historic 1846 **First Parish Church,** 223 Maine St. at Bath Rd., Brunswick 04011, tel. (207) 729-7331, a Gothic Revival (or carpenter Gothic) board-and-batten structure crowning the rise at the head of Maine Street. Scores of celebrity preachers have ascended this pulpit, and Harriet Beecher Stowe was inspired to write *Uncle Tom's Cabin* while listening to her husband deliver an antislavery sermon here. If you're a fan of organ music, arrive here before noon any Tuesday, early July to early August (or call ahead for details), when guest organists present 40-minute lunchtime concerts (12:10-12:50 p.m.) on the 1883 Hutchings-Plaisted tracker organ. Admission is free, but a small donation is requested. Stick around for the postconcert church tour. At other times, the church is open by appointment.

Brunswick's Noted Women

With more than 20 points of interest, the **Bruns-**

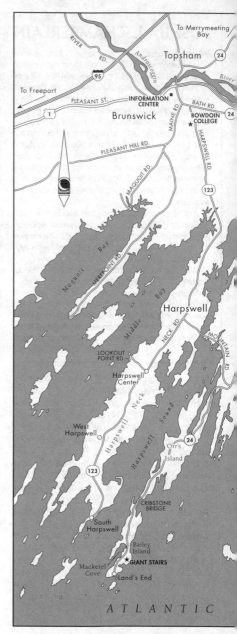

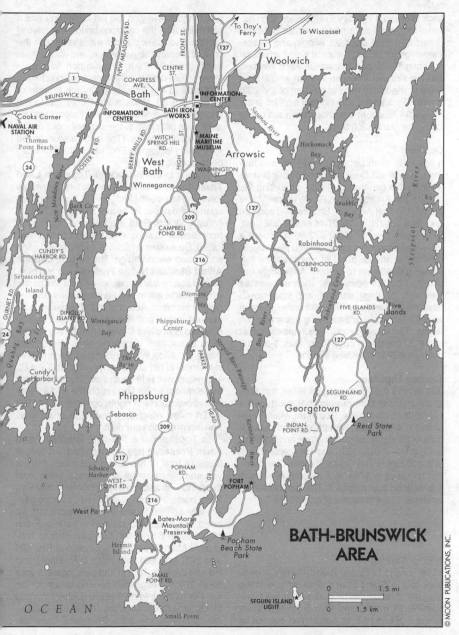

BATH-BRUNSWICK AREA

wick **Women's History Trail** covers such national notables as authors Harriet Beecher Stowe and Kate Douglas Wiggin and lesser-known lights including naturalist Kate Furbish, pioneering Maine pediatrician Dr. Alice Whittier, and the Franco-American women who slaved away in the textile mills at the turn of the 20th century. Pick up the walking-tour booklet at the Pejepscot Museum gift shop. Then set out to follow the fascinating story.

Go, Fish!

If you're in town between mid-May and late June, plan to visit Central Maine Power's **Brunswick Hydro** generating station, straddling the falls on the Androscoggin River, Lower Maine St., next to Fort Andross, Brunswick-Topsham town line, tel. (207) 729-7644 or 623-3521 ext. 2116 weekdays, or (800) 872-9937, where a glass-walled viewing room lets you play voyeur during the annual ritual of anadromous fish heading upstream to spawn. Amazingly undaunted by the obstacles, such species as alewives (herring), salmon, and smallmouth bass make their way from salt water to fresh via a 40-foot-high, 570-foot-long manmade fish ladder. The viewing room, which maxes out at about 20 people, is open Wed.-Sun. 1-5 p.m., during the brief spawning season.

Touring Topsham

Just across the Androscoggin River, the Topsham Historic Commission has produced a handy illustrated guide, *Topsham, Maine, Historical Walking Tour,* with photos and descriptions of 35 significant architectural and historical landmarks—mostly 18th- and 19th-century Federal and Greek Revival residences. Topsham, incorporated in 1764, is a sleeper of a town; this walking tour proves it. The free booklet is available at the chamber of commerce.

RECREATION

Hiking/Walking

In the village of Bailey Island, there's a mini-walk to the **Giant Stairs,** a waterfront stone stairway of mammoth proportions. To get there, take Rt. 24 from Cooks Corner toward Bailey Island and Land's End, keeping an eye out for

Washington Ave., on the left about one and a half miles after the cribstone bridge. (Or drive to Land's End, park the car with the rest of the crowds, survey the panorama, and walk .8 mile back along Rt. 24 to Washington Ave. from there.) Turn onto Washington Ave., go .1 mile, and park at the Episcopal Church (corner of Ocean Street). Walk along Ocean St. to the shorefront path. Watch for a tiny sign. Don't let small kids get close to the slippery rocks on the surf-tossed shoreline. (The same advice, by the way, holds for Land's End, where the rocks can be treacherous.)

Thanks to the **Brunswick-Topsham Land Trust,** founded in 1985, two nature preserves (one on Harpswell Neck, one in Topsham) are open to the public for hiking, birding, and cross-country skiing. Both are free and accessible from sunrise to sunset; no bikes or pets are allowed. Be a conscientious trail-keeper and carry a litter bag when you go. The 11-acre **Captain Alfred Skolfield Nature Preserve** has two blue-blazed nature-trail loops; one skirts a saltmarsh, where you're apt to see egrets, herons, and osprey in summer. Adjacent to the preserve is an ancient Indian portage site that linked Middle Bay and Harpswell Coves when Native Americans spent their vacations here. (No dopes, they!) Dr. Alice Whittier donated the preserve in memory of her seafaring grandfather. Take Rt. 123 (Harpswell Rd.) south from Brunswick about three miles; when you reach the Middle Bay Rd. intersection (on right), continue on Rt. 123 for 1.1 miles. Watch for a small sign, and a small parking area, on your right.

In Topsham, the 163-acre **Bradley Pond Farm Preserve** has two well-laid-out nature loops (a total of two and a half miles) that let you sample marshes, woodlands, fields, and the pond—all astonishingly close to civilization. Farm owners Florence and Fred Call have generously agreed to share their special turf, so heed the rules and stay on the trails. From Maine St. in Brunswick, cross the river to Topsham's Main Street. At the junction of Rts. 196 and 201, take 201 four miles to Bradley Pond Rd. (on the left). Turn in and park (or leave your bike) in the designated parking areas on the left. For further info on these and other reserved lands, or even to volunteer some trail-maintenance time, contact the Brunswick-Topsham

Land Trust, 83 Maine St., Brunswick 04011, tel. (207) 729-7694.

In the communities to the north (Bath) and south (Freeport) are several more nature preserves well worth visits.

Cycling

Maine's Green Party launched an ambitious **Bike-Share Program** starting in Brunswick in early 1997. Thanks to generous cash and in-kind donations, party members and supporters collected and repaired more than 200 bikes; volunteers set up bike racks at Brunswick's Curtis Memorial Library, Fort Andross (next to the river), and the Tontine Mall. Everything's on the honor system. From spring until early December, help yourself to one of the bright-green single-gear bikes, pedal around as long as you like, then return it to the most convenient rack. The bikes are best for local transport—you'll want higher-tech wheels for cycling outside of town, especially if you're headed to the Harpswells.

As in so many other parts of Maine, roads in the Harpswells rate poor-to-zero for biking, so you'll want a mountain bike or hybrid to negotiate the crummy shoulders. But the scenic rewards erase any inconvenience. Al Taber's **Center Street Bicycles**, 11 Center St., just off Maine St., Brunswick 04011, tel. (207) 729-5309, a local institution since 1981, rents mountain bikes ($24 a day, including helmet), does repairs, and sells a good range of accessories. The staff also provides route info. Open Mon.-Fri. 9 a.m.-5:30 p.m., Saturday 9 a.m.-4 p.m.; closed January.

An ambitious but not difficult **50-mile loop** starts and ends at Cooks Corner, Rt. 24, east of downtown Brunswick, where you can leave your vehicle in the shopping-center parking lot. Take Rt. 24 south about 14 miles to Land's End, en route crossing bridges to Great (Sebascodegan), Orr's, and Bailey Islands. Backtrack as far as Mountain Rd. and head west 2.6 miles (several scenic viewpoints) to Rt. 123 on Harpswell Neck. Turn left and go all the way down Rt. 123 to Potts Point, then return all the way up Rt. 123 to Bath Rd. in downtown Brunswick. Turn right to go back to Cooks Corner. Lodgings and restaurants are all along this route, so you can easily break it up into a two-day (or more) jaunt. You can also do one segment at a time—just Harpswell Neck, or just the islands—to rack up less mileage. Since the roads are narrow, and weekend traffic is the heaviest, try to schedule these treks for weekdays.

Swimming

Thomas Point Beach, 29 Meadow Rd., Brunswick 04011, tel. (207) 725-6009, is actually 64 acres of privately owned parkland with facilities for swimming (lifeguard on duty; bathhouses), fishing, field sports, picnicking (500 tables), and camping (75 tent and RV sites at $16; no water hookups; $4 for electricity). The sandy beach is tidal, so the swimming "window" is about two hours before high tide until two hours afterward; otherwise, you're wallowing in mudflats. (The same rule holds for kayakers or canoeists.) There's a big playground with lots of room to run that's perfect for toddlers. Teenagers gravitate to the arcade and the ice cream parlor; for adults, there's a gift shop (which also carries paper plates and such). The park is also the site of several annual events: the Maine Festival of the Arts, the Maine Highland Games, and the Bluegrass Festival. Parking is ample. At Cooks Corner, where Bath Rd. meets Rt. 24 south, take the Thomas Point Rd. southwestward about two miles to the park. Open Memorial Day weekend to Labor Day, 9 a.m.-sunset. Admission is $2.50 adults, $2 children under 12.

If the tide is low and freshwater swimming appeals, head to town-owned **Coffin Pond,** River Rd., Brunswick, tel. (207) 725-6656, a manmade swimming hole with a sandy beach, lifeguards, water slide, picnic tables, playground, changing rooms, and snack bar. Kids' swimming lessons (ages 5-14) are held in August. It's a popular spot, so expect plenty of company. Open mid-June to Labor Day, 10 a.m.-7 p.m. Nonresident admission is $3.50 adults, $2 children 12 and under. Heading west on Rt. 1 (Pleasant St.), turn right onto River Rd. and go about a mile to the parking area (on the right).

Another terrific but nonsecret spot for freshwater swimming is **White's Beach,** White's Beach & Campground, Durham Rd., Brunswick 04011, tel. (207) 729 0415. The sandy-bottomed pond maxes out at nine feet, so it's particularly good for small kids. Admission is $2.50 adults, $1.50 kids 12 and under. Campsites (45) are $13-17 a night. Open mid-May to mid-October.

From Rt. 1 just south of the I-95 exit into Brunswick, take Durham Rd. 2.2 miles northwest.

Golf

Established in 1901 primarily for Bowdoin College students, the **Brunswick Golf Club,** River Rd., Brunswick 04011, tel. (207) 725-8224, is now an especially popular 18-hole public course, so you'll need to call for a starting time. Heading west on Rt. 1 (Pleasant St.), turn right onto River Rd. and go three quarters of a mile. Open early April to mid-November. If you can stand the runway backdraft challenging your swing, the nine-hole **Brunswick Naval Air Station Golf Club,** Bath Rd., Brunswick, tel. (207) 921-2155, is open to the public. You'll have access to the pro shop, snack bar, and driving range; moderate greens fees.

Getting Afloat

Departing at noon from the Cook's Lobster House Wharf in Bailey Island (end of Rt. 24), a large, sturdy **Casco Bay Lines ferry** does a one-and-a-half-hour nature-watch circuit of nearby islands, including Eagle Island, the onetime home of Adm. Robert Peary (there are no stopovers on these circuits; for excursions to Eagle Island, see "Getting Afloat" under "Greater Portland" in the South Coast/Portland chapter). The nature-watch cruise operates daily except Saturday, late June through Labor Day, then Sunday only through mid-October. Reservations aren't needed. Cost is $8 adults, $6.75 seniors, $3.25 children 5-9; under five are free. To confirm the schedule when weather is iffy, call Casco Bay Lines, (207) 774-7871, or Cook's Wharf, (207) 833-6641.

For a more intimate excursion in a smaller boat, Capt. Les McNelly, owner of **Sea Escape Charters,** Box 7, Bailey Island 04003, tel. (207) 833-5531, operates two-hour on-demand sightseeing cruises throughout the summer (weather permitting) for $40 pp (two persons) or $25 pp (four persons). Or he'll take you out to Eagle Island for $30 a couple (lower rate for more passengers). Call to schedule a trip.

For **sea kayaking,** contact H2Outfitters, P.O. Box 72, Orr's Island 04066, tel. (207) 833-5257 or (800) 649-5257 in Maine, a thriving operation since 1978. Based in a red-painted wood building on the Orr's Island side of the famed cribstone bridge, the company provides basic group instruction ($25 pp, two hours) and clinics ($35 pp, two hours) and offers half-day ($50 pp), day-long ($75 pp), and multiday ($100/day pp) trips; all gear is included.

If you're an experienced sea kayaker, consider exploring Harpswell Sound from the boat launch on the west side of the cribstone bridge; kayaks can also put in at Mackerel Cove, near Cook's Lobster House.

Hazel-Bea House and The Captain's Watch (see "B&Bs" under "Accommodations," below) both offer sailing excursions but are far enough off the beaten track that most of their customers tend to be their guests.

ENTERTAINMENT

There's no lack of classical music in Brunswick each summer, but for lighter fare, the **Maine State Music Theatre,** Pickard Theatre, Bowdoin College, mailing address 14 Maine St., Suite 109, Brunswick 04011, tel. (207) 725-8769, fax 725-1199, has been a summer tradition since 1959. The theater brings real pros to the Brunswick stage for five musicals (mid-June to late August). Loyal subscribers book the same seats year after year, and performances tend to sell out, so call ahead for the schedule and reservations. (Nonsubscription tickets go on sale May 1.) Performances are at 8 p.m. Tues.-Sat.; matinees are staged at 2 p.m. Tuesday, Thursday, and Friday. No kids under four. Ticket range is $15-30. Budget hint: Two preview performances precede each opening; balcony seats are $15.

Brunswick's liveliest club is the downtown **Barking Spider,** 94 Maine St., beneath Kingsfords Restaurant, tel. (207) 721-9662, with jam sessions, cribbage tournaments, darts, jukebox, laser karaoke, and about seven dozen beer choices. Often there's no cover for live entertainment. Open all year.

First-run films, and at least one kiddie flick, are on offer at Hoyt's **Brunswick Cine 10,** 19 Gurnet Rd., Cooks Corner, tel. (207) 798-3995, a multiplex that opens about 11:30 a.m. and closes about 12 hours later. Call for a schedule or check Brunswick's *Times Record* or the *Portland Press Herald.*

Eveningstar Cinema, Tontine Mall, Brunswick, tel. (207) 729-5486, catering to the college crowd, screens lesser-known art and second-run films. It also offers inexpensive matinees ($3) of PG-rated kids' movies. Open all year.

FESTIVALS AND EVENTS

From late June through early August, the **Bowdoin Summer Music Festival** is a showcase for musical talent of all kinds. Guest artists, faculty, and music students perform classical and contemporary concerts Wednesday and Friday evenings (Wednesday tickets are less expensive). Friday faculty recitals (8 p.m., $17.50) are in the state-of-the-art Crooker Theater at Brunswick High School. Wednesday Upbeat! concerts ($6) are in Kresge Auditorium at Bowdoin College. The festival also includes other special performances on other evenings, so check with the festival office, tel. (207) 725-3895, or the chamber of commerce.

Wednesday evenings (Thursdays if it rains) July and August, **Music on the Mall** presents family band concerts at 7 p.m. on the Brunswick Mall.

The Maine Festival, the first weekend in August, is a huge, eclectic showcase of Maine's cultural talent, with back-to-back performances, artistic happenings, and plenty of interesting ethnic food well into the evening at Thomas Point Beach, in Brunswick. The first week of August, the **Topsham Fair** is a week-long agricultural festival with exhibits, demonstrations, live music, ox pulls, contests, harness racing, and fireworks at the Topsham Fairgrounds. The third Saturday of the month, the **Maine Highland Games** mark the annual wearing of the plaids—but you needn't be Scottish to join in the games or watch the highland dancing or browse the arts and crafts booths. (Only a Scot, however, can appreciate that unique concoction called haggis.) If you're seeking your clan roots, this is the place; lots of genealogical networking goes on here. It all happens at Thomas Point Beach; tickets are $8 adults, $4 kids 6-12.

Also at Thomas Point Beach, September's **Annual Bluegrass Festival** is a three-day event with nonstop bluegrass, including big-name

artists. Tickets run $20-24 per day, $55 for the whole works. Kickoff is Friday noon.

SHOPPING

More than a dozen small shops are part of the **Tontine Mall,** 149 Maine St., Brunswick; the mall entrance is right in the middle of downtown.

Art, Craft, and Antiques Galleries

Since 1985, Ray Farrell's **O'Farrell Gallery,** 58 Maine St., Brunswick 04011, tel. (207) 729-8228, has been mounting six superb shows annually, specializing in contemporary American artists. Gallery regulars are Neil Welliver, Robert Indiana, Alex Katz, and Marguerite Robichaux. Open all year, Mon.-Sat. 10 a.m.-5 p.m.

Next door, **Connections: Objects and Images,** 56 Maine St., Brunswick 04011, tel. (207) 725-1399, with a year-round schedule of changing contemporary-art exhibits, is open Mon.-Sat. 10 a.m.-6 p.m. (to 8 p.m. Friday) in summer, shorter hours in winter.

Less than a block away is **ICON,** 19 Mason St., Brunswick 04011, tel. (207) 725-8157, another showcase for contemporary Maine art. Open Mon.-Fri. 1-5 p.m., Saturday 1-4 p.m. in summer, shorter hours in winter.

Stone Soup Artisans, 102 Maine St., Brunswick 04011, tel. (207) 798-5841, a cooperative gallery affiliated with the Society of Southern Maine Craftsmen, markets high-quality work by dozens of artisans. Open all year, Mon.-Sat. 9:30 a.m.-5:30 p.m. (to 8 p.m. Thursday and Friday in summer), and Sunday noon-4 p.m. in summer.

Facing the Mall, **Day's Antiques,** 153 Park Row, Brunswick 04011, tel. (207) 725-6959, occupies five rooms and the basement of the handsome historic building known as the Pumpkin House. Quality is high, prices are fair. Open all year, Mon.-Sat. 10 a.m.-5 p.m.

Along Rt. 123 in South Harpswell, south of Mountain Road, watch for distinctive blue-heron signs that mark the studios of **Harpswell Craft Guild** members—a half-dozen or so artisans who welcome visitors to see (and buy) their pottery, sculpture, jewelry, and chocolate (yes!). Appointments are necessary for some studios.

memorial to Maine's fishermen,
Land's End, Bailey Island

Membership varies from year to year, so call (207) 833-6004 (Ash Cove Pottery) or (207) 833-6081 (Widgeon Cove Studios) for details.

Bookstores
Bet you can't leave Brunswick without buying a book! Bookstores are plentiful. In addition to the ones described below, there's also the Bowdoin College Bookstore, located in the campus's new David Saul Smith Student Union.

With an eclectic new-book inventory that includes lots of esoterica, **Gulf of Maine Books,** 134 Maine St., Brunswick 04011, tel. (207) 729-5083, has held the competition at bay since the early 1980s. Poet/publisher/Renaissance man Gary Lawless oversees everything.

Upstairs from Gulf of Maine is Clare Howell's **Old Books,** 136 Maine St., Brunswick 04011, tel. (207) 725-4524, another longstanding operation, specializing in literary classics and other out-of-print titles. Count on her prices

being fair. Open Mon.-Sat. (except Thursday) 10 a.m.-5 p.m.; call ahead to be sure.

If you're looking for Maine books, **Maine Writers and Publishers Alliance,** 12 Pleasant St., Brunswick 04011, tel. (207) 729-6333, fax 725-1014, is the place. Primarily a networking and professional-development organization for the poetry and publishing set, it has a retail shop where you can buy just about everything in print by Maine authors. Open Mon.-Fri. 9 a.m.-5 p.m., Saturday 10 a.m.-1 p.m.

Bookland of Maine, Cooks Corner Shopping Center, corner of Bath Rd. and Rt. 24 south, Brunswick 04011, tel. (207) 725-2313, a Maine-headquartered chain, was the largest bookstore north of Boston when it opened in 1994. That's no longer true, but no matter. This is a terrific store with an especially helpful staff. Inside the 20,000-square-foot emporium are a zillion books (plus CDs and cards) as well as the Hardcover Cafe. At *least* try one of their desserts. Open Mon.-Sat. 9 a.m.-10 p.m. (to 11 p.m. Friday and Saturday) and Sunday 9 a.m.-6 p.m.

Natural Foods/Farmers' Market
Morning Glory Natural Foods, 64 Maine St., Brunswick 04011, tel. (207) 729-0546, stocks a health-food inventory ranging from the typical to the unusual. Plus it's open every day and weekday evenings.

One of Maine's best farmers' markets is the **Brunswick Farmers' Market,** which sets up, rain or shine, on the Mall (village green) Tuesday and Friday 8 a.m.-3 p.m., May-Nov. (Friday is the bigger day). Produce, cheeses, crafts, condiments, live lobsters, and serendipitous surprises—depending on the season. Brunswick's market inspired the 1991 publication of Sandra Garson's *How to Fix a Leek . . . And Other Fresh Food from Maine Farmers' Markets,* providing month-by-month recipes for preparing all the stuff you'll pick up. Copies are usually available at the market or at the Maine Writers and Publishers Alliance bookshop.

ACCOMMODATIONS

Hotels, Motels, Inns
Combining a Federal-style manse with a new hotel wing, **The Captain Daniel Stone Inn,** 10

Water St., Brunswick 04011, tel. (207) 725-9898 or (800) 267-0525, fax (207) 725-9898, has 34 guest rooms and suites with reproduction furnishings and a country-hotel feel. Private baths, a/c, phones, cable TV; no pets. Doubles are $109-175, including continental breakfast; special packages are available. The inn's casually elegant **Narcissa Stone Restaurant,** open daily year-round for dinner (and weekdays for lunch), serves a mean Sunday brunch 10 a.m.-2 p.m. for $10.95 pp. Light (prices and food) meals are available in the lounge and on the veranda.

Part of the reliable national chain, the 80-room **Comfort Inn,** 199 Pleasant St., Rt. 1, Brunswick 04011, tel. (207) 729-1129 or (800) 228-5150, fax (207) 725-8310, is one of the town's newest hostelries. Located at the southern end of Brunswick, on busy Rt. 1, it's wisely set back a bit from the road, but ask for a rear-facing room if you're sensitive to traffic noise. Facilities include a/c, cable TV (free movies), and free continental breakfast. No pets. Rates run $70-80 d, July-Oct.; $50-75 d other months. Open all year.

As its name suggests, **The Atrium Inn,** 21 Gurnet Rd., Rt. 24, Cooks Corner, Brunswick 04011, tel. (207) 729-5555, fax 729-5149, wraps its 161 rooms and 25 suites around a huge enclosed space—partly occupied by a heated pool. Kids love this place, and pool noise usually quiets down early. The only drawback is a whiff of chlorine. Rooms have microwaves, cable TV, a/c; there's also a health club. Doubles are $65-100 May to mid-September, $55-65 other months, including continental breakfast. The inn's restaurant, adjacent to the lobby, is open daily 6 a.m.-10 p.m. (Sunday from 7 a.m.) For the sports-starved, the inn has **Winner's,** tel. (207) 725-6500, a sports grill with more than a dozen TVs, a six-foot screen, off-track betting (and an ATM), and lunch and dinner daily.

A dozen miles down Rt. 24 from Cooks Corner is the turnoff for the **Little Island Motel,** RD 1, Box 15, Orr's Island 04066, tel. (207) 833-2392 or 833-7362 guest phone, a nine-unit complex on its own spit of land with deck views you won't believe. Basic rooms have cable TV and small fridge. Doubles go for $110-114 (mid-summer) and $84-88 (early and late season), including buffet breakfast (homemade muffins) and use of bikes, boats, and a little beach. No pets, no credit cards. Open mid-May to mid-October.

Continue another mile down Rt. 24, cross the cribstone bridge, and you'll come to the **Bailey Island Motel,** Rt. 24, P.O. Box 4, Bailey Island 04003, tel. (207) 833-2886, a congenial, clean, no-frills waterfront spot with 10 rooms that go for $85 d mid-June through September, and $65 early and late in the season. Kids under 10 are free, continental breakfast is included, and rooms have cable TV. No pets. Open early May to late October.

Looking rather like an old-fashioned tear-jerker film set, the family-run **Driftwood Inn,** P.O. Box 16, Bailey Island 04003, tel. (207) 833-5461, has 28 basic rooms in three buildings, a saltwater pool, a stunning view, a dining room (open to the public), and a determinedly rustic ambience. Nearby are the Giant Stairs. Rooms are $65-70 d; all meals are extra, but MAP rates are available. Open mid-May to mid-October.

B&Bs

Right downtown, facing the tree-shaded Mall, is Mercie and Steve Normand's **Brunswick Bed & Breakfast,** 165 Park Row, Brunswick 04011, tel. (207) 729-4914 or (800) 299-4914, a handsome, 30-room Greek Revival mansion built in 1849. Special touches are the twin parlors (with fireplaces), lots of antiques, and the Normands' collection of antique and modern quilts. Four of the five elegant second-floor guest rooms have private baths; the fifth shares a bath with an extra third-floor room rented only in summer. Breakfast is a treat. No smoking, no pets. No minimum stay except for special Bowdoin College occasions (graduation, parents' weekend). Doubles are $75-95. Open all year, but call ahead off season.

Diving into a multi-year project to restore the 1761 **Harpswell Inn,** 141 Lookout Point Rd., RR 1, Box 141, South Harpswell 04079, tel. (207) 833-5509 or (800) 843-5509, hospitable hosts Susan and Bill Menz created a comfortable, welcoming, antiques-filled oasis on three and a half secluded acres. It's tough to break away from the glass-walled great room, but Middle Bay sunsets from the porch can do it. And just down the hill is Allen's Seafood, where you can watch lobstermen unload their catch in a gorgeous cove. In fall, the foliage on two little islets in the cove turns brilliant red. The B&B has 13 rooms (five with private bath, seven with water views) at $59-116 d. Just behind the main building are two luxury suites ($150 d or $900 a week) with cathedral ceilings and kitchens. Two-night minimum for all rooms July, August, and October weekends. No children under 10; limited access for pets; smoking only on the porch. From Bath Rd., in Brunswick, take Rt. 123 eight miles to Lookout Point Rd. (on right). Open all year.

Overlooking Quahog Bay on Great (officially Sebascodegan) Island, **Hazel-Bea House,** Fire Rd. 280, Sebascodegan Island, mailing address RR 2, Box 2233, Brunswick 04011, tel. (207) 725-6834, is just off Rt. 24, about six miles from Cooks Corner or Land's End. Three rooms (one with private bath) are $75 d. Chuck and Roberta Hammond get high marks for hospitality and sundeck breakfasts. No pets; smoking outside only. Open May through October, sometimes also at Thanksgiving. By prior arrangement, Capt. Chuck offers daysails and charters aboard his handsome 38-foot pilothouse ketch *Winnower.* Maximum of six for daysails, three for overnights. Cost depends on the schedule; he'll gladly suggest an itinerary.

Another bed-and-breakfast-cum-boat operation is a mouthful: **The Captain's Watch at Cundy's Harbor B&B and Sail Charter,** 2476 Cundy's Harbor Rd., Cundy's Harbor, mailing address RR 5, Box 2476, Brunswick 04011, tel. (207) 725-0979. Based in the National Historic Register Cupola House—an inn since Civil War days—the B&B has five guest rooms, including a suite, all with private baths and unusual features (two share access to the head-swiveling octagonal cupola). Energetic hosts Donna Dillman and Ken Brigham, innkeepers since 1986, took the reins here in 1996. Ken captains the 37-foot sloop *Symbion* for daysails ($40 pp for four hours, $100 pp overnight); Donna produces the gourmet breakfasts and goes sailing off season. Doubles are $95-140. No smoking, no pets, no small children. Open all year, by reservation off season. From Cooks Corner, go four and a half miles on Rt. 24, turn left and go another 4.4 miles to Cundy's Harbor, near the "fingertips" of Great Island's easternmost "arm."

While most Maine B&Bs operate out of older homes (or lookalike older homes), **Orr's Island Bed & Breakfast,** Rt. 24, Box 561, Orr's Island 04066, tel. (207) 833-2940 or (800) 550-2940, is an attractive modern house with two second-floor rooms (private baths) overlooking tidal

Long Cove. Breakfast on the deck is as good as it gets, the gardens are outstanding, and you can swim in the cove when the tide's in. Bring your kayak or rent one—you can launch it near H2Outfitters, just down the road. No pets; smoking permitted only on the deck. Rates are $85 d in season, $65 d off season. Open all year. From Cooks Corner, go 10.2 miles on Rt. 24.

Retired Bowdoin professor William Whiteside and his wife, Susan, a former commercial pilot, have been the congenial hosts at **Tower Hill Bed and Breakfast,** Rt. 24, RFD 1, Box 688, Orr's Island 04066, tel. (207) 833-2311, fax 833-6256, since 1994. Antiques are everywhere in their casually elegant 19th-century home, including fascinating specimens from travels in China. Birders, take note: Outside are four acres of lawns and gardens, plus trails to a marsh and Harpswell Sound. Four suites (two with private baths) are $68-130 d. No smoking, no children under eight. Cancellation policy strictly enforced. Open April-November.

After many years as an extremely popular dining destination 13 miles south of Cooks Corner, **The Log Cabin,** Rt. 24, P.O. Box 41, Bailey Island 04003, tel. (207) 833-5546, fax 833-7858, in 1996 added lodging to its repertoire. Three rooms are over the restaurant, two rooms and a suite are in a nearby building. All rooms are newly decorated, with private baths, phones, TV/VCR, and private decks facing the bay and, weather permitting, splendid sunsets over the White Mountains. Rates are $99-109 d ($150 d for a suite) in midsummer, lower early and late in the season. Full breakfast is included. No pets, no smoking. The restaurant—serving first-rate regional specialties in an informal setting—is open 11:30 a.m.-2 p.m. and 5-8 p.m. daily. Reservations are a must: this family-run operation draws crowds. Both B&B and restaurant are open mid-March through October.

Seasonal Rentals and Campgrounds

For weekly and monthly rentals in Great, Orr's, and Bailey Islands, contact Becky-Sue Betts at **Your Island Connection,** P.O. Box 300, next to the cribstone bridge, Bailey Island 04003, tel. (207) 833-7779. Extremely knowledgeable and helpful about her turf and the various types of lodgings, she manages more than five dozen homes, cottages, and apartments ($475-2,000 a week). The Bath-Brunswick chamber of commerce also keeps a list of seasonal cottage rentals.

On Harpswell Neck, contact Sue and Bill Menz at the **Harpswell Inn,** tel. (207) 833-5509 or (800) 843-5509, for information about the four weekly-rental cottages they manage (occasionally, they're available for stays as short as two nights).

Campsites are available at Thomas Point Beach and White's Beach.

FOOD

Local wisdom holds that this college town has relatively few restaurants per capita because Bowdoin College—unlike most higher-learning institutions—actually serves good food. If you want to find out for yourself, stop in at the college's David Saul Smith Student Union or the café at Coles Tower, both open to the public.

Brunswick and Topsham

Mediterranean sandwiches and salads are specialties at **Pane Vino,** 153 Park Row, Brunswick 04011, tel. (207) 729-0339; the $5.95 antipasto is one of the best values. But it's hard to decide; everything's delicious. This bright spot in the historic Pumpkin House, across from the lovely Mall, is open all year, Tues.-Sat. 8:30 a.m.-3 p.m. (lunch begins at 11:30). In summer, make a dash for the patio. During the theater and music-festival season, Pane Vino serves pre-performance suppers.

At the upper end of the downtown drag is **Scarlet Begonias,** 212B Maine St., Brunswick 04011, tel. (207) 721-0403, an especially cheerful place with a bistro-type pizza-and-pasta menu. How could anyone resist a $7.50 pasta puttanesca dubbed Scarlet Harlot? Open Mon.-Fri. 11 a.m.- 8 p.m. (to 9 p.m. Friday), Saturday noon-9 p.m.

If Chinese appeals, head for **China Rose,** 42 Bath Rd., Brunswick 04011, tel. (207) 725-8813, a clone of the superb Freeport restaurant of the same name. Sichuan, Hunan, Cantonese, and Mandarin are all on on the extensive lunch and dinner buffets. Adults can do the dinner buffet for only $10.95 pp. Buffet hours are limited (11 a.m.-2:30 p.m., 5-8:30 p.m.), but the restaurant is open daily 11 a.m.-9:30 p.m. (to 10:30 p.m. Friday and Saturday).

If you'd rather go a bit more ethnic, try **Rosita's,** 212 Maine St., Brunswick, tel. (207) 729-7118, a Mexican restaurant with a veggie emphasis. Order at the counter and grab a table. Prices are incredibly reasonable (combo platter is under $6) and beans are lard- and oil-free. No smoking, no credit cards; beer license only. Open daily 11 a.m.-9 p.m. (to 9:30 p.m. Friday and Saturday).

Generous portions, moderate prices, efficient service, and narrow aisles are the story at **The Great Impasta,** 42 Maine St., Brunswick 04011, tel. (207) 729-5858, an informal eatery where the garlic meets you at the door. No reservations, so expect to wait, although you can call ahead and add your name to the waiting list. Small but varied wine list; no smoking; "bambino menu" for the kids. Open Mon.-Sat. 11 a.m.- 9 p.m. (to 10 p.m. Friday and Saturday), Sunday 5-9 p.m.

Wild Oats Bakery and Cafe, 149 Maine St., Tontine Mall, Brunswick 04011, tel. (207) 725-6287, turns out terrific made-from-scratch breads and pastries, especially the breakfast kind, in its cafeteria-style place. Outside tables, moderate prices, good-for-you salads and sandwiches. No credit cards, no smoking. Open Mon.-Sat. 7:30 a.m.-5 p.m., Sunday 8 a.m.-2 p.m.

After the healthful stuff, there's always **Ben & Jerry's,** 96 Maine St., Brunswick 04011, tel. (207) 725-2723, purveyors of upscale ice cream and T-shirts to match, open daily 11:30 a.m.-midnight.

Fat Boy Drive-In, Bath Rd., Old Rt. 1, Brunswick, tel. (207) 729-9431, is a genuine throwback—a landmark since 1955 boasting carhops, window trays, $1.25 cheeseburgers, and a menu guaranteed to clog your arteries. Fries and frappés are specialties. If you insist, there are five booths indoors. No credit cards. Open—get this—the third Tuesday in March to the second Sunday in October, daily 10:55 a.m.-8:55 p.m. (to 9:25 p.m. weekends). The second Saturday in August, about 700 people show up, many in 1950s get-ups, for the annual sock hop. Tickets are $7 pp. Only pre-1970 cars can park in the lot that night (if you have one, stop in ahead of time for a pass).

For food-on-the-run—no-frills hot dogs straight from the cart—head for Brunswick's Mall, the village green where **Danny's On the Mall** (no telephone) has been cooking up dirt-cheap tube steaks since the early 1980s. Open mid-May to mid-October. There's also a "branch," **Danny's Off the Mall,** at 89 Harpswell Rd., Rt. 123, Brunswick, tel. (207) 721-0022, with a more extensive array of fast food.

The area's best pizza is at **Benzoni's Brick-Oven Pizza & Italian Café,** 11 Town Hall Place, Brunswick, tel. (207) 729-2800, a newish operation that also serves calzones, pasta entrées, and soup-and-salad combos—indoors or on the deck. A large Benzoni's original pizza is $11.95. Full liquor license. Open 11 a.m.-10 p.m. daily in summer, shorter hours off season. The café is next to the fire station.

After you've hit a couple of galleries on lower Maine Street, a New York-style deli might be just the ticket. The **Big Top Deli,** 70 Maine St., Brunswick 04011, tel. (207) 721-8900, carries out its theme beautifully, with circus-act photos on the blue walls and even a circus burger (with avocado and salsa, $3.75) on the menu. No credit cards, no smoking. The deli is open Mon.-Fri. 6 a.m.-8 p.m., Saturday 8 a.m.-7 p.m., and Sunday 8 a.m.-4 p.m.

Just across the river from downtown Brunswick, is the **Cross Street Cafe,** 2 Cross St., Topsham 04086, tel. (207) 721-0556, a magnet for breakfast. But you won't go wrong for lunch, either. The Philly steak bomb goes for $5.25. No smoking, no credit cards, no bar. Open Tues.-Sat. 7 a.m.-2 p.m., Sunday 7:30 a.m.-2 p.m.

The Harpswells
Everything's homemade at **J. Hathaways' Restaurant and Tavern,** Rt. 123, Harpswell Center, tel. (207) 833-5305, Jean and Jeff Hathaway's attractive place in a converted barn attached to their house. Entrées run $5.95-13.95; a specialty is authentic fish 'n chips. Smoking is allowed in the tavern, not in the dining room. Open March-Dec., Tues.-Sun. 5-8 p.m. (to 9 p.m. on weekends and all summer). The restaurant is on Harpswell Neck, 10 miles south of downtown Brunswick.

Arguments rage endlessly about who makes the best chowder in Maine, but **The Dolphin Restaurant,** Dolphin Marina, Basin Point, South Harpswell, tel. (207) 833-6000, heads lots of lists for its fish chowder, served with each entrée. Plus you can't beat the scenic 13-mile drive south from Brunswick and the spectacular water

views at the tip of Harpswell Neck. The decor is '50s-ish in this popular spot, and the breakfast menu has barely changed since then. The blueberry pancakes and bacon are famous—never mind the cholesterol count. Open daily 8 a.m.-8 p.m., Memorial Day weekend to Labor Day.

Another super-popular lobster-in-the-rough site, located two fingers to the east of the Dolphin, is **Holbrook's Lobster Wharf,** Cundy's Harbor, tel. (207) 725-0708. Order one of their well-stuffed lobster rolls, or some fried clams, and relax on the deck overlooking the picturesque harbor. Perfection. Burgers are on the menu for fish-phobes. BYOL. Open daily 11 a.m.-8 p.m., Memorial Day weekend to Labor Day. Holbrook's is at the end of Cundy's Harbor Rd., at the end of the earth, about 10 miles south of Cooks Corner.

A Bailey Island landmark since the 1950s, the sprawling **Cook's Lobster House,** Rt. 24, Bailey Island 04003, tel. (207) 833-2818, is one of the most reliable of several seafood places near the peninsula's tip. The fish is predictably fresh, service is efficient, and the view is unbeatable. Besides, you can even order a steak. The restaurant overlooks the hamlet's unique cribstone bridge—a massive latticelike structure that's been allowing tides to ebb and flow since 1928. Open all year, daily 11:30 a.m.-9 p.m. in summer, reduced hours in winter. The Casco Bay Lines summertime nature cruise (see "Getting Afloat" under "Recreation," above) departs from the restaurant's dock.

INFORMATION AND SERVICES

Contact the **Chamber of Commerce of the Bath-Brunswick Region,** 59 Pleasant St., corner of Spring St., Brunswick 04011, tel. (207) 725-8797, for info on lodgings, restaurants, and area activities. The staff is particularly helpful. Request a copy of the free *Intown Brunswick Walking Map.* Open weekdays 8:30 a.m.-5 p.m. year-round, plus some Saturdays in summer. On weekends, local innkeepers maintain a lodging referral service to make sure every visitor finds a bed.

The **Curtis Memorial Library,** 23 Pleasant St., Brunswick 04011, tel. (207) 725-5242, with all the normal adult features, also has an especially friendly children's department. Open Mon.-Fri. 9:30 a.m.-6 p.m. (to 8 p.m. Mon.-Wed.), Saturday 9:30 a.m.-5 p.m. The all-volunteer Friends of the Curtis Memorial Library has produced the *Children's Resource Handbook,* a periodically updated booklet containing dozens of well-organized ideas for entertaining the under-14 set. Copies are available free at the library and the chamber of commerce.

Newspapers
Brunswick's *Times Record,* tel. (207) 729-3311, published weekdays, runs extensive arts and entertainment listings in its Thursday edition. The paper also produces a summer vacation supplement available free at the chamber of commerce and at restaurants and lodgings. The weekly *Coastal Journal,* tel. (207) 443-6241, a free tabloid paper available throughout the Brunswick/Bath area, has extensive calendar listings and periodic *Summer in Maine* supplements.

Emergencies
Mid-Coast Hospital, 58 Baribeau Dr., Brunswick 04011, tel. (207) 729-0181, has a 24-hour emergency department. Also maintaining round-the-clock emergency service is **Parkview Hos-**

pital, Maine St., a mile south of Bowdoin College, Brunswick, tel. (207) 729-1641, a Seventh Day Adventist facility. For **police, fire, and ambulance,** dial 911.

Veterinarians/Kennels
The **Bath-Brunswick Veterinary Associates,** Bath Rd., Brunswick 04011, a quarter-mile east of Cooks Corner, is an especially well-run full-service facility with a boarding kennel. Rates are $10-12 a night for cats or dogs. Open Mon.-Fri. 8 a.m.-7 p.m. (to 6 p.m. Friday) and 9 a.m.-1 p.m. Saturday.

Photo Services
A branch of the first-rate Bath firm by the same name, **Kennebec Camera and Darkroom,** Tontine Mall, 149 Maine St., Brunswick, tel. (207) 721-0598, provides one-hour photo service as well as custom work, including black and white.

Laundromat
Sunshine Center has a coin-operated laundromat at each end of Brunswick: 87-A Pleasant St., Rt. 1, tel. (207) 729-1564, and 200 Bath Rd., tel. (207) 729-6072. Both are open daily 7 a.m.-9 p.m., all year.

BATH AREA

One of the smallest of Maine's cities, Bath—with a population of about 9,500 in only nine square miles—like Brunswick, sits astride Rt. 1 and a river, counts on modern military dollars, yet has centuries of tradition. The defense part is impossible to ignore, since giant cranes dominate the riverfront cityscape at the huge Bath Iron Works complex—source of state-of-the-art warships. Less evident (but not far away) is the link to the past: just south of Bath, in Popham on the Phippsburg Peninsula, is a poorly marked site where a trouble-plagued English settlement predated the Plymouth Colony by 13 years. (Of course, Champlain arrived before that, and Norsemen left calling cards even earlier.) In 1607 and 1608, settlers in the Popham Colony managed to build a 30-ton pinnace, *Virginia of Sagadahoc,* designed for transatlantic

trade, but they lost heart during a bitter winter and abandoned the site.

Bath is the jumping-off point for two peninsulas to the south—Phippsburg (of Popham Colony fame) and Georgetown—both dramatically scenic, with glacier-carved farms and fishing villages. Drive or cycle a dozen miles down any of these fingers and you're in different worlds, ones where artists and photographers, hikers and historians go crazy with all the possibilities.

Across the soaring Carlton Bridge from Bath is Woolwich, from which you can continue northeastward along the coast or detour northward on Rt. 128 to the hamlet of Day's Ferry. Named after 18th-century resident Joseph Day, who shuttled back and forth in a gondola-type boat across the Kennebec here, the picturesque vil-

lage has a cluster of 18th- and 19th-century
homes and churches—all part of the Day's Ferry
Historic District. And the village's Old Stage
Road saw many an old stage in its day—passengers would ferry from Bath and pick up the
stage here to continue onward.

SIGHTS

Bath Iron Works

Only during one of its relatively infrequent
launchings is Bath Iron Works (BIW) open to
the public, and then it's a mob scene, with
hordes of politicos, townsfolk, and military
poohbahs in their scrambled eggs and brass.
But the launchings are exciting occasions, with
flags flying everywhere. BIW, under the umbrella of giant defense contractor General Dynamics, employs more than 8,500 in its Bath
and smaller Brunswick sites. When BIW talks,
everyone listens. And when BIW's afternoon
shift changes, everyone within 10 miles suffers
from the gridlock. In fact, anyone who shows
up in Bath on a weekday between 3:25 and 4
p.m. lives to rue it. Be forewarned and plan your
schedule around the witching hour.

Maine Maritime Museum

Spread over 10 acres on the Kennebec River is
the state's premier marine museum, the Maine
Maritime Museum, 243 Washington St., Bath
04530, tel. (207) 443-1316, fax 443-1665. On
the grounds are relics of the 19th-century Percy
& Small Shipyard and a hands-on lobstering
exhibit, but the first thing you see is the architecturally dramatic Maritime History Building,
locale for permanent and temporary displays of
marine art and artifacts and a shop stocked with
nautical books and gifts. Bring a picnic and let
the toddlers loose in the children's play area.
Then join up with one of the twice-daily, hour-
long guided shipyard tours. In summer, weather permitting, the museum sponsors a variety of
special river cruises; call for info. Open 9:30
a.m.-5 p.m. daily, year-round; Percy & Small
Shipyard is open late spring through Thanksgiving weekend. Admission is $7.50 adults,
$6.75 seniors, $4.75 children 6-16, free for kids
under six. Family rate (two adults, two kids) is
$21. The museum is 1.6 miles south of Rt. 1.

Bath History Preserved

Sagadahoc Preservation Inc. (SPI), founded in
1971 to rescue the city's architectural heritage,
has produced *Architectural Tours: Walking
& Driving in the Bath Area,* a terrific foldout
brochure (with maps) to guide you—via car,
ankle express, or bicycle—around Bath, Phippsburg, and Day's Ferry (in Woolwich). Pick up a
copy at the chamber of commerce or contact
SPI, Box 322, Bath 04530.

Also available at the chamber of commerce is
*An Historical Walking Tour through Down-
town Bath, Maine,* a foldout brochure produced
in early 1996 by seventh-graders at Bath Middle
School. The youngsters have done a fine job
covering 17 highlights of the city's waterfront
area.

For a different spin on the self-guided-tour
concept, and a great way to see the city from a
botanical perspective, request yet another
brochure: *Historic Bath Seen Through Its
Trees.* The Bath Community Forestry Committee has identified more than three dozen significant trees—from ash to zelkova—in Bath's
urban forest. You can follow the trail by bike or
car, or do sections of it on foot.

Phippsburg Peninsula

Thanks to an impressive map/brochure produced by the Phippsburg Historical Society and
the Phippsburg Business Association, you can
spend a whole day—or, better still, several days
—exploring the peninsula that drops down from
Bath. Along the way are campgrounds, B&Bs, a
resort, restaurants, a unique state park, hiking
trails, secluded coves, spectacular scenery, and
tons of history.

About two miles south of Bath is a causeway
known as **Winnegance,** an Abnaki name usually translated as "short carry" or "little portage."
Native Americans crossed here from the Kennebec to the New Meadows River. Early settlers erected nearly a dozen tide-powered mills
to serve the shipbuilding industry, but they're
long gone. Just before the causeway, on the
Bath-Phippsburg boundary, is the **Winnegance
General Store,** 36 High St., Bath 04530, tel.
(207) 443-9805, a local favorite for the miscellanea that general stores offer. About one and a
half miles farther is a left turn onto Fiddler's
Reach Rd., leading to the **Morse Cove Public**

Launching Facility, one of the state's most scenic boat-launch sites. If you have a kayak, plan to go downriver on the ebb tide and return on the flow (otherwise, you'll be battling the Kennebec River current). There's plenty of paved parking here, plus a restroom.

Back on Rt. 209, it's another 1.3 miles to the **Dromore Burying Ground** (on the right), with great old headstones—the earliest dated 1743. The next mile opens up with terrific easterly views of Dromore Bay. Right in the line of sight is 117-acre Lee Island (which the owners sold to the state in 1995). From May through mid-July, the island is off-limits to protect nesting eagles and waterfowl.

Next you're in **Phippsburg Center,** alive with shipbuilding from colonial days to the early 20th century. Hang a left onto Parker Head Rd. (but avoid this side trip if you're cycling; it's too narrow and winding). After the Phippsburg Historical Museum (in an 1859 schoolhouse) and the Alfred Totman Library, turn left onto Church Lane to see the **Phippsburg Congregational Church,** built in 1802. Out front is a "Constitution Tree," a huge English linden allegedly planted in 1775. (Beyond the church is the Riverview Bed and Breakfast.)

Parker Head Rd. continues southward and meets up with Rt. 209, which takes you to **Popham Beach State Park.** Continue to the end of Rt. 209 for **Fort Popham Historic Site,** where parking is woefully inadequate in summer (and costs an exorbitant $5 at nearby Percy's Store). But youngsters love this place—they can fish from the rocks, climb to the third level of the 1865 stone fortress (though the chicken-wire fencing ruins photos), picnic on the seven-acre grounds, and create sand castles on the tiny beach next to the fort. Resist the urge to swim, though; the current is dangerous, and there's no lifeguard. Across the river is Bay Point, a lobstering village at the tip of the Georgetown Peninsula. **Percy's Store,** tel. (207) 389-2010, by the way, with a handful of tables, is the best place down here for pizza, picnic fare, and fishing tackle. On weekends, if your arteries can tolerate it, sample their fried dough.

Across from the fort is a narrow, winding road leading to the poorly marked shorefront site of the 1607 Popham Colony. Climb the path up Sabino Hill to World War I-era **Fort Baldwin,** the best vantage point for panoramic photos.

Backtrack about four miles on Rt. 209, turn left onto Rt. 216, and head toward **Small Point.** On the left, watch for the sign marking the tiny (eight cars) parking area for the **Bates-Morse Mountain Preserve.** Farther south are Head Beach and Hermit Island.

Returning northward on Rt. 216, you'll hook up with Rt. 209 and then see a left turn (Rt. 217) to Sebasco Harbor Resort. Take the time to go beyond the Sebasco resort area. When the paved road goes left (to the Water's Edge Restaurant), turn right at a tiny cemetery and continue northward on the Old Meadowbrook Road, which meanders for about four miles along the west side of the peninsula. About midway along is **the Basin,** regarded by sailors as one of the Maine coast's best "hurricane holes" (refuges in high winds). As you skirt the Basin and come to a fork, bear right to return to Rt. 209; turn left and return northward to Bath.

Woolwich Historical Society Museum
Next to a Rt. 1 flashing caution light, two and a half miles north of Bath, the two-story Woolwich Historical Society Museum, Rt. 1 at Nequasset Rd., P.O. Box 98, Woolwich 04579, tel. (207) 443-4833, admirably well organized, has rooms full of early 19th- to early 20th-century quilts, clothing, tools, and tradesmen's wares. The oldest part of the building dates from the early 19th century. Open daily 10 a.m.-4 p.m., July through Labor Day. Admission is $2 adults, $1 children over six.

PARKS, PRESERVES, AND RECREATION

In-Town Parks
An old-fashioned gazebo, just right for hanging out with a book (bring a cushion), is the centerpiece of **Library Park,** the manicured space fronting the Patten Free Library, Summer and Washington Streets. In summer, the park is the site of weddings, concerts, art exhibits, and children's story hours.

Waterfront Park, bordering the Kennebec on Commercial St., has covered picnic tables, restrooms, and Friday-night concerts in summer. After years of neglect, the waterfront area is undergoing a long-overdue renaissance, with shops, restaurants, and even more green space.

For the kids, there's a particularly creative playground at **Fischer-Mitchell Elementary School,** 597 Hyde St., across from the Hyde School.

Hamilton Sanctuary

Owned by Maine Audubon Society, Hamilton Sanctuary, Foster Point Rd., West Bath, no telephone, is a great birding spot on the New Meadows River with one and a half miles of trails winding through meadows and forests and along the Back Cove shoreline. From Rt. 1 between Bath and Brunswick, take the New Meadows Rd. exit. Head south on New Meadows. When it becomes Foster Point Rd., go four miles to the sanctuary entrance. Open all year, sunrise to sunset; free admission. For more information, contact **Maine Audubon Society,** Gilsland Farm, 118 Rt. 1, Falmouth 04105, tel. (207) 781-2330, fax 781-6185.

Popham Beach State Park

On hot July and August weekends, the parking lot at Popham Beach State Park, Rt. 209, Phippsburg 04562, 14 miles south of Bath, tel. (207) 389-1335, fills up by 10 a.m., so plan to arrive early at this huge crescent of sand backed by sea grass, beach roses, and dunes. Facilities include changing rooms, outside showers, restrooms, seasonal lifeguards. Admission is $2 adults, 50 cents children 5-11, free for seniors and kids under five. Officially open April 15-Oct. 30, but the beach is accessible all year (no winter contact number).

A mile down the road, at the end of Rt. 209, is the seven-acre **Fort Popham Historic Site,** where kids of all ages can explore the waterfront tower and bunkers of a 19th-century granite fort. No swimming here—the current is dangerous—but there's fun fishing from the rocks (no license needed), plus picnic tables and restrooms.

Bates-Morse Mountain Conservation Area

Consider visiting the lovely, 600-acre Bates-Morse Mountain Conservation Area, Rts. 209 and 216, Small Point, Phippsburg Peninsula, *only* if you are willing to be extra-conscientious about the rules for this private preserve. A rela-tively easy four-mile roundtrip hike takes you through marshland (you'll need insect repellent) and to the top of 210-foot Morse Mountain, with panoramic views, then down to privately owned Seawall Beach. On a clear day, you can see New Hampshire's Mt. Washington from the summit. No dogs or vehicles; no recreational facilities; stay on the preserve road and the beach path at all times (side roads are private). Least terns and piping plovers—both endangered species—nest in the dunes, so avoid this area, especially mid-May to mid-August. Birding hint: Morse Mountain is a great locale for spotting hawks during their annual September migration southward. Pick up a map (and the rules) from the box in the small (eight cars max) parking area on Rt. 216 (just under a mile south of the Rt. 209 turnoff to Popham Beach). Roadside parking is also allowed, but pull as far off the road as possible, and don't block access. No admission fee; open sunrise to sunset. For more information, contact the Bates College Department of Biology, tel. (207) 786-6109.

Head Beach

Just off Rt. 216, about two miles south of the Rt. 209 turnoff to Popham Beach, is Head Beach, a sandy crescent that's open until 10 p.m. A minimal day-use fee is payable at the small gatehouse; there's a restroom on the path to the beach.

Reid State Park

Reid State Park, on the Georgetown Peninsula, Seguinland Rd., Georgetown 04548, tel. (207) 371-2303, is no secret, so plan to arrive early on summer weekends, when parking is woefully inadequate. Highlights of the 765-acre park are one and a half miles of splendid beach (in three distinct sections), marshlands, sand dunes, and tidepools. Kids love the tidepools, treasure troves left by the receding tide. Facilities include changing rooms (with showers), picnic tables, restrooms, and snack bars. Test the water before racing in; even in midsummer, it's breathtakingly cold. In winter, bring cross-country skis and glide along the shoreline. The park—14 miles south of Rt. 1 (Woolwich) and two miles off Rt. 127—is open daily all year. Admission is $2.50 adults, 50 cents children 5-11, free for kids under five.

Just a half a mile beyond the Reid State Park entrance is **Charles Pond,** where the setting is unsurpassed for freshwater swimming in the long, skinny pond. You'll wish this were a secret, too, but it isn't. No facilities.

Josephine Newman Sanctuary
A must-see for any nature lover, the 119-acre Josephine Newman Sanctuary, Rt. 127, Georgetown, no telephone, has two and a half miles of blazed loop trails winding through 110 wooded acres and along Robinhood Cove's tidal shoreline. Josephine Oliver Newman (1878-1968), a respected naturalist, bequeathed her family's splendid property to the Maine Audubon Society, which maintains it today. The .6-mile Self-Guiding Trail is moderately difficult, but the rewards are 20 informative markers highlighting special features: glacial erratics, reversing falls, mosses, and marshes. Easiest route is the three-quarter-mile Horseshoe Trail, which you can extend for another mile or so by linking into the Rocky End Trail. The sanctuary is open daily, all year, sunrise to sunset; free admission. No pets or bikes. The best way to appreciate it is to buy *Forests, Fields, and Estuaries,* a 60-page sanctuary guide ($3.50), with lots of natural-history info useful for other preserves. Contact the Maine Audubon Society, Gilsland Farm, 118 Rt. 1, Falmouth 04105, tel. (207) 781-2330, fax 781-6185, or stop in at the society's gift shop in Falmouth. To reach the Newman sanctuary, take Rt. 127 from Rt. 1 in Woolwich (the road to Reid State Park) for 9.1 miles. Turn right at the sanctuary sign and continue to the small parking lot. A map of the trail system is posted at the marsh's edge.

Montsweag Preserve
Owned by The Nature Conservancy, 45-acre Montsweag Preserve, Montsweag Rd., Woolwich, no telephone, is a peaceful estuarine microcosm on the shore of tidal Montsweag Brook. A one-and-a-half-mile, blue-blazed loop trail meanders through fields and woods, tidal frontage and salt marsh. Wear long pants and waterproof shoes or boots. Open all year, sunrise to sunset. From Bath, take Rt. 1 northwest about six and a half miles, to Montsweag Road (not well marked). Turn right and go 1.3 miles to the preserve, on the left (also not well marked).

Park alongside the road and do the trail clockwise. For more information, contact the The Nature Conservancy, Maine Chapter, tel. (207) 729-5181.

Golf
The 18-hole **Bath Country Club,** Whiskeag Rd., Bath, tel. (207) 442-8411, has a fairly new back nine, moderate greens fees, a particularly well-stocked pro shop, and a restaurant serving lunch and dinner. Starting times needed on weekends. Open early April to mid-October. From Rt. 1 in West Bath, take New Meadows Rd., then Ridge Rd., north two miles to Whiskeag Rd. and the club.

The Sebasco Harbor Resort has a nine-hole course.

Cycling
Bath-area headquarters for anything to do with bikes is **Bath Cycle and Ski,** Rt. 1, opposite Rt. 127 north, Woolwich 04579, tel. (207) 442-7002, fax 442-0936. Rentals are $18 a day (including helmet and lock), route maps are available, and the shop sponsors weekly road and mountain-bike rides (Monday, Tuesday, Sunday at 6 p.m.). Stop here, too, for in-line skates and snowboards. Open Mon.-Fri. 9 a.m.-6 p.m. (to 8 p.m. Friday), Saturday 9 a.m.-5 p.m.

A relatively easy nine-mile loop recommended by the bike shop begins at the downtown Bath post office (750 Washington St.; parking available). Go north on Washington St. to North St., turn left and go one-half mile to Oak Grove Avenue. Turn sharp right (five-way intersection) and continue about one mile to Whiskeag Rd.; turn left. Go another .7 mile and turn right, continuing for 1.6 miles. Turn left at Hawkes Farm and go about two miles (part unpaved) to Old Brunswick Rd.; turn left. Continue 2.3 miles back toward town (Old Brunswick becomes Lincoln St.) to Centre St.; turn left and continue down the hill to Washington Street. Turn right to return to the post office.

Canoeing
Close to civilization, yet amazingly undeveloped, 392-acre **Nequasset Lake** is a great place to canoe. You'll see a few fishermen, a handful of houses, and near-wilderness along the shoreline. Personal watercraft (jet skis) and

motors under 10 hp are banned. Take Rt. 1 from Bath across the bridge to Woolwich. Continue to the flashing caution light at Nequasset Rd.; turn left and continue to Rt. 127. Turn right and go about one and a half miles to Old Stage Road. Turn right and go about one-half mile to the Nequasset Brook bridge. The hand-carry launch is west of the bridge, the trailer launch is east of the bridge; parking is limited. Canoe the lake itself and/or paddle upstream along Nequasset Brook for a mile or so until you reach a small waterfall.

In 1996, town fathers in their wisdom established an even more convenient launch site, close to Rt. 1. At the flashing caution light described above, turn *right* and go .1 mile. Turn left, and left again, into the parking area for the Nequasset Stream Waterfront Park. Launch your canoe and head upstream, under Rt. 1, to the lake.

Excursion Boats

The 50-foot *Yankee* operates out of Small Point's Hermit Island Campground Mon.-Sat. throughout the summer. You can go on nature cruises, enjoy the sunset, or visit Eagle Island; the schedule is different each day. Costs range from $7-20 adults, $5-15 kids. For reservations, call (207) 389-1788.

The M/V *Ruth,* a 38-foot excursion boat, runs cruises out of Sebasco Harbor Resort from late June through September. The schedule changes weekly, but possible options are a harbor cruise (one and a half hours), nature cruise (two hours), lobstering demos (one hour, 15 minutes), and Eagle Island (four and a half hours). Costs range from $8-15 adults, $5-10 kids 5-12. Call the resort, (207) 389-1161, for the schedule, which is available a week in advance. You don't need to be a Sebasco guest, but reservations are essential.

For on-demand trips to Seguin Island and its two-century-old lighthouse—about 20 minutes each way—contact Howie and Linda Marston at **Kennebec Charters,** Popham Beach, Phippsburg 04562, tel. (207) 389-1883. From late May to Labor Day, weather permitting, Howie takes six passengers at a time from the Fort Popham dock to the 64-acre island, where you can climb the hill to the lighthouse, then climb the 53-foot

light tower for a fabulous view from the deck. Afterward, visit the small Seguin Museum, loaded with lighthouse memorabilia. The non-profit Friends of Seguin, Inc., maintains the island's buildings and subsidizes the summertime caretakers; the Coast Guard maintains the automated light, which has an 18-mile range. There's no dock, so you'll be offloaded by dinghy —not recommended for the unsteady. Cost is $35 an hour for the boat, no matter how many passengers; allow at least two hours for the trip. Call the Marstons to schedule a time, on a first-come, first-served basis. They're also available for sightseeing and sportfishing charters.

The Maine Maritime Museum (see "Sights," above) also runs excursion boats in summer, weather permitting.

ENTERTAINMENT

Bath's most diversified entertainment setting is the **Center for the Arts at the Chocolate Church,** 804 Washington St., Bath 04530, tel. (207) 442-8455—a chocolate-brown board-and-batten structure built in 1846 as the Central Congregational Church. Year-round activities at the arts center include music and dance concerts, dramas, exhibits, and children's programs. Check local papers for listings or call ahead for a schedule. The art gallery is open Tues.-Fri. 9 a.m.-4 p.m., Saturday noon-4 p.m.

Throughout the summer, the **Maine Maritime Museum,** tel. (207) 443-1316, schedules special events, often hinging on visits by tall ships and other vessels. Some boats are open to the public for an extra fee. Call the museum to check.

FESTIVALS AND EVENTS

Happenings in Boothbay Peninsula and the Brunswick area are also nearby.

Every Friday, June through Labor Day, the **Downtown Concert Series** brings live entertainment to Waterfront Park and outside City Hall. The week of the Fourth of July, **Bath Heritage Days** fills three or four days with art exhibits, a carnival, a parade, and fireworks.

SHOPPING

Antiques

Three antiques shops lined up along Front Street are all worth a visit. At **Front Street Antiques,** 190 Front St., Bath 04530, tel. (207) 443-8098, a group shop, china is a specialty, as are quilts and Victoriana. Open Mon.-Sat. 10 a.m.-5 p.m., Sunday 11 a.m.-3 p.m. **Pollyanna's Antiques,** 182 Front St., Bath, tel. (207) 443-4909, is a good bet for Civil War items, vintage clothing, and old tools. Open daily 10 a.m.-5 p.m. **Brick Store Antiques,** 143 Front St., Bath, tel. (207) 443-2790, also open daily 10 a.m.-5 p.m., has a particularly wide variety of country and formal pieces.

Gifts, Crafts, and Clothing

Right in the shadow of the Rt. 1 overpass is an incredible resource for knitters and weavers. **Halcyon Yarn,** 12 School St., Bath 04530, tel. (207) 442-7909 or (800) 341-0282, a huge warehouse of a place, carries domestic and imported yarns, looms, spinning wheels, how-to videos, kits, and pattern books. Open year-round, Mon.-Sat. 10 a.m.-4 p.m. (to 8 p.m. Wednesday).

A long-established (since 1970) crafts cooperative, **Yankee Artisan,** 56 Front St., Bath 04530, tel. (207) 443-6215, maintains extremely high standards among its members, who staff the shop Mon.-Sat. 9 a.m.-5 p.m. year-round, plus Sunday 11 a.m.-3 p.m. in summer. And, while you're in town, there's the well-stocked, marine-oriented gift shop at the Maine Maritime Museum.

For adult and kids' sportswear bargains, check out **Goodwill Industries Retail Store,** Bath Shopping Center, Rt. 1, Bath 04530, tel. (207) 443-4668. A big-name sports outfitter distributes its overstocks to Goodwill stores, whose proceeds benefit people with disabilities. Open all year, Mon.-Sat. 9 a.m.-9 p.m., Sunday noon-5 p.m.

About nine miles down Rt. 127, you'll come to **Georgetown Pottery,** Rt. 127, Georgetown 04548, tel. (207) 371-2801, a top-quality ceramics studio/shop. Open daily 8:30 a.m.-5 p.m.

Flea Market

One of Maine's biggest and most-enduring flea markets is right on Rt. 1 north of Bath, often creating near-accidents as rubbernecking motorists slam to a halt. Montsweag Flea Market, Rt. 1 at Mountain Rd., P.O. Box 252, Woolwich 04579, tel. (207) 443-2809, is a genuine treasure trove, located about seven miles northeast of the Bath bridge. Open weekends in May, September, and October; open Wednesday, Friday, Saturday, and Sunday June through August. Sales begin at 6:30 a.m.

Farmers' Market

Next to City Hall in Bath, the **Bath Farmers' Market** operates every Saturday 9 a.m.-1 p.m., mid-June to Labor Day, featuring crafts, plants, and cheeses in addition to seasonal produce.

ACCOMMODATIONS

Most of Bath's inns and B&Bs are located in historic residences built by shipping magnates and their families, giving you a chance to appreciate the quality of craftsmanship they demanded in their ships and their homes alike.

Phippsburg Peninsula

At the end of a tiny lane off Parker Head Rd.—just behind the historic Phippsburg Congregational Church, stands the **Riverview Bed & Breakfast,** Church Lane, HC 31, Box 29, Phippsburg 04562, tel. (207) 389-1124, a 19th-century Cape-style house on the banks of the Kennebec. The two second-floor rooms share a bath. Ask innkeeper Alice Minott for advice on where to hike, swim, and sightsee—she knows the area well. Doubles are $40-50; no credit cards. Children are welcome; no pets. Two-night minimum on summer weekends. Open May through October.

Sebasco Harbor Resort, Rt. 217, Sebasco Estates 04565, tel. (207) 389-1161 or (800) 225-3819, fax (207) 389-2004, on the New Meadows River, is a self-contained, 664-acre seaside resort 12 miles south of Bath. Families come here year after year. Ninety-six widely varying rooms are scattered among nearly two dozen buildings, some decidedly old-fashioned. Most intriguing is The Lighthouse, a four-story, multisided, cupola-topped structure right on the harbor. In July and August, room rates range $87-

BATH B&BS

Rates listed here are for doubles, including full breakfast. To write to any of the following add Bath, ME 04530 to the street address. All are open year-round unless indicated otherwise. A two-night minimum may be required on midsummer weekends.

The Bath Bed and Breakfast, 944 Middle St., tel. (207) 443-4477 or (800) 524-7042. 19th-century ship-captain's home; $75-95; three rooms, private baths; no smoking; no pets; children welcome; intown location.

Elizabeth's B&B, 360 Front St., tel. (207) 443-1146. Informal ambience; $55-65; four rooms, shared baths, river views; no pets, limited smoking; intown location. Open mid-April to mid-November.

The Fairhaven Inn, No. Bath Rd.; tel. (207) 443-4391. 18th-century clonial on over 20 acres; $60-90 peak season, lower off season; eight rooms, private and shared baths; no smoking; rural location near Bath Country Club.

The Front Porch B&B, 324 Washington St., tel. (207) 443-5790. $50-75; three rooms, private and shared baths; no smoking; pets welcome; intown location near Maine Maritime Museum. Open March-December.

The Galen C. Moses House, 1009 Washington St., tel. (207) 442-8771. Elaborate Italianate Victorian in Historic District; $65-95; three rooms, private baths; no smoking; no pets; no credit cards; intown location.

Garden Street Bed & Breakfast, 30 Garden St., tel. (207) 443-6791. Antiques-filled Federal home in Historic District; $65-95; two rooms, private baths; no smoking; no pets.

The Inn at Bath, 969 Washington St., tel. (207) 443-4294, fax 443-4295. Outstanding Greek Revival in Historic District; $65-150; five rooms, one suite, private baths, water views; no smoking; pets welcome; wheelchair accessible; a/c; cable TV; phones; intown location.

The Packard House B&B, 45 Pearl St., tel. (207) 443-6069 or (800) 516-4578. 18th-century home in Historic District; $60-90; three rooms, private baths; no smoking; no pets; quiet intown side street.

RiverSide Bed & Breakfast, No. Bath Rd., tel. (207) 443-2898. Modern timber-frame home in splendid rural setting; $80; two guest rooms, private baths, river views; no small children. Open mid-April through October.

122 pp a day, MAP (jackets encouraged for dinner), and depend on your lodging choice. Most guests stay by the week; special packages are available in spring and fall, when rates range $70-112 pp, MAP. No pets. Recreational facilities include tennis courts (extra fee), nine-hole golf course (extra fee), saltwater pool, bowling, horseshoes, a playground, and lots of organized activities. See "Excursion Boats," above, for info on cruises in the M/V *Ruth.* Sebasco Harbor Resort is open Memorial Day weekend to early October, with highest rates late June through Labor Day.

Next to Popham Beach State Park is the **Popham Beach Bed & Breakfast,** HC 31, Box 430, Popham Beach, Phippsburg 04562, tel. (207) 389-2409, a unique hostelry in a partly restored 1883 Coast Guard station. Peggy Johannessen, innkeeper of this "work in progress," takes guests to the rooftop lookout tower and shares the building's history as a maritime life-saving center. Three huge rooms, each with private bath, go for a steep $145 d in midsummer; request The Library if it's in your budget. Another room with private bath is $95 d; a small room with shared bath is $80 d. All have lower rates off season. You're paying for the terrific location here. A two-course breakfast is served in the dining room each morning, and guests can hang out in the large oceanfront living room. No pets, no smoking; children are welcome. Open early May through October.

Just south of the turnoff to Popham Beach, and close to the access for Morse Mountain is **Edgewater Farm Bed & Breakfast,** Rt. 216, Box 464, Small Point 04565, tel. (207) 389-1322, Carol and Bill Emerson's restored 19th-century farmhouse. Six rooms, most with private baths, go for $75-85 d. A brunch-size breakfast benefits from lots of organic produce grown on the four-acre grounds. By prior arrangement, Carol makes delicious dinners for guests ($15-30 pp, depending on menu). No smoking, no pets, kids welcome. Open Memorial Day weekend to mid-October.

David and Jan Tingle, ensconced with their small daughter after years of Caribbean and Mediterranean chartering, operate **Small Point Bed & Breakfast,** Rt. 216, HC 32, Box 250, Sebasco Estates 04565, tel. (207) 389-1716, a late-19th-century farmhouse with three guest rooms (one with private bath). In summer, the Tingles move to the barn, and guests have the run of the house; in winter, only one room (with private bath) is available. Limited facilities for children and dogs; no smoking. Off season, by prior arrangement, Jan will prepare dinner (extra charge). Rates are $40-120 d, depending on season. The B&B is one and a half miles south of the Rt. 209 turnoff to Popham Beach.

Georgetown Peninsula

Staying at **The Grey Havens Inn,** Seguinland Rd., P.O. Box 308, Georgetown 04548, tel. (207) 371-2616, winter tel. (517) 439-4115, is like holing up at a classic seacoast summer home: National Historic Register Shingle-style building, huge screened veranda, tongue-and-groove paneling, lounge decorated in "early relative," honor bar, optional dinner (Tues.-Sat.). There's 10 rooms; water views are especially spectacular from the more pricey turret rooms. Two-night minimum summer weekends. Doubles are $100-220 in midsummer, $50-110 off season; private and shared baths. No pets, no small children. The inn adjoins Reid State Park and is a quarter-mile off Rt. 127. Open April-December.

Campgrounds

You'll need to book a site by February if you want to camp in midsummer at the Phippsburg Peninsula's **Hermit Island Campground,** Small Point 04567, tel. (207) 443-2101, winter mailing address 42 Front St., Bath 04530, same phone. With 275 campsites (no vehicles larger than pickup campers; no hookups) spread over a 255-acre causeway-linked island, this is oceanfront camping at its best. Prime sites surround Sunset Lagoon. The well-managed operation has a store, snack bar, post office, boat rentals, boat excursions, trails, and seven private beaches. No washing machines, but dryers are available. Rules are strictly enforced (no visitors al-

lowed in the camping area). Open and wooded sites run $24-34 (two people) mid-June to Labor Day, $20 early and late in the season. Open mid-May through Columbus Day. The campground is at the tip of the Phippsburg Peninsula.

At **Ocean View Park Campground,** Rt. 209, Phippsburg 04562, tel. (207) 389-2564, winter address P.O. Box 107, Phippsburg 04562, tel. (207) 443-1000, adjacent to Popham Beach State Park, the 48 sites are small, but many are right next to the sandy beach. Hookups are available. Sites are $18-21. Open mid-May through mid-September.

Over on the Georgetown Peninsula, well-managed **Camp Seguin,** Seguinland Rd., Georgetown 04548, tel. (207) 371-2777, adjoins Reid State Park and has 30 wooded and oceanfront sites (some tent platforms) at $15-21. Maximum RV size is 30 feet. Open Memorial Day weekend to Columbus Day.

FOOD

Miscellanea

Bath's best pizza comes from **The Cabin,** 552 Washington St., Bath 04530, tel. (207) 443-6224—a local landmark since 1973. The white garlic sauce is outstanding, and the cheese steak is about the best outside of Philly. A large three-topping pizza is only $10.95. Order food to go or eat in at this decidedly casual place across from Bath Iron Works. Beer and wine license only. Reservations are wise Friday and Saturday evenings. Open all year, Mon.-Fri. 10 a.m.-10 p.m. (to 11 p.m. Thursday and Friday), Saturday 11:30 a.m.-11 p.m., Sunday noon-10 p.m.

A newer branch of the superb Wiscasset restaurant of the same name, **Sarah's Cafe,** Old Customs House, 1 Front St., Bath 04530, tel. (207) 442-0996, serves the same delicious home-made goodies (soups, sandwiches, desserts), plus you can take it outside and eat on the lawn overlooking the Kennebec River. No liquor license; no credit cards. Open for lunch weekdays 10 a.m.-2 p.m.

Moderate to Expensive

J.R. Maxwell & Co., 122 Front St., Bath 04530, tel. (207) 443-2014, fits right in with Bath's maritime tradition; lots of nautical stuff everywhere you look. Thanks to a loyal clientele, dinner reservations are advisable. Basic meat-and-seafood menu ($9-17 for dinner entrées), well prepared. Open all year, Mon.-Sat. 11:30 a.m.-2:30 p.m. and 5-9 p.m. (to 10 p.m. Saturday), Sunday noon-9 p.m. Wednesday is twofer night.

Known all over Maine for its fabulous baked goods, **Kristina's Restaurant & Bakery,** 160 Centre St., at High St., Bath, tel. (207) 442-8577, packs 'em in for weekend brunches, so reservations are essential. Reserve, too, on summer weekends. Entrées ($13-19) are especially creative, with Mediterranean influences and lower-priced light fare. Breakfasts are the best in the area. Rotating art exhibits add to the imaginative ambience here. Wheelchair accessible. No smoking after 5 p.m. Open daily Feb.-December. Summer hours are Mon.-Fri. 8 a.m.-9 p.m., Saturday 9 a.m.-9 p.m., Sunday 9 a.m.-2 p.m. and 5-9 p.m.; winter hours are Mon.-Fri. 8 a.m.-8:30 p.m. (to 9 p.m. Thursday and Friday), Saturday 9 a.m.-9 p.m., Sunday 9 a.m.-2 p.m.

Worthwhile Wallet-Cruncher

The building alone is worth a visit to the **Robinhood Free Meetinghouse,** Robinhood Rd., HC 33, Box 1469A, Georgetown 04548, tel. (207) 371-2188, a multi-star restaurant in a beautifully restored 1855 building on the Georgetown Peninsula. Most tables are on the main floor; overflow diners go to the second floor, where many of the pews remain. The huge, high-quality menu makes it even more enticing. Noted chef Michael Gagne presides over the kitchen. Creativity is the menu byword for Gagne, who gained fame during eight years as the innovative chef of Robinhood's nearby Osprey Restaurant. Entrées are in the $16-23 range, and portions are large. No smoking; reservations essential. Open daily 5:30-9 p.m., plus 10 a.m.-2 p.m. Sunday for brunch, May-Oct. Other months, hours and days are limited; call to check. The restaurant is on the left, about a mile east of Rt. 127.

Natural Food/Farmers' Market

Center Street Grainery, 36 Centre St., Bath 04530, tel. (207) 442-8012, carries all the usual health-food items, plus jewelry, baked goods, books, clothes, and delicious sandwiches and soups. Open all year, Mon.-Sat. 9 a.m.-5:30 p.m. (to 6 p.m. Friday, to 5 p.m. Saturday).

The **Bath Farmers' Market** sets up each Saturday 9 a.m.-1:30 p.m., mid-May through October, in the lot next to City Hall on Front Street. Wares include produce, crafts, and flowers.

Lobster-in-the-Rough

Phippsburg Peninsula: Overlooking the New Meadows River, **The Water's Edge Restaurant,** Freezer Rd., off Rt. 217, Sebasco Estates 04565, tel. (207) 389-1803, is aptly named—and well worth a bit of effort to find it. The unassuming red-shingled place has indoor and deck dining, plus waterside picnic tables. Mahogany quahogs are a specialty, and desserts are great. Unlike many lobster places, Water's Edge serves beer and wine and takes credit cards. Dining-room reservations are wise on weekends. Open daily 11 a.m.-9 p.m., mid-May to Labor Day. Take Rt. 209 south from Bath 11 miles, then turn right onto Rt. 217. Continue beyond Sebasco Harbor Resort and make two left turns to the restaurant.

Back on Rt. 209, continue south and pick up Rt. 216. About two and a half miles south of the Rt. 217 turnoff stands the rustic, buoy-draped **Lobster House,** Rt. 216, Small Point, tel. (207) 389-1596 or 389-2178. The windowed eating area, with open beams, overlooks a scenic tidal cove; the view's best when the tide's in. Open Tues.-Sat. 5- 9 p.m., Sunday noon-8:30 p.m., mid-May to Labor Day.

Georgetown Peninsula: Just over a mile beyond the turnoff to Reid State Park, you'll reach the end of Rt. 127—at Five Islands. Here you'll find **The Love Nest,** run by the Georgetown Fishermen's Co-op, Rt. 127, Five Islands, Georgetown 04548, tel. (207) 371-2950, where you can pig out on lobster rolls and fried onion rings, 8 a.m.-8 p.m., mid-May to mid-October. Dress down, BYOL, and enjoy the end-of-the-road ambience. No credit cards.

INFORMATION AND SERVICES

The Bath branch of the **Chamber of Commerce of the Bath-Brunswick Region,** 45 Front St., Bath 04530, tel. (207) 443-9751, is open weekdays, 8:30 a.m.-5 p.m., with occasional Saturday hours in summer. The chamber's seasonal **information center** on Rt. 1 at Witch Spring Hill (right side northbound from Brunswick to Bath, about a mile south of Bath) is open weekends in May and daily all summer. Request copies of the *City of Bath Downtown Map and Guide* and the *Bath-Brunswick Region Map & Guide.*

Bath's **Patten Free Library,** 33 Summer St., Bath 04530, tel. (207) 443-5141, has one of the state's most comfortable and elegant library reading rooms. It's entirely too easy to spend a rainy day hanging out here with the huge supply of newspapers and magazines. The library's outstanding Sagadahoc History and Genealogy Room draws genealogists from all over (open Tues.-Fri. noon-4 p.m.), and the Children's Room is especially kid-friendly. The library is open Mon.-Fri. 10 a.m.-5 p.m. (to 8 p.m. Tuesday and Thursday).

Newspapers
Brunswick's *Times Record,* tel. (207) 729-3311, published weekdays, runs extensive arts and entertainment listings in its Thursday edition. The paper also produces a summer vacation supplement available free at the chamber of commerce and at restaurants and lodgings. The weekly *Coastal Journal,* tel. (207) 443-6241, a free tabloid available throughout the Brunswick/Bath area, has extensive calendar listings and special *Summer in Maine* supplements. The *Portland Press Herald,* published daily and covering most of southern Maine, covers Bath cultural activities in its *Go* supplement each Thursday.

Emergencies
Because of hospital restructuring and a new facility in the planning stages, medical emergencies in Bath are handled by the **Bath Urgent Care Center,** 1356 Washington St., Bath 04530, tel. (207) 443-5524, which is open daily 7 a.m.-10 p.m., all year. The nearest hospital with 24-hour emergency-room care is 10 miles south of Bath, at **Mid-Coast Hospital,** 58 Baribeau Dr., Brunswick 04011, tel. (207) 729-0181. For **police, fire, and ambulance,** dial 911.

Public Restrooms
Public restrooms are at **Bath City Hall,** 55 Front St., **Patten Free Library,** 33 Summer St., **Sagadahoc County Courthouse,** 752 High St., and (summer only) **Waterfront Park,** Commercial Street.

Photo Services
With branches in Bath and Brunswick, and an excellent reputation, **Kennebec Camera & Darkroom,** 160 Front St., Bath 04530, tel. (207) 442-8628, does professional color and black-and-white work as well as one-hour photo processing.

Laundromat
Best self-service facilities are at the **Centre Street Laundry,** 28 Centre St., Bath 04530, tel. (207) 443-8801.

Special Courses
In 1974, enterprising entrepreneurs Pat and Patsy Hennin jumped on the do-it-yourself bandwagon and established the **Shelter Institute,** 38 Centre St., Bath 04530, tel. (207) 442-7938, in downtown Bath, to train neophytes in energy-efficient home design and construction techniques. Since then, some 20,000 students have taken one- to three-week courses here, and enthusiastic alumni span the globe. Students range in age from late teens to early 80s. Visitors are welcome any time, and anyone who appreciates fine woodworking tools *has* to visit the **Woodbutcher Tools** retail shop and bookstore, open Mon.-Fri. 8 a.m.-4:30 p.m., Saturday 9 a.m.-3 p.m.

Getting Around
Bath Taxi, tel. (207) 443-4009, maintains round-the-clock radio-dispatched taxis. **Drew's Taxi,** tel. (207) 443-9166, operates Mon.-Wed. 7 a.m.-11 p.m. and Thurs.-Sat. 7 a.m.-1 a.m. **Mid-Coast Limo,** tel. (800) 937-2424, based in Camden, provides service between Portland International Jetport and the Bath area by reservation.

WISCASSET AREA

Billing itself "The Prettiest Village in Maine," Wiscasset (pop. 3,500) works hard to live up to its slogan, with quaint street signs, well-maintained homes, and an air of attentive elegance. Behind the scenes, however, it's actually a rather workaday community—not overrun with deep-pocketed retirees. The interesting mix includes artists, antiques dealers, worm diggers, and blue-collar types. And it seems to work.

Wiscasset (meeting place of three rivers), incorporated as part of Pownalborough in 1760, has had its current name since 1802. In the late 18th century, it became the shire town of Lincoln County and the largest seaport north of Boston. Countless tall-masted ships sailed the 12 miles up the Sheepscot River to tie up here, and shipyards flourished, turning out vessels for domestic and foreign trade. The 1807 Embargo Act and the War of 1812 delivered a one-two punch that shut down trade and temporarily squelched the town's aspirations, but Wiscasset yards soon were back at it, producing vessels for the pre-Civil War clipper-ship era—only to face a more lasting decline with the arrival of the railroads and the onset of the Industrial Revolution.

From the 1930s to the mid-1990s, two derelict four-masted wooden ships, the *Hesper* and the *Luther Little,* reminders of the town's heyday, languished in Wiscasset Harbor, providing a distinctive landmark and photo ops for locals and visitors. But years of storms, and even a fire, took their toll, eventually reducing the boats to little more than piles of toothpicks.

Just east of Wiscasset, across the Donald Davey Bridge, is Edgecomb, a tiny town that primarily serves as a funnel to the Boothbay Peninsula. (Except for Rt. 1 Edgecomb locations, most of Edgecomb's handful of attractions and facilities are described in the "Boothbay Peninsula" section.)

The Donald Davey Bridge, built in 1983, is the most recent span over the Sheepscot. The earliest, finished in 1847, was a toll bridge that charged a horse-and-wagon 15 cents to cross, pedestrians three cents each, and pigs one penny apiece. Prior to that, ferries carried passengers, animals, and vehicles between Wiscasset and Edgecomb's Davis Island (then named Folly Island).

North and a bit east of Wiscasset are the lovely rural communities of Sheepscot and Alna, definitely worth the detour.

Wiscasset was long known as the site of the controversial Maine Yankee nuclear-power plant, built in 1973 on Montsweag Bay, six miles south of town. Maine's first and only nuclear facility, plagued by problems and protesters, suspended operations in 1997 to begin the long-term process of decommissioning. During its lifetime, Maine Yankee was a cash cow, allowing Wiscasset to have all the civic benefits of a huge tax base. The plant's closure has been a major blow to the town's economy, but Wiscasset will survive.

Whether it will survive its notoriety for midsummer gridlock is another matter. Especially on weekends, traffic backs up on Rt. 1 for miles in both directions—to the frustration of drivers, passengers, and Wiscasset merchants. When you stop in town, try to park pointed in the direction you're going.

SIGHTS

In 1973, a large chunk of downtown Wiscasset was added to the National Register of Historic Places, and a walking tour is the best way to appreciate the Federal, classical revival, and even pre-Revolutionary homes and commercial buildings in the Historic District. Below are a few of the prime examples. If you do nothing else, be sure to swing by the homes on High Street.

Castle Tucker

Once known as the Lee-Tucker House, Castle Tucker, Lee and High Sts., Wiscasset 04578, tel. (207) 882-7364, is a must-see. Built in 1807 by Judge Silas Lee, and bought by sea captain Richard Tucker in 1858, the imposing mansion has Victorian wallpaper and furnishings, Palladian windows, an amazing elliptical staircase, and a dramatic view over the Sheepscot River. In early 1997, Jane Tucker, Richard's granddaughter, magnanimously deeded the house to the Society for the Preservation of New England Antiquities (SPNEA). Open July and August, Thurs.-Sat.; tours begin on the hour, noon-4 p.m. SPNEA anticipates expanding the schedule into June and September, so inquire locally. Admission is $4 adults, $3.50 seniors, $2 children 6-12.

Nickels-Sortwell House

Also owned by SPNEA, the three-story Nickels-Sortwell House, Main St. (Rt. 1), Wiscasset 04578, tel. (207) 882-6218, looms over Rt. 1, yet it's so close to the road many motorists miss it. Don't. Sea captain William Nickels commissioned the mansion in 1807 but died soon after its completion. For 70 or so years, it became the Belle Haven Hotel, prior to Alvin and Frances Sortwell's meticulous colonial revival restoration in the early 20th century. Today, the house is open June 1-Sept., Wed.-Sun.; tours begin on the hour, noon-4 p.m. Admission is $4 adults, $3.50 seniors, $2 children 6-12.

Lincoln County Jail and Museum

Wiscasset's Old Jail, completed in 1811, was the first prison in the District of Maine (then part of Massachusetts). Amazingly, it remained a jail—mostly for short-termers—until 1953. Two years after that, the Lincoln County Historical Association took over, so each summer you can check out the 40-inch-thick granite walls, floors, and ceilings; the 12 tiny cells; and historic graffiti penned by the prisoners. Attached to the prison is the 1837 jailer's house, now the Lincoln County Museum, containing antique tools, the original kitchen, and various temporary exhibits. The complex is open Tues.-Sun. 11 a.m.-4:30 p.m., in July and August. Admission is $2 adults, $1 children under 13. A Victorian gazebo, overlooking the Sheepscot River, is a great place for a picnic. From Rt. 1 (Main St.) in downtown Wiscasset, take Federal St. (Rt. 218) 1.2 miles. For more information, contact **Lincoln County Historical Association**, P.O. Box 61, Wiscasset 04578, tel. (207) 882-6817.

Ride the Rails

Twice daily, the **Maine Coast Railroad**, Water St., P.O. Box 614, Wiscasset 04578, tel. (207) 882-8000 or (800) 795-5404, fax (207) 882-7699, makes a one-and-a-half-hour roundtrip over the river and through the woods to nearby Newcastle, giving you a chance to see herons, a huge osprey nest, maybe a bald eagle or a moose—and wildflowers galore. Fall-foliage runs are outstanding. No smoking. Next to the Wiscasset depot are riverview tables for a pre- or post-ride picnic; inside are restrooms. The depot is two blocks south of Rt. 1, below Le Garage restaurant. Tickets are $10 adults, $9 seniors, $5 children 5-12; a $25 family rate covers two adults and up to four kids. Reservations aren't needed, but the fall trips are especially popular, so arrive early at the depot. Trains operate daily at 11 a.m. and 1 p.m., late June to late September; weekends and holidays from Memorial Day weekend to late June and late September to late November. Special events—including longer trips, lobsterbakes, fall-foliage tours—occur periodically during the season; call for schedule.

Musical Wonder House

The treasures in The Musical Wonder House, 18 High St., P.O. Box 604, Wiscasset 04578, tel. (207) 882-7163 or 882-6373, an 1852 sea captain's mansion, are indeed astonishing, and eccentric Austrian-born museum founder Danilo Konvalinka delights in sharing them—for a price. The best way to appreciate the collection of hundreds of 19th-century European music boxes, player pianos, and musical rarities is to take an on-demand one-and-a-half-hour guided tour of the first floor, including two dozen player-piano and music-box demonstrations. Cost is $10 adults, $7.50 seniors and kids under 12 (don't bring small children). Admission to the building and gift shop is $1 adults, 50 cents kids—providing access to about 20 coin-operated music boxes. The museum is open daily 10 a.m.-5 p.m., Memorial Day weekend to Oct. 15; guided tours are limited after Labor Day. A mail-order sideline, tel. (800) 336-3725, offering music-box and player-piano cassettes and CDs, continues year-round.

Head Tide Village

Follow Rt. 218 north from Wiscasset for about eight miles to Head Tide Village, an eminently picturesque hamlet at the farthest reach of

*historical
Head Tide Village*

Sheepscot River tides. From the late 18th century to the early 20th, Head Tide (now part of the town of Alna) was a thriving mill town, a source of hydropower for the textile and lumber industries. All that's long gone, but hints of that era come from the handful of well-maintained 18th- and 19th-century homes in the village center.

Up the hill, the stunning 1838 **Head Tide Church,** another fine example of local prosperity, is open Saturday 2-4 p.m., in July and August (or by appointment; contact the Alna Store, Rt. 218, tel. 207-586-5515). Volunteer tour guides point out the original pulpit, a trompe l'oeil window, a kerosene chandelier, and walls lined with historic Alna photographs. An annual service is held at the church—usually the first Sunday in August.

Head Tide's most famous citizen was the poet **Edwin Arlington Robinson,** born here in 1869. His family home, at the bend in Rt. 194 and marked by a plaque, is not open to the public. Perhaps his Maine roots inspired these lines from his poem *New England:* "Here where the wind is always north-north-east/And children learn to walk on frozen toes."

Just upriver from the bend in the road is a favorite swimming hole, a millpond where you can join the locals on a hot summer day. Not much else goes on here, and there are no restaurants or lodgings, so Head Tide can't be termed a destination, but it's a village frozen in time—and an unbeatable opportunity for history buffs and shutterbugs.

Pownalborough Court House
Prepare to enter a pre-Revolutionary riverfront courthouse where President John Adams once handled a trial—in a mid-18th-century frontier community (named Pownalborough) established by French and German settlers. During the 30-minute tour of the three-story Pownalborough Court House, River Rd., Rt. 128, Dresden 04342, guides delight in pointing out the restored beams, paneling, and fireplaces—as well as the on-site tavern that catered to judges, lawyers, and travelers. Walk a few hundred feet south of the dramatically sited courthouse and you'll find a cemetery with Revolution-era graves. Along the river is a nature trail developed by local Eagle Scouts. Admission is $3 adults, $1 kids under 13. Open July and August, Wed.-Sat. 10 a.m.-4 p.m., Sunday noon-4 p.m. For more information, call or write **Lincoln County Historical Association,** P.O. Box 61, Wiscasset 04578, tel. (207) 882-6817. From Rt. 1 in Wiscasset, take Rt. 27 about nine miles north to the junction with Rt. 128. Turn left (south) and go two and a half miles to the courthouse sign. The courthouse is also an easy drive from Bath or Augusta.

PARKS AND RECREATION

Across Federal Street from the Nickels-Sortwell House in downtown Wiscasset is the lovely **Sunken Garden,** an almost-unnoticed pocket park created around the cellar hole of a long-gone inn. Bring a picnic or a book and ignore the traffic streaming by on Main Street.

Around the corner from the Town Wharf, more or less at the end of Pleasant St., is the foot-bridge to tiny **White's Island,** where you can take a picnic and get away from it all.

Morris Farm

In 1995, a group of civic-minded citizens managed to stave off developers and buy the Morris Farm, Rt. 27, P.O. Box 136, Wiscasset 04578, tel. (207) 882-4080. Thanks to the energy of Morris Farm Trust members and the resident caretakers, the 60-acre property has become a community center for agriculture-related education and recreation, including a summer day-camp program and several summer festivals. Every Wednesday at 4:30 p.m., early July to late August, the farm directors lead hour-long tours of the property (suggested donation is $4 adults, free for kids under 18). And always, dawn to dusk, the farm is open for walking, hiking, and picnicking. The Morris Farm is three quarters of a mile from Rt. 1 (turn onto Rt. 27 next to the Wiscasset Municipal Building).

If you're traveling with kids, continue along Rt. 27, about a quarter of a mile farther, to the creative playground on the right, run by the Wiscasset Recreation Department.

Sherman Lake Rest Area

About four miles east of Wiscasset (in the town of Newcastle) is the state-operated Sherman Lake Rest Area, a scenic spot along Rt. 1 with picnic tables, outhouses, and a dog-walking area. Bring a kayak or canoe and paddle around the mile-long lake. Birders should have good luck spotting waterfowl. Open all year.

FESTIVALS AND EVENTS

Wiscasset's day-long **Annual Strawberry Festival and Country Fair** celebrates with tons of strawberries, plus crafts and an auction at St. Philip's Episcopal Church, Hodge St., tel. (207) 882-7184, the last Saturday in June.

In early July, the day-long **Morris Farm Fair** takes place at the nonprofit community Morris Farm on Rt. 27, and includes animal exhibits,

farm tours, crafts, games, and food. St. Philip's Episcopal Church is the site of **Monday-night fish-chowder suppers,** early July to mid-August. Reservations are advised for the 5:30 p.m. suppers.

SHOPPING

Antiques and Collectibles

It's certainly fitting that a town filled end-to-end with antique homes should have nearly 20 solo and group antiques shops. Most are located at the eastern end of town, between High Street and the Sheepscot River; a few are at the western end of town. Most do cooperative advertising, so newspapers and shops have ads and brochures listing them all.

On the southwestern outskirts of Wiscasset, in two low-slung, nondescript buildings (called North Building and South Building), **Parkers of Wiscasset,** Rt. 1, P.O. Box 273, Wiscasset 04578, tel. (207) 882-5520, is a high-quality group shop with an eclectic inventory ranging from folk art and paintings to quilts, furniture, and jewelry. Open daily 9 a.m.-5 p.m., mid-April to mid-October; 10 a.m.-4 p.m., mid-October to late December.

Right downtown, **The Marston House,** Main and Middle Sts., Wiscasset 04578, tel. (207) 882-6010, specializes in Americana and caters to serious dealers and collectors. Hours are 10 a.m.-5 p.m. daily, April-Dec., but it's often open off season; call ahead to be sure.

High-quality American antiques are also the specialty at **Priscilla Hutchinson,** Pleasant St., Wiscasset 04578, tel. (207) 882-4200, located in an attractive carriage house half a block from Rt. 1. Open daily 10 a.m.-5 p.m., June-Sept., other months by appointment.

Eclectic is the theme at **Nonesuch House,** 1 Middle St., Wiscasset 04578, tel. (207) 882-6768, a group shop that created an international stir in 1996 when one of the dealers decided to sell an unwrapped Egyptian mummy he'd purchased years earlier. The shop is open daily 10 a.m.-5 p.m., April-Nov., other months by appointment.

Even more eclectic and mostly lower on the price scale is Richard Plunkett's **Wizard of Odds . . . and Ends,** 7 Main St., Wiscasset 04578, tel. (207) 882-7870, where you'll find everything from early primitives to fine paintings in seven rooms of a 1790 building. Open daily 10 a.m.-5 p.m., late May through October. Closed one or two weekdays in October; call ahead to be sure.

Art Galleries

European and American 19th- and 20th-century painters are the broad focus at **Wiscasset Bay Gallery,** Main St. (Rt. 1), P.O. Box 309, Wiscasset 04578, tel. (207) 882-7682, which schedules high-quality rotating shows throughout its season. Open daily 10:30 a.m.-5 p.m., mid-May to mid-October.

Located in the handsome open spaces of an early-19th-century brick schoolhouse, the **Maine Art Gallery,** Warren St., P.O. Box 315, Wiscasset 04578, tel. (207) 882-7511, was founded in 1957 as a nonprofit corporation to showcase contemporary Maine artists. Rotating exhibits occur throughout the season, March to November. The gallery is open Mon.-Sat. 10 a.m.-4 p.m., Sunday 1-4 p.m. Memorial Day weekend through Columbus Day; other months, it's open only Friday, Saturday, and Sunday.

Gifts, Crafts, and Miscellanea

The oldest commercial building in town is **Wiscasset Hardware,** Water St., Wiscasset 04578, tel. (207) 882-6622, built in 1797 as a ship chandlery on the east side of Water Street. Since 1949, the Stetson family has run this hardware-plus business. Request a free town map and check out the great view from the riverview deck, where you can buy sandwiches, hot dogs, ice cream, and coffee. While you're at it, do your Wiscasset gift shopping here, too; there's plenty of variety. The store is open all year, Mon.-Sat. 7:30 a.m.-5 p.m. and Sunday 9 a.m.-1 p.m.

Stop in at **Area's Jewelry and Gifts,** Water St., Wiscasset 04578, tel. (207) 882-7755, not just for the tasteful selection of books, cards, jewelry, crafts, and candles—the 1870 Customs House alone is worth the visit. Open daily 10 a.m.-5 p.m., June-Sept.; Tues.-Sat. the rest of the year.

The Butterstamp Workshop, Middle St., Wiscasset 04578, tel. (207) 882-7825, not only creates and sells designs copied from antique molds, but is also a source of hard-to-find gravestone-rubbing supplies. Plus you can watch the workshop operation, which produces butter, cookie, and candle molds; muffin pans and gingerbread boards; beeswax ornaments; even magnets. Open daily 10 a.m.-5 p.m., Memorial Day weekend through Columbus Day.

Sinks, serving bowls, vases, and lamps are just some of the finely glazed objects available at **Sheepscot River Pottery,** Rt. 1, Davis Island, Edgecomb 04556, tel. (207) 882-9410 or (800) 659-4794 outside Maine, just across the river from Wiscasset. The Maine Island pattern is especially striking. Located in a handsome modern roadside building (opposite the Muddy Rudder restaurant), the shop also accepts commissions. Open daily 9 a.m.-6 p.m., Memorial Day weekend through September, and 9:30 a.m.-5:30 p.m. the rest of the year. There's a small branch shop on Main Street in Damariscotta.

Discount Shopping

Carving out its own unique niche is **Big Al's Super Values,** Rt. 1, Wiscasset 04578, tel. (207) 882-6423, a catchall emporium specializing in odd lots, closeouts, funky souvenirs, and half-price birthday cards. Bargains galore, plus free coffee and a free gift. Lots of tourism brochures are also available here. Three miles south of Wiscasset, across from the Sea Basket Restaurant, Big Al's is open April to Christmas Eve, Mon.-Sat. 9 a.m.-8 p.m. and Sunday 10 a.m.-5:30 p.m.

Farmers' Market

The fledgling **Wiscasset Farmers' Market,** sponsored by Morris Farm (see "Parks and Recreation," above), operates Saturday 9 a.m.-noon, mid-May to Labor Day, in the parking lot of the Lincoln County Courthouse on Rt. 1.

ACCOMMODATIONS

B&Bs

Wiscasset isn't loaded with B&Bs, but the choices are intriguing. One is downtown and two are within easy walking distance of antiques shops and the waterfront. Two others are farm B&Bs with their own special charm.

Named after a famous Maine clipper ship, the **Snow Squall B&B,** Rt. 1 at Bradford Rd., P.O. Box 730, Wiscasset 04578, tel. (207) 882-6892 or (800) 775-7245, fax (207) 882-6832, has four lovely rooms and three suites, all with private baths for $85-195 d. Rooms are named for clipper ships, and the gathering room even has a glass case with a *Snow Squall* relic, retrieved from the ship's Falkland Islands wreckage. Mary Lou and Bob Madsen are avid sailors; Mary Lou manages Caribbean yacht charters based in St. Thomas. The B&B is open all year, but only by reservation off season (two-night minimum). No smoking, no pets.

On the other side of Rt. 1, **Highnote Bed & Breakfast,** 36 Lee St., Wiscasset 04578, tel. (207) 882-9628, is a splendid Victorian on a quiet side street. John and Marie Reinhardt (he's an opera singer, hence the name) serve a European-style breakfast, including Marie's world-class scones. Three rooms (shared bath) are $65 d. No smoking, no pets, no credit cards. Open all year.

Attached to The Marston House antiques shop, **The Marston House B&B,** Main and Middle Sts., Wiscasset 04578, tel. (207) 882-6010, has two good-size rooms for $95 d in the carriage house out back (away from Rt. 1 traffic noise). Each has a fireplace, private bath, and private entrance on Middle Street. No smoking, no pets. Open May through November.

Then there's a major getaway—**The Squire Tarbox Inn,** Rt. 144, Westport Island, mailing address Box 1181, Westport Island, Wiscasset 04578, tel. (207) 882-7693, fax 882-7107, an elegantly casual B&B/inn that also happens to be a purebred-goat dairy farm. Eleven lovely rooms (all private baths) are divided between the late-18th-century main house and the early-19th-century carriage house. Five-course dinners (open to the public by reservation—one seating, 7 p.m.; $31) are memorable, preceded by samples of the inn's excellent gourmet goat cheese as diners gather. Doubles are $85-166, including breakfast, or $139-220 MAP. Bikes and boats are available for guests. No pets, no children under 14; smoking outdoors only. Open mid-May to late October. From downtown Wiscasset, head southwest four miles on Rt. 1 to Rt. 144. Turn left and go about eight and a half scenic miles to the inn.

On the Alna/Whitefield line, nine and a half miles from Rt. 1 in Wiscasset, 43-acre **Anniversary Farm Bed & Breakfast,** 2282 Alna Rd., Alna 04535, tel. (207) 586-5590, fax 586-5108, is an answer to prayer for gardeners, gourmets, and wildlife enthusiasts. Hiking trails wind through the property, canoeing waters are nearby, and innkeepers Ellin and Stephen Sheehy can arrange for llama walks. Two elegant rooms in their historic home are $85 d (fireplace and private half bath) and $65 d (shared bath); two-night minimum. The Sheehys bought their certified organic farm to celebrate their 25th anniversary; Ellin now coordinates several farmers' markets, does catering, and runs her own gourmet take-out farmstand (Tues.-Sun. 10 a.m.-6:30 p.m.). On their front porch, a lovely tearoom is open to the public Wed.-Sat. 3:30-5:30 p.m. in summer. Dinner is available to guests by prior arrangement (extra charge). No smoking, no pets, no small children. Open June through October.

Motels

One Wiscasset-area motel is on the southwestern outskirts of town; the other two are in Edgecomb, just over the bridge from Wiscasset, making them convenient to the Boothbay Peninsula as well.

Fairly close to Rt. 1 but buffered a bit by century-old hemlocks, the **Wiscasset Motor Lodge,** Rt. 1, RR3, Box 911, Wiscasset 04578, tel. (207) 882-7137 or (800) 732-8168, is a comfortable, well-maintained motel/cottage colony. The 10-acre complex, open April-Nov., has six tiny cottages that go for $40 d summer, $32-37 spring and fall, and 19 motel rooms for $49-60 in summer, $36-52 other months. Extra persons (only in motel rooms) are $8 in summer, $6 other months. Cable TV in all units, a/c in some units, phones in motel rooms; free breakfast buffet in summer.

The 40-room **Edgecomb Inn,** Rt. 1, Box 51, Davis Island, Edgecomb 04556, tel. (207) 882-6343, connected to The Muddy Rudder, has the same view as the restaurant and is just far enough off the highway to be quiet. Doubles are $71-99 July and August, $44-80 other months. Facilities include tennis court, laundry, and a nature trail to nearby Fort Edgecomb. Pets are allowed. At the corner of Shore Rd., the inn is open all year.

Newest, spiffiest motel in the area is the gray-shingled **Cod Cove Inn,** Rts. 1 and 27, P.O.

Box 36, Edgecomb 04556, tel. (207) 882-9586 or (800) 882-9586, fax (207) 882-9294, perched high on a hill overlooking tidal Cod Cove and Wiscasset beyond. Thirty rooms have balcony or patio, a/c, cable TV, and telephone. Best views are from second-floor rooms. Rates are $95-125 d in peak season, including continental breakfast; off-season doubles are $60-110. No pets. The inn is a mile east of Wiscasset, at the turnoff to the Boothbay Peninsula. Open late April through October.

Campgrounds

On little-developed, spring-fed Gardiner Pond, four miles north of Wiscasset, 400-acre **Down East Family Camping**, Rt. 27, RR 3, Box 223, Wiscasset 04578, tel. (207) 882-5431, has 43 wooded tentsites ($16-20 for two persons), a few hookups (22-foot RV limit), and facilities for swimming, fishing, and boating. Pets are allowed, and there's a playground. Open Memorial Day weekend to Columbus Day.

Geared more toward RV and seasonal campers, well-managed **Chewonki Campgrounds**, Box 261, Wiscasset 04578, tel. (207) 882-7426, has 47 sites that go for $18-25 mid-June through Labor Day, less early and late in the season. Many sites are close to tidal Montsweag Bay. Facilities include a pool, rec hall, small store, games, and canoe and boat rentals. Leashed pets are welcome. Open mid-May to mid-October. From downtown Wiscasset, head southwest four miles on Rt. 1 to Rt. 144. Turn left, then turn right onto Chewonki Neck Rd., past the airport, to the campground.

FOOD

Lunch and Miscellanea

Yes, **Red's Eats**, Main and Water Sts., Wiscasset 04578, tel. (207) 882-6128, is a take-out stand, but don't let that dissuade you. It's been here for decades (starting as Al's Eats), and there's always a line for hot dogs, lobster rolls, pocket sandwiches, and more. The few tables on the sidewalk and behind the building, overlooking the river, are seldom empty (except in bad weather), but it's only a two-block walk across Main Street to picnic tables (and a public restroom) on the Town Wharf. Open daily, early May to mid-October—until 2 a.m. on sum-

mer weekends. No credit cards.

Back up the street, across from the post office, is **Treat's**, Main St., Box 156, Wiscasset 04578, tel. (207) 882-6192, source of gourmet picnic fixings: wine, cheese, condiments, and home-made bread. Open all year, Mon.-Sat. 10 a.m.-6 p.m., plus Sunday noon-5 p.m. April through December.

Two miles southwest of downtown Wiscasset, **The Sea Basket Restaurant**, Rt. 1, Wiscasset 04578, tel. (207) 882-6581, has been serving up hearty bowls of lobster stew and good-size baskets of eminently fresh seafood since 1981. There's always a crowd—locals eat here, too—so expect to wait. Picnic tables outside; no smoking at inside tables. Best plan is to order lunch to go, wait for your number to be called, and head for the picnic tables on the Wiscasset waterfront. Open daily except Tuesday 11 a.m.-8 p.m., late February to mid-December.

Moderate

Three waterfront restaurants get high marks for their views.

In a high-visibility location across Rt. 1 from Red's, **Sarah's Cafe**, Main and Water Sts., Wiscasset 04578, tel. (207) 882-7504, is the home of huge nautical-theme sandwiches, homemade soups (self-serve), pizza (try the lobster), vegetarian specials, and an ice cream fountain. A branch serves lunch in downtown Bath. Beer and wine license, a/c. Open all year for lunch and dinner, Sun.-Thurs. to 8 p.m., Friday and Saturday to 9 p.m.

Overlooking the remnants of what used to be picturesque derelict schooners, **Le Garage**, Water St., Wiscasset 04578, tel. (207) 882-5409, claims one of the best downtown harbor views from its upper and lower enclosed porch/decks. (Smoking only on the lower level.) Request a porch/deck table, and dine by candlelight. Lamb is a specialty, service is good, and light suppers are thrifty choices. Reservations are wise on weekends. The restaurant is two blocks off Rt. 1. Open Feb.-December. Hours are Mon.-Sat. 11:30 a.m.-3 p.m. and 5-9:30 p.m. (to 10 p.m. Friday and Saturday), Sunday 11 a.m.-9:30 p.m., Memorial Day weekend to Labor Day. Off-season hours are Tues.-Sat. 11:30 a.m.-2:30 p.m. and 5-8:30 p.m. (to 9:30 p.m. Friday and Saturday), Sunday 11 a.m.-8:30 p.m.

Directly across the river is **The Muddy Rudder,** Rt. 1, Edgecomb 04556, tel. (207) 882-7748, where you can watch the sunset over Wiscasset (request a window table). Service is efficient, prices are reasonable, the children's menu has plenty of choices, and a subdued piano accompanies dinner and brunch. Open daily 11 a.m.-11 p.m., all year, for lunch, dinner, and Sunday brunch.

INFORMATION AND SERVICES

The **Wiscasset Regional Business Association** (WRBA), P.O. Box 150, Wiscasset 04578, tel. (207) 882-9617, fax 882-9086, is the local information clearinghouse. Since there's no official information center, the best place to find WRBA brochures is the display rack at Big Al's Super Values, three miles southwest of downtown. Once you get into town, stop at Wiscasset Hardware for a free walking map of the downtown area.

For a copy of *Wiscasset Invites You,* a free booklet, contact the **Wiscasset Town Office,** Rt. 1, Wiscasset 04578, tel. (207) 882-8205. The office, in the brick municipal building at the western end of town, is open weekdays.

The brick **Wiscasset Public Library,** High St., Wiscasset 04578, tel. (207) 882-7161, built as a bank in 1805, is a lively year-round operation, with book-discussion groups, children's story hours, a small art collection, and an annual used-book sale. Hours are Tues.-Fri. 10 a.m.-5 p.m. (to 7 p.m. Wednesday), Saturday 10 a.m.-3 p.m.

Newspapers
The best coverage of local news and events appears in the *Wiscasset Newspaper,* tel. (207) 882-6355 or 633-4620, under the same ownership as the *Boothbay Register.* It's published each Thursday. (The *Register* also carries Wiscasset-area news and listings.) The daily *Portland Press Herald* includes Wiscasset in its coverage, particularly the Thursday *Go* entertainment supplement.

Emergencies
The nearest full-service hospital is **St. Andrews Hospital and Healthcare Center,** 3 St. An-

drews Lane, Boothbay Harbor 04538, tel. (207) 633-2121 (ext. 368 for the emergency room). The **Family Care Center North,** Rt. 1, Edgecomb, tel. (207) 882-9858, a division of St. Andrews across from The Muddy Rudder restaurant, accepts walk-in patients for noncritical care weekdays 2-7 p.m., Saturday 8 a.m.-1 p.m.

For **police, fire, and ambulance** in Wiscasset, Alna, or Edgecomb, dial 911.

Public Restrooms
The **Town Wharf,** Water St., and the **Lincoln County Court House,** on Rt. 1 next to the sharp curve, have public facilities.

Laundromat
At the **Wiscasset Home Laundromat,** Water St., tel. (207) 882-9389, you can do your own laundry or they'll do it for you. Hours are 8 a.m.-9 p.m. daily, all year.

Special Tours, Programs, and Courses
For a bird's-eye view of the Wiscasset area, try getting up with the birds. Operating out of Wiscasset Airport, about a quarter of a mile off Rt. 1, **Downeast Flying Service,** Chewonki Neck Rd., Wiscasset 04578, tel. (207) 882-9401, does on-demand scenic flights throughout the year. Pemaquid Light, Boothbay Harbor, and the islands of Sheepscot Bay are on a typical route, but you can specify your own tour. Fall-foliage flights are fantastic. Cost for a 30-minute sweep is $50 for up to three people. Reservations aren't required, but you'll get what you want if you call ahead. From Wiscasset, head southwest on Rt. 1 to Rt. 144. Turn left and cross the railroad tracks, then bear right onto Chewonki Neck Road. The airport is on the left.

The **Chewonki Foundation,** RR 2, Box 1200, Wiscasset 04578, tel. (207) 882-7323, fax 882-4074, is the umbrella group for an impressive nonprofit educational organization begun as a summer boys' camp in 1915. The late birding guru Roger Tory Peterson, a Chewonki counselor in the 1920s, wrote the first edition of his *A Field Guide to the Birds* here and dedicated it to Clarence Allen, Chewonki's founder. The philosophy of Chewonki (which predates Outward Bound) emphasizes personal growth, group interaction, and sensitivity to the natural world. In addition to the summer camp (boys only; $2,400 for three weeks), programs now include the Maine Coast Semester (for 11th-graders), short-term residential programs at the Environmental Education Center, Elderhostel programs, wilder-

ness trips for school kids, and, for whole families, 3- to 10-day wilderness expeditions in the United States and Canada ($150-1,800 per adult).

BOOTHBAY PENINSULA

East of Wiscasset, en route to Damariscotta, only a flurry of signs along Rt. 1 in Edgecomb (pop. 1,000) hints at what's down the peninsula bisected by Rt. 27. Drive southward between Memorial Day and Labor Day and you'll find yourself in one of Maine's longest-running summer playgrounds.

The three peninsula towns of Boothbay (pop. 2,600), Boothbay Harbor (pop. 2,220), and, connected by a bridge, Southport Island (pop. 620) have sightseeing and whalewatching excursions, a first-rate small aquarium, an antique-railway museum, wall-to-wall shops, scads of restaurants and beds, and quiet preserves for escaping the inevitable midsummer crowds.

When Rt. 27 arrives at the water, having passed through Boothbay Center, you're at the hub, Boothbay Harbor ("the Harbor"), scene of all the action. The harbor itself is a boat fan's dream, loaded with working craft and pleasure yachts. Ashore, you'll face one-way streets, traffic congestion, and pedestrians everywhere. But there's plenty in this area to appreciate. Parking areas are noted on the Boothbay Harbor Region Chamber of Commerce's walking map.

Try to save time for quieter spots: East Boothbay, Ocean Point, Southport Island, or even just over the thousand-foot-long footbridge stretching across one corner of the harbor. Cross the bridge and walk down Atlantic Avenue to the Fishermen's Memorial, a bronze fishing dory commemorating the loss of hardy souls who've earned a rugged living here by their wits and the sea. Across the street is Our Lady Queen of Peace Catholic Church, with shipwright-quality woodwork and its own fishing icon—a lobster trap next to the altar.

Peak season in the Boothbay Region kicks off each year with Windjammer Days, a two-day midweek celebration in late June, when more than a dozen antique and replica windjammer schooners parade into the harbor under full sail, followed by concerts, fireworks, and a big, old-fashioned street parade.

Despite Boothbay Harbor's distinctly contemporary, tourist-oriented veneer, plenty of history lies below the surface. The English productively worked fishing grounds around Damariscove Island, just offshore, as far back as the early 17th century, when settlers established a fishing entrepôt on Cape Newagen. Conflicts between settlers and Indians scattered the newcomers, and 40 years passed before the next wave of settlers put down roots around present-day Boothbay Harbor. Established as Townsend in 1730, it was incorporated as the town of Boothbay in 1764. Southport spun off into a separate town in 1842, and Boothbay Harbor in 1889.

During the War of 1812, the area gained some renown for the U.S. Navy brig *Enterprise*'s capture of the Royal Navy brig *Boxer* offshore between Damariscove and Monhegan Islands. Damariscove's residents had front-row seats.

In the 1870s, when many scenic coastal areas experienced an influx of steamboat-borne rusticators from the Boston area and beyond, the Boothbay region entered its tourism phase— an era that shows no indication of coming to a close.

In fact, a pioneering summer colony chartered in 1871, 130-acre **Squirrel Island,** at the mouth of the harbor, remains an exclusive yet low-key enclave with about one hundred sizable Victorian cottages, no cars or bikes, no private phones, and a wonderfully relaxed pace. The squirrel motif is everywhere, though you won't see many examples of the real thing. Still controlled by the members-only Squirrel Island Village Corporation, message center tel. (207) 633-4715, the island is officially part of the town of Southport. The island has no interest in tourism, and there are no public facilities, but visitors are permitted on the island's paved perimeter path; allow at least an hour for the circuit, taking in open ocean, a sandy beach, rugged cliffs, and dense woods. It's a window on another era. Balmy Days Cruises operates the

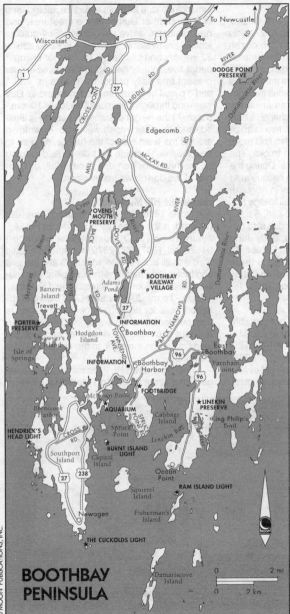

BOOTHBAY PENINSULA

© MOON PUBLICATIONS, INC.

seasonal Squirrel Island ferry from Boothbay Harbor, tel. (207) 633-2284, landing on the northwest corner of the island.

SIGHTS

Before turning off Rt. 1 for the Boothbay Peninsula, make a quick, interesting detour in Edgecomb, immediately east of the Wiscasset bridge, to historic Fort Edgecomb—perfect for a riverfront picnic. Afterward, back roads can connect you to Rt. 27 for Boothbay and Boothbay Harbor, but it's less confusing to return to Rt. 1, continue a bit east, and turn onto Rt. 27. (You can stock up on picnic fodder at Sarah's or Red's Eats, in Wiscasset.)

Fort Edgecomb

Built in 1808 to protect the Sheepscot River port of Wiscasset, the Fort Edgecomb State Historic Site, Eddy Rd., RR 1, Box 89, Edgecomb 04556, tel. (207) 882-7777, occupies a splendid, three-acre riverfront spread ideal for picnicking and fishing (no swimming). Many summer weekends, the Revolutionary encampments on the grounds of the octagonal blockhouse make history come alive with reenactments, period dress, craft demonstrations, and garrison drills. Admission is $1 adults, 50 cents children 5-11, free for seniors and kids under five. The fort officially is open daily 9 a.m.-5 p.m., Memorial Day weekend to Labor Day, but the grounds are easily accessible all year. From Rt. 1 at the Edgecomb Inn, take Eddy Rd. and go half a mile to Fort Road.

Ride the Rails
Boothbay Railway Village, Rt. 27, P.O. Box 123, Boothbay 04537, tel. (207) 633-4727, feels like a life-size train set. More than two dozen old and new buildings have been assembled here since the museum was founded, in 1964, and a restored narrow-gauge steam train makes a one-and-a-half-mile, 20-minute circuit throughout the day. Among the structures are a toy shop, a one-room schoolhouse, a chapel, a barbershop, a 19th-century town hall, two railroad stations, and a firehouse. You'll also find more than four dozen antique cars and trucks. The gift shop stocks train-oriented items. During the summer, special events include an antique auto meet, Children's Day (third Sunday in August), and the Columbus Day weekend fall foliage festival. The village is open daily 9:30 a.m.-5 p.m., mid-June to Columbus Day; train rides also operate on Memorial Day weekend, early June weekends, and the last weekend in October (a ghostly Halloween ride). The village is three and a half miles north of downtown Boothbay Harbor, seven and a half miles south of Rt. 1.

Feel the Fish
A 20-foot touch tank, with slimy but pettable specimens, is a major kid magnet at the **Marine Resources Aquarium,** McKown Point Rd., West Boothbay Harbor 04538, tel. (207) 633-9542, operated by the state Department of Marine Resources. Exhibits in the hexagonal aquarium include rare lobsters (oversize, albino, and blue) and other Gulf of Maine creatures, and new residents arrive periodically. Self-guiding leaflets are available. Admission is $2.50 adults, $2 seniors and children 5-18, free for children under five. In July and Aug., marine scientists present free daily programs at 11 a.m. and 1 and 3 p.m. The aquarium is open Memorial Day weekend through Columbus Day, daily 10 a.m.-5 p.m. At the height of summer, parking is limited, and it's a fairly long walk from downtown around the west side of the harbor, so plan to take the free Rocktide Inn trolleybus, departing on the half-hour from the Small Mall, or from one of the downtown trolley stops.

Hendricks Hill Museum
A historic 1810 Cape-style building, carefully restored, is the home of the Hendricks Hill Museum, Rt. 27, P.O. Box 3, West Southport 04576, tel. (207) 633-2370, a community attic filled with all kinds of workaday tools and utensils and fascinating maritime memorabilia. The museum is open Tuesday, Thursday, and Saturday 11 a.m.-3 p.m., July to Labor Day. During September, call for an appointment. Admission is free, but donations are welcomed. The museum is about two miles south of the Southport Island bridge, on the right, in the center of West Southport.

Continuing down Rt. 27 toward Cape Newagen, stop at the **Southport Memorial Library,**

clapboard Hendricks Hill Museum

tel. (207) 633-2741. It's a rare, surprising treat: a huge collection of beautifully mounted butterflies once owned by Dr. and Mrs. Stanley Marr. The library is open all year, Tuesday and Thursday 1-4 and 7-9 p.m., plus Saturday 1-4 p.m.

Nicholas T. Knight House

After more than a dozen years of neglect, the handsome 18th-century Nicholas T. Knight House, 2 Corey Lane, P.O. Box 457, Boothbay 04537, tel. (207) 633-6619, meticulously restored and now a private residence, is open for hour-long tours by reservation, June-Oct. and during the Christmas season. Cost is $2 pp. Anyone intrigued by old-house transformations, as well as lovely perennial gardens, has to see Jeff and Melinda Browne's National Historic Register home. Together with nearby MacNab's Tea Room—run by Jeff's mother—the Brownes also organize elegant special-event teas at the Knight House, which is just beyond the Rt. 27 monument in Boothbay Center.

PARKS AND PRESERVES

Courtesy of the very active **Boothbay Region Land Trust** (BRLT), more than 700 acres on the peninsula and nearby islands have been preserved for wildlife, residents, and visitors. About 10 miles of trails are open to the public in six preserves. Individual preserve maps, as well as a general brochure/map with driving directions, are available at the information centers or at the BRLT office, 2 McKown St., 2nd floor, P.O. Box 183, Boothbay Harbor 04538, tel./fax (207) 633-4818, open all year, Monday, Wednesday, and Friday 9 a.m.-noon. (Inquire at the office about summertime guided walks in the various preserves.) Kiosks at the trailheads hold preserve maps. There are no trash receptacles, so carry a litterbag and help the BRLT and everyone who follows you. To do even more, make a cash donation to the BRLT (any amount is welcome).

In East Boothbay, on the way to Ocean Point, is the 94.6-acre **Linekin Preserve,** stretching from Rt. 96 to the Damariscotta River. The 2.1-mile, white-blazed River Loop (best done clockwise) takes in an old sawmill site, a beaver dam, and great riverfront views. You'll meet a couple of moderately steep sections on the eastern side, near the river, but otherwise it's relatively easy.

On the west side of the peninsula, at the southern end of Barters Island, is the wooded, 19-acre **Porter Preserve,** with two loop trails that get you to great views over the Back and Sheepscot Rivers. From the trailhead, you can do a clockwise half-mile loop (red- and white-blazed) or stop midway for an added .4-mile (yellow-blazed) trail that rejoins the first loop. Next to the yellow trail is a tiny sandy beach.

Other BRLT holdings open to the public are the 146-acre **Ovens Mouth Preserve** with 4.7 miles of trails (wear insect repellent), 12-acre **Kitzi Colby Wildlife Preserve** off the River Rd., 22.5-acre **Marshall E. Saunders Memorial Park** in Boothbay, and 16-acre **Singing Meadows.**

Besides the BRLT preserves on the Boothbay Peninsula, see Damariscotta/Newcastle for info on the Dodge Point Preserve, on River Rd. in Newcastle (geographically on Boothbay's peninsula, but maintained by the Damariscotta River Association) and several other special locales on the Pemaquid Peninsula.

Damariscove Island

Summering Wabanakis knew it as Aquahega, but Damerill's Cove was the first European name attributed to the secure, fjordlike harbor at the southern tip of 209-acre Damariscove Island in 1614, when Capt. John Smith of the Jamestown Colony explored the neighborhood. By 1622, Damerill's Cove fishermen were sharing their considerable codfish catch with starving Plimoth Plantation colonists desperate for food. Fishing and farming sustained resident Damariscovers during their up-and-down history, and archaeologists have found rich deposits for tracing the story of this early island settlement about seven miles south of Boothbay Harbor.

Rumors persist that the ghost of Capt. Richard Pattishall, decapitated and tossed overboard by Indians in 1689, still roams the island, accompanied by the spectre of his dog. The fog that often overhangs the low-slung, bleak, almost-treeless island makes it easy to fall for the many ghost stories about Pattishall and other onetime residents. In summer, the island is awash with wildflowers, bayberries, raspberries, blackberries, and Rugosa roses.

Since 1966, most of 1.7-mile-long Damaris-cove has been owned by The Nature Conservancy. Day-use visitors are welcome on the island anytime, but the northern section (called Wood End) is off limits March 15-Aug. 15, to protect the state's largest nesting colony of eiders—nearly 700 nests. Damariscove Island became a National Historic Landmark in 1978. Dogs are not allowed.

Access to the island is most convenient if you have your own boat. Enter the cove at the southern end of the island and disembark at The Nature Conservancy dock on the west side of the harbor. Summertime caretakers live in the small cabin above the dock, where a trail map is available. Stay on the trails (watch out for poison ivy) or on the shore and away from any abandoned structures; the former Coast Guard station is privately owned.

For information about Damariscove Island, contact **The Nature Conservancy**, Fort Andross, 14 Maine St., Suite 401, Brunswick 04011, tel. (207) 729-5181, fax 729-4118.

RECREATION

The **Boothbay Region YMCA**, Rt. 27, Boothbay Harbor 04538, tel. (207) 633-2855, has an Olympic pool, fitness center, sauna, racquetball courts, and aerobics classes. Scuba certification classes are held in June and July, and the summer sports camps for kids (preregistration required) are terrific. Call the Y for racquetball reservations, as well as to reserve one of the municipal tennis courts, located just south of the Boothbay Region High School. Daily and weekly Y memberships are available for visiting adults ($7 pp) and families ($10). The Y is open Mon.-Fri. 5:30 a.m.-9 p.m. and Saturday 8 a.m.-1 p.m., June-August. Hours are Mon.-Fri. 5:30 a.m.-9:30 p.m. and Saturday 7:30 a.m.-6 p.m., Sept.-May. It's also open Sunday 1-5 p.m., Jan.-March. Stop in at the Y, or call, to check on the pool schedule.

To unwind toddlers, or even the grammar-school set, take them to the marvelously creative **Harold B. Clifford Community Playground** on Back River Rd., just north of Rt. 27 near Boothbay Center; turn right at the monument. Pack a picnic and eat it here; kids love it.

Cycling

If you haven't brought your own bike, the best local source is **Harborside Bike Rentals,** Boothbay House Hill, Boothbay Harbor 04538, tel. (207) 633-4303, across from the Town Landing. Full-day rental (secured by credit card) is $14, including helmet. The shop, a division of Augusta's AuClair Cycle and Ski, tel. (800) 734-7171, is open daily 10 a.m.-6 p.m., Memorial Day weekend to Labor Day. Some years, when the weather cooperates, the shop stays open into September; call ahead to check. In mid-summer, it's wise to call ahead and reserve a bike; this is a popular operation. The shop also has tandem bikes, child trailers, and family rates. You can also rent from **Tidal Transit,** 49 Townsend Ave., Boothbay Harbor 04538, tel. (207) 633-7140, for $20 a day, $12 a half-day.

At the chamber of commerce information centers, pick up a copy of the bike route for the 31-mile Barters Island/Southport loop (also a fine driving itinerary). Pack a picnic. Allow a full day to bike it, including stops and detours. The terrain is mostly easy and relatively level, but many stretches are narrow and winding, with poor shoulders, so it's *essential* to follow biking rules and exercise caution.

An alternate loop route, about 15 miles long, follows only the Southport Island section, from downtown Boothbay Harbor. If you're biking with kids, opt for this itinerary—but make sure they know the rules of the road, too. Again, take a picnic, or plan to stop at the Southport General Store, Rt. 27, tel. (207) 633-6666, about two miles south of the bridge. Also check out the nearby historic cemetery, the Hendricks Hill Museum, and the Hendricks Head Light (go west on Beach Rd. from the general store).

When crossing the swing bridge that spans Townsend Gut, between West Boothbay Harbor and Southport Island, be especially cautious. The surface can be a bear trap for bike tires.

Another good biking (and driving) route begins at the junction of Rts. 27 and 96, going through East Boothbay, then on down to **Ocean Point,** where the Shore Road loop skirts the rocky shoreline. (Ocean Point is about six miles from the Rt. 27/96 crossroads.) About halfway down Linekin Neck toward Ocean Point, hang a left onto King Philip's Trail, then left onto the loop road, clockwise, through the hamlet of Little

River, returning to Rt. 96. Like the Southport Island route, the roads are narrow and winding along Linekin Neck, and traffic can be heavy at the height of summer. Early morning is a great time to bike here; park your car in the Shop 'n Save supermarket lot, the Small Mall, or the YMCA, back up Rt. 27.

Getting Afloat

The Boothbay Harbor region is prime territory for getting out on the water; don't miss an opportunity, whether it's a harbor cruise, sunset cruise, whalewatching or sportfishing trip, or Monhegan Island excursion.

Cabbage Island Clambakes, Pier 6, Fisherman's Wharf, Boothbay Harbor, tel. (207) 633-7200, mailing address P.O. Box 21, East Boothbay 04544, deserves a category all its own. Touristy, sure, but it's a delicious adventure. You board the 126-passenger excursion boat *Argo* at Pier 6 in Boothbay Harbor; cruise for about an hour past islands, boats, and lighthouses; and disembark at five-and-a-half-acre Cabbage Island. Watch the clambake in progress, if you like, explore the island, or play volleyball. When the feast is ready, pick up your platter, find a picnic table, and dig in. A cash bar is available in the lodge, as are restrooms. When the weather's iffy, the lodge and covered patio have seats for a hundred. For $37.50 pp, you'll get two lobsters (or half a chicken), chowder, clams, corn, potatoes, dessert, beverage, and the boat ride. For children under 12, a boat-ride-plus-hot-dog option goes for $14. No credit cards. Clambake season is late June through Labor Day. The three-and-a-half-hour trips depart Mon.-Fri. at 12:30; Saturday trips depart at 12:30 and 5 p.m., Sunday trips are 11:30 a.m. and 1:30 p.m.

During the same season, the *Argo* also does two-hour **harbor cruises** on a varying itinerary, departing at 10 a.m. No reservations are needed; just show up at Pier 6 in time to find a seat. Cost is $8 pp; children under 13 are free.

Excursions

Boothbay Harbor's veteran excursion fleet is **Cap'n Fish's Cruises,** Pier 1, Wharf St., Boothbay Harbor 04538, tel. (207) 633-3244 or 633-2626 or (800) 636-3244. In addition to whale-watching trips, Cap'n Fish's 150-passenger boats do two-hour **nature cruises** ($7-12) and three-hour **puffin-watching trips** ($15-25; mid-June through July), plus **seal-watching trips** and **sunset cruises.** Pick up a schedule at one of the information centers and call for reservations.

The harbor's other big fleet is **Balmy Days Cruises,** Pier 8, Commercial St., P.O. Box 535, Boothbay Harbor 04538, tel. (207) 633-2284, operating four vessels on a variety of excursions. Two-hour **picnic supper cruises** aboard the *Balmy Days II* depart at 5:30 p.m. Tuesday, Thursday, and Saturday in July and Aug.; reservations are necessary. Cost is $17-27 adults (depending on food choice) or $13 just for the cruise. The *Novelty* does hour-long **harbor tours** on a varying schedule, 7 a.m.-9:30 p.m.; cost is $8 adults, $4 children. The 31-foot Friendship sloop *Bay Lady* does four one-and-a half-hour **sailing trips** daily in summer. Cost is $18 pp. Reservations are wise for the *Bay Lady* as well as for the fleet's most popular cruise, a day-long trip to Monhegan Island on the *Balmy Days II,* departing daily at 9:30 a.m. and returning at 4:15 p.m., early June through September, plus weekends in May and October. The three-hour roundtrip allows about three and a half hours ashore on idyllic Monhegan Island. Cost is $28 adults, $18 children 3-9. You're headed 12 miles offshore on this trip, so be sure to dress warmly, wear sturdy walking/hiking shoes, and take a camera and binoculars.

If you're addicted to lobster and yearn to see how they're caught, take one of the **lobster-trap-hauling excursions** aboard the 30-passenger converted lobsterboat *Miss Boothbay,* Pier 6, Fisherman's Wharf, Boothbay Harbor 04538, tel. (207) 633-6445. Veteran lobsterman Dan Stevens shows you how he retrieves a trap, removes the unlucky lobsters, secures their flailing claws, and rebaits the trap for the next unsuspecting crustaceans. You'll return with a whole new appreciation for the rugged routine of these hardworking fishermen. From mid-June to Labor Day, one-hour, 15-minute trips operate Tues.-Sat. at 9:30 and 11:30 a.m. and 1:30 and 3 p.m., weather permitting. The schedule occasionally varies, so reservations are advisable. Cost is $10 adults, $5 children.

Whalewatching

Variations in Gulf of Maine whale-migration patterns have added whalewatching to the list of Boothbay Harbor boating options as the massive mammals travel northeastward within reasonable boating distance. **Cap'n Fish's**, Pier 1, Wharf St., Boothbay Harbor 04538, tel. (207) 633-3244, 633-2626, or (800) 636-3244, is the best choice. Three- to four-hour trips depart daily, mid-June to mid-October. Cost is $15-25, with a raincheck if the whales don't show up. Reservations are advisable, especially early and late in the season and on summer weekends. No matter what the weather on shore, dress warmly and carry more clothing than you think you'll need. Motion-sensitive children and adults need to plan ahead with appropriate medication.

Sea Kayaking

From Memorial Day weekend through September, **Tidal Transit**, 89 Townsend Ave., Boothbay Harbor 04538, tel. (207) 633-7140, near the footbridge, will get you afloat with a two-and-a-half-hour **sealwatching** or **sunset tour** for $30 pp, or a **full-day tour with lunch** for $70 pp. No experience is necessary. For do-it-yourselfers, Tidal Transit rents single kayaks for $50 a day, tandems for $75. Their bike rentals are $20 a day, $12 a half-day.

ENTERTAINMENT

For nightlife, **Gray's Wharf**, Pier One, Boothbay Harbor 04538, tel. (207) 633-5629, is an unfancy, fun hot spot, with live entertainment and dancing most weekends all year, and weeknights during the summer. Happy hour is Mon.-Fri. 4-6 p.m., best enjoyed on the deck, almost *in* the harbor. Pool tables and giant TVs enhance the din inside.

Across from the Boothbay Region Chamber, the **Harbor Lights Cinema**, Small Mall, Rt. 27, Boothbay Harbor 04538, tel. (207) 633-3799, screens first-run films daily, Memorial Day weekend to Labor Day. Most popular night is Tuesday, when you'll get two tickets for the price of one.

FESTIVALS AND EVENTS

The **Fishermen's Festival** is a locally colorful early-season celebration, held the third weekend of April, beginning with a Friday Miss Shrimp Princess pageant. Saturday brings a lobster-crate race and afternoon contests such as trap hauling, scallop- and clam-shucking, fish-filleting, and net mending (plus a real steal—a lobster-eating contest you can enter for $5). Saturday night, church suppers feature fish and shellfish, and Sunday, a chowder luncheon precedes the blessing of the fleet to ensure a successful summer season.

June is the month for **Windjammer Days**, two days of festivities centering on traditional windjammer schooners. Highlights are the Windjammer Parade, harborfront concerts, plenty of food, and a fireworks extravaganza. The **Lincoln Arts Festival** presents six concerts—classical, pops, choral, and jazz—at various locations on the Boothbay Peninsula from late June to early September. Tickets are $12-16 adults, $9-10 students.

Early July through August is a great time for music in Boothbay Harbor. Free Thursday night **band concerts** at 8 p.m. are performed by the Hallowell Community Band. Bring a blanket or folding chair to the Memorial Library lawn, Boothbay Harbor. And the **Cormorant Chamber Players of Maine** present three or four first-rate professional concerts at the Congregational Church, Eastern and Townsend Aves.; info: tel. (207) 633-3936.

Columbus Day weekend marks the **Fall Foliage Festival**, featuring craft and food booths, a petting zoo, live entertainment, train rides, and more at Boothbay Railway Village.

SHOPPING

Art Galleries

A handsome 1807 brick building is the eight-room home of **Gleason Fine Art**, 15 Oak St., Boothbay Harbor 04538, tel. (207) 633-6849, one of Maine's top retail venues for 20th-century painting and sculpture. The gallery is open Tues.-Sat. 10 a.m.-5 p.m., April-Dec., other times by appointment.

Formerly housed at the Gleasons' location, the nonprofit **Boothbay Region Art Foundation,** 7 Townsend Ave., P.O. Box 124, Boothbay Harbor 04538, tel. (207) 633-2703, founded in the 1960s, moved in 1993 to its present high-visibility site. From mid-April to mid-October, the gallery mounts five juried shows of members' work, plus a student art show. Hours are Mon.-Sat. 11 a.m.-5 p.m., Sunday noon-5 p.m.

Books, Etc.

You're bound to find something at the two-story **Sherman's Book & Stationery (& Music) Store,** 7 Commercial St., Boothbay Harbor 04538, tel. (207) 633-7262 or (800) 371-8128, fax (207) 633-6630. Cards and cassettes, games and gifts, books and more books, kitchenware and kitsch. The shop is open all year, daily 9 a.m.-10 p.m. in summer, daily to 5:30 p.m. in winter.

Craft Galleries/Gift Shops

If pottery is high on your shopping list, plan an attack on the Edgecomb/Boothbay Peninsula area. Several talented ceramicists have long-established reputations, and there's enough variety to cover every interest.

The area's veteran craft shop is **Abacus,** 8 McKown St., Boothbay Harbor 04538, tel. (207) 633-2166 or (800) 206-2166 outside Maine, which has expanded from the original 1971 Boothbay Harbor store (seasonal) to year-round stores in Freeport, Portland, and Kennebunkport. Great stuff—functional items, wearable art, and charming doodads—high-end American crafts from several hundred artisans. The shop is open daily, Memorial Day through October. At the height of summer, it's open to 9:30 or 10 p.m., only to 6 p.m. in shoulder periods.

Also downtown is the **Gold/Smith Gallery,** 41 Commercial St., Boothbay Harbor 04538, tel. (207) 633-6252, featuring intriguing gold jewelry and contemporary paintings. The gallery is open Mon.-Sat. 10 a.m.-6 p.m. and Sunday noon-5 p.m., mid-May to Christmas. Off season, owners John Vander and Karen Swartsberg regroup at their home in the Tuscan hills—a recurring theme in some of their exhibits.

Back up the peninsula, in Edgecomb, Pat Hannigan produces brilliantly glazed, Japanese-influenced porcelain in whimsical (and functional) shapes. Her studio/shop, **Hannigan Pottery,** 65 Dodge Rd., Edgecomb 04556, tel. (207) 882-6430, in a gray-shingled converted barn, is open all year, Mon.-Sat. 10 a.m.-5 p.m. And don't miss the gardens. Dodge Rd. is off Rt. 1, about a mile east of the Rt. 27 turnoff for Boothbay.

Also relatively close to Rt. 1 is the **Iron and Silk Forge and Gallery,** Rt. 27, P.O. Box 163, Edgecomb 04556, tel. (207) 882-4055, the 400-square-foot retail shop for Elizabeth Derecktor's hand-painted silk scarves and clothing and Peter Brown's high-end handwrought weathervanes, chandeliers, and fireplace tools. The gallery, three miles south of Rt. 1, is open all year, Mon.-Sat. 9:30 a.m.-5 p.m.

Fresh and dried herbs are the overriding theme at Mel and Evelyn Shahan's **Sweet Woodruff Farm,** Rt. 27, Boothbay 04537, tel. (207) 633-6977, 5.3 miles south of Rt. 1, but the 1767 barn also has an interesting inventory of moderately priced country antiques. The shop is open daily 10 a.m.-5 p.m., May to late December.

General Store

At the blinking light in East Boothbay, stop in at the eclectic **East Boothbay General Store,** Rt. 96, Ocean Point Rd., East Boothbay 04544, tel./fax (207) 633-4503, source of lobster rolls, take-out sandwiches, snacks, beer, wine, and—yes—*electric trains*. The store is open all year, daily 6 a.m.-6 p.m. (to 9 p.m. in summer). No credit cards.

Farmers' Market

Lots of variety is the key at the excellent Boothbay Farmers' Market, operating from mid-June to early September, each Thursday 9 a.m.-noon. Set up at Conley's Garden Center on Rt. 27 in Boothbay Harbor (across from the Shop 'n' Save supermarket), 10 or 12 vendors have goat cheese, lamb, preserves, breads, and of course fresh produce. While you're here, check out the Maine-products gift section at Conley's, an especially fine greenhouse/nursery.

ACCOMMODATIONS

Boothbay Harbor's longevity as a holiday destination means beds galore—more than anyone cares to count. Even so, from late June to mid-

August, you'll meet a blur of No Vacancy signs. If that's when you decide to show up here, make reservations ahead. There's also several lodging choices in nearby Wiscasset.

Classic Inns with Restaurants

To get away from it all, book in at the **Newagen Seaside Inn,** Rt. 27, P.O. Box 68, Southport Island, Cape Newagen 04552, tel. (207) 633-5242 or (800) 654-5242 outside Maine, a full-service, unstuffy inn with casual fine dining and views that go on forever from the 85-acre grounds. Plus there's a mile-long rocky shore, a nature trail, tennis courts, oceanfront saltwater pool, guest rowboats, game room, and porches just for relaxing. Honeymooners and seniors head the guest list, but it's also a great spot for a family vacation. Twenty-six rooms and suites (private baths) are $100-150 d, including generous buffet breakfast, mid-July to Labor Day; $75-110 d early and late in the season. Several cottages are available by the week. The dining room is open to the public by reservation for breakfast, buffet lunch, and dinner Wed.-Mon.; entrées run $11-22. Smoking is allowed only in the bar and the Great Room. No pets. Open mid-May to Columbus Day. The inn is six miles south of downtown Boothbay Harbor.

Another getaway, on a peninsula jutting into the harbor, is the **Spruce Point Inn,** Atlantic Ave., P.O. Box 237, Boothbay Harbor 04538, tel. (207) 633-4152 or (800) 553-0289, which has grown topsy-turvy in recent years, adding modern condos to its already extensive complex of traditional inn rooms and cottages. Last count was 75 rooms/suites/cottages/condos (all with private baths, phones, and cable TV), with more to come. Attentive staffers, creative cuisine, a homey lounge, and a knockout setting create a big demand for rooms at Spruce Point. Reserve well ahead, especially in midsummer, and request a water-view room. Inn rooms and suites are $264-396 d, MAP, mid-July to late August; off-season rates are $190-388 d, MAP. Rustic cottages are $479-532 a day, MAP (four persons). Children's MAP rates (ages 4-14) are also available. Pets are allowed only in one cottage. Special packages are available for festival weekends and shoulder seasons. Amenities at the 15-acre resort include freshwater and saltwater pools, tennis court, fitness center, rocky

shorefront, and a shuttle bus to downtown (about one and a half miles). The 200-seat **harborview dining rooms** are open to the public for breakfast (7:30-9:30 a.m.) and dinner (6-9 p.m.); entrée range is $15-27. Jackets are required for dinner in the main dining room (they usually have some spares); casual dress is fine in the Patriots' Room. Thursday is buffet night in July and August; Tuesday is clambake night, when the dining rooms are closed. The inn is open Memorial Day weekend to mid-October.

Across the harbor from Spruce Point, the **Lawnmeer Inn,** Rt. 27, Southport Island, tel. (207) 633-2544 or (800) 633-7645, mailing address P.O. Box 505, West Boothbay Harbor 04575, is only two miles from downtown Boothbay Harbor. Built in 1898 on Southport Island, overlooking Townsend Gut, the traditional inn has 13 comfortable rooms (no smoking) about half with water views. A separate modern motel building has 18 rooms. All have private baths. From late June to Labor Day and fall weekends, rooms are $68-168 d; other months, $58-158 d. Children are welcome. Pets are a steep $25 per night (see "Kennels" under "Information and Services," below for a better option). Beginning mid-June, the inn's multi-star, **waterview restaurant** is open to the public for breakfast (Mon.-Sat. 7:30-10 a.m., Sunday to 11 a.m.) and dinner (daily 6-9 p.m.). After Labor Day, it's closed Monday night. Seafood is predominant on the extensive menu, which is imaginative and well prepared; entrées run $13-22. Dessert specialty is Key lime pie. Reservations are essential; it's a popular spot. The inn is open mid-May through Columbus Day.

B&Bs

Close to the head of the Boothbay Peninsula, half a mile south of Rt. 1, **Cod Cove Farm Bed and Breakfast,** Rt. 27, P.O. Box 94, Edgecomb 04556, tel. (207) 882-4299, is an artist's or photographer's dream. Set in an apple orchard, overlooking a farm pond, the mid-19th-century Cape-style home on five acres grabs your attention the minute you see it. Enthusiastic innkeepers Charlene ("Charley") and Don Schuman have four intriguingly decorated rooms, all with a/c; two have private baths and all have in-room sinks. Guests have the run of the historic home, even access to the Steinway baby grand in the living room. Rates are $85-105 d May-Oct., $65-85 d other months, including full breakfast and afternoon tea. No pets, no smoking, no children under 14. Credit cards are accepted, but cash or checks are preferred. Open early January to late November.

About nine and a half miles south of Rt. 1, in the heart of Boothbay Center and close to the picturesque Town Common, **Kenniston Hill Inn,** Rt. 27, P.O. Box 125, Boothbay 04537, tel./fax (207) 633-2159 or (800) 992-2915, has 10 lovely rooms, all with private baths; half have fireplaces. Trees and the lawn buffer the handsome, late-18th-century inn from traffic, but request a rear or side room if you're extremely noise-sensitive. Rates are $69-120 d, including David and Sue Straight's hearty country breakfast and afternoon tea. No smoking, no pets, no children under 10. Open all year.

All 15 rooms have Linekin Bay views and private baths (five have fireplaces) at the **Five Gables Inn,** Murray Hill Rd., P.O. Box 335, East Boothbay 04544, tel. (207) 633-4551 or (800) 451-5048, which began life as a no-frills summer hotel in the late 19th century. She's gone steadily upmarket since then, and well-traveled innkeepers De and Mike Kennedy, owners since 1995, have added their own unique touches. The living room is congenial, the gardens are gorgeous, and the porch goes on forever. Rates are $90-140 d (one room with a king-size bed and fireplace is $160 d), including Mike's gourmet buffet breakfast. No smoking, no pets, no children under eight. Book well ahead at this popular spot. The inn, on a side road off Rt. 96 in the traditional boatbuilding hamlet of East Boothbay, is three and a half miles from downtown Boothbay Harbor. Two moorings are available for guests. Open mid-May through October.

Square in the middle of downtown, overlooking the harbor and close to everything, **Admiral's Quarters Inn,** 71 Commercial St., Boothbay Harbor 04538, tel. (207) 633-2474, fax 633-5904, is an 1830 sea captain's home that's had a recent makeover courtesy of personable innkeepers Les and Deb Hallstrom. Four two-room suites and two double rooms have private baths, cable TV, water views, and private decks and entrances. Forget about lunch after the killer breakfast buffet. Rates are $85-135 d in summer, $75-105 off season. No pets or smoking,

no children under 12. Open mid-February to mid-December.

Campgrounds

With 150 well-maintained wooded and open sites on 45 acres, **Shore Hills Campground,** Rt. 27, P.O. Box 448, Boothbay 04537, tel. (207) 633-4782, is a popular destination where reservations are essential in midsummer. Rates are $14 for tents and $18-21 for hookup locations (two adults, two kids); cable TV is $1 extra. Leashed pets are allowed. Facilities include coin-operated showers and laundry. Located on the tidal Cross River, about eight miles south of Rt. 1 and close to the Boothbay Railway Village, Shore Hills is open mid-April to mid-October.

Seasonal Rentals

For a long-term rental, start with the **Cottage Connection of Maine,** P.O. Box 51, Boothbay Harbor 04538, tel. (207) 633-6545 or (800) 823-9501, fax (207) 633-3043, which has a free catalog of more than 150 rental properties. The annual tourism booklet published by the Boothbay Harbor Region Chamber of Commerce includes several pages of cottage-rental listings.

FOOD

No one starves in the Boothbay area, thanks to food emporia ranging from sidewalk hot-dog vendors to sandwich shops to pizza palaces to tearooms, lobster wharves, and upscale dining rooms. This is merely a sampling.

Watch local papers and bulletin boards for notices of **public suppers** and **chowder suppers,** great opportunities for sampling local home cooking and local color. Most start relatively early, do not include liquor, and cost under $6 for all you can eat. Such a deal.

Miscellanea

A foot-long overstuffed lobster roll ($10.95) is the summertime best-seller at **Hungry Dan's,** Rt. 27, Boothbay 04537, tel. (207) 633-3063, a deservedly popular spot across from Adams Pond, about eight and a half miles south of Rt. 1. Superb meatball or sausage subs, with tasty sauce, are also in demand; sandwiches are in the $1.95-4.95 range. Eat at one of the picnic tables or get it to go. No credit cards. Dan Carroll's eatery is open all year, Mon.-Sat. 6 a.m.-2 p.m.

Close to the harbor, **Eastside Market and Deli,** 32 Atlantic Ave., Boothbay Harbor 04538, tel. (207) 633-4616, is an old-fashioned Maine market morphed into a New York deli selling thick sandwiches (Boar's Head meats; average $3.95), creative salads, veggie items, wine, and everything you need for a chic picnic. No credit cards. The market is at the end of the footbridge from downtown. It's open Mon.-Sat. 8 a.m.-9 p.m. and Sunday 8 a.m.-6 p.m., May through mid-October.

Since 1943, no-nonsense Brud Pierce has been the "Duke of Dogs" in Boothbay Harbor, setting up his **Brud's Hot Dogs** wagon across from the Boothbay Harbor Memorial Library. Summer hours are daily 10 a.m.-5 p.m., to 9:30 p.m. Thursday—a boon for concertgoers. Occasionally, he even deserts his cart and joins the band with his rhythmic spoons.

A longtime landmark once known as Porter's Drug Store, **Downeast Pharmacy,** 27 Townsend Ave., Boothbay Harbor 04538, tel. (207) 633-4311, steadfastly refuses to sell cigarettes and provides the best of service for medications and sundries—right down to the old-fashioned soda fountain in the back. Ice-cream sodas are still only $1. Summer hours are Mon.-Sat. 8 a.m.-7 p.m., Sunday 8 a.m.-4 p.m. Winter hours (after Labor Day) are Mon.-Sat. 8 a.m.-6 p.m., Sunday 8 a.m.-3 p.m.

Inexpensive to Moderate
Jump-start the day with a moon muffin from the **Blue Moon Café,** 84 Commercial St., Boothbay Harbor 04538, tel. (207) 633-2349, or lunch on the deck with homemade soups and salads, great sandwiches, and sinful pastries. If you're headed out for a picnic, a $6 box lunch special can tide you over. "The Moon" is open Mon.-Sat. 8 a.m.-4 p.m. and Sunday 8 a.m.-2 p.m., mid-April to late November.

Another breakfast-and-beyond choice is **Andrews' Harborside Restaurant,** at the footbridge, Boothbay Harbor 04538, tel. (207) 633-4074, a bright blue-and-white place where Lisa Andrews and her chef-husband, Craig, concentrate on hearty starter-uppers in the morning then turn out pasta, steak, and fish specialties

(as well as Saturday night prime rib). Open daily 7:30-11:30 a.m. for breakfast, 11:30 a.m.-3 p.m. for lunch, and 5:30-8:30 p.m. for dinner, May to mid-October. On Friday and Saturday, dinner usually continues to 9 p.m.

The **Black Orchid,** 5 By-Way, Boothbay Harbor 04538, tel. (207) 633-6659, has been an always-reliable Italian seasonal standby since 1986; entrée range is $11-22. No reservations, so you may have to wait (enjoy drinks on the deck). Open Wed.-Mon. 5-9 p.m., May-Oct.; in spring and fall, it's sometimes also closed Sunday or Monday.

Over in East Boothbay, the cozy, inn-like **Carriage House Restaurant,** Ocean Point Rd., Rt. 96, East Boothbay 04544, tel. (207) 633-6025, has earned a reputation for its daily all-you-can-eat fish fry. Beyond the seafood specialties, steaks turn out just right, portions are ample, and prices are reasonable. Even in summer, there's usually a twofer night (two entrées for the price of one). The Carriage House, three and a half miles south of the Rt. 27/96 junction, is open all year, Mon.-Sat. 11 a.m.-9 p.m., Sunday 8 a.m.-9 p.m. The owners whimsically term their neighborhood the Costa Plenta Peninsula.

Tearooms
The Boothbay region has not one but *two* tearooms—one English, the other distinctly Scottish. Not far from the harbor, **Crumps,** 20 McKown St., Boothbay Harbor 04538, tel. (207) 633-7655, includes pub lunches, cappuccino, and retail teapots in its offerings (which also include Devonshire cream teas). No smoking. It's open daily 10 a.m.-5 p.m., Memorial Day weekend to Columbus Day.

Tea: A Magazine gives a thumbs-up to **MacNab's Tea Room,** Back River Rd., P.O. Box 206, Boothbay 04537, tel. (207) 633-7222 or (800) 884-7222, fax (207) 633-4691, near the center of Boothbay (not the harbor). Tartans and terriers are the dominant motifs in this informal, folksy place, where Frances Browne inquires about your tea choice as soon as you settle in. Homemade soups, Highland pie, open-faced scone sandwiches, and typically Scottish sweets are all on the lunch menu. High tea, available by prior arrangement, includes a tour of the Nicholas T. Knight House. Even if you can't get here, send for the entertaining mail-order catalog. Located in an antique Cape-style farmhouse .4 mile off Rt. 27, MacNab's is open Tues.-Sat. 11 a.m.-6 p.m.

Lobster-in-the-Rough

Boothbay Harbor and East Boothbay seem to have more eat-on-the-dock lobster shacks per square inch than almost anywhere else on the coast. If you're a lobster fanatic, you've reached nirvana, heaven, ground zero, whatever. Two excellent choices are Robinson's Wharf and Lobsterman's Wharf. On the Southport Island side of the harbor, overlooking Townsend Gut next to the swing bridge, **Robinson's Wharf,** Rt. 27, Southport Island, tel. (207) 633-3830, mailing address P.O. Box 544, West Boothbay Harbor 04575, is a sprawling place with tons of indoor and outdoor seating. Lobster dinners, lobster stew, fried seafood, steamed clams, mussels—it's all here. Plus burgers, dogs, fries, pasta salad, even BLTs and grilled cheese sandwiches. Save room for homemade pie with Round Top ice cream. Beer and wine are available. The restaurant is open daily 11:30 a.m.-7:45 p.m., mid-June to Labor Day (to 8:45 p.m. July and August).

Around the other side of the harbor, facing the Damariscotta River in East Boothbay, is the **Lobsterman's Wharf,** Rt. 96, East Boothbay 04544, tel. (207) 633-5481 or 633-3443. Everything from ties to T-shirts adorns the clientele, usually a mix of locals and flatlanders. The lobsters are great; so are the steaks and fries; dinner entrées range $11-19. Nearly 200 seats inside and out, and most of 'em fill up on Sunday, when there's live jazz, sometimes blues. Smoking is allowed only in the unique bar—the ex-pilothouse of a locally built minesweeper. Midsummer hours are daily 11:30 a.m.-10 p.m. (with lighter fare at the bar until midnight); in spring and fall, it closes at 9 p.m. and all day Tuesday. From the junction of Rts. 27 and 96 in Boothbay Harbor, take Rt. 96 three miles to the wharf, on the left.

AISLINN RACE

INFORMATION AND SERVICES

The **Boothbay Harbor Region Chamber of Commerce,** Rt. 27, P.O. Box 356, Boothbay Harbor 04538, tel. (207) 633-2353, fax 633-7448, maintains one seasonal and one year-round information center. The seasonal center is on Rt. 1, next to the Bay View Inn, at the Rt. 27 turnoff. Hours are Mon.-Thurs. and Saturday 10 a.m.-7 p.m., Friday 10 a.m.-9 p.m., and Sunday 10 a.m.-5 p.m. Down Rt. 27, 10.8 miles from Rt. 1, is the chamber's main office, across from the Small Mall and just south of the Carousel Music Theatre. It's open Mon.-Fri. 8 a.m.-5 p.m., all year.

About eight miles south of Rt. 1, in between the two centers above, is the **Boothbay Chamber of Commerce Information Center,** Rt. 27, Boothbay Center 04537, tel. (207) 633-4743. It's open weekends Memorial Day to mid-June, then Mon.-Sat. 9 a.m.-9 p.m. and Sunday 11 a.m.-6 p.m., mid-June to Labor Day. From Labor Day to Columbus Day, it's open Mon.-Sat. 10 a.m.-6 p.m., Sunday 11 a.m.-4 p.m. Debbie Peters is the third generation in her family to run this operation, and there's almost nothing she can't handle.

All three centers stock brochures for the entire peninsula; wherever you stop, be sure to request the handy annual *Boothbay Harbor walking map,* the Boothbay Region Land Trust hiking brochure, and the useful tourism booklet covering the whole peninsula.

The handsome Greek Revival **Boothbay Harbor Memorial Library,** Oak St., Boothbay Harbor 04538, tel. (207) 633-3112, holds Friday morning story hours for kids, and the library's summertime "used bookstore" is a magnet for everyone else. Summer library hours are Tuesday 10 a.m.-4:30 p.m., Wednesday 10 a.m.-7 p.m., and Thurs.-Sat. 10 a.m.-4:30 p.m. Bookstore hours are Mon.-Sat. 10:30 a.m.-4:30 p.m., mid-June to mid-September. Thursday evenings, there are band concerts on the lawn.

Newspapers

Best local news and feature coverage is provided by the ***Boothbay Register,*** tel. (207) 633-4620, published every Thursday since 1876. Other newspapers with Boothbay news, ads, and calendar items are the ***Lincoln County Weekly*** and the ***Lincoln County News.*** The ***Portland Press Herald,*** published daily, includes the Boothbay region in its news and cultural sections.

Each summer, the *Boothbay Register* publishes a free tabloid, *Summertime,* filled with features, touring suggestions, ads, and calendar listings. It's available at all information centers as well as local shops, lodgings, and restaurants. The off-season version, aptly named *Wintertime,* covers winter events and year-round attractions.

Emergencies

For fire, police, and ambulance services, dial 911 in **Boothbay, Boothbay Harbor, and Southport.** In **Edgecomb,** call (207) 882-7712 for fire and ambulance, (207) 882-7332 for police.

Round-the-clock emergency care is available at **St. Andrews Hospital and Healthcare Center,** 3 St. Andrews Lane, Boothbay Harbor 04538, emergency room tel. (207) 633-2121 ext. 368, which has great views over Mill Cove.

Public Restrooms

At the municipal parking lot on Commercial St. (next to Pier 1), and at the municipal lot on Howard St., are public restrooms. St. Andrews Hospital and the Marine Resources Aquarium also have restrooms.

Kennels

Haggett Hill Boarding Kennel, 93 Dodge Rd., Edgecomb 04556, tel. (207) 882-6709, boards dogs for $10 a day, cats for $5.50. Reserve well ahead for this popular, attentive operation. No credit cards. Year-round hours are Mon.-Sat. 7 a.m.-6 p.m., Sunday 8-9 a.m. and 5-7 p.m. In summer, the kennel often opens at 6 a.m. Mon.-Saturday. It's located half a mile south of Rt. 1, not far beyond Hannigan Pottery.

Laundromat

Harbor Village Cleaners and Wash & Dry, Harbor Village Plaza, Townsend Ave., Boothbay Harbor 04538, tel. (207) 633-3891, with coin-operated washers and dryers, is open daily 7:30 a.m.-7:30 p.m.; in summer, it's usually open until 8:30 p.m. weekdays.

Getting Around

Two Boothbay Harbor motel complexes, the Rocktide Inn and Cap'n Fish's Motel, operate free trolleybuses on continuous scheduled routes during the summer. Approaching Boothbay Harbor on Rt. 27, you can pick up a trolley at the Flagship Motor Inn or at the Small Mall, across from the Boothbay Harbor Region Chamber of Commerce. The Rocktide trolley makes special hourly trips from the Small Mall to the Marine Resources Aquarium, alleviating the parking problem there. Check at any of the information centers to confirm the trolleybus schedule, usually mid-June to Labor Day, 8:30 a.m.-5 p.m. (aquarium runs begin later and end earlier).

DAMARISCOTTA/NEWCASTLE

At the head of the Pemaquid Peninsula, the two riverfront towns of Damariscotta (pop. 1,900) and her Siamese twin, Newcastle (pop. 1,600), serve as the gateway to New Harbor (probably Maine's most photographed fishing village), Pemaquid Point (site of one of Maine's most photographed lighthouses), and historic ports reputedly used by Capt. John Smith, Capt. Kidd, and assorted less-notorious types. Here, too, are a restored fortress, Native American historic sites, craft shops galore, a thriving cultural center, boat excursions to offshore Monhegan, and one of the best pocket-size sand beaches in Mid-Coast Maine.

On Christmas Day 1614, famed explorer Capt. John Smith anchored on Rutherford Island, at the tip of the peninsula, and promptly named the spot Christmas Cove. And thus it remains today; Christmas Cove is one of three villages belonging to the town of South Bristol, the southwestern finger of the Pemaquid Peninsula. South Bristol and Bristol (covering eight villages on the bottom half of the peninsula) were named after the British city.

As early as 1625, settler John Brown received title to some of this territory from the Abnaki sachem (chief) Samoset, an agreeable fellow who learned snippets of English from British codfishermen. Damariscotta (dam-uh-riss-COT-ta), in fact, is Abnaki for "plenty of alewives [herring]." The settlement here was named Walpole but was incorporated, in 1847, under its current name.

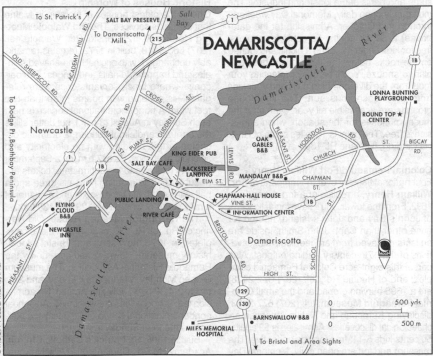

Newcastle, incorporated in 1763, earned fame and fortune from shipbuilding and brickmaking —which explains the extraordinary number of brick homes and office buildings throughout the town. In the 19th century, Newcastle's shipyards sent clippers, Downeasters, and full-rigged ships down the ways and around the world.

SIGHTS

Pemaquid Light/Fishermen's Museum

There's something irresistible about lighthouses, and the setting here makes it even more so. Commissioned in 1827, **Pemaquid Light** stands sentinel over some of Maine's nastiest shoreline—rocks and surf that can reduce any wooden boat to kindling. Now automated, the light tower is not accessible, but the adjacent **Fishermen's Museum,** in the former lightkeeper's house, tel. (207) 677-2494, points up the pleasures and perils of the lobstering industry. The museum is open daily, Memorial Day weekend through mid-October. Admission (at the gatehouse) is $1 for adults, 50 cents for seniors, free for kids under 12. Bring a picnic and lounge on the rocks below the light tower, but don't plan to snooze. You'll be busy protecting your food from the dive-bombing gulls and your kids from the treacherous surf. The lighthouse grounds are accessible all year, even after the museum closes for the season, when admission is free. The point is 15 miles south of Rt. 1, via winding, two-lane Rt. 130.

Colonial Pemaquid/Fort William Henry

Four national flags fly over the ramparts of **Fort William Henry,** a replica of a fort dating from 1692. From the tower, you'll have fantastic views of John's Bay and John's Island, named for none other than Capt. John Smith; inside are artifacts retrieved from archaeological excavations of the 17th-century trading outpost. Also part of this eight-acre Colonial Pemaquid complex, end of Huddle Rd., tel. (207) 677-2423, are a 1695 burying ground and the small **Colonial Pemaquid Museum,** tel. (207) 677-2423, displaying European and Native American archaeological discoveries. Admission is $2 adults, 50 cents kids 5-11; free for kids under five. The museum and fort are open daily, Memorial Day

weekend to Labor Day. The surrounding park, sloping down to John's Bay, is a great picnic spot, accessible all year. (During blackfly season, a reliable sea breeze keeps the insects away.) Colonial Pemaquid is 14 miles south of Rt. 1 and one mile west of Rt. 130.

Chapman-Hall House

Damariscotta's oldest surviving building is the Cape-style Chapman-Hall House, Main St., no telephone, built in 1754 by Nathaniel Chapman, whose family tree includes the legendary John Chapman—"Johnny Appleseed." Highlights are a 1754 kitchen and displays of local shipbuilding memorabilia. The National Historic Register house, meticulously restored by the Chapman-Hall House Preservation Society in the styles of three different eras, is open July and August, Tues.-Sun. 1-5 p.m. Admission is $1. Don't miss the antique roses in the back garden.

Historic Houses of Worship

One of the oldest houses of worship in Maine that still holds services, **The Old Walpole Meeting House,** Rt. 129, Bristol Rd., Walpole, tel. (207) 563-5318, built in 1772, remains remarkably unchanged, with original hand-shaved shingles and handmade nails and hinges. The balcony—where black servants once were relegated—is paneled with boards more than two feet wide. A nondenominational service is held each Sunday in August (3 p.m.), but better still is the annual candlelight concert, a dramatic occasion in this building with no electricity and splendid acoustics. It's at 7 p.m. on a September Sunday (call ahead to confirm date; tickets are about $13). The meeting house is three and a half miles south of Damariscotta and a quarter of a mile south of where Rts. 129 and 130 fork.

The **Harrington Meeting House,** Old Harrington Rd., off Rt. 130, begun in 1772 and completed in 1775, now serves as Bristol's local-history museum—town-owned and run by the Pemaquid Historical Association. The museum is open Monday, Wednesday, Friday, and Saturday 2-4:30 p.m., July and August. No admission fee, but donations are welcomed. An annual nondenominational service, with guest speaker, occurs the third Sunday in August.

Built in 1808, **St. Patrick's Catholic Church,** Academy Hill Rd., Damariscotta Mills, Newcas-

St. Patrick's Church, Newcastle

tle 04553, tel. (207) 563-3240, a solid brick structure with one-and-a-half-foot-thick walls and a Paul Revere bell, is New England's oldest surviving Catholic church. Open daily 9 a.m. to sundown. Academy Hill Road starts at Newcastle Square, downtown Newcastle; the church is two and a quarter miles from there, and one mile beyond Lincoln Academy.

St. Andrew's Episcopal Church, Glidden St., Newcastle 04553, tel. (207) 563-3533, built in 1883, is nothing short of exquisite, with carved-oak beams, stenciled ceiling, and, for the cognoscenti, a spectacular Hutchings organ.

Darling Marine Research Center
Not far beyond the Old Walpole Meeting House is the turnoff to the **Ira C. Darling Oceanographic Center,** 25 Clark's Cove Rd., off Rt. 129, Walpole 04573, tel. (207) 563-3146, part of the University of Maine System. Generally known as the Darling Center, it's the hands-on laboratory for the university's marine-biology students. From mid-July to late August, the cen-

ter sponsors a weekly lecture series, sometimes even a concert. Held in the center's Kresge classroom, the programs (Wednesday at 7:30 p.m.) focus on maritime history, ecology, and marine biology. Suggested donation is $3; call ahead for schedule details. The best chance to tour the 136-acre campus is during the center's annual open house; the date varies, so call for info. From downtown Damariscotta, take Rt. 130 two miles to Rt. 129. Continue five miles on Rt. 129 to Clark's Cove Rd.; turn right and go about one mile to the campus.

The Iceman Cometh
On a late-February Sunday morning (weather permitting), several hundred helpers and onlookers gather at Thompson Pond, next to **The Thompson Ice House,** Rt. 129, South Bristol 04568, tel. (207) 644-8551 or 644-8120, for the annual ice harvest. Festivity prevails as a crew of robust fellows marks out a grid and saws out 12-inch-thick ice cakes, which are pushed up a ramp to the ice-storage house. More than 60 tons of ice are harvested each year. Sawdust-insulated 10-inch-thick walls keep the ice from melting in this National Historic Register building first used in 1826. In 1990, the house became part of a working museum. The grounds are accessible free all year, including a photographic display board depicting a 1964 harvest. The museum (with ice tools and a window view of the stored ice cakes) is open Wednesday, Friday, and Saturday 1-4 p.m., July and August. Suggested donation is $1 adults, 50 cents kids. The site is on Rt. 129, 12 miles south of Damariscotta. Roadside parking is allowed.

The Gut
At the foot of a hill on Rt. 129 is the tiny community of **South Bristol,** the heart of the town that stretches along the western edge of the Pemaquid Peninsula. In the village center is a green-painted swing bridge (swinging sideways) spanning a narrow waterway quaintly named The Gut. Separating the mainland from Rutherford Island, The Gut is a busy thoroughfare for local lobsterboat traffic, so the bridge opens and closes (a 10-minute procedure) often. No one is in much of a hurry in this sleepy hamlet, so the frequent stoppages never seem to bother anyone, and the scenery is worth it all. So be patient.

PARKS AND PRESERVES

Residents of the Pemaquid Peninsula are incredibly fortunate to have several foresighted local conservation organizations, each with its own niche and mission: Damariscotta River Association, Pemaquid Watershed Association, and Damariscotta Lake Watershed Association. In addition, The Nature Conservancy, Maine Audubon Society, and National Audubon Society all have holdings on the peninsula, a natural-resource bonanza.

Salt Bay Farm

Headquarters of the **Damariscotta River Association** (DRA), founded in 1973, is the Heritage Center, a late-18th-century farmhouse on 90-acre DRA Salt Bay Farm, Belvedere Rd., P.O. Box 333, Damariscotta 04543, tel. (207) 563-1393. Here you can pick up maps, brochures, and other info on the hundreds of acres of land protected and managed by the DRA—notably the Dodge Point Preserve, Menigawum (Stratton Island) Preserve, and the Salt Bay Preserve. Salt Bay Farm's fields, saltmarsh, and shore frontage are open to the public daily, year-round, from sunrise to sunset; the office is open weekdays, usually 8 a.m.-4 p.m. No camping or fires. To reach the farm from downtown Newcastle, take Mills Rd. (Rt. 215) to Rt. 1. Turn right (north) and go 1.4 miles to the blinking light (Belvedere Road). Turn left and go .4 mile; park in the grassy area on the right.

Salt Bay Preserve Heritage Trail

Across Salt Bay from the DRA Salt Bay Farm is the trailhead for the Salt Bay Preserve Heritage Trail, a relatively easy three-mile loop around Newcastle's Glidden Point that touches on a variety of habitat and also includes several areas of major historical interest going back 2,500 years. Part of the trail is protected by the feds, do *not* disturb or remove anything. Better still, carry a litterbag and help maintain the path.

This is a super family hike, and leashed dogs are allowed. Along the trail, watch for eagles, osprey, herons, several stands of rare white oaks, and open views of Great Salt Bay. Best time to come is close to low tide, as some parts of the trail require slight detours at high tide—es-

pecially during the new or full moon. In any case, rubberized shoes or boots are a good idea. To reach the preserve from Newcastle Square, take Mills Rd. (Rt. 215) about two miles to the offices of the *Lincoln County News* (just after the post office). Go inside and request permission to park in their lot (park to the right, as far away from the buildings as possible). Walk across Rt. 215 to the trailhead, and pick up a brochure/map.

Dodge Point Preserve

In 1989, the state of Maine acquired the 506-acre Dodge Point Preserve—one of the stars in its crown—as part of a $35 million bond issue. The Damariscotta River Association (DRA), which initiated its protection, helps manage and maintain the property. To sample what the Dodge Point Preserve has to offer, pick up a map at the entrance and follow the Loop Road counterclockwise, then hook into the Discovery Trail, heading clockwise, with several dozen highlighted sites. Consider stopping for a riverside picnic and swim at Sand Beach before continuing back to the parking lot. Hunting is permitted in the preserve, so November isn't the best time for hiking here. Winter brings out ice-skaters and cross-country skiers. The Dodge Point parking area is on River Rd., 2.6 miles southwest of Rt. 1 and three and a half miles southwest of downtown Newcastle. Open all year for day use only, closing at sunset. Admission is free. For more information, contact the DRA.

Menigawum Preserve (Stratton Island)

Owned by the Damariscotta River Association, 30-acre Stratton Island is also known locally as Hodgdon's Island. You'll need your own small boat, canoe, or kayak to get here—it's at the entrance to Seal Cove on the west side of the South Bristol peninsula. Closest public boat launch is at The Gut, about four miles downriver—a trip better done *with* (in the same direction as) the tide. Best place to land is in the northeast corner—also a great spot for shelling. Pick up a map in the small box at the north end of the island and follow the perimeter trail clockwise. At the northern end, you'll see osprey nests; at the southern tip are Native American shell middens—discards from hundreds of years of marathon summer lunches. (Needless to say, do *not* disturb or remove anything.) You can picnic in the pasture, but no fires or camping. Stay clear of the abandoned homesite on the island's west side. The preserve is accessible from sunrise to sunset.

Witch Island Preserve

Named for a 19th-century local woman dubbed "The Witch of Wall Street" for her financial wizardry, Witch Island Preserve is owned by the Maine Audubon Society. The wooded, 18-acre island has two beaches, a perimeter trail, and the ruins of the "witch's" house. Located a quarter of mile offshore, it's accessible by canoe or kayak from the South Bristol town landing, just to the right after the swing bridge over The Gut. Put in, paddle under the swing bridge, and go north to the island. For more information, contact Maine Audubon Society, Gilsland Farm, 118 Rt. 1, Falmouth 04105, tel. (207) 781-2330, fax 781-6185.

Rachel Carson Salt Pond/ La Verna Preserve

If you've never spent time studying the variety of sealife in a tidal pool, the Rachel Carson Salt Pond is a great place to start. Named after the famed author of *Silent Spring* and *The Edge of the Sea,* who summered in this part of Maine, the salt pond was a favorite haunt of hers. The whole point of visiting a tidepool is to see what the tide leaves behind, so check the tide calendar (in local newspapers, or ask at your lodging) and head out a few hours after high tide. Wear rubber boots and beware of slippery rocks and rockweed. Among the many creatures you'll see in this quarter-acre pond are mussels, green crabs, periwinkles, and starfish. Owned by The Nature Conservancy, the salt pond is on Rt. 32 in the village of **Chamberlain,** about a mile north of New Harbor. Parking is limited. Across the road is a trail into a 78-acre inland section of the preserve—most of it wooded. Brochures are available in the registration box.

About two miles farther north on Rt. 32 (or four miles south of Round Pond) is the 119-acre **La Verna Preserve,** also owned by The Nature Conservancy. Behind the 3,600-foot-long Muscongus Bay shorefront are woodlands, marshlands (wear insect repellent and rubber-

ized shoes or boots), and old cellar holes. Park on Rt. 32 and walk into the preserve on half-mile-long Tibbitts Road, an unpaved private road that begins opposite the red North Country barn. (Keep right when Tibbitts Rd. forks.) A trail leads through woodlands to the shore, with intriguing geological formations and spectacular views.

For additional information about both preserves, which are accessible from sunrise to sunset year-round, contact The Nature Conservancy, Maine Chapter, 14 Maine St., Fort Andross, Brunswick 04011, tel. (207) 729-5181.

Todd Wildlife Sanctuary

The mainland section of a 345-acre National Audubon Society complex, the Todd Wildlife Sanctuary, Keene Neck Rd., HC 60, Box 102, Medomak 04551, includes a visitor's center and gift shop (open daily 10 a.m.-4 p.m., June through August, tel. 207-529-5148; off season, 207-529-5880), and the **Hockomock Nature Trail,** winding through the woods and down to the shore (open year-round). Pick up a trail guide at the center and follow the informative signs. Allow about an hour. Don't forget a picnic so you can have lunch on the beach. Just offshore is 333-acre **Hog Island,** site of the summertime **National Audubon Ecology Camp** for teenagers and adults. Each July, Hog Island holds an open house, a three-hour weekday-afternoon program including boat trip, guided tour, and refreshments. Cost is about $5, and reservations are required. It's an excellent chance to get the lay of the place, maybe even consider a future workshop. Call to find out the date. At other times, if you have your own boat, you can roam Hog Island during daylight hours (no camping). Just check in at the office near the dock at the north end of the island.

RECREATION

For the kids, there's a great creative playground —the **Lonna Bunting Playground,** built by local volunteers—on Business Rt. 1 next to the **Central Lincoln County YMCA,** tel. (207) 563-3427, which has inexpensive one-day memberships for access to tennis courts and fitness facilities.

Golf

The nine-hole **Wawenock Country Club,** Rt. 129, Walpole, tel. (207) 563-3938, established in the 1920s, is a challenging and very popular public course about midway down the Pemaquid Peninsula from Damariscotta. The par-three eighth hole features a treacherous bunker named Big Bertha. Starting times are needed on summer weekends.

Cycling

Portland's **Maine Bicycle Trail Association,** 43 Carleton St., Portland 04102, tel. (207) 879-7440, has produced a well-planned bicycling map of the Damariscotta area. The map also covers Boothbay, Damariscotta Lake, and Waldoboro. It's well worth the $1 it costs. As with so many other parts of Maine, bike lanes on the Pemaquid Peninsula are poor to nonexistent, so exercise the utmost caution. Roads are narrow, winding, and poorly shouldered. (The association, linked with the Bicycle Transportation Alliance of Portland, tel. (207) 773-3053, led by enthusiast Sandy Vogels, has also produced bike maps, at $1 each, of Casco Bay Islands, Cape Elizabeth, and Historic Portland.)

Swimming

Best bet (but also most crowded) on the peninsula for saltwater swimming is town-owned **Pemaquid Beach Park,** a lovely, tree-lined sandy crescent. No lifeguard, but there are showers (cold water) and bathrooms, and the snack bar serves decent food. No alcohol allowed on the beach. Admission is $1 for anyone over 12, free for anyone younger. At 7 p.m., the gates close (restrooms close at 5). The beach is just off Snowball Hill Rd., west of Rt. 130.

A much smaller beach is the pocket-size sandy area in Christmas Cove, on Rutherford Island. Take Rt. 129 around the cove and turn to the right, then right again down the hill.

One of the area's most popular freshwater swimming holes is **Biscay Pond,** a long, skinny body of water in the peninsula's center. From Business Rt. 1 at the northern edge of Damariscotta, take Biscay Rd. (turn at McDonald's) three miles to the pond (on the right, heading east). On hot days, this area sees plenty of cars; pull off the road as far as possible. In summer, the YMCA offers swimming lessons here (pre-registration required).

Farther down the peninsula, on Rt. 130 in **Bristol Mills,** is another roadside swimming hole, between the dam and the bridge.

GETTING AFLOAT

Boat Excursions

At 9 a.m. each day between mid-May and mid-October, the 60-foot powerboat *Hardy III* departs for **Monhegan,** a Brigadoon-like island a dozen miles offshore, where passengers can spend the day hiking the woods, picnicking on the rocks, birding, and inhaling the salt air. At 2:30 p.m., everyone re-boards, arriving in New Harbor just over an hour later. The boat has toilets and a snack bar. Dress warmly and wear rubber-soled shoes. Cost is $26 adults, $15 children under 12. Reservations are required, and they're held until 20 minutes before departure. Trips operate rain or shine, but heavy seas can affect the schedule. Go light on breakfast before boarding. From mid-June through September, the *Hardy III* also operates daily one-and-a-half-hour puffin tours, one-hour seal-watching tours, and one-hour lighthouse tours. **Hardy Boat Cruises** is 19 miles south of Rt. 1, based at Shaw's Fish and Lobster Wharf, Rt. 32, New Harbor 04554, tel. (207) 677-2026 or (800) 278-3346.

Canoeing

Experienced canoeists may want to take the **Damariscotta-Pemaquid River Canoe Trail,** a 40-mile clockwise loop that begins in Damariscotta and follows some of the region's traditional Indian canoe routes. Although few portages are required, one, fairly close to the beginning, is about a mile long over private land. For a route map, contact Mike Krepner at **Native Trails,** P.O. Box 240, Waldoboro 04572, tel. (207) 832-5255.

A great resource for canoeing in this area is Ralph Webber at **Pemaquid River Canoe Rental,** P.O. Box 46, Bristol 04539, tel. (207) 563-5721, in Bristol Mills. He's been renting canoes—17-foot Grummans—since 1978 and knows everything about the routes and the turf. His barn-based shop backs up to the Bristol dam; watch for his roadside sign on a portable trailer (east side of Rt. 130, five miles south of Damariscotta). You can put in right from his back

lobsterboat at The Gut, South Bristol

yard and go 14 miles north to the top of Lake Pemaquid, via the Pemaquid River and Biscay Pond. It's all flatwater, so paddling is easy in both directions, and much of the shoreline is undeveloped (it's private, though; no camping). For a less-ambitious trek, paddle six miles (two hours) to the beach at the top of Biscay Pond, have a swim, and return. Canoes are $20 a day, or $5 an hour if less than four hours. Open daily 7 a.m.-7 p.m.

If you have your own canoe, or just want to paddle the three-mile length of **Biscay Pond,** you can park at the beach area and put in there (see "Swimming" under "Recreation," above). Another good launching site is right next to Rt. 1 in **Nobleboro,** at the head of eight-mile-long **Lake Pemaquid.**

ENTERTAINMENT

The hub of culture on the Pemaquid Peninsula is the **Round Top Center for the Arts,** Business Rt. 1, Damariscotta 04543, tel. (207) 563-1507. This energetic association, staffed largely by volunteers, seems to have no limits. Classes, concerts, workshops, and exhibits go on throughout the year; call for schedule.

FESTIVALS AND EVENTS

Every Thursday in July, the **Lunch at the Library Lecture Series** combines brown-bag lunches and lectures at the Skidompha Library, Damariscotta, noon-1 p.m. The last Saturday in the month brings the 6:30 p.m. **Annual Concert on the Lawn.** Take a picnic and a cushion to Round Top Center for the Arts.

The second weekend in August, **Olde Bristol Days** features a craft show, a parade, road and boat races, live entertainment, and fireworks. At Fort William Henry, in Pemaquid, it's a summer highlight on the peninsula.

SHOPPING

Since many of the shops listed below are downtown, a parking advisory is in order. Downtown parking in summer is a major headache; the municipal lot, behind the storefronts, has a three-hour limit, and it's almost always full. (On weekends, head just up the hill to the Bath Savings Institution, on Church St., opposite Bristol Rd.; the bank is closed on weekends, so there's ample space in its parking lot.)

Antiques/Antiquarian Books
Kaja Veilleux Antiques, Newcastle Sq., Business Rt. 1, Newcastle 04553, tel. (207) 563-1002 or (800) 924-1032 in Maine, fax (207) 563-3445, is one of the area's venerable dealers in art and antiques. He also does free verbal appraisals every Thursday and organizes periodic auctions. The shop is open Mon.-Sat. 9 a.m.-5 p.m. (and Sunday noon-4 p.m. in summer).

Round Pond Village Antiques, Village Center, Round Pond 04564, tel. (207) 529-5592, zeroes in on country furniture, porcelain, and brassware, all in very good condition. Open Wed.-Sat. 11 a.m.-4 p.m., or by appointment.

Based in a screen-fronted antique carriage house just south of Round Pond village, **Jean Gillespie Books,** Rt. 32, HC 61, Box 71, Round Pond 04564, tel. (207) 529-5555, has separate rooms and alcoves, all very user-friendly. Specialties are cookbooks, nautical and Maine titles, and illustrated children's books; the "Royalty" category fills six shelves. Open daily noon-5 p.m., July and August; other months, open by appointment.

Art Galleries

Worth a visit for the building alone, the **Victorian Stable Gallery,** Water St., P.O. Box 728, just off Main St., Damariscotta 04543, tel. (207) 563-1991, was built in the 19th-century clipper-ship era and still has original black-walnut stalls—providing a great foil for the work of dozens of Maine craftsmen. Lining the walls are paintings and prints from the gallery's large "stable" of artists. Prices are moderate. Open June-Oct., Mon.-Sat. 10 a.m.-5 p.m.

In his **River Gallery,** Main St., P.O. Box 805, Damariscotta 04543, tel. (207) 563-6330, dealer Geoff Robinson specializes in 19th- and early-20th-century European and American fine art—a connoisseur's inventory. Open Mon.-Sat. 10 a.m.-3 p.m.; call ahead off season.

On the outskirts of Nobleboro, three miles north of Damariscotta, is the **Gallery House at Holly Hill,** Rt. 1, Box 047A, Nobleboro 04555, tel. (207) 563-8466. Rotating shows of contemporary New England artists are hung on the walls of a lovely antique Cape-style house; the gallery represents several dozen artists. The hilltop complex also includes a garden shop with unusual gifts, and greenhouses with antique roses, black petunias, and other atypical specimens. Open daily 8:30 a.m.-5 p.m., all year (except major holidays).

Books, Gifts, Crafts, and Clothing

The Pemaquid Peninsula is fertile ground for crafts and gifts, and many of the shop locations provide opportunities for exploring off the beaten path.

One of the state's "top 10" independent bookstores is in downtown Damariscotta. The inventory at the **Maine Coast Book Shop,** Main St., P.O. Box 309, Damariscotta 04543, tel. (207) 563-3207, fax 563-3243, always seems to anticipate customers' wishes, so you're unlikely to walk out empty-handed. Superb children's section; large selection of magazines; helpful staff.

Whimsy is the theme at **2fish,** 44 Main St., P.O. Box 114, Damariscotta, tel. (207) 563-

2220, a small gift shop stocked with appealing jewelry, clothing, and trinkets from here and abroad. Open Mon.-Sat. 9:30 a.m.-5 p.m., Sunday 11 a.m.-3 p.m., shorter hours off season.

Back behind the Main Street businesses is **Seasoned Artisans,** Nathaniel Austin House, Main St., Damariscotta, tel. (207) 563-3699, a cooperative gallery filled with Maine crafts. Open Mon.-Sat. 10 a.m.-5 p.m.

Close to Seasoned Artisans, and also just off Main Street (turn at Reny's), is **Weatherbird,** Elm St., P.O. Box 1168, Damariscotta, tel. (207) 563-8993, a terrifically eclectic shop with an inventory that defies description. Housewares, wines, toys, cards, gourmet specialties, and intriguing women's clothing are all part of the mix. Weatherbird is open Mon.-Sat. 8:30 a.m.-5:30 p.m., year-round. In July and August, it's also open Sunday 11 a.m.-3 p.m.

Formerly at the Gallery House at Holly Hill, **Brambles,** Main St., P.O. Box 1089, Damariscotta 04543, tel. (207) 563-2800, now has a high profile downtown. Six rooms filled with wonderful wares make all those upscale home-and-garden catalogs come to life: unusual birdhouses, whimsical garden ornaments, wind chimes, great garden tools, plus books and cards. Summer hours are Mon.-Sat. 8:30 a.m.-6 p.m. (to 8 p.m. Friday and Saturday) and Sunday 10 a.m.-6 p.m.

The **Round Top Center for the Arts,** Business Rt. 1, Damariscotta 04543, tel. (207) 563-1507, in addition to putting on all kinds of cultural activities (see "Entertainment," above) has a gift shop with especially unusual arts and crafts (including Hmong tapestries). It's open Mon.-Sat. 11 a.m.-4 p.m., Sunday 1-4 p.m.

Down the peninsula, there's no question that the **Granite Hall Store,** Backshore Rd., Rt. 32, P.O. Box 92, Round Pond 04564, tel. (207) 529-5864, is unique. Eric and Sarah Herndon's eclectic inventory is tough to describe. The first floor of this mid-19th-century emporium carries pottery, CDs, paper dolls, fudge, baskets, even catnip mice and cookie cutters. The old-fashioned peanut-roasting machine snares the kids. Upstairs, their parents usually succumb to books, antiques, and stunning handwoven Scottish and Irish woolens. Adding to the flavor are old ship models, hardwood floors, and a ship's bell that tolls the time. Open daily 10 a.m.-8:30

p.m., May to Christmas Eve; closed Monday in May and November. The shop is in "downtown" Round Pond, 11 miles south of Rt. 1.

Jenny Cleaves and Phyllis Leck are the incredibly talented artisans sharing the studio/shop at **Village Weavers,** Village Center, Round Pond 04564, tel. (207) 529-5523 or 529-5796. Phyllis specializes in Early American table linens and pillow covers, Jenny designs contemporary clothing and rugs. Both accept commissions. The shop is open Mon.-Sat. noon-5 p.m. (11 a.m.-4 p.m. in summer) or by appointment.

Also in Round Pond, on Rt. 32, is the **Scottish Lion Blacksmith,** P.O. Box 8, Round Pond 04564, tel. (207) 529-5523, where skilled smith Andrew Leck turns out all kinds of attractive wrought-iron accessories: wall brackets, fireplace tools, and more. Open by appointment; some of his work is available at the Village Weavers.

A nifty touch at the **Old Post Office Shop,** Village Center, New Harbor 04554, tel. (207) 677-3339, is the do-it-yourself gift-wrapping corner. The shop supplies free paper, tape, scissors, and a flat surface; you do the rest (and buy whatever ribbon you need). The atmosphere is friendly and quality is high here: locally made Sandcastle pottery, imported cards, decent T-shirts. Open daily 9 a.m.-5 p.m., May-December. Across the street, and under the same ownership, is the **Sandcastle Toy Shop,** tel. (207) 677-3339, with made-to-last toys designed to outsmart destructive kids.

Only a tenth of a mile off Rt. 1, Marion Berry's **Country Mouse Collectibles,** Hopkins Hill Rd., P.O. Box 272, Newcastle 04553, tel. (207) 563-8975, specializes in exquisite Ukrainian wax-resistant eggs *(pysanky)*—a traditional craft you can watch when you visit the shop (in the barn attached to a yellow Cape-style house). Also here are handknits, quillwork, wreaths, glassware, and other Maine crafts. Open Wed.-Sat. noon-5 p.m., May-October.

Natural Foods/Farmers' Market
Rising Tide Natural Foods Market, Business Rt. 1, Damariscotta 04543, tel. (207) 563-5556, has been a thriving co-op organization since 1978. Bulk items are available, plus books, cosmetics, and all kinds of preservative-free organic food. Located at the northern end of town,

next to Round Top Center for the Arts, the market is open Mon.-Sat. 9 a.m.-5:30 p.m. (to 7 p.m. Thursday).

From mid-May through October, the **Damariscotta Area Farmers' Market** sets up at R.L. Foster's Antiques parking lot, Rt. 1, Newcastle, two and a half miles south of Damariscotta, 9 a.m.-noon. Condiments, baked goods, cheeses, local shellfish, Chinese dumplings, and crafts are always available, and you never know what else will turn up at this major market. From late June through August, 9 a.m.-noon on Monday, a smaller market operates at the Reny's Warehouse ballfield, School St., just off Business Rt. 1, Damariscotta.

ACCOMMODATIONS

Inns and B&Bs
Commemorating the legendary, mid-19th-century globe-circling clipper ship, **The Flying Cloud Bed & Breakfast,** River Rd., P.O. Box 549, Newcastle 04553, tel. (207) 563-2484, fax 563-8640, is Alan and Jeanne Davis's exquisitely restored home with five guest rooms named after the ship's ports of call. The Melbourne Room, for instance, has fascinating Australian artifacts (and a fine view of the Damariscotta River). All rooms have private baths. Rates are $75-95 d, including superb Pennsylvania Dutch breakfasts; lower rates off season. No smoking, no pets, no children under eight. Open all year.

Just down the road from The Flying Cloud is **The Newcastle Inn,** River Rd., Newcastle 04553, tel. (207) 563-5685 or (800) 832-8669, fax (207) 563-6877, where Howard and Rebecca Levitan picked up the reins in 1995. Ideal for a romantic getaway, the lovely hostelry has 15 guest rooms with private baths (some with fireplaces), riverfront gardens, and an upscale country-inn ambience. Doubles are $95-175 June-Oct., $75-150 other months, including a huge breakfast. Special packages available off season. No smoking, no pets, no small children. The inn restaurant, open to the public by credit-card reservation, serves three- and five-course dinners ($30 and $37.50 pp). The inn is open all year; the restaurant is open Tues.-Sun. in summer, Thurs.-Sun. in winter.

Martha Scudder runs a nursery school in her basement, and she mothers her B&B guests like prized students at **Oak Gables Bed & Breakfast,** Pleasant St., P.O. Box 276, Damariscotta 04543, tel. (207) 563-1476. At the end of a pretty lane, this 13-acre hilltop estate overlooks the Damariscotta River. Despite a rather imposing setting, everything's homey, informal, and hospitable. Four second-floor rooms ($65 d) share a bath; a lower-level summertime room ($95 d) has a private bath and separate entrance. The heated swimming pool is a huge plus, and guests can harvest blackberries from scads of bushes. Also on the grounds are a three-bedroom cottage and two attractive riverfront apartments ($550-750 a week in summer, $500-650 a week off season), usually booked up well ahead. No pets, no smoking, no credit cards. Open all year.

Around the corner from Oak Gables, on a quiet side street, **Mandalay Bed & Breakfast,** Church St., RR 2, Box 005, Damariscotta 04543, tel. (207) 563-2260, has three comfortable bedrooms (sharing two baths) in a small, antiques-furnished, Cape-style home. Rooms go for $50-60 d, with an ample breakfast. No smoking, no pets, no credit cards.

Just 1.6 miles beyond downtown Damariscotta, **Barnswallow Bed & Breakfast,** 362 Bristol Rd., Rt. 130, Damariscotta 04543, tel. (207) 563-8568, is Rachael Sherrill's lovely 1835 Cape-style home with lots of fireplaces, formal and informal guest parlors, and an elegant Colonial breakfast room. (Breakfast is generous continental.) Three comfortable guest rooms (private baths) are $60-80 d in summer, slightly less in winter. No smoking, no pets, no children under 12. Open all year, but call ahead off season.

Joe Hovance, innkeeper at the historic **Brannon-Bunker Inn,** Rt. 129, Walpole 04573, tel. (207) 563-5941 or (800) 563-9225, is an avid collector/dealer in political and military memorabilia, and the inn's upper halls are a virtual gallery of World War I posters, medals, and photos. Lots of character and informality here, and the whole family pitches in: Jeanne Hovance makes the breakfast muffins and the children help with chores. Five rooms with homemade quilts and stenciling on the walls (private and shared baths; $55-70 d) and a three-room suite ($75 d). No smoking, no pets. Kids are

welcome, and the well-equipped kitchen even has a lobster pot for guests' eat-in convenience. Open April through November.

On Rutherford Island, just off the end of the South Bristol peninsula, **Coveside,** Christmas Cove, South Bristol 04568, tel. (207) 644-8282, fax 644-8204, has been in the Mitchell family since 1968. The red-clapboard main building, built in the 1880s, has five rooms (private baths attached or across the hall). Across the lawn is the 10-room motel-style Shorefront building, with skylights, private decks, and unbeatable views of the cove. Coveside caters to yachtsmen, providing guest moorings ($15 a night), dock space, and fuel; the pennant-draped Dory Bar and the 84-seat restaurant attract a steady stream of boaters during the cruising season. The inn is open mid-June to mid-September; rates there run $65-75 d. Shorefront is open mid-May to mid-October; rooms are $70-95 d, depending on season. The restaurant, serving breakfast, lunch, and dinner daily during the season, closes Labor Day.

Within easy walking distance of Pemaquid Light and 16 miles south of Rt. 1, **The Bradley Inn,** Rt. 130, Pemaquid Point, New Harbor 04554, tel. (207) 677-2105, fax 677-3367, is a well-maintained, century-old building with 13 guest rooms (private baths and phones) and lovely gardens—a great location for a quiet weekend getaway. The **Ships Restaurant,** overlooking the gardens and open to the public, has an ambitious, mostly seafood menu (entrées $15-22). Check out the granite bar in the adjoining pub. Rooms (with continental breakfast) are $100-195 d June through October, $85-125 d other months. A suite and a garden cottage are available by the week. No smoking, no pets. The inn is open April through December.

Even closer to Pemaquid Light is the rambling **Hotel Pemaquid,** Rt. 130, HC 61, Box 421, New Harbor 04554, tel. (207) 677-2312. Seventeen miles south of Rt. 1 but just 450 feet from the lighthouse, the hotel has been welcoming guests since 1900, and you can peruse the old guest registers. Hang out in the large, comfortable parlor or the wraparound veranda. The inn building has six rooms (private and shared baths; $55-70 d in August, less other months) and three suites ($115-125 d in August). Other buildings have motel-style units with private baths, some with kitchen facilities ($60-115 d in August). For the Victorian flavor of the place, request an inn room or suite. No smoking, no pets, no credit cards, no small children in the inn building. No restaurant, but The Bradley Inn and The Sea Gull Shop (see "Lunch and Miscellanea" under "Food," below) are nearby. Open mid-May to mid-October.

Up the eastern side of the peninsula, in the middle of New Harbor, **The Gosnold Arms,** HC 61, Box 161, New Harbor 04554, tel. (207) 677-3727, off season tel. (407) 575-9549, has been here since 1925 and remains deliberately old-fashioned, with pine-paneled rooms and a country-cottage common room. Customers return year after year. The family-owned operation includes the inn building and eight other buildings (with 14 units), so there's variety in layout, location, and decor. Many of the 11 inn rooms (private baths) include water views, but the loudspeaker at the lobster wharf across the street (Shaw's) can preclude an afternoon nap in front rooms. Cottage units are $95-135 d. Inn rooms are $80-95 d, including breakfast, late June through Labor Day, lower off season. Guests receive a 10% dinner discount in the inn restaurant, which has a fantastic harbor view and is open to the public. No pets. The restaurant is open daily 5:30-8:30 p.m., mid-May to mid-October.

The Briar Rose, Rt. 32, P.O. Box 27, Round Pond 04564, tel. (207) 529-5478, is an especially homey B&B in a minuscule Pemaquid Peninsula village. Two rooms and a suite (private baths) are $65-75 d; two-night minimum on summer holiday weekends. Innkeepers Anita and Fred Palsgrove provide hospitality baskets in each room; books, games, puzzles, and antiques are everywhere. Lawn chairs let you watch the world go by. No smoking, no pets, no credit cards, no kids under 10. Eleven miles south of Rt. 1. Open all year.

Just two and a half miles west of Rt. 1, but a world away, is **Shangri-La,** Sheepscot Rd., P.O. Box 266, Newcastle 04553, tel. (207) 586-5305, Lee and Alan Brown's lovely hideaway. An authentic Cape-style replica (built in 1985) with three rooms (and private baths), the B&B sits on 14 acres of gardens, wildflower meadows, and a beaver pond. The huge common room is a congenial gathering spot, and breakfast includes such specialties as Denver scramble and a unique French toast. Rooms are $75 d in summer, $60 d without breakfast. No smoking, no pets, no small children. Open all year, but be sure to call ahead off season.

Motels

Families gravitate to **The Oyster Shell Motel,** Business Rt. 1, RR 1, Box 267, Damariscotta 04543, tel. (207) 563-3747 or (800) 874-3747 outside Maine, at the northern edge of Damariscotta. One- and two-bedroom motel/condo-type units have a/c and cooking facilities. There's also a pool, continental breakfast (mid-June through Labor Day), and free lodging for kids. One-bedroom suites range from $59-85, depending on the season; two-bedroom suites are $75-99.

Campgrounds

The area's best-run campground is 150-acre **Lake Pemaquid Camping,** off Biscay Rd., P.O. Box 967, Damariscotta 04543, tel. (207) 563-5202, with 225 tent and RV sites, many right on the seven-mile-long lake. It's a lively operation, well managed, with tennis, pool and lake swimming, fishing (licenses available), playground, game room, store (lobsters available), laundry, sauna, and canoe and boat rentals. Some sites can be rented only by the week, mid-June to Labor Day; rates are lower other times. Sites (five people) are $22-35 weeknights, $24-37 weekends, mid-June to Labor Day; $20 a night off season. Rustic cabins and cottages are available by the week. The campground is open mid-May to Columbus Day.

FOOD

Lunch and Miscellanea

Looking like a transplanted Turkish coffeehouse, the **River Café,** Main St., P.O. Box 972, Damariscotta 04543, tel. (207) 563-6611, is located downtown, in the Damariscotta Center. Filled with Turkish, Afghan, and Central Asian carpets and kilims (all for sale—and at reasonable prices), the café carries designer coffees, cambric tea, and terrific pastries. Open all year, Mon.-Fri. 8 a.m.-5 p.m., Saturday 8 a.m.-4 p.m., occasionally on Sunday in summer. Every second and fourth Wednesday 7-9 p.m., there's Celtic music.

On the grounds of Round Top Center for the Arts, at the northern edge of Damariscotta, is the area's best homemade ice cream, in unusual flavors you'd never dream up. Never mind that **Round Top Ice Cream,** tel. (207) 563-5307, in business since 1924, is next door to the health-food store; just go for it. Open daily 11:30 a.m.-10 p.m. in summer.

A New Harbor landmark since 1928, **C.E. Reilly & Son,** Village Center, New Harbor 04554, tel. (207) 677-2321, is one of those local markets that has nearly everything: pizza, sandwiches, meat, first-rate produce, roast chicken, baked goods, liquor, lottery tickets, video rentals, upscale goodies, a few hardware items, and daily New York and Boston newspapers. Open daily 8 a.m.-6 p.m. (to 8 p.m. Friday and Saturday).

Close to Pemaquid Beach, **Mike's Captain's Catch,** Pemaquid Beach Rd., New Harbor 04554, tel. (207) 677-2396, is a chummy, unassuming place with four tables and placemat menus. Lobster and clam cookers steam away outside and "yesterday's chowder" (superb seafood stew, $4.25 a cup) bubbles away in the kitchen. Seafood is all fresh off the boat. After 4 p.m., order pizza by Rosario (a legendary New Harbor baker). Every Friday night, crowds gather for the fish fry. Open Thurs.-Sun. 11:30 a.m.-8:30 p.m.

Right next to Pemaquid Light (and with free parking) is **The Sea Gull Shop,** Pemaquid Point, tel. (207) 677-2374, an oceanfront place with touristy prices ($13.95 for a lobster roll) but decent food—pancakes and muffins, for instance, overflowing with blueberries. Open the second Sunday in May to Columbus Day, 8 a.m.-7:30 p.m. (to 8 p.m. July and August).

Inexpensive to Moderate

A reliable standby in downtown Damariscotta, next to the Damariscotta Bank & Trust, the **Salt Bay Café,** Main St., Damariscotta 04543, tel. (207) 563-1666, has a loyal following—thanks to its imaginative, reasonably priced menu and cheerful, plant-filled setting. No smoking; liquor license. Open daily for lunch and dinner; closed Monday off season.

Just down the street, family-run **King Eider's Pub,** 2 Elm St., Damariscotta 04543, tel. (207) 563-6008, acquired the status of local hangout soon after it opened in 1996. Chalk that up to host Larry Schneider. The first-floor pub, all wood and brick, serves up designer beers and snacks; the bright restaurant upstairs has a small oyster bar and a moderately priced menu focusing on local produce and seafood. Late in the evening, there's "after-theater fare" (appetizers and sandwiches). Open daily 11 a.m.-11 p.m.

Behind Main Street and right on the Damariscotta River, **Backstreet Landing,** Elm St., Damariscotta, tel. (207) 563-5666, has a far better view than Salt Bay and King Eider's (which have none) and a creative menu as well. Soups and sandwiches are predictably good. Open daily for lunch and dinner.

Opposite the post office in New Harbor is the unfussy **Samoset Restaurant,** Rt. 130, New Harbor 04554, tel. (207) 677-2142, a longtime favorite among families and seniors. In 1996, they added a pub to tempt a younger crowd (they succeeded). The restaurant is open all year, Sun.-Thurs. 6 a.m.-8 p.m., Friday and Saturday 5 a.m.-8:30 p.m.

One of the best meal deals in the area is the **Anchor Inn,** Harbor Rd., Round Pond 04564, tel. (207) 529-5584, tucked away on the picturesque harbor in Round Pond, on the eastern side of the peninsula. Informal and rustic, with a menu that'll surprise you, the place always attracts a crowd. Lobster is available, but why eat it here when you have more interesting choices? If lobster's your obsession, go to one of Round Pond's lobsteries (see "Lobster-in-the-Rough," below). No reservations for fewer than six, so you may have to wait. Open 11 a.m.-9 p.m. Memorial Day weekend to Columbus Day; after Labor Day, call to confirm hours.

Moderate to Expensive

Most of the restaurants in this category are eateries located in lodgings. The Bradley Inn, Coveside, The Gosnold Arms, and The Newcastle Inn are all excellent choices. See "Inns and B&Bs" under "Accommodations," above, for descriptions and more information.

Lobster-in-the-Rough

The Pemaquid Peninsula must have more lobster-in-the-rough places per capita than any-place in Maine. Some are basic, no-frills operations, others are big-time commercial concerns. Each has a loyal following.

The biggest and best-known lobster wharf is **Shaw's Fish and Lobster Wharf,** Rt. 32, New Harbor, tel. (207) 677-2200 or (800) 772-2209, where you place your order, take a number, and wait for it to come booming back at you over the loudspeaker. (You can also order steak here. And margaritas.) Open Sun.-Thurs. 11 a.m.-8 p.m., Fri.-Sat. to 9 p.m., mid-May to mid-October.

Facing each other across the dock in the hamlet of Round Pond are the **Round Pond Lobster Co-Op,** tel. (207) 529-5725, and **Muscongus Bay Lobster,** tel. (207) 529-5528. Hard to say which is better; both are good. If you're in a rush, look for the smallest crowd. Round Pond is open 10 a.m.-6 p.m.; Muscongus stays open to 7 p.m.

Other seasonal lobster wharves on the peninsula are the **New Harbor Co-Op,** Rt. 32, New Harbor, tel. (207) 677-2791, **Pemaquid Fishermen's Co-Op,** Pemaquid Harbor Rd., Pemaquid Harbor, tel. (207) 677-2801, **South Bristol Fishermen's Co-Op,** Thompson Inn Rd., South Bristol, tel. (207) 644-8224 or 644-8246, and **Broad Cove Marine Services,** off Rt. 32, Medomak, tel. (207) 529-5186.

INFORMATION AND SERVICES

The **Damariscotta Information Bureau,** P.O. Box 217, Damariscotta 04543, a private organization established in 1935, has two seasonal offices, one in downtown Damariscotta, Business Rt. 1 at Church St., tel. (207) 563-3175, and a more visible one on Rt. 1, about one and a half miles south of downtown Newcastle, tel. (207) 563-3176. The Newcastle office, a small, square roadside building on the right (northbound) side, is open mid-June to mid-September on a rather erratic schedule—usually Monday, Friday, and Saturday, beginning at 10 a.m. Hours at the Damariscotta office, open early June through September, are Mon.-Sat. 10 a.m.-5 p.m. (to 6 p.m. July and August). Veteran staffers and volunteers in both locations are especially helpful, and you can contact the organization year-round by phone or mail.

The **Damariscotta Region Chamber of Commerce,** P.O. Box 13, Damariscotta 04543, tel. (207) 563-8340, publishes a free annual information booklet about the area, and the **Pemaquid Area Association,** Chamberlain 04541, no telephone, produces a very useful annotated map covering the lower half of the Pemaquid Peninsula. Both publications are available by mail and at the information bureaus.

The best local library is the **Skidompha Library,** Main St., Damariscotta, tel. (207) 563-5513. Where *did* they get that name? In summer, the library sponsors Discovery Days for kids, who can spend a few hours doing painting, pottery, photography, and more. Call for a schedule. For adults, there's a brown-bag lecture series every Thursday in July, noon-4 p.m. Also in summer, the library's secondhand-book room has lots of bargain books for sale, all to benefit library projects. The library is open Mon.-Fri. 10 a.m.-5 p.m., Saturday 10 a.m.-1 p.m.

Newspapers
Rival newspapers, both published every Thursday, cover the territory and include lots of local listings. The *Lincoln County Weekly,* tel. (207) 563-5006, is on Main St. in Damariscotta. The *Lincoln County News,* tel. (207) 563-3171 or (800) 339-5818, older of the two, is on Mills Rd. (Rt. 215) in Newcastle.

The largest daily paper serving the area is the *Portland Press Herald,* tel. (800) 442-6036, which includes the Damariscotta/Newcastle area in the *Go* supplement of its Thursday edition.

Emergencies
Just south of downtown Damariscotta, the respected **Miles Memorial Hospital,** Bristol Rd., Rt. 130, Damariscotta 04543, tel. (207) 563-1234, has 24-hour emergency-room services. For **police, fire, and ambulance,** dial 911.

Laundromat
The **Tri-Bay Laundromat,** Business Rt. 1, Damariscotta, tel. (207) 563-1865, is open daily 6 a.m.-10 p.m.

Photo Services
Main Street Photo, Main St., Damariscotta 04543, tel. (207) 563-2111, is a well-stocked shop with one-hour photo service. Open Mon.-Saturday.

Special Courses
Watershed Center for the Ceramic Arts, 19 Brick Hill Rd., Newcastle 04553, tel. (207) 882-6075, a nationally known summer residency retreat for ceramic artists, offers fall and winter community pottery courses for adults, children, and families. No experience is necessary for off-season programs. The center also organizes therapeutic workshops for AIDS patients, at-risk juveniles, and senior citizens. Call or write for course information.

WALDOBORO AREA

Just east of the Pemaquid Peninsula and the Damariscotta/Newcastle area, Rt. 1 cuts a commercial swath through Waldoboro without revealing the attractive downtown—or the lovely Friendship Peninsula, south of the highway. Duck into Waldoboro, then follow Rt. 220 south 10 miles to Friendship.

Waldoboro's heritage is something of an anomaly in Maine—predominantly German, thanks to 18th-century Teutons who swallowed the blandishments of Gen. Samuel Waldo, holder of a million-acre "patent" stretching as far as the Penobscot River. In the cemetery at the Old German Church, on Rt. 32, is a 19th-century marker whose inscription sums up the town's early history: "This town was settled in 1748, by Germans who emigrated to this place with the promise and expectation of finding a populous city, instead of which they found nothing but a wilderness; for the first few years they suffered to a great extent by Indian wars and starvation. By perseverance and self-denial, they succeeded in clearing lands and erecting mills. At this time [1855] a large proportion of the inhabitants are descendants of the first settlers." (Makes you wonder why Waldo's name stuck to the town.)

After the mill era, the settlers went into shipbuilding in a big way, establishing six shipyards and producing more than 300 wooden vessels, including the first five-masted schooner, the 265-foot *Governor Ames,* launched in 1888. Although the *Ames*'s ill-supported masts collapsed on her maiden voyage, repairs allowed her to serve as a coal hauler for more than 20 years, and many more five-masters followed in her wake. It's hard to believe today, but Waldoboro once was America's sixth-busiest port. At the Town Landing, alongside the Medomak River, a marker describes the town's shipyards and shipbuilding heritage.

With a population of about 4,800, Waldoboro's major draws now are the world headquarters of the *Maine Antique Digest,* a clutch of unusual shops, the handsomely restored Waldo Theatre, and the springtime alewife fishery in the Medomak River. Commercial clamming is a thriving industry. Most of the time, it's a quiet place with a lot of character (and characters—one admirer described it as a "Down East Lake Wobegon").

Down Rt. 220 from Waldoboro, the town of **Friendship** (pop. 1,100) is best known as the birthplace of the Friendship Sloop—a distinctive traditional sailing vessel formerly used as a fishing workhorse and now dedicated to recreational purposes. Lobstering is the major industry here these days; beyond the busy workboat harbor, everything's mighty quiet—a picturesque place to relax and watch the world go by.

Back up the peninsula and across Rt. 1, Rt. 32 leads north and a bit west to Jefferson, a pastoral community settled in the late 18th century—and the site of Damariscotta Lake State Park.

SIGHTS

Historic Sites
The **Waldoborough Historical Society Museum,** Washington Rd., Rt. 220, Waldoboro 04572, no telephone, is a three-building roadside complex just one-tenth of a mile south of Rt. 1, at the eastern end of town. On the grounds are the one-room 1857 **Boggs Schoolhouse,** the 1819 **Town Pound** (to detain stray livestock), and two buildings filled with antique tools, toys, and utensils, plus period costumes, antique fire engines, and artifacts from the shipbuilding era. The museum is open daily 1-4:30 p.m., July through Labor Day, as well as occasional week-

Boggs School House, Waldoboro

ends in September and October. While you're here, ask about the nature trail out back.

A remnant of the German connection is the **Old German Church** and its cemetery, Rt. 32, Waldoboro 04572, tel. (207) 832-5369 or 832-7742. The Lutheran church, built in 1772 on the opposite side of the Medomak River, was moved across the ice in the winter of 1794. Inside are box pews and a huge hanging pulpit. One of the three oldest churches in Maine, it lost its flock in the mid-19th century, when new generations no longer spoke German. The church is open daily 1-3 p.m. in July and August.

Maine Antique Digest

Believe it or not, the home of the nationally renowned *Maine Antique Digest,* 911 Main St., P.O. Box 1429, Waldoboro 04572, tel. (207) 832-7534, is a modern, solar-heated structure just off the main drag in downtown Waldoboro. Founded by Sam and Sally Pendleton, it's a busy operation, not geared up for squads of vis-

itors, but you can stop in on a weekday, admire the William Zorach sculpture, and buy a copy of the fat monthly tabloid.

PARKS, PRESERVES, AND RECREATION

Damariscotta Lake State Park

As opposed to the chilly ocean, the water here is warmer. There's also a lovely sand beach, a lifeguard, changing rooms, and picnic tables with hibachis. The only problem is that 17-acre Damariscotta Lake State Park, Rt. 32, Jefferson 04348, tel. (207) 549-7600, is no secret to area residents—so arrive early on hot summer days; the parking lot fills up quickly. Officially open Memorial Day weekend to Labor Day, the park is accessible in winter for ice-skating, snowmobiling, and cross-country skiing. Admission in season is $2 adults, 50 cents kids 5-11, and free for kids under five. From Rt. 1, take Rt. 32 north about eight miles to the park entrance.

Osborn Finch Preserve

Even if you can't squeeze in a visit to the Osborn Finch Preserve, Dutch Neck Rd., Waldoboro, no telephone, at least allow time for a drive down **Dutch Neck.** If you can hike the 11-acre preserve, so much the better, as you'll end up on the shores of the Medomak River (bring a picnic and enjoy it on the rocks). Terrain is easy, through fields and woods. To reach the preserve—owned by the Pemaquid Watershed Association—from Rt. 1, go 2.7 miles south on Rt. 32 and turn left onto Dutch Neck Road. Continue 3.1 miles to the small preserve sign (on left). Park along the road, pulling off as far as possible.

About 500 feet before you reach the preserve, you'll see a public boat landing—a fine place to launch a sea kayak or other small boat. Check the tide calendar in a local newspaper and ride with the tide.

Nelson Nature Preserve

Owned by the Mid-Coast Audubon Society, the Nelson Nature Preserve, Rt. 97, Friendship 04547, no telephone, is a rectangular property between Rt. 97 and the Goose River. A network of seven short trails totals about four miles. Much of the terrain is marshy, so wear rubberized boots and insect repellent. The trailhead is just off Rt. 97, a mile north of Friendship's village center (you'll need to walk about 300 feet in from the highway).

Post-Exertion Massage
Students come from all over New England to attend the year-long courses at the **Downeast School of Massage,** Rt. 220, P.O. Box 24, Waldoboro 04572, tel. (207) 832-5531, and the school's graduates are much in demand for their skill and professionalism. Between June and August, students have to rack up many practice hours, so they offer $10 hour-long massages—a great way to undo the knots from hiking or biking. Contact the school for details.

ENTERTAINMENT AND SHOPPING

The center of local entertainment is the neoclassic **Waldo Theatre,** 916 Main St., P.O. Box 587, Waldoboro 04572, tel. (207) 832-6060, built as a cinema in 1936. Restored in the mid-1980s, it now operates as a nonprofit organization, presenting first-rate concerts, plays, films, lectures, and other year-round community events.

Antiques/Art Gallery
Bill Miller at **Ram Pasture Antiques,** 1069 Main St., Waldoboro 04572, tel. (207) 832-7044, .3 mile south of Rt. 1, always has unusual finds at very reasonable prices. Open daily 9 a.m.-5 p.m. in summer, by appointment in winter.

The **Eliza Sweet Gallery,** 218 Kaler's Corner Rd., Rt. 32, Waldoboro 04572, tel. (207) 832-4969, sponsors rotating group shows by contemporary Maine artists. Don't miss the sculpture garden. The gallery, .4 mile south of Rt. 1, is open Wed.-Sun. 11 a.m.-5 p.m., mid-May to mid-October.

Gifts and Miscellanea
On the western outskirts of Waldoboro, **The Well-Tempered Kitchen,** 122 Atlantic Hwy., Rt. 1, Waldoboro 04572, tel. (207) 563-5762, can furnish your kitchen with gourmet gadgets, coffees and teas, pots and pans, cards and cookbooks. Sunday afternoon, stop in for coffee or tea and pastries. The shop, based in a renovated barn at the end of a long driveway, is

open all year, Mon.-Sat. 9 a.m.-5 p.m., Sunday noon-5 p.m. It's closed Sunday Jan.-March. Look for a large Open pennant on the north side of Rt. 1, .3 mile east of the Nobleboro Dinner House.

Central Asian Artifacts, Main and Jefferson Sts., Waldoboro, mailing address 108 Patterson Mill Rd., Warren 04864, tel. (207) 832-4003 or 273-2490, connects Mid-Coast Maine to the Silk Road. Owner Jeff Evangelos treks annually to Pakistan and beyond, bringing back fascinating new objets: carpets, antique brass, textiles, furniture, and jewelry. The shop is open all year, Tues.-Sat. 10 a.m.-5 p.m., plus Monday in summer.

For the hops- and grapemeisters on your shopping list, **The Purple Foot Downeast,** 116 Main St., Waldoboro 04572, tel. (207) 832-6286, carries a complete line of supplies for creating beer and wine. The downtown shop also organizes classes and takes mail orders. Open all year, Tues.-Sat. 9:30 a.m.-4:30 p.m.

Rose fans will flip out at **The Roseraie at Bayfields,** Rt. 32, P.O. Box R, Waldoboro 04572, tel. (207) 832-6330. Old roses, English roses, hardy roses, shrub roses—all labeled "practical roses for hard places." The nursery has a free mail-order catalog (fax 800-933-4508), but you have to visit the "catalog in the ground" to appreciate the scope of this incredible operation. It's open Mon.-Sat. 10 a.m.-5 p.m. and Sunday 8:30 a.m.-noon, mid-April through September. From Rt. 1, take Rt. 32 south 1.7 miles.

The **Waldoboro 5&10,** Friendship St., Waldoboro 04572, tel. (207) 832-4624, is one of those old-fashioned, little-of-everything variety stores that disappeared ages ago. Check this one out while it's still here, in the middle of downtown, and you'll probably spot something you need. Open all year, Mon.-Sat. 9 a.m.-5:30 p.m. (to 8 p.m. Friday). Also open Sunday 10 a.m.-3 p.m., July through December.

If you're in the market for really good fabric gear, custom made, you'll want to get in touch with Mike Krepner at **Igas Island,** P.O. Box 240, Waldoboro 04572, tel./fax (207) 832-5255. Working in a solar-powered shop (when he's not trekking or testing gear in Siberia, Belize, or northern Maine), Mike makes backpacks, all kinds of luggage, canoe packs, raingear, and a handy carryall ($12.50) for your *Maine Atlas* *and Gazetteer.* His gym bag ($55) even has an outside mesh pocket for wet towels and stinky socks. He'll do custom work and mail order (the flyer/catalog is entertaining itself), and you can visit his shop by appointment. Mike is also president of **Native Trails,** a national organization working to revive and map trails used by our Native American forerunners. They already have maps for three routes in coastal and woodland Maine.

ACCOMMODATIONS

The lodgings in Waldoboro, Friendship (10 miles south), and Jefferson (10 miles north) are all B&Bs or weekly-rate cottages.

Waldoboro
Globetrotters Robin and Bill Branigan have made the in-town Victorian **Roaring Lion Bed and Breakfast,** 995 Main St., P.O. Box 756, tel. (207) 832-4038, an informal home away from home for their many guests. Three rooms share a bath (with clawfoot tub); the Rose Room has a private bath. Doubles are $50-75, depending on the season. Bill's hearty breakfasts (often lion eggs—a secret recipe) are served in the tin-walled, tin-ceilinged dining room; he's a whiz with vegetarian/macrobiotic diets. Maine crafts, paintings, and Bill's superb photos are sold in the screened-porch "gallery." No smoking, no pets; children are welcome. Open all year.

Just up the hill from the Waldo Theatre, hospitable Libby Hopkins has been running the **Broad Bay Inn and Gallery,** 1014 Main St., P.O. Box 607, tel. (207) 832-6668, since 1984, and she's an energetic breakfast chef. Five antiques-filled rooms share three baths—$55-75 pp, including afternoon tea or sherry. Guests can play the piano, browse through the huge art-book collection, or watch old films. No smoking, no pets, no kids under 10. The barn gallery—stocked with watercolors and some crafts—is open by appointment in summer, when Libby also organizes art workshops run by professional teachers. The B&B is open all year, by reservation off season.

Green-thumbers and cyclists should stay at **Le Va Tout Bed & Breakfast,** 218 Rt. 32, tel. (207) 832-4969, which gardener/biker/art en-

thusiast Eliza Sweet took over in 1996. Two rooms have private baths ($75 d), three share a bath ($65 d); breakfast is cooked to order. Touring cyclists receive discounts. In the stunning gardens behind the 1830 house is a hot tub, and there's plenty of green space for kids (Eliza has two). No smoking; children are welcome, as are well-mannered dogs.

Friendship and Jefferson
The Outsiders' Inn Bed & Breakfast, Rts. 97 and 220, Box 521A, Friendship 04547, tel. (207) 832-5197, is the destination of choice for sea kayakers. Bill and Debbie Michaud have converted an 1830 home (once a doctor's office) into a comfortable village-based getaway about 10 miles south of Rt. 1. Tin ceilings, stenciled walls, flower-filled vases, and a woodstove all add to the cozy ambience. Four rooms share two baths; the elegant Chamberlain Room has a private bath. Doubles are $50-65; an efficiency cottage is $350 a week. Breakfast is always special. No smoking, no pets, children welcome. There's no TV. Open all year. In summer, Debbie carries a selection of reasonably priced Maine crafts. Bill, a Registered Maine Guide, rents kayaks (single or double), gives instructions, and leads tours.

Delicious Scandinavian breakfasts, lovely gardens, and a harbor-view terrace are the special features at Liga and Len Jahnke's **Harbor Hill Bed & Breakfast,** Town Landing Rd., P.O. Box 35, Friendship 04547, tel. (207) 832-6646, off season (203) 647-1368. Three comfortable rooms with private baths go for $85-90 d; a separate cottage is $500 a week. No smoking, no pets, no credit cards; children welcome. Open June through Labor Day, plus spring and fall weekends by prior arrangement.

And then there's the 60-acre waterfront complex on Friendship's Flood's Cove—a vacation tradition since the turn of the century. Now run by the third generation of Floods (and patronized by the third generation of guests), it's part B&B and part cottage colony—particularly good for families. Mary Flood Thompson runs the B&B, **Cap'n Am's,** tel. (207) 832-5144; three large guest rooms share two baths. Nightly rates are $65-75 d ($10 each extra person), including full breakfast; kids are welcome. No smoking, no credit cards. It's open Memorial Day weekend to

Labor Day. John Flood, Mary's brother, manages **Flood's Cove,** tel. (207) 832-6237, the cottage colony surrounding the B&B. Obviously he does it well; it's tough to get a reservation, what with all the repeats. Eight rustic cottages have 2-5 bedrooms, for $550-800 a week. Each has an ocean view and a fireplace or woodstove; guests bring sheets and towels. All have hot water except Defiance, perched on an oceanfront rock. The cottage season extends through September. What else is here? A mile of shorefront, sandy beaches, free use of rowboats and kayaks, a blueberry field, tennis court, clamflats, and low-tide access to offshore Pa's Island for exploring and picnicking. Information: P.O. Box 639, Friendship 04547.

Less than half a mile northeast of Jefferson, **The Jefferson House Farm Bed & Breakfast,** Rt. 126, Jefferson 04348, tel. (207) 549-5768, gets you away from it all on 12 acres bordering Davis Stream. Since 1987, Jim and Barbara O'Halloran have welcomed guests to their mid-19th-century farmhouse with three second-floor rooms (sharing one bath). Rates are $50 d. Settle on the deck overlooking a millpond and waterfall, or walk the farm's nature trail, or launch one of their canoes and paddle down to Damariscotta Lake. In winter, bring cross-country skis. No smoking, no credit cards; well-behaved pets are welcome. Open all year, but call ahead off season.

Just around the head of the lake from the Jefferson House (and the state park), **Damariscotta Lake Farm Cottage Colony,** Rts. 32 and 126, Jefferson 04348, tel. (207) 549-7953, has 20 one-, two-, and three-bedroom red-painted cottages—cascading stairlike down to the shore—available by the week ($290-410). Kitchens are fully equipped; guests need to bring towels, sheets, and blankets. On the well-maintained premises are a marina (boats for rent) and a sandy beach. No credit cards. Open late May to mid-September.

FOOD

Three miles west of downtown Waldoboro, the Civil War-era **Nobleboro Dinner House,** Rt. 1, Nobleboro 04555, tel. (207) 563-8506, provides a chuckle with ironic names (changed monthly) for its entrées ($10-13)—the green party and pork barrel in November, for example, lame duck a month later. Prime rib is the regular Friday special. Portions are huge. No smoking, no credit cards; beer and wine only. Reservations advisable midsummer weekends and off season. Open Wed.-Mon. 5-9 p.m., all year except March.

The **Pine Cone Café,** 13 Friendship St., Waldoboro 04572, tel. (207) 832-6337, is a casual, chummy place with booths and tables in downtown Waldoboro. Order breakfast or lunch at the counter. Service is sometimes slow, but the superbly creative food is always worth any wait. Unusual soups, fantastic pastries, vegetarian specials, great sandwiches. In summer, a second-floor deck overlooks the Medomak River. Open most of the year, Tues.-Sat. 7:30 a.m.-9 p.m. and Sunday 10 a.m.-2 p.m. for brunch.

Truck drivers, tourists, locals, and notables have been flocking to **Moody's Diner,** Rts. 1 and 220, Waldoboro 04572, tel. (207) 832-7785, since the early 1930s, when the Moody family established this classic diner on a Waldoboro hilltop. The antique neon sign has long been a Rt. 1 beacon, especially on a foggy night, and the crowds continue, with new generations of Moodys and considerable expansion of the premises. Expect hearty, no-frills fare and such calorific desserts as peanut-butter pie. After eating, you can buy the cookbook ($8.95). No smoking, no credit cards, a/c. Open round-the-clock weekdays. Closes 11 p.m. Friday and Saturday nights, opening at 5 a.m. Saturday and 7 a.m. Sunday. Closed Christmas Day.

About three miles west of downtown Waldoboro, in an area known as Moose Crossing (you might see one, but don't count on it), **Bullwinkle's Family Steak House,** Rt. 1, Waldoboro 04572, tel. (207) 832-6272, is exactly as described—a reliable source of reasonable, homemade grub for the whole family. The dining-room menu centers on steaks, seafood, and barbecue. The Bog Tavern has microbrews galore. Open Tues.-Sun. 11 a.m.-8 p.m. (to 9 p.m. Friday and Saturday). Live entertainment Friday nights.

Specialty Foods

Each fall, around mid-September, a tiny, cryptic display ad appears in local newspapers. It reads:

"Kraut's Ready." Savvy readers recognize this as the announcement of the latest batch of **Morse's sauerkraut.** This has been an annual ritual since 1918. The homemade kraut is available in stores and by mail order, but it's more fun (and cheaper) to visit the shop, the **Kraut House,** 3856 Washington Rd., Rt. 220, Waldoboro 04572, tol. (207) 832-5569 or (800) 486-1605, where you can pick up a three-pound bucket for about $6.50. The red-painted farm store also carries Aunt Lydia's Beet Relish, baked beans, mustard, maple syrup, and other Maine foods. Located eight miles north of Rt. 1, it's open Mon.-Fri. 8 a.m.-4 p.m. and Saturday 10 a.m.-4 p.m., mid-August through April.

At the corner of Rts. 1 and 220, opposite Moody's Diner, is the warehousey blue building that turns out superb **Borealis Breads,** 1860 Atlantic Hwy., Rt. 1, Waldoboro 04572, tel. (207) 832-0655. Using sourdough starters (and no oils, sweeteners, eggs, or dairy products), owner Jim Amaral and his crew produces baguettes, olive bread, lemon fig bread, rosemary focaccia, and about a dozen other inventive flavors (each day has its specialties). Borealis distributes to retail outlets and sandwich shops over a 60-mile radius, but patronize the source—a refrigerated case holds a small selection of picnic fixings (sandwich spreads, juices). Open Mon.-Fri. 7:30 a.m.-6:30 p.m., Saturday 7:30 a.m.-4:30 p.m. The shop occasionally closes earlier when all the bread sells out.

INFORMATION AND SERVICES

Waldoboro has no active chamber of commerce, hence no centralized information source. Once you get here, the best resource is Waldoboro Town Clerk Becky Maxwell. She's in the Waldoboro Town Office, 1600 Atlantic Hwy, Rt. 1, P.O. Box J, Waldoboro 04572, tel. (207) 832-5369. It's staffed weekdays 8:30 a.m.-5 p.m., all year. In Friendship, the best source of local info (besides B&B proprietors) is the **Friendship Market,** right in the village, tel. (207) 832-4283. While you're at it, they also have pizza and all kinds of sandwiches. Open all year, Mon.-Sat. 8 a.m.-8 p.m., Sunday 9 a.m.-8 p.m.

Next door to the Waldo Theatre is the similarly imposing **Waldoboro Public Library,** Main St., Waldoboro 04572, tel. (207) 832-4484, an 1855 Italianate building that once was a thriving customs house. It's open Monday 9:30 a.m.-6 p.m., Wed.-Fri. 9:30 a.m.-4:30 p.m. and Saturday 9:30 a.m.-noon.; closed Tuesday and Sunday.

Emergencies
The closest **hospital** with a round-the-clock emergency room is **Miles Memorial Hospital,** down Rt. 1 in Damariscotta. For **police, fire, and ambulance,** dial 911.

THOMASTON AREA

Thomaston is a little gem of a town bookended by two eyesores—the state's only maximum-security prison and a giant cement factory. Ignore the blights and explore the gem. Thomaston is also the gateway to two lovely fingers of land bordering the St. George River and jutting into the Gulf of Maine—the Cushing and St. George Peninsulas.

In 1605, British adventurer Capt. George Waymouth sailed up the river now named after him (it was originally called the Georges River). A way station for Plymouth traders as early as 1630, Thomaston was incorporated in 1777 and officially named after Gen. John Thomas, a Revolutionary War hero.

Industry began with the production of lime, which was used for plaster. A growing demand for plaster, and the frequency with which the wooden boats were destroyed by fire while carrying loads of extremely flammable lime, spurred the growth of shipbuilding and all its related infrastructure. Thomaston's slogan became "the town that went to sea." Seeing the sleepy harborfront today, it's hard to visualize the booming era when dozens of tall-masted wooden ships slid down the ways. But architecture in town is a testament and tribute to the prosperous past—all those splendid homes on Main and Knox Streets were funded by wealthy shipowners and shipmasters who well understood how to occupy the idle hands of off-duty carpenters.

SIGHTS

Montpelier

As you head out of Thomaston on Rt. 1, toward Rockland, you'll come face to face with an imposing Colonial hilltop mansion at the junction with Rt. 131 South. Dedicated to the memory of Gen. Henry Knox, President George Washington's secretary of war, Montpelier, Rts. 1 and 131, Thomaston 04861, tel. (207) 354-8062, is a 1930s replica of Knox's original Thomaston home. The mansion today contains Knox family furnishings and other period antiques—all described with great enthusiasm during the hour-long tours. A gift shop run by the Friends of Montpelier carries books and other relevant items. Concerts and other special events occur here periodically throughout the summer; General Knox's birthday is celebrated with considerable fanfare in early July. Open Tues.-Sat. 10 a.m.-4 p.m. and Sunday 1-4 p.m., Memorial Day weekend to mid-October. Admission is $4 adults, $3 seniors, $2 children 5-11, and free for kids under five. For more information, contact the **Friends of Montpelier,** P.O. Box 326, Thomaston 04861.

Down near Thomaston's waterfront is the site of Gen. Knox's original Montpelier. The complex of eight or nine buildings, in decrepit condition, was razed in 1871 when the railroad came through. Only a late-18th-century brick farmhouse remains—today the headquarters of the **Thomaston Historical Society,** Knox St., Thomaston 04861, tel. (207) 354-2295. Special local-interest exhibits are held here each summer; open Tuesday and Thursday afternoons, June to mid-September.

National Historic District

Montpelier is the starting point for a walking, cycling, or, if you must, driving tour (about three miles) of nearly 70 sites in Thomaston's National Historic District. Pick up a copy of the tour brochure at one of the local businesses or in the info kiosk at the Exxon station in the center of town. Included are lots of stories behind the facades of the handsome 19th-century homes that line Main and Knox Sts.; the architecture here is nothing short of spectacular.

If you're in the area in December, another treat's in store: Thomaston's holiday decorations are stunning. All over town, but especially in the Historic District, huge wreaths, tiny white lights, and (usually) a blanket of snow create a scene lifted right out of a Currier & Ives print.

Classic Wooden Boats

Just down the street from the historical society building is the **Maine Watercraft Museum,** 4 Knox St. Landing, Thomaston 04861, tel. (207) 354-0444 or (800) 923-0444, home of more than 130 classic Maine boats, many in mint condition—canoes, peapods, duckboats, and what-have-you. Wooden-boat nut John Shelley, who's been collecting boats since 1970, founded the two-acre museum in 1994. It's quickly become a

MAINE OFFICE OF TOURISM

Montpelier, historic home of General Henry Knox

must-see for kindred spirits. Best of all, these are boats you can borrow, for $10 an hour, and find out why they're classics. Admission is $4 adults, $2 seniors and students, free for kids under five. Open daily 10 a.m.-5 p.m., Memorial Day weekend to mid-October.

RECREATION

The nearest **golf courses** are in Rockland. For **bicycling, sea kayaking,** and **tennis,** try the St. George Peninsula. Best nearby **hiking** is in Camden.

ENTERTAINMENT

A new multiplex cinema is changing Thomaston's nightlife outlook. The seven-screen **Flagship Cinema,** Rt. 1, Thomaston 04861, tel. (207) 594-4705, opened its doors in the fall of 1997 and draws customers from a wide area (competing mightily with downtown Rockland's two-screen Strand Cinema).

FESTIVALS AND EVENTS

Thomaston's **Fourth of July,** an old-fashioned hometown celebration reminiscent of a Norman Rockwell painting, draws huge crowds. A spiffy parade—with bands, veterans, kids, and pets—starts off the morning (11 a.m.), followed by races, craft and food booths, and lots more. If you need to get *through* Thomaston on July 4th, do it well before the parade or well after noon, as the marchers go right down Main St., Rt. 1, and gridlock forces a detour.

SHOPPING

Thomaston has a block-long shopping street (on Rt. 1), with ample free parking out back behind the stores. No big businesses here, but you'll find an especially choice collection of book, antiques, gift, and craft shops.

Books
Don't be misled by the relatively small quarters of **Thomaston Books & Prints,** 105 Main St., Rt. 1, Thomaston 04861, tel. (207) 354-0001 or (800) 300-3008. This respected independent bookstore compensates for the lack of space with excellent service and a well-chosen inventory. A former children's librarian selects the kids' books. Open Mon.-Sat. 9:30 a.m.-5:30 p.m., year-round; open Sunday 10 a.m.-3 p.m., in summer.

Gifts—From Behind Bars
Next door to Maine's only maximum-security prison, the **Maine State Prison Showroom Outlet,** Main St., Rt. 1, corner of Wadsworth St., Thomaston 04861, tel. (207) 354-2535, ext. 272, markets the handiwork of inmate craftsmen. Some of the souvenirs verge on kitsch; the bargains are wooden bar stools, toys (including dollhouses), and chopping boards. You'll need to carry your purchases with you; prison-made goods cannot be shipped. Open daily 9 a.m.-5 p.m., all year.

Farmers' Market
An offshoot of Rockland's farmers' market sets up shop in Thomaston, behind the Rt. 1 downtown brick business block, 4-6 p.m. each Tuesday, early July through August.

ACCOMMODATIONS

For other nearby lodgings, see "St. George Peninsula" section. The only campground is on the Thomaston/Cushing town line.

At the southern edge of town, **Cap'n Frost's Bed and Breakfast,** 241 W. Main St., Rt. 1, Thomaston 04861, tel. (207) 354-8217, has three rooms, one with private bath, all facing away from street noises. Doubles are $45-50. Innkeepers Arlene and Harold Frost have filled their lovely Cape-style home with country antiques—and "Arlene's Closet" has others for sale. Guests have use of the book-lined sitting room and the manicured backyard (with croquet set and picnic table). Each morning, Cap'n Harold creates the breakfasts and serves them in one of the friendliest dining rooms you'll find. No smoking, no pets; well-behaved kids are welcome. Open all year, but call ahead off season.

The best local camping is at **Saltwater Farm Campground,** Wadsworth St./River Rd., Cushing, mailing address P.O. Box 165, Thomaston 04861, tel. (207) 354-6735, a 35-acre Good Sampark one and a half miles south of Rt. 1. Thirty open and wooded tent and RV sites ($18-20, for four) overlook the St. George River. Facilities include a bathhouse, freshwater pool, laundry facilities, store, and a play area. The river is tidal, so swimming there is best near high tide; otherwise, you're dealing with mudflats. Open mid-May to mid-October.

FOOD

Often overlooked by visitors (but certainly not by locals) is casual **Thomaston Café & Bakery,** 88 Main St., Rt. 1, Thomaston 04861, tel. (207) 354-8589. German-born chef Herb Peters is one of Mid-Coast Maine's best-known culinary pros. He and his wife, Eleanor, produce superb pastries, breads, and desserts (eat here or take out). Everything's homemade, there are childrens' options, the café uses only organic poultry, and prices are very reasonable. Beer and wine only. Open all year, Mon.-Sat. 7 a.m. to 2 p.m.; in summer, there's Sunday brunch 9 a.m.-1:30 p.m. No credit cards.

Hidden away on Thomaston's waterfront is the **Harbor View Tavern,** Thomaston Landing, Water St., Thomaston 04861, tel. (207) 354-8173. Try for a table in the back, where you'll have a front-row seat on the harbor. The ambience is informal and seafood is the specialty here (entrées $13-15); the French owner adds his own flair to escargots, mussels, and scallops. From Rt. 1 in Thomaston, take Knox St. to Water Street. The restaurant is a half mile off Rt. 1. Open daily 11:30 a.m.-2:30 p.m. and 5-9 p.m., year-round; call ahead off season.

When the kids are hungry and the wallet is thin, the solution is **Dave's Restaurant,** Rt. 1 South, Thomaston 04861, tel. (207) 594-5424, a Thomaston eatery that everyone assumes is in Rockland (it's on the boundary line). Good, solid home cooking with a big emphasis on seafood. Friendly service, no frills, local color. No smoking. The restaurant complex also includes a well-stocked fish market and a summer-only driving range, go-carts, and batting cages. Open daily in summer 6 a.m.-10 p.m., shorter hours in winter. Next door is the Flagship Cinema multiplex.

INFORMATION AND SERVICES

Thomaston and its two peninsulas come under the umbrella of the **Rockland-Thomaston Area Chamber of Commerce,** based in downtown Rockland, Harbor Park, P.O. Box 508, Rockland 04841, tel. (207) 596-0376. The only Thomaston clearinghouse for visitors' information is an outside, brochure-filled kiosk at the Exxon station on Main Street.

The **Thomaston Public Library,** 42 Main St., Thomaston 04861, tel. (207) 354-2453, occupies part of the Greek Revival Thomaston Academy, once the town's elementary school (until 1982). Now the library shares the space with the Thomaston branch of the University of Maine at Augusta; college classes are held here throughout the school year.

Emergencies
For anyone in Thomaston, or on the Cushing and St. George Peninsulas, the nearest hospital is **Penobscot Bay Medical Center** in Rockport, Rt. 1, tel. (207) 596-8000, where there is 24-hour emergency-room care. For **police, fire, and ambulance,** dial 911.

CUSHING PENINSULA

Cushing's recorded history goes back at least as far as 1605, when someone named "Abr [maybe Abraham] King"—presumably a member of explorer George Waymouth's crew—inscribed his name on a ledge (now private property) here. Since 1789, settlers' saltwater farms have sustained many generations, and the active Cushing Historical Society keeps the memories and memorabilia from fading away. But the outside world knows little of this—Cushing is better known as "Wyeth country," the terrain depicted by the famous artistic dynasty of N.C., Andrew, and Jamie Wyeth (and assorted talented other relatives).

Even though several Wyeths still spend time here, you're not likely to meet any members of the family (unless you hang out near Fales's Store for days on end). However, if you're an Andrew Wyeth fan, visiting Cushing will give you the feeling of walking through his paintings. The flavor of Maine is here—rolling fields, wildflower meadows, rocky tidal coves, broad vistas, character-filled farmhouses, and some well-hidden summer enclaves. The only retail businesses are a general store, a few farmstands, and a seasonal takeout—plus a campground on the Thomaston/Cushing town line.

SIGHTS

Cushing's town line begins 1.3 miles south of Rt. 1 (take Wadsworth St. at the Maine State Prison Showroom Outlet). Two miles farther, you'll pass giant wooden sculptures in the yard of the late artist **Bernard Langlais.** Before Langlais died in 1977, his roadside pond held a huge, sinking carving of Richard Nixon in the "I am not a crook" pose. It brought many a car to a screeching halt.

Six miles from Rt. 1 is the **A.S. Fales & Son Store** (locally, just "Fales's Store"), Cushing's heart and soul—source of fuel, film, gossip, and groceries. Built in 1889, the store has been in the Fales family ever since. Just beyond the store, take the left fork, continuing down the peninsula toward the Broad Cove Church and the Olson House.

Broad Cove Church

Wyeth aficionados will recognize the Broad Cove Church as one of his subjects—alongside River (Cushing) Road en route to the Olson House. Most days, it's open, so step inside and admire the classic New England architecture. The church is also well known as the site of one of the region's best beanhole bean suppers, held on a mid-July Saturday and attracting several hundred appreciative diners. Bear left at the fork after Fales's Store; the church is .4 mile farther, on the right.

The Olson House

Many an art lover makes the pilgrimage to the Olson House, a famous icon near the end of Hathorn Point Road. The early-19th-century farmhouse appears in Andrew Wyeth's 1948 painting *Christina's World* (which hangs in New York's Museum of Modern Art), his best-known image of the disabled Christina Olson, who died in 1968. In 1991, two philanthropists donated the Olson House to the Farnsworth Art Museum, which has retained the house's sparse, lonely, and rather mystical ambience. The clapboards outside remain unpainted, the interior walls bear only a few Wyeth prints (hung close to the settings they depict), and it is easy to sense Wyeth's inspiration for chronicling this place. The house is open daily 11 a.m.-4 p.m., Memorial Day weekend through Columbus Day. Admission is $3 adults and seniors, $1 kids 8-18; children under eight are free. Combination tickets are sold at the Farnsworth Museum, where you can also pick up a map for getting to the Olson House. From Rt. 1 in Thomaston, at the Maine State Prison Showroom Outlet, turn onto Wadsworth St. and go six miles to Fales's Store. Take the left fork after the store, go one and a half miles, and turn left onto Hathorn Point Road. Go another 1.9 miles to the house.

The Georges River Bikeways

The Cushing Peninsula is the endpoint for The Georges River Bikeways, bicycle routes meandering through three sections of the St. George River watershed, beginning near Liberty. Organized by the Georges River Land Trust (GRLT), the routes follow mostly side roads (some unpaved) rather than major highways, reaching salt water near the tip of the Cushing Peninsula. A mountain bike is your best choice—for the hilly terrain and unpaved roads in the upper regions and the shoulderless roads along the whole route. You'll need a GRLT map as well as a copy of the DeLorme *Maine Atlas and Gazetteer* (see the Booklist).

ST. GEORGE PENINSULA

Even though the Cushing and St. George Peninsulas face each other across the St. George River, they differ dramatically. Cushing is far more rural, seemingly less approachable—with little access to the surrounding waters; St. George has a whole string of things to do and see, and places to sleep and eat—plus shore access in various spots along the peninsula.

The St. George Peninsula is actually better known by some of the villages scattered along its length: Tenants Harbor, Port Clyde, Wiley's Corner, Spruce Head—plus the smaller neighborhoods of Martinsville, Smalleytown, Glenmere, Long Cove, Hart's Neck, and Clark Island. Each has a distinct personality, determined partly by the different ethnic groups—primarily Brits, Swedes, and Finns—who arrived to work the granite quarries in the 19th century. Wander through the Seaview Cemetery in Tenants Harbor and you'll see the story: row after row of gravestones with names from across the sea.

A more famous former visitor was 19th-century novelist Sarah Orne Jewett, who holed up in an old schoolhouse in Martinsville, paid a weekly rental of 50 cents, and penned *The Country of the Pointed Firs,* a tale about "Dunnet's Landing" (Tenants Harbor). The schoolhouse, tel. (207) 372-8012, is still on the rental market, but it's been refurbished and now goes for $100 a night, $500 a week.

Today the picturesque peninsula has saltwater farms, tidy hamlets, a striking lighthouse, spruce-edged tidal coves, an active yachting harbor, and, at the tip, a tiny fishing village (Port Clyde), which serves as the springboard to offshore Monhegan Island.

Port Clyde, in fact, may be the best-known community here. (It is, fortunately, no longer called by its unappealing 18th-century name—Herring Gut.) George Waymouth explored Port Clyde's nearby islands in 1605, but you'd never suspect its long tradition. It's a sleepy place, with a general store, an inn, a couple of galleries, and expensive parking. (Enterprising locals charge $4 a day, mostly for visitors heading to car-less Monhegan.)

Marshall Point Light

SIGHTS

Marshall Point Lighthouse Museum
Not many settings can compare with the spectacular locale of the Marshall Point Lighthouse Museum, Marshall Point Rd., P.O. Box 247,

Port Clyde 04855, tel. (207) 372-6450, a distinctive 1857 lighthouse and park overlooking Port Clyde, the harbor islands, and the passing lobsterboat fleet. Bring a picnic and let the kids run on the lawn (but keep them well back from the shoreline). The tiny museum, in the 1895 keeper's house, displays local memorabilia. Admission is free, but donations are welcomed. Open Tues.-Sun. 1-5 p.m., Memorial Day weekend through September, and occasional weekend afternoons in May and October. The grounds are accessible year-round. Take Rt. 131 to Port Clyde and watch for signs to the museum.

Georges River Scenic Byway
The brainchild of energetic members of the Georges River Land Trust, the Georges River Scenic Byway is a 50-mile auto route along the St. George River (a.k.a. Georges River) from its inland headwaters to the sea in Port Clyde. You can follow the trail in either direction, or pick it up anywhere along the way, but first obtain a map/brochure at a chamber of commerce or other information locale. You can also contact **The Georges River Land Trust** (GRLT), 328 Main St., Rockland 04841, tel. (207) 594-5166. Better still, support the GRLT and become a member; the basic rate is $35 a year. The land trust also maintains bicycle routes through the St. George River watershed to Cushing. Following mostly side roads (some unpaved) rather than major highways, the routes reach salt water near the tip of the Cushing Peninsula. A mountain bike is your best choice—for the hilly terrain and unpaved roads in the upper regions and the shoulderless roads along the whole route.

RECREATION

Swimming, Beachcombing
Drift Inn Beach, on Drift Inn Beach Rd. (also called Candy's Cove Rd.), isn't a big deal as beaches go, but it's the best public one on the peninsula, so it gets busy on hot days. The name comes from the Drift Inn, a summer hotel located here early in the century. Drift Inn Beach Road parallels Rt. 131, and the parking lot is accessible from both roads. Heading south on the peninsula, about three and a half miles after

the junction with Rt. 73, turn left at Drift Inn Beach Road. The sign frequently disappears; watch for a square granite house and a red farm. Go .2 mile from the turn.

Cycling
A popular local bicycling route follows Rt. 131 south from Thomaston (Rt. 1) to Port Clyde (14 miles)—with a side trip along Rt. 73 to Spruce Head for the ambitious. Another option—a 35-mile loop—is to take Rt. 131 south from Thomaston, then turn left at Rt. 73, continue on Rt. 73 through Spruce Head and South Thomaston to Rockland, where Rt. 1 loops back to Thomaston. Be forewarned, however, that these roads are narrow and at times rather heavily traveled, especially in July and August, and shoulders are poor-to-nonexistent. Route 1 has some shoulders (breakdown lanes) but a great deal of traffic. If you need a rental bike, contact **Maine Sport Outfitters,** Rt. 1, Rockport 04856, tel. (207) 236-7120, about 10 miles north of Thomaston.

Tennis
Public courts, available on a first-come, first-served basis, are located behind the municipal building in **South Thomaston,** Rt. 73, about three-quarters of a mile south of the Keag Store, Rt. 73, Village Center, South Thomaston.

Getting Afloat
If you have your own sail- or powerboat, there are moorings in Tenants Harbor (near the East Wind Inn), Port Clyde (near the Port Clyde General Store), and Spruce Head (at Merchants Landing).

The St. George Peninsula is especially popular for **sea kayaking,** with plenty of islands to add interest and shelter. If you need a rental kayak, contact **Maine Sport Outfitters,** Rt. 1, Rockport, tel. (207) 236-7120, about 10 miles north of Thomaston, or **Mount Pleasant Canoe & Kayak,** 650 Mt. Pleasant Rd., West Rockport, tel. (207) 785-4309. Both will supply you with charts and all necessary gear. If you're a novice, both offer lessons. If you've had experience, you can launch on the ramp just before the causeway that links the mainland with Spruce Head Island, in Spruce Head (Island Rd., off Rt. 73). Parking is limited. A great paddle goes clockwise around Spruce Head Island and nearby Whitehead (there's a lighthouse on its south-eastern shore) and Norton Islands. Duck in for lunch at Waterman's Beach Lobster. Around new moon and full moon, plan your schedule to avoid low tide near the Spruce Head cause-way, or you may become mired in mudflats. Spruce Head's postmaster, Dana Winchenbach, is a kayaking pro. Contact him weekdays 10 a.m.-1 p.m. and 2-4 p.m., tel. (207) 594-7647, if you need advice; at lunchtime, he's out on the water.

The best boating experience on this peninsula is a passenger-ferry trip to offshore **Monhegan Island**—for a day, overnight, or longer. Per-haps because the private ferry company has a monopoly on this harbor, the trip isn't cheap, and parking adds to the cost, but it's a "must" ex-cursion, so try to factor it into the budget. Port Clyde is the nearest mainland harbor to Mon-hegan; this service operates all year. **Mon-hegan-Thomaston Boat Line,** P.O. Box 238, Port Clyde 04855, tel. (207) 372-8848, fax 372-8547, uses two boats, the *Laura B.,* 70 minutes each way, and the newer *Elizabeth Ann,* 50 minutes. Roundtrip tickets are $25 adults, $12 kids 12 and under, $2 pets. (Leave your bicycle in Port Clyde; you won't need it on the island.) Reservations are essential in summer, espe-cially for the 10:30 a.m. boat; a $5 pp fee holds the reservation until 45 minutes before depar-ture. No deposit is needed for other boats, but show up 30 minutes before departure. Secure parking in Port Clyde is $4 a day. If a summer day-trip is all you can manage, aim for the first or second boat and return on the last one; don't go just for the boat ride.

In May, before Memorial Day weekend, there's only one daily boat, so you'll need to stay overnight. There are two boats daily in June, then three trips July through Labor Day. From Labor Day to mid-October, there are two daily trips, then one trip the rest of October. Trips are only Monday, Wednesday, and Fri-day (except postal holidays), Nov.-April.

Shepherd-for-a-Day

It's not everyone's dream job, but you can try your hand at herding sheep on Allen Island if you arrive at the right time of year. Each spring, the call goes out for a Saturday in early June, when several dozen sturdy volunteers are need-ed on offshore Allen Island, in Muscongus Bay, to help round up the resident flock for shear-ing. Port Clyde is the mainland departure point for the boat to the island, owned by Betsy and Andrew Wyeth. The all-day project is moder-ately strenuous; the rewards are plenty of exer-cise and an all-you-can-eat midday feast. To join the herding party, contact the nonprofit **Is-land Institute,** 410 Main St., Rockland 04841, tel. (207) 594-9209, fax 594-9314. Call by mid-May to be sure of the date.

SHOPPING

Art Galleries

The St. George Peninsula has been attracting artists for decades, so it's no surprise that gal-leries seem to be everywhere you look. Some have been here for years, others started yes-terday; most are worth a stop, so keep an eye out for their signs.

The Drawing Room Gallery, Rt. 131, Wi-ley's Corner, St. George 04860, tel. (207) 372-6242, mounts several theme-based group shows each summer. Philip and Barbara An-derson's gallery is just north of the junction with Rt. 73, about five miles south of Rt. 1. Open Tuesday, Thursday, and Saturday 10 a.m.-5 p.m., Sunday 2-5 p.m., or by appointment.

Established in 1996 by mixed-media pho-tographer Cindy McIntyre, **Scalawags,** Main St., Rt. 131, Tenants Harbor 04860, tel. (207) 372-0614, features her work and those of other photographers and artists. The gallery, across from Farmer's Restaurant, is open in summer, Tues.-Sat. 10 a.m.-6 p.m., Sunday noon-5 p.m.

Founded in 1955, the **Port Clyde Arts and Crafts Society,** a nonprofit artists' cooperative with more than 60 members, wandered from one location to another before finally erecting its own building in 1997. Now, rotating summer shows are held in the rustic new space sur-rounded by lovely gardens. Hours are seasonal: Thurs.-Sun. 10 a.m.-5 p.m., July and August; Fri.-Sun. 10 a.m.-5 p.m. June, September, and October. The gallery is on Rt. 131, about three and a half miles south of the junction with Rt. 73 and across from a sturdy granite building and a large red barn.

Sally MacVane calls her **Gallery-by-the-Sea,** Rt. 131, Port Clyde 04855, tel. (207) 372-8671, "the biggest little gallery in Maine." After careers as newspaper editor and drama teacher, her artistic bent has led her here—close to Monhegan, where she's spent many a year. She's filled five rooms with a wide variety of wall-hung work and puts on several shows each summer. The gallery is open early June through September, Tues.-Sat. 10 a.m.-5:30 p.m., Sunday noon-5 p.m., Monday by appointment.

Overlooking the reversing falls in downtown South Thomaston, **The Old Post Office Gallery,** Rt. 73, P.O. Box 356, South Thomaston 04858, tel. (207) 594-9396, focuses on marine art: ship models, prints, paintings, sculpture, scrimshaw, and jewelry. The price range is broad. Open Tues.-Sat. 10 a.m.-4 p.m.

Crafts

Across from the general store in downtown Tenants Harbor is a discreet sign for **Roy Daniel, Tinsmith,** Main St., Rt. 131, P.O. Box 133, Tenants Harbor 04860, tel. (207) 372-8587. And what a craftsman he is, one of the nation's few dozen practicing tinsmiths. He turns out masterful replicas of Colonial chandeliers, lanterns, and even Christmas ornaments. Stop in his shop most days, or call ahead for an appointment.

Since 1972, Tony Oliveri has been the inspiration and the artisan behind **Keag River Pottery,** Westbrook St., P.O. Box 227, South Thomaston 04858, tel. (207) 594-7915, a small shop attached to his home just .1 mile off Rt. 73 (or 2.2 miles east of Rt. 131). He produces brilliantly glazed functional wares, such as bowls, dishes, and lamps, and readily accepts commissions. Open July to Labor Day, Tues.-Sat. 9 a.m.-5 p.m., other seasons by appointment.

Used Books

Drive up to the small parking area at **Lobster Lane Book Shop,** Island Rd., Spruce Head 04859, tel. (207) 594-7520, and you'll see license plates from everywhere. Owner Vivian York's tiny shop, a crammed but well-organized shed that's been here since the 1960s, has 50,000 or so treasures for used-book fans. For a few dollars, you can stock up on a summer's worth of reading. Open Thurs.-Sun. afternoons,

June through September. The shop is just under a mile east of Rt. 73, with eye-catching vistas in several directions (except, of course, when Spruce Head's infamous fog sets in).

Miscellanea

For honest-to-goodness, old-country-style wurst —and lots of other goodies, too—stop at **Kohn's Smokehouse,** Rt. 131, St. George, mailing address Box 160, Thomaston 04861, tel. (207) 372-8412, fax 372-0506. Since 1979, German-born Ute Kohn has been smoking mussels, pheasant, fish, bacon, even eel, and prices are reasonable. You're in for a treat. The shop, next to her house, is four and a half miles down the St. George Peninsula from Rt. 1. Open daily in summer 9 a.m.-6 p.m.; after Labor Day, it's closed Sunday.

Despite periodic ownership changes, **Port Clyde General Store,** Rt. 131, Port Clyde 04855, tel. (207) 372-6543, remains a characterful destination, a two-century-old country store with a few yuppie touches. Stock up on groceries, pick up a newspaper, order a pizza, or buy a sweatshirt (you'll need it on the Monhegan boat). Open daily 7 a.m.-8 p.m., year-round. Out back is the Dip Net Restaurant.

ACCOMMODATIONS

Inns

The East Wind Inn, Rt. 131, P.O. Box 149, Tenants Harbor 04860, tel. (207) 372-6366 or (800) 241-8439, fax (207) 372-6320, is the perfect rendition of an old-fashioned country inn. Built in 1860 and originally used as a sail loft, it has a huge veranda, a cozy parlor, harbor-view rooms, and a quiet dining room with a creditable menu. Of the 16 traditional rooms in the main inn building, six have private baths; the others share four baths. Rates are $82-120 d mid-June to Labor Day, $55-108 d other months (April and November are lowest rates). Next door, the inn's spiffed-up 19th-century Meeting House, a former sea captain's home, has 10 rooms and suites, all with great views and private baths ($120 d in midsummer, $80-108 d other months, higher for suites). Also on the premises, the Ginny Wheeler Cottage has three superb lodging options ranging $165-260 d in midsummer, $115-

234 d other months. Everyone gets a full breakfast. From April to November, the water-view dining room is open to the public for breakfast (7:30-9:30 a.m., to 10 a.m. in July and August), Sunday brunch (11:30 a.m.-2 p.m.), and dinner (5:30-8:30 p.m., to 9:30 p.m. in July and August). Reservations are wise. No smoking in the dining room. Children are welcome. Inquire at the inn about three-hour daysails ($25-30 pp) aboard the traditional Friendship sloop *Surprise*. Located nine and a half miles south of Rt. 1, the inn is open April-Nov., other months for groups by special arrangement.

If you stay at the **The Ocean House,** Rt. 131, P.O. Box 66, Port Clyde 04855, tel. (207) 372-6691 or (800) 269-6691, plan to roll out of bed, eat breakfast, and roll down the hill to the Monhegan boat (see "Getting Afloat" under "Recreation," above). It's ultraconvenient, and you can leave your car here (free). Several of the nine unpretentious inn rooms (seven with private bath) have great harbor views (especially number 11). Owner Bud Murdock also operates the **Seaside Inn,** across the street, with eight rooms (private and shared baths). Doubles in both rooms are $56-66, plus $5 for a single-night stay. No credit cards. Open mid-May through October. Breakfast, served 7 a.m.-noon, is a big deal in the 40-seat dining room, and Sundays it's filled with locals. Before the boat, try the Monhegan quickie, a variation on an Egg McMuffin. Family-style dinner is served weekdays by reservation, at 6:30 p.m. only. The set menu (around $15) focuses on seafood; lobster is always available and desserts are delicious. BYOL.

B&Bs

Convenient for catching the early morning Monhegan boat (four miles away), **Church Hill Bed & Breakfast,** Rt. 131, P.O. Box 126, Tenants Harbor 04860, tel. (207) 372-6256, has a two-room Victorian-style suite (with bath), ideal for families or two couples traveling together. Breakfast is hearty continental; carry it to the sunporch out back and enjoy the village view. Cost is $85 (for five) July-Sept., $65 other months. No smoking, no pets. In the garage, Norman and Judy Grossman operate the **Golden Hand Gift Shop,** specializing in baskets. The gift shop is open daily in summer 10 a.m.-6 p.m.; the B&B is open all year, but call ahead off season.

Newest B&B on the peninsula is the **Blue Lupin,** Waterman's Beach Rd., South Thomaston 04848, tel. (207) 594-2673, in an off-the-beaten-track locale with an out-of-this-world view. Three rooms and a suite, all with private bath and TV/VCR, go for $65-125 d, mid-May through October, less off season. Breakfast is a feast. You're right on the water, so bring a sea kayak and launch it from the beach. Or bring a bicycle to explore the area. Next door is Waterman's Beach Lobsters. No smoking, no pets, no children under 12. Open all year. The B&B is seven miles from Rockland, slightly farther from Thomaston.

In the center of South Thomaston village but overlooking the reversing falls on the tidal Wessaweskeag River, the 1830 **Weskeag at the Water,** Rt. 73, P.O. Box 213, South Thomaston 04858, tel. (207) 596-6676 or (800) 596-5576, has five second- and third-floor rooms and a suite (private and shared baths) for $65-135 d. This place is especially relaxing; congenial innkeepers Gray and Lynne Smith provide guests with games, puzzles, books, a huge video library, a great deck, and a lawn stretching to the river. Bring your sea kayak and bicycles. It's one and a half miles from the Owls Head Transportation Museum (the Smiths love vintage cars) and a few more miles from the restaurants of downtown Rockland. No smoking and no pets, but kids are welcome. Open all year.

Seasonal Rentals

Lots of **rental cottages** are tucked into secluded coves throughout the St. George Peninsula. Many of the owners advertise in the classified pages of *Down East* magazine, usually the March and April issues. In addition, the Rockland-Thomaston Area Chamber of Commerce, based in downtown Rockland, Harbor Park, P.O. Box 508, Rockland 04841, tel. (207) 596-0376, maintains a listing of cottage-rental opportunities in the area—especially in **Tenants Harbor, Port Clyde, Spruce Head,** and **Owls Head.**

FOOD

The wide range of interesting restaurants in the Rockland area is close enough to sample conveniently.

Lunch and Miscellanea

Don't be surprised to see the handful of tables occupied at the **Keag Store,** Rt. 73, Village Center, South Thomaston, tel. (207) 596-6810, one of the most popular lunch stops in the area. (Keag, by the way, is pronounced "gig"—short for "Wessaweskeag.") Roast-turkey sandwiches are a big draw, as is the pizza, which verges on the greasy but compensates with its flavor—no designer toppings, just good pizza. Order it all to go and head across the street to the public wharf, where you can hang out and observe all the comings-and-goings. Open daily, all year.

Other good spots for picnic fare are the **Port Clyde General Store** Rt. 131, Port Clyde 04855, tel. (207) 372-6543; the **Schoolhouse Bakery,** Rt. 131, Tenants Harbor, tel. (207) 372-9608; and the **Off Island Store,** Island Rd., Spruce Head, tel. (207) 594-7475.

Inexpensive to Moderate

Farmer's Restaurant, Main St., Rt. 131, Tenants Harbor 04860, tel. (207) 372-9642, a longtime neighborhoody place, underwent an ownership change in 1997, quickly attracting a loyal following for all three meals. The dinner menu is unfancy but solid, with fresh seafood, steaks, and such. Open daily 7 a.m.-8 p.m. (to 9 p.m. Friday and Saturday), all year. The restaurant is in Tenants Harbor Village.

Seafood is everything at **The Harpoon,** Drift Inn and Marshall Point Rds., Port Clyde 04855, tel. (207) 372-6304, and it's about as fresh as it gets. Steaks are also on the menu, along with Cajun dishes. Lobster's available, but save that for an outdoor deck (see "Lobster-in-the-Rough," below). Rebuilt from the ashes of an early 1990s fire, the informal restaurant is just over a low hill from the center of Port Clyde. Open daily 5-9 p.m. (to 10 p.m. Friday and Saturday), mid-May to mid-October.

Lobster-in-the-Rough

These open-air lobster wharves are the best places in the area to get down and dirty and manhandle a steamed or boiled lobster.

With outside picnic tables overlooking the harbor, **Cod End,** next to the town dock, Tenants Harbor 04860, tel. (207) 372-6782, is the right kind of rustic. Dig into lobster, fried clams, chowders, and delicious homemade pies; beer and wine available. Lobster-dinner discount for seniors Mon.-Thursday. Open daily 7 a.m.-9 p.m., July and August, shorter hours June, September, and October. Take Rt. 131 south nine and a half miles from Rt. 1 in Thomaston; turn left about 30 yards beyond Hall's Market.

Out back behind the Port Clyde General Store, and overlooking the Port Clyde lobsterboat fleet, are the picnic tables of the **Dip Net,** Rt. 131, Port Clyde 04855, tel. (207) 372-6543, open June to early October for breakfast, lunch, and dinner 7 a.m.-8 p.m.

A broad view of islands in the Mussel Ridge Channel is the bonanza at **Waterman's Beach Lobsters,** Waterman's Beach Rd., South Thomaston 04858, tel. (207) 594-2489 or 594-7518. This tiny operation turns out well-stuffed lobster and crabmeat rolls and superb pies. Step up to the window and place your order. Service can be slow, but why rush with a view like this? Choose a good day; there's no real shelter from bad weather. BYOL; no credit cards. Open daily 11 a.m.-7 p.m., Memorial Day weekend to Labor Day. Located next door to the **Blue Lupin** B&B, the wharf is on a side road off Rt. 73 between Spruce Head Village and South Thomaston; watch for signs on Rt. 73.

Atwood's Cooker, Spruce Head Island, tel. (207) 594-9266, doesn't have the sweeping vistas you'll get at Waterman's Beach, but you'll be sitting at lobsterland's ground-zero. The small restaurant (with a few tables indoors and a tree-shaded outside deck) adjoins one of Maine's largest lobster wholesalers—and it's right across the road from the bustling commercial wharf. Open daily in summer, Mon.-Sat. 11 a.m.-8 p.m., Sunday noon-8 p.m. From Rt. 73 in Spruce Head, take Island Rd. about one and a half miles to a stop sign; turn right and go downhill toward the wharf.

MONHEGAN: OFFSHORE IDYLL

Eleven or so miles from the mainland lies a unique island community with gritty lobstermen, close-knit families, a can-do spirit, a longstanding summertime artists' colony, no cars, astonishingly beautiful scenery, and some of the best birding on the eastern seaboard. Until the 1980s, the island only had radiophones and generator power; with the arrival of electricity and real phones, the pace has quickened a bit—but not much. Welcome to Monhegan Island.

But first a cautionary note: Monhegan has remained idyllic largely because generations of residents, part-timers, and visitors have been ultrasensitive to its fragility. When you buy your ferry ticket, you'll receive a copy of the regulations, all very reasonable, and the captain of your ferry will reiterate them. *Heed them or don't go.*

Many of the regulations have been developed by The Monhegan Associates, an island land trust founded in the 1960s by Thomas Edison, son of the inventor. Firmly committed to preservation of the island in as natural a state as possible, the group maintains and marks the trails, sponsors natural-history talks, and insists that no building be allowed beyond the village limits.

The origin of the word Monhegan remains up in the air; it's either a Maliseet or Micmac name meaning "out-to-sea island" or an adaptation of the name of a French explorer's daughter. In any case, Monhegan caught the attention of Europeans after English explorer John Smith stopped by in 1614, but the island had already been noticed by earlier adventurers including John Cabot, Giovanni da Verrazano, and George Waymouth. Legend even has it that Monhegan fishermen sent dried fish to Plimoth Plantation during the Pilgrims' first winter on Cape Cod. Captain Smith returned home and carried on about Monhegan, snagging the attention of intrepid souls who established a fishing/trading outpost here in 1625. Monhegan has been settled continuously since 1674, with fishing as the economic base.

In the 1880s, lured by the spectacular setting and artist Robert Henri's enthusiastic reports, gangs of artists began arriving, lugging

their easels here and there to capture the surf, the light, the tidy cottages, the magnificent headlands, fishing boats, even the islanders' craggy features. American, German, French, and British artists have long (and continue to) come here; well-known signatures associated with Monhegan include Rockwell Kent, George Bellows, Edward Hopper, James Fitzgerald, Andrew Winter, Alice Kent Stoddard, Reuben Tam, William Kienbusch, and Jamie Wyeth.

Officially called Monhegan Plantation (part of Lincoln County), the island has about 85 year-rounders. Several hundred others summer here. A handful of students attend the tiny school through eighth grade; high-schoolers have to pack up and move "inshore" to the mainland during the school year.

At the schoolhouse, the biggest social event of the year is the Christmas party, when everyone brings casseroles, salads, and desserts to complement a big beef roast. Kids perform their Christmas play, Santa shows up with presents, and dozens of adults look on approvingly. The

---

RULES FOR MONHEGAN VISITORS

1. Smoking is banned everywhere except in the village.

2. Rock climbing is not allowed on the wild headlands on the back side of the island.

3. Preserve the island's wild state—do not remove flowers or lichens.

4. Bicycles and strollers are not allowed on island trails.

5. Camping and campfires are forbidden island-wide.

6. Swim only at Swim Beach, just south of the ferry landing (if your innards can stand the shock). Wait for the incoming tide, when the water is warmest (and this warmth is relative). It's wise not to swim alone.

A suggestion: Carry a trash bag, use it, and take it off the island when you leave.

islanders turn out en masse for almost every special event at the school, and the adults treat the island kids almost like common property, feeling free to praise or chastise them any time it seems appropriate—a phenomenon unique to isolated island communities.

As if the isolation weren't rigorous enough, Monhegan's lobster-fishing season—a legislatively sanctioned period—perversely begins on January 1 (locally known as Trap Day). An air of nervous anticipation surrounds the dozen or so lobstermen after midnight on New Year's Eve, as they prepare to steam out to set their traps on the ocean floor. Of course, with the lack of competition from mainland fishermen that time of year, and a supply of lobsters fattening up since the previous June, there's a ready market for their catch. But success still depends on a smooth "setting." Meetings are held daily between Christmas and New Year's to make sure everyone will be ready to "set" together. The season ends on June 25. It has been thus since 1906.

March brings the annual town meeting, an important community event that draws every able-bodied soul and then some. The island's entire annual budget is only about $160,000.

Almost within spitting distance of Monhegan's dock (but you'll still need a boat) is **Manana Island,** once the home of an ex-New Yorker named Ray Phillips. Known as the Hermit of Manana, Phillips lived a solitary sheepherding existence on this barren island for more than half a century, until his death in 1975. His story had spread so far afield that even *The New York Times* ran a front-page obituary when he died. (Photos and clippings are displayed in the Monhegan Museum.) In summer, youngsters with skiffs often hang around the harbor, particularly Fish Beach and Swim Beach, and you can usually talk one of them into taking you over, for a fee. (Don't try to negotiate too much or he may not return to pick you up.) Some curious inscriptions on Manana (marked with a yellow X near the boat landing) have led archaeologists to claim that Vikings even made it here, but cooler heads attribute the markings to Mother Nature.

When to Go
If a day-trip is all your schedule will allow, visit

Monhegan between Memorial Day weekend and mid-October, when ferries from Port Clyde, New Harbor, and Boothbay Harbor operate daily, allowing 5-9 hours on the island—time enough to do an extensive trail loop, visit the museum and handful of shops, and picnic on the rocks. Other months, there's only one ferry a day from Port Clyde (only three a week Nov.-April), so you'll need to spend the night—not a hardship, but definitely requiring planning ahead.

Almost any time of year, but especially in spring, fog can blanket the island, curtailing photography and swimming (although not the ferries). A spectacular sunny day can't be beat, but the fog lends an air of mystery you won't forget, so don't be deterred. Rain, of course, is another matter; some island trails can be perilous even in a drizzle.

Other Points to Consider
Monhegan has no bank, and credit cards are not widely accepted. Personal checks, traveler's checks, or cash will do. The few **public telephones** in the village require phone credit cards.

The only **public restroom** unconnected to a restaurant or lodging is on Horn Hill, at the southern end of the village (near the Monhegan House), and it will cost you $1 to use it. Outrageous, yes, but the restroom was installed to protect the woods and trails and deter day-trippers from bothering innkeepers. Unfortunately the fee inspires some people to spurn these facilities and go elsewhere. Spend the dollar and preserve the island.

If you're staying overnight, be sure to bring a flashlight for negotiating the unlighted island walkways, even in the village. Birders and hikers in particular should be aware that Monhegan's whitetail deer herd has contributed to a relatively high incidence of **Lyme disease,** transmitted via deer ticks. Even on hot days, opt for long cotton pants rather than shorts, and be sure to tuck pant legs inside socks.

SIGHTS AND RECREATION

Monhegan is a getaway destination, a relaxing place for self-starters, so don't anticipate entertainment beyond the occasional lecture or narrated nature tour. Bring sturdy shoes (maybe even an extra pair in case trails are wet), a windbreaker, binoculars, a camera, and a journal. If you're staying overnight, bring a book. (If you forget, there's an amazingly good library.) In winter, bring ice skates for use on the Ice Pond.

Sights and Shopping

The National Historic Register **Monhegan Lighthouse**—activated in July 1824 and automated in 1959—stands at the island's highest point, Lighthouse Hill, an exposed summit that's also home to the **Monhegan Museum,** tel. (207) 596-7003, in the former keeper's house and adjacent buildings. Overseen by the **Monhegan Historical and Cultural Museum Association,** Monhegan 04852, the museum contains an antique kitchen, lobstering exhibits, and a fine collection of paintings by noted and not-so-noted artists. Two outbuildings have tools and gear connected with fishing and ice-cutting, traditional island industries. A volunteer usually is on hand to answer questions. Museum hours, coordinated with the ferry runs, are 11:30 a.m.-3:30 p.m., July through September. Admission is technically free, but donations are encouraged. Funds are being collected for restoration of the assistant lightkeeper's house, a long-term project that will provide a climate-controlled environment for the museum's impressive art collection.

Close to 20 **artists' studios** are open to the public during the summer (usually July and Au-gust), but not all at once. At least five are open most days—some in the morning but more in the afternoon. Wednesday and Saturday tend to have the most choices. Sometimes it's tight time-wise for day-trippers who also want to hike the trails, but most of the studios are relatively close to the ferry landing. An annually updated map/schedule details locations, days, and times.

Galleries and shops in the village include **Winter Works** (craft co-op), **Lupine Gallery,** tel. (207) 594-8131 (art, some crafts), **Black Duck** (gifts), and the **Carina Shop** (bread, produce, coffee, newspapers, books, gourmet specialties).

Hiking/Walking

Just over half a mile wide and 1.7 miles long, barely a square mile in area, Monhegan has 18 numbered hiking trails, most easy to moderate, covering about 17 miles. All are described in the *Monhegan Associates Trail Map,* available at mainland ferry offices and island shops and lodgings. (The map is not to scale, so the hikes can take longer than you think.)

Dress in layers, including long pants, and wear hiking boots or sturdy walking shoes. Even if you're warm in the village, you'll feel the wind on the island's backside and up at the lighthouse.

The footing is uneven everywhere, so Monhegan can present major obstacles to the physically challenged, even on the well-worn but unpaved village roads. Maintain an especially

"communications central," Monhegan Island

healthy respect for the ocean here, and don't venture too close; over the years, rogue waves on the island's backside have claimed victims young and old.

A relatively easy **day-tripper loop** (with a couple of moderate sections along the backside of the island) that takes in several of Monhegan's finest features starts at the southern end of the village, opposite the church. To appreciate it, allow at least two hours. From the Main Rd., go up Horn Hill, following signs for the **Burnthead Trail** (no. 4). Cross the island to the **Cliff Trail** (no. 1). Turn north on the Cliff Trail, following the dramatic headlands on the island's backside. Lots of great picnic rocks in this area. Continue to Squeaker Cove, where the surf is the wildest, but be cautious. Then watch for signs to the **Cathedral Woods Trail** (no. 11), carpeted with pine needles and leading back to the village.

When you get back to Main Rd., detour up the **Whitehead Trail** (no. 7) to the museum. If you're spending the night and feeling energetic, consider circumnavigating the island via the **Cliff Trail** (nos. 1 and 1-A). Allow at least five hours for this route; don't rush it.

Birding

One of the East Coast's best birding sites during spring and fall migrations, Monhegan is a migrant trap for exhausted creatures winging their way north or south. Avid birders come here to add rare and unusual species to their life lists, and some devotees return year after year.

Predicting exact bird-migration dates can be dicey, since wind and weather aberrations can skew the schedule. Generally, the best times are mid- to late May and most of September, into early October. If you plan to spend a night (or more) on the island during migration seasons, don't try to wing it—reserve a room well in advance.

No birder should come here without a copy of the superb *Birder's Guide to Maine* (see the Booklist). Jan Erik Pierson, one of the book's three coauthors, also leads an annual four-day **birding tour** to Monhegan in late September. Cost is under $600 pp, not including transportation to Maine; maximum 12 people. For tour information, contact **Field Guides**, tel. (800) 728-4953.

ACCOMMODATIONS

The island has a variety of lodgings from rustic to comfortable; none qualify in the multistar category. Best is Philip Truelove and Howard Garrett's **Island Inn**, Monhegan 04852, tel. (207) 596-0371 or (800) 722-1269, an imposing three-story mid-19th-century building with a veranda and lawns overlooking the ferry landing. Thirty-six basic harbor- and meadow-view rooms (shared baths) start at $98 d, including full breakfast. The inn's restaurant is open to the public for breakfast, lunch, and dinner; credit cards accepted. Open late May to early October.

In the heart of the village, **Monhegan House,** Monhegan 04852, tel. (207) 594-7983 or (800) 599-7983, built in 1870, is a large four-story building with 32 rooms (shared baths), which go for $75 d. No smoking, no pets, credit cards accepted. Islanders and visitors flock to the inn's airy **Monhegan House Café** for breakfast, dinner, and take-out lunches. Open mid-May to mid-October.

A more modernized hostelry, **Shining Sails,** P.O. Box 346, Monhegan 04852, tel. (207) 596-0041 or (800) 606-9497, fax (207) 596-7166, lacks the quaintness of the other inns, but it's convenient to the dock, stays open all year, and has private baths. Breakfast (included only in season) is continental. Seven first- and second-floor rooms and efficiencies (some with water views) go for $70-85 d, May to mid-October; lower rates for multiple nights and off season stays. No pets, credit cards accepted.

Funkiest lodging is **The Trailing Yew,** Monhegan 04852, tel. (207) 596-0440, owned for eons by colorful islander Josephine Davis Day, who remained omnipresent until 1996, when she died at the age of 99. Spread among five rustic buildings south of the village on the road to Lobster Cove, the 55 rooms are $56 d (shared baths, not always in the same building), including breakfast and dinner. Inn guests pay an extra $9 for a lobster dinner. The old-fashioned, low-key dining room is also open to the public for dinner at 5:45 p.m., served family-style by reservation ($13 pp; $22 if you order lobster), and for breakfast ($6) at 7:45 a.m. Bring a sleeping bag in spring or fall; rooms are unheated. Only the main building has electricity. No credit cards. Open late May to early October.

Seasonal Rentals

About two dozen weekly-rental cottages and apartments—categorized as very rustic, fair, very good, and excellent—are managed by **Shining Sails Real Estate,** P.O. Box 346, Monhegan 04852, tel. (207) 596-0041 or (800) 606-9497, fax (207) 596-7166. About half have electricity; the others have gas lights and appliances. Some sleep up to six people; kids, pets, and smoking may be limited. Peak-season (July and August) weekly rates range $400-1,100, lower off season. A few are available by the night, space permitting, especially off season. To rent one of the better seasonal places, you may be asked for at least a two-week commitment.

FOOD

Don't visit Monhegan for fussy gourmet cuisine; everything is quite casual here, and food is hearty and ample. None of the eateries have liquor licenses, so purchase beer or wine at the Monhegan Store. All of the restaurants and food sources are in or close to the village.

As you disembark from the ferry, you'll see **The Barnacle,** tel. (207) 596-0371, under the same ownership as the nearby Island Inn. From June to early October, this casually upscale operation is open daily 8 a.m.-5 p.m., offering picnic-ready sandwiches and salads, plus croissants, scones, and designer coffees.

The **Monhegan Store,** tel. (207) 594-4126, hub of the village and source of picnic fare, groceries, and local tidbits, is open Mon.-Sat. 11 a.m.-6 p.m., Sunday noon-6 p.m.

NOT North End Pizza, tel. (207) 594-5546, dishes up pizza (whole or by the slice) only on Sunday. Other days, this tiny place features a variety of sandwiches, salads, and soups plus red beans and rice. It's a popular day-trippers' lunch spot, so beat the crowd by making this your first stop after getting off the ferry. Go up the hill from the wharf and turn right; NOT North End is ahead on your left. You can always backtrack to the galleries afterward. It's open daily in summer only. (NOT North End got its current name and menu when owner Katy Boegel developed carpal tunnel syndrome after a dozen years of pizza-making.)

Also open seasonally is **The Periwinkle,** tel. (207) 594-5432, doing burgers ($5-7), subs, onion rings, and salads—marginally healthy since they fry with vegetable oil. The island's only coin-operated phone is here.

Also see "Accommodations," above, for info on meals served at Monhegan House, The Island Inn, and The Trailing Yew.

OTHER PRACTICALITIES

Getting There and Getting Around

See "Getting Afloat" under "Recreation" in the St. George Peninsula section, above, for details on cost and schedule of the year-round Monhegan ferries from Port Clyde. Seasonal service to the island is provided from **New Harbor** by Hardy Boat Cruises and from **Boothbay Harbor** by Balmy Days Cruises.

Part of the daily routine for many islanders and summer folk is a stroll to the harbor when the ferry comes in, so don't be surprised to see a good-size welcoming party when you arrive. You're the live entertainment.

Monhegan's only vehicles are li'l ol' trucks used by **Monhegan Trucking.** If you're staying a night or longer and your luggage is too heavy to carry, request their service when you arrive at the island wharf.

Information

Several free brochures and flyers, revised annually, will answer most questions about planning a day-trip or overnight visit to Monhegan. At the ferry ticket office in Port Clyde, pick up the 12-page *Visitor's Guide to Monhegan Island,* as well as the *Monhegan Associates Trail Map.* Both are also available at island shops, galleries, and lodgings, as well as at the New Harbor and Boothbay Harbor ferry offices. To obtain copies beforehand, contact **Monhegan-Thomaston Boat Line,** P.O. Box 238, Port Clyde 04855, tel. (207) 372-8848, fax 372-8547, around mid-April. Also request a copy of the **ferry schedule.** For fastest service, send a self-addressed stamped envelope. When you reach the island, the Monhegan Store, in the heart of the village, is the easiest place to find the map of *Monhegan Artists Studio Locations.*

The **Rockland-Thomaston Area Chamber of Commerce,** Harbor Park, off So. Main St., P.O. Box 508, Rockland 04841, tel. (207) 596-0376 or (800) 562-2529, fax (207) 596-6549, also has information about lodgings and other facilities on Monhegan.

Monhegan's nice little library, the **Jackie and Edward Library,** was named after two children who drowned in the surf in the 1920s. The fiction collection is especially extensive, and it's open to everyone. At the head of Wharf Hill, it's usually open Tuesday, Thursday, and Saturday 1-4 p.m., plus two or three evenings a week; check when you arrive.

Also check the **bulletin board** on the old rope shed next to the meadow, right in the village. Monhegan's version of a bush telegraph, it's where everyone posts flyers and notices about nature walks, lectures, excursions, and other special events.

Emergencies

Monhegan has an **emergency rescue squad,** tel. 911, but the island has no doctor or medical facility, so watch your step while hiking—broken bones can make the boat ride to the mainland excruciating. Locations of several **fire boxes** are noted on the island's trail map.

ROCKLAND AREA

A "Share the Pride" campaign—kicked off in the 1980s to boost sagging civic self-esteem and the local economy—has succeeded in transforming Rockland. Once a run-down county seat best known for the aroma of its fish-packing plants, the city has undergone a sea change—benches and plants line Main Street (Rt. 1), stores offer appealing wares, coffeehouses and art galleries attract a diverse clientele, and Rockland Harbor boasts more windjammer cruise schooners than neighboring Camden (which had long claimed the title of "Windjammer Capital").

Foresighted entrepreneurs had seen the potential of the bayside location in the late 1700s and established a tiny settlement here called "Shore Village" (or "the Shore"). Today's commercial-fishing fleet is one of the few reminders of Rockland's past, when multimasted schooners lined the wharves, some to load volatile cargoes of lime destined to become building material for cities all along the eastern seaboard, others to head northeast—toward the storm-racked Grand Banks and the lucrative cod fishery there. Such hazardous pursuits meant an early demise for many a local seafarer, but Rockland's 5,000 or so residents were enjoying their prosperity in the late 1840s. The settlement was home to more than two dozen shipyards and dozens of lime kilns, was enjoying a construction boom, and boasted a newspaper and regular steamship service. By 1854, Rockland had become a city.

Today, Rockland remains a commercial hub—with Knox County's only shopping plazas (not quite malls, but Wal-Mart has arrived), a fishing fleet that heads far offshore, ferries that connect nearby islands, and firms that manufacture clothing, snowplows, and leather goods. Rockland also claims the title of "Lobster Capital of the World"—thanks to Knox County's shipment nationally and internationally of some 10 million pounds of lobster each year. (The weathervane atop the police and fire department building is even a giant copper lobster.)

Present-day entrepreneurs, carried along on a whole new wave of enthusiasm, are quickly making Rockland an interesting place to live, work, and play. And, with just under 8,000 souls, Rockland is more year-round community than tourist town. But visitors pour in during two big summer festivals—Schooner Days, in early July, and the Maine Lobster Festival, in early August. Centerpiece of Schooner Days is the day-long Great Schooner Race in Penobscot Bay; highlight of the Lobster Festival is King Neptune's coronation of the Maine Sea Goddess—carefully selected from a bevy of local young women—who then sails off with him to his watery domain.

SIGHTS

The Farnsworth Art Museum

Anchoring downtown Rockland is the nationally respected Farnsworth Art Museum, 352 Main

Sculpture by Louise Nevelson stands outside the Farnsworth Art Museum.

St., P.O. Box 466, Rockland 04841, tel. (207) 596-6457, fax 596-0509, established in 1948 through a trust fund set up by Rocklander Lucy Farnsworth. With an ample checkbook, the first curator, Robert Bellows, toured the country, accumulating a splendid collection of 19th- and 20th-century Maine-related American art—the basis for the permanent *Maine in America* exhibition. The collection today includes work by Fitz Hugh Lane, Gilbert Stuart, Eastman Johnson, Childe Hassam, John Marin, Maurice Prendergast, Rockwell Kent, George Bellows, and Marsden Hartley. Best known are the paintings by three generations of the Wyeth family (local summer residents) and sculpture by Louise Nevelson, who grew up in Rockland. Sculpture, jewelry, and paintings by Nevelson form the core of the third-floor Nevelson-Berliawsky Gallery for 20th Century Art. (The only larger Nevelson collection is in New York's Whitney Museum of American Art.) Andrew Wyeth's work occupies a new wing behind the original building; his father, N.C. Wyeth, and son Jamie are rep-

resented in the **Wyeth Center,** across Union St. in a former church.

In the Farnsworth's library—a grand, high-ceilinged oasis akin to an English gentleman's reading room—browsers and researchers can explore an extensive collection of art books and magazines. The museum's hyperactive education department annually sponsors hundreds of lectures, concerts, art classes for adults and children, poetry readings, and field trips. Most are open to nonmembers; some require an extra fee. A glitzy gift shop stocks posters, Wyeth prints, notecards, imported gift items, and art games for children.

Next door to the museum is the mid-19th-century Greek Revival **Farnsworth Homestead,** with original high-Victorian furnishings. Looking as though William Farnsworth's family just took off for the day, the house has been preserved rather than restored.

The Farnsworth also owns the Olson House, 14 miles away in nearby Cushing, where the whole landscape looks like a Wyeth diorama. Pick up a map at the museum to help you find the house—definitely worth the side trip.

The Farnsworth is open all year, including summer holidays; the Homestead and the Olson House are open Memorial Day weekend to mid-October. Summer museum hours: Mon.-Sat. 9 a.m.-5 p.m., Sunday noon-5 p.m. Homestead hours: Mon.-Sat. 10 a.m.-5 p.m., Sunday 1-5 p.m. Winter museum hours: Tues.-Sat. 10 a.m.-5 p.m., Sunday 1-5 p.m. Admission is $5 adults, $4 seniors, $3 children 8-18, free for kids under eight. A special Olson Package ticket covers the museum, homestead, and Olson House for $7 adults, $6 seniors, $4 children 8-18.

Main Street Historic District

Rocklanders are justly proud of their Main Street Historic District, lined with 19th- and early-20th-century Greek and Colonial Revival structures, as well as examples of mansard and Italianate architecture. Most now house retail shops on the ground floor; upper floors have offices, artists' studios, and apartments. The district starts at the corner of Winter and Main Sts. and runs north to the alley just after Kelsey's Appliances. The chamber of commerce has a map and details.

Lighthouse Museum

Three blocks west of Union Street (Rt. 1 South), the **Shore Village Museum,** 104 Limerock St., Rockland 04841, tel. (207) 594-0311, claims to have the nation's largest collection of lighthouse and Coast Guard memorabilia: foghorns, ships' bells, nautical books and photographs, marine instruments, ship models, scrimshaw, even a giant lens built for Maine's tallest lighthouse. Nor is the collection only maritime—over the years, various local groups and individuals have donated doll collections, Civil War uniforms and diaries, and other odd bits and pieces. The eclectic flavor makes it fun for children, especially since lights and noisemakers still work. The price is right: there's no admission fee, although donations are welcomed. In the gift shop, the lighthouse motif adorns almost everything—postcards and T-shirts, buttons and bookends. The museum is open daily 10 a.m.-4 p.m., June 1 to mid-October; by appointment the rest of the year.

Owls Head Transportation Museum

Don't miss this place, even if you're not an old-vehicle buff. A generous endowment has made The Owls Head Transportation Museum, Rt. 73, P.O. Box 277, Owls Head 04854, tel. (207) 594-4418, fax 594-4410, a premier facility for celebrating wings and wheels; it draws more than 75,000 visitors a year. Scads of eager volunteers help restore the vehicles and keep them running. On weekends, May-Oct., the museum sponsors airshows (including aerobatic displays) and car and truck meets for hundreds of enthusiasts. Season highlight is the annual rally and aerobatic show (early August), when more than 300 vehicles gather for two days of festivities. Want your own vintage vehicle? Attend the antique, classic, and special-interest auto auction (third Sunday in August). The gift shop carries transportation-related items. If the kids get bored (unlikely), there's a play area outside, with picnic tables. In winter, groomed cross-country-skiing trails wind through the museum's 60-acre site. (Ask for a map at the information desk.) The museum, two miles south of Rockland, is open daily 10 a.m.-5 p.m., April-Oct.; weekdays 10 a.m.-4 p.m., weekends 10 a.m.-3 p.m., Nov.-March. Admission is $5 adults, $4.50 seniors, $3 ages 5-11. (Special events are extra.)

PARKS AND RECREATION

Rockland Breakwater

Protecting the harbor from wind-driven waves, the 4,346-foot-long Rockland Breakwater took 18 years to build, with 697,000 tons of locally quarried granite. In the late 19th century, it was piled up, chunk by chunk, from a base 175 feet wide on the harbor floor (60 feet below the surface) to the 43-foot-wide cap. The Breakwater Light—now automated and maintained by the U.S. Coast Guard—was built in 1902 and added to the National Historic Register in 1981. The breakwater provides unique vantage points for photographers, and a place to picnic or catch sea breezes or fish on a hot day, but it is extremely dangerous during storms. Anyone on the breakwater risks being washed into the sea or struck by lightning (ask the local hospital staff: it *has* happened!). Do not take chances when the weather is iffy.

To reach the breakwater, take Rt. 1 north to Waldo Ave. and turn right. Take the next right onto Samoset Rd. and drive to the end, to Marie Reed Memorial Park (tiny beach, benches, limited parking). Or go to the Samoset Resort and take the path to the breakwater from there.

Harbor Park

If you're looking for a park with more commotion than quiet green space, spend some time at Harbor Park. Boats, cars, and delivery vehicles come and go; the chamber of commerce office has a steady stream of visitors; and you can corner a picnic table or a patch of grass and watch all the action. Public restrooms are in the left side of the chamber office. The park is just off Main Street, below the *Courier-Gazette* newspaper offices.

Creative Play

Kids have a great time at the **Rockland Community Playground,** just behind the Rockland Recreation Center, Union and Limerock Sts. (enter on Limerock). The layout is especially imaginative, with castles, swings, and even a boat. Parents can watch from convenient benches; two-hour parking. Open sunrise to sunset.

Parks in the South End

From S. Main St. (Rt. 73), take Ocean St. to **Sandy Beach Park**—not a large recreation area, but another vantage point for boatwatching and picnicking. If you see swimmers here, resist the urge to join them—Rockland Harbor isn't certifiably pollution-free.

Half a dozen blocks farther south on S. Main St. is Mechanic Street. Turn left and continue to **Snow Marine Park,** with picnic tables and a boat landing. In winter, the park attracts kids for ice-skating and sledding.

Owls Head Light State Park

On Rt. 73, about a mile past Rockland's south-end parks, you'll reach North Shore Rd., in the town of Owls Head. Turn left, toward Owls Head Light State Park. Located 3.6 miles from this turn, Owls Head Light occupies a dramatic promontory with panoramic views over Rockland Harbor and Penobscot Bay. Don't miss it. The keeper's house and the light tower are off limits, but the park surrounding the tower has easy walking paths, picnic tables, and a pebbly beach where you can sunbathe or check out Rockland Harbor's boating traffic. (If it's foggy or rainy, don't climb the steps toward the light tower: the view evaporates in the fog, the access ramp can be slippery, and the foghorn is dangerously deafening.) Follow signs to reach the park. From North Shore Rd., turn left onto Main St., then left onto Lighthouse Rd., and continue along Owls Head Harbor to the parking area. This is also a particularly pleasant bike route—about 10 miles roundtrip from downtown Rockland—although, once again, the roadside shoulders are poor.

Swimming

"Lucia Beach" is the local name for **Birch Point State Park,** one of the best-kept secrets in the area (mostly because self-appointed "protectors" keep removing the official brown signs). Located in Owls Head, just south of Rockland—and not far from Owls Head Light—the spruce-lined sand crescent (free; outhouses but no other facilities) has rocks, shells, and tidepools. There's ample room for a moderate-size crowd, although parking and turnaround space can get a bit tight on the access road. From downtown Rockland, take Rt. 73 one mile to North Shore

Dr. (on your left). Take the next right, Ash Point Dr., and continue past Knox County Regional Airport to Dublin Road. Turn right, go .8 mile, then turn left onto Ballyhac Rd. (opposite airport landing lights). Go another .8 mile, fork left onto an unpaved road, and continue .4 mile to the parking area.

If chilly ocean water doesn't appeal, head for freshwater **Chickawaukee Lake,** on Rt. 17, two miles from downtown Rockland. Don't expect to be alone, though; on hot days, **Johnson Memorial Park**'s pocket-size sand patch is a major attraction. A lifeguard holds forth, there are restrooms, picnic tables, a snack bar, and a boat-launch ramp. (In winter, iceboats, snow-mobiles, and ice-fishing shacks take over the lake.) A signposted bicycle path runs alongside the busy highway, making the park an easy pedal from town.

Golf

At par 69 and 5,549 yards, the **Rockland Golf Club,** 606 Old County Rd., .2 mile northeast of Rt. 17, Rockland 04841, tel. (207) 594-9322, ranks high on many a Maine golfer's list. Established in 1932, the 18-hole public course is open April through October. In July and August, you'll need to reserve a starting time if you plan to tee off anytime after 7 a.m. The modern clubhouse—rebuilt after a disastrous fire in the late 1980s—has a full bar and serves breakfast and lunch at reasonable prices. Parking is plentiful.

Bike and Sea Kayak Rentals

Maine Sport Outfitters, Rt. 1, Rockport 04856, tel. (207) 236-8797, (800) 722-0826, fax (207) 236-7123, just north of Rockland, is the best local source for renting bikes and kayaks. For suggested cycling and sea kayaking routes, see the Thomaston Area and Camden-Rockport Area sections.

GETTING AFLOAT

Rockland has a variety of ways to get afloat: windjammer cruises, excursion boats, and the Maine State Ferry Service. Plus the yachting fraternity has discovered Rockland Harbor, and mooring space has mushroomed. If you're arriving aboard your own boat, the Rockland harbormaster, operating out of the chamber of commerce building, Harbor Park, tel. (207) 594-0314, can provide details on guest moorings. Inside the building are pay showers.

Other nearby anchorages with facilities for boaters are Spruce Head, Tenants Harbor, and Port Clyde.

Windjammer Cruises

Ten traditional windjammer schooners and one restored motor yacht call Rockland home; all but one head out for 3-6 days, late May to mid-October, tucking into coves and harbors around Penobscot Bay and its islands. The mostly engineless craft set their itineraries by the wind, propelled by stiff breezes to Bucks Harbor, North Haven, and Deer Isle—where passengers can hike, shop, and sightsee. Then it's back to the boat for chow—windjammer cooks are legendary for creating three hearty, all-you-can-eat meals daily, including at least one lobster feast! Everything's totally informal, geared for relaxing.

Down below, cabins typically are small and basic, with paper-thin walls—sort of a campground afloat (earplugs are available for light sleepers). Romantic it isn't, although some captains keep track of post-cruise marriages. Most boats have shared showers and toilets. If you're Type-A, given to pacing, don't inflict yourself on the cruising crowd. If you're flexible, ready for whatever, sign on. You can help with the sails, eat, curl up with a book, inhale salt air, shoot photos, eat, sunbathe, birdwatch, eat, chat up fellow passengers, sleep, or just settle back and enjoy spectacular sailing you'll never forget.

The best-known boats in Rockland's fleet are three schooners based at **North End Shipyard,** P.O. Box 482, Rockland 04841, tel. (800) 648-4544, fax (207) 594-8015. Captain John Foss skippers the 92-foot, 28-passenger *American Eagle* (three or six days; no kids under 12; $395-715 pp), Capts. Doug and Linda Lee operate the 94-foot, 33-passenger *Heritage* (six days; no kids under 16; $595-675 pp), and Capt. Ed Glaser runs the 65-foot, 20-passenger *Isaac H. Evans* (three or six days; no kids under eight; $335-675 pp).

Built in 1900, and largest in the fleet, is the three-masted, 132-foot, 44-passenger *Victory Chimes* (three or six days; kids welcome; $375-

725 pp), skippered by Capt. Kip Files, P.O. Box 1401, Rockland 04841, tel. (207) 594-0755 or (800) 745-5651. The *Chimes,* an especially elegant vessel with all sails set, is listed on the National Register of Historic Places.

Other schooners sailing out of Rockland are the 26-passenger *J. & E. Riggin,* P.O. Box 571, Rockland 04841, tel. (207) 594-2923 or (800) 869-0604 (six days; no kids under 16; $550-650 pp); the 12-passenger, three-masted *Kathryn B.,* P.O. Box 133, Hope 04847, tel. (207) 763-4109 or (800) 500-6077, fax (207) 763-4255 (three or six days; no kids under 10; $475-1,000 pp); the 24-passenger *Nathaniel Bowditch,* P.O. Box 459, Warren 04864, tel. (207) 273-4062 or (800) 288-4098 (three, four, or six days; no kids under 10; $335-675 pp); the seven-passenger *Summertime,* 115 S. Main St., Rockland 04841, tel. (800) 562-8290 (three or six days; kids only on special charters; $415-550 pp); and the 22-passenger *Stephen Taber,* P.O. Box 1050, Rockland 04841, tel. (207) 236-3520 or (800) 999-7352, fax (207) 236-0585 (three, four, or six days; no kids under 12; $380-720 pp).

If you can't spare three days or, ideally, a week, the 67-foot, 14-passenger schooner-yacht *Wendameen,* P.O. Box 252, Rockland 04841, tel. (207) 594-1751, does one-night sails (2 p.m.-10 a.m.) out of Rockland's Tillson Avenue Wharf. Cost is $155 pp, including dinner and breakfast.

On the summer cruising schedule, several weeks are particularly popular because they coincide with special windjammer events, so you'll need to book a berth far in advance for these: last week in June (Windjammer Days), Fourth of July week (Great Schooner Race), first week in August (Swans Island Sweet Chariot Music Festival), second week in September (WoodenBoat Sail-In).

Three of Rockland's schooners (*Riggin, Bowditch, Chimes*) and seven of Camden-Rockport's are members of **The Maine Windjammer Association,** P.O. Box 1144, Blue Hill 04614, tel. (800) 807-9463, fax (207) 374-2952, a one-stop resource for vessel and schedule information.

Excursions and Daysailing

Based at Rockland's Harbor Park, near the chamber of commerce, Capt. Ray Remick's 270-passenger M/V *Monhegan,* 655 Main St., Rockland 04841, mailing address P.O. Box 187,

Glen Cove 04846, tel. (207) 596-5660, does 40-minute summer noontime cruises departing at 12:10 p.m., including a light lunch, for $11.95. The rest of the schedule varies; call ahead for info.

Maine State Ferry Service

In 1996, a fancy new ferry terminal opened on Rockland's waterfront, serving regular car and passenger ferries headed for the islands of Vinalhaven, North Haven, and Matinicus. (See the On the Road chapter for ferry schedules.) The Vinalhaven and North Haven routes make fantastic day-trips (especially with a bike), or you can spend the night; the Matinicus ferry is much less predictable.

ENTERTAINMENT

Rockland's downtown movie house—an old-fashioned sort of place with first-run flicks—is the two-screen **Strand Cinema,** Main St., Rockland 04841, tel. (207) 594-7266. The Strand offers two showings a night and occasional 2 p.m. Sunday matinees; films change weekly, usually on Friday. Open all year. The nearest theater showing art films is in Camden.

The competition is the seven-screen Flagship Cinema, out on Rt. 1, just over the Rockland line in Thomaston and next to Dave's Restaurant.

Prime locales for live entertainment are **Waterworks Pub** and **Second Read Books & Coffee** and the **Breakwater Lounge,** part of the Samoset Resort.

FESTIVALS AND EVENTS

The week of July Fourth, **Schooner Days** means three days of festivities focusing on windjammers and featuring music, a sailboat parade, seafood, fireworks, and an all-day Great Schooner Race. Occasionally, this festival occurs the second week in July; check in advance with the chamber of commerce (see "Information and Services," below).

August's **Maine Lobster Festival** is a four-day lobster extravaganza, with live entertainment, the Maine Sea Goddess pageant, a lob-

ster-crate race, craft booths, boat rides, a parade, lobster dinners, and mega-crowds (the hotels are full for miles in either direction). About eight tons of lobsters bite the dust during the weekend.

SHOPPING

Art Galleries

Piggybacking on the fame of the Farnsworth Museum, or at least working symbiotically, more than half a dozen art galleries have opened in Rockland since 1990, with more likely to come. Ask around and look around.

Across from the Farnsworth's side entrance, the **Caldbeck Gallery,** 12 Elm St., Rockland 04841, tel. (207) 594-5935, has gained a top-notch reputation as a "must-see" (and "must-be-seen") space. Featuring the work of contemporary Maine artists, the gallery mounts more than half a dozen solo and group shows each year, May through September. Open Mon.-Sat. 11 a.m.-5 p.m., Sunday 1-5 p.m.

Next door to the Caldbeck, across a lovely little patio (mews?) is **Between the Muse Gallery,** 8 Elm St., P.O. Box 666, Rockland 04841, tel. (207) 596-6868, also with rotating summer shows. Open Mon.-Sat. 11 a.m.-6 p.m. and Sunday noon-5 p.m., April-December.

Other eminently browsable downtown-Rockland galleries are **Atlantis Gallery,** 30 Elm St., tel. (207) 596-6509; **The Gallery at 357 Main,** 357 Main St., tel. (207) 596-0084; **Gallery One,** 365 Main St., tel. (207) 596-0059, above Huston Tuttle; **Harbor Square Gallery,** 374 Main St., tel. (207) 594-8700; and **Elements Gallery,** 431 Main St., tel. (207) 596-6010. The **Islands of Maine Gallery,** 412 Main St., tel. (207) 596-0701, also has artistic offerings.

Books, Crafts, Gifts, and Clothing

An independent bookstore with excellent inventories of best-sellers, cookbooks, kids' books, remainders, magazines, and CDs, **The Reading Corner,** 408 Main St., Rockland 04841, tel. (207) 596-6651, occupies two full rooms in downtown Rockland. Open all year, Mon.-Saturday.

Next door is the four-story **Island Institute,** 410 Main St., Rockland 04841, tel. (207) 594-9209, fax 594-9314, nonprofit steward of Maine's

4,617 offshore islands. The ground-floor **Islands of Maine Gallery,** 412 Main St., P.O. Box 1104, tel. (207) 596-0701, opened in 1996, is an attractive retail outlet for talented craftspeople from 14 year-round islands. Open April-Jan., Mon.-Sat. 10 a.m.-6 p.m. and Sunday noon-4 p.m.

Left (south) of The Reading Corner is **The Grasshopper Shop,** 400 Main St., Rockland 04841, tel. (207) 596-6156, an eclectic emporium filled with jewelry, clothing, accessories, and unusual gifts, all tastefully displayed beneath a handsome antique tin ceiling. An updated version of a Camden shop that closed in the mid-1990s, The Grasshopper is open all year, Mon.-Sat. 9:30 a.m.-7 p.m. (to 8 p.m. Friday and Saturday) and Sunday 11 a.m.-5 p.m.

Appropriately labeling its wares "elegant necessities and practical indulgences," **Peabody & King,** 373 Main St., Rockland 04841, tel. (207) 596-6781, has all those splurge items you'd love to own but can't quite bring yourself to buy. So you could spring for a wedding gift and hope they cancel the ceremony. Lamps, ties, leather items, jewelry, even furniture—it's all here. The shop is open Mon.-Sat. 10 a.m.-5:30 p.m. and Sunday noon-5 p.m. in summer; off season, it's closed on Sunday.

A family-run department store with a respected local reputation and an especially helpful staff, **Coffin's,** 384 Main St., Rockland 04841, tel. (207) 596-6441, carries men's and women's clothes and shoes. Open Mon.-Sat. 8:30 a.m.-5:30 p.m.

Discount Shopping
Rockland has several outlets for real bargains on new and used clothing and footwear. **Nautica,** 87 Camden St., Rockland 04841, tel. (207) 596-7713, is a factory outlet for locally made brand-name sportswear. Open daily, mid-May to mid-October. **J.S. Puddleduck's Thrift Boutique,** 150 Union St., Rockland 04841, tel. (207) 596-0791, is a consignment shop for used infants' and children's clothing and maternity wear. Open all year but on an unpredictable schedule. **Ravishing Recalls,** 389 Main St., Rockland 04841, tel. (207) 596-6164, is a high-quality consignment shop. Open all year. **Goodwill Industries Retail Store,** Harbor Plaza, Camden St., Rockland 04841, tel. (207) 594-2419, carries hand-me-downs plus overstocks from a big-name

sportswear outfitter; proceeds benefit people with disabilities. Open all year.

In Rockport, less than a mile north of Rockland's city limits, you'll find the **Dexter Shoe Factory Outlet,** 1070 Commercial St., Rockport 04856, tel. (207) 594-2001, where you can buy casual and dress shoes at reduced rates. The store is open daily most of the year.

Natural Foods/Farmers' Market
An old-fashioned cooperative where members "do time" in return for reduced rates, the **Good Tern Co-op,** 216 S. Main St., Rockland 04841, tel. (207) 594-9286, carries lots of bulk grains and nuts, plus organic produce and frozen foods. Nonmembers pay slightly higher prices. Open Mon.-Sat. 9:30 a.m.-6 p.m. (to 5 p.m. Saturday). Several other good sources of natural foods and vitamins are a few miles up Rt. 1 in Rockport and Camden.

The **Rockland Farmers' Market** gets underway each Thursday 9 a.m.-noon, June-Sept., in the side parking lot at Harbor Plaza, opposite Shaw's Supermarket, Rt. 1, Rockland. Wares include produce, crafts, baked goods, cheeses, and occasionally a llama or goat for the kids to pet.

ACCOMMODATIONS

If you're planning an overnight stay in the Rockland area the first weekend in August—during the Maine Lobster Festival—*be sure* to make reservations well in advance. Festival attendance runs well over 50,000, No Vacancy signs extend from Waldoboro to Belfast, and there just aren't enough beds or campsites to go around.

Samoset Resort
The 230-acre waterfront Samoset Resort, 220 Warrenton St., Rockport 04856, tel. (207) 594-2511 or (800) 341-1650 outside Maine, straddles the boundary between Rockland and Rockport, the next town to the north. Built on the ashes of a classic, 19th-century summer hotel, the Samoset is a top-of-the-line modern resort with knockout ocean views from most of its 150 rooms and suites, plus separate condos. Conferences go on here throughout the year, but

it's also a great family place—with special-package rates, indoor and outdoor swimming pools, fitness center, lighted tennis courts, cross-country skiing, kids' programs, golf simulator, and a fabulous 18-hole waterfront golf course. The elegant, bay-view Marcel's Restaurant has an ambitious, pricey menu; jackets are required for dinner, and reservations are a good idea. It's open for breakfast, lunch, and dinner. The best deal is Sunday brunch—a huge, all-you-can-eat buffet. Marcel's is open Mon.-Sat. 7-11 a.m., 11:30 a.m.-2 p.m., and 6-9 p.m.; Sunday hours are 7-11 a.m., noon-2 p.m., and 6-9 p.m. More casual is the Breakwater Lounge, with a good selection of light fare, live entertainment, and a fabulous water-view patio area (weather permitting). The lounge is open 11:30 a.m.-10 p.m. for lunch and dinner, to 12:30 a.m. for drinks.

Peak-season (early July-Labor Day) doubles are $220-305, off-season rates (late Oct.-mid-May) are $105-150. Rooms have phones, cable TV, a/c, and lots of other amenities; no pets. Modern condos and townhouses are available by the day or week.

Motels

Directly opposite the ferry terminal for boats going to the islands of Vinalhaven, North Haven, and Matinicus, the 80-room **Navigator Motor Inn,** 520 Main St., Rockland 04841, tel. (207) 594-2131, fax 594-7763, is a five-story shingled place with cable TV, a/c, phones, and laundry facilities. Upper-floor rooms have plenty of space and good views of the harbor, but be prepared for traffic noise from the parking lot and street. Rates are $35-95 d, depending on the season. A bright, modern restaurant serves good, reasonably priced food, 6:30 a.m.-2 p.m. and 5-9:30 p.m. Open all year.

Rockland abuts Rockport, and several Rockport motels are close to Rockland's city limits.

B&Bs

Across the street from the ferry terminal (and next door to the Navigator Motor Inn), the turn-of-the-19th-century **Old Granite Inn,** 546 Main St., Rockland 04841, tel. (207) 594-9036 or (800) 386-9036, is a downright fun place to stay, thanks to congenial innkeepers Stephanie and John Clapp. John's a sculptor, Stephanie's an accomplished chef, and both are longtime

sailors. Quilts, plants, artwork, books, and wonderful family antiques give the 11 rooms their homey and whimsical touches. The inn is on Rt. 1, but thick granite walls subdue traffic noise, so rooms are quiet. (Request a back or side room if you're worried.) Several rooms are wheelchair-accessible. For island-goers, the Clapps know Vinalhaven (and Rockland) inside-out. Breakfast is "heavy continental"; no one goes hungry. No smoking, no pets; three-day minimum during the Maine Lobster Festival. Rates are $60-120 d (mostly private baths). Open all year.

Filled with reproduction furnishings and unusual touches, **The LimeRock Inn,** 96 Limerock St., Rockland 04841, tel. (207) 594-2257 or (800) 546-3762, is an 1890s National Historic Register mansion on a quiet street. Each of the eight rooms has its own distinctive flavor—such as the Turret Room with a wedding canopy bed and the Island Cottage Room with a private deck overlooking the back gardens. No pets, no smoking. Rooms go for $85-180 d, including breakfast in the Victorian dining room. Open year-round, but call ahead in midwinter.

Opened in 1996, the **Capt. Lindsey House Inn,** 5 Lindsey St., Rockland 04841, tel. (207) 596-7950 or (800) 999-7352, fax (207) 236-0585, dates back to 1837. The Barnes family (owners of the adjacent Waterworks Pub and two local cruise boats) gutted the handsome brick structure and restored it dramatically, adding such modernities as phones, a/c, and TV. The library has a desk and computer port. Antiques fill the nine comfortable rooms, all with private baths. Rates are $95-160 d, including breakfast. Combination inn/boat/dinner packages are available. No smoking, no pets, no kids under 12. Open all year.

Campgrounds

There are no campgrounds in Rockland; the closest good ones are in Rockport, Camden, and Thomaston.

FOOD

Breakfast, Lunch, and Miscellanea

It used to be tough to find anything more than run-of-the-mill lunch fare in Rockland; now it's tough to make a decision. The prize for most-creative breakfasts and lunches goes to **The Brown Bag,** 606 Main St., Rockland 04841, tel. (207) 596-6372, bakery tel. (207) 596-6392, which has grown from a single room in 1987 to two rooms and a bakery (plus a branch in Brewer). Operated by a team of energetic sisters, The Brown Bag is *the* place for breakfast, especially weekends, with fantastic baked goods and a full blackboard of other options. Lunches include a half-dozen veggie choices and imaginative salads. This is a great place to assemble a picnic. Order at the counter; no table service, no credit cards, no smoking. Open Mon.-Sat. 6:30 a.m.-4 p.m., Sunday 7 a.m.-2 p.m. The bakery is open Mon.-Sat. 6:30 a.m.-5:30 p.m. (to 4 p.m. Saturday).

Backed up against an outside wall of The Brown Bag is a longstanding Rockland lunch landmark—**Wasses Hot Dogs,** 2 N. Main St., Rockland 04841, tel. (207) 594-7472, source of great chili dogs and creative ice cream (in waffle cones). This onetime lunch wagon is now a permanent modular building—only for takeout, though. It's open all year, Mon.-Sat. 10:30 a.m.-6 p.m. and Sunday 11 a.m.-4 p.m. Branch "wagons" carry on the tradition in Camden, Belfast, Thomaston, and the south end of Rockland.

Lots of Rockland-watchers credit **Second Read Books & Coffee,** 328 Main St., Rockland 04841, tel. (207) 594-4123, with sparking the designer-food renaissance in town. In 1995, it outgrew its original space and moved into this high-ceilinged room in a historic downtown block. Whether it's a panini sandwich for lunch, a scone, or just a latte, you won't be rushed. Order at the counter, then peruse the shelves of "preread books" while you wait. In a very short time, Second Read has become an institution. Open all year, Mon.-Sat. 7:30 a.m.-5:30 p.m. (to 10 p.m. Friday and Saturday), Sunday noon-5 p.m. Check local papers (or call) for a schedule of live entertainment, including Irish music, acoustic acts, and poetry readings.

Two other popular lunch spots are the bayview patio at the **Samoset Resort's Breakwater Lounge** and the casual restaurant at the Navigator Motor Inn. The Navigator and The Brown Bag are especially convenient to the Maine State Ferry Service terminal and the Concord Trailways bus stop.

Inexpensive to Moderate

When you're *really* famished, the place to go is **Conte's Fish Market & Restaurant,** Harbor Park, off Main St., Rockland 04841, tel. (207) 596-5579, where portions are humongous and prices are not. John Conte moved here from New York in 1995, bringing his family's century-old restaurant tradition. Specialties are pasta and seafood—Italian all the way, loaded with garlic. Beer and wine only. The decor is wildly funky—fishnets, marine relics, old books, even stacks of canned plum tomatoes—all with a terrific view of Rockland Harbor. Menus are hand-written, table coverings are yesterday's newspapers, and operatic arias sometimes play in the background. Reservations only for six or more, so you may have to wait on summer weekends. Open daily for lunch and dinner, all year.

Moderate to Expensive

For a front-row seat on the harbor, try for an outdoor table at **The Landings Restaurant,** 1 Commercial Dr., Rockland 04841, tel. (207) 596-6563, where seafood is the prime matter but you can get everything from blueberry pancakes to hefty sandwiches to lobster dinners. Prices are reasonable. Open 7 a.m.-9 p.m., mid-May to Columbus Day.

Cleverly retrofitted from an old brick garage, **The Waterworks Pub and Restaurant,** 5 Lindsey St., Rockland 04841, tel. (207) 596-7950, serves up good pub fare—fish 'n' chips and shepherd's pie—plus fish cakes, burgers, and a broad selection of designer brews. Eat at long tables in the pub or small tables in the more sedate dining area. Open Mon.-Sat. 11 a.m.-10 p.m., Sunday noon-10 p.m. The pub is next door to the owners' Capt. Lindsey House Inn.

Café Miranda, 15 Oak St., Rockland 04841, tel. (207) 594-2034, is summed up in its slogan, "We do not serve the food of cowards." This popular, casual place is terrific—and moderately priced—if a bit avant-garde for kids and timid adults. Lots of pastas, smoked items, veggies, olive oil, greens, and way-out combinations. Focaccia comes with every meal. If you sit at the counter, you can watch the creations emerging from the brick oven. Beer and wine only. No smoking. Reservations advisable in summer, on weekends, and whenever a good flick is playing at the nearby cinema. Open early Feb.-Dec., Tues.-Sun. 5:30-9 p.m.

Swiss chef Hans Bucher has a Midas touch that keeps the customers coming to **Jessica's: A European Bistro,** 2 S. Main St., Rt. 73, Rockland 04841, tel. (207) 596-0770, one of Maine's best restaurants—set up in five rooms of an air-conditioned Victorian home. Specialties include veal Zurich, lamb Provençale, and a variety of pasta and focaccia entrées. Reservations essential July and August, recommended other times. There's a children's menu, but squirmy children may be uncomfortable in these relatively small rooms. Open all year, 5:30-9 p.m. Closed Tuesday off season.

Also see "Samoset Resort," above, under "Accommodations," for info about **Marcel's.**

Lobster-in-the-Rough

Although several Rockland restaurants serve lobster dinners, the best, closest alfresco spots for pigging out on the delicious crustaceans are several wharves on the St. George Peninsula.

INFORMATION AND SERVICES

The **Rockland-Thomaston Area Chamber of Commerce,** Harbor Park, off S. Main St., P.O. Box 508, Rockland 04841, tel. (207) 596-0376 or (800) 562-2529, fax (207) 596-6549, with a very welcoming staff, occupies its own little cupola-topped building on Rockland's waterfront. It's open daily in summer, weekdays off season.

The handsome stone **Rockland Public Library,** Union St., Rockland 04841, tel. (207) 594-0310, has been a local landmark since 1904, when townsfolk received a $20,000 Carnegie grant to jump-start its construction. The library is open Mon.-Tues. 9 a.m.-8 p.m., Wed.-Fri. 9 a.m.-5:30 p.m. Best time to visit is Tuesday or Thursday afternoon (1-5 p.m.) or Saturday morning (9 a.m.-noon), when you can pick up real used-book bargains at the library's lower-level **Book Stop** and help out the library at the same time.

Newspapers

The only statewide daily newspaper with a Rockland office is the *Bangor Daily News,* 7 Limerock St., Rockland 04841, tel. (207) 596-6688.

Local news, features, and calendar listings appear in Rockland's *Courier-Gazette,* published three times weekly, tel. (207) 594-4401. *The Free Press,* a free weekly, tel. (207) 596-0055, has even more extensive calendar listings.

Emergencies

The closest hospital is on the Rockland/Rockport boundary. **Penobscot Bay Medical Center,** Rt. 1, Rockport 04856, tel. (207) 596-8000, has round-the-clock emergency-room care and all private rooms. For minor emergencies, **Qwik Care,** 231 Main St., Rockland 04841, tel. (207) 596-7838, a walk-in clinic, is open Wednesday 6-7 p.m. and Sat.-Sun. 9 a.m.-noon. For **police, fire, and ambulance,** dial 911.

Public Restrooms

You'll find public restrooms at the **chamber of commerce building,** the **Knox County Court House,** Union and Masonic Sts., the **Rockland Recreation Center,** across from the court house, next to the playground, Union and Limerock Sts., and the **Maine State Ferry Service terminal.**

Special Courses

Part of the international Outward Bound network, **Hurricane Island Outward Bound School,** P.O. Box 429, Rockland 04841, tel. (207) 594-5548 or (800) 541-1744, was founded in 1964 as a maritime adjunct to the national program. Maine sea courses take place on offshore Hurricane Island, a former granite-quarrying site; land-based courses are held around Newry, in western Maine's mountains. An extensive course catalog is available.

Begun in 1986 to provide language classes for adults, **Penobscot School,** 28 Gay St., Rockland 04841, tel. (207) 594-1084, fax 594-1067, has become a multicultural clearinghouse with ties around the globe. School founder Julia Schulz, always alert to new opportunities, has managed to heighten cultural awareness among statewide corporations, state government, and local service organizations. In fall, winter, and spring, the school offers day and evening courses in 6-10 languages, sponsors ethnic dinners and festivals, organizes language-immersion weekends, and puts on international study programs in local schools. From July to September, international students (ages 18-65) arrive at the school for intensive three-week English-language courses. So many alumni have talked up the summer program that every opening has a waiting list. On summer weekdays, visitors are often invited for lunch at the school to interact with students practicing their English. Call for information.

Bay Island Sailing School, 120 Tillson Ave., Rockland 04841, tel. (207) 596-7550 or (800) 421-2492, is an American Sailing Association-approved summer program that has weekday, weekend, and live-aboard learn-to-sail classes —and special courses for teenagers and women. Contact the school for a course catalog.

Photo Services

Two local firms sell film and provide one-hour photo services. **P.D.Q.** (Prints Done Quickly), 491 Main St., Rockland 04841, tel. (207) 594-5010, close to the Maine State Ferry Service terminal, also does passport photos. Near McDonald's, **Thuss Photo & Video** formerly Take One Photo & Video, 80 Camden St., Rockland 04841, tel. (207) 594-4310, also rents videos and offers drive-up service. Open Mon.-Sat. 9 a.m.-9 p.m., Sunday 11 a.m.-9 p.m.

Laundromats

Across from the fire station, **Park St. Laundromat & Dry Cleaners,** 117 Park St., Rockland 04841, tel. (207) 594-9393, lets you do your own or they'll do it for you. Open daily 7 a.m.-9 p.m. Across from McDonald's, **Garden Island Cleaners and Laundry,** 44 Maverick St., Rockland 04841, tel. (207) 596-0001, with plenty of self-service machines, is open daily 7 a.m.-9 p.m. (to 7 p.m. Sunday).

Getting Around

Coastal Trans, tel. (207) 596-6605, a nonprofit organization, operates a weekday, wheelchair-accessible van service throughout Rockland, 8:15 a.m.-3:30 p.m., with a dozen regular stops (signposted Rockland Shuttle). One-way fare is $1.50; roundtrip (good for unlimited rides all day) is $3 (exact change required). Other special intown services are available, as well as transport from outlying communities. Call for a schedule.

Two efficient **taxi** services are active in Rockland and the surrounding areas. Telephone for a pickup. **Ben's Windjammer Taxi,** tel. (207) 594-4545, operates daily until 2:30 a.m. **Schooner Bay Taxi,** tel. (207) 594-5000 or (800) 539-5001, fax (207) 594-4999, provides round-the-clock service. Taxis usually are available at the Maine State Ferry Service terminal (where Concord Trailways buses from Boston and Portland also stop), but there's no outside pay phone when the ferry terminal shuts down for the night. The Rockland taxis are accustomed to making runs to Port Clyde for the ferry to Monhegan.

Camden-based **Mid-Coast Limo,** tel. (800) 937-2424, provides van service, by reservation, between Rockland and Portland International Jetport.

Besides connecting Rockland with Vinalhaven, North Haven, and Matinicus, the **Maine State Ferry Service** has car ferries to Islesboro, Swans Island, and Frenchboro. For private passenger ferries to Monhegan, see the St. George Peninsula section. (Longer passenger-ferry trips to Monhegan depart from New Harbor and Boothbay Harbor.)

ROCKLAND'S FERRY-LINKED ISLANDS

Penobscot Bay's three major year-round islands are Vinalhaven, North Haven, and Matinicus. Each has its own distinct personality. To generalize, Vinalhaven is the largest and busiest, while North Haven is sedate and exclusive. Matinicus is a bit frontier-like. The Rockland terminal of the Maine State Ferry Service serves all three of the islands, although service to Matinicus operates only a few times a month in summer. Charter air service (not inexpensive) is available to the islands via Penobscot Air Service (PAS) from Knox County Regional Airport in Owls Head, just south of Rockland. (PAS also provides grocery delivery from Shaw's Supermarket in Rockland.)

VINALHAVEN

Five miles wide, seven and a half miles long, and covering some 10,000 acres, Vinalhaven is 13 miles off the coast of Rockland—a 75-minute ferry trip. The shoreline has so many zigs and zags that no place on the island is more than a mile from water.

With a full-time population of about 1,200 souls, Vinalhaven is a serious working community, not primarily a playground. Nearly 200 fishermen bring in lobsters, urchins, shrimp, and scallops; shopkeepers cater to locals as well as visitors; and increasing numbers of artists and artisans beaver away in their studios. For day-trippers, there's plenty to do—shopping, picnicking, hiking, biking, swimming—but an overnight stay provides a chance to sense the unique rhythm of life on a year-round island.

The Maine State Ferry Service, tel. (207) 596-2202, operates six roundtrips daily to Vinalhaven in summer ($9 adults, $4 kids, roundtrip), fewer runs in winter. The ferry takes cars, but a bicycle ($8 roundtrip per adult bike, $4 for a child's bike) will do fine unless you have the time or inclination to see every corner of the island. Besides, getting car space on the ferry during high season can be a frustrating experience. If you're not spending the night on the island, watch the clock so you don't miss the last

boat back to Rockland.

There's no official ferry service between Vinalhaven and North Haven, even though the two islands are almost within spitting distance. An informal on-demand service was shut down by the Coast Guard in 1996, so you'll need to inquire in Rockland, or when you get to the islands. Don't let anyone convince you to return to Rockland for the ferry to the other island. If nothing else, ask around at the dock in Carver's Harbor.

History

Vinalhaven and neighboring North Haven have been known as the Fox Islands ever since 1603, when English explorer Martin Pring sailed these waters and allegedly spotted gray foxes in his search for sustenance. Nowadays, you'll find reference to that name only on nautical charts, identifying the passage between the two islands as the Fox Islands Thorofare—and there's nary a fox in sight.

Vinalhaven's earliest known resident was one David Wooster, in 1762, but the first permanent non-Indian settlement here seems to have sprung up around 1765. The Thaddeus Carver family—for whom Carver's Harbor is named—arrived a few years later, and as the population increased, lumbering became the major industry. In 1789, the town was incorporated, and soon thereafter, residents were collecting taxes, subsidizing the indigent, and hiring a minister and a schoolteacher.

Vinalhaven granite first headed for Boston around 1826, and within a few decades, quarrymen arrived from as far away as Britain and Finland to wrestle out and shape the incredibly resistant stone. Schooners, barges, and "stone sloops" left Carver's Harbor carrying mighty cargoes of granite destined for government and commercial buildings in Boston, New York, and Washington, D.C. In the 1880s, nearly 4,000 people lived on Vinalhaven, North Haven, and Hurricane Island. After World War I, demand declined, granite gave way to concrete and steel, and the industry petered out and died. But Vinalhaven has left its mark—ornate columns, paving

blocks, and curbstones in communities as far west as Kansas City.

Sights

One Main Street landmark that's hard to miss is the three-story, cupola-topped **Odd Fellows Hall,** a Victorian behemoth with assorted gewgaws in the streetfront display windows. Artist Robert Indiana, who first arrived as a visitor in 1969, owns the structure, built in 1885 for the IOOF Star of Hope Lodge. Other artists have come to Vinalhaven in Indiana's footsteps, either as summer folk or year-rounders, including Pat Nick, whose **Vinalhaven Press,** renowned for its printmaking expertise, attracts master printers and prominent artists to a topflight summer program.

At the top of the hill just beyond Main Street (corner of School and East Main Sts.) is a greenish-blue replica **galamander,** a massive reminder of Vinalhaven's late-19th-century granite-quarrying era. Galamanders, hitched to oxen or horses, carried the stone from island quarries to the finishing shops. (by the way, the origin of the name remains unexplained.) Next to the galamander is a colorful wooden bandstand, site of very popular evening band concerts held sporadically during the summer.

The unusually energetic **Vinalhaven Historical Society,** tel. (207) 863-4410 or 863-4318, operates a museum in the onetime town hall on High St., just east of Carver's Cemetery. The building itself has a tale, having been floated across the bay from Rockland, where it served as a Universalist church. The museum's documents and artifacts on the granite industry are particularly intriguing, and special summer exhibits add to the interest. Open daily 11 a.m.-3 p.m., mid-June to mid-September, by appointment other times until mid-October. Admission is free, but donations are welcomed. At the museum, request a copy of *A Self-Guided Walking Tour of the Town of Vinalhaven and Its Granite-Quarrying History,* a handy little brochure that details 17 intown locations related to the late-19th and early-20th-century industry.

Built in 1832 and now owned by the town of Vinalhaven, **Brown's Head Light** guards the southern entrance to the Fox Islands Thorofare. To reach the grounds (no access to the light itself; the keeper's house is a private residence), take the North Haven Rd. about six miles, at which point you'll see a left-side view of the Camden Hills. Continue to the second road on the left, Crockett River Road. Turn and take the second road on the right, continuing past the Brown's Head Cemetery to the hill overlooking the lighthouse.

Parks and Preserves

No, you're not on the Devonshire moors, but you could be fooled in the 45-acre **Lane's Island Preserve.** Masses of low-lying ferns, Rugosa roses, and berry bushes cover the granite outcrops of this sanctuary—and a foggy day makes it even more moorlike and mystical, a Brontë novel setting. Best (albeit busiest) time to come is early August, when you can compete with the birds for blackberries, raspberries, and blueberries. Easy trails wind past old stone walls, an aged cemetery, and along the surf-pounded shore. The preserve is a 20-minute walk (or five-minute bike ride) from Vinalhaven's ferry landing. Set off to the right on Main St., through the village. Turn right onto Water St., then right on Atlantic Avenue. Continue across the causeway on Lane's Island Rd. and left over a saltmarsh to the preserve. The large white house on the harbor side of Lane's Island, formerly an inn, is privately owned.

Next to the ferry landing in Carver's Harbor is **Grimes Park,** a wooded, vest-pocket retreat with a splendid view of the harbor. Owned by the American Legion, the two-and-a-half-acre park is perfect for picnics or for hanging out (especially in good weather) between boats.

Just behind the Island Community Medical Center, close to downtown, is 30-acre **Armbrust Hill Town Park,** once the site of granite-quarrying operations. Still pockmarked with quarry pits, the park has beautifully landscaped walking paths and native flowers, shrubs, and trees—much of it thanks to late island resident Betty Roberts, who made this a lifelong endeavor. From the back of the medical center, follow the trail to the summit for a southerly view of Matinicus and other offshore islands. If you're with children, be especially careful about straying onto side paths, which go perilously close to old quarry holes. Before the walk, lower the children's energy level at the large playground off to the left of the trail. The creative climbing structure is bound to wear 'em down.

Recreation

Vinalhaven is loaded with wonderful hikes and walks, some deliberately unpublicized. Since the mid-1980s, the foresighted **Vinalhaven Land Trust,** P.O. Box 268, Vinalhaven 04863, tel. (207) 863-2543, has expanded the opportunities. When you reach the island, inquire at the land trust's seasonal office at **Skoog Memorial Park,** Sands Cove Rd., west of the ferry terminal, or at the town office or the Paper Store. Some hiking options are the **Perry Creek Preserve** (terrific loop trail), **Middle Mountain, Tip-Toe Mountain, Polly Cove Preserve, Arey's Neck Woods,** and **Sunset Rock Park.** Even better, join the land trust and support its efforts; annual dues are only $5.

The Maine chapter of **The Nature Conservancy,** 14 Maine St., Fort Andross, Brunswick 04011, tel. (207) 729-5181, owns or manages several islands and island clusters near Vinalhaven. **Big Garden** (formerly owned by Charles and Anne Morrow Lindbergh) and **Big White Islands** are easily accessible and great for shoreline picnics if you have your own boat. Other Conservancy holdings in this area are fragile environments, mostly nesting islands off-limits from mid-March to mid-August. Contact the Conservancy for specifics.

Swimming: Abandoned quarries are all over the island, and most are on private property, but two town-owned ones are easy to reach from the ferry landing. **Lawson's Quarry,** on the North Haven Rd., is about a mile from downtown; **Booth's Quarry** is on Pequot Rd., one and a half miles from downtown. Both are signposted. You'll see plenty of swimmers and sunbathers-on-the-rocks on a hot day, but there are no lifeguards, so swimming is at your own risk. There are no restrooms or changing rooms.

Down the side road beyond Booth's Quarry is **Narrows Park,** a town-owned space looking out toward Narrows Island, Isle au Haut, and, on a clear day, Mount Desert Island.

For saltwater swimming, continue along Pequot Rd. about one and a half miles beyond Booth's Quarry. At the crossroads, you'll see a whimsical bit of local folk art—the Coke lady sculpture. Turn right (east) and go half a mile to **Geary's Beach** (also called **State Beach**), where you can picnic and scour the shoreline for shells and sea glass.

Cycling: Even though Vinalhaven's 40 or so miles of public roads are narrow, winding, and poorly shouldered, they're relatively level, so a bicycle is a fine way to tour the island. Bring your own ($8 roundtrip on the ferry) or rent one at the **Tidewater Motel,** on Main St. near the ferry landing, tel. (207) 863-4618. You'll need to supply your own helmet. For repairs, track down **Pete Gasperini,** tel. (207) 863-4837. A wide selection of rental bikes (including helmets) is available on the mainland in Rockport at **Maine Sport Outfitters** Rt. 1, Rockport 04856, tel. (207) 236-8797, (800) 722-0826, fax (207) 236-7123.

A 10-mile, two-and-a-half-hour bicycle route begins on Main St. and goes clockwise out the North Haven Rd., past Lawson's Quarry, to Round the Island Rd., then Poor Farm Rd. to Geary's Beach and back to Main St. via Pequot Rd. and School Street. Carry a picnic and enjoy it on Lane's Island; stop for a swim in one of the quarries; or detour down to Brown's Head Light. If you're here for the day, keep track of the time so you don't miss the ferry.

Entertainment

No one visits Vinalhaven for nightlife, but you can get in some bowling or pool at **Candlepin Lodge,** Roberts Cemetery Rd., tel. (207) 863-2730, a log cabin about half a mile from the ferry wharf. Live music is occasionally on the agenda, and dinners are served Friday and Saturday 6-9 p.m. For the kids, there are burgers, fries, and ice cream. Open all year, Tues.-Fri. 5-10 p.m. and Sunday noon-10 p.m.

Shopping

The Paper Store, Main St., tel. (207) 863-4826, carries newspapers, gifts, film, and odds and ends. **Carver's Harbor Market,** Main St., tel. (207) 863-4319, is a full-service supermarket and the only island source for bottled liquor. Take-out sandwiches are available in summer. Both stores are open all year.

Next to Carver's Cemetery and the Vinalhaven Historical Society, **Vinalhaven Grocery,** High St., tel. (207) 863-4301, stocks an amazing selection of fresh produce and meat, plus baked goods and take-out food. Open daily Mon.-Fri. 7 a.m.-6 p.m., Saturday 8 a.m.-6 p.m., and Sunday 9 a.m.-4 p.m., all year. On winter weekends, the store sometimes closes a bit earlier.

Interesting year-round shops on Main Street include **Island Home and Garden,** tel. (207) 863-2020, carrying garden gear, vegetables, antiques, and beautiful sweaters; and **L.R. Smith Co.,** tel. (207) 863-4655, which sells clothing, including Vinalhaven T-shirts.

Seasonal shops worth a stop are **Winter-Long Herbs,** tel. (207) 867-9978, and **Everything Country,** tel. (207) 863-9934 or 863-4819.

Midway between the ferry landing and the downtown area is the eminently browsable **Harbor Wharf** complex, an eclectic handful of low-key shops, art galleries, and eateries.

Accommodations

Vinalhaven isn't overrun with spare beds, so if you plan to spend the night (or stay longer), especially between mid-July and mid-August, be sure to make a reservation. If you're going for the day, pay attention to the ferry schedule and allow enough time to get back to the boat. Islanders may be able to find you a bed in a pinch, but don't count on it. There are no campsites on the island.

B&Bs: Informality is the key at **The Fox Island Inn,** Carver St., P.O. Box 451, Vinalhaven 04863, tel. (207) 863-2122, winter phone (904) 878-2643, a comfortable B&B on a quiet side street. Innkeeper Gail Reinertsen, a dedicated marathoner, has several bicycles available for guests, who can also use the kitchen for packing a picnic or fixing a snack. Four first-floor rooms share one and a half baths; upstairs is a suite (or two separate rooms). Doubles go for $45-55; the two room suite is $65. No smoking, no pets, no credit cards, no children under eight. The inn is a 12-minute walk from the ferry landing, so if your luggage is heavy, ask Gail about taxi service. From the ferry, go right, through the village on Main St., then take a left onto Carver Street. Open June through September.

Other seasonal B&Bs, both convenient to downtown, are **The Libby House,** Water St., Vinalhaven 04853, tel. (207) 863-4696; $60-100 d, open summer only; and the **Payne Homestead at the Moses Webster House,** Atlantic Ave., Box 216, Vinalhaven 04863, tel. (207) 863-9963 or (888) 863-9963; $75-100 d; open May-Oct.; no credit cards.

Motels: Your feet practically touch the water when you spend the night at the **Tidewater Motel,** Main St., Carver's Harbor, P.O. Box 29, Vinalhaven 04863, tel. (207) 863-4618, a well-maintained, modernized building cantilevered over the harbor. Owned by Phil and Elaine Crossman, the 11-room motel (with private baths) was built by Phil's parents in 1970. It's a great place to sit on the deck and watch the lobsterboats do their thing. Be aware, though, that commercial fishermen are early risers, and lobsterboat engines can rev up as early as 4:30 on a summer morning—all part of the pace of Vinalhaven. Doubles are $55-95, depending on the season; kids 10 and under are free; five units are efficiencies. No smoking, no pets, no credit cards. Rental bikes are available for $10 a day or $5 a half-day; you'll need your own helmet. Open all year.

Seasonal Rentals: The best resource for weekly and monthly "camp," cottage, and village house rentals is **Vinalhaven Rentals,** RR 1, Box 792, Vinalhaven 04863, tel. (207) 863-2241, fax 863-2763, run by Frank and Ada Thompson.

Food

The island's best dinner spot is **The Haven,** Main St., tel. (207) 863-4969, with a great harbor view and a creative menu that changes nightly in summer. Two seatings—6 and 8:15 p.m.—by reservation, Tues.-Saturday. The restaurant's streetside room, serving Tues.-Sat. 6-9 p.m., is more casual and less creative; no reservations, so you may need to wait, especially on summer weekends. No smoking in either section.

When The Haven is closed (Sunday and Monday), head for Candlepin Lodge or **The Sand Dollar,** Main St., tel. (207) 863-9937, an unpredictable sort of place that dishes up huge portions. It's open 5:30-8:30 p.m. (to 9 p.m. Friday and Saturday). Saturday is prime-rib night; BYOL.

Opposite the municipal parking lot, the **Harbor Gawker,** Main St., tel. (207) 863-9365, is a tiny, hole-in-the-wall take-out stand that's been a local landmark since 1975. On the menu are burgers, lobster rolls, sandwich baskets, terrific fish chowder (by the cup, pint, or quart), and soft ice cream. Open daily 10:30 a.m.-8 p.m. (to 9 p.m. July and August), early May into October.

Also on Main Street is **The Islander Restaurant,** tel. (207) 863-2028, open daily 5-10 a.m. for breakfast, Mon.-Fri. 11 a.m.-2 p.m. for lunch, and Tues.-Sat. 6-9 p.m. for dinner. The **Pizza Pit,** Harbor Wharf, tel. (207) 863-4311, serves a full menu Wed.-Sun. 4-9 p.m. Each year, one or two take-out wagons also dish out food-on-the-run.

Information and Services

Vinalhaven's version of a chamber of commerce is the **Vinalhaven Community Council,** P.O. Box 548, Vinalhaven 04863, which, along with the Tidewater Motel, produces a helpful little island booklet full of facts, tips, maps, and dates. For a copy, write the council or call the **Vinalhaven Town Office,** tel. (207) 863-4471 or 863-4393. It's also available at the Rockland-Thomaston Area Chamber of Commerce.

Vinalhaven's weekly newsletter, *The Wind,* P.O. Box 194, Vinalhaven 04863, tel. (207) 863-2158, named after the island's original newspaper, first published in 1884, is loaded with island flavor: news items, public-supper announcements, editorials, and ads. A year's subscription is $25; single copies are available in several downtown locales.

The **Vinalhaven Public Library,** E. Main and Chestnut Sts., tel. (207) 863-4401, a distinctive, Carnegie-funded granite building built in 1906, is open Tuesday and Thursday 1-5 p.m. and 6-8 p.m., Wednesday and Friday 9 a.m.-noon and 1-5 p.m., Saturday 9 a.m.-1 p.m.

The **Maine State Ferry Service** office on Vinalhaven is at the Carver's Harbor ferry landing, tel. (207) 863-4421, or call the Rockland terminal, (207) 596-2202.

There's a **bank** with an ATM on the island. **Public restrooms** are at the ferry landing and the town office, but the town office is only open a few hours on weekdays.

Emergencies
The **Island Community Medical Center,** Armbrust Hill, Vinalhaven 04863, tel. (207) 863-4341, on the hill just beyond the downtown area, coordinates medical facilities on the island and has a full-time doctor. Critical cases are ferried or airlifted from the island's tiny airstrip to Rockland or Portland. To report a **fire,** call (207) 863-2255.

NORTH HAVEN

Eight miles long by three miles wide, North Haven is 12 miles off the coast of Rockland—an hour by ferry. The island boasts sedate summer homes, open fields where hundreds of sheep once grazed, about 350 year-round residents, a yacht club called the Casino, and a village gift shop that's been here since 1954.

Originally called North Island, North Haven had much the same settlement history as Vinalhaven, but, being smaller (about 5,280 acres) and more fertile, it has developed—or not developed—differently. It was one of the landforms dubbed the Fox Islands by explorer Martin Pring in 1603. David Wooster, considered Vinalhaven's earliest white settler, is accorded the same distinction for North Haven. But carbon dating of shell middens (mounds) piled up by Native Americans has shown that Pring's and Wooster's precursors were here as early as 3300 B.C.

In 1846, North Haven was incorporated and severed politically from Vinalhaven, and by the late 1800s, the Boston summer crowd began buying up traditional island homes, building tastefully unpretentious new ones, and settling in for a whole season of sailing and socializing. Several generations later, "summer folk" now come for weeks rather than months, often rotating the schedules among slews of siblings. Informality remains the key, though—now more than ever.

The island has two distinct hamlets—North Haven Village, on the Fox Islands Thorofare, where the state ferry arrives, and Pulpit Harbor, particularly popular with the yachting set.

North Haven Village
Fanning out from the ferry landing is a delightful cluster of substantial, year-round clapboard homes—a marked contrast to the weathered-shingle cottages typical of so many island communities. It won't take long to stroll Main Street, but you'll want a camera.

Anchoring the cluster of shops "downtown" is the **North Haven Gift Shop,** Main St., tel. (207) 867-4444, a rabbit warren of rooms that June Hopkins has been running since 1954. No problem spending money here—everything's tastefully selected, from the pottery to the notecards to the books, jewelry, and gourmet condiments. One room is a gallery, with work by Maine artists. Open Mon.-Sat. 9:30 a.m.-5 p.m.

Next door (connected via an elevated corridor) is the **Eric Hopkins Gallery,** Main St., tel. (207) 867-2229 or 867-4401, owned by June Hopkins's son, a megatalented painter who's gained a repute far beyond Maine. If you can't spring for an original (figure on several thousand dollars), his distinctive work—luminous bird's-eye views of island, sea, and forest—now appears also on notecards, postcards, T-shirts, and one-of-a-kind sweaters. Open daily 10 a.m.-5 p.m., July and August, other times by appointment.

Just down the street is **Brown's Market,** Main St., tel. (207) 867-9933, a chummy sort of general store/coffeehouse where you can pick up almost anything imaginable, including picnic supplies and local gossip. A store specialty for anyone staying overnight (or longer) is the "welcome back sack": phone, fax, or mail your food order two weeks ahead and they'll have it ready when you get off the ferry. A free bag of cookies goes with the deal. The store is open all year, Mon.-Sat. 7 a.m.-6:30 p.m. and Sunday 10 a.m.-2 p.m.

Across the street is four-story, early-20th-century **Calderwood Hall,** Main St., tel. (207) 867-2265, artist Herb Parsons's eclectic gift shop/art gallery/entertainment center. It's open Memorial Day weekend to Columbus Day, Mon.-Sat. 10 a.m.-5 p.m. and Sunday 10:30 a.m.-4 p.m., and evenings when concerts, slide shows, poetry readings, and other events are on the agenda.

Golf
The nine-hole **North Haven Golf Club,** Waterman Cove, tel. (207) 867-2061, established in 1932, is open to the public June through September. Tee times usually aren't necessary, but you might want to call ahead to check. The scenic, well-maintained course overlooks Waterman Cove, about a 10-minute stroll from the North Haven Village ferry landing. If you don't take your car on the ferry, you'll need to walk to the links (unless someone gives you a lift), so keep your bag light.

Cycling
North Haven has about 25 miles of paved roads, but, just as on most other islands, they are narrow, winding, and nearly shoulderless. Starting near the ferry landing in North Haven Village, take South Shore Rd. eastward, perhaps stopping en route for a picnic at town-owned Mullin's Head Park (also spelled Mullen Head) on the southeast corner of the island. Then follow the road around, counterclockwise, to North Shore Rd. and Pulpit Harbor.

Sailing
If you have your own boat, this area is a sailor's nirvana. Be sure to have on board a copy of *A Cruising Guide to the Maine Coast* (see the Booklist).

Boat fanatics will enjoy peeking into the **J.O. Brown & Sons** boatshop, tel. (207) 867-4621, on the Thorofare in North Haven Village. It's a remnant of a bygone era, with the scents and feel of traditional craftsmanship. In the late 19th century, Brown's built the first **North Haven Dinghy,** a 14.5-foot wooden sailboat, and followed it with dozens more. The fleet has had a summer racing season here since the 1880s. The boatyard, by the way, has a laundromat and showers and also rents moorings. If you

need boat transportation across the Thorofare to Vinalhaven, someone at the shop may be able to help you out. It's open all year.

Accommodations and Food
Guest beds are scarce on North Haven; other than the summer folk, most visitors are day-trippers. The only inn/B&B is the **Pulpit Harbor Inn,** North Haven 04853, tel. (207) 867-2219, a small, veteran hostelry that's had an up-and-down track record in recent years.

Food choices are all in the middle of North Haven Village; the two seasonal restaurants always seem to be busy. Picnic fixings are available at Brown's Market. For a sit-down lunch (or breakfast or dinner), head for **Cooper's Landing,** Main St., tel. (207) 867-2060, where you can eat on the deck if the weather cooperates. It's open daily 7 a.m.-9 p.m., in July and August, weekends May-June and Sept.-October. Reservations are a good idea. No smoking, no credit cards. The **Coal Wharf Restaurant,** Main St., tel. (207) 867-4739, next to Brown's Boatshop, is a rustic seasonal eatery that can serve 60 at a time. It's open daily 6-9 p.m. in July and August, weekends in June and September. Reservations are wise. No smoking, no credit cards.

Information and Services
The best source of information is the **North Haven Town Office,** Upper Main St., North Haven 04853, tel. (207) 867-4433, fax 867-2207. It's open weekdays, all year. The shops closest to the ferry landing are accustomed to fielding questions, so try them for answers.

The **Maine State Ferry Service** office on North Haven is at the North Haven Village ferry landing, tel. (207) 867-4441, or call the Rockland terminal, tel. (207) 596-2202.

Emergencies
To reach the island's **doctor or physician's assistant,** call (207) 867-2021. Critical cases are airlifted from the island airstrip to a hospital in Rockland or Portland.

Getting There
The **Maine State Ferry Service,** tel. (207) 596-2202, operates three roundtrip car ferries a day, year-round, between Rockland and North Haven

Village. Roundtrip tickets are $9 adults, $4 kids, $8 adult bicycles. Even though the ferry carries cars, it can be tough to get space at peak times (midsummer and holiday weekends), so consider taking a bike instead. No rental bikes are available on the island. If you're not spending the night, watch the clock so you don't miss the last boat back to Rockland.

North Haven is also accessible via **Penob-scot Air Service,** P.O. Box 1286, Rockland 04841, tel. (207) 596-6211 or (800) 780-6071, fax (207) 594-8329, operating a fleet of six-passenger twin-engine planes out of the Knox County Regional Airport in Owls Head. One-way fare to North Haven is $50 for a single passenger, $75 for a family of five. The service operates all year, but weather can cancel a trip; call or write for details.

CAMDEN-ROCKPORT AREA

Driven apart by a local squabble in 1891, Camden and Rockport have been separate towns for a century, but they're inextricably linked. They share school and sewer systems and an often-hyphenated partnership. On Union St., just off Rt. 1, a white wooden arch reads Camden on one side and Rockport on the other. These days, this area is one of the Mid-Coast's —even Maine's—prime destinations.

Camden—the better known of the two—has a year-round population of about 5,000, but that triples during the summer months; Rockport, with a much lower profile, doubles in summer from about 2,900 year-round. While Rockport's harbor is relatively peaceful—with yachts, lobsterboats, and a single windjammer schooner—Camden Harbor is a summer-long madhouse, jammed with dinghies, kayaks, windjammers, megayachts, minor yachts, and a handful of fishing craft.

Much of Camden's appeal is its drop-dead-gorgeous setting—a deeply indented harbor with parks, a waterfall, and a dramatic backdrop of low mountains. It is views of Camden that typify Maine nationwide, even worldwide, on calendars and postcards, in photo books, you name it. This is one of those places seemingly created for summer tourism, but it's far more than that. An influx of well-situated retirees has tipped the median age balance in recent years, and the arrival of credit-card giant MBNA in 1993 created controversy that still simmers just beneath the surface. MBNA painted its many buildings an unsubtle dollar green and the suits are omnipresent, but MBNA funds have bolstered the coffers of towns and nonprofits throughout the area. So the jury's still out on the company's impact on the area, which extends to Lincolnville and Belfast.

HISTORY

Not very long ago—as recently as the 1970s, in fact—Camden was a sleepy mill town still reminiscing about its shipbuilding heyday at the turn of the century. The Holly M. Bean Shipyard had turned out stoutly crafted multimasted vessels, including the nation's first six-masted schooner, the 300-foot *George W. Wells,* which weighed nearly 3,000 tons when she was launched here, in 1900. During World War II, the Camden Shipbuilding yard was a hive of production for military tugs and minesweepers. Nowadays, Wayfarer Marine, a giant yachting enterprise, sprawls along the prime harborfront real estate.

In the late 1880s, Camden's proximity to steamer transport made it a destination of choice for urban industrialists scouting for summer retreats. Camden became a fair-weather colony for families with names such as Watson, Curtis, Bok, and Dillingham. Their handsome shingled "cottages" still line the outer harbor and the outer reaches of Chestnut and Bay View Sts.; many are occupied year-round.

Rockport has its own workaday heritage as the site of 19th-century kilns used to burn lime for the construction industry. Ship after ship took on the volatile powder and carried it off to cities all along the eastern seaboard. With the death of wooden ships and the decline of the lime industry, Rockport saw the birth of a summer music colony—prominent musicians who have left their considerable mark on the town. The Bay Chamber Concerts organization, founded in the 1960s, and Camden's Salzedo Harp Colony are impressive legacies of this tradition.

SIGHTS

Historical Tour
The **Camden-Rockport Historical Society** has produced a handy little brochure, *A Visitor's Tour,* detailing more than 50 significant historic sites in downtown Camden, Camden's High Street and Chestnut Street Historic Districts, and downtown Rockport. To cover it all, you'll want a car or bike; to cover segments—and really appreciate the architecture—don your walking shoes. Pick up a copy of the brochure at the chamber of commerce.

Old Conway Homestead and Museum
Just inside the Camden town line from Rockport, the Old Conway Homestead and Museum, Conway Rd., Camden, mailing address P.O. Box 747, Rockport 04856, tel. (207) 236-2257, is a five-building complex owned and run by the Camden-Rockport Historical Society. The 18th-century Cape-style **Conway House,** on the National Register of Historic Places, contains fascinating construction details and period furnishings; in the barn are carriages and farm tools. Two other buildings—a blacksmith shop and a 19th-century sap house, used for making maple syrup—have been moved to the grounds

Camden Harbor

and restored. In the contemporary **Mary Meeker Cramer Museum** (named for the prime benefactor) are displays from the historical society's collection of ship models, old documents, and period clothing. For local color, don't miss the Victorian outhouse. The complex is open early July through August, Tues.-Fri. 10 a.m.-4 p.m. Admission is $3 adults, $1.50 seniors, $1 teenagers, 50 cents kids 6-12. The museum and sap house are also open for maple-syrup demonstrations on Maine Maple Sunday (fourth Sunday in March).

Vesper Hill
Built and donated to the community by a local benefactor, the rustic, open-air **Vesper Hill Children's Chapel** is dedicated to the world's children. Overlooking Penobscot Bay and surrounded by gardens and lawns, the nondenominational chapel is an almost mystical oasis in a busy tourist region. Except during weddings or memorial services, there's seldom a crowd, and you might have the place to yourself. From Central St. in downtown Rockport, take Russell Ave. east to Calderwood Ln. (fourth street on right). On Calderwood, take the second right (Chapel St.) after the golf course. If the sign is down, look for a large rock with Vesper Hill carved in it. From downtown Camden, take Chestnut St. to just past Aldermere Farm; turn left at Calderwood Ln. and take the second right after the golf course.

Aldermere Farm, by the way, is the home of America's original herd of Belted Galloway cattle—Angus-like beef cattle with a wide white midriff. First imported from Scotland in 1953, the breed now shows up in pastures all over the United States. The animals' startling "oreo-cookie" hide pattern never fails to halt passersby—especially in spring and early summer, when the calves join their mothers in the pastures.

Maine Coast Artists
Once a local firehouse, this attractive building has been totally rehabbed to provide display space for the work of Maine's best contemporary artists. Nonprofit Maine Coast Artists, 162 Russell Ave., P.O. Box 147, Rockport 04856, tel. (207) 236-2875, fax 236-2490, mounts as many as a dozen shows each summer, along with special lectures, a wildly popular art auction (early August), an annual juried art exhibition featuring more than 100 selections, and an annual juried craft show (mid-October) spotlighting several dozen artisans. The prime exhibit season runs from early April to early November. Open Mon.-Sat. 10 a.m.-5 p.m. (to 8 p.m. Thursday), and Sunday noon-5 p.m., except Fourth of July and Labor Day. Admission is $2.

PARKS AND PRESERVES

For more than a century, the Camden-Rockport area has benefited from the providence of conscientious year-round and summertime conservationists. Thanks to their benevolence, countless acres of fragile habitat, woodlands, and scenic viewpoints have been preserved. Nowadays, the most active organization is the **Coastal Mountains Land Trust,** 18 Central St., P.O. Box 101, Rockport 04856, tel. (207) 236-7091, fax 236-0612, founded in 1986. Maps and information about trails open to the public are available at the office (open 8 a.m.-5 p.m.

weekdays, all year). Better still, join up; annual dues are $25.

Camden Hills State Park
A five-minute drive and a $2 pp fee gets you to the top of **Mount Battie**, centerpiece of 5,650-acre Camden Hills State Park, Belfast Rd., Rt. 1, tel. (207) 236-3109, and the best place to see why Camden is "where the mountains meet the sea." The summit panorama is, well, breathtaking, and reputedly the inspiration for Edna St. Vincent Millay's poem "Renascence" (a bronze plaque marks the spot); information boards identify the offshore islands. Climb the summit's stone tower for an even better view. The 20 miles of hiking trails (some for every ability) include two popular routes up Mt. Battie—an easy, hour-long hike from the base parking lot (Nature Trail) and a more strenuous 45-minute one from the top of Mt. Battie Street in Camden (Mount Battie Trail). Or drive up the paved Mount Battie Auto Road. The park has plenty of space for picnics, and the 112-site camping area (no hookups) is wheelchair-accessible. In winter, ice climbers use a rock wall near the Maiden's Cliff Trail, reached via Rt. 52 (Mountain Street). The park entrance is two miles north of downtown Camden—next to the long-term lot for The Camden Shuttle. Day-use admission is $2 adults, 50 cents children 5-11, free for children four and under. The nonresident camping fee is $15 per site per night; two-night minimum. Request a free trail map. The park is open mid-May to mid-October. Hiking trails are accessible all year, weather permitting.

Merryspring Park
Straddling the Camden-Rockport boundary, 66-acre Merryspring Park, Conway Rd., P.O. Box 893, Camden 04843, tel. (207) 236-2239, is a magnet for nature lovers. More than a dozen well-marked trails wind through woodlands, berry thickets, and wildflowers; near the preserve's parking area are lily, rose, and herb gardens. Admission is free, but donations are welcomed. Special programs (fee charged) include lectures, demonstrations, and a summer Ecology Camp for youngsters. Most programs are held in the park's modern new Ross Center, named for Merryspring founders Mary Ellen and

Ervin Ross. The entrance is on Conway Rd., .3 mile off Rt. 1, at the southern end of Camden. Open dawn to dusk, year-round.

Parks in Town
Just east of the Camden Public Library is the **Camden Amphitheatre** (also called the Bok Amphitheatre, after a local benefactor), a sylvan spot resembling a set for *A Midsummer Night's Dream* (which, yes, has been performed here). Concerts, weddings, and all kinds of other events take place in the park. Across Atlantic Avenue, sloping to the harbor, is **Harbor Park,** with benches, a couple of monuments, and some of the best waterfront views in town. The noted landscape firm of Frederick Law Olmsted designed the park.

Rockport's intown parks include **Marine Park,** off Pascal Ave., at the head of the harbor; **Walker Park,** on Sea St., west side of the harbor; **Mary-Lea Park,** overlooking the harbor next to the Rockport Opera House; and **Cramer Park,** alongside the Goose River just west of Pascal Avenue. At Marine Park are the remnants of 19th-century lime kilns, an antique steam engine, picnic tables, a boat-launching ramp, and a polished granite sculpture of André, a harbor seal adopted by a local family in the early 1960s. André had been honorary harbormaster, ring-bearer at weddings, and the subject of several books and a film—and even did the honors at the unveiling of his statue—before he was fatally wounded in a mating skirmish in 1986, at the age of 25.

Curtis Island
Marking the entrance to Camden Harbor is town-owned Curtis Island, with a 26-foot automated light tower (and adjoining keeper's house) facing out into the bay. Once known as Negro Island, it's a sight (and site) made for photo ops; the views are stunning in every direction. A kayak or dinghy will get you out to the island, where you can picnic (take water; there's no facilities), wander around, gather berries, or just watch the passing fleet. Land on the Camden (west) end of the island, allowing for tide change when you beach your boat. Respect the privacy of the keeper's house in summer; it's occupied by volunteer caretakers.

G.W. Hodson Park

Another good picnic spot is a tiny little town park just outside of Camden, overlooking the Megunticook River outlet from Megunticook Lake. G.W. Hodson Park is a serene, pine-needled space with a riverfront picnic table. It's open daily 6 a.m.-10 p.m. From downtown Camden, take Rt. 105 (Washington St.) 2.6 miles to Molyneaux Road. Turn right and go half a mile to the park, on the right. Alternatively, take Rt. 52 (Mountain St.) 1.8 miles to Beaucaire Rd.; turn left and go .6 mile to the park.

Fernald's Neck

Three miles of Megunticook Lake shoreline, groves of conifers, and a large swamp ("the Great Bog") are features of 315-acre Fernald's Neck Preserve, on the Camden-Lincolnville line (and the Knox-Waldo County line). Shoreline and mountain views are stupendous, even more so during fall-foliage season. Easiest trail is the Blue and White Loop, at the northern end of the preserve; the longer Orange Loop begins at the same point, goes past the Great Bog, and loops around the southern end of the preserve. Yellow Trails connect the loops. While on the Blue and White Loop, take the Green offshoot for a great view of the lake and hills. Some sections can be wet; wear boots or rubberized shoes, and use insect repellent. From Rt. 1 in Camden, take Rt. 52 (Mountain St.) about four and a half miles to Fernald's Neck Rd., about .2 mile beyond the Youngtown Inn. Turn left, then bear left at next fork. Continue past the gray farmhouse at the road's end, continue into the hayfield, and park near the woods. Head into the woods (look for signs bearing The Nature Conservancy oak leaf) and pick up a map/brochure at the trailhead register. A map is also available at the chamber of commerce office.

RECREATION

Local entrepreneurs Stuart and Marianne Smith have made **Maine Sport Outfitters,** Rt. 1, Rockport 04856, tel. (207) 236-8797, (800) 722-0826, fax (207) 236-7123, a major destination for anyone interested in outdoor recreation. The knowledgeable staff can lend a hand and steer you in almost any direction, for almost any summer or winter sport.

Kudos to the town of Rockport for establishing a first-rate recreation area, with ballfields, a playground, picnic tables, basketball court, and tennis courts. The **Rockport Recreation Park** is on Rt. 90, 1.2 miles west of Rt. 1 (watch for the sign on right).

Cycling

Despite a scarcity of designated bike routes, cycling is popular in the Camden-Rockport area. It's partly the scenery, partly exercise, and partly a solution to summer auto gridlock. At the chamber of commerce, pick up a bike-route map, which has lots of suggestions for short and long rides. Here's an easy option for a start. A short, mostly level, **eight-mile loop** begins in downtown Camden on the Bay View Street side of Camden National Bank (a busy, five-way intersection). Continue along Bay View until it dead-ends at Upper Chestnut St. (next to the cemetery). Turn left (the street becomes Russell Ave. and you're in Rockport), continue past Aldermere Farm, then turn left onto Calderwood Lane. At a cluster of mailboxes, leave the unpaved road and bear right, pedaling around Beauchamp Point to Mechanic St. (paved). Turn left onto Russell Ave. and continue to the Rockport Public Library. Bear right onto Union St., returning to Camden and Rt. 1.

Maine Sport Outfitters Rt. 1, Rockport 04856, tel. (207) 236-8797, (800) 722-0826, fax (207) 236-7123, purveyors of just about anything sporting, rents bikes for $15-20 a day and provides info on biking routes. **Fred's Bikes,** 53 Chestnut St., Camden 04843, tel. (207) 236-6664, is a full-service rental (and sales) shop in downtown Camden; they'll even deliver the wheels to your lodging. All-day rentals (including helmets) are $15; a car rack is $5 extra. Fred's also does repairs and sponsors group rides.

Hiking

There's enough hiking in **Camden Hills State Park** to fill any vacation, but many other options exist as well. For instance, there's **Bald Mountain,** northwest of downtown Camden, for magnificent views of Penobscot Bay. From Rt. 1 at the center of town, take Mechanic St. until it forks at the edge of town; bear right onto Melvin Heights Rd. (left goes to the Snow Bowl). Continue to the next fork and bear left onto West Fork Rd. (right is East Fork Road). Continue to Molyneaux Rd., take a quick left then an immediate right onto Howe Hill Road. Drive uphill .8 mile, at which point you'll see a tiny gravel clearing at the beginning of a woods road on the left. Park as far off the road as possible. The blue-blazed trail is moderate, requiring about one and a half hours on the ascent; the summit views are well worth the trek, especially in fall. Avoid it in late May and early June, when the blackflies take command. Depending on the season, you may encounter squishy areas, so wear rubberized shoes or waterproof boots.

An excellent resource for hiking info in the Camden-Rockport area is the **West Bay Outing Club,** which organizes hikes of varying skill levels throughout the year, usually on Sunday afternoons. Check newspaper calendar listings or contact the spearhead of the club, Jack Williams, at (207) 236-2354. (He's also the driving force behind Camden's toboggan chute.)

Swimming

The Camden area is blessed with several locales for freshwater swimming—a real boon, since Penobscot Bay can be mighty chilly, even at summer's peak. **Shirttail Point,** with limited parking, is a small sandy area on the Megunticook River. It's shallow enough for young kids and has picnic tables and a play area. From Rt. 1 in Camden, take Rt. 105 (Washington St.) 1.4 miles; watch for a small sign on the right. **Barrett's Cove,** on Megunticook Lake, has more parking space, usually more swimmers, and restrooms, picnic tables and grills, as well as a play area. Diagonally opposite the Camden Public Library, take Rt. 52 (Mountain St.) about three miles; watch for the sign on the left. To cope with the parking crunch on hot summer days, bike to the beaches. You'll be ready for a swim after the uphill stretches, and it's all downhill on the way back.

Camden and Rockport both have saltwater swimming but no sandy beaches. In Camden, it's **Laite Memorial Park** (also called Laite Beach), on Bay View St. about one and a half miles from downtown Camden. Right on Camden Harbor, the park has great views, a strip of sand, picnic tables, a playground, and live music each Wednesday at 1 p.m. in July and August.

Rockport has **Walker Park,** tucked away on the west side of the harbor. From Pascal Ave., take Elm St., which becomes Sea Street. Walker Park is on the left, with picnic tables, a play area, and a small, pebbly beach.

Indoor-pool options are the **Camden YMCA,** 50 Chestnut St., Camden, tel. (207) 236-3375, and the **Samoset Resort,** on the Rockport-Rockland boundary.

Golf

On a back road straddling the Camden-Rockport line, the **Goose River Golf Club,** Simonton Rd., RFD Box 4820, Camden 04843, tel. (207) 236-8488, competes with the best for outstanding scenery. A second set of tees in the nine-hole layout makes the course virtually an 18-holer. Starting times are needed on weekends and holidays. Snack bar; cart and club rentals; moderate greens fees. Open mid-May through late October. Simonton Road is roughly parallel to Rt. 1, and you can reach it several ways. Easiest is to take John St. from Rt. 1 in Camden, next to Subway. Continue to Simonton Rd. and turn left. The clubhouse is roughly two miles from downtown Camden or Rockport.

For an 18-hole course in an unsurpassed waterfront setting (but steeper rental and greens fees), check out the links at the **Samoset Resort.** Resort guests receive golf discounts, and the course often has a longer season than Goose River.

Playgrounds

Two creative playgrounds will give the kids a chance to defuse some excess energy. Since they're both on the grounds of elementary schools, don't go when school is in session. In Camden, head for the Elm Street School, a big old wooden building at the corner of Rt. 1 (Elm St.) and Union Street. In Rockport, an even more elaborate playground is at the Rockport Elementary School, corner of Rts. 1 and 90.

Winter Sports

With the Gulf Stream not far offshore, winters can be unpredictable in the Camden-Rockport area—as well as in many other Maine coastal communities. Still, the snow gods often do cooperate. The town-owned **Camden Snow Bowl,** P.O. Box 1207, Camden 04843, tel. (207) 236-

3438, snow phone (207) 236-4418, is a family-friendly ski area that has provided a jump-start for many a budding alpine standout. Besides, where else can you begin a downhill run with a panoramic view of ocean and islands?

On Ragged Mountain, the Snow Bowl has nine trails (easy to difficult), two T-bars, a double chairlift, and snowmaking and floodlights on major runs. Best of all, the lift tickets are outrageously reasonable compared to prices at the major ski areas. Vertical drop is 950 feet. The Ragged Mountain Ski School offers lessons for every age and skill level; equipment rentals are available; and the cozy A-frame lodge has a snack bar. There's skating on adjacent Hosmer Pond in winter; when the pond is frozen, the unique **toboggan chute** also is open—weekends and holidays 9 a.m.-4 p.m. Cost is $1 a run on a Snow Bowl toboggan, 50 cents if you bring your own. The Snow Bowl is three miles west of Camden; turn off Rt. 1 at John Street.

You'll find **cross-country ski trails** in nearby Lincolnville and the Thomaston area.

GETTING AFLOAT

There's no excuse for staying ashore in Camden and Rockport. Take your pick from week-long windjammer cruises, windjammer daysails, powerboat excursions, and sea kayak rentals.

The yachting crowd is drawn here by the Camden Yacht Club (private) as well as Wayfarer Marine, tel. (207) 236-0353 (primarily sailing yachts); and P.G. Willey, tel. (207) 236-3256 (primarily luxury power yachts). If you're aboard your own boat and looking for a mooring, Camden has more than 400 of them—albeit not always available. Camden's harbormaster, operating out of a small signposted building near the head of the harbor, tel. (207) 236-7966, can provide details

Rockport Marine, tel. (207) 236-9651, specializing in wooden boats, is the draw in that harbor; the private Rockport Boat Club is a deliberately laid-back version of the tony Camden Yacht Club.

Other nearby anchorages with facilities for boaters are Rockland, Spruce Head, Tenants Harbor, and Port Clyde. Offshore options are in North Haven and Vinalhaven.

If you have your own canoe, kayak, rowboat, or whatever, there are a number of boat-launching sites, both saltwater (Eaton Point, at the end of Sea St., in Camden; and, even better, Marine Park, in Rockport) and freshwater (Megunticook Lake, west and east sides; Bog Bridge, on Rt. 105, about three and a half miles from downtown Camden; and Barrett's Cove, on Rt. 52, also about three and a half miles from Camden).

Windjammer Cruises

In 1936, Camden became the home of the "cruise schooner" (sometimes called "dude schooner") trade when Capt. Frank Swift restored a creaky wooden vessel and offered sailing vacations to paying passengers. He kept at it for 25 years—gradually adding other boats to the fleet—and the rest, as they say, is history. Windjammers have become big business on the Maine coast, with Camden and Rockland sparring for the title of Windjammer Capital. Rockland wrested it from Camden in the mid-1990s.

Seven traditional windjammer schooners homeported in Camden, and one in Rockport, head out for two-, three-, six-, or eight-day cruises, late May to mid-October. Relax and do nothing or pitch in and help—the choice is yours. The camaraderie is tangible, the food is extraordinarily satisfying, and the sailing is unsurpassed. Costs depend on accommodation type, cruise length, and time of year.

Heir to Frank Swift's original Camden fleet is the three-vessel **Maine Windjammer Cruises,** P.O. Box 617, Camden 04843, tel. (207) 236-2938 or (888) 692-7245, which includes the 29-passenger *Grace Bailey* (six days; kids welcome; $495-725 pp); 26-passenger *Mercantile* (four days or weekends; kids welcome; $295-525 pp); and the six-passenger *Mistress* (four or six days or weekends; kids welcome; the vessel is usually chartered by a group; $315-785 pp). The *Merc* has the longest season.

Others sailing out of Camden are the 22-passenger *Lewis R. French*, P.O. Box 992, Camden 04843, tel. (207) 236-2463 or (800) 469-4635, (four or six days; no kids under 16; no smoking; $325-695 pp); the 29-passenger *Mary Day*, P.O. Box 798, Camden 04843, tel. (207) 236-2750 or (800) 992-2218 (three, four, or six days; no kids under 15; $350-700 pp); the 36-

passenger *Roseway,* P.O. Box 696, Camden 04843, tel. (207) 236-4449 or (800) 255-4449 (three, six, or eight days; no kids under 13; $300-700 pp); and the 31-passenger steel gaff-topsail ketch *Angelique,* P.O. Box 736, Camden 04843, tel. (207) 236-8873 or (800) 282-9989 (three, four, or six days; no kids under 16; $385-710 pp).

Rockport is home to the 14-passenger *Timberwind,* P.O. Box 247, Rockport 04856, tel. (207) 236-0801 or (800) 759-9250 (three or six days; no kids under six; $339-650 pp).

All of the above windjammers are members of the **Maine Windjammer Association,** P.O. Box 1144, Blue Hill 04614, tel. (800) 807-9463, fax (207) 374-2952, a helpful one-stop resource for vessel and schedule information.

On the summer cruising schedule, several weeks coincide with special windjammer events, so you'll need to book a berth far in advance for these: last week in June (Boothbay Harbor's Windjammer Days), July Fourth week (Great Schooner Race), first week in August (Swans Island Sweet Chariot Music Festival), and second week in September (WoodenBoat Sail-In).

Daysails and Excursions

You can't compare a two-hour daysail to a week-long cruise, but at least you get a hint of what could be—and it's a far better choice for most kids. Several daysailing schooners operate out of Camden in summer. Most weekdays, you can just show up at the dock and find a space, but on weekends, better call for a reservation. Several are based at Bay View Landing, formerly known as Sharp's Wharf.

The historic 55-foot *Olad* and the new, 75-foot steel-hulled *North Wind,* both owned by accomplished skipper John Nugent, do two-hour sails from Camden's public landing (Bay View Landing), weather permitting, June to October. Between them, his boats go out eight or nine times a day. Call (207) 236-2323 to check on the schedule and/or make reservations. *Olad* tickets are $15 adults, $10 kids; *North Wind* tickets are $20 adults, $10 kids; children under six are $5; snacks are served.

Another historic Camden daysailer is the 57-foot schooner *Surprise,* built in 1918 and skippered by congenial educator Jack Moore. He and his wife, Barbara, do four two-hour sails

daily, departing from Camden's public landing. Cost is $20-25, including snacks. No smoking, no kids under 12. For info, call (207) 236-4687.

The 86-foot *Appledore,* built in 1978 for round-the-world cruising, sails from Bay View Landing three or four times daily, June to October, beginning around 10 a.m. Cruises last two hours and cost $20-25 pp. Beer, wine, and sodas are available. Call (207) 236-8353 for information or reservations.

Over in Rockport, the only daysailer is not a schooner; she's the 40-foot sloop *Shantih II,* requiring a bit more planning. Carrying only six passengers, the *Shantih* goes out for a full day (up to six hours), May-Oct., for $75 pp, including lunch. Half a day is $50 pp with snacks; a sunset cruise is $25 pp with snacks. The hourly rate is $12.50 pp. Special family rates are available, but the cockpit is relatively small, so don't plan to take toddlers. Call (207) 236-8605 or (800) 599-8605.

For an even shorter cruise—but a great way to see Camden and Rockport, their lighthouses and shorelines—head down to the Camden public landing and buy a ticket for the 30-passenger converted lobsterboat *Betselma.* Reservations usually aren't needed. Retired schooner captain Les Bex knows these waters, the wildlife, and the history. His tours last an hour and cost $10 adults, $5 children, free for kids under three. Some days, he also does two-hour trips, out into the bay and around Islesboro ($20 adults, $10 kids), departing at 9:15 a.m. and 4 p.m. Weather permitting, June-Sept., *Betselma* makes eight hour-long trips daily, beginning at 10:30 a.m. and ending with a 7:30 p.m. trip. For information, call (207) 236-4446.

Sea Kayaking

Sea kayaking has mushroomed in the 1990s. If you've brought your own craft, head for the boat-launching ramps listed above. Otherwise, stop in or call **Maine Sport Outfitters** Rt. 1, Rockport 04856, tel. (207) 236-8797, (800) 722-0826, fax (207) 236-7123, which rents (and sells) kayaks and organizes guided kayak tours and lessons. Kayak rentals require previous paddling experience.

Another contact for guided tours is **Mount Pleasant Canoe & Kayak,** 650 Mt. Pleasant Rd., P.O. Box 86, West Rockport 04865, tel.

(207) 785-4309. Owner Don Peckham leads day trips but also organizes three-night inn-to-inn sea-kayaking tours, Spruce Head to Rockland, for about $650 pp, everything included.

BOB RACE

Three miles south of Camden, **Megunticook Campground by the Sea,** Rt. 1, P.O. Box 375, Rockport 04856, tel. (207) 594-2428 or (800) 884-2428, fax (207) 594-0549, provides shuttle service and rents Sit On Top kayaks ($40 double, $25 single, for all day).

ENTERTAINMENT

Thursday and Friday evenings in July and August, and each month the rest of the year, **Bay Chamber Concerts** draw sell-out audiences to the beautifully restored (and air-conditioned) Rockport Opera House. Founded in the 1960s as a classical series, the summer concerts feature a resident quartet, prominent guest artists, and outstanding programs. The first week in August ("Next Generation Week") is devoted to classes and concerts for and by teenagers. Seats are reserved for summer concerts ($16 for adults); open seating is the rule in winter, when tickets are less expensive and programs vary from classical to pops to jazz. (Season tickets and flex passes are available.) For information, or an advance copy of the schedule, call or write Bay Chamber Concerts, P.O. Box 191, Camden 04843, tel. (207) 236-2823.

Fans of art flicks would scream if the **The Bayview Street Cinema,** 10 Bay View St., Camden, tel. (207) 236-8722, ever closed its doors, but there's seldom a mob at this second-floor movie house in downtown Camden. The quirky management screens all sorts of interesting esoterica, as well as films already available at the local video store. Biggest turnouts are for movies filmed in the area—*Peyton Place, Man Without a Face, Thinner.* Two screenings nightly, usually 7 and 9 p.m.; some Sunday matinees (3 p.m.). Tickets are $5.50 adults, $4 seniors, $3 children. Headphones are available for the hearing impaired. Nearest cinemas for first-run films are in Rockland and Belfast.

Founded in the 1970s, the **Camden Civic Theatre** presents impressively creditable performances, thanks to lots of fine local talent. Musicals and dramas are mounted primarily in summer at the Camden and Rockport Opera Houses. Call (207) 236-2281 for schedule info.

FESTIVALS AND EVENTS

The first full weekend of February is given over to the **Camden Conference,** an annual three-day foreign-affairs conference boasting nationally known speakers. That same weekend also marks the **National Toboggan Championships,** two days of races and fun at the nation's only wooden toboggan chute—Camden Snow Bowl.

Classical **Bay Chamber Concerts** are offered Thursday and Friday evenings (8:15 p.m.) early July through late August in the Rockport Opera House. Adults $17, students $7. Third Thursday of the July is declared **House and Garden Day,** on which you can take a self-guided tour (10 a.m.-4:30 p.m.) of significant homes and gardens in Camden and Rockport. Proceeds benefit the Camden Garden Club. And the **Annual Arts and Crafts Show,** on the third weekend in July, draws dozens of artists and craftspeople displaying and selling their wares at the Camden Amphitheatre, Harbor Park. (It coincides with the Camden Library book sale.)

The week-long **Union Fair** is a country fair with a carnival, agricultural exhibits, harness racing, food booths, and a focus on blueberries. At the Union Fairgrounds, Union (Rt. 17, west of Camden-Rockport), the third week of August.

Labor Day weekend is also known as **Windjammer Weekend** here, with cruises, windjammer open houses, fireworks, and live entertainment in Camden Harbor.

Dozens of artists and craftspeople display and sell their wares at the **Fall Festival and Arts and Crafts Show,** the first weekend in October at the Camden Amphitheatre, Harbor Park.

Christmas by the Sea is a family-oriented early-December weekend featuring open houses, special sales, a Santa Claus visit, and concerts.

SHOPPING

Downtown Camden is a tough place to find socks or thread, but it's a boutique-shopper's paradise if gifts are your goal. Rockport has a handful of unusual gift and antiques shops and galleries.

Antiques

Located in an upscale Rt. 1 carriage house, **Schueler Antiques,** 10 High St., Camden 04843, tel. (207) 236-2770, off season (617) 738-8309, has been one of Camden's finest antiques shops since the mid-1940s. Specialties are furniture and accessories, plus some paintings, with a good selection of decoys. Open mid-May to mid-October, Tues.-Sat. 10 a.m.-5 p.m., Sunday 1-5 p.m., and by appointment on Monday.

In downtown Rockport, **Katrin Phocas, Ltd.,** 19 Main St., Rockport 04856, tel. (207) 236-8654, carries an exquisite selection of high-end antiques, accessories, and paintings. Open June-Sept., Mon.-Sat. 10 a.m.-5 p.m.

New and Old Books

The Owl and Turtle Bookshop, 8 Bay View St., Camden 04843, tel. (207) 236-4769 or (800) 876-4769, fax (207) 236-2113, has two floors of books, CDs, and cards, plus a convenient special-order service. Specialties? Marine and children's books. Summer hours are Mon.-Sat. 9 a.m.-5:30 p.m. and Sunday noon-5 p.m.; shorter hours off season.

Across the street is an even older Camden landmark, in a funky building that complements its inventory. **ABCDef Books,** 23 Bay View St.,

Camden 04843, tel. (207) 236-3903, changed hands in 1995 but maintains its excellent stock of rare books and first editions (prices are a bit steep). Open Mon.-Sat. 10 a.m.-9 p.m. and Sunday noon-6 p.m. in July and August; Tues.-Sat. 10 a.m.-5 p.m., April-June and Sept.-December.

Gifts and Crafts

You'll need to wander the streets to take in all the gift and craft shops, particularly in Camden—some are obvious, others are tucked away on side streets and back alleys. Explore.

Planet Emporium, 31 Main St., Camden 04843, tel. (207) 236-9022, fax 236-9025, and **Planet Kids,** 10 Main St., face each other across Main Street in downtown Camden. The former features ecosensitive gifts, books, and clothing; the latter is a gold mine of educational toys, including books and software. Guard your wallet—lots of tempting stuff here. Open all year, daily to 10 p.m. in summer.

A downtown-Camden landmark since 1940, **The Smiling Cow,** 41 Main St., Camden, tel. (207) 236-3351, is as good a place as any to pick up Maine souvenirs—a few slightly kitschy, but most reasonably tasteful. Before or after shopping here, head for the rear balcony, where there's free coffee and a knockout view of the harbor and the Megunticook River waterfall. Open daily 8 a.m.-9 p.m., April-October.

The name tells it all at **Once a Tree,** 46 Bay View St., Camden, tel. (207) 236-3995. Wood is everywhere: cutting boards, clock faces, vases, game boards, spoons, furniture. It's an education in the versatility of wood. The shop is open all year, daily in summer.

Anne Kilham Designs, 165 Russell Ave., Rockport 04856, tel. (207) 236-0962, stocks the entire line of prints, cards, T-shirts, placemats, and Advent calendars created by talented local artist Anne Kilham. Plus original watercolor and oil paintings. The bright, spacious shop is open daily 10 a.m.-5 p.m. in summer, shorter hours off season, often closed in winter.

Gifts, crafts, and clothing from exotic locales (Bali, Lombok, Morocco, Zimbabwe, Turkey) fill the shelves, walls, and floors at **L.E. Leonard,** 67 Pascal Ave., Rockport, tel. (207) 236-0878. Lots of unusual one-of-a-kind stuff. Open May-Dec., weekdays 11 a.m.-5 p.m., weekends

10:30 a.m.-5 p.m. The shop is at the end of West St. (Rt. 90), a block from Rt. 1.

Follow West St. (Rt. 90) straight from L.E. Leonard for almost three miles and you'll come to **Danica Candleworks,** Rt. 90, West Rockport 04865, tel. (207) 236-3060, producers of the loveliest candle colors you've ever seen. Owner Erik Laustsen learned the hand-dipping trade from his Danish relatives, and Danica now ships its work all over the country. The Scandinavian-style shop, which carries other gift items, is open all year, Mon.-Fri. 10 a.m.-5 p.m. and Saturday 10 a.m.-4 p.m.

Clothing and Sporting Gear

Established in 1976, **The Admiral's Buttons,** 36 Bay View St., Camden 04843, tel. (207) 236-2617, fax 236-4475, stocks a carefully selected line of classic, high-end men's and women's clothing and accessories (bowties, foulweather gear, cufflinks, Tilley hats, great sweaters), plus Maine-created Shard pottery and Thomas Moser furniture. Open April-Jan., daily 10 a.m.-5 p.m. in summer, Mon.-Sat. other months.

Sturdy, well-designed, homemade (by knitting machine) wool and cotton sweaters are the specialty at **Unique One,** 2 Bay View St., Camden 04843, tel. (207) 236-8717. Or you can pick out yarn and make your own. Open spring through fall, daily 9 a.m.-7 p.m. in summer.

A manageable microcosm of giant outfitter L.L. Bean, **Maine Sport Outfitters,** Rt. 1, P.O. Box 956, Rockport 04856, tel. (207) 236-7120 or (800) 722-0826, fax (207) 236-7123, sells and rents canoes, kayaks, bikes, skis, and tents, plus all the relevant clothing and accessories. The savvy staff is especially helpful, willing to demonstrate everything—even skating and kayaking on the tiny pond outside the modernistic building. **Maine Sport Outdoor School,** same address, tel. (207) 236-8797, has a full schedule of canoeing, kayaking, and camping trips. A snack bar, in-line-skating rink, and public restrooms make the store a destination in itself. The store is half a mile north of the junction of Rts. 1 and 90. Open all year, daily 8 a.m.-9 p.m. mid-June through August.

Discount Shopping

With a name like **Heavenly Threads,** 47 Elm St., Rt. 1, Camden 04843, tel. (207) 236-3203, how can anyone resist this thrift shop? Established by Camden's community-oriented First Congregational Church (next door to the shop), Heavenly Threads carries high-quality preowned clothing, books, and jewelry. Staffed by volunteers, with proceeds going to such local ecumenical causes as Meals-on-Wheels, the shop is open all year, Tues.-Fri. 10 a.m.-4 p.m. and Saturday 10 a.m.-1 p.m.

Natural Foods/Farmers' Market

The best source for health foods, homeopathic remedies, and fresh, seasonal produce is **Fresh Off the Farm,** Rt. 1, Rockport 04856, tel. (207) 236-3260, an inconspicuous red-painted roadside place that looks like an overgrown farmstand (it is). Watch for one of those permanent/temporary signs highlighting latest arrivals (Native Blueberries, Native Corn, etc.). The shop is 1.3 miles south of the junction of Rts. 1 and 90. Open daily in summer, Mon.-Sat. off season.

The **Camden Farmers' Market,** one of the best in the state, holds forth in a parking lot at Colcord and Limerock Sts., across from Tibbetts Industries. Temporary signs are posted on Rt. 1 on market days—Wed. 4:30-6:30 p.m., Saturday 9 a.m.-noon. The market goes on, rain or shine, late May through October. Besides an unusually good selection of produce, you'll find jams, cheeses, plants, crafts, and sometimes even a petting zoo.

ACCOMMODATIONS

The Camden-Rockport area (including Lincolnville) is loaded with lodgings—from basic motels to cottage complexes to elegant inns and B&Bs. Many of Camden's finest accommodations (especially B&Bs) are located on Rt. 1 (variously disguised as Elm St., Main St., and High St.), heavily trafficked in summer. If you're unusually sensitive to nighttime noises, request a room facing away from the street.

The chamber of commerce is very helpful with lodging information and also maintains a lengthy list of **seasonal rentals.** A private firm, **Camden Accommodations,** 77 Elm St., Rt. 1, Camden 04843, tel. (207) 236-6090 or (800) 236-1920, fax (207) 236-6091, arranges reservations at all kinds of lodgings in Camden and surrounding communities—for one night or all summer. For July and August weekends, it's best to reserve rooms well in advance. Toughest time to find a last-minute bed is the first weekend in August, when the Maine Lobster Festival is underway in next-door Rockland.

Camden

Maine's most unusual (and priciest) B&B, **Norumbega**, 61 High St., Rt. 1, tel. (207) 236-4646, fax 236-0824, is an 1886 turreted stone castle overlooking Camden's outer harbor. Provided your wallet can stand the crunch, splurge

CAMDEN-ROCKPORT ACCOMMODATIONS

In addition to the lodgings noted in the accompanying text, Camden and Rockport have enough B&Bs to satisfy every taste—if not every budget. The only relative bargains are off season, when rates drop dramatically. Rates listed here are for peak-season doubles (including full breakfast at B&Bs unless indicated otherwise). All are open year-round unless indicated otherwise. A two-night minimum may be required on some midsummer weekends.

B&Bs

All of the B&Bs listed here are in Camden (zip code 04843) and have private baths unless indicated otherwise; none allow smoking in guest rooms.

A Little Dream, 66 High St., tel. (207) 236-8742. Turreted frilly Victorian with especially hospitable innkeepers; $95-159; seven rooms and suites (five with private bath), some fireplaces; a/c; TV; phones; no pets or children; about a mile uphill from the harbor.

The Blue Harbor House, 67 Elm St., tel. (207) 236-3196 or (800) 248-3196, fax (207) 236-6523. Carefully decorated intown house; $85-135; 10 rooms and suites; pets and children welcome; gourmet (or lobster) dinner for guests ($30 pp) by reservation.

Captain Swift Inn, 72 Elm St., tel. (207) 236-8113 or (800) 251-0865. Elegantly restored intown 1810 Federal house; $85-110; four rooms; a/c; TV; phones; wheelchair access; no pets, no children under four; back deck has an away-from-it-all feel.

Edgecombe-Coles House, 64 High St., HC 60, Box 3010, tel. (207) 236-2336 or (800) 528-2336, fax (207) 236-6227. Large, rambling country-inn-type place, meticulously decorated, with water and wooded views; $80-185; six rooms; no pets, no children under eight; set back and buffered from Rt. 1 traffic; about half a mile uphill from downtown.

The Elms, 84 Elm St., tel. (207) 236-6250 or (800) 755-3567. Lovely 1806 Federal on the edge of com-

mercial district; $85-95; six rooms; phones; no pets, no children under 12; congenial innkeepers are maritime history (especially lighthouse) fans.

Hawthorn Inn, 9 High St., tel. (207) 236-8842. Large, gracious Victorian backed up to the harbor; $90-185; 10 rooms and efficiencies (in inn and carriage house); extensive buffet breakfast; no pets, no children under 12.

Owl and Turtle Guest Rooms, 8 Bay View St., tel. (207) 236-9014. Modern harbor-view rooms in the heart of downtown; $80-90; three rooms; a/c; TV; phones; continental breakfast; no pets, children welcome; located above The Owl and Turtle Bookshop.

Swan House, 49 Mountain St., tel. (207) 236-8275 or (800) 207-8275. Elegant 1870 Victorian on Rt. 52 next to one of the Mt. Battie hiking trails; $85-120; six rooms and suites; phones; no pets, no children under 12.

Windward House, 6 High St., tel. (207) 236-9656. Restored Greek Revival with dramatically lighted English gardens; $100-175; eight rooms; no pets, no children under 12; close to harbor and downtown.

Motels/Cottage Complexes

The following are also in Camden (zip code 04843).

Cedar Crest Motel, 115 Elm St., tel. (207) 236-4839 or (800) 422-4964, fax (207) 236-6719. Family-run two-story motel at the southern edge of Camden; $92-115; 37 rooms; a/c; TV; phones; coffee shop (open Tues.-Sun.); heated outdoor pool; laundry facilities; playground; smoking permitted; children welcome, no pets, .8 mile from downtown. Open mid-April through October.

Country Inn at Camden/Rockport, Rt. 1, P.O. Box 277, tel. (207) 236-2725. Spiffy modern all-suite motel next to Camden Shuttle parking lot on the Camden-Rockport boundary; $99-200 (kids under five free); 25 suites; a/c; TV; phones; free continental breakfast; indoor pool; health club; laundry; no pets; set back and buffered from Rt. 1 traffic.

for a night (or two) here—if only to feel like temporary royalty. Honeymooners are frequent guests. Twelve strikingly decorated rooms and suites (with private baths) are $195-450 d, including gourmet breakfast and afternoon tea, lower rates and special packages off season. No pets, no smoking, no children under seven. Open all year.

Opened for guests in 1901 and operated since the 1970s by the Dewing family, the **Whitehall Inn,** 52 High St., Rt. 1, P.O. Box 558, tel. (207) 236-3391 or (800) 789-6565, fax (207) 236-4427, retains its century-old genteel air. Lovely gardens, rockers on the veranda, a tennis court, and attentive service all add to the appeal of this historic country inn. Ask to see the Millay Room, commemorating famed poet Edna St. Vincent Millay, who graduated from Camden High School and first recited her poem "Renascence" to Whitehall guests in 1912. Fifty comfortable, unpretentious rooms (45 with private baths) in the inn and two separate buildings (Maine House and Wicker House). Doubles are $75-170. No pets. The bright dining room is open to the public for breakfast (8-9:30 a.m.) and dinner (6-8 p.m.); dinner entrées are $15-18. Open mid-May to late October.

The three hospitable hosts at **Maine Stay,** 22 High St., Rt. 1, tel. (207) 236-9636, do everything right, from the attractive decor to the delicious breakfasts to the welcoming window candles. The stunning residence, built in 1802 and known as the Bass-Huse House, faces busy Rt. 1 and is close to downtown, but inside and out back, behind the carriage house and barn, you'll feel worlds away. (Request a rear room if you're worried about traffic noise.) Eight doubles (six with private bath) are $75-125. No smoking, no children under 10. Open all year.

Just off busy Rt. 1 and two blocks from downtown Camden, in the National Historic District, **The Nathaniel Hosmer Inn,** 4 Pleasant St., tel. (207) 236-4012 or (800) 423-4012, fax (207) 236-3651, built in the early 1800s, earns high marks for comfort, convenience, and quiet ambience. Seven guest rooms (private baths) go for $95-125 d June-Oct., less off season; two rooms have a/c. Breakfast is a feast, served under a real chandelier, and innkeepers Rich and Dodie Schmidgall can accommodate special diets. They're also wonderful day-trip planners. No

smoking, no pets. Two-night minimum midsummer and holidays. Open all year.

Closest motel to downtown Camden (two blocks), the **Towne Motel,** 68 Elm St., Rt. 1, tel. (207) 236-3377 or (800) 656-4999, fax (207) 236-0075, is a longtime landmark. Nineteen clean, comfortable, basic rooms have cable TV, a/c, phones, and free continental breakfast. Doubles are $75-105. The two-story building is at a 90-degree angle from Rt. 1, minimizing noise. (If you're worried, request a room toward the rear.) Owners Hal and Barbara Smith, active community volunteers, can provide all kinds of local info. Open all year.

About midway between two clusters of B&Bs, **The Lord Camden Inn,** 24 Main St., Rt. 1, tel. (207) 236-4325 or (800) 336-4325, fax (207) 236-7141, is a hotel alternative in a historic, four-story downtown building (with elevator). Decor is reproduction Colonial with exposed brick walls and scads of old framed photos in rooms and hallways. (The brick moderates the noise level.) Rooms are pricey ($128-178 d, late June through August, lower rates other months), but kids under 16 stay free, and continental-plus breakfast is included. All 31 rooms and suites have phones, a/c, and cable TV. Top-floor rooms have harbor-view balconies. No pets. Inn staffers are especially helpful. Open all year.

A fine choice for families is **The Lodge at Camden Hills,** Rt. 1, P.O. Box 794, tel. (207) 236-8478 or (800) 832-7058, fax (207) 236-7163, with 20 modern suites and cottages in an especially attractive enclave a mile uphill from downtown Camden. Doubles are $99-195 in midsummer, lower by the week and off season; children under 12 stay free. Facilities include a/c, phones, cable TV, some kitchens. No pets, no smoking. Open all year.

A hybrid of an inn, B&B, motel, and cottage three miles north of town, **The High Tide Inn,** Rt. 1, tel. (207) 236-3724 or (800) 788-7068, has enough variety for every budget—all in an outstanding, seven-acre oceanfront setting with a private pebbly beach. The two-story, eight-unit "Oceanfront" motel unit is closest to the water and farthest from Rt. 1. Thirty rooms (with private bath) are $55-135, including continental breakfast on the water-view porch. Open spring through fall.

In a town full of high-end lodgings, **The Good House,** 50 Elm St., Rt. 1, tel. (207) 236-2139, may be the biggest bargain. Two no-frills rooms (private baths) are $35-55 d, without breakfast (plenty of breakfast spots close by). Pets and children are welcome; no smoking, no credit cards. Located right downtown, it's open April through November.

Rockport
One of the area's spiffiest motels also has terrific Penobscot Bay views. In the Glen Cove section of Rockport (three miles south of downtown Rockport, three miles north of downtown Rockland; next door to Penobscot Bay Medical Center), the **Glen Cove Motel,** Rt. 1, P.O. Box 35, Glen Cove 04846, tel. (207) 594-4062 or (800) 453-6268, sits on a 17-acre bluff with a lovely trail leading to the rocky shore. Many of the 34 units boast water views; all have a/c, phones, cable TV. There's also a heated pool. No pets. Request a room set back from Rt. 1. Doubles are $79-129 mid-June through August, $59-109 other months; open all year.

Megunticook Campground by the Sea, Rt. 1, P.O. Box 375, Rockport 04856, tel. (207) 594-2428 or (800) 884-2428, fax (207) 594-0549, is the area's best-run commercial campground, a 17-acre facility with 85 wooded sites. Amenities include hot showers, playground, snack bar, heated pool, laundry, and bike and kayak rentals. Noise rules are strictly enforced; pets are allowed. Sites are $20-28 a night (four persons), $18-20 early and late in the season. Open mid-May to mid-October. The campground is three miles south of Camden, five miles north of Rockland.

FOOD

Lunch and Miscellanea
The **Camden Bagel Cafe,** Highland Mill, Mechanic St., Camden, tel. (207) 236-2661, has a hugely loyal clientele, drawn by *real* coffee, fresh bagels, fast service, daily newspapers, and a casual air. No smoking, no credit cards. Open all year, Mon.-Sat. 6:30 a.m.-5 p.m., Sunday 7:30 a.m.-2 p.m.

Good coffee is also a draw at the **Camden Deli,** 37 Main St., Camden, tel. (207) 236-8343, in the heart of downtown, but its biggest asset is the windowed seating area overlooking the Megunticook River waterfall. The view doesn't get much better than this. Made-to-order sandwiches, homemade soups, veggie burgers, and subs (try the Deli Lama) all add to the mix. Beer and wine only. No credit cards, no smoking. Open all year, weekdays 7 a.m.-9:30 p.m., weekends 7 a.m.-10 p.m.

Just down the street, **The Village Restaurant,** 7 Main St., Camden, tel. (207) 236-3232, gets raves for an equally fine view and, say aficionados, the town's best chowder. At lunchtime, locals throng to this longtime standby, along with the tour-bus crowd. Try to hold out for a window table. No smoking. Open all year for lunch and dinner.

Since the early 1970s, **Scott's Place,** 85 Elm St., Rt. 1, Camden, tel. (207) 236-8751, a roadside lunch stand near Harbor Audio-Video, has been dishing up inexpensive burgers and dogs, nowadays adding veggie burgers ($2.25) and salads. Call ahead and it'll be ready. Open all year, Mon.-Fri. 10 a.m.-7 p.m., Saturday to 4 p.m., shorter hours in winter.

Wasses Hot Dogs, Union and Limerock Sts., Camden, tel. (207) 236-6551, formerly the Sea Gull, is the Camden "branch" of a Rockland landmark. Bacon chili cheese dogs go for $1.75, and you can even get BLTs here. Open for lunch all year, Mon.-Sat.; a few picnic tables are the only seating.

Zaddik's, 20 Washington St., Rt. 105, Camden, tel. (207) 236-6540, a kid-friendly place, has one foot in Mexico and one in Italy—an extensive menu with pizza, fajitas, calzones, and quesadillas. The New York-style pizza is tops; Starbucks coffee, Celestial Seasonings teas, and Fresh Samantha juices. Free delivery in town. No smoking. Open Tues.-Sun. 5-9 p.m. (to 10 p.m. Friday and Saturday), shorter hours off season.

Facing downtown Camden's five-way intersection, **French & Brawn,** 1 Elm St., Camden, tel. (207) 236-3361, is an independent market that earns the description *super.* It's gourmet heaven—exotic produce, oven-ready take-out meals, high-cal frozen desserts, esoteric meats, and a staff with a can-do attitude. Loyal longtime customers even have charge accounts. Open all year, Mon.-Sat. 6 a.m.-8 p.m. and Sunday 8 a.m.-8 p.m.

The **Rockport Corner Shop,** Main and Central Sts., Rockport, tel. (207) 236-8161, a bright, clean, airy place, is the ultimate local hangout, so seats can be hard to come by. Lunch menu is basic American, always reliable—sandwiches, burgers, soups, salads. No smoking. Open all year, Mon.-Fri. 6:30 a.m.-3 p.m., Saturday 7 a.m.-2 p.m. and Sunday 7 a.m.-1 p.m.

Inexpensive to Moderate

Run by a couple of culinary-school graduates, the cheerful **Frogwater Cafe,** 31 Elm St., Rt. 1, Camden, tel. (207) 236-8998, gets right out there with an adventurous menu specializing in smoked items. (Ask the origin of the cafe's name.) Prices are moderate, but service can be uneven. Beer and wine only. Open all year, Tues.-Sun. 5-9 p.m.; call ahead off season.

Next door to the Frogwater is **Hi Bombay!,** 31 Elm St., Camden, tel. (207) 230-0434, whose name origin you'll figure out from the curry aroma drifting down the street. Opened in 1996, this branch of a Portland restaurant is Camden's first taste of the Eastern Hemisphere—and a respectable representative it is. The tiny winter restaurant expands in summer with an enclosed rear patio—a more spacious setting. Beer and wine only. Open all year for lunch and dinner, but call ahead off season.

In the heart of Camden, **Cappy's,** 1 Main St., tel. (207) 236-2254, is small, a bit cramped, reliably good, and very popular with locals and out-of-towners alike. In summer, ask for a table in the second-floor Crow's Nest. There's a children's menu, but kids seem just as content with the burger-and-sandwich adult fare. Seafood chowder is a specialty. Open daily 7:30 a.m.-midnight, most of the year except midwinter, when it's apt to close earlier.

A glass-walled microbrewery adjoins Maine's most picturesque brewpub at the **Sea Dog Tavern & Brewery,** 43 Mechanic St., Camden, tel. (207) 236-6863. Housed in a tastefully restored section of a onetime woolen mill, with gears and pulleys still hanging from the ceiling, the restaurant overlooks the waterfalls that once powered the Knox Mill. On tap are the brewery's award-winning Penobscot Maine Lager and Old Gollywobbler Brown Ale, plus several other selections. The menu has basic-to-average tavern fare, with lunch and dinner specials. Open daily 11:30 a.m.-3 p.m. and 5-9:30 p.m., June-Oct.; 11:30 a.m.-2 p.m. and 5-9 p.m. other months. Half-hour brewery tours are presented daily at 11 a.m., June-Oct., and Saturday at 3:30 p.m., Nov.-May.

Five miles south of Camden and 2.3 miles west of Rt. 1, **The Haven,** Rt. 90, Rockport, tel. (207) 236-2232, *always* has a well-filled parking lot—and well-filled customers of every age. Homestyle cooking, family management, ample portions, and reasonable prices do the trick. Open mid-March to mid-November, Tues.-Fri. 11:30 a.m.-2:30 p.m. and 4:30-8:30 p.m. (to 9 p.m. Friday), Saturday and Sunday 11:30 a.m.-9 p.m.

Moderate to Expensive

Since 1974, **Peter Ott's,** 16 Bay View St., Camden, tel. (207) 236-4032, has been a mainstay of the Camden restaurant scene—an informal spot where you can count on excellent steaks, seafood, heart-healthy entrées, and heart-unhealthy (but award-winning) desserts. No reservations, so expect to wait in July and August, but the comfortable lounge eases the anxiety. The bar is also a local watering hole for the after-work crowd. Open daily 5:30-9:30 p.m., early May through December; open Wed.-Sun., January through mid-February.

Across the street from Peter Ott's is **The Marigold Grille,** 21 Bay View St., Camden, tel. (207) 236-3272, formerly O'Neil's. The new incarnation has been a hit from the start, featuring elegantly rustic Italian cuisine (not an oxymoron, even if it sounds like it). Dinner entrées range from $9-16. Service is especially attentive in this informal spot. Try for a table on the airy, second-floor deck (no water view). No smoking. Open all year, daily 11 a.m.-2 p.m. and 4:30-11 p.m.

Down on the harbor behind Peter Ott's is the informal, art-filled **Atlantica Grille,** 3 Bay View

Landing, Camden, tel. (207) 236-6011, two floors of creativity in the seafood and veggie department; fresh fish tacos are a specialty. No smoking. Open all year for lunch 11:30 a.m.-2:30 p.m., dinner 5:30-8:30 p.m., and Sunday brunch. Closed Sunday in midwinter.

The Waterfront Restaurant, Bay View St., Camden, tel. (207) 236-3747, has the best waterside dining in town, but arrive early for a table on the deck. Lunches are the most fun, overlooking lots of harbor action; the restaurant is open daily in summer for lunch 11:30 a.m.-2:30 p.m. and dinner 5-10 p.m. The lounge and oyster bar are open 11:30 a.m.-midnight. Winter hours can be unpredictable; call ahead.

Housed in a former sailmaker's shop with a stunning view of a standout harbor, the **Sail Loft,** public landing, Rockport, tel. (207) 236-2330, specializes in seafood, but there's no problem satisfying anyone who wants chicken, beef, or vegetarian fare. Blueberry muffins accompany every meal, and service is superb. Especially popular with middle-agers and beyond, the Sail Loft keeps youngsters happy with crayons and a clever kids' menu. Reservations advisable in July and August. No smoking; wheelchair-accessible. Open all year, Mon.-Sat. 11:30 a.m.-2:30 p.m. and 5:30-9 p.m., Sunday noon-8 p.m.

In summer, another option in this category is the sedate dining room at the elegantly old-fashioned **Whitehall Inn** (see above, under "Accommodations"). Year-round, another inn with a dining room open to the public is the **Youngtown Inn** (see "Lincolnville," below).

Lobster-in-the-Rough
Capt'n Andy's, Upper Washington St., Camden, tel. (207) 236-2312, isn't an eat-in place, but it's a great source for a bucket of clams, live or cooked lobsters, or a container of cooked lobster meat. Arthur, Marlene, and Cheryl Andrews even take credit cards, and they'll deliver your order in the Camden-Rockport area. Their house is 1.2 miles out Washington St. (Rt. 105) from downtown Camden.

Lincolnville and Thomaston-area lobster-in-the-rough choices are also convenient.

INFORMATION AND SERVICES

One of Maine's busiest local tourism offices is the **Camden-Rockport-Lincolnville Chamber of Commerce,** public landing, P.O. Box 919, Camden 04843, tel. (207) 236-4404. They've heard every possible question by now, so don't hesitate to ask. The chamber sponsors a number of special events each year, so it's a lively operation. The gray building, facing the parking lot and the harbor at Camden's public landing, is open daily in summer, Mon.-Sat. the rest of the year.

Both Camden and Rockport have undertaken major expansions of their libraries in the last several years—and the results themselves are worth a visit. A $2.3 million expansion at the **Camden Public Library,** Main St., Rt. 1, Camden 04843, tel. (207) 236-3440, created a state-of-the-art facility with subterranean lecture room, computer setup, and outside children's garden. Open Mon.-Saturday. The **Rockport Public Library,** Russell Ave., Rockport 04856, tel. (207) 236-3642, is a smaller but very user-friendly oasis at the head of Rockport's main drag. Even the gardens are conducive to a good read. Open Mon.-Saturday.

Newspapers
The beat for the *Camden Herald,* tel. (207) 236-8511, is Camden, Rockport, Lincolnville, Appleton, and Hope. Published every Thursday, the paper carries calendar listings and, in summer, a waterfront info section. The weekly *Free Press,* tel. (207) 596-0055, based in Rockland, has the area's most extensive calendar listings. The only statewide daily newspaper paying attention to this part of the Mid-Coast is the *Bangor Daily News,* 7 Limerock St., Rockland, tel. (207) 596-6688.

Emergencies
The closest hospital is on the Rockport/Rockland boundary. **Penobscot Bay Medical Center,** Rt. 1, Rockport 04856, tel. (207) 596-8000, has 24-hour emergency-room care and all private rooms. For minor medical problems, **Qwik Care,** 45 Park St., corner of Rt. 1, Camden 04843, tel. (207) 236-8586, a walk-in clinic, is open week-

days 2-4 p.m. For police, call 911 in **Camden,** (207) 236-2027 in **Rockport,** (207) 338-2040 in **Lincolnville.** For the fire department, call (207) 236-2000 in **Camden,** (207) 236-3517 in **Rockport,** and 911 in **Lincolnville.** For an ambulance, call (207) 236-2000 in **Camden, Rockport, and Lincolnville.**

Public Restrooms

With the number of visitors who arrive in Camden each summer, merchants and restaurateurs tend to be reluctant to allow use of their restrooms to noncustomers. Fortunately, the town provides public facilities—in the gray building across the parking lot from Camden's chamber of commerce.

Photo Services

Maine Coast Photo, 23 Elm St., Camden, tel. (207) 236-1010, does one-hour print processing and stocks an extensive array of slide and print film. In summer, it's open daily.

Laundromats

In downtown Camden, there's **Clothes Care Unlimited,** 19 Mechanic St., tel. (207) 236-3332, behind the Lord Camden Inn. Summer hours are 7:30 a.m.-9 p.m. daily. **Bishop's Store Laundromat,** 96 Washington St., Rt. 105, Camden, tel. (207) 236-3339, is .6 mile off Rt. 1; it's open weekdays 5:30 a.m.-10 p.m. and Sunday to 9 p.m. Do your own laundry or drop it off and they'll do it for you.

Special Courses

Students come from all over the world to the prestigious **Maine Photographic Workshops,** 2 Central St., P.O. Box 200, Rockport 04856, tel. (207) 236-8581, fax 236-2558, where international photo luminaries teach one- and two-week courses, summer and fall, to neophytes and professionals. A degree-granting program, called **Rockport College,** continues during the winter. Courses are fairly pricey; evening slide lectures are open to the public.

Alumni of the one-, two-, and 12-week workshops at the **Center for Furniture Craftsmanship,** 25 Mill St., Rockport 04856, tel. (207) 594-5611, rave about their experiences. Courses are for various skill levels, from beginner to pro. The center can arrange for lodging and meals.

Getting Around

Downtown Camden, at the height of summer, is a traffic nightmare. Route 1 bisects the village, and getting across it on foot or by car can be perilous. It's not Boston or Rome, but it's still aggravating. The scarcity of parking creates a musical cars situation with drivers circling endlessly to find a space. At the chamber of commerce, be sure to request local maps, which show locations of two-hour and all-day parking areas.

Better still, bring or rent a bike and use that to get around. There are few bike lanes, so safety is an extra concern, but bike enthusiasts have placed racks at strategic locations around town. Take advantage of them.

In 1996, town fathers introduced **The Camden Shuttle,** a free park-and-ride service between two outlying parking lots and downtown Camden. The shuttle makes about 20 daily runs, mid-June to Labor Day, 7:30 a.m.-6:30 p.m., with several stops along Rt. 1. The parking lots are at Camden Hills State Park (two miles north of Camden) and next to the Country Inn at Camden-Rockport (southern end of Camden). North-lot departures are on the half hour and south-lot departures are on the quarter hour. Call (207) 596-6605 with questions.

LINCOLNVILLE

Since the early 1990s, the town of Lincolnville, just north of Camden, has outpaced all the surrounding communities in population growth. An influx of new residents has pushed the census over the 2,000 mark. Two distinct enclaves make up the town—oceanfront Lincolnville Beach ("the Beach") and, about five miles inland, Lincolnville Center ("the Center"). Lincolnville is laid-back and mostly rural; the major activity center is a short strip of shops and restaurants at the Beach, and few visitors realize there's anything else.

About a mile north of Lincolnville Beach is a part of town with the quaint name of Ducktrap. Near the mouth of the Ducktrap River, where shoreline trees screen the water, ducks used to gather as ducks do. During moulting season, when the ducks shed their feathers and were unable to fly, foraging Native Americans would sneak up on them and capture them for dinner.

Directly offshore from Lincolnville Beach, almost within spitting distance, is the island of Islesboro, a fine day-trip destination from Lincolnville and the Camden-Rockport areas. The car ferry departs from the southern end of Lincolnville Beach.

SIGHTS

Kelmscott Farm

Cotswold and Shetland sheep, Kerry cattle, Gloucester Old Spots pigs, Nigerian dwarf goats, and a llama security patrol are among the unusual creatures filling the barns and fields at Kelmscott Farm, RR 2, Box 365, Lincolnville 04849, tel. (207) 763-4088, fax 763-4298. Established as a nonprofit foundation by Robyn and Bob Metcalfe (inventor of Ethernet) to preserve rare livestock breeds, the wonderful farm encourages visitors to meet the critters, walk a nature trail, bring a picnic, stroll the fabulous gardens, take a wagon ride, and browse a gift shop stocked with high-quality woolen goods. Special events are held almost every weekend. It's open Thurs.-Sun. 11 a.m.-4 p.m., Memorial Day weekend to Labor Day weekend. Admission

is $5 adults, $3 children 5-18, free for kids under five, and $8 for families. From downtown Camden, take Rt. 52 (Mountain St., a back road from Camden to Belfast) to Lincolnville Center (junction of Rts. 52, 235, and 173). Bear right, staying on Rt. 52 another 4.2 miles to Vancycle Road. Turn left to the farm (signposted).

Lincolnville's Microbrewery

A ride into rural country inland from Camden ends up at Andrew Hazen's farm-cum-brewery, **Andrew's Brewery,** High St., RFD 1, Box 4975, Lincolnville 04849, tel. (207) 763-3305. Except for major national holidays, Andrew will give a free, 15-minute tour by appointment any time of year. While you tour the brewery, the kids can visit the donkeys in the barn. Brewery specialties are Andrew's Old English Ale, Andrew's Brown Ale, and Ruby's Golden Pale Ale. From Camden, take Washington St. (Rt. 105) to Rt. 235. Go .6 mile and turn left onto Moody Mountain Road. Continue 1.6 miles and turn right onto High Street. The brewery is one mile ahead, on the left.

RECREATION

Swimming

Penobscot Bay flirts with Rt. 1 at **Lincolnville Beach,** a sandy stretch of shorefront in the congested hamlet of Lincolnville Beach. This is about as close as the road gets to the ocean. On a hot day, the sand is wall-to-wall people; during one of the coast's legendary northeasters, it's quite a wild place. There's **freshwater swimming** at several area ponds (most people would call them lakes). On Rt. 52 in Lincolnville Center, there's a small town-owned swimming/picnic area on **Norton Pond.** Other swimming ponds are **Coleman Pond, Pitcher Pond,** and **Knight's Pond.**

Sea Kayaking/Canoeing

Ducktrap Sea Kayak Tours, Rt. 1, Lincolnville Beach, mailing address HC 60, Box 3315, Camden 04843, tel. (207) 236-8608, runs two-hour harbor tours for $25 pp; a half-day guided tour is $50. No experience is needed, but be sure to call for reservations.

Best places to canoe are Norton Pond and Megunticook Lake, and you can even canoe (or kayak) all the way from the head of Norton Pond to the foot of Megunticook Lake.

Hiking

The boundaries of both Camden Hills State Park and Fernald's Neck extend into Lincolnville, where the major state-park hike follows the **Ski Shelter Trail** to the **Bald Rock Trail.** From Rt. 1 in Lincolnville Beach, take Rt. 173 west about two and a half miles to the marked parking area just beyond the junction of Youngtown Road. The 1,200-foot summit—with great views of Penobscot Bay (weather permitting)—is about two miles one way, easy to moderate hiking. The route links up with the rest of the state-park trail network, but unless you've arranged for a shuttle, it's best to do Bald Rock as a roundtrip hike.

Cross-Country Skiing

Also part of the state park—but leased to the University of Maine Cooperative Extension for environmental conferences and experiential ecology programs—is 830-acre **Tanglewood 4-H Camp and Learning Center,** Lincolnville, tel. (207) 789-5233 or 789-5868, mailing address 375 Main St., Rockland 04841, tel. (207) 596-0063. In winter, Tanglewood has more than 10 miles of cross-country trails, the best network in this part of the Mid-Coast. Some winters, Mother Nature provides scanty snow cover here, but when she obliges, the trails are superb. Some trails are also used by snowmobiles. No pets. To reach Tanglewood from Rt. 1, continue .8 mile north of Lincolnville Beach and turn left at the Tanglewood sign; go .7 mile and turn right onto an unpaved road; continue .8 mile to the camp and park on the right side. At the gate, pick up a trail map.

SHOPPING

Art, craft, and souvenir shops are clustered along the Rt. 1 strip at Lincolnville Beach; just north of town are several unusual shops and galleries worth a visit.

Handsome, dark wood buildings .2 mile north of the Beach are home to **Windsor Chairmakers,** Rt. 1, RR 2, Box 7, Lincolnville Beach 04849, tel. (207) 789-5188 or (800) 789-5188. You can observe the operation, browse the display area, or order some of their well-made chairs, cabinets, and tables. Open daily 8 a.m.-5 p.m., June-Oct.; open weekdays Nov.-May.

Professional boatbuilder Walt Simmons has branched out into decoys and wildlife carvings, and they're just as outstanding as his boats. Walt and his wife, Karen, run **Duck Trap Decoys,** Duck Trap Rd., Lincolnville 04849, tel. (207) 789-5363, a three-room gallery/shop that also features the work of nearly five dozen other woodcarvers. Open Mon.-Sat. 9 a.m.-5 p.m., April through December; also open Sunday 1-5 p.m., early May through September. Call for appointment Jan.-March.

Two miles north of Lincolnville Beach, **Maine's Massachusetts House,** Rt. 1, Lincolnville 04849, tel. (207) 789-5705, has been a reliable source of crafts and gifts since the early 1950s—long before a slew of souvenir shops invaded this area. Behind the main building, the gallery spotlights Maine artists and also carries Inuit soapstone carvings. Open Mon.-Sat. 9 a.m.-5 p.m., Sunday noon-5 p.m., May-Dec.; open weekends March and April. It's closed January and February.

ACCOMMODATIONS

B&Bs

About four miles north of Camden and a mile south of Lincolnville, **The Victorian by the Sea,** Rt. 1, Lincolnville Beach 04849, tel. (207) 236-3785 or (800) 382-9817, fax (207) 236-0945, mailing address P.O. Box 1385, Camden 04843, overlooks the bay at the end of a winding lane from Rt. 1. Six Victorian-style rooms with private baths—some with fireplaces, two with water views—are $135-245 d in summer, lower off season. Access is through the Water's Edge Motel. No smoking, no pets, no children under 10. Open all year.

About midway between Camden and Lincolnville, down an oceanward lane, **The Inn at Sunrise Point,** Rt. 1, Lincolnville, mailing address P.O. Box 1344, Camden 04843, tel. (207)

236-7716 or (800) 435-6278, fax (207) 236-0820, has three handsome rooms in the main lodge and four separate cottages. Rates run $150-350 d. Decor is tastefully elegant; breakfast in the solarium is spectacularly good. Each cottage has a double jacuzzi, phone, fireplace, TV/VCR, mini-bar, and private bay-view deck. No smoking, no pets, no children. Open late May to late October.

Located at Lincolnville Beach's ground zero—close to shops and across the street from the ferry dock, the beach, and the Lobster Pound—**The Spouter Inn,** Rt. 1, P.O. Box 270, Lincolnville Beach 04849, tel. (207) 789-5171, is the best place to overnight before or after an Islesboro day-trip. Ask the hospitable innkeepers—Paul and Catherine Lippman—about rental bikes. The inn, built in 1832, has been beautifully restored and expanded. Seven rooms (all with private baths, most with fireplaces and bay views) are $75-175 d in summer; breakfasts are memorable. No smoking, no pets, no children under seven. Open all year.

Motels and Cottages

Motels and cottage complexes are strung all along Rt. 1 between Camden and Lincolnville Beach. Rates vary widely, depending on amenities; most are not fancy.

Pine Grove Cottages, Rt. 1, HC 60, Box 585, Lincolnville 04849, tel. (207) 236-2929 or (800) 530-5265, is a neat, comfortable, no-frills cottage complex with bay views. Eight one- and two-bedroom cottages are $85-115 d (less by the week), including kitchen, phone, and cable TV. No smoking. Children are welcome and pets are allowed ($7 fee). Pine Grove is four miles north of Camden, set back from the highway. Open mid-April to mid-November.

The family-run **Mount Battie Motel,** Rt. 1, HC 60, Box 570, Lincolnville Beach 04849, tel. (207) 236-3870 or (800) 224-3870, a particular favorite of Islesboro residents, charges $50-85 d for its 23 rooms with a/c, TV, phones, and generous continental breakfast. No smoking, no pets. Four miles north of Camden, and fairly close to the highway, it's open mid-April to mid-November.

Snow Hill Lodge, Rt. 1, HC 60, Box 550, Lincolnville Beach 04849, tel. (207) 236-3452 or (800) 476-4775, fax (207) 236-8052, is a basic,

well-maintained motel with a knockout view of Penobscot Bay. Thirty rooms are $60-70 d (lower off season), with TV, phones, and free continental breakfast. No pets. It's four and a half miles north of Camden, less than a mile south of Lincolnville Beach, fairly near the highway, and open all year.

Campgrounds

Named for an early-18th-century house located on its 60 acres, **The Old Massachusetts Homestead Campground,** Rt. 1, P.O. Box 5, Lincolnville Beach 04849, tel. (207) 789-5135 or (800) 213-8142, has 68 well-spaced RV and tentsites ($18 for four people) as well as five tiny cabins. Located two miles north of Lincolnville Beach, the well-managed campground has a pool, playground, laundry facilities, and nature trails. Pets welcome. Open May through October.

FOOD

Miscellanea

The **Center General Store,** Rt. 52, Lincolnville Center, tel. (207) 763-3666, is more than just a market—it's an experience. At this old-fashioned, early-19th-century place, you can pick up baked goods, ice-cream cones, animal feed, liquor, fuel, lottery tickets, bait, and a fishing license. Stock up for a picnic or eat it here and watch the comings-and-goings. Open daily all year, except Christmas, Mon.-Fri. 6 a.m.-9 p.m., Saturday 7 a.m.-9 p.m., Sunday 8 a.m.-8 p.m.

Moderate to Expensive

Chef Manuel Mercier gives his French cuisine a Maine twist at the **Youngtown Inn,** Rt. 52 and Youngtown Rd., Box 4246, Lincolnville 04849, tel. (207) 763-4290 or (800) 291-8438, an early-19th-century restaurant and inn four and a half miles northwest of Camden. Ambience is low-key yet elegant. Specialties include rack of lamb and lobster ravioli (entrées $14-22). Open for dinner Tues.-Sun. year-round, but call ahead in winter. Upstairs are six country-French guest rooms with private baths for $85-100 d, including breakfast. Children are welcome; no smoking.

Lobster-in-the-Rough

Across the street from Chez Michel is Lincolnville's best-known landmark—**The Lobster Pound Restaurant,** Rt. 1, P.O. Box 118, Lincolnville Beach 04849, tel. (207) 789-5550. About 300 people—some days, it looks like more than that—can pile into the main restaurant, an enclosed patio, and a separate oceanfront eating area, so be sure to make reservations on summer weekends. Despite the crowds, food and service are reliably good. Lobster, of course, is king, and unless you're allergic, it's crazy not to order it here. Poultry and steaks are also available. Request a patio table. Open late April to late October for lunch and dinner; breakfast is also available in July and August.

INFORMATION

Lincolnville is part of the **Camden-Rockport-Lincolnville Chamber of Commerce,** and most of its visitor info is channeled through the chamber office in Camden—public landing, P.O. Box 919, Camden 04843, tel. (207) 236-4404. You can call in advance for the *Lincolnville Welcomes You* map/brochure, published annually by the Lincolnville Business Group, P.O. Box 202, Lincolnville 04849.

ISLESBORO

Lying three miles offshore from Lincolnville Beach, via 20-minute car ferry, is 12-mile-long Islesboro, a year-round community with a population of almost 650—beefed up annually by a sedate summer colony. Time was when islanders and summer rusticators barely intermingled—except that many islanders served as caretakers, kitchen staff, and general gofers for wealthy visitors in their grand mansions, primarily in the enclave of Dark Harbor. The summer social scene remains exhaustingly active, and many islanders still have jobs as caterers and property managers, but apartheid has diminished. Year-rounders and summer folk roll up their sleeves and work together for worthy island causes—land trust, churches, school, library, and historical society—and there's even gentle joshing about the island culture. A 1996 talent show, for example, featured the song "I Wanna Go Back to My 40-Room Shack in Dark Harbor."

Islesboro's first white settlers put down their roots in the late 1760s, taking up fishing and farming, then some shipbuilding, including boats for the giant Pendleton fleet sailing out of Searsport, across the bay. The town—covering about 6,000 acres on this and adjacent islands—was incorporated in 1788. In the 1860s, population peaked at about 1,200; grand estates and resort hotels began sprouting in the 1890s.

Nowadays, besides the service industry, the major employment options are construction and maritime trades. There are three boatyards, and

more than 30 lobsterboats are homeported here. A 1990s phenomenon is an expanding crop of high-tech freelancers living here and commuting to work via the information highway.

Car ferries are frequent enough to make Islesboro an ideal day-trip destination—and that's the choice of most visitors, partly because there's only one inn (pricey and seasonal). The only camping is on nearby Warren Island State Park—and you have to have your own boat to get there. If you're not spending the night, keep an eye on the time so you don't miss the last ferry—4:30 p.m.—back to the mainland.

SIGHTS

View from the Road

The best way to get an island overview (besides flying into the tiny airstrip) is to do an end-to-end auto tour. You won't see all the huge "cottages" tucked down long driveways, and you won't absorb island life and its rhythms (that requires a longer stay), but you'll scratch the surface of what Islesboro has to offer. Drive off the ferry, which docks about a third of the way down the island, and go one mile to a stop sign. Turn right and go 1.2 miles to another stop sign. Turn right, onto Main Rd., and go 4.3 miles south to the Town Beach at the bottom of the island. Then backtrack on Main Rd., past the turnoff to the ferry dock, heading "up island" (as it's known locally) and covering 12 miles to

Grindle Point Light and Museum, Islesboro

northernmost Pripet and Turtle Head. En route, you'll pass exclusive summer estates, workaday homes, spectacular seaside vistas, and a smattering of shops for crafts, books, and take-out food. On the up island circuit, watch for a tiny marker on the west side of the road. It commemorates the 1780 total eclipse witnessed here—the first recorded in North America. At the time, British loyalists still held Islesboro, but they temporarily suspended hostilities, allowing Harvard astronomers to lug their instruments to the island and document the eclipse.

Sailors' Memorial Museum

As the ferry glides into the western side of Gilkey Harbor, you can't miss the squat little **Grindle Point Light,** tel. (207) 734-2253, built in 1850, rebuilt in 1875, and now automated. Next to it, in the former keeper's house, is the town-owned Sailors' Memorial Museum, filled with seafaring memorabilia acquired in the 1970s. The volunteer-staffed museum is open Tues.-Sun. 9 a.m.-4:30 p.m., July through Labor Day (closed for lunch at midday). Admission is free.

Islesboro Historical Society

Right about the center of the island, 3.8 miles from the ferry and just south of the aptly named Narrows, stands the two-story Islesboro Historical Society, corner of Main and West Side Rds., tel. (207) 734-6733, in the former town hall. On the first floor are rotating temporary exhibits, throughout the summer, while the second-floor museum contains the permanent collection of island memorabilia. The society also sponsors program/meetings with guest lecturers at 8 p.m. the last Wednesday of the month. The building generally is open five days a week, 12:30-4:30 p.m., July to Labor Day, usually Sun.-Thurs.,

but call ahead to be sure. Or call for an appointment; volunteers often are in the building even when it's closed. Admission is free, but donations are welcomed.

PARKS AND RECREATION

Warren Island State Park

Why is 70-acre Warren Island State Park the most underutilized of Maine's state parks? There's no organized transportation to the island. If you want to hike, camp, or picnic on Warren, you'll need a boat—but it's well worth the effort. Besides, it'll give you a chance to see some of Islesboro's shorefront homes. A painless way to do this is to lash a kayak, canoe, or skiff atop your vehicle, take the ferry from Lincolnville Beach, park at the Islesboro ferry landing, and paddle the protected quarter mile to the east side of the island. There are nine well-spaced, wooded campsites with picnic tables and plenty of potable water and firewood; no reservations accepted. For information, contact the Camden Hills State Park manager, tel. (207) 236-3109. Day-use fees are $2 adults, 50 cents children 5-11, free for seniors and children four and under. Camping is $15 pp per site per night for nonresidents. The park is open Memorial Day weekend to September 15.

Town Beach

At Pendleton Point, Islesboro's southern tip, the Town Beach has two sandy pockets, tidepools, unique rock formations, wooded paths, well-spaced picnic tables, blackberry bushes (in season), and great views. The beach is two and a half miles south of Dark Harbor Village.

Cycling/Hiking

Islesboro is fairly level, and walking end to end is unrealistic for a day-trip, so a bicycle would seem to be the perfect solution. Not exactly. Bicycles are very controversial here—hardly surprising, since the shoulderless roads are narrow and too many cyclists have failed to heed commonsense rules. A safer solution is to take leisurely drives to both ends of the island, then park the car (in summer, there's room near the handsome stone Islesboro Central School, which also has two creative playgrounds) and walk along the road through Dark Harbor Village to the Town Beach at the southern end of the island.

ENTERTAINMENT

Churches, the library, and the historical society manage to organize impressive schedules of concerts, lectures, craft fairs, public suppers, and other events during July and August—when the population is at its height and fundraising is most successful. Check the *Islesboro Island News* for listings. The **Performing Arts Series** of the Society for the Preservation of the Free Will Baptist Church includes classical, jazz, vocal, and steel-band music. Concerts are at 8 p.m., usually Thursday or Saturday, at the church (also known as the Up Island Church).

SHOPPING

Art, Antiques, and Gifts

The well-connected **Double Door Gallery,** Main Rd., P.O. Box 271, Islesboro 04848, tel. (207) 734-6507, just south of the library, mounts rotating art exhibits throughout its season: late June to mid-September. The gallery is open Tues.-Sat. 10 a.m.-3 p.m.

Since 1992, Diane Pendleton has been dealing in country antiques (and decorative painting) at **Pentimento,** West Shore Rd., P.O. Box 296, tel. (207) 734-6515, obtaining much of her inventory at auctions. Open Tues.-Sat. 10 a.m.-5 p.m., early June to mid-October. In the same building is **Islesboro Realty,** tel. (207) 734-6488, one of the island's clearinghouses for seasonal rentals.

Island **gift shops** worth a look-see are **Apples,** tel. (207) 734-9727, **Sundry Scents,** tel. (207) 734-9704, **Popcorn Tree Gifts,** tel. (207) 734-6411, and **Island Designs,** tel. (207) 734-8809 or 734-6901.

ACCOMMODATIONS AND FOOD

Unless you have island pals, a seasonal rental, or a boat anchored in the harbor, the only place to stay in Islesboro is the bright yellow **Dark Harbor House,** P.O. Box 185, Dark Harbor, Islesboro 04848, tel. (207) 734-6669—but what a place it is. Built in the late 19th century by a Philadelphia banker, the Georgian Revival mansion (on the National Historic Register) has 10 rooms, all with private baths, some with fireplaces and balconies. Despite the pomp, the ambience is casual. Breakfast and dinner (open to the public by reservation) are served in the oval dining room. Rooms are $110-245 d, including full breakfast, worth the splurge if you can swing it; two-night minimum on holiday weekends. No smoking, no pets, no children under 12. The inn has bikes for guests to use, and they'll arrange access to the island's private golf club. Open mid-May to mid-October.

The Dark Harbor Shop, Dark Harbor, tel. (207) 734-8878, fax 734-8883, is the hub for local gossip over breakfast, lunch, snacks, sandwiches, or just an ice-cream cone. Kids love the penny candy, and there's a selection of gifts. When the late Sen. Margaret Chase Smith cruised to Islesboro on her namesake ferry, she lunched at the counter here. Open daily 8 a.m.-5 p.m. (to 7 p.m. in July and August). Bill Warren, the Dark Harbor Shop's owner, also operates **Warren Realty,** tel. (207) 734-8857; if you're interested in a **seasonal rental,** check with him.

Best place for a quickie snack is **The Islander,** a tiny takeout right at the ferry landing, tel. (207) 734-2270. The breakfast menu (40 cents-$4) includes a Texas scramble; the lunch/dinner menu ($1-6) has daily specials, plus lobster rolls, burgers, and fish 'n chips. How about homemade pie for $1.50? Open daily 7 a.m.-5 p.m., Friday and Saturday to 7 p.m.

Islesboro's two markets both sell sandwiches and other picnic fare in summer—much easier than packing lunch ahead of time. **Durkee's**

General Store, Main Rd., corner of Ryder's Rd., tel. (207) 734-2201, sells a full line of groceries, plus hardware, fuel, newspapers, T-shirts, and liquor. Open Mon.-Sat. 8 a.m.-6 p.m. (to 7 p.m. Friday and Saturday) and Sunday 10 a.m.-2 p.m. Near the post office and the municipal building, **The Island Market,** tel. (207) 734-6672, carries a similar inventory (beer and wine, but no liquor), plus terrific baked goods, and is open Mon.-Sat. 6 a.m.-5:30 p.m., plus Sunday 9 a.m.-1 p.m. July and August.

For designer take-out food—gourmet picnic goodies such as pâté, smoked fish, and breads —head for Betty Ann Boucher's **Four Shades of Purple,** Dark Harbor, tel. (207) 734-9702. Open late May to mid-October. July and August hours are Mon.-Sat. 7 a.m.-3:30 p.m. (to 5:30 Friday and Saturday), Sunday 10 a.m.-2 p.m. Early in the season, and after Labor Day, hours are 9:30 a.m.-2:30 p.m. except Sunday and Wednesday.

INFORMATION AND SERVICES

There's no chamber of commerce on the island, so the best source of information is a free annual map/brochure called *The Island of Islesboro,* available at the ferry landing in Lincolnville Beach, and the **Town Office,** Municipal Building, Main Rd., P.O. Box 76, Islesboro 04848, tel. (207) 734-2253, which is open weekdays 8:30 a.m.-4:30 p.m.

The handsome stone **Alice L. Pendleton Memorial Library,** corner of Main and Hewes Point Rds., tel. (207) 734-2218, is open Wednesday, Saturday, and Sunday 1:30-4:30 p.m. The local newspaper is the chatty *Islesboro Island News,* HC 60, Box 227, Islesboro 04848, tel. (207) 734-6745, an ad-filled tabloid published about six times a year.

For **ambulance, fire, and police,** call (800) 660-3398 (toll-free connection to the Waldo County Sheriff's office). Only in July and August does Islesboro have a resident police officer—an arrangement islanders refer to as "rent-a-cop." A physician's assistant is based at the **Islesboro Health Center** in the municipal build-

ing, tel. (207) 734-2213. Health Center hours are 9 a.m.-4 p.m.; critical cases are ferried to mainland hospitals.

There are **public toilets** at the ferry terminal in Gilkey Harbor and at the Town Beach.

GETTING THERE

The car ferry *Margaret Chase Smith* departs Lincolnville Beach almost every hour on the hour, 8 or 9 a.m. to 5 p.m., and Islesboro on the half hour, 7:30 a.m.-4:30 p.m. Roundtrip fares are $13 for car and driver, $4.50 adults, $2 children, $4 adult bicycles, $2 kids' bikes. Reservations are $5 extra. A slightly reduced schedule prevails late October to early May. The 20-minute trip crosses a stunning three-mile stretch of Penobscot Bay, with views of islands and the Camden Hills. In summer, avoid the biggest bottlenecks: Friday afternoon (to Islesboro), Sunday afternoon and Monday holiday afternoons (from Islesboro). The *Smith* remains on Islesboro overnight, so don't miss the last run to Lincolnville Beach. For more information contact **Maine State Ferry Service,** P.O. Box 214, Lincolnville 04849, tel. (207) 789-5611, Islesboro tel. (207) 734-6935.

Since ferry service ends in the late afternoon, Capt. Earl MacKenzie has established a water taxi to help islanders and mainlanders attend evening programs, meetings, and social events. The 28-passenger *Quicksilver* operates Thursday and Saturday, departing Islesboro at 9:40 p.m. and Lincolnville Beach at 10 p.m. Cost is $5 pp. He'll also do special charter runs for $60 per boatload. You can reach him at tel. (207) 734-6984, onboard cellular phone (207) 557-0197.

Small-plane air-charter companies serving Islesboro are **Ace Aviation,** Belfast Airport, tel. (207) 338-2970 or (800) 338-2970, and **Penobscot Air Service** (PAS), Knox County Regional Airport, Owls Head, tel. (207) 596-6211 or (800) 780-6071. The PAS fare from Owls Head to Islesboro is $70 pp; a planeload (five persons) is $105.

BELFAST AREA

With a population of 6,300, Belfast is relatively small as cities go, but changes have been occurring at lightning speed—courtesy of gigantic credit-card company MBNA (the nation's second-largest in credit cards and largest in affinity cards), which established a major presence here in 1996. Even before MBNA arrived, Belfast was becoming one of those off-the-beaten-track destinations popular with tuned-in visitors. Chalk that up to its status as a magnet for leftover back-to-the-landers and enough artistic types to earn the city a nod for cultural cool. Belfast boasts a curling club, meditation centers, a clutch of art galleries and boutiques, dance and theater companies, the oldest shoe store in America, and half a dozen different 12-step self-help groups.

This eclectic city is a work in progress, a study in Maine-style diversity. It's also a gold mine of Federal, Greek Revival, Italianate, and Victorian architecture—some of it occasionally on the market for only a tad more than the proverbial song (although that, too, is changing). Take the time to stroll the well-planned back streets, explore the shops, and hang out at the newly cleaned-up waterfront.

Down at the harbor, a visitor's first question is likely to be, "Good grief! How do you say the name of that river?" Separating Belfast from East Belfast, the Passagassawaukeag River is pronounced "Puh-sag-gus-uh-WAH-keg," but it is known more familiarly as "the Passy." The Indian name has been translated as both "place of many ghosts" and the rather different "place for spearing sturgeon by torchlight."

Native Americans, of course, were here long before the first Scotch-Irish settlers, who put down roots in 1765 and soon named their village for the Irish city. After the Revolutionary War, development began in earnest, with shipbuilding remaining the major enterprise well into the 20th century. Most of the workers lived along Bay View Street, a district leveled by fire in 1873; the prosperous ship owners and other entrepreneurs built grand mansions on Church Street, High Street, and Primrose Hill.

Following World War II, the economy shifted, and poultry eclipsed shipbuilding. At one point, Belfast was the largest chicken processor in the world. The annual July Broiler Festival celebrated the industry with a marathon chicken barbecue (although the chickens have flown the coop, the barbecue is still a highlight of the successor Belfast Bay Festival).

As the hub of 724-square-mile Waldo County, which has a population of about 35,000, Belfast draws its traffic and talent from many surrounding communities—Northport, Searsmont, Liberty, Freedom, Thorndike, Unity, Brooks, Waldo, Swanville, and Monroe.

SIGHTS

Historic Walking Tour

No question, the best way to appreciate Belfast's fantastic architecture is to tour by ankle express. At the Belfast Area Chamber of Commerce, pick up the well-researched *Belfast Historic Walking Tour* map/brochure. Among the 43 highlights on the mile-long, self-guided route are the 1818 Federal-style **First Church,** handsome residences on **High** and **Church Streets,** and the 1840 **James P. White House** (corner of Church St. and Northport Ave., not open to the public), New England's finest Greek Revival residence. Amazing for a community of this size, the city actually has three distinct National Historic Districts: Belfast Commercial Historic District (47 downtown buildings), Church Street Historic District (residential), and Primrose Hill Historic District (also residential).

Bayside

Continuing the focus on architecture, just south of Belfast, in Northport, is the Victorian enclave of Bayside, a neighborhoody sort of place with small, well-kept, gingerbreaded cottages cheek by jowl on pint-size lots. Formerly known as the Northport Wesleyan Grove Campground, the village took shape in the mid-1800s as a summer retreat for Methodists. In the 1930s, the retreat was disbanded and the main meeting hall was razed, creating the waterfront park at the heart of the village. Today, many of the colorfully painted homes are rented by the week, month, or summer, and their tenants now indulge in athletic rather than religious pursuits. The camaraderie remains, though, and a stroll (or cycle or drive) through Bayside is like a visit to another era. Bayside is four miles south of Belfast, just east of Rt. 1.

Temple Heights

Continue south on Shore Rd. from Bayside to **Temple Heights Spiritualist Camp,** Shore Rd., Northport, tel. (207) 338-3029, mailing address P.O. Box 311, Lincolnville 04849, yet another religious enclave—this one still going. Founded in 1882, Temple Heights has become a shadow of its former self, reduced to the funky, 12-room Nikawa Lodge on Shore Road, but the summer program continues, thanks to prominent mediums from all over the country. Even a temporary setback in 1996—when the camp president was suspended for allegedly putting a hex on Northport's town clerk—failed to derail the operation. Camp programs, late June through Labor Day, are open to the public; a schedule is published each spring. Spiritualist services and group healing sessions are free; day-long Saturday seminars are $25 and Monday-night classes (including one that teaches mediumship) are $5. Better yet, sign up for a one-and-a-half-hour **group message service,** when you'll sit in a circle with a medium and a dozen or so others and receive insights—often uncannily on-target—from departed relatives or friends. Message services occur Wednesday and Saturday at 7:30 p.m.(arrive a half-hour early). Cost is $8 pp and reservations are necessary. Private readings can be arranged for $25, or a mini-reading for $15.

The Bull Moose Railroad

And now for something completely different. On the Belfast waterfront, climb aboard the **Belfast and Moosehead Lake Railroad,** 43 Front St., Belfast, mailing address 1 Depot Sq., Unity 04988, tel. (207) 948-5500 or (800) 392-5500, fax (207) 948-5903, and chug off into the countryside. Affectionately called the Bull Moose Railroad, the B&ML has been operating excursion trains through rural Waldo County for decades—and since the late 1980s in its most recent incarnation. From mid-May through October, a diesel engine does a one-and-a-half-hour Belfast-to-Waldo route ($14 adults, $7 kids). In Unity, about 20 miles west and north of Belfast, the B&ML operates a Swedish steam train on a Unity-to-Burnham route Thurs.-Sun. ($14 adults, $7 kids). Each has a dining car serving subs, chips, cookies, soda, and wine. A kitschy extra is a "surprise" train robbery on each route; kids love it. In Unity, you can watch the steam engine being turned on the round-table. Fall-foliage season is far and away the most popular, so book well ahead to ensure a seat. The schedule is intricate, so it's best to call for a copy. In June, both routes run weekends only. In summer, the train links up with a one-and-a-half-hour Belfast-based cruise ($14 adults, $7 kids) aboard the *Voyageur,* a Mississippi riverboat gone astray. Combo tickets and overnight packages are also available.

Gull's-Eye View

Based at Belfast Municipal Airport, **Ace Aviation,** Rt. 1, P.O. Box 457, Belfast 04915, tel. (207) 338-2970 or (800) 338-2970, operates scenic flights by reservation Feb.-December. Best time to go is late September to early October, when the foliage is spectacular. For a 30-minute tour (the most popular)—taking in islands, the Camden Hills, the bay, or your own requested route—cost is $50 pp (maximum three persons). A 15-minute flight is $25 per person.

A Little-of-Everything Museum

Stop here before or after the Unity-to-Burnham rail excursion—it's only three miles southeast of Unity. **Bryant Stove and Music Museum,** Rts. 139 and 220, Rich Rd., Box 2048, Thorndike 04986, tel. (207) 568-3665, fax 568-3666, the creation of Joe and Bea Bryant, started out as a woodstove business. Now it's an eclectic collection of antique woodstoves, player pianos, nickelodeons, and cars, plus an incredible doll circus. Bring the old folks, bring the kids—everyone finds this barn of a place (and its owners) fascinating. (The owners also operate a mail-order business; send for the catalog.) Open Mon.-Sat. 8 a.m.-5 p.m., all year. Admission is $4 adults, $2 children 8-18, free for kids under eight. The museum is 30 miles northwest of Belfast.

PARKS AND RECREATION

One of the state's best municipal parks is just on the outskirts of downtown. Established in 1904, **Belfast City Park**, 87 Northport Ave., tel. (207) 338-1661, has lighted tennis courts, an outdoor pool, a pebbly beach, plenty of picnic tables, an unusually creative playground, lots of green space for the kids, and fantastic views of Isles-boro, Blue Hill, and Penobscot Bay. The park is the site of the annual Belfast Bay Festival. For more action, right in the heart of Belfast, head for **Heritage Park**, with front-row seats on waterfront happenings. Bring a picnic, grab a table, and watch the yachts, tugs, and lobsterboats.

Lake St. George State Park

Along the lake's western shore, 360-acre Lake St. George State Park, Rt. 3, Liberty 04949, tel. (207) 589-4255, is another of Maine's secret treasures—known best to local residents. The spring-fed lake tends to be cool, but not as cold as the ocean, so a warm day brings out the crowds. Wooded picnic sites border the lake, as do some of the 38 campsites, which go for $16 for nonresidents. (Try for a waterfront site; those nearer the highway can be noisy.) Pack your fishing gear and a small boat—or rent one here for $10 a day. Across Rt. 3 are hiking trails, easy to moderately strenuous. Admission is $2 adults, 50 cents kids 5-11. Open May 15-Sept. 30, but since the park is alongside Rt. 3, it's accessible all year. The park entrance is two miles west of downtown Liberty, 19 miles west of Belfast.

Swan Lake State Park

Lovely name, this one—and a lovely 67-acre park for a picnic and swim: Swan Lake State Park, Frankfort Rd., Swanville 04915, tel. (207) 525-4404. Admission is $2 adults, 50 cents kids 5-11. Open Memorial Day weekend to Labor Day, but accessible all year. Swanville is six miles north of Belfast. To reach the park, take Rt. 141 about three miles north of town and turn right (sign-posted) onto Frankfort Road. Continue to the park access road (on the right).

Hiking

Belfast and the rest of Waldo County have some fine hiking spots, but for serious hikes, drive to Camden Hills State Park. An excellent hiking resource for the entire state, but especially for Waldo County, is *Hiking Maine,* by Tom Seymour (see the Booklist), who lives in the Belfast area. He describes hikes along the two B&ML excursion railbeds, plus Frye Mountain (with an abandoned fire tower), Mt. Waldo and Howard Mendall Marsh (near Frankfort), Halfmoon Pond (near Brooks), and Lake St. George State Park.

Golf

Just south of Belfast is the nine-hole **Northport Golf Club,** 581 Bluff Rd., Northport, mailing address RR 1, Belfast 04915, tel. (207) 338-2270, established in 1916. Operating out of a classic shingled clubhouse, the club is open mid-April to mid-October. Snacks and carts are available; starting times usually aren't necessary.

Much newer (opened in 1963) and less fussy is the aptly named **Country View Golf Club,** Rt. 7, Brooks 04921, tel. (207) 722-3161. No starting times are needed at this well-maintained, family-run club. Rural vistas are fabulous on the nine-hole course, especially in spring and fall. Snacks and carts are available. Open early April through October. The club is a mile north of Brooks, 12 miles northwest of Belfast.

Georges River Scenic Byway

Seventeen miles west of Belfast, in Liberty, is the beginning of the Georges River Scenic Byway, a 50-mile auto route along the St. George River (a.k.a. Georges River) from its inland headwaters to the sea in Port Clyde. The official start is at the junction of Rts. 3 and 220 in Liberty, but you can follow the trail in either direction, or pick it up anywhere along the way. Road signs are posted, but it's far better to obtain a map/brochure at a chamber of commerce or other information locale. Or contact the architects of the route: **The Georges River Land Trust** (GRLT), 328 Main St., Rockland 04841, tel. (207) 594-5166.

Still in the fledgling phase are the Georges River Bikeways, one of which also goes through this head-waters area east and north of Liberty. Two other routes begin around Searsmont and include Union, Warren, and Thomaston. To follow these routes, you'll need a mountain bike, the GRLT map, and a copy of the DeLorme *Maine Atlas and Gazetteer.* Contact the GRLT for its bike-ways map.

Getting Afloat

Until the early 1990s, pleasure boats were scarce in Belfast Harbor. Tugboats, however, were abundant—sturdy workhorses based here and used for heavy-duty towing all along the coast. But, as with Rockland to the south, polluting industry has declined in Belfast, the waterfronts have been upgraded, and yachts have moved in.

The retired New Orleans riverboat *Voyageur* is the "sail" part of rail-and-sail trips organized by the Belfast and Moosehead Lake Railroad, but you can also book a one-and-a-half-hour cruise and skip the train ride. Cost is $14 adults, $7 kids.

If you don't have your own kayak, Harvey Schiller's **Belfast Kayak Tours,** RR 1, Box 715, Freedom 04941, tel. (207) 382-6204, based at Belfast's public landing, operates hour-long, three-mile harbor excursions. Hours are 9 a.m.-6 p.m. daily, weather permitting, mid-June to Labor Day. Cost is $15 adults, $10 kids 10-15. Longer trips can be arranged. Reservations aren't required, but it's worth calling to confirm the schedule and weather conditions. If you're at all squeamish, go in the morning—the harbor tends to be less choppy then.

If you've brought your own kayak or canoe, several lakes and ponds inland from Belfast are prime destinations (with boat-launching sites): Freedom Pond (officially, Sandy Pond), Unity Pond, Quantabacook Lake, Levenseller Pond, and the lakes at the two state parks (see above).

Searsmont, southwest of Belfast, is the starting point for the annual St. George River Canoe Race, one of the earliest spring whitewater races. Once summer arrives, there's great canoeing on this river, a real pastoral experience. The *AMC River Guide: Maine* (see the Booklist) has details.

Winter Sports

Nearest downhill ski area is the Camden Snow Bowl, and the best cross-country skiing is at Tanglewood 4-H Camp and Learning Center in Lincolnville. In Belfast itself there's **ice-skating** at "The Muck," a pond at the edge of town (corner of Lincolnville Ave. and Miller St.), east of the Rt. 1 bypass.

The Scottish national sport of curling has dozens of enthusiastic supporters at Maine's only curling rink, the **Belfast Curling Club,** Belmont Ave., Rt. 3, Belfast 04915, tel. (207) 338-9851 or 548-0142, an institution here since the late 1950s. Leagues play regularly on week-nights, and the club holds tournaments *(bonspiels)* and open houses several times during the season, which runs early November to early April.

ENTERTAINMENT

It's relatively easy to find nightlife in Belfast—not only are there theaters and a cinema, but there's usually a bar open at least until midnight, and sometimes later. Some spots also feature live music, particularly on weekends.

If you don't feel like searching out a newspaper to check the entertainment listings, just go to the Belfast Co-op Store, 123 High St., tel. (207) 338-2532, and study the bulletin board. You'll find notices for more activities than you could ever squeeze into your schedule.

An old-fashioned downtown cinema—recently restored to its art deco splendor—shows first-run films for moderate ticket prices. The **Colonial Theatre,** 163 High St., Belfast, tel. (207) 338-1930, has twin screens, each with one or two showings a night and 2 p.m. matinees Saturday and Sunday. Open all year.

Check local papers for the schedule of the **Belfast Maskers,** a community theater group that never fails to win raves for its interpretations of contemporary and classical dramas and musicals. Performances are held throughout the year in the waterfront Railroad Theater, 43 Front St., Belfast, tel. (207) 338-9668. In winter, wear an extra pair of socks; the floor is drafty.

Just south of Belfast, the funky **Blue Goose Dance Hall,** Rt. 1, Northport, tel. (207) 338-3003, has to be seen to be believed. This low-slung roadside establishment is the site of folk concerts, contra dances, auctions, and more. Most events occur Saturday nights. Check local papers or the Belfast Co-op Store bulletin board.

FESTIVALS AND EVENTS

Belfast is a hive of activity, but lots of the surrounding Waldo County communities also put on some ambitious fairs, festivals, and public suppers. Check the newspapers for schedules.

Taking place in Brooks Village, **Brooks Field Days** is a four-day rural-village festival tied to the Fourth of July. Featured are food and craft booths, fireworks, kids' events, and a demolition derby. The **Annual Garden Walk,** usually the second weekend of the month, offers two days (10 a.m.-4 p.m.) of self-guided access to some of Belfast's loveliest horticulture. Proceeds benefit Waldo County General Hospital. Tickets are $8. The third week in July, the **Belfast Bay Festival** is the highlight of the summer—five days of fun including a carnival, live music, kids' games, bingo, fireworks, a parade, craft booths, and a chicken barbecue in Belfast City Park.

Labor Day weekend brings the **Annual Maine Healing Arts Festival** to Hidden Valley Camp in Freedom. The three-day New Age get-together includes workshops, meditations, sweat-lodge ceremonies, gourmet vegetarian meals, firewalking, and a full program for children. Lodging is in cabins, or you can bring a tent. Advance registration is required; call (207) 336-2065; brochure available. Cost is about $260 pp, much less for children. The third weekend in September is the unique **Common Ground Country Fair** in Unity, featuring hayrides, ethnic- and wholesome-food booths, country dancing, folk art and craft demonstrations, exotic animals, world music, books, and alternative-lifestyle booths. Sponsored by Maine Organic Farmers and Gardeners Association.

Downtown Belfast comes alive the first Saturday in October with the **Church Street Festival** and its food booths, art and craft exhibits and sales, unique parade, and kids' events. Hours are 9 a.m.-5 p.m.

SHOPPING
Antiques

Searsport, just east on Rt. 1, holds the Mid-Coast "antiques capital" title, but Belfast has several fine antiques sources. Outlying **Liberty** gets the prize for being the best area source of antique tools.

Avis Howells Antiques, 21 Pearl St., corner of Court St., Belfast 04915, tel. (207) 338-3302, specializes in high-quality Canton ware and Shaker items, with prices to match. Her inventory is superb. Open all year by appointment.

Downtown, in a wonderful Victorian Gothic building with tin ceilings and unusual wainscoting, **Landmark Architectural Antiques,** 4 Main St., Belfast, tel. (207) 338-4933, provides the setting for **The Gothic,** a Lilliputian coffeehouse. Both enterprises are equally casual, and sometimes it's hard to figure out where one ends and the other starts. Maybe that's the point. The antiques are eccentric, the sandwiches and pastries are fabulous. No smoking. Credit cards accepted for antiques only. Open Mon.-Sat. 8 a.m.-8 p.m., in summer. Spring and fall hours are Mon.-Fri. 8 a.m.-5 p.m., Saturday 9 a.m.-3 p.m. Closed mid-December through April.

It's a store! It's a museum! It's amazing! More than 10,000 "useful" tools—plus used books and prints and other tidbits—fill the three-story **Liberty Tool Company,** Main St., Liberty 04949, tel. (207) 589-4771. Drawn by nostalgia and a compulsion for handmade adzes and chisels, thousands of vintage-tool buffs arrive at this eclectic emporium each year; few leave empty-handed. No credit cards. Open daily 9 a.m.-5 p.m., June 1 to mid-October; open Thurs.-Sun. 9 a.m.-5 p.m. mid-October to late December and early March through May. From the Rt. 1 bypass, take Rt. 3 west, 17 miles, then turn left at the signs for Liberty village.

Across the street is Liberty Graphics (see below), and just down Main Street is the old **Liberty Post Office,** a unique octagonal structure that looks like an oversized box. Built in 1867 as a harnessmaker's shop and later used as the town's post office, it's now the headquarters/museum of the Liberty Historical Society, tel. (207) 589-4393. In July and August, the museum is open Saturday and Sunday 1-4 p.m.

Art Galleries

Artfellows Cooperative Gallery, 104B Main St., Belfast 04915, tel. (207) 338-5776, exhibits the work of nearly two dozen jury-selected artists. Much of the art is experimental and non-traditional; prices are moderate. The gallery is open May-Dec., Wed.-Fri. 11 a.m.-4 p.m. (to 7 p.m. Friday) and Saturday 10 a.m.-4 p.m. Many of the Artfellows members (and some non-members) also have **studios** regularly or periodically open to the public. Ask for details at the gallery.

Exactly midway between Lincolnville Beach and Belfast (five miles in each direction), **The Studio at Saturday Cove,** 608 Atlantic Hwy., Rt. 1, Northport, mailing address 608 Atlantic Hwy., Lincolnville 04849, tel. (207) 338-3654, is a retired post office/gas station transformed into a cheerful gallery. Featuring Maine artists in excellent rotating exhibits, the gallery is open Tues.-Sat. 9 a.m.-5 p.m. and Sunday noon-5 p.m. in summer, shorter hours off season.

Books

Belfast's two independent bookstores are friendly places with good intentions but not huge inventories. **Canterbury Tales,** 52 Main St., Belfast 04915, tel. (207) 338-1171 or (888) 338-1171, also carries topo maps and recorded books. It's open Mon.-Sat. 9 a.m.-6 p.m., Sunday 11 a.m.-5 p.m. Farther up the hill, the quaintly named **Fertile Mind Bookshop,** 105 Main St., tel. (207) 338-2498, has a particularly good children's section and also carries magazines. It's open Mon.-Sat. all year.

For **used books,** there are two good options: **Frederica de Beurs Books,** 42 Cedar St., Belfast, tel. (207) 338-4122, specializes in art books, music, and Maine authors; open all year, Wed.-Sun. 10 a.m.-5 p.m. The entrance is around the corner on Grove Street. **The Booklover's Attic,** Searsport Ave., RFD 2, Box 8, Belfast, tel. (207) 338-2450, carries children's and military books plus lots of old LP recordings; open May-Oct., Mon.-Sat. 10 a.m.-5 p.m., Sunday 11 a.m.-4 p.m.

Clothing, Gifts, and Crafts

With historic brick buildings, eclectic boutiques, art galleries, cafes, and even a few Joe-Six-pack stores, downtown Belfast is a fun place to shop and window-shop.

Even if shoes aren't on your shopping list, stop in at "the oldest shoe store in America." Founded in the 1830s (!), **Colburn Shoe Store,** 79 Main St., Belfast 04915, tel. (207) 338-1934 or (800) 286-8613, may be old, but it isn't old-fashioned—all the latest brands and styles are here. Open all year, Mon.-Sat. 9 a.m.-5 p.m. (to 7 p.m. Thursday and Friday) and Sunday 11 a.m.-4 p.m., June-Dec. Hours are the same Jan.-May, except the store closes at 5 p.m. on Thursday and Friday.

Coyote Moon, 54 Main St., Belfast, tel. (207) 338-5659, is an especially attractive New Age-y boutique carrying natural-fiber clothing, jewelry, recycled-paper items, and, of course, incense. Open all year. In summer hours are Mon.-Thurs. 9 a.m.-7 p.m., Fri.-Sat. 9 a.m.-8 p.m., and Sunday 10:30 a.m.-6 p.m. Off season it's open Mon.-Sat. 9:30 a.m.-6 p.m., Sunday 11 a.m.-5 p.m.

Even more exotic wares fill the walls and shelves across the street at **Timelines,** 61 Main St., Belfast, tel. (207) 338-6884, focusing on Third World crafts. Open all year, Mon.-Fri. 10 a.m.-6 p.m., Saturday 9 a.m.-6 p.m., and Sunday noon-5 p.m.

Gourmets should just head straight for **The Good Table,** 68 Main St., Belfast, tel. (207) 338-4880 or (800) 588-7591, source of cookbooks galore and almost any kitchen tools and gadgets you can think of. Open all year, Mon.-Sat. 10 a.m.-5 p.m. Between Thanksgiving and Christmas, The Good Table also opens on Sunday 1-4 p.m.

About two miles east of Belfast's bridge, on the right, is the small roadside shop of **Mainely Pottery,** Searsport Ave., Rt. 1, Belfast, tel. (207) 338-1108. Since 1988, Jeannette Faunce and Jamie Oates have been marketing the work of two dozen Maine potters, each with different techniques, glazes, and styles. It's the perfect place to select from a wide range of reasonably priced work. Peek into the adjacent studio and you'll find Jamie, who specializes in lamps (under the name of Pequog Pottery) and is happy to answer questions. Don't miss Jeannette's garden out back. The shop is open daily, June to mid-October. Off season, they're at P.O. Box 123, Brooks 04921, tel. (207) 722-3567.

Natural Foods/Farmers' Market

The **Belfast Co-op Store,** 123 High St., Belfast 04915, tel. (207) 338-2532, is an experience in itself. You'll have a good impression of Belfast after one glance at the clientele and the bulletin board. Open to members and nonmembers alike (with lower prices for members), the co-op store has local organic produce, fresh and frozen pesto, baked goods, bulk grains and nuts, a great deli, meat and fish, cheeses, camping foods, wine and beer, and a chummy cafe. Hours are Mon.-Fri. 8 a.m.-7 p.m., Saturday 9 a.m.-7 p.m., Sunday 10 a.m.-5 p.m. Lunch is available in the café weekdays 11 a.m.-2 p.m.; Saturday and Sunday brunches are 10 a.m.-2 p.m.

A fixture since 1980, the **Belfast Farmers' Market** sets up, rain or shine, in Belfast Plaza ("Reny's Plaza" locally), junction of Rts. 1 and 3, Tuesday 3:30-6:30 p.m. and Fri.-Sat. 9 a.m.-1 p.m., May through October. Among the goodies are maple syrup, crafts, cheeses, organic herbs, and Chinese food.

If you're in the area between late June and mid-July, head out to **Schartner's Mt. View Fruit & Berry Farm,** Rt. 220, Thorndike 04986, tel. (207) 568-3668, and pick your own strawberries on their 20 acres—cheaper and tastier than buying them at the market. Go early—you'll still have plenty of company; Schartner's is legendary. Feel free to sample as you work (in moderation, of course). It's open daily 5 a.m.-8 p.m.; they even provide drinking water, picnic tables, portable toilets, and strawberry recipes. In mid-September, when their acres of pick-your-own apple trees are ready, Schartner's is open Tues.-Sun. 9 a.m.-5 p.m. On fall weekends, there are horse-drawn hayrides, 10 a.m.-3 p.m. Thorndike is about 30 miles from Belfast, a fun detour.

Discount Shopping
Bargains are here to be had, but caveat emptor—check items carefully before you plunk down your cash.

With designs heavy on wildlife and the environment, the **Harborside Graphics Factory Store,** Belfast ("Reny's") Plaza, Rts. 1 and 3, Belfast, tel. (207) 338-4551, carries sweatshirt and T-shirt closeouts and seconds. A percentage of profits goes to environmental causes. Open daily (except major winter holidays) all year.

Across the street from the Liberty Tool Company is the **Liberty Graphics Outlet Store,** 1 Main St., P.O. Box 5, Liberty 04949, tel. (207) 589-4035, fax 589-4415, selling the ecosensitive company's overstocks, seconds, and discontinued-design T-shirts. Outstanding silkscreened designs are done with water-based inks, and many of the shirts are organic cotton. Also available in this old-fashioned shop are Maine-made craft items and good-for-you snacks., It's open daily 9 a.m.-5 p.m., April-Dec.; March hours are weekends 9 a.m.-5 p.m.; it's closed January and February. Liberty is 17 miles west of Belfast.

ACCOMMODATIONS

B&Bs
Located on a quiet side street, **The Jeweled Turret,** 16 Pearl St., Belfast 04915, tel. (207) 338-2304 or (800) 696-2304, is one of Belfast's pioneer B&Bs. Carl and Cathy Heffentrager understand the business and go out of their way to make guests comfortable. The 1898 Victorian inn is loaded with handsome woodwork and Victorian antiques—plus an astonishing stone fireplace. Carl can even fix your bike, if necessary, and he's up on all the local byways. Seven rooms (with private baths) are $70-95 d, $60-85 d off season. No smoking, no pets. Open all year.

One of Belfast's prized historic properties, the 1812 Admiral Pratt House (also called the Pratt-Johnson House), is now **The Inn on Primrose Hill,** 212 High St., Belfast, tel. (207) 338-6982 or (888) 338-6982, an especially attractive B&B with four guest rooms (three with private bath) at $75-85 d (including tax). Pat and Linus Heinz serve breakfast and afternoon tea at one end of the barrel-ceilinged living room, overlooking outstanding gardens (including a Zen-style garden). Children welcome; no pets, no smoking, no credit cards. Open all year.

Marble fireplaces, tin ceilings, and ornate woodwork fill the public and guest rooms of the 1840 **Alden House Bed & Breakfast,** 63 Church St., Belfast, tel. (207) 338-2151 or (800) 335-2151, in the Church Street Historic District. Marla Stickle and Jessica Jahnke, enthusiastic innkeepers and cooks, have seven rooms (most with private baths) for $65-95 d. They also have a huge video library; some rooms have VCRs. No smoking, no pets. Open all year.

Motels

Most of the Belfast-area motels are on the Rt. 1 stretch just to the east of town, toward Searsport. Some have been here for decades, others are brand new; prices and quality vary widely. Below are some good choices.

Belfast's flagship motel is the **Comfort Inn,** Rt. 1, Belfast 04915, tel. (207) 338-2090 or (800) 228-5150, opened in 1996 with 52 ocean-view rooms and suites. All have a/c, cable TV, and phones. The motel has an indoor pool, sauna, wheelchair access, and free continental breakfast. Doubles are $115 in summer, $65-79 off season. Pets and children are welcome. On the road to Searsport, east of Belfast, the motel is open all year.

Not far from the Comfort Inn is the **Belfast Harbor Inn,** Rt. 1, RR 2, Box 21, Belfast 04915, tel. (207) 338-2740 or (800) 545-8576, fax (207) 338-5205, not quite as fancy but certainly comfortable. Rooms have cable TV, a/c, and phones; there's an outdoor pool. Doubles are $85-95 in summer, $35-45 off season. Open all year. The motel is close to the highway, so request a room facing the bay. Adjacent to the inn on the six-acre site is **Chelsea's By the Sea,** tel. (207) 338-5939, a summertime restaurant with terrific water views; weather permitting, you can dine on the deck. Specialties are seafood (including lobster) and steaks. It's open 6 a.m.-9 p.m.; no reservations, so you may have to wait on midsummer weekends.

Campgrounds

East of Belfast, **The Moorings,** Searsport Ave., Rt. 1, RR 1, Box 69, Belfast 04915, tel. (207) 338-6860, opened in 1993 with 51 sites, all with hookups. Views are fabulous, and the rocky beach has a pocket of sand; swimming is only for the hardy. Sites in midsummer are $25 (two adults plus two kids under 18), $22 early and late in the season. Facilities include laundry, play area, and game room. Extra fees for a/c or heat hookup, pumpout, and day or overnight visitors. Open mid-May to mid-October.

Seasonal Rentals

Most of the Belfast area's seasonal rentals are in Northport, specifically the charming Victorian enclave of Bayside (see "Sights," above), where the **Blair Agency,** Bayside, mailing address

P.O. Box 368, Belfast 04915, tel. (207) 338-2257, fax 338-3166, has cornered the market in sales and rentals. Contact them in spring for their free booklet of 40 or so rental properties.

FOOD

Miscellanea

Judy's Eggroll, Lincolnville Ave., Rt. 52, Belfast 04915, tel. (207) 338-1400, operates out of a small prefab building next to Judy's house, a mile south (feels like west) of the Rt. 1 bypass. Plastic is the dominant theme (as in flowers, tablecloths, menus), but this folksy place has homemade Chinese and Korean sauces (no MSG), top-notch eggrolls (and other Asian goodies), large portions, and down-to-earth prices. Eat in or order to go. No smoking. Open Wed.-Sun. 11:30 a.m.-9 p.m.

Ducktrap River Fish Farm, 57 Little River Dr., Industrial Park So., Belfast 04915, tel. (207) 338-6280, has become a global corporation, shipping European-style smoked seafood and seafood pâtés worldwide. Stop in at the high-tech smokehouse and pick up a supply. (The smoked tuna pâté is fantastic, as is the mustard dill sauce.) The shop is open all year, Mon.-Fri. 8 a.m.-4:30 p.m.; no tours. The Industrial Park is south of the Rt. 1 bypass, east of the Belfast Municipal Airport.

Old-fashioned general stores are always an adventure, and one of the best is the red-clapboard **Fraternity Village General Store,** Rt. 173, Searsmont 04973, tel. (207) 342-5866, near the beginning of two Georges River Bikeway routes. Early-20th-century author Ben Ames Williams set some of his short stories in Searsmont, dubbing it Fraternity Village; the

BOB RACE

shop trades on the connection. Inventory is all the usual country-store hodgepodge—apples to zippers. Load up on snacks here before heading out on your bike. It's open all year, Mon.-Fri. 5:30 a.m.-8 p.m. (to 9 p.m. Friday), Saturday and Sunday 7 a.m.-9 p.m.

Inexpensive to Moderate

A longtime standby for creative (including vegetarian) cuisine, **Darby's Restaurant & Pub,** 155 High St., Belfast, tel. (207) 338-2339, had tofu before tofu was cool. This place has been serving food and drink since just after the Civil War; the tin ceilings and antique bar are reminders of that. Reservations are wise on weekends and Belfast Maskers performance nights. Open daily, year-round, for lunch (at 11:30 a.m.) and dinner (at 5 p.m.).

In the heart of downtown Belfast, **90 Main Street,** 90 Main St., Belfast, tel. (207) 338-1106, is another longtime standby, although several owners have rotated through. Ambience is strictly casual, the menu is creative, and there's live music Thursday and Friday all year (9 p.m.-1 a.m.); cover charge is seldom more than a dollar. Open daily in summer, from 6 a.m. for the bakery section, 11 a.m.-4 p.m. for lunch, 5-10 p.m. for dinner. Weather permitting, you can eat on the deck out back, but bring a hat—there's no shelter. In winter, 90 Main Street is closed Tuesday and serves no lunch on Wednesday.

Lobster pie and fried Maine shrimp are the specialties at the **Maine Chowder House,** Rt. 1, East Belfast, tel. (207) 338-5225, a modernistic eatery with spectacular panoramic views of Penobscot Bay. There's also a fixed-price ($3.25) children's menu. Dine on the deck or even order takeout and eat at picnic tables. The Steel's Ledge Lounge features live music nightly in summer. Under the same ownership as Darby's, the Chowder House is about two miles from downtown Belfast (one and a half miles east of the bridge), en route to Searsport. Open April through November, daily 11 a.m.-9 p.m. (to 8 p.m. spring and fall).

Who'd expect big crowds at an unpretentious, brightly painted building advertising south-of-the-border cuisine alongside Rt. 1? **Dos Amigos' Mexican Restaurant and Cantina,** Rt. 1, 144 Bayside Rd., Northport, tel. (207) 338-5775, has earned its reputation as purveyor of the area's best Tex-Mex cuisine. (There's also a branch in Bangor.) Margaritas are jumbo; nachos are loaded. Thirteen miles north of Camden, about three miles south of Belfast; open Wed.-Sun. 11 a.m.-9:30 p.m. (to 10:30 Friday and Saturday), April to mid-December.

Lobster-in-the-Rough

Young's Lobster Pound, Mitchell St., Box 4, East Belfast, tel. (207) 338-1160, fax 338-3498, is a classic eat-on-the-dock lobster place overlooking the bay. Dress down, relax, and pile into the crustaceans. BYOL. From downtown, cross the bridge to East Belfast and turn right at Jed's Restaurant. Continue to the end of Mitchell Street. Open daily 7:30 a.m.-8 p.m., May through November.

Pubs

Belfast's first brewpub opened in 1996. Belfast Bay Brewing Co. produces its own beers and ales and serves 'em up in the **Port Authority Brewpub,** 100 Searsport Ave., Rt. 1, East Belfast, tel. (207) 338-2662. Located about two miles east of downtown Belfast, next to Th' Ice Cream Barn and across from the Belfast Harbor Inn, the pub is open 11 a.m.-midnight (food served until 10:30 p.m.), with plenty of live entertainment. Free brewery tours daily at 4:30 p.m. in summer, or call for an appointment. Open all year.

Not a brewpub, but certainly a pub, **Logos Pub & Grill,** 121 Main St., Belfast 04915, tel. (207) 338-0300, is the newest entry in Belfast's nightlife stakes—and a hit since the minute it opened. The recipe for success includes a great rehab job on the historic building, creditable menus for lunch and dinner, live music Friday and Saturday nights, and game tables for cribbage, Scrabble, chess, and backgammon. Logos is open daily 11 a.m.-1 a.m., all year.

INFORMATION AND SERVICES

The information center of the **Belfast Area Chamber of Commerce,** 1 Main St., P.O. Box 58, Belfast 04915, tel. (207) 338-5900, with an especially cheerful staff, is conveniently located in the Consumers Fuel building, near the public landing and Heritage Park and close to the municipal parking lot. Open mid-May to mid-October, daily 9 a.m.-6 p.m., other months Mon.-Fri. 9 a.m.-3 p.m. The chamber's annual visitors' booklet is an especially useful compendium, with lodging and dining directories.

Founded in 1888, the **Belfast Free Library,** 106 High St., Belfast 04915, tel. (207) 338-3884, in addition to normal library activities, has Internet access and an active community-service program with terrific lectures and concerts in the 200-seat Abbott Auditorium. On summer Thursdays, there are children's story hours. The library is open Mon.-Sat., all year.

Newspapers
Belfast's dueling weekly newspapers keep residents acutely attuned to local happenings. The grande dame is *The Republican Journal,* tel. (207) 338-3333, published every Thursday since 1829. The scrappy, widely read upstart, speaking right up since 1985, is *The Waldo Independent,* tel. (207) 338-5100, also published Thursday. Both papers have extensive calendar listings.

Emergencies
A round-the-clock emergency room is only one of the convenient features at the first-rate **Waldo County General Hospital,** 118 Northport Ave., P.O. Box 287, Belfast 04915, tel. (207) 338-2500 or (800) 649-2536, a community-oriented private (despite its name) institution with Maine's first inpatient hospice beds. For **police, fire, and ambulance** in Belfast, dial 911. In outlying communities, contact the **Waldo County sheriff,** tel. (800) 660-3398.

Public Restrooms
You won't have much trouble finding public restrooms in Belfast. Facilities are at the waterfront **public landing,** in the **railroad station,** and at the **Waldo County General Hospital.**

Sauna
The **Belfast Dance Studio,** 55 High St., Belfast 04915, tel. (207) 338-5380, opens its sauna (and showers) to the public. The sauna schedule is erratic, so you'll need to call for details. The studio also offers classes in all kinds of movement (African dance to yoga) and gives periodic performances and recitals (check local papers).

Veterinarian/Kennels
Little River Veterinary Hospital, Rt. 1, Northport, tel. (207) 338-2909, with a fine reputation for animal care, has a new kennel facility with heated indoor runs. Located close to Belfast's southern boundary, it's open Mon.-Fri. 8 a.m.-5 p.m. and Saturday 8 a.m.-noon.

Six miles northwest of Belfast, **Sunlight Boarding Kennels,** Rt. 7, Waldo, mailing address Morrill 04952, tel. (207) 722-3351, is a first-class boarding operation with canine day care.

Special Courses
Linked to the National Audubon Society and Lesley College, the **Audubon Expedition Institute** (AEI), P.O. Box 365, Belfast 04915, tel. (207) 338-5859, fax 338-1037, is an extraordinary traveling environmental-education program that just happens to be based in Belfast. Ranging ages 18-40, students board buses for semester-long, hands-on experiences in various parts of the United States. Founded in 1978, AEI offers college credit and two-year AA (liberal arts) and MS (environmental education) degrees.

Getting Around
Downtown Belfast parking is limited to two hours, so if you're hanging around longer, head for the municipal parking lot on lower Main Street, convenient to the waterfront and the chamber of commerce.

For taxis, contact the **Belfast Taxi Company,** tel. (207) 338-2943.

Waldo County Transportation, tel. (207) 338-4769 or (800) 439-7865, a nonprofit bus/van service designed primarily for seniors and other nondrivers, is open to anyone who needs a ride. Except for the Belfast Shopper, which follows a set intown route on weekdays, you'll need to reserve a seat at least a day in advance; most trips operate only one or two days a week (no weekends). One-way fares range from 75 cents to $2.50. Routes go to communities all over Waldo County, as well as to Augusta, Bangor, Waterville, and Rockland.

For information on car ferries to **Islesboro,** see "Getting There," under "Islesboro," above. Ace Aviation, Rt. 1, P.O. Box 457, Belfast 04915, tel. (207) 338-2970 or (800) 338-2970, provides (expensive) charter service from Belfast Municipal Airport to Islesboro.

SEARSPORT AREA

Five miles northeast of downtown Belfast, you're in the heart of Searsport, a name synonymous with the sea, thanks to an enduring seafaring tradition that's appropriately commemorated here in the state's oldest maritime museum. The seafaring heyday occurred in the mid-19th century, but white settlers from the Massachusetts Colony had already made inroads here 200 years earlier. By the 1750s, Fort Pownall, in nearby Stockton Springs, was a strategic site during the French and Indian War (the American phase of Europe's Seven Years' War).

Shipbuilding was underway by 1791, reaching a crescendo between 1845 and 1866, with six year-round shipyards and nearly a dozen more seasonal ones. Incredibly, by 1885, 10% of all full-rigged American-flag ships on the high seas were under the command of Searsport and Stockton Springs captains—many bearing the name of Pendleton, Nichols, or Carver. Many of these were involved in the perilous China trade, rounding notorious Cape Horn with great regularity.

All this global contact shaped Searsport's culture, adding a veneer of cosmopolitan sophistication. Imposing mansions of seafaring families were filled with fabulous Oriental treasures, many of which eventually made their way to the Penobscot Marine Museum. Brick-lined Main Street is more evidence of the mid-19th-century wealth, and local churches reaped the benefits of residents' generosity—the First Congregational Church, patronized by captains and shipbuilders (most ordinary seamen attended the Methodist church), boasts Tiffany windows and a Christopher Wren steeple.

Another inkling of this area's oceangoing superiority comes from visits to local burial grounds: check out the headstones at Gordon, Bowditch, and Sandy Point cemeteries. Many have fascinating tales to tell.

Near the peak of its prosperity, Searsport incorporated in 1845, deriving its name from David Sears, a summer resident and wealthy Boston merchant active in the China trade.

In the late 19th and early 20th centuries, when summering in Maine became "in," the Eastern Steamship Line brought passengers from Boston to Searsport (Maine's second-largest deep-water port) for the princely sum of $5.70. All that ceased in the 1920s, with the advent of the automobile and the Great Depression.

Today, with a population of 2,700, the Searsport area's major draws are the Penobscot Marine Museum, the still-handsome brick Historic District, a slew of B&Bs, a couple of special state parks, and wall-to-wall antiques shops and flea markets.

SIGHTS

Penobscot Marine Museum

Exquisite marine paintings, ship models, and unusual China-trade objets are just a few of the 10,000 treasures at the Penobscot Marine Museum, Rt. 1 at Church St., P.O. Box 498, Searsport 04974, tel. (207) 548-2529, fax 548-2520, Maine's oldest maritime museum—founded in 1936. Plan to spend several hours exploring the old and new buildings lining Church Street, just east of downtown. Check out the exhibits, visit the unusual gift shop, and picnic on the grounds next to the shop. Pick up tickets at the Museum Education Center (restrooms are also available here), first building on your left on Church Street. Call or write for the schedule of lectures, concerts, and temporary exhibits. Admission is $5 adults, $4 seniors, $2 children 7-15, free for kids six and under. Open Memorial Day weekend to October 15, Mon.-Sat. 10 a.m.-5 p.m., Sunday noon-5 p.m.

Historic District

The Maine Historic Preservation Commission considers the buildings in Searsport's Main Street Historic District the best examples of their type outside of Portland—a frozen-in-time, mid-19th-century cluster of brick and granite structures. The ground floors of most of the buildings are shops or restaurants; take time to stop in and admire their interiors.

Lupine Landscape

If you happen to be here in late June and early July, take a quickie detour onto **Prospect Street,**

flea market, Searsport

MAINE OFFICE OF TOURISM

off Rt. 1 at the southern end of Searsport (turn at the Victorian Inn). Just after the inn, off to the east, the landscape is a blanket of purple lupines—with a few pink and white ones thrown in for good measure. In the distance, the distinctive white spire of the First Congregational Church pokes up from the center of town—all in all, a perfect Kodak moment.

PARKS AND RECREATION

Moose Point State Park

Here's a smallish park with a biggish view—183 acres wedged between Rt. 1 and a dramatic Penobscot Bay panorama. Moose Point State Park, Rt. 1, Searsport, tel. (207) 548-2882, is one and a half miles south of downtown Searsport. Bring a picnic, let the kids hang out and play (there's no swimming), walk through the woods. Moose-crossing signs are posted on the highway, but don't count on seeing one. Open Memorial Day weekend to October 1, but since it's alongside the highway, the park is accessible, weather permitting, all year. Admission is $1 adults, 50 cents children 5-11, free for kids under five.

Mosman Park

Southeast of busy Rt. 1, four-acre Mosman Park, a town-owned facility, has picnic tables, a traditional playground, lots of grassy space, a pocket-size pebbly beach, seasonal toilets, and

fabulous views of the bay. Turn off Rt. 1 at Water St. and continue to the end.

Sears Island

After years of heavy-duty squabbling over a proposed cargo port on Searsport's Sears Island, plans have been suspended, leaving this lovely, causeway-linked island in limbo. The only improvement is a road, but it's sometimes gated (the island is officially private property—owned by a subsidiary of the Bangor and Aroostook Railroad). From downtown Searsport, continue northeast on Rt. 1 two miles to a right turn signposted Dead End. Turn right and go 1.2 miles to the gate. Another one and a half miles will take you to the parking area, overlooking Mack Point and hills off to the left. Bring a picnic and binoculars—and, if you're hardy, a swimsuit. Before driving or cycling to the island, check access status by calling the **Searsport Town Office**, tel. (207) 548-6372, open weekdays all year.

Fort Point State Park

Continuing northeast on Rt. 1 from Sears Island will get you to the turnoff for Fort Point State Park, Fort Point Rd., Stockton Springs 04981, tel. (207) 567-3356, on Cape Jellison's eastern tip. Within the 154-acre park are the earthworks of 18th-century **Fort Pownall** (a British fortress built in the French and Indian War), **Fort Point Light** (a square, 26-foot, 19th-century tower guarding the mouth of the Penobscot River), shoreline trails, and a 200-foot pier where you can fish-, bird-, or boat-watch. (Birders can spot waterfowl—especially ruddy ducks, but also eagles and osprey.) Bring picnic fixings, but stay clear of the keeper's house—it's private. At the Rt. 1 fork for Stockton Springs, bear right onto Main St. and continue to Mill Rd., in the village center. Turn right and then left onto East Cape Rd., then another left onto Fort Point Rd., leading to the parking area. Officially, the park is open Memorial Day weekend through Labor Day, but it's accessible all year, weather permitting. Admission is $1 adults, 50 cents children 5-11, free for kids under five.

Cycling

One of the state's most hyperactive bicycle shops is about a mile north of downtown Searsport. **Birgfeld's Bike Shop,** Rt. 1, Searsport 04974, tel. (207) 548-2916 or (800) 206-2916, fax (207) 548-0372, in business since the 1970s, is a mandatory stop for any cyclist, novice or pro. Rentals, local info, supplies, maps, weekly group rides, sales, and repair services are all part of the Birgfeld's mix. Mountain-bike rental is $15 daily or $80 weekly (cheaper than in Bar Harbor); bikes are in good condition. There's free parking behind the shop. This family-run operation also includes an upstairs hobby shop for kids and an adjacent yarn shop. The bike shop is open all year, daily 9 a.m.-5:30 p.m. (to 5 p.m. Saturday and Sunday).

An especially good ride in this area is the **Cape Jellison** loop, in Stockton Springs, even though it means biking from Birgfeld's about four miles along congested Rt. 1. If you have your own bike or care to transport the rental, park at Stockton Springs Elementary School and do the loop from there. Including a detour to Fort Point, the ride totals less than 10 miles from downtown Stockton Springs.

FESTIVALS AND EVENTS

The fourth Saturday in August, a day-long series of **Lobsterboat Races,** with a dozen classes, is the last event on the annual Maine lobsterboat racing circuit. Races take place in Searsport Harbor, starting off Mack Point. Best place to spectate is Mosman Park, site of a chicken barbecue and live entertainment.

Also in late August is the **Lobster Stew and Blueberry Pie Supper.** Residents and savvy visitors arrange their schedules around this annual feast, usually held midweek, at the First Congregational Church, Searsport, 5-7 p.m. (arrive early). Cost is $9.50 adults, $6.50 kids under 12.

SHOPPING

The word shopping in Searsport usually applies to antiques—from 25-cent flea-market collectibles to antique tools to high-end china, furniture, and glassware. The town has more than a dozen separate businesses—and some of *those* are group shops with multiple dealers. Searsport is definitely Maine's "Antiques Capital."

More than two dozen dealers supply the juried inventory for Bob and Phyllis Sommer's **Pumpkin Patch,** Rt. 1, P.O. Box 178, Searsport 04974, tel. (207) 548-6047—with a heavy emphasis on Maine antiques. Specialties, priced reasonably, include quilts (at least 80 always on hand), silver, paint-decorated furniture, nautical and Native American items, and Victoriana. Open daily 9:30 a.m.-5 p.m., April-Oct., weekends in November, by appointment Dec.-March.

Maine's mother lode of antique tools is **Liberty Tool Company,** west of Belfast. But you can sample the wares at the company's sister shop, **Captain Tinkham's Emporium,** 34 Main St., Searsport 04974, tel. (207) 548-6465. It's open all year, daily 9 a.m.-5 p.m., sometimes closed Wednesday off season.

Crafts and Gifts

Close to the highway in a farmstand-style building about a mile east of downtown Searsport, the **Waldo County Craft Co-op,** Rt. 1, Searsport 04974, tel. (207) 548-6686, features the work of more than two dozen Mainers: quilts, jams, jewelry, baskets, pottery, and lots else. Open daily 9 a.m.-5 p.m., mid-May to mid-October.

If you're into Victorian and country gifts and crafts, stop at **Silkweeds,** 191 E. Main St., Searsport, tel. (207) 548-6501, in the midst of antiques shops and flea markets at the eastern end of town. Don't miss the potpourri corner—where you serve yourself from a clawfoot tub. Open daily 9 a.m.-5 p.m., Feb.-December.

Marine Hardware

You may not *think* you're in the market for marine gewgaws, but wait till you get a load of this shop. Almost everyone who walks into **Hamilton Marine,** Rt. 1, P.O. Box 227, Searsport 04974, tel. (207) 548-6302, walks out with a purchase—and often lots of them. Filling 8,000 feet in a former trucking warehouse, Hamilton Marine is the largest ship chandlery north of Boston—a candy store for boatbuilders and recreational and commercial nautical types. Prices are especially moderate. There's also a 200-page mail-order catalog. The store is about .8 mile east (actually northeast) of downtown Searsport, close to the Searsport Antique Mall. Open Mon.-Sat. 8 a.m.-5 p.m., all year; also open Sunday April-June.

Used Books

A local fixture in Stockton Springs since 1960, the **Victorian House/Book Barn,** E. Main St., P.O. Box 397, Stockton Springs 04981, tel. (207) 567-3351, is an especially welcoming shop with well-organized shelves. Open daily 8 a.m.-8 p.m., April-Dec.; 8 a.m.-dark, Jan.-March.

Discount Shopping

Dakin's Gift and Collectibles Outlet Store, Main St., Rt. 1, Searsport, tel. (207) 548-9925, carries its own Dakin toy line, plus such other noted brands as Playmobil, Brio, Steiff, and Lionel. Bringing kids in here may crunch your wallet. Open daily 9 a.m.-5 p.m., all year.

ACCOMMODATIONS

B&Bs

Searsport's B&Bs have banded together in an unusually amiable association that includes a well-organized summer referral service. The owners make every effort to help visitors find beds in town. For the association brochure, contact **Searsport B&B Association,** P.O. Box 787, Searsport 04974, or the **Waldo County Chamber of Commerce,** P.O. Box 577, Unity 04988, tel. (207) 948-5050.

The veteran B&B in town is **The Homeport Inn,** Rt. 1, P.O. Box 647, Searsport 04974, tel. (207) 548-2259 or (800) 742-5814, a fabulous 1861 sea captain's mansion presided over since 1978 by genial Edith Johnson. Her fascination with antiques and British royalty is evident everywhere, creating an unstuffy, user-friendly museum of a place: four-poster and canopied beds, fireplaces, Spode pottery, Oriental carpets, even wallpaper copied from Queen Victoria's bedroom. Breakfast is served on the glassed-in porch overlooking gardens beautifully landscaped by Edith's dentist husband. Guests can play darts or do puzzles in The Mermaid, a pub-style family room on the lower level. Six first-floor rooms (with private baths) and four second-floor rooms (sharing one bath) are $60-85 d May-Oct., lower other months. No pets, limited smoking. No children under two, but bear in mind that unruly kids of any age could threaten the treasures. Open all year.

Across Rt. 1 from The Homeport Inn, and buffered from the highway on two landscaped acres, is **The Carriage House Inn,** Rt. 1, P.O. Box 238, Searsport 04974, tel. (207) 548-2289, a sprawling Victorian complex that once was the summer home of Maine artist Waldo Peirce. Built in 1874 by one of Searsport's famed clipper-ship captains, the National Historic Register mansion also served as officers' quarters during World War II. Three handsome, second-floor rooms (private baths) and a third-floor room (shared bath) are $85-95 d. Breakfasts are huge. No smoking, no pets. Open all year.

At the other end of town, Ed and Judie Upham's **Victorian Inn,** Rt. 1, P.O. Box 807, Searsport 04974, tel. (207) 548-0044 or (800) 943-0044, was built in 1886 by yet another sea captain. Wallpaper and woodwork are 90% original, and astonishing Victorian touches are everywhere. Four guest rooms (private baths) are $65-95 d. No smoking, no pets; children are welcome. Open all year, but call ahead off season; reservations are advisable even in summer.

On a quiet side street near the Victorian Inn is Karen Kropewnicki's (CROW-puh-nicky) homey **Flowering Plum,** 28 Prospect St., P.O. Box 259, Searsport 04974, tel. (207) 548-2610. The turn-of-the-20th-century farmhouse has two second-floor rooms (one with four-poster) sharing a large bath for $50 d. Outside are croquet and badminton setups; inside is a cozy den with cable TV, plus tons of games and books. No smoking; well-behaved pets are welcome (there's a resident cat). Open May through October.

Farther west along Rt. 1, on two beautifully landscaped acres, the elegant brick Colonial **Old Glory Inn B&B,** Rt. 1, P.O. Box 461, Searsport 04974, tel. (207) 548-6232, has two guest rooms ($55 and $65 d) superbly and comfortably furnished with quilts, rag rugs, stenciling, canopied beds, and other fabulous antiques. There's also an antiques shop on the premises. Each room has a designated private bath down the hall; robes are provided. An expanded continental breakfast is served on antique dishes in the former keeping room. Bruce and Rita Huddleston, transplants from Little Rock, Arkansas earn raves for their hospitality. No pets, no young children, no credit cards. No smoking in guest rooms. Open mid-May through November.

Near the Old Glory, at the western end of Searsport, is Lee and Wilson Flight's 1830s **Capt. Butman Homestead,** Rt. 1, P.O. Box 306, Searsport 04974, tel. (207) 548-2506, off season tel. (508) 433-2145. Three second-floor guest rooms, furnished with antiques and sharing a bath, are $45 d. No smoking, no pets, no credit cards. Open late June to Labor Day, weekends off season by prior arrangement.

In **Stockton Springs,** about five miles northeast of downtown Searsport, the **Whistlestop B&B,** Maple St., RFD 2, Box 639, Stockton Springs 04981, tel. (207) 567-3726, is an oasis well worth the half-mile detour off Rt. 1. David and Katherine Wilson named their Cape-style waterfront home for an elegant old Pullman car once "parked" here and used as a summer "cottage." Nowadays, you'll hear the twice-daily whistle of the Bangor and Aroostook Railroad. Relax on the bayview deck or down on the lawn; pick berries in season; play the grand piano in the comfortable living room. It all feels miles from everywhere. Two rooms (private baths) are $75 d in summer, $60 off season. No smoking, no pets. Open all year, but call ahead off season.

Campgrounds

How can you beat 1,100 feet of tidal oceanfront and unobstructed views of Islesboro, Castine, and Penobscot Bay? **Searsport Shores Camping Resort,** 216 W. Main St., Rt. 1, Searsport 04974, tel. (207) 548-6059, gets high marks for its fabulous six-acre setting. One hundred sites (including a wilderness camping area) go for $15-27 a day. Facilities include a laundry, private beach, small store, free showers, play areas, new recreation hall, nature trails, and volleyball court. Request a site away from organized-activity areas. Bring a sea kayak and launch it here. Leashed pets are allowed. The campground is slightly more than a mile southwest of downtown Searsport, about four miles east of downtown Belfast. Open mid-May to Columbus Day.

FOOD

Whether you're up for a splurge or hunting for a bargain, restaurants in Searsport and Stockton Springs run the gamut. A couple of the low-end places are notably unpretentious (almost off putting, in fact), but don't be fooled. They'll fix you up with hearty New England cooking, hefty portions, local color, no frills, and a bill that won't dent your wallet.

Here are four of them. **Jordan's Restaurant,** Main St., Rt. 1, Searsport, tel. (207) 548-2555, right downtown, draws big crowds for its Friday night buffet 5-8 p.m.—all you can eat, even dessert, for $8.95. Call for a reservation. Otherwise, it's open daily, all year, 7 a.m.-9 p.m. (to 8 p.m. Sunday), with senior discounts Tuesday. The take-out window is open 11 a.m.-9 p.m. daily (Sunday to 8 p.m.). **Fillmore's Restaurant,** 161 E. Main St., Rt. 1, Searsport, tel. (207) 548-6652, specializing in seafood (great fried clams), is open daily 6 a.m.-8 p.m. (to 9 p.m. Friday and Saturday). Eat indoors or on the deck. Less than a mile from downtown Searsport, it's in the heart of the flea market and antiques area. **Light's Restaurant,** Rt. 1, Searsport, tel. (207) 548-2405, is probably the least assuming and one of the most popular, particularly for its twin lobster entrée (about $17, including salad bar). Other big favorites are fish chowder and lobster rolls. Connected to a 14-room '50s-style roadside motel, the restaurant is one and a half miles northeast of downtown Searsport. Open April to mid-November. Summer hours are daily 7 a.m.-8:45 p.m.; off-season hours are Mon.-Fri. 11 a.m.-7:45 p.m. (to 8:45 p.m. Friday), and 7 a.m.-7:45 p.m. Saturday and Sunday. The motel ($38-46 d in July and August) is open May through October. **Just Barb's,** Main St., Rt. 1, Stockton Springs, tel. (207) 567-3886, at the Rt. 1 turnoff to Stockton Springs, is a funky, nondescript place with a Friday-night fish fry loaded with haddock ($6.95). No credit cards. Open daily, all year, 6 a.m.-8 p.m. (to 7 p.m. in winter).

In downtown Searsport, the best menu is at the reasonably priced **Seafarer's Tavern,** 23 E. Main St., Searsport, tel. (207) 548-2465, a onetime pool hall that's been a popular watering hole since 1986. Kites, boat models, and a canoe hang from the ceiling; paintings (for sale) cover the walls. Specialties are calzones, pizza-by-the-slice, crab cakes, hearty sandwiches, and homemade desserts. Children's portions are available, and everything can be prepared to go. No a/c, no reservations, no credit cards. Open all year, Mon.-Sat. 11 a.m.-9 p.m. (to 11 p.m. Friday and Saturday).

About 1.4 miles south of downtown Searsport, **Periwinkles Bakery,** 227 W. Main St., Rt. 1, Searsport, tel. (207) 548-9910, is an upscale source of scones, croissants, outrageously good walnut squares, and other unusual pastries—plus designer coffees and teas, sandwiches, quiche, and soups. Based in the back section of a lovely old house, the bakery has a handful of tables inside, plus some outside chairs—although most of the clientele picks up goodies to go. No credit cards. Open daily 8 a.m.-6 p.m., Feb.-Dec.; closed Monday and Tuesday in winter.

In the top price bracket is **Nickerson Tavern,** Rt. 1, Searsport 04974, tel. (207) 548-2220, on the ground floor of a handsome, 1838 mustard-yellow house. Under new ownership since 1993, the restaurant has been working hard to retain the five-star reputation earned by former chef Tom Weiner. Specialties are duckling, veal, and hazelnut chicken; prices range $14-20. No smoking. Reservations advisable on midsummer and holiday weekends. Open Thurs.-Sun. 5:30-9 p.m., April-Dec.; daily in July and August. Nickerson Tavern is almost three miles northeast of Searsport, about halfway to Stockton Springs.

Tucked into the village in Stockton Springs is **The Griffin House Cafe and Espresso Bar,** Main St., Stockton Springs, tel. (207) 567-3057, an airy, friendly place that holds only about two dozen people. Order at the counter, grab a newspaper, and settle into one of the captain's chairs. The French toast is stupendous. No smoking, no credit cards. Open all year, Wed.-Sun. 7 a.m.-2 p.m., with occasional special dinners by reservation (call to inquire).

INFORMATION AND SERVICES

In 1996, Searsport joined forces with other area communities and became part of the **Waldo County Chamber of Commerce,** P.O. Box 577, Unity 04988, tel. (207) 948-5050, which has produced a helpful visitors brochure and installed information corners in multiple business locations around the county. Even though brochures and maps are readily available, the sites are not always staffed, so you may need to ask around a bit to get questions answered. Searsport's most obvious info location, and the one likeliest to be open at odd hours, comes up after you've been through town—at the **Steamboat Texaco** gas station on Rt. 1, tel. (207) 548-2728. While you're at it, you can stock up on snacks and use the restrooms and the ATM. It's across Rt. 1 from a gray-shingled lighthouse.

The handsome fieldstone **Carver Memorial Library,** Mortland Rd. at Union St., Searsport 04974, tel. (207) 548-2303, was built in 1910. From June to August, hours are Monday, Thursday, Friday 1-5 p.m., Tuesday 1-8 p.m., Wednesday 10 a.m.-5 p.m., and Saturday 10 a.m.-1 p.m. Hours are the same Sept.-May, except it's closed Monday. The library is a block off Rt. 1.

Emergencies
The nearest hospital is **Waldo County General Hospital,** Northport Ave., Belfast 04915, tel. (207) 338-2500, a community facility with round-the-clock emergency-room care. For **police, ambulance, and fire,** dial 911 in Searsport and Stockton Springs.

BOB RACE

ACADIA REGION

Stretching from the banks of the Penobscot River to the eastern border of Hancock County, and inland to Bangor, this region takes its appellation from Acadia National Park, a gem of a natural resource that dangles like a pendant just south of the mainland.

Surrounding the national park on Mount Desert Island are Bar Harbor (the area's commercial center), Northeast Harbor, Southwest Harbor, Bass Harbor, and a couple of smaller enclaves. Offshore are the Cranberry Isles and Swans Island, accessible by ferry.

Stringing the region together is slow-moving Rt. 1, and the prime locales for exploring are handsome historic towns and villages lying seaward from the highway. The vital coastal artery is only two lanes wide, and summertime traffic creates frustrating delays (hardly surprising, given that some three million visitors descend on Acadia each year), often doubling the off-season travel time. But a widening of the highway could spoil this area forever.

Most of this region will never be spoiled—maybe overappreciated, but not spoiled. There's beauty enough to go around. Consider the Acadia region a transition zone—a place where you begin to decompress as you edge slowly Down East from the more congested South Coast and Mid-Coast regions. Here, you can watch the sunset from atop Blue Hill Mountain, or the sun*rise* from Cadillac Mountain; join kayakers surf-ing through Blue Hill Falls; stroll through the village of Castine (charming verging on precious), whose streets are lined with dowager-like homes; discover America's largest yellow-birch tree (on Deer Isle); visit *WoodenBoat* magazine's world headquarters in tiny Brooklin; stretch out on the beach at Lamoine State Park, across the bay from Acadia's mountains; show up at tony Northeast Harbor's May azalea extravaganza; surf-watch from the rocks at Schoodic Point; or hang out on the fishermen's wharves in Stonington or Corea.

An essential key to understanding this special region is its islands—each, like people, with a distinct personality. Some are linked to the mainland by causeways or bridges, others are reachable only by ferry. Mount Desert Island heads almost anyone's list, but it's so eminently accessible that it almost doesn't qualify as an "island." Farther south is Deer Isle, a unique agglomeration of craftspeople and fisherfolk; offshore is Isle au Haut—part hamlet, part national park.

The 2,040-foot-long, bright green Waldo-Hancock Bridge, built in 1931 at a cost of $850,000, links Waldo and Hancock Counties and introduces you to the Bucksport area (in midsummer, watch as you cross for the resident osprey nesting on the northernmost bridge tower). Working hard and well to gentrify its longtime rough-and-ready river-port image, Bucksport changes even as you watch.

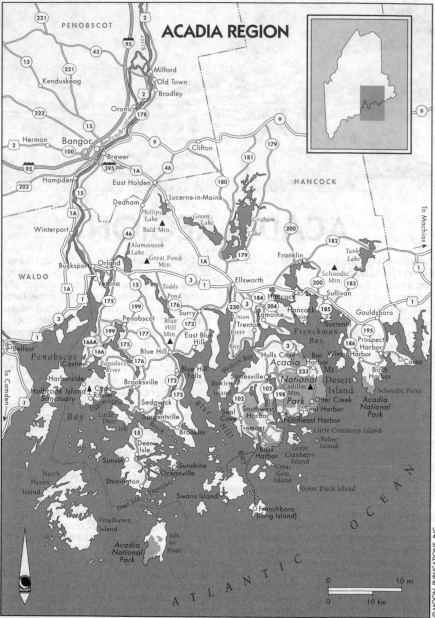

ACADIA REGION

From Bucksport, Rt. 1 makes a 20-mile run, flanked by blueberry fields that flame red in the fall, to Ellsworth. Off to the south is the smattering of very attractive communities that make up the Blue Hill Peninsula.

In the northeastern corner of the region, up the mighty Penobscot, a dose of reality intrudes in the form of metropolitan bustle in Bangor, a city shifting in the late 20th century from a frontier-style scrappiness to a newfound sophistication (we're still not talking Big Apple trendiness, but rather a greater openness to the world beyond). Bangor is the state's third-largest city

and the commercial hub for all of northern and eastern Maine. The antique brick and wooden buildings provide a serious sense of history, and the stream bisecting the streets downtown lends an aura of surprising calm.

On the peaceful eastern fringe of Hancock County, at the tip of the Schoodic Peninsula, a stunning pocket of Acadia National Park sees only a fraction of the visitors who descend on the main part of the park. And towns lining the eastern shore of Frenchman Bay have some of the best views of all: front-row seats facing the peaks of Mount Desert Island.

BUCKSPORT TO ELLSWORTH

When Bar Harbor is filled to overflowing, especially in July and early August, this area provides a buffer on the fringes, still conveniently close to Acadia National Park and the Blue Hill Peninsula. Between Bucksport and Ellsworth you can explore a fort, hike a mountain, visit a fish hatchery and a bird sanctuary, tour a paper mill and an elegant mansion, and do some shopping.

Anchoring Rt. 1 at the western edge of Hancock County and dominated by the giant Champion International paper mill, Bucksport has in recent years striven to become more than a mill town—and it's succeeding. New businesses have arrived, a marina is underway, and a new local newspaper has improved communications and sparked community spirit. With a population of just under 4,900, it's the county's second-largest town (edged out only by Ellsworth, with 6,200).

Bucksport is no upstart. Native Americans first gravitated to these Penobscot River shores in summers, finding here a rich source of salmon for food and grasses for basketmaking. In 1764, it was officially settled by Col. Jonathan Buck, a Massachusetts Bay Colony surveyor who modestly named it Buckstown and organized a booming shipping business here. His remains are interred in a local cemetery, where his tombstone bears the distinct outline of a woman's leg; this is allegedly the result of a curse by a witch Buck ordered executed, but in fact it's probably a flaw in the granite. Most townsfolk prefer not to discuss the matter, but the myth re-

fuses to die—and it has immortalized a man whose name might otherwise have been consigned to musty history books. (The monument is across Rt. 1 from the Shop 'n Save supermarket; a small sign tells the tale.)

By the 1840s, steamships were already carrying vacationers between Boston and Bangor, via Bucksport. The town is still a major port, receiving large tankers bringing in heating oil for the region and jet fuel for Bangor International Airport.

Papermaking came to Bucksport in 1930, and more than 1,200 employees now staff the Champion International mill on Indian Point (you can watch the action on tours).

Just south of Bucksport, at the bend in the Penobscot River, Verona Island (pop. 500 or so) is best known as the mile-long link between Prospect and Bucksport. Just before you cross the bridge from Verona to Bucksport, hang a left, then a quick right to a small municipal park with a boat launch and broad views of Bucksport Harbor (and the paper mill). In the Buck Memorial Library is a scale model of Adm. Robert Peary's arctic exploration vessel, the Roosevelt, built on this site.

Route 1 east of Bucksport leads to Orland, whose idyllic setting on the banks of the Narramissic River makes it a magnet for shutterbugs. It's also the site of a unique service organization called h.o.m.e. (Homeworkers Organized for More Employment). East Orland (officially part of Orland) claims the Craig Brook National Fish Hatchery and Great Pond Mountain (which juts out from the landscape on your left as you drive east on Rt. 1).

Twenty miles east of Bucksport on Rt. 1, Ellsworth—Hancock County's shire town—unfortunately has earned its reputation as the summertime bottleneck to Bar Harbor. In fact, there's much more here, including handsome architectural remnants of the city's 19th-century lumbering heyday (which began shortly after its incorporation in 1800). Brigs, barks, and full-rigged ships, built in Ellsworth and captained by local fellows, loaded lumber here and carried it round the globe. Despite a ruinous 1855 fire that swept through downtown, the lumber trade thrived until late in the 19th century, along with factories and mills turning out shoes, bricks, boxes, and butter.

SIGHTS

The *Other* Fort Knox

Looming over Bucksport Harbor, Fort Knox, Rt. 174, Prospect, mailing address RR 1, Box 1316, Stockton Springs 04981, tel. (207) 469-7719, a 125-acre state historic site, actually is in adjoining Waldo County. However, it's only a few hundred feet from the intimidating, 137-foot-high Waldo-Hancock Bridge on Rt. 1, linking Prospect, Verona Island, and Bucksport. Named for Maj. Gen. Henry Knox, George Washington's first secretary of war, the sprawling granite fort was begun in 1844. Built to protect the upper Penobscot River from attack, it was never finished and never saw battle. To explore the underground passages, wear rubberized shoes and bring a flashlight; you can set the kids loose. Bring a picnic. Open May-Oct., 9 a.m.-4 p.m. (to 8 p.m. in July and August). Memorial Day weekend through Labor Day, the ranger gives free guided tours daily, and Civil War reenactments occur here several times a summer (check with the chamber of commerce). The grounds are accessible all year. Admission is $2 adults, 50 cents children 5-11. Children under five and seniors are free.

Paper Mill Tours

From mid-June to late August, **Champion International,** Main St., P.O. Box 1200, Bucksport 04416, tel. (207) 469-1700 or 469-1482, offers free, hour-long guided tours of its riverfront

coated-paper mill. No open-toed shoes, cameras, or children under 12 are allowed. You'll be issued a hard hat and earplugs. Tours run Monday, Wednesday, and Friday 9 a.m.-3 p.m. (on the hour; no noon tour); 10 people to a tour. If it's raining, go early or late in the day or you'll find a long wait. Check in at the brick security office on the south side of Water St., .9 mile west of Rt. 1. Limited streetside parking; the municipal lot is .4 mile east of the mill.

Old-Time Flicks

Phoenix-like, the 1916 **Alamo Theatre,** 379 Main St., P.O. Box 900, Bucksport 04416, tel. (207) 469-0924 or (800) 639-1636, fax (207) 469-7875, has been retrofitted for a new life—focusing on films about New England produced and/or revived by unique **Northeast Historic Film** (NHF), which is headquartered here. Stop in, survey the restoration, visit the displays (free), and browse the Alamo Theatre Store for antique postcards, T-shirts, toys, and reasonably priced videos on ice harvesting, lumberjacks, maple sugaring, and other traditional New England topics. Located half a mile west of Rt. 1, it's open weekdays 9 a.m.-4 p.m. all year, and on Saturday June through Labor Day. There's a minimal fee for family-oriented summertime matinees (Saturday, 2 p.m.) in the 120-seat theater. Continue the fun by joining NHF ($25 annual membership; $15 for students and teachers), so you can borrow by mail from the NHF video collection.

Historical Museums

Two small, volunteer-staffed local-history museums in Bucksport and Orland are open briefly in summer. No admission fees, but donations are welcomed. A preserved 1874 Maine Central Railroad station is home to the **Bucksport Historical Society Museum,** Main St., P.O. Box 798, Bucksport 04416, tel. (207) 567-3623 or 469-2591, open Wed.-Fri. 1-4 p.m. in July and August. The onetime depot is slightly below street level, adjoining Bucksport's waterfront walkway. **Orland Historical Society Museum,** Main St., Rt. 175, P.O. Box 97, Orland 04472, tel. (207) 469-2476, containing collections of minerals, Native American artifacts, antique photos, and military uniforms, is open Wednesday and Saturday 2-4 p.m. and by appointment, in July, August, and September.

h.o.m.e.

Located adjacent to the flashing light on Rt. 1 in Orland, h.o.m.e. is tough to categorize. Linked with the international Emmaus Movement founded by a French priest, h.o.m.e. (Homeworkers Organized for More Employment) was started in 1970 by Lucy Poulin, still the guiding force, and two nuns at a nearby convent. The quasi-religious organization shelters refugees and the homeless, operates a soup kitchen and a car-repair service, runs a day-care center, and teaches work skills in a variety of hands-on cooperative programs. Seventy percent of its income comes from sales of crafts, produce, and services. At the Rt. 1 store (corner of Upper Falls Rd.; open daily 9 a.m.-4:30 p.m.), you can buy handmade quilts, organic produce, maple syrup, and jams—and support a worthwhile effort. To volunteer time in the sawmill, store, or learning center, write P.O. Box 10, Orland 04472, or call (207) 469-7961.

Colonel Black Mansion

Very little has changed at Woodlawn, the Colonel Black Mansion in Ellsworth, West Main St./Surry Rd., Rt. 172, Ellsworth 04605, tel. (207) 667-8671, since George Nixon Black donated it to the town in 1928. Completed in 1828, the Geor-

Colonel Black Mansion, Ellsworth

MAINE OFFICE OF TOURISM

gian house is a marvel of preservation, one of Maine's best, filled with Black-family antiques and artifacts. Enthusiastic docents lead hour-long tours ($5 adults, $2 children under 12), beginning on the hour and half-hour, to point out the circular staircase, rare books and artifacts, canopied beds, a barrel organ, and lots more. Even kids appreciate all the unusual stuff. Afterward, plan to picnic on the manicured grounds, then explore two sleigh-filled barns, the Memorial Garden, and the three miles of mostly level trails in the woods up beyond the house. Restrooms are next to the parking area. There's an elegant tea each Wednesday afternoon (2-4 p.m.), late June through Labor Day, in the garden (or the carriage house if it's raining). China, silver, linens, special-blend tea, sandwiches, pastries, and live music—all for $6 a person. Call for reservations. The house is open June 1-Oct. 15, weekdays 10 a.m.-5 p.m. (last tour at 4 p.m.). In winter, there's cross-country skiing on the trails. On Rt. 172, a quarter of a mile southwest of Rt. 1, watch for the small sign and turn into the winding uphill driveway.

For the Birds

Just beyond Ellsworth, en route to Bar Harbor, watch carefully on the right for the tiny, hedge-crowded sign that marks **Birdsacre,** Rt. 3, Bar Harbor Rd., P.O. Box 485, Ellsworth 04605, tel. (207) 667-8460, a 130-acre urban sanctuary. Wander the trails in this peaceful preserve—spotting wildflowers, birds, and well-labeled shrubs and trees—and you'll have trouble believing you're surrounded by prime tourist territory. The sanctuary is open all year, sunrise to sunset; admission is free, but donations are welcomed. At the sanctuary entrance is the 1850 **Stanwood Homestead Museum,** with period furnishings and wildlife exhibits. Once owned by noted ornithologist Cordelia Stanwood, the museum is open daily 10 a.m.-4 p.m., mid-May to mid-October. Admission is $2.50 adults, 50 cents for kids under 12. Birdsacre is also a wildlife rehab center, so expect to see all kinds of winged creatures in various stages of rescue from oblivion. Some will be returned to the wild.

PARKS AND RECREATION

For a day of hiking, picnicking, swimming, canoeing, and a bit of natural history, pack a lunch and head for 135-acre **Craig Brook National Fish Hatchery,** 120 Hatchery Rd., East Orland 04431, tel. (207) 469-2803, on Alamoosook Lake. Turn off Rt. 1 six miles east of Bucksport and continue 1.4 miles north to the parking area just above the small visitor center (open daily 8 a.m.-5 p.m., May-Nov.; no charge; maps and restroom). Except on special occasions, you won't be allowed in the hatchery's raceway building. The grounds are accessible all year, daily 8 a.m.-8 p.m. Established in 1871, the U.S. Fish and Wildlife Service hatchery raises Atlantic salmon for stocking Maine rivers. The birch-lined shorefront has picnic tables and grills, a boat-launching ramp, Atlantic salmon display pool, additional parking, and a spectacular cross-lake view. Watch for eagles, osprey, and loons. Hiking options include a mile-long nature trail loop partly bordering Craig Brook, a two-mile (roundtrip) walking path to scenic, swimmable Craig Pond, and an easy-to-moderate two-hour (roundtrip) hike up Great Pond Mountain.

Called "Great Hill" in the *AMC Maine Mountain Guide,* 1,038-foot **Great Pond Mountain**'s biggest asset is its summit, with 360-degree views and lots of space for panoramic picnics. On a clear day, Baxter State Park's Katahdin is visible from Great Pond Mountain's north side. In fall, watch for migrating hawks. Access to the mountain is via gated private property beginning about a mile north of the hatchery parking area. Roadside parking is available near the trailhead; during fall-foliage season, you may need to park at the hatchery. Pick up a brochure from the box at the trailhead, stay on the trail, and respect the surrounding private property; in winter, snowmobilers use the trail. The **Great Pond Mountain Conservation Trust,** P.O. Box 266, Orland 04472, tel. (207) 469-2476 or 469-2819, acts as conscientious local steward for Great Pond Mountain and surrounding wild lands.

Contact the **Bucksport Parks and Recreation Department,** tel. (207) 469-3518, weekdays 8 a.m.-5 p.m., for year-round information on facilities they supervise: first-come, first-served lighted municipal tennis courts next to Buck-sport High School; a municipal swimming pool, with open swims daily 1-4:30 p.m. and some evening hours, mid-June to late August, next to Jewett School, Broadway Extension; and an outdoor skating/hockey rink, with a warming house, on Broadway Extension behind the health center. Parks and Rec also maintains the half-mile walkway along the restored Bucksport waterfront—a great place to relax on a bench and enjoy the expansive view of the harbor, Fort Knox, and the Waldo-Hancock Bridge.

Bike Rentals

In Ellsworth, on the way to Mount Desert Island, **Bar Harbor Bicycle Shop,** 193 Main St., Ellsworth 04605, tel. (207) 667-6886, is a branch of the Bar Harbor firm. The shop has full-day bike rentals for $15; half-day (four hours) rentals are $10. Open all year, Mon.-Fri. 10 a.m.-6 p.m. (to 8 p.m. Friday), Saturday 9 a.m.-6 p.m., and Sunday 10 a.m.-5 p.m. in summer.

Golf

Bucksport Golf and Country Club, Rt. 46, one and a half miles north of Rt. 1, tel. (207) 469-7612, prides itself on having Maine's longest nine-hole course. Moderate greens fees; pro shop; snack bar; driving range; carts. Open mid-April through October. On Rt. 1, one and a half miles east of Ellsworth, the **White Birches** motel complex, tel. (207) 667-3621 or (800) 660-3621 in Maine, also has a nine-hole course (free with lodging). Moderate fees; carts; restaurant.

Kids' Stuff

If the kids need some unwinding, the answer to parents' prayers is the creative playground on Elm Street in Bucksport, across from the Jewett School (make sure they see the dragon).

If you're in the area as long as a week, contact the **Down East Family YMCA,** Rt. 1A, Upper State St., Ellsworth 04605, tel. (207) 667-3086, for its schedule of fitness, swim, and outdoor programs for kids, teens, adults, and families. Most popular is the activity-filled day camp, mid-June to mid-August ($75 a week for nonresidents); reserve well ahead if you plan to take advantage of it.

A full-size dory and beanbag seats in three rooms of well-displayed children's books make the **Ellsworth Public Library,** State St., Ellsworth 04405, tel. (207) 667-6363, one of the kid-friendliest around. Open Tues.-Fri. 10 a.m.-5 p.m. (to 8 p.m. Wednesday), Saturday 10 a.m.-1 p.m.

Along Rt. 3 (Bar Harbor Road), en route from Ellsworth to Mount Desert Island, is a whole string of commercial attractions to keep kids entertained (and your wallet drained).

ENTERTAINMENT

The carefully restored art deco **Grand Auditorium of Hancock County,** 100 Main St., Ellsworth 04405, tel. (207) 667-9500, is the year-round site of films, concerts, plays, and art exhibits. Most films are at 7:30 p.m. Call for schedule.

First-run films, usually showing twice a night, plus bargain matinees in midsummer, are on the docket at **Maine Coast Mall Cinemas 2,** High St., Rt. 1, Ellsworth 04405, tel. (207) 667-3251. Bucksport residents also patronize the **Colonial Theatre** in Belfast.

A summer highlight is the **Ellsworth Concert Band** concert series, held three Wednesday evenings in July in the plaza outside Ellsworth City Hall (an imposing building just north of Main Street). Practice begins at 6:30 p.m., concerts start at 8 p.m., and the 50-member community band even welcomes visitors with talent and instruments. Just show up at practice time. The repertoire is mostly marches and show music; a prize goes to the person who correctly identifies a mystery tune.

FESTIVALS AND EVENTS

Early July's **Annual Antiques Show and Sale,** at the Franklin Street Methodist Church, in Bucksport, runs 9 a.m.-3 p.m. and offers a varied selection and excellent lunches.

Ellsworth is home to the **Annual Rotary Club All-You-Can-Eat Blueberry Pancake Breakfast,** 6-10:30 a.m. the second Saturday in August on the city hall lawn.

Also see the Castine and Blue Hill sections for other nearby events.

SHOPPING

Antiques, Art Galleries, Books
You're unlikely to meet a single soul who has left the **Big Chicken Barn,** Rt. 1, Box 150A, Ellsworth 04605, tel. (207) 667-7308, without buying *something.* You'll find every kind of collectible on the vast first floor, courtesy of four dozen dealers. Climb the stairs for books, magazines, old music, and more. With 21,000 square feet, this place is addictive. Free coffee, hassle-free browsing. Open daily, all year. Big Chicken is 11 miles east of Bucksport, eight and a half miles west of Ellsworth.

In downtown Ellsworth, the **Union River Gallery,** 92 Main St., Ellsworth 04605, tel. (207) 667-7700, showcasing two dozen or so artists, plus posters, photos, and antique prints, is open all year, Tues.-Fri. 10 a.m.-6 p.m. and Saturday 10 a.m.-5 p.m.

Clothing, Gifts, Crafts
In Bucksport, check out **The Vineyard,** Main St. at Third St., Bucksport 04416, tel. (207) 469-7844, based in three rooms of a yellow house. Since 1989, owner Barbara Vittum has carried an eclectic mix of wine, beer, cheese, and gourmet goodies, plus high-quality local crafts and paintings. Somehow the combination works. Open all year, Mon.-Fri. 9 a.m.-6 p.m. and Saturday 9 a.m.-1 p.m. No credit cards.

Surry Gardens, Rt. 172, Surry 04684, tel. (207) 667-4493, is a flower fan's paradise, with knowledgeable staff and hundreds of plant varieties—many geared for northern climes. For $2, they'll send their 80-page mail-order catalog. Open all year, Mon.-Sat. 8 a.m.-5 p.m. and Sunday 9 a.m.-5 p.m.

Don't miss **Rooster Brother,** 18 W. Main St., Rt. 1, Ellsworth 04605, tel. (207) 667-8675, for gourmet cookware, cards, and books on the main floor; coffee, candy, condiments, and fresh breads in the basement. Open all year, the shop is in a handsome old riverside building on busy Rt. 1; access can be tricky at times, so be cautious and patient.

The Grasshopper Shop, 124 Main St., Ellsworth 04605, tel. (207) 667-5816, appeals primarily to those under 40, with eclectic clothes, unusual gifts, and great cards. The two-story emporium is open daily year-round, also evenings in summer. The deeper-pocket crowd shops at **Beal's Jewelry Store,** 97 Main St., Ellsworth 04605, tel. (207) 667-2161, for upscale jewelry, clothing, and gifts. Open all year.

For an extensive sporting-gear inventory, plus advice on outdoors activities, stop in at **Cadillac Mountain Sports,** 34 High St., Rt. 1, Ellsworth 04605, tel. (207) 667-7819. Open daily year-round.

Discount Shopping

You can certainly find bargains at the **L.L. Bean Factory Store,** 150 High St., Rt. 1, Ellsworth 04605, tel. (207) 667-7753, but this is an outlet, so scrutinize the goods for flaws and blemishes before buying. Open all year, Mon.-Sat. 9 a.m.-9 p.m. and Sunday 9 a.m.-6 p.m.

Across the road is **Reny's Department Store,** Ellsworth Shopping Center, High St., Rt. 1, Ellsworth 04605, tel. (207) 667-5166, a Maine-based discount operation with a you-never-know-what-you'll-find philosophy. It's open Mon.-Sat. 8 a.m.-8 p.m. and Sunday 10 a.m.-5 p.m., mid-April to Thanksgiving. Other months, it's open Mon.-Sat. 9 a.m.-7 p.m. (Friday to 8 p.m.) and Sunday 10 a.m.-5 p.m.

Maine Coast Mall, High St., Rt. 1, Ellsworth, tel. (207) 667-9905, has several outlet stores, in addition to fast-food meccas, retail shops, a bank, a cinema, and the Holiday Inn. Also along this commercial strip are towel, shoe, and housewares outlets. Across from the mall, Rt. 1 bears off toward Eastport and Calais, while Rt. 3 continues on to Mount Desert Island.

Health Foods/Farmers' Market

Down East Maine's biggest selection of health foods is at **John Edwards Market,** 158 Main St., Ellsworth 04605, tel. (207) 667-9377. Organic produce, fresh breads, wines, and self-help books are also in the inventory. Stop in for a cup of coffee or tea and some healthful go-withs. It's open all year, Mon.-Thurs. 9 a.m.-5:30 p.m., Friday 9 a.m.-8 p.m., Saturday 9 a.m.-5 p.m., and Sunday noon-5 p.m.

Ellsworth Farmers' Market gets underway at 85 High St. (Rt. 1, next to Irving Mainway) mid-June to late October, Monday and Thursday 2-5:30 p.m. and Saturday 9:30 a.m.-12:30 p.m. There's also a farmers' market in nearby Blue Hill.

ACCOMMODATIONS

B&Bs

The most attractive B&B in this area is **The Sign of the Amiable Pig,** Rt. 175, Castine Rd., P.O. Box 232, Orland 04472, tel. (207) 469-2561, once a hideout on the Underground Railroad. Three rooms (private and shared baths) are $60-65 d, including an imaginative breakfast. A separate guest house, sleeping five, goes for $400 a week. Guests have the run of Charlotte and Wes Pipher's very comfortable home with parlor, keeping room, and lots of fireplaces. The oldest house section dates from 1765. Oriental carpets and fresh flowers are everywhere. No pets, credit cards, or smoking. The Amiable Pig (named for the weathervane atop the barn) is open all year, but be sure to call ahead and reserve space off season. It's located .3 mile east of Rt. 1.

Not far from the Amiable Pig but well off Rt. 1, **Alamoosook Lodge,** P.O. Box 16, Orland 04472, tel. (207) 469-6393, fax 469-2528, is a comfortably rustic inn with six ground-floor rooms (private baths) overlooking 1,100-acre Alamoosook Lake. Rates are $85 d June-mid-Oct., $65 d other months, including full breakfast. Each room has its own journal, full of rave reviews. Children over 12 are welcome; families can swim, canoe, fish, play lawn games, or just relax on the five and a half acres. In winter, there's ice fishing, ice-skating, and cross-country skiing. Complimentary wine and cheese are served at 5 p.m., but dinner is available only on holidays and for group functions; nearest restaurants are in Bucksport and down the Blue Hill Peninsula. No smoking, no pets; open all year.

Motels

In downtown Bucksport, the award for best view goes to the **Jed Prouty Motor Inn,** Main St., P.O. Box 826, Bucksport 04416, tel. (207) 469-3113, a four-story Best Western motel nudged right up to the harbor's edge. Forty modern rooms have phones, a/c, and cable TV. Be sure to request a water view, or you'll be facing a parking lot. Doubles are $89 July to mid-October, $79 the rest of the year.

National chain and independent motels line High Street (Rts. 1 and 3), a densely commercial stretch in Ellsworth, and continue southward toward Mount Desert Island. (Bar Harbor is 20 miles from downtown Ellsworth.) If you can handle sleeping in the middle of a shopping mall, the best of these is the **Holiday Inn,** High St., Rt. 1, Ellsworth 04605, tel. (207) 667-9341 or (800) 401-9341, fax (207) 667-7294. Request a room facing the mall, not the highway. The 103-room facility has a/c, phones (and dataports), cable TV, laundry, serious fitness center, indoor tennis courts, and heated indoor pool. Doubles are $119-140 in July and August, $69-100 other months. Kids and pets are welcome. Open all year.

About one and a half miles east of the Holiday Inn, heading Down East, **White Birches,** Rt. 1, P.O. Box 743, Ellsworth 04605, tel. (207) 667-3621 or (800) 660-3621 in Maine, (800) 435-1287 outside Maine, is a clean, generic motel with 70 rooms ($60-80 d July to Labor Day, $40-50 other months), but the biggest plus for golfers is free use of the nine-hole course. Request a room overlooking the course. The motel's **Czy Gil's Restaurant** does a breakfast buffet for $4.50 pp, as well as lunch and dinner. Rooms have phones and cable TV but no a/c. Pets and kids are welcome. Open all year.

Campgrounds

The rivers, lakes, and ponds in the area between Bucksport and Ellsworth make it especially appealing for camping, and sites tend to be cheaper than in the Bar Harbor area. During July and August, especially weekends, reservations are wise. On Rt. 1, the first campground you'll encounter is just below the Waldo-Hancock Bridge. The well-maintained **Flying Dutchman Campground,** Verona Island, P.O. Box 549, Bucksport 04416, tel. (207) 469-3256, dramatically situated on 10 acres bordering the tidal Penobscot River, has 35 tent and RV sites, some wooded. Cost is $15-18 (four persons). Facilities include a laundry, creative playground, rec room, free movies, and heated outdoor pool. Pets are allowed. Open May to mid-October.

Six miles east of Bucksport, across from Craig Pond Rd., is Back Ridge Rd., leading to **Balsam Cove Campground,** P.O. Box C, East Orland 04431, tel. (207) 469-7771 or (800) 469-7771 in Maine. From Rt. 1, take Back Ridge Rd. one and a half miles to the left turn for the

campground, on the shores of 10-mile-long Toddy Pond. Facilities on the 50 acres include 60 wooded tent and RV sites ($15-20 for four), dump station, store, laundry, free showers, boat rentals, and freshwater swimming. Open late May to late September. The same season holds for 10-acre **Whispering Pines Campground,** Rt. 1, East Orland 04431, tel. (207) 469-3443, also on Toddy Pond but accessed directly from Rt. 1. Facilities include 45 tent and RV sites (request one close to the lake), free use of canoes and rowboats, free showers, freshwater swimming, and rec hall. Cost is $16-18 for two persons. Whispering Pines is six and a half miles east of Bucksport.

Seasonal Rentals

For cottages and homes available by the week, month, or season, contact Karen Sullivan at **Coastal Cottage Rental Company,** RR1, Box 123-1A, Surry 04684, tel. (207) 667-0100.

FOOD

Breakfast, Lunch, and Miscellanea

Order breakfast anytime at **The Riverside Café,** 42 Main St., next to the Union River, Ellsworth 04605, tel. (207) 667-7220. Juices are fresh (if a bit pricey), buckwheat pancakes ($1.10 each) are outstanding, but try The Riverside ($3.95), a bowl of mixed fruit and granola-topped yogurt. Lunch menu includes homemade soups, salads, sandwiches, grilled burgers, and high-cal desserts; skip the fried-seafood platters. Sunday brunches (summer and fall only) are legendary. Box lunches ($5.75) are available Memorial Day weekend to mid-October (order by 11 a.m.). No credit cards. Open all year, Mon.-Fri. 5 a.m.-3 p.m., Saturday 7 a.m.-3 p.m.; it's also open Sunday 7 a.m.-2 p.m. June to mid-October.

Bucksport House of Pizza (BHOP), Main St., Bucksport 04416, tel. (207) 469-3974, vies with **Gobbi's Pizza,** Rt. 1, Verona Island, tel. (207) 469-3319, for claim to the best pizza in Bucksport. Both are open daily 11 a.m.-9 p.m., all year; BHOP stays open to 10 p.m. Friday and Saturday.

Seven miles east of Bucksport, the **East Orland Country Store,** Rt. 1, East Orland 04431, tel. (207) 469-7658, dishes out subs, burgers, dogs, pizzas, videos, and stamps (it's the local post office). The store, which also carries groceries, beer, and wine, is open daily, all year, 6:30 a.m.-9 p.m. in summer, 7 a.m.-8 p.m. in winter.

On the Main Street spur heading east from Ellsworth (also called Washington Junction Road), **Larry's Pastry Shop,** 241 Main St., Ellsworth 04605, tel. (207) 667-2557, may look unassuming, but *everyone* goes there for bread, rolls, pies, and Saturday night's baked beans. No preservatives are used. Open all year, Mon.-Sat. 6 a.m.-5 p.m.

Moderate

All of the restaurants in this category are likely to please both palate and wallet. However, if you're looking for more elegance and creativity (and higher prices), drive a bit farther to Blue Hill, Castine, Deer Isle, or even Mount Desert Island.

MacLeod's, Main St., Bucksport 04416, tel. (207) 469-3963, is Bucksport's most popular restaurant. The menu is varied, children are welcome, it has a liquor license, and it's air-conditioned. French chocolate silk pie is a specialty. Open daily, all year, Mon.-Fri. 11 a.m.-9 p.m., Saturday and Sunday 5-9 p.m.

In Ellsworth, go to **Frankies Café & Good Stuff,** 40 High St., Rt. 1, in the Cadillac Mountain Sports building, tel. (207) 667-7701, for excellent Mediterranean/vegetarian specialties ($3.50-5) —veggie-rice pie, spanakopita, brie pasta pie, sesame-butter-topped bagels. Pâté and meat sandwiches are available. Everything's very casual. Owner Rosemary Foreman formerly cooked at Deer Isle's Haystack Mountain School of Crafts. Only six tables, so order food to go if it's crowded. Open for lunch and dinner Mon.-Saturday. It closes Monday and Saturday at 5 p.m., Tues.-Thurs. at 6 p.m., and Friday at 7 p.m.

The Mex, 185 Main St., Ellsworth, tel. (207) 667-4494, has been a popular local eatery since 1979. The menu is punnily entertaining ("Juanderful Beginnings"), service is good, and you won't go hungry. Lots of vegetarian choices. Take home a bottle of their fiery hot sauce. Open all year, daily 11 a.m.-9 p.m. (to 10 p.m. weekends).

There's even a Thai restaurant in Ellsworth, and it's a good one. **The Bangkok Restaurant,**

Rt. 3, Bar Harbor Rd., Ellsworth, tel. (207) 667-1324, does a creditable job, and the always-popular pad thai is a winner. No smoking, no MSG. Open all year, Mon.-Sat. 11 a.m.-9 p.m. and Sunday 4-9 p.m.

INFORMATION AND SERVICES

The **Bucksport Bay Area Chamber of Commerce,** Main St., P.O. Box 1800, Bucksport 04416, tel. (207) 469-6818, is right next to the municipal office in downtown Bucksport. Office hours are Mon.-Fri. 9 a.m.-1 p.m., but the side door is open afternoons and weekends for access to an extensive array of brochures, newspapers, and other publications, plus bulletin-board notices. Bucksport information is also available at the **Gateway Mobil Station,** at the traffic light on the corner of Rt. 1, between the bridge and the Shop 'n Save supermarket.

It can be hard to spot the **Ellsworth Area Chamber of Commerce,** P.O. Box 267, Ellsworth 04605, tel. (207) 667-5584, amid the malls and fast-food places lining High Street (Rt. 1). Watch for a small gray building topped by an Information Center sign (on the right, close to the road, when heading toward Bar Harbor). Open Mon.-Fri. 9 a.m.-4:30 p.m. mid-September to mid-June; Mon.-Sat., mid-June to mid-September; daily, with extended hours, July and August.

Don't miss a chance to visit one of the state's loveliest libraries, the **Ellsworth Public Library,** 46 State St., Ellsworth, tel. (207) 667-6363. The National Historic Register Federalist building was donated to the city in 1897 by George Nixon Black, grandson of the builder of Woodlawn. Services include photocopies, computer and Internet access, lectures, art exhibits, and a popular paperback exchange (take one and leave one). Open Tues.-Fri. 10 a.m.-5 p.m. (Wednesday to 8 p.m.), Saturday 10 a.m.-5 p.m. in winter, 10 a.m.-1 p.m. in summer.

The **Buck Memorial Library,** Main St., P.O. Box DD, Bucksport 04416, tel. (207) 469-2650, established in 1887, has Wednesday and Saturday morning story hours and free Internet access. The library is open Mon.-Fri. 10 a.m.-5 p.m. and Saturday 10 a.m.-noon.

Newspapers

The *Bangor Daily News,* is Down East Maine's daily resource, presenting some local news but also state, national, and international stories. Bucksport's community-spirited local paper, *The Enterprise,* 346 Main St., P.O. Box 829, Bucksport 04416, tel. (207) 469-6722, appears every Thursday, with news, features, calendar info, and local ads. The *Enterprise* also produces a very helpful local-resource booklet, *The Enterprise SourceBook,* available at its office or the chamber of commerce. The respected *Ellsworth American,* tel. (207) 667-2576, also published weekly, has been around since the mid-19th century. The *Ellsworth Weekly,* a newcomer, appears every Saturday, tel. (207) 667-5514 or 667-1219. In summer and fall, the *Ellsworth American* publishes *Out & About in Downeast Maine,* a free monthly vacation supplement in tabloid format.

Community Radio

Founded in 1985, **WERU 89.9 FM,** Maine's only community radio station, in 1997 moved its headquarters from a converted henhouse in East Blue Hill to a converted restaurant in East Orland, Rt. 1, P.O. Box 170, East Orland 04431, tel. (207) 469-6600, fax 469-8961. Tune in for an eclectic array of contemporary music, as well as liberal commentary and interviews. Featured big-name performers at the Left Bank Bakery & Café often manage to squeeze in a WERU broadcast. The station's major fund-raiser is the annual **Full Circle Fair,** an extraordinary cultural festival held on a mid-July weekend. The fair location rotates, so contact the station or watch newspapers.

Emergencies

In **Bucksport, Verona Island, and Orland,** call 911 for fire and ambulance; in **Orland,** call (207) 667-7575 for police. In **Ellsworth,** call (207) 667-2525 for fire, (207) 667-2133 for police, and (207) 667-3200 for ambulance.

Maine Coast Memorial Hospital, 50 Union St., Ellsworth 04605, emergency room tel. (207) 667-4520, the largest hospital in the area, has 24-hour emergency-room service.

Area residents also patronize Blue Hill Memorial Hospital in Blue Hill and the giant Eastern Maine Medical Center in Bangor.

Veterinarian/Kennel

Dr. John Hunt's **Bucksport Veterinary Hospital,** Rt. 1, Bucksport 04416, tel. (207) 469-3614, provides medical care as well as cat and dog boarding facilities year-round. Drop-off hours are liberal (Mon.-Sat.), and rates are especially reasonable. The hospital/kennel is about two miles east of downtown Bucksport, on the right.

Laundromat

Hanf Laundrymat, 151 High St., Ellsworth 04605, tel. (207) 667-4428, has self-service machines and is open 24 hours.

Public Restrooms

In Bucksport, public restrooms next to the **town dock** (behind the Bucksport Historical Society) are open spring, summer, and fall. There are year-round restrooms in the **Gateway Mobil gas station** (at the Rt. 1 traffic light next to the Bucksport bridge) and in the **Bucksport Municipal Office** on Main Street.

Getting Around

Ellsworth Taxi, tel. (207) 667-2722, is on call round-the-clock every day, providing in-town Ellsworth and out-of-town service. **Superior Limousine and Taxi Service,** tel. (207) 469-1155 or (800) 340-1155, provides service around Bucksport and to the Bangor International Airport.

MACKIE FOLKS

BANGOR AREA

Lumber Capital of the World in the 19th century, Bangor (BANG-gore), with a population approaching 33,000, is still northern Maine's magnet for commerce and culture—the big city for the northern three-quarters of the state. Chief draws now in this region are the 80-store Bangor Mall (and surrounding shops), Bangor International Airport, and the academic, athletic, and artistic activities of the flagship University of Maine campus, in Orono, a few miles north-

east. The county seat for Penobscot County, downtown Bangor is awakening from a 1960s slump typical of many urban areas, and today you can stroll alongside Kenduskeag Stream, cruise the Penobscot River, duck into shops and restaurants, and spend a comfortable night in the city's heart.

Bangor incorporated in 1791, but when, in 1604, explorer Samuel de Champlain landed here (an event commemorated by a plaque

downtown, next to Kenduskeag Stream), the Queen City bore the Native American name of Kenduskeag, meaning "eel-catching place."

In the late 19th century, when the lumber trade moved westward, smaller industries moved into greater Bangor to take up the slack, but a disastrous fire on April 30, 1911, leveled 55 acres of Bangor's commercial and residential neighborhoods, retarding progress for several decades.

Plenty of elegant architecture from Bangor's lumbering heyday escaped incineration, so you can still appreciate it by wandering around with a walking-tour brochure available at the Bangor Region Chamber of Commerce, or take a one-hour Best of Bangor bus tour through the city's seven historic districts, featuring a giant statue of legendary lumberjack Paul Bunyan, the home of noted author Stephen King, and fine specimens of Victorian, Italianate, Queen Anne, and Greek Revival architecture.

SIGHTS

Walk the Walk
If time allows, explore the city by picking up the Bangor Historical Society's free walking-tour brochure at the chamber of commerce and following the signs. Numbered signs mark stops on the east side tour, lettered signs mark those on the west side tour. The west side tour takes slightly longer and is more spread out; Stephen King's Italianate villa (not identified by name in the brochure) is one of the stops. Another distinctive west side landmark is the National Historic Register **Thomas Hill Standpipe**, a squat 1897 water tower on one of the city's highest points. It's seldom open to the public, unfortunately—there's a great view from the observation platform.

Best of Bangor Bus Tours
If time is limited, at least try to catch one of the Best of Bangor narrated bus tours through the city's historic districts, which the **Bangor Historical Society** sponsors each Thursday morning and the first Saturday of each month (10:30-11:30 a.m.), July through September. Cost is $5 adults, free for kids under 12 with an adult. Buses depart from the **Bangor Region Chamber of Commerce** information center, 519 Main Street. Contact the chamber, tel. (207) 947-0307, or the historical society, tel. (207) 942-5766, for details.

Paul Bunyan, Native Son?
On Main Street, next to the chamber of commerce office and across from the Holiday Inn, stands a 31-foot-tall statue of the mythical lumberjack Paul Bunyan, allegedly born in Bangor on February 12, 1834. Weighing 3,200 pounds, the colorful statue was erected on a 12-foot-high base in 1959, during the city's 125th anniversary. Inside the base is a time capsule due to be opened in 2084. Kids can run and play in adjacent **Paul Bunyan Park.**

Stephen Kingdom
Maine native and naturalized hometown boy, horror honcho Stephen King is anything but a myth. Born in Portland, he's lived in Bangor since 1980, and you may spot him around town (especially at baseball and basketball games). His rambling mansion, at 47 West Broadway, looks like a set from one of the movies based on his novels and stories—complete with a wrought-iron front gate and fence festooned with iron bats and cobwebs. Heed the No Trespassing sign; the best-selling author has had his share of odd encounters with off-the-wall devotees. King fans should be sure to visit **Betts Bookstore,** downtown. If you'd like the author to autograph one of your books, just send it with a self-addressed, stamped envelope, and a note indicating the recipient, to Stephen King, P.O. Box 1186, Bangor 04402. And be patient.

Museums
The Greek Revival **Thomas A. Hill House,** 159 Union St., Bangor 04401, tel. (207) 942-5766, built by a wealthy attorney in 1836, is the headquarters of the **Bangor Historical Society.** Listed on the National Register of Historic Places, the handsome brick building on the corner of High Street has been restored to Victorian elegance, with period furnishings, Maine paintings, and special exhibits. Hour-long guided tours occur noon-4 p.m. Open Tues.-Fri., mid-March to mid-December, as well as Sunday, July through September. Admission is $2 adults, 50 cents for kids 11 and under (little kids may get squirmy here).

*Bangor home of
horror novelist
Stephen King*

On the other hand, children *love* the **Cole Land Transportation Museum,** 405 Perry Rd., P.O. Box 1166, Bangor 04401, tel. (207) 990-3600, fax 990-2653, a sprawling facility founded by Bangor trucking magnate Galen Cole. More than 200 19th- and 20th-century vehicles—just about anything that has ever rolled across Maine's landscape—fill the museum. Besides vintage cars, there are fire engines, tractors, logging vehicles, baby carriages, even a replica railroad station. A gift shop stocks transportation-related items. Admission is $2 adults, $1 seniors, free for those under 19. The museum, located near the junction of I-95 and I-395, is open daily 9 a.m.-5 p.m., May to mid-November.

Winterport

In Waldo County, 12 miles downriver from Bangor, is Winterport, a sleeper of a town. It earned its name as the limit of winter navigation for Bangor's lumber trade; ice blocked shipping traffic from proceeding farther upriver. The National Register **Winterport Historic District** includes splendid 19th-century Greek Revival homes and commercial buildings on Rt. 1A and the short side streets descending to the river. To appreciate what's here, pick up the free *Walking Tour of Winterport* brochure at the Colonial Winterport Inn, on Rt. 1A, and pace off the 13-stop route.

PARKS AND RECREATION

Parks pop up everywhere in Bangor—from vest-pocket oases to a downtown pedestrian mall to a sprawling garden cemetery. Beyond the city in all directions (but particularly north) lie preserves and countless recreational opportunities.

In a state where burial grounds almost invariably command views to die for, the standout is **Mount Hope Cemetery,** consecrated in 1836 and easily the state's loveliest. Among the prominent Mainers interred here is Civil War-era U.S. Vice President Hannibal Hamlin. Inspired by the design of Mt. Auburn Cemetery in Cambridge, Massachusetts, 254-acre Mount Hope is more park than cemetery—with gardens, ponds, bridges, paved paths, lots of greenery, a few picnic tables, and wandering deer. Roller-bladers consider it paradise. Open daily 7:30 a.m. to sunset, all year. The Bangor Historical Society, tel. (207) 942-5766, sponsors an hour-long guided walking tour of the cemetery on the first Saturday of the month at 10 a.m., June-September. Cost is $5. The entrance to the green-fenced cemetery is at 1038 State St. (Rt. 2), about a quarter of a mile east of Hogan Road.

Built over the meandering Kenduskeag Stream, right downtown, are two block-long parks: **Norumbega Parkway,** with a war memorial and benches, and **Hamlin Mall,** with cannons, the Champlain landing plaque, and a statue of Hannibal Hamlin.

A waterfall and a fountain are the focus at **Cascade Park,** State St., Rt. 2, .3 mile east of Eastern Maine Medical Center, where you can collapse on a bench or grab a picnic table and chill out.

The best kid place is **Hayford Park,** 115 13th St., off Union St., northwest of downtown, where the Gothic-looking **Bangor Creative Playground,** designed by Robert Leathers, has a maze of entertaining wooden structures to climb in, on, and around. Next to it is the state-of-the-art, 1,500-seat Shawn T. Mansfield baseball stadium, underwritten by baseball super-enthusiast Stephen King (who annually abandons his computer to attend Boston Red Sox opening day).

With parks and recreation sites spotted all over the city, the best way to check on locations and opening times for municipal swimming pools, tennis courts, and skating rinks is to contact the **Bangor Parks and Recreation Department,** tel. (207) 947-1018.

Golf

Considered a standout among public courses, the **Bangor Municipal Golf Course,** 280 Webster Ave., Bangor 04401, tel. (207) 941-0232, has 18 holes dating from 1964 and a newer (and tougher) nine holes. Stretching over both sides of Webster Avenue, the course is also on the Bangor Airport flight path; don't flinch when a jet screams overhead. Tee times are needed only for the newer nine, but plan to arrive early in midsummer (the course opens at 7 a.m.). Open mid-April to mid-November. The clubhouse (with pro shop and snack bar) is .4 mile south of Hammond St. (Rt. 2), on the southwest side of town.

Twelve miles southeast of Bangor, next to the Lucerne Inn, the nine-hole **Lucerne Hills Golf Club,** Rt. 1A, Lucerne-in-Maine 04429, tel. (207) 843-6282, is worth a visit just for the spectacular view. The course is open mid-April through October, the fall foliage is fabulous, and greens fees are moderate.

Cycling

Three Bangor-area bike shops (and one in Searsport) spearhead the bicycling activity in this part of Maine. They publicize group rides via the newsletters and flyers of **The Maine Freewheelers,** P.O. Box 2037, Bangor 04402. The shops sponsor road and offroad group rides, most briskly paced, April-Oct., in the Bangor area. During the same months, Maine Freewheelers, open to members and nonmembers, schedules weekend rides, mostly beyond the Bangor area, with options for different skill levels. Nature preserves, swim breaks, and picnics are often built into the plans. Helmets are required. North of I-95 (and east of the Bangor Mall), next to the Olive Garden, is **Ski Rack Sports,** 24 Longview Dr., Bangor, tel. (207) 945-6474 or (800) 698-6474 in Maine, with a huge selection of mountain bikes and fast repair service. If you haven't brought your bike, this is the best place to rent one—for a half-day, day, or week. The shop is open all year, Mon.-Sat. 10 a.m.-6 p.m. (to 8 p.m. Friday) and Sunday noon-4 p.m. Group rides are Monday and Wednesday at 6 p.m. Across the Penobscot River is well-stocked **Pat's Bike Shop,** 373 Wilson St., Rt. 1A, Brewer 04412, tel. (207) 989-2900, which has no rentals but sponsors group rides Mon.-Thurs. and Sunday. It's open Mon.-Fri. 10 a.m.-6 p.m. and Saturday 9 a.m.-5 p.m. Upriver is **Rose Bicycle,** 9 Pine St., Orono 04473, tel. (207) 866-3525 or (800) 656-3525 in Maine, catering to the university crowd. In summer, the shop is open Monday and Friday 9 a.m.-5 p.m., Tues.-Thurs. 9 a.m.-7 p.m., and Saturday 9 a.m.-4 p.m. The shop is closed Sunday and Monday in winter. Group rides are Monday, Wednesday, and Friday. No rentals, but there are free route maps.

Spectator Sports

Most spectator sports are affiliated with the University of Maine at Orono, where the **Bangor Blue Ox** independent professional baseball team also plays.

Downtown at Bass Park, the **Bangor Auditorium,** 100 Dutton St., Bangor 04401, tel. (207) 941-9711, is the site of other sporting events, with high-school basketball taking the lead in winter. Call for a schedule.

Hiking

After you've done the walking tour of Bangor, and cruised the Bangor Mall (if you're so inclined), you'll need to get out of town for anything in the way of hiking. In Dedham, 12 miles southeast of Bangor, a favorite hike goes up **Bald Mountain** (sometimes called Dedham Bald Mountain) to the disused fire tower on the bald summit. On a clear day, climb the tower for panoramic views to both Katahdin and Cadillac Mountain. Allow about two hours roundtrip if you plan to picnic and climb the tower. To reach the trailhead from downtown Bangor, take Rt. 1A (Wilson St.) about eight and a half miles from the Penobscot River bridge to the Rt. 46 junction. Just beyond the junction, turn right onto Upper Dedham Road. Go about two and a half miles and, just after a stream, bear left onto Dedham Road. Continue about three and a half miles to the parking area (on left). The trail leads up from here, over a few steep, ledgy spots. It's well worth the climb, especially during fall-foliage season.

Getting Afloat

During the summer and fall, the beautifully restored 83-foot motor yacht *Pauline* (once a sardine carrier) cruises the Penobscot River southward. Trips operate four times daily, starting at 10 a.m., the first three weeks in June, the last two weeks in July, the first two weeks in September, and late September to mid-October. Cruises are 1-2 hours (including a basic lunch or dinner buffet on the latter), and tickets range $10-30 (the sunset dinner cruise is the most expensive). The *Pauline* is berthed at the municipal dock next to the Sea Dog Restaurant. Reservations required; call (207) 990-3385 or (800) 999-7352.

ENTERTAINMENT

More than a century ago, when cabin-feverish lumberjacks roared into Bangor for R&R, they were apt to patronize Fan Jones's "establishment" on Harlow Street. Adult entertainment is still available in the city, but so is higher-brow stuff. The **Bangor Symphony Orchestra,** established in 1896, has an enviable reputation as one of the country's oldest and best community orchestras. Call (207) 942-5555 or (800) 639-3221 for a schedule. During the regular season, Oct.-April, monthly concerts are pre-

sented weekends at the University of Maine's Maine Center for the Arts, in Orono. *The Nutcracker* is often the December offering.

The professional **Penobscot Theatre Company,** P.O. Box 1188, Bangor 04401, tel. (207) 942-3333, fax 947-6678, performs five or six classic and contemporary comedies and dramas early October to mid-May. Curtains are Thursday 7 p.m., Friday 8 p.m., Saturday 5 and 8:30 p.m., and Sunday 2 p.m. Tickets are $15-19. From late July to mid-August, the company presents the **Maine Shakespeare Festival,** performing three classics in repertory, on the Bangor waterfront, next to the Joshua Chamberlain Bridge. Preperformance entertainment includes madrigals, juggling, and Renaissance dancing. Bring a blanket, mat, or folding chair; performances are Wed.-Sun. at 8 p.m. Tickets cost $10.

The local film multiplex is **Hoyts Cinemas,** 557 Stillwater Ave., Bangor 04401, next to the Bangor Mall, tel. (207) 942-1303, with a choice of 10 screens. Three or four usually have matinees, with lower prices than evening flicks.

For the ultimate in down-home live entertainment (a locally colorful country-and-western spot), head for **Stacey's Lounge,** 420 Wilson St., Rt. 2, Brewer 04412, tel. (207) 989-4940, where 200 or so singles and couples pile in on Friday and Saturday nights, pay a $2-4 cover charge, keep the cocktail waitresses hopping, and live it up on and off the dance floor until 1 a.m. College kids, middle-agers, bikers, chain smokers, and Canadian swingers are all part of the mix. It's definitely an adventure. The lounge, open daily all year—Mon.-Thurs. from 6 p.m., Fri.-Sun. from 5 p.m.—is attached to Stacey's Brewer Motel, just across the river from downtown Bangor. No cover charge Monday night.

FESTIVALS AND EVENTS

In April (usually the third Saturday), the **Kenduskeag Stream Canoe Race** is an annual 16.5-mile spring-runoff race sponsored by Bangor Parks and Recreation, tel. (207) 947-1018. It draws upwards of 700 canoes and thousands of spectators and finishes in downtown Bangor. The best location for spotting action is

Six Mile Falls—take Broadway (Rt. 15) about six miles northwest of downtown. Registration for canoeists is $15 in advance, $25 on race day.

June is the month for the **World's Largest Garage Sale.** All-day (9 a.m.-4 p.m.) the third or fourth Saturday of the month, the sale, sponsored by WLBZ-TV and held at the Pickering Square Parking Garage in downtown Bangor, is a benefit for local charities.

Late July into early August, the **Bangor State Fair** is a huge 10-day affair with agricultural and craft exhibits, a carnival, fireworks, sinful food, and big-name live music. This is a big deal and attracts thousands from all over northern Maine. It's held in Bass Park.

SHOPPING

The largest mall north of Portland is the 80-store **Bangor Mall,** Hogan Rd. and Stillwater Ave., just north of I-95 Exit 49, with such household names as J.C. Penney, Porteous, and Sears. The mall is open Mon.-Sat. 9:30 a.m.-9 p.m., Sunday noon-5 p.m. When the mall closes at 9 p.m., lots of shoppers head nearby to the giant **Borders** bookstore, Bangor Mall Blvd., Bangor, tel. (207) 990-3300, which has live entertainment, coffee, and night-owl hours on Friday and Saturday.

New and Used Books
Three independent bookstores in downtown Bangor have carved out their own niches, helping them compete with Borders.

Betts Bookstore, 26 Main St., Bangor 04401, tel. (207) 947-7052, fax 947-6615, a local landmark since 1938, specializes in Stephen King. All of his books are here (and available by mail), including autographed copies and $7,500 limited editions, plus King posters and models of his house. The **Second Story** (upstairs, natch) has a large stock of used books. The first floor is open all year, weekdays 7 a.m.-5 p.m., Saturday 8 a.m.-5 p.m., Sunday and 8 a.m.-4 p.m. Second Story hours are weekdays noon-4 p.m. and weekends 10 a.m.-4 p.m.

Where is human nature so weak as in a bookstore? reads a sign at **BookMarc's Bookstore and Café,** 78 Harlow St., Bangor 04401, tel. (207) 942-3206, northern Maine's largest independent bookstore. Indulge your literary weakness with lots of children's and young adult titles, esoteric journals, and almost everything by Stephen King. After that, sit down in the adjoining café and succumb to gourmet coffee, vegetarian lunches, and pastries. The store, located opposite Bangor City Hall, is open all year, weekdays 9:30 a.m.-5:30 p.m., weekends 10 a.m.-4 p.m. The café is open weekdays 7:30 a.m.-4 p.m. and Saturday 10 a.m.-2 p.m.

Just around the corner from BookMarc's is **Lippincott Books,** 32 Central St., Bangor 04401, tel. (207) 942-4398, a longtime antiquarian-book resource, with about 20,000 preowned books. Specialties are Maine titles and nonfiction volumes on Native Americans and Canada, but you'll find lots of surprises. The eclectic shop is open May-Feb., Mon.-Sat. 10 a.m.-5:30 p.m. (Saturday to 5 p.m.), and occasionally (or by appointment) in March and April.

Also in downtown Bangor is **Pro Libris,** 12 Third St., Bangor 04401, tel. (207) 942-3019, billing itself as a "readers' paradise." With 30,000 used paperbacks and hardcovers, that's just about right.

Gifts and Clothing
Believe it when **The Grasshopper Shop** claims to be the state's largest boutique—it sprawls over three floors in two buildings (dubbed The Grasshopper Shop and The Hop) in downtown Bangor, 1 W. Market Sq., Bangor 04401, tel. (207) 945-3132. Steer kids toward The Hop for T-shirts, music, and toys. Across the street, adults will find unstodgy imported clothing, housewares, jewelry, gifts, and cards. (Another branch is located in downtown Ellsworth, near Bar Harbor.) The shops are open daily, all year, with varying hours depending on the season.

ACCOMMODATIONS

Downtown
The **Phenix Inn,** 20 Broad St., Bangor 04401, tel. (207) 947-0411, fax 947-0255, is a National Historic Register hostelry in downtown Bangor. Built in 1873, the four-story hotel underwent extensive restoration in the 1980s. Walls are thick, furnishings are tasteful replicas, and the lobby feels like an English gentlemen's reading room.

Request a room overlooking Kenduskeag Stream. Thirty-five doubles (private baths, a/c) go for $75 in summer, $57 off season, including continental breakfast. Two suites are $90 d in season, $70 other months. Children under 12 stay free. Open all year.

Many of the guests at the **Riverside Inn,** 495 State St., Bangor 04401, tel. (207) 947-3800 or (800) 252-4044, fax (207) 947-3591, have business at Eastern Maine Medical Center, next door, but the inn is open to everyone (as is the hospital's 24-hour cafeteria). Inn rooms—54 total, including 15 suites—are several notches above generic motel decor. Request one overlooking the Penobscot River; avoid rooms overlooking the hospital parking lot. Prices are moderate ($60-100 d in summer, less off season) and special discounts are available; no charge for an under-18 child who doesn't need a cot. Phones, a/c, and cable TV. No pets. Access to Bangor Athletic Club facilities is included with the room, as is a continental breakfast. Open all year.

Bangor Airport/Bangor Mall
Your choice of airport-area motel may depend on your frequent-flyer memberships. There are lots of options. Linked to the terminal by a skyway, the **Bangor Airport Marriott,** 308 Godfrey Blvd., Bangor 04401, tel. (207) 947-6721 or (800) 228-9290, at ground zero, has 103 rooms, an average restaurant, and an outdoor pool. Next closest (two miles) to the airport are Marriott's **Fairfield Inn,** 300 Odlin Rd., Bangor 04401, tel. (207) 990-0001 or (800) 228-2800, with reasonable family rates; **Ramada Inn,** 357 Odlin Rd., Bangor 04401, tel. (207) 947-6961 or (800) 228-2828, with an indoor pool; and the 200-room **Holiday Inn,** 404 Odlin Rd., Bangor 04401, tel. (207) 947-0101 or (800) 914-0101, with a terrific fitness center. The **Comfort Inn,** 750 Hogan Rd., Bangor 04401, tel. (207) 942-7899 or (800) 289-6469, and the **Hampton Inn,** 10 Bangor Mall Blvd., Bangor 04401, tel. (207) 990-4400 or (800) 426-7866, near the Bangor Mall and about five miles from the airport, have free shuttle services. **Motel 6,** tel. (207) 947-6921, and **Super 8 Motel,** tel. (207) 945-5681 or (800) 800-8000, are also on this side of the city.

South and Southeast of Bangor
About midway between Bangor and coastal Rt.

1 is the Penobscot River community of Winterport. In the center of the town's historic district, the 1834 **Colonial Winterport Inn,** Main St., Rt. 1A, P.O. Box 525, Winterport 04496, tel. (207) 223-5307, fax 223-5864, is only one of dozens of stunning architectural specimens here. Duncan and Judie Macnab produce outstanding prix-fixe dinners ($14-18), Tues.-Sat. 6-8 p.m. by reservation only, and an extremely popular Sunday breakfast buffet. Lunch is served 11:30 a.m.-2 p.m., May to mid-October. (Canadian-born Duncan has Cordon Bleu degrees.) A one-night MAP package is available year-round. Five rooms (private baths) are $60-65 d in summer, less off season. Two mini-suites are also available. Request a back or side room; Rt. 1A is a busy highway. Children are welcome.

Route 1A runs between Winterport and Bangor, then turns southeast and goes back down to the coast. Twelve miles southeast of Bangor (and 25 miles northwest of Ellsworth) is **The Lucerne Inn,** Bar Harbor Rd., Rt. 1A, RR 3, Box 540, Lucerne-in-Maine 04429, tel. (207) 843-5123 or (800) 325-5123, fax (207) 843-6138, a retrofitted early-19th-century stage-coach hostelry on a 10-acre hilltop overlooking Phillips Lake and the hills beyond. The fall panorama is spectacular. Thanks to a 1920s tourism scheme, the area is known, with a bit of stretching, as Little Switzerland—hence the Lucerne designation. Despite the highway out front, noise is no problem in the antiques-filled, rear-facing rooms. Twenty-one rooms and four suites ($99-129 d July-mid-Oct., $59-109 other months) have a/c, phones, cable TV, and working fireplaces. Outside there's a pool. The Sunday brunch buffet in the inn's dining room (where moderately priced dinners are served nightly, 5-9 p.m.) is a big draw, as is the adjacent golf course.

Campgrounds
On Bangor's western perimeter are two clean, well-managed campgrounds convenient to I-95 and Bangor. Closest to the city is the 52-site **Paul Bunyan Campground,** 1862 Union St., Rt. 222, Bangor 04401, tel. (207) 941-1177, about three miles northwest of I-95 Exit 47. Facilities at this attractive Good Sampark include a rec hall and huge outdoor pool; activities are offered most weekends. Leashed pets are wel-

come and noise rules are strictly enforced. Sites (for two adults, two children) are $12.50 with no hookup, $23.75 with full hookup. For early birds and late-season campers, Paul Bunyan is open all year, but full hookups are only available May through October.

About two miles farther out on Rt. 222, **Pleasant Hill Campground,** Union St., Rt. 222, RFD 3, Box 180A, Bangor 04401, tel. (207) 848-5127, also a Good Sampark, has 105 sites on 60 acres. Facilities include mini-golf, laundry, play areas, rec room, and a small store. Pets are welcome. Rates are $13-20, and the campground is open May to mid-October.

FOOD

Breakfast Bites
A downtown landmark since 1978, **The Bagel Shop,** 1 Main St., Bangor 04401, tel. (207) 947-1654, is a convenient central spot facing West Market Square to meet, greet, and grab some really good bagels and other Jewish-deli specialties. It's closed Saturday but open Mon.-Thurs. 6 a.m.-6 p.m., Friday 6 a.m.-5:30 p.m., and Sunday 6 a.m.-2 p.m. No credit cards.

Downtown
Serendipity and creativity are the bywords at **The Lemon Tree,** 167 Center St., Bangor 04401, tel. (207) 945-3666, a casual, 13-table restaurant-cum-art gallery near St. Joseph Hospital. Owner Scott Feeney weaves Southwest flavors into his eclectic menu, which includes seafood and vegetarian selections. Pecan-breaded chicken is a specialty. A private baker supplies designer breads and outstanding desserts. No smoking. Lemon Tree packs 'em in; call for reservations. Open all year, Mon.-Sat. 10:30 a.m.-3 p.m., Tues.-Thurs. 5-9:30 p.m., Fri.-Sat. 5-11 p.m., and Sunday 9 a.m.-2 p.m. and 5-9 p.m.

Reservations are also essential at **Thistle's,** 175 Exchange St., Bangor 04401, tel. (207) 945-5480, a winner since it moved to downtown Bangor (Maliseet Gardens Plaza) from Dover-Foxcroft in the early 1990s. Creative, moderately priced continental entrées, plus excellent homemade breads and desserts, have drawn the crowds, especially at lunchtime. No smoking.

Open all year, Mon.-Sat. 11 a.m.-2:30 p.m. and 4:30-8 p.m. (to 9 p.m. Friday and Saturday).

As the name suggests, plants and windows are everywhere at **The Greenhouse,** 193 Broad St., Bangor 04401, tel. (207) 945-4040, a popular local watering hole next to the Joshua Chamberlain Bridge. At night, you'll have a front-row seat for city lights; in summer, dine on the deck overlooking the river. The ambience is upscale casual. Carnivores should try the Greenhouse lamb. A children's menu is available, but this is no place for restless kids. Open all year, Tues.-Fri. 11:30 a.m.-10 p.m. and Saturday 5-10 p.m.

A prime spot for view-and-brew is the riverfront **Sea Dog Brewing Co.,** 26 Front St., Bangor 04401, tel. (207) 947-8004, where you can dine on the deck in summer. The menu can be uneven, but the award-winning lagers and ales are superb. Attractively decorated with tongue-and-groove pine on the inside, the brewpub serves lunch and dinner daily 11:30 a.m.-1 a.m. Live music Thurs.-Sat. ($1 cover charge after dinner). Each Saturday, at 2:30 p.m., there's a free, one-hour **brewery tour,** including samples. Reservations aren't needed, but call the brewery, (207) 947-8009, for information.

The major claim to fame at **Miller's,** 427 Main St., Bangor 04401, tel. (207) 942-6361, is a 200-item salad bar—all you can eat for $6.95 at lunch, $10.95 at dinner. (It's not included with all entrées.) This veteran restaurant is open all year, daily 11 a.m.-10 p.m.

Maine's relative scarcity of ethnic restaurants makes cheerful, family-owned **Bahaar Pakistani Restaurant,** 23 Hammond St., Bangor 04401, tel. (207) 945-5975, especially welcome. Vegetarians find lots of options among the 70-plus reasonably priced appetizers, biryanis, and curries, which you can order hot, hotter, and hottest. No smoking; takeout available; full liquor license. Reservations are advisable Friday and Saturday. Open Mon.-Sat. 11 a.m.-10 p.m., Sunday 5-10 p.m.

Three blocks from Bahaar, another downtown ethnic option is **Taste of India,** 68 Main St., Bangor 04401, tel. (207) 945-6865, an enduring South Asian favorite. It's open Mon.-Sat. 11 a.m.-10 p.m. and Sunday 5-10 p.m., May-December. No smoking, no reservations; beer and wine only.

Bangor Airport/Bangor Mall
Best known for its seafood, **Captain Nick's,** 1165 Union St., Rt. 222, Bangor 04401, tel. (207) 942-6444, across from the airport, also serves up steak, chicken, and pasta. There's live entertainment at 7 p.m. Saturday in the lounge. Reservations are a good idea on summer weekends. Open all year, Mon.-Thurs. 11 a.m.-9:45 p.m., Fri.-Sat. 11 a.m.-10:45 p.m., and Sunday 11 a.m.-9 p.m. (to 10 p.m. in summer).

Granddaddy of Bangor-area restaurants is the **Pilots Grill Restaurant,** 1528 Hammond St., Rt. 2, Bangor 04401, tel. (207) 942-6325 or (800) 963-6325 in Maine, a landmark since 1940. We're not talking fancy—just predictably good food, generous portions, efficient service, and dinner entrées in the $9-15 range (except for lobster). Located two miles west of I-95, Pilots is open all year, Mon.-Sat. 11:30 a.m.-9:30 p.m. and Sunday 11:30 a.m.-8 p.m. Reservations are advisable on summer weekends. If you'd rather just tackle a good pizza, **Feta's Bar and Brick Oven Pizza** is in the same building. It's open Mon.-Sat. 11:30 a.m.-2 p.m. and 4-9:30 p.m., and Sunday noon-8 p.m.

Amazingly, the Bangor area supports more than half a dozen Chinese restaurants, of which the best known is **Oriental Jade,** 55 Stillwater Ave., Bangor 04401, tel. (207) 947-6969, next to the multiplex cinema in the Bangor Mall area. Established in the late 1970s, Oriental Jade has developed a loyal year-round clientele. Ever amenable, the restaurant even accepts ATM cards. No reservations are needed, and it's open 10:30 a.m.-10:30 p.m. In 1996, the owners opened a branch on Wilson Street (Rt. 1A) across the river in Brewer.

Brewer
A relative newcomer at Brewer's Twin City Plaza, **Brown Bag of Brewer,** 272 State St., Brewer, tel. (207) 989-9980, was an immediate hit. Chalk it up to the owners' phenomenal success at their Brown Bag Cafe in Rockland. Some patrons never make it past the homemade muffins and cookies. Eat in or order a creative meal to go. No credit cards, no smoking. Open all year, Mon.-Sat. 6:30 a.m.-6 p.m., Sunday 7 a.m.-2 p.m.

Local Color
Convenient to I-95 Exit 44, **Dysart's,** Coldbrook Rd., Hermon 04401, tel. (207) 942-4878, is a truckers' destination resort—you can grab some grub, shower, shop, phone home, play video games, fuel up, and even sneak a bit of shuteye. For real flavor, opt for the truckers' dining room, where the air is smoky, the music is country, and dozens of bleary-eyed drivers have reached the end of their transcontinental treks. If you're here with a carload, order an 18-Wheeler—18 scoops of ice cream with a collection of toppings. No question, Dysart's is unique, and it's open 24 hours, every day, all year.

INFORMATION AND SERVICES

The **Greater Bangor Chamber of Commerce,** 519 Main St., P.O. Box 1443, Bangor 04401, tel. (207) 947-0307, fax 990-1427, is an especially active outfit. Located next to the Paul Bunyan statue, the office is open weekdays 8 a.m.-5 p.m., all year. The information center, in the same building, is open Mon.-Sat. 8 a.m.-7 p.m. and Sunday noon-5 p.m., June-September.

Two **Maine Information Centers** are located just south of Bangor on I-95, one on each side of the highway. The modern gray-clapboard buildings have racks of statewide information, agreeable staffers, clean restrooms, vending machines, and covered picnic tables. Northbound, the center is at mile 169, tel. (207) 862-6628; southbound, it's at mile 172, tel. (207) 862-6638. They're open 9 a.m.-5 p.m. all year, with later hours in summer.

Claiming one of the state's best reference sections, with a staff of librarians fielding about 30,000 questions a year, the **Bangor Public Library,** 145 Harlow St., Bangor 04401, tel. (207) 947-8336, also provides interlibrary loans throughout the state. A large, metered parking lot is just across the street. The handsome 1912 structure, built after the 1911 fire and renovated at a cost of $8.5 million in the mid-1990s, is open Mon.-Sat. all year.

Newspapers
The *Bangor Daily News,* tel. (207) 990-8000 or (800) 432-7964, carries the densest coverage of Bangor and northern Maine, plus national and in-

MAINE OFFICE OF TOURISM

Horses pull a wagon tour across the covered bridge at Leonard's Mills, Bradley.

ternational news. The Thursday edition has extensive calendar listings.

Emergencies

Maine's second-largest medical center is **Eastern Maine Medical Center,** 489 State St., P.O. Box 404, Bangor 04402, tel. (207) 973-7000. Round-the-clock emergency-room service, tel. (207) 973-8000, a walk-in clinic, tel. (207) 973-8030, and a state-of-the-art children's wing are among the first-rate features here. **St. Joseph Hospital,** 360 Broadway, Bangor, tel. (207) 262-1000, a Catholic facility, also has a 24-hour emergency department.

For **police, fire, and ambulance** in Bangor, Orono, and Old Town, dial 911.

Photo Services

Bangor Photo, 315 Harlow St., Bangor 04401, tel. (207) 942-6728, in business since 1976, has a wide range of services, including passport photos, one-hour print and E-6 slide processing, and new and used gear. The shop, a little tricky to find, is open all year, Mon.-Fri. 8:30 a.m.-6 p.m. and Saturday 9 a.m.-4 p.m.

Getting There and Getting Around

If you're headed for Maine's North Woods, Bar Harbor and Acadia National Park, or the Down East counties of Washington and Hancock, Bangor is the handiest large airport. Incredibly, nearly half a million passengers annually move through **Bangor International Airport** (BIA),

tel. (207) 947-0384, a user-friendly state-of-the-art facility on the outskirts of the city. Major scheduled airlines with frequent service are **Delta, Continental Express, US Airways, Business Express,** and New England-oriented **Downeast Air.** International charter planes regularly refuel here and discharge their passengers to clear customs before heading on to points south and west. Bad weather in Portland or Boston often creates unexpected arrivals at Bangor's less-foggy airfield.

Concord Trailways, 1039 Union St., Rt. 222, Bangor 04401, tel. (207) 945-4000 or (800) 639-3317, operates three **express buses** daily to and from Boston's Logan Airport and downtown Boston, with a stop in Portland. Concord's coastal route operates twice daily between Brunswick and Bangor, making nine stops and connecting with buses to Portland and Boston. The Concord Trailways stop is near I-95 Exit 47.

Vermont Transit Co., 158 Main St., Bangor 04401, tel. (207) 945-3000 or (800) 894-3355, stopping in downtown Bangor, operates daily service and connects with **Greyhound bus** routes.

Avis, Budget, Hertz, and **National** car rental companies all have desks at Bangor International Airport. **Thrifty** car rental is about two miles away.

In downtown Bangor, the inexpensive **Pickering Square Parking Garage,** tel. (207) 941-1654, alongside Kenduskeag Stream, is especially convenient for downtown shopping and dining. Many of the merchants will stamp your parking ticket to void the fee. Parking is free on Saturday; the garage is closed Sunday.

Round-the-clock **taxi service** is provided by Airport/River City Taxi, tel. (207) 947-8294 or (800) 997-8294, and AAA Yellow Cab, tel. (207) 945-6441.

ORONO AND VICINITY

Home of the University of Maine's flagship campus, Orono is part college town, part generic Maine village—and a fine example of the tail wagging the dog. Nearly 15,000 university students converge on this Bangor suburb every year, fairly overwhelming the 9,200 year-round residents.

Called Stillwater when it was settled by Europeans in the 1770s, the town adopted the name of Penobscot Indian chief Joseph Orono and incorporated in 1806. By 1840—as with Bangor, eight miles to the southwest—prosperity descended, thanks to the huge Penobscot River log drives spurring the lumber industry's heyday. A stroll along Orono's Main Street Historic District, especially between Maplewood Avenue and Pine Street, attests to the timber magnates' success; the gorgeous homes are a veritable catalog of au courant architectural styles: Italianate, Greek Revival, Queen Anne, Federal, and Colonial Revival. Contact Orono's municipal office for a free copy of *A Walking Tour of Orono,* a dated but still useful booklet on the town's cultural and architectural history.

Old Town (pop. 8,200) gained its own identity in 1840, after separating from Orono. ("Old Town" is the English translation of the settlement's Abnaki name.) In those days, sawmills lined the shores of the town's Marsh Island, between the Stillwater and Penobscot Rivers—the end-of-the-line for the log drives and the backbone of Old Town's economy. That all crumbled in 1856, though, when a devastating fire swept through the area. Occurring as residents exited from memorial services for Abraham Lincoln, it was called the "Lincoln Fire." Several decades later, Old Town finally regained its economic footing, thanks to factories making shoes, canoes, and paper products.

Under separate tribal administration and linked to Old Town by a bridge built in 1951, Indian Island Reservation is home to about 500 Penobscot Indians. Since the 1980 resolution of an enormous land-claims case, providing Maine's Indians with reparations, many of the island village's residents have managed to broaden their horizons and improve their living conditions. A new school and a health clinic have been built, most houses have been rehabbed, and dozens of island residents are pursuing college degrees. But controversy surfaces periodically over Indian Island's state-sanctioned high-stakes bingo operation, bringing in gamblers by the busload, and social-welfare problems still need resolution. It's been no easy road, and more bumps lie ahead.

SIGHTS

Orono's major sights are on the 600-acre **University of Maine** (UMO) campus, a venerable institution founded in 1868 as the State College of Agriculture and Mechanical Arts. It received its current designation in 1897 and now awards bachelor's, master's, and doctoral degrees. Oldest building on campus is North Hall, an updated version of the original Frost family farmhouse.

One of the newest buildings, built in 1986, is the architecturally dramatic **Maine Center for the Arts,** scene of year-round activity. Cleverly occupying part of the center is the small **Hudson Museum,** 5746 Maine Center for the Arts, Belgrade and Beddington Rds., University of Maine, Orono 04469, tel. (207) 581-1901, spotlighting traditional and contemporary world cultures in a series of well-designed galleries on three floors. Frequent special exhibits augment an eclectic ethnographic collection that includes Peruvian silver stickpins, African fetish dolls, Navajo looms, and the superlative Palmer Gallery of Pre-Hispanic Mexican and Central American Culture. An interactive corner lets visitors learn a few words in the Penobscot (Native American) language, and a small shop, tel. (207) 581-1903, stocks unusual global gifts. Admission is free. The museum is open Tues.-Fri. 9 a.m.-4 p.m. and Saturday and Sunday 11 a.m.-4 p.m. It's also open about an hour prior to performances in the adjoining Hutchins Concert Hall.

The solar system takes center stage at the **Maynard F. Jordan Planetarium,** 5781 Wingate Hall, Munson Rd., University of Maine, Orono 04469, tel. (207) 581-1341, fax 581-1314, hotline tel. (207) 581-1348, on the second floor of Wingate Hall. Multimedia presentations and laser-light shows, usually lasting an hour under a 20-foot dome, help explain the workings of our universe and bring astronomy to life. Comet collisions and rocketing asteroids keep the kids transfixed. Program scheduling tends to be unpredictable, especially in summer, so you'll need to call ahead to confirm the schedule and reserve space in the 45-seat auditorium. Most programs are on weekends; no programs in May, June, or during university holidays. Admission to scheduled events is $4 adults, $3 seniors and students.

At the eastern edge of the campus, the six-acre **Lyle E. Littlefield Ornamental Trial Garden,** Rangeley Rd., University of Maine, Orono 04469, tel. (207) 581-2918, contains more than 1,200 plant species, many being tested for winter durability. Best time to come is early June, when crabapples and lilacs put on their perennial show. The garden is open daily; bring a picnic.

Other UMO sites for horticulture fans are the 10-acre riverside **Fay Hyland Arboretum,** on the western edge of campus, tel. (207) 581-2976, and the **Roger Clapp Greenhouses,** in the center of campus, open weekdays, tel. (207) 581-3112.

Campus **parking** is a major sticking point at UMO, so you'll need to have a parking decal for most areas except the Maine Center for the Arts and the sports complex. Free permits and maps are available at the UMO visitors' center, Chadbourne Hall, Munson Rd., tel. (207) 581-3740.

Old Town Museum

Located in the former St. Mary's Catholic Church, the Old Town Museum, 138 S. Main St., P.O. Box 375, Old Town 04468, tel. (207) 827-7256, has well-organized exhibit areas focusing primarily on Old Town's pivotal role in the 19th-century lumbering industry. Other displays feature woodcarvings by sculptor Bernard Langlais, an Old Town native, and an excellent collection of Native American sweetgrass baskets. Each year, temporary exhibits add to the mix. Try to attend one of the regular Sunday afternoon (2 p.m.) programs—anything from carving, weaving, beadwork, and quilting demonstrations to handbell concerts and historical lectures. Admission is free. The museum is open Wed.-Sun. 1-5 p.m., June-Sept., except for the week of July Fourth.

Penobscot Nation Museum

Indian Island's Penobscot Nation Museum, 5 Center St., Indian Island 04468, tel. (207) 827-4153 or 827-7776, a fledgling facility, has exhibits of baskets, beadwork, tribal dress, antique tools, and birchbark canoes. The museum theoretically is open weekdays 10 a.m.-4 p.m., but the schedule seems hopelessly unpredictable, so call ahead to check on opening hours.

In the island's Protestant cemetery is the grave of **Louis Sockalexis,** the best Native American baseball player at the turn of the 20th century. Allegedly, his acceptance onto Cleveland's baseball team spurred management to dub them the Indians—a name that evidently has stuck.

Leonard's Mills

Officially known as the **Maine Forest and Logging Museum,** 265-acre Leonard's Mills re-creates a late-18th-century logging village, with a sawmill, blacksmith shop, covered bridge, a log cabin, and other buildings. The site is accessible May-Nov., sunrise to sunset, but the best times to visit are during the museum's special-events days—each Saturday 10 a.m.-3 p.m., July-Sept. —when dozens of museum volunteers don period dress and bring the village to life. Demonstrations, beanhole bean dinners, hayrides, antique games, and even 1790s political debates are all part of the mix. The season's grand finale is **Living History Days,** a two-day festival the first weekend in October. Admission to special programs is $5 adults, $3 children 12 and under; other times, admission is $2, payable on the honor system. For more info, contact Maine Forest and Logging Museum, P.O. Box 456, Orono 04473, tel. (207) 581-2871 or 866-0811, fax 827-3641. The museum is on Penobscot

Experimental Forest Rd., in Bradley, 1.3 miles southeast of Rt. 178. It's directly across the river from Orono, but the only bridges are north (Old Town/Milford) and south (Bangor/Brewer).

PARKS AND PRESERVES

Sunkhaze Meadows National Wildlife Reserve

The best time to visit Sunkhaze Meadows National Wildlife Refuge, Milford, mailing address 1033 S. Main St., Rt. 2, Old Town 04468, tel. (207) 827-6138, is during the fall waterfowl migration, but hunting is allowed then, so wear a blaze-orange hat and/or vest. More than 200 bird species have been spotted here; moose and beaver are common. Best way to see them is to paddle the five-mile stretch of Sunkhaze Stream that bisects the refuge. Allow a day for this expedition, putting in on Stud Mill Road and taking out on Rt. 2. Don't forget insect repellent. Access is via the unpaved Stud Mill Rd. or County Rd., north of Milford. No staff or facilities are available at the 9,337-acre refuge; visit or call the Old Town office for information and a map. The office is open Mon.-Fri. 7:30 a.m.-4 p.m.

RECREATION

At the University of Maine's **Maine Bound Outdoor Equipment Rental Center,** 5748 Memorial Union, Orono 04469, tel. (207) 581-1794, you can rent camping gear, touring and telemark skis, snowshoes, mountaineering and ice-climbing equipment, canoes, kayaks, and all kinds of accessories. Very reasonable rates are charged by the day, weekend, or week. A ski-touring package, for example, is less than $20 for a weekend. During the academic year, hours are Mon.-Fri. 9 a.m.-9 p.m. and Saturday and Sunday noon-9 p.m. During summer and school vacations, hours are less predictable, so be sure to call ahead—not a bad idea in any case, to be sure the equipment you need is on hand. A 10% reservation fee will hold your stuff.

Canoeing

Besides canoeing at Sunkhaze, paddlers can join the area's annual rite of spring, the 16.5-mile **Kenduskeag Stream Canoe Race,** a chilly challenge held in late April (usually the third Saturday) with a Bangor finish line.

Savvy canoeists will want to check out the wares at the **Old Town Canoe Factory,** 130 N. Main St., Old Town 04468, tel. (207) 827-5513.

Spectator Sports

Operating from an impressive athletic complex, the University of Maine has turned out national champions in several sports, including women's basketball. To check on current schedules and ticket availability during the academic year, call (207) 581-2327.

The **Bangor Blue Ox** independent professional baseball team has been sparking enthusiasm ever since arriving in town in 1996. Represented by antic mascot Babe the Blue Ox, the team plays about three dozen home games at UMO's Mahaney Diamond, off College Ave., mid-June to late August. Game times are 7:30 p.m. weekdays and Saturday, 1:30 p.m. Sunday. Tickets are $4-6 adults, $3 for kids under 12. Call (207) 941-2337 for the schedule.

ENTERTAINMENT

On the UMO campus, the **Maine Center for the Arts** is the year-round site of concerts, dramas, and other events with big name performers. The box office for the 1,629-seat Hutchins Concert Hall is open weekdays 9 a.m.-4 p.m., tel. (207) 581-1744 or (800) 622-8499. Call for schedule information.

Catering to the college audience with $2.50 tickets ($1 on Tuesday) is the six-screen **Spotlight Cinemas,** 8 Stillwater Ave., Orono 04473, tel. (207) 827-7411. First-run films begin about noon daily, all year, with last showings about 9 or 9:30 p.m. In spring and fall, the cinema puts on art and foreign film festivals. Spotlight is in University Mall, behind Burger King.

Anything happening in the Bangor area is also close enough to attend conveniently.

SHOPPING

Carrying a superbly selective line of gifts, wine, and gourmet goodies (including baked goods and Nilsdotter packaged soups, which are created right here), **The Store—Ampersand,** 22 Mill St., Orono 04473, tel. (207) 866-4110, just off Main St., is a very easy place to drop a few bucks. Open all year, Mon.-Sat. 7 a.m.-7 p.m. and Sunday 9 a.m.-4 p.m.

On the UMO campus, on the north side of the Memorial Union, ground floor, the **University Bookstore,** tel. (207) 581-1700, besides handling routine textbook business, is the source of logo-printed gifts and clothing, plus cards and a good general-book selection. Open all year, with reduced hours during the summer.

The **Orono Farmers' Market** has a particularly fine reputation for selection and quality. You'll find everything from organic produce to fresh and dried herbs, seasonal berries, cheeses, baked goods, and unusual condiments. Hours are Tuesday and Saturday 8 a.m. until sold out, late May through September. The market is set up at the university heating-plant parking lot, College Ave., Rt. 2A, at the western edge of the UMO campus.

The world's oldest continuously operating canoe manufacturer, **Old Town Canoe Company,** still has its big old factory on Middle Street, close to the Penobscot River in downtown Old Town. Incorporated in 1904, the company was turning out as many as 400 boats a month two years later. In 1915, the list of dealers included Harrod's in London and the Hudson's Bay Company in far northern Canada, and Old Town had supplied canoes to expeditions in Egypt and the Arctic. Quality is high at Old Town, so their boats are pricey, but you can visit the **Old Town Canoe Factory Outlet,** 130 N. Main St., Old Town 04468, tel. (207) 827-5513, and look over the supply of "factory-blemished" canoe and kayak models. You may end up with a real bargain. The shop is open all year, Mon.-Sat. 9 a.m.-6 p.m., and on Sunday 10 a.m.-3 p.m., in summer.

ACCOMMODATIONS

Six columns frame the entrance to the **High Lawn Bed & Breakfast,** 193 Main St., Orono 04473, tel. (207) 866-2272 or (800) 297-2272, an elegant early-19th-century mansion set back from the street on four acres. An early-20th-

century classics professor, yearning for a Greek facade, added the columns. Convenient to the University of Maine campus, High Lawn has attracted an international clientele since 1984. Three antiques-filled rooms (private baths) are $55-65 d, with overflow rooms available as needed. Guests relax in the fireplaced living room, or in the den, and innkeeper Betty Lee Comstock prepares an impressive breakfast. No smoking, no children under 12. Limited access for pets. Two-night minimum on special university weekends. The B&B is .8 mile from I-95 Exit 50 (Kelly Road). Open all year.

Even closer to the university is the three-story **Best Western Black Bear Inn,** 4 Godfrey Dr., Orono 04473, tel. (207) 866-7120 or (800) 528-1234, fax (207) 866-7433. Opened in 1990, it has 68 motel-style rooms with private baths and cable TV. Depending on season, rates are $54-89 d, including continental breakfast; highest rates are July through October. Concertgoers, sports fans, and university visitors fill up the rooms during the school year, so book well ahead to get in here then. Open all year.

FOOD

Catering to the notoriously slim budgets of college students, eating establishments in Orono all range from inexpensive to moderate. Three of the most popular spots are on Mill Street, just off Rt. 2 (Main Street).

Orono's veteran restaurant is **Pat's Pizza,** 11 Mill St., Orono 04473, tel. (207) 866-2111, a statewide family-owned chain founded in Orono in July 1931 by C.D. "Pat" Farnsworth. Then known as Farnsworth's Café, it became Pat's Pizza in 1953. Pizza toppings are endless, even pineapple, sauerkraut, and capers. Subs, calzones, burgers, and "tomato Italian" entrées are also on the menu. Open all year, Mon.-Sat. 6 a.m.-1 a.m. and Sunday 7 a.m.-1 a.m

Tex-Mex is the rule at **Margarita's,** 15 Mill St., Orono 04473, tel. (207) 866-4863, sibling of three other Maine restaurants turning out some of the state's best—you guessed it—margaritas. This popular student hangout is open all year, daily 4 p.m. to 1 a.m. Busiest time is happy hour, weekdays 4-7 p.m. Dinner reservations are advisable on weekends during the school year.

Across the street from Margarita's is **Jasmine's,** 28 Mill St., Orono 04473, tel. (207) 866-4200, where the signature dish is calamari (squid), served every Wednesday (reservations essential). "Calamari Club" members get frequency discounts. This friendly, informal spot near the university also features creative variations of veal, eggplant, chicken, pizza, and pasta; plenty of vegetarian options. Kids' menu items are under $4. No smoking. Dinner reservations are wise. Open all year, Mon.-Fri. 11 a.m.-2 p.m. and 5-9 p.m., and Saturday 5-9 p.m.

Even though the drinking age is 21, every college town manages to have a variation on the pub theme. At the **Bear Brewpub,** 36 Main St., Orono 04473, tel. (207) 866-2739, try a mug of Crow Valley Blonde, Midnight Stout, or I'll Be Darned Amber Ale. The menu changes daily; try the ribs. No smoking. On request, they'll give you a free, 10-minute brewery tour. The Bear is open all year, daily 11:30 a.m.-11 p.m.

The color doesn't get much more local than at the **Oronoka Restaurant,** Bangor Rd., Orono 04473, tel. (207) 866-2169, although the "locals" tend to be college students, airline pilots, and anyone else looking for the funkiest experience in the area. Word-of-mouth does the trick. Service can be slow, but steaks are humongous in this barn of a place. For a special occa-

sion, call ahead and you'll have a free cake for dessert. The restaurant is open all year, Mon.-Fri. 5 p.m.-midnight and Saturday and Sunday 1 p.m.-midnight. After 9 p.m., it can get pretty smoky.

INFORMATION AND SERVICES

The best source of information on Orono and Old Town is the **Greater Bangor Chamber of Commerce,** 519 Main St., P.O. Box 1443, Bangor 04402, tel. (207) 947-0307, fax 990-1427. Also helpful is the **Orono Town Office,** 59 Main St., P.O. Box 130, Orono 04473, tel. (207) 866-2556, which has free copies of *A Walking Tour of Orono.* The office is open all year, Mon.-Fri. 8:30 a.m.-4:30 p.m.

Information about the University of Maine campus, including guided tours, is available from the **UMO visitors' center,** Chadbourne Hall, Munson Rd., University of Maine, tel. (207) 581-3740, in the same building as the Admissions Office. The center is open Mon.-Fri. 8 a.m.-5 p.m. and Saturday 10 a.m.-3 p.m. Guided campus tours occur Mon.-Sat. at 9:15 and 11:15 a.m. and 1:15 p.m., during the academic year. In summer, there's no 9:15 a.m. tour.

BLUE HILL PENINSULA

When a 1995 magazine article dubbed the Blue Hill Peninsula "The Fertile Crescent," local residents winced—they'd been discovered. Few other Maine locales harbor such a high concentration of artisans, musicians, and on-their-feet retirees juxtaposed with top-flight wooden boat builders, lobstermen, and umpteenth-generation Mainers. Perhaps surprisingly, the mix seems to work.

The peninsula comprises several enclaves with markedly distinctive personalities: Blue Hill, Castine, Deer Isle and Isle au Haut, and Brooklin, Brooksville, and Sedgwick.

BLUE HILL

Twelve miles south of Rt. 1 is the hub of the peninsula, Blue Hill (pop. 2,010), exuding charm from its handsome old homes to its waterfront setting to the shops, restaurants, and galleries that boost its appeal.

Eons back, Native American summer folk gave the name Awanadjo ("small, hazy mountain") to the mini-mountain that looms over the town and draws the eye for miles around. The first permanent settlers arrived after the French and Indian War, in the late 18th century, and established mills and shipyards. More than a hundred ships were built here between Blue Hill's incorporation, in 1789, and 1882—bringing prosperity to the entire peninsula.

Critical to the town's early expansion was its first clergyman, Jonathan Fisher, a remarkable fellow who's been likened to Leonardo da Vinci. In 1803, Fisher founded Blue Hill Academy (predecessor of today's George Stevens Academy), then built his home (now a museum), and eventually left an immense legacy of inventions, paintings, engravings, and poetry.

Throughout the 19th century and into the 20th, Blue Hill's granite industry boomed, reaching its peak in the 1880s. Scratch the Brooklyn Bridge and the New York Stock Exchange and you'll find granite from Blue Hill's quarries. Around 1879, the discovery of gold and silver brought a flurry of interest, but little came of it.

Copper, too, was found here, but quantities of it, too, were limited.

At the height of industrial prosperity, tourism took hold, attracting steamboat-borne summer boarders. Many succumbed to the scenery, bought land, and built waterfront summer homes. Thank these summer folk and their offspring for the fact that music has long been a big deal in Blue Hill. The Kneisel Hall Chamber Music School, established in the late 19th century, continues to rank high among the nation's summer music colonies. New York City's Blue Hill Troupe, devoted to Gilbert and Sullivan operettas, was named for the longtime summer home of the troupe's founders.

Sights

A few of Blue Hill's elegant houses have been converted to museums, inns, restaurants, even some offices and shops, so you can see them from the inside out. To appreciate the private residences, you'll want to walk, bike, or drive around town.

Named for a brilliant Renaissance man who arrived in Blue Hill in 1794, the 1814 **Parfon Fifher Houfe** immerses visitors in period furnishings and Jonathan Fisher lore. And Fisher's feats are breathtaking: a Harvard-educated preacher who also managed to be an accomplished painter, poet, mathematician, linguist, inventor, farmer, architect, and engraver. In his spare time, he fathered nine children. Fisher also pitched in to help build the yellow house on Tenney Hill, Rt. 15/176, Mines Rd., Blue Hill 04614, tel. (207) 374-2459 or 374-2161, which served as the Congregational Church parsonage. Now it contains intriguing items created by Fisher, memorabilia that volunteer tour guides delight in explaining. Don't miss it. Open July-mid-Sept., Mon.-Sat. 2-5 p.m. Admission is $2.

In downtown Blue Hill, a few steps off Main Street, stands the **Holt House,** Water St., Blue Hill 04614, no telephone, home of the Blue Hill Historical Society. Built in 1815, the Federal-style building contains restored stenciling, period decor, and masses of memorabilia contributed by local residents. Open July and August, Tuesday and Friday 1-4 p.m. Requested donation is $1.

At the foot of Greene's Hill in Blue Hill stands one of Maine's more unusual institutions, a library where you can borrow by mail or in person from a collection of 625,000 scores and sheet music. Somehow this seems so appropriate for a community that's a magnet for music lovers. Annual membership is $10 ($5 for students); the library publishes nine catalogs of its holdings ($6-20); fees range from 50 cents for a single work to $5 for a full score—and you can keep it

for up to three months. The **Bagaduce Music Lending Library,** Rt. 172, P.O. Box 829, Blue Hill 04614, tel. (207) 374-5454, is open all year, Tuesday, Wednesday, and Friday 10 a.m.-3 p.m., or by appointment.

Walk or drive up Union St. (Rt. 177), past George Stevens Academy, and wander **The Old Cemetery,** established in 1794. If gnarled trees and ancient headstones intrigue you, there aren't many good-size Maine cemeteries older than this one.

© MOON PUBLICATIONS, INC.

Parks and Recreation

Blue Hill Mountain: Mountain seems a fancy label for a 943-footer, yet Blue Hill stands alone, visible from Camden and even beyond. On a clear day, head for the summit and take in the wraparound view. Climb the fire tower and you'll see even more. In fall, the colors are spectacular—with reddened blueberry barrens added to the variegated foliage. Go early in the day; it's a popular easy-to-moderate hike, 1.5-2 hours roundtrip. The trailhead is on Mountain Rd., just north of town off Rt. 15. Watch for the Firetower sign on the north side of the road, about .4 mile east of Rt. 15. Parking is allowed along Mountain Road, but you can also walk (uphill) the mile from the village. The trail can be squishy, especially in the wooded sections, so you'll want rubberized or waterproof shoes or boots.

If upscale group hiking appeals, **Country Walkers,** P.O. Box 180, Waterbury, VT 05676, tel. (802) 244-1387, fax 244-5661, offers ecosensitive six-day hiking tours that cover Blue Hill, Castine, and Acadia National Park. Lodging and dinners are at inns. Cost is under $1,000 pp, not counting airfare. Age range tends to be 35-70, group size 14-20. Hikers do 4-10 miles a day, toting only a day pack. Conscientious owners Cindy and Bob Maynard contribute 10% of their profits to conservation organizations.

Parks/Playgrounds: At the end of Water Street, just beyond the hospital, **Blue Hill Town Park** has picnic tables, an incredibly creative playground (including little houses), and a terrific view. Pick up picnic fixings and bring it all here. There's also a playground next to the **Blue Hill Consolidated School** (off High Street).

Scenic Routes: Parker Point Road (turn off Rt. 15 at the Blue Hill Library) takes you from Blue Hill to Blue Hill Falls the back way, with vistas en route toward Acadia National Park. For other great views, drive the length of **Newbury Neck,** in nearby Surry, or head west on Rt. 15/176 toward Sedgwick, Brooksville, and beyond.

Golf and Tennis: The golf course at the Blue Hill Country Club is private; nearest public courses are the nine-hole Island Country Club (Deer Isle), the nine-hole Castine Golf Club (Castine), and the nine-hole Bucksport Golf Club (Bucksport). Both Castine Golf Club and Island Country Club also have public tennis courts.

Cycling: Again, most of Maine's side roads are not bike-friendly, so be super-cautious, alert to traffic, and wary of soft shoulders. **Vermont Bicycle Touring,** P.O. Box 711, Bristol, VT 05443, tel. (800) 245-3868, fax (802) 453-4806, in business since the mid-1970s, offers five-day tours of the Blue Hill Peninsula (including Castine and Blue Hill) with dinners and overnights at inns. The route is easy to moderate, covering 20-30 miles a day. About a dozen trips operate early June to mid-October, for under $1,000 pp, not counting bike rental, beverages, or cost of getting here. (The early June trips are about $100 cheaper.)

Winter Sports: There's **cross-country skiing** on the Blue Hill Country Club golf course (Parker Point Rd.), also on the relatively level trails at Holbrook Island Sanctuary and on the carriage roads in Acadia National Park. For winter **sleigh rides,** as well as summer hayrides, contact Paul and Mollie Birdsall at Horsepower Farm, just north of Blue Hill on Rt. 15 in North Penobscot, tel. (207) 374-5038. There's no schedule; it's all "on demand," so don't count on a ride unless you make arrangements in advance.

Getting Afloat

Canoeing/Kayaking: The **Phoenix Centre,** Rt. 175, Blue Hill Falls 04615, tel. (207) 374-2113 or (800) 879-5483, fax (207) 374-5709, is owned and run year-round by the Ensworth family. Founded in 1993, this very active, ecosensitive operation has become the premier resource for local paddling. There are plenty of entry-level canoeing and kayaking options June-Sept.; you can join a beginners' half-day ($50) or all-day ($75) sea-kayak tour (one guide for six kayakers), or sign up for multi-day expeditions. All gear is supplied. Located on a 48-acre site bordering the Salt Pond, the Phoenix Centre also offers private and group kayaking and canoeing instruction, rock climbing, family camping, plus canoeing and backpacking trips.

A favorite spot for kayakers and canoeists is **Blue Hill Falls** (not far from the Phoenix Centre), which churns with whitewater when the tide turns. Check for times of high and low tide. Roadside parking is very limited and the Rt. 175 bridge is narrow, so be cautious here.

Native Trails, Inc., based in Waldoboro, Box

Blue Hill Falls

SHERRY STREETER

240, Waldoboro 04572, tel. (207) 832-5255, is currently working to re-create the ancient **Min-newokun Canoe Trail,** a 25-mile circuit of the southeast corner of the Blue Hill Peninsula—including the Bagaduce River and Eggemog-gin Reach—used by Native Americans to tap the fisheries of the Bagaduce Estuary.

Sailing: Unless you own a boat or know a member of the Kollegewidgwok Yacht Club, in East Blue Hill, tel. (207) 374-5581, there's no sailing out of Blue Hill. If you're trailing a boat, there's a public boat launch down on the harbor. Kollegewidgwok, incidentally, is a Penobscot Indian word meaning "blue hill on shining green water."

Entertainment and Events
Variety and serendipity are the keys here. Check local calendar listings and tune in to radio station **WERU** (89.9 FM), the peninsula's own community radio; there might be announcements of concerts by local resident pianist Paul Sullivan or the Bagaduce Chorale, or maybe a contra dance or a tropical treat from Carl Chase's Atlantic Clarion Steel Band or Flash-in-the-Pans Community Band. WERU's program guide, *Salt Air,* is available free in shops, restaurants, and lodgings. In 1997, after nearly 10 years in a converted henhouse in East Blue Hill, the station moved its headquarters to East Orland.

Kneisel Hall Chamber Music Festival: For nearly a century, chamber-music students have been spending summers perfecting their skills and demonstrating their prowess at the **Kneisel Hall Chamber Music School** on Rt. 15, P.O. Box 648, Blue Hill 04614, tel. (207) 374-2811. Faculty concerts run Friday evening (8:15 p.m.) and Sunday afternoon (4 p.m.), late June to mid-August. Single tickets are $19, but you can take a chance on unreserved veranda seats ($10), available an hour before each concert. The likelihood of getting in depends on the popularity of the program. If you are determined to see a particular program, spring for a reservation. The schedule is published in the spring, and tickets (nonrefundable) can be ordered by phone. A less-expensive option is a $5 unreserved ticket for one of the FanFare events: seven student-artist concerts (three in July and four in August, usually 7:30 p.m.), open rehearsals on Friday (9 a.m.) for faculty concerts, and evening master classes.

Blue Hill Concert Association: Chamber music continues in winter thanks to this active volunteer group. Five or six concerts are performed between January and March at the Congregational Church, a handsome, traditional New England spired edifice on Main Street. For the schedule, contact the Blue Hill Concert Association, P.O. Box 140, Blue Hill 04614.

The Left Bank: A chunk of New York, a slice of Paris, a whiff of London—it's all here in an offbeat, wildly popular establishment alongside Rt. 172. The Left Bank Bakery & Café, Rt. 172, Blue Hill 04614, tel. (207) 374-2201, is open all day, turning out baked goods and doing breakfast and lunch, but evening is when everything comes alive. Go for dinner (served only on performance nights) and stay for the entertainment (most nights in summer, weekends in winter)—top names in folk, jazz, and blues, with an occasional classical night. A few past headliners: Deidre McCalla, Trout Fishing in America, Tom Rush, Gordon Bok, Dave Van Ronk, Arlo Guthrie, Maria Muldaur, Cheryl Wheeler, Jean Redpath. Tickets are $12, discounted $2 if you have dinner. Sellouts are common, so call ahead for a schedule and reserve in advance if you can.

Blue Hill Fair: Held at the Blue Hill Fairgrounds, Rt. 172, Blue Hill, tel. (207) 374-9976, during the extended Labor Day weekend (first weekend in September), the Blue Hill Fair is one of the state's best agricultural fairs. Besides the food booths (good-for-you fare competes with fried dough), a carnival, fireworks, sheepdog trials, and live musical entertainment, you can check out the blue-ribbon winners for finest quilt, beefiest bull, or largest squash.

Shopping
Antiques/Art Galleries: If folk art is your interest, stop in at **Anne Wells Antiques,** Rt. 172, Blue Hill 04614, tel. (207) 374-2093, where painted furniture is a specialty. Open Mon.-Sat. 10:30 a.m.-5 p.m., Sunday by appointment. **Antiques at 8/Barteau Antiques,** 8 Water St., Blue Hill 04614, tel. (207) 374-2199 or 326-4973, fax (207) 326-9772—specializing in Windsor furniture, French country antiques, and antique art and photography—attracts a high-end clientele. Open Tues.-Fri. 10 a.m.-5 p.m., otherwise by appointment. The same patrons seek out Brad Emerson's **Emerson Antiques,** Main St., Blue Hill 04614, tel. (207) 374-5140, concentrating on early Americana, such as hooked rugs and ship models. Open Mon.-Sat. 10 a.m.-5 p.m., May to mid-October; Wed.-Fri. 11 a.m.-4:30 p.m. mid-October through December; by appointment Jan.-April.

The **Liros Gallery,** Main St., Blue Hill 04614, tel. (207) 374-5370 or (800) 287-5370 in Maine, has been dealing in Russian icons since the mid-1960s. Prices are high, but the icons are fascinating. The gallery also carries Currier & Ives prints, antique maps, and 19th-century British and American paintings. Since the Blue

Hill Chamber has no information office, Serge Liros stocks a good supply of local brochures and maps in his downtown shop. Open Mon.-Fri. 9 a.m.-5 p.m., Saturday 10 a.m.-5 p.m., and Sunday noon-5 p.m.

If bronze sculpture appeals, the **Jud Hartmann Gallery,** Main St. at Rt. 15, Blue Hill 04614, tel. (207) 374-9917 or 359-2544, carries Hartmann's figures as well as paintings by Maine and non-Maine artists. The well-lighted gallery is open daily 10 a.m.-5 p.m., late June to early September.

Count on seeing outstanding contemporary art at the **Leighton Gallery,** Parker Point Rd., Blue Hill 04614, tel. (207) 374-5001. Owner Judith Leighton has built a reputation as one of Maine's best art connoisseur/dealers. Don't miss the sculpture garden. Open mid-May to mid-October, Mon.-Sat. 10:30 a.m.-5 p.m., Sunday noon-5 p.m.

Watercolorist **Lee Clark Allen** specializes in still lifes at her garden studio at the Levy House on Main St. in Blue Hill, tel. (207) 374-8894. Open June-Oct., Mon.-Sat. 11 a.m.-5 p.m.

Books: Blue Hill's literate population manages to support two full-service, year-round, independent bookstores. Best selection is at **Blue Hill Books,** 2 Pleasant St., Rt. 15, Blue Hill 04614, tel. (207) 374-5632, thanks to owners Nick Sichterman and Mariah Hughs. Downstairs, the café serves up cappuccino while you browse. Open Mon.-Sat. 9:30 a.m.-5:30 p.m., also Sundays in July and August.

Gifts, Crafts, and More: Blue Hill also has two noted, year-round pottery workshops, both turning out wheel-thrown ware with distinctive lead-free glazes—not surprising, since one evolved from the other. First came **Rowantrees Pottery,** Union St., Rt. 177, Blue Hill 04614, tel. (207) 374-5535, then **Rackliffe Pottery,** Surry Rd., Rt. 172, Blue Hill 04614, tel. (207) 374-2297. Rowantrees is open June-Sept., weekdays 7 a.m.-5 p.m. and Saturday 8:30 a.m.-5 p.m. Winter hours are weekdays 7 a.m.-3:30 p.m. Rackliffe is open Mon.-Sat. 8 a.m.-4 p.m., plus Sunday noon-4 p.m. in July and August.

On Main Street in Blue Hill, **North Country Textiles,** tel. (207) 374-2715, and **Handworks Gallery,** tel. (207) 374-5613, are seasonal (May-Dec.) craft galleries featuring high-quality work by Maine artisans. Handworks is open daily in summer, Wed.-Sat. in spring and fall. North Country is open daily in July and August, Mon.-Sat. other months.

The Himalayas meet Blue Hill at Jeff Kaley's **Options from the World Marketplace,** Pleasant St., Rt. 15, P.O. Box 1234, Blue Hill 04614, tel./fax (207) 374-2284. A Nepal Peace Corps veteran, Kaley seeks out ecosensitive suppliers using fair-trade practices, bringing back custom-made Nepalese, Tibetan, Indian, and Thai clothing, jewelry, and artifacts, as well as organic Himalayan tea. Open late May to early September, Mon.-Sat. 10 a.m.-5 p.m., other months by chance or appointment. Jeff also leads small-group cultural tours and treks in Nepal and Tibet; contact him for details.

Need a winter dog parka or an orange dog vest for walking the woods during hunting season? Or cat and bird gear? Or aquarium doodads? It's all available at **Blue Hill Pets,** 8 Water St., Blue Hill 04614, tel. (207) 374-5724. Open Mon.-Fri. 10 a.m.-5 p.m., Saturday 10 a.m.-3 p.m.

Blue Hill Tea and Tobacco Shop, Main St., Blue Hill 04614, tel. (207) 374-2161, tucked into a converted horse barn, carries teas, coffees, and a huge selection of wines, plus blended tobaccos and unusual pipes for diehard, upscale smokers. Open all year, Mon.-Sat. 10 a.m.-5:30 p.m.

Farmers' Market/Natural Foods: Local gardeners, farmers, and craftspeople peddle their wares at the Blue Hill Farmers' Market, set up at the Blue Hill Fairgrounds (Rt. 172, just north of downtown) every Saturday 9-11:30 a.m., late June through September. For info, call (207) 374-5038.

The **Blue Hill Co-Op,** Greene's Hill, Rt. 172, Blue Hill 04614, tel. (207) 374-2165, sells organic and hydroponic produce and grains, cheeses, organic coffee, and more. Steve Lanzalotta, founder of the Pain de Famille bakery (see "Food" under "Brooklin/Brooksville/Sedgwick," below), creates his terrific breads here; sandwiches and soups are also available. Winter hours are Mon.-Sat. 9 a.m.-6 p.m. and Sunday 10 a.m.-4 p.m.; summer hours are Mon.-Sat. 8 a.m.-8 p.m. and Sunday 10 a.m.-6 p.m. The market is open to the public; co-op members receive a discount.

Among the many farmstands in this area, **Haight Farm,** Rt. 175, HC 64, Box 192, Blue Hill Falls 04615, tel. (207) 374-2840, is best known for exotic hydroponic greens, herbs, fresh lamb (in season), and handwoven woolen items. Courtenay and Woody Haight's farm, two miles south of Blue Hill Falls, is open in summer and fall; call or drop by if you're headed from Blue Hill to Brooklin.

Accommodations
Don't visit Blue Hill for cheap sleeps or eats; visit for the handful of select inns and B&Bs. It's tough to go wrong here. Remember, though, that rooms are scarce in July and August, as well as on summer and fall holiday weekends (Memorial Day, Labor Day, Columbus Day). Reserve ahead or show up during quieter times.

Two miles north of town, at the **Blue Hill Farm Country Inn,** Rt. 15, P.O. Box 437, Blue Hill 04614, tel. (207) 374-5126, a huge refurbished barn serves as the gathering spot for guests. If the weather is lousy, you can edge toward the oversize woodstove and start in on cribbage or other games. Antique-sleigh-runner banisters lead to the barn's seven second-floor rooms—all with private baths, skylights, hooked rugs, and quilts ($85 d, lower off season). During the summer, visiting jazz or classical musicians sometimes entertain in the barn, but it all eases off early. A wing of the farmhouse has seven more rooms with shared baths and more quilts ($70 d, lower off season; a cozy single is $60, lower off season). On the inn's 48 acres are well-cleared nature trails, an 18th-century cellar hole, and a duck pond. Limited accommodations for kids under 12. No minimum stay, no TV, no smoking, no pets. Open all year.

On a quiet side street close to town, the **Blue Hill Inn,** Union St., Rt. 177, P.O. Box 403, Blue Hill 04614, tel. (207) 374-2844 or (800) 826-7415, fax (207) 374-2829, has been welcoming guests since 1840. Stay here if you enjoy antiques, attentive service, classic New England inns, and five-course candlelight dinners; don't stay if you're on a tight budget or have small children. Nine rooms and two suites, all with private baths, boast real chandeliers, four-posters, down comforters, fancy linens, working fireplaces, braided and Oriental rugs. The third-floor garret suite is ideal for families with well-behaved children; a first-floor room is wheelchair-accessible. Rear rooms overlook the extensive cutting garden, with chairs and a hammock. The library, dominated by a Persian chandelier, has masses of local information on an old country-store counter. Nonalcoholic refreshments are available all day; complimentary hors d'oeuvres are served 6-7 p.m. in two elegant parlors or the garden. Doubles are $120-170 (MAP, including dinner and full breakfast). A double without dinner is $30 less, but try to indulge at least once. Special packages—wine-tasting, inn/schooner overnights, kayaking or concert weekends—are attractive bargains. Innkeepers Mary and Don Hartley will arrange for Kneisel Hall tickets, kayak rentals, cruises, massages, and more. Two-day minimum on summer weekends; no TV, no smoking, no pets, no children under 10. Open April-Nov., plus Christmas and New Year's holidays.

Just half a mile east of town, off Morgan Bay Road (Rt. 176), rises the white-pillared **John Peters Inn**, Peters Point, P.O. Box 916, Blue Hill 04614, tel. (207) 374-2116, like something out of *Gone With the Wind*. Set on 30 acres bordering Blue Hill Bay, the 1815 brick mansion has eight rooms, all with private baths ($95-160 d). The second-floor Blue Hill Room tops the list, with a four-poster king bed, a private deck overlooking Blue Hill village, a fireplace, and a wet bar. The modern Carriage House has six more rooms, also with private baths ($95-145 d). Rick and Barbara Seeger purchased the National Historic Register property in 1985 and keep it open May through October before heading south in their sailboat. Nine of the elegantly decorated rooms have fireplaces, six have outside decks; four Carriage House rooms have kitchens and telephones. In the parlor are two fireplaces and a grand piano; outside is a 40-foot swimming pool. The breakfast choices include a legendary lobster omelette with artichoke hearts and Hollandaise sauce—served in the inn's solarium. No one leaves hungry—or thinner. No minimum stay, no pets, no smoking, no children under 12, no arrivals after 9 p.m. Guests can use the Seegers's canoe, daysailer, and two rowboats.

For less-expensive B&B lodgings, contact the **Mountain Road House**, Mountain Rd., RR 1, Box 2040, Blue Hill 04614, tel. (207) 374-2794, which has three bay- or mountain-view

rooms ($55-85 d) with private baths. It's as close as you can get to the Blue Hill Mountain trail-head, and an easy walk from the Blue Hill Fairgrounds. Or try **Ken-Rose Farm B&B**, RR 1, Box 1035, Blue Hill 04614, tel. (207) 374-2468, on busy Rt. 15, six miles north of Blue Hill. An 1850 farmhouse owned by Kendall and Flossie Howard, the B&B has three $50 rooms with shared bath.

Blue Hill's only motel is the **Heritage Motor Inn**, Rt. 172, P.O. Box 453, Blue Hill 04614, tel. (207) 374-5646, a clean, no-frills, 23-room year-round place on Greene's Hill. Rooms have cable TV, coffeemakers, and great views of Blue Hill Bay, but no phones or a/c. Doubles are $79-85 in summer, $49-72 other months.

The nearest **campgrounds** are actually in East Orland, not far away.

Seasonal Rentals: Weekly rentals (or longer) can pay off if you have a large family or are doing a group vacation. The Blue Hill Peninsula has lots of rental cottages, camps, and houses, but the trick is to plan ahead: this is a popular area in summer, and many renters sign up for the following year before they leave town. For information, contact Emily Hawkins at **Peninsula Property Rentals**, Main St., P.O. Box 611, Blue Hill 04614, tel. (207) 374-2428, fax 374-5496. Other realtors handling seasonal rentals are **Mountain View Realty**, Main St., Blue Hill 04614, tel. (207) 374-2000 or 374-2091, fax 374-5714, and **Saltmeadow Properties**, Main St., Blue Hill 04614, tel. (207) 374-5010, fax 374-5124.

Food

Lunch and Miscellanea: Picnic fare is available at **Merrill & Hinckley**, a quirky, 150-year-old, family-owned grocery store, Union St., Blue Hill 04614, tel. (207) 374-2821; open Mon.-Sat. 7 a.m.-9 p.m., Sunday 8 a.m.-9 p.m. M&H carries liquor and wine and has a **photo-developing** service.

The **Left Bank Bakery & Café**, Rt. 172, tel. (207) 374-2201, has a small lunch menu with reasonable prices. It's open daily, all year (except two weeks in February), 7 a.m.-3 p.m. **Jean-Paul's Bistro**, Main St., P.O. Box 612, tel. (207) 374-5852, offers lunch and tea, 11 a.m.-5 p.m., in a Federal-style house with a fantastic harborfront terrace. The menu is creative, service is good, but alas, its season is short: mid-June to Labor Day. In the fall, Jean-Paul LeComte doffs his toque and dons his teacher hat in New York.

Local Color: For Maine home-style cooking, try **Sarah's Restaurant,** Main St., Blue Hill, tel. (207) 374-5181, which serves lunch and dinner (to 9 p.m. in summer, 8 p.m. in winter) year-round, plus weekend breakfasts (7-11 a.m.) May through October. Friday is all-you-can-eat fish-fry night. Smoking is allowed in the back, near the bar.

Moderate to Expensive: Save your pennies and splurge on dinner in Blue Hill. Two restaurants in this category are outstanding—the Firepond and the Blue Hill Inn. If you can't try them both, flip a coin. It's a tough call.

At the moderate end of the scale is **The Captain Isaac Merrill Inn Café,** 1 Union St., Blue Hill 04614, tel. (207) 374-2555, based in a lovely 1830 sea captain's home next door to the Merrill & Hinckley market. Dinner entrées are mostly American (turkey, steak, ham; $12-15), followed by apple pie and bread pudding. House specialty is Portuguese seafood stew. Lunch sandwiches and chowders are superb. Beer and wine license. Open all year for lunch, Mon.-Sat. 11:30 a.m.-2:30 p.m., and dinner, Fri.-Sat. 5:30 p.m.-9 p.m. Dinner reservations are advisable in midsummer. Designer coffees and teas, seltzers, and light fare are available all day.

Dinner is served promptly at 7 p.m. in the windowed dining room at the **Blue Hill Inn,** Union St., Blue Hill 04614, tel. (207) 374-2844, where the five-course meal (over $30) includes outrageous desserts. The menu changes daily and always includes a seafood selection. In summer, music students often serenade guests during preprandial hors d'oeuvres (6-7 p.m.). Special dinner arrangements can be made for Kneisel Hall concertgoers. Open daily by reservation late May-Nov., then weekends and holidays only; closed the first two weeks in December and all of January. Reservations are essential; no smoking.

Firepond, Main St., Blue Hill 04614, tel. (207) 374-9970, serves the priciest fare in town (entrées $16-21), but you won't forget or regret it. In business since the 1970s, the restaurant is now in its finest incarnation. The two-story wooden

building huddled almost unobtrusively next to the millstream in the village center has three distinct dining areas, including a romantic, candlelit screened porch. Try the lobster Firepond, made with a three-cheese cream sauce, or any of the veal or lamb dishes. Open daily for dinner, mid-May through New Year's Eve, and for lunch Memorial Day to Labor Day. Reservations are essential; no smoking.

Information and Services
Unfortunately, there's no local information office, but lodgings maintain racks of brochures covering area activities, as does the Liros Gallery, on Main Street, in the center of town. Don't hesitate to ask shopkeepers for information—they're a helpful bunch. To plan ahead, write to the **Blue Hill Chamber of Commerce,** P.O. Box 520, Blue Hill 04614. The **Blue Hill Public Library,** Main St., tel. (207) 374-5515, is open Mon.-Sat. 10 a.m.-5 p.m. (to 8 p.m. Thursday).

Newspapers: Useful local publications are Blue Hill's *Weekly Packet,* the *Ellsworth American,* and the *Ellsworth Weekly,* all published every Thursday. The *Packet* carries extensive events listings and lots of local ads. The *Bangor Daily News,* published daily, covers some local news but also carries state, national, and international stories.

Emergencies: The deputies of the Hancock County Sheriff's Department in Ellsworth, tel. (207) 667-7575, serve as Blue Hill's **police** force. The Blue Hill **Fire Department** is on Water St., tel. (207) 374-2435. To contact the **Peninsula Ambulance Corps,** call (207) 374-9900. The respected **Blue Hill Memorial Hospital,** Water St., Blue Hill 04614, tel. (207) 374-2836, has 24-hour emergency-room service. A two-page list of crisis hotlines and community-service phone numbers appears in the front of the local phone book.

Veterinarians/Kennels: Maine Coast Veterinary Hospital, South St., Rt. 172, Blue Hill 04614, tel. (207) 374-2385, has two veterinarians, boarding facilities, and emergency service. (The hospital maintains a clinic in Deer Isle.) For other nearby kennels, see the Deer Isle and Bucksport to Ellsworth sections.

Laundromat: The Blue Hill Laundry, Main St., Blue Hill, tel. (207) 374-2777, is open all year, daily 7 a.m.-6 p.m. (to 9 p.m. in summer).

Public Restrooms: There are no public restrooms, and restaurant owners don't appreciate noncustomers asking to use their facilities. Public buildings that have restrooms are the Blue Hill Town Hall (Main St.), Blue Hill Public Library (Main St.), and Blue Hill Memorial Hospital (Water Street).

Getting There and Getting Away
There is no public transportation, nor are there taxis, within Blue Hill; nearest transportation hub is Ellsworth, 14 miles away. **Airport & Harbor Taxi Co.,** Bar Harbor Rd., Trenton, tel. (207) 667-5995, provides service from Blue Hill and other peninsula communities to Bar Harbor and Bangor International Airports. **G&M Taxi,** 203 Main St., Ellsworth, tel. (207) 667-7030, is on 24-hour call and provides service to Bar Harbor and Bangor airports. Major car-rental agencies have offices at Bangor International Airport.

BROOKLIN/BROOKSVILLE/SEDGWICK

Nestled near the bottom of the Blue Hill Peninsula and surrounded by Castine, Blue Hill, and Deer Isle, this often-missed area offers superb hiking, kayaking, and sailing, plus historic homes and unique shops, studios, lodgings, and personalities.

Best-known town is Brooklin (pop. 785), thanks to two magazines: *The New Yorker* and *WoodenBoat.* Wordsmiths extraordinaire E.B. and Katharine White "dropped out" to Brooklin in the 1930s and forever afterward dispatched their splendid material for *The New Yorker* from here. (The Whites' former home, a handsome Colonial not open to the public, is on Rt. 175 in North Brooklin, six and a half miles from the Blue Hill Falls bridge.) In 1977, *WoodenBoat* magazine moved its headquarters to Brooklin, where its 60-acre shoreside estate attracts builders and dreamers from all over the globe. Nearby Brooksville (pop. 770) drew the late Helen and Scott Nearing, whose *Living the Good Life* made them role models for back-to-the-landers. Buck's Harbor, a section of Brooksville, is the setting for *One Morning in Maine,* one of Robert McCloskey's beloved children's books.

Oldest of the three towns is Sedgwick (pop. 903, incorporated in 1789), which once included all of Brooklin and part of Brooksville. Now wedged between Brooklin and Brooksville, it includes the hamlet of Sargentville, the Caterpillar Hill scenic overlook, and a well-preserved complex of historic buildings. The flow of pilgrims continues in this area—many of them artist wannabes bent on capturing the spirit that has proved so enticing to creative types.

Sights
On Naskeag Pt. Road, 1.2 miles from downtown Brooklin (Rt. 175), a small sign marks the turn to the world headquarters of the **WoodenBoat** empire. (Also based here is the bimonthly *Hope* magazine.) Buy magazines and books at the office, stroll the grounds, or sign up for one of the dozens of one- and two-week spring, summer, and fall courses in seamanship, navigation, boatbuilding, sailmaking, marine carving, and more. Special courses are geared to kids, women, pros, and all-thumbs neophytes; the camaraderie is legendary. One-week tuition runs $420-500, plus about $275 for room and board. School visiting hours are Mon.-Sat. 8 a.m.-5 p.m., June to October. For more info, contact WoodenBoat School, Naskeag Pt. Rd., P.O. Box 78, Brooklin 04616, tel. (207) 359-4651, fax 359-8920.

Now used as the museum/headquarters of the Sedgwick-Brooklin Historical Society, the 1795 **Rev. Daniel Merrill House,** Rt. 172, P.O. Box 171, Sedgwick 04676, tel. (207) 359-2547 or 359-8977, was the parsonage for Sedgwick's first permanent minister. Inside the house are period furnishings, old photos, toys, and tools; a few steps away are a restored 1874 schoolhouse, an 1821 cattle pound (for corralling wandering bovines), and a hearse barn. The complex, a mile north of the junction with Rt. 175, is open Sunday 2-4 p.m. in July and August, or by appointment. Admission is free but donations are welcomed. Pick up a brochure during open hours and guide yourself around the buildings and grounds. The **Sedgwick Historic District,** crowning Town House Hill, comprises the Merrill House and its outbuildings plus the imposing 1794 Town House and the 23-acre Rural Cemetery (oldest headstone dates from 1798) across Rt. 172.

Forest Farm, home of the late Helen and Scott Nearing, is now the site of **The Good Life Center,** Cape Rosier, Box 11, Harborside 04642, tel. (207) 326-8211. Advocates of simple living and authors of 10 books on the subject, the Nearings created a trust to perpetuate their farm and philosophy. Resident stewards lead tours daily 1-5 p.m., and copies of Nearing books are available for sale. From early June to late August, "Monday Night Meetings" (7:30 p.m.) at the farm feature gardeners, philosophers, musicians, and other guest speakers. Occasional work parties and conferences are also on the center's schedule. For additional information, contact the Trust for Public Land, 33 Union St., Boston, MA 02108, tel. (617) 367-6200. The farm is on an unpaved road on Orr's Cove in Harborside, not the easiest place to find. Call for directions. If you're hiking in Holbrook Island Sanctuary (see below), relatively close to the farm, ask there for directions.

Parks, Preserves, and Recreation
In the early 1970s, foresighted benefactor Anita Harris donated to the state 1,230 acres in Brooksville that would become the **Holbrook Island Sanctuary,** Box 280, Brooksville 04617, tel. (207) 326-4012. From Rt. 176, between West Brooksville and South Brooksville, head west on Cape Rosier Rd., following brown-and-white signs for the sanctuary. Go first to the headquarters, about two and a half miles in, and pick up a trail map and bird checklist from the box next to the door. Park across the dirt road (next to the outhouse). The easy Backshore Trail (about 30 minutes) starts here, or go back a mile and climb the steepish trail to **Backwoods Mountain,** for the best vistas. Also here are shorefront picnic tables and grills, four old cemeteries, a beaver flowage, and super birding during spring and fall migrations. Leashed pets are allowed; no bikes on the trails; no camping. Officially open May 15-Oct. 15, but the access road and parking areas are plowed for cross-country skiers.

Or you can take a picnic to the **Bagaduce Ferry Landing,** in West Brooksville, off Rt. 176, where there are picnic tables and cross-river vistas toward Castine.

A small, relatively little-known beach is Brooklin's **Pooduck Beach.** From the Brooklin General Store (Rt. 175), take Naskeag Pt. Rd. about half a mile, watching for the Pooduck Rd. sign on the right. Drive to the end. You can also launch a sea kayak into Eggemoggin Reach here.

For both **golf** and **tennis,** the best and closest choice is the Island Country Club, on Deer Isle.

Cycling: Roads here are particularly narrow and winding, with poor shoulders, so be especially attentive; mountain bikes are a wise idea. Bring your own bike if you can; rentals are hard to find here. If you're up to a 40-plus-mile circuit of low-to-moderate difficulty, start in Blue Hill (check with the town office or the hospital about parking) and go counterclockwise, following Rts. 15, 176, and 175 through West and South Brooksville (Buck's Harbor), Brooksville, Sargentville, Sedgwick, Brooklin, and back to Blue Hill. The same circuit makes a good day trip by car from Blue Hill, or a variation from Castine. See below for food and lodging possibilities en route. Carry a water bottle and arm yourself with a picnic lunch.

Kids' Stuff: To unwind the kids, head for the **playgrounds** at the new Brooklin Elementary School (Rt. 175, not far from the center of town) and Sedgwick Elementary School. A great way to raise kids' environmental consciousness is to enroll them in summer activities sponsored by the **MERI Community Resource Center** on Rt. 175 in the center of Brooklin, P.O. Box 300, Brooklin 04616, tel. (207) 359-8078, fax 359-8079. MERI (Marine Environmental Research Institute), a nonprofit organization, offers daylong island boat trips and island walks, plus a variety of naturalist-led morning (ages 6-9) and afternoon (ages 10-14) programs at the center itself. Special family activities occur two days a week. The MERI center's gift shop and marine-oriented library are open Tuesday and Thursday in June and Mon.-Sat. in July and August (10 a.m.-4 p.m.).

Scenic Routes: No one seems to know how **Caterpillar Hill** got its name, but its reputation comes from a panoramic vista of water, hills, and blueberry barrens—with a couple of convenient picnic tables where you can stop for lunch, photos, or a ringside view of sunset and fall foliage. The signposted rest area is on Rt. 175/15, between Brooksville and Sargentville, next to a small gift shop; watch out for the blind curve when you pull off the road. Between Sargentville and Sedgwick, Rt. 175 offers nonstop views of Eggemoggin Reach, with shore access to the Benjamin River just before you reach Sedgwick village. The 40-mile cycling circuit described above includes both Caterpillar Hill (the only really tough section) and the Sedgwick area.

Two other scenic routes, via car or bike, are **Naskeag Point,** in Brooklin, and **Cape Rosier,** westernmost arm of the town of Brooksville. Naskeag Pt. Rd. begins off Rt. 175 in "downtown" Brooklin, heads down the peninsula for 3.7 miles past the entrance to WoodenBoat Publications, past Amen Farm (home of the late author Roy Barrette), to a small shingle beach (limited parking) on Eggemoggin Reach where you'll find picnic tables, a boat launch, a seasonal toilet, and a marker commemorating the 1778 Battle of Naskeag, when British sailors came ashore from the sloop *Gage,* burned several buildings, and were run off by a ragtag band of local settlers. Cape Rosier's roads are poorly marked, perhaps deliberately, so keep your DeLorme atlas handy. The Cape Rosier loop takes in Holbrook Island Sanctuary, Goose Falls, the hamlet of Harborside, and plenty of water and island views.

Getting Afloat
Captain Gil Perkins, tel. (207) 326-4167, operates the sailboat *2nd Fiddle* out of Buck's Harbor, in South Brooksville. Half-day (1-4 p.m.) cruises are $35 pp. Full-day (10 a.m.-4 p.m.)

trips are $65, including a box lunch. For details on overnight charter cruises aboard the classic yacht *Senta,* see the "Castine" section below.

Native Trails, Inc., based in Waldoboro, Box 240, Waldoboro 04572, tel. (207) 832-5255, and headed by Mike Krepner, is working to recreate the ancient Minnewokun Canoe Trail, a 25-mile circuit of the southeast corner of the Blue Hill Peninsula—including the Bagaduce River and Eggemoggin Reach—used by Native Americans to tap the fisheries of the Bagaduce Estuary. The name allegedly means "many-angled route," and that it is. The 15-mile section between Castine and Walker Pond is already a popular (mostly flatwater) paddling route. Contact Native Trails for a map and an update on the project's status.

Entertainment and Events
Nightlife is mostly catch-as-catch-can in this area (it's not why most people are here). Head for Blue Hill or Castine if you feel the urge for live music. Or, if you're a fan of steel-band music, arrange to be in downtown South Brooksville, Buck's Harbor, when Carl Chase's **Flash-in-the-Pans Community Steel Band** takes over the street outside the Buck's Harbor Market every other Monday night (7:30-9 p.m.) mid-June to early September. These musicians aren't professionals, but you'd never know it. Local papers carry the summer schedule for the two-dozen-member band, which performs in

Eggemoggin Reach, Sedgwick

various area locales and deserves its devoted following; or call (207) 667-5973 or 667-5447.

Wooden boats are big attractions hereabouts, so when a huge fleet sails in for the **Eggemoggin Reach Regatta** (usually the first Saturday in August, but the schedule can change), crowds gather. Don't miss the parade of wooden boats. Best locale for watching the regatta itself is on or near the bridge to Deer Isle, or near the Bridge Inn grounds on Little Deer Isle. Contact *WoodenBoat* magazine, P.O. Box 78, Brooklin 04616, tel. (207) 359-4651, for details.

Nearest cinemas are the Grand Auditorium in Ellsworth and the Criterion in Bar Harbor.

Shopping

Antiques: When you need a slate sink, a claw-foot tub, brass fixtures, or a Palladian window, **Architectural Antiquities,** Harborside 04642, tel. (207) 326-4938, on Cape Rosier, is just the ticket—a restorer's delight. Prices are reasonable for what you get, and they'll ship your purchases. Open all year by appointment; ask for directions. Painted country furniture, decoys, and unusual nautical items are specialties at Peg and Olney Grindall's **Old Cove Antiques,** Rt. 15/175, Reach Rd., Sargentville 04673, tel. (207) 359-2031 or 359-8585. The weathered-gray shop, across from the Eggemoggin Country Store, is open daily 10 a.m.-5 p.m., May-Sept., other times by appointment. Low-key **Pineflower Antiques, Handcrafts, and Flowers,** Naskeag Pt. Rd., Box 102, Brooklin 04616, tel. (207) 359-4627, is a good bet for antique lamps and jewelry, vintage clothing and games, dried-flower wreaths, nautical doodads, and local handcrafts. Open mid-May to mid-September, Sun.-Fri. 10 a.m.-5 p.m.

Used Books: Whimsical signs—Unattended Children Will Be Sold as Slaves; Jackets Please, Gentlemen—adorn the walls of **Wayward Books,** Rt. 15, RFD 26B, Sargentville 04673, tel. (207) 359-2397, a user-friendly shop housed in an unassuming gray building just north of the suspension bridge to Little Deer Isle. Owned by Sybil Pike, a Library of Congress retiree, Wayward has 15,000 or so "medium-rare" titles in such creative categories as "civil liberties" and "books on books." Open mid-May-Dec., Mon.-Fri. 10 a.m.-5 p.m., Saturday noon-5 p.m.

Gifts, Crafts, Art Galleries: Transplanted from downtown Stonington to downtown Brooklin, Kate FairChild's **Eastern Bay Gallery,** Rt. 175, Brooklin 04616, tel. (207) 359-8045, continues a fine track record of displaying and marketing high-end contemporary Maine crafts: jewelry, pottery, clocks, textiles, and calligraphy. Sharing a building with the MERI Community Resource Center, the gallery is open Tues.-Sat. 10 a.m.-6 p.m. Memorial Day weekend through Columbus Day.

Long an eyesore in downtown Brooklin, the handsome old Oddfellows Hall has been spiffed up as the home of the cooperative **Baker Gallery,** Rt. 175 and Center Harbor Rd., Brooklin 04616, tel. (207) 359-2714. The wide-open ground floor serves as exhibit space for pottery, paintings, and prints; the gallery is open only in summer.

If you like folk art, check out the Noah's Arks at George, Georgene, and Kathy Allen's **Creeping Thyme Farm,** Rt. 175, North Brooklin 04616, tel. (207) 359-2067. As you drive from Blue Hill toward Brooklin, watch for a sign and an Open banner; turn down the unpaved road to the shop. Open mid-June through September weekdays, some weekends.

On Rt. 175 (Reach Rd.) in Sedgwick, watch for a small sign for **Mermaid Woolens,** Reach Rd., Sedgwick 04676, tel. (207) 359-2747, source of Elizabeth Coakley's wildly colorful handknits—vests, socks, and sweaters. They're pricey but worth every nickel. The shop is open Tues.-Sat. 10 a.m.-5 p.m. in summer, by appointment in winter.

Scott Goldberg and Jeff Oestreich—Potters produce a huge variety of dark-glazed pots, pitchers, and platters in their studio on Rt. 176, RR 1, Box 147A, North Brooksville 04617, tel. (207) 326-9062, one and a half miles west of the Bagaduce River's reversing falls. Open daily 10 a.m.-6 p.m., mid-June to mid-October.

Three varieties of English-style hard cider are specialties at **The Sow's Ear Winery,** Rt. 176 at Herrick Rd., RR 1, Box 24, Brooksville 04617, tel. (207) 326-4649, a minuscule operation in a funky, gray-shingled building. Winemaker Tom Hoey also produces sulfite-free blueberry and rhubarb wines; he'll let you sample it all. Ask to see his cellar, where everything happens. No credit cards. Open early May through December, Tues.-Sat. noon-5 p.m., or by appointment; it's best to call ahead in any case.

Nautical books, T-shirts, gifts, and boat gear line the walls of the tiny shop at **Buck's Harbor Marine,** on the dock, South Brooksville 04617, tel. (207) 326-8839. Operated by boating author Jerry Kirschenbaum and his wife, Lois, the marina is open daily 8:30 a.m.-5:30 p.m. (8 a.m.-7 p.m. in August), Memorial Day to Columbus Day.

In tiny downtown South Penobscot, **North Country Textiles,** junction of Rts. 175 and 177, South Penobscot 04476, tel. (207) 326-4131, is the outlet version of the topnotch Blue Hill shop by the same name. Hard-to-resist and reasonably priced baby blankets, jackets, and placemats are specialties of this veteran enterprise owned by a trio of weavers. Open June-Sept., Mon.-Sat. 10 a.m.-5 p.m. Upstairs via the outside stairway is **Larson Fine Art,** Box 176, Penobscot, tel. (207) 326-8222, David Larson's studio and gallery. Open June-Sept., daily 10 a.m.-5 p.m. Rumor has it that Duncan Hines Blueberry Muffin Mix was invented in this building.

Accommodations

B&Bs: Susie and Mike Canon have created a mini-Shangri-la at the end of a secluded driveway off Herrick Road: **Eggemoggin Reach Bed and Breakfast,** Winneganek Way, RR 1, Box 33A, Brooksville 04617, tel. (207) 359-5073 or (888) 625-8866, fax (207) 359-5074. The options here are two romantic, king-bedded cottages in the woods ($135 d) and six modern efficiency studios with dramatic water views ($150 d). You can hike private nature trails, lounge on the shorefront boulders at sunset, canoe or row in Eggemoggin Reach, or hang out on the covered porch. Magazines, books, and bouquets are everywhere. Smoking outside only; no pets; deepwater guest moorings. Shorefront lobsterbakes can be arranged Wednesday and Saturday evenings. Open mid-May to mid-October.

Buck's Harbor Inn, Rt. 176, P.O. Box 268, South Brooksville 04617, tel. (207) 326-8660, fax 326-0730, a rambling, gambrel-roofed, three-story building dating from 1901, occupies a corner lot at the crossroads just up Steamboat Wharf Road from picturesque Buck's Harbor. Renovated by Peter and Ann Ebeling in 1982,

the informal inn has six rooms sharing two full baths and two half-baths ($65 d, including full breakfast cooked to order); a suite is $75 d. No pets, no smoking. The harbor is one of the coast's most secure anchorages, and the private yacht club is Maine's third oldest, so don't be surprised to see yachting types hanging around the inn. Close by are The Landing restaurant and the Buck's Harbor Market. Open all year.

Cottage Colonies: The two operations in this category feel much like informal family compounds—where you quickly become an adoptee. Don't even think about dropping in, however; successive generations of hosts have catered to successive generations of visitors, and far-in-advance reservations are essential for July and August. Many guests book for the following year before they leave. We're not talking fancy; cottages are old-shoe rustic, of varying sizes and decor. Most of the cottages have cooking facilities, although both colonies offer a MAP in July and August. Both also have hiking trails, playgrounds, rowboats, and East Penobscot Bay on the doorstep.

Jim and Sally Littlefield are the genial fourth-generation hosts at **Oakland House Seaside Inn and Cottages,** Herrick Rd., RR 1, Box 400, Brooksville 04617, tel. (207) 359-8521 or (800) 359-7352, a sprawling complex of 15 wooded and waterfront cottages, as well as Shore Oaks, a 10-bedroom stone mansion a few steps from the half-mile-long shorefront. Lots of history here: Much of this land was part of the original king's grant to Jim's ancestors. Thursday is lobster-picnic night. Weekly rates mid-June to early September: $826-1,386 d, MAP; lower rates for children. Shore Oaks rooms, mid-June to early September, go for $392-497 pp weekly, MAP. Biggest bargains are early May to mid-June and Sept.-Oct., when you can rent a whole cottage, without meals, for $50-115 daily and $250-575 weekly. Smoking permitted in cabins; leashed dogs are allowed, but no cats.

The fourth generation also manages the **Hiram Blake Camp,** Weir Cove Rd., Harborside P.O., Cape Rosier 04642, tel. (207) 326-4951, but with a difference: the second and third generations still pitch in and help with gardening, lobstering, maintenance, and kibitzing. Fourteen cottages line the shore of this 100-acre complex. Don't bother bringing reading matter:

the dining room has ingenious ceiling niches lined with countless books. Open mid-May to mid-October. One-week minimum (beginning Saturday or Sunday) July and August, when cottages go for $400-700 a week; meals for the week are $120 per adult, $70 per child. Off-season rates (no meals, but cottages have cooking facilities) are $250-450 a week; you'll need to bring your own linens or rent them ($15 pp). Best chances for getting a reservation are in June and September. Pets allowed; smoking permitted in cabins.

Seasonal Rentals: For information on one-week or longer cottage rentals, contact **Mountain View Realty,** Main St., Blue Hill 04614, tel. (207) 374-2000, fax 374-5714, **Peninsula Property Rentals,** Main St., Blue Hill, tel. (207) 374-2428, or **Saltmeadow Properties,** Main St., Blue Hill, tel. (207) 374-5010, fax 374-5124.

Food

Breakfast, Lunch, and Miscellanea: Competition is stiff for lunchtime seats at the **Morning Moon Café,** in the center of Brooklin, junction of Rt. 175 and Naskeag Pt. Rd., Brooklin 04616, tel. (207) 359-2373, mostly because *WoodenBoat* staffers consider it an annex to their offices. "The Moon" is a friendly hangout for coffee, pizza, or great sandwiches (specialty is the roast-beef-filled Adam Bomb) and salads—or order it to go. Open all year, Tues.-Sun. 7 a.m.-2 p.m. (Also open for dinner, 5-8 p.m., but days change by the season.)

Across the street from the Morning Moon, the **Brooklin General Store,** junction of Rt. 175 and Naskeag Pt. Rd., tel. (207) 359-2373, vintage 1872, carries groceries, newspapers, take-out sandwiches, and local chatter. It's open Mon.-Sat. 5:30 a.m.-7 p.m. and Sunday 8 a.m.-5 p.m. On Rt. 175 in Sedgwick, the **Sedgwick Store,** tel. (207) 359-6689, has similar inventory, plus such goodies as smoked salmon, in a modern building overlooking the Benjamin River. It's open all year, Mon.-Sat. 6 a.m.-6 p.m.

Sargentville's center has the well-stocked **Eggemoggin Country Store,** Sargentville 04673, tel. (207) 359-2125 or (800) 409-5552, source of everything from meat and muffins to beer, wine, fresh breads, lobster pizza, spit-grilled chicken—and public restrooms. The warehousey place is open all year, Mon.-Sat. 6

a.m.-9 p.m. and Sunday 7 a.m.-9 p.m. (to 8 p.m. off season).

Box lunches and boat lunches are specialties at the **Buck's Harbor Market,** Rt. 176, South Brooksville 04617, tel. (207) 326-8683, fax 326-9577, a low-key, marginally yuppified general store popular with yachties in summer. Breakfast, above-average pizza, quiche, exotic condiments, live lobsters, and round-the-clock fax service. Open all year, Mon.-Sat. 7 a.m.-8 p.m., Sunday 8 a.m.-8 p.m. Tucked behind the market, next to a small sculpture garden, is the **Pain de Famille Bakery,** Rt. 176, South Brooksville 04617, tel. (207) 326-9160, where dozens of different kinds of bread emerge from the brick oven. Spring for a whole loaf or part of one, or fabulous cookies, panettone, biscotti, and seasonal sweets. They also do mail orders; call for a list. In summer, the bakery is open daily 8 a.m.-5 p.m.; the winter schedule is Wednesday and Sunday 9 a.m.-2 p.m., and Thurs.-Sat. 9 a.m.-5 p.m. Bakery founder Steve Lanzalotta now spends most of his time at his other branch, at the Blue Hill Co-op. With the café here at the market and summertime steel-band street concerts outside, this is a busy corner.

In North Brooksville, where Rt. 175/176 crosses the Bagaduce River, stands the **Bagaduce Lunch,** a popular take-out stand open daily 11 a.m.-8 p.m., early May to mid-September. Check the tide calendar and go when the tide is changing; order a lobster roll ($5.95), settle in at a picnic table, and watch the reversing falls. The food is so-so, the setting is tops.

Here's a surprise: On Rt. 175, a mile south of downtown South Penobscot (crossroads of Rts. 175 and 177), you'll come upon **The Real Thing!** (no telephone), a recycled red double-decker bus. The cook can be a bit grumpy, but he has no problem frying up batches of honest-to-goodness fish 'n' chips. Open afternoons, summer only. In South Penobscot village, the **Northern Bay Market,** tel. (207) 326-8606, is another little-of-everything country store that's open daily 7 a.m.-8:30 p.m. Lobsters and pizza are specialties.

Inexpensive to Moderate: If elegant (read "expensive") dining is on your mind, head for Blue Hill, Deer Isle, or Castine. For easy-on-the-budget prices in off-the-beaten-track locales, try one of the following. In the back room of the

Buck's Harbor Market is the cleverly named **Café Out Back,** Rt. 176, South Brooksville 04617, tel. (207) 326-8683, serving superb homemade pot pies, lasagne, pizza, and daily specials. The congenial café—including a bar seating an extra 18—is open all year, Saturday and Sunday 11:30 a.m.-3 p.m. for lunch, and Wed.-Sun. 5-10 p.m. for dinner. No smoking.

The dining room at **Oakland House Seaside Inn & Cottages,** Herrick Rd., Brooksville, tel. (207) 359-8521, is open to the public by reservation in July and August for its daily breakfast buffet, Sunday brunch, Wednesday buffet lunch, Thursday night shoreside lobster picnic, and dinner other nights. In Brooklin, at the tip of Flye Point, **The Lookout** restaurant, Flye Point Rd., off Rt. 175, North Brooklin, tel. (207) 359-2188, has a knockout view of Herrick Bay. Dinner is served daily in summer, occasionally off season. Quality can be inconsistent, but you can't beat the scenery.

The Landing Restaurant, Steamboat Wharf Rd., off Rt. 176, South Brooksville 04617, tel. (207) 326-8483, owned by a Swiss couple, features American regional cuisine with a continental flair in a spectacular harborfront setting. Entrées (moderate to expensive) include Australian lamb, Atlantic salmon, and usually a vegetarian choice. Guest moorings are available for sailors. After an up-and-down track record in recent years, The Landing now is on a roll. Reservations are advisable on midsummer weekends; request a window table. Open Memorial Day weekend to mid-Oct., Tues.-Sun. 5-9:30 p.m.

Information and Services

Finding tourism information about this area can be frustrating. The best general source for brochures and maps is the **Liros Gallery,** Main St., Blue Hill 04614, tel. (207) 374-5370, but once you've landed on Rt. 172 or 175, pop into one of the small roadside convenience stores and start asking questions. The clerks (often they're the owners) know it all cold, and these markets always have a fair share of local color. Of course, they won't object if you also buy something while you're there.

Since most visitors in this area start in Blue Hill, see that section for more advice—as well as for information on coping with any **medical emergencies.**

Libraries: The public libraries in this area are small and welcoming, but hours are limited. The **Friend Memorial Library,** Rt. 175, Brooklin 04616, tel. (207) 359-2276, is open Tues.-Sat. 10 a.m.-4 p.m. (to 9 p.m. Wednesday and 6 p.m. Thursday) in summer; closed Wednesday in winter. The library's lovely Circle of Friends Garden, with benches and brick patio, is dedicated to the memory of longtime Brooklin residents E.B. and Katharine White. Other area libraries are the **Free Public Library,** Rt. 176, Brooksville 04617, tel. (207) 326-4560, open Monday and Wednesday 9 a.m.-5 p.m., Saturday 9 a.m.-2 p.m.; **Sargentville Library,** Sargentville 04673, tel. (207) 359-5066, open Saturday 2-4 p.m. all year, plus Monday and Friday 2-4 p.m. and Wednesday 7-8:30 p.m. in summer; and **Sedgwick Village Library,** Sedgwick 04676, tel. (207) 359-2177, open Saturday 2-4 p.m. all year, plus Wednesday and Saturday 7-9 p.m. in summer.

CASTINE

Castine (pop. 1,170) is a gem of a place—a serene New England village with a tumultuous past. Once beset by geopolitical squabbles, saluting the flags of three different nations—France, Britain, and Holland—its only crises now are local political skirmishes. This is an unusual community, a National Historic Register enclave that many people never find. The town celebrated its bicentennial in 1996. If you're staying in Blue Hill or even Bar Harbor, spend a day here. Or bunk here and use Castine as a base for exploring here and beyond. Either way, you won't regret it.

Originally known as Fort Pentagoet, Castine received its current name courtesy of Jean-Vincent d'Abbadie, Baron de St.-Castin. A young French nobleman manqué who married a Wabanaki princess named Pidiwamiska, d'Abbadie ran the town in the second half of the 17th century, and eventually returned to France.

A century later, in 1779, occupying British troops and their reinforcements scared off potential American seaborne attackers (including Col. Paul Revere), who turned tail up the Penobscot River and ended up scuttling their more than 40-vessel fleet—a humiliation known as the Penobscot Expedition and still regarded as one of America's worst naval defeats.

During the 19th century, peace and prosperity became the bywords for Castine—with lively commerce in fish and salt—but it all collapsed during the California Gold Rush and the Civil War trade embargo, leaving the town fresh out of luck.

Today a major presence is Maine Maritime Academy, yet Castine remains the quietest imaginable college town. Students in search of a party school won't find it here; naval engineering is serious business.

What visitors discover is a year-round community with a busy waterfront, an easy-to-conquer layout, a handful of hostelries and boutiques, wooded trails on the outskirts of town, and an astonishing collection of splendid Georgian and Federalist architecture.

Of the many historical landmarks scattered around town, one of the most intriguing must be the sign on "Wind Mill Hill," at the junction of Rt. 166 and State Street: "On Hatch's Hill there stands a mill. Old Higgins he doth tend it. And every time he grinds a grist, he has to stop and mend it." In smaller print, just below the rhyme, comes the drama: "Here two British soldiers were shot for desertion." Castine has quite a history.

Sights

To appreciate Castine fully, you need to arm yourself with the Castine Merchants Association's visitors' brochure/map (all businesses and lodgings in town have copies) and follow the numbers on bike or on foot. With no stops, walking the route takes less than an hour, but you'll want to read dozens of historical plaques, peek into public buildings, shoot some photos, and perhaps even do some shopping.

Highlights of the tour include the late-18th-century **John Perkins House,** moved to Perkins Street from Court Street in 1969 and restored with period furnishings. It's now open July and August for guided tours Sunday and Wednesday 2-4:45 p.m.; admission is $4.

Next door, **The Wilson Museum,** Perkins St., tel. (207) 326-8545, founded in 1921, contains an intriguingly eclectic two-story collection of prehistoric artifacts, ship models, dioramas, baskets, tools, and minerals assembled over a lifetime by John Howard Wilson, a geologist/anthropologist who first visited Castine in 1891 (and died in 1936). Among the exhibits are Balinese masks, ancient oil lamps, cuneiform tablets, Zulu artifacts, pre-Inca pottery, and assorted local findings. Don't miss this, even though it's a bit musty. (The only comparable Maine institutions are the Nylander Museum, in Caribou, and the L.C. Bates Museum, in Hinckley.) Open late May to late September, Tues.-Sun. 2-5 p.m.; free admission. Next door,

John Perkins House

and open the same hours (free admission), are the **Blacksmith Shop,** where a smith does demonstrations, and the **Hearse House,** containing Castine's 19th-century winter and summer funeral vehicles. The nonprofit **Castine Scientific Society,** P.O. Box 196, Castine 04421, operates the four-building complex. A 1779 **windmill** on Madockawando St., now a private residence, once was a six-gun battery.

At the end of Battle Avenue stands the 19th-century **Dyce's Head Lighthouse,** privately owned and no longer operating. Alongside it is a public path (signposted) leading via a wooden staircase to a tiny patch of rocky shoreline and the beacon that has replaced the lighthouse.

Maine Maritime Academy, the state's only merchant-marine college (and one of only seven in the nation), founded in 1941, offers undergraduate and graduate degrees in such areas as marine engineering, ocean studies, and marina management, preparing 650 or so men and women for careers as ship captains, naval architects, and marine engineers. The academy owns a fleet of 90 vessels, including the historic research schooner *Bowdoin,* flagship of arctic explorer Adm. Donald Macmillan, and the 498-foot training vessel TV *State of Maine,* berthed down the hill at the waterfront. In 1996-97, the *State of Maine,* formerly the U.S. Navy hydrographic survey ship *Tanner,* underwent a $12-million conversion for use at the academy. Midshipmen conduct free 30-minute tours of the vessel on weekdays in summer (about mid-July to late August). The schedule is posted at the dock, or call (207) 326-4311 to check. Tours of the 50-acre campus can be arranged through the Admissions Office, Castine 04420, tel. (207) 326-2206 or (800) 227-8465 outside Maine. Campus highlights include three-story Nutting Memorial Library, in Platz Hall (open daily during the school year, weekdays in summer and during vacations); the Henry A. Scheel Room, a cozy oasis in Leavitt Hall containing memorabilia from late naval architect Henry Scheel and his wife, Jeanne; and the well-stocked bookstore, tel. (207) 326-9333, in Curtis Hall.

Highest point in town is **Fort George State Park,** site of a 1779 British fortiftcation. Nowadays, little remains except grassy earthworks, but there are interpretive displays and picnic tables. Taking advantage of the setting, Cold Comfort Productions (see "Entertainment," below) occasionally performs here in the summer.

Main Street, descending toward the water, is a feast for historic-architecture fans. Artist Fitz Hugh Lane and author Mary McCarthy once lived in elegant houses along the elm-lined street (neither building is open to the public). On Court Street between Main and Green stands turn-of-the-20th-century **Emerson Hall,** site of Castine's municipal offices. Since Castine has no official information booth, you may need to duck in here for answers to questions.

Across Court Street, **Witherle Memorial Library,** a handsome early-19th-century building on the site of the 18th-century town jail, looks out on the Town Common. Also facing the Common are the Adams and Abbott Schools, the former still an elementary school. The **Abbott School,** built in 1859, has been carefully restored for use as a museum/headquarters for the **Castine Historical Society,** P.O. Box 238, Castine 04421. A big draw at the volunteer-run museum, tel. (207) 326-4118 in summer, is the 24-foot-long Bicentennial Quilt, assembled for Castine's 200th anniversary in 1996. The museum is open early July to Labor Day, Tues.-Sat. 10 a.m.-4 p.m. and Sunday 1-4 p.m. From Memorial Day weekend to July, and Labor Day to Columbus Day, there's a reduced schedule. Admission is free, but donations are welcomed. The historical society, founded in 1966, organizes lectures, exhibits, and special events (some free) in various locations around town. For off-season information, call (207) 326-8786.

Across the narrow neck between Wadsworth Cove and Hatch's Cove stretches a rather overgrown canal scooped out by the occupying British during the War of 1812. Effectively severing land access to the town of Castine, the Brits thus raised havoc, collected local revenues for eight months, then departed for Halifax with enough funds to establish Dalhousie College (now Dalhousie University). Wear waterproof boots to walk the canal route; best time to go is at low tide.

Parks, Preserves, and Recreation
Witherle Woods, a 96-acre preserve owned by Maine Coast Heritage Trust and managed by

the Castine Conservation Trust, is a popular walking and cycling area with a maze of numbered trails. Adjacent property is privately owned, so carry a trail map and stick to it. Access is via a shaded path, signposted Hatch Natural Area, from Battle Avenue. Several lodgings keep a supply of maps, or contact the **Castine Conservation Trust** (CCT), Main St., Box 421, Castine 04421, tel. (207) 326-9711. The CCT has been protecting the natural resources of Castine, Penobscot, and Brooksville since the early 1980s. Also ask the CCT for information about the **Henderson Natural Area** and other public-access preserves, some accessible only by boat.

If a waterfront picnic sounds appealing, purchase the fixings at Bah's Bakehouse, the Tarratine Market, or the Castine Co-op (see "Food," below) and settle in on the grassy earthworks along the harborfront at **Fort Madison**, site of an 1808 garrison (then Fort Porter) near the corner of Perkins and Madockawando Streets. The views from here are fabulous, and it's accessible all year.

Golf and Tennis: The **Castine Golf Club**, Battle Ave. and Wadsworth Cove Rd., Castine 04421, tel. (207) 326-8844, dates back to 1897, when the first tee required a drive from a 30-step-high mound. Redesigned in 1921 by Willie Park, Jr., the nine-hole course is open May 15-Oct. 15. Starting times are seldom required, and greens fees are reasonable. The club also has four clay tennis courts. Call to schedule court time.

Swimming: Backshore Beach, a crescent of sand and gravel on Wadsworth Cove Road (turn off Battle Ave. at the Castine Golf Club), is a favorite saltwater swimming spot, with views across the bay to Stockton Springs. Be forewarned, though, that ocean swimming in this part of Maine is not for the timid. Best time to try it is on the incoming tide, after the sun has had time to heat up the mud. At mid- to high tide, it's also the best place to put in a sea kayak. Park alongside the road.

If a pool sounds more attractive, you can swim in the Cary W. Bok indoor pool at Maine Maritime Academy. A daily fee of $4 also includes use of a workout room, an indoor track, and racquetball and squash courts. Call (207) 326-2450 for hours.

Getting Afloat
Eaton's Boatyard, P.O. Box 123, Castine 04421, tel. (207) 326-8579, fax 326-4727, owned by Ken Eaton, tel. (207) 326-4916, is a full-service marina renting moorings and outboards by the day or week. You can also buy live lobsters May-Oct. or order them shipped anywhere year-round.

If comfortable cruising appeals, Jeff and Micki Colquhoun ("ca-HOON"), a marine artist and town official and a retired private-school administrator, respectively, will welcome you aboard *Senta,* their classic 53-foot, Philip Rhodes-designed wooden yacht. For two or more days (at $500 a day, including wine and beer), you and three friends can luxuriate with comfortable bunks, gourmet meals and snacks served in crystal and on linens, and matchless cruising among the islands. Contact the Colquhouns at Box 18, Castine 04421, tel. (207) 326-4135, fax 326-4051.

For **canoeing and kayaking** rentals, advice, and tours, see "Getting Afloat," under "Blue Hill," above.

Entertainment
Best place for live music is **Dennett's Wharf,** Sea St., next to the town dock, tel. (207) 326-9045. Some performances require a ticket, seldom more than $5. Open daily, May-Columbus Day.

Using the slogan "We do theater," **Cold Comfort Productions,** P.O. Box 259, Castine 04421, tel. (207) 326-8830, puts semiprofessionals in front of the footlights during July and August. The 8 p.m. performances (and occasional matinees) are mostly in Maine Maritime Academy's Delano Auditorium, but try to catch an outdoor one, at Fort George.

Festivals and Events
The **Castine Summer Festival** fills Water Street the last Saturday of June with a sidewalk craft show, food booths, live music, and kids' activities.

Demonstrations, slide shows, lectures, and kayak and accessory sales are the highlights of the **Atlantic Coast Sea Kayak Symposium,** at Backshore Beach (Wadsworth Cove) and the Maine Maritime Academy (lodging is available at the academy) the middle weekend of July.

The Maine Maritime Academy's Smith Gym is the site of a **used-book sale** benefiting Witherle Memorial Library the first Saturday of August.

Shopping

Antiques and Galleries: Chris Murray Gallery of Wildlife Art, Main St., P.O. Box 630, Castine 04421, tel. (207) 326-9033, filled with Murray's award-winning basswood carvings, is downright astonishing. The specimens are understandably pricey—songbirds run $400-500, decorative decoys are $1,000-1,500—but you'll be able to afford one of his handmade feather pins. Open May-Oct., daily 10 a.m.-5 p.m.

Tucked into the back of the 1796 Parson Mason House, one of Castine's oldest residences, **Leila Day Antiques,** Main St., Box 200, tel. (207) 326-8786, is a must for anyone in the market for folk art, period furniture, quilts, and unusual contemporary Shard pottery (from Dover-Foxcroft). The shop, established in 1978, is open daily 10 a.m.-5 p.m., Memorial Day weekend to Labor Day, by chance or appointment the rest of the year.

McGrath Dunham Gallery, Main St., tel. (207) 326-9175 or 326-9416, a well-lighted, two-story space, shows work by painter Greg Dunham and more than two dozen other artists. Open May-Oct., Mon.-Sat. 10 a.m.-5 p.m.

Books: Driving toward Castine on Rt. 166, watch on your right for a small sign for **Dolphin Books and Prints,** P.O. Box 225, Castine 04421, tel. (207) 326-0888 or 326-4467, where Pete and Liz Ballou have set up their antiquarian business after a dozen years in Camden and decades in the publishing world. Specialties are botanical prints, first editions, biographies, and maritime books. Open all year, Mon.-Sat. 10 a.m.-5 p.m., but call ahead to be sure. Another out-of-downtown purveyor of used books is **Barbara Falk—Bookseller,** who carries a good inventory of poetry, women writers, and children's literature. Her shop is on Rt. 166A, two miles north of Castine. Look for the mailbox with her name, P.O. Box 356, Castine 04421, tel. (207) 326-4036. Open all year, Tues.-Sat. 10 a.m.-5 p.m., but call to be sure.

In downtown Castine, tucked into the left side of the *Castine Patriot* building, **The Compass Rose,** Main St., tel. (207) 326-9366 or (800) 698-9366, carries a small but discerning selection of new books, cards, prints, and classical music chosen by British-born owner Frances Kimball, whose previous shop was in Bermuda. Open all year, Mon.-Sat. 9 a.m.-5 p.m.

Gifts and Crafts: Water Witch, Main St., Castine 04421, tel. (207) 326-4884, specializes in Indonesian batik and Liberty fabric, clothing, and accessories. Buy off the rack or choose a fabric and a style and Jean de Raat will have it made up flawlessly within a few days. Don't expect a bargain—a made-to-order dress can cost $150—but it's cheaper than flying to London or Jakarta. Just down the street, close to the harbor, **Four Flags,** Main St., P.O. Box 232, tel. (207) 326-8526, carries high-quality Maine and nautical gifts, plus an excellent card selection. The staff is particularly friendly. Open daily 9:30 a.m.-5 p.m., April-Dec., reduced schedule Jan.-March.

Accommodations

Inns and B&Bs: The three-story **Castine Inn,** Main St., P.O. Box 41, Castine 04421, tel. (207) 326-4365, fax 326-4570, earns a stellar rating for its stunning semiformal gardens, mural-lined dining room, and extremely helpful staff. The 20 rooms are simply furnished, updated from their 1890s origins, with twin or queen beds, private baths, and good lighting ($85-135 d, with full breakfast, lower rates off season). There's lots of interesting artwork everywhere and a very simpatico and unpretentious air, encouraged by enthusiastic young innkeepers Amy and Tom Gutow. In the small, English-style pub, hikers, cyclists, kayakers, and less energetic guests mingle with a devoted local clientele. No pets, no kids under five, no smoking in dining room or lobby. Open early May to late December; two-night minimum July-Labor Day.

Music gets top billing at the three-story, century-old **Pentagöet Inn,** Main St., P.O. Box 4, Castine 04421, tel. (207) 326-8616 or (800) 845-1701, fax (207) 326-9382, where transplanted Georgians Lindsey and Virginia Miller schedule evening recitals by pianists, chamber and folk musicians, vocalists, and sometimes even a storyteller. For those in the know, the library boasts a Bosendorfer piano. Decor is Victorian in the 16 rooms, with antique furnishings, lots of pastels, and even pillows needlepointed by Lindsey's mother. Doubles (all with private baths) are $95-130, including breakfast. The windowed dining room is open to the public for dinner by reservation, but the clientele is primarily inn guests. Open late May to late October. No pets, no smoking, no children under 12.

Castine's least-fancy rooms are at the **Village Inn,** set back from Main and Water Sts., Castine 04421, tel. (207) 326-9510, where summer rates are $55 d (shared bath) to $75 d (private bath). The inn is above Bah's Bakehouse, but noise doesn't seem to be a problem. Open all year, with lower rates off season.

Seasonal Rentals: Perched in a field along the edge of Hatch's Cove, with terrific views, are the six two-bedroom **Castine Cottages,** Rt. 166, P.O. Box 224, Castine 04421, tel. (207) 326-8003, operated by Alan and Diana Snapp. Weekly rentals ($500) in summer (mid-June to Labor Day); nightly rates available ($80, two-night minimum) off season (May to mid-June and Labor Day to late October). You'll need to provide your own sheets and towels. Several Castine realtors have listings for summer cottage rentals, but you won't go wrong if you start with **Saltmeadow Rentals,** Main St., P.O. Box 718, Castine 04421, tel. (207) 326-9116, fax 326-9126.

Food

Lunch and Miscellanea: On lower Main Street is a tiny sign for **Bah's Bakehouse,** Water St., Castine 04421, tel. (207) 326-9510, a higgledy-piggledy eatery of three rooms and a deck at the end of an alleyway beneath the Village Inn. Its slogan is "creative flour arrangements," and creative it is. Stop here for morning coffee, cold juices, interesting snacks and salads, home-made soups, wine or beer, and the best sandwiches in town (eat in or take-out). They'll pack a picnic basket for you or deliver an order dockside. Open all year. Summer hours: Mon.-Sat. 7 a.m.-9 p.m. and Sunday 7 a.m.-8 p.m.

Tarratine Market, corner of Main and Water Sts., tel. (207) 326-4818, is the second-best picnic source, and they'll deliver your order if you're aboard a boat or just don't feel like budging. Open all year. Summer hours: Sun.-Wed. 7 a.m.-8 p.m. and Thurs.-Sat. 7 a.m.-9 p.m.

Across Main Street from the market, natural foods, vitamins, fabulous breads, fresh produce, and picnic fare are all available at the **Castine Co-op,** corner of Main and Water Sts., tel. (207)

326-8760. If you're doing your own cooking, pick up some organic chicken or lamb, plus a selection of superb fresh pastas and sauces created by Mainstay Pasta, a local caterer. The co-op is open all year, Mon.-Sat. 10 a.m.-2 p.m. and Monday, Tuesday, Thursday, and Friday 4-6 p.m.

Down on Castine's town dock is **The Breeze,** tel. (207) 326-4032, a Lilliputian snack bar that serves up predictable and reasonably priced fast food: fried clams, hamburgers, ice cream, and an excellent crab roll. Settle in at one of the nearby picnic tables and watch the waterfront goings-on. Open May-September.

Inexpensive to Moderate: Dennett's Wharf, Sea St., next to the Town Dock, tel. (207) 326-9045, is a colorful barn of a place with outside deck and front-row windjammer-watching seats on summer Mondays and Tuesdays. The service is particularly cheerful, and kids are welcomed. Best sandwich is grilled crabmeat. The crayoned kids' menu—$4 prix fixe—includes all the usual favorites, such as mac-'n-cheese and gummy dinosaurs for dessert. Try attaching a dollar bill to the soaring ceiling; countless others have. Open daily 11 a.m.-midnight, May-Columbus Day.

Moderate to Expensive: Wrestle with your schedule and make reservations at the **Castine Inn,** Main St., Castine 04421, tel. (207) 326-4365, for the Tuesday-night buffet 5:30-8:30 p.m. Memorial Day-Labor Day (regular menu Wed.-Mon.). Business is brisk and reservations are even advisable off-season (7 p.m. dinner in May; 6-7:30 p.m. Labor Day through October). Other nights, the entrée range is $15-26. Inn specialties are seafood, game, and award-winning crab cakes with almost no filler. Appetizers and meals are also available in the pub.

Although the **Pentagöet Inn,** Main St., tel. (207) 326-8616, focuses on its houseguests, the attractive dining room is open to the public every evening, late May-mid-Oct., by reservation. Cocktails and complimentary hors d'oeuvres are served at 6 p.m., four-course dinner ($30) at 7. You can opt for lobster or one of three other entrées; be ready to make these decisions when you call to reserve.

Information and Services

Castine has no local information office, but all businesses and lodgings in town have copies of the Castine Merchants Association's visitors' brochure/map. For additional info, go to the **Castine Town Office,** Emerson Hall, Court St., Castine 04421, tel. (207) 326-4502. It's open Mon.-Thurs. 9 a.m.-4 p.m., Friday 9 a.m.-3 p.m.

Witherle Memorial Library, Court St., Box 202, tel. (207) 326-4375, is open Monday 4-8 p.m., Tues.-Fri. 11 a.m.-5 p.m., and Saturday 10 a.m.-2 p.m. Also accessible to the public is the **Nutting Memorial Library,** in Platz Hall on the Maine Maritime Academy campus. It's open Mon.-Fri. 8 a.m.-4:30 p.m. during the summer, longer hours during the school year.

Newspapers: The *Castine Patriot,* published every Thursday, has the best local coverage, including calendar listings. The *Bangor Daily News,* published daily, carries local, state, and a smidgen of international news. The *Ellsworth American* and *Ellsworth Weekly* are published every Thursday. From June through September, the *Ellsworth American* publishes *Out & About in Downeast Maine,* a free monthly vacation supplement in tabloid format. *Preview!,* a free tabloid focusing on arts and entertainment along the coast between Bar Harbor and Rockland, appears weekly in summer. Rely on the latter two for staying abreast of the area's many events and activities.

Emergencies: Castine's police are deputies in the **Hancock County Sheriff's Department,** in Ellsworth, tel. (207) 667-7575. The **Castine Fire Department** is on Court St., tel. (207) 326-4322. **Castine Community Health Services,** Court and Dyer Sts., tel. (207) 326-4348, has 24-hour emergency service, as well as X-ray and lab facilities. Contact the volunteer-operated **Bagaduce Ambulance Corps** at (207) 374-9900. The nearest acute-care hospital is Blue Hill Memorial Hospital.

Veterinarians/Kennels: Nearest boarding facilities are in Bucksport and Deer Isle. For animal emergencies, most Castine residents rely on the Bucksport Veterinary Hospital.

Other Services: The Castine **post office,** Main St., between Court and Perkins Sts., Castine 04421, tel. (207) 326-8551, reportedly is the nation's oldest continuously used post office, dating from 1815. There are **public restrooms** on the town dock, at the foot of Main Street.

Getting Around
There is no public transportation within Castine, but the village itself is easily walkable or bikeable.

DEER ISLE

"Deer Isle is like Avalon," wrote John Steinbeck in *Travels with Charley*—"it must disappear when you are not there." Deer Isle (the name of both the island and its midpoint town) has been romancing authors and artisans for decades, but it's unmistakably real to the quarrymen and fishermen who've been here for centuries. These long-timers are a sturdy lot—as even Steinbeck recognized: "I would hate to try to force them to do anything they didn't want to do."

Early-18th-century maps show no name for the island, but by the late 1800s, nearly a hundred families lived here, supporting themselves first by farming, then by fishing. In 1789, when Deer Isle was incorporated, some 80 local sailing vessels were scouring the Gulf of Maine in pursuit of mackerel and cod, and Deer Isle men were circling the globe as yachting skippers and merchant seamen. At the same time, in the once-quiet village of Green's Landing (now called Stonington), the shipbuilding and granite industries boomed, spurring development, prosperity, and the kinds of rough hijinks typical of commercial ports the world over.

Green's Landing became the "big city" for an international crowd of quarrymen carving out the terrain on Deer Isle and nearby Crotch Island, source of high-quality granite for Boston's Museum of Fine Arts, the Smithsonian Institution, a humongous fountain for John D. Rockefeller's New York estate, and less showy projects all along the eastern seaboard. The heyday is long past, but the industry did extend into the 20th century (including a contract for the pink granite at President John F. Kennedy's Arlington National Cemetery gravesite). Today, Crotch Island is the site of Maine's only operating island granite quarry.

Measuring about nine miles north to south (plus another three miles for Little Deer Isle), the island of Deer Isle today has a handful of hamlets (including Sunshine, Sunset, Mountainville, and Oceanville) and two towns—Stonington and Deer Isle—with a population just topping 3,000. Road access is via Rt. 15 on the Blue Hill Peninsula. A huge suspension bridge, built in 1939 over Eggemoggin Reach, links the Sargentville section of Sedgwick with Little Deer Isle; from there, a sinuous, .4-mile causeway connects to the northern tip of Deer Isle.

Eight miles off Stonington lies 4,700-acre Isle au Haut, roughly half of which belongs to Acadia National Park. Pronounced variously as "ill-a-HO" or "ILL-a-ho," the island has nearly 20 miles of hiking trails, excellent birding, a tiny village, and one rustic, romantic, and pricey inn.

Sights

Sightseeing on Deer Isle means exploring back roads, browsing the galleries, walking the trails, hanging out on the docks, soaking in the ambience. The only museum per se is the 1830 **Salome Sellers House**, Rt. 15A, Sunset Village, tel. (207) 348-2886 or 348-2513, a repository of local memorabilia and headquarters of the **Deer Isle-Stonington Historical Society.** Volunteer guides love to provide tidbits about various items; seafarers' logs and ship models are particularly intriguing. Located just north of the Island Country Club and across from Eaton's Plumbing, the house is open Wednesday and Friday 2-5 p.m., early July to early September.

A unique downtown Stonington attraction is a Lilliputian complex known hereabouts as the "Miniature Village." Some years ago, the late Everett Knowlton created a dozen and a half replicas of local buildings and displayed them on granite blocks in his yard. Since his death, they've been restored and put on display each summer in town—along with a donation box to support the upkeep. The village is set up on E. Main St. (Rt. 15), across from Bartlett's Supermarket.

Parks and Preserves

Foresighted benefactors have managed to set aside precious acreage for respectful public use on Deer Isle. The Nature Conservancy owns two properties, **Crockett Cove Woods Preserve** and **Barred Island Preserve.** For information, contact the Conservancy, 14 Maine St., Fort Andross, Brunswick 04011, tel. (207) 729-5181, fax 720-4118. The conscientious steward of other local properties is the **Island Her-**

itage Trust (IHT), Atlantic Ave., P.O. Box 369, Stonington 04681, tel. (207) 367-6599, with a seasonal office in the Atlantic Hardware building on the Stonington harborfront. When the office is open (usually July and August weekdays 10 a.m.-4 p.m. and Saturday 10 a.m.-noon), you can pick up note cards, photos, T-shirts, and maps and information on hiking trails, nature preserves, and boat excursions. Proceeds benefit the IHT's efforts, including the purchase of 51 acres of the abandoned **Settlement Quarry** on Webb Cove (off Oceanville Road) in Stonington. Inquire about the Holt Mill Pond and Tennis Preserves. Several of the preserves have limited parking, so don't try to squeeze in if there isn't room.

Crockett Cove Woods Preserve: Donated to The Nature Conservancy by benevolent, eco-conscious local artist Emily Muir, 98-acre Crockett Cove Woods Preserve is Deer Isle's natural gem—a coastal fog forest laden with lichens and mosses. Four interlinked trails cover the whole preserve, starting with a short nature trail. Pick up the helpful map/brochure at the registration box. Wear rubberized shoes or boots and respect adjacent private property. The preserve is open daily, sunrise to sunset, all year. Admission is free; no camping. From Deer Isle Village, take Rt. 15A to Sunset Village. Go two and a half miles to Whitman Rd., then to Fire Lane 88. The local contact phone number is (207) 367-2674.

Ames Pond: Ames Pond is neither park nor preserve, but it might as well be. On a back road close to Stonington, it's a mandatory stop in July and August, when the pond wears a blanket of pink and white water lilies. From downtown Stonington, take Indian Point Rd. east, just under a mile, to the pond. There's no official parking, so if you're shooting photos, pull off the road as far as possible, respecting private property.

Recreation

The **Deer Isle Walking Trails Group,** tel. (207) 367-2448, has produced a handy map—*Walking Trails of Deer Isle*—available for $1 at most island lodgings and the Island Heritage Trust office on Atlantic Ave., in Stonington, tel. (207) 367-6599. The map shows major and secondary roads, scenic biking and walking paths, birding areas, nature preserves, and boat-launching sites.

Cycling: As with so many other parts of Maine, the roads on Deer Isle are narrow and winding, with inadequate shoulders for bikes, so be particularly cautious. In general, Deer Isle is fairly level, so we're not talking rigorous. Route 15, the major north-south artery, has the heaviest traffic, so plan to cycle on the less-busy side routes.

There are no rental bikes on the island (some lodgings provide them for guests), but if you've brought your own, an easy, five-mile roundtrip starts at the Chamber of Commerce information booth on Little Deer Isle. Park your car there and head northwest along Eggemoggin Rd. to the tip of Little Deer Isle. From the turnaround at road's end, there's a splendid view of **Pumpkin Island Light** and Cape Rosier (Brooksville) in the distance. If you plan this spin for late afternoon, you can backtrack on Eggemoggin Rd. and detour down Blastow's Cove Rd. to Eaton's Lobster Pool for dinner and a sunset.

From Deer Isle village, a seven-mile route (14 miles roundtrip) goes east along the Sunshine Rd., through Mountainville, to Sunshine and south to the Haystack Mountain School of Crafts. On the way, stop at Nervous Nellie's. If you're staying at the Sunshine Campground, you can do the route in reverse.

Swimming: The island's only major freshwater swimming hole is the **Lily Pond,** northeast of Deer Isle village. Just north of the Shakespeare School, turn into the Deer Run Apartments complex. Park and take the path to the pond, which has a shallow area for small children.

Golf and Tennis: About two miles south of Deer Isle village, watch for the large sign (on the left) for the **Island Country Club,** Rt. 15A, Sunset, tel. (207) 348-2379, a nine-hole public course that's been here since 1928. Starting times aren't needed, and greens fees are moderate; no rental carts. Open late May to late September. Also at the club are three beautifully maintained tennis courts. Or just commandeer a rocking chair and watch the action from one of the porches. The club's cheeseburgers and crab rolls are among the island's best bargain lunches.

Sea Kayaking: With lots of islets and protected coves in the waters around Deer Isle, especially off Stonington, sea kayaking has come up fast in the recreation department. The nearest place to rent a kayak is the Phoenix Centre, Rt. 175, Blue Hill Falls, tel. (207) 374-2113, but you'll need to backtrack to the Blue Hill Peninsula to pick up the boat. If you sign up with the Maine Island Trail Association, you'll receive a handy manual that steers you to more than a dozen islands where you can camp, hike, and picnic—ecosensitively—in the Deer Isle archipelago. Boat traffic can be a bit heavy at the height of summer, so if you'd like to appreciate the tranquility of this area, try this in September, after the Labor Day holiday. Nights can be cool, but days are likely to be brilliant. See "Accommodations," below, for info on a couple of B&Bs that specially cater to sea kayakers.

Getting Afloat
From mid-June to Labor Day, the excursion boat *Miss Lizzie* departs at 2 p.m. daily from the Isle au Haut/Stonington Dock on Sea Breeze Avenue in Stonington for a narrated trip among the islands. Cost of the memorable hour-long trip is $12 adults, $5 kids under 12. Reservations are essential, tel. (207) 367-5193 days, 367-2355 evenings. *Miss Lizzie* is owned by the Isle au Haut Company, operator of the regular mailboat/passenger-ferry service to offshore Isle au Haut.

Captain Reggie Greenlaw will keep you totally entertained with stories that won't quit and answers for everything during his two-hour tour of the bay aboard the *Palmer Day IV*. The 49-passenger boat—with shelter for misty weather—covers a 16-mile circuit, departing at 2 p.m. daily, July and August, weather permitting. Cost is $10 adults, $5 children under 10. Each Thursday, a five-and-a-half-hour excursion goes to **Vinalhaven and North Haven,** departing 8 a.m. Cost is $12 adults, $8 children under 10. Trips depart from the east side of Stonington Harbor, off Bayview Street. Reservations required, tel. (207) 367-2207.

About two and a half miles west of Deer Isle, in East Penobscot Bay, lies **Eagle Island,** a longtime farming community that lost most of its year-round residents at the onset of World War II. For $15 pp, you can go along on the two-hour Eagle Island **mailboat run,** departing Mon.-Sat. at 8:30 a.m., mid-June to mid-September. Contact the **Sunset Bay Company** tel. (207) 348-9316, for details. The mailboat departs from the Deer Isle Yacht Club on Sylvester's Cove in Sunset, southwest of Deer Isle village.

Festivals And Events

From early June to late August, the **Haystack Lecture Series** includes evening slide programs, lectures, and concerts starting at 8 p.m. at the Haystack Mountain School of Crafts, in Sunshine.

July brings the **Stonington Lobsterboat Races,** very popular competitions held in the harbor, with lots of possible vantage points. Stonington is one of the major locales in the lobsterboat race circuit.

An annual highlight is the August **Flash-in-the-Pans Steel Band Concert** in downtown Stonington. An annual event, complete with street dancing, the concert benefits the active Fishermen's Wives organization. Also in Stonington in August—usually on the second weekend—the **Round-the-Island Sailboat Race** doesn't offer much for spectators except the spectacle of a fleet of billowing sails, but there are other related activities.

Shopping

Antiques/Antiquarian Books: A big, old, white, clapboard house and barn are the home of **Belcher's Antiques and Gifts,** Reach Rd., RR 1, Box 359, Deer Isle 04627, tel. (207) 348-9938, just .2 mile off Rt. 15. The emphasis here is on the antiques, and it's pretty tough not to find something. The shop corners the market on Victorian twig furniture reproductions. Open daily 10 a.m.-5 p.m., late May through Thanksgiving. (There's also a branch Belcher's on Water St. in Blue Hill, tel. 207-374-5769.)

When you head south, toward Deer Isle village, you'll come to **Old Deer Isle Parish House Antiques,** Church St., P.O. Box 445, Deer Isle 04627, tel. (207) 348-9964 or 367-2455, a funky shop heavy into vintage clothing, antique kitchen utensils, and other collectibles. No credit cards. Open mid-June through October, Mon.-Fri. 11 a.m.-6 p.m. and Saturday and Sunday 2-6 p.m.

In Deer Isle village, Stan Clifford hangs out at **Skeans & Clifford, Booksellers,** Main St., P.O. Box 725, Deer Isle 04627, tel. (207) 348-2660. The classy but not overpriced shop specializes in first editions and books on the arts. Open

Mon.-Fri. 12:30-6 p.m. in summer, but, as Stan says, "don't cut it too close at either end." Other times, he's open by appointment.

Anyone on the trail of rare books should also be sure to stop en route to Deer Isle at Wayward Books, in Sargentville, just the other side of the Deer Isle bridge.

Art and Craft Galleries: Thanks to the presence and influence of Haystack Mountain School of Crafts, supertalented artists and artisans lurk in every corner of the island. Most are tucked away on back roads, so watch for roadside signs and pick up a free copy (available in shops and galleries statewide) of the Maine Crafts Association's annual *Maine Cultural Guide.* Not surprisingly, the statewide organization is headquartered on Deer Isle.

Name a craft and Mary Nyburg probably has an example in her high-ceilinged barn, the **Blue Heron Gallery & Studio,** Church St., Deer Isle 04627, tel. (207) 348-2940. Formerly a Haystack board member and currently an honorary trustee, her gallery provides a retail outlet for the work of the school's topflight faculty—printmakers, blacksmiths, potters, weavers, papermakers, glassworkers, and more. Prices are reasonable. The gallery is open Mon.-Sat. 10 a.m.-6 p.m. and Sunday noon-6 p.m., early June to mid-October, but hours are less predictable after Labor Day, so call ahead.

The **Maine Crafts Association** (MCA), P.O. Box 228, Deer Isle 04627, tel. (207) 348-9943, and the **Deer Isle Artists Association** (DIAA) are headquartered together less than a mile northwest of Deer Isle village at 6 Dow Rd., Deer Isle. The DIAA's co-op gallery (no telephone) features two-week exhibits of paintings, prints, drawings, and photos by local pros. Open daily 1-5 p.m., mid-June through Labor Day. The MCA gift shop—marketing the work of 70 or so members—is open all year, Mon.-Sat. 10 a.m.-5 p.m. and Sunday 1-5 p.m. in summer; Mon.-Fri. 10 a.m.-5 p.m. other months. Many of Deer Isle's MCA members have studios open to the public, often on an unpredictable schedule; inquire at the MCA or the Blue Heron Gallery.

One of the island's premier galleries gained a larger home in 1996. Elena Kubler moved **The Turtle Gallery,** Rt. 15, P.O. Box 219, Deer Isle 04627, tel. (207) 348-9977, to a handsome space formerly known as the Old Centennial

House Barn (owned by retired Haystack director Francis Merritt). Group and solo shows of contemporary paintings, prints, and crafts are hung upstairs and down, and there's usually sculpture in the garden. Just north of Deer Isle village—across from the Shakespeare School, oldest on the island—the gallery is open Memorial Day weekend through September, Mon.-Sat. 10 a.m.-5:30 p.m. and Sunday 2-6 p.m.

Here's an interesting juxtaposition—in a lovely setting—**William Mor Stoneware and Oriental Rugs,** 409 Reach Rd., Deer Isle 04627, tel. (207) 348-2822. Bill Mor has been throwing pottery since the 1970s, and there's plenty of it here, but he also imports natural-dyed Afghan and Tibetan rugs via the nonprofit Cultural Survival organization—stunning work for a worthy cause. The shop is open daily 10 a.m.-5 p.m., mid-May through October. Reach Road is a mile south of the Rt. 15 Little Deer Isle-Deer Isle causeway; the shop is 3.3 miles down Reach Road.

On Rt. 15, about 500 feet south of Reach Road and almost across from the Holden Homestead, is the compact home of **George Hardy,** tel. (207) 348-2885, a self-taught folk carver who's been featured in a solo video and turns out incredibly imaginative carved and painted animals. George is here most days. Watch for the Hardy Folk Carving sign, bring your wallet (cash only), and carry home an unusual treasure.

Gifts: If you're looking for Maine pottery, weaving, metalwork, pewterware, tiles, or walking sticks, go directly to **Harbor Farm,** Rt. 15, P.O. Box 64, Little Deer Isle 04650, tel. (207) 348-7755 or (800) 342-8003, fax (207) 348-7713, one of the state's best gift shops. Based in a mid-19th-century schoolhouse a mile south of the Deer Isle suspension bridge, Lee and Richard McWilliams carry thousands of very unusual, high-quality items, and it's all available by mail as well. Hours are Mon.-Sat. 10 a.m.-5 p.m. and Sunday noon-5 p.m., Memorial Day weekend to mid-October; Mon.-Sat. 10 a.m.-5 p.m., mid-October through December; Mon.-Fri. 10 a.m.-5 p.m., January to Memorial Day weekend.

Also well stocked with Maine-made gifts and crafts is **The Rugosa Rose,** Main St., Deer Isle 04627, tel. (207) 348-6615, on the grounds of The Pilgrim's Inn. Jean and Dud Hendrick do everything tastefully, so you can't go wrong; nearly 40 artisans have their work here. The small, two-story shop is open daily 8 a.m.-8 p.m., mid-May to mid-October.

Now for a bit of whimsy. From Rt. 15 in Deer Isle village, take the Sunshine Rd. east three miles to **Nervous Nellie's Jams and Jellies,** Sunshine Rd., RFD 474A, Deer Isle 04627, tel. (800) 777-6845. Outstandingly creative condiments are the rule here; sample hot pepper jelly or blackberry peach conserve or ginger syrup. The promotional brochures are hilarious. Best time to come is July and August, 10 a.m.-5 p.m., when the shop operates the **Mountainville Café,** serving tea, coffee, and delicious scones —with, of course, Nervous Nellie's products. While you're at it, the surrounding meadow teems with whimsical wooden sculptures (all for sale) by Nellie's owner Peter Beerits. The condiments are available by mail, but that's missing half the fun. The shop is open daily 10 a.m.-5 p.m., mid-June to Columbus Day.

In downtown Stonington, **Dockside Books & Gifts,** W. Main St., P.O. Box 171, Stonington 04681, tel. (207) 367-2652, carries just what its name promises, with a specialty in marine and Maine books. The shop is open daily 9 a.m.-5:30 p.m., May to mid-October.

Accommodations

Inns/B&Bs: The most elegant place to sleep on Deer Isle is the **Pilgrim's Inn,** Main St., Deer Isle 04627, tel. (207) 348-6615, fax 348-7769, smack in the middle of Deer Isle village. Amiable innkeepers Jean and Dud Hendrick have 13 antiques-filled rooms (private or shared baths; no smoking) in their beautifully restored Colonial inn overlooking the peaceful Mill Pond. Doubles are $150-175, including breakfast and dinner (MAP), in July and August, $145-170 other months. They also have two waterview units in the building next door. The National Historic Register inn began life in 1793 as a boardinghouse named The Ark; be sure to check out the fascinating guestbook, with names dating to 1901. The inn has sloping lawns, bikes for guests, an adjacent gift shop, and a fine dining room serving dinner to guests and the public by reservation. No pets, no children under 10. Open mid-May to mid-October.

Just when you're convinced you're lost, and the paved road has turned to dirt, you arrive at **Goose Cove Lodge,** Goose Cove Rd., P.O. Box 40, Sunset 04683, tel. (207) 348-2508 or (800) 728-1963 outside Maine, fax (207) 348-2624, a 20-acre hillside complex of rustic and modern cottages and main-lodge rooms and suites—all with private baths, most with fireplaces, and many with stunning views of secluded Goose Cove. Request one of the seven older "secluded cottages," with cove-facing decks. Rates vary widely here, depending on lodging choice, and the cost can add up; one-week minimum and MAP are required from late June to Labor Day. Some cottages also require a three-person minimum rate during the same period. High-season MAP ranges $85-130 pp per day; off-season MAP is in the $75-110 pp range. B&B rates (available mid-May to mid-June and after Labor Day) are $90-170 d; two-night minimum. Goose Cove innkeepers Joanne and Dom Parisi organize nature walks and astronomy talks and provide maps and descriptions of local trails, including The Nature Conservancy's Barred Island Preserve, close to the lodge property. Bikes, boats, and games are available for guests. The dining room, open to the public by reservation for dinner and Sunday brunch, has a reputation well beyond Deer Isle. The inn is open mid-May to mid-October; one-week minimum in July and August, two-night minimum other months. No pets. Children are welcome at this family-oriented spot; there's even a kids' activity director, and children eat together on midsummer evenings. The lodge is four and a half miles from Rt. 15, via Deer Isle village.

In 1995, a longtime downtown-Stonington landmark known as the Captain's Quarters changed hands, became **The Inn on the Harbor,** Main St., P.O. Box 69, Stonington 04681, tel. (207) 367-2420 or (800) 942-2420, fax (207) 367-5165, and headed a bit upscale. But not totally; the updated 1880s complex still has an air of unpretentiousness. Most of the 13 rooms and suites (private baths) have harbor views and private or shared decks where you can keep an eye on lobsterboats, small ferries, windjammers, and pleasure craft. An espresso bar is open noon-4 p.m.; wine and sherry are served 5-6 p.m. Nearby are antiques, gift, and craft shops;

guest moorings are available. Rates are $100-125 d, including breakfast and aperitifs; special packages are available off season. No pets, no children under 12; smoking only on decks. Open early April through December.

Eggemoggin Reach is almost on the doorstep at **The Inn at Ferry Landing,** Old Ferry Rd., RR 1, Box 163, Deer Isle 04627, tel. (207) 348-7760, fax 348-5276, overlooking the abandoned Sargentville-Deer Isle ferry wharf. The view is wide open from the inn's "great room," where guests gather to read, play games, talk, and watch passing windjammers. Professional musician Gerald Wheeler has installed two grand pianos in the room; it's a treat when he plays. His wife, Jean, is the hospitable innkeeper. Three water-view guest rooms ($95 d in summer, lower off season) and a suite ($135 d) have private baths. An annex, sleeping seven, is rented by the week ($1,000, without breakfast). No smoking, no pets, no children under 10 in the main building; kids are welcome in the annex. The inn is open all year.

On Little Deer Isle, just north of the causeway and close to Harbor Farm, **The Red House,** Rt. 15, Little Deer Isle 04650, tel./fax (207) 348-5234, is one of the least pricey Deer Isle B&Bs. Genial hosts Lou and Sally Cooper, former innkeepers at Ferry Landing, have two comfortable, informal second-floor rooms sharing a bath ($55 d, including full breakfast and tax). The smaller room has a water view; a cranberry bog covers part of the 1.4-acre property. No smoking, no pets (cats in residence), no credit cards. Open all year, but be sure to call ahead off season.

In downtown Stonington, convenient for walking, is **Près du Port,** W. Main St. and Highland Ave., P.O. Box 319, Stonington 04681, tel. (207) 367-5007, a bright, comfortable B&B run by Charlotte Casgrain, who's been on the island since 1955 and becomes a Connecticut French teacher in winter. Two rooms share a bath, one has a private bath ($60-80 d). Children are welcome; there's even a toy cupboard to entertain them. No credit cards. Open May 1-Nov. 1. Charlotte also manages a four-person water-view cottage across the street ($75 a night or $400 a week). When Deer Isle beds are scarce in the height of summer, Charlotte is the best resource for dozens of overnight rooms in local homes.

Especially popular with hikers, sea kayakers, and birders, **Burnt Cove Bed & Breakfast,** Whitman Rd., RFD 1, Box 2905, Stonington 04681, tel. (207) 367-2392, is about two miles west of downtown Stonington. The entrance to Crockett Cove Woods Preserve is a few minutes' walk from Bob Williams and Diane Berlew's modern house, and kayakers can launch into Burnt Cove from the gravel beach. Views from the waterfront deck are extraordinary. Two second-floor rooms share a bath ($60 d); a large first-floor room has a water view, private bath, and private entrance ($85 d). Breakfast is hearty continental, with homemade goodies. No smoking, no pets, no kids under 12. Open early May through October.

Also geared to sea kayakers and the low-key boating set is **Oceanville Seaside Bed & Breakfast,** Oceanville Rd., RR 1, Box 890, Stonington 04681, tel. (207) 367-2226, Tim and Kathy Emerson's mid-19th-century Cape-style home at 44°11' N, 68°37' W. It's tough to find a more idyllic setting for a paddling or sailing rest stop—a secluded, pink-granite-lined cove overlooking ocean and islands. The kitchen and living room in this informal spot have tin ceilings and great views. Nearby are miles of trails. A first-floor room (shared bath) is $65 d; the second-floor suite (private bath), sleeping five, is $80 d ($20 per extra person). Kathy's fabulous breakfasts are included; she'll prepare dinner ($10 pp; BYOL) by prior arrangement. No smoking, no credit cards, no children under five. A mooring is available for guests; kayakers can paddle in and paddle out on any tide. As if all that isn't enough, the Emersons can send you off to spruce-covered Sheep Island, owned by their family, for hiking, birding, and picnicking. The B&B, east of Stonington in the hamlet of Oceanville, is open all year by reservation.

Seasonal Rentals: For house and cottage rentals by the week, month, or season, contact Alice Gross at **Island Vacation Rentals,** RFD, Box 615, Stonington 04681, tel. (207) 367-5095, fax 367-6335. Plan well ahead, as the best properties get snapped up as much as a year in advance. Other rental agencies are **Deer Isle Rental Co.,** P.O. Box 446, Stonington 04681, tel. (207) 367-5994, and **Sargent's Rentals,** P.O. Box 115, Stonington 04681, tel. (207) 367-5156, fax 367-2444.

Fire Chief Richard Haskell and his wife Candy own **Haskell's Cottages,** Dow Rd., P.O. Box 625, Deer Isle 04627, tel. (207) 348-2843, two clean, unadorned two-bedroom cabins in a convenient location about a mile northwest of Deer Isle village. The reasonable weekly rate is $350 in July and August, $300 in June and September. Bring your own sheets and towels; everything else is provided. No pets. Open June through September.

Campgrounds: There's only one small private campground on Deer Isle, in the village of Sunshine, so plan ahead if you're thinking about camping. Offshore, on Isle au Haut, are a few lean-tos managed by Acadia National Park and available only by reservation.

Sunshine Campground, RR1, Box 521D, Deer Isle 04627, tel. (207) 348-6681, has 24 wooded RV (maximum 40 feet) and tentsites for $10-15 a night. Facilities include laundry, firewood, and a small store. No credit cards; leashed pets are allowed. Open Memorial Day weekend to mid-October. From Deer Isle village, the campground is on the Sunshine Rd., 5.7 miles east of Rt. 15.

Food
Miscellanea: Bread mavens head for **Penobscot Bay Provisions,** W. Main St., P.O. Box 68, Stonington 04681, tel. (207) 367-2920, to capture the freshly baked rosemary focaccia soon after it emerges from the ovens. Other special breads appear too, including out-of-this-world olive rolls. The tiny upscale shop produces great salads, soups, and sandwiches and will pack up a picnic for you. No credit cards. Open mid-May to early October. Summer hours (late May to Labor Day) are Tues.-Sat. 8 a.m.-5 p.m., Sunday 10 a.m.-2 p.m.; hours are shorter in spring and fall.

Equally creative is the menu at **Lily's Café,** Rt. 15, Stonington 04681, tel. (207) 367-5936, in a cute house at the corner of the Airport Road. Eat here or assemble a *haut gourmet* picnic: veggie and meat sandwiches (Stan's Pig with an Apple is great), Mediterranean salads, cheeses, and homemade soups and breads. Lily's is open Mon.-Sat. 10 a.m.-8 p.m. and Sunday 10 a.m.-2 p.m.

Best pizza on the island? Head for **Joey's,** Church St., Deer Isle village, tel. (207) 348-2911, where you can have lunch, dinner, Green Mountain coffee, and from-scratch pizza. Jackie Cobb is in charge. There are a few tables, but most customers do takeout. No credit cards. Open March-Dec., Tues.-Sat. 11 a.m.-8 p.m. Running a close second (or, according to some, tied for first) is **Burnt Cove Market,** Rt. 15, Stonington, tel. (207) 367-2681. Besides pizza, you can get fried chicken and sandwiches. The store is open all year, Mon.-Sat. 6 a.m.-8 p.m. (to 9 p.m. Friday and Saturday) and Sunday 9 a.m.-8 p.m.

Inexpensive to Moderate: In July or August, don't show up at **Finest Kind Dining,** Joyce's Cross Rd., P.O. Box 388, Deer Isle 04627, tel. (207) 348-7714, without a dinner reservation. This log-cabin family restaurant is no longer a secret. Nothing fancy—just good, homemade all-American food served conscientiously in a come-as-you-are setting. Pizza, pasta, prime rib, seafood. And save room for dessert. Wheelchair access; liquor license. Open May-Oct., daily 11 a.m.-9 p.m. The restaurant, owned by the Perez family, is halfway between Rt. 15 and Sunset Road (Rt. 15A). The Perezes also own the adjacent **Round the Island Mini Golf** (same phone, open the same months).

The Fisherman's Friend Restaurant, School St., Rt. 15A, Stonington 04681, tel. (207) 367-2442, run by Jack and Susan Scott, gets high marks for respectable food, generous portions, fresh seafood, and outstanding desserts. BYOL. All day Friday, the popular fish fry goes for $6.50. Located across from the elementary school, it's open daily 11 a.m.-8 p.m. (to 9 p.m. Friday and Saturday), April to late October. Just up the street is **Connie's Restaurant,** School St., Rt. 15A, Stonington, tel. (207) 367-2742, another spot for daily specials and local flavor. It's open all year, daily 7 a.m.-8 p.m. No credit cards; smoking allowed at one table.

Moderate to Expensive: Both restaurants in this category are conveniently linked to lodgings, and MAP packages are available. If you have the time, and your wallet and waistline will stand it, be sure to try them both.

At Jean and Dud Hendrick's **Pilgrim's Inn,** Main St., Sunset Rd., Deer Isle Village 04627, tel. (207) 348-6615, fax 348-7769, dinner is a scheduled affair, elegantly casual, in the restored barn. At 6 p.m., delicious hors d'oeuvres are served in the common room; at 7 p.m., the multicourse dinner begins, featuring an entrée-of-the-day (call ahead to hear the selection). The 1997 publication of *The Pilgrim's Inn Cookbook* focused even more attention on the inn and its award-winning chef, Terry Foster. Reservations are required; prix-fixe tab is $30 (plus tax, tip, wine); the restaurant has a liquor license. No smoking in the dining room. This is a grown-up kind of place, so don't bring children unless they qualify as angelic. Open mid-May to mid-October.

Running head-to-head with the Pilgrim's Inn in the culinary department is **Goose Cove Lodge,** Goose Cove Rd., P.O. Box 40, Sunset 04683, tel. (207) 348-2508, fax 348-2624, where superbly creative four-course dinners are served to guests and the public in the attractive main lodge by reservation Sat.-Thurs. at 6:30 p.m. Friday night, weather permitting, there's a lobster feast on the beach at 6 p.m.—all you can eat plus make-your-own sundaes. Each night there's also a special children's menu; entertainment follows dinner three nights a week. The Sunday buffet brunch (10 a.m.-1 p.m.; $16 pp) is justifiably popular, a major treat (pray for a sunny day; the tables have a spectacular view of the gorgeous cove). The lodge also serves breakfast and lunch in the dining room, and lunch on the terrace in season. Call well ahead for holiday and weekend reservations; Goose Cove may be remote, but it's no secret. Open mid-May to mid-October.

Lobster-in-the-Rough: Eaton's Lobster **Pool,** Blastow's Cove, Little Deer Isle, tel. (207) 348-2383, qualifies in this category because you can order your crustaceans by the pound, but it's a bit more gussied up than the eat-on-the-dock places. You'll find more interesting food and faster service at other island restaurants, but you'd be hard put to find a better view than here on Blastow's Cove. Dramatic sunsets can even subdue the usual din in the rustic dining room. BYOL; no credit cards; smoking only outside. Reservations are advisable, especially on weekends. Open daily 5-9 p.m., mid-June to mid-September; open Fri.-Sun., mid-May to mid-June and mid-September to early October. Look for signs across from the Chamber of Commerce information booth.

In downtown Stonington, a good bet for fresh-out-of-the-water seafood is **The Lobster Deck,**

Sea Breeze Ave., Stonington, tel. (207) 367-6526, in the North Atlantic Seafood building, heart of the fishing docks. Burgers are also available, and there's indoor seating. This casual spot is open Mon.-Tues. 6 a.m.-2 p.m., Wed.-Sat. 6 a.m.-7 p.m., and Sunday 6 a.m.-noon.

Information And Services
The **Deer Isle-Stonington Chamber of Commerce,** P.O. Box 459, Stonington 04681, tel. (207) 348-6124, has a summer information booth on a grassy triangle on Rt. 15 in Little Deer Isle, a quarter of a mile after crossing the bridge from Sargentville (Sedgwick). Staffed by volunteers, the office has a rather erratic schedule, allegedly weekdays 10 a.m.-4 p.m. and Sunday 11 a.m.-5 p.m.

Across from the Pilgrim's Inn, the **Chase Emerson Memorial Library,** Main St., Deer Isle Village 04627, tel. (207) 348-2899, is open Monday and Wednesday 11 a.m.-3 p.m. and Saturday 9 a.m.-noon. The **Stonington Public Library,** Main St., Stonington 04681, tel. (207) 367-5926, is open Tuesday and Friday 12:30-4:30 p.m. and Saturday 10 a.m.-noon.

Emergencies: The **Island Medical Center,** Airport Rd., South Deer Isle, tel. (207) 367-2311, a division of Blue Hill Memorial Hospital, handles minor medical problems. The nearest round-the-clock emergency room is at Blue Hill Memorial Hospital, Water St., Blue Hill 04614, tel. (207) 374-2836. Throughout Deer Isle, contact the **police** (actually the Hancock County Sheriff) at (207) 667-7575. To report a fire or summon an ambulance, call (207) 367-2655 in **Stonington** or (207) 348-2325 in **Deer Isle village.**

Newspapers: *Island Ad-Vantages,* tel. (207) 367-2200, published every Thursday, includes the *Compass* supplement, listing area events and activities. Regular features are "The Fisheries Log" (going rates for seafood, including lobsters and crabmeat) and "Laurels and Lemons" (praise and pans for good and bad deeds). The same publisher also owns the *Castine Patriot* and Blue Hill's *Weekly Packet.*

The Ellsworth American, 63 Main St., Ellsworth 04605, tel. (207) 667-2576, published every Thursday, produces a monthly summer tabloid supplement, *Out and About in Downeast Maine,* with feature articles, maps, ads, and calendar listings that include Deer Isle. The supplement is available free at shops, lodgings, and restaurants throughout the area.

Public Restrooms: There are public restrooms at the Atlantic Avenue Hardware pier and at the Stonington Town Hall, Main St. (open Mon.-Fri. 8 a.m.-4 p.m.), as well as at the Chase Emerson Library in Deer Isle village.

Kennels: Karen Weed's **Ranga Kennels** ("RAIN-ja"—a Maine-ification of the name Ranger), P.O. Box 266, Deer Isle 04627, tel. (207) 348-6159, takes in dogs and cats, by prior appointment, for daytime, overnight, or long-term stays. She's extremely amenable to odd schedules, and she provides daily dog walks for "people contact." One-night lodging is $10 for dogs, $5 for cats, lower rates for longer stays. Open all year. Watch for a sign at the northern tip of Deer Isle, just south of the causeway from Little Deer Isle.

Special Courses: Internationally famed artisans—sculptors and papermakers, weavers and jewelers, potters and printmakers—become the faculty each summer for the unique **Haystack Mountain School of Crafts,** Sunshine Rd., P.O. Box 518, Deer Isle 04627, tel. (207) 348-2306, fax 348-2307. Chartered in 1950, the school has weekday classes and round-the-clock studio access for the adult students, ranging from beginners to advanced professionals. Portfolio review is required for advanced courses. Two or three evenings a week (8 p.m.), between late June and early August, faculty and visiting artists present slide/lecture programs open to the public. An hour-long Wednesday-afternoon (1 p.m.) tour of the architecturally and scenically dramatic 40-acre shorefront campus usually includes visits to some of the studios. None of the work is for sale. Haystack is seven miles east of Deer Isle village.

Getting Around
Nancy Brooks runs the very efficient **A-Z Taxi & Tours,** P.O. Box 184, Stonington 04681, tel. (207) 348-6186, van number (207) 460-0758; call her year-round for tours of the island or trips to the Bangor or Bar Harbor airports.

ISLE AU HAUT

Half a hundred souls call 5,800-acre Isle au Haut home year-round, most of them eking out a living from the sea. Each summer, the population temporarily swells with day-trippers, campers, and cottagers—then settles back in fall to the measured pace of life on an island six miles offshore.

Samuel de Champlain, threading his way through this archipelago in 1605 and noting the island's prominent central ridge, came up with the name of Isle au Haut—High Island. Appropriately, the tallest peak (543 feet) is now named Mt. Champlain. Incorporated in 1868, Isle au Haut became, courtesy of political horse-trading, part of Knox County, whose shire town (Rockland) is nearly four hours away—by boat and car.

Most of the southern half of the six-mile-long island belongs to Acadia National Park, thanks to the wealthy summer visitors who began arriving in the 1880s—it was their heirs who, in the 1940s, donated valuable acreage to the federal government. Today, this offshore division of the national park has a well-managed 20-mile network of trails, a few lean-tos, several miles of unpaved road, and summertime ferry service to the park entrance.

In the island's northern half are the private residences of fisherfolk and summer folk, a mi-nuscule village (including a market and post office), a four-mile paved road, and the only inn. The only vehicles on the island are owned by residents.

If spending the night on Isle au Haut sounds appealing (it is), you'll need to plan well ahead; it's no place for spur-of-the-moment sleepovers. (Even spontaneous day-trips aren't always possible.)

The most exotic and priciest overnight option is **The Keeper's House,** P.O. Box 26, Lighthouse Point, Isle au Haut 04645, off-island tel. (207) 367-2261, Maine's only light-station inn. Attached to Robinson's Point Light (automated) and within night sight of three other lighthouses, the six-room inn gets booked up months ahead. Judi Burke, daughter of a Cape Cod lightkeeper, bought the 1907 National Historic Register building with her husband, Jeff, in 1986. The top-floor Garret Room has the only private bath. Best view is from The Keeper's Room, overlooking the light tower and Isle au Haut Thorofare. The main house has two other rooms. Two more are in outbuildings; most rustic of these is the Oil House, with a solar shower and private outhouse. Rooms are $250-285 d, covering three meals, including candlelight gourmet dinners. BYOL and pack light. A two-night minimum in July and August (and all weekends) escalates the tab. The ferry operates Mon.-Sat. all year, and Sundays and holidays from late June through Labor Day. Single-speed

welcome to Isle au Haut

SHERRY STREETER

bikes are available for guests. If you're going hiking or biking, the Burkes will pack you a lunch. No electricity, no phones, no smoking, no credit cards, no pets. Nirvana. Open May through October.

Getting There
Unless you have your own vessel, the only access to Isle au Haut's town landing is via the private boat owned by the **Isle au Haut Company,** Sea Breeze Ave., Stonington 04681, tel. (207) 367-5193 days, 367-2355 evenings, which generally operates three daily trips, Mon.-Sat., between early April and mid-October, plus once-a-day Sunday and holiday trips from late June to Labor Day. Best advice is to call for a copy of the current schedule, covering dates, variables, fares, and extras.

In spring, summer, and fall, weekday roundtrips are $24 adults, $10 kids under 12 (two bags each). Adult weekend roundtrips are $28. Surcharges: bikes ($14 roundtrip), boats and canoes ($24 minimum), pets ($6), credit cards ($2 pp). Winter rates are half-price. Weather seldom affects the schedule, but be aware that ultraheavy seas could cancel a trip.

From late June to Labor Day, Mon.-Sat., there is twice-daily ferry service from Stonington to Duck Harbor, at the edge of Isle au Haut's Acadia National Park campground. For a day-trip, the schedule allows you seven hours on the island. Roundtrip fares are $20 adults, $10 kids under 12, $6 pets. No boats or bikes are allowed on this route, and no dogs are allowed in the campground. A ranger boards the boat at the town landing and goes along to Duck Harbor to answer questions and distribute maps. Before mid-June and after Labor Day, as well as on Sundays in the peak season, you'll be offloaded at the Isle au Haut town landing, about five miles from Duck Harbor. The six-mile passage from Stonington to the Isle au Haut town landing takes 45 minutes; the trip to Duck Harbor tacks on 15 minutes more.

Ferries depart from the **Isle au Haut/Stonington Dock,** Sea Breeze Ave., off E. Main St. in downtown Stonington. Parking (for a fee) is available next to the ferry landing, but you can also unload your gear at the dock and arrange to park (for a fee) at **Steve's Garage,** Weedfield Rd., Stonington, tel. (207) 367-5548. Arrive an

hour early to get all this settled so you don't miss the boat. Better yet, spend the night on Deer Isle before heading to Isle au Haut.

A note on the weather: Fog is no stranger to Isle au Haut (or, for that matter, many other Maine islands and coastal areas), so keep in mind that even though it doesn't halt boat service, it can affect what you see. Fog shouldn't faze hikers or walkers, but it certainly affects photographers. Then again, moody fog shots have their own special appeal. There's nothing you can do about fog, so make the best of it.

Recreation
Hiking on national park trails is the major recreation on Isle au Haut, and even in the densest fog, you'll see valiant hikers going for it. **Biking** is a bit iffier, limited to the 12 or so miles of paved and unpaved roads. If you're staying at The Keeper's House, they're handy around the village and for going swimming. Mountain bikes are not allowed on the park's hiking trails, and rangers try to discourage park visitors from bringing them to the island. The mailboat carries bikes only to the town landing, not to the park's Duck Harbor Landing.

For **freshwater swimming,** head for Long Pond, a skinny, one-and-a-half-mile-long swimming hole running north-south on the east side of the island. You can bike over there, clockwise along the road, almost five miles, from the town landing. Or bum a ride from an island resident. If you're only here for the day, though, there's not enough time to do this *and* get in any hiking. Opt for the hiking.

Acadia National Park
Mention Acadia National Park and most people think of Bar Harbor and Mount Desert Island, where more than three million visitors arrive each year. The Isle au Haut section of the park sees maybe 5,000 visitors a year—partly because only 48 people a day (not counting campers) are allowed to land here. But the remoteness of the island and the scarcity of beds and campsites also contribute to the low count.

Near the town landing, where the year-round mailboat docks, is the **Park Ranger Station,** where you can pick up trail maps and park information—and use the island's only public facilities (outhouses).

A loop road circles the whole island; an unpaved section goes through the park, connecting with the paved nonpark section. Walking is easy. Beyond the road, none of the park's 20 miles of trails could be labeled "easy"; the footing is rocky, rooty, and often squishy. But the trails *are* well marked, and the views—of islets, distant hills, and ocean—maximize the effort.

The most-used park trail is the 4- to 5-mile (one way) **Duck Harbor Trail,** connecting the town landing with Duck Harbor. Figure about two hours each way. (You can use this route or follow the road to get to the campground when the summer ferry ends its Duck Harbor run.) Toughest trail is probably **Duck Harbor Mountain,** about 1.2 miles (one way) that'll take you about three hours roundtrip. For terrific shoreline scenery, take the **Western Head** and **Cliff Trails,** at the island's southwestern corner. If the tide is out (and *only* if it's out), you can walk across the tidal flats to the quaintly named Western Ear for views back toward the island. Western Ear is private, so don't linger. The **Goat Trail** adds another four miles (roundtrip) of moderate hiking east of the Cliff Trail; views are fabulous and birding is good, but you'll need to decide whether there's time to catch the return mailboat.

Of course, there's much less pressure if you're camping, but you'll need to get your bid in early to reserve one of the five six-person lean-tos

at **Duck Harbor Campground,** open May 15-Oct. 15. Before April 1, contact the park for a reservation request form. Write to Acadia National Park, P.O. Box 177, Bar Harbor, 04609. Anytime from April 1 on *(not before),* return the completed form, along with a check for $25, covering camping for up to six persons for a maximum of five nights May 15-June 15, three nights June 15-Sept. 15, and five nights again Sept. 15-Oct. 15. Competition is stiff in the height of summer, so list alternate dates. The park refunds the check if there's no space; otherwise, they'll send you a special use permit (don't forget to bring it along). There's no additional camping fee.

Unless you don't mind backpacking nearly five miles to reach the campground, try to plan your visit between mid-June and Labor Day, when the mailboat stops in Duck Harbor. It's wise to call for the current ferry schedule before choosing dates for a lean-to reservation.

Trash policy is carry-in-carry-out, so bring a trash bag. Also bring a container for carting water from the campground pump, since it's .3 mile from the lean-tos. It's a longish walk to the general store for food—when you could be off hiking the island's trails—so bring enough to cover your stay.

The best part about staying overnight on Isle au Haut is that you'll have so much more than seven hours to enjoy this idyllic island.

MOUNT DESERT ISLAND

Summer folk have been visiting Mount Desert Island (MDI) for millennia. The earliest Native Americans discovered fabulous fishing and clamming, good hunting and camping, and invigorating salt air here; today's arrivals find variations on the theme: thousands of lodgings and campsites, hundreds of restaurant seats, dozens of shops, plus 40,000 acres of Acadia National Park.

It's no coincidence that artists were a large part of the 19th-century vanguard here: the dramatic landscape, with both bare and wooded mountains descending to the sea, still inspires everyone who sees it. Once the word got out, painterly images began confirming the reports, and the surge began. Even today, no saltwa-

ter locale on the entire eastern seaboard can compete with the variety of scenery on Mount Desert Island.

Those pioneering artists brilliantly portrayed this area, adding romanticized touches to landscapes that really need no enhancement. From the 1,530-foot summit of Cadillac Mtn., preferably at an off hour, you'll sense the grandeur of it all—the slopes careening toward the bay and the handful of islands below looking like the last footholds between Bar Harbor and Bordeaux.

For nearly four centuries, controversy has raged about the pronunciation of the island's name, and we won't resolve it here. French explorer Samuel de Champlain apparently gets

*Stanley Brook
Bridge*

AISLINN RACE

credit for naming it l'Île des Monts Déserts, "is-land of bare mountains," when he sailed by in 1604. The accent in French would be on the second syllable, but today Mount De-SERT and Mount DES-ert both have their advocates, al-though the former seems to get the most use.

However, either way, the island is anything but deserted today. Even as you approach the is-land, via Trenton on Rt. 3, you'll run the gauntlet of a minor-league Disneyland, with water slides, bumper cars, and enough high-cholesterol eater-ies to stun the surgeon general. Don't panic. Acadia National Park lies ahead. My own first in-stinct is to head straight for the park, for the less commercial air and the incredible vistas.

As you drive or bike around the island—vaguely shaped like a lobster claw and indented by Somes Sound (the only fjord on the United States' east coast)—you'll cross and re-cross the national-park boundaries, reminders that Acadia National Park, covering a third of the is-land, is indeed the major presence here. It af-fects traffic, indoor and outdoor pursuits, and, in a way, even the climate.

The other major presence is Bar Harbor, largest and best-known of the island's commu-nities. It's the source of just about anything you could want (if not need), from T-shirts to tacos,

books to bike rentals. The contrast with Acadia is astonishing, as the park struggles to main-tain its image and character.

Bar Harbor shares the island with Southwest Harbor, Tremont, and a number of smaller vil-lages: Bass Harbor, Bernard, Northeast Har-bor, Seal Harbor, Otter Creek, Somesville, and Hall Quarry. From Bass, Northeast, and South-west Harbors, private and state ferries shuttle car, bike, and foot traffic to offshore Swans Is-land, Frenchboro (Long Island), and the Cran-berry Isles.

If time permits, spend a week on the island (longer would be even better) and squeeze in as much hiking, biking, kayaking, whalewatching, birdwatching, pub-crawling, and grub-grazing as you can manage.

Trenton: Gateway to Mount Desert Island
Unless you're arriving by boat, you can't get to Mount Desert Island without first going through Trenton, straddling Rt. 3 from Ellsworth south-ward. Restaurants, motels, amusements, and gift shops line the congested six-mile strip, and some are worth at least a genuflect. If you're traveling with children, count on being begged to stop.

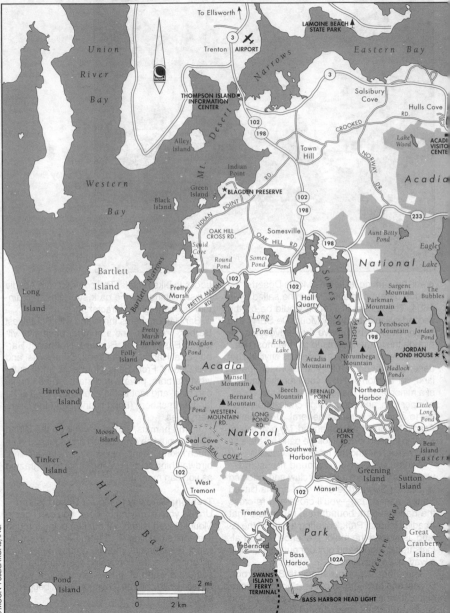

© MOON PUBLICATIONS, INC.

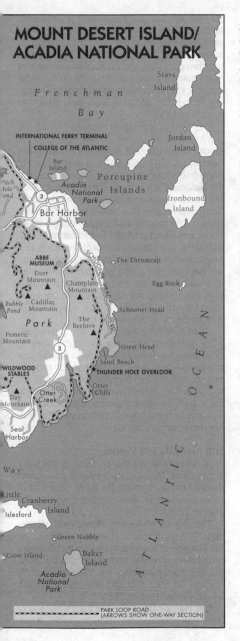

MOUNT DESERT ISLAND/ ACADIA NATIONAL PARK

Frenchman

Bay

Stave Island

INTERNATIONAL FERRY TERMINAL
COLLEGE OF THE ATLANTIC

Jordan Island

Bar Island

Porcupine

Acadia National Park

Islands

itch ole ond

Bar Harbor

Ironbound Island

ABBE MUSEUM

The Thrumcap

Dorr Mountain

Champlain Mountain

Egg Rock

Bubble Pond

Cadillac Mountain

SCHOONER HEAD RD

Schooner Head

Park

The Beehive

Pemetic Mountain

Great Head

Sand Beach

WILDWOOD STABLES

THUNDER HOLE OVERLOOK

Day Mountain

Otter Creek

Otter Cliffs

Seal Harbor

O C E A N

Way

Little Cranberry Island

Islesford

Green Nubble

A T L A N T I C

Crow Island

Baker Island

Acadia National Park

PARK LOOP ROAD
(ARROWS SHOW ONE-WAY SECTION)

Before or after visiting Mount Desert Island, if you're headed farther Down East—to Lamoine, the eastern side of Hancock County, and beyond—there's a good shortcut from Trenton. About five miles south of Ellsworth on Rt. 3, just north of the Acadia Zoo, turn east onto Rt. 204.

Attractions: What kid doesn't like water slides, mini-golf, and go-karts? Indulgent parents can join in the fun at **Seacoast Fun Park,** Bar Harbor Rd., Rt. 3, Trenton, tel. (207) 667-3573, mailing address P.O. Box 5193, Ellsworth 04605, or settle in at one of the picnic tables overlooking the monstrous blue water slides. Good thing here is that there are options for a range of ages—even a video arcade (popular with teenagers, as is the sand-volleyball court). A snack bar serves typical snack-bar fare. General admission ($15) covers all day on the water slide, plus one round each of golf and go-karts. Separate fees are available for individual activities. The park, 2.8 miles south of downtown Ellsworth, is open daily, Memorial Day to Labor Day. In spring and fall, it's also open weekends, when water-slide water is heated.

Roaming the 30 acres at the **Acadia Zoo,** Bar Harbor Rd., Rt. 3, Trenton, tel. (207) 667-3244, mailing address Box 113, RFD 1, Ellsworth 04605, a nonprofit educational facility, are more than 100 exotic and not-so-exotic creatures—reindeer, bison, wolves, moose, and more. Enter the barn and—voilà—you're in a simulated rain forest populated with monkeys, Amazon fishes, and tropical birds and reptiles. Little tykes love the petting zoo, where pony rides are offered during July and August. Admission is $5 adults and $4 seniors and children 3-12; no charge for children under three. The zoo is open daily at 9:30 a.m., early May to mid-October.

Since 1982, **Acadia Air,** Bar Harbor Rd., Rt. 3, Trenton, tel. (207) 667-5534, mailing address Ellsworth 04605, has been providing low-level flightseeing service in the Mount Desert Island region. Seven options range $15-37 pp for 10- to 45-minute flights. Everyone has a window seat in the three-passenger Cessna 172. Children under two are free if seated in an adult's lap. Most popular is the 22-minute Somes Sound route ($22 adults, $11 children under 75 pounds; minimum two adult fares), offering glimpses of lighthouses, mountains, harbors, and islands—

plus the entire length of five-mile Somes Sound. The appeal to small children depends on parents, kids, and their relevant experience. Some kids love these flights, others would be terrified. Acadia Air is based at a roadside booth next to Hancock County/Bar Harbor Airport, just north of Mount Desert Island and 12 miles north of downtown Bar Harbor. Flights are first-come, first-served; the wait is seldom longer than 20 minutes. Planes operate daily, weather permitting, mid-May through October (fall foliage flights are fabulous); winter flights can be arranged by appointment.

Lodgings and Lobster: As you make your way from Ellsworth to Mount Desert Island along Rt. 3 (Bar Harbor Road), you'll pass plenty of **motels and cabins.** If you're sensitive to highway noise and/or want to be closer to Bar Harbor and Acadia National Park, keep going. If your budget is tight, you may want to stop along here —and at the height of summer, when No Vacancy signs sprout all around Bar Harbor, these lodgings sometimes have the only remaining beds for travelers who haven't planned ahead.

Route 3 (Bar Harbor Road) is lined with eateries, including several lobster "pounds" that deserve a stop. One of the best-known and longest-running (since 1956) is **Trenton Bridge Lobster Pound,** Rt. 3, Bar Harbor Rd., Trenton, tel. (207) 667-2977, on the right, next to the bridge leading to Mount Desert Island. Watch for the "smoke signals"—steam billowing from the huge vats; the lobster couldn't be much fresher. The pound is open daily, May to mid-October.

Four miles southwest of Rt. 3, on Rt. 230, **Oak Point Lobster Pound,** tel. (207) 667-8548, is another popular spot where chowder, lobsters, and steamed clams pack 'em in. Be prepared to wait—Oak Point is no secret. Kick back and enjoy the fabulous waterfront view. Steaks are available for those who shun seafood. In August, save room for the blueberry pie. Wheelchair accessible; liquor license. Oak Point opens at 5 p.m. daily, mid-June to mid-September.

Mount Desert Island Information
Trenton is home to two information centers designed to orient you to Mount Desert Island.

A for-profit operation that sounds like it's connected to Acadia National Park but isn't, the **Acadia Information Center,** Rt. 3, Bar Harbor

Rd., Trenton, tel. (207) 667-8550 or (800) 248-9250, fax (207) 244-3020, is the first info center you'll encounter along the way. Clean restrooms, a new building, telephones, some high-tech interactive gadgetry, and racks of brochures and maps make it worth stopping. It's on the right, only a thousand feet before the bridge to Thompson Island. The center is open daily 10 a.m.-8 p.m., May 1-Oct. 15.

The best independent resource for all the communities of Mount Desert Island is the **Mount Desert Island Regional Information Center,** tel. (207) 288-3411, a joint project of the island's four chambers of commerce and the National Park Service. There's information here on the park and its campground vacancies (but be sure to stop also at the park's visitor center). The modern building, on bridge-linked Thompson Island in Mount Desert Narrows, has restrooms, pay phones, scads of brochures and maps, and particularly congenial staffers who will help you find a bed or campsite and plan your visit. Across the road is an attractive picnic spot overlooking the Narrows. The center is open May 15 to Columbus Day, daily 9 a.m.-6 p.m. (to 8 p.m. in July and August).

Acadia Weekly Magazine, tel. (207) 288-9025, published each week from mid-June to Columbus Day, is a useful 50-page booklet emphasizing Acadia National Park but also carrying ads and features for other parts of the island. It's available free, almost everywhere you look on the island. The same publisher also produces a free annual menu booklet, primarily for Bar Harbor restaurants.

MDI Festivals and Events
This list only skims the surface of the busy schedule on Mount Desert Island; check with the information centers for up-to-date lists of other happenings. Also check the weekly *Bar Harbor Times.*

The year-round **Arcady Music Festival** presents 8 p.m. concerts Thursday evenings on the College of the Atlantic campus, offering a broad array of music, from ragtime to classical. For information, write or call the festival at 93 Cottage St., P.O. Box 780, Bar Harbor 04609, tel. (207) 288-2141 or 288-3151.

Bar Harbor Days fills the third weekend of June with special events including races, a barbecue, a parade, and more in downtown Bar Harbor. A highlight is the Lobster Race, a crustacean competition drawing contestants such as Lobzilla and Larry the Lobster in a four-lane saltwater tank on the Village Green.

The **Fourth of July** is always a big deal in Bar Harbor, celebrated with a blueberry-pancake breakfast (6 a.m.), a parade (10 a.m.), a seafood festival (11 a.m. on), a band concert, and fireworks. And Independence Day celebrations in the smaller villages evoke a bygone era. Concerts, workshops, and display booths are all parts of the **Downeast Dulcimer and Folk Harp Festival,** organized by Bar Harbor's Song of the Sea music shop, tel. (207) 288-5653, the second weekend in July at St. Saviour's Church and Agamont Park, Bar Harbor. In even-numbered years, the **Mount Desert Garden Club Tour** presents a rare chance to visit some of Maine's most spectacular private gardens the second or third Saturday in July (confirm the date in advance with Bar Harbor Chamber of Commerce). The **Bar Harbor Music Festival,** a summer tradition since 1967, emphasizes up-and-coming musical talent in a series of classical, jazz, and pops concerts, usually Fridays and Sundays, at various island locations early July through early August. Reservations are wise: tel. (207) 288-5744 in July and August, (212) 222-1026 off season. Tickets are $15. For more music, the **Bar Harbor Town Band** performs free Monday and Thursday evening (8 p.m.) on the Village Green, Main and Mt. Desert Sts., Bar Harbor, throughout July and August.

The Abbe Museum and Maine Indian Basketmakers Alliance sponsors the **Indian Basketmakers' Sale and Evening of Story, Song, and Dance** 10 a.m.-4 p.m., the first Saturday of August. Free admission at Gates Auditorium, College of the Atlantic, Bar Harbor.

The **Sweet Chariot Music Festival,** tel. (207) 526-4443, is a unique three-day midweek festival of folk singing and traditional sea music. Windjammers and other traditional and modern vessels converge on Swans Island from all over the Gulf of Maine for jampacked concerts ashore each evening at 7:30 p.m. in Burnt Coat Harbor the first or second week of August. The **Directions Craft Show** fills the second or third weekend of August with extraordinary displays and sales of crafts by members of Directions.

You'll find it at the Maine Crafts Guild Friday 5-9 p.m., and at MDI High School, Rt. 233, Saturday and Sunday 10 a.m.-5 p.m.

Emergencies

Mount Desert Island's only full-service hospital is **Mt. Desert Island Hospital,** 10 Wayman Ln., Bar Harbor 04609, tel. (207) 288-5081, with a 24-hour emergency room, tel. (207) 288-8439. The next-closest facility is in Ellsworth, and the nearest major medical center is Eastern Maine Medical Center, in Bangor.

For ambulance service, and police and fire emergencies, call 911 in **Bar Harbor,** and (207) 276-5111 in the towns of **Northeast Harbor and Mount Desert.** Within the town of **Southwest Harbor,** call (207) 244-5030 for the ambulance, (207) 244-5233 for the fire department, and (207) 244-5552 for the police department.

Getting There and Away

The **Bar Harbor Airport,** Rt. 3, Bar Harbor Rd., Trenton, 12 miles from downtown Bar Harbor, is centrally located for anyone headed for Mount Desert Island. **Continental Connection** (formerly Colgan Air), tel. (800) 525-0280, operates daily commuter-plane service from Boston to Bar Harbor Airport, with a stop in Rockland (Knox County Municipal Airport). Flight time is about 80 minutes. The airline will also arrange other connections beyond Boston. Larger jets (usually less expensive) arrive at Bangor International Airport, 50 miles away. Hertz and Budget have rental-car offices at the Bar Harbor Airport; in summer, be sure to reserve a car well in advance. By car, Bar Harbor is 268 miles from Boston.

Bar Harbor is the starting point for the summertime car-and-passenger ferry to Yarmouth, Nova Scotia, which shaves 600 miles off the driving route. From early June to mid-October, the ferry departs each day at 8 a.m., stops briefly in Yarmouth, and returns to Bar Harbor. The midsummer day-cruise roundtrip fare is $45 adults, $40 seniors, $20 children. Normal one-way summer rates are $42 adults, $38 seniors, $21 children 5-12. A car is $55 one-way in summer. Reservations are wise, especially if you're taking a car. For a current schedule and other fare information, call (888) 249-7245. From July to mid-October, the **Yarmouth County Tourism**

Association, tel. (207) 288-9432 or (902) 742-5355, staffs an information office at the ferry terminal (Rt. 3, Bar Harbor).

ROUTE 3 TOWARD BAR HARBOR

Just after the Thompson Island information center, you're faced with a choice—Rt. 3 toward the Acadia National Park Visitor Center and Bar Harbor or Rt. 102/198 toward Southwest Harbor and lesser-known parts of the island's "quiet side." Here's what you'll first encounter if you head toward the Bar Harbor side.

Shopping: On Rt. 3, one and a half miles east of Thompson Island, watch for the gray building of the **MDI Workshop,** RFD 1, Box 2042, Bar Harbor 04609, tel. (207) 288-5252. Developmentally disabled adults have made everything in the well-stocked shop—quilts, chairs, note cards, birdhouses, and more—and they benefit from all proceeds. The shop is open all year, Mon.-Sat. 9 a.m.-5 p.m.; there's a seasonal branch in Northeast Harbor.

Accommodations: Staying in the northern end of the island means informality, less hubbub than in Bar Harbor, and relatively lower prices. **The Cove Farm Inn Bed & Breakfast,** Crooked Rd., RFD 1, Box 420, Bar Harbor 04609, tel. (207) 288-5355 or (800) 291-0952, run by the Keene family, is a great place to bring the kids and let down your hair. Everyone mixes in. There's a guest refrigerator, a guest vegetable patch, and you can even use the kitchen to pack picnics. The farm has resident roosters, ducks, and geese. Jerry Keene, an island expert, loves sharing his local knowledge. No smoking, no pets. Eleven basic rooms (some private baths, some shared) go for $40-115 d July to mid-October, lower rates off season. Two separate housekeeping cottages, each sleeping eight, are $125-205 a week in summer, $85 d per night off season. The B&B is open May-Feb., the cottages are open all year. Cove Farm is a quarter of a mile west of Rt. 3, near Hulls Cove and the Acadia visitor center.

Within two miles of Thompson Island are two well-sited **campgrounds,** both fairly large and well maintained. Next to the causeway, and 10 miles northwest of Bar Harbor, **Barcadia Campground,** RFD 1, Box 2165, Bar Harbor 04609,

tel. (207) 288-3520, occupies 40 acres with 200 open and wooded tent and RV sites. Views are terrific. Facilities include coin showers and laundry, playground, beach, game areas, small shop, and a shuttle bus to Bar Harbor. Pets are allowed. Rates are $17-30 a night (four persons) late June to Labor Day, $14-26 (two persons) other months. Open mid-May to mid-October.

Mt. Desert Narrows Camping Resort, RR1, Box 2045, Bar Harbor 04609, tel. (207) 288-4782, one and a half miles east of the causeway, has a fantastic view over Thomas Bay and the Narrows. The 40-acre campground has 210 wooded and open tent and RV sites, heated pool, convenience store, canoe rentals, playground, coin laundry, shuttle bus to Bar Harbor, and live entertainment mid-June to Labor Day. Pets are allowed. Sites are $20-39 per night (two persons) mid-June to Labor Day, $17-30 other months. Open May 1 to late October.

ACADIA NATIONAL PARK

America's first national park east of the Mississippi River, and the only national park in the northeastern United States, Acadia National Park covers more than 40,000 acres on Mount Desert Island, the neighboring Schoodic Peninsula, and several islands close by and farther offshore. Within the boundaries of this splendid space are mountains, lakes, ponds, trails, fabulous vistas, and several campgrounds. Each year, some three million visitors bike, hike, and drive into and through the park. Yet even at the height of summer, when the whole world seems to have arrived here, it's possible to find peaceful niches and less-trodden paths.

History
Thanks to the incredible drive and determination of a handful of astute environmentalists, Acadia National Park became reality on January 19, 1929, after previous incarnations as Sieur de Monts National Monument (1916) and Lafayette National Park (1919). Inspired and prodded by dedicated conservationist George B. Dorr, benevolent summer and year-round citizens donated land and campaigned for federal recognition of the park. Starting as the Hancock County Trustees of Public Reservations, the group

ACADIA NATIONAL PARK HIGHLIGHTS

The highlights listed here are within the park territory on Mount Desert Island.

Cadillac Mountain: Acadia's prime highlight is the tallest point on the eastern seaboard, allegedly where the sun's first rays land. You can drive, bike, or hike to the 1,530-foot summit for head-swiveling vistas, and a gift shop and restrooms. Be sure to walk the paved, .3-mile Summit Trail loop for the full effect.

Carriage Roads: On the eastern side of Mount Desert Island, some 57 miles of meandering, crushed-stone paths, crossing 17 handsome stone bridges, welcome walkers, bikers, horseback riders, snowshoers, and cross-country skiers.

Hiking Trails: Besides the carriage roads, the park has more than 120 miles of easy, moderate, and rugged trails just for hikers.

Naturalist Programs: Park rangers present lectures and lead 1- to 3-hour walks and hikes throughout the summer season. Most are free, some require reservations; many are specially geared to children and families. For reservations call (207) 288-5262. Park rangers also accompany several natural and cultural history cruises, all requiring reservations and fees.

Park Loop Road: If you have only a few hours for exploring Acadia, the best capsule experience is the paved, 20-mile Park Loop Road, followed clockwise. (The road to the Cadillac Mountain summit adds another seven miles, roundtrip, to this total.)

Bass Harbor Head Light: This cliffside lighthouse within park boundaries at the southern tip of Mount Desert Island is a prime photo-op site.

acquired land parcel by parcel, eventually turning it over to federal jurisdiction. Corporate giant John D. Rockefeller, Jr., owner of a sprawling summer estate on Mount Desert Island, was responsible for securing nearly a third of the park's acreage, as well as building the unique 57-mile carriage-road system. In 1935, his contribution was valued at $4 million. Even today, the park continues to expand as philanthropic individuals donate more land to benefit future generations.

Information

To plan a park visit, write or call Information, Acadia National Park, P.O. Box 177, Bar Harbor, ME 04609, tel. (207) 288-3338. Be sure to request a park map, a carriage-road map, a hiking-

trail list, and camping information. The park also publishes an access guide, detailing wheelchair accessibility of information centers, campgrounds, shops, cruises, museums, and trails. Other flyers worth requesting cover geology, plants, birds, mammals, and the park's history.

Once you arrive on the island and head toward Bar Harbor, make your first stop the modern **visitor center,** tel. (207) 288-3338, on Rt. 3 in Hulls Cove, eight miles southeast of the causeway to the island. Here you can rendezvous with pals, make reservations for natural and cultural history programs, watch a short park presentation, rent or buy cassette guides, admire the view of Frenchman Bay, and use the restrooms. Pick up a copy of the summertime *Beaver Log,* a tabloid listing the schedule of park activities.

Parking is ample, although the lot gets mighty full in midsummer, when 9,000 people a day visit the center. Ascend a stairway from the parking lot to the center, which is open May-Oct., 8 a.m.-4:30 p.m., to 6 p.m. July through August. From November to April, information is available daily at **Acadia National Park Headquarters,** Rt. 233, about three and a half miles west of downtown Bar Harbor. The office is closed only Thanksgiving, Christmas, and New Year's Day.

Friends of Acadia

One of the park's greatest assets today is an energetic membership organization called Friends of Acadia (FOA), founded in 1986 to preserve and protect the park for resource-sensitive tourism and myriad recreational uses. You can join FOA and support the cause—$25 a year; Box 725, 43 Cottage St., Bar Harbor 04609, tel. (207) 288-3340, or just lend a hand while you're here. FOA organizes volunteer work parties for Acadia trail and road maintenance three times weekly between May and mid-October: Tuesday, Thursday, and Saturday 9 a.m.-1 p.m. Call (207) 288-3340 for the work locations. This is a terrific way to give something back to the park, and the camarad-

Sand Beach

SHERRY STREETER

erie is contagious. Be sure to take your own water.

Even if you don't have time to join a work party, be a conscientious trailkeeper as you hike, and carry a small trash bag.

Park Loop Road

The best way to fully appreciate Acadia is to hike the trails, bike the carriage roads, canoe and swim the ponds, and camp overnight. But if your time is limited, the 20-mile Park Loop Road covers scenic highlights, including access to the summit of Cadillac Mountain. (Going to the summit adds another seven miles.) A drive-it-yourself tour booklet ($1) is available at the park's visitor center. Start at the parking lot below the visitor center and follow the signs pointing in a clockwise direction; part of the loop is one-way. Traffic gets heavy at midday in midsummer, so aim for an early morning start. Maximum speed is 35 mph, but be alert for gawkers and photographers stopping without warning. Along the route are lots of trailheads, scenic overlooks, Sand Beach, Thunder Hole, Otter Cliffs, Jordan Pond House, and Eagle Lake, plus the Cadillac summit. Between Schooner Head overlook and Sand Beach is the park's entrance station. The park admission fee is $5 per vehicle (valid for one day), $3 per cyclist or pedestrian (valid for four days), or $10 for a four-day vehicle pass. An annual pass is $20. To drive up Cadillac without doing the rest of the Park Loop Road, take the Cadillac Mountain access road off Rt. 233, west of Bar Harbor. It's three and a half miles to the top.

The road is also open to bicyclists (as are the carriage roads, unlike the hiking trails). While the carriage roads are more scenic (and don't permit cars), the Park Loop Road provides an excellent workout and sightseeing opportunity for mountain bikers. (But get an early start or go late in the day to minimize breathing automobile exhaust fumes.)

Recreation

The Carriage-Road System: John D. Rockefeller, Jr., began laying out the 57-mile carriage-road system in 1913, overseeing the project through the 1940s. Motorized vehicles have never been allowed on these lovely graded byways, making them real escapes from the auto world. Devoted now to multiple uses, the "Rockefeller roads" see hikers, bikers, baby strollers, horse-drawn carriages, even wheelchairs. Busiest times are 10 a.m.-2 p.m.

Pick up a free copy of the carriage-road map at the visitor center; road maintenance is ongoing, a constant battle, so be sure to inquire about any road closings.

The most crowded carriage roads are those closest to the visitor center—the Witch Hole Loop, Duck Brook, and Eagle Lake. Avoid these, opting instead for roads west of Jordan Pond, or go early in the morning or late in the day. Better still, go off season, when you can enjoy the fall foliage (late September/early October) or winter's cross-country skiing.

If you need a bicycle to explore the carriage roads, see the "Bar Harbor" and "Southwest Harbor" sections for rental information. Be forewarned that hikers are allowed on the carriage roads that spill over onto private property south of the Jordan Pond House, but cyclists are not. *Bikers must be especially speed-sensitive on the carriage roads, keeping an eye out for hikers, small children, and the hearing impaired.*

To recapture the early carriage-roads era, take one of the horse-drawn open-carriage tours run by **Wildwood Stables,** a mile south of the Jordan Pond House, on the Park Loop Rd., P.O. Box 241, Seal Harbor 04675, tel. (207) 276-3622. Six one- and two-hour trips start at 9:30 a.m. daily, mid-June to Columbus Day. Reservations are not required, but they're a good idea, especially in midsummer. Best outing is the two-hour **Sunset at the Summit** to the top of Day Mountain, departing at 6:30 p.m. in June, 6:15 p.m. in July and 6 p.m. in August. Cost is $15 adults, less for seniors and children. Other routes are $12 and $13 per adult. (Besides the horse-carriage tours based in the park itself and ranger-accompanied cruises, a couple of bus-tour firms operate out of Bar Harbor. See the "Bar Harbor" section for information on boat, bus, and trolleybus tours.)

Hikes: If you're spending more than a day on Mount Desert Island, plan to buy a copy of *A Walk in the Park: Acadia's Hiking Guide,* by Tom St. Germain, which details more than 60 hikes, including some outside the park. Remember that pets are allowed on park trails, but only on leashes no longer than six feet. Here's a handful of personal favorite Acadia hikes, ranging from easy to rugged.

• **Jordan Pond Nature Trail:** Start at the Jordan Pond parking area; easy, one-mile wooded loop trail; pick up a brochure. Include Jordan Pond House in your schedule.

• **Ship Harbor Nature Trail:** Start at the Ship Harbor parking area, on Rt. 102A between Bass Harbor and Seawall Campground, in the southwestern corner of the island; easy, 1.3-mile loop trail leading to the shore; pick up a brochure at the trailhead. Ship Harbor is particularly popular among birders seeking warblers, and you just might spot an eagle while you picnic on the rocks. An even easier trail, with its parking area just east of the Ship

Harbor parking area, is **Wonderland.** It's 1.4 miles roundtrip. Across Rt. 102A from Wonderland is **Seawall Bog,** attractive primarily to birders. Be sure to stay on the trails (worn but not marked); the peat underfoot is especially fragile.

• **Great Head Trail:** A moderate, 1.4-mile loop trail starts at the eastern end of Sand Beach, off the Park Loop Road. Park in the Sand Beach parking area and cross the beach to the trailhead. Or take Schooner Head Rd. from downtown Bar Harbor and park in the small area where the road dead-ends. There are actually two trail loops here, both of which have enough elevation to provide terrific views.

• **Beech Mountain:** Also a moderate hike, Beech Mountain's summit has an abandoned fire tower, from which you can look out toward Long Pond and the Blue Hill Peninsula. Roundtrip on the wooded route is about 1.2 miles, although a couple of side trails can extend it. You'll have less competition here, in a quieter part of the park. Take Rt. 102 south from Somesville, heading toward Pretty Marsh. Turn left onto Beech Hill Rd. and follow it to the parking area at the end.

• **Beehive Trail** and **Precipice Trail:** These two are the park's toughest routes, with sheer faces and iron ladders; Precipice often is closed (usually mid-April through August) to protect nesting peregrine falcons. If challenges are your thing and these trails are open (check beforehand at the visitor center), go ahead. But a fine alternative in the difficult category is the **Beachcroft Trail** on Huguenot Head. Also called the Beachcroft Path, the trail is best known for its 1,500 beautifully engineered granite steps. Roundtrip is about 2.2 miles, or you can continue a loop at the top, taking in the Bear Brook Trail on Champlain Mtn., for about 4.4 miles. The parking area is just north of Rt. 3, near the Abbe Museum and Sieur de Monts Spring, and just west of the Park Loop Road, near the Jackson Memorial Laboratory.

Rock Climbing: The park's only approved rock climbing areas are Otter Cliffs and the south wall of Champlain Mountain. Sadly, rope friction and overuse have led to receding vegetation on Otter Cliffs. Registration boxes exist at both locations. Unless you're a pro, the best advice is to contact an outfitter in Bar Harbor and sign on for a half-day climbing experience, including professional lessons and at least one rappel. From mid-May to September, **Acadia Mountain Guides Climbing School,** 137 Cottage St., P.O. Box 937, Bar Harbor 04609, tel. (207) 288-8186, off season P.O. Box 121, Orono 04473, tel. (207) 866-7562, offers all levels of instruction and guided climbs for individuals and families in Acadia as well as in Camden, Clifton, and Baxter State Park. All gear is provided. Costs vary widely, depending on site, number of climbers, and session length.

Swimming: Sand Beach, next to the Park Loop Road and south of the entrance station, is the park's only sandy beach on salt water. Lifeguards are on duty during the summer, and even then, the biggest threat can be hypothermia. The water is terminally glacial, and even though kids seem not to notice, they can become chilled quickly. The best solution is to walk to the far end of the beach, where a warmer, shallow stream meets the ocean. On a hot August day, arrive early; the parking lot fills up. Bring a picnic.

A less-crowded saltwater beach, not in the park, is at the head of the appealing harbor in chic Seal Harbor, a few miles east of Northeast Harbor.

Don't assume you can swim in any freshwater pond or lake you encounter. Six island locations—Upper and Lower Hadlock Ponds, Bubble and Jordan Ponds, Eagle Lake, and the southern half of Long Pond—are reservoirs where swimming is banned (but not boating).

The most popular freshwater swimming site, staffed with a lifeguard and inevitably crowded on hot days, is **Echo Lake,** south of Somesville on Rt. 102. If you have a canoe, kayak, or rowboat, you can reach swimming holes in **Round, Seal Cove,** or **Somes Pond** (all on the western side of Mount Desert). The eastern shore of **Hodgdon Pond** (also on the western side of the island) is accessible by car (via Hodgdon Road and Long Pond Fire Road). **Lake Wood** (at the northern end of Mount Desert) has a small beach and auto access. To get to Lake Wood from Rt. 3, head west on Crooked Rd. to unpaved Park Road. Turn left and continue to the parking area, which will be crowded on a hot day, so arrive early.

The best guide to the entire island's freshwater attractions is *The Lakes and Ponds of Mt. Desert,* by William V. P. Newlin (see the Booklist).

Accommodations and Food
The only accommodations within Acadia National Park are two **campgrounds,** Seawall and Blackwoods, neither of which has RV hookups. In addition, the park operates a handful of lean-to campsites, at its Duck Harbor location on Isle au Haut. Commercial campgrounds and a variety of other lodgings are located all over Mount Desert Island.

Both campgrounds have seasonal restrooms (no showers) and dumping stations. Both also have amphitheaters, where park rangers present free, hour-long evening programs (usually at 9 p.m.) during the summer on a variety of natural- and cultural-history topics. Noncampers are also welcome at these events.

With more than 300 campsites, **Blackwoods Campground,** just off Rt. 3, five miles south of Bar Harbor, is open all year. Reservations are required only between June 15 and Sept. 15, tel. (800) 365-2267; have your credit card handy. Cost is $16 per site per night. Camping is free Dec.-March, and no reservations are necessary; off-season facilities include pit toilets, fire rings, and a hand-operated water pump. When bathrooms are open off season, the campsite fee is $8 a night.

No reservations are required at **Seawall Campground,** on Rt. 102A, four miles south of Southwest Harbor, but you'll need to arrive as early as 8 a.m. in midsummer to secure one of the 200 or so sites. Seawall is open Memorial Day weekend through September. Cost is $14 per night for drive-up sites and $10 per night for walk-in sites.

The only full-service restaurant within the park is the **Jordan Pond House,** tel. (207) 276-3316, a modern facility in a spectacular waterside setting. Jordan Pond House is a destination—an oasis for indulging in tea, popovers, and extraordinary strawberry jam, served on the lawn each summer and fall afternoon 2:30-5:30 p.m., weather permitting. Not exactly a bargain at $5.50, but it's worth it. However, Jordan Pond is far from a secret, so expect to wait for seats at the height of summer. (You *can* call ahead to put your name on the waiting list for seats.)

Jordan Pond House began life as a rustic 19th-century teahouse; wonderful old photos still line the walls of the current incarnation, which went up following a disastrous fire in 1979. The restaurant is open daily 11:30 a.m.-8 p.m., mid-May to mid-October (to 9 p.m. July and August). Although the menu is unstartling ($10-18 for dinner entrées), you'll need reservations for lunch and dinner, and it's a good idea to call at least an hour in advance for afternoon-tea reservations.

Emergencies

If you have an emergency while in the park, call (207) 288-3369 or 288-3360. The nearest hospital is in Bar Harbor. The nearest major medical center is in Bangor, via a congested route that can take well over an hour at the height of summer. Best advice for averting emergencies: Be cautious and sensible in everything you undertake in the park. Don't hike alone or go off the trails—people are seriously injured or killed falling from the cliffs nearly every year.

BAR HARBOR AND VICINITY

In 1996, Bar Harbor celebrated the bicentennial of its founding (as Eden). In the late 19th century and well into the 20th, the town grew to become one of the east coast's fanciest summer watering holes.

In those days, steamboats arrived from points south, large and small resort hotels sprang up, and exclusive mansions (quaintly dubbed "cottages") were the venues of parties thrown by resident Drexels, DuPonts, Vanderbilts, and prominent academics, journalists, and lawyers. The "rusticators" came for the season, with huge entourages of servants, children, pets, and horses. The area's renown was such that by the 1890s, even the staffs of the British, Austrian, and Ottoman embassies retreated here from summers in Washington, DC.

The establishment of the national park, in 1919, and the arrival of the motorcar changed the character of Bar Harbor and Mount Desert Island; two world wars and the Great Depression took an additional toll in myriad ways; but the

coup de grâce for Bar Harbor's era of elegance came in 1947.

Nothing in the history of Bar Harbor and Mount Desert Island stands out like the Great Fire of 1947, a wind-whipped conflagration that devastated more than 17,000 acres on the eastern half of the island and leveled gorgeous mansions, humble homes, and more trees than anyone could ever count. Only three people died, but property damage was estimated at $2 million. Whole books have been written about the October inferno; fascinating scrapbooks in Bar Harbor's Jesup Memorial Library dramatically relate the gripping details of the story. Even though some of the elegant cottages have survived, the fire altered life here forever.

Bar Harbor Today

Land in Bar Harbor in mid-July and you'll find it tough to believe that the year-round population is only 4,700. Bar Harbor is liveliest (in both positive and negative senses) in July and August, but the season keeps stretching. Many clued-in travelers try to take advantage of September's prime weather, relative quiet, and spectacular foliage, although even September activity has stepped up in recent years. In the dead of winter, the town is close to moribund, kept alive by devoted year-rounders; the students and faculty of the College of the Atlantic, a unique four-year liberal-arts college geared to environmental studies; and the staff of the internationally recognized Jackson Laboratory for Mammalian Research.

If you're traveling with children, Bar Harbor can be a very convenient base of operations, comprising a smallish downtown area where kids can walk around, play in the parks, hang out at the waterfront, buy ice cream, and hit the movies. It's also a source for sporting-gear rentals and the starting point for boat, bus, and kayaking tours. Staying downtown and not having to rely totally on a car in summer can be a real plus, but the high cost of even ordinary lodging—especially for families—is a minus. Bar Harbor Chamber of Commerce staffers are particularly adept at rounding up rooms, but don't abuse their helpfulness—contact them early and plan well ahead for a height-of-summer holiday.

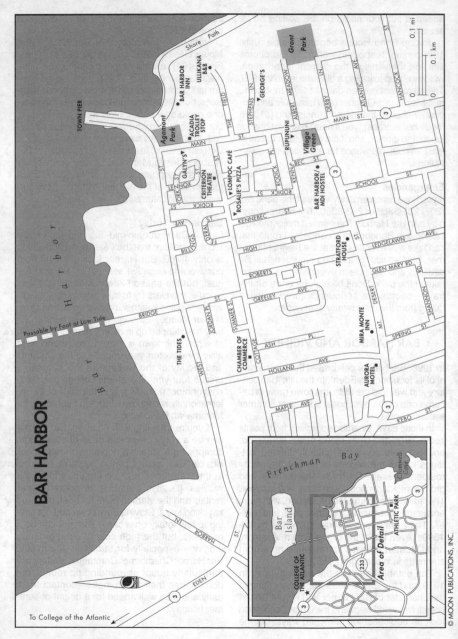

BAR HARBOR

© MOON PUBLICATIONS, INC.

To College of the Atlantic

Sights

Acadia National Park comes right up to the edge of town, providing enough sights and activities to fill weeks, but the Bar Harbor area has attractions of its own.

World renowned in genetic research, **The Jackson Laboratory for Mammalian Research,** 600 Main St., Rt. 3, Bar Harbor 04609, tel. (207) 288-3371, breeds special mice used to study cancer, diabetes, muscular dystrophy, and other diseases—with considerable success. From early June to late September (except the middle week of August), a lively audiovisual program explains the lab's impressive work. The free, hour-long program, Tuesday and Thursday only, begins at 3 p.m. in the lab's auditorium. The lab is one and a half miles south of downtown Bar Harbor.

St. Saviour's Episcopal Church, 41 Mt. Desert St., Bar Harbor 04609, tel. (207) 288-4215, close to downtown Bar Harbor, boasts Maine's largest collection of Tiffany stained-glass windows. In July and August, volunteers conduct free tours of the Victorian-era (1878) church Mon.-Sat. at 11 a.m. and 3 p.m., and Sunday at 3 p.m. The church is open daily, dawn to dusk. Off season, call to arrange a tour. If you're intrigued by old cemeteries, spend time wandering the old town graveyard next to the church. St. Saviour's is also the site of a summertime hostel.

At the northern edge of Mount Desert Island, eight and a half miles northwest of downtown Bar Harbor, is the **Bar Harbor Oceanarium,** Rt. 3, Bar Harbor 04609, tel. (207) 288-5005, one of the island's two related aquariums. As with its sister site (in Southwest Harbor), this low-tech, high-interest operation awes the kids—with a tank full of live harbor seals, a marsh walk to check out tidal creatures and vegetation, and a lobsterman who answers all their questions and explains lobstering life and lore. At the aquarium's adjacent lobster hatchery, visitor can view thousands of tiny lobster hatchlings. The Oceanarium and the hatchery building are open Mon.-Sat. 9 a.m.-5 p.m., mid-May to late October. Oceanarium tickets are $6 adults, $4.50 children 4-12; hatchery tickets are $3.95 adults, $2.75 children. This gets rather pricey, but combination tickets, covering these two sections and the Oceanarium in Southwest Harbor, are $11.95 adults, $8.75 children.

Located on the College of the Atlantic campus (but scheduled to move into dedicated quarters of its own in early 1999), the **Natural History Museum,** 105 Eden St., Rt. 3, Bar Harbor 04609, tel. (207) 288-5015, showcases regional birds and mammals in realistic dioramas. Biggest attraction for children is the Discovery Room, with a please-touch philosophy. Tickets are $2.50 adults, $1.50 seniors and students (13-18), and $1 children (3-12); no charge for children under three. The museum is open daily 9 a.m.-5 p.m., mid-June to Labor Day. A daily interpretive program (11 a.m.) focuses on the museum collection; a Wednesday lecture series (8 p.m.) runs throughout July and August. The museum gift shop has a particularly good collection of books and gifts for budding naturalists. The college and its museum are located one-half mile northwest of downtown Bar Harbor.

About 2.3 miles south of Bar Harbor, at Sieur de Monts Spring, where Rt. 3 meets the Park Loop Road, is the **Abbe Museum,** Rt. 3, P.O. Box 286, Bar Harbor 04609, tel. (207) 288-3519, a superb place to introduce children (and adults) to prehistoric and historic Native American tools, crafts, and other cultural artifacts. Everything about this privately funded museum, established in 1927, is tasteful, including the park setting, a handsome National Historic Register building, and displays from a 50,000-item collection. Museum-sponsored summer events include craft workshops, hands-on children's programs, an **Indian Basketmakers' Sale** (held at the College of the Atlantic), and archaeological field schools. The museum is open mid-May to mid-October, 10 a.m.-4 p.m. (9 a.m.-5 p.m. in July and August). Tickets are $2 adults, 50 cents for kids under 12.

While you're at the Abbe Museum, take the time to wander the adjacent **Wild Gardens of Acadia,** an incredible .75-acre microcosm of more than 300 plant species native to Mount Desert Island. Nine separate display areas, carefully maintained and labeled by the Bar Harbor Garden Club, represent native plant habitats; pick up the map/brochure that explains each.

Historical Walking Tours

Calling their enterprise **Legends, Lies, & Local History,** Richard Sassaman and Susan Gross lead fascinating two-hour historical walking tours of downtown Bar Harbor. After combing local archives and culling reminiscences, the husband-and-wife writer/architect team started the business in 1995, following two different one-and-a-half-mile routes from the Village Green on Main Street. Wear comfortable shoes and just show up under the Centennial clock; no reservations needed. Bring questions; they have answers—and not canned ones (Richard is the author of the hilarious book *Bar Harbor Police Beat,* a collection of tidbits from the police blotter column in the *Bar Harbor Times*). Tours begin at 10 a.m. Tues.-Sat., mid-June to mid-September, except during downpours. Cost is $12.50 adults, $5 children 6-11, free for kids under six. For details, call (207) 288-5949.

Park Tours

The veteran of the Bar Harbor-based bus tours is **Acadia National Park Tours,** Bayside Landing, 53 Main St., P.O. Box 52, Bar Harbor 04609, tel. (207) 288-3327, operating Memorial Day weekend to mid-October. A two-and-a-half-hour, naturalist-led tour of Bar Harbor and Acadia departs at 10 a.m. and 2 p.m. daily from downtown Bar Harbor (look for the green-and-white bus across from Testa's). Reservations are wise in midsummer and during fall-foliage season (late September and early October); pick up reserved tickets 30 minutes before departure. Cost is $15 adults, $5 children 12 and under.

The same owners also operate a one-hour trolleybus tour, five times daily (between 10 a.m. and 6 p.m.), early July through October, including Bar Harbor mansion drive-bys and the Cadillac summit. Starting point and phone number are the same as for the bus. Dress warmly; it's an open-air trolley. Cost is $10 adults, $5 children. The bus and trolley routes both include potty stops.

For private tours of the park and other parts of the island, contact Michael Good at **Down East Nature Tours,** P.O. Box 521, Bar Harbor 04609, tel. (207) 288-8128. A biologist with a special interest in birds, he'll take neophyte birders on a four-hour tour they won't forget; tours happen 8 a.m.-noon or 1-5 p.m. What better place to begin a life list than Acadia National Park? Birding tours occur daily, rain or shine, starting at $15; maximum group is eight persons. Lodging pickup is available. Bring your own binoculars, but

Michael supplies a spotting scope. Other options, on demand, are two-hour wetland tours, Cadillac sunrise and sunset trips, and one-day excursions Down East to Washington County.

Recreation

Although Acadia steals the limelight for much of the island's recreation, Bar Harbor has its own pursuits—plus several outfitters for anyone headed to the park.

A real treat is a stroll along downtown Bar Harbor's **Shore Path,** a well-trodden, granite-edged byway built around 1880. Along the craggy shoreline are granite-and-wood benches, town-owned **Grant Park** (great for picnics), birch trees, and several handsome mansions (two of them now inns) that escaped the 1947 fire. Offshore are the four Porcupine Islands. The path is open 6:30 a.m.-dusk, and leashed pets are okay. Allow about 30 minutes for the mile loop beginning next to the Town Pier and the Bar Harbor Inn and returning via Wayman Lane. There's also access to the path next to the Balance Rock Inn.

Check the *Bar Harbor Times* or the Bar Harbor Chamber of Commerce visitor booklet for the times of low tide, then walk across the gravel bar (wear hiking boots or rubberized shoes) to wooded **Bar Island** (formerly Rodick's Island) from the foot of Bridge St. in downtown Bar Harbor. Shell heaps recorded on the eastern end of the island indicate that Native Americans enjoyed this turf in the distant past. You'll have the most time to explore the island during new-moon or full-moon low tides, but no more than three hours—an hour or so before and after low tide. Be sure to wear a watch so you don't get trapped (for up to 10 hours). The foot of Bridge Street is also an excellent kayak launching site.

Golf: Duffers first teed off in 1891 at **Kebo Valley Golf Club,** 100 Eagle Lake Rd., Rt. 233, Bar Harbor 04609, tel. (207) 288-3000, one of Maine's oldest clubs. The 17th hole is legendary; it took President William Howard Taft 27 tries to sink the ball in 1911. Kebo is very popular, with a gorgeous setting, an attractive clubhouse, and decent food service, so tee times are essential; greens fees ($34 in July and August) are the highest on the island. Open daily, May-Oct., the 18-hole course is a mile west of downtown Bar Harbor.

Bike Rentals: With all the great biking options, including 57 miles of carriage roads and some of the best roadside bike routes in Maine, you'll want to bring a bike or rent one here. Two firms are based in downtown Bar Harbor. **Acadia Bike & Canoe,** 48 Cottage St., Bar Harbor 04609, tel. (207) 288-9605 or (800) 526-8615 outside Maine, rents adult bikes for $16 a day, kids' bikes for $10; reserve with a credit card, preferably at least a day ahead. Helmets and maps are included. The shop opens at 8 a.m. daily in spring, summer, and fall. Down the street, at the National Park Outdoor Activities Center, the **Bar Harbor Bicycle Shop,** 141 Cottage St., Bar Harbor 04609, tel. (207) 288-3886, has earned a reputation for well-maintained bikes, renting for $9 a half-day and $14 all day; tandems are $18 and $25. Price includes a helmet, map, and optional child carrier. Hours in summer are 8 a.m.-8 p.m. daily, other months Tues.-Sat. 9 a.m.-5:30 p.m. The shop stays open March through Christmas.

Getting Afloat

Bar Harbor has so many ways for you to get out on the water that it would be a shame not to do it at least once. In addition to the whale-watching, lobster-fishing, sailing, and kayaking options, see "Getting There and Away" in the "Mount Desert Island" introduction for information on the car-and-passenger ferry service between Bar Harbor and Yarmouth, Nova Scotia.

Whalewatching/Lobstering Excursions: Whalewatching boats go as much as 20 miles offshore, so no matter what the weather in Bar Harbor, dress warmly and bring more clothing than you think you'll need—even gloves if you're especially sensitive to cold. Motion-sensitive children and adults should plan ahead with appropriate medication.

Humpback, finback, right, and minke whales are prime targets of Bar Harbor's oldest whale-watching firm, **Whale Watcher, Inc.,** 1 West St., P.O. Box 153, Bar Harbor 04609, tel. (207) 288-3322 or (800) 508-1499, which takes its sturdy, 105-foot *Whale Watcher* 20 miles offshore to spot the huge mammals. A naturalist provides commentary during the three-and-a-half-hour trip. Sightings usually occur, but the company offers a rain-check guarantee. No pets; wheelchair accessible; snack bar with beer and wine. Whalewatching trips operate June to late October; reservations are not needed after Labor Day, but the fall schedule tends to be less predictable. Headquartered in the same office, next to the Town Pier, are one- and two-hour nature/sightseeing excursions aboard the *Acadian,* one-and-a-half-hour lobstering excursions aboard the *Katherine,* and two-hour sailing trips aboard the 85-foot schooner *Bay Lady.* An Acadia National Park ranger narrates the *Acadian*'s 10 a.m. run. All trips are weather-dependent. Discount prices are available for two or more boat trips; children five and under are free on all boats, but kids tend to prefer the lobstering and whalewatching trips. Adult tickets are $10 (one-hour sightseeing) to $28 (whalewatching).

Bar Harbor Whale Watch Co., Rt. 3, Bar Harbor 04609, tel. (207) 288-2386 or (800) 942-5374, based at the Bar Harbor Regency Holiday Inn, northwest of downtown Bar Harbor, operates a 200-seat catamaran, *Friendship V,* which remains stable—a plus when you meet offshore swells. Downside is there isn't as much open deck space as on other boats. One sailing (at noon) early and late in the season; two or three sailings mid-June to late September. Tickets are $30 adults, $18 ages 6-14, free for children five and under; a downtown ticket office is located at 39 Cottage Street.

Sailboat and Powerboat Cruises: Captain Steve Pagels, under the umbrella of **Downeast Windjammer Cruises,** tel. (207) 288-4585 or 288-2373, mailing address P.O. Box 8, Cherryfield 04622, offers two-hour daysails on the 155-foot steel-hulled *Margaret Todd,* a gorgeous four-masted schooner built in 1997. Three or four daily trips, beginning around 8 a.m., mid-May to mid-October (weather permitting), depart from the Bar Harbor Inn pier, just east of the Town Pier in downtown Bar Harbor. A sunset cruise often includes live music; bring a picnic supper. Cost is $20 adults, $14 children under 12.

Under the same ownership is the 1920s-era, 65-foot motor vessel *Chippewa,* which hugs the shore and cruises past lighthouses and elegant mansions, doing three or four trips daily. Cost is $16 adults, $10 children under 12. The *Chippewa* is a handsomely restored classic, with an open upper deck and an enclosed cabin.

Sea Kayaking: Sea kayaking is wildly popular along the Maine coast, and Bar Harbor has become a mecca for practitioners. No experience is necessary to join tours operated by either of the firms in Bar Harbor. Half-day ($43), full-day ($65), and multi-day ($175-599) seakayak tours are on the schedule organized by **Coastal Kayaking Tours,** 48 Cottage St., P.O. Box 405, Bar Harbor 04609, tel. (207) 288-9605 or (800) 526-8615 outside Maine, a spirited operation that also rents kayaks, canoes, mountain bikes, camping equipment, and lots of related accessories. By prior arrangement, special half-day family tours can handle kids eight and over. A three-hour sunset cruise begins at 5 p.m. Other kayak trips are offered mid-May through September. All trips are weather-dependent, and reservations are essential. If you want to go it alone, solo kayaks rent for $35 a day.

Down the street, at the National Park Outdoor Activities Center, **National Park Sea Kayak Tours,** 137 Cottage St., Bar Harbor 04609, tel. (207) 288-0342 or (800) 347-0940 outside Maine, runs half-day coastal trips in two-person kayaks (six-boat maximum). Cost is $45 pp; children must be taller than four feet eight inches. The skilled guides (equipped with cell phones) hug the shoreline to point out birds, seals, and other wildlife. Each trip includes an island stopover to stretch your legs (bring a snack). All trips are weather-dependent, and reservations are advised, but the shop opens at 8 a.m. in summer if you want to take a chance. The shop also has full-day double-kayak rentals for do-it-yourselfers; map, compass, and advice are included. Even if you've brought your own kayak, stop in here for local advice. The season runs late May through September; the shop is open until 8 p.m. in summer.

Entertainment

At the height of the summer season, there's plenty of live entertainment, ranging from pub music to films to classical concerts.

Cinema: First- and second-run films are on the schedule at the beautifully refurbished National Historic Landmark **Criterion Theatre,** 35 Cottage St., Bar Harbor 04609, tel. (207) 288-3441 or 288-5829, built in 1932. Adults soak up the nostalgia of this art deco classic with nearly 900 seats; kids just call it "awesome."

The season is early May to early October; daily screenings begin at 7 p.m. or later, depending on film length. When it's raining at noon in Bar Harbor, the cinema adds a 2 p.m. matinee. Adult tickets are $7 for the balcony, $6 downstairs (try for the balcony); children 11 and under get in for $3.50.

You can enjoy pizza with your picture show at **Reel Pizza Cinerama,** 33B Kennebec Pl., Bar Harbor 04609, film tel. (207) 288-3811, food tel. (207) 288-3828.

Shopping

Bar Harbor's boutiques are indisputably visitor-oriented—many shut down for the winter, even removing or covering their signs and blanketing the windows. Fortunately, the island has enough of a year-round community to support the cluster of loyal shopkeepers determined to stay open all year, but shop-till-you-droppers will be happy here only between Memorial Day weekend and Columbus Day. (Remember, too, that Bar Harbor isn't MDI's only shopping area.)

Galleries: Birdsnest Gallery, 12 Mt. Desert St., Bar Harbor 04609, tel. (207) 288-4054, has a quarter-century reputation for a fine selection of paintings, sculpture, and prints. Prices match the quality. Open daily 10 a.m.-10 p.m. in summer, lesser hours other months, mid-May through October. **Spruce Grove Gallery,** 29 Cottage St., Bar Harbor 04609, tel. (207) 288-2002, run by gemcutter Sean Sweeney, represents a handful of well-chosen artists and jewelers. You can watch Sean ply his trade—often on Maine tourmaline. The gallery is open daily 10 a.m.-5 p.m. (sometimes to 10 p.m. in July and August), Memorial Day to Columbus Day, by appointment or by chance other months.

Books: Toys, cards, and newspapers blend in with the new-book inventory at **Sherman's Book Store,** 56 Main St., Bar Harbor 04609, tel. (207) 288-3161. There's even some funky clutter here, but it's all user-friendly. Sherman's is just the place to pick up maps and trail guides for fine days and puzzles for foggy days. Open daily 9 a.m.-5:30 p.m. (to 10:30 p.m. in summer), all year.

Souvenir Gifts/Crafts: Souvenir shops are *everywhere* on Mount Desert Island, so why single out the Acadia Shops? If you need Maine-made mementos for Uncle Harry and Aunt Mary, if the kids need trinkets for friends back home, the main downtown Bar Harbor operation (part of a multi-store chain on the island) can cover it all. Price range is broad, quality is high, and clerks are especially friendly at **The Acadia Shop & Bookloft Gallery,** 85 Main St., Bar Harbor, tel. (207) 288-5600. It's open daily 8 a.m.-11 p.m. in midsummer, 9 a.m.-5 p.m. off season. At 45 Main St., another branch, **Acadia Outdoors,** tel. (207) 288-2422, features sportswear and kids' games. The parent corporation also has three seasonal satellite shops: at Jordan Pond House, on the Cadillac Mountain summit, and at Thunder Hole on Acadia National Park's Park Loop Road.

Musical Instruments: Most vacationers don't expect to shop for musical instruments, but everyone with an affinity for folkloric music gravitates toward **Song of the Sea,** 47 West St., Bar Harbor 04609, tel. (207) 288-5653, a unique, jampacked harborfront shop where you can find guitars, banjos, harmonicas, and tin whistles—but also such esoterica as hammered dulcimers, bagpipes, and psalteries. Ed and Anne Damm—founders of Bar Harbor's July Dulcimer and Folk Harp Festival—are incredibly knowledgeable and helpful, even to the point of playing instruments over the phone for call-in orders. Hours are Mon.-Sat. 10 a.m.-9 p.m., Sunday noon-8 p.m. mid-May to mid-October. Off season, the shop is open Mon.-Fri. 11 a.m.-2:30 p.m., Saturday 10 a.m.-4 p.m.

Accommodations

Bar Harbor alone has thousands of hotel, motel, inn, and B&B rooms—and the rest of the island adds to the total. Nonetheless, lodgings can be scarce at the height of summer (particularly the first two weeks in August), also the outrageous peak period for room rates. Off season, there's plenty of choice, even after the seasonal places shut down, and rates are always lower—often dramatically so.

Hotels/Motels: One of the town's best-known, most-visible, and best-located hotels is the **Bar Harbor Inn,** Newport Drive, Box 7, Bar Harbor 04609, tel. (207) 288-3351 or (800) 248-3351, a sprawling complex on eight acres overlooking the harbor and Bar Island. The 153 rooms vary considerably in style, from traditional inn to motel, in three different buildings; rates are $115-265 d mid-June to mid-October, $59-189 d other

months. Continental breakfast is included and special packages are available—a plus if you have children. Rooms in the Oceanview Lodge are good choices, with reasonable rates and terrific views. No pets. Service is attentive. Open all year.

At the opposite end of the budgetary scale is the **Aurora Motel,** 51 Holland Ave., Bar Harbor 04609, tel. (207) 288-3771 or (800) 841-8925, a clean, no-frills, family-run motel from which you can walk everywhere. Nine first-floor rooms ($80-95 d in high season, $45 and up off season) have private baths, phones, a/c, and cable TV. No pets. Open all year.

Inns and B&Bs: A dozen of Mount Desert Island's most attractive B&Bs (most in the Bar Harbor area, two in Southwest Harbor) have banded together as **Inns of the Island,** insisting on high standards of service and comfort (and, of course, rather high prices). You get what you pay for, however, so you won't go wrong with any of them. For Inns of the Island brochures, call (207) 288-3131; for availability and referral May-Oct., call (207) 288-9439.

If money is no object, spring for one of the six rooms at the **Breakwater 1904,** 45 Hancock St., Bar Harbor 04609, tel. (207) 288-2313 or (800) 238-6309, fax (207) 288-2377, an elegantly refurbished turn-of-the-20th-century summer "cottage" on four beautifully landscaped waterfront acres. Second-floor rooms in the Tudor-style mansion are huge, and so is the breakfast. Rates are $185-335 d in summer, $145-265 off season. No smoking, no pets, no small children. Open mid-April to mid-November. An adjacent carriage house, open all year, has two-bedroom efficiency apartments going for $1,200-1,500 a week in peak season.

Three gorgeous water-view suites on a quiet side street are big draws at **The Tides,** 119 West St., Bar Harbor 04609, tel. (207) 288-4968, a handsome Greek Revival manse overlooking the bay. Joe and Judy Losquadro do everything right, down to the multi-star breakfast, so it's not easy to get a reservation at this National Historic Register inn. Access to Bar Island is right around the corner. Peak-season rates are $225-265 d Memorial Day weekend and mid-June to mid-October, $125-165 d other months. No pets, no smoking, no children under 12. Open all year.

Also heavily booked up, the updated Tudor-style **Inn at Canoe Point**, Rt. 3, Box 216, Bar Harbor 04609, tel. (207) 288-9511, is tucked along the shoreline two miles from downtown Bar Harbor (and close to the Acadia National Park visitor center). It's a romantic spot, with fireplaces, balconies, and bay views—plus a lovely waterfront deck. Five beautifully furnished rooms and suites go for $135-245 d in summer, $90-160 off season. No smoking, no small children. Open all year.

Even the address is appealing at **Ullikana Bed & Breakfast**, 16 The Field, Bar Harbor 04609, tel. (207) 288-9552, a Victorian Tudor house close to Bar Harbor's Shore Path. Everything blends beautifully here, even the modern-art collection. Ten comfortable rooms, all with private baths and some with water views, are $115-195 d in midsummer, lower early and late in the season. A hearty breakfast is served on the water-view patio. No smoking, no pets, no children under eight. Open May through October.

Energetic Marian Burns, a former math/science teacher and 1994 Maine Innkeeper of the Year, is the reason everything runs smoothly at **Mira Monte Inn,** 69 Mt. Desert St., Bar Harbor 04609, tel. (207) 288-4263 or (800) 553-5109, fax (207) 288-3115, close (but not too close) to downtown. Born and raised here, and an avid gardener, Marian's a terrific resource for island exploring. Try to capture her during wine and cheese (5-7 p.m.), and don't miss her collection of antique Bar Harbor hotel photos. The 15 Victorian-style rooms have a/c, cable TV, and other nice touches ($120-180 d mid-June to mid-October; two-night minimum); two suites ($180) in a separate building are ideal for families. Early and late in the season, Marian organizes special-rate theme weekends. Open early May through October.

Just down the street from Mira Monte, **Stratford House**, 45 Mt. Desert St., Bar Harbor 04609, tel. (207) 288-5189, is a turn-of-the-20th-century Tudor-style home conveniently close to downtown. Leave the car and walk to shops and restaurants, or pedal to the national park carriage roads. This handsome "cottage," built by a Boston publisher boasts brass beds, a music room, and a library. Hospitable innkeeper Barbara Moulton serves continental breakfast in the elegant dining room. Ten rooms (eight have

private baths) are $75-150 July to Labor Day (two-night minimum), $55-130 other months. No smoking, no pets, children welcome. Open mid-May to mid-October.

Hostel: Affiliated with Hostelling International, the **Bar Harbor/Mount Desert Island Hostel,** 27 Kennebec St., P.O. Box 32, Bar Harbor 04609, tel. (207) 288-5587 or 288-9336, is in the parish hall of St. Saviour's Episcopal Church. Twenty beds in two dorm-style rooms are $10 each; kitchen facilities are available. Hostel hours are 4:30 p.m.-9 a.m.; there's no daytime access. The hostel is open mid-June through August. Reservations (best by mail) are essential, as this is a popular location. Visa cards are accepted.

Campgrounds: There are no campsites within Bar Harbor's town limits, but there are plenty nearby; for a selection, see the "Mount Desert Island," "Southwest Harbor and Vicinity," and "Acadia National Park" sections.

Seasonal Rentals: Contact The Swan Agency, 43 Cottage St., P.O. Box 46, Bar Harbor 04609, tel. (207) 288-5818, fax 288-2151, for listings of cottages available by the week or month. In high season (June to Labor Day), rates run $700-6,000 a week.

Food

You won't go hungry in Bar Harbor, but you also won't find chain fast-food places. The summer tourism trade and the College of the Atlantic students have created a demand for pizzerias, vegetarian bistros, brewpubs, and a handful of creative restaurants. And even if you're using Bar Harbor as a base of operations, don't miss opportunities to explore restaurants elsewhere on the island.

Miscellanea: An unscientific but reliable local survey gives the best-pizza ribbon to **Rosalie's Pizza & Italian Restaurant,** 46 Cottage St., Bar Harbor 04609, tel. (207) 288-5666, where the Wurlitzer jukebox churns out tunes from the 1950s. This family-owned standard gets high marks for consistency with its homemade pizza (by the slice or in four sizes), calzones, and subs—lots of vegetarian options. Rosalie's is open daily from 11 a.m., all year. Beer and wine are available.

Combine a pizza with an art or second-run flick at **Reel Pizza Cinerama,** 33B Kennebec

Pl., Bar Harbor 04609, film tel. (207) 288-3811, food tel. (207) 288-3828, where you order your pizza, relax in an easy chair, and watch the show (at 6 and 8:30 p.m.). Pizzas ($9-15) have cinematic names—Zorba the Greek, How Green Was My Valley, The Godfather. Film tickets are $4. Reel Pizza opens daily at 5 p.m. and offers occasional Saturday matinees.

Efficient, friendly, cafeteria-style service makes **EPI Sub and Pizza Shop,** 8 Cottage St., Bar Harbor 04609, tel. (207) 288-5853, an excellent choice for picnics or a quick break from sightseeing. The dozen-plus sub-sandwich choices at EPI's (short for epicurean) are bargains (try the Cadillac), and the pizza is right up there. If the weather closes in, there are always the pinball machines in the back room. No credit cards. Open daily 10 a.m.-8 p.m. (to 9 p.m. July and August), early Feb.-December. Closed Sunday in November, December, and from February to mid-May.

Brewpubs and Microbreweries: Bar Harbor's longest-lived brewpub is the **Lompoc Café & Brew Pub,** 32 Rodick St., Bar Harbor 04609, tel. (207) 288-9392, serving creative lunches and dinners daily 11:30 a.m.-9 p.m., late April to mid-December. (Try the Indonesian peanut chicken.) After 9 p.m., there's just beer and pizza. The congenial pub has a beer garden, a bocce court, and live entertainment nightly during the summer. The pub's signature Bar Harbor Ale, plus five or six others, are brewed next door at **Atlantic Brewing Company,** 30 Rodick St., tel. (207) 288-9513. Free half-hour tours, including tasting, are given daily at 4 p.m., Memorial Day weekend to mid-October; reservations aren't needed.

Bar Harbor Brewing Company & Soda Works, Otter Creek Rd., Rt. 3, HC 30, Box 61, Bar Harbor 04609, tel. (207) 288-4592, begun in 1990 by Tod and Suzi Foster as a mom-and-pop operation, remains a small, friendly, hands-on enterprise producing five kinds of beer and ale in a basement microbrewery. Start off at the log-cabin tasting room/gift shop, where kids can sample Old Bar Harbor Root Beer, Suzi Foster's specialty. Free 15-minute tours are given about every 20 minutes between 3:30 and 5 p.m. Tuesday, Thursday, and Friday, early June to mid-October (tours Mon.-Fri. during July and August). Call ahead in June and after Labor

Day. The brewery is four and a half miles east of downtown Bar Harbor.

Inexpensive to Moderate: Once a Victorian boarding house and later a 1920s speakeasy, **Galyn's Galley,** 17 Main St., Bar Harbor 04609, tel. (207) 288-9706, has been a popular year-round eatery since 1986. Lots of plants, modern decor, reliable service, a great downtown location, and several indoor and outdoor dining areas contribute to the steady clientele. The cuisine is consistently good if not outstandingly creative (dinner entrées $10-17). Reservations advisable in midsummer. Open daily for lunch and dinner (to 11 p.m. in July and August), except major national holidays.

Blue-corn crab cakes and A-plus margaritas are specialties at **Miguel's Mexican Restaurant,** 51 Rodick St., Bar Harbor 04609, tel. (207) 288-5117, home of "The Picasso of Picante" and the island's best Tex-Mex food. In midsummer, try for the patio (there's no air-conditioning). Expect to wait; this is a popular spot. No smoking. Open daily for dinner 5-10 p.m., April-Oct.; closed on Monday after Labor Day.

Just down the street from Galyn's and Miguel's, **Rupununi,** 119 Main St., Bar Harbor 04609, tel. (207) 288-2886, gets its name from a river in Guyana—the inspiration of owner Mike Boland, a College of the Atlantic grad. Billed as "an American bar and grill," Rupununi draws a lively, fun crowd for great burgers (platters for $6.95), veggie and meat dinner entrées ($10-16), and some Caribbean and Mediterranean touches. The daily poacher's special always features game (buffalo, ostrich, venison, or even more unusual items). On Sunday, jazz is part of the mix. Open daily 11 a.m.-1 a.m. (food stops at midnight). Upstairs is **Carmen Verandah,** Rupununi's even livelier nightclub, with darts, pool, and plenty of space for dancing to blues, rock, or funk groups. Latest addition to the ever-expanding Rupununi empire is **Joe's Smoke Shop,** an upscale cigar bar in a former gallery next door.

Moderate to Expensive: One of Bar Harbor's fine longtime reliables, **George's,** 7 Stephens Ln., Bar Harbor 04609, tel. (207) 288-4505, occupies four attractively laid-out rooms in a restored home on a downtown side street. Specialties are wild game, Greek-inspired lamb, seafood, and outrageous desserts. "Grazers"

($8.50 each) are seafood and Mediterranean oriented. Entrées are $20; prix-fixe menus are $29 and $31. Reservations are essential in July and August. There's terrace dining when weather permits. No smoking, except on the terrace. Open at 5:30 p.m. daily, mid-June through October.

The view's the thing at the Bar Harbor Inn's **Reading Room Restaurant,** Newport Dr., Bar Harbor, tel. (207) 288-3351; request a window seat. Once the stuffy Bar Harbor Reading Room, a gentlemen's club, the dining room still has an incredible sweeping curve of windows overlooking Bar Island and Frenchman Bay. Dinner entrées, emphasizing meat and seafood, are commendably creative ($16-22), the wine list is good, desserts are so-so. Despite the elegant setting, dress is informal, and there's a children's menu. Brunch is extremely popular; in good weather, it's also served on the terrace. Reservations are essential. Breakfast (mid-April through October) is 7-10:30 a.m., lunch (on the terrace, weather permitting) is 11:30 a.m.-9:30 p.m., dinner is 5:30-9:30 p.m.

Five miles south of Bar Harbor is the nondescript-looking **Burning Tree,** Rt. 3, Otter Creek 04665, tel. (207) 288-9331, where reservations are essential in summer. One of Mount Desert Island's best restaurants, it's bright and airy inside. Specialties are imaginative seafood entrées ($15-20)—such as stuffed calamari, cioppino, Maryland (yes!) crab cakes—and vegetarian dishes made from organic produce. Scallop kebabs have *lots* of scallops, and edible flowers garnish the entrées. The homemade breads and desserts are incredible. At the height of summer, service can be a bit rushed and the kitchen runs out of popular entrées. Solution: Just plan to eat early. The Burning Tree is open for dinner Wed.-Mon., late June to early October (plus Tuesday in August).

Ice Cream: Only a masochist could bypass **Ben and Bill's Chocolate Emporium,** 66 Main St., Bar Harbor 04609, tel. (207) 288-3281 or (800) 806-3281, a long-running taste-treat-cum-experience in downtown Bar Harbor. The homemade candies and more than 50 ice cream flavors (including a dubious lobster flavor, $33 a bucket to go) are nothing short of outrageous; the whole place smells like the inside of a chocolate truffle. The shop, a cousin of three Massa-chusetts ice cream parlors, is open March-Dec. daily at 9 a.m.-10 p.m. spring and fall, 9 a.m.-midnight in summer.

Information and Services
The **Bar Harbor Chamber of Commerce,** 93 Cottage St., Bar Harbor 04609, tel. (207) 288-5103 or (800) 288-5103, recorded message tel. (207) 288-3393, close to the downtown action, has an especially helpful staff accustomed to a steady stream of summer traffic. The office is open daily 8 a.m.-5 p.m. in summer, weekdays 8 a.m.-4:30 p.m. off season. The only drawback is a certain myopia: there's little information here on other parts of the island, so you'll need to remedy that by stopping at one of the information centers near the bridge from the mainland. Bar Harbor's annual visitor information booklet usually is off the presses in January, so you can plan ahead for a summer vacation. If you've managed to bestir yourself early enough to catch sunrise on the Cadillac summit, stop in at the chamber of commerce office and request an official membership card for the **Cadillac Mountain Sunrise Club** (they'll take your word for it).

Jesup Memorial Library, 34 Mt. Desert St., Bar Harbor 04609, tel. (207) 288-4245, is open all year, Tues.-Sat. 10 a.m.-5 p.m. (to 7 p.m. Wednesday). On the lower level, the **Bar Harbor Historical Society**—with fascinating displays, stereopticon images, and scrapbooks about the 1947 fire—is open mid-June to early October, Mon.-Sat. 1-4 p.m. It's open by appointment in winter. Free admission.

Newspapers: The *Bar Harbor Times,* 76 Cottage St., Bar Harbor 04609, tel. (207) 288-3311, published each Thursday, carries extensive calendar listings. The paper also produces four summer issues of *Acadia Visitor,* a free newsprint booklet containing features, ads, events listings, and other helpful touring tidbits for Acadia National Park and the rest of Mount Desert Island.

Public Restrooms: Downtown Bar Harbor has public restrooms at the town pier and on the School Street side of the athletic field, where there is RV parking. There are also restrooms at the Mount Desert Island Hospital and the International Ferry Terminal.

Photo Services: Across from the Village Green, **First Exposure USA,** 156 Main St., P.O. Box 6, Bar Harbor 04609, tel. (207) 288-5868, provides one-hour photo service and rents cameras and camcorders. Open daily 9 a.m.-9 p.m., May through October.

Getting Around

In the summer, driving and parking can be hellacious in Bar Harbor. Several campgrounds have shuttle-bus services, which relieve some of the pressure, but a bike can come in very handy.

On weekends, be creative: use bank parking lots on Main Street and the town-office lot on Cottage Street. RVs are not allowed to park near the town pier; designated RV parking is alongside the athletic field, Lower Main and Park Sts., about eight blocks from the center of town.

NORTHEAST HARBOR AND VICINITY

Some sort of Northeast Harbor bush telegraph must have been operating in the Philadelphia area in the late 19th century, because Main Liners from the City of Brotherly Love have been summering in and around this village since then. Sure, they also show up in other parts of Maine, but it's hard not to notice the preponderance of Pennsylvania license plates surrounding Northeast Harbor's elegant "cottages" from mid-July to mid-August. (In the last several years, the Pennsylvania plates have been joined by growing numbers from the District of Columbia, New York, and Texas.)

Actually, even though Northeast Harbor is a well-known name with special cachet, it isn't even an official township; it's a zip-coded village within the town of Mount Desert.

The small downtown area's attractive boutiques and eateries cater to a casually posh clientele, while the well-protected harbor attracts a tony crowd of yachties. For their convenience, a palm-size annual directory, *The Redbook,* discreetly lists owners' summer residences and winter addresses—but no phone numbers. The directory also includes listings for the village of Seal Harbor—an even more exclusive village a few miles east of Northeast Harbor where style maven Martha Stewart purchased a palatial estate in 1997, much to the chagrin of long-timers.

Except for two spectacular public gardens and two unusual museums, not much here is geared to budget-sensitive visitors—but there's no charge for admiring the scenery.

Sights

Somes Sound: As you head toward Northeast Harbor on Rt. 198 from the northern end of Mount Desert Island, you'll begin seeing cliff-lined Somes Sound on your right. This glacier-sculpted fjord juts five miles into the interior of Mount Desert Island from its mouth, between Northeast and Southwest Harbors. Watch for the right-hand turn for Sargent Drive (no RVs allowed), and follow the lovely, granite-lined route along the east side of the sound. Halfway along, a marker explains the geology of this natural fjord—the only one on the eastern seaboard. There aren't many pullouts en route, and traffic can be fairly steady in midsummer, but don't miss it. An ideal way to appreciate Somes Sound is from the water—sign up for an excursion out of Northeast or Southwest Harbor.

Asticou and Thuya Gardens: If you have the slightest interest in gardens (even if you don't, for that matter), allow time for Northeast Harbor's two marvelous public gardens. Information about both is available from the local chamber of commerce. If gardens are extra-high on your priority list, inquire also about visiting the private Rockefeller garden, accessible on a very limited basis.

Maine's best spring showcase is the Asticou Azalea Garden, a three-acre pocket where 50 or 60 varieties of azaleas, rhododendrons, and laurels—many from the classic Reef Point garden of famed landscape designer Beatrix Farrand—burst into bloom. Oriental serenity is the key—with a Japanese sand garden, stone lanterns, granite outcrops, pink-gravel paths, and a tranquil pond—so try to visit early in the season, early in the morning, to savor the effect. The garden is on Rt. 198, at the northern edge of Northeast Harbor, immediately north of the junction with Peabody Drive (Rt. 3). Watch for a tiny sign on the right, marking access to the parking area. Although Asticou is open daily, all year, prime time for azaleas is mid-May to mid-June.

excursion boat
Islesford Ferry

MAINE OFFICE OF TOURISM

Behind a carved wooden gate on a forested hillside not far from Asticou lies an enchanted garden inspired by Beatrix Farrand and designed by Charles K. Savage. Special features of Thuya Garden are perennial borders, sculpted shrubbery, and Oriental touches. On a misty summer day, when few visitors appear, the colors are brilliant. Adjacent to the garden is **Thuya Lodge,** tel. (207) 276-5130, former summer cottage of Joseph Curtis, donor of this awesome municipal park. The lodge, with an extensive botanical library and quiet rooms for reading, is open daily 10 a.m. to 5 p.m., late June to Labor Day. The garden is open 7 a.m.-7 p.m., July through September. A collection box next to the front gate requests a $2 donation. To reach Thuya, continue on Rt. 3 beyond Asticou Garden and watch for the Asticou Terraces parking area (no RVs, two-hour limit) on the right. Cross the road and climb the Asticou Terraces Trail (.4 mile) to the garden. Or drive .2 mile beyond the Rt. 3 parking area, watching for a minuscule Thuya Garden sign on the left. Go half a mile up the driveway to the parking area.

Eliot Mountain Trail: After you've visited Thuya Garden, go outside the back gate, where you'll see a sign for the Eliot Mountain Trail, a 1.4-mile moderately difficult (lots of exposed roots) roundtrip. Near the summit, Northeast Harbor spreads out before you. If you're here in August, sample the wild blueberries. Eliot Mountain is not an Acadia trail, and much of it is on private land, so stay on the path and be respectful of private property.

Petite Plaisance: On Northeast Harbor's quiet South Shore Road, Petite Plaisance is a museum commemorating noted Belgian-born author and college professor Marguerite Yourcenar (pen name of Marguerite de Crayencour), first woman elected to the prestigious Académie Française. From the early 1950s to 1987, Petite Plaisance was her home, and it's hard to believe she's no longer here; her intriguing possessions and presence fill the two-story house. Free, hour-long tours of the first floor are given in French or English, depending on visitors' preferences. French-speaking visitors often make pilgrimages here. The house is open daily, June 15-Aug. 31. No children under 12. Call (207) 276-3940 at least a day ahead, between 9 a.m. and 4 p.m., for an appointment and directions, or write: Petite Plaisance Trust, P.O. Box 403, Northeast Harbor 04662. Yourcenar devotees should request directions to Brookside Cemetery in Somesville, seven miles away, where she is buried.

Great Harbor Maritime Museum: Nautical buffs and kids of all ages will thrill to the model ships, small boats, historic naval equipment (including a 1908 gasoline engine six feet long and four feet tall), and exhibits on the maritime history of the Mount Desert Island area in the small, eclectic Great Harbor Maritime Museum ("Great Harbor" refers to the Somes Sound area—Northeast, Southwest, and Seal Harbors, as well as the Cranberry Isles), Main St. (P.O. Box 145), Northeast Harbor 04662, tel. (207) 276-5262 (housed in the old village fire station and municipal building). Yachting, coastal trade, and fishing receive special emphasis. What else is here? Antique photos and tools, furniture and clothing—even an old player piano, which works. Special programs and exhibits are held during the summer. The museum is open Mon.-Sat. 10 a.m.-5 p.m., late June to Columbus Day, but you may be able to get in at other times by appointment, too, so call ahead. Admission is $1 per person, $2 per family.

Getting Afloat
Northeast Harbor is the starting point for most of the boats headed for the **Cranberry Isles.** The vessels depart from the commercial floats at the end of the concrete Municipal Pier on Sea Street.

Captain Rob Lievow's 75-foot *Sea Princess,* tel. (207) 276-5352, carries visitors as well as an Acadia National Park ranger on a three-hour morning trip around the mouth of Somes Sound and out to Little Cranberry Island (Islesford) for a 50-minute stopover. The boat leaves Northeast Harbor daily at 9:45 a.m., mid-May to mid-October. Cost is $13 adults, $9 children under 12. The *Sea Princess* also does a scenic one-and-a-half-hour Somes Sound cruise, departing daily at 3:45 p.m., late June to early September. Cost is $11 adults, $7 children. The same months, there's also a three-hour sunset/dinner cruise, departing 5:30 p.m. for the Islesford Dock Restaurant on Little Cranberry. Cost is $10 adults, $7 children (not including dinner). Reservations are advisable for all trips.

The **MDI Water Taxi,** tel. (207) 244-7312, a converted lobsterboat home-ported in Northeast Harbor, provides on-demand trips anywhere you'd like to go, mid-May to Thanksgiving. Captain Wes Shaw, an accommodating fellow, will run a daytime boatload to Islesford for $60 roundtrip. Other trips are $55 an hour per boatload. Reservations are wise.

Shopping
Gifts and Clothing: Two upscale shops here are worth a visit (if you have the money) and maybe even a major splurge.

Early and late in the season, the summer crowd shops at **The Kimball Shop & Boutique,** Main St., Northeast Harbor 04662, tel. (207) 276-3300, to stock up on wedding and Christ-

mas gifts. It's all very tasteful. In June, it's open Mon.-Sat. 9:30 a.m.-5:30 p.m.; July and August, Mon.-Sat. 9 a.m.-6 p.m. and Sunday noon-5 p.m.

At **Local Color,** Main St., Northeast Harbor 04662, tel. (207) 276-5544, you'll find stunning silk and chenille sweaters, needlepoint rugs, and finely crafted pottery and jewelry. Most is locally made. Nothing is cheap—in quality or price. The shop is open Mon.-Sat. 9 a.m.-5 p.m., May to Christmas (to 6 p.m. July and August). Local Color also has a branch in downtown Camden.

Luxuries and Laundry: Consider it a yuppie adventure to visit the **Pine Tree Market,** Main St., Northeast Harbor 04662, tel. (207) 276-3335, fax 276-0542, where you'll find gourmet goodies, a huge wine selection, resident butcher, fresh fish, and homemade croissants. A landmark here since 1921, the market is open daily 7 a.m.-7 p.m.; free delivery to your yacht. Below the store is the Downtown Laundry Cellar, with coin-operated machines. The laundromat is open 7 a.m.-9 p.m.

Accommodations
Unless you're celebrating a landmark occasion, Northeast Harbor's lodgings may be a little too pricey, but if money's no object and a haute ambience appeals, spring for the **Asticou Inn,** Rt. 3, Northeast Harbor 04662, tel. (207) 276-3344 or (800) 258-3373, fax (207) 276-3373. Built in 1883 and refurbished regularly, the classic old inn has 27 rooms and 23 suites, plus several modern cottages. Facilities include tennis courts, outdoor pool, and access to the Northeast Harbor Golf Club. The elegant, mural-lined dining room, open to the public for Sunday brunch and dinner (6:30-10 p.m.) by reservation, has fabulous views of the harbor. Jackets and ties are advised for dinner. Lunch is also open to the public, served 11:30 a.m.-5 p.m.; reservations aren't needed. The inn is open mid-June to mid-September, when rates are $225-300 d, MAP; two-night minimum. A B&B rate ($160-220 d) is optional mid-June to mid-July and in early September. The best bargain is off season at the inn's Victorian-style **Cranberry Lodge,** across the road ($80-140 d, including breakfast, mid-September through January and May to mid-June), when the inn itself is closed. Plan a late-May or early-June visit; you're prac-

tically on top of the Asticou Azalea Garden, and Thuya Garden is a short walk away.

Food

Lobster-in-the-Rough: At the edge of Somes Sound, five miles north of downtown Northeast Harbor, **Abel's Lobster Pound,** Rt. 198, Mount Desert, tel. (207) 276-5827, prides itself on a knockout view, super-fresh lobster, and the island's best "steamers" (steamed clams). Outdoor or indoor dining; liquor license. You can also order crustaceans cooked to go. Abel's is open late May through Columbus Day: noon-9 p.m. late May through June, noon-10 p.m. July and August, 5-9 p.m. September to mid-October. Reservations are wise between 5 and 9 p.m. in July and August.

Ice Cream: Northeast Harbor Café and Ice Cream Parlor, Main St., Northeast Harbor 04662, tel. (207) 276-4151, has soup, sandwiches, and pizza on the menu, but the cognoscenti show up for the superb ice cream, a summer tradition. Island maps and pricey prints line the walls. The café is open daily 11 a.m.-8 p.m.

Inexpensive: Real Local Color and crab cakes and crab sandwiches are the *best* at the **Docksider,** Sea St., Northeast Harbor 04662, tel. 276-3965, a low-key, family-friendly, unassuming, hole-in-the-wall place inevitably jammed with devoted locals and summer folk. Located just up the hill from the chamber office, the Docksider has a couple of veteran (since forever) waitresses, no view, and a reputation far and wide. If you're smitten, buy one of their T-shirts, featuring an upright lobster announcing, "Frankly, I don't give a clam." Closed off season.

Expensive: Spicy crab cakes, rare lamb, and smoked-oyster Caesar salad are specialties at the very popular **Redfield's,** Main St., Northeast Harbor 04662, tel. (207) 276-5283. The extensive wine list—heavy on the French—suits the topnotch dinner fare (entrées $15-22). No smoking; reservations are essential in July and August. In summer, Redfield's opens in late afternoon for aperitifs and appetizers. Closed Sunday year-round; closed Sun.-Thurs. early November to late May; and closed two weeks in March.

In exclusive Seal Harbor, a few miles east on Rt. 3 from Northeast Harbor, is one of the is-

land's best and priciest restaurants. Getting a reservation at one of its half-dozen tables is no easy feat, but if you can manage it, by all means go. **The Bistro at Seal Harbor,** Main St., P.O. Box 247, Seal Harbor 04675, tel. (207) 276-3299, founded in 1993, does everything right: pasta and seafood are fresh, desserts are outstanding, the wine list is choice. Entrées run $16-22, with appetizers $6-8. No smoking. Open Tues.-Sun. 6-10 p.m., early June to mid-October.

Information

The harborfront information center (also called the Yachtsman's Building) of the **Mount Desert Chamber of Commerce,** Sea St., Northeast Harbor 04662, tel. (207) 276-5040, 244-7843 off season, is open daily 9:30 a.m.-4:30 p.m., mid-June to mid-October. The extremely cordial staff can provide information on Northeast Harbor's gardens, museums, and trails, in addition to food and lodging. Coin-operated ($1, quarters only) hot showers, designed primarily but not exclusively for the boating crowd, are available here round the clock (after office hours, pick up the key at the harbormaster's office, just to the right of the Yachtsman's Building). They even rent towels and a hair dryer. Request a free copy of the annual *Mt. Desert Chamber of Commerce Guide & Northeast Harbor Port Directory.* To obtain a copy early in the year, call (207) 244-7312, fax 244-0331.

ROUTE 102/198 TOWARD THE ISLAND'S WESTERN SIDE

Just after the Thompson Island information center, if you don't take Rt. 3 toward the Acadia National Park Visitor Center and Bar Harbor, your other choice is Rt. 102/198, toward Southwest Harbor and lesser-known parts of the island's "quiet side." Here's what you'll first encounter if you bear right at the fork.

Indian Point/Blagden Preserve: It's an easy side trip from the fork to a lovely preserve owned by The Nature Conservancy. From the junction of Rts. 3 and 102/198, continue 1.8 miles to Indian Point Rd. and turn right. Go 1.7 miles to a fork and turn right. Watch for the preserve entrance, marked by a Nature Conservancy oak leaf.

Five trails wind through forested, 110-acre Indian Point/Blagden Preserve, local caretakers' tel. (207) 288-4838, a rectangular Nature Conservancy parcel with island, hill, and bay vistas. Sealwatching and birding are popular—harbor seals on offshore rocks and woodpeckers (plus 130 other species) in blowdown areas. To spot the seals, plan your hike around low tide, when they'll be sprawled on the rocks close to shore. Wear rubberized shoes, and be sure to bring binoculars. To keep from disturbing the seals, watch quietly and avoid jerky movements. Park near the preserve entrance and follow the Big Woods Trail, running the length of the preserve. There's a second parking area farther in, but then you'll miss much of the preserve. When you reach the second parking area, just past an old field, bear left along the Shore Trail to see the seals. Register at the caretakers' house (just beyond the first parking lot, where you can pick up bird and flora checklists), and respect private property on either side of the preserve. Open daily dawn to 6 p.m., all year.

Shopping: Roughly midway between Thompson Island and Somesville, in the Town Hill area, **Aquarius Artifacts,** Rt. 102, Town Hill, tel./fax (207) 288-4143, mailing address Box 2485, Bar Harbor 04609, delivers an armchair adventure—and you might even find the armchair. Drums, dolls, jewelry, baskets, pottery, cabinets, Japanese stone lanterns, carousel horses, and medicine bags are just some of the funky shop's global folk art and architectural leftovers. Prices are amazingly reasonable. Aquarius is open daily 10 a.m.-4 p.m., late June to Columbus Day, or by appointment.

SOUTHWEST HARBOR AND VICINITY

From Town Hill drive south toward Somesville and then on to Southwest Harbor, which considers itself the hub of Mount Desert Island's quiet side. In fact, in summer, Southwest Harbor's tiny downtown district is probably the busiest spot on the whole western side of the island (west of Somes Sound), but that's not saying a great deal. It has the feel of a settled community, a year-round flavor that Bar Harbor sometimes lacks. And it competes with the best

in the scenery department. The Southwest Harbor area deserves the nod as a very convenient base for exploring Acadia National Park, the island's less-crowded villages, and offshore Swans Island.

Officially, the town of Southwest Harbor only includes the village of Bass Harbor, but the island's lovely western-side village of Somesville is nearby, as is the neighboring town of Tremont, which includes the villages of Bernard and Seal Cove.

Be sure to drive or bike around the smaller villages, especially Somesville, Bass Harbor, and Bernard. Views are fabulous, the pace is slow, and you'll feel you've stumbled upon "the real Maine." The Somesville Historic District, with its distinctive arched white footbridge, is especially appealing, but traffic gets congested here along Rt. 102, so plan to stop and walk around.

A broad swath of Acadia National Park cuts right through the center of this side of the island, and many of its hiking trails are far less congested than elsewhere in the park.

Sights

Museums: In the center of Southwest Harbor, the **Wendell Gilley Museum,** Herrick Rd., corner of Rt. 102, P.O. Box 254, Southwest Harbor 04679, tel. (207) 244-7555, was established in 1981 to display the life's work of local woodcarver Wendell Gilley (1904-83). The modern, energy-efficient museum houses more than 200 of his astonishingly realistic bird specimens. Don't miss it. Special summer exhibits feature other wildlife artists. Many days, a local artist gives woodcarving demonstrations, and the gift shop carries an ornithological potpourri—books to binoculars to carving tools. Kids over eight appreciate this more than younger ones. Wheelchair access. Tickets are $3 adults, $1 children 5-12. Open Tues.-Sun. 10 a.m.-4 p.m., June-Oct. (to 5 p.m. in July and August), Fri.-Sun. in May, November, and December.

Touching a sea cucumber or a starfish may not be every adult's idea of fun, but kids sure enjoy the hands-on experience at the **Southwest Harbor Oceanarium,** Clark Point Rd., Southwest Harbor 04679, tel. (207) 244-7330, sister-site to the Bar Harbor Oceanarium. A knowledgeable naturalist introduces creatures from a watery touch tank during a tour of the facility. Twenty other exhibits line the walls of this intriguing, low-tech museum located next to the Coast Guard station. It's open Mon.-Sat. 9 a.m.-5 p.m., mid-May to late October. Oceanarium tickets are $6 adults, $4.50 children 4-12; combination tickets, covering this and the Oceanarium in Bar Harbor, are $11.95 adults and $8.75 children.

On the westernmost side of the island, a nondescript blue building camouflages **The Seal Cove Auto Museum,** Pretty Marsh Rd., Rt. 102, Seal Cove 04674, tel. (207) 244-9242, a fantastic collection of more than 100 antique autos and several dozen antique motorcycles. It's easy for kids of any age to spend an hour here, reminiscing and/or fantasizing. Tickets are $5 adults, $2 children under 12. Open daily 10 a.m.-5 p.m., June 1-Sept. 15, the museum is about six miles southwest of Somesville. Or, if you're coming from Southwest Harbor, take the Seal Cove Rd. (partly unpaved) west to Rt. 102 and go north about one and a half miles.

Bass Harbor Head Light: At the southern end of Mount Desert's western "claw," follow Rt. 102A to the turnoff toward Bass Harbor Head. Drive or bike to the end of Lighthouse Rd., walk down a steep wooden stairway, and look up and to the right. Voilà! Bass Harbor Head Light—its red glow automated since 1974—stands sentinel at the eastern entrance to Blue Hill Bay. Built in 1858, the 26-foot tower and lightkeeper's house are privately owned, but the dramatic setting is a photographer's dream. Winter access to the parking lot may be limited, but otherwise the area is open all year. Not far from the light (east along Rt. 102A) are the trailheads for the easy Ship Harbor and Wonderland nature trails (see "Recreation" under "Acadia National Park," above).

Recreation
Acadia National Park is the recreational focus throughout the island; on the western side of the island, the main nonpark recreational activities are bike-, boat-, and picnic-related.

Picnic spots are everywhere on this side of the island, but an Acadia National Park site that many people miss is the Pretty Marsh Picnic Area, overlooking Pretty Marsh Harbor. Dense woods shelter grills and tables, and you can walk down to the shoreline and even launch a

sea kayak. Kids love this place, but be prepared with insect repellent. The picnic area is just west of Rt. 102, on the westernmost side of Mount Desert Island.

Bicycling: Southwest Cycle, Main St., Southwest Harbor 04679, tel. (207) 244-5856 or (800) 649-5856 in Maine, rents bikes by the day ($16 adults, $12 children) and week and is open all year. From June to September hours are Mon.-Sat. 8:30 a.m.-5:30 p.m. and Sunday 10 a.m.-4 p.m.; Oct.-May, it's open Mon.-Sat. 9 a.m.-5 p.m. See "Islands near Mount Desert," below for planning a biking day-trip from Bass Harbor to Swans Island or Southwest Harbor to the Cranberry Isles. The staff at Southwest Cycle will fix you up with maps and lots of good advice for three loops (10-30 miles) on the western side of Mount Desert.

Getting Afloat
Southwest Harbor is the home of one of the nation's best boatbuilders, **The Hinckley Company,** Shore Rd., P.O. Box 699, Southwest Harbor 04679, tel. (207) 244-5531, fax 244-9833, a name with stellar repute since the 1930s. There are no tours of the Hinckley complex, but most yachtsmen can't resist the urge to look in at the yard. Plus you can stop in at the **Hinckley Ship'-Store,** tel. (207) 244-7100 or (800) 446-2553 outside Maine, and pick up books, charts, and all sorts of Hinckley-logo gear. The shop is open Mon.-Fri. 7:30 a.m.-5 p.m., Saturday 8 a.m.-4 p.m., and Sunday 8 a.m.-1 p.m.

Schooner *Rachel B. Jackson:* Eighth-generation islander Jeff Crafts is skipper of the 67-foot wooden schooner *Rachel B. Jackson,* P.O. Box 131, Southwest Harbor 04679, tel. (207) 244-7813, sailing out of the Manset Town Dock, near the XYZ Restaurant. Departures for the two-and-a-half-hour cruises are 10 a.m. and 1, 4, and 7 p.m., mid-May to Columbus Day. Tickets are $18 adults, $12 children. Or you can try the B&B (boat and breakfast) option—a sunset sail, an overnight at anchor in Somes Sound, and morning repast. Cost is $75 pp, maximum eight persons. No credit cards. Reservations are advisable for all cruises, and required for the B&B. Tickets can be purchased in downtown Southwest Harbor at the Seafaring Crafts shop, across from the post office.

Canoeing: Across the road from Long Pond, the largest lake on Mount Desert Island, **National Park Canoe Rentals**, Rt. 102, Mount Desert 04660, tel. (207) 244-5854, makes canoeing a snap; it's even easier if you're staying at the adjoining Long Pond Inn. Just rent the canoe, carry it across to Pond's End, and launch it. Be sure to pack a picnic. Morning (8:30 a.m.-12:30 p.m.) rate is $18, afternoon (1-5 p.m.) rate is $22, and all day is $28. Reservations are advisable, and essential in July and August. Open mid-May through mid-October.

If you've brought your own canoe (or kayak), launch it here at Pond's End and head off. It's four miles to the southern end of the lake. If the wind kicks up, skirt the shore; if it *really* kicks up from the north, don't paddle too far down the lake, as you'll have a devil of a time getting back.

You can swim at Pond's End, and in the upper half of the lake, but swimming is banned in the lower half, as it's used for drinking water. Almost the entire west side of Long Pond is national park property, so plan to picnic and swim along there; tuck into the sheltered area west of Southern Neck, a crooked finger of land that points northward from the western shore. Stay clear of private property on the east side of the lake.

Entertainment

It's not too far to drive from Southwest Harbor to Bar Harbor for evening entertainment, but Southwest has a cabaret theater that even draws customers in the reverse direction. After a 21-year run on a side street in Bass Harbor, **The Deck House Restaurant and Cabaret Theater** moved in 1997 to a new, high-profile location at the Hinckley Great Harbor Marina, Rt. 102, Southwest Harbor 04679, tel. (207) 244-5044. Lunch is served Mon.-Sat. 11 a.m.-2 p.m., with no entertainment. Sunday brunch, 10:30 a.m.-1 p.m., includes entertainment. And then there's dinner, served daily. Try to arrive by 6:30 p.m. to enjoy the spectacular view and order your meal (entrées are $18; appetizers and salads are à la carte). The cathedral-ceilinged dining room holds 140, and the table is yours for the evening (reservations are essential in midsummer). No smoking. Just after sunset (about 8:15 p.m.), the young waitstaff, chameleonlike, unveils its other talents—singing, dancing, even story-

telling. After hearing the 13 numbers, you won't be surprised to learn that many Deck House staff have moved on to Broadway and beyond. The theater "house charge" is $6 pp. The Deck House is open mid-June to mid-September.

Since the early 1970s, the **Acadia Repertory Theatre**, Rt. 102, Somesville, mailing address P.O. Box 106, Mount Desert 04660, tel. (207) 244-7260, has been providing first-rate thespian repertory on the stage of Somesville's antique Masonic Hall. Classic plays by Wilde, Goldsmith, even Molière, have been staples, as has the annual Agatha Christie mystery. Performances run early July to mid-September, Tues.-Sun. at 8:15 p.m., with occasional 2 p.m. Sunday matinees. Tickets are $15 adults, $12 seniors and students, $10 children 16 and under. Special children's programs, such as *Charlotte's Web*, occur Wednesday and Saturday at 10:30 a.m.; tickets are $6 adults, $4 children.

Shopping

The best shopping locales on this side of the island are Southwest Harbor and the villages of Somesville and Bernard. Mind you, there aren't *lots* of shops, but the small selection is interesting.

Antiques: It's hard to label **Nancy Neale Typecraft**, Steamboat Wharf Rd., Bernard 04612, tel. (207) 244-5192, fax 244-5090. Museum? Shop? Gallery? Right on Bernard Harbor, Nancy and Irving Silverman have assembled the nation's largest collection (three million pieces) of wooden printing type. Stop in, browse through the goodies (some not for sale), and create your own type art (at no charge). The shop theoretically is open daily 10 a.m.-6 p.m., June to mid-October, but if you're making a special detour, it's best to call ahead. From downtown Southwest Harbor, it's four miles. Take Rt. 102, through the center of Tremont, and turn left onto Bernard Road. Continue to Steamboat Wharf Rd. and turn right. You can't miss the shop, covered with a wall of lobster buoys and next to the Silvermans' private lighthouse. It's a shutterbug's delight. And while you're at it, have lunch or dinner here at Thurston's Lobster Pound.

Stop in at **E.L. Higgins**, Bernard Rd., P.O. Box 69, Bernard 04612, tel. (207) 244-3983. In two former classrooms from an 1890s schoolhouse, Edward Higgins has the state's best collection of antique wicker furniture. His shop is open May-Sept., usually daily 10 a.m.-5 p.m., but call ahead to be sure.

High-end (and high-quality) American antiques fill the shop at **Marianne Clark Fine Antiques,** Main St., Rt. 102, Southwest Harbor 04679, tel. (207) 244-9247. Specialties are 18th- and 19th-century furniture and folk art. The shop is open most of the year, Mon.-Sat. 10 a.m.-5 p.m., but again, call ahead to be sure.

Books: The two-story **Port in a Storm Bookstore,** Main St., Rt. 102, Somesville, Mount Desert 04660, tel. (207) 244-4114 or (800) 694-4114, fax (207) 244-7998, named "Best Bookstore in Maine" by *The Maine Times,* is totally seductive, guaranteed to lighten your wallet. High ceilings, comfortable chairs, whimsical floor sculptures, open space, and Somes Cove views all contribute to the ambience. Inventory is not huge, but it's well selected—especially nature and children's books—and the staff is very knowledgeable. Especially in summer, noted authors often appear to lecture or sign their books. The shop is open all year, Mon.-Sat. 9:30 a.m.-5:30 p.m., and Sunday 1-5 p.m.

Everything's purple at **Oz Books,** Main St., Rt. 102, P.O. Box 125, Southwest Harbor 04679, tel. (207) 244-9077 or (800) 241-9077, fax (207) 244-7249, a cheerful children's bookstore owned by a former social-studies teacher. While parents browse through a wisely chosen collection of books and games, their offspring head right for a kid-friendly, pillow-lined alcove. Allow extra time for convincing them to leave. Open Mon.-Sat. 9:30 a.m.-5:30 p.m., plus Sunday 1-5 p.m. in summer and December. Open until 8 p.m. Friday in summer and December.

Accommodations

As the Asticou Inn is to Northeast Harbor, so is the Claremont to Southwest Harbor. On the other end of the lodging scale, there are several commercial campgrounds in this part of the island, plus an Acadia National Park campground.

When you're ready to splurge, **The Claremont,** P.O. Box 137, Southwest Harbor 04679, tel. (207) 244-5036 or (800) 244-5036, fax (207) 244-3512, may well be your choice, but you'll have to plan a year ahead to land a room in July or August. Most popular time is the first

week in August, during the annual Claremont Croquet Classic. This grand old yellow-clapboard hostelry dominating a five-acre hilltop overlooking Somes Sound caters to honeymooners, yuppies, and gentrified folk. Service is impeccable; enjoy it.

The Claremont Dining Room, with a view from every table, is open to the public for breakfast and dinner (jackets and ties requested for dinner). Dining-room service can be slow; reservations are advisable in midsummer. Informal lunches and cocktails are held in the shorefront Boat House, also open to the public, as is the Thursday lecture series (8:15 p.m. mid-July to late August) featuring noted speakers. Dating from 1884, the main building has 24 rooms (with bath and phones), most recently refurbished. Other accommodations are in 12 cottages and two other buildings, with a wide range of daily and weekly rates; cottages can go as high as $1,200 a week in midsummer. Main-building rooms, July to Labor Day, are $130 d (including breakfast) or $195 d MAP, plus a hefty 22% service and lodging tax. No pets, no credit cards, no smoking in rooms. The hotel and dining room are open mid-June to mid-October; cottages are open early May to late October.

B&Bs: In the center of Somesville, marked by a millstone but no sign, is Binnie and Stan MacDonald's charming **MacDonald's B&B,** Rt. 102, Somesville, P.O. Box 52, Mount Desert 04660, tel. (207) 244-3316. You'll never be bored here, with tons of games and books, a quiet garden with Adirondack chairs, a music room, water views, easy access to Acadia National Park, and very congenial hosts. (Stan is a jazz musician.) Across the road is the Port in a Storm Bookstore. All three rooms in the 19th-century house have private baths; two have water views. Rates are $75-85 d mid-June to mid-October, $50-60 off season. Two-night minimum in summer. No smoking, no pets, no children under six. Open all year.

Around the corner from MacDonald's is **Reibers' Bed and Breakfast,** Rt. 198, Somesville, P.O. Box 163, Mount Desert 04660, tel. (207) 244-3047, with a discreet sign attached to a lamppost set back from the street. Four acres of lovely lawns stretch to a tidal creek outside Gail and David Reiber's handsome mid-19th-century antiques-filled home. (Across the street is former Secretary of Defense Caspar Weinberger's estate.) The Reibers have lots of touring ideas. Two second-floor rooms go for $75 d (private bath) or $65 (shared bath) in summer, less off season. No smoking, no pets; children are welcome. Open all year.

Between Somesville and downtown Southwest Harbor is **The Heron House,** 1 Fernald Point Rd., HC 33, Box 101, Southwest Harbor 04679, tel. (207) 244-0221, Sue and Bob Bonkowski's Victorian B&B at the corner of Rt. 102. Antique St. Bernard prints are a dominant theme, and a live St. Bernard greets you at the door. Three second-floor rooms ($60 d May-Oct., $50 Nov.-April) share two bathrooms; kimonos are provided. It's all relaxed and informal; guests can use the refrigerator or grill dinner outside. A former wildlife rehabber and dedicated hiker, Sue has countless suggestions for area hiking. Her hearty breakfasts include edible flowers and unusual herbs. No pets, no smoking, no credit cards. Open all year.

Just down the side road from Heron House is **The Birches,** Fernald Point Rd., P.O. Box 178, Southwest Harbor 04679, tel. (207) 244-5182, Dick and Rocky Homer's waterfront home on five acres .4 mile east of Rt. 102. Outside are gardens and a croquet court. Three lovely rooms (two with water views) have private baths; $90 d. No pets. Open all year; two-night minimum.

In downtown Southwest Harbor, the following three B&Bs stand cheek-by-jowl—two moderately expensive ones and an inexpensive one.

The only amenity innkeeper Jill Lewis doesn't provide in her tasteful Victorian **Inn at Southwest,** 371 Main St., Rt. 102, Box 593, Southwest Harbor 04679, tel. (207) 244-3835, is a TV, but no one misses it. Guests gather for games, reading, conversation, and afternoon tea in a huge living room with fireplace and comfortable couches. Nine second- and third-floor guest rooms—named for Maine lighthouses and full of character—are fitted out with wicker furniture, ceiling fans, down comforters, and lots more. All have private baths. Rates are $90-135 d mid-June to late October, $60-95 other months. No pets, no children under 12; smoking only on the veranda. Open May through October.

Across the street, **The Kingsleigh Inn,** 373 Main St., P.O. Box 1426, Southwest Harbor 04679, tel. (207) 244-5302, is a very attractive Victorian with eight well-thought-out rooms (private baths) on three floors. If you're sensitive to street noise, request a back-facing (harborview) room, although air-conditioners muffle the sound in summer. Tea and coffee are always available in the kitchen, there's a separate guest phone, and wine and cheese are served in the living room each afternoon at 5. Rates are $95-105 d July to mid-September, $55-85 d other months. The turret suite, with fireplace, TV, and telescope, is $95-165 d, depending on the season. No children under 12; smoking only on the veranda. Open all year.

Across Rt. 102 from the above two B&Bs is the far more casual **Penury Hall,** Main St., Box 68, Southwest Harbor 04679, tel. (207) 244-7102, fax 244-5651, run by Toby and Gretchen Strong since 1982. Three second-floor rooms in the 1830 house share two baths (one up, one down). Rates are $70 d June-Oct. (two-night minimum), $50-60 d other months. Mature children are welcome, but no more than two persons to a room. No smoking, no pets (coon cats in residence). Free sauna for guests. Open all year; a surrogate innkeeper takes charge when the Strongs head to the Bahamas in winter.

On a quiet side street close to the water in Southwest Harbor is Ann and Charlie Bradford's **Island House,** Clark Point Rd., Box 1006, Southwest Harbor 04679, tel. (207) 244-5180, filled with exotic paintings and furniture from Ann's youth in Singapore, Malaysia, and India. Their hospitality and breakfasts are memorable. Four rooms share two baths ($65 d mid-June to mid-October, $50-55 d other months; $5 surcharge for a one-night stay). The Birch Room boasts a skylight. A separate carriage-house apartment is $95 for two, $135 for four. A double with private bath is $10 extra Nov.-May. No smoking, no pets. Open all year. The Bradfords also rent a summer cottage, $550-650 a week, near Bass Harbor Head Light.

In nearby Bass Harbor, **Pointy Head Inn and Antiques,** Rt. 102A, HC 33, Box 2A, Bass Harbor 04653, tel. (207) 244-7261, is as quirky—and entertaining—as its name. Doris Townsend keeps everything shipshape in the comfortable, three-story 18th-century house overlooking Bass Harbor; husband Warren regales the guests and creates woodcarvings for the adjoining antiques/gift shop. Four rooms share two baths;

two rooms have private baths. Rates are $55-95 d, depending on the season; two-night minimum in summer. No smoking, no small children, no pets. This is a perfect base for anyone going to Swans Island; the ferry landing is almost within spitting distance.

Campgrounds: A smallish, low-key campground in an outstanding setting, **Somes Sound View Campground,** Hall Quarry Rd., Mount Desert 04660, tel. (207) 244-3890, has 60 tent and RV sites on the edge of the eponymous quarry. Facilities include hot showers; nearest store is two miles. Sites are $15-18 (two adults and two children) in July and August, $12 early and late in the season. Open late May to mid-October. The campground is two miles south and east of Somesville and a mile east of Rt. 102.

On the eastern edge of Somesville, just off Rt. 198 at the head of Somes Sound, the **Mount Desert Campground,** Rt. 198, Somesville, mailing address Mount Desert 04660, tel. (207) 244-3710, is especially centrally located for visiting Bar Harbor, Acadia, and the whole western side of Mount Desert Island. The campground has 152 wooded RV and tentsites, about 45 on the water; hookup sites are in the minority. Reservations are advisable for this popular campground, which gets high marks for its maintenance, noise control, and convenient tent platforms. Rates are $20-27 a night ($22 for a tent platform, $27 for the waterfront sites). No pets July, August, and Labor Day weekend. No trailers over 20 feet. Keowee kayak rentals are $6 an hour, $15 for four hours. Open Memorial Day weekend through September.

Seasonal Rentals: Martha Dodge, at **L.S. Robinson Real Estate,** 337 Main St., Southwest Harbor 04679, tel. (207) 244-5563, commands an inventory of 500 seasonal (and yearround) rentals, most on the western side of Mount Desert Island. She can also assist with rentals in other parts of the island.

Food
Kids (and wannabe kids) flock to the old-fashioned soda counter at **Mrs. McVety's Ice Cream Shoppe,** Main St., Southwest Harbor, tel. (207) 244-7015, which amiable former schoolteacher Judy McVety has been running since 1988. Homemade cones, ice cream floats, whoopie pies, and mega-sundaes are big draws, although you can also order chowder, a crab roll, or pie. World and U.S. wall maps pinpoint hometowns of enthusiastic customers. In summer, the ice cream parlor is open daily 9 a.m.-9 p.m.

The gorp is the greatest at **Burdock's Natural Foods,** Main St., Rt. 102, P.O. Box 176, Southwest Harbor 04679, tel. (207) 244-0108, so stock up here with pound-size packets of interesting trail mixes. No credit cards. Open all year, Mon.-Fri. 9 a.m.-5:30 p.m. and Saturday 9:30 a.m.-4 p.m., plus Sunday 9 a.m.-5:30 p.m. in summer.

Lobster-in-the-Rough: It's really tough to top the experience at **Thurston's,** Steamboat Wharf Rd., Bernard 04612, tel. (207) 244-7600, probably the best lobster-alfresco deal on the island. Family-oriented Thurston's also has chowders, sandwiches, and terrific desserts. The screened dining room practically sits in the water. Beer and wine available. Open Memorial Day weekend to Columbus Day, daily: 11 a.m.-8 p.m. early and late in the season, 7 a.m.-8:30 p.m. in July and August.

Inexpensive to Moderate: Some of the island's most creative sandwiches and pizza toppings emerge from Arthur and Kate Jacobs's **Little Notch Café,** 340 Main St., P.O. Box 1295, Southwest Harbor 04679, tel. (207) 244-3357, next to the library in Southwest Harbor's downtown. How about a small broccoli, sausage, and black-olive pizza for $9? Freshly baked breads, outrageous desserts, a couple of dinner entrées, and homemade soups, stews, and chowders make the Little Notch a winner. No credit cards. Open all year, Mon.-Sat. 11 a.m.-8 p.m.

Don't be intimidated by the unprepossessing exterior of **Keenan's,** Rt. 102A, Bass Harbor 04653, tel. (207) 244-3403—and arrive early or late to get a seat. Liz and Frank Keenan operate one of Mount Desert Island's "in" spots. Among their specialties are seafood gumbo (including a lobster tail, $4 a bowl), barbecue ribs ($13), seafood pasta, and excellent homemade cornbread. Kids can order inexpensive burgers and hot dogs. Wine and beer license only. No credit cards. Open all year, Tues.-Sun. 5:30-10 p.m. in summer, Thurs.-Sat. in winter. Keenan's is at the triangle where Rts. 102 and 102A meet, across from Harbor Divers.

Restaurant XYZ, Shore Rd., Manset, Southwest Harbor 04679, tel. (207) 244-5221, specializing in "classical food of the Mexican interior," focuses on unusual entrées ($10-14) from Xalapa, Yucatán, and Zacatecas (hence, XYZ). The margaritas are classic. For dessert, try the exquisite XYZ pie. The harbor view is spectacular; stroll the Shore Road after dinner. A small adjacent gallery features art and folk crafts by Maine and Mexican artists. Open for dinner mid-May through mid-October. Reservations are advisable in July and August. XYZ is across from the Manset town dock.

Moderate to Expensive: After earning a stellar reputation in Bar Harbor with his FinBack Restaurant, now closed, Terry Preble opened the superb Preble Grille, 14 Clark Point Rd., Southwest Harbor 04679, tel. (207) 244-3034, in 1995, quickly making it a culinary favorite. His angle is Mediterranean with a Maine twist—ultrafresh seafood and creative pasta specialties. A fireplace adds to the ambience, and there's a small bar. No smoking. Don't arrive without a reservation during July and August. Open daily 5:30-10 p.m., Memorial Day weekend to late October; open Thurs.-Sat. in November and December and mid-April to late May.

Information and Services
Based at Harbor House, a town-owned multipurpose facility, the Southwest Harbor/Tremont Chamber of Commerce, Main St., P.O. Box 1143, Southwest Harbor 04679, tel. (207) 244-9264 or (800) 423-9264 outside Maine is open on an erratic schedule, but you can usually find someone here weekdays in summer. The information center at Thompson Island has more predictable and longer hours.

The Southwest Harbor Public Library, Main St., Southwest Harbor 04679, tel. (207) 244-7065, is open Mon.-Fri. 9 a.m.-5 p.m. (to 8 p.m. Wednesday).

Public Restrooms: In downtown Southwest Harbor, public restrooms are located at the southern end of the parking lot behind Carroll's Drug Store (Main Street). Across Main Street, Harbor House, locale of the chamber of commerce, also has a restroom, as does the Swans Island ferry terminal in Bass Harbor.

ISLANDS NEAR MOUNT DESERT

The most popular island day-trip destinations from Mount Desert Island are the Cranberry Isles and Swans Island. Most commercial and mailboats for the Cranberries depart from Northeast Harbor, although one line originates in Southwest Harbor (both carry bikes but no cars); state car ferries for Swans Island depart from Bass Harbor, south of Southwest Harbor.

The Maine State Ferry Service also operates a ferry to Long Island (referred to as Frenchboro, the name of the village on the island) from Bass Harbor, but the schedule doesn't lend itself to day-trips or convenient visits. But this may change in the next several years.

CRANBERRY ISLES

The Cranberry Isles, south of Northeast and Seal Harbors, comprise Great Cranberry, Little Cranberry (called Islesford), Sutton, Baker, and Bear Islands. Islesford and Baker include Acadia National Park property. Bring a bike and explore the narrow, mostly level roads on the two largest islands (Great Cranberry and Islesford), but remember to respect private property. Unless you've asked permission, don't cut across private land to reach the shore.

The Cranberry name has been attributed to 18th-century loyalist governor Francis Bernard, who received these islands (along with all of Mount Desert) as a king's grant in 1762. Cranberry bogs (now long gone) on the two largest islands evidently caught his attention. Permanent European settlers were here in the 1760s, and there was even steamboat service by the 1820s.

Lobstering and other fishing industries are the commercial mainstay, boosted in summer by the various visitor-related pursuits. Artists and writers come for a week, a month, or longer; day-trippers spend time on Great Cranberry and Islesford.

Largest of the islands is Great Cranberry, first stop on the mailboat route. You can even spend the night at **The Red House,** P.O. Box 164, Cranberry Isles 04625, tel. (207) 244-5297 or (407) 664-1757 in winter, a rustic, six-room B&B with kitchen facilities. The late-18th-century cottage, facing the peaks of Mount Desert, is open Memorial Day to Columbus Day. Innkeepers John and Dorothy Towns will prepare dinner (extra charge) if you forewarn them. Rooms are $70-80 d (private bath), $60 d (shared bath) late June to Labor Day; $55-65 d (private bath), $50 d (shared bath) other months. Reservations are essential.

Also on Great Cranberry are the **Cranberry General Store,** near the dock, tel. (207) 244-7972, for picnic fixings, and the **Whale's Rib Gift Shop,** about midway along the main road, tel. (207) 244-5153.

The second-largest island is **Little Cranberry,** locally known as **Islesford.** Close to the dock is **The Islesford Historical Museum,** operated by the National Park Service, tel. (207) 288-3338. The exhibits focus on local history, much of it maritime, so displays include ship models, household goods, fishing gear, and other memorabilia. The museum is open daily 10:45 a.m.-noon and 12:30-4:30 p.m., mid-June to Labor Day. Free admission. (Restrooms are next door, in The Blue Duck, a mid-19th-century building once operated as a chandlery and now owned by the Park Service.) **Islesford Artists,** tel. (207) 244-3145, is a small but excellent gallery specializing in local artists' depictions of local sites (lots of landscapes, naturally). Run by Danny and Katy Fernald, the gallery is open daily 10 a.m. to 5 p.m., in July and August; weekdays 10 a.m.-4 p.m. or by appointment the rest of the season, closed in winter.

At dockside is **The Islesford Dock,** tel. (207) 244-7494, serving lunch and dinner daily 10 a.m.-3 p.m. and 5-9 p.m., June through Labor Day. Prices are moderate, food is home-cooked, and views are incredible. If the weather's good, eat on the deck. Reservations are wise in mid-summer. Water taxis are available for returning to Northeast Harbor after dinner. Also on the dock is **Islesford Pottery,** Islesford 04646, tel. (207) 244-5686, Marian Baker's summertime ceramic studio. Her functional pieces are particularly attractive. The shop is open daily 10 a.m.-4 p.m., June to Labor Day.

Islesford's imaginative postmaster, Joy Sprague, has brought the island a bit of postal fame by creating Maine's busiest stamps-by-mail operation—$57,000 worth of stamp orders in 1996. Her customers, who do their ordering from as far away as Turkey, receive her two-page personal island newsletter in appreciation for their support. And every 25th express mail customer at the Islesford post office receives a batch of her homemade cream puffs. Now *that's* service. Use Postal Service form 3227 if you'd like to join the ordering club; her address is U.S. Post Office, Islesford 04646.

Getting to the Cranberries

Decades-old, family-run **Beal & Bunker, Inc.,** P.O. Box 33, Cranberry Isles 04625, tel. (207) 244-3575, provides year-round mailboat/passenger service to the Cranberries from Northeast Harbor. The ferries don't carry cars, but you can bring a bike. Or just plan to explore on foot. The summer season, with more frequent trips, runs mid-June through Labor Day. The first boat departs Northeast Harbor's Municipal Pier Mon.-Sat. at 7:30 a.m.; first Sunday boat is 10 a.m.; the last boat for Northeast Harbor leaves Islesford at 6:30 p.m. and Great Cranberry at 6:45 p.m. The boats do a bit of zigging and zagging on the three-island route (including Sutton in summer), so be patient as they make the circuit. It's a people-watching treat. If you just did a roundtrip and stayed aboard, the loop would take about an hour and a half. Roundtrip tickets (covering the whole loop, including intra-island if you want to visit both Great Cranberry and Islesford) are $10 adults, $5 kids under 12 (free for kids under three). Bicycles are $2 roundtrip. The off-season schedule operates early May through mid-June and early September through late October; the winter schedule runs late October through early May. In winter, the boat company advises phoning ahead on what Mainers quaintly call "weather days."

Cranberry Cove Boating Company, Upper Town Dock, Clark Point Rd., Southwest Harbor 04679, tel. (207) 244-5882, operates a summertime ferry service to the Cranberries, mid-June to mid-September, aboard the 47-passenger *Island Queen.* First departure from Southwest Harbor is 9:30 a.m.; last departure from Great Cranberry is 5:15 p.m. Roundtrip fares are $10 adults, $5 children under 12 (free for kids under three). Bikes are $2 roundtrip. Off season, call to check on the schedule.

The best way to visit beautiful, uninhabited **Baker Island,** part of Acadia National Park, is to take the Baker Island cruise operated by the **Islesford Ferry Co.,** Box 451, RFD 2, Ellsworth 04605, tel. (207) 276-3717 or 422-6815 off season, which is based at the municipal pier in Northeast Harbor. The four-and-a-half-hour trip starts at 1 p.m. daily, June-Sept., and a park naturalist accompanies the 72-passenger boat in July and August to describe the human and natural history of the island; other months, Capt. Bill Barter, a real pro, does the explaining. Wear sturdy shoes; you'll be offloaded by small boat and the terrain is uneven. Cost is $16 adults, $15 seniors, $8 children 4-11, free for kids under four. Reservations are advisable, and are held until 10 minutes before departure. The Islesford Ferry Co. also has a two-and-a-half-hour Cranberries nature cruise, departing from Northeast Harbor daily at 10:05 a.m. and stopping in Islesford long enough for lunch or a visit to the museum. Cost is $11 adults, $10 seniors, $6 kids 4-11.

The **MDI Water Taxi,** a converted lobsterboat, makes frequent on-demand trips to the Cranberries (a daylight run to Islesford costs $60 for a boatload). Call (207) 244-7312.

SWANS ISLAND

Six miles off Mount Desert Island lies scenic, 6,000-acre Swans Island (pop. about 350), named after Col. James Swan, who purchased it and two dozen other islands as an investment in 1786. As with the Cranberries, fishing—especially lobstering—is the year-round way of life here; summer sees the arrival of artists, writers, and other seasonal visitors.

With plenty of relatively level terrain (but narrow roads), and a not-impossible amount of real estate to cover, Swans is ideal for a bicycling day-trip. The island has no campsites, no public restrooms, and one tiny B&B. Visitors who want to spend more than a day tend to rent cottages by the week.

If you can be flexible, wait for a clear day, then catch the first ferry (7:30 a.m.) from Bass

Hockamock Head Light, Swans Island

Harbor. At the ferry office in Bass Harbor, request a Swans Island map (and take advantage of the restroom). Keep an eye on your watch so you don't miss the last ferry (4:30 p.m.) back to Bass Harbor.

Pack a picnic or plan to stop for picnic fixings at the **General Store** in Minturn, one of the island's three villages, on the east side of Burnt Coat Harbor. Then pedal around to the west side of the harbor and down the peninsula to **Hockamock Head Light** (officially, Burnt Coat Harbor Light). From the ferry landing, Hockamock Head is about five miles.

The distinctive square lighthouse, built in 1872 and now automated, sits on a rocky promontory overlooking Burnt Coat Harbor, Harbor Island, lobsterboat traffic, and crashing surf. The keeper's house is unoccupied; the grounds are great for picnics.

If it's hot, ask for directions to one of two prime island swimming spots **Fine Sand Beach** (salt water) or **Quarry Pond** (fresh water). Fine

Sand Beach is on the west side of Toothacher Cove; you'll have to navigate a short stretch of unpaved road to get there, but it's worth the trouble. Be prepared for chilly water, however. Quarry Pond is in Minturn, not far from the post office.

On the east side of the island is the weaving barn of the **Atlantic Blanket Company,** Swans Island 04685, tel. (207) 526-4492, fax 526-4174, where John and Carolyn Grace and Carol Loehr produce exquisite undyed handwoven blankets from local white, black, brown, and gray wool. A summer-weight twin-bed blanket runs $265; quality is flawless. The barn, overlooking the sheep pastures, is open all year, Mon.-Sat. 2-5 p.m., other times by appointment. They also do mail order (with a credit card).

A Swans Island summer highlight is the **Sweet Chariot Music Festival,** a three-night midweek extravaganza in early August. Windjammers arrive from Camden and Rockland, enthusiasts show up on their private boats, and the island's Oddfellows Hall is SRO for three evenings of folk singing, storytelling, and impromptu hijinks. In midafternoon of the first two days (about 3:30 p.m.), musicians go from boat to boat in Burnt Coat Harbor, entertaining with sea chanteys. Tickets for evening concerts (7:30 p.m.) are $10. Along the route from harbor to concert, enterprising local kids peddle lemonade, homemade brownies, and kitschy craft items. It's all very festive, but definitely a "boat thing," not very convenient for anyone without waterborne transport. Info is available from festival founder Doug Day, P.O. Box 129, Swans Island 04685, tel. (207) 526-4443.

Getting to Swans Island

Swans Island is a 40-minute trip on the car ferry *Captain Henry Lee.* Between mid-April and mid-October, the ferry makes 5-6 roundtrips a day, the first from Bass Harbor at 7:30 a.m. (9 a.m. Sunday) and the last from Swans Island at 4:30 p.m. Other months, the first and last runs are the same, but there are only 4-5 trips. For more information, contact **Maine State Ferry Service,** P.O. Box 114, Bass Harbor 04653, tel. (207) 244-3254; P.O. Box 158, Swans Island 04685, tel. (207) 526-4273. Roundtrip fares are $6 adults, $3 children 5-11. Bikes are $5 roundtrip per adult, $2 per child. Parking across the road from the Bass Harbor ferry terminal is $4 a day. Roundtrip for vehicle and driver is $18. Reservations are accepted only for vehicles.

To reach the Bass Harbor ferry terminal on Mount Desert Island, follow the distinctive blue signs, marked Swans Island Ferry, along Rts. 102 and 102A.

Southwest Cycle, Main St., Southwest Harbor 04679, tel. (207) 244-5856 or (800) 649-5856 in Maine, rents bikes by the day ($16 adults, $12 children) and is open all year. Hours are Mon.-Sat. 8:30 a.m.-5:30 p.m. and Sunday 10 a.m.-4 p.m., June-Sept.; Mon.-Sat. 9 a.m.-5 p.m., Oct.-May. They also have ferry schedules and Swans Island maps. (For the early-morning ferry, you'll need to pick up bikes the day before; reserve them in advance if you're doing this in July or August.)

EASTERN HANCOCK COUNTY

Sneak around to the eastern side of Frenchman Bay and you'll see this region from a whole new perspective. One hour from the Acadia National Park visitor center, you'll find Acadia's mountains silhouetted against the sunset, the surf slamming onto Schoodic Point, the peace of a calmer lifestyle.

If you're coming from Trenton—the funnel to Mount Desert—duck east via Rt. 204 toward Lamoine and its state park. From Ellsworth, follow Rt. 1 toward Hancock, Sullivan, Sorrento, Gouldsboro, and Winter Harbor.

Winter Harbor (pop. 1,250), the only separate town on the Gouldsboro Peninsula, is known best as the gateway to the Schoodic Peninsula, Acadia National Park's only mainland acreage. A highly classified U.S. Navy communications operation (officially, Naval Security Group Activity, NSGA) in Winter Harbor keeps a relatively low profile, as does the old-money, Philadelphia-linked summer colony on exclusive Grindstone Neck. But little clues hint at the presence of both of them.

Winter Harbor's summer highlight is the annual Lobster Festival, second Saturday in August. The gala day-long event includes a parade, live entertainment, games, and more crustaceans than you could ever consume.

Gouldsboro (pop. 2,100)—including the not-to-be-missed villages of Birch Harbor, Corea, and Prospect Harbor—earned its own minor fame from Louise Dickinson Rich's 1958 book *The Peninsula,* a tribute to her summers on Corea's Cranberry Point—"a place that has stood still in time." Since 1958, change has crept into Corea, but not so's you'd notice. It's still the same quintessential lobster-fishing community, perfect for photo ops.

SIGHTS

The biggest attractions in Eastern Hancock County are the spectacular vignettes and vistas—of offshore lighthouses, distant mountains, close-in islands, and unchanged villages. Check out each finger of land: Lamoine, Hancock Point, Sorrento, and Winter Harbor's Grindstone Neck. Loop around the Schoodic Peninsula, circle the Gouldsboro Peninsula, and detour to Corea. Then head inland and follow Rt. 182, a designated Scenic Highway, from Hancock to Cherryfield. Accomplish all this and you'll have a fine sense of place. (Make sure to stock up on film, and remember that a wide-angle lens or a panoramic camera is a major asset.)

Bartlett's Winery
German and Italian presses, Portuguese corks, and Maine fruit all go into the creation of Bob and Kathe Bartlett's award-winning dinner and dessert wines: apple, pear, blueberry, raspberry, blackberry, strawberry, and loganberry. Founded in 1983, Bartlett Maine Estate Winery, Chicken Mill Pond Rd., RR 1, Box 598, Gouldsboro 04607, tel. (207) 546-2408, produces nearly 20,000 gallons annually in a handsome wood-and-stone building designed by the Bartletts. On-demand tours take about 20 minutes, after which you can buy single bottles and gift packages. Bartlett's, a mile south of Rt. 1 in Gouldsboro, is open Memorial Day weekend to Columbus Day, Mon.-Sat. 10 a.m.-5 p.m., or by appointment off season.

PARKS, PRESERVES, AND RECREATION

Acadia National Park
Slightly more than 2,000 of Acadia National Park's acres are on the mainland, and they're all here on the **Schoodic Peninsula.** Along the six-mile one-way (counterclockwise) road that loops through the park are picnic spots, a few hiking trailheads, an offshore lighthouse, and scenic turnouts. There's no camping in the park, but Ocean Wood Campground, tel. (207) 963-7194, on the Schoodic Peninsula, is convenient and beautiful. The world-class scenery, free admission, and the general lack of congestion make Schoodic the preferred Acadia destination of many a savvy visitor. Note: If you're driving and see a viewpoint you like, stop; it's a long way around to return.

To reach the park boundary from Rt. 1 in Gouldsboro, take Rt. 186 south to Winter Harbor. Continue through town, heading east, then turn right after Schoodic Snacks and continue to the park-entrance sign, just before the bridge over Mosquito Harbor.

Just after the bridge, the first landmark is **Frazer Point Picnic Area,** with lovely vistas, picnic tables, and convenient outhouses. Other spots are fine for picnics, but this is the only official one. If you've brought bikes, leave your car here and do a counterclockwise loop through the park and back to your car via Birch Harbor and Rt. 186. It's a fine day-trip.

From the picnic area, the **Park Loop Road** becomes one-way. Go about two and a half miles and watch for a narrow, unpaved road on the left, leading a mile up to the open ledges on 440-foot Schoodic Head. (Don't confuse it with Schoodic Mountain, which is well north of here.) For exercise, hike up, although you'll need to keep an eye out for cars.

Continue on the Park Loop Road, past the sprawling, secretive U.S. Navy base, and hang a right onto a short, two-way spur to **Schoodic Point,** where the parking lot seldom fills up. Check local newspapers for the time of high tide and try to arrive here then; the word "awesome" is overused, but it sure fits Schoodic Point's surf performance on the rugged pink granite. **Caution:** If you've brought children, keep them well back from the water; a rogue wave can sweep them off the rocks all too easily. Picnics are great here (make sure you bring a litter bag), and so are the tidepools. Birding is spectacular during spring and fall migrations.

Return to the Park Loop Road and go about a mile to the Blueberry Hill parking area. Across the road is the trailhead to the 180-foot-high **Anvil** headland, and then on up to Schoodic Head. Allow 2-3 hours for the clockwise Schoodic Head-Anvil loop back to your car.

From Blueberry Hill, continue another two miles to the park exit, just before Birch Harbor.

Lamoine State Park

In July and August, when every single campsite on Mount Desert Island is booked solid, those in the know go eight miles southeast of Ellsworth to the wooded, no-frills campground at 55-acre Lamoine State Park, Rt. 184, Lamoine 04605, tel. (207) 667-4778. Park facilities include a pebble beach and picnic area with a spectacular view, a boat-launch ramp, and a children's play area. Day-use admission is $2 adults, 50 cents children 5-11. Camping (61 sites) is $15 per site per night for nonresidents; no hookups; two-night minimum. The park is open daily, mid-May to mid-October, and accessible off season for daytime activities.

Donnell Pond Public Reserved Land

More than 14,000 acres have been preserved for public access in a huge mountain-and-lake area north and east of Sullivan. Developers had their eyes on this gorgeous real estate in the 1980s, but preservationists fortunately rallied to the cause. Outright purchase of 7,316 of the acres, in the Spring River Lake area, came through the foresighted Land for Maine's Future program. Route 182, an official Scenic Highway, cuts right through the Donnell Pond preserve.

Major water bodies here are **Donnell Pond** (big enough by most gauges to be called a lake) and **Tunk** and **Spring River Lakes;** all are accessible for boats (even, alas, powerboats and jet skis). Tunk Lake has a few campsites in its southwestern corner. The eastern and southern shores of Donnell Pond have primitive, first-come, first-served sites (no charge), which are snapped up quickly on midsummer weekends. Schoodic Beach, the prime swimming area, is in the southeastern corner of Donnell Pond.

By boat, trailheads at Schoodic Beach as well as Black Beach provide access to **Caribou, Black,** and **Schoodic Mountains,** all tied together by connector trails. None are easy but it's great hiking—and there's a tower on 1,069-foot Schoodic. The Caribou-Black Mountain Loop, clockwise, is about a seven-mile roundtrip from the Black Beach boat-access trailhead.

To reach the boat-launching area for Donnell Pond from Rt. 1 in Sullivan, take Rt. 200 north to Rt. 182. Turn right and go about one and a half miles to a right turn just before Swan Brook. Turn and go not quite two miles to the put-in; the road is poor in spots but adequate for a regular vehicle. The Narrows, where you'll put in, is lined with summer cottages ("camps" in the Maine vernacular); keep paddling eastward to the more open part of the lake.

To reach the vehicle-access trailhead for Schoodic Mountain from Rt. 1 in East Sullivan, drive just over four miles northeast on Rt. 183 (Lake Road). Cross the Maine Central Railroad tracks and turn left onto an unpaved road (marked as a jeep track on the USGS map). Continue to the parking area and trailhead. Follow the Schoodic Mountain Loop clockwise, heading westward first. To make a day of it, pack a picnic and take a swimsuit (and don't forget a camera and binoculars for the summit views). On a brilliantly clear day, you'll see Baxter State Park's Katahdin, the peaks of Acadia National Park, and the ocean beyond. For such rewards, this is a popular hike, so don't expect to be alone on summer and fall weekends.

Still within the preserve boundaries, but farther east, you can put in a canoe at the northern end of Long Pond and paddle southward into adjoining Round Pond. In early August, Round Mountain, rising a few hundred feet from Long Pond's eastern shore, is a great spot for gathering blueberries and huckleberries. The put-in for Long Pond is on the south side of Rt. 182 (park well off the road), about two miles east of Tunk Lake.

Golf

Play a nine-hole round at the **Grindstone Neck Golf Course,** Grindstone Ave., Winter Harbor 04693, tel. (207) 963-7760, just for the dynamite scenery, and for a glimpse of this exclusive, late-19th-century summer enclave. Established in 1895, the public course attracts a tony crowd; 150-yard markers are cute little bird-houses. Tee times usually aren't needed, but call to make sure. The course is open early June through September.

Getting Afloat

You'll soon be a **sea kayaking** convert if you take a lesson/tour with dedicated ecologists Don and Mary Alice Bruce of **Schoodic Tours,** Sand Cove Ln., Corea 04624, tel. (207) 963-7958. Experienced paddlers, people with disabilities, and children are all welcome. Reservations are required; group maximum is eight. Cost is $40 pp for a three-hour stint; special rates for families. No credit cards. Tours go out daily, early June to late September. Three or four times weekly, special trips venture beyond the Corea Peninsula. All excursions are weather-dependent, and sometimes tide-dependent. The Bruces also rent sea kayaks and mountain bikes and organize guided ecology walks. They're just off Rt. 195, west of Corea's center.

Registered Maine Guide Danny Mitchell operates **Moose Look Guide Service,** HC 35, Box 246, Gouldsboro 04607, tel. (207) 963-7720, with three-hour kayak tours departing at 9 a.m. and 5:30 p.m. Cost is $35 pp. Moose Look also rents kayaks ($25 a day), canoes ($20 a day), and mountain bikes ($15 a day; $1 extra for a car rack). Kayak tours are weather-dependent.

On-your-own paddling possibilities are described above under "Donnell Pond Public Reserved Land."

ENTERTAINMENT

The **Pierre Monteux School for Conductors and Orchestra Musicians,** Rt. 1, Hancock 04640, tel. (207) 422-3931, a prestigious summer program founded in 1943, presents two well-attended concert series between late June and early August. Known also as the Domaine School or the Pierre Monteux School, it has an internationally renowned faculty and has trained dozens of national and international classical musicians. Five Wednesday concerts (8 p.m.) feature chamber music; six Sunday concerts (5 p.m.) feature symphonies. An annual children's concert usually is held on a Monday (1 p.m.) in mid-July. Tickets are $12 adults, less for

students. Concerts are held in the School Hall on Rt. 1.

Nearest cinemas are in Ellsworth and Bar Harbor, as are lots of other entertainment possibilities.

SHOPPING

Zero in on Eastern Hancock County to shop for everyone on your list who appreciates unusual crafts and gifts. Hancock, Sullivan, and Gouldsboro are loaded with great gallery-shops.

Art and Craft Galleries

Maine art and crafts—textiles, jewelry, glasswork, baskets, and pottery—fill the **Sugar Hill Gallery,** Rt. 1, P.O. Box 96, Hancock 04640, tel. (207) 422-8207, a lovely space nine miles northeast of Ellsworth. Opened in 1995, the gallery has a soupçon of Southern flavor, thanks to Georgia-born owner Cynthia Perkins. The gallery is open daily 10 a.m.-5 p.m., June-mid-Oct.; Thurs.-Sat. in May and mid-Oct.-Dec.; unpredictable hours Feb.-April. In the fall, the gallery creates mail-order Christmas wreaths, call (800) 572-0488 for a catalog.

Bet you can't keep from smiling at the whimsical animal sculptures of talented sculptor/painter Philip Barter. His work is the cornerstone of the eclectic, two-room **Barter Family Gallery,** Shore Rd., Box 102, Sullivan 04664, tel. (207) 422-3190, on a back road in Sullivan. But there's more: Barter's wife and seven children have put their considerable skills to work producing braided rugs, jewelry, and other craft items sold here at moderate prices. No credit cards. Located two and a half miles northwest of Rt. 1, the gallery is signposted soon after you cross the bridge from Hancock. It's open daily, all year; the family home is attached. Summer hours are Mon.-Sat. 10 a.m.-5 p.m. and Sunday noon-5 p.m.

On an even farther-back road (unpaved), the Buell family carries on a variety of enterprises at **The Granite Garden Gallery,** FR 10, North Sullivan 04664, tel. (207) 422-6885, a magical, almost-mystical place supervised by a giant Philip Barter sculpture—Quarrysaurus, mascot-in-residence. Gibran Buell quarries granite on a small scale; a stone sculptor often is working away at his craft in the open-air gallery artfully littered with whimsical granite compositions; a tiny shed-shop features polished stones and cedar boxes. In addition, there are miles of mountain-bike trails and some dirt-cheap primitive accommodations. No credit cards. The gallery area is open Mon.-Sat. 9 a.m.-5 p.m., mid-July to mid-September. From Rt. 1 in Sullivan, take Shore Rd. to FR 10; watch carefully for signs. Total distance is about two miles.

Artist Paul Breeden, best known for the remarkable illustrations, calligraphy, and maps he's done for *National Geographic,* Time-Life Books, and other national publications, displays and sells his paintings at the **Spring Woods Gallery,** Rt. 200, Box 40A, Sullivan 04664, tel. (207) 422-3007. Also filling the handsome modern gallery space are paintings by Ann Breeden, metal sculptures and silk scarves by the talented Breeden offspring, and Pueblo artifacts from the American Southwest. The beautifully landscaped gallery, .2 mile north of Rt. 1, is open Mon.-Sat. 10 a.m.-6 p.m., Memorial Day weekend through October.

Gifts and More Crafts

Blue-and-white Japanese-style motifs predominate at **Gull Rock Pottery,** 325 Eastside Rd., Hancock 04640, tel. (207) 422-3990, Torj and Kurt Wray's studio and shop one and a half miles south of Rt. 1 (the driveway is another half a mile). They'll also do special orders of their wheel-thrown, hand-painted, dishwasher-safe pottery. No credit cards. The shop is open all year, Mon.-Sat. 9 a.m.-5 p.m.

Overlooking Hog Bay, 3.6 miles north of Rt. 1, Charles and Susanne Grosjean have been the key players at **Hog Bay Pottery,** Rt. 200, Box 175, Franklin 04634, tel. (207) 565-2282, since 1974. Inside the casual, laid-back showroom are Charles's functional, nature-themed pottery and Susanne's stunning handwoven rugs. They produce a mail-order catalog and often fill custom orders. The shop, next to their house, is open daily May-Oct.; call ahead other months.

Chickadee Creek Stillroom, Rt. 186, P.O. Box 220, W. Gouldsboro 04607, tel. (207) 963-7283 or (800) 969-4372, is the Toys R Us of herb fanciers. Jeanie and Fred Cook seem to have thought of everything—potpourri, teas, wreaths, fresh herbs for cooking. The barn-shop, 1.7 miles south of Rt. 1, is open daily 10 a.m.-4 p.m., May to mid-October, plus Saturday and Sunday 10 a.m.-4 p.m., mid-October to Christmas. Request a copy of the mail-order catalog.

Visiting the **U.S. Bells Foundry and Store,** West Bay Rd., Rt. 186, P.O. Box 73, Prospect Harbor 04669, tel./fax (207) 963-7184, is a treat for the ears, as browsers try out the many varieties of cast-bronze bells made in the adjacent foundry by Richard Fisher. If you're lucky, he may have time to explain the process—particularly intriguing for children, and a distraction from their instinctive urge to test every bell in the shop. The store also carries a tasteful selection of handmade quilts, Shaker items, pottery, and jewelry. It's open all year, Mon.-Fri. 8 a.m.-5 p.m. and Saturday 8 a.m.-noon. Summer Saturdays, it's open until 5 p.m. U.S. Bells is a quarter of a mile up the hill from Prospect Harbor's post office.

Just up the road (toward Rt. 1) from U.S. Bells, Cindy and Bill Thayer's enthusiasm is contagious as they explain their incredibly prolific organic farm—home to hairy Scotch Highland cattle, turkeys, sheep, pigs, and border collies. At **Darthia Farm,** West Bay Rd., Rt. 186, Box 520, Gouldsboro 04607, tel. (207) 963-7771, kids love feeding the pigs and riding on the hay wagon; parents can check out Hattie's Shed for Cindy's outstanding ikat weavings. Farm tours occur each Tuesday and Thursday at 2 p.m., mid-May to late October. Cost is $2 pp. The farmstand is open daily 8 a.m.-6 p.m. If you can't visit Hattie's Shed, request a mail-order catalog. The farm is 1.7 miles south of Rt. 1.

ACCOMMODATIONS

Country Inns with Restaurants

Follow Hancock Point Rd. 4.8 miles south of Rt. 1 to the three-story, gray-blue **Crocker House Country Inn,** Hancock Point Rd., Hancock 04640, tel. (207) 422-6806, fax 422-3105, Rich and Liz Malaby's antidote to Bar Harbor's summer traffic. Built as a summer hotel in 1884, the inn underwent total rehabbing a century later. Eleven rooms (private baths) are $90-130 d in summer, $75-95 d off season, including breakfast. Guests can hang out in the comfortable common room or reserve spa time in the carriage house. Nearby are clay tennis courts, quiet walking routes past Hancock Point's elegant seaside "cottages," and a unique octagonal public library. The Malabys will even lend bicycles or pack picnic lunches (extra charge) for day-trips to Campobello Island, Acadia, or Lamoine State Park. If you're arriving by boat, request a mooring. Two dining rooms are open to the public for dinner (5:30-9 p.m. daily; entrées $16-20) and Sunday brunch (11 a.m.-2 p.m. Memorial Day weekend through Labor Day); reservations are essential. The well-prepared, unpretentious continental cuisine, emphasizing local produce, draws a crowd all season long. The inn is open daily, mid-April through October, then weekends in November and December.

Le Domaine, Rt. 1, Box 496, Hancock 04640, tel. (207) 422-3395 or 422-3916 or (800) 554-8498, fax (207) 422-2316, has gained a five-star reputation for its restaurant, founded by the mother of present owner/chef Nicole Purslow in 1946—long before fine dining had cachet here. But that's only part of the story. Above the restaurant is a charming, seven-room, country-French inn, buffered from the highway by hedges. The 80-acre inn property, nine miles east of Ellsworth, is virtual Provence, an oasis transplanted magically to Maine. On the garden-view balconies, or on the lawn out back, you're oblivious to the traffic whizzing by. Better yet, follow the lovely wooded trail to a quiet pond. Seven guest rooms (private baths, several sharing the balconies), all named after herbs, are $200 d, MAP. (Best room is Rosemary.) A lower rate is available early and late in the season. Continental breakfast, usually including croissants, can be served in your room or on the balcony. Alert the inn if you'll be arriving after 5:30 p.m., when the staff has to focus on dinner. The ultra-French restaurant with a 5,000-bottle wine cellar is open to the public Wed.-Mon. 6-9 p.m. (in August, it's open daily). No smoking. Reservations are essential, especially in July and August. The tab may dent your budget (entrées $21-26), but stack it up against plane fare to France. Le Domaine's season is Memorial Day weekend to mid-October.

B&Bs

Set back from the highway 12 miles east of Ells-

worth, **Sullivan Harbor Farm B&B,** Rt. 1, P.O. Box 96, Sullivan 04664, tel. (207) 422-3735 or (800) 422-4014, fax (207) 422-8229, is an unpretentious 19th-century farmhouse with spectacular sea and mountain views. Across the road from a lovely cove, the driveway curves through two giant outcrops higher than a car—great spots for watching the passing scene. Three second-floor rooms (two with private baths) go for $75 d in summer, less off season. In summer, two cottages (Milo and Cupcake) are available by the week ($575 and $700, respectively, with a two-day off-season minimum); cottage guests need to make special arrangements for breakfast. The B&B rooms are available all year. Ask innkeepers Joel Frantzman and Leslie Harlow to steer you toward their favorite ponds and hiking trails—they'll even lend you a canoe. Or grab a book from their eclectic library and hang out in the peaceful backyard. Or visit their spotless **Sullivan Harbor Smokehouse** and ship your pals some fantastic cold-smoked salmon. Each night, Joel parks his truck at the end of the driveway; about 2 a.m., a refrigerator truck from Eastport, Maine, offloads a batch of the freshest-possible fish. Next morning, the smoking process begins. The results speak for themselves.

Just down the road is the **Island View Inn,** Rt. 1, HC 32, Box 24, Sullivan 04664, tel. (207) 422-3031, its name the height of understatement. Spread before you are the peaks of Mount Desert, a remarkable panorama. Three of the six rooms (all private baths; $60-90 d) capture the view from this updated turn-of-the-century summer home. The Island View has its own private beach, but the water is terminally chilly. No smoking; children and pets are welcome. Open Memorial Day weekend to mid-October.

Sorrento is such a low-key place that lots of people don't realize it has a B&B. **Bass Cove Farm,** Eastside Rd., Rt. 185, Box 132, Sorrento 04677, tel./fax (207) 422-3564, was opened in 1992 by spinner/weaver/gardener/editor Mary Ann Solet and her husband Michael Tansey, a group-home supervisor whose resume also includes the Harry S. Truman Manure Pitchoff Championship at the annual Common Ground Country Fair. Mary Ann can rattle off dozens of ideas for exploring the area, particularly in the craft department, and she raids her garden to produce a hearty, healthful breakfast. Two first-floor rooms (one with private bath; $50 and $70 d) and a second-floor suite ($70 d, plus $10 for kitchen use) have quilt-covered beds and other homey touches. No smoking, no pets; well-behaved children are welcome. The B&B is open all year, but be sure to call ahead off season.

Aptly named, **The Sunset House Bed & Breakfast,** Rt. 186, HC 60, Box 62, Gouldsboro 04607, tel. (207) 963-7156 or (800) 233-7156, overlooks the setting sun off to the west and water from more than one angle. Most of the seven rooms (shared and private baths) in Carl and Kathy Johnson's charming three-story Victorian home have water views. Jones Pond, Gouldsboro's swimming hole, borders the property; bring a canoe and launch it here—but not before launching into Carl's generous breakfast. Rates are $59-69 d July to mid-September, $39-59 d other months; two-night minimum on weekends July through October. No smoking, no children under 12, no pets. Open all year. In winter, there's ice-skating and cross-country skiing. Sunset House is a quarter of a mile south of Rt. 1, in the village of West Gouldsboro.

Overlooking the Gouldsboro Peninsula's only sandy saltwater beach, **Oceanside Meadows Inn,** Rt. 195, Corea Rd., P.O. Box 90, Prospect Harbor 04669, tel. (207) 963-5557, is a jewel of a place on 200 acres with fabulous gardens and wildlife habitat. The elegant 1860s main house has seven attractive rooms (private baths; $85-95 d); next door are three suites ($675-775 a week) in a recently renovated 1830s farmhouse. Breakfast is an event, staged by innkeepers Sonja Sundaram and Ben Walter. Children are welcome; no smoking. Open all year. Oceanside Meadows is six miles off Rt. 1.

Even more of a detour, and definitely worthwhile, is Bob Travers and Barry Canner's **Black Duck Inn on Corea Harbor,** Crowley Island Rd., P.O. Box 39, Corea 04624, tel. (207) 963-2689, fax 963-7495, literally the end of the line on the Gouldsboro Peninsula. (Nearest ATM is in Winter Harbor.) Set on 12 acres in this timeless fishing village, the B&B has four handsomely decorated rooms (private and shared baths) for $65-95 d ($140 d for a suite), depending on the season. Across the way are two little seasonal cottages, one rented by the day (three-night minimum) and one by the week

($625 d). The inn and Corea are geared to wanderers, readers, and people seeking serenity (who isn't?). Rocky outcrops dot the property and a nature trail meanders to a mill pond; in early August, the blueberries are ready. If the fog socks in, the large parlor has comfortable chairs and loads of books. No pets (Dolly Bacon, a potbellied pig, resides out back), no children under 10, no smoking. Three of the rooms are open all year.

Something of a categorical anomaly, **The Bluff House Inn,** Rt. 186, Gouldsboro 04607, tel. (207) 963-7805, is part motel, part hotel, part B&B—a successful mix in a contemporary building overlooking Frenchman Bay on the west side of the Gouldsboro Peninsula. Verandas wrap around the first and second floors, so bring binoculars for osprey and bald eagle sightings. The eight second-floor rooms (private baths; $75-85 d) are decorated "country" fashion, with quilts on the very comfortable beds. (In hot weather, request a corner room.) Breakfast is generous continental. In summer, walk the steep path to the shore; in winter, you can cross-country ski on the owner's 400 acres across the road. No smoking, no pets. Open all year.

Campgrounds

On a wooded finger of land projecting eastward from the Schoodic Peninsula, **Ocean Wood Campground,** P.O. Box 111, Birch Harbor 04613, tel. (207) 963-7194, gets kudos for eco-sensitivity, noise control, and 16 fantastic wilderness sites, most on the ocean. Don't expect frills; nature provides the entertainment. The 70 campsites (some with hookups) range $12-25, depending on location. Pets (leashed) and guests are allowed at regular sites, but not at the wilderness ones. Hot showers are free, 7 a.m.-9 p.m. No credit cards. Open early May to late October, the campground is a terrific base for exploring the Schoodic section of Acadia National Park.

Seasonal Rentals

Next to their Black Duck Inn, Barry Canner and Bob Travers operate **Black Duck Properties,** Crowley Island Rd., P.O. Box 39, Corea 04624, tel. (207) 963-2689, fax 963-7495, handling both home sales and seasonal rentals. Corea is their primary focus, with harborfront cottages a specialty, but they can suggest suitable spots anywhere on the Gouldsboro Peninsula. Weekly-rental range is $475-900, with $675 being a fairly typical rate.

FOOD

Make a point to attend one of the many **public suppers** held throughout the summer in this area and so many other rural corners of Maine. Typically benefiting a worthy cause, these usually feature beans or spaghetti and the serendipity of plain potluck. Everyone saves room for the homemade pies. High on the lists of the savvy are the bean suppers (under $6 pp) put on by the **Union Congregational Church in Hancock,** Rt. 1, tel. (207) 422-3100 or 422-9127. Crowds begin lining up by 4:30 p.m. for the 5 p.m. start on summer Saturdays, and most everything is scarfed up before the official 6:30 p.m. finish. Call ahead to confirm the dates. If you end up hungry, you're either too timid or you arrived too late.

General Stores
By definition, old-fashioned country stores are eclectic sources of local color, last-minute items, and plenty of answers for which you probably have questions. Three good examples are right in this area.

Lots of people stop at **Dunbar's Store,** Rt. 1,

Sullivan 04664, tel. (207) 422-6844, just to admire the view. Then they go inside the old-fashioned market and almost always manage to make a purchase—maybe compensation of sorts for the scenery. Some even offer to buy the place. More of a grocery store than a fast-food source, Dunbar's is open all year, Mon.-Sat. 8 a.m.-9 p.m. and Sunday 9 a.m.-6 p.m.

Farther east on Rt. 1, in a new building that replaced a half-century-old country store, **Young's Market,** Rt. 1, Gouldsboro 04607, tel. (207) 963-7774, also has a fabulous view—along with pizza, gasoline, ATM, fishing gear, auto parts, and more. It's open all year, daily 5 a.m.-9 p.m.

Ice cream from the traditional soda fountain is the specialty at **Gerrish's Store,** Main St., Winter Harbor 04693, tel. (207) 963-5575, officially the J.M. Gerrish Store. Only hitch is that it's seasonal, open May to mid-October. And it's become a bit yuppified, so penny candy and postcards coexist with gourmet goodies and designer coffee. But no matter; it's fun.

Lobster-in-the-Rough
For some peculiar reason, eat-on-the-wharf lobster shacks become scarce as you head Down East into Washington County. Odd, because the Sunrise Coast's prime geography deserves dining-on-the-dock, even when the fog sweeps in. Sure, you can buy fresh lobsters, but you'll usually have to cook 'em yourself. Or go to a regular restaurant, where it's awkward to be messy. So

local humor in Corea

before you drive any farther northeast, take advantage of this area's "last chances." A good choice is the **Tidal Falls Lobster Pound,** Tidal Falls Rd., Hancock 04640, tel. (207) 422-6818, where two dozen tables stretch down toward the water and you can watch the "falls" if the tide is turning. (Inside are 11 more tables.) From Rt. 1, on a fairly sharp curve, take East Side Rd. and follow signs to "The Pound," on the east side of Sullivan Harbor. It's open daily 5-9 p.m., June to Labor Day. BYOL.

Inexpensive

Don't be put off by the lobster "sculpture" outside **Ruth & Wimpy's Kitchen,** Rt. 1, Hancock 04640, tel. (207) 422-3723; you'll probably see a crowd as well. This family-fare standby serves hefty dinner sandwiches ($4-7), seafood and steak ($7-13), and exotic cocktails, as well as lobster dinners, pizza, and a sense of humor. Bring the kids. Located five miles east of Ellsworth, close to the Hancock Point turnoff, Ruth & Wimpy's is open all year, Mon.-Thurs. 11 a.m.-8 p.m., Fri.-Sat. 7 a.m.-9 p.m., and Sunday 8 a.m.-9 p.m.

Best place for grub and gossip in Winter Harbor is **Chase's Restaurant,** 193 Main St., Winter Harbor 04693, tel. (207) 963-7171, a seasoned, no-frills booth-and-counter operation that turns out first-rate fish chowder, fries, and onion rings. No credit cards. It's open all year for breakfast, lunch, and dinner.

Inexpensive to Moderate

Intriguingly, two restaurants in this category share their profits with charitable organizations; by all means, encourage their efforts—and enjoy the cuisine while you're at it.

Oceanwood Gallery and Restaurant, Birch Harbor 04613, tel. (207) 963-2653, on the eastern side of the Schoodic Peninsula about two and a half miles east of the center of Winter Harbor, commands a lovely location overlooking quiet Birch Harbor and the eponymous trees. The creative menu features seafood, organic produce, and vegetarian, pork, and beef entrées (up to $18). No smoking. The gallery combines local paintings with ethnic basketwork and woodcarvings. Profits support the conservation-focused Pajaro Jai Foundation. Ocean Wood is open mid-June through Labor Day, daily 10 a.m.-9 p.m. Reservations are essential for dinner, and wise for lunch on midsummer weekends.

A relative newcomer, **The Olde Post Office Restaurant,** Rt. 186, HC 60, Box 174, Gouldsboro 04607, tel. (207) 963-5900, has taken over South Gouldsboro's retired post office, cleverly incorporating tables for 20 diners into the space. The small but select menu emphasizes seafood, fresh ingredients, and careful preparation over flashiness and exotica; dinner entrées run $9-15. Owner Steve Rumpel donates five percent of his profits to local charities. Beer and wine only; no smoking. Reservations are essential. Open all year, Wed.-Sun. 5-9 p.m.

INFORMATION AND SERVICES

For advance information, contact the **Schoodic Peninsula Chamber of Commerce,** P.O. Box 381, Winter Harbor 04693, tel. (207) 963-7658 or (800) 231-3008 outside Maine, and request its handy map/brochure, revised annually. The nearest convenient **information center** is run by the Ellsworth Area Chamber of Commerce, P.O. Box 267, Ellsworth 04605, tel. (207) 667-5584, on the Rt. 1/3 commercial strip, close to where the highway forks toward Mount Desert Island and Eastern Hancock County. It's open daily in July and August; Mon.-Sat. from mid-June to mid-September; and weekdays 9 a.m.-4:30 p.m., the rest of the year.

BOB RACE

THE SUNRISE COAST

"Down East," people say, is the direction the wind blows—the prevailing southwest wind that powered 19th-century sailing vessels along this rugged coastline. But to be truly Down East, in the minds of most Mainers, you have to be physically here, in Washington County—a stunning landscape of waterways, forests, blueberry barrens, rocky shoreline, and independent, pocket-size communities.

At one time, *most* of the Maine coast used to be as underdeveloped as this portion of it. You can set your clock back a generation or two while you're here, but don't bet on time's standing still for much longer.

Where eastern Hancock County meets western Washington County, you're on the Sunrise Coast. From Steuben eastward to Jonesport, Machias, and Lubec, then "around the corner"—inland to Eastport, Calais, and Grand Lake Stream—Washington County is twice the size of Rhode Island, covers 2,528 square miles, has about 35,000 residents, and stakes a claim as the first U.S. real estate to see the morning sun. The Sunrise Coast also includes handfuls of offshore islands—some accessible by ferry, charter boat, or private vessels. (Some, with sensitive bird-nesting grounds, are off limits.) Conveniently linked to Lubec by a bridge, New Brunswick's Campobello Island is home to Franklin D. Roosevelt's summer retreat and a popular day-trip destination. Other attractions include festivals, concert series, art and antique galleries, lighthouses, two Native American reservations, and all the outdoors for hiking, biking, birding, sea kayaking, whalewatching, camping, swimming, and fishing.

One of the Sunrise Coast's 1990s buzzwords has been ecotourism, and local conservation organizations and chambers of commerce have targeted and welcomed visitors willing to be careful of the fragile ecosystems here—visitors who will contribute to the economy while respecting the natural resources and leaving them untrammeled, visitors who know how not to cross the fine line between light use and overuse.

One natural phenomenon no visitor can affect is the tide—the inexorable ebb and flow, predictably in and predictably out. If you're not used to it, even the 6- to 10-foot tidal ranges of southern Maine may surprise you. But here, along the Sunrise Coast, they're astonishing—as much as 26 feet of difference in water-level within six hours. Old-timers tell stories of big money lost betting on horses racing the fast-moving tides.

Another distinctive natural feature of Washington County is its blueberry barrens (fields). Depending on the time of year, the fields will be black (torched by growers to jump-start the

SUNRISE COAST

To Houlton

Forest City

Spednic Lake

Vanceboro

6

Baskahegan Lake

1

WASHINGTON

NEW BRUNSWICK

St. Croix River

CANADA

To I-95

6

Sysladobsis Lake

West Grand Lake

Peter Dana Point

Grand Falls Flowage

St. Stephen

Grand Lake Stream

Princeton

Calais

Fourth Machias Lake

Big Lake

Pocomoonshine Lake

Baileyville (Woodland)

Baring

Red Beach

Third Machias Lake

MILL RD.

Meddybemps Lake

Moosehorn National Wildlife Refuge

Robbinston

STUD

9

214

Meddybemps

Charlotte

Boyden Lake

Passamaquoddy Bay

Wesley

192

Cathance Lake

191

Dennys River

Pennamaquan Lake

Pembroke

Perry

Pleasant Point

9

Machias River

Moosehorn National Wildlife Refuge

West Pembroke

Shackford Head State Park

Cobscook Bay

Eastport

To Bangor

193

Beddington

Dennysville

Edmunds

North Lubec

Campobello Island

Deblois

Hadley Lake

Cobscook Bay State Park

189

Quoddy Head State Park

Lubec

Narraguagus River

Gardner Lake

Whiting

South Trescott

Marshfield

East Machias

Bailey's Mistake

To Ellsworth

Whitneyville

Machias

1A

1

Muchiasport

191

Columbia Falls

Indian River

Jonesboro

Bucks Harbor

Machias Bay

Cutler

Western Head

Cherryfield

Harrington

1

Addison

Roque Bluffs

Starboard

★JASPER BEACH

1A

187

Roque Bluffs State Park

Roque Island

Englishman Bay

Cross Island

Milbridge

West Jonesport

Jonesport

Beals

Chandler Bay

Steuben

Pleasant Bay

Cape Split

South Addison

Western Great Wass Island

Machias Seal Island

ATLANTIC OCEAN

Petit Manan ★ National Wildlife Refuge

0   15 mi

0   15 km

© MOON PUBLICATIONS, INC.

*a long way down
at low tide*

SHERRY STREETER

crop), blue (ready for harvest), or maroon (fall foliage, fabulous for photography). In early summer, a million rented bees set to work pollinating the blossoms. By August, when a blue haze forms over the knee-high shrubs, bent-over bodies use old-fashioned wooden rakes to harvest the ripe berries. It's backbreaking work, but the employment lines form quickly when newspaper ads announce the advent of the annual harvest.

Although most Down East barren barons harvest their blueberries for the lucrative wholesale market—averaging 65 million pounds annually—a few growers advertise pick-your-own blueberries in mid-August. Watch the local newspapers and go for it. Or, as you hike the county's public-access trails, just help yourself to any wild blueberries you find (Moosehorn National Wildlife Refuge, near Calais, is prime blueberrying turf).

Whenever possible, venture off Rt. 1. In part, this is so you don't miss the scenery. Also, though, it's wise in summer to avoid this major (albeit two-lane) artery, which can become congested, although nowhere near as static as farther south. Taking this into account, you'll find that local residents often estimate distances in time rather than miles. The only thing that makes travel slower in winter than in summer is blizzard conditions. I once conducted an unscientific survey and quizzed five separate Machias resi-

dents on how long it would take to reach Jonesport; four differed by as much as 45 minutes, and the fifth refused to play the game.

Visitor Information (and Two Caveats)

For general information about Washington County, and a helpful county map, contact the **Washington County Promotions Board** (WCPB), P.O. Box 605, Machias 04654, tel./fax (800) 377-9748. The WCPB maintains a round-the-clock answering service, promises a response within 24 hours, and handles liaison with all of the county's chambers of commerce.

One bit of advice you might not receive from the board is that warm clothing is essential in this corner of Maine. It may be named the Sunrise Coast, but it also gets plenty of fog, rain, and cool temperatures. Temperatures tend to be warmer, and the fog diminishes, as you head toward the inland parts of the county, but you can *never* count on that—Mother Nature is an accomplished curveball pitcher, and El Niño periodically provides an assist.

Note, too, that Maine has tough drunk-driving laws, and enforcement seems to be especially rigid in Washington County, where police and county sheriffs patrol major roads diligently—particularly on weekends—and hand out frequent citations for operating under the influence. You can find much better souvenirs.

WESTERN WASHINGTON COUNTY

The pace begins to slow a bit by the time you reach western Washington County, the beginning of the Sunrise Coast. In this little pocket are the towns of Steuben, Milbridge, Cherryfield, and Harrington.

Life can even be tough here nowadays, where once great wooden ships slid down the ways and brought prosperity and trade to shippers, builders, and barons of the timber industry. Cherryfield's stunning houses are evidence enough. The barons now control the blueberry fields, covering much of the inland area of western Washington County and annually shipping millions of pounds of blueberries out of headquarters in Milbridge (pop. about 1,300) and Cherryfield (pop. about 1,200). The big names here are Jasper Wyman & Sons and Cherryfield Foods.

Milbridge straddles Rt. 1, as well as the Narraguagus River (Nar-ra-GWAY-gus, a Native American name meaning "above the boggy place"), once the state's premier source of Atlantic salmon. Cherryfield is at the tidal limit of the Narraguagus. Even though Rt. 1A trims maybe three miles off the trip from Milbridge to Harrington (pop. 900), resist the urge to take it. Take Rt. 1 from Milbridge to Cherryfield—the Narraguagus Highway—and then continue on to Harrington. You just shouldn't miss Cherryfield.

SIGHTS

Local History
A group of energetic residents worked tirelessly to establish the **Milbridge Historical Society Museum,** Main St., P.O. Box 194, Milbridge 04658, tel. (207) 546-4471, which opened its new Rt. 1 building in 1996. Displays in the large exhibit room focus on Milbridge's essential role in the shipbuilding trade, but kids will enjoy such oddities as an amputation knife used by a local doctor, and a re-created country kitchen. The volunteer-staffed museum, next to the Schoodic Insurance office, is open Memorial Day weekend through September.In July and August, hours are Tuesday, Saturday, and Sunday 1-4 p.m.; other months, Saturday and Sunday 1-4 p.m.

Admission is free but donations are welcomed.

Scenic Fall-Foliage Routes
In fall—roughly early September to early October in this part of Maine—the post-harvest blueberry fields take on brilliant scarlet hues, then maroon. They're gorgeous. The best barren-viewing road is **Route 193** between Cherryfield and Beddington, via Deblois, the link between Rts. 1 and 9—21 miles of granite outcrops, pine windscreens, and fiery-red fields.

Also in fall, consider taking a lovely alternate route from Hancock into western Washington County. A few miles east of Ellsworth, Route 182 veers northeast off Rt. 1 to Franklin and on to Cherryfield, a 25-mile stretch of sparkling ponds, brilliant colors, and no civilization. Schoodic Mountain, Donnell Pond, and Tunk Lake are just three of the natural treasures along the way. As you enter Washington County and land in Cherryfield, you're brought gently back to civilization by a whole town full of architectural treasures.

Cherryfield Historic District
Imagine a little town this far Down East having a 75-acre National Register Historic District with 52 architecturally significant buildings. If architecture appeals, don't miss Cherryfield. The **Cherryfield-Narraguagus Historical Society,** P.O. Box 96, Cherryfield 04622, has produced a free brochure/map, *Guide to the Cherryfield Historic District,* which you can obtain in advance or pick up once you get here. Architectural styles included on the route are Greek Revival, Italianate, Queen Anne, Colonial Revival, Second Empire, Federal, and Gothic Revival—dating from 1803 to 1940, with most being late 19th century.

PARKS, PRESERVES, AND RECREATION

Petit Manan National Wildlife Refuge
Occupying a 2,166-acre peninsula in Steuben with 10 miles of rocky shoreline (and three offshore islands), outstandingly scenic Petit Manan

National Wildlife Refuge, Pigeon Hill Rd., Steuben, mailing address P.O. Box 279, Milbridge 04658, tel. (207) 546-2124, sees only about 15,000 visitors a year. The moderately easy, three-mile Birch Point Trail and easy, one-mile Shore Trail provide splendid views and opportunities to spot wildlife alongshore and in the fields, forests, and marshland. This is foggy territory, but on clear days, you can see the 123-foot lighthouse on Petit Manan Island, two and a half miles offshore. From Rt. 1, on the east side of Steuben, take Pigeon Hill Rd. six miles south to the refuge parking lot; space is limited. The refuge is open daily sunrise to sunset, all year; cross-country skiing is permitted in winter.

Milbridge's McClellan Park

As you enter Milbridge on Rt. 1 from the west and south, turn right onto Wyman Rd. and drive down the peninsula to McClellan Park, an outstanding town-owned park on Narraguagus Bay with picnic tables, restrooms, hiking trails, and even a handful of campsites.

Getting Afloat

Between June and December, Capt. Bob Cordier skippers the 45-foot *Idle Ours* out of Milbridge Harbor, doing three-hour **lighthouse cruises** past Petit Manan and Pond Island Lights ($35 pp) and two-and-a-half-hour **wildlife-and-islands cruises** ($30 pp). Weather permitting, trips operate Mon.-Sat., plus Sunday afternoon. Departure time depends on tide levels, so reservations are essential; call no later than a day ahead. The boat has a heated cabin; four-passenger minimum, six-passenger max. Contact **Eastern Isles Charter Co.**, P.O. Box 272, Milbridge 04658, tel. (207) 546-2136.

ENTERTAINMENT

The only cinema in western Washington County is the updated, air-conditioned **Milbridge Theatre,** Main St., Rt. 1, Milbridge 04658, tel. (207) 546-2038, a classic movie house that's been here since 1937. First-run films, with a good sound system, go on at 7:30 p.m.; all seats are $3.75. It's open daily, Memorial Day weekend through October; weekends in April, November, and December; closed Jan.-March.

Occasionally there are Saturday or Sunday matinees at 2 p.m.

Check locally for the concert schedule of the **Cherryfield Band,** an impressive community group with about three dozen enthusiastic members. They're in demand from May to December, but best of all are their concerts in the lovely downtown bandstand, overlooking the Narraguagus River.

FESTIVALS AND EVENTS

The biggest event in this end of Washington County, and even beyond, is the **Milbridge Anniversary Celebration,** the last weekend in July, drawing hundreds of visitors. Saturday-afternoon highlight is the codfish relay race—hilarious enough to have been featured in *Sports Illustrated* and on national television. The runners, clad in slickers and hip boots, *really do* hand off a greased cod instead of the usual baton. Team prize is $100. Race rules specify that runners must be "reasonably sober" and not carry the codfish between their teeth or legs. Also on the schedule are blueberry pancake breakfasts, a fun parade, kids' games, auction, dance, beano and cribbage tournaments, craft booths, and a lobsterbake. You have to be there. The relay race has been going since the mid-1980s; the festival has been going for a century and a half.

SHOPPING

Gifts and Crafts

Hands On!, Rt. 1, P.O. Box 262, Milbridge 04658, tel. (207) 546-2682 or 288-5478 off season, one of Down East Maine's oldest and best craft galleries, occupies a small building on Rt. 1 at the eastern entrance to Milbridge. Owned by the husband-and-wife team of Carol Shutt and Rocky Mann, the bright, modern display space showcases high-quality, high-end jewelry, pottery, metal sculpture, basketry, and weaving—the work of more than two dozen Maine artisans. The gallery is open mid-June through Labor Day, Mon.-Sat. 10 a.m.-5 p.m.

Just down the road, in town, is Milbridge's answer to Camden's Smiling Cow. The **Sea Witch,** Main St., Rt. 1, Milbridge 04658, tel. (207) 546-

7495, has three rooms of just about anything
you could want in the inexpensive gift and souvenir category; blueberry and lobster themes
dominate. It's open April-Dec.: daily 9 a.m.-6
p.m. in midsummer; Wed.-Sat. noon-5 p.m. off
season.

ACCOMMODATIONS

B&Bs
One of Cherryfield's 52 Historic Register buildings, the 1803 **Ricker House,** Park St., P.O.
Box 256, Cherryfield 04622, tel. (207) 546-2780,
borders the Narraguagus River and makes a
superb base for exploring inland and Down East
Maine. Jean and Bill Conway keep coming up
with unending lists of things to do—after a huge
breakfast, maybe a loll on the lovely sunporch,
then a stroll to the river, where there's a canoe.
Three second-floor bedrooms ($50 d) share a
bath. Bicycles are available for guests; tennis
courts are across the street. No pets, no smoking, no credit cards. Open May through November. Ricker House is a block off Rt. 1, near
the center of town.

At the **Moonraker Bed & Breakfast,** Main
St., Rt. 1, Milbridge 04658, tel. (207) 546-2191,
kids make a beeline for the red-stained-glass
cupola atop Ingrid and Bill Handrahan's three-
story Queen Anne Victorian mansion in the middle of tiny Milbridge. Five second- and third-
floor rooms (private and shared baths) are $50-
60 d. No pets, no smoking. Open all year. Ingrid
also runs a gift shop on the premises.

Campgrounds
Covering seven acres on the tidal Harrington
River, small, low-key **Sunset Point Campground,** Marshville Rd., P.O. Box 102, Harrington 04643, tel. (207) 483-4412, has 30 open
sites ($11-14 for two), a playground, and salt-
water swimming. Leashed pets are allowed.
Open mid-May to mid-October. From Rt. 1, east
of Harrington, take the road toward Marshville for
2.8 miles; the campground is on the right.

Town-owned **McClellan Park,** in Milbridge,
has a handful of campsites for about $5 a night,
on a first-come, first-served basis. Make inquiries and arrangements at the Milbridge Town
Office.

FOOD

Miscellanea
Best place in Milbridge for pizza—and a lot else
—is the **Milbridge Market,** Main St., Milbridge
04658, tel. (207) 546-3410, a local landmark
once known as Frankenstein's. You'll find magazines, beer, wine, fishing gear, even a laundromat. It's open all year, daily 6:30 a.m.-9 p.m.

Moderate to Expensive
After six years of restoring their antique Cape-
style house and surrounding it with fabulous
gardens, Jessie King and Alva Lowe opened
the six-table **Kitchen Garden Restaurant,** 335
Village Rd., Steuben 04680, tel. (207) 546-2708,
in the first floor of their home. Imaginative dinners, all homemade and conscientiously organic, include jerk chicken, thanks to Alva's Jamaican ancestry. The five-course dinners (four
entrée choices) are $22-24, with the menu
changing monthly. Bring your own wine or beer.
The charming restaurant, a quarter of a mile off
Rt. 1, is open 5:30-9:30 p.m., Wed.-Sat. in summer and Fri.-Sat. in winter. Reservations are
required. No credit cards, no smoking.

Seven miles to the east, and far more casual,
is the aptly named **Red Barn Restaurant,** Main
St., Milbridge 04658, tel. (207) 546-7721, a locally popular spot for breakfast, lunch, and dinner, featuring ample portions of down-home
chowder, fried seafood ($9-14), and steaks.
Open all year, Sun.-Thurs. 7 a.m.-8 p.m., Fri.-
Sat. 7 a.m.-9 p.m. The restaurant is set back a
bit from Main St., easiest to access from Bridge
St. (just off Rt. 1).

INFORMATION AND SERVICES

Information centers are scarce in this part of
Maine, so you'll need to plan ahead or ask questions in restaurants, lodgings, and town offices.
In advance, the **Washington County Promotions Board,** P.O. Box 605, Machias 04654,
tel. (800) 377-9748, is the best source of general
information.

To reach the **Milbridge Town Office,** School
St., Milbridge 04658, tel. (207) 546-2422, from
the south, turn right onto Bridge St. from Rt. 1,

then turn right onto School Street. The office is open weekdays 8 a.m.-4 p.m., all year. The office has a useful free map of the Milbridge area, although some of its listings are dated; call ahead and they'll send it.

JONESPORT/BEALS AREA

Between western Washington County and the Machias Bay area is the molar-shaped Jonesport Peninsula, reached from the west via the attractive little town of Columbia Falls, bordering Rt. 1. Down the peninsula are the picturesque towns of Addison, Jonesport, and Beals Island. First settled around 1762, Columbia Falls (pop. about 550) still has a handful of houses dating from the late 18th century, but its best-known structure is the early-19th-century Ruggles House.

On the banks of the Pleasant River, just south of Columbia Falls, Addison (pop. about 1,100) once had four huge shipyards cranking out wooden cargo vessels that circled the world. Since that 19th-century heyday, little seems to have changed, and the town today may be best known as the haunt of painter John Marin, who first came to Maine in 1914. His onetime home and studio, on outstandingly scenic Cape Split, at the bottom of Addison's peninsula, is not open to the public, but it's worth driving there to understand his inspiration.

Jonesport and Beals Island, with a combined population of about 2,200, are traditional hardworking fishing communities—old-fashioned, friendly, and incredibly photogenic. Beals, connected to Jonesport via an arched bridge over Moosabec Reach, is named for Manwarren Beal, Jr., and his wife, Lydia, who arrived around 1773 and quickly threw themselves into the Revolutionary War effort. But that's not all they did—the current phone book covering Jonesport and Beals Island lists dozens of Beal descendants (as well as dozens of Alleys and Carvers, other early names).

Even more memorable than Manwarren Beal was his six-foot seven-inch son Barnabas, dubbed "Tall Barney" for obvious reasons. The larger-than-life fellow became the stuff of legend all along the Maine coast—and a popular Jonesport restaurant preserves his name.

Also legendary here is the lobsterboat design known as the Jonesport hull. People from away won't recognize its distinctive shape, but count on the fishing pros to know it. The harbor here is jam-packed with Jonesport lobsterboats, and souped-up versions are consistent winners in the summertime lobsterboat-race series held in Jonesport, Stonington, and Winter Harbor.

The finest natural treasure in this part of Maine, a must-see, is the Great Wass Archipelago, partly owned by The Nature Conservancy. Some areas are open to the public, notably the Great Wass Island preserve and Mistake Island.

SIGHTS

Ruggles House
Behind a picket fence on a quiet street in Columbia Falls stands the remarkable Ruggles House, Main St., Columbia Falls 04623, tel. (207) 483-4637. Built in 1818 for Judge Thomas Ruggles—lumber baron, militia captain, even postmaster—the tiny house on a grand scale boasts a famous flying (unsupported) staircase, intricately carved moldings, Palladian window, and unusual period furnishings. Rescued in the mid-20th century and maintained by the Ruggles House Society, this gem has become a magnet for savvy preservationists. Located a quarter of a mile east of Rt. 1, it's open for hour-long guid-

Ruggles House, Columbia Falls

ed tours June 1-Oct. 15, daily 9:30 a.m.-4:30 p.m. Suggested donation is $3 adults, $1.50 children; $10 family maximum.

At the house, pick up a copy of the Columbia Falls **walking-tour brochure,** which details the intriguing history of other houses in this hamlet.

Sandy River Model Railroad

Here's Nirvana for model-train enthusiasts. Retired Coast Guardsman Harold ("Buzz") Beal and his wife, Helen, have created a fantastic model railroad layout—the Sandy River Railroad—covering 750 square feet in a building next to their house. Buzz Beal figures railroading is in his blood; his grandfather was a Canadian Pacific engineer. Visitors are welcome any day of the year, but it's best to call ahead to be sure someone's home. On Rt. 187, about four miles northeast of downtown Jonesport, watch for the Church Enterprises sign on the right, then take the next left to the Beals' house. There's no charge, but donations are welcomed.

Beals Island Regional Shellfish Hatchery

Welcome to the world's only soft-shell clam hatchery. The Beals Island Regional Shellfish Hatchery, Beals Island 04611, tel. (207) 497-5769 or 255-1314 off season, is also Maine's only public shellfish hatchery, and visitors are welcome daily 9 a.m.-4 p.m., June through September. The annual aquaculture process begins in mid-March; by November millions of tiny soft-shell clams *(Mya arenaria)* are transplanted into Maine coastal clam flats from Kittery to Eastport. The **Dana E. Wallace Education Center** next to the hatchery has microscopes, explanatory videos, walls lined with wonderful old clam-industry photos, and a staff member to answer questions and guide you through the hatchery. Admission is free. To reach the hatchery, take Rt. 187 from Rt. 1, continuing through Jonesport and across the arched bridge to Beals Island. Turn left, and left again, at the next paved road.

PRESERVES AND RECREATION

Great Wass Island

Allow a whole day to explore 1,579-acre Great Wass Island, an extraordinary preserve, even

when it's drenched in fog—a not-infrequent event. Owned by The Nature Conservancy, the preserve is at the tip of Jonesport's peninsula. Easiest hiking routes are the wooded, two-mile Little Cape Point and one-and-a-half-mile Mud Hole Trails, retracing your path for each. (Making a loop by connecting the two along the rocky shoreline adds considerably to the time and difficulty, but do it if you have time; wear waterproof footwear.) Expect to see beach-head iris (like blue flag) and orchids, jack pine, a peat bog, seals, pink granite, pitcher plants, and lots of warblers. Carry water and a picnic; wear bug repellent. No camping, fires, or pets; no toilet facilities. Daytime access only. To reach the preserve from Rt. 1, take Rt. 187 to Jonesport (12 miles), then cross the arched bridge to Beals Island. Continue across Beals to the Great Wass causeway (locally called "the Flying Place"), then go three miles on Black Duck Cove Rd. to the parking area (on the left). Watch for The Nature Conservancy oak-leaf symbol. At the parking area, pick up a trail map and a bird checklist.

Also owned by The Nature Conservancy is 21-acre **Mistake Island,** accessible only by boat. Low and shrubby, Mistake has a Coast Guard-built boardwalk from the landing at the northwest corner to **Moose Peak Light,** standing 72 feet above the water at the eastern end of the island. The only negative on this lovely island is rubble left behind when the government leveled the keeper's house.

For more information about the Great Wass Archipelago, contact **The Nature Conservancy, Maine Chapter,** Fort Andross, 14 Maine St., Brunswick 04011, tel. (207) 729-5181, fax 729-4118.

Golf and Swimming

You can play golf and swim (in salt or fresh water) on the adjoining **Roque Bluffs Peninsula.** On the east side of the Jonesport peninsula, there's saltwater swimming at **Sandy River Beach,** but be prepared for glacial temperatures. Bring a picnic—it's a lovely spot—but respect private property here. From Rt. 187, take Beach Ln. (signposted Church Enterprises), about four miles northeast of downtown Jonesport.

GETTING AFLOAT

A great-grandson of legendary local "Tall Barney" Beal, Capt. Barna Norton began offering puffin-watching trips to Machias Seal Island (MSI) in 1940 in a 33-foot boat incautiously named *If*. Now his son, Capt. John, has taken over the helm, in a 40-footer heading 20 miles offshore to an island claimed by both the U.S. and Canada—a colorful saga. To preserve the fragile nesting sites of Atlantic puffins and arctic terns, access to the 15-acre island is restricted. Passengers are offloaded into small boats, but sea swells sometimes prevent landing. (The captain supplies wrist bands to queasy passengers.) The trip is not appropriate for small children or unsteady adults. The boat departs Jonesport around 7 a.m., allowing 2-3 hours on MSI before returning about 1 p.m. Cost is $50 pp; reservations are necessary. Wear waterproof hiking boots and pack some munchies. The Nortons have very casual accommodations available in their **Puffin House** at $50 d. Trips begin Memorial Day weekend and end by Labor Day. For information and reservations, contact **Norton of Jonesport,** RR 1, Box 990, Jonesport 04649, tel. (207) 497-5933.

Captain Laura Fish, Kelley's Point Rd., RR 1, Box 1360, Jonesport 04649, tel. (207) 497-3064, offers daily (weather permitting) three-hour cruises in her 23-foot powerboat *Aaron Thomas*. Among the sights are Great Wass Island and Mistake Island. Cost is $20 adults, $15 children under 18; six-person maximum. Reservations are essential. Trips depart from Jonesport and operate May to mid-October.

FESTIVALS AND EVENTS

The biggest annual event hereabouts is the wingding Jonesport **Fourth of July** celebration, with several days of special activities, including barbecues, beauty pageant, kids' games, fireworks, and the famed **Jonesport Lobsterboat Races** in Moosabec Reach.

The August **Maine Wild Blueberry Festival,** in neighboring Machias, is an easy jaunt from the Jonesport/Beals area.

SHOPPING

Gifts and Crafts

Flower-design majolica pottery and whimsical terra-cotta items are specialties at **Columbia Falls Pottery,** Main St., P.O. Box 235, Columbia Falls 04623, tel. (207) 483-4075 or (800) 235-2512, fax (207) 483-2905, an appealing shop in a rehabbed country store next to the Ruggles House. Veteran potter April Adams keeps the inventory fresh, and the company does a hefty mail-order business. The shop, half a mile east of Rt. 1, is open daily 9 a.m.-5 p.m., June-Dec.; Tues.-Sat. 10 a.m.-5 p.m., Jan.-May.

In downtown Jonesport, **Church's True Value,** Main St., Rt. 187, Jonesport 04649, tel. (207) 497-2778, carries all the usual hardware items, plus gifts, souvenirs, and sportswear. Helpful owners John and Sharon Church can also answer any question and solve most any problem. The store is open all year, Mon.-Sat. 7 a.m.-5 p.m.

Multitalented Laura Fish produces an attractive line of stenciled canvas gift items—handbags, ditty bags, and tote bags—marketing them at **Canvas Creations,** Kelley's Point Rd., RR 1, Box 1360, Jonesport 04649, tel. (207) 497-3064. Her season is June to Christmas, but you'll need to call to check hours.

ACCOMMODATIONS

B&Bs

How about staying in a beautiful, modern farmhouse overlooking the water—with llamas named Enchilada, Fajita, and Figaro llolling outside? At **Pleasant Bay Bed & Breakfast and Llama Keep,** West Side Rd., Box 222, Addison 04606, tel. (207) 483-4490, Joan and Lee Yeaton manage to pamper four-legged beasts as well as two-legged guests. Three miles of trails wind through the 110 acres, and a canoe is available for guests. Three lovely rooms (private and shared baths) are $45-65 d. No pets, no smoking. Well-behaved children are welcome; arrange in advance for a llama walk. Open all year. The farm borders Pleasant Bay, 3.9 miles southwest of Rt. 1.

In the early 1980s, congenial innkeeper Charlotte ("Tootsie") Beal opened Washington County's first bed and breakfast, and she's still going strong. (Her late husband, by the way, was a great-grandson of the famous "Tall Barney" Beal, and Tootsie herself was born in Barna Norton's Puffin House.) **Tootsie's Bed & Breakfast,** Trynor Sq., RR 1, Box 575, Jonesport 04649, tel. (207) 497-5414, is a beautifully maintained Victorian with three cozy second-floor rooms (water views; one and a half baths). The rate is $40 d, and Tootsie's is open all year. No credit cards.

In the middle of Jonesport, Dick Deegan's relaxed **Jonesport By-the-Sea B&B,** 1 Main St., Rt. 187, P.O. Box 541, Jonesport 04649, tel. (207) 497-2590, has five first- and second-floor rooms (private and shared baths) for $40-60 d in summer, $40-50 d off season. Breakfast is generous continental. No smoking, no credit cards. Open all year. The inn's antiques shop, open May-Oct. (other times by appointment), specializes in nautical items.

More elaborate is Jeri Taylor's **Raspberry Shores Bed and Breakfast,** 97 Main St., Rt. 187, P.O. Box 217, Jonesport 04649, tel. (207) 497-2463, a century-old intown house overlooking Moosabec Reach. Innkeeper Geri Taylor, who's dealt in antiques and real estate here, has three second-floor rooms, one with a turret (all three share a bath) at $50 d, including full breakfast or an extensive buffet. Outside are steps to the water, and a picnic table; great spot. If you're taking a puffin cruise or hiking Great Wass, Geri prepares generous picnic baskets, with Cornish hen or vegetarian items, for $20—ample for two. No smoking, no pets. The B&B is open April through October, other months by special arrangement.

Motels/Cabins

Convenient for Great Wass hikers is **Rosemarie's Motel,** Black Duck Cove Rd., Great Wass Island, P.O. Box 21, Beals 04611, tel. (207) 497-2511, a tiny new roadside motel with six basic efficiency units. Rooms ($40 d) have cable TV, but no phones (pay phone in the office). No pets; nonsmokers preferred. Open all year. Rosemarie's is at the northern end of Great Wass, a quarter of a mile from the Beals Island causeway.

Seasonal Rentals

Close to the best sandy beach on the peninsula, the **Church Family Cottages,** Rt. 187, Sandy River Beach, RR1, Box 2220, Jonesport 04649, tel. (207) 497-2829, managed by Keith Church, are three rustic, well-maintained cottages available by the week. Best view is from Sandpiper, which sleeps six and rents for $700 a week; the others (Linnet and Lemon Drop) are $420 and $490 a week. Pets only by prior arrangement. Bring your own sheets and towels. Open May through October. The cottages are seven miles south of Rt. 1 and four miles northeast of downtown Jonesport. Keith also manages a fourth cottage, Harbor View ($350 a week), an eccentric little place with a spectacular panoramic view, in downtown Jonesport.

The seasonal-rental brochure produced by the Machias Bay Area Chamber of Commerce usually includes Jonesport-area cottages. See "Information and Services" under "Machias Bay Area" for details.

Campgrounds

The town of Jonesport operates the low-key, no-frills **Jonesport Campground,** Henry Point, Kelley's Point Rd., Jonesport 04649, tel. (207) 497-2804 or 497-5926, about two acres with fabulous views over Sawyer's Cove and Moosabec Reach. Basic facilities include outhouses, picnic tables, and fire rings; three power poles provide hookups. Showers and washing machines are available across the cove at Jonesport Shipyard, tel. (207) 497-2701. The campground is exposed to wind off the water, so expect nights to be cool. Sites, on a first-come, first-served basis, are a bargain-basement $8 a night. Open early May to Labor Day. Avoid the campground during July Fourth festivities; it's jam-packed. From Rt. 187 at the northeastern edge of Jonesport, turn right onto Kelley Point Rd., then right again to Henry Point.

FOOD

Lunch and Miscellanea

For local color, start at **Tall Barney's,** Main St., Rt. 187, Jonesport 04649, tel. (207) 497-2403, where you'll find homemade baked beans and chowders, pizza, and more—and you won't break the bank. Sit back and watch the servers chat up the lobstermen regulars camped out at the big center table. The air gets a bit smoky at times. Open all year, 5:30 a.m.-7 p.m. in summer, to 6 p.m. in winter. No credit cards. The restaurant is just before the bridge to Beals Island; watch for the statue of Barney.

If you're anywhere near Jonesport in August, head for Lois Hubbard's home bakery, called **The Farm,** Mason's Bay Rd., Rt. 187, RR 1, Box 3115, Jonesport 04649, tel. (207) 497-5949. For $1 each, you can pick up a couple of—get this—wild blueberry whoopie pies. Other months, she'll make these items only on request. Carrot cake and specialty breads are available all year. The bakery, signposted 3.1 miles south of the Jonesboro end of Rt. 1, is open Monday, Wednesday, and Friday 8:30 a.m. 5:30 p.m., Tuesday 1-5:30 p.m., and Saturday 8:30 a.m.-noon.

Lobster-in-the-Rough

Lobster-in-the-rough places are scarce in Washington County, so Maureen and Gene Hart's **Harbor House on Sawyer Cove,** Sawyer Sq., Rt. 187, P.O. Box 468, Jonesport 04649, tel. (207) 497-5417, is a welcome new addition. Open 11 a.m.-8 p.m., May through October, the Harbor House café is attractively rustic, with open beams and poster-size historic fishing prints. Eat on the 60-foot screened porch, or on the lawn overlooking the cove. BYOL. No smoking in the café. On the right side of the building, the Harts operate an antiques shop, selling what they call "curiosities." Wonderful old woodwork remains from its 19th-century days as Jonesport's first telegraph office.

Inexpensive to Moderate

About midway between Harrington and Columbia Falls, near the turnoff for Addison, **Perry's Seafood,** Rt. 1, Columbia 04623, tel. (207) 483-2953, is your basic no-frills roadside seafood restaurant with everything fresh and homemade. Steaks are also available. In summer, it's open daily 6 a.m.-9 p.m.; winter hours are daily 7 a.m.-8 p.m.

Ready for "Far East Down East" dining? The **Red Lantern,** Ruggles House Sq., Columbia Falls 04623, tel. (207) 483-2426, serves four-course gourmet Chinese dinners ($13-19, all

inclusive) in a refurbished country store across from the lovely Ruggles House (be patient; the food is all prepared to order). Two entrée choices are vegetarian. The restaurant seats only 25, so reservations are essential. BYOL. Open all year, Tues.-Sun. 5-9 p.m.

No sooner did Faye Carver open **The Seafarer's Wife,** Rt. 187, Jonesport 04649, tel. (207) 497-2365, in 1994 than tables were hard to come by—her culinary reputation did the trick. By 1997, she had a new building, in a new location, with two distinct restaurant operations. Colonial-costumed wait staff—all family members—serve the carefully paced, creative five-course meals. Specialties, not surprisingly for this seafaring family, are such entrées as baked haddock and baked stuffed lobster tails ($14-20, all inclusive). Allow two hours, enjoy the gracious ambience, and BYOL. No smoking. Open daily 5:30-8:30 p.m., all year. Reservations are essential in midsummer, and often other times as well. The restaurant is about three miles northwest of downtown Jonesport, just south of the sign for the Jonesport schools.

On the other side of the building, a much more casual (and less expensive) atmosphere prevails in the Carvers' **Ol' Salt** restaurant (same phone). It's open daily 11 a.m.-9 p.m., all year.

INFORMATION AND SERVICES

The **Machias Bay Area Chamber of Commerce** handles inquiries for the Jonesport/Beals Area, which has no official information center. In downtown Jonesport, the best source of local information is **Church's True Value,** Main St., Rt. 187, Jonesport 04649, tel. (207) 497-2778.

Newspapers

Newspapers that cover the Jonesport/Beals Area are the competing *Machias Valley News Observer,* tel. (207) 255-6561, fax 255-4058, published every Wednesday, and the Cutler-based *Downeast Coastal Press,* tel./fax (207) 259-7751, published every Tuesday. The daily of choice is the *Bangor Daily News.*

Emergencies

The county sheriff handles police-type emergencies for **Jonesport,** tel. (800) 432-7303; the state police handle calls for **Addison, Columbia, and Columbia Falls.** For fire emergencies, call (207) 483-2993. For an ambulance, call (207) 497-2385 in **Jonesport,** and (207) 546-7718 in **Addison, Columbia, and Columbia Falls.**

The nearest hospital is **Down East Community Hospital** in Machias.

Public Restrooms

There are restrooms at the CITGO station at the Four Corners Shopping Center, Rt. 1 in **Columbia,** midway between Harrington and Columbia Falls. This minimall also has an ATM machine, supermarket (picnic fare available), drugstore, sportswear shop, and department store.

MACHIAS BAY AREA

The only negative thing about Machias (Muh-CHY-us; pop. 2,600) is its Micmac Indian name, meaning "bad little falls" (even though it is accurate—the midtown waterfall here *is* treacherous). A contagious local esprit pervades this shire town of Washington County, thanks to antique homes, a splendid river-valley setting, Revolutionary War monuments, and a small but busy university campus.

If you regard crowds as fun, an ideal time to land here is during the renowned annual Machias Wild Blueberry Festival, third weekend in August, when harvesting is underway in Washington County's blueberry fields and you can stuff your face with blueberry-everything—muffins, jam, pancakes, ice cream, pies. You can also collect blueberry-logo napkins, T-shirts, magnets, pottery, and jewelry; then top it off with a tour of the Maine Wild Blueberry processing plant. The menu at the local McDonald's even lists blueberry pancakes and sundaes that weekend. Among the other summer draws are a chamber-music series, art shows, and semiprofessional theater performances. Within a few miles are day-trips galore—options for hiking, biking, golfing, swimming, and sea kayaking.

English settlers, uprooted from communities farther west on the Maine coast, put down permanent roots here in 1763, harvesting timber to ensure their survival. Stirrings of revolutionary discontent surfaced even at this remote outpost, and when British loyalists in Boston began usurping some of the valuable harvest, Machias patriots plotted revenge. By 1775, when the armed British schooner *Margaretta* arrived as a cargo escort, local residents aboard the sloop *Unity,* in a real David-and-Goliath episode, chased down and captured the *Margaretta.* On June 12, 1775, two months after the famed Battles of Lexington and Concord (and five days before the Battle of Bunker Hill), Machias Bay was the site of what author James Fenimore Cooper called "The Lexington of the Sea"—the first naval battle of the American Revolution. The name of patriot leader Jeremiah O'Brien today appears throughout Machias—on a school, a street, a cemetery, and a state park. In 1784, Machias was incorporated; it became the shire town in 1790.

Timber remained a valuable resource for this area well into the 20th century. Fed with timber headed downriver by courageous log drivers, sawmills lined the banks of the Machias River in the 19th century, and trains hauled timber from mills to harbors as early as 1842. The locomotive Lion, a Machias-area workhorse 1846-83, now greets visitors to the Maine State Museum in Augusta. The last log drive on the Machias River occurred as recently as the 1970s.

Also included within the Machias sphere are the towns of Roque Bluffs, Jonesboro, Whitneyville, Marshfield, East Machias, and Machiasport. Just to the east, between Machias and Lubec, are the towns of Whiting and Cutler.

SIGHTS

History is a big deal in this area, and since Machias was the first settled Maine town east of the Penobscot River, lots of enthusiastic amateur historians have helped rescue homes and sites dating from as far back as the Revolutionary era.

Museums

One-hour guided tours vividly convey the atmosphere of the 1770 **Burnham Tavern,** Main St., Rt. 192, Machias 04654, tel. (207) 255-4432, where upstart local patriots met here in 1775 to plot revolution against the British. Job and Mary Burnham's tavern/home next served as an infirmary for casualties from the Revolution's first naval battle, just offshore. Lots of fascinating history in this National Historic Site maintained by the Daughters of the American Revolution. Hanging outside is a sign reading, "Drink for the thirsty, food for the hungry, lodging for the weary, and good keeping for horses, by Job Burnham." Admission is $2 adults, 25 cents for kids under 12. It's open Mon.-Fri. 9 a.m.-5 p.m., mid-June through September, and by appointment off season. If you're here in early August, you can join in the museum's annual **lawn party,** including lunch, tours, and handicraft sales.

Headquarters for the Machiasport Historical Society and one of the area's three oldest residences, the 1810 **Gates House,** Rt. 92, P.O. Box 301, Machiasport 04655, tel. (207) 255-8461, was snatched from ruin and restored in 1966. The National Historic Register building overlooking Machias Bay contains fascinating period furnishings and artifacts—many related to the lumbering and shipbuilding era. The museum, four miles southeast of Rt. 1 in downtown Machias, is open Tues.-Sat. 12:30-4:30 p.m., mid-June to mid-September. Admission is $1. Limited parking on a hazardous curve.

Centre Street Congregational Church

Machias's most distinctive landmark is the steeple of the 1836 Gothic Revival Centre Street Congregational Church, Center St., Machias 04654, tel. (207) 255-6665, paradoxically located on *Center* Street. The community-oriented parishioners spearhead the annual Maine Wild Blueberry Festival, and the church is the site of the July and August Machias Bay Chamber Concerts.

O'Brien Cemetery

Old-cemetery buffs will want to stop at O'Brien Cemetery, resting place of the town's earliest settlers. It's next to Bad Little Falls Park, close to

downtown. Take Rt. 92 toward Machiasport, hang a left onto Avery Street. A big plus here is the view, especially in autumn, of blueberry barrens, the waterfall, and the bay.

Maine Wild Blueberry Company

Continue a short distance down Rt. 92 beyond the cemetery turnoff and you'll see (on the left) the Maine Wild Blueberry Company, Elm St., Rt. 92, P.O. Box 278, Machias 04654, tel. (207) 255-8364. Free half-hour tours are available only by reservation in August. At the plant, you can buy gift packages of canned, frozen, or dried blueberries (great munchies), as well as blueberry-logo souvenirs.

University of Maine at Machias

Founded in 1909 as Washington State Normal School, University of Maine at Machias (UMM), 9 O'Brien Ave., Machias 04654, tel. (207) 255-1200, is now part of the state university system. UMM has 1,000 students, eastern Maine's biggest gym, impressive degree programs in marine biology, recreation management, and teacher education, and a popular summer institute in ornithology. During the summer, the **UMM Art Galleries,** in Powers Hall, feature works from the university's expanding permanent collection of Maine painters—including John Marin, William Zorach, Lyonel Feininger, and Reuben Tam. Rotating exhibits occur throughout the school year. Summer hours for the two galleries are Mon.-Fri. 10 a.m.-noon and 1-4 p.m., or by appointment.

SCENIC ROUTES

The drives described below can also be bike routes (easy to moderately difficult), but be forewarned that the roads are narrow and shoulderless, so caution is essential. Heed biking etiquette.

Route 191, the Cutler Road

Never mind that Rt. 191, between East Machias and West Lubec is one of Maine's most stunning coastal drives, you can still follow the entire 27-mile stretch and meet only a handful of cars. **East Machias** even has its own historic district, with architectural gems dating from the late 18th century along High and Water Streets. Farther along Rt. 191, you'll find fishing wharves, low moorlands, a hamlet or two, and islands popping over the horizon. The only peculiarly jarring note is the 26-tower forest of North Cutler's Naval Computer and Telecommunications Station, nearly a thousand feet high—monitoring global communications—but you see this only briefly. (At night, the skyscraping red lights are really eerie.) Off Rt. 191 are minor roads and hiking trails worth exploring, especially the Bold Coast Trail. About three miles south of the Rt. 191 terminus, you can also check out **Bailey's Mistake,** a hamlet with a black-sand (volcanic) beach. And the name? Allegedly it stems from one Capt. Bailey who, misplotting his course and thinking he was in Lubec, drove his vessel ashore here one night in the late 19th century. Unwilling to face the consequences of his lapse, he and his crew offloaded their cargo of lumber and built themselves dwellings. Whether true or not, it makes a great saga. Even though it's in the town of **Trescott,** and the hamlet is really South Trescott, everyone knows this section as Bailey's Mistake.

Route 92, Starboard Peninsula

Pack a picnic and set out on Rt. 92 (beginning at Elm St. in downtown Machias) down the 10-mile length of the Starboard Peninsula to a stunning spot known as the Point of Maine. Along the way are the villages of Larrabee, Bucks Harbor, and Starboard, all part of the town of Machiasport. In Bucks Harbor is the turnoff (a short detour to the right) to **Yoho Head,** a controversial upscale development overlooking Little Kennebec Bay.

South of the Yoho Head turnoff is the sign for **Jasper Beach,** described below under "Parks, Preserves, and Recreation." From the Jasper Beach sign, continue 1.4 miles to two red buildings (the old Starboard School House and the volunteer fire department). Turn left onto a dirt road, continue to a sign reading Driveway, go around the right side of a shed, and park on the beach. (Keep track of the tide level, though.) You're at **Point of Maine,** a quintessential Down East panorama of sea and islands. On a clear day, you can see offshore **Libby Island Light,** the focus of Philmore Wass's en-

tertaining narrative *Lighthouse in My Life* (see the Booklist).

PARKS, PRESERVES, AND RECREATION

Just as dedicated as the historical preservationists are the hikers, birders, and other ecosensitive outdoors enthusiasts who've helped preserve thousands of acres in this part of Maine for public access and appreciation.

An especially active local organization in eastern Washington County is the **Quoddy Regional Land Trust** (QRLT), Rt. 1, P.O. Box 49, Whiting 04691, tel. (207) 733-5509, which has secured conservation easements on hundreds of acres and several miles of shoreline. In 1997, the QRLT published the *Cobscook Trails* hiking guide (see the Booklist), and it's actively involved in a variety of other projects. If you'd like to support their efforts, individual memberships start at $10 a year.

Bad Little Falls Park

At Bad Little Falls Park, alongside the Machias River, stop to catch the view from the footbridge overlooking the roiling falls (especially in spring). Bring a picnic and enjoy this midtown oasis tucked between Rts. 1 and 92.

Mill Memorial Park

On the east bank of the East Machias River, at the edge of the East Machias Historic District, Mill Memorial Park is a great, grassy place for the kids to let off steam. A large sign here shows the locations of 13 grist and sawmills once powered by the river.

Fort O'Brien State Memorial

The American Revolution's first naval battle was fought just offshore from Fort O'Brien in June 1775. Now a State Historic Site, the fort was built and rebuilt several times—originally to guard Machias during the Revolutionary War. Only Civil War-era earthworks now remain, plus well-maintained lawns overlooking the Machias River. Steep banks lead down to the water; keep small children well back from the edge. No restrooms or other facilities, but there's a playground at the Fort O'Brien School, next door. Officially, the park is open Memorial Day weekend to Labor Day, but it's easily accessible all year. Admission is free. Take Rt. 92 from Machias about five miles toward Machiasport; the parking area is on the left.

Jasper Beach

Thanks to a handful of incredibly foresighted year-round and summer residents, spectacular, crescent-shaped Jasper Beach—piled high with ocean-polished jasper and other rocks—has been preserved by the town of Machiasport. No sand here, just stones, in intriguing shapes and colors. Resist the urge to fill your pockets with souvenirs, maybe settling for just a single special rock. Parking is limited; no facilities. From Rt. 1 in downtown Machias, take Rt. 92 (Machias Rd.) nine and a half miles southeast, past the village of Bucks Harbor. Watch for a large sign on your left. The beach is on Howard's Cove, .2 mile off the road and accessible all year.

Roque Bluffs State Park

Southwest of Machias, six miles south of Rt. 1, is 275-acre Roque Bluffs State Park, Roque Bluffs Rd., Roque Bluffs 04648, tel. (207) 255-3475. Saltwater swimming this far north is for the young and brave, but this park also has a 60-acre freshwater pond—warm and shallow enough for toddlers and the old and timid. Facilities include primitive changing rooms, outhouses, a play area, and picnic tables—no food or lifeguards—but views go on forever from the wide-open, mile-long sweep of sand beach. Admission is $1 adults, 50 cents children 5-11. The fee box relies on the honor system. The park is open daily, May 15-Sept. 15, but the beach is accessible all year.

Bold Coast Trail

On Rt. 191, about four and a half miles northeast of the center of Cutler, watch for the parking area (on the right) and trailhead sign (including map) for the extraordinary Bold Coast Trail, a spectacular five-mile loop in the 2,115-acre state-owned **Cutler Coast Preserve.** Follow the blue-blazed loop clockwise, allowing an easy start for about a mile before a stretch of moderately rugged hiking southward along dramatic, tree-fringed shoreline cliffs.

Bring plenty of film; the views from this wild coastline are fabulous. Also bring insect repellent—inland boggy stretches are buggy. Bring a picnic and commandeer a granite ledge overlooking the surf. Precipitous cliffs and narrow stretches can make the shoreline section of this trail perilous for small children or insecure adults, so use extreme caution and commonsense. There are no facilities in the preserve. If you're here in August, you can stock up on blueberries, and even some wild raspberries. Allow at least four hours for the loop. An extension of the trail, southward along the shoreline another 2.2 miles, leads to three primitive campsites (stoves only, no fires); the return is via the same route. Information on the preserve is available from the **Maine Bureau of Parks and Lands,** 22 State House Station, Augusta 04333, tel. (207) 287-3821.

In 1997, several donors, primarily the Richard King Mellon Foundation, deeded to the state 10,055 acres of fields and forests across Rt. 191 from the Cutler Coast Preserve, creating a phenomenal tract that now runs from the ocean all the way back to Rt. 1. Located mostly in Cutler but also in Whiting, it's Maine's second-largest public-land gift—after Baxter State Park. Plans are underway to manage the land for hiking and hunting; the Bureau of Parks and Lands will oversee it.

Golf

With lovely water views, and tidal inlets serving as obstacles, the nine-hole **Great Cove Golf Course,** Roque Bluffs Rd., Jonesboro 04648, tel. (207) 434-7200, is a good challenge. Reasonable greens fees, carts, and a snack bar; you can also rent clubs. From Jonesboro (Rt. 1), go three and a half miles east and south on Roque Bluffs Road. Open May through October.

BOB RACE

Llama Llunch Hikes

Four miles from Rt. 1, **Steeplebush Farm**, RR 1, Box 285, Machias 04654, tel./fax (207) 255-4244, a llama-breeding enterprise since 1988, offers llama lunch hikes, by reservation only, on weekends from late August to mid-October. Hikes are relatively easy, lasting 3-6 hours. Cost ranges $20-45 pp (2-6 people), depending on the route, lunch arrangements, and hiker and llama headcounts. Call to reserve and arrange logistics. Farm owners Jane Heart and Belden Morse (respectively, an anthropologist/social worker and a restorer of antique buildings) are real enthusiasts for llamas and their Latin American cultural trappings. They also generously share the animals with the community: schoolchildren, nursing-home patients, and group-home residents. A portion of their proceeds goes to Percent for Peace.

GETTING AFLOAT

If you've brought your own **sea kayak**, there are public launching ramps in Bucks Harbor (east of the main Machias Rd.) and at Roque Bluffs State Park. You can also put in at Sanborn Cove, beyond the O'Brien School on Rt. 92, where there's a small parking area. Before setting out, be sure to check the tide calendar and plan your strategy so you don't have to slog through acres of muck when you return. Or contact Machias Bay Boat Tours and Sea Kayaking.

Bold Coast Charter Company

Andy Patterson, skipper of the 40-footer *Barbara Frost,* operates the Bold Coast Charter Company, P.O. Box 364, Cutler 04626, tel. (207) 259-4484, homeported in Cutler Harbor. Andy provides knowledgable narration, answers questions in depth, and shares his considerable enthusiasm for this pristine corner of Maine. His two-hour Bold Coast cruises depart in early afternoon, mid-May through October, swing around Little River Light (invisible from the mainland), and move in close to Cutler's fish-farming pens, where Andy explains the fascinating aquaculture process.

Bold Coast is best known for its five-hour **puffin-sighting trips** to Machias Seal Island (mid-May through August, departing about 7 a.m.), but there are also half-day and full-day trips several times a week to **Cross Island.** All trips are dependent on weather and tide conditions. Reservations are essential, especially for the very popular Machias Seal Island trip; seats are easiest to come by in May or mid- to late August. Cost for the Bold Coast trip is $20 adults, $10 children 14 and under. Cost for MSI trips is $50 adults, $25 kids (but don't bring small children). Daily access to the island is restricted, and swells can roll in, so passengers occasionally cannot disembark, but the curious puffins often surround the boat, providing plenty of photo opportunities. No matter what the air temperature on the mainland, be sure to dress warmly, and wear sturdy shoes. The *Barbara Frost*'s wharf is on Cutler Harbor, across from the Methodist Church on Rt. 191 in downtown Cutler.

Lobstering and Sea Kayaking Excursions

Captain Martha Jordan operates **Machias Bay Boat Tours and Sea Kayaking,** P.O. Box 42, Machias 04654, tel. (207) 259-3338, skippering the 34-foot *Martha Ann* on lobstering excursions in July and August (also weekends in April, May, September and October). You'll see lighthouses, aquaculture pens, seals, and the rugged coast, and you'll see how the pros haul lobster traps. Departing from Holmes Bay, about four miles east of East Machias on Rt. 191 (the Cutler road), the morning and afternoon trips last about three and a half hours, depending on weather. Reservations are required; six-person maximum. Cost is $50 per adult, $35 for children under 10.

The fledgling company also offers sea kayaking trips in Machias Bay, May through October. On the most popular excursions, you'll paddle in two-person kayaks past Indian petroglyphs estimated at 1,700 years old. Hourly rate is $15 per person. Do-it-yourself rentals are not available.

Canoeing

The spectacular **Machias River,** one of Maine's most technically demanding canoeing rivers, is a dynamite trip mid-May to mid-June, but no beginner should attempt it. Best advice is to sign on with an outfitter/guide who will get you through. The run lasts 3-8 days, the latter if you start from Fifth Machias Lake. Expect to see such wildlife as osprey, eagles, ducks, loons, moose, deer, beaver, and snapping turtles. Be aware, though, that the Machias is probably the buggiest river in the state, and blackflies will form a welcoming party. Bring khaki duds; the bugs are attracted to colors. The major portage is at Upper Holmes Falls; trying to run the half-mile-long rips buys you a ticket to the morgue. Two companies experienced on the Machias are **Sunrise County Canoe Expeditions,** Cathance Lake, Grove Post Office 04638, tel. (800) 748-3730 or (207) 454-7708, fax (207) 454-3315, and **Wilds of Maine,** 2 Abby Ln., Yarmouth 04096, tel. (207) 846-9735. All-inclusive cost is $100-150 per day. Sunrise County, based not far away at Cathance Lake, can arrange a shuttle if you're determined to go guideless.

ENTERTAINMENT

The University of Maine at Machias is the cultural focus in this area, particularly during the school year, but two active theater groups—**Downriver Theatre Company** and **Rubicon Playhouse**—mount summer productions. Check newspapers or the chamber of commerce for schedules.

For slightly noisier nightlife, stop in at **The Dubliner Pub,** 36 Main St., Machias 04654, tel. (207) 255-0654. Here you'll find suds, plus a basic menu (beef stew, meatballs, and the like). During the day, it's quieter. No credit cards. It's open daily 11 a.m.-1 p.m., all year.

FESTIVALS AND EVENTS

Throughout the school year, **Stage Front: The Arts Downeast** puts on an annual series of concerts, plays, recitals, and other events in the Performing Arts Center at the University of Maine at Machias. Contact UMM, tel. (207) 255-1200, for schedule information.

Tuesday-evening **Machias Bay Chamber Concerts** are offered mid-July to mid-August at 8 p.m. at the Centre Street Congregational Church.

The **Maine Wild Blueberry Festival** is a summer highlight, running Fri.-Sun. the third weekend in August, featuring a pancake break-

fast, road races, concerts, a craft show, a baked-bean supper, and more. The blueberry motif is everywhere. Organized by Centre Street Congregational Church, in downtown Machias.

SHOPPING

Gifts, Crafts, Clothing
Maine-made crafts and clothing, a select book inventory, ecosensitive toys, and unusual greeting cards fill the two rooms at **The Sow's Ear,** 7 Water St., Machias 04654, tel. (207) 255-4066, the oddest-named but nicest shop in Machias. The Sow's Ear also carries intriguing "things from away" (also known as "imports"), and the staff is especially helpful. Open Mon.-Sat., Feb.-December.

For some great prices and a blast of local color, stop in at the **Down East 5 & 10 Cent Store,** Main St., Machias 04654, tel. (207) 255-8850. It's open all year, Mon.-Thurs. 8 a.m.-5:30, Friday 8 a.m.-6 p.m., and Saturday 8 a.m.-5 p.m.

Influenced by traditional Japanese designs, Connie Harter-Bagley markets her dramatic ceramics at **Connie's Clay of Fundy,** Rt. 1, Box 345, East Machias 04630, tel. (207) 255-4574, on the East Machias River. If she's at the wheel, you can also watch her work. The shop, four miles east of downtown Machias, is open daily 10 a.m.-4 p.m., all year.

ACCOMMODATIONS

B&Bs
Victoriana rules at the **Riverside Inn,** Rt. 1, P.O. Box 373, East Machias 04630, tel. (207) 255-4134, a meticulously restored sea captain's home with lots of unusual doodads that Tom and Carol Paul enjoy explaining. Relax on the deck overlooking the East Machias River and you'll forget you're a few steps from a busy highway. Two rooms, two suites (all with private baths), and the popular dining room also face the river—a hangout for osprey and eagles. (The suites have riverfront balconies.) Rooms are $68 d, suites are $78-85 d, July-Oct.; lower rates off season. No smoking, no pets, no children. Open all year. The inn is four miles northeast of downtown Machias.

Overlooking scenic Cutler Harbor, **Little River Lodge,** Rt. 191, P.O. Box 251, Cutler 04626, tel. (207) 259-4437, under Gary Sego's ownership since 1995, has six basic guest rooms, one with a private bath. Rates are $45-70 d, including early breakfast for anyone heading out on a puffin trip. Picnic lunches ($3-5) are also available. Family-style dinners, $10-15, are served to guests on request, to the public by reservation. No smoking, no pets, no credit cards. Yachtsmen anchored in Cutler Harbor can take showers at the lodge: $6 if you need a towel, $5 if you bring your own. The B&B is open Memorial Day weekend to Labor Day, with future plans to remain open through Columbus Day.

Motels
The second generation now runs **The Bluebird Motel,** Rt. 1, Box 45, Machias 04654, tel. (207) 255-3332, a clean, upgraded-1950s-style motel, and Peter and Sharon Stackpole are especially knowledgeable about the area. Forty pine-paneled rooms (15 are nonsmoking) have cable TV, phones, a/c, and large baths. The motel is set back from Rt. 1 enough to keep down noise, but request a room in the rear section if you're a light sleeper. The motel, a mile south of downtown, has two wheelchair-accessible rooms. Children are welcome; pets are allowed in some units. Rooms are $56 d mid-June to mid-September, $48 d other months. Open all year.

The best feature of the two-story **Machias Motor Inn,** 26 E. Main St., Rt. 1, Machias 04654, tel. (207) 255-4861, is its location overlooking the tidal Machias River; sliding doors open onto decks-with-a-view. Twenty-nine guest rooms and six efficiencies have extra-long beds, plus cable TV, a/c, and phone. Room rate ($60 d mid-June to mid-September, $50 d other months; $80 d for efficiencies in summer, $65 d in winter) includes free use of the heated indoor pool, open to nonguests for $5 pp a day ($10 per family). Next door is Helen's Restaurant—famed for seasonal fruit pies and an all-you-can-eat weekend breakfast buffet. Children and pets ($5 fee) are welcome; small kids are free. The motel is within easy walking distance to downtown. Open all year.

Campgrounds and Seasonal Rentals
Campgrounds close to Machias are near Lubec

and at Cobscook Bay State Park. The Machias Bay Area Chamber of Commerce produces an annual flyer listing weekly and monthly summer rentals. Weekly rates average $400-800.

FOOD

Watch the local papers for listings of **public suppers, spaghetti suppers,** or **baked bean suppers,** a terrific way to sample the culinary talents of local cooks. Most begin at 5 p.m., and it's worth arriving early to get near the head of the line. The suppers often benefit needy individuals or struggling nonprofits—always worth supporting—and where else can you eat nonstop for well under $10?

Breakfast, Lunch, and Miscellanea
It's a toss-up which Machias pizza parlor to choose—this college town supports two good ones, and they're both open all year. Neither delivers. **Machias House of Pizza,** 15 Main St., Machias 04654, tel. (207) 255-6410, is open daily 11 a.m.-10 p.m. Calzones, pasta, salad, and beer are also available. Just down the street, **Murphy's Pizza,** 50 Main St., Machias, tel. (207) 255-3733, is open Mon.-Sat. 11 a.m.-10 p.m. and Sunday 2-9 p.m. Their grinders are also good.

Biggest treat at **Sam's Country Café,** Rt. 1, Jonesboro 04648, tel. (207) 434-2300, a roadside log cabin, is finding grits on the menu—grits and biscuits with sausage gravy no less, for under $4. This bright, folksy spot is open Tues.-Sun. 5 a.m.-2 p.m., all year; breakfast is served all day. Sam's is .2 mile south of the Rt. 187 turnoff to Jonesport.

If you're headed along the shoreline toward Cutler, pick up picnic fare at the **Village Market,** Rt. 191, Cutler 04626, tel. (207) 259-3922, a locally colorful emporium with made-to-order sandwiches and subs, plus burgers, dogs, pizza, wine, beer, and even fishing gear. It opens Mon.-Sat. at 6 a.m., and Sunday at 8 a.m., all year. Closing time is 6 p.m. in winter, later in summer.

Inexpensive to Moderate
Don't expect fancy at **Joyce's Lobster House,** Rt. 1, East Machias 04630, tel. (207) 255-3015

—just respectable home cooking heavy on seafood and steaks. Efficient service bogs down a bit at lunchtime in this popular local spot. The children's menu has plenty of reasonable options. Open daily 11 a.m.-8 p.m., May-Oct. (to 9 p.m. July to mid-September), the restaurant is next to the Maineland Motel, a mile east of downtown Machias.

Also family-owned, and very popular all day long, is **The Blue Bird Ranch**, 3 E. Main St., Rt. 1, Machias 04654, tel. (207) 255-3351, named for the Prout family's other enterprise, Blue Bird Ranch Trucking. Service is efficient, food is hearty, portions are ample. One dining room serves smokers, two are for nonsmokers. Liquor license. The restaurant is open all year, Mon.-Sat. 5 a.m.-8:30 p.m. and Sunday 6 a.m.-8:30 p.m.

Moderate to Expensive
Choose from four or five well-prepared entrées and settle in for candlelight dining at **Micmac Farm**, Rt. 92, P.O. Box 336, Machiasport 04655, tel. (207) 255-3008, Barbara Dunn's 1776 Cape-style house overlooking the Machias River. Dinners ($16-18, depending on entrée) include superb homemade breads and soups. BYOL. No smoking. Reservations are required. Open all year, Tues.-Sat. 6-8:30 p.m. From May 1 to mid-October, Mrs. Dunn also rents three comfortable, moderately-priced **cabins**—by the day ($50-60) or week ($300-375)—with kitchen facilities, heat, and river views. Micmac Farm is just off Rt. 92, two and a half miles south of downtown Machias.

Patterned hardwood floors, tin ceilings, and Victoriana provide the warm atmosphere at the **Riverside Inn** dining room, overlooking the East Machias River. Five-course dinners (three entrée selections) are $14-16. BYOL; no smoking. Reservations essential. Open for dinner Mon.-Sat., all year. The first Sunday in December, the inn holds a Victorian Christmas Tea ($5 pp), transforming the whole building into a Victorian Christmas wonderland.

Farmers' Market
The **Machias Valley Farmers' Market** sets up shop on "the dike" (Rt. 1, near the Machias Motor Inn) each Saturday 8 a.m.-noon, May to mid-October. There aren't many farmers' markets in this part of Maine; this is a good one to patronize.

INFORMATION AND SERVICES

Based at the 19th-century railroad station alongside Rt. 1 at the junction of Rt. 1A, the **Machias Bay Area Chamber of Commerce**, 23 E. Main St., P.O. Box 606, Machias 04654, tel./fax (207) 255-4402, stocks brochures, maps, and information on area hiking trails. The office is generally open Mon.-Fri. 10 a.m.-3 p.m. Once linked to the Maine Central Railroad system, the station is undergoing rehabbing to serve as a railroad museum, community building, and tourism information center.

Summer hours at the handsome stone **Porter Memorial Library**, Court St., Machias 04654, tel. (207) 255-3933, built in 1892, are Monday 11 a.m.-4 p.m., Tuesday and Friday 11 a.m.-5 p.m., and Wednesday 11 a.m.-8 p.m.

Summer hours at the University of Maine's **Merrill Library**, on the UMM campus, tel. (207) 255-1284, which is open to the public, are Mon.-Fri. 8 a.m.-4:30 p.m.

Newspapers
Two dueling weeklies cover coastal Washington County, with a wide range of local news, features, ads, and calendar listings. *Machias Valley News Observer*, tel. (207) 255-6561, fax 255-4058, based in Machias, is published every Wednesday; the *Downeast Coastal Press*, tel./fax (207) 259-7751, in Cutler, comes out every Tuesday. Since Washington County's major shopping hub is Bangor, the *Bangor Daily News* has a grip on readership in this part of Maine.

Emergencies
To reach the police, call (207) 255-4033 in **Machias;** (207) 255-4422 in **East Machias and Machiasport;** and 911 in **Jonesboro.** For an ambulance, call (207) 255-3535 in **Machias, East Machias, and Machiasport,** and 911 in **Jonesboro.** In case of fire, call (207) 255-3535 in **Machias;** (207) 255-3939 in **East Machias;** (207) 255-4041 in **Machiasport;** and 911 in **Jonesboro.**

Down East Community Hospital, Upper Court St., Rt. 1A, Machias 04654, tel. (207) 255-3356, has a 24-hour emergency room. Machias residents also patronize hospitals in Ellsworth, Bangor, and Calais.

Laundromat
Machias Cleaning and Laundry Center, 9 Water St., Machias 04654, tel. (207) 255-6639, with coin-operated machines, is open all year, weekdays 8 a.m.-6 p.m., Saturday and Sunday 8 a.m.-5 p.m.

Getting There and Getting Around
The nearest major airport is Bangor International Airport.

Machias Taxi, tel. (207) 255-4157 or (800) 348-2947, is on call round-the-clock, all year, and makes trips to and from Bangor International Airport.

LUBEC AND VICINITY

Literally the beginning of America—at the nation's easternmost point—Lubec (pop. 1,800) makes an ideal base for exploring New Brunswick's Campobello Island, the Cutler coastline, and territory to the west. With several appealing B&Bs, more than 90 miles of meandering waterfront, and a harbor ever so slowly on the upswing, Lubec conveys the aura of realness: a hardscrabble fishing community that extends a warm welcome to visitors.

Settled in 1780 and originally part of Eastport, Lubec was split off in 1811 and named for the German port of Lübeck (for convoluted reasons still not totally clear). The town's most famous resident was Hopley Yeaton, first commandant of the U.S. Coast Guard (originally the U.S. Revenue-Marine), who retired here in 1809.

Along the main drag (Water Street), a row of shuttered buildings reflects the town's rollercoaster history. Once the world's sardine capital, Lubec today has only two packing plants (no tours), but aquaculture has come to the forefront, and new businesses are arriving—including a commercial and pleasure-boat marina opened in 1997.

In summer, a free public concert series (Wednesday evenings) is part of the schedule for SummerKeys, 6 Bayview St., Lubec 04652, tel. (207) 733-2316, (201) 451-2338 off season, an unusual music school run by Bruce Potterton, a New York music-school teacher in his other life. Limited to 12 adults, the school can handle any skill level from rank beginner to rusty professional. Practice studios in the former Masonic Hall are all soundproofed. The camaraderie and enthusiasm are contagious. Tuition runs $200-260 a week.

SIGHTS AND RECREATION

If walking and hiking are on your Lubec (and Washington County) agenda, be sure to send for a copy of *Cobscook Trails,* published by the Quoddy Regional Land Trust (see the Booklist). The parks and preserves described below, and many others in eastern Washington County, are included in the QRLT booklet.

And if time allows, tag along with Lubec's **Pathfinders Walking Group,** tel. (207) 733-2129—enthusiastic area residents who go exploring every Sunday, year-round, 1-3 p.m. in winter, 2-4 p.m. in summer. Nonmembers are welcome, there's no fee, and you'll see a Lubec (and more) that most visitors never encounter.

Even the humongous tides and dramatic sunsets over Johnson Bay can get your attention if you hang out at the **Lubec breakwater.** Across the channel, on Campobello Island, is redcapped **Mulholland Point Lighthouse,** an abandoned beacon built in 1885. As the tide goes out—18 or so feet of it—you'll also see hungry harbor seals dunking for dinner. And if you're lucky, you might spot the eagle pair that nests on an island in the channel (bring binoculars).

Quoddy Head State Park
Beachcombing, hiking, picnicking, and an up-close look at Maine's only red-and-white-striped lighthouse are the big draws at 480-acre Quoddy Head State Park, W. Quoddy Head Rd., Lubec 04652, tel. (207) 733-0911, the easternmost point of U.S. land. The cliffs of Canada's Grand Manan Island are visible from the grounds

of West Quoddy Head Light, located just out-side the park boundary. A 1.75-mile, moderate-ly difficult trail follows the 90-foot cliffs to Carrying Place Cove, and an easy, mile-long boardwalk winds through a unique moss and heath bog designated as a National Natural Landmark. The park opens daily at 9 a.m., mid-May to mid-Oc-tober. Be forewarned that the park gate is locked at sunset. Admission is $1 adults, 50 cents chil-dren 5-11. In winter, the park is accessible for snowshoeing. From Rt. 189 on the outskirts of Lubec, take S. Lubec Rd. (well signposted) to W. Quoddy Head Road. Turn left and continue to the parking area.

West Quoddy Head Light, towering 83 feet above mean high water, was built in 1808. (Its counterpart, East Quoddy Head Light, is on New Brunswick's Campobello Island.) Views from the lighthouse grounds are fabulous, and whale sightings are common in summer.

Flightseeing
From May through October, retired Maine game warden Gray Morrison, P.O. Box 264, Lubec 04652, tel. (207) 733-2124, offers **scenic flights** in his four-passenger Cessna based at the Lubec Municipal Airport (the well-maintained grassy strip behind the Eastland Motel), flying low over lighthouses, islands, and the coast-line. Fall-foliage trips are spectacular. All flights are by reservation; he also shuttles visitors to and from offshore Grand Manan Island. A typical sightseeing flight lasts 20-30 minutes, with a fare as low as $10 pp if the plane is full; hourly rate for the plane is $60. No credit cards.

FESTIVALS AND EVENTS

In Lubec, free **Mary Potterton Memorial Piano Concerts** take place at Sacred Heart Church Parish Hall at 7:30 p.m. Wednesday evenings mid-July through August.

Lubec's old-fashioned **Annual Country Fair** includes art and craft booths, kids' games, a rummage sale, food booths, fish-chowder lunch, live entertainment, and an auction. Proceeds benefit the Regional Medical Center at Lubec (RMCL). The fair starts at 9 a.m. on the third Saturday in July.

SHOPPING

Flower fans should definitely make the short detour, four and a half miles north of Rt. 189, to the **Cottage Garden,** N. Lubec Rd., Lubec 04652, tel. (207) 733-2902, a lovely oasis de-veloped by Gretchen and Alan Mead. Bring a picnic and stroll through the perennial, herb, and alpine gardens. There's no charge for wan-dering, but you'll probably be tempted by the small print, craft, and gift shop on the premises—not to mention the pots of perennials for sale. Cottage Garden is open only in summer, Wed.-Sat. 10 a.m.-4 p.m., or by appointment.

ACCOMMODATIONS

Many visitors use Lubec as a base for day-trips to Campobello Island or Machias Seal Island, so it's essential to reserve rooms ahead at the height of summer. Several lodgings are also available on Campobello.

B&Bs
Count on warm Gemütlichkeit at the **Lübecker Gast Haus B&B,** 31 Main St., Lubec 04652, tel./fax (207) 733-4385, where German-born Ir-mgard Swiecicki and her husband settled in 1994, when he retired from the U.S. Public Health Service. Comfortable, unfussy rooms boast European comforters and some water views; three second-floor rooms share a bath ($65 d). No pets, no children; limited smoking. The B&B is open early June to late September. On weekend afternoons year-round, Irmgard operates a European coffeehouse—**Cafe Kon-tinental**—serving outrageous Sachertorte, black forest cherry cake, and her specialty, marzipan torte. Dieters beware!

Built in 1860 by a British sea captain, **Pea-cock House Bed and Breakfast,** 27 Summer St. at Church St., Lubec 04652, tel. (207) 733-2403, has long been one of Lubec's most pres-tigious residences. Veda Childs and her daugh-ter, Debra Norris, have restored it to perfection, and their hospitality tops it all off. They'll pack pic-nic lunches, produce tea and scones in midafter-noon, and steer you toward their antique bar (BYOL). Breakfast is an event. Four rooms ($70

d) and the Margaret Chase Smith suite (named after its most famous overnighter; $80 d) have private baths. One room is wheelchair-accessible. No pets, no smoking, no children under seven. Open mid-May to mid-October.

Unusual antiques fill the guest and sitting rooms of Miyoko and Tim Carman's 19th-century **Home Port Inn,** 45 Main St., P.O. Box 50, Lubec 04652, tel. (207) 733-2077 or (800) 457-2077 outside Maine, ensconced on a Lubec hilltop. Seven outside rooms (private baths) are $60-80 d, including generous continental breakfast. No smoking, no pets, no small children. Miyoko runs a tiny in-house emporium with tasteful local crafts. Reservations are wise for the inn's very popular restaurant—a sunken dining room with tables for 30. Specialty is seafood; creative entrées run $9-14. The B&B and its dining room are open late May to mid-October. The Carmans also own the Waterside Restaurant and have a thriving wreath-making business.

Motels

If you're traveling with small children, the **Eastland Motel,** County Rd., Rt. 189, RR1, Box 6915, Lubec 04652, tel. (207) 733-5501, is Lubec's best bet, and owner Lee Aragon is a helpful Lubec booster. Located four miles southwest of town, near the Lubec Municipal Airport (used infrequently), the motel has 20 clean rooms at $52-62 d May-Oct., $40-50 d other months. Children under 17 are only $2 extra; small pets are $3. Rooms have cable TV. No a/c, but window fans do the job, since heat waves seldom hit this part of Maine. Request one of the 12 rooms in the newer section. Free morning coffee. The motel is open all year.

FOOD

Phinney's Seaview, County Rd., Rt. 189, P.O. Box 110, Lubec 04652, tel. (207) 733-0941, Lubec's best family restaurant—not at all fancy—starts with a stunning view of Johnson Bay. If weather permits, settle on the deck and enjoy one of their seafood specialties. Air-conditioned; children's menu; beer and wine license only. In summer, you can pick up fresh fish and lobsters at the adjacent fish market. Open daily 6:30 a.m.-9 p.m., late May through September;

Fri.-Tues. 7 a.m.-8 p.m., the rest of the year. Occasionally closed in January. Phinney's is 1.2 miles southwest of downtown Lubec.

Depending on whom you talk to, **Uncle Kippy's,** County Rd., Rt. 189, Lubec 04652, tel. (207) 733-2400, gets high and higher marks in Lubec for wholesome cooking. A sign out front announces, Stop in or we'll both starve. Steak and seafood are specialties—at unfancy prices —and the pizza is the area's best. Beer and nonvintage wine are available. Video games and pool tables provide diversion for those who need it. Located half a mile southwest of downtown Lubec, it's open daily 11 a.m.-8 p.m., all year.

Lobster-in-the-Rough

Best place to dine with a view is one of the picnic tables on the Eastern Steamship Deck of **The Waterside,** Lubec Landing, Lubec 04652, tel. (207) 733-2500—a retrofitted warehouse right on the harbor. This casual barn of a place serves up lobster rolls ($6), steamed clams, even hot dogs and chili. Big lobster tanks keep the kids amused. No credit cards. Open daily 11 a.m. to sunset, Memorial Day weekend to mid-September.

INFORMATION AND SERVICES

The **Lubec Chamber of Commerce** is a small, volunteer-staffed operation, so it helps to write ahead for information. Send requests to P.O. Box 123, Lubec 04652, or call (207) 733-4522 (you may need to leave a message). Once you're here, stop on the outskirts of town at the **Eastland Motel,** County Rd., Rt. 189, for brochures and advice.

The **Lubec Memorial Library,** 10 School St., Lubec 04652, tel. (207) 733-2491, is open all year, Monday and Saturday 10 a.m.-2 p.m., Wednesday and Friday 10 a.m.-4 p.m., and Tuesday 6-8 p.m.

Newspapers

Best local coverage appears in the twice-monthly Eastport-based *Quoddy Tides,* tel. (207) 853-4806, fax 853-4095, and the weekly Cutler-based *Downeast Coastal Press,* tel./fax (207) 259-7751. Both carry tide tables—critical information in this part of Maine. The only daily paper covering this area is the *Bangor Daily News.*

Emergencies

For **police, fire, and ambulance** in Lubec, call (207) 733-4321. The **Regional Medical Center at Lubec** (RMCL), S. Lubec Rd., Lubec 04652, tel. (207) 733-5541, can handle minor medical and dental emergencies weekdays 8 a.m.-5 p.m., and a doctor is on call for emergencies around the clock, but the nearest 24-hour emergency room is at Machias's Down East Community Hospital.

Getting There

Lubec is about two and a half hours by car from Bangor International Airport, the nearest major airport.

CAMPOBELLO ISLAND

Just over the Franklin D. Roosevelt Memorial Bridge from Lubec lies 10-mile-long Campobello Island, in Canada's New Brunswick province. Since 1964, 2,800 acres of the island have been under joint United States and Canadian jurisdiction as **Roosevelt Campobello International Park,** commemorating U.S. President Franklin D. Roosevelt. FDR summered here as a youth, and it was here that he contracted infantile paralysis (polio) in 1921. The park, covering most of the island's southern end, has well-maintained trails, picnic sites, and dramatic vistas, but its centerpiece is the imposing Roosevelt Cottage, a mile northeast of the bridge.

Roosevelt Cottage/Visitor Centre

Little seems to have changed in the 34-room red-shingled Roosevelt "Cottage" overlooking Passamaquoddy Bay since President Roosevelt last visited in 1939. The grounds are beautifully landscaped, and the many family mementos—especially those in the late president's den—bring history alive. It all feels very personal, far less stuffy than most presidential memorials.

Stop first at the park's Visitor Centre, where you can pick up brochures (including a trail map), use the restrooms, and see a short video setting the stage for the cottage visit. Then walk across to the house/museum, which is open daily, Memorial Day weekend to Columbus Day (Canadian Thanksgiving). Hours are 10 a.m.-6 p.m. Atlantic daylight time (9 a.m.-5 p.m. eastern daylight time). Admission is free. For more information, contact **Executive Secretary, Roosevelt Campobello International Park,** P.O. Box 97, Lubec 04652, or P.O. Box 9, Welshpool, Campobello, NB, Canada E0G 3H0. Seasonal phone (in Canada) is (506) 752-2922.

The Park by Car

If time is short, or you're unable to hike, at least take some of the park's driving routes—**Cranberry Point Drive,** 5.4 miles roundtrip from the Visitor Centre, **Liberty Point Drive,** 12.4 miles roundtrip, via Glensevern Rd., from the Visitor Centre, and **Fox Hill Drive,** a 2.2 mile link between the other two main routes. Even with the car, you'll have access to beaches, picnic sites, spruce and fir forests, and incredible views of lighthouses, islands, and the Bay of Fundy.

Just west of the main access road from the bridge is the **Mulholland Point Picnic Area,** where you can spread out your lunch next to the distinctive red-capped lighthouse overlooking the Lubec Narrows.

Hiking/Picnicking

Within the international park are eight and a half miles of walking/hiking trails, ranging from dead easy to moderately difficult. Easiest is the 1.4-mile (roundtrip) walk from the Visitor Centre to **Friar's Head Picnic Area,** named for its distinctive promontory jutting into the bay. For the best angle, climb up to the observation deck on the "head." Grills and tables are here for picnickers. (If you haven't packed a picnic, nearest source of the makings is the town of Welshpool.)

The most difficult—and most dramatic—trail is a 1.9-mile stretch from **Liberty Point to Raccoon Beach,** along the southeastern shore of the island. Precipitous cliffs can make parts of this trail chancy for small children or insecure adults, so use caution. Liberty Point is incredibly rugged, but observation platforms make it easy to see the tortured rocks and wide-open Bay of Fundy. At broad Raccoon Beach, you can walk the sands, have a picnic, or watch for whales, porpoises, and osprey. To avoid returning via the same route, park at Liberty Point and walk back along Liberty Point Drive from Raccoon Beach. If you're traveling with nonhikers, arrange for them to meet you with a vehicle at Con Robinson's Point.

You can also walk the park's perimeter, including just over six miles of shoreline, but only if you're in good shape, have waterproof hiking boots, and can spend an entire day on the trails. Before attempting this, however, inquire at the Visitor Centre about trail conditions and tide levels.

CAMPOBELLO BEYOND THE INTERNATIONAL PARK

Take a day or two and explore Campobello beyond the park; overnighters have several lodging and food options. You can also continue on by ferry from here to New Brunswick's Deer Island.

Herring Cove Provincial Park

New Brunswick's provincial government does a conscientious job of running Herring Cove Provincial Park, tel. (506) 752-2396 or (800) 561-0123, with picnic areas, 91 campsites (tel. 506-752-7010), a four-mile trail system, a mile-long sandy beach, freshwater Glensevern Lake, and the nine-hole championship-level **Herring Cove Golf Course** (tel. 506-752-2467). The club restaurant, overlooking the cove and open to the public, has the same phone as the park; it's open 11 a.m.-9 p.m. (Atlantic time). The course is open daily 8:30 a.m.-9 p.m. (Atlantic time). The park is open early June through September.

East Quoddy Head Light

Consult the tide calendar before planning your assault on East Quoddy Head Light (also known as Head Harbour Light), at Cam-

West Quoddy Head Light, Lubec

pobello's northernmost tip. It's on an islet accessible only at low tide. The distinctive lighthouse has a huge red cross painted on its white tower. (You're likely to pass near it on whale-watching trips out of Eastport.) From the Roosevelt cottage, follow Rt. 774 through the village of Wilson's Beach and continue on an unpaved road to the parking area. A stern Canadian Coast Guard warning sign tells the story: *Extreme Hazard. Beach exposed only at low tide. Incoming tide rises 5 feet per hour and may leave you stranded for 8 hours. Wading or swimming are extremely dangerous due to swift currents and cold water. Proceed at your own risk.* So there. It's definitely worth the effort for the bay and island views from the lighthouse grounds, often including whales and eagles. Allow about an hour before and after dead low tide (be sure your watch coincides with the Atlantic-time tide calendar).

ACCOMMODATIONS AND FOOD

In midsummer, if you'd like to overnight on the island, be sure to reserve lodgings well in advance; Campobello is a popular destination. Nearest backup beds are in Lubec, and those fill up, too.

B&Bs

The Owen House, North Rd., Welshpool, Campobello Island, NB, Canada E0G 3H0, tel. (506) 752-2977, is the island's best address, an elegant early-19th-century inn on 10 acres overlooking the bay. Nine guest rooms (private and shared baths) are about US$45-55 per double. Just north of the inn is the Deer Island ferry landing. Open mid-May through September.

The Lupine Lodge, P.O. Box 91, Lubec, 04652, tel. (207) 853-6036, or P.O. Box 2, Welshpool, Campobello Island, NB, Canada E0G 3H0, tel. (506) 752-2555, an updated summer estate of Roosevelt kin, is only a quarter of a mile from the Roosevelt cottage. Bay views from the 11-acre grounds are terrific. Eleven rooms in two buildings (private baths, some fireplaces) go for about US$35-60 d, a pet is around $11 extra. No smoking in rooms. The adjacent restaurant serves breakfast, lunch, dinner, and Sunday brunch, plus tea on Tuesday 2-4 p.m. Open early June through mid-October.

Don't expect culinary creativity on Campobello, but you won't starve—at least during the summer season. Best choice is the **Herring Cove Restaurant.** Shortly before you reach the restaurant, you'll see the **Jolly Roger Takeout,** tel. (506) 752-2399, rigged with all kinds of pirate gear; it's always popular with the kids, and you can get subs, ice cream, and more. Open summer only, 11 a.m.-9 p.m. Atlantic time (10 a.m.-8 p.m. eastern time).

INFORMATION AND SERVICES

If you're planning to visit Campobello Island, you'll have to pass Customs checkpoints on the Lubec, U.S., tel. (207) 733-4331, and Campobello, Canada, tel. (506) 752-2091, fax 752-1080, ends of the Franklin D. Roosevelt Memorial Bridge. **U.S. citizens** need some form of identification, typically a driver's license, although you may not even need to show it. You'll be asked your purpose in going to the island, and the length of your stay. Most clearances are perfunctory, but be sure you are not carrying any live plant material; it will be confiscated.

Even for a day trip to Campobello, **non-U.S. citizens** need to show a valid passport; citizens of most non-European countries must also have a Canadian visa, obtained in advance. **U.S. resident aliens** must be prepared to show a valid green card.

Be aware that crossing this short little bridge takes an hour, because there's a one-hour time difference between Lubec and Campobello. Lubec (like the rest of Maine) is on eastern standard time; Campobello, like the rest of Canada's Maritime Provinces, is on Atlantic time, an hour later.

There is no need to convert U.S. currency to Canadian for use on Campobello; U.S. dollars are accepted everywhere on the island, but prices everywhere tend to be quoted in Canadian dollars. The exchange rate fluctuates, but figure on getting about $1.35 Canadian for a U.S. dollar.

Just after Canadian Customs waves you through from Lubec, stop at the **Tourist Information Centre,** tel. (506) 752-2997, on your right. The staff can fix you up with trail maps of the international park and New Brunswick propaganda, then steer you toward the Roosevelt property. To contact the **Campobello Island Chamber of Commerce** (the Campobello Gift House, on Rt. 774), call (506) 752-2233 or (207) 752-2513.

Getting Away
A funky, bargelike car ferry runs between Welshpool on Campobello and lovely **Deer Island,** where you can explore, picnic, or camp (even without a car). You can also board another ferry from Deer Island to Eastport (every hour on the hour, beginning at 9 a.m. Atlantic time, 8 a.m. EST). Operated by **East Coast Ferries Ltd.,** tel. (506) 747-2159, the ferry does six or seven daily roundtrips to Deer Island from Welshpool, mid-June to late September, beginning at 10 a.m. Atlantic time (9 a.m. EST). The Welshpool dock is on North Road, near The Owen House. One-way ticket for car and driver is about US$8; children under 12 are free.

EASTPORT AND VICINITY

Settled in 1772, the city (yes, it's officially a city) of Eastport (pop. 2,000) has had its ups and downs. Now it's mostly up, with only an occasional sideslip, thanks to an influx of commercial development and a tangible optimism among natives and newcomers. Aquaculture is big business; the commercial port has expanded; and new restaurants, galleries, and B&Bs have opened. But no one goes to Eastport for bright lights and nightlife; it's more to explore a Down East community with a genuine history and a can-do attitude.

In 1780, the first European settlement here was named Freetown; 19 years later, it became incorporated as Eastport. Until 1811, the town also included Lubec, which is about two and a half miles across the water in a boat, but 40 or so in a car.

Eastport is on Moose Island, connected by causeway to the mainland at Pleasant Point. Views are terrific on both sides, especially at sunset, as you hopscotch from one blob of land to another and finally reach this mini-city, where the sardine industry was introduced as long ago as 1875. Five sardine canneries once operated here, employing hundreds of local residents who snipped the heads off herring and stuffed them into cans—one of those skills not easily translatable to other tasks. The focus now is on fish farming; many of hilly Eastport's vantage points overlook the salmon nurseries floating in the bay. Aquaculture has brought jobs and money to Eastport.

Also bringing jobs and money is the deepwater port for oceangoing vessels. Not everyone appreciates the large, noisy trucks that descend Washington Street to the harbor early in the morning when cargo carriers are in port, but no one complains about their benefit to the local economy.

Periodically, a plan surfaces to establish a ferry linking Eastport and Lubec, but now most everyone approaches Eastport from the southwest, via coastal Rt. 1, curving inland east of Machias. Along the way are the towns of Whiting, Edmunds Township, Dennysville, and Pembroke.

Edmunds Township's claims to fame are its splendid public lands—Cobscook Bay State Park and a unit of Moosehorn National Wildlife Reserve. Just past the state park, loop along the scenic shoreline before returning to Rt. 1.

Pembroke, once part of adjoining Dennysville, claims Reversing Falls Park, where you can watch (and hear) ebbing and flowing tides draining and filling Cobscook Bay.

If time allows a short scenic detour, especially in fall, turn left (northwest) on Rt. 214 and drive 10 miles to quaintly named Meddybemps, allegedly a Passamaquoddy word meaning "plenty of alewives [herring]." Views over Meddybemps Lake, on the north side of the road, are spectacular, and you can launch a canoe or kayak into the lake here, less than a mile beyond the junction with Rt. 191 (take the dead-end unpaved road toward the water).

Backtracking to Rt. 1, heading east from Pembroke, you'll come to Perry, best known for the Pleasant Point Indian Reservation, a Passamaquoddy settlement, two miles east of Rt. 1, that's been here since 1822. If there's time, stop at the small Waponahki Museum. Or plan a visit around the reservation's August Indian Days celebration.

SIGHTS

Historic Walking Tour

The best way to appreciate Eastport's history is to pick up and follow the route in *A Walking Guide to Eastport,* available at many local locations. The handy map/brochure spotlights the city's 18th-, 19th-, and early-20th-century homes, businesses, and monuments, many now on the National Register of Historic Places. Among the nearly 20 highlights are historic homes converted to B&Bs, two museums, and a large chunk of downtown Water Street.

Raye's Mustard Mill Museum

How often do you have a chance to watch mustard being made in a turn-of-the-20th-century mustard mill? Drive by J.W. Raye & Co., Outer Washington St., Rt. 190, P.O. Box 2, Eastport

04631, tel. (207) 853-4451 or (800) 853-1903, at the edge of Eastport, and stop in for a free tour if the yellow flag is flying—that means they're grinding mustard. But stop in regardless—the gift shop stocks all of Raye's mustard varieties, plus other Maine-made food items. In summer, the shop is open Mon.-Sat. 9 a.m.-5 p.m. and Sunday noon-5 p.m.; in winter, it's open Mon.-Sat. 9 a.m.-3 p.m.

Maine's Native Americans
Baskets, tools, beadwork, a birch-bark canoe, and photo-lined walls are all part of the **Waponahki Museum,** Pleasant Point Reservation, P.O. Box 295, Rt. 190, Perry 04667, tel. (207) 853-4001, a small collection dedicated to preserving the history and culture of Maine's Passamaquoddy Indians. The museum has spurred revival of the Passamaquoddy language, now being taught and written. The most interesting time to visit is in August, during Pleasant Point Reservation's annual **Indian Days** celebration. The museum—two miles east of Rt. 1 and seven miles north of Eastport—is open all year, Mon.-Fri. 8:30-11 a.m. and noon-4 p.m., but the schedule can be erratic, so call ahead to be sure. Admission is free, but donations are welcomed.

Getting Airborne
The whole business about this region's humongous tidal changes becomes so much clearer during a flightseeing excursion with **Quoddy Air,** Eastport Municipal Airport, Airport Rd., RR 1, Box 69, Eastport 04631, tel. (207) 853-0997. Try to schedule a low-tide trip, when you'll see boats lying in mud, docks high and dry, and gulls searching for lunch. In August, you can watch for whales; in mid-September, you'll see splendid foliage. At any time of year, it's a great adventure. For three passengers, a 20-minute flight costs $30, an hour-long flight is $90. Flights, of course, are weather-dependent, but pilots are available daily, all year.

PARKS, PRESERVES, AND RECREATION

If walking and hiking are on your agenda here—and they should be—send for a copy of *Cob-*

scook Trails, published by the Quoddy Regional Land Trust (see the Booklist). The parks and preserves described below, and many others in eastern Washington County, are included in the QRLT booklet.

One section of Moosehorn National Wildlife Refuge adjoins Cobscook Bay State Park, but the headquarters and major recreational tracts are located near Calais.

Shackford Head
The highlight of 90-acre Shackford Head, Deep Cove Rd., Eastport, is an easy, half-mile-long wooded trail leading to a headland with wide-open views of Eastport, salmon aquaculture pens, and—depending on weather—Campobello Island, Lubec, and Pembroke. This state preserve is a particularly good family hike. Use bug repellent and carry binoculars and a camera. There's a toilet near the parking area, but no other facilities. Even in winter, trail access is not difficult. The trailhead and parking area are just east of the Washington County Technical College Marine Technology Center, at the southern end of town.

Cobscook Bay State Park
A two-and-a-half-mile network of nature trails, picnic spots, great birding and berry-picking, usually hot showers, and wooded shorefront campsites make 888-acre Cobscook Bay State Park, Rt. 1, Edmunds Township, P.O. Box 51, Dennysville 04628, tel. (207) 726-4412, one of Maine's most spectacular state parks. It's even entertaining just to watch the 24-foot tides surging in and out of this area at five or so feet an hour; there's no swimming because of the undertow. And get in the shower line early; the hot water tends to run out. Even though the park tends to be underutilized, and you can usually find a site even at the height of summer, reserve ahead to get a place on the shore. To guarantee a site in July and August, using MasterCard or Visa, call (207) 287-3824; reservation fee is $2 per site per night; two-night minimum. The park is open daily, mid-May to mid-October; trails are groomed in winter for cross-country skiing, and one section goes right along the shore. Summer day-use fees are $2 adults, 50 cents children 5-11; children under five are free. Nonresident camping fees are $15 per site per

night; fees for Maine residents are $11.50. The park entrance is just off Rt. 1, about six miles south of Dennysville.

Reversing Falls Park

There's plenty of room for adults to relax and kids to play at the 140-acre Reversing Falls Park in West Pembroke—plus picnic tables, restrooms, shorefront ledges, and a front-row seat overlooking a fascinating tidal phenomenon. Pack a picnic, then check newspapers or information offices for the tide times, so you can watch the saltwater surging through a 300-yard-wide passage at about 25 knots, creating a whirlpool and churning "falls." The park is at Mahar Point in West Pembroke, 7.2 miles south of Rt. 1. Coming from the south (Dennysville), leave Rt. 1 in West Pembroke when you see the Triangle Store. Turn right and go .3 mile to Leighton Point Rd., where you'll see a sign saying, Shore Access 5.5 miles. Turn right and go 3.8 miles, past gorgeous meadows, low shrubs, and views of Cobscook Bay. Turn right at a very tiny Reversing Falls sign. After about one and a half miles, turn left onto a gravel road and continue two miles to the park. The zigzagging is worth it. The park is open all year, except when snow blocks car access.

Eco-Tours and More

On the way to Reversing Falls Park, just a mile off Rt. 1, **Tidal Trails,** Leighton Point Rd., P.O. Box 321, Pembroke 04666, tel. (207) 726-4079, is an energetic new outfitter providing more recreational options than you could possibly choose. Anxious for visitors to appreciate their stunning corner of Maine, Amy and Tim Sheehan (he's a biology teacher and Master Maine Guide) lead eight different day-long natural-history tours ($10-40 pp) and organize day-long and week-long canoeing, sea kayaking, and birding trips. If you prefer to do it yourself, they have all the rental equipment needed for canoeing ($30 a day), sea kayaking ($40 a day), mountain biking ($20 a day), and clamming ($6 a day). As if all that weren't enough, they manage a number of weekly and monthly saltwater rental cottages, so you can hang out in the area before and after their tours. The Sheehans also make a unique offer: after one of their tours, if you've managed to fill a 30-gallon trash bag

with shoreline plastic dreck, they'll give you a voucher for a free trip or rental (one voucher per family). Makes you want to run right out and start collecting.

GETTING AFLOAT

Whalewatching

Crusty Eastporter Butch Harris loads his passengers onto the 56-foot *Janna Marie* and heads out into the prime whale-feeding grounds of Passamaquoddy Bay—passing the Old Sow whirlpool (largest tidal whirlpool in the Northern Hemisphere), salmon aquaculture pens, and Campobello Island. En route, you'll see bald eagles, porpoises, and more. Best months are July and August, when sightings are frequent, but Butch is a skilled spotter, so if they're there, he'll find them. Dress warmly and wear sunscreen—there's no shelter on board. Daily departures, mid-June to mid-September, are at 1:30 p.m.; trips last 3-4 hours. Reservations are wise, especially early and late in the season. Contact **Harris Whale Watching,** Harris Pt. Rd., Eastport 04631, tel. (207) 853-2940 or 853-4303. (The first number is at the Harborside Clipper beauty salon at 104 Water St., where you can get information, make reservations, or buy tickets Tues.-Sat. 9 a.m.-5 p.m.) Cost is $15 adults, $7.50 children 12 and under.

Ferries to Deer and Campobello Islands

In July and August, **East Coast Ferries Ltd.,** Deer Island, New Brunswick, tel. (506) 747-2159, operates flatbed car ferries between Eastport and Deer Island, and then on to Campobello Island.

The ferry schedule lists both eastern standard time and Atlantic time, since Eastport is on the former and the two Canadian islands are on the latter. Eastport departures are on the half-hour, beginning at 8:30 a.m. EST (9:30 a.m. Atlantic time). Check the schedule carefully to avoid missing the last boat back to Eastport. (If you take a car, you can drive back to Eastport from Campobello. It's one and a half miles by water and almost 50 miles by road.) The ferry landing in Eastport is just off Water Street, .3 mile north of Washington Street. It all seems very informal, and the trip is an adventure, but remember that you're crossing the Canadian border. U.S. citizens need valid identification (such as a driver's license); non-U.S. citizens need a passport; most non-Europeans also need a Canadian visa.

ENTERTAINMENT

An enthusiastic local theater group, **Stage East,** mounts three or four productions between April and Christmas at the **Eastport Arts Center,** the onetime Masonic Hall in downtown Eastport. Most performances are at 7:30 p.m., but there are occasional matinees. Check newspapers for schedule information, or call the box office at The Motel East, (207) 853-4747.

The **Eastport Arts Center,** Water and Dana Sts., P.O. Box 153, Eastport 04631, tel. (207) 853-4133, is also the locale for concerts, films, summer art classes and workshops, and other cultural events throughout the year.

For **live music,** find out what's happening at La Sardina Loca, 28 Water St., tel. (207) 853-2739.

FESTIVALS AND EVENTS

For a small community, Eastport manages to pull together and put on plenty of successful events during the year. Besides the celebrations listed below, popular nearby events are the Calais International Festival, the first week in August and the Maine Wild Blueberry Festival, held in Machias the third weekend in August.

Eastport's annual four-day **Fourth of July— Old Home Week** extravaganza includes a parade, pancake breakfasts, barbecues, a flea market, an auction, races, live entertainment, and fireworks. This is one of Maine's best July Fourth celebrations and attracts a crowd of more than 10,000.

Indian Days, a three-day Native American celebration includes children's games, canoe races, craft demos, talking circles, fireworks, and traditional food and dancing at the Pleasant Point Indian Reservation, in Perry, the second weekend in August. **Moose Island Antique Show** is an all-day (10:30 a.m.-3:30 p.m.) show and sale, plus lunch, at Washington County Technical College, Deep Cove Rd., Eastport, the second Saturday in August.

Eastport Salmon Festival celebrates the area's aquaculture industry. If you like salmon, you'll *love* this event, which combines a salmon barbecue, craft booths, live entertainment, and boat trips at the Eastport breakwater 11 a.m.-4 p.m. the Sunday after Labor Day.

SHOPPING

Art, Crafts, and Antiques

Eastport has long been a magnet for artists and craftspeople yearning to work in a supportive environment, but the influx has increased in recent years. Proof of this is **The Eastport Gallery,** 69 Water St., Eastport 04631, tel. (207) 853-4166, a cooperative whose works line the walls of a handsome two-story downtown building. While you're here, grab a chair on the second-floor deck and watch the waterfront action. In summer, the gallery is open Mon.-Thurs. 10:30 a.m.-5:30 p.m., Friday 1-8 p.m.; off season, the schedule is erratic and it's usually closed, but try calling.

Up the street, next to the pizza parlor, is **Purple Lake Gallery,** 38 Water St., Eastport, Richard Netzband's eclectic antiques shop with lots of whimsical collectibles. Between Memorial Day and late October, the shop usually is open Mon.-Sat. noon-6 p.m.; to be sure, call (207) 733-2891 for an appointment.

Just around the corner, in the same building as the Eastport Arts Center, is **Earth Forms,** 5 Dana St., Eastport 04631, tel. (207) 853-2430, featuring ceramicist Donald Sutherland's intriguing wheel-thrown work—self-described as functional, nonfunctional, and dysfunctional pottery. The shop is open most of the year, daily 9 a.m.-4:30 p.m. (and some evenings in summer), but he's a solo show, so call ahead to be sure.

Up the hill a few blocks from the Deer Island ferry landing is the studio of **Elizabeth Drinker Woodworking,** 4 Favor St., Eastport 04631, tel./fax (207) 853-4560, source of astonishing hand-turned bowls, furniture, and objets—some decorative, most functional, all stunning. Her studio is open daily, all year, by appointment; evening is the best time to call.

Books

Here's a treat. **Fountain Books,** 58 Water St., Eastport 04631, tel. (207) 853-4519, using the slogan, "Life the Way It Used to Be," has a fantastic old-fashioned soda fountain upmarketed with cappuccino, late-breakfast goodies, and creative sandwiches. Plus you can browse the interesting inventory of books (including Maine and Native American titles) and CDs. From Memorial Day to Labor Day, it's open 9 a.m.-9 p.m., other months on a less predictable schedule.

Farmers' Market

The **Sunrise County Farmers' Market** sets up its tables at the Perry Municipal Building on Rt. 1 every Saturday 9 a.m.-5 p.m., mid-June to mid-September. On Wednesday, the market is held in Robbinston. Except for Machias, these are the only farmers' markets in Washington County.

ACCOMMODATIONS

Lodgings in Eastport can fill up in summer, and since it's literally the end of the road, it's wise to reserve ahead. Fortunately, choices include an excellent selection of B&Bs, plus a good motel, so it's a great place to spend the night.

B&Bs

Two large parlors and a back-deck hot tub are magnets for guests at **The Inn at Eastport,** 13 Washington St., Eastport 04631, tel. (207) 853-4307, fax 853-6143, Bob and Brenda Booker's congenial, Federal-style B&B. Four rooms (private baths) are $55-65 d, depending on the season. Breakfast specialty is apricot French toast stuffed with cream cheese. If you're a light sleeper, ask for a side room, as this is Eastport's busiest street. When ships are in port, traffic begins early. No pets; children are welcome; smoking only on porches. Open all year.

Tasteful antiques are everywhere at **The Milliken House Bed & Breakfast,** 29 Washington St., Eastport 04631, tel. (207) 853-2955, Joyce and Paul Weber's very comfortable Victorian home. Artists have free use of the skylighted garret studio, and flower fans will drool over the gardens. Locally smoked salmon often

appears at breakfast, served in the elegant dining room. Five attractive rooms share two baths ($60 d in summer, lower off season). Traffic sometimes begins early on Washington Street, so request a side or back room if you're noise-conscious. Children are welcome; smoking only on the back deck. Open all year.

At the 1775 **Todd House,** Todd's Head, Eastport 04631, tel. (207) 853-2328, Eastport native Ruth McInnis converts guests willingly into instant history buffs. The National Historic Register Cape-style house has character, from the book and arrowhead collections to the beautiful quilts and a resident cockatiel named Bird. Six first- and second-floor rooms (two with private baths) are $45-80 d, lower off season. A generous continental breakfast is served in the lovely common room. Guests can grill dinner in the backyard fireplace. No smoking; well-behaved pets and children are welcome. Open all year.

In 1833, noted artist John James Audubon stayed at the elegant **Weston House,** 26 Boynton St., Eastport 04631, tel. (207) 853-2907 or (800) 853-2907, so one of the five guest rooms bears his name—and walls lined with Audubon bird prints. Rates are $60-75 d (two and a half shared baths). Family antiques fill the house, which is on a quiet side street two blocks above the waterfront. Breakfast is an event, accompanied by a candelabra and classical music. Outside are croquet and badminton facilities, plus a lovely garden with chairs and table. No smoking, no pets; well-behaved children welcome. Open all year.

Motels

Enthusiastic about his adopted community, host Owen Lawlor at **The Motel East,** 23A Water St., Eastport 04631, tel./fax (207) 853-4747, shares all kinds of advice and guarantees you'll enjoy the area. Got a problem? Owen solves it. His modern, three-story hostelry looks unassuming from the street, but guests have front-row seats on Passamaquoddy Bay, overlooking Campobello Island, and you can walk to everything downtown. Six rooms and eight efficiency suites ($90-95 d) have phones and cable TV. Request a balcony room. No pets, children welcome. Free coffee in the lobby. Open all year.

FOOD

Gourmet Seafood

Jim Blankman's seafood business—started and continuing in the back of his house—just keeps growing! Word has spread about his superb applewood-smoked salmon ($12 a pound), smoked mussels in salsa, even smoked salmon roe. He'll ship anywhere, and you can call and get on his mailing list, but it's fun to stop by and check out his sideline: beautifully crafted musical instruments and wooden boxes with understandably sizable price tags. No credit cards. **Jim's Smoked Salmon**, 37 Washington St., Eastport 04631, tel. (207) 853-4831, is open all year, except Christmas Day.

Lunch and Miscellanea

The best pizza in Eastport comes from **Frank's Pizzaria and Deli**, 33 Water St., Eastport 04631, tel. (207) 853-2709, where you can also get calzones, pasta, and deli sandwiches. Only a dozen seats, so grab your stuff and eat it elsewhere. Frank's is open all year, Mon.-Sat. 10 a.m.-8 p.m. (to 9 p.m. July and August). No credit cards.

When you're wandering around the Eastport breakwater, you'll notice the line at **Rosie's Hot Dogs**, municipal pier, Eastport, no telephone, a veteran take-out stand open only in summer. Rosie's tube steaks are the best around. Open Mon.-Sat. at 11 a.m., Sunday at noon.

Inexpensive to Moderate

A popular roadside eatery with a well-deserved reputation, the aptly named **New Friendly Restaurant**, Rt. 1 at Shore Rd., Perry 04667, tel. (207) 853-6610, lays on breakfast until 11 a.m., then launches into home-cooked offerings for "dinnah" (a Maine-ism meaning lunch), specializing in steak and seafood. Don't be surprised to find it crowded. Liquor license, a/c. Open daily 8 a.m.-8 p.m., all year. The New Friendly is just north of the Rt. 190 turnoff to Eastport.

A downtown-Eastport institution since 1924, the **Wa-Co Diner** (WHACK-o, short for Washington County), at Bank Square on Water St., tel. (207) 853-4046, is a must-do local-color stop with diner-style booths and counter, friendly service, and unremarkable but inexpensive and filling food. Some days, it gets a bit smoky. For even more local color, the bar stays open 7 p.m.-midnight Thurs.-Saturday. It's open all year, Mon.-Sat. starting at 6 a.m., for breakfast, lunch, and dinner, plus breakfast on Sunday. No credit cards.

And there's another funky place almost across the street. How many restaurants keep Christmas lights going year-round—on an upside-down Christmas tree? How many places open for dinner and serve breakfast fare as well? In downtown Eastport, **La Sardina Loca** ("the crazy sardine"), 28 Water St., tel. (207) 853-2739, bills itself as the easternmost Mexican restaurant in the United States. It's not the most authentic Tex-Mex (no sangria or guacamole), but it's good enough—and the place will keep you entertained (some nights with live music). Enchiladas are $6-8. Opt for the dining room and leave the bar to the locals. Open all year, at 4 p.m. daily June-Sept., and Thurs.-Sun. Oct.-May. After New Year's, the schedule can be unpredictable, so call ahead or take your chances.

Overlooking Eastport Harbor and the harborfront path, the **Baywatch Café**, 75 Water St., Eastport, tel. (207) 853-6030, is the newest restaurant incarnation in this historic brick building. Homecooked dinner entrées (mostly steaks and seafood) are $8-15. In summer, the deck seats 50, but the view is almost as good inside by the windows. Full liquor license; tiny smoking area. Open all year, daily 6 a.m.-9 p.m.

When the Cannery Wharf restaurant closed several years back, everyone bemoaned its loss. Now the two-story building, close to the Deer Island ferry landing, has been revived and rehabbed as **The Eastport Lobster and Fish House**, 167 Water St., Eastport 04631, tel. (207) 853-6006 or (888) 327-8767. Seafood, natch, is the specialty, with entrées in the $9-18 range. Huge windows overlook the bay from the second-floor dining area; the bar/lounge is below. It's open daily 11 a.m.-9 p.m., Memorial Day weekend through October. The restaurant's adjacent gift shop stocks Maine-made items.

INFORMATION AND SERVICES

The volunteer-run **Eastport Area Chamber of Commerce**, P.O. Box 254, Eastport 04631, tel. (207) 853-4644, produces *The Eastport Area*

Guide, a useful directory/map of places to sleep, eat, shop, and play. It's available at **Quoddy Crafts,** 72 Water St., along with other brochures, but the hours are unpredictable. Best to write or call ahead for information. Be sure also to request a copy of *A Walking Guide to Eastport.*

If you haven't planned ahead, stop in at the conveniently located **Motel East,** 23A Water St., tel./fax (207) 853-4747. Owner Owen Lawlor, an active chamber member, can set you up and steer you in the right direction. He also handles advance ticket purchases for performances by Stage East.

The handsome stone **Peavey Memorial Library,** Water St., Eastport 04631, tel. (207) 853-4021, built in 1893, is named after the inventor of the Peavey grain elevator. It's open Mon.-Sat. 1:30-5 p.m., plus Wednesday 10 a.m.-noon.

Next to the breakwater is the office of the *Quoddy Tides* newspaper and the **Quoddy Tides Foundation Marine Library,** 121 Water St., Eastport 04631, tel. (207) 853-4806, a jumble of books, periodicals, charts, and newspapers related to seafaring and the sea. Unfortunately, the library is only open Thursday morning. In the basement is the minuscule **Quoddy Tides Aquarium,** which has a fascinating scale model of Passamaquoddy Bay, plus an assortment of local marine-life specimens. It's open July-Sept., Mon.-Fri. 8:30 a.m.-5 p.m. Suggested donation is $1 adults, 50 cents children.

Newspapers

The best coverage of Eastport news appears in the twice-monthly *Quoddy Tides,* 123 Water St., Eastport 04631, tel. (207) 853-4806, billing itself as the "most easterly newspaper published in the United States." Check the paper for tide tables, usually listed in Atlantic time (subtract an hour); the paper also carries ads and features on

TIDES

Nowhere in Maine is the adage "Time and tide wait for no man" more true than along the Sunrise Coast. They don't wait for women or kids, either. The nation's most extreme tidal ranges occur in this area, so the hundreds of miles of tidal shore frontage between Steuben and Calais provide countless opportunities for observing tidal phenomena. Every six hours or so, the tide begins either ebbing or flowing. The farther Down East you go, the higher (and lower) the tides. Although tides in Canada's Bay of Fundy are far higher, the highest tides in New England occur along the St. Croix River, at Calais.

Tides govern coastal life—particularly Down East, where average tidal ranges may be 10-20 feet and extremes approach 28 feet. Everyone is a slave to the tide calendar, which coastal-community newspapers diligently publish. Boats tie up with extra-long lines; clammers and wormdiggers schedule their days by the tides; hikers have to plan ahead for shoreline exploring; and kayakers need to plan their routes to avoid getting stuck in the muck.

Tides, as we all learned in grade school, are lunar phenomena, created by the gravitational pull of the moon; the tidal range depends on the lunar phase. Tides are most extreme at new and full moons—when the sun, moon, and earth are all aligned. These are **spring tides,** supposedly because the water springs upward (they have nothing to do with the season). And tides are smallest during the moon's first and third quarters—when the sun, earth, and moon have a right-angle configuration. These are **neap tides** ("neap" comes from an Old English word meaning "scanty"). Other lunar/solar phenomena, such as the equinoxes and solstices, can also affect tidal ranges.

The best time for shoreline exploration is on a new-moon or full-moon day, when low tide exposes mussels, sea urchins, sea cucumbers, periwinkles, hermit crabs, rockweed, and assorted nonbiodegradable trash. Rubber boots or waterproof, treaded shoes are essential on the wet, slippery terrain.

Caution is also essential in tidal areas. Unless you've carefully plotted tide times and heights, don't park a car or bike on a beach; make sure a sea kayak is lashed securely to a tree or bollard; don't take a long nap on shoreline granite; and don't cross a low-tide land spit without an eye on your watch.

A perhaps-apocryphal but almost believable story goes that one flatlander stormed up to a ranger at Cobscook Bay State Park one bright summer morning and demanded indignantly to know why they had had the nerve to drain the water from her shorefront campsite during the night.

Canada's Campobello and Grand Manan Islands.

The only statewide daily newspaper covering Washington County is the *Bangor Daily News*, but it's used mostly by Eastporters headed for shopping or movies in Bangor.

Emergencies

In Eastport, contact the **police** at (207) 853-2544, the **fire department** at (207) 853-4221, and the **ambulance** at (207) 853-2771.

The nearest 24-hour emergency room is 27 miles away at **Calais Regional Hospital,** 50 Franklin St., Calais 04619, tel. (207) 454-7521, Washington County's largest hospital.

Laundromat

Boone's Eastport Maytag Laundromat, Boynton and Middle Sts., Eastport 04631, no telephone, with coin-operated machines, is open daily 7 a.m.-9 p.m.

Public Restrooms

In summer, there are portable toilets on Eastport's breakwater.

Getting Around

Sunrise Taxi, 39 Adams St., Eastport 04631, tel. (207) 853-6162, with moderate rates, covers the Eastport area and beyond.

CALAIS AND VICINITY

Europeans showed up in the Calais area (CALus) as early as 1604, when French adventurers established an ill-fated colony on St. Croix Island in the St. Croix River—16 whole years before the Pilgrims even thought about Massachusetts. After a winter-long debacle, all became relatively quiet until 1779, when the first permanent settler arrived. By 1851, Calais was incorporated as a city, and shipping was the biggest industry in this head-of-tide port. In August 1870, a fire devastated Calais, sparking the construction of today's Main Street Historic District.

Today, the city is quiet again, almost dormant, and dependent on a single industry. The lifeblood of the Calais area is pulp and paper giant Georgia-Pacific Corporation (G-P), whose forest and mill jobs, headquartered in nearby Baileyville (Woodland), prop up the economy. Any hint of instability at G-P sends immediate shivers down the local spine.

The most interesting time to show up in Calais (pop. 4,100) is during the International Festival, the first or second week in August, when the city and neighboring St. Stephen, New Brunswick, go all out with dances, concerts, races, barbecues, and fireworks—reinforcing the trans-border cooperation that has long benefited both communities.

After that, head north and west to Princeton, then 10 miles into the woods west of Rt. 1, where the tiny town of Grand Lake Stream has long beckoned visitors for legendary sportfishing and hunting, plus family-oriented canoeing, swimming, and birding vacations.

Southeast of Calais is tiny Robbinston, a booming shipbuilding community in the 19th century but today little more than a 500-person blip on the map. Highlights nowadays are a great B&B, a wonderful chocolate shop, and the Calais-Robbinston "milestones."

Calais is the eastern terminus for a 98-mile section of Maine Rt. 9 quaintly known as "The Airline." Connecting Bangor and Calais (actually, Eddington and Baring), it's this area's major inland artery, a two-lane highway used by a colorful array of commuters, visitors, sportsmen, and truck drivers. Mostly it's a convenient shortcut, and sometimes not even that, since there are few restaurants, shops, or lodgings along the way—only well-known magnets such as the Airline Snack Bar, in Beddington, and the Cloud 9 Diner, in Wesley. And then there are the winter perils of Dunker Hill, Day Hill, Hardwood Hill, and Breakneck Hill. In the fall, though, it's a delight, with gorgeous colors as far as you can see, especially in the elevated blueberry barrens closer to Bangor. The road, built for postal stagecoaches in the mid-19th-century, trimmed nearly 60 miles off the longer coastal Rt. 1. Hazards in those days were bad weather, wolves, and marauding bandits; today, they are bad weather, moose, and barreling fuel and lumber trucks.

SIGHTS

St. Croix Island

Unless you have your own boat, you can't get over to six-and-a-half-acre St. Croix Island, an International Historic Site under joint U.S. and Canadian jurisdiction. The current in the St. Croix River is strong, and tidal ranges can be as high as 28 feet, so neophyte boaters shouldn't even attempt a crossing, but local residents often picnic and swim off the island's sandy beach on the southern end. Long-range plans call for a mainland visitor center and ferry service to the island, but for now, you can see the island from an attractive 16-acre roadside rest area on Rt. 1 at **Red Beach Cove,** eight miles southeast of Calais. Here you'll find picnic tables, restrooms, a gravel beach, a boat launch, and a small parking lot. It's a great place to stop for a picnic.

The island is the site of the pioneering colony established by French explorers Samuel de Champlain and Pierre du Gua (Sieur de Monts) in 1604. Doomed by disease, mosquitoes, lack of food, and a grueling winter, 35 settlers died; in spring, the emaciated survivors abandoned their effort and moved on to Nova Scotia. In 1969, archaeologists found graves of 23 victims, but the only monument on the island is a commemorative plaque dating from 1904.

Whitlock Mill Lighthouse

From the lovely Pikewoods Rest Area, beside Rt. 1, about four miles southeast of Calais, there's a prime view of 32-foot-high Whitlock Mill Lighthouse, on the southern shore of the St. Croix River. Built in 1892, the green-flashing light is only accessible over private land, so check it out from this vantage point. Besides, you can also have a picnic break here.

Calais-Robbinston Milestones

A quirky little local feature, the Calais-Robbinston milestones are a dozen red-granite chunks marking each of the 12 miles between Robbinston and Calais. Presaging today's highway mileage markers, late-19th-century entrepreneur and journalist James S. Pike had the stones installed on the north side of Rt. 1 to keep track of the distance while training his pacing horses.

PARKS, PRESERVES, AND RECREATION

Moosehorn National Wildlife Refuge

More than 50 miles of trails and disused roads wind through the 17,257-acre Baring Unit of the Moosehorn National Wildlife Refuge, Charlotte Rd., P.O. Box 1077, Calais 04619, tel. (207) 454-3521 or 454-7161, on the outskirts of Calais. Start with the 1.2-mile **nature trail** near the refuge headquarters, and get ready for major-league wildlife-watching: 35 mammal and 220 bird species have been spotted in the refuge's fields, forests, ponds, and marshes. Wear waterproof shoes and insect repellent. In August, help yourself to wild blueberries. During November deer-hunting season, either avoid the refuge Mon.-Sat. or wear a blaze-orange hat and vest. The refuge is open daily, all year, sunrise to sunset; trails are accessible by snowshoes, snowmobile, or cross-country skis in winter. Admission is free. To reach refuge headquarters, take Rt. 1 west and south from downtown Calais (it's called Rt. 1 north because eventually it goes that way) about three miles. Turn left onto the Charlotte Rd. and go 2.4 miles to the headquarters sign. The office is open Mon.-Fri. 7:30 a.m.-4 p.m., all year (except major national holidays); you can pick up free trail maps, bird checklists, and other informative brochures.

If you don't have time to walk the trails, watch for the elevated manmade nesting platforms, avian highrises for bald eagles, outside of Calais alongside Rt. 1 north (near the junction with the Charlotte Road). Depending on the season, you may spot a nesting pair or even a fledgling. The chicks (usually twins but occasionally triplets) hatch around mid-May and try their wings by early August. A 400-square-foot observation deck across Rt. 1 is the best place for eagle-watching.

Continuing on the Charlotte Road past the Moosehorn refuge headquarters, you'll come to **Round Lake** (locally called Round Pond), a lovely spot where you can picnic, swim, or put in a kayak or canoe. Across the road, with a great lake view, is the interesting old Round Pond Cemetery, dating from the early 19th century. (Why do graveyards always have the best views?) Just after the cemetery, a left turn puts you on Pennamaquam Lake Rd. (or Charlotte

Rd.) toward Perry; a right turn takes you to Rt. 214, near Pembroke.

Golf

At the nine-hole **St. Croix Country Club,** River Rd., Rt. 1, P.O. Box 294, Calais 04619, tel. (207) 454-8875 or 454-7970, the toughest and most scenic hole is the seventh, one of five holes on the river side of Rt. 1. Starting times usually aren't needed for the course, located on the southeastern outskirts of Calais. It's open late April to late October.

Bicycling

If you've brought your own bike, shoulders are wide enough along most of Rt. 1 in this area for comfortable cycling. You'll need to figure on 26-28 miles each way between Eastport and Calais, perhaps a bit long for a one-day roundtrip. If you're staying in Robbinston, figure on a 25-mile roundtrip to peddle to Calais and cross over to St. Stephen. Robbinston is also a good base for biking to Eastport—about 30 miles roundtrip, slightly longer if you take the more scenic **Shore Road,** east of and parallel to Rt. 1, between Perry and North Perry.

Getting Afloat

Headquartered on a back road (Rt. 191), about midway between Calais and Machias, **Sunrise County Canoe Expeditions** (SCCE), Cathance Lake, Grove Post Office 04638, tel. (207) 454-7708, is one of the state's premier canoeing outfitters—and the local expert on the St. Croix River, the boundary between Maine and New Brunswick. ESPN even covered SCCE on the river, designated a Canadian Heritage River. SCCE does guided four-day trips on the St. Croix, typically putting in below the dam at Vanceboro and taking out 33 miles later at Grand Falls Flowage (longer trips are also possible). Along the way, with Class I and II water, you'll see bald eagles, loons, and moose. You can canoe the dam-controlled river from spring through fall, but the best time to go is September, for the fantastic fall foliage. Cost for four days is under $500 pp, including everything but transportation to base camp.

SCCE also offers canoe rentals and shuttle service if you want to use the Appalachian Mountain Club's *AMC River Guide* and do it yourself. SCCE was established in 1973 and

now does rivers in Iceland, Canada, the Arctic, and the U.S. Southwest, in addition to several other rivers in Maine.

Canoe rentals are also available at Long Lake Camps. From the Calais area, the nearest **whalewatching** excursions depart from Eastport.

ENTERTAINMENT

First-run films show at the three-screen **State Cinemas,** 79 Main St., Calais, tel. (207) 454-8830, open all year.

FESTIVALS AND EVENTS

Nearby Eastport and the Machias Bay area are good for additional summertime celebrations.

The two-day **Grand Lake Stream Folk Art Festival,** the last weekend in July, features a juried craft show, canoebuilding demonstrations, live entertainment, sporting-camp open houses, and dinner at Grand Lake Stream, tel. (207) 796-8199.

Calais, Maine, and St. Stephen, New Brunswick, collaborate the first or second weekend of August for the four-day (Thurs.-Sun.) **International Festival** of dinners, concerts, dances, a craft fair, ball games, and cross-border parade and road race. Newspapers carry schedules (just be sure to note which events are on eastern time and which are on Atlantic time).

SHOPPING

Gifts

If you stop in at **Katie's on the Cove,** Rt. 1, Mill Cove, Box 237, Robbinston 04671, tel. (207) 454-3297 or (800) 494-5283, do it at your own risk. Chocoholics may need a restraining order. Joseph and Lea Sullivan's family operation, begun in 1982, produces several dozen varieties of homemade fudge, truffles, caramels, peanut brittle, even marzipan. Quality and prices are high. The candies are available in Washington County gift shops, even elsewhere in Maine, and the Sullivans do mail orders, but the aroma alone is worth a trip to the source. The shop, 12 miles southeast of Calais and about 15 miles west of Eastport, is open all year,

Tues.-Fri. 10 a.m.-5 p.m. and Sat.-Sun. 10 a.m.-3 p.m. This is no place for unruly or demanding kids—space is limited and the candy is pricey.

ACCOMMODATIONS

B&B
After 30 years as a Chicago antiques dealer, Estelle Holloway has found a perfect outlet for her expertise—an 1820s National Register Greek Revival mansion perched dramatically on a rural hillside. At **Brewer House B&B,** Rt. 1, P.O. Box 94, Robbinston 04671, tel. (207) 454-2385, Estelle and husband David provide superb hospitality, gourmet breakfasts (not a muffin in sight), and even shuttle service if you're biking or canoeing. Four character-filled rooms and a suite go for $55-85 d (shared and private baths). No pets, no children under 12; limited smoking. Open all year, but be sure to call ahead in winter. Their well-stocked antiques shop, **The Landing,** in the carriage house, is open March through mid-October. Brewer House is 12 miles southeast of Calais.

If Brewer House is filled, the nearest B&Bs are about 15 miles back down the road in Eastport.

Motels/Cottages
At the gingerbread-trimmed **Redclyffe Shore Motel & Dining Room,** Rt. 1, P.O. Box 53, Robbinston 04671, tel. (207) 454-3270, fax 454-8723, 16 motel units are $55-65 d (cable TVs, phones, and sunset-facing river views). No pets. Redclyffe is locally popular for its dining room, serving moderately priced entrées daily 5-9 p.m. Dinner reservations are a good idea in July and August, especially during the International Festival. It's located .2 mile northwest of the Brewer House B&B. The motel is open mid-May through October; the restaurant is open mid-May through December.

Continuing toward Calais, you'll soon come to **Brooks Bluff Cottages,** Rt. 1, Box 393, Robbinston 04671, tel. (207) 454-7795, on 25 acres with knockout river views. Sixteen rustic cottages, half with kitchens and most with heat, are $275-400 a week. No pets, but smoking is allowed. The complex is open late June to mid-September.

About five and a half miles southeast of Calais, family-run **Heslin's Motel and Cottages,** Rt. 1, RR 1, Box 111, Calais 04619, tel. (207) 454-3762, has 15 clean, basic rooms and 10 rustic cottages on 60 acres alongside the St. Croix River. Rates are $58-62 d (no phones). A big plus is a heated swimming pool. No pets. In the motel's informal river-view restaurant, broiled and fried seafood ($9-14) are the specialties, served daily 5-9 p.m., plus brunch on Sunday, June through October. Small portions are available for kids and seniors. The cocktail lounge draws a loyal local clientele.

Sporting Camps
Thirteen American Plan (three meals daily) or housekeeping log cabins are part of the lakeside complex at **Long Lake Camps,** West St., P.O. Box 807, Princeton 04668, tel. (207) 796-2051 or (800) 435-0212, built on a lovely wooded peninsula in the 1940s. Housekeeping rates are $65 d a night (less by the week); AP is $150 d (also less by the week); pets are $5 extra; no charge for kids two and under. This is a great family locale, with facilities for fishing (catch-and-release preferred), canoeing, and swimming.

Long Lake Camps serves hearty, home-cooked dinners to its guests and the public in **The Lodge**—a good chance to sample the Maine sporting-camp atmosphere even if you aren't sleeping here. Pizza is always available, entrées are $9-16, Saturday special is prime rib ($17), and Sunday dinner is buffet-style ($11). Dinner reservations are advisable in July and August. BYOL. The restaurant is open Tues.-Sun. 4:30-8:30 p.m., mid-May to late October. From Rt. 1 in Princeton (25 miles northwest of Calais), go one mile southwest on West St. and hang a right onto an unpaved road after the tiny airport.

For other nearby sporting camps, see "Accommodations and Food" under "Grand Lake Stream," below.

Campgrounds
High enough for a great view of the St. Croix River, **Hilltop Campground,** Ridge Rd., RR 1, Box 298, Robbinston 04671, tel. (207) 454-3985 or (888) 454-3985, has 84 tent and RV sites on 100 wooded and open acres, plus a pool, a pond, a small store, and laundry facilities. Sites

are $13-18 a night. Small cabins are also available at this well-maintained place. Open mid-May to mid-October, the campground is on Ridge Road, a mile west of Rt. 1 (turn at Mill Cove).

FOOD

Miscellanea

If you're near downtown Calais, order picnic sandwiches to go at **The Sandwich Man,** 206 North St., Rt. 1, Calais 04619, tel. (207) 454-2460, a reliable local favorite since the late 1970s. Lots of choices, including vegetarian, and three sandwich lengths. It's open all year, Mon.-Sat. 9 a.m.-9 p.m. and Sunday 9 a.m.-6 p.m.

Farmers' Market

The **Sunrise County Farmers' Market** sets up shop along Rt. 1 at Mill Cove (near Katie's on the Cove) in Robbinston each Wednesday 9 a.m.-5 p.m., mid-June to early September.

INFORMATION AND SERVICES

On the banks of the St. Croix River, near the Ferry Point Bridge just off Rt. 1 (Main Street) in downtown Calais, is an especially convenient and attractive **Maine Information Center,** 7 Union St., Calais 04619, tel. (207) 454-2211, with clean restrooms and scads of brochures, including those produced by the **Greater Calais Area Chamber of Commerce,** tel. (207) 454-2308. The Information Center is open daily 9 a.m.-5 p.m., all year (and some evening hours in summer).

Next door to the Information Center is the imposing stone **Calais Free Library,** Union St., Calais 04619, tel. (207) 454-2758, open Mon.-Wed. noon-8 p.m., Thursday 9 a.m.-6 p.m., and Friday 9 a.m.-5 p.m.

Newspapers

The Calais Advertiser, tel. (207) 454-3561, published every Wednesday, carries features, ads, and local events listings. The statewide daily for this area is the *Bangor Daily News.*

Emergencies

In Calais, contact the **police, fire department, and ambulance** at 911. **Calais Regional Hospital,** 50 Franklin St., Calais 04619, tel. (207) 454-7521, has round-the-clock emergency-room care.

Public Restrooms

The **Maine Information Center,** 7 Union St., Calais, has restrooms; the headquarters of the **Moosehorn National Wildlife Refuge** has portable toilets.

Getting Around

Bailey's Taxi, 34 Garfield, Calais 04619, tel. (207) 454-7157, is on call all year.

Crossing into Canada

If you plan to cross into Canada, you'll have to pass Customs checkpoints on both the Calais (U.S., tel. 207-454-3621) and St. Stephen (Canada, tel. 506-466-2363) ends of the bridges. U.S. citizens need some form of identification, typically a driver's license, although you might not have to show it. You'll be asked your purpose in going to Canada, and the length of your stay. Most clearances are perfunctory, but if you are carrying any live plant material, Canadian Customs will confiscate it.

Even for a day trip to St. Stephen, non-U.S. citizens need to show a valid passport; citizens of most non-European countries must also have a Canadian visa (which must be obtained in advance). U.S. resident aliens must be prepared to show a valid green card.

Pay attention to your watch, too—Calais is on eastern time, St. Stephen (as well as the rest of Canada's Maritime Provinces) is on Atlantic time.

GRAND LAKE STREAM

For a tiny community of under 200 year-rounders, Grand Lake Stream has a well-deserved, larger-than-life reputation. It's the center of a vast area of rivers and lakes, ponds and streams—a recreational paradise.

The famous stream is a narrow, three-mile neck of prime scenic and sportfishing water connecting West Grand Lake and Big Lake. A dam spans the bottom of West Grand, and just downstream is a state-run salmon hatchery. Since the mid-19th century, the stream and its lakes have been drawing fishing fans to trout and landlocked salmon spawning grounds, and fourth and fifth generations now return here each year.

Fly fishermen arrive in May and June for landlocked salmon and smallmouth bass (the stream itself is fly-fishing only); families show up in July and August for canoeing, birding, swimming, fishing, and hiking; hunters arrive in late October for game birds and deer; and snowmobilers, snowshoers, and cross-country skiers descend as the snow piles up.

A great time to visit the village is the last weekend in July, for the annual Grand Lake Stream Folk Art Festival. Traditional crafts, such as canoebuilding and basketmaking, are the focus. Other activities are hatchery tours, lodge open houses, and dinners. For more info, contact Grand Lake Stream Festival Committee, P.O. Box 1, Grand Lake Stream 04637.

Canoebuilding, in fact, has contributed to the area's mystique. The distinctive Grand Lake canoe (or "Grand Laker"), a lightweight, square-sterned, motorized 20-footer, was developed in the 1920s specifically for sportfishing in these waters. In the off season, several villagers still hunker down in their workshops and turn out these stable cedar beauties.

In the early 1990s, the spectre of development galvanized lodge owners, guides, and the environmental community to preserve most of the land bordering Grand Lake Stream itself; their efforts permanently preserved four miles of stream frontage and 271 acres, now managed by the Maine Department of Inland Fisheries and Wildlife.

Recreation

If you're only in Grand Lake Stream for the day, head for the **public landing,** just north of the main road into town, where you'll find a big parking area, pontoon boats, a dock, beach, restrooms, and a boat launch. A small take-out stand may or may not be open. You can also walk the path on the western shore of the stream.

If you're here longer, reserve a date with **Randy McCabe,** a Master Maine Guide who arranges all-day wildlife canoe and/or hiking trips. About a fourth of Grand Lake Stream's residents are Registered Maine Guides, most specializing in fishing and hunting outings. Randy focuses on ecotours. Tailoring the schedule to his customers' interests, he'll point out beaver dams, bald eagles, and moose. He'll take you out at 4 a.m. for great birding, or early afternoon so you can listen for loons and stargaze after sunset. To keep the noise level down and the quality up, ideal maximum is five persons, in two canoes. All-inclusive cost is around $150 a day for two, including packed lunches; special rates for families (no credit cards). Bring binoculars and a camera. If you need Randy on a specific day, reserve as far ahead as possible. Canoeing trips begin early May and run into November; fall trips are gorgeous. In winter, he's available for snowshoe walks. Contact him at **Maine Wilderness Trips,** P.O. Box 295, Princeton 04668, tel. (207) 796-7926.

ACCOMMODATIONS AND FOOD

Cabin accommodations, with or without meals, are the lodgings of choice in Grand Lake Stream, and there's enough variety for every taste and budget. Few guests stay one night; most stay several days or a week. Rates quoted below are for two; many cabins can sleep more than that, and rates may be lower for extra persons. Some housekeeping cabins require your own sheets and/or towels. Most camps have boat rentals for $15-20 a day (motor additional).

American Plan Only

Weatherby's Camps, Grand Lake Stream 04637, tel. (207) 796-5558, tel. (207) 246-7391 off season, is the veteran here, with 15 log cottages. MAP daily rate is $130-170 d. Open May to mid-October.

Leen's Lodge, Box 40, Grand Lake Stream 04637, tel. (207) 796-5575, off season P.O. Box 92, Newport 04953, tel. (207) 368-5699, has 11 small and large cabins on West Grand Lake. MAP daily rate (three-day minimum) is $180 d. Open May through October.

American Plan or Housekeeping

Indian Rock Camps, Grand Lake Stream 04637, tel. (207) 796-2822 or (800) 498-2821, has five rustic two-bedroom log cabins, plus a lodge where everyone gathers for some fine home cooking. Open all year; snowmobilers are welcome.

Almost 12 miles west of Grand Lake Stream, via an unpaved road, **The Pines,** P.O. Box 158, Grand Lake Stream 04637, tel. (207) 796-5006 or 825-4431 off season, is a special gem, a family-oriented oasis on the shore of Sysladobsis (Sis-la-DOB-sis) Lake. Five log cabins and five second-floor rooms in the main lodge; two remote island cabins. Open early May through September.

Housekeeping Only

Grand Lake Lodge, P.O. Box 8, Grand Lake Stream 04637, tel. (207) 796-5584, on the shore of West Grand Lake and two blocks from the village center, is a particularly good choice for families, with a nice swimming area. Weekly rates in July and August are $220-380; other months, about $50 d per night. Open late April to mid-November.

Food

If you opt for housekeeping arrangements, you'll want to provision before you get here, but you can pick up pretty much anything at Kurt and Kathy Cressey's **Pine Tree Store,** Water St., P.O. Box 129, Grand Lake Stream 04637, tel. (207) 796-5027, in the heart of the village. This '90s-era mom-'n'-pop emporium is open daily 6:30 a.m.-8 p.m. April-Nov., and 8 a.m.-6 p.m. other months. You can buy maps and postcards, frozen meat and fishing licenses, and lots more. Or order pizza or a meatball sub (no fried food) and chow down at the picnic table outside.

INFORMATION

The volunteer-run **Grand Lake Stream Chamber of Commerce,** P.O. Box 124, Grand Lake Stream 04637, produces a brochure listing accommodations, shops, and services. The **Pine Tree Store,** Water St., P.O. Box 129, Grand Lake Stream 04637, tel. (207) 796-5027, is also

Grand Lake Stream Folk Art Festival

a good source of local information, since it is open long hours. Another option is the **Grand Lake Stream Town Office,** 4 Water St., Grand Lake Stream 04637, tel. (207) 796-2001.

Getting There
On Rt. 1 north, about two miles northwest of Princeton, turn left (west) onto Grand Lake Stream Rd. (also called Princeton Road). Continue about 10 miles to the village.

BOB RACE

KATAHDIN/MOOSEHEAD REGION

Named for Maine's highest mountain and largest lake, the Katahdin/Moosehead Region—covering all of Piscataquis County and the northern two-thirds of Penobscot County—typifies Maine's rugged North Woods. Within Piscataquis County are 40-mile-long Moosehead Lake, the appealing frontier town of Greenville, the headwaters of the Allagash Wilderness Waterway, and the controlled wilds of Baxter State Park.

Sportsmen have always frequented the North Woods, and they still do. But hunters, sportfishermen, and back-to-the-landers increasingly have to share their untamed turf with a new generation of visitor. Sporting camps originally built for rugged fishermen and hunters now welcome photographers, birders, and families; whitewater rafting, canoeing, and snowmobiling are all big business; and hikers have found nirvana in a vast network of trails—particularly the huge, carefully monitored trail system in Baxter State Park, my own favorite destination for peace, renewal, and old-fashioned vertical exercise.

In the 1970s, paper companies were forced by environmental concerns to halt the perilous river-run log drives that took their products to market. This cessation not only cleaned up the

rivers, but also spared the lives of the hardy breed of men who once made a living unjamming the logs in roiling waters. The alternative now is roads, lots of them, mostly unpaved—a huge network that has opened up the area to more and more outdoors enthusiasts. (Fortunately, despite some resentment and grumbling among outdoorsfolk about user fees, the paper companies allow public recreation on their roads and lands.) These timber-company throughways are there for all to use, but never forget that the logging trucks *own* them—in more ways than one. As they barrel along, give them room —and some slack as well; you may even be glad they're there. I've been lost on some of these roads and wound up eternally grateful to loggers who have stopped to help. The *DeLorme Atlas* is essential for exploring the area, but every time the loggers begin working a new patch, they open new roads, so the cartographers can barely keep up.

The area is rich in aquatic possibilities, too. Maine's best-known, classic canoe trips follow the Allagash and St. John Rivers northward, but no one can even begin to count the other lakes, rivers, and streams that have wonderful canoeing. Among the best are Lobster, Allagash,

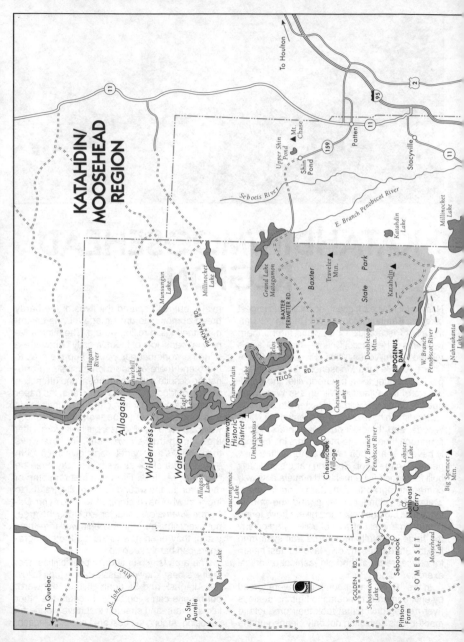

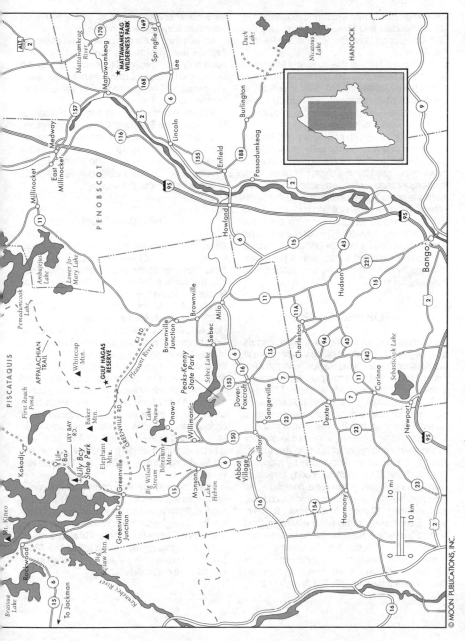

© MOON PUBLICATIONS, INC.

Caucomgomoc, Ambajejus, and Chesuncook Lakes; Seboeis and Pleasant Rivers, plus the East and (upper) West Branches of the Penobscot River.

The largest town in this region is Millinocket, home to fewer than 7,000 souls (almost outnumbered by lumber trucks). Stay at one of the primitive forest campsites and you'll really sense the wilderness—owls hoot, loons cry, frogs croak . . . and, oh yes, insects annoy.

No matter how much civilization intrudes, it's still remote and wild. As one writer put it, "Trees grow, die, fall, and rot, never having been seen by anyone. They litter the shores of lakes, form temporary islands, block streams, and quickly eradicate paths." Don't underestimate the North Woods: bring versatile clothing (more than you think you'll need), don't strike out alone without telling anyone, stock up on insect repellent and water, use a decent vehicle (4WD if possible), and carry a flashlight, maps, and a compass. Perhaps most important, be a conscientious, ecosensitive visitor.

SPORTING CAMPS

Although dozens of traditional sporting camps exist all over Maine, most of the veterans are in the Katahdin/Moosehead Region, with the Kennebec Valley and western mountains running a close second. Almost all are north of Bangor.

Sporting camps are unique, and so varied that it's impossible to paint them with one broad brush. They're so much more than a place to stay—they're an experience, often a throwback to the 19th century, or at least to the earlier 20th. All but a few are accessible by road, but the "road" might be a rutted, muddy tank trap, making passengers yearn for a floatplane. All are rustic, no-frills operations, some much more so than others. (If you're a frill-seeker, forget it; seek elsewhere.) Some have electricity and flush toilets; others have kerosene lanterns and private or shared outhouses. All are on or close to fresh water, meant to be convenient for fishing. Some offer American Plan rates, serving three meals a day, usually family-style; others

have housekeeping facilities, where you're on your own; some let you choose.

About a third of the camps are open all year to capture the snowmobile trade, but most are open only May through November, during the fishing and hunting seasons. All but a few sporting camps sell resident and nonresident fishing and hunting licenses.

If all this sounds intriguing, request a brochure from the **Maine Sporting Camp Association,** P.O. Box 89, Jay 04239, a group with over 50 members founded in 1987. Then check your bookstore for a copy of *In the Maine Woods,* by Alice Arlen (see the Booklist), a helpful guide to traditional sporting camps.

INFORMATION

Besides the chambers of commerce in Millinocket, Greenville, and Dover-Foxcroft, and Baxter State Park Headquarters, regional recreational information is available from **Bowater/Great Northern Paper,** Public Relations Dept., 1 Katahdin Ave., Millinocket 04462, tel. (207) 723-2229, and **North Maine Woods** (NMW), P.O. Box 421, Ashland 04732, tel. (207) 435-6213. Both have very helpful maps (small fee). North Maine Woods will send you an order form listing publications for sale as well as free brochures covering use of logging roads, campsites, and other relevant information. The eminently useful 12-page *North Maine Woods Atlas,* with a scale of an inch to three miles, shows locations of checkpoints, campsites, sporting camps, ranger stations, and more. Cost is $3. NMW also sells a blaze-orange hat ($6), required gear in the woods during hunting season (late Oct.-late November).

You, too, can be an information source—extra eyes and ears for the understaffed warden service. If you're out and about and spot poachers harassing, wounding, or killing game, you can assist **Operation Game Thief** and report them anonymously by calling (800) 253-7887. Do not intervene; merely supply descriptions or any other relevant details.

MILLINOCKET AND VICINITY

Crucial to the timber industry, Millinocket (pop. 6,600) is not exactly a hot vacation spot—but since it's the closest civilization to Baxter State Park's southern entrance, most Baxter visitors find themselves here at some time or other. Food, lodging, books, auto fuel, and other essentials are all available in Millinocket—so don't be surprised to see ruddy-cheeked families chowing down at McDonald's here before heading for Baxter's wilderness.

Giant, smoke-belching stacks owned by Bowater/Great Northern Paper dominate the skyline in Millinocket and adjoining East Millinocket (pop. 2,000), providing the major support for the local economy. Nearly 20% of the nation's newsprint comes out of these plants, built at the turn of the 20th century.

The town of Medway links I-95 with the two mill towns; just to the north on Rt. 11 are the communities of Sherman, Sherman Station, Patten, and Shin Pond, providing access to the less-used northeast entrance (Matagamon Gate) of Baxter State Park.

SIGHTS

Besides the sights described below, try to squeeze in a visit to The Museum of Vintage Fashion in Island Falls, about 48 miles northeast of Millinocket in Aroostook County. One of Maine's unique museums, it's an easy run from Millinocket, partly via I-95.

Patten Lumberman's Museum

About 40 miles northeast of Millinocket, half a mile west of downtown Patten, and about 25 miles southeast of Baxter State Park's Matagamon Gate, is a family-oriented museum commemorating the lumberman's grueling life. The 10 buildings at the open-air Patten Lumberman's Museum, Shin Pond Rd., Rt. 159, Patten 04765, tel. (207) 528-2650 or 528-2547, tell the tale of timber in the 19th and early 20th centuries: cramped quarters, hazardous equipment, rugged terrain, nasty weather. Lots of working gear and colorful dioramas appeal to children,

and there are picnic tables, a snack bar, and room to roam. The reception center has a craft shop and restrooms. Summer highlight is the annual **beanhole bean dinner** (beans baked underground overnight), held the second Saturday in August. The museum is open Memorial Day through September, Tues.-Sat. 9 a.m.-4 p.m. and Sunday 11 a.m.-4 p.m. It's also open Monday in July and August, plus weekends in early October. Admission is $2.50 adults, $1 kids 6-12, free for kids under six.

Ambajejus Boom House

You'll need either a boat or a snowmobile to get to the Ambajejus Boom House, Ambajejus Lake, eight miles northwest of Millinocket, no telephone, but once you get there, it's always open, and filled with incredible lumbering-era artifacts. Sign the register and jot down the weather conditions. The boom house, erected here in 1906, was used as a rest stop for 65 years by rugged river drivers, lumbermen who "boomed out" (collected with immense chains) and actually rode logs downstream to the sawmills. As many as 14 could sleep and eat here. Listed on the National Historic Register, the boom house is owned by Bowater/Great Northern Paper, but the meticulous restoration of the once-derelict house has been done as a personal project by Chuck Harris, a onetime river driver. Launch your boat in Spencer Cove, near Katahdin Air Service, on the west side of the Golden Road, and paddle or motor out and around to the right, to the head of the lake. Stay close to shore, as the wind can pick up unexpectedly. (If you need a canoe, you can rent one across the road at the Big Moose Inn.)

The Golden Road

On the outskirts of Millinocket is the eastern end of The Golden Road, best-maintained logging route in the North Woods and the lifeline for Bowater/Great Northern Paper Company. Running 96 mostly unpaved miles from here, across the top of Moosehead Lake to the Quebec border, the private wilderness road reputedly earned its name from the mega-cost ($3.2 million) of construction, completed in 1975. Red-and-white mile markers tick off the distance. Logging trucks have the right-of-way, moose frequently stray onto the road, the scenery is captivating, and you'll need to sign in and out at paper-company checkpoints en route—not a big deal. The non-resident user fee is $8 a day per vehicle, $6 a day if you're planning to camp. Bicycles are *not* allowed on the road.

The Golden Road has seen a huge surge in use in recent years, particularly the section between Baxter State Park and Moosehead Lake. More than 160,000 visitors passed through the checkpoints in 1995. It's also the major access route for the beginning of the Allagash Wilderness Waterway as well as whitewater-rafting trips on the West Branch of the Penobscot River. Even though you'll never see a traffic jam (unless a moose creates it), and the road has no visitor facilities, one driver sighted a *Bangor Daily News* vending box along the roadside. What next?

The Golden Road is the most scenic link between Millinocket and Greenville, a 71-mile trip, two-thirds unpaved. You'll exit the Golden Road after about 48 miles, then drive along Moosehead Lake's east shore to Greenville.

Flightseeing
Based at Ambajejus Lake, about eight miles northwest of Millinocket, on the road to Baxter State Park, **Katahdin Air Service** (KAS), Box 171, Millinocket 04462, tel. (207) 723-8378 or

(888) 742-5527, provides access to wilderness locations in every direction, but even if you have no particular destination, the scenic seaplane flights are fabulous. Fall-foliage trips are beyond fabulous. Three short options, ranging 15-30 minutes, cost $15-30 pp (three-person minimum). You'll fly over Katahdin and the Penobscot River's West Branch, perhaps spotting a moose en route. KAS also offers a two-person canoe-'n'-fly day trip to Lobster Lake for $85 pp. Flights operate daily, late May through October, weather permitting.

PARKS AND RECREATION

Besides the recreational opportunities in the Millinocket area, the town is also the site of **Baxter State Park Headquarters,** 64 Balsam Dr., Millinocket 04462, tel. (207) 723-5140, just off Central St., Rt. 157. Day-use park visitors don't need to stop at the headquarters, since there are information centers at both park gates, but it's a convenient meeting place, close to food and shopping sites, and you'll have to come here if you're planning to drive up in January for summer camping reservations. For details on the park, see "Baxter State Park," below.

Mattawamkeag Wilderness Park
Talk about a well-kept secret that shouldn't be! Check out 1,000-acre, town-owned Mattawamkeag Wilderness Park, Rt. 2, P.O. Box 5, Mat-

Pockwockamus Rock, en route to Baxter State Park

tawamkeag 04459, tel. (207) 736-4881, about an hour's drive southeast of Baxter State Park's southern gate. The park's well-run facilities include 15 miles of trails, picnic tables, restrooms, free hot showers, recreation hall, playground, sand beach (on the Mattawamkeag River), and fishing for bass, salmon, and trout. There's also access to fine canoeing, including flatwater and Class V whitewater, on one of northern Maine's most underutilized rivers. And you can stay the night at one of the 52 wooded campsites and 11 lean-tos. Entrance is nine miles east of Rt. 2, on an unpaved logging road locally called "the park road"; it's signposted on Rt. 2. Admission is $1 pp, maximum $4 per car for day use. Camping fees are $11-15 per site per night. The park is open daily, late May to mid-September. If someone else's cooking sounds more appealing than camping cuisine, the Keag Market and Cafe is on Rt. 2, near the park access road.

New England Outdoor Center

Maine's biggest whitewater-rafting area is around The Forks, where the Kennebec and Dead Rivers meet, but the second-largest area is along the West Branch of the Penobscot River, near Millinocket. Class IV and V rapids named Exterminator, Bone Cruncher, and Cribwork make the Penobscot River trip a real challenge and a terrific adventure.

The primary rafting outfitter here, as well as a major player in The Forks, is the New England Outdoor Center (NEOC), Rice Farm Rd., Millinocket 04462, tel. (207) 723-5438 or (800) 766-7238, based in a huge new complex on the eastern outskirts of Millinocket. NEOC's Rice Farm headquarters organizes whitewater rafting on the West Branch ($79-109 pp, depending on day and month); multiday canoeing and kayaking courses ($199-429); clinics and rescue courses. No children under 16 on Penobscot trips. For lodging, NEOC has 40 campsites ($8 pp) and cabin tents ($17-22 pp) at its Rice Farm location and traditional sporting-camp log cabins ($35 pp) at its Twin Pine Camps on Millinocket Lake, eight miles northwest of Millinocket. No pets at either location. Lots of special packages are available, including breakfasts and dinners. The River Drivers' Restaurant at Rice Farm has a great deck overlooking the Penobscot. To reach the Rice Farm from I-95, take Exit 56,

head west on Rt. 157 toward Millinocket for eight miles. After the causeway over Dolby Pond, turn left (south) and go 1.2 miles to the NEOC.

Canoeing and Kayaking

This part of Maine is a canoeist's paradise, well known as the springboard for Allagash Wilderness Waterway and St. John River trips.

Close to Millinocket, experienced canoeists and kayakers may want to attempt sections of the **East and West Branches of the Penobscot River,** but no neophyte should try them. We're talking Big Water. Refer to the *AMC River Guide* (see Booklist) for details. Or contact one of the local outfitters, such as New England Outdoor Center or Penobscot River Outfitters at Katahdin Shadows Campground (see "Campgrounds and Campsites" under "Accommodations," below).

A veteran operation providing comprehensive equipment rental and transportation service is **Katahdin Outfitters Inc.,** P.O. Box 34, Millinocket 04462, tel. (207) 723-5700 or (800) 862-2663. Eddie Raymond ("Crazy Eddie"), their best-known driver, is a third-generation local resident; his grandfather was here in 1899, even before Millinocket was built. There's nary a corner of the North Woods Eddie hasn't seen. Delivering you to a West Branch put-in runs $80-90, plus $5 per passenger; East Branch put-ins are $50-80. Old Town Canoe rentals are $20 a day, less for multiple days. The firm also rents camping gear ($6 per day for a two-person tent). From June to mid-October, Katahdin Outfitters operates from a trailer behind the North Woods Trading Post at Millinocket Lake, eight miles north of Millinocket and close to the Big Moose Inn.

For recorded information on the **water flow** on the West Branch of the Penobscot River, regulated by Bowater/Great Northern Paper, call (207) 723-2328, April to mid-October. The message is updated daily at 5:30 and 8 a.m. The flow also affects whitewater rafters, but all the rafting outfitters are tied into this communications network and already will have the latest info.

A relatively gentle, early-summer canoe trip ideal for less-experienced paddlers is on the **Seboeis River,** between the Shin Pond/Grand Lake Rd. and Whetstone Falls, about 24 miles.

Even easier, and a good family trip, is the flat-water run putting in below Whetstone Falls (west of Stacyville) and taking out before Grindstone Falls. Shuttle service is available from Penobscot River Outfitters at Katahdin Shadows Campground and Katahdin Outfitters. During the summer, try to figure out your shuttle needs a day or two in advance, as the campground is a multi-faceted operation with lots of demands.

If you launch your canoe early in the day on **Sawtelle Deadwater,** near Shin Pond, west of Patten, you're bound to see moose. From Shin Pond, head northwest, crossing the Seboeis River at about six miles, then turn right onto the next unpaved road and continue less than two miles to the water. You can also reach the Deadwater off the parallel, paved Huber Road.

Canoe rentals are also available at Shin Pond Village (see "Campgrounds and Campsites" under "Accommodations," below).

Katahdin View Pontoon Boat Rides

Docked in Millinocket Lake, eight miles north-west of Millinocket, Katahdin View Pontoon Boat Rides, 210 Morgan Ln., Millinocket 04462, tel. (207) 723-5211, must be the least strenuous recreation in the whole area. Weather permitting, the 24-foot *Morning Star* departs every two hours, daily 7 a.m. to sunset, mid-May to mid-October. Daytime trips last one and a half hours; the sunset cruise is two and a half hours. The boat skirts the shoreline in Katahdin's shadow, scouting for moose and other creatures; loons are common. Bring binoculars and a camera. Cost of the day cruise is $12 adults, $8 children 5-12, $3 kids under three. Sunset trip is $15 adults, $12 children. (Take the kids on the shorter day cruise.) No credit cards.

Hiking

The area's best hiking, hands down, is in Baxter State Park, but experienced hikers should also consider the Gulf Hagas Reserve and Borestone Mountain Sanctuary, both described in the Dover-Foxcroft Area section, below.

WINTER SPORTS

The north country gets socked with snow more often than not, so winter recreation provides a major boost for the local economy. Among the winter sports in the Millinocket area are snowmobiling, snowshoeing, cross-country skiing, and ice fishing. To accommodate winter-sports enthusiasts, several sporting camps in the area remain open all year.

Snowmobiling

Motels in Millinocket fill up fast in snow season, so you'll need to plan ahead to try this sport. More than 350 miles of the Interconnecting Trail System (ITS) crisscross the Millinocket area, including some that run right through town. Local snowmobile clubs produce trail maps available from the Katahdin Area Chamber of Commerce.

Snowmobile rentals are available from **Sport Shop Express,** 23 Katahdin Ave. Ext., Millinocket 04462, tel. (207) 723-5333, at $95 a day. The shop is open Mon.-Sat. 8 a.m.-5:30 p.m. Mt. Chase Lodge and Shin Pond Village also rent snowmobiles. The New England Outdoor Center, based near ITS-86 in Millinocket, rents snowmobiles and also offers guided all-day snowmobile trips.

If you've never tried snowmobiling, a one-day guided trip is the safest, sanest way to begin, even if it's not the cheapest.

FESTIVALS AND EVENTS

Millinocket is widely known for its week-long **Fourth of July** celebration (the fireworks display is outstanding). Every fifth year, there's also a giant homecoming celebration, bringing several thousand former residents back to their roots.

Patten's **Annual Bean-Hole Bean Dinner** is a great celebration featuring good food (and a fascinating culinary tradition) at the Patten Lumberman's Museum the second Saturday in August.

BOB RACE

Labor Day weekend marks the **Olde Home Days Celebration** in Sherman with a parade, chicken barbecue, food booths, children's games, and lobster boil.

ACCOMMODATIONS

Lodgings in Millinocket itself cater primarily to pre- and post-Baxter visitors, Appalachian Trail through-hikers, and paper-industry executives in town for meetings—a rather disparate clientele.

Millinocket is also the springboard for a number of wilderness sporting camps, some of which are inaccessible, or nearly so, by road. Small planes equipped with skis or pontoons ferry clients to the remote sites—not an inexpensive undertaking.

B&Bs

The two B&Bs in Millinocket are ultra-casual, congenial, and inexpensive. Most popular is the intown **Sweet Lillian Bed and Breakfast,** 88 Pine St., Millinocket 04462, tel. (207) 723-4894, where seven comfortable rooms (shared baths) go for $30-50 d. Arrange in advance for a superb spaghetti dinner (extra fee), and finish off the evening with a game of cribbage. Appalachian Trail hikers frequently decompress here, thanks to innkeeper Donna Cogswell's noted warmth. No smoking, no small children, no pets, no credit cards. Open May through October. A few blocks away is the **Katahdin Area B&B,** 94-96 Oxford St., Millinocket 04462, tel. (207) 723-5220 or (800) 275-5220, an unpretentious green house with a view of Katahdin down Oxford Street from the front steps. Two suites and a single are $40-50 d, including the propietors' legendary breakfast. No smoking, no pets, no credit cards; children are welcome.

Motels/Inns

As its name indicates, 72 rooms and 10 suites at the three-story **Atrium Motel,** 740 Central St., Rt. 157, Millinocket 04462, tel./fax (207) 723-4555, wrap around an enclosed space—partly occupied by a heated pool, wading pool, hot tub, and a couple of caged parrots. Don't be put off by the warehouselike exterior; it's cheerier inside. Kids love this place, and pool noise usually quiets down early. The only drawback is a

scent of chlorine. Amenities include an exercise room, coin-operated laundry, and bar. Rates are $65-90 d; children under 18 stay free; special discounts for snowmobilers and whitewater rafters. Pets are allowed. The free breakfast is more than ample. The motel is next to the Northern Plaza shopping center at the eastern edge of Millinocket, 10 miles west of I-95. Open all year.

The two-story, 59-room **Heritage Motor Inn,** 935 Central St., Rt. 157, Millinocket 04462, tel. (207) 723-9777, part of the Best Western chain, sees steady business in winter from snowmobilers, plus a full house in early January when diehard Baxter State Park campers show up to make their summer reservations (see "Baxter State Park," below). The motel is unpretentious, on a busy highway; request a back-facing room. Rates are $62-79 d, mid-May through Labor Day, $59-69 other months. Free continental breakfast, cable TV. Pets are allowed for a fee ($15). Open all year.

Close to I-95, Exit 56, is the **Gateway Inn,** Rt. 157, P.O. Box 360, Medway 04460, tel. (207) 746-3193, fax 746-3430, a 30-room motel opened in 1995. Rooms on the west side have decks and great views of Katahdin (weather permitting), for $65 d; standard rooms are $50 d. Eight suites are $60-100 d. Special rates for snowmobilers; pets are welcome. Free continental breakfast, a/c, phones, cable TV, and indoor pool. Open all year.

Hardest to characterize is the **Big Moose Inn,** Millinocket Lake, Box 98, Millinocket 04462, tel. (207) 723-8391, midway between Millinocket and Baxter State Park's southern boundary. It's part inn, part sporting camp, part campground. In the main lodge are 11 basic rooms ($52 d; three shared baths). Guests hang out in the common room, with a huge fireplace. On the grounds are 36 tentsites and screened leantos, plus four good-size cabins. The dining room is open to the public by reservation, Wed.-Sat. 5:30-10 p.m., May through Columbus Day; food is first-rate and moderately priced. No smoking, no credit cards. Canoe rentals are $15 a day. The lodge, cabins, and campground are open May through Columbus Day.

Sporting Camps

At the eastern side of Baxter State Park, in the Patten area, are two road-accessible sporting camps: Mt. Chase Lodge and Bowlin Camps. Roughly midway between Patten and the northeast gate of Baxter State Park, **Mt. Chase Lodge**, Shin Pond Rd., Box 281, Patten 04765, tel. (207) 528-2183, is an especially congenial operation thanks to owners Rick and Sara Hill. Old-timers and globetrotters hang out together in the huge, wood-paneled common room overlooking Mt. Chase and the thoroughfare between Upper and Lower Shin Ponds. Eight second-floor rooms (one with private bath) in the main lodge are $48-55 d in summer, $39-45 d off season; MAP rates are also available. Five cabins ($65-75) vary in size and quality; request a newer one. Sara's cooking earns raves; in summer, the dining room is open to the public for dinner by reservation. Rick guides canoe trips ($75 for two) on Sawtelle Deadwater, a premier moosewatching site. Canoes, boats, snowmobiles, and cross-country skis are available for rent. Mt. Chase is open all year except December and April.

Closer to Baxter is **Bowlin Camps**, P.O. Box 251, Patten 04765, tel. (207) 528-2022, run by genial hosts Jon and Betty Smallwood since 1968. This traditional fishing/hunting camp on the shore of the Penobscot's East Branch now also welcomes family groups, especially in July and August. Kids love the Smallwoods' suspension bridge across the river, and there are trails to ponds and two waterfalls. An easy, 16-mile canoe run starts here (rentals are available), and Jon will meet you at the other end. Cabins are rustic, heated with woodstoves; two have bathrooms and six share the clean bathhouse. Summer rates are $385 pp a week (AP); the family-style meals are superb. Family rate for housekeeping cabins (no meals) is $50 a day per family with kids under 12. Linens included in spring, summer, and early fall; other times, bring a sleeping bag. Snowmobiling is huge here, and there are 12 miles of cross-country trails; Bowlin is open all year. From Patten, take Rt. 159, then the Shin Pond/Grand Lake Rd. about five miles west of the Seboeis River. At Hay Lake (on the right), turn south and continue eight miles to Bowlin Camps.

Two fine sporting camps off to the north, with longstanding reputations, are Libby Camps and Bradford Camps. Both require arduous, one-and-a-half-hour drives, so plan to arrive by float-plane (see "Getting Around" under "Information and Services," below). About 150 miles north of Bangor, **Libby Camps**, Millinocket Lake, Township 8, Range 9, mailing address P.O. Box Drawer V, Ashland 04732, tel. (207) 435-8274 (radiophone) or 435-6233, on the east shore of a different Millinocket Lake than the one near Millinocket, is flanked by Baxter State Park and the Allagash Wilderness Waterway. Matt and Ellen Libby are the third generation to run this fishing and hunting camp, and it's a serious business. Salmon and brook trout are prime targets. If you catch a trophy, they'll even skin it for the taxidermist. Seven rustic cabins have flush toilets, propane-fired lights, and quilt-topped beds. Weekly rates for adults are $550 pp (AP), less for seniors and children; special family rates are available. Meals are served in the log-beamed lodge, close to an enormous fireplace. Grumman canoes are available for rent. The Libbys also own nine "outcamps," single cabins on wildly remote ponds. Libby Camps is open May through November; most convenient air service (20-minute flight) is through Katahdin Air Service.

Higher on the sporting-camp scale is **The Bradford Camps**, Munsungan Lake, P.O. Box 729, Ashland 04732, tel. (207) 746-7777, in winter P.O. Box 778, Kittery 03904, tel. (207) 439-6364, owned by Igor and Karen Sikorsky. The scenery and sunsets are magnificent, the loons are mystical, and moose sightings are frequent. Fishing has high priority. Eight bathroom-equipped log cabins are $100 a day pp (AP), less for children; excellent meals are served family-style in the lake-view lodge. Family rates are available July and August. Open May-Nov.; most October and November guests are hunters seeking deer, bear, moose, and grouse. Roundtrip flight from Patten (15 minutes each way) via Scotty's Flying Service runs about $100 pp.

Among the more remote sporting camps is **Katahdin Lake Wilderness Camps**, Box 398, Millinocket 04462, tel. (207) 723-4050, just east of Baxter State Park. Why remote? Access is only via floatplane, pack horses ($50 roundtrip), ankle express, snowshoes, or cross-country skis. As you might suspect, the place is utterly simple, a quiet outpost on the shores of four-and-a-half-square-mile Katahdin Lake. The view of Katahdin is so dramatic here that painter Marsden Hartley once captured it on canvas. Ten rustic cabins have woodstoves, kerosene lamps, linens, and outhouses. Several rate options are available, depending on length of stay, meal plan, and season. From July through Labor Day, the family cabin rate is $600 a week (housekeeping cabin for seven; no meals). The daily AP rate (three meals, served in the main lodge) for five days or more is $65 pp. Canoe rentals are $20 a day. The camp is open all year. Trail access is south of Roaring Brook Campground in Baxter State Park.

Campgrounds and Campsites
Hundreds of wilderness campsites sprinkled throughout Maine's North Woods—many accessible from Millinocket—are part of the recreational-management program overseen by North Maine Woods (NMW), the umbrella organization based in Ashland.

The best-run commercial campground in the Millinocket area is 32-acre **Katahdin Shadows Campground**, Rt. 157, P.O. Box H, Medway 04460, tel. (207) 746-9349 or (800) 794-5267, a Good Sampark where owner Rick LeVasseur works like an octopus to keep tabs on cabins, campsites, canoeing expeditions, and more pet rabbits than you could ever count. Kids are never bored here, with such features as basketball, horseshoes, heated pool, playground, arcade, pool table, and all those bunnies to feed (bring your own carrots). Parents get free morning coffee and hot showers. Tentsites are $16 a day (two adults); wooden hutniks are $19; cabins are $21-39. Kids 17 and under are free; leashed pets are allowed. Canoe rentals are $16 a day. The campground, 1.7 miles west of I-95 Exit 56, is open all year. This place is so popular you'll need to reserve well in advance for any holiday weekend. Also based here is **Penobscot River Outfitters**, providing guided canoe trips, Old Town canoe rentals and sales, and shuttle service.

Between Upper and Lower Shin Ponds, 100-acre **Shin Pond Village**, Shin Pond Rd., Rt. 159, RR1, Box 280, Patten 04765, tel. (207) 528-2900, is much more than a campground. It's a multifaceted operation with 30 campsites ($15-19 a site), six one- and two-bedroom cottages ($49-89 a night), a lunch counter (open daily

7:30 a.m.-9 p.m.), and other facilities such as laundry room, public restrooms, gift shop, canoe and boat rentals, and a swimming hole in the nearby brook. In winter, there are snowmobile rentals. Most RV sites are ample but provide little privacy; the dozen tentsites are nicely wooded. Shin Pond Village is 10 miles northwest of Patten and 15 miles east of Baxter State Park's northeast (Matagamon) entrance. Cabins are open all year; laundry facilities and restrooms are only open May through November.

FOOD

Lunch and Miscellanea
Millinocket House of Pizza, Northern Plaza, 782 Central St., Millinocket 04462, tel. (207) 723-4528, always busy, includes Greek salad, gyro sandwiches, and Greek pizza on its menu. Order at the stand-up counter and grab a Formica-topped table. Or get it all to go. It's open daily 11 a.m.-10 p.m., all year; free delivery until 9 p.m. if you're staying nearby.

Plenty of local color is your reward at the **Patten General Store & Sporting Goods**, Rt. 11, P.O. Box 479, Patten 04765, tel. (207) 528-2549, one of those old-fashioned, little-of-everything emporia. Food (eat here or take out), ammo, bait, blaze-orange hats, newspapers, and, if you hang around long enough, plenty of local gossip. The store is open daily 10 a.m.-10 p.m., all year.

Close to Mattawamkeag Wilderness Park access road is the **Keag Market and Café**, Rt. 2, P.O. Box 39, Mattawamkeag 04459, tel. (207) 736-7333, open for breakfast, lunch, and dinner all year, Mon.-Sat. 5 a.m.-8 p.m. and Sunday 7 a.m.-8 p.m. Baked goods are excellent, as is the ice cream.

Inexpensive to Moderate
A huge stone fireplace dominates the dining room of **The Hotel Terrace**, 52 Medway Rd., Millinocket 04462, tel. (207) 723-4525, Millinocket's most congenial restaurant. It's hard to beat a prime-rib dinner, with all the extras, for under $12. The wine list is small but well chosen; the lounge is a local watering hole. No problem bringing kids to this informal spot. Located just off Rt. 157, on a hill above downtown, it's open

all year, daily 5:30 a.m.-10 p.m. Also here are 11 motel rooms at $30-50 d, including a/c, phones, and cable TV. No pets. Open all year.

Steaks, pizza, calzones, and seafood are the specialties at the **Scootic In,** 70 Penobscot Ave., Millinocket 04462, tel. (207) 723-4566, along with big-screen TV and a good-size local crowd. A more sedate group patronizes the adjoining **Penobscot Room,** where the menu is more creative and prices are marginally higher. Kids' menu entrées run $4-6. Save room for homemade desserts. The Scootic In is open Mon.-Sat. at 11 a.m., Sunday at noon, and closes daily at 1 a.m. The Penobscot Room is open for lunch weekdays only, open for dinner at 4 p.m. daily.

INFORMATION AND SERVICES

The **Katahdin Area Chamber of Commerce,** 1029 Central St., Rt. 157, Millinocket 04462, tel. (207) 723-4443, based in a small prefab building at the eastern edge of Millinocket, is open daily 9 a.m.-4 p.m. Memorial Day weekend through Labor Day; the rest of the year, it's open Mon.-Fri. 9 a.m.-2 p.m.

The **Millinocket Memorial Library,** 5 Maine Ave., Millinocket 04462, tel. (207) 723-7020, is open all year, Monday and Thursday 9 a.m.-8 p.m., Tuesday and Wednesday 1-8 p.m., and Friday and Saturday 1-5 p.m. (closed Saturday in summer).

Newspapers

For thorough coverage of local information and events listings, the *Katahdin Times,* tel. (207) 723-8118, fax 723-4434, is published every Tuesday. The daily newspaper covering the Millinocket area is the *Bangor Daily News,* tel. (800) 432-7964.

Emergencies

For police, fire, and ambulance service in **Millinocket, East Millinocket, and Medway,** call 911. In **Patten,** call (207) 528-2220 for an ambulance or to report a fire; call (800) 432-7911 for the county sheriff.

The 50-bed **Millinocket Regional Hospital,** 200 Somerset St., Millinocket 04462, tel. (207) 723-5161, has 24-hour emergency care. The nearest major medical facility is **Eastern Maine Medical Center,** in Bangor, nearly 70 miles to the south via I-95.

Public Restrooms

Just east of Northern Plaza in Millinocket, **Baxter State Park Headquarters,** open weekdays, has public restrooms, as does Millinocket's **municipal building,** 197 Penobscot Ave., on the lower level.

Laundromats

In a region where backpackers abound, laundromats are popular spots. The **Downtown Laundromat,** 55 Penobscot Ave., Millinocket 04462, tel. (207) 723-5825, is open all year, Mon.-Fri. 8 a.m.-6 p.m., and Saturday and Sunday 9 a.m.-4 p.m. At **Shin Pond Village,** Shin Pond Rd., Rt. 159, Patten 04765, tel. (207) 528-2900, close to Baxter State Park's northeast gate, you can use the laundry room even if you aren't spending the night. The machines are accessible until 8 p.m.

Kennels

If you're headed with your pet for Baxter State Park, you'll need a kennel, as pets are not allowed in the park. For $7-9 a day, Joyce Landry's **North Ridge Boarding Kennel,** Jones Rd., Medway 04460, tel. (207) 746-9537, takes superb care of dogs, cats, and whatever else you consider a pet. Capacity here is 15, and they walk dogs three times a day, so call at least two weeks in advance for a reservation—farther ahead for July and August weekends. To avoid disrupting the animals, kennel hours are limited to Mon.-Sat. 9-10 a.m. and 6-7 p.m., all year. No credit cards. The kennel is on Rt. 116, four miles south of Rt. 157.

Getting Around

Two firms beyond Millinocket's town lines provide **floatplane** and **skiplane** access to remote campsites and sporting camps. **Katahdin Air Service,** Box 171, Millinocket 04462, tel. (207) 723-8378 or (888) 742-5527, has an excellent half-century reputation, offering charter floatplane flights between May and November. **Scotty's Flying Service,** Shin Pond, Patten 04765, tel. (207) 528-2626 or 528-2528, based close to Baxter State Park's northeast entrance, does charter flights at roundtrip rates ranging $50-200 pp. Scotty's also offers hour-long scenic flights, at $150 for three persons.

Taxi service in the Millinocket area is provided by Tom's Taxi, tel. (207) 723-4133, and Katahdin Taxi, tel. (207) 723-2000. Both are on call 6 a.m.-1 a.m., all year.

BAXTER STATE PARK

Consider the foresight of Maine Governor Percival Proctor Baxter. After years of battling the state legislature to protect the area around Katahdin, Maine's highest mountain, he bade good-bye to state government in 1925 and proceeded on his own to make his dream happen. Determined to preserve this chunk of real estate for Maine residents and posterity, he pleaded the cause with landowners and managed to accumulate an initial 5,960-acre parcel—the nucleus of today's 204,733-acre Baxter State Park—and donated it to the state in 1931. From then on, he acquired and donated more and more bits and pieces (adding his last 7,764-acre parcel in 1962, just seven years before his death at the age of 90). The governor's prescience went far beyond mere purchases of land; his deed of gift carried stiff restrictions that have been little altered since then. And interest from his final bequest has allowed park authorities to add even more acreage since his death.

Today this fantastic recreational wilderness has 46 mountain peaks and 175 miles of trails. One rough, unpaved road (20 mph limit) circles the park; no pets, radios, or cellular phones are allowed; no gasoline or drinking water is available; camping is carry-in, carry-out.

Camping, in fact, is the only way to sleep in Baxter—at tentsites, lean-tos, bunkhouses, or rustic log cabins. Competition for sleeping space is fierce on midsummer weekends; it's pure luck to find an opening, so you need to plan ahead. Guaranteeing a spot, particularly one of the coveted 23 cabins, means reserving in January (no refunds). The rewards are rare alpine flowers, unique rock formations, pristine ponds, waterfalls, wildlife sightings (especially moose), dramatic vistas, and, in late September, spectacular fall foliage.

The hiking here is incomparable. Peak-baggers accustomed to 8,000-footers (or more) may be unimpressed by the altitudes, but no one should underestimate the ruggedness of Baxter's terrain.

Percival Baxter was by no means the first to discover this wilderness. His best-known predecessor was author Henry David Thoreau, who climbed Katahdin in 1846 from what's now Abol Campground but never reached the summit. He didn't even reach Thoreau Spring (4,636 feet), named in his honor, but he *did* wax eloquent about the experience: "This was that Earth of which we have heard, made out of Chaos and Old Night . . . It was the fresh and natural surface of the planet Earth, as it was made forever and ever . . . so Nature made it, and man may use it if he can."

Locked in what he called "a cloud factory," Thoreau declined to approach the summit: "Pomola [Pamola, the Penobscot Indians' malevolent spirit of Katahdin] is always angry with those who climb to the summit of Ktaadn." And Native Americans traditionally stayed below treeline, fearing the resident evil spirits. They all had a point. The current trail system didn't exist in the Native Americans' or Thoreau's days, of course (the first recorded summiteer was Charles Turner, Jr., in 1804), so fatalities were probably more frequent, but in this century climbers have died on Katahdin, and difficult rescues occur every year.

Regulations

The list of rules is long at Baxter—and enough park rangers make the rounds to ensure enforcement. It's not unusual to hear complaints that there's too much regimentation here, but Park Director Irvin ("Buzz") Caverly is a kind of one-man Supreme Court, interpreting Governor Baxter's stipulations. He's backed up by the Baxter State Park Authority, an autonomous board comprising three state officials who have ultimate park power.

• The park's **entrance gates** are staffed only until 9 p.m. (Matagamon Gate) and 10 p.m. (Togue Pond Gate); campers must arrive at one of the gates by 8:30 p.m.

• **No pets.** This rule is so strict that a blind

THE UNGAINLY, BELOVED MOOSE

Everyone loves Maine's state animal, *Alces alces americana*. The ungainly moose, bulbous-nosed and topheavy, stops traffic and brings out the cameras. It also stops cars literally, usually creating a lose-lose situation. The moose's long legs put its head and shoulders about windshield level, and a collision can propel the animal head-first through the glass. Human and animal fatalities are common.

State biologists estimate that Maine has nearly 30,000 moose, most in the North Woods, so it's pretty hard not to encounter one if you're driving the roads or hiking the trails in the Katahdin/Moosehead region.

Moose pay no heed to those yellow-and-black, diamond-shaped moose-crossing signs, but officials post them near typical moose hangouts, so *slow down* when you see them. During daylight hours, especially early and late in the day, keep your binoculars and camera handy. In late spring and early summer, pesky flies and midges drive the moose from the deepest woods, so you're more likely to see them close to the roadside. At night, be even more careful, as moose eyes don't reflect headlights.

Moose are vegetarians, preferring new shoots and twigs in aquatic settings, so the best places to see them are ponds fringed with grass and shrubs. These spots are likely to be buggy, too, so slather yourself with insect repellent.

Moose hunting, officially sanctioned, is somewhat controversial—partly because the creatures seem to present little sporting challenge. But they are a challenge—not because of wile or speed but because of heft. Imagine dragging one of these fellows out of the woods to a waiting truck; it's no mean feat. In Maine's annual Moose Lottery—a herd-thinning scheme concocted by the Department of Inland Fisheries and Wildlife—2,000 hunters receive permits to shoot moose in early October. At official state weighing stations, the hapless moose are strung up, weighed, tested for parasites, and often butchered on the spot by freelance meat packagers. Moose meat is actually tasty—especially if you try not to think about where it came from.

Moose Trivia

• Typical height for an adult bull moose is seven feet at the shoulders; typical weight is about 1,000 pounds, with 1,400-pounders also recorded. Cow moose run about 800 pounds.

• Moose usually lumber along, seemingly in no hurry, but they've been known to run as fast as 35 mph.

• The bull moose's rack of antlers can measure six feet across; the largest recorded was a hair under seven feet.

• Moose give birth in late May or early June, after a 35-week pregnancy; singles are normal, twins are less common, triplets are very rare. A newborn calf weighs 20-30 pounds, occasionally 35 pounds.

• Moose have extremely acute senses of hearing and smell, but their eyesight is pitiable. If you're utterly quiet and stay downwind of them, they probably won't spot you.

• Moose have no history of harming humans, but stay out of their way during "the rut," when they're charging around the woods looking for females in heat. This usually occurs between mid-September and mid-October, when the foliage is at its peak, hikers are out and about, and moose-lottery winners are in hot pursuit.

Moosewatching Hot Spots (Katahdin/Moosehead Region)
• Sandy Stream Pond, Baxter State Park
• Grassy Pond, Baxter State Park
• Russell Pond, Baxter State Park
• Sawtelle Deadwater, off Shin Pond Road, about seven miles northwest of Shin Pond
• Lazy Tom Bog, off Lily Bay Road, about 19 miles north of Greenville
• Rt. 6/15, between Greenville Junction and Rockwood, on the west side of Moosehead Lake
• The Golden Road, between Ripogenus Dam and Pittston Farm

BOB RACE

Appalachian Trail through-hiker was forbidden to bring his seeing-eye dog into the park to finish his trek. Maine's governor, unable to dissuade park officials, later welcomed the hiker and his dog at the governor's mansion in Augusta.

- **Water quality** cannot be guaranteed in the park, so you'll need to carry in all your drinking water or boil it for 20 minutes before drinking it or bring bleach or iodine to purify it. A small-pore filter will also work.

- **No motorcycles, motorbikes, or ATVs** are allowed in the park; **bicycles** are allowed only on maintained roads, not on trails, but the narrow, rough Perimeter Road is not particularly bike-friendly. **Snowmobiles** are restricted to certain areas; check with park rangers.

- As mentioned above, the park bans operation of **cell phones, TVs, radios, and CD or cassette players.** Noise levels in the park are strictly monitored by the rangers. There are no pay phones in the park, but all park rangers have radiophones.

Baxter in Winter

The roads aren't plowed, campgrounds are closed, and the lakes and ponds are frozen solid, but Baxter authorities allow winter use of the park—with a long list of rigid restrictions. If this sounds appealing, contact the Baxter State Park Authority for winter information.

DAY USE

Most day-use visitors are here to hike; on summer and fall weekends, you'll need to arrive early—even if you're not climbing Katahdin—because the day-use parking areas fill up. Between 7 and 8 a.m. on weekends, a long line forms at the Togue Pond gatehouse. A notice board at each gatehouse specifies which day-use parking areas are closed and which are open; there's always someplace to park (though *never* alongside the Perimeter Road or campground access roads), and zillions of trails to hike, but it may not be what you had in mind. So plan ahead and arrive early (no later than 7 a.m. to hike Katahdin) or be prepared to be totally flexible.

The northern end of the park is much less utilized than the southern end, so consider entering via the Matagamon Gate and hiking the wonderful trails in that part of Baxter. From I-95 Exit 56 (Medway; the exit for Millinocket and the southern park entrance), it's 19 miles to Exit 58 (Sherman), then another 33 miles to Matagamon Gate, via Patten and Shin Pond.

Picnicking

Picnic areas, some with only a single table, are spotted throughout the park; most of the vehicle-accessible campgrounds (except Kidney and Daicey Ponds) also have picnic areas where noncampers are welcome. At the campgrounds, park in the day-use parking area, not the campers' area.

HIKING

Baxter's 175 miles of trails can occupy hikers for their entire lives. There's no such thing as "best" hikes, but some are indeed better (for various reasons) than others. Below is a range of options; consult Stephen Clark's *Katahdin* guide (see the Booklist) for details and more suggestions.

Hikes originating at campgrounds all have registration clipboards; sign-in is requested for all hikes and *required* for Katahdin hikes. All trails are blue-blazed, except for ones that are part of the Appalachian Trail, with white blazes. Carved brown signs appear at all major trail junctions. All hikers are required to carry a flashlight—which any hiker should know enough to do anyway.

Wear Polartec, polypropylene, Gore-tex, or wool clothing, not cotton. Jeans can be a real drag if you get soaked in a stream or rainstorm. If you're planning to hike Katahdin, bring more layers than you think you'll need. Bring plenty of insect repellent, especially in June, when the blackflies are on the rampage. In June, you'll be best off with 100% DEET bug dope; wear long pants and a long-sleeved shirt/sweater with tight-fitting wrists and a snug collar.

Nature Trails and Other Family Hikes

Baxter has three easy nature trails that make ideal hikes for families with a range of age and skill levels. Nature-trail maps are available at park headquarters, the park entrance gates, and the nearest ranger stations to the trailheads. The 1.8-mile **Daicey Pond Nature Trail,** beginning at Daicey Pond Campground, circumnavigates the pond counterclockwise, taking about an hour. In August, help yourself to the raspberries near the end of the circuit. Best of all, you can extend the hike at the end by renting a canoe ($1 an hour) at the campground's ranger station, in the shadow of Katahdin's west flank. After that, take the easy l.2-mile roundtrip hike from the campground to Big Niagara Falls for a swim, or at least some photographs.

The other nature trails are the **South Branch Nature Trail,** a .7-mile walk starting at South Branch Campground, in the northern part of the park, and **Roaring Brook Nature Trail,** a .75-mile walk starting near Roaring Brook Campground, in the southeastern corner of the park, with dramatic views of Katahdin's eastern flank.

Other good family hikes, easy to moderate, are Trout Brook Mountain, Burnt Mountain, and Howe Brook Trail—all in the northern section of the park. Burnt Mountain has a firetower at the top, and you'll need to climb it to see the view; the summit itself is quite overgrown. In the southern end of the park, a short, easy trail leads from Upper Togue Pond to **Cranberry Pond.** An easy, 5.2-mile roundtrip from Daicey Pond Campground goes to **Lily Pad Pond,** then via canoe to **Windy Pitch Ponds.** Plan to picnic en route alongside Big Niagara Falls. (Before departing, stop at the Daicey Pond office and pick up the keys for the canoe locks.)

Howe Brook Trail, departing from South Branch Campground, requires fording the brook several times in summer, so wear waterproof footgear. The reward, higher up, is a series of waterfalls and little pools where the kids can swim (the water is frigid)—and flat boulders where you can picnic and sunbathe. In the fall, the foliage on this hike is especially colorful. For the six-mile hike, allow about four hours roundtrip—time for lunch, a swim, and dawdling. Afterward, rent a canoe at the campground ($1 an hour) and paddle around scenic Lower South Branch Pond, in the shadow of North Traveler Mountain.

Moderate Hikes
Good hikes generally classified as moderate are Doubletop Mountain, Sentinel Mountain,

Mt. OJI, and The Owl. If you decide to hike **Doubletop Mountain,** start at the Nesowadnehunk (Ne-SOWD-na-hunk) Field trailhead and go south to Kidney Pond Campground, an eight-mile one-way trek, up and over and down. It's much less strenuous this way; allow about six hours.

Allow about six hours also for the **Sentinel Mountain Trail** from Daicey Pond Campground (6.6 miles roundtrip) or Kidney Pond Campground (four miles roundtrip). It's not difficult; the only moderate part involves a boulder field about midway up. Take a picnic and hang out at the top; the view of Katahdin, The Owl, and Mt. OJI, across the way, is splendid. With binoculars, you'll probably spot moose in the ponds below. Keep one eye on your lunch, however; a resident Canada jay at the summit has an aggressive streak.

If weather has been rainy, *do not* consider hiking Mt. OJI or The Owl. Both verge on being strenuous even under normal conditions, and the rock slide areas on OJI are especially treacherous when wet.

Katahdin
Mile-high Katahdin, northern terminus of the Appalachian Trail, is the Holy Grail for most Baxter State Park hikers—and certainly for Appalachian Trail through-hikers, who have walked 2,158 miles from Springer Mountain, Georgia, to get here. Thousands of hikers scale Katahdin annually via several different routes. The climb is strenuous, requires a full day, and is not suitable for small children; kids under six are banned above treeline. You'll be a lot happier and a lot less exhausted if you plan to camp in the park before and after the Katahdin hike.

"Katahdin," by the way, is a Native American word meaning "greatest mountain"—hence no need to refer to it as *Mount* Katahdin. The Katahdin massif actually comprises a single high point (Baxter Peak, 5,267 feet) and several neighboring peaks (Pamola Peak, 4,902 feet; Hamlin Peak, 4,756 feet; and the three Howe Peaks, 4,734 to 4,612 feet).

Even though Thoreau never made it to Katahdin's summit (Baxter Peak), countless others have, and the mountain sees a virtual traffic jam in summer and fall—particularly late in the season, when most of the through-hikers tend to show up. Some hikers make the summit an annual ritual; others consider it a onetime rite of passage, then opt for less-trodden paths and less-strenuous climbs.

Weather reports are posted every morning at all the campgrounds. Katahdin has its own biome, and weather on the summit can be dramatically different from that down below. At times, especially in high-wind and blowing-snow conditions, park officials close trails to the summit. They don't do it frivolously; Katahdin is a killer, literally.

There are six major **access trails** up Katahdin: Northwest Basin, North Peaks, Chimney Pond/Cathedral, Helon Taylor, Abol, and Hunt Trails.

Besides the requisite photo next to the Baxter Peak summit sign, Katahdin's other "been there, done that" is a traverse of the aptly named **Knife Edge,** a treacherous, 1.1-mile-long granite spine (minimum width three feet) between Baxter and Pamola Peaks. If you can stand the experience, hanging on for all you're worth, next to a 1,500-foot drop, go for it; the views are incredible. But don't push beyond your personal limits; you're hours from the nearest hospital.

The most-used route to Baxter Peak is the **Hunt Trail,** a 10-mile roundtrip that coincides with the Appalachian Trail from Katahdin Stream Campground; allow 7-8 hours. Other routes start from Russell Pond, Chimney Pond, Roaring Brook, and Abol Campgrounds. See Stephen Clark's *Katahdin* guide for specific route information.

CAMPING

Facilities at 10 campgrounds range from cabins to tentsites, lean-tos, and bunkhouses; there are also several wilderness campsites supervised by the nearest campground rangers.

The campgrounds close Oct. 15, and open at various times, beginning May 15. Two hike-in campgrounds open June 1. Fees range from $6 per person per night in lean-tos (two-person minimum) to $17 per person in cabins (minimums depend on cabin size). Fees must be prepaid and are not refundable.

The 23 cabins are at **Daicey Pond Campground** and **Kidney Pond Campground,** in the park's southwest corner. Daicey Pond has

the best views—Katahdin from every cabin, and the sunrises are matchless. With two exceptions, Kidney Pond cabins overlook the pond and surrounding woods, but not the mountains; Doubletop Mountain is in back of the campground. All cabins have woodstoves (for heating only), propane lanterns, outhouses, outside fireplaces, and beds; bring your own linens and everything else.

Chimney Pond and Russell Pond Campgrounds are hike-in campgrounds. Distance from the Roaring Brook parking area to Chimney Pond is 3.3 miles; to Russell Pond is seven miles. Chimney Pond has a bunkhouse and nine four-person lean-tos. Russell Pond has a bunkhouse, four lean-tos, and four tentsites—all arranged around the pond, where you can also rent canoes ($1 an hour).

South Branch Pond Campground, close to Matagamon Gate, has a bunkhouse, 12 lean-tos, and 20 tentsites in an especially idyllic setting; nine of the lean-tos are right next to the pond.

From June through August, bring fabric screening if you're staying in a lean-to; a tarp may foil the blackflies, mosquitoes, and no-see-ums, but you don't want to suffocate.

Getting Reservations

Camping reservations must be made by mail or in person; no phone reservations. July gets booked up first, then August; weekends are more crowded than weekdays.

As early as December, contact the **Baxter State Park Authority,** 64 Balsam Dr., Millinocket 04462, tel. (207) 723-5140, for a reservation form. On the form, list your preferred dates and sites and return it with your check (payable to "Baxter State Park") so it arrives on January 2. Enclose a self-addressed, stamped envelope. Clerks will process your application and return any overpayment, along with a reservation confirmation. About 700 mailed-in requests show up on January 2.

Several hundred diehard campers, especially ones hoping for midsummer cabin reservations, actually drive to park headquarters in Millinocket on January 2, when processing begins. Some even spend the night in town to be there when the door opens at 7 a.m.; since Millinocket is in Maine's snow belt, the trek becomes something of an adventure. The absence of computers and a convoluted system—including a limit on cabin reservations—make this a lengthy but oddly enjoyable process.

If you can't plan that far ahead but can be fairly flexible, send in your request later in the spring, or even take a chance on showing up at the last minute. Except on weekends from July to mid-August, a tentsite can usually be found. But be sure to have a fallback plan.

If you make a reservation and can't keep it, be considerate and call to cancel, even though you won't receive a refund. It will give someone else a chance to enjoy the beauty of Baxter.

PARK ACCESS, INFORMATION, AND SERVICES

Unless you're hiking the Appalachian Trail (AT), the only way to enter the park is via one of two gates. **Togue Pond Gate**, at the southern end of the park, is the choice for visitors from Greenville or Millinocket and the most-used gate. At the northeast corner of the park is **Matagamon Gate**, accessed via I-95, Patten, and the Shin Pond Road. Togue Pond Gate is open 6 a.m.-10 p.m. May 15-Oct. 15; Matagamon Gate is open 6 a.m.-9 p.m. the same months.

Note: Before you enter the park, check your fuel gauge and fill up your tank; there are no fuel facilities in the park.

Be sure that you are not arriving at the park with more people than your reservations indicate; the rangers at the gate check this, and the campground rangers even do body counts to be sure you haven't stuffed extra people into cabins or lean-tos.

Appalachian Trail hikers are required to register at Daicey Pond Campground, closest ranger station to the park's AT entrance.

Maine residents have free daytime use of the park—one of Governor Baxter's stipulations. At the gates, **nonresidents** pay $8 per vehicle per day; a nonresident season pass is $25. A rental car with Maine plates qualifies in the resident category. Everyone must pay for camping.

There is no public transportation to or within Baxter State Park, so you'll need a car, truck, or

bicycle. RVs are also allowed, but maximum size is nine feet high and 22 feet long (or 44 feet for car-and-trailer). Baxter is not a drive-through park. The 43-mile unpaved park **Perimeter Road**, connecting Togue Pond and Matagamon Gatehouses, is narrow and corrugated, deliberately so; it's designed for access, not joyriding.

A few trail loops include the Perimeter Road, but avoid walking on it if possible. In wet weather, you'll be splashed by cars navigating the potholes; in hot weather, the gritty dust gets in your teeth. Hitchhiking is discouraged, but you can usually get a ride if you need it.

Information

Books, maps, and information are available at **Baxter State Park Headquarters,** 64 Balsam Dr., Millinocket 04462, tel. (207) 723-5140, open Mon.-Fri. 9 a.m.-5 p.m., all year, at campground ranger stations, and at information centers close to the two entrance gates. (Camping reservations must be made by mail or in person.)

Available in the same locations, as well as in bookstores throughout Maine, is the essential handbook for the park: *Katahdin: A Guide to Baxter State Park & Katahdin,* by Stephen Clark (3d ed., $16.95; see the Booklist). It's loaded with trail details, park history, and camping information and has a convenient foldout map. Despite an appalling number of spelling errors, it's the sine qua non for park hiking and camping.

If you don't have the *Katahdin* guide, pick up a *Day Use Hiking Guide* ($1) at the park gate or park headquarters. The foldout map, quite sketchy, also has basic info on major park trails.

Helping Hands

The Boston-based **Appalachian Mountain Club** (AMC), established in 1876, organizes summer **trail-maintenance programs** at Baxter State Park, usually in August. The six-day projects, including a weekend at Roaring Brook Campground to hike Katahdin, cost $70 for AMC members, $75 for nonmembers. No experience is necessary. For details and schedule, contact the AMC's White Mountains Trails Program, tel. (603) 466-2721.

ALLAGASH AND ST. JOHN CANOEING

Maine's two classic canoe trips—routes traceable to our Native American predecessors—are on the Allagash and St. John Rivers.

With headwaters in Somerset and Piscataquis Counties and flowing northward, the St. John and Allagash Rivers meet at the top of Maine, in Aroostook County.

The St. John, undammed and therefore runnable only in spring, is much wilder and less crowded than the Allagash, which has three dams and sees canoeists from mid-May to mid-October. About 15,000 people canoe the Allagash each year. Depending on where you put in and take out, figure on 4-8 days for the St. John and 5-10 days for the Allagash.

Respect Private Property

Both rivers run through working forest lands, so it's crucial for canoeists to respect private property and remember that logging trucks have the right-of-way on these roads. Paper companies don't own the rivers, but you'll be crossing their turf (and paying for it) to access the rivers. Abuse of private property will only restrict the opportunities for future recreation. Be ecosensitive and future-sensitive on the rivers: don't take more fish than you'll eat; keep noise levels down; consider the rights of other canoeists; and be a low-impact camper. Although paper companies have created token "beauty strips" to preserve the rivers' wilderness aura—250 feet on each side of the St. John, 500 feet on each side of the Allagash—don't be surprised to hear the intrusive buzz of logging machinery in the near distance.

Maps and Information

A useful, accurate map covering both rivers is *Allagash & St. John,* published by DeLorme Mapping, 2 DeLorme Dr., Yarmouth 04096, tel. (800) 452-5931. Cost of the foldout version is $4.95 (plus $1 shipping).

Both rivers are well covered in the best-available canoeing handbook, the *AMC River Guide: Maine,* published by the Appalachian Mountain Club (see the Booklist).

Canoeing Guides

Neophyte canoeists should think twice before setting out without a guide on multiday canoe trips. You should have experience with Class II whitewater before attempting either of these rivers. Even experienced paddlers who are unfamiliar with Maine's rivers ought to assess the pluses and minuses of a do-it-yourself expedition versus a guided trip. It's rare to find a deserted campsite. The costs of provisioning, arranging shuttles, camping fees, and gear rental can add up—and guides spare you from cooking and cleanup. Not a bad tradeoff.

Most guide services have their specialties, but few specialize in only one river. Some arrange trips all over the state; others go to Canada, Alaska, and beyond. Veteran guide services that offer trips on both the St. John and the Allagash include Mike Patterson and Edgar Eaton's **Wilds of Maine Guide Service,** 2 Abby Lane, Yarmouth 04096, tel. (207) 846-9735; **Gil Gilpatrick,** P.O. Box 461, Skowhegan 04976, tel. (207) 453-6959; the Cochrane family's **Allagash Canoe Trips,** P.O. Box 713, Greenville 04441, tel. (207) 695-3668; Blaine Miller's **Allagash Guide Inc.,** Box 3210, Rt. 1, Norridgewock 04957, tel. (207) 634-3748; and Rick and Judy Givens's **Allagash Wilderness Outfitters,** HC 76, Box 620, Greenville 04441, radiophone (207) 695-2821, 36 Minuteman Drive, Millinocket 04462, tel. (207) 723-6622, Dec.-April.

Two guide services well known for small groups and a special love of traditional woods lore and gear are Garrett and Alexandra Conover's **North Woods Ways,** RR 2, Box 159A, Willimantic, Guilford 04443, tel. (207) 997-3723, and Ray and Nancy Reitze's **Earthways,** RFD 2, Box 2757, Canaan 04924, tel. (207) 426-8138. The Conovers run the Allagash early and late in the season, and the St. John in late May, but they provide woodstove-heated tents to combat the chill.

Costs vary for guided trips, usually including everything except transportation to Maine; figure on $80-120 a day per person.

THE ALLAGASH WILDERNESS WATERWAY

In 1966, the state established a 92-mile stretch of the Allagash River as **The Allagash Wilderness Waterway** (AWW), a collection of lakes, ponds, and streams starting at Telos Lake and ending at West Twin Brook, about six miles before the Allagash meets the St. John River. Also recognized as a National Wild and Scenic River, the waterway's habitats shelter rare plants, 30 or so mammal species, and more than 120 bird species. You'll spot plenty of wildlife along the way.

Arranging a flexible schedule to do the Allagash gives you enough slack to wait out strong winds on the three largest lakes. Such a schedule also allows time for a leisurely pace, side trips, and fishing along the way.

Information
The Maine **Bureau of Parks and Lands,** in the Department of Conservation, manages operations on the Allagash Wilderness Waterway. During the season, rangers are stationed at key sites all along the route. For general information, including a useful free map, call (207) 941-4014 Mon.-Sat. 8 a.m.-5 p.m. For seasonal water-level information, call (207) 435-7963 daily 8 a.m.-5 p.m., late April to mid-December.

A particularly lovely pictorial overview of the waterway is naturalist Dean Bennett's excellent book, *Allagash: Maine's Wild and Scenic River* (see the Booklist).

ALLAGASH WATERWAY HIGHLIGHTS

Allagash Lake, one of the state's most pristine lakes, feeds into Chamberlain Lake from the west, via Allagash Stream. No motors are allowed on Allagash Lake, making it especially tranquil. The side trip is six miles one-way, and water levels (too high or too low) can make it a rough go. At Lock Dam, ask about conditions.

Between Chamberlain and Eagle Lakes, on a narrow spit of land seemingly in the middle of nowhere, stand two of the waterway's oddities— two old **steam engines,** relics rusted out and long abandoned. Once linked to the Eagle Lake and West Branch Railroad, the short-run locomotives operated round-the-clock, six days a week, between 1927 and 1933, hauling pulpwood for the timber industry. The nonprofit **Allagash Alliance Group,** tel. (207) 929-8245, has begun long-range restoration of the engines and the site, known as the **Tramway Historic District.**

Allagash Falls, eight miles before the end of the waterway and six miles before the river meets the St. John, has a dramatic, 40-foot drop. Needless to say, you'll need to portage here— but only a third of a mile.

When to Go
Canoeing season on the AWW usually runs late May (after "ice-out") to early October. Water and insect levels are high and water temperature is low in May and June; July and August are most crowded but have better weather; September can be chilly, but the foliage is fabulous. Average annual temperature in this area is 40° F; winter temperatures average 20° F. The AWW is accessible in winter for snowmobiling and ice fishing. Winter camping is permitted at the Chamberlain Thoroughfare Bridge parking lot, on a first-come, first-served basis.

Campsites
There's 80 signposted campsites along the waterway; all are first-come, first served. In July and August, when canoe traffic is fairly heavy, don't wait too late in the day to set up camp. Sites are $5 a day (including tax) for nonresi-

dents, $4 a day for residents. Children under 10 are free. Fees are payable in advance at the ranger station where you enter the waterway. Theoretically, you're expected to stay only one night at any site, but an extension usually isn't a big problem.

Sporting Camps Along the Waterway

Close to one of the major waterway access points, and roughly 50 miles north of Millinocket, **Nugent's Chamberlain Lake Camps,** Chamberlain Lake, mailing address HC 76, Box 632, Greenville 04441, tel. (207) 944-5991, is reachable only by boat, plane, or snowmobile. You can drive as far as Chamberlain Thoroughfare Bridge, park, and arrange for Nugent's staff to pick you up ($20 per boatload). Built in 1936, the 12 clean cabins are determinedly rustic, without bathrooms; a common bathhouse serves the camps. Although housekeeping rates are available (bring your own linens; no meals; $22 pp a night), opt for American Plan ($60 pp a day, including linens and meals) to take advantage of the hearty family-style meals in the character-full main lodge. Kids 12 and under stay for half price. Boat rentals are $35 a day (plus gas). Owners John Richardson and Regina Webster keep Nugent's open all year, catering to snowmobilers in winter.

Nearly 70 miles downriver, on the east shore of Round Pond, is one of Maine's legendary sporting camps. **Willard Jalbert Camps,** Round Pond, T13, R12, mailing address 6 Winchester St., Presque Isle 04769, tel. (207) 764-0494 or (718) 858-4496, started in the 1940s, is still almost as rustic as when it was built. Owner Phyllis Jalbert is the granddaughter of the late Maine Guide Willard Jalbert, whose best-known client was Supreme Court Justice William O. Douglas. Three log cabins, sleeping a total of 22, have woodstoves and gas lights; guests use a common outhouse. A sauna is a terrific plus. From the camps, a four-and-a-half-mile hike will take you to the abandoned Round Pond fire tower, with a fabulous view of the area. Best access to the camps is via floatplane. Open mid-May to mid-November.

Getting There

The Allagash Wilderness Waterway is accessible by private logging roads at specified points. You can get here from Greenville or Millinocket, or from the Aroostook County community of Ashland. Official **access points** with parking areas are Chamberlain Thoroughfare Bridge, Churchill Dam, Umsaskis Thoroughfare, and Michaud Farm. Winter access sites are different.

THE ST. JOHN RIVER

Like the Allagash, the St. John has long been associated with the timber industry—and the spring log drives when huge loads of giant logs were

St. John River

driven *upstream* and eventually to the mills. The history of the late-19th- and early-20th-century lumbering era is especially colorful, loaded with tales of unbelievably rugged conditions and equally rugged characters. It's only a memory now that the log drives have ended, but you'll see remnants of the industry along the way.

Information

North Maine Woods (NMW), P.O. Box 421, Ashland 04732, tel. (207) 435-6213, the non-profit recreational manager for this area, produces a handy 24-page booklet, *Pocket Guide for the Canoeist on the St. John River,* containing almost everything you need to know about canoeing the St. John: access points, campsites, river descriptions, and the river's lumbering history. Cost is $3.

When to Go

The prime season for canoeing the St. John River is May and early June, although most years there's enough water until late June. North Maine Woods monitors daily water levels on the river, so you'll need to call a day in advance, tel. (207) 435-6213, to confirm that water flow is adequate, especially after mid-June. NMW suggests that 3,000 cfs (cubic feet per second) is the minimum for enjoyable canoeing—to avoid grounding out or extensive portaging—but experienced canoeists recommend a minimum of 2,000 cfs.

June brings out the blackflies at campsites, so be sure you are well prepared to combat them with high-powered bug dope and tight-fitting, light-colored clothing.

Campsites

Between Baker Lake and Allagash village, there are 28 riverside camping areas with a total of more than 60 sites. All are signposted. Most are on the left (west) side of the St. John; some require climbing the bank to reach level ground. Campsites are first-come, first-served. If a site is filled, you'll have to move on, anywhere from 2-5 more miles. Camping is allowed only at designated sites. About half of the sites have at least one sheltered picnic table, a real plus that saves rigging tarps for meals in rainy weather. Other facilities are outhouses and fire rings. Campsites are $5 per person per night (plus tax); fees are payable at the checkpoint where you enter North Maine Woods territory.

Note: Even though the St. John has no dams, a heavy rainstorm can swell the water level, causing the river to rise as much as three feet overnight. Keep this in mind when lashing your canoe for the night; secure it well, as high as possible.

Getting There

There are four main access points for the St. John, plus the final takeout point downriver at the top of Maine. From the southernmost point, **5th St. John Pond,** it's 143 miles to the town of Allagash. The easiest way to get here is via one of Greenville's two flying services. Downstream are **Baker Lake** and **Moody Bridge,** the latter being best for low-water conditions; drive in via Ashland (about three and a half hours on the American Realty Road). By the time you get to **Priestly Bridge,** you're more than halfway downriver—almost not worth the trip. Opt instead for starting at Baker Lake or Moody Bridge—or, if you're going with a guiding service, wherever your guides prefer to start. Shuttle arrangements can be complicated for St. John trips. If you're on your own hook, be sure all details are worked out in advance, and include logging-road user fees in your budget.

GREENVILLE AND VICINITY

Greenville (pop. 1,900) is the jumping-off point for the North Woods—ground zero for float- and skiplanes maintaining contact with remote hamlets and sporting camps. It's the big city for tinier communities in every direction, but it's a bit like a frontier town itself. Greenville looks out over Moosehead Lake—Maine's largest—from its southern end. Moosehead is 40 miles long and covers 117 square miles, but counting all the niches and notches, its shoreline runs to more than 400 miles.

The origin of the lake's name *has* to be from the large number of antlered critters hereabouts, especially along the shore toward Rockwood or Kokadjo. In addition to moosewatching, you can wear yourself out with all the recreational choices: swimming, boating, fishing, camping, hiking, whitewater rafting, golfing, picnicking, birding, skiing, snowshoeing, and snowmobiling. In spring, summer, and fall, you can also join the fire warden in his floatplane or cruise the lake in an antique steamer.

The most distinctive landmark here, at the lake's "waistline," is Mount Kineo, a 763-foot-high chunk of green-tinged rhyolite or felsite that erupted from the bowels of the earth about 425 million years ago. Smoothed by glacial activity on the west side, Kineo has sharp cliffs on its east side. The chert-like volcanic stone (not flint—Maine has no native flint) was a major reason Native Americans glommed on to the Moosehead area thousands of years ago—its hardness served them well for weapons and fishing and hunting tools. The surrounding woodlands yielded prime birchbark, supplying raw material for canoes, carry-alls, and even shelters. Stone tools and arrowheads still turn up occasionally, especially along the shore when the water level is low, but most have been carted off by amateur collectors. *Resist the urge to take home samples.*

Moosehead has been attracting outdoors enthusiasts, primarily hunters and fishermen, since the 1880s. The long haul from lower New England—ending with the passenger train from Bangor—apparently was worth it for the clean air, prime angling, and chance to rough-it. That

era has long passed, and the clientele has changed noticeably, but Greenville's downtown still has a rustic air, and the outlying hamlets even more so.

Greenville was incorporated in 1836, just before the timber industry began to take off. Steamboats hauled huge corrals ("booms") of logs down the lake to the East Outlet of the Kennebec River (East and West Outlets are both on the west side of Moosehead), where river drivers took over. All that ended fairly recently, in the 1970s. The steamer *Katahdin* is a relic of that colorful era.

Greenville's lakeshore Siamese twin, Greenville Junction, once a busy rail crossroads, now has become one of those blink-and-you'll-miss-it places, but you can still eat and sleep there. Twenty miles northwest of Greenville, on Rt. 6/15, is the small and somewhat crowded hamlet of Rockwood, closest spot to Kineo, a scenic viewpoint for lakeside lodgings. One of the best views is from the public boat landing, on a loop road just off Rt. 6/15. Route 6/15 then continues west, along Brassua Lake and the aptly named Moose River, to Jackman—a lovely 30-mile drive popular with moosewatchers.

From Greenville, it's easy to access the fabled Golden Road, the 96-mile unpaved timber superhighway from Millinocket to the Quebec border. To enter the road on Moosehead's east side, at Bowater/Great Northern's Sias Hill Checkpoint, take the Lily Bay Rd. north from Greenville for 23 miles; the last section is unpaved but well maintained. The gate is staffed 4 a.m.-11 p.m.; nonresidents pay $8 per vehicle for using the road; Maine-plated cars pay $4.

To reach the Golden Road via Moosehead's west shore—the route to Pittston Farm—take Rt. 6/15 northwest of Greenville for 20 miles to Rockwood. Then go another 18 or so unpaved miles northwest to Bowater/Great Northern's Twenty-Mile Checkpoint, staffed 4 a.m.-11 p.m., and pay the user fee: $8 for nonresident vehicle, $4 for Maine plates. It's only a few more miles to Pittston Farm, just south of the Golden Road.

Don't be surprised, when you make inquiries about the Moosehead area, to hear lots of references to ice-out. It's almost a season—the time when winter's ice releases its grip on the lake and spring and summer activities can begin. Depending on the severity of the winter, ice-out occurs anywhere from early to late May. Fishermen arrive, plumbing begins to work, and a few weeks later, the blackfly larvae start to hatch. Spring is underway.

SIGHTS

Lake Cruises

A turn-of-the-century wooden vessel once used in the lumber industry, the steamboat *Katahdin* (locally called the *Kate*) has been converted to diesel and now runs cruises on 40-mile-long Moosehead Lake. The best trip for children is the regular three-hour run, departing Tuesday, Wednesday, Saturday, and Sunday at 12:30 p.m. Tickets are $13 adults, $6 kids 5-15; kids under five are free. A six-and-a-half-hour **Mount Kineo cruise** ($19 adults, $10 kids, plus $6 for buffet lunch) operates each Thursday, and all-day head-of-lake trips ($32 adults, $16 kids) operate the last Sunday of July, August, and September. The fall foliage is fantastic on the September trip. Indoor and outdoor seating; snack bar on board. No smoking or high-heeled shoes; the boat is wheelchair accessible. Cruises operate on a regular schedule July-Sept., but only on weekends Memorial Day weekend through June. Reservations are a good idea for the longer cruises; contact **Katahdin Cruises,** N. Main St., P.O. Box 1151, Greenville 04441, tel. (207) 695-2716.

The 48-foot *Socatean,* Jolly Roger's Moosehead Cruises, Roger Lane, P.O. Box 35, Rockwood 04478, tel. (207) 534-8827 or 534-8817, based at the mouth of the Moose River, on Moosehead's west shore, runs narrated cruises Memorial Day weekend to Columbus Day. (Her name, by the way, is pronounced "so-CAT-ee-an.") Reservations are wise but not required; call if the weather is iffy. The three-hour Mount Kineo cruise departs weekends at 11 a.m. from Memorial Day weekend through late June, and Labor Day to mid-October. From late June to Labor Day, cruises run daily. Cost is $17 adults, $12 children 12 and under, including lunch. From late June to Labor Day weekend, a one-

and-a-half-hour sunset cruise departs each Saturday night (7 p.m. until mid-August, then 6:30 p.m.). Dress warmly and bring libations; the cruise attracts a lively crew. Cost is $12 adults. Children 12 and under are $7, but they'll be happier on the daytime cruise.

Flightseeing

Moosehead Lake from the air during fall-foliage season is incomparable—you'll bank over Mount Kineo, survey a palette of autumn colors, and very possibly see a moose or two. (They're easiest to spot in the sad-looking tracts clear-cut by the paper companies.) Most fun is the lakefront takeoff and landing. **Currier's Flying Service,** Pritham Ave., Rt. 6/15, Greenville Junction 04442, tel. (207) 695-2778, offers a whole slew of on-demand trips over the Allagash Wilderness Waterway, Mount Kineo, and Mount Katahdin. Costs range $15-80 pp (two-person minimum). Call to arrange flight schedule; planes depart from Greenville Junction, where the Currier family also operates a small gift shop. Roger Currier also does occasional fire-patrol trips, covering an even wider route; cost is $35 pp.

Folsom's Air Service, P.O. Box 507, Greenville 04441, tel. (207) 695-2821, fax 695-2434, also does daily flightseeing trips ($20-85 pp), weather permitting, including a 4:30 p.m. dinner flight to Pittston Farm ($50 pp). Folsom's, Currier's, and another local firm are available year-round for flights to remote wilderness camps.

PARKS AND RECREATION

Lily Bay State Park

Lining the eastern shore of Moosehead Lake, 925-acre Lily Bay State Park, Lily Bay Rd., HC 76, Box 425, Greenville 04441, tel. (207) 695-2700, is the place to go for moosewatching, fishing, picnicking, hiking, canoeing, swimming, birding, and camping at some of Maine's most desirable waterfront sites. On July and August weekends, campsite reservations are essential; two-night minimum. Call (207) 287-3824, and have a MasterCard or Visa ready. Only the lucky will find a last-minute space, even though there are 93 sites in two clusters; no hookups. Park admission (for daytime use) is $2 adults, 50

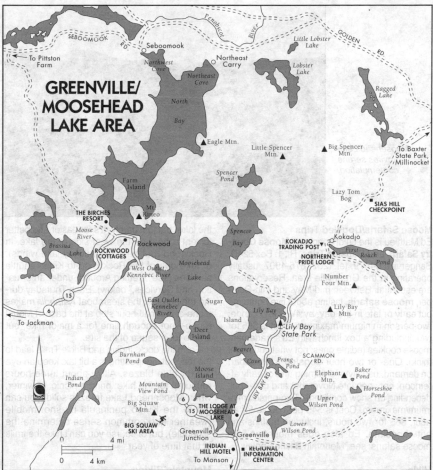

GREENVILLE/ MOOSEHEAD LAKE AREA

© MOON PUBLICATIONS, INC.

cents children 5-11; seniors and kids under five are free. Nonresident camping fees are $15 per site per night, plus the reservation fee of $2 per site per night. The park is open daily 7 a.m.-11 p.m., May-Oct. 15, but it's accessible in winter for excellent cross-country skiing and snowmobiling. From Greenville, head north on Lily Bay Rd. for eight miles; the park is on the left.

Lazy Tom Bog

Swampy Lazy Tom Bog is one of the region's best moosewatching haunts. Plan to go soon

after sunrise or just before sunset. From Greenville, take Lily Bay Rd. north to Kokadjo, 18 miles. A mile later, when the road forks, take the left fork (signposted Spencer Pond Camps). Continue half a mile to a small bridge. Park on either side of the bridge and have your camera ready, preferably with a long lens. If you want to emerge from your car, or even stick your lens through the open window, you may need to douse yourself with insect repellent. And try to keep the kids quiet. For other moosewatching tips, see the special topic "The Ungainly, Beloved Moose."

Moosehead Lake invites serene contemplation.

Moose Safaris/Dogsled Trips

Ed Mathieu is the chief honcho of **Moose Country Safaris and Dogsled Trips,** Rt. 1, Box 524D, Sangerville 04479, tel. (207) 876-4907, usually operating in the Greenville area. Reservations are essential. Between mid-May and mid-October, **moose safaris,** lasting about five hours, go out early or late in the day, by 4WD and canoe; two-person minimum/maximum. Cost is $95 for two, including a box lunch with Ed's trademark moose cookies (edible ones; not what you might think). One- or two-hour **dogsled trips** depart on demand, usually midmorning and/or early afternoon, between late November and mid-April, depending on snow conditions. Two-person minimum/maximum. Cost is $45 per couple for an hour, $65 for two hours, including muffins and hot chocolate. Ed also does mountain-bike moose safaris; see "Mountain Biking," below.

Hiking

Except for early June, when blackflies torment woodland hikers as well as moose, the Greenville area is sublime for hiking. The chamber of commerce has a list that includes hiking directions for **Number Four Mountain, Big and Little Squaw Mountains, Big and Little Spencer Mountains,** and **Elephant Mountain** (a B-52 wreck site).

Mount Kineo

A hike up Mount Kineo is a must. Kineo is accessible by rough roads, via the east side of the lake, but just barely. It's far easier and better to rent a boat on the west side of the lake, in Rockwood (but beware of flukey lake winds), or take one of the Rockwood-to-Kineo shuttle services (see "Getting Around" under "Information and Services," below). Each Thursday during the season, the steamboat *Katahdin* makes a one-and-a-half-hour stop at the base of Mount Kineo—not enough time for a major hike, but ample for a sense of the site.

From the dock, Indian and Bridle Trails lead to the top, but signposting is a bit lax; keep an eye out for blue blazes. Allow about three hours roundtrip for the hike; bring a picnic. In winter, when Moosehead Lake freezes solid, you can get to the Kineo peninsula by snowmobile (weather and common sense determine the schedule), but of course you can't hike the trails at that time of year.

Mountain Biking

The Moosehead area's hottest new sport is mountain biking. You can bring a bike and strike out on your own, rent a bike, or go with a guide or group. Remember, however, that bicycles are *not* allowed on logging roads; the huge lumber trucks are intimidating enough for passenger vehicles, never mind bicycles.

Mountain bike **rentals** are available from **Northwoods Outfitters,** Main St., P.O. Box 160, Greenville 04441, tel. (207) 695-3288, for $20-25 a day. The shop is open daily 9 a.m.-7 p.m. in summer, Wed.-Mon. 8 a.m.-5:30 p.m.

in winter. They're helpful with trail information and will deliver free to Lily Bay State Park.

Twenty miles north of Greenville, **The Birches Resort,** P.O. Box 41, Rockwood 04478, tel. (207) 534-7305, rents mountain bikes and sends you off on their 50-mile network of mountain-bike trails. An all-day guided mountain-bike tour starts at $55 pp.

Ed Mathieu, owner of Moose Country Safaris and Dogsled Trips, Rt. 1, Box 524D, Sangerville 04479, tel. (207) 876-4907, also leads half-day and all-day **mountain-bike moose safaris** from late April through October in the Greenville area. Ed entertains with lots of Indian lore along the way. Reservations are required. Cost is $50 pp for a half-day, $100 pp for the day, including lunch and beverages.

Canoeing

If you're not an experienced paddler, be cautious about canoeing on Moosehead Lake. The sheltered bays and coves are usually all right, but you can have serious trouble in the open areas. At Lily Bay State Park, you can launch a canoe from the waterfront campsites and easily make it to Sugar Island.

The **Maine Guide Fly Shop and Guide Service,** Main St., Box 1202, Greenville 04441, tel. (207) 695-2266, in addition to being the best local resource for fly fishermen, organizes eight-hour family canoe trips on the Penobscot River's Upper West Branch. No serious water here, no experience necessary. It's a chance for enjoyable canoeing in major moose country; carry binoculars and a camera (in waterproof bags). Trips operate May through late September, departing about 7 a.m.; two-person minimum. Cost is $150 pp, including canoe, gear, and lunch. The shop is open daily 7 a.m.-5:30 p.m., mid-April through September; Thurs.-Sun. 5 a.m.-5 p.m., mid-December to mid-April.

If you're on your own and need gear, **Northwoods Outfitters,** Main St., P.O. Box 160, Greenville 04441, tel. (207) 695-3288, has canoe rentals for $15-20 a day, kayaks for $15 (single) or $50 (tandem) a day. They offer free delivery to Lily Bay State Park. They also rent tents and provide shuttle service. Open daily 9 a.m.-7 p.m. in summer, Wed.-Mon. 8 a.m.-5:30 p.m. off season.

Whitewater Rafting

The major whitewater rafting operator in the Greenville area is Wilderness Expeditions, one of the many enterprises based at The Birches Resort, in Rockwood. **Wilderness Expeditions,** P.O. Box 41, Rockwood 04478, tel. (800) 825-9453, fax (207) 534-8835, runs 14- to 16-mile one-day trips on the **Dead, Kennebec,** and **Penobscot Rivers,** between early May and Columbus Day. Costs range $40-99 pp, depending on the river and trip date. Overnight packages start at $165 pp for the Kennebec, $195 pp for the Penobscot. A bus shuttles rafters from Rockwood to the put-in points, or you can stay at the Wilderness Expeditions outpost lodges on the Kennebec (at The Forks) or the Penobscot's West Branch. No kids under 12 are allowed on the Kennebec or the Penobscot's Lower West Branch; no kids under 15 on the Dead or the Penobscot's Upper West Branch. Call for the brochure, with dates and details.

Golf

The most popular, most scenic, and most windswept course in the area is the nine-hole **Kineo Golf Club,** built for the 500 or so guests at the turn-of-the-20th-century Mount Kineo House. At every turn, you'll see Mount Kineo or Moosehead Lake, or both. Dynamite views. The course is open June to mid-October, and you'll need to get there by boat.

Built in the 1920s, nine-hole **Squaw Mountain Village Golf Course,** Rt. 6/15, Greenville Junction 04441, tel. (207) 695-3609, is now part of a modern condo complex. Greens fees are low, the pace is unhurried. The course is open May through October.

Snowmobiling

The biggest winter pursuit hereabouts is snowmobiling, thanks to an average 102-inch annual snowfall and 300 miles of Greenville-area trails connecting to the entire state network. It's pretty competitive trying to get a bed in winter if you don't plan ahead; be forewarned. Incidentally, if you're curious about the influence of snowmobiling in northern Maine, check out the parking lot at the Greenville school complex (Pritham Avenue) in winter; the transport of choice is the snowmobile.

A particularly popular loop trail is the 160-mile **Moosehead Trail,** which circumnavigates Moosehead Lake—Greenville to Rockwood to Pittston Farm, Seboomook, Northeast Carry, Kokadjo, and back to Greenville. Or start at any access point along the route and go in either direction.

The chamber of commerce has snowmobile trail maps and can put you in touch with local snowmobile clubs. Thanks to these energetic clubs, trails are well maintained and signposted. **Snowmobile rentals** are available at The Birches Resort, Box 41, Rockwood 04478, tel. (207) 534-7305, but it's wise to call ahead and reserve; cost is $100-150 a day, including helmets and handlebar and thumb warmers.

Downhill Skiing

Compared to the world-class ski resorts south and west of here, the **Big Squaw Mountain Resort,** Rt. 6/15, P.O. Box 430, Greenville 04441, tel. (207) 695-1000, is small potatoes, but if slopeside frills and mega-prices don't fit your budget, here's your ticket. Best of all, we're not talking wimpy bunny slopes; there's a challenge for every alpine skill level. Summit views of Moosehead Lake are fantastic. Eighteen trails are served by a triple chairlift, a double chair, and a T-bar. Vertical drop is 1,750 feet. Snowmaking covers a third to half of the mountain. Big Squaw has had a roller-coaster career in recent years, and it's still in a transitional phase, but equipment maintenance has had high priority. The hotel decor is still leftover '60s, but how can you beat a cafeteria (open 9 a.m.-4 p.m.) with 25-cent sodas and $1.50 hot dogs? And more than 250 beds in slopeside lodging at $50 d on weekends. And—get this—weekday adult lift tickets for $15.

In summer, the double chairlift whisks you up for that terrific view, but the lift tends to operate on a rather erratic schedule. You'll need to call to check or ask at the chamber of commerce. The ski area is just off Rt. 6/15, on the west side of Moosehead Lake.

Cross-Country Skiing

The Birches Resort, Box 41, Rockwood 04478, tel. (207) 534-7305, has 30 miles of groomed cross-country-ski trails winding through an 11,000-acre nature preserve. Cost is $8 adults,

$5 kids under 10. Ski rentals are available at The Birches Ski Touring Center. For lodging at The Birches, see "Sporting Camps" under "Accommodations," below—or escape to one of their remote, heated trailside yurts for $15-20 pp.

SHOPPING

If you're entering Greenville from the south, cresting the last hill you'll see on your right the **Indian Hill Trading Post,** Rt. 15, Greenville 04441, tel. (207) 695-2104, a frontier minimall with camping gear, an ATM machine, fishing and hunting licenses, souvenirs, and an IGA supermarket that sells ice, liquor, groceries, even live lobsters. It's open daily 7 a.m.-8 p.m., all year. It's right next to the chamber of commerce information center, where you'll want to stop anyway.

In downtown Greenville, **Maine Street Station,** Main St., Greenville 04441, tel. (207) 695-2375, carries a tasteful line of gifts, crafts, and souvenirs, including baskets and Adirondack furniture. You can't miss it: there's a giant moose sculpture out front. It's open daily 8 a.m.-5 p.m., mid-May to mid-October. In winter, it's mostly open weekends.

FESTIVALS AND EVENTS

Late January's **Down East Sled Dog Races** brings two days of races, plus special sideline activities, to Greenville.

Moosemainea, an annual, month-long, moose-oriented festival sponsored by the Moosehead Lake Region Chamber of Commerce, combines canoe, rowboat, and mountain-bike races; family events; a parade; a craft fair; moose safaris; even a best-moose-photo contest. Register your own moose sightings on a huge map at the chamber of commerce. Events take place in Greenville and Rockwood mid-May to mid-June.

Greenville's **Fourth of July** celebration includes a huge fireworks display capping daytime community events.

The first full weekend in September, the **International Seaplane Fly-In Weekend** is a four-day event drawing seaplanes from all over New England for public breakfasts, a two-day craft fair, flightseeing, and more. At Greenville and Greenville Junction.

ACCOMMODATIONS

The Greenville area has about 2,000 beds for visitors, so even if you arrive on the spur of the moment, you're likely to find a place to sleep as long as you're flexible. August is a busy month; the September fly-in weekend is crowded, as is the fall-foliage season. Winter brings out snowmobilers by the dozens; rooms can be scarce. From mid- to late May, before the black-flies emerge, Greenville is uncrowded; some back roads may still be tank traps, and the weather will be cool, but it's a peaceful time to be here.

Country Inns

Talk about an oasis! Elegance and comfort are bywords at Roger and Jennifer Cauchi's **The Lodge at Moosehead Lake,** Lily Bay Rd., Greenville 04441, tel. (207) 695-4400, fax 695-2281, but the most astonishing feature is the furniture. Each of the five guest rooms in the main building has a theme—Trout, Loon, Moose, Totem, and Bear—and each has hand-carved beds and mirrors, plus lots of accessories, to carry it out. All but the Trout have dramatic views of Moosehead Lake. Jacuzzis and camouflaged VCRs are in each room, as well as in the three bi-level carriage-house suites—Allagash, Baxter, and Katahdin. In Allagash and Baxter, lumber-era boom chains hold swaying queen-size beds with incredible lake views; lots of elegantly rustic twig furniture completes the picture. Don't worry—it works. No smoking, no small children. All this of course comes with a price: lodge rooms are $175-250 d, suites are $250-350 d. In winter, gourmet dinners are included. The inn, open all year, is two and a half miles north of downtown Greenville.

Pretend you're the guest of a lumber baron at the **Greenville Inn,** Norris St., P.O. Box 1194, Greenville 04441, tel./fax (207) 695-2206 or (888) 695-6000, a gray-blue Victorian occupying a prime intown hilltop. Completed in 1895, the building has incredible woodwork, Tiffany-style lamps, and myriad other elegant details on the ground floor. Five second-floor rooms and a

suite (private baths), a more rustic Carriage House suite, and six cottages are $115-185 d late June to late September, $125-195 d late September to mid-October, and $85-165 d other months. Cottages have mountain views; several inn rooms have water views. No smoking, no pets. No children under seven in inn rooms. The generous breakfast buffet has a European flair. The inn's cuisine deserves the raves it receives; entrées are $16-20. Specialties are seafood and game—all superbly prepared and served in three lovely dining rooms (two with views of the sunset). Dinner is 6-9 p.m., May through October. Be sure to reserve ahead, especially in midsummer and fall, and save room for dessert. The inn is open all year; dinner is available for guests off season only by advance reservation.

On First Roach Pond in downtown Kokadjo ("population not many"), **Northern Pride Lodge,** Lily Bay Rd., HC 76, Box 588, Kokadjo 04441, tel. (207) 695-2890, was built by a lumber magnate in 1896. Common areas have handsome woodwork, antiques, and a slate floor; less ornate are the five first- and second-floor guest rooms ($80 d, including breakfast; shared baths; kids 12 and under are half price). Opt for the American Plan ($35 extra pp). Barb Lucas prepares superb gourmet dinners. Jeff Lucas is a skilled fly fisherman, and both are attentive yet informal hosts. The attractive dining room is open to the public by reservation Fri.-Mon. 5-9 p.m. Waterfront campsites on the five-acre grounds are $16 d, $2 extra for dogs. Canoe rentals are $16 a day, mountain bikes are $35 a day. Eighteen miles north of Greenville and across from the Kokadjo Trading Post, Northern Pride is open all year.

B&Bs

With much the same spectacular lake view as The Lodge at Moosehead, but in a lower price range, **The Devlin House,** Lily Bay Rd., P.O. Box 1102, Greenville 04441, tel. (207) 695-2229, is a comfortable, air-conditioned three-room bed-and-breakfast with private baths and TVs. Rates are $75-125 d; pets and children are allowed. No smoking. Open all year, but call ahead off season.

Half a block from Main Street is the turreted Victorian **Pleasant Street Inn,** Pleasant St.,

P.O. Box 1261, Greenville 04441, tel. (207) 695-3400. Eight rooms (private baths) are $75 d mid-May through October and $65 d November to mid-May; breakfast is a treat. No pets, no children under 12; smoking only on the expansive porch. Open all year.

Views are fabulous from **The Lakeview House Bed and Breakfast,** Lakeview Ave., East Cove, P.O. Box 524, Greenville 04441, tel. (207) 695-3543, run by longtime Greenville innkeepers Dick and Concetta Edwards. In 1997, they restored this 1887 Victorian farmhouse to provide three attractive guest rooms with private baths ($85-105 d). No pets, no smoking, no children under 12 without prior approval. Open May through October.

Motels

The **Kineo View Motor Lodge,** Rt. 15, P.O. Box 514, Greenville 04441, tel. (207) 695-4470 or (800) 659-8439, three miles south of Greenville, sits on a prime hilltop with a dead-on view of Mount Kineo and gorgeous sunsets. Opened in 1993, the modern, three-story motel has 12 good-size rooms for $65-75 d, including free continental breakfast Memorial Day weekend to mid-October; $59-69 d (no breakfast) other months. Innkeepers Diane and George Edmondson are especially cordial, and this is a great place to bring kids—lots of acreage to run around, including nature trails. Rooms have phones, TV, and private decks. Outside are picnic tables and a grill; the windowed ground floor has a hot tub for guests' use. Kineo View, open all year, is half a mile east of Rt. 15.

Two miles closer to Greenville than Kineo View, with the best hilltop view of Moosehead Lake itself, the **Indian Hill Motel,** Rt. 15, P.O. Box 327, Greenville Junction 04442, tel. (207) 695-2623 or (800) 771-4620, is a more typical one-story motel with 15 rooms for $50-60 d. Good-size rooms have phones, cable TV, and that splendid view. In the commercial complex across Rt. 15 are a supermarket and the chamber of commerce. Open May to mid-November.

You're practically *in* the lake at **Chalet Moosehead,** Birch St., P.O. Box 327, Greenville Junction 04442, tel. (207) 695-2950 or (800) 290-3645. The two-story motel has seven standard rooms at $65 d in season, $60 d off season; eight two-room efficiencies are $72 d in

season, $65 d off season. Kids five and under stay free; pets are $5. All rooms have cable TV, phones, and views of the lake. Dock space is free if you bring your own boat, and guests have access to canoes, a paddleboat, gas grills, and a private swimming area. Open all year.

Small Cottage Colonies

In Rockwood, 20 miles north of Greenville, on Moosehead's west shore, are three well-run small cottage colonies—nothing fancy, but well sited. **Abnaki Housekeeping Cottages,** P.O. Box 6, Rockwood 04478, tel. (207) 534-7318, fax 534-7434, has five white two- and three-bedroom housekeeping cottages for $342-510 a week, including linens; one-week minimum in July and August, two-day minimum other months. Open mid-May through September. **Rockwood Cottages,** Rt. 6/15, Box 176, Rockwood 04478, tel. (207) 534-7725, has eight two-bedroom housekeeping cottages, also painted white and fully equipped (even cable TV). Weekly rate in summer is $390 d; half price for kids under six. Daily rate is $65 d. Canoe rentals are $15 a day. Waterfront sauna, picnic tables, and swimming area. Open all year. The six modern cottages at **Sundown Cabins,** Rt. 6/15, Box 129, Rockwood 04478, tel. (207) 534-7357, fax 534-2285, are close to the road yet comfortably quiet. Weekly rates for one- and two-bedroom units are $350-395 d; large two- and three-bedroom cottages are $495-595 for four. One-week minimum July, August, and November; three-night minimum other months. Open all year.

Sporting Camps

Nailing down a category for **The Birches Resort,** P.O. Box 41, Rockwood 04478, tel. (207) 534-7305 or (800) 825-9453, isn't easy, because this family-owned operation has a finger in every pie—from lodging to first-rate dining to year-round recreational activities. The views, over the lake and Mount Kineo, are fantastic. Set the alarm to catch the sunrise.

The **main lodge** has four small, attractive second-floor rooms (shared baths; two rooms have water-view decks) at $40-75 d June-Sept., $35-70 other months. Fifteen rustic, sporting-camp-style **log cabins** (one, two, or four bedrooms), most with lakeside porches, are $90-

210 per cabin June-Sept., $75-180 other months. Pets in cabins are $5 extra. **Cabin tents and yurts** are $15-22 pp and share a shower house. From Memorial Day weekend through Columbus Day, American Plan rates are available for cabin, lodge, and cabin-tent guests—a good idea. You're a healthy drive from Greenville's restaurants, but the cuisine here competes favorably.

The lake-view **dining room**—featuring a humongous moose head, a stone fireplace, and a cedar-strip canoe suspended from the rafters—is open to guests and the public May-Oct. for breakfast and dinner (dinner reservations are essential; this place packs 'em in.) Prime ribs are a specialty. A limited lunch menu is served from the patio grill. From January through March, snowmobile season, buffet dinners are served daily; breakfast and lunch can be ordered ahead.

Besides whitewater rafting, snowmobiling, and cross-country skiing, The Birches organizes Sport-Yak excursions, ropes course, lake cruises, kayak lessons, gear rentals, sea-kayak ecotours, and ice fishing. By the time you arrive, they'll have added something else. Send for the current brochure. The Birches Resort is on an unpaved road beyond the center of Rockwood; turn right off Rt. 6/15 at the Moose River, cross the river and watch for signs on the right.

Genial hosts Andy and Carol Stirling are the third generation now running **West Branch Ponds,** Kokadjo, mailing address Box 1153, Greenville 04441, tel. (207) 695-2561, one of the quintessential old-time sporting camps. Lining the shore of First West Branch Pond, overlooking White Cap Mountain, are eight classically rustic cabins that have seen better days. But there *is* indoor plumbing. When the bell rings for meals, guests head to the 1890 lakeside lodge and vacuum up the hearty cuisine described in one upscale national magazine as "simple, soulful Yankee cooking." Thursday nights, the prime-rib dinner ($12 pp) is open to the public by reservation. Most guests stay for a week, and the many repeats make it tough to book space, but the daily rate is $60 pp American Plan. Fly fishing, hiking, and canoeing are the major pursuits here; the Stirlings don't stay open for hunting season. Take Lily Bay Rd. from Greenville 17 miles; turn right onto an unpaved road (signposted for West Branch Ponds)

and go 10 more miles. It's open May through September.

Campgrounds and Campsites

The **Maine Forest Service** supervises and maintains free campsites, with fireplaces and outhouses, many on the shores of Moosehead Lake. Most are accessible only by boat—first come, first served. For information, contact the Maine Forest Service office in downtown Greenville, tel. (207) 695-3721.

At the northern end of Moosehead Lake, about five and a half miles south of the Golden Road, **Seboomook Wilderness Campground,** Seboomook Village, mailing address HC 85, Box 560, Rockwood 04478, tel. (207) 534-8824, has 84 wooded and open tent, RV, and cabin sites, many right on the water. All are very rustic. Request a site on the eastern side, away from the longterm RV area. Facilities include a small, shallow beach, free hot showers, and a grocery store/lunch counter. Campsites are $8 a day (per family, or four adults), lean-tos are $10 (same head count), RV sites are $12. Gas-lighted log cabins (bring your own linens) are $45-55 a day May-Sept., $55-60 a day the rest of the year. Two-night minimum on weekends; weekly rates are lower. Seboomook's cabins and store are open all winter for snowmobilers and cross-country skiers. The campground is about 28 unpaved miles north of Rockwood; you'll need to pay a user fee ($8 for non-Maine plates, $4 for Maine plates) at Bowater/Great Northern's Twenty-Mile Checkpoint just before Pittston Farm.

Seasonal Rentals

Sharon Pelletier's **Vacation Rentals, Inc.,** P.O. Box 1346, Greenville 04441, tel. (207) 695-2327, has an especially wide selection of weekly and monthly rentals—remote log cabins, comfortable cottages, and modern condos. Weekly cabin and cottage rates range $350-1,500, depending on amenities; condos are $400-1,000, depending on bedroom count. Most accept pets.

Folsom's Air Service, P.O. Box 507, Greenville 04441, tel. (207) 695-2821, fax 695-2434, rents rustic housekeeping cottages and camps on remote fishing ponds, and they'll fly you in with your gear.

FOOD

The range of dining experiences in and near Greenville is amazingly broad. From pure rustic to local color to upwardly mobile to gourmet cuisine—take your pick. No need to starve here.

Inexpensive to Moderate

Across from the *Katahdin* steamboat dock, **Auntie M's Family Restaurant,** N. Main St., Greenville 04441, tel. (207) 695-2238, is a throwback to the 1950s—a locally colorful, casual hangout with booths and tables. A peanut butter and jelly sandwich goes for $1.50, a hearty bowl of homemade chili for $3.25, a side order of gravy for 50 cents. Breakfast is served all day. For something really different, order a stack of chocolate-chip pancakes ($3.95). Open all year, 5 a.m.-9 p.m. in summer, to 7 p.m. in winter.

Also popular among local residents for breakfast and lunch is the **Boom Chain Restaurant,** Main St., Greenville 04441, tel. (207) 695-2602, named after part of the gear that hauled timber down the lake. Ever had beans-and-toast ($1.25) for breakfast? No liquor license. It's open all year, daily 6 a.m.-2 p.m.

The emphasis at **Flatlander's,** Pritham Ave., Greenville 04441, tel. (207) 695-3373—a bright, clean, modern place—is on creative home cooking. Kids go for the 12-inch "long dogs," their parents might prefer Flatlander's ribs. The specialty is marinated, steam-roasted chicken—and there are vegetarian and heart-healthy options. Open May through March, daily 11 a.m.-9 p.m. In midwinter, it's usually closed Monday.

In Kokadjo, eighteen miles up the east side of the lake, is the **Kokadjo Trading Post,** Lily Bay Rd., Kokadjo, mailing address Box 1210, Greenville 04441, tel. (207) 695-3993, where a sign next to the door reads Parking for Italians Only. Fred and Marie Candeloro opened this chummy Italian-restaurant-cum-convenience-store in 1993, and they've gained a loyal following. In winter, the parking lot is wall-to-wall snowmobiles. Marie's fantastic seafood chowder isn't always on the menu, but order it if it is. The operation is open all year: Mon.-Thurs. 6 a.m.-8 p.m. and Fri.-Sun. 6 a.m.-11 p.m. in summer; Sun.-Thurs. 8 a.m.-8 p.m. and Fri.-Sun. 7 a.m.-11 p.m. in winter.

And then there's Maine's original **Road Kill Café,** Rt. 6/15, P.O. Box 1307, Greenville Junction 04442, tel. (207) 695-2230, on the other side of the lake. Started in 1992, it's maintained its wacky sense of humor with a zany waitstaff and a menu and decor to match. The sign in the restroom ("The Bushes") says, Employees and raccoons must wash hands. Smiling all the way to the bank, the owners have created clones in half a dozen other New England locations. The food is average, but what the heck—for $8 you get a burger-and-fries billed as The Interstate Pile-Up and a Pail o' Nightcrawlers. There's lots of logo merchandise, or order it by mail. The café is open daily 11:30 a.m.- 10 p.m. in summer, 11:30 a.m.-8:30 p.m. the rest of the year.

Also in Greenville Junction, with fantastic lake views, is **Kelly's Landing,** Rt. 6/15, P.O. Box 336, Greenville Junction 04442, tel. (207) 695-4438 or (800) 498-9800 in Maine. Hearty home cooking is the rule, and you can eat on the deck in good weather. The big, open dining room, its walls lined with hunting trophies, is open daily, all year, for breakfast, lunch, and dinner. Entrées run $6-15, with a kids' menu available. The Sunday breakfast buffet is a mega-bargain at $6. There's always a crowd here, and boaters can tie up at the dock.

Trust me. If you continue on up Rt. 6/15 from Greenville, 20 miles to Rockwood, and then another 20 miles on an unpaved road, you're guaranteed to have an adventure at **Pittston Farm,** Seboomook Rd., T2 R4, mailing address P.O. Box 525, Rockwood 04478, radiophone (207) 695-2821. You may even spot some moose on the way; drive defensively. (A few miles before the farm, you'll need to stop at the Bowater/ Great Northern checkpoint and pay the road fee: $4 for Maine plates, $8 for non-Maine plates.) This unincorporated territory, officially called the Pittston Academy Grant, once was a major center for timber operations along the Penobscot River. Now the 100-acre riverside farm is known as *the* place to go—by car, flying service, or snowmobile—for meals fit for lumberjacks. Dress down (suspenders will fit right in) and prepare to line up for dinner and eat at a big table; buffet-style meals start daily at 5 and 6:30 p.m., all year. Cost is $8.95, and plates are huge; seconds are allowed. BYOL. It's hearty home cooking, definitely meat-oriented, and you won't eat alone. Owner Ken Twitchell and his helpers feed as many as 300 people a day on a holiday weekend; snowmobilers pile in here by the dozens. Reservations are advisable. Breakfast (great doughnuts) and lunch (buffet on Friday and Saturday in summer) are also available. Basic accommodations in the farmhouse (shared baths) go for $40 pp, including meals. Don't miss the resident tropical birds, and don't fall for the $10 bill polyurethaned to the floor.

INFORMATION AND SERVICES

The regional information center is the **Moosehead Lake Region Chamber of Commerce,** Indian Hill, Rt. 15, P.O. Box 581, Greenville 04441, tel. (207) 695-2702, fax 695-3440, on a panoramic hilltop as you enter Greenville from the south. The modern office has **public restrooms** and a gift shop stocked with such moose-erie as T-shirts, moose magnets, bumper stickers, and boxer shorts. It's open daily 10 a.m.-4 p.m., Memorial Day through September, then Monday and Thurs.-Sat. 10 a.m.-4 p.m., October to May. The chamber annually publishes a very helpful, free *Visitors Guide.* The Greenville Downtown Merchants Association produces a map showing locations of shops, restaurants, and lodgings in the small downtown area.

DeLorme Mapping produces a widely available foldout *Map & Guide of Moosehead Lake* ($5.95) with excellent detail and information on sightseeing and recreational pursuits.

The **Shaw Public Library,** N. Main St., Greenville 04441, tel. (207) 695-3579, its archives loaded with North Woods lore, is open all year, Mon.-Wed. 2-5 p.m., Thursday 6-8 p.m., Friday 10 a.m.-6 p.m., and Saturday 10 a.m.-2 p.m.

Newspaper
The Moosehead Messenger, tel. (207) 695-3077 or (800) 696-3077, published every Wednesday, covers Greenville and points north.

Emergencies
Greenville is on the boundary of Penobscot and Piscataquis Counties; the Piscataquis County Sheriff, tel. (800) 432-7372, handles **police** duties. For an **ambulance,** call (207) 695-2223. To report a **fire,** call (207) 695-2570. In **Rockwood,** dial 911 for all three services.

State agencies with offices in Greenville are the **Maine Warden Service** (MWS), tel. (207) 695-3756, and the **Maine Forest Service** (MFS), Lakeview St., Greenville 04441, tel. (207) 695-3721. The Greenville MWS office, with jurisdiction for a fourth of Maine's acreage, undertakes at least one search-and-rescue mission a week. The MFS, besides fire-spotting duty, also is responsible for a number of public campsites in the region.

The **Charles A. Dean Memorial Hospital,** Pritham Ave., Greenville 04441, tel. (207) 695-2223, maintains a round-the-clock emergency room. Although the hospital is small, it's the first stop for remote-area trauma cases, such as injured hikers and snowmobile accident victims, so the staff is accustomed to emergency situations.

Public Restrooms
The Greenville area is more considerate than most in the matter of public restrooms. In Greenville, the **chamber of commerce office** has restrooms; in Greenville Junction, there are restrooms at **Junction Wharf;** in Rockwood, there are restrooms at the **public boat landing.** Lily Bay State Park has outhouses, but of course you'll have to pay the day-use fee to enter the park.

Getting Around
Three separate **flying services** operating small pontoon- or ski-equipped planes act as the lifelines to remote North Woods sporting camps, campsites, rivers, lakes, and ponds inaccessible overland. In some cases, road access exists, but you'll jeopardize your vehicle and your innards along the way. Veteran of them all is **Folsom's Air Service,** P.O. Box 507, Greenville 04441, tel. (207) 695-2821, fax 695-2434, based at the southeastern corner of Moosehead Lake. Founded in 1946, when everyone walked, canoed, or flew, Folsom's had a huge clientele. The Folsom's headquarters radiophone was their only link to the outside world. Now, with roads (albeit bumpy), snowmobiles, and cellular phones, the business has changed markedly,

but many visitors still opt for the convenience of the planes. Roundtrip rates to more than 60 locations range $50-300 pp; they'll even fly to Augusta, Bangor, and Portland. Canoe transport is also available (extra charge). **Currier's Flying Service,** Pritham Ave., Rt. 6/15, Greenville Junction 04442, tel. (207) 695-2778, and **Jack's Air Service,** Pritham Ave., Greenville 04441, tel. (207) 695-3020, based in downtown Greenville, also provide on-demand charter service to remote locales. All three firms have flat hourly rates if you want to create your own itinerary.

You don't need a plane to get to Kineo, but you will need a boat. First, drive the 20 miles along Rt. 6/15 to Rockwood, where the lake is narrowest—about 4,000 feet across. The *Kineo Launch,* a sturdy transport vessel, has been operating since the spring of 1997. It runs back and forth continuously from the Rockwood pub-

lic landing (on the village loop just off the highway) to Kineo. Just show up and climb aboard. Cost is $3 pp. **Rockwood Cottages,** tel. (207) 534-7725, operates an on-demand boat shuttle to Kineo for $5 pp roundtrip (two-person minimum). Call to arrange. Shuttle services operate late May to mid-October.

Many of the **roads** in the Greenville area are unpaved; paper-company roads tend to be the best maintained, because access is essential for their huge log trucks and machinery. But others, especially roads leading to sporting camps, can become tank traps in spring—April and May—and after a heavy downpour. Before setting out during those times—especially if you don't have a 4WD vehicle—be sure to check on road conditions. Ask the chamber of commerce, the Maine Forest Service, the county sheriff, or the sporting camp owners.

DOVER-FOXCROFT AREA

Located at the bottom of Piscataquis (Piss-CAT-uh-kwiss) County, Dover-Foxcroft is the county seat, hub for the surrounding towns of Milo, Brownville Junction, Sangerville, Guilford, Abbot, and Monson. Here's an area that's often overlooked—probably because Greenville, Moosehead Lake, and Baxter State Park are just up the road. But it's easy to spend a couple of exploring days here—notably for dramatic Gulf Hagas Reserve and Borestone Mountain Sanctuary, but also for a handful of out-of-the-way towns few visitors get to appreciate.

One town growing steadily in renown is Monson (pop. about 725), 20 miles northwest of Dover-Foxcroft and 15 miles south of Greenville. Incorporated in 1822, Monson has an old reputation and a new one. The old one comes from its slate quarries, first mined in the 1870s, which shipped slate around the nation for sinks, roof tiles, blackboards, and even urinals. A considerable Finnish community grew up here to work the quarries; their descendants still celebrate traditional holidays. Although the industry has declined, and only two companies still operate, Monson slate monuments adorn the gravesites of John F. Kennedy and Jacqueline Kennedy Onassis. You can still see an abandoned quarry pit on Pleasant Street, near Lake Hebron, on

the western side of town.

Monson's current fame comes from Appalachian Trail through-hikers, whose energetic grapevine carries the word about the town's hospitality to the rugged outdoorsfolk nearing the end of their arduous trek from Springer Mountain, Georgia. The Monson stopover comes just before the AT leg known as the "100 Mile Wilderness," so it's a place to regroup, clean up, and rev up for the isolated week or 10 days ahead.

Sangerville (pop. 1,375), incorporated in 1813, is the birthplace of the infamous Sir Harry Oakes, a colorful adventurer who acquired a fortune in Canadian gold mining. Murdered in bed in his Nassau (Bahamas) mansion in 1943, gazillionaire Oakes was interred in Dover-Foxcroft. His killer was never found. Also born in Sangerville was Sir Hiram Maxim, inventor of the Maxim gun.

SIGHTS, PARKS, PRESERVES, AND RECREATION

Low's Covered Bridge
In 1987, the raging Piscataquis River, swollen by spring rains, wiped out 130-foot-long Low's Covered Bridge, near Sangerville. Named after

settler Robert Low, the original bridge was built in 1830 and replaced in 1843 and 1857. The current incarnation, a well-made replica, reopened in 1990, at a cost of $650,000. It's one of only nine covered bridges now in Maine. Close to Rt. 16/6/15, the bridge is 3.7 miles east of Guilford and four and a half miles west of Dover-Foxcroft.

Katahdin Iron Works

Only a lonely stone blast furnace and a charcoal kiln remain at Katahdin Iron Works, the site of a once-thriving 19th-century community where iron mining produced 2,000 tons of ore a year and steam trains brought tourists to the three-story Silver Lake House to "take the waters" at Katahdin Mineral Springs. Today most visitors drive down the unpaved six and a half miles from Rt. 11 and stop just across the road, at the North Maine Woods **KI Checkpoint**, for hiking in Gulf Hagas Reserve. Entrance to the KI site (as it's known locally) is free, but the best way to appreciate the site and its fascinating history is to contact local historian/author Bill Sawtell, a fount of information, to schedule one of his fact-filled, 45-minute, $10-a-carload tours: **Bill Sawtell**, P.O. Box 272, Brownville 04414, tel. (207) 965-3971; best to call in the morning. Wear sturdy shoes to follow him around. The site is officially open Memorial Day to Labor Day. Katahdin Iron Works is 11.5 miles northwest of Brownville Junction.

Gulf Hagas Reserve

Hiking in and around Gulf Hagas Reserve, a spectacular 400-foot-high, three-and-a-half-mile-long wooded, rocky gorge along the West Branch of the Pleasant River, requires registering first at the **KI Checkpoint,** tel. (207) 965-8135, operated by North Maine Woods, the forest recreation-management association. (KI is short for Katahdin Ironworks.) The checkpoint is one of the entrances into the **KI Jo-Mary Multiple Use Forest,** a working forest over 200,000 acres. (Jo-Mary is the name of a legendary Indian chief.) The checkpoint is open 6 a.m.-8 p.m. (sometimes later on midsummer weekends), early May to Columbus Day. The staffers have maps of the reserve ($1) and KI Jo-Mary ($2). Access is $7 for nonresidents, $4 for Maine residents; seniors and kids under 15 are free. No

bikes or ATVs can go beyond this point. Camping at one of the 60 scenic primitive sites In this area costs an extra $5 per night (residents or nonresidents). It's wise to call the checkpoint ahead of time to reserve one of the sites, which have outhouses, picnic tables, and fire rings. The policy is carry-in, carry-out. There's also a commercial campground here.

Drive about seven miles from the checkpoint to one of the two parking areas; remember that logging trucks have the right-of-way on this road. As you walk from your vehicle toward the gulf, you'll go through **The Hermitage,** a 35-acre Nature Conservancy preserve of old-growth pines. Gulf Hagas Reserve, a National Natural Landmark, is no cakewalk. Almost weekly, rangers have to rescue injured or lost hikers who underestimate the terrain. Ledges are narrow, with 100-foot dropoffs, and rain can make them perilous. Leave rambunctious children at home; the section beyond **Screw Auger Falls** is particularly dangerous for kids under 12. Wear waterproof boots—you have to cross a stream to gain access to the reserve.

Caveats aside, the hike is fantastic—especially mid-September to early October, when the leaves are gorgeous and the bugs have retreated. Carry a compass and a flashlight and allow 6-8 hours for the 8.3-mile canyon circuit (although there are shortcuts if you tucker out before the end). Most hikers do the loop clockwise. North Maine Woods trails are blue-blazed; a spur of the AT is white-blazed. The trails are open mid-May to late October, but atypical weather can affect the schedule. The checkpoint is 11.5 miles northwest of Brownville Junction (six and a half miles northwest of Rt. 11).

Peaks-Kenny State Park

Get organized to arrive at Peaks-Kenny State Park, Sebec Lake Rd., Dover-Foxcroft 04426, tel. (207) 564-2003, well before 11 a.m. on weekends in June, July, and August—after that, you may be turned away or have to wait. This particularly scenic park on 14-mile-long Sebec Lake has 50 picnic sites, a playground, lifeguard-staffed sand beach, nine miles of hiking trails, an amphitheater for special nature programs, and 56 campsites. On July and August weekends, camping reservations are essential (two-night minimum). Call (207) 287-3824, using

MasterCard or Visa. Day-use admission is $2 adults, 50 cents children 5-11; seniors and kids under five are free. Nonresident camping fees are $16 per site per night, plus the reservation fee of $2 per site per night; no hookups. Leashed pets are allowed. The park is open 7 a.m.-10 p.m., May 15-Sept. 30. Take Rt. 153 north from Dover-Foxcroft, about six miles, following signs for the park.

Borestone Mountain Sanctuary

Owned and maintained by the National Audubon Society, Borestone Mountain Sanctuary, Elliotsville Rd., Elliotsville Township, mailing address P.O. Box 112, Monson 04464, tel. (207) 631-4050, is an easy-to-moderately difficult family climb with ample rewards at the top: wildflowers, space for a picnic, and full-circle views, including Lake Onawa, from twin peaks a quarter of a mile apart. Foliage season is especially dramatic in the 1,600-acre sanctuary (it's some-

Appalachian Trail marker

times erroneously spelled Boarstone). Allow four hours for the four-mile roundtrip, including a halfway-up stop at the Sunrise Pond visitor center. Ahead are the quaintly named Midday and Sunset Ponds. Pets are not permitted. Admission is $2 adults, $1 children 6-18. The sanctuary is officially open June-Oct., 8 a.m. to sunset. From Rt. 15 at the northern edge of Monson, take the Elliotsville Rd. (partly unpaved) northeast eight and a half miles to the trailhead.

Lake Onawa

Four-mile-long Lake Onawa is the mountain-ringed setting for the charming hamlet of **Onawa,** once linked to civilization only by train. Then came the road, and passenger service ceased, leaving Onawa as a summer colony with a year-round population of three. A prime attraction here is an incredible 126-foot-high wooden railroad trestle (pronounced "trussel" around here) that challenges even bravehearted souls. Acrophobes, forget it. There's a walkway alongside, but it's still scary; don't attempt it on a windy day. Bungee jumpers haven't yet discovered the trestle, but it *was* featured in one of Stephen King's films. During World War II, the trestle was protected by black security guards, among them Edward Brooke. The 1,400-foot-long trestle, officially the Ship Pond Stream Viaduct, soars over Ship Pond Stream, at the southern end of the lake, about half a mile beyond the cluster of cottages. To reach Onawa, follow directions (above) for Borestone Mountain, but turn right off Elliotsville Rd. at the Big Wilson Stream bridge, then the next left onto Onawa Road. Continue about three miles to the settlement.

Northern Maine Riding Adventures

Under the heading of Northern Maine Riding Adventures, Notch Rd., P.O. Box 16, Dover-Foxcroft 04426, tel. (207) 564-3451, Maine Guides Judy Cross-Strehlke and Bob Strehlke operate pack trips, summer camps, a riding school, and a therapeutic program out of their 65-acre farm. The most popular day-trip is the Hi-Cut Trail Ride ($100 pp), suitable for every level of rider (age nine and above) and ascending 900 feet to panoramic views. The ride takes five or six hours, including time to down a box lunch along the way. Group minimum is two; maximum is 10. Campsites are available on the farm. No credit cards. Prices for other trips range from $55 (half day) to $1,080 (five days, including lodging). It's pricey, since kids pay as much as adults, but you'll have a well-run adventure. Reservations are required for the trips, which operate mid-May to late October, depending on weather and demand. The farm is six miles southeast of Dover-Foxcroft and six miles northeast of Dexter, off Rt. 7.

FESTIVALS AND EVENTS

The last Saturday in April, the early-season **Piscataquis River Canoe Race** covers eight miles of mostly flat water, between Guilford and Dover-Foxcroft. An hour-long, family-oriented race goes under Low's Covered Bridge. Start time is 11 a.m., next to the Guilford Industries factory.

The **Piscataquis Valley Fair** takes place the fourth weekend in August. A family-oriented traditional county fair, it features agricultural exhibits, a pig scramble, a homemade ice-cream parlor, fireworks, and a carnival. At the Piscataquis Valley Fairgrounds, Fairview Ave. (just south of Rt. 6/15, east side of town), in Dover-Foxcroft.

SHOPPING

Three miles south of Dover-Foxcroft is the outlet shop for Victoria Rattigan's **Shard Pottery,** 10 Ames Rd., Rt. 15, Dover-Foxcroft 04426, tel. (207) 564-8687. The hand-thrown, hand-painted stoneware, sold in exclusive shops all over the country, comes in a dozen different designs—all with a Colonial flavor. Major colors are blue and green. The outlet adjoins the potterymaking operation. It's open Mon.-Fri. 8 a.m.-4 p.m. and Saturday 9 a.m.-3 p.m.

In the category of unconventional shopping is the downtown Dover-Foxcroft manufacturing operation for nationally renowned **Borealis Yurts,** 16 Vaughn St., P.O. Box 362, Dover-Foxcroft 04426, tel. (207) 564-3355, fax 564-2159. There are no factory tours, but if you envision a yurt in your future, be sure to call (weekdays 8 a.m.-4 p.m.) and ask to see one here. Manufacturing is done in the funky old brick Brown's Mill, once a hotbed for alternative-energy projects. Borealis owners John ("Bo") and Jeffrey Norris produce four different sizes (12-24 feet in diameter) of fabric-sided yurts, their designs a variation on the Mongolian/Kazak theme. Costs are in the $2,500-6,000 range. For the do-it-yourselfer, yurt kits are $2,300-5,300. Shipping is extra. The eco-conscious Norrises recycle their wood waste to local gardeners and craftspeople. Request a copy of their interesting brochure/newsletter.

ACCOMMODATIONS

B&Bs

Three second-floor guest rooms share one and a half baths at **The Foxcroft Bed & Breakfast,** 25 W. Main St., Rt. 15, Dover-Foxcroft 04426, tel. (207) 564-7720, Marie and Vaughn Fuller's comfortable 13-room 1847 Colonial home in downtown Dover-Foxcroft, centrally located between Bangor and Greenville. Marie and Vaughn are Maine natives, very knowledgeable about the area. Vaughn is an artist and former bush pilot. Count on meeting repeat customers here. Rooms are $50 d, including a full breakfast in the spacious kitchen. No pets. The Foxcroft is open all year.

The Carousel Bed & Breakfast, Back Brownville Rd., RFD 1, Box 81, Brownville 04414, tel. (207) 965-7741, an ideal base for hiking Gulf Hagas Reserve, has three first- and second-floor rooms (private and shared baths) for $40-45 d. Innkeeper Betty Friend also operates a bakery/café serving breakfast, lunch, dinner, and Sunday brunch in her comfortable hilltop home. Open all year.

Just beyond the Dover-Foxcroft area, but close enough, the **Brewster Inn,** 37 Zions Hill, Dexter 04930, tel. (207) 924-3130, is an attractively updated 19-room National Historic Register mansion once owned by Maine Governor Ralph Brewster. The B&B's six rooms and suites (private baths; $52-72 d) all have stories to tell. The knotty-pine Game Room Suite was the governor's private hideout, and guess who once slept in the Truman Room? Innkeepers Roberta Caswell and Mary Ellen Beal have done wonders with the gardens. Breakfast is generous continental. No pets, no smoking. Open all year. Dexter is 13 miles south of Dover-Foxcroft.

Hostel

Headquarters for Appalachian Trail through-hikers, a home-away-from-home, is the legendary **Shaw's Boarding Home,** Pleasant St., Monson 04464, tel. (207) 997-3597. To weary hikers, Pat and Keith Shaw's welcoming, no-frills operation feels like the Hyatt Regency. Short-haul hikers are also welcome, and snowmobilers in winter; couch potatoes will feel out of place. The Shaws can accommodate 26 guests in varied arrangements—private rooms in the main house ($20 pp), bunkhouse beds ($15 pp), and bunks in the adjoining barn ($12 pp). A lumberjack-quality breakfast is $4.50, supper is $8. For a fee, the Shaws provide shuttle and maildrop service and laundry facilities. The hostel is a block west of Main Street (Rt. 15). Open all year.

Sporting Camps

Amanda and Jerry Packard are the fourth generation now running the show at **Packard's Camps,** Sebec Lake, RFD 2, Box 176, Guilford 04443, tel. (207) 997-3300, making this the state's oldest sporting-camp dynasty. It's yet another classic sporting camp, begun in 1894 and now covering 100 acres at the northwest corner of Sebec Lake. Linens are provided in the 18 rustic one- to three-bedroom housekeeping cabins, but no meals are served. Weekly rates are $300-450; daily rates are $25 pp (two-night minimum) off season. Don't expect to drop by, though. You'll need to call months in advance for space in July and August, and you still might not get it. Some guests have been coming here for 60 years, and they book their next year's visit before they go out the door. Fifteen campsites ($15 a night) are available on the grounds. Motorboat rentals are $30 a day. No credit cards, no pets. Open early May through November. Take Rt. 150 to its end, 13 miles north of Guilford.

Camping

Within the boundaries of the KI Jo-Mary Multiple Use Forest is a single commercial campground, the **Jo-Mary Lake Campground,** Upper Jo-Mary Lake, TB R10 WELS, mailing address P.O. Box 329, Millinocket 04462, tel. (207) 723-8117 or 746-5512, located on the southern shore of five-mile-long Upper Jo-Mary Lake. Despite being remote, the campground has 60 sites, flush toilets, hot showers, laundry facilities, a snack bar, plenty of play space for kids, and a sandy beach. Sites are about $15 a night per family. In July and August, there's a Wednesday night beanhole bean supper (beans baked underground). The campground, open mid-May through September, is 15 miles southwest of Millinocket and 20 miles north of Brownville. From Brownville Junction, take Rt. 11 northwest about 15 miles, turn left onto an unpaved road and stop at the Jo-Mary Checkpoint. After paying the user fee ($7 for nonresidents, $4 for Maine residents; seniors and kids under 15 are free), continue six miles northwest to the campground.

FOOD

A popular local favorite, **The Covered Bridge Restaurant,** Rt. 15, RR 2, Box 2060, Dover-Foxcroft 04426, tel. (207) 564-2204, is just across the street from Low's Covered Bridge, midway between Dover-Foxcroft and Guilford. Dinner entrées—hearty home cooking—run $6-12. No liquor license, no credit cards. Open Tues.-Sun. 7 a.m.-7 p.m., all year.

If you feel like rubbing shoulders with AT through-hikers—especially in September, when they're close to finishing up—plan to have breakfast or lunch at the chummy **Appalachian Station Restaurant,** 1 Tenney Hill Rd., Rt. 15, Monson 04464, tel. (207) 997-3648. Plenty of local color here, too—what one patron calls "the real goddam thing." No smoking (natch), no liquor license, no credit cards. Open all year, Mon.-Fri. 6 a.m.-2 p.m., Saturday 6 a.m.-noon, Sunday 7 a.m.-12:30 p.m., as well as Friday for dinner 5-7 p.m.

INFORMATION AND SERVICES

Based in a riverside log cabin, the **Southern Piscataquis County Chamber of Commerce,** 100 South St., Rt. 7, P.O. Box 376, Dover-Foxcroft 04426, tel. (207) 564-7533, is open daily 9 a.m.-4 p.m., June through August; weekdays 9 a.m.-4 p.m. other months.

For information about Gulf Hagas Reserve and the KI Jo-Mary Multiple Use Forest, contact **North Maine Woods,** P.O. Box 421, Ashland 04732, tel. (207) 435-6213.

Newspapers

The *Piscataquis Observer,* tel. (207) 564-8355, published weekly in Dover-Foxcroft, covers this area thoroughly. The *Bangor Daily News* is the daily newspaper focusing on this area.

Emergencies

In **Dover-Foxcroft, Guilford, and Monson,** dial 911 for police, fire, or ambulance services. **Mayo Regional Hospital,** 75 W. Main St., Dover-Foxcroft 04426, tel. (207) 564-8401, has round-the-clock emergency care. The nearest major medical facility is **Eastern Maine Medical Center,** emergency room tel. (207) 973-8000, in Bangor.

Kennels

All Breed Groom and Board, Downs Rd., RFD 2, Box 640, Dover-Foxcroft 04426, tel. (207) 564-3656, boards both dogs ($7 a day) and cats ($4 a day). The kennel is open all year, Tues.-Sat. 8 a.m.-6 p.m., Sunday and Monday 8-10 a.m. and 4-6 p.m. It's on a side road north of Rt. 6/16, about midway between Dover-Foxcroft and Milo.1

AROOSTOOK COUNTY

Night Loon

Cry, loon, cry; we share the night
And your lone wailing over an empty lake
speaks for us all.

~Lucy Bell Sellers

BOB RACE

AROOSTOOK COUNTY

This is the Crown of Maine—at 6,500 square miles, Maine's largest county. When Mainers refer to "The County," this is the one they mean. Although Aroostook (a Micmac Indian word meaning "bright" or "shining") has plenty of wide-open space for its 82,000 residents, fully a fourth of them live in only two smallish cities, Presque Isle and Caribou.

Neat farmhouses and huge, half-buried potato-storage barns anchor vast, undulating patches of potatoes, broccoli, and barley. The sky seems to go on forever. Potato fields define The County—bright green in spring, pink and white in summer, dirt-brown and gold just before the autumn harvest. Native to South America, the potato is king here, where 92% of Maine's spuds grow on 78,000 acres. Maine is America's fifth- or sixth-largest producer (depending on the harvest), and Aroostook sod annually yields more than two billion pounds of the tubers, destined for shipment "downstate" and beyond.

Annual festivals in Fort Fairfield and Houlton celebrate the blossoms and the harvest; potatoes appear on every restaurant menu and family table; countless roadside stands peddle them by the bag; and high schools still close for two or three weeks in September so students (and teachers) can assist with the harvest. Even grade-schoolers used to fan out over the fields, though these days you'll find more teachers than students in the fields, since federal regulations require students to be over 16 to operate harvesting machines (tedious hand-digging is rare nowadays). No matter, though—to the younger kids, it still means school's out.

Aroostook County, like the rest of Maine, has its share of hills, forests, and waterways, but the most significant hills here—Quaggy Jo, Mars, Debouillie, Haystack, Number Nine—are startling. Almost accidental, they appear out of nowhere—chunks the glaciers seem to have overlooked. Thanks to them, you'll find authentic vertical hiking—although Aroostook's trails are more often horizontal, through marshlands and woodlands, and along abandoned railbeds.

Snowmobiling is a big deal here (one national magazine ranked The County's snowmobile trails second best in the country), and a huge boost to the local economy. Legions of snowmobilers (often called "sledders" locally) crisscross The County every winter, exploring 1,600 miles of the incredible Interstate Trail System (ITS). Lodgings and restaurants fill up and the fields and woods hum with horsepower. The region is enough to tempt almost anyone onto a snowmobile—for the chance to see and perhaps capture on film the beauty of a rural winter. Time was when snowmobilers had less-than-attractive reputations and accidents were rampant. Today, sledders span the social strata, and safety holds high priority (although serious accidents do still occur). For me, the primary drawback is still the engine noise, an inevitably irritating whine.

The County's agricultural preeminence sets it apart from the rest of Maine, but so does the Acadian culture of the northernmost St. John Valley, where the French dialect is unlike anything you'll ever hear in language classes (or even in France). Islands of Acadian or French culture exist in other parts of Maine, but it's in "the Valley" that you'll be tempted to pile on the pounds with such Acadian specialties as *poutine* (French fries with cheese and gravy), *tourtiere* (pork pie), and *tarte au saumon* (salmon tart).

Another unique ethnic enclave is Aroostook's pocket of Swedish culture, centered about eight miles northwest of Caribou, in New Sweden, and dating from the late 19th century. If you didn't realize you were driving out of Caribou, you'd know that you'd landed in New Sweden—the homes have a distinctly Scandinavian look, mailboxes carry Swedish names, and if you've traveled in Nordic countries, you'll feel instantly at home. But most visitors don't arrive here by accident. The last time I visited the historical museum, I encountered two Swedish descendants of local settlers. In the midst of a pilgrimage they'd been planning for years, they were excitedly poring over town documents for mention of their relatives.

Aroostook County's major brush with historic notoriety occurred in 1839, with the skirmish known as the Aroostook War. Always described by the adjective bloodless—since there were no casualties (other than a farmer accidentally downed by friendly fire)—the war was essentially a boundary dispute between Maine and New Brunswick that had simmered since 1784, when New Brunswick was established. The 1783 Treaty of Paris had set the St. Croix River as the Washington County line, but loopholes left the northernmost border ill-defined. Maine feared losing timber-rich real estate to Canada, and matters heated up when 200 burly militiamen descended on the region in early 1839 to defend the young state's territory. Some 3,000 troops ended up defending the Maine cause, and legendary war hero Gen. Winfield ("Old Fuss and Feathers") Scott was sent to Augusta for three weeks in March 1839 to negotiate the success-

ful truce. Following the "war," Aroostook was incorporated as a county, and by 1842 the Webster-Ashburton Treaty (sometimes also called the Treaty of Washington), negotiated by Daniel Webster and Lord Ashburton, brought a long-awaited peace that opened the area for stepped-up settlement. Among the remnants of the Aroostook War is a wooden blockhouse, now a National Historic Site, on the banks of the St. John River in Fort Kent.

As often occurs with remote rural areas, The County sometimes gets a bum rap (never from the snowmobiling crowd) among downstaters and others who've never been here. But it deserves notice—for the scenery if nothing else. Admittedly, it's a long haul—it's about as far as you can get from the rockbound coast—but you're guaranteed a totally different Maine experience.

FESTIVALS AND EVENTS

As with other parts of Maine, Aroostook County has frequent **public suppers** throughout the summer. Visitors are welcome, even encouraged (most suppers benefit a good cause), so check the papers, line up early, and enjoy the local food and color.

A snowmobile parade kicks off Fort Kent's five-day February **Can Am Crown International Sled Dog Races.** Special locations offer vantage points for watching teams competing in 60- and 250-mile races. A mushers' banquet is the finale. Fort Kent also hosts a Maine-style **Mardi Gras** in February or March (depending on the date of Ash Wednesday), four or five days of pre-Lenten festivities, including a snowmobile parade, dances, and family fun.

Everyone arrives at Island Falls the first Saturday in March on snowmobiles or cross-country skis for the **Log Drivers' Beanhole Bean Cookout,** a torchlight parade and cookout at Mud Pond, which is more popular than you'd expect.

Spring runoff generates the thrills for Houlton's **Meduxnekeag River Race,** usually the last Saturday in April.

New Sweden's Scandinavian **Midsommar** festival features music and dancing, Swedish food, and other Nordic events on the weekend closest to June 21. And Madawaska hosts the Franco-American **Acadian Festival,** with Acadian food, music, and dancing the last weekend in June.

The four-day **Houlton Fair** includes a carnival, a pig scramble, truck pulling, and craft and agricultural exhibits right around the Fourth of July. Ashland's Union Congregational Church hosts a hugely popular (two seatings) **Salmon Supper** the second Friday of July. Third week of July, Fort Fairfield's **Potato Blossom Festival** combines games, a raft race, a potato supper,

mashed-potato wrestling, a street dance, and a parade—all celebrating the surrounding fields carpeted with potato blossoms.

Agriculture exhibits, harness racing, live entertainment, and fireworks are all part of Presque Isle's **Northern Maine Fair,** the biggest country fair in this part of Maine, the first full week of August. Another celebration of the spud is Houlton's **Potato Feast,** featuring potato games, a doll parade, art and craft booths, a potato barrel rolling contest, and gala supper the last full weekend in August.

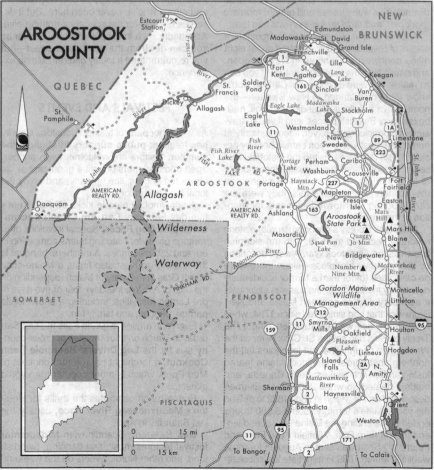

© MOON PUBLICATIONS, INC.

Sherman celebrates **Olde Home Days** on Labor Day weekend with an old-fashioned celebration including a parade, a chicken barbecue, and games.

INFORMATION

Besides individual chambers of commerce in half a dozen towns and cities, Aroostook Coun-

ty maintains a central information resource: **Northern Maine Development Commission,** P.O. Box 779, 2 S. Main St., Caribou 04736, tel. (888) 216-2463.

Information on the potato industry is available from the **Maine Potato Board,** 744 Main St., P.O. Box 669, Presque Isle 04769, tel. (207) 769-5061 or (800) 553-5516 in Maine, fax (207) 764-4148, the industry clearinghouse.

SOUTHERN AROOSTOOK COUNTY

Driving north on I-95, you find the interstate petering out at Houlton, about 120 miles northeast of Bangor. That may make this feel like the end of the earth, but it's actually just the beginning of Aroostook County.

Southern Aroostook, centered on Houlton, is a narrow north-south corridor, roughly straddling Rt. 1 from Danforth to Presque Isle. Among its communities are Island Falls, Oakfield, Bridgewater, and Mars Hill.

Hard by the New Brunswick border, Houlton (pop. about 6,800) has carved out its own niche as the shire town—and, according to the local historical society, "history's hiding place." Some of it is well hidden indeed, but not the Market Square Historic District, with its 28 turn-of-the-century National Historic Register buildings. Incorporated in 1834, Houlton is quiet and not often considered a "destination," but the county courts and other government offices are all located here, so there's a fair amount of activity—at least during the week.

North, south, and west of Houlton, you can canoe, swim, and fish in lakes, ponds, streams, and rivers; you can go golfing, birding, or camping; and you can visit small museums, shops, and the state's northernmost and easternmost covered bridge.

Less than 30 miles north of Houlton, Mars Hill is a strategic link in the International Appalachian Trail (IAT), a planned 600-mile extension of the Appalachian Trail from Katahdin in Baxter State Park to Mt. Carleton in New Brunswick and on to 4,160-foot Mt. Jacques Cartier, highest peak in Quebec province, ending at Cap Gaspé, on the Gulf of St. Lawrence. Parts of the trail have already been cut and blazed; much remains to be done, including approval

of rights-of-way. (For information on the IAT, call the trail's godfather, conservationist Richard Anderson, at (207) 774-2458.)

From Houlton, you can traverse Southern Aroostook, via Rts. 2 and 212, to reach north-south Rt. 11, but the best way to "do" Rt. 11 is to begin in Fort Kent and head south.

SIGHTS

Historic Houlton
Pick up the *Walking Guide to Market Square Historic District* at the Houlton chamber and wander the downtown, being sure to expand the route to include **Pierce Park.**

At the edge of the district is the 1903 White Memorial Building, a Colonial Revival residence that now houses Houlton's chamber of commerce and the **Aroostook County Historical and Art Museum,** 109 Main St., Houlton 04730. The museum—containing photos, books, vintage clothing, antique tools and housewares—is open mid-May to Labor Day, daily 11 a.m.-3 p.m. Other times, contact the chamber office, tel. (207) 532-4216, for an appointment.

Watson Settlement Bridge
About six miles north of Houlton, amid typical Aroostook farmland, stands Maine's northernmost covered bridge, the Watson Settlement Bridge, Carson Rd., Littleton 04730, built in the early 20th century and last used in 1985. The wood-truss bridge, straddling a branch of the Meduxnekeag River, feels quite forlorn, a remnant of the past just sitting here unused. Maine once had 120 or so covered bridges; only nine remain. To reach the bridge, take Foxcroft Rd.

from Rt. 2 and continue 6.1 miles; turn left onto Carson Road. If you're on your way north to Presque Isle, continue westward on Carson Rd. after the bridge to meet up with Rt. 1.

Flightseeing

Since 1966, **Larson Flying Service,** Houlton International Airport, Airport Rd., Houlton 04730, tel. (207) 532-9489 or (800) 696-3572, has had an efficient operation here. Professional pilot Terry Larson flies a four-seater Cessna low enough to spot wildlife, photograph the landscape, and survey fall foliage. Off to the west, you'll see Katahdin. Headphones allow passengers to hear his commentary over the noisy engine. Flights are weather-dependent and on demand. The office is open weekdays 7 a.m.-5 p.m., plus weekends during fall-foliage season. Cost is $75 an hour per planeload; 20-minute foliage flights are $45 per planeload. Parents will have to make a judgment call on this; most kids love it, some don't.

During World War II, Houlton's airport was the site of Maine's largest German POW camp —4,000 prisoners lived here in barracks while doing forced labor in lumber camps, canneries, potato farms, and paper mills.

On your way to or from the airport, notice the pond near the U.S. Customs office—linger here a bit, especially early or late in the day, and you may spot a moose.

Oakfield Railroad Museum

Seventeen miles west of Houlton, off I-95 Exit 60, is the Oakfield Railroad Museum, Station St., Oakfield 04743, tel. (207) 757-8575. Housed in a 1910 Bangor and Aroostook Railroad station and run by the Oakfield Historical Society, the museum contains an impressive collection of iron-horse memorabilia—guaranteed to fascinate kids of any age. Wheelchair-accessible. It's easy to get caught up in the enthusiasm of the railroad buffs who staff the museum. The gift shop carries all kinds of railroad-logo items. The museum, next to the fire station in Oakfield, is open Memorial Day weekend to Labor Day, Saturday noon-4 p.m. and Sunday 1-4 p.m. Admission is free, but donations are welcomed.

The Height of Fashion

Nostalgia reigns at the **John E. and Walter D. Webb Museum of Vintage Fashion,** Sherman St., Rt. 2, Island Falls 04747, tel. (207) 463-2404, off season P.O. Box 18, Hampden 04444, tel. (207) 862-3797, an unlikely hamlet where Frances Webb Stratton exhibits her lifetime accumulation of antique clothing and accessories —including 700 hats!—in a 14-room Victorian house. This museum is a sleeper, worth a detour. Docents (sometimes Mrs. Stratton) lead hour-long tours pitched to seniors and children. Kids love the "dress-up" children's clothes, antique toys, and military uniforms. Call ahead to reserve for afternoon tea and crumpets (extra charge). The museum is open June to early October, Mon.-Thurs. 10 a.m.-4 p.m., or by appointment. Admission is $3 adults, $2 seniors, $1 children under 12. Island Falls is about 25 miles southwest of Houlton.

Trolley Rides

Each Friday from Memorial Day weekend to Labor Day, beginning at noon, Shiretown Livery, tel. (207) 532-2242, operates free, one-hour horse-drawn trolley rides along Rt. 1 and into downtown Houlton. Two hefty Clydesdales pull the 12-passenger trolley—an unusual contraption resembling a pontoon boat on wheels. Look for the trolley at the state rest area on North St. (Rt. 1, at the edge of town) or flag it down anywhere along the route.

PARKS, PRESERVES, AND RECREATION

For canoeists and kayakers, the year's biggest event is the eight-mile spring-runoff **Meduxnekeag River Race,** held on a Saturday in late April or early May. Beginning in New Limerick, west of town, the route includes a short stretch of Class III rapids. Registration is $5 ($9 to get a souvenir T-shirt); fees benefit local Boy Scouts.

Pierce Park

Near downtown Houlton, mystery surrounds the origins of Pierce Park's quaint fountain with a centerpiece statue usually called "The Boy with the Leaking Boot." Donated to the town in 1916, it's one of two dozen or so similar statues in the United States and Europe. Legends have it coming from Germany or Belgium or Italy, but no record exists. Lower- and upper-level troughs provide fresh water for pets and their owners.

Benches surround the fountain. The Houlton Garden Club maintains the flowers in the park—a popular local spot for photographs, picnics, and coffee breaks.

Community Park
Also close to Houlton's downtown, Community Park has a great playground, tennis courts, picnic tables, and plenty of space for kids to run. The park is the venue for major outdoor concerts and the July Fourth fireworks extravaganza.

Garrison Park
Another picnic location is Garrison Park, off Upper Military St., Houlton, a reminder of the troops garrisoned here at the time of the 1838-39 Aroostook War. Only a few rundown buildings remain, but it's a fine place for a picnic. Take Rt. 2 toward the airport and turn left onto Garrison Rd., across from Drake's Dairy Bar.

Art Howell's Wildlife Refuge
At the **A.E. Howell Wildlife Conservation Center & Spruce Acres Refuge,** Lycette Rd., HC 61, Box 6, North Amity 04471, tel. (207) 532-6880 or 532-0676, Art Howell and his family have dedicated their land (64 acres) and their lives to conservation and wildlife rehabilitation, and their enthusiasm is contagious. Most creatures in the nonprofit refuge will be cared for and released, but permanent residents include a great horned owl and two bald eagles. The refuge layout is a bit higgledy-piggledy, but that adds to its charm. Kids under 12 can fish in stocked trout ponds, and families can explore five and a half miles of trails. If you have time, volunteer to lend a hand; there's always a need, and it's a rewarding experience. A gift shop carries T-shirts and posters. Admission is $3 adults, $2 seniors, and free for kids under 16. The season is May 1-Nov., but trails are open all year, for hiking or cross-country skiing. The refuge is just west of Rt. 1, 14 miles south of Houlton.

Gordon Manuel Wildlife Management Area
Just south of Houlton, the Gordon Manuel Wildlife Management Area, Hodgdon, no telephone, covers 5,592 acres of fields, woods, and marshland along the Meduxnekeag River. From Rt. 1, turn right (west) onto Hodgdon Rd.

and watch for Layton's Dairy Bar. Take the first left after Layton's onto the unpaved Horseback Road. Continue 1.7 miles and turn left at a narrow dirt road. Wind through the trees, about .2 mile, to a small parking area on the Meduxnekeag River. Watch for osprey, green herons, even bald eagles. You can launch a canoe or kayak (no motors allowed) and explore the area. The setting is particularly gorgeous during the fall-foliage season, but be forewarned that hunting is allowed here, so wear a blaze-or-ange vest and/or hat from mid-October through November.

If you don't have a canoe or kayak, and just want to do some birding, this is a particularly relaxing bike ride, even from Houlton. If you haven't packed a picnic, **T and S Market,** tel. (207) 532-6672, on Main St. in Hodgdon, has the best pizza in the whole area.

Golf
On a clear day, Baxter State Park's Katahdin is visible from **Va-Jo-Wa Golf Club,** 142-A Walker Settlement Rd., Island Falls 04747, tel. (207) 463-2128, a scenic 18-hole, par-72 course named after Vaughn, John, and Warren Walker. No starting times are needed and greens fees are moderate. Facilities include a restaurant and bar, plus a driving range. Open May-Oct., Va-Jo-Wa is five miles north of I-95, off Rt. 2, between Pleasant and Upper Mattawamkeag Lakes.

Southwest of Houlton is the nine-hole **Houlton Community Golf Club,** Drew's Lake Rd., New Limerick 04761, tel. (207) 532-2662, built on onetime potato fields in 1921. The setting is lovely, on the shores of Nickerson Lake; the lakefront clubhouse has a snack bar. Call for a starting time and bring a swimsuit; a dip in the lake feels great after a round of golf. The course is open mid-May to mid-October. Take Rt. 2A (Bangor Rd.) west and south of Houlton about three miles to Drew's Lake Rd. (also known as Nickerson Lake Rd.), continuing two and a half miles to the club.

A much newer nine-hole course is in Mars Hill, 28 miles north of Houlton, near the Bigrock ski area. The **Mars Hill Country Club,** York Rd., Mars Hill 04758, tel. (207) 425-4802, built in 1991, has a restaurant and is open June to mid-October. From Rt. 1A in Mars Hill, take Boynton Rd. east to York Road.

Fitness Center
Gym rats as well as neophytes will appreciate **Guiod's Fitness Center,** 70 Main St., Houlton 04730, tel. (207) 532-6905, equipped with stair steppers, treadmills, Nautilus machines, free weights, and lots more. The daily rate is $5 pp, $15 for a family of four. There's no pool, but showers and tanning are available. Open all year.

Winter Sports
Houlton is at the fringe of prime **snowmobiling** country. The crowds tend to head up the road to Presque Isle, Caribou, and the St. John Valley, but there are plenty of trails here, as well. For information on snowmobiling in the Houlton area, contact the chamber of commerce or the **Maine Snowmobile Association,** tel. (207) 622-6983, which can put you in touch with local snowmobile clubs. For information on **snowmobile trail conditions,** call (800) 880-7669.

When snowmobiling in the Houlton area, you'll notice on trail maps that some routes cross into Canada. Be sure you are carrying valid identification when you are anywhere near the border. The Houlton border crossing is open 24 hours.

On Mars Hill Mountain, about 28 miles north of Houlton, **Bigrock,** P.O. Box 518, Mars Hill 04758, tel. (207) 425-6711, 429-9743 or (800) 416-4339, is a small, family-oriented ski area with one chairlift, three Poma lifts, and 15 trails with a maximum elevation of 980 feet. Rentals, lessons, and lift tickets are a fraction of the prices in western Maine; nothing fancy here, but a fun place to play. Bigrock is signposted off Rt. 1, but you can't miss the mountain—a giant eruption on an otherwise-flat landscape.

ENTERTAINMENT

Presque Isle has a movie multiplex, but Houlton has the historic **Temple Cinema,** Market Sq., Houlton 04730, tel. (207) 532-3756, a two-screen (side-by-side) complex in the 1918 Masonic Hall.

First-run films are $4.50 adults, $2.50 seniors and children under 12; Tuesday night is bargain night ($2.50 for all tickets). Open all year.

SHOPPING

Not far from downtown Houlton, **Brown's Trading Post,** Ludlow Rd., Box 337, Houlton 04730, tel. (207) 532-2534, is an adventure in itself. This rustic grab bag of fishing, camping, and hunting gear has been a local landmark since 1973. George and Mary Brown are friendly sorts who can put their fingers on just the right rod or lure or topo map. Plus they have freeze-dried food and jelly beans. Not to mention horseshoeing services. It's open all year, Mon.-Thurs. 7 a.m.-7 p.m., Friday and Saturday 7 a.m.-9 p.m., and Sunday 10 a.m.-2 p.m. (closed Sunday in summer). Considered The County's largest sporting-goods store, Brown's is 1.7 miles west of Rt. 1; turn at Wal-Mart.

Just north of the Shiretown Motor Inn is **Volumes,** North Rd., Rt. 1, Houlton 04730, tel. (207) 532-7727, an especially user-friendly used-paperback emporium. Besides the 40,000 or so books, well categorized, you'll find Maine-made everything: jewelry, wooden items, T-shirts, wind chimes, condiments, and even music. Volumes is open daily all year, Mon.-Sat. 9 a.m.-6 p.m. (to 8 p.m. Friday) and Sunday noon-5 p.m.

About 22 miles north of Houlton, a small showroom piled high with variations on the barrel theme is the retail shop for the **Bradbury Barrel Company,** Rt. 1, P.O. Box A, Bridgewater 04735, tel. (207) 429-8141 or (800) 332-6021, a decades-old firm with an international clientele. The hand-built white-cedar products make great planters, storage bins, toy buckets, or catchalls. The showroom is open all year, Mon.-Thurs. 7 a.m.-4 p.m. Call a few days ahead to schedule a half-hour tour of the company's operations.

BOB RACE

ACCOMMODATIONS

Lodgings are not Houlton's strong suit, but at least there are a couple of choices. Close to downtown Houlton, the 52-room **Shiretown Motor Inn,** North Rd., Rt. 1, RR 3, Box 30, Houlton 04730, tel. (207) 532-9421 or (800) 441-9421, fax (207) 532-3390, lacks atmosphere, but it's convenient to I-95, Rt. 1, and the Trans-Canada Highway. Health-club facilities, including an indoor pool, are free for guests and open 10 a.m.-9:45 p.m. Rooms have phones, cable TV, and a/c; $50-74 d. No pets. Request a back-facing room if you're particularly noise-sensitive. The adjoining **Atrium Restaurant,** tel. (207) 532-4085, serving reasonably priced continental fare (entrées $10-17) amid lots of greenery, is open Mon.-Fri. 11 a.m.-2 p.m. and Mon.-Sat. 5-10 p.m.; the lounge stays open until 12:45 a.m. Dinner reservations are a good idea, as this is Houlton's best all-around restaurant. The complex is open all year.

A smaller, less expensive operation on the same stretch of Rt. 1 is **Ivey's Motor Lodge,** Rt. 1, P.O. Box 241, Houlton 04730, tel. (207) 532-4206 or (800) 244-4206 in Maine, with 24 good-size rooms ($46-56 d) and cable TV. It's open all year.

If you're headed from Houlton to Presque Isle, need a really cheap sleep, and are male, stop at **Smith's Farm,** Rt. 1, Blaine, tel. (207) 429-8549 or 429-9410, mailing address P.O. Box 1014, Mars Hill 04758, 26 miles north of Houlton (and just south of Mars Hill). This is essentially a truck stop with a clean upstairs bunkroom; eight beds go for $10 each. Showers are available round-the-clock ($1 with your own towel, $2 if you use theirs), as is a coin-operated washer. An adjacent restaurant serves up hearty, trucker-endorsed food—open Mon.-Sat. 5 a.m.-11 p.m., Sunday 7 a.m.-11 p.m. And in late summer, a fill-up at the gas pump will net you a bonus: free broccoli.

FOOD

Miscellanea

It was no great loss when Dunkin Donuts left Houlton in 1996; **Donut Country,** 79 Bangor St., Rt. 2A, Houlton 04730, tel. (207) 532-7386, was still there. And still making the *best* blueberry doughnuts. This mom-and-pop operation is open Mon.-Sat. 5:30-11 a.m.

In downtown Houlton, the **Shiretown Bakery and Coffee Shoppe,** 53 Main St., Houlton 04730, tel. (207) 532-2218, draws a loyal local crowd, especially around coffee-break time. It's open Mon.-Fri. 6 a.m.-5 p.m. and Saturday 7 a.m.-3 p.m. (lunch is served 11 a.m.-2 p.m.).

For some unexplained reason, the Houlton area seems to have more dairy bars (ice-cream takeouts) per capita than anywhere else in Maine. The best is **Drake's Dairy Bar,** Upper Military St., Rt. 2, Houlton 04730, tel. (207) 532-7481, open daily 10:30 a.m.-9 p.m. (to 10 p.m. in midsummer), mid-April to Labor Day. Hot dogs are also available. Alongside it are a driving range and a mini-golf course. An added advantage is its prime hilltop location close to Garrison Park.

Farmers' Market

The Houlton Farmers' Market sets up shop daily, late May to mid-Oct., next to McDonald's on Rt. 1, just south of I-95 Exit 62.

Inexpensive to Moderate

For large portions, home cooking, good service, and local color, the **Elm Tree Diner,** Bangor St., Rt. 2A, Houlton 04730, tel. (207) 532-3181, is Houlton's place to go. Nothing fancy, mind you, and not a diner in the strict sense—a sprawling, one-story, modern building—but this is a good spot to fill up the kids. Save room for dessert. No credit cards. Located one and a half miles south of I-95 Exit 62, the Elm Tree is open all year, Mon.-Sat. 5 a.m.-10 p.m. and Sunday 6 a.m.-10 p.m.

Where can you find a grilled-cheese sandwich on homemade bread for $1.90 or a nine-inch cheese pizza for $2.70? In Mars Hill, 28 miles north of Houlton. For a guaranteed dose of local color—and decent food besides—pull up at the antique neon sign outside **Al's Diner,** 87 Main St., Rt. 1, Mars Hill 04758, tel. (207) 429-8186, a friendly village eatery. Started as an ice cream shop in 1937, it has booths, a counter, a nonsmoking back room, and air-conditioning. The third generation is now running the place. No credit cards. Open all year, Mon.-Sat. 5 a.m.-9 p.m. and Sunday 7 a.m.-8 p.m.

Just inside the southern boundary of Aroostook County, in tiny Weston, is the vista known locally as the **Million Dollar View,** with a 180-degree panorama over the U.S.-Canadian Chiputneticook Lakes. Perched on the best elevation is a small seasonal restaurant named—why not?—**The Million Dollar View,** Rt. 1, Weston 04424, tel. (207) 448-7013. Serving breakfast, lunch, and dinner daily from the second Sunday in May to Labor Day, and lunch and dinner until Columbus Day, the informal eatery draws a crowd for its burger- and seafood-centric menu, but mostly for that view. It's open to 10 p.m. in summer, to 7:30 p.m. after Labor Day. Weston is 30 miles south of Houlton.

INFORMATION AND SERVICES

The **Greater Houlton Chamber of Commerce,** 109 Main St., Houlton 04730, tel. (207) 532-4216, in the same 1903 Colonial Revival building as the Aroostook Historical and Art Museum, is open weekdays all year, 9 a.m.-5 p.m. Be sure to request the *Walking Guide to Market Square Historic District.*

Next door is the **Cary Memorial Library,** 107 Main St., Houlton 04730, tel. (207) 532-1302. In winter, it's open Mon.-Thurs. 9 a.m.-6 p.m., Friday 9 a.m.-5 p.m., and Saturday 9 a.m.-1 p.m. In summer, the hours are Monday, Wednesday, Thursday, Friday 9 a.m.-5 p.m., Tuesday 9 a.m.-8 p.m., and Saturday 9 a.m.-1 p.m.

The Maine Publicity Bureau's **Maine Information Center,** Ludlow Rd., Houlton 04730, tel. (207) 532-6346, with brochures and maps covering the entire state, is open weekdays 9 a.m.-5 p.m., all year, with weekend and extended hours in summer.

Newspapers

The best source for calendar listings is the *Houlton Pioneer Times,* tel. (207) 532-2281, published every Wednesday under the endearing slogan, "The only newspaper in the world interested in Houlton, Maine." The *Bangor Daily News* covers the rest of the world.

Emergencies

In Houlton, call (207) 532-3751 to report a **fire,** (207) 532-6694 for an **ambulance,** and (207) 532-2287 for **police.** To reach the state-police barracks in Houlton, call (207) 532-2261 or (800) 924-2261.

Houlton Regional Hospital, 20 Hartford St., Houlton 04730, tel. (207) 532-9471, has round-the-clock emergency-room coverage.

Photo Services

Right downtown, **Houlton Photo Labs,** 1 Kendall St., Union Sq., Houlton 04730, tel. (207) 532-3631, provides efficient, reliable one-hour photo service. Open Mon.-Fri. 9 a.m.-5:30 p.m. and Saturday 9 a.m.-3 p.m.

Laundromat

The **Military Street Laundromat,** 35 Military St., Rt. 2, Houlton 04730, tel. (207) 532-2898, with coin-operated machines, is open daily 8 a.m.-9 p.m. It's also air-conditioned, so the dryer heat won't fry you.

Getting Around

Houlton has two competing taxi services: **Houlton Cab,** tel. (207) 532-6116, and **Shiretown Taxi,** tel. (207) 532-7173.

CENTRAL AROOSTOOK COUNTY

At the heart of central Aroostook are the cities of Presque Isle and Caribou, their downtowns separated by 13 miles of Rt. 1. The cities have long enjoyed a friendly rivalry—and distinct personalities. Both are at the hub of The County's potato industry and miles of snowmobile trails; each has a weekly newspaper; both are less than 15 miles from the Canadian border.

Presque Isle (pop. 10,500) boasts a University of Maine branch, a 577-acre state park, the Aroostook Centre Mall, a six-mile multiuse trail (and access to a larger network), TV and radio stations, and The County's largest hospital. Caribou (pop. 9,500) has a unique natural-history museum, a respected performing-arts center, an energetic recreation department, and a sleepy downtown.

Maine Senator Susan Collins comes from Caribou, and legions of Aroostook County supporters turned out to help send her to Washington in 1996. No wonder—several generations of her family have been prominent local and state leaders.

Northwest of Caribou are the Swedish-American communities of New Sweden, Stockholm, and Westmanland. Off to the east and west—creating a sort of geographical diamond shape—are the towns of Fort Fairfield (pop. 4,000) and Washburn (pop. almost 2,000). We're massaging the geometry a bit here: three of these communities—Presque Isle, Caribou, and Fort Fairfield—usually are known collectively as the Potato Triangle.

Presque Isle, incorporated in 1859, received electricity in 1887, welcomed the Bangor and Aroostook Railroad in 1895, and became The County's first city in 1940.

Caribou, incorporated in 1859 as Lyndon, received its present name in 1877. Agriculture, mainly potatoes, has always been the mainstay of the local economy. Caribou has the dubious distinction of being the third-coldest and fifth-snowiest city in the United States, with an average annual temperature of 39° F and an average annual snowfall (snowmobilers, take note) of 110.4 inches.

Scenic Routes

With so much open space in The County, particularly in the Potato Triangle, drivers and cyclists can enjoy great long vistas. One route, a favorite of Sen. Susan Collins, who ought to know, is **Route 164** between Caribou and Presque Isle, half of it along the Aroostook River. (Locals call it the Back Presque Isle Road.) On the way, you can check out the museums in Washburn, detour on the multiuse trail, and visit the Woods Edge Gallery in Perham.

Another scenic drive is **Route 167,** between Presque Isle and Fort Fairfield; the 12-mile stretch is especially dramatic in mid-July, when the rolling fields are draped with pink and white potato blossoms and Fort Fairfield puts on its annual Potato Blossom Festival.

PRESQUE ISLE AREA SIGHTS

University of Maine at Presque Isle

Established in 1903 as the Aroostook State Normal School, for training teachers, the University of Maine at Presque Isle (UMPI), 181 Main St., Rt. 1, Presque Isle 04769, tel. (207) 768-9400, now has more than 1,500 two- and four-year students on its 150-acre campus at the southern end of the city. The school is noted for its training in physical education and recreation. In the Campus Center is the **Reed Art Gallery,** where rotating exhibits spotlight Maine and Canadian artists. During the school year, the gallery is open Mon.-Fri. 10 a.m.-5 p.m. and Saturday 1-5 p.m.; the summer schedule tends to be less predictable.

Salmon Brook Historical Society Museums

Here's a worthwhile two-for-one deal, with lots of charm and character: in tiny, downtown Washburn, across from the First Baptist Church, the **Salmon Brook Historical Society,** P.O. Box 71, Washburn, 04786, tel. (207) 455-4339, operates the **Benjamin C. Wilder Homestead,** an 1852 National Historic Register farmhouse, and the **Aroostook Agricultural Museum** in the adjacent red barn. The well-restored 10-room house has period furnishings and displays; the barn contains old tools and antique cookware. The museums, on two and a half acres at 17 Main St. (Rt. 164), are open Saturday and Sunday 1-4 p.m., mid-June to mid-September, other times by appointment, tel. (207) 455-8110. Admission is free, but donations are welcomed. Washburn is 11 miles northwest of Presque Isle and 10 miles southwest of Caribou.

Also in Washburn (next to Perham Road, Rt. 228) is a convenient parking lot for access to the region's multiuse trail network.

CARIBOU AREA SIGHTS

Nylander Museum

If you were an eccentric, self-educated geologist and needed a place to display and store everything you'd accumulated, you'd create a place like the **Nylander Museum**, 393 Main St., P.O. Box 1062, Caribou 04736, tel. (207) 493-4209. Swedish-born Olof Olssen Nylander traveled the world collecting specimens, settled in Caribou, and bequeathed his work—including 6,000 fossils and 40,000 shells—to the city. Since his 1943 death, the museum has acquired other collections: butterflies, mounted birds, and additional geological specimens. The dinosaur displays particularly appeal to kids. A small gift shop has nature-related items. The museum is open Wed.-Sun. 1-5 p.m., Memorial Day weekend to Labor Day.; Saturday and Sunday 1-5 p.m., Labor Day through December and March through May. Admission is free, but donations are welcomed.

PARKS AND RECREATION

Presque Isle

Parks: Hiking, picnicking, swimming, fishing, and camping are among the options at 577-acre **Aroostook State Park**, State Park Rd., Presque Isle 04769, tel. (207) 768-8341, on the shores of Echo Lake. Twin-peaked **Quaggy Jo Mountain**, accessible via park trails beginning in the camping area, juts from the landscape and provides superb views from the summit, especially North Peak. A three-mile easy-to-moderate

clockwise loop starts next to campsite 18 and goes first to South Peak. Allow 2-3 hours. Quaggy Jo comes from the Micmac word *quaquajo,* meaning either "boundary mountain" or "twin-peaked." Canoe rentals are available; check with the ranger. Park admission is $2 adults, 50 cents children 5-11. Campsites are $10 per site per night (including tax); facilities are basic, but sites are wooded, close to Echo Lake. To be sure of a campsite on summer weekends, call (207) 287-3824 (MasterCard or Visa needed), at least two weeks ahead; two night minimum for reservations. The park is open daily, mid-May to mid-October, and accessible in winter for cross-country skiing and snowmobiling. A tiny, rustic day-use lodge is open weekends in winter. The gate is one and a half miles west of Rt. 1, five miles south of downtown Presque Isle.

Double Eagle Park, Spragueville Rd., Presque Isle 04769, featuring a replica of the helium balloon *Double Eagle II,* was the launch site of the first transatlantic balloon flight in August 1978. A three-man crew made the Presque Isle-to-France passage in less than a week. There's room here for kids to run, and the state park is nearby. The access road is the same as for the state park: just off Rt. 1, five miles south of downtown Presque Isle. (The first *solo* transatlantic balloon flight, six years later, took off from Caribou.)

Canoe Rentals: About a mile before you reach the Aroostook State Park gate from Rt. 1, watch for Leslie Cronin's **Partners in Sports,** 74 Spragueville Rd., Presque Isle 04769, tel. (207) 764-4562 or (800) 764-4562, source of rental canoes as well as archery equipment. Rates vary, so you'll need to call or stop in. She lives next to the shop, so hours are fairly flexible.

Rentals are also available at the state park, but only for use in Echo Lake.

Bike Rentals: Aroostook Bicycle and Sport, 690 Main St., Presque Isle 04769, tel. (207) 764-0206, rents bikes by the half-day and full day; you'll need to call to check the price scale. The shop also can handle almost any bike repair. It's open all year, Mon.-Sat. 9 a.m.-5 p.m.

Golf: The 18-hole **Presque Isle Country Club,** Parkhurst Siding Rd., P.O. Box 742, Presque Isle 04769, tel. (207) 764-0430 or 769-7431, established in 1958, was The County's first 18-

hole course. Facilities include a restaurant, driving range, cart and club rentals, and lessons. The course is open May through October. Take Rt. 163/167, Fort Fairfield Rd., east from downtown Presque Isle to Rt. 205, Parkhurst Siding Road. Turn left and go about a mile to the club, on the right.

Caribou Recreation

The **Caribou Parks & Recreation Department,** 59 Bennett Dr., Caribou 04736, tel. (207) 493-4224 or 493-4225, hotline (207) 496-5180, is an especially dynamic municipal operation with a huge variety of programs open to Caribou residents (free) and nonresidents (small charge). The office is open weekdays 8 a.m.-noon and 1-5 p.m. Among the offerings are ski rentals and groomed cross-country trails at the Caribou Country Club; fitness classes; indoor walking; pickup basketball; outdoor community pool (at Teague Park, across the street from the office); children's arts and crafts classes. Many of the programs require preregistration. The department also supervises development and maintenance of the huge network of multiuse trails for biking and hiking. Pick up a free trail map and a Parks & Rec schedule at the office. (Or call in advance if you want to plan ahead.)

The prettiest and most rural section of this impressive **rails-to-trails network** begins in Washburn and ends in Stockholm, including a short stretch through the Woodland Bog. Park in downtown Washburn. Be sure to carry plenty of water. Other trails go from Caribou to Van Buren, 25 miles (about two and a half hours one-way), and Washburn to New Sweden.

Woodland Bog Preserve: About 11 miles west of Caribou, Woodland Bog Preserve, a 200-acre Nature Conservancy property, is home to several rare orchid species and dozens of bird species (nearly 90 have been banded here). From mid-May through mid-July, Perham resident Richard Clark, the Conservancy's on-site steward—and donor of the nearby 10-acre **Perham Bog Preserve**—leads fascinating free walks through the bog (technically, a calcareous fen surrounded by a cedar swamp). To set up a time, call him at (207) 455-8359 days or 455-8060 evenings. Wear waterproof shoes and insect repellent. Richard and his wife, Susan, have also donated a 135-acre conservation easement for **Salmon Brook Lake Bog,** also in this area. **Note:** These preserves have extremely fragile ecosystems, so don't even consider visiting them on your own.

Multiuse Trails: Spearheaded by the Caribou Parks & Recreation Department, several volunteer groups have worked to open up more than 70 miles of abandoned railroad beds for year-round use by bikers, hikers, and snowmobilers. The trails are mostly packed gravel, so you'll want a mountain bike. ATVs (all-terrain vehicles) also use the trails, creating a certain amount of racket, but otherwise they're great. From Caribou, you can go to Stockholm and on to Van Buren (29 miles one-way). Or start in Washburn and go to Stockholm and Van Buren (40 miles one-way). Or begin in Carson (just west of Caribou) and go to New Sweden (nine miles one-way).

Kids' Stuff: Teague Park, Bennett Dr., Caribou, tel. (207) 493-4239, across from Caribou Recreation Center, has a terrific creative playground—a great place to let the kids loose and wind them down. It's open to the public any time school is not in session.

Mike Bosse is the second-generation owner of **Funland Amusement Park,** Rt. 1, Presque Isle Rd., Caribou 04736, tel. (207) 493-3157, a family-oriented park with activities for every age level. It's no competition for Disneyland, but it will keep the kids occupied for hours. Options include go-carts, mini-golf, driving range, water slide, video-game room, giant sand box, and a gift shop with every imaginable kind of souvenir. Open May 1 to Labor Day: weekends until Memorial Day weekend, then daily, from 11 a.m. or noon to 8 or 9 p.m. Each activity at the park is "pay as you go" and varies widely. The park is three miles south of downtown Caribou.

Almost qualifying as an amusement park as well, **Goughan's Berry Farm,** Rt. 161, RFD 2, Caribou 04736, tel. (207) 498-6565, has a bit of everything, depending on when you show up. Open April through Christmas, Mon.-Sat. 8 a.m.-5 p.m., Sunday noon-5 p.m., Goughan's (GAWNS) has maple syrup in spring; pick-your-own strawberries, raspberries, and veggies in summer; choose-your-own pumpkins in fall; and Christmas wreaths in winter. Kids can feed and pet the farm animals and get delicious homemade ice cream at the dairy bar in the grainery. Also in the grainery is a gift shop with Maine-made goodies. The farm is three miles southeast of Caribou, on the Fort Fairfield Road (Rt. 161).

Snowmobile Tours: If you've never tried snowmobiling (a.k.a. sledding) and want to test the waters (not literally) without investing in a lot of expensive gear, contact **Crystal Snowmobile Tours,** P.O. Box 1448, Caribou 04736, tel. (207) 498-3220 or 492-7471, for information about their weekend snowmobile tours. They also rent snowmobiles if you want to try it yourself, but *do not* go snowmobiling without local advice, detailed maps, and adequate clothing.

Snowmobile **rentals** are also available at **The Sled Shop,** 108 Main St., Presque Isle 04769, tel. (207) 764-2900, next to Keddy's Motor Inn.

ENTERTAINMENT

Caribou and Presque Isle have plenty of movie screens. The **Aroostook Centre Cinemas,** Aroostook Centre Mall, 830 Main St., Presque Isle 04769, tel. (207) 764-8506, have eight screens showing first-run flicks day and night, usually including at least one child-approved film. Reduced prices before 6 p.m. Open all year. The **Caribou Cinema Center,** 126 Sweden St., Caribou 04736, tel. (207) 493-3013, has four screens and cheaper tickets, but only evening shows. It's also open all year.

Throughout the year, concerts, plays, and other live events occur at the 800-seat **Caribou Performing Arts Center,** Caribou High School, 410 Sweden St., Rt. 161, Caribou 04736, tel. (207) 493-4278. Check the newspapers or ask at the Caribou Chamber of Commerce.

SHOPPING

The major shopping destination in the Presque Isle-Caribou area is Presque Isle's Aroostook Centre Mall, but both cities have other shops worth patronizing.

Presque Isle
On the banks of the Aroostook River, the 40-store **Aroostook Centre Mall,** N. Main St., Rt. 1, Presque Isle 04769, tel. (207) 764-2616 or 764-

2633, has all the usual suspects: department stores, book and card shops, drugstores, a food court, a good restaurant, and an eight-screen cineplex. Amenities include an ATM machine, public restrooms, and free use of strollers and wheelchairs. This largest mall north of Bangor is open Mon.-Sat. 9:30 a.m.-9 p.m., Sunday noon-6 p.m.

Caribou Area
Customers trek from all over Maine to wander through Swedish-born Monica Soderberg's two-story shop. At **Monica's Scandinavian Gift Shop,** 12 Prospect St., Caribou 04736, tel. (207) 498-8861, you'll find Scandinavian embroidery and greeting cards, Swedish crystal and clogs, Finnish dinnerware, Icelandic sweaters, Danish figurines, Norwegian pewter, and an entire room devoted to Christmas items. The shop is open Mon.-Sat. 9:30 a.m.-5 p.m., April-Dec., and 10 a.m.-5 p.m. Jan.-March.

Tucked away in downtown Caribou, **The Northland Studio,** 112 Sweden St., Caribou 04736, tel. (207) 493-4430, exhibits and sells the work of a broad spectrum of Northern Maine artists—paintings, photographs, pottery, and prints. The shop also offers T-shirt printing and other graphic-design services. Located in a building called the Sweden Street Mall, it's open all year, Mon.-Fri. 10 a.m.-5 p.m.

About 11 miles west of Caribou, the **Woods Edge Gallery,** High Meadow Rd., P.O. Box 77, Perham 04766, tel. (207) 455-8359 or 455-8060, devotes almost a thousand feet of exhibit space to watercolor and acrylic landscapes, plus photography—most by Aroostook County artists. Located 1.25 miles west of Rt. 228, the gallery is open all year, Tues.-Sat. 1-5 p.m. Gallery owner Richard Clark, steward for The Nature Conservancy's nearby Woodland Bog, also leads seasonal nature tours there.

ACCOMMODATIONS

Hotels/Motels
University professors, snowmobilers, and traveling salespeople all gravitate to the 153-room **Keddy's Motor Inn,** Rt. 1, P.O. Box 270, Presque Isle 04769, tel. (207) 764-3321 or (800) 561-7666, fax (207) 764-5167—atop a hill over-

looking Presque Isle and beyond. Decor is motel-modern at the only Maine hostelry of a 15-branch Canadian chain. Amenities include a health club, indoor pool, on-site coin laundry, and cable TV. The Old Jail Bar is a popular local rendezvous spot, and there's live entertainment weekends in the Connections Lounge. The motel is close to the University of Maine's Presque Isle campus. In winter, when the parking lot has more snowmobiles than cars, don't even think about arriving sans reservation. Rooms are $54 d; children under 18 stay free.

Patronized primarily for its convenient downtown site, **The Northeastland Hotel,** 436 Main St., Presque Isle 04769, tel. (207) 768-5321 or (800) 244-5321 in Maine, fax (207) 764-1720, caters to business travelers but also offers good value for families, with inexpensive meals available on the premises. Fifty rooms ($51-56 d) are motel-style modern, with a/c. No pets; children 12 and under stay free. Open all year. Located here since 1934, the two-story Northeastland is a central Aroostook tradition, with agreeable staffers; the informal restaurant is a popular local lunch spot.

Considered the best all-round lodging in the area, the **Caribou Inn and Convention Center,** Rt. 1, RFD 3, Box 25, Caribou 04736, tel. (207) 498-3733, fax 498-3149, has 73 large, comfortable rooms and suites with a/c, cable TV, and refrigerators (suites have kitchenettes). Pool and health-club facilities, free to guests, are open 17 hours daily. (Request a room away from the pool area.) Rooms are $52-72 d; children 12 and under stay free. The attractive **Greenhouse Restaurant** serves breakfast, lunch, and dinner Mon.-Sat (no dinner Sunday); dinner entrées are $9-15. As with Keddy's in Presque Isle, snowmobilers end up here, so be sure to reserve well in advance in winter. The Caribou Inn is three miles south of downtown Caribou, junction of Rts. 1 and 164.

B&Bs

Art professor Clifton Boudman puts out an unforgettable spread—a Scottish breakfast—when you stay at the **Rum Rapids Inn,** Rt. 164, Rum Rapids Dr., Crouseville 04738, tel. (207) 455-8096, a beautifully furnished 1839 house. By prior arrangement, he'll also produce an elegant multicourse dinner (extra charge; BYOL),

served at 7 p.m. Specialties include baked trout Italiano, grilled and limed steak, and penne Medici. In summer, relax on the deck overlooking Rum Rapids; in winter, cross-country ski on the Boudmans' 15 acres. Two rooms (private baths) are $48 d. No smoking, no pets; one room suits children. Open all year. The inn is five miles northwest of Presque Isle; watch for a tiny sign on the left.

Close to downtown Caribou, the **Old Iron Inn B&B,** 155 High St., Caribou 04736, tel./fax (207) 492-4766, comes by its name honestly. Hundreds of antique irons are displayed through this turn-of-the-20th-century house, and geology professor Kevin McCartney can recount the background of each one. Four rooms ($39-49 d), comfortably furnished with quilts and antiques, share two and a half baths. Guests can use the office and fax machine or browse through the McCartneys' book and magazine collection. Smoking only on the porch. No children, no pets. Known for her culinary talent, Kate McCartney serves a delicious breakfast in the Victorian dining room. Open all year.

Campgrounds

Registered Maine Guide Mike Bouchard and his wife, Jan, own **Aroostook River Camping & Recreation,** Rt. 1, RFD 3, Box 40, Caribou 04736, tel. (207) 498-6969, three miles south of downtown Caribou on the banks of the Aroostook River. The smallish campground, open all year, has 20 RV sites, a tenting area, and basic cabins. Four nature trails wind through the property, and the snowmobile trail system is accessible here. Mike Bouchard, a Fort Kent native, is especially knowledgeable about outdoors pursuits in the region; he also rents canoes and provides a canoe shuttle service.

There's also camping at Aroostook State Park. For details see "Presque Isle" under "Parks and Recreation," above.

FOOD

Presque Isle

Where can you get a $7 lobster roll in February? **Winnie's Dairy Bar III,** 79 Parsons St., Presque Isle 04769, tcl. (207) 769-4971, owned by Patty LeBlanc (Winnie was the first owner, in the

1940s). And LeBlanc's gourmet lobster stew has become so famous for being "the real thing" (no fillers) that Patty's crew ships nearly 200 pints a day all over the country ($9.99 a pint; overnight delivery). The ultra-casual restaurant, also known for its Winnie's burgers, is open all year, daily 10 a.m.-8 p.m. in winter, to 10 p.m. in summer. In winter, snowmobilers arrive here en masse, so be prepared to wait.

Also popular is the **Riverside Inn Restaurant,** 399 Main St., Presque Isle 04769, tel. (207) 764-1447, a small place with zero ambience but reliable, inexpensive food (entrées $3-6). No credit cards. Located in downtown Presque Isle, close to Riverside Park, the restaurant is open all year, Mon.-Sat. 5 a.m.-10 p.m. and Sunday 6 a.m.-10 p.m.

For a taste of the Southwest, go directly to **Ruby Tuesday,** 830 Main St., Aroostook Centre Mall, Presque Isle 04769, tel. (207) 764-2874, where specialties are steaks, ribs, fajitas, and more ($6-13). As the name (after a Rolling Stones song) suggests, it's a hip place, and service is excellent. Reservations are advisable on weekends. Open all year, Sun.-Thurs. 11 a.m.-10 p.m., Friday and Saturday 11 a.m.-11 p.m. Ruby Tuesday is near the K-mart end of the mall.

Caribou

Breakfast is served all day at the first-rate **Mainer's Omelette Trap,** 7 Prospect St., Caribou 04736, tel. (207) 496-8727. Don't be put off by the corny name; there's real creativeness here. One specialty is a four-egg omelette ($7.95, enough for two) filled with lobster, shrimp, and crab and served with *rösti* potatoes (the Swiss national starch). The weekend dinner menu includes lobster stew, prime rib, and Creole and Cajun dishes. Top it all off with a cappuccino. The Trap is open all year, Tues.-Fri. 11 a.m.-2 p.m., Saturday and Sunday 7:30 a.m.-2 p.m., plus Friday and Saturday 5:30-8:30 p.m. It's at the corner of Herschel Street, across from Monica's Scandinavian Gift Shop.

An informal setting, excellent service, and top-quality beef and seafood are the hallmarks of **Joe Hackett's Steak & Seafood,** Rt. 1, Presque Isle Rd., Box 1034, Caribou 04736, tel. (207) 496-2501, Caribou's most popular restaurant. Entrées are $8-14. Also on the menu

are Joey chips (French fries), Atlantic Belly Dancers (clams), and American Girls (poached chicken). Children's menu features Dinosaur Nests (spaghetti and meatballs) and Buckaroo's Wallet with a Cow's Blanket (cheeseburger). Covering all bases, vegetarian and "heart-healthy" items are also available. The wine list is basic but adequate. Located three miles south of downtown Caribou, across from the Caribou Motor Inn, Joe Hackett's opens for dinner Mon.-Sat. at 5 p.m., Sunday at noon.

An extremely loyal clientele makes unpretentious **Frederick's Southside,** 217 S. Main St., Caribou 04736, tel. (207) 498-3464, busy most of the time. Inexpensive home cooking is the draw. It's open all year, Mon.-Sat. 5 a.m.-8 p.m. and Sunday 6:30 a.m.-8 p.m.

INFORMATION AND SERVICES

Presque Isle, Caribou, and Fort Fairfield all have their own chambers of commerce. The **Presque Isle Area Chamber of Commerce,** 3 Houlton Rd., Rt. 1, P.O. Box 672, Presque Isle 04769, tel. (207) 764-6561, at the southern outskirts of the city, is open Mon.-Fri. 8 a.m.-5 p.m.; it may be closed 12:30-1:30 p.m. for lunch. On weekends and after hours, brochures and maps are available at the Aroostook Centre Mall, N. Main St., Rt. 1, Presque Isle. The **Caribou Chamber of Commerce,** 111 High St., P.O. Box 357, Caribou 04736, tel. (207) 498-6156, with an especially helpful staff, is open Mon.-Fri. 7:30 a.m.-4:30 p.m. The office is close to downtown Caribou. Hardest to find is the **Fort Fairfield Chamber of Commerce** 121 Main St., P.O. Box 607, Fort Fairfield 04742, tel. (207) 472-3802, in a poorly signposted second-floor office in the municipal complex along the main drag. It's open weekdays 8 a.m.-5 p.m., all year.

The **Mark and Emily Turner Memorial Library,** 39 Second St., Presque Isle 04769, tel. (207) 764-2571, is open all year. Winter hours are Mon.-Thurs. 10 a.m.-8 p.m. (kids' section closes at 7 p.m.), Friday 10 a.m.-5:30 p.m., and Saturday 10 a.m.-4 p.m. Summer hours are the same, except for Saturday, when the library is closed. The **Caribou Public Library,** 30 High St., Caribou 04736, tel. (207) 493-4214, is open Mon.-Fri. noon-8 p.m. and Saturday 10 a.m.-4 p.m. in winter; summer hours (June-Aug.) are Mon.-Fri. noon-8 p.m.

Emergencies
In **Presque Isle,** call (207) 764-4476 for police, (207) 764-6363 for an ambulance, and (207) 768-7411 to report a fire. In **Caribou,** call (207) 493-3301 for police, and (207) 493-3306 for fire and ambulance services. The nearest state police barracks is in Houlton.

Aroostook County's largest hospital is **Gould Memorial Hospital,** a division of The Aroostook Medical Center, 140 Academy St., Rt. 10, Presque Isle 04769, emergency room tel. (207) 768-4100, with round-the-clock emergency-room care. The **Cary Medical Center,** 37 Van Buren Rd., Caribou 04736, tel. (207) 498-3111, has medical staff on call round the clock.

Newspapers
Presque Isle's hometown paper is *The Star-Herald,* tel. (207) 768-5431, published every Wednesday; Caribou's paper, under the same ownership, is the *Aroostook Republican and News,* tel. (207) 496-3251, also published Wednesday. Both carry local calendar listings. The *Bangor Daily News* is the daily paper for local residents.

GETTING THERE

Based at Northern Aroostook Regional Airport in Frenchville, **Pine State Airlines,** tel. (800) 353-6334, provides twice-daily commuter service between Portland and Presque Isle, stopping in Augusta and Bangor. No tickets are issued; you'll receive a confirmation number when you reserve. Be sure to carry a photo ID. As with larger airlines, costs vary widely; supersaver fares offer good discounts. A 21-day advance-purchase roundtrip ticket on the Portland-Presque Isle run averages $250.

NEW SWEDEN

On July 23, 1870, a determined and dynamic fellow named William Widgery Thomas, Jr., a Portland native and Bowdoin College graduate, arrived in the wilds of Aroostook County with 50 sturdy Swedish farmers and their families. This was the first wave of "a noble experiment," which grew to 600 Swedes within three years and to 1,400 in 25 years. By 1895, the New Sweden area had 689 buildings on more than 7,500 productive acres.

The inspiration for the settlement came from Thomas, who had been trained as a diplomat. After posts in Constantinople and Moldavia, he went to Sweden, where he fell right in, learning the language and marrying a Swedish woman. Returning to Maine in the late 1860s, he was asked to help reverse the state's tide of outmigration, so he devised a unique plan to encourage Swedish farmers to come to a wilderness not unlike their own land. After three or four years of wheedling, Thomas won approval, cornered enough acreage, and sailed for Sweden to deliver his sales pitch. Within only six weeks, he had assembled his core group, and the adventure began.

It wasn't easy, and Aroostook was no paradise on earth. The families cleared the land, built log houses and churches, spun wool for clothing, and kept on keeping on, apparently undaunted by subzero temperatures, sickness, and unpredictable crops. After this feat, William Widgery Thomas became U.S. Minister to Sweden and Norway in 1883, serving for more than a dozen years. He died in 1927, but residents still honor "Father Thomas," who called those early settlers "my children in the woods."

One of the little-recognized contributions made by New Sweden's settlers was the introduction of skiing to Maine during that first winter. Nordic skiing, of course, was as natural as breathing for the Swedes, and the town even had something of a ski jump on Ringdahl Hill.

Today, Swedish culture survives among the thousand or so residents of the towns of New Sweden and Stockholm and the hamlet of Westmanland. The phone book lists dozens of Thomases, plus plenty of Soderbergs, Nelsons, Carlsons, Petersons, and Andersons—all blended in among the Franco-Americans and Yankees who earlier had settled this area.

Around Town
New Sweden is eight miles northwest of downtown Caribou, via Rt. 161. At the **New Sweden Historical Museum,** Capitol Hill and Station Rds., New Sweden 04762, tel. (207) 896-
3018, three floors of memorabilia reflect the
rugged life in this frontier community. An exact
replica of the colony's "Kapitoleum" (capitol),
the museum was built in 1971 after fire leveled
the original structure. Check out the museum's
guestbook: visitors have come from all over
Scandinavia to see this cultural enclave. The
museum, half a mile north and east of Rt. 161,
is open early June to mid-September, Tues.-
Sat. noon-4 p.m. and Sunday 2-5 p.m. Off season, call (207) 896-5843 for an appointment.
Admission is free, but donations are welcomed.
Next door, in the **Capitol Hill School,** a gift
shop carries Swedish items. Out back is a monument with the list of the original settlers.
  Continuing east on Station Road, you'll pass
W.W. Thomas Memorial Park on the left, a
great spot for a picnic, with a play area for kids
and a dramatic vista over the rolling countryside. Concerts occur periodically in the bandshell. About .2 mile farther, also on the left, is the
shingled **Lars Noak Blacksmith and Woodworking Shop,** another remnant of the early
settlers.
  A fun time to visit New Sweden is during the
Midsommar festival, on the closest weekend
to Midsummer Day (June 21), when residents
don traditional Swedish costumes and celebrate
the year's longest day. Activities include deco-
ration of a Maypole, Swedish dancing, a smorgasbord, concerts, and a prayer service. Non-
Scandinavians are welcome to join in.
  New Sweden has no accommodations, but
Caribou is only eight miles away. Information
on the festival is available from the Caribou
Chamber of Commerce or the New Sweden
Town Office, tel. (207) 869-3306.
  While you're in the area, continue another
eight miles up Rt. 161 to the edge of Madawaska
Lake, site of the legendary **Stan's Grocery,** Rt.
161, Madawaska Lake, Stockholm 04783, tel.
(207) 896-5645. Why legendary? Check the sign
outside: Home of 10¢ Coffee. Enter this old-fashioned country store and luncheonette, run by la-
conic Stan Thomas, and set your watch back 50
years. Then spring for bait, sweatshirts, maybe
some lunch, and 11-cent (including tax) coffee. A
large table collects regulars who discuss world affairs and profess to come up with solutions. On
the back wall is Stan's father's collection of 300
spoons. Stan's is open all year, Mon.-Sat. 7:30
a.m.-10:30 p.m. and Sunday 9 a.m.-10:30 p.m.
  Continuing on Rt. 161 after Stan's will get
you to Fort Kent and the rest of the St. John
Valley, but unless time demands the shortcut,
you'll see more of the Valley by taking Rt. 1
north to Van Buren from Caribou.

Information
The best place in town for general information is
the museum, Capitol Hill and Station Rds., New
Sweden, tel. (207) 896-3018, where you can
pick up a map and a New Sweden brochure.
Or try the New Sweden Town Office on Station
Road.

THE ST. JOHN VALLEY

Plan to visit The Upper St. John River Valley
from east to west, counterclockwise, from Van
Buren to Fort Kent, and perhaps on to Allagash,
giving yourself a buildup to this unique cultural
region settled by Acadians in 1785.
  Van Buren calls itself "The Gateway to the St.
John River Valley," and you begin to notice here
the change of cultural pace. Valley hallmarks are
huge Roman Catholic churches, small riverside
communities, unfancy but tidy homes, an eclectic French patois, and a handful of unique culinary
specialties—all thanks to a twist of fate.
  Henry Wadsworth Longfellow's immortal epic
poem *Evangeline* relates a saga of *le grand
dérangement,* when more than 10,000 French-
speaking Acadians tragically lost their lease on
Nova Scotia after the British expelled them for
disloyalty in 1755—a date engraved ever since
in the minds of their thousands of descendants
now living on the American and Canadian sides
of the St. John River. (Thousands more of their
kin ended up in Louisiana, where Acadian traditions also remain strong.)
  In this part of Maine, Smiths and Joneses are

few—countless residents bear such names as Cyr, Daigle, Gagnon, Michaud, Ouellette, Pelletier, Sirois, and Thibodeau. In Van Buren, Grand Isle, Madawaska, St. Agatha, and Frenchville, French is the mother tongue for 97% of the residents, who refer to the Upper St. John Valley as *chez nous* ("our house"), their homeland. Many roadside and shop signs are bilingual—even the nameboard for the University of Maine branch in Fort Kent.

Religion is as pervasive an influence as language. When a Madawaska beauty represented Maine in the Miss America contest in 1995, the local *St. John Valley Times* admonished its readers: "Keep your fingers crossed and your rosaries hot."

Since the 1970s, renewed local interest in and appreciation for Acadian culture has spurred cultural projects, celebrations, and genealogical research throughout the valley, with the eventual goal of a National Park Service Acadian culture center. "Valley French," a unique, archaic patois long stigmatized in Maine schools, has undergone a revival. Since the 1970s, several valley schools have established bilingual programs, and a 1991 survey estimated that 40% of valley schoolchildren speak both English and French.

Controversy erupts periodically over whose lineage is "true" Acadian (as opposed to Quebecois—although many Acadians also fled to Quebec), but valley residents all turn out en masse for the summer highlight: Madawaska's multiday Acadian Festival, centered on Acadian Day, June 28. It's a local festival unlike any other in Maine.

Between Madawaska and Fort Kent, detour off Rt. 1 into the lovely lake district—locally known as the "back settlements"—through the town of St. Agatha and the village of Sinclair, on Rt. 162, entering Fort Kent on Rt. 161 from the southeast. Better still, after reaching the end of Rt. 162, turn northwest onto Rt. 161 and meander through the back roads off to the east and north before landing in Fort Kent. (Use Map 68 in the DeLorme *Maine Atlas and Gazetteer*.)

West of Fort Kent are the tiny and tinier riverside communities of St. John, St. Francis, Allagash, and Dickey, the latter serving as endpoints for two of Maine's most popular long-distance canoe routes: the St. John River and the Allagash Wilderness Waterway.

Heading out of Aroostook County, via Rt. 11 south from Fort Kent, be prepared for stunning scenery and lakes, ponds, and rivers off to the right and left.

VAN BUREN

Twenty-five miles north of Caribou, Van Buren isn't the end of Rt. 1, but Rt. 1 takes a sharp turn and follows the St. John River to Fort Kent—terminus of the long, long road running from Florida to Maine. Named after President Martin Van Buren, the town of Van Buren (pop. about 2,800) has lovely, long views but a not-too-promising short-term outlook. Unemployment is high, and many youngsters escape soon after high school (if not before). Life isn't easy on this frontier.

In the hamlet of Keegan, about two miles northwest of downtown Van Buren, is a prominent reminder of the heritage in this valley—Acadian settlement in 1785. Begun as a small-scale bicentennial project in 1976, the **Acadian Village**, Rt. 1, Van Buren 04785, tel. (207) 868-5042, is a two-and-a-half-acre open-air museum that has collected 16 antique and replica buildings in an A-shaped layout. Included are a country store, forge, schoolhouse, chapel, and several residences. Maintenance has fallen slightly behind, but a self-guided tour vividly conveys the daily struggles for 18th- and 19th-century Acadians in the valley. Kids particularly enjoy the schoolhouse and the barbershop; outside, there's plenty of letting-off-steam room. Admission is $3 adults, $1.50 children. When you buy the tickets, pick up a "tour book," which you'll turn in at the end. The museum is open daily noon-5 p.m., mid-June to mid-September.

GRAND ISLE

As with the other religion-dominated communities in the valley, the most prominent landmark in Grand Isle (pop. 550) is the Catholic church, a twin-towered building undergoing long-term restoration as a museum/cultural center: **Le Musée et Centre Culturel du Mont-Carmel.** Built in 1909 in the section of town known as Lille, Our Lady of Mount Carmel Church last held services in 1978. Since historian/preservationist Don Cyr bought the wooden church in 1984, he's organized concerts and other events under the aegis of L'Association Culturelle et Historique du Mont-Carmel. Each Labor Day weekend, the center sponsors the **Lille Classical Impressionist Music Festival.** For information on the project, or the festival, contact Cyr, tel. (207) 895-3339, or the **Greater Madawaska Chamber of Commerce,** 378 Main St., Rt. 1, Madawaska 04756, tel. (207) 728-7000, fax 728-4696. There's no schedule of visiting hours, but if you're interested in seeing the interior, check at the former rectory behind and to the left of the church.

About four miles farther northwest on Rt. 1, on the Grand Isle-Madawaska town line, you'll come to the state-run **Mount Carmel Rest Area,** with picnic tables and an outhouse. If you've brought the fixings, it's a good spot for a picnic. Across the road is a monument to Acadian pioneers.

MADAWASKA

Bounced back and forth in a U.S.-Canada border dispute, Madawaska (pop. 4,800) finally was incorporated with its present boundaries in 1869. The name allegedly is Micmac, "where one river runs into another"; the Madawaska and St. John Rivers meet here.

Fort Kent may be the head of the valley, the site of the official Acadian Archives, but Madawaska is its heart. You'll understand why if you arrive for the annual **Acadian Festival.** Each year, Maine's governor recognizes June 28 as **Acadian Day,** so the heritage celebration always wraps around this date, usually four or five days. The festival includes bike races, a parade, petting zoo, food and craft booths, cow-chip roulette, potato-peeling contest, and traditional Acadian music and dance. Each day has a special theme. A highlight is the **Acadian Supper,** usually a Friday night, featuring such Acadian specialties as *pâté chinois* (shepherd's pie), *fougères* (fiddleheads), *ployes* (buckwheat cakes), *pot-en-pot* (meat pie), and *tourtiere* (pork pie). Most of the events occur at the Mid-Town Shopping Center on St. Thomas Street, a block south of Rt. 1. Plan ahead if you want to be there; the festival fills lodgings throughout the valley.

As you reach the eastern edge of Madawaska, you can't help but notice the bell tower of the imposing brick **St. David Catholic Church,** established in 1871 and still holding services in French. The National Historic Register building, usually open, has a high arched ceiling, a domed altar, and stained-glass windows.

Just to the right (east) of St. David's is the one-room **Tante Blanche Museum,** Rt. 1, St. David Parish, Madawaska 04756, tel. (207) 728-4518, containing Acadian artifacts. Run by the **Madawaska Historical Society,** P.O. Box 258, Madawaska 04756, the log museum commemorates **Marguerite Blanche Thibodeau Cyr** ("Tante Blanche"), an Acadian heroine during a 1797 famine. The museum is open June 10-Aug. 10, Mon.-Fri. 10 a.m.-3 p.m. and Sunday 1-3 p.m. Next door to the museum, kids enjoy the hands-on exhibits in **School House #1.** Beside the museum (to the right), take the half-mile gravel road leading down to the shore, where a 14-foot-high marble cross marks the reputed 1785 landing spot of Acadians expelled by the British from Nova Scotia and New Brunswick. An Acadian flag flies here, near memorials to the original settlers.

As you approach central Madawaska, you'll see (on your right), the **Northern Trading Company,** 190-202 E. Main St., P.O. Box 250, Madawaska 04756, tel. (207) 728-4273, a sprawling complex that turns out perfumes and body lotions. Summer is especially busy at the plant, so call a day or two ahead to schedule a free, 45-minute tour. You may even get a free sample. The plant operates all year.

In downtown Madawaska, **Fraser Paper Ltd.,** 25 Bridge St., Madawaska 04756, tel. (207) 728-8200, is the only American plant in Canada's Fraser Paper network. French is as common as English among the 1,100 or so employees, who each day produce 1,200 tons of paper. Knowledgeable staff members conduct free, hour-long factory tours. You have to don a hard hat and earplugs, so the machinery noise can drown out the narrative, but it's worth it to see the operation. No children under 12, no open-toed shoes. Tour hours are weekdays 9 a.m.-4 p.m., all year, but avoid arriving near the end of the day. You don't need a reservation, but you might have to wait a few minutes.

Madawaska is a major border crossing to New Brunswick—one of only three in the St. John Valley—so the two-lane bridge to Edmundston (on Bridge Street, of course) gets incredibly backed up, especially during paper-mill shift changes. If you go across, be sure to carry proper identification (photo ID for U.S. citizens, passport and Canadian visa for non-U.S. citizens). The **U.S. Customs office** in Madawaska, tel. (207) 728-4376, is open round-the-clock. Remember, also, that New Brunswick is on Atlantic time, an hour later than eastern time.

Fine dining isn't Madawaska's long suit, but you won't starve. Four pizzerias and several fast-food outlets will take care of that.

The **Greater Madawaska Chamber of Commerce,** 378 Main St., Rt. 1, Madawaska 04756, tel. (207) 728-7000, fax 728-4696, between N. 6th and N. 7th Aves., is open weekdays 9 a.m.-5 p.m. The *St. John Valley Times,* tel. (207) 728-3336, published every Wednesday in Madawaska, provides local coverage for the area.

FRENCHVILLE

Eleven miles roughly west of Madawaska, on Rt. 1 North, you'll find Frenchville (pop. about 1,300). If you arrive in time for lunch or dinner, stop off at **Rosette's Restaurant,** 240 Main St., Rt. 1, Frenchville 04745, tel. (207) 543-7759, a favorite from Madawaska to Fort Kent. Everything's homemade, prices are very reasonable, and the color is local. Rosette's is open Tues.-Sun. 7 a.m.-9 p.m., all year.

Headquartered at Frenchville's Northern Aroostook Regional Airport is **Aroostook Aviation, Inc.,** 74 Airport Ave., P.O. Box 88, Frenchville 04745, the parent company of Pine State Airlines, a scheduled service with two flights daily from Portland to Augusta, Bangor, Presque Isle, and Frenchville. Aroostook Aviation also operates on-demand **sightseeing flights** in three-passenger Cessnas. Fall-foliage flights are the most spectacular, but summer trips run a close second, and they'll even do night flights over the valley. The one-hour **Fish River Chain** flight makes a clockwise circuit over Long Lake, Square Lake, and Eagle Lake; watch for moose on this route. The **Valley and Allagash Run,** lasting about 70 minutes, follows the St. John from east to west, Madawaska to Allagash and back. Cost is $59 an hour per planeload (1-3 persons). Aroostook Aviation is open daily 6 a.m.-7 p.m. The airport is about three miles east of Rt. 1.

ST. AGATHA

From Rt. 1 in Frenchville, instead of continuing directly to Fort Kent, take the long, scenic route by detouring first down Rt. 162 to the town of St. Agatha (often pronounced the French way—"Saint a-GAHT"), on Long Lake, about four and a half miles from Rt. 1. T-shaped **Long Lake** is the northernmost of the Fish River Chain of Lakes, extending southwest to Eagle Lake.

About halfway between Frenchville and St. Agatha, watch for a small sign for **Spare Moments,** 140 Main St., Rt. 162, St. Agatha 04772, tel. (207) 543-6150. Here's where stained-glass pro Lisa Myers runs her home-based business. Her sculptured glass is incredible; she also restores old glass and sells stained-glass supplies. Open all year by chance or appointment.

Auberge du Lac Bed & Breakfast, Birch Point Rd., RR 1, Box 142-1, St. David 04773, tel. (207) 728-6047, on the east side of Long Lake, is not in St. Agatha itself, but it's close enough—about seven miles. Enthusiastic innkeeper Grace Ouellette has three comfortable rooms ($55-65 d; private and shared baths) in a ranch-style house overlooking the lake and its sunsets. Breakfast always includes an Acadian treat, and Grace will pack a picnic lunch if you notify her in advance. No smoking, no pets, no children under 14. Open all year.

Across the lake is another overnight option, the **Long Lake Motor Inn,** Rt. 162, St. Agatha 04772, tel. (207) 543-5006, Ken and Arlene Lerman's clean, modern motel. All 18 rooms have phones and cable TV; 11 rooms have lake views (and great sunrises). Continental breakfast is included. Rates run $46 d in winter, $42-45 d in summer. If you're here in winter, reserve well ahead or the snowmobilers will beat you to it. Open all year.

When it's time for a meal, head up the hill for the best view in town, at **The Lakeview Restaurant,** 7 Lakeview Dr., St. Agatha 04772, tel. (207) 543-6331. An awning-covered deck overlooks Long Lake; indoor booths and tables have plenty of visibility. Reasonably priced steak and seafood ($7-17) are dinner specialties. The Lakeview is open all year, daily 6 a.m.-1 a.m. Take Rt. 162 to Flat Mountain Rd. to Lakeview Drive.

For something a little different, the best view in the village of **Sinclair,** about six miles down the road from St. Agatha, is at the **Long Lake Sporting Club Resort,** Rt. 162, Sinclair 04779, tel. (207) 543-7584 or (800) 431-7584. In the middle of nowhere, this informal place is almost always crowded. In summer, guests come by boat or car; in winter, by snowmobile. The deck has a fabulous view over Long Lake. Huge steaks and giant lobsters are specialties, and all meals come with *ployes,* Acadian buckwheat pancakes (adding syrup is considered gauche). Settle in the lounge, choose from six entrées ($9-19, except lobster), and they'll usher you to your table when it's all ready. Open Mon.-Sat. 5-9 p.m. and Sunday noon-8 p.m. in July and August; Tues.-Sat. 5-9 p.m. and Sunday

noon-8 p.m. the rest of the year. If you're ready to party, there's live music Saturday night, but be prepared for smoke and noise.

For **picnicking, swimming, and canoeing** in the St. Agatha area, head for **Birch Point Beach,** Chapel Rd., St. David, on the east side of Long Lake. The turnoff to the beach (at St. Michael's Chapel), is 1.3 miles south of the Auberge du Lac B&B. There's a small grassy area, plus picnic tables, and the lake views are fantastic.

Less than a mile south of the Birch Point Beach turnoff is the nine-hole **Birch Point Country Club,** Birch Point Rd., St. David 04773, tel. (207) 895-6957. Ultra-casual, it's a perfect place for amateur golfers out for exercise and fun; no starting times are needed. The clubhouse has a bar and basic menu; cart rentals are available. The course is open May to mid-October.

On the western shore of Long Lake, Rt. 162 in St. Agatha, is a lovely picnic and recreation area, plus a boat launch.

FORT KENT

In the middle of downtown Fort Kent, close to the bridge to Canada, is an almost offhand roadside sign with an impressive message: This Site Marks the Northern Terminus of Historic U.S. Rt. 1 Originating in Key West, Florida. You're 318 miles north of Portland, 368 miles north of the New Hampshire border at Kittery, and 2,209 miles north of Key West.

Fort Kent (pop. 4,300) was incorporated in 1869, after the dust settled from the 1839 Aroostook War. Named for Edward Kent, Maine governor at the time of the border skirmish, the town is the largest in the St. John Valley, occupying a strategic and attractive site on the southern banks of the St. John River, just across from Clair, New Brunswick.

SIGHTS

Fort Kent Blockhouse
Built in 1839 during the decades-long U.S.-Canada border dispute known as the Aroostook War, the National Historic Register Fort Kent Blockhouse, Blockhouse Rd., Fort Kent

04743, is the only remnant of a complex that once included barracks, a hospital, and an ammunition hoard. On the second floor are historic artifacts—unfortunately, not well labeled—plus information about the curious "bloodless" bordier skirmish over timber rights. Bring a picnic and commandeer a table in the pretty little riverside park just below the fort. Early in the summer, before the river dwindles, you can also launch a canoe or kayak here. The Fort Kent Boy Scouts, tel. (207) 834-3866, maintain and staff the blockhouse and the nearby log-cabin gift shop, which are open daily 9 a.m. to sunset, Memorial Day weekend to Labor Day. Admission is free.

University of Maine at Fort Kent
Founded in 1878 as a teacher-training school, the University of Maine at Fort Kent (UMFK) 25 Pleasant St., Fort Kent 04743, tel. (207) 834-7500, still prides itself on the quality of its teacher-education program. Because of its location in the Upper St. John Valley, UMFK also offers a B.S. degree in bilingual/bicultural studies, and the school's **Acadian Archives,** tel.

(207) 834-7535, are the state's best resource on Maine's Acadian heritage. The campus, just off Rt. 1, has a bucolic feel.

Maine's Iditarod

The **Can Am Crown International Sled Dog Races** are a multi-sight, multi-sound experience for spectators as well as participants. Maine's version of the Iditarod, the Can Am 60 (a one-day sprint, 60 miles) and the Can Am 250 (two or three days) are held in mid-February. More than 50 teams usually sign on for the races, which start on Fort Kent's Main Street. (The Can Am 250 also ends there; the 60 ends at Lonesome Pine Trails, at the edge of town.) More than 5,000 people line Main Street for the race starts. The Fort Kent Chamber of Commerce provides maps showing a half-dozen spectator vantage points. Nonparticipants are welcome at the two mushers' awards banquets —a bargain at $6 and $10.

Children, in particular, are not allowed near the sled dogs, but race organizers set aside a special petting area with kid-friendly huskies and mushing gear.

As with Madawaska's Acadian Festival, you'll have to book lodgings well ahead if you want to get in on the action. In February, you're competing for beds with snowmobilers, so don't wait till the last minute. And don't forget to bring far more warm clothing than you think you'll ever need.

RECREATION

The Bangor & Aroostook Railroad line runs right through the first and ninth holes at the **Fort Kent Golf Club**, St. John Rd., Rt. 161, Fort Kent 04743, tel. (207) 834-3149, but that never seems to bother anyone. The meticulously groomed, hilly course has dynamite views of the St. John River. Call for a tee time on weekends; cart rentals are available. The attractive clubhouse has a bar and light meals. The club, three miles west of town (toward Allagash), is open May through October.

Fort Kent's chamber of commerce can dispense information on guided or do-it-yourself **fishing and canoeing,** as well as offer **snowmobiling** advice in winter.

ACCOMMODATIONS AND FOOD

Close to downtown Fort Kent, **Daigle's Bed & Breakfast,** 96 E. Main St., Rt. 1, Fort Kent 04743, tel. (207) 834-5803, is a clean, homey place run by Doris and Elmer Daigle. Four second-floor rooms share a bath ($50 d), and a suite has a private bath and phone ($75 d); two first-floor rooms share a bath ($50 d). A hearty breakfast is served in a two-story glassed-in dining area overlooking the town, the river, and New Brunswick beyond. No smoking, no pets. Open all year.

The best place to eat in Fort Kent is **Sirois' Restaurant,** 84 W. Main St., Rt. 1, Fort Kent 04743, tel. (207) 834-6548, a bright, friendly, family-run operation with creative nightly specials, steaks, pizzas, burgers, a handful of Italian entrées, and first-rate prime ribs ($8-16). (The name is pronounced "CY-russ.") The only Acadian menu item is *poutine,* a cholesterol-loaded

Fort Kent blockhouse

pile of french fries topped with gravy and cheese. Small no-smoking section; limited wine list but full liquor license. On weekends, reservations are a good idea. Open all year, Tues.-Fri. 11 a.m.-9 p.m., Saturday 3-10 p.m., and Sunday 9 a.m.-9 p.m.

INFORMATION AND SERVICES

The **Fort Kent Chamber of Commerce,** 54 W. Main St., Rt. 1, P.O. Box 430, Fort Kent 04743, tel. (207) 834-5354 or (800) 733-3663, serves as a clearinghouse for much of the Upper St. John

Valley. The downtown office, across from Roger's Sport Center, is open weekdays 9 a.m.-5 p.m. On weekends, stop in at the log cabin near the Fort Kent Blockhouse, where area brochures and maps are available.

Customs note: Carry proper identification (passport or photo ID) if you plan to cross into Canada at Fort Kent. The **U.S. Customs** office here, tel. (207) 834-5255, is open round-the-clock. Remember that New Brunswick is on Atlantic time, an hour later than eastern time.

The **Northern Maine Medical Center,** 143 E. Main St., Rt. 1, Fort Kent 04743, tel. (207) 834-3155, has round-the-clock emergency-room care.

SOUTH FROM THE PEAK OF THE CROWN

FORT KENT TO ALLAGASH

It's 30 miles from Fort Kent southwest to Dickey (just west of Allagash)—a scenic riverside drive or pedal on Rt. 161. The first 20 miles is comfortably level; beyond St. Francis, it becomes more winding and hilly. Pack up a picnic, allow a couple of hours, and head out. In mid-September, one of the best times to be here, the hills on your left are a riot of color, all the way to Allagash. On your right, the river usually dribbles along this time of year, exposing gravel bars much of the way. A far cry from late winter and spring, when ice jams and spring runoff are the rule.

St. Francis (pop. 650) is a good spot for a lunch break; the rest area here, overlooking the river, has covered picnic tables, grills, a pit toilet, and a boat-launching ramp. If you're up for an easy, 40-mile bike ride, pedal here from Fort Kent, stop for lunch, and return.

Twenty-three miles from Fort Kent, you'll see the **Welcome to Allagash** sign, announcing a tiny town (about 350 residents) and a legendary waterway (the 92-mile Allagash Wilderness Waterway). Just before the sign is a minuscule riverview rest area with a picnic table and limited parking (a steep bank prevents river access).

The town of **Allagash,** curiously enough, was settled by Irish and English immigrants, so it's not unusual to find lots of Irish surnames in this part of the valley. Contemporary author Cathie

Pelletier grew up in Allagash, called "Mattagash" in her entertaining novels of life in northern Maine. Townspeople love identifying each of the characters. Allagash town manager Roy Gardner and his wife, Maude, operate **Gardner Sporting Camps,** Box 127, Allagash 04774, tel. (207) 398-3168, a collection of rustic cabins, in a knockout setting on the banks of the St. John. Some guests have been returning for years. Average nightly rate is $20 pp, but there's a three-night minimum in October and a one-week minimum in November for hunters. The Gardners arrange shuttle service for canoeists exiting from the Allagash Waterway, and they'll provide meals if you forewarn them. Open mid-May to mid-December.

Route 161 ends in the hamlet of **Dickey,** best known for the frontier-style **Dickey Trading Post,** tel. (207) 398-3157, source of odds and ends, basic lunch fare, and just enough groceries to keep you going.

Allagash and St. John Canoeing

Shuttles, pickups, food, and very basic lodgings are all available in Allagash and Dickey, the endpoints for many Allagash and St. John paddlers. Information on outfitters, guides, and access appears in the Katahdin/Moosehead Region chapter, where these trips begin. Willard Jalbert Camps, a veteran sporting camp along the Allagash Wilderness Waterway, is located in the wilds of Aroostook County, with an office in Fort Kent.

SOUTH ON ROUTE 11

If you took a poll among those who know, especially photographers, Route 11 southbound from Fort Kent to Portage probably would rank near the top as a favorite fall-foliage drive. What's so appealing along this 37-mile Scenic Highway? Brilliant colors, rolling hills, open vistas, and a smattering of lakes and ponds. It's really stunning, either by car or bike.

Eagle Lake

A good stopping point is Eagle Lake (pop. 860), about 18 miles south of Fort Kent. The official rest area, overlooking the lake, has picnic tables and plenty of parking. Many a photo has been snapped here. If it's a typically bright fall day, you'll see why: a prime hilltop with a pristine lake surrounded by multicolored foliage. Eighteen-mile-long, L-shaped Eagle Lake is a key link in the Fish River Chain of Lakes, starting at Long Lake in St. Agatha. In winter, the lake supports wall-to-wall ice-fishing shacks.

Eagle Lake's **town park,** down at lake level, has shorefront picnic tables and grills. The wind kicks up wildly at times, but on a calm day, this is a fine place to launch a canoe. From Rt. 11, turn at Old Main St. and go .6 mile; there's plenty of parking.

If you'd like to overnight along Route 11, opt for the immaculately maintained **Overlook Motel,** N. Main St., Rt. 11, Eagle Lake 04739, tel. (207) 444-4535, fax 444-4571, with the same dramatic view as the official rest area. Opened in 1995, it's become one of Rt. 11's most popular lodgings. Rooms include three singles ($42 s), two doubles ($48 d), four efficiencies ($58 d), two hot-tub suites ($68 d), and an apartment that sleeps six ($94); amenities include phones, a/c, cable TV, and free continental breakfast. Even the singles have a microwave and refrigerator. In winter, snowmobilers pile in here.

About one and a half miles east of Rt. 11, on Old Main Street beyond the town park, is **Camps of Acadia,** Box 202, Eagle Lake 04739, tel. (207) 444-5207—less remote than most sporting camps, but just as rustic. Established in 1931, Camps of Acadia is open all year. In the 8 cabins you can choose housekeeping facilities ($55 a day for four) or American Plan (AP) with three meals in the lodge ($60 a day pp; chil-

dren under 10 are $30). In July and August, family rates are $50 a day AP for adults, $25 for kids 6-12; housekeeping rates those months are $45 for four. Meals are also available separately for housekeeping guests. Boat and canoe rentals are $15 a day ($30 for boat and motor). Just east of the camps is the 23,000-acre Eagle Lake unit of public reserved land, terrific for fishing, camping, and boating.

Over the years, Eagle Lake has benefited heavily from being the hometown of John Martin, one of Maine's most influential politicians, now playing a rearguard role. The town just really looks as though someone has been paying attention.

About eight miles south of Eagle Lake is the wooded **Hedgehog Mountain Rest Area,** trailhead for Hedgehog Mountain. It's not your most exciting climb, and the summit view is so-so, but it's easy exercise for an hour or so. The trail is just over a mile roundtrip.

Portage

The end of the officially designated Scenic Highway, but not the end of the scenery, Portage (pop. 440) is particularly popular as a summer playground, and many County residents have built or rented camps on the shores of Portage Lake.

Golfers may want to play a round at nine-hole **Portage Hills Country Club,** Portage 04768, tel. (207) 435-8221, where the challenges come with the rolling terrain. Starting times aren't needed; the course is open Memorial Day weekend through September.

Need a bite to eat? The dining room at **Dean's Motor Lodge,** Rt. 11, Portage 04768, tel. (207) 435-3701 or 435-6840, specializing in steaks and seafood, is open all year for breakfast, lunch, and dinner.

From Rt. 11, turn west at W. Cottage Rd. and go half a mile to reach the Portage **town beach.** The view is fabulous and parking is ample; there are picnic tables, a grill, and a grassy "beach."

Route 11 in Portage provides access to **Moose Point Camps,** Fish River Lake, P.O. Box 170, Portage 04768, tel. (207) 435-6156, an idyllic spot with 10 rustic cabins on the shore of five-mile-long Fish River Lake (a.k.a. Fish Lake). Rates are $280 a week pp, AP (all meals), $75 a week for children under 12. BYOL. Motorboat rentals are $35 a day, canoes are

$10 a day. In the main lodge are games, books, and a huge fireplace. Open early May through August. Watch for the sign on Rt. 11 and turn west. About four miles from Portage, you'll reach the Fish River Checkpoint, the toll booth for entering the logging area. Roundtrip fee is $18 for non-Maine residents; seniors and kids under 15 are free. **Note:** Don't expect to be alone with the moose and other wildlife out here; logging trucks legally own the road, and they know it, so give them a wide berth.

A mile south of Portage is **North Woods Saddle Expeditions,** Rt. 11, Nashville Plantation, mailing address P.O. Box 39, Portage 04768, tel. (207) 435-4371, Sarah Brooks and Mike Boulier's working horse farm. Lots of options here: half-day and all-day guided trail rides with a steak feed ($70-90 pp); carriage, hay, and sleigh rides; and a three-room farmhouse B&B ($40 d; shared bath). You can combine any of the above and even help with the chores. No trail rides during hunting season (late October to late November). Third weekend in September is an Operation Liftoff benefit, a gala festival, including a wagon train, to raise funds for terminally ill children.

Ashland

Considered the "Gateway to the North Maine Woods," Ashland (pop. 1,600) is the home of **North Maine Woods,** P.O. Box 421, Ashland 04732, tel. (207) 435-6213, a private organization charged with managing recreational use of about 4,400 square miles of northern Maine's working timberlands. North Maine Woods publishes maps, newsletters, and serves as an information resource for camping, fishing, hunting, hiking trails, and logging roads. Call (weekdays only) for a free packet of regulations and list of outfitters, plus an order form for maps and other publications.

The open-air **Ashland Logging Museum,** Garfield Rd., Ashland 04732, tel. (207) 435-6039, has six buildings containing a blacksmith shop, old woods rigs, and other gear—a taste of what the timber industry was like. The museum is open Memorial Day weekend to Labor Day, daily 10 a.m.-6 p.m. Admission is free. Just before Ashland, when Rt. 11 takes a sharp left, turn right onto Garfield Rd. and go a little less than a mile. (You'll get an even better taste of the trade at the Patten Lumberman's Museum in Patten, east of Baxter State Park.)

About 10 miles east of Ashland on Rt. 163 (Presque Isle Road) is the trailhead (on the left) for **Haystack Mountain,** a short, steep climb—easy to moderate—to a fairly bald summit. Pack a picnic so you can enjoy the almost-360-degree view.

Roughly midway between Ashland and Masardis, in the town of Masardis, is an access road to the boat landing for **Squa Pan Lake,** probably the oddest-shaped lake in the state—V-shaped, tongue-shaped, you-name-it. One wag alleges the name comes from a squaw who married a French man named Pan, and if you believe that, there's this bridge. . . .

Route 11 continues southward and out of Aroostook County, to Patten, Medway, and Millinocket.

BOB RACE

THE KENNEBEC/ MOOSE RIVER REGION

The mighty Kennebec, Maine's fourth-largest river, defines this region. The river wends its way through Somerset and Kennebec Counties from Jackman through Bingham, Skowhegan, Waterville, Augusta, and Richmond, and then on toward the sea at Bath. Many of these inland communities seldom see out-of-towners, since most visitors tend to concentrate on the region's lovely lakes districts—Belgrade Lakes, China Lakes, and Winthrop Lakes, all favorite summer destinations for as long as anyone can remember.

In 1976, timber companies stopped floating logs down the Kennebec to their lumber mills. Since then, whitewater rafting has mushroomed, focusing long-overdue attention on the beautiful Upper Kennebec Valley and creating a whole new crowd of enthusiasts for this region. And there's no sign of a let-up. When I first rafted the Kennebec, in 1985, it was still a rather volatile yet unsophisticated business; regulations were still a bit loose, and the competition was scrappy. Since then, however, a number of fly-by-night firms have gone belly-up, and those that remain range from deliberately small operations to four-season enterprises with a variety of other sports options and all the amenities

anyone could want. Visit The Forks and you'll understand.

When you see the terrain, you'll also begin to understand some of the awful rigors endured by Col. Benedict Arnold (before his change of heart and alliance) and his men when they chose a route through the Kennebec Valley to attack the British in Quebec City in 1775.

The Arnold Trail

"A tragic masterpiece of bad timing, bad maps, and bad luck" is author Ogden Tanner's summation of the "March on Quebec" spearheaded by Col. Benedict Arnold. Although he later betrayed the Revolutionary cause, Arnold was in good graces when he set out that fall with 1,100 adventurers to remove the English from their Quebec stronghold. In Pittston (six miles south of Augusta), the expedition assembled 220 locally made bateaux, then continued up the Kennebec River to Augusta, Skowhegan, and Norridgewock—cutting a swath through the Kennebec/Moose River region before portaging westward at Carrying Place Township to the Western Lakes and Mountains region and on into Canada. Afflicted by disease, hunger, cold, insects, and unforgiving terrain, the group was devastated before dragging into Quebec City in December 1775. From Pittston to The Carrying Place (10 miles north of Bingham), Arnold Trail historical markers note the expedition's rest stops, obstacles, and other details. Even though Arnold's expedition has been little more than a footnote to history, it's an incredible story, and one best appreciated during a visit to this region.

AUGUSTA AND VICINITY

As the state capital, Augusta is where everything is supposed to happen. A lot does happen here, but don't be surprised to find the imposing State House and lovely governor's mansion the centerpieces of a relatively sleepy city. With a population of only 21,000, Augusta is the seventh-largest city in Maine and no megalopolis, but it *is* the heart of state government and central Maine.

Pilgrims first settled here on the banks of the Kennebec River in the 17th century (in 1997, the city celebrated its bicentennial with considerable fanfare), and Boston merchants established Fort Western in the mid-18th century. Augusta was named the capital in 1827.

Preparations for the bicentennial provided the spark for a healthy turnaround in attitudes about Augusta. Such pejoratives as "Disgusta" seem to have dwindled, and the city is on an upswing. Housing costs are low, and the population is particularly diverse for Maine. The only remaining eyesores are some of the older buildings at one end of Water Street, along the west bank of the Kennebec.

The three best-known communities south of Augusta—Hallowell, Gardiner, and Richmond—all scale down hillsides to the river, making their settings especially attractive. In Hallowell (pop. 2,600), settled in 1762, the main thoroughfare still retains the air of its former days as a prosperous port and source of granite and ice. The entire downtown, with brick sidewalks and attractive shops and restaurants, is a National Historic District.

Six miles south of Augusta, Gardiner (pop. 6,780), the "Tilbury Town" of noted author Edwin Arlington Robinson, claims more National Historic Register buildings than any of its neighbors. The Gardiner Historic District includes more than 45 downtown buildings; lots more are beyond the district. Besides Robinson, another prominent Gardiner resident was Laura

Howe Richards, author of *Captain January* and daughter of Julia Ward Howe, who wrote "The Battle Hymn of the Republic." (The yellow Federal-style home where Richards and her husband raised seven children, at 3 Dennis St., is not open to the public.) Most outstanding of Gardiner's mansions (also not open to the public) is "Oaklands," a Gothic Revival home built in 1836 by the grandson of founding father Dr. Sylvester Gardiner, a wealthy land speculator.

Just over the border in Sagadahoc County, Richmond (pop. 3,085), also flush with handsome buildings, was the site of a Russian émigré community in the 1950s. Here's a town that awaits rediscovery.

West of Augusta, the town of Monmouth (pop. 3,500) is the site of Cumston Hall, a dramatic, turn-of-the-20th-century structure that now houses The Theater at Monmouth as well as the municipal offices and public library.

SIGHTS

Maine State House

From almost every vantage point in Augusta, your eye catches the prominent dome of the Maine State House, centerpiece of the government complex on the west side of the Kennebec River. Occupying the corner of State and Capitol Sts., the State House dates originally from 1832, when it was completed to the design of famed Boston architect Charles Bulfinch, who modeled it on his Massachusetts State House design. Only a dozen years had passed since Maine had separated from Massachusetts, and Augusta became the state capital in 1827. Granite for the building came from quarries in nearby Hallowell; total construction cost was $139,000. Atop the oxidized copper dome stands a gold-plated sculpture of Minerva, goddess of Wisdom. In the early 20th century, space needs

forced a major expansion of the building, leaving only the front portico as today's Bulfinch legacy.

Visitors are welcome to wander around the State House, but check first to see whether the legislature is in session. If so, parking becomes scarce, the hallways become congested, and access may be restricted. Best place to enter the building is on the first floor at the south end (close to the State Street parking lot). Pick up the useful brochure for a self-guided tour, or, better still, take a free guided tour, available weekdays 9 a.m.-1 p.m. Call ahead, (207) 287-1408, to arrange it, or use one of the red phones close to where you entered. There's a cafeteria on the first floor.

Maine State Museum

If the Smithsonian is the nation's attic, welcome to Maine's attic—and a well-organized one at that. At the Maine State Museum, State House Complex, Augusta 04333, tel. (207) 287-2301, fax 287-6633, gears and tools spin and whir in the intriguing *Made in Maine* industrial exhibits—focusing on quarrying, ice harvesting, fishing, agriculture, lumbering, and shipbuilding. A spiraled archaeological exhibit covers the past 12 millennia of Maine's history. Some displays are interactive and all exhibits are wheelchair-accessible. During the winter, the museum sponsors a free Sunday afternoon (2 p.m.) lecture series. A small gift shop stocks historical publications. The museum is part of the state government complex that includes the State House and the Maine State Library. The museum and library share a building, separated by a parking lot from the State House. The museum is open all year, Mon.-Fri. 9 a.m.-5 p.m., Saturday 10 a.m.-4 p.m., and Sunday 1-4 p.m. Best of all, admission is free.

Each summer, the **Friends of the Maine State Museum,** 83 State House Station, Augusta 04333, tel. (207) 287-2304, sponsors a field school in archaeology, with two six-day sessions, usually in June. Locations vary, but it's always remarkable—past sites have been a Paleo-Indian village in Searsmont and a prehistoric village on Blue Hill Bay. Cost is $600

pp ($500 for museum members); each session is limited to 12.

The Blaine House
In 1833, a year after the State House was ready for business, retired sea captain James Hall finished his elegant new home across the street. But it was not until 29 years later, when prominent politico James G. Blaine assumed ownership, that the house became the hotbed of state and national political ferment. No underachiever, Blaine was a Maine congressman and Senator, Speaker of the U.S. House, U.S. secretary of state under two presidents, and

THE RUSSIANS WERE COMING

In the 1950s, the sleepy Kennebec River town of Richmond, 12 miles south of Maine's state capital, became the center of a unique and unlikely colony, as several hundred Russian-speaking refugee families settled among the area's villages and rolling farmland. The Kennebec Valley, economically depressed and remote from other Russian immigrant centers in the United States, seems an improbable choice for a Slavic enclave. Yet Richmond soon boasted a Russian restaurant, a Russian bootmaker's shop, and even onion domes—on St. Alexander Nevsky, Maine's first Russian Orthodox church. For the first time, Russian was heard on Richmond's streets, and Russian-speaking children enrolled in local schools.

The settlement was the brainchild of Baron Vladimir von Poushental, a swashbuckling veteran of the tsar's World War I air force. Fleeing the Bolshevik Revolution, he landed in New York, where his personality and family connections gained him entrée to a series of managerial jobs, if not to the wealth he had enjoyed as a Russian noble. An expert marksman and dedicated hunter, von Poushental in 1947 decided to retire to a modest cabin in the Kennebec Valley, where he had hunted and fished for many years. There he began buying up abandoned farms and promoting the valley's attractions to fellow Russian émigrés. The climate and countryside resembled Russia's, he said, and land was cheap. For a few thousand dollars, a refugee could buy a house and 30 acres. To create a nucleus for the settlers, the baron donated a 400-acre farm to the aging veterans of Russia's White armies, and he helped them es-

tablish a retirement home and an Orthodox chapel.

And so they came: Ukrainians, Russians, Byelorussians, and Cossacks; professors, farmers, artists, and carpenters. Some came directly from Europe's displaced-persons camps, others from homes and jobs in U.S. cities where they had lived for years. The settlers shared a common language, their Orthodox faith, a zest for life, and a hatred of the Soviet regime. The younger émigrés worked, raised families, and became part of the larger American community around them. Their elderly parents felt more comfortable associating with other Russian-speakers.

Today the bootmaker and restaurant are gone. Most of the elderly—the old émigrés from pre-Communist Russia—are dead, their Cyrillic gravestones dotting the Richmond cemetery. A few old-timers, still hardy, stand each Sunday through the long Orthodox service, and they bake *pirozhki* or sweets for church sales on special occasions, like the town's late-July celebration of Richmond Days.

Their grandchildren, Russian-Americans, have merged successfully into mainstream America. Most have married outside their ethnic group, and many have taken jobs outside the Kennebec Valley, not necessarily by choice. Yet a fair number still live and work in the area. In a way that might have surprised even von Poushental (who died in 1978), the colony he sponsored took root and flourished in a part of America he loved.

—Robert S. Jaster, author of a forthcoming book on Richmond's Russian colony

Republican candidate for the presidency. Two decades after his death, Blaine's widow donated the family home to the state of Maine; it's been the **governor's mansion** ever since.

Free, half-hour guided tours of the ground-floor public areas of The Blaine House, State and Capitol Sts., Augusta 04333, tel. (207) 287-2121, occur Tues.-Thurs. 2-4 p.m., all year. A special event could cancel the tour schedule, so it's wise to call ahead to avoid being disappointed.

Old Fort Western

Built in 1754 for the French and Indian Wars and restored as recently as 1988, Old Fort Western, 16 Cony St., Augusta 04330, tel. (207) 626-2385, fax 626-2304—reputedly the nation's oldest remaining stockaded fort—has witnessed British, French, and Native Americans squabbling over this Kennebec riverfront site. Benedict Arnold and his troops camped here during their 1775 march on Quebec. Today, costumed interpreters help visitors travel through time to the 18th century; hands-on demonstrations—butter churning, musket drill, barrel building, weaving, even vinegar making—occur daily from July Fourth to Labor Day. Admission is $4.50 adults, $2.50 children 6-16; kids under six are free. Open daily 1-4 p.m., Memorial Day weekend to July Fourth; weekdays 10 a.m.-4 p.m. and weekends 1-4 p.m., July Fourth to Labor Day; weekends only 1-4 p.m., Labor Day to Columbus Day. From November through May, the fort is also open the first Sunday of the month, 1-3 p.m. The museum is on the east bank of the Kennebec in downtown Augusta, next to Augusta City Hall.

PARKS AND PRESERVES

On the east side of State Street, between the State House and the river, is 10-acre **Capitol Park,** a great place for a picnic after visiting the Maine State Museum, the State House, and the Blaine House. In the park is the **Maine Vietnam Veterans Memorial,** a dramatic, you-are-there, walk-through monument erected in 1985.

On the east side of the Kennebec River, across from Augusta Mental Health Institute, is a wonderful oasis. The **Pine Tree State Arbo-retum,** 153 Hospital St., Rt. 9, P.O. Box 344, Augusta 04332, tel. (207) 621-0031, devotes 224 acres to more than 600 trees and shrubs. Bring a picnic (carry-in, carry-out) and wander the three-and-a-half-mile trail network. If you're a birder, bring binoculars. Well-designed planting clusters include hosta and rhododendron collections, a rock garden, an antique apple orchard, and the Governors Grove—with a white pine dedicated to each Maine governor. Stop first at the Viles Visitor Center to pick up a trail map and a flora and fauna list. The grounds are open daily sunrise to sunse, all yeart; the visitor center is open Mon.-Fri. 8 a.m.-4 p.m. Leashed pets are allowed; no smoking on the grounds. During the winter, the trails are groomed for cross-country skiing; an additional 12-mile loop trail continues from the arboretum to the Togus Veterans' Hospital east of Augusta.

Next to the arboretum parking lot is **Cony Cemetery,** one of Augusta's oldest, with gravestones dating from the late 18th century. Old-cemetery buffs will want to check it out, but rubbings are not permitted.

About 12 miles south of Augusta, 100-acre **Peacock Beach State Park,** Rt. 201, Richmond 04357, tel. (207) 582-2813, on long, narrow Pleasant Pond, is an underutilized pocket park great for swimming and picnicking; a lifeguard is on duty in summer. Admission is $1 adults, 50 cents children 5-11; free for kids under five. Open Memorial Day through Labor Day.

The Maine Department of Inland Fisheries and Wildlife (IF&W) has used a somewhat complicated reservation system to limit visitors to its **Steve Powell Wildlife Management Area** on 1,750-acre, four-mile-long **Swan Island,** in the middle of the Kennebec River. Don't be daunted; it's worth the effort. Well-marked trails cover the island; one trail takes 30 minutes, another takes three hours and goes the length of the lovely wooded island. Plan to take the free, hour-long ranger-guided tour. No license is needed for fishing, but even private boats need permission to land here (near the campground). Bikes are not allowed. The island is accessible only by 15-passenger boat from a dock in Richmond, directly north of the town-owned Waterfront Park on Rt. 24. The boat operates May through the third week in September. You'll need to make reservations for a specific departure time, preferably two weeks ahead, *in writing*, through the IF&W office. Maximum daily headcount is 60. Call for a reservation form and informational flyer, tel. (207) 547-4167, Mon.-Fri. 8 a.m.-noon, fax 547-4035. When you reserve, you'll need to include a $5 reservation fee, applicable toward your admission fees. Admission is $3 pp for day use; children five and under are free. Request the earliest boat (9 a.m.), so you can spend the whole day. Also request a copy of the IF&W's island history booklet. Pack a picnic lunch; day visitors can use the fireplaces at the campground, but bring tinfoil for cooking.

The island, settled in the early 1700s, once had as many as 95 resident farmers, fishermen, ice-cutters, and shipbuilders. Now there are derelict antique houses, a herd of whitetail deer, wild turkeys, nesting bald eagles, plenty of waterfowl and other birds, and the primitive campground. No liquor or pets are allowed on the island.

Swan Island's campground has 10 well-spaced lean-tos with picnic tables, fireplaces, and outhouses; firewood and bottled water are provided. Cost is $5 pp per night; two-night maximum. A rickety flatbed truck with benches meets campers at the island dock and transports them the one and a half miles to the campground. The same truck does the island tour.

RECREATION

Bicycling
Bike routes with decent shoulders are all too rare in Maine, so take advantage of Rt. 27 between Augusta and Belgrade Lakes. It's mostly wide, flat, and fairly open, making an easy 18-mile one-way trip to Belgrade Lakes village.

Golf
Ten miles north of Augusta and 12 miles south of Waterville, the highly rated 27-hole **Natanis Golf Club,** Webber Pond Rd., RR 1, Box 6820, Vassalboro 04989, tel. (207) 622-3561, has been the site of many a Maine golf tournament. Named after a trusted Indian guide, the Natanis club calls its three nines Arrowhead, Tomahawk, and Indian Territory. The attractive new

clubhouse has a pro shop, café/lounge, and wraparound veranda. Tee times are required on weekends; the course is open April to mid-November. On the east bank of the Kennebec in Augusta, take Rt. 201 eight miles to Webber Pond Rd. and continue to the club entrance.

Kids' Stuff
"Small is beautiful" fits the **Children's Discovery Museum,** 265 Water St., Vickery Building, P.O. Box 5056, Augusta 04330, tel. (207) 622-2209, with interactive activities and imaginative playthings for kids to age 10. Besides the five display rooms, there's a communications center with computers and a ham radio. Adults must accompany all children. Admission is $3 pp; children under one are free. The museum is open Mon.-Fri. 9 a.m.-4 p.m. in summer. Other months, it's open Mon.-Fri. 9 a.m.-2 p.m., Saturday 10 a.m.-4 p.m., and Sunday 1-4 p.m. On the ground floor of the same building is the **Vickery Café,** 261 Water St., Augusta 04330, tel. (207) 623-7670, serving up PB&J sandwiches and lots of other child-friendly fare. It's open all year, Mon.-Fri. 7 a.m.-2:30 p.m., but unfortunately not on weekends.

Richmond Sauna
Meriting a recreational category of its own—or maybe it should qualify as entertainment—the **Richmond Corner Sauna,** Dingley Rd., Richmond 04357, tel. (207) 737-4752 or (800) 400-5751, is one of those funky places you either like or you don't. But it's been here since 1976. And you'll probably like it. Finnish-American owner Richard Jarvi has built up a loyal clientele for his authentic, wood-heated sauna house—six private rooms and a group one. In between and afterward, there's a pool and hot tub. If nudity bothers you, don't come, but no one seems to gawk. If you're too relaxed to drive after the sauna, the informal main house, built in 1831, has five B&B rooms at $60 d (sauna included). The sauna is open all year, Tues.-Sun. 5-9 p.m. Cost is $15 pp. From downtown Richmond, take Rt. 197 west about five miles and turn left (south) onto Rt. 138. Take an immediate left onto Dingley Rd., where you'll see the sign.

ENTERTAINMENT

On the northern edge of Augusta, across from the Augusta Civic Center (Rt. 27), is the 10-screen **Hoyts Cinema,** 23 Marketplace Dr., Augusta 04330, tel. (207) 623-8183. Something for everyone, and matinees as well. Close to downtown Augusta, the five-screen **State Street Cinema,** 290 State St., Augusta 04330, tel. (207) 622-9848, has cheaper seats and summer matinees starting as early as 1 p.m. Check local newspapers or call for schedules.

The **Gaslight Theater,** a talented community-theater group, performs periodically throughout the year at the **Hallowell City Hall Auditorium,** Winthrop St., Hallowell 04347, tel. (207) 626-3698. Call for schedule, or stop in at the town office.

Six miles south of Augusta, the 1864 **Johnson Hall,** Water St., Gardiner 04345, tel. (207) 582-7144, is the year-round site of just about anything anyone wants to present—plays, lectures, classes, concerts, vaudeville shows, and more. Call for a current schedule.

Maine's enduring Shakespearean theater is **The Theater at Monmouth,** Main St., Rt. 132, P.O. Box 385, Monmouth 04259, box office tel. (207) 933-9999 or (800) 769-9698 in Maine, based in Monmouth's architecturally astonishing Cumston Hall. Completed in 1900, the Romanesque Victorian structure has columns,

cutout shingles, stained glass, and a huge square tower. The interior is equally stunning, with frescoes and a vaulted ceiling. The theater's summer season, performed by professionals in rotating repertory, runs early July through August. Shakespeare gets the nod for at least two of the four plays. Tickets are $20 adults, $18 seniors, less for matinees and the annual children's play.

FESTIVALS AND EVENTS

During the school year, the **University of Maine at Augusta** campus on the outskirts of the city schedules lectures, concerts, and other performances. Check with the school, tel. (207) 621-3000 or (800) 696-6000, for current information.

The Augusta area seems to claim more country fairs than any other part of the state; don't miss an opportunity to attend at least one. Each has a different flavor, but there are always lots of animals and junk food, often a carnival, and sometimes harness racing.

The small, four-day **Pittston Fair** features agricultural exhibits, a carnival, and even a pig scramble at the Pittston Fairgrounds, East Pittston the third weekend of June. The huge **Whatever Family Festival** runs for a week late June to the Fourth of July with races, live entertainment, a carnival, fireworks, and several river-related events in Augusta and Gardiner. Late June to mid-August, free **New England**

Cumston Hall,
Monmouth

MAINE OFFICE OF TOURISM

Music Camp Concerts are offered by students Saturday and Sunday (3 p.m.), with chamber-music recitals by faculty on Friday (8 p.m.). Student concerts are at the outdoor "Bowl-in-the-Pines" (bring a blanket or chair); faculty recitals take place in Alumni Hall. The famed camp was founded in the 1930s. New England Music Camp, Lake Messalonskee, Sidney, tel. (207) 465-3025.

Augusta's annual three-day Franco-American **Festival de la Bastille** celebrates French independence with French food, music, dancing, children's events, a bean supper, and fireworks at Le Club Calumet, Old Belgrade Rd., tel. (207) 623-8211, on the weekend nearest July 14. The third Saturday in July, **Old Hallowell Day** includes a craft fair, a parade, food booths, games, and fireworks 10 a.m.-10 p.m. in downtown Hallowell. The **Monmouth Fair** fills four days with agricultural exhibits, live entertainment, a carnival, and a special children's day the last weekend of July or first weekend in August.

The last week of August, the Windsor Fairgrounds come alive with the week-long **Windsor Fair**'s agricultural exhibits, harness racing, parade, beauty pageant, and carnival.

Litchfield's three-day **Litchfield Fair** has farm exhibits, a carnival, craft demos, and more the first weekend in September.

SHOPPING

Augusta has two major shopping areas—not exactly malls, but clusters of stores—**Capitol Shopping Center,** intown on Western Avenue, and **The Mall at Augusta,** across from the Augusta Civic Center on Rt. 27 north of the city.

For a different kind of shopping experience, head a mile south of Augusta to Hallowell, where boutiques, restaurants, and nearly a dozen antiques shops line historic Water Street. It's a prime destination for anyone in search of anything from gifts to collectibles to fine antiques.

Art Galleries
The **Harlow Gallery,** 160 Water St., P.O. Box 213, Hallowell 04347, tel. (207) 622-3813, headquarters for the Kennebec Valley Art Association, serves as a magnet not only for its member artists but also for poets and jazz musicians.

It's a happening place. Open limited hours: Friday 7-9 p.m., Saturday noon-9 p.m., and Sunday 10 a.m.-3 p.m.

Established in 1973, **The Talent Tree Art Gallery,** Hospital St., Rt. 9, Augusta 04330, tel. (207) 623-8018, is a high-end, low-profile gallery with a first-rate reputation and changing monthly exhibits. On the first floor is Maine's best art-conservation lab, where museum pieces get a new lease on life. The gallery is open Mon.-Fri. 9 a.m.-5:30 p.m. in summer, plus Saturday 9 a.m.-1 p.m. in winter. It's on the east side of the Kennebec, one and a half miles south of the junction of Rts. 9 and 17.

New and Used Books
The megabookstores, following the Wal-Mart trend, have entered Maine like gorillas, so underdog defenders are quick to lambaste them, but it's impossible to ignore the quality, value, and service at **Barnes & Noble Booksellers,** 9 Marketplace Dr., Augusta 04330, tel. (207) 621-0038. Besides, with its heavy schedule of special events, it even qualifies in the entertainment category in a community not overloaded with evening options. In addition to carrying about 150,000 titles, Barnes & Noble stocks an excellent selection of Maine books, even self-published ones. The "woody" decor, random easy chairs, café, and large public restrooms encourage browsing and lingering. The store is open all year, Mon.-Sat. 9 a.m.-11 p.m. and Sunday 10 a.m.-9 p.m. It's at the northern edge of Augusta, just off Rt. 27 on the hill across from the Augusta Civic Center.

The apt slogan at **Merrill's Bookshop,** 108 Water St., Hallowell 04347, tel. (207) 623-2055, is "Good literature from Edward Abbey to Leane Zugsmith." John Merrill has an eye for unusual rare and used books, so you may walk out with a personal treasure. The shop is open Tues.-Sat. 10 a.m.-5 p.m., all year.

Fine Jewelry
Half a dozen goldsmiths market their exquisite jewelry at **David-Brooks Goldsmiths,** 190 Water St., Hallowell 04347, tel. (207) 622-9895 or (800) 734-2666, fax (207) 622-7607, and they'll also accept custom orders. Prices are high, but definitely worth it. Open Mon.-Sat. 9 a.m.-5 p.m., all year.

Hussey's General Store

What do power tools, fishing gear, and bridal gowns have in common? Not what you may think. They're all in the front window at Hussey's General Store, Rt. 32, Windsor 04363, tel. (207) 445-2511, a country store with a difference. There isn't much that Hussey's doesn't have, and that bridal department does a steady business. Hussey's is open all year: May-Dec., Mon.-Sat. 8 a.m.-8 p.m. and Sunday 9 a.m.-5 p.m.; Jan.-April, Mon.-Sat. 8 a.m.-6 p.m. and Sunday 9 a.m.-5 p.m. From Augusta, take Rt. 105 about 11 miles east to Rt. 32; Hussey's is on the corner. If you're at the Windsor Fairgrounds, the store is only about two miles farther north on Rt. 32.

Farmers' Markets

At the Capitol Shopping Center on Western Avenue, the **Augusta Farmers' Market** operates Wednesday 9 a.m.-1 p.m. and Saturday 9 a.m.-1 p.m., mid-May to late October.

West of Augusta, the **Winthrop Farmers' Market** begins in March (or when the snow stops) and ends in October or November (when the snow returns), setting up at the municipal building parking lot (Main St. in Winthrop) each Tuesday and Saturday 9 a.m.-2 p.m.

South of Augusta, the smallish **Gardiner Farmers' Market** is located on Water Street each Friday 3-6 p.m., early June to mid-October.

ACCOMMODATIONS

Most of the lodgings in the Augusta area are motels; chain motels are well represented. The emphasis seems to be on convenience, efficiency, and anonymity. Close to the Augusta Civic Center, on the northern outskirts of town, recommended chain motels are the **Comfort Inn,** 281 Civic Center Dr., Augusta 04330, tel. (207) 623-1000 or (800) 808-1188, and the **Holiday Inn,** 110 Community Dr., Augusta 04330, tel. (207) 622-4751 or (800) 694-6404. Both have on-site restaurants. **Alfred's,** tel. (207) 621-0100, at the Comfort Inn, is a good choice, especially for nonsmokers. On the western edge of the city, close to I-95 Exit 30, are the **Best Western Senator Inn,** Outer Western Ave., Augusta 04330, tel. (207) 622-5804 or (800) 528-1234, **Augusta Hotel,** 390 Western Ave., Au-

gusta 04330, tel. (207) 622-6371 or (888) 636-2463, and the **Super 8 Motel,** 395 Western Ave., Augusta 04330, tel. (207) 626-2888. At these three motels, request a room farthest from traffic noise. The Senator and Augusta Hotel have on-site restaurants; **Margarita's,** tel. (207) 622-7874, at the Augusta Hotel, is one of several in a good New England Tex-Mex chain.

B&Bs

On a back road only 10 minutes from the State House, 62-acre **Maple Hill Farm Bed and Breakfast Inn,** Outlet Rd., RR 1, Box 1145, Hallowell 04347, tel. (207) 622-2708 or (800) 622-2708, fax (207) 622-0655, feels like worlds away. Six rooms and a suite ($50-110 d, with a/c and in-room phones) in the informal, renovated 1890s farmhouse overlook woods, fields, gardens, and even the Camden Hills. Innkeeper Scott Cowger —a state legislator, avid cyclist, and Hallowell enthusiast—pays close attention to guests' needs. His favorite line is, "I can customize your day," specializing in outdoor activities and day-trips. Three rooms share a bath; all others have private baths. Smoking only outside; no children under eight; no pets. Maple Hill Farm is three miles west of downtown Hallowell.

About 15 miles west of Augusta, Arn and Leda Sturtevant are the genial sixth-generation owners of **Home-Nest Farm,** Baldwin Hill Rd., Fayette, mailing address Box 2350, Kents Hill 04349, tel. (207) 897-4125, a 200-acre, 18th-century tree and sheep farm with a fabulous 65-mile view. Two suites are in a wing of the farmhouse; two cottages are separate—one is a restored red schoolhouse. Daily rates start at $80 d, two-night minimum July through September. Amenities include woodstoves or fireplaces, kitchens in two cottages and one of the suites, plus enough provisions for do-it-yourself breakfasts. Discounts for extended stays. Book well ahead. No smoking, no pets, no credit cards; children are welcome. Open May through February. The B&B is 1.7 miles southeast of Rt. 17, well signposted.

Cottage Colony

A cross between a cottage colony and a sporting camp, **Echo Lake Lodge & Cottages,** Rt. 17, Fayette, mailing address P.O. Box 528, Readfield 04355, tel. (207) 685-9550; off season RR

2, Box 2720, Norridgewock 04957, tel. (207) 362-5642, has occupied these 20 wooded acres since 1937. All of the 15 rustic white cottages ($250-580 a week, including continental breakfast) have kitchen facilities; bring your own sheets and towels or rent them here for $10 pp a week. This is an especially kid-friendly place, and families have been repeating here for years, so reserve well ahead. Request a cottage with a screened porch to ward off mosquitoes. The main lodge has seven B&B rooms rented by the night (private baths; $59 d and up). Occasionally, usually at the last minute, you can rent a cottage on a daily basis. Canoes and kayaks are available for guests. Open May to mid-October, Echo Lake is 15 miles west of Augusta.

FOOD

Special Bakeries

Hand-in-hand with the microbrewery explosion in Maine has come a microbakery explosion—a feast of designer bread and pastries. Run, don't walk, to sample their ethnic specialties, incredible flatbreads, and unique, just-invented combinations. Two super examples are on the outskirts of Augusta. Chris Szigeti-Johnson's **Upper Crust Bakery**, Rt. 202, Manchester 04351, tel. (207) 622-5333, features 18 different kinds of Western and Central European baked goods and lots of pastry choices. Her Linzertorte is beyond delicious, and they'll fill mail orders. The shop is open all year, Mon.-Fri. 6 a.m.-6 p.m., Saturday 6 a.m.-5 p.m., and Sunday 6 a.m.-2 p.m. (to 4 p.m. in summer). If it's closed and there's a vehicle out front, knock on the door. The Upper Crust is three miles west of I-95 Exit 30.

The specialty at **Black Crow Bakery**, Plains Rd., RR 1, Box 1550, Litchfield 04350, tel. (207) 268-9927, is a Tuscan loaf that's as pretty as it is tasty. Except for onion focaccia, all their other exotic breads are sourdough-based—200-300 loaves a day. A modern mixer is Mark and Tinker Mickalide's only high-tech tool; they operate a very traditional bakery in their 1810 farmhouse's former summer kitchen, even grinding their own grains on Maine granite. The shop is open all year, Tues.-Sat. 7 a.m.-7 p.m. It's across from the Legion Hall, between I-495 and the Litchfield Fairgrounds.

While you're on an upscale-bread kick, **Slates**, 161 Water St., Hallowell 04347, tel. (207) 622-9575, also has an excellent bakery, open daily 7 a.m.-6 p.m.

If you'd rather have old-fashioned high-cal fare, head for **MacDonald's Bakery**, 339 Water St., Gardiner 04345, tel. (207) 582-5450, where hundreds of doughnuts disappear out the door before 10 a.m. and the most popular item is a six-inch eclair for 85 cents. Under new ownership since 1997, the bakery is open all year, Tues.-Sat. 6 a.m.-6 p.m. On Monday, it's open only 10 a.m.-noon, when everything in the store is half-price.

Lunch and Miscellanea

Not noted for gourmet cuisine, but an okay stop for a quick, convenient, inexpensive fix is the cafeteria on the first floor of the **State House** in the capitol complex. Officially called Filibuster's, but fondly known as the Bay of Pigs, it's open to the public weekdays, 8 a.m.-2 p.m. Among the choices are sandwiches, burgers, and daily hot-dish specials. When the legislature is in session, the crowds pour in, so assess the situation before you enter.

A block away from the State House is the alternative, a veteran take-out establishment. High-profile politicos get their names attached to the delicious bulging sandwiches at **Burnsies Sandwich Shop**, 1 Hichborn St., Augusta 04330, tel. (207) 622-6425; coincidentally (?), many are heavy on ham and turkey. Watching the lined-up lobbyists and pols makes the wait go quickly, but try to avoid high noon, the busiest time. If you're Irish, you'll love the decor. Assemble your picnic goodies here and lug everything over to Capitol Park for a river view. Or take it across the river to the Pine Tree State Arboretum. Burnsies is open all year, Mon.-Fri. 7:30 a.m.-3 p.m. No credit cards.

Along Augusta's downtown waterfront, **Java Joe's Café**, 275 Water St., Augusta 04330, tel. (207) 622-1110, serves great creative sandwiches—call 'em "progressive American." And of course it's coffee heaven. No smoking. The café is open all year, Mon.-Sat. 7 a.m.-4 p.m.

Inexpensive to Moderate

If you're traveling with children, **The Ground Round**, 110 Community Dr., Augusta 04330, tel. (207) 623-0022, is better than McDonald's at keeping them distracted, although the atmosphere is a bit frenetic. One or two days a week (it varies), kids get weighed as they enter and pay a penny a pound for their entrées. Such a deal. The menu is burger-centric, always reliable. The waitresses know how to finesse the kids. Part of the Holiday Inn complex at the Augusta Civic Center, the Ground Round is open daily 6:30 a.m.-11 p.m., all year.

The best grownup food in the Augusta area is at **Slates,** 161 Water St., Hallowell 04347, tel. (207) 622-9575, the Energizer bunny of local restaurants. Founded in 1979, it just keeps improving. Dinner entrées—mostly creative seafood and chicken, and a few token tournedos—are in the $10-16 range. The Saturday and Sunday brunches are fabulous: grilled fish and meats, unique omelets and benedicts, huevos rancheros, stuffed croissants, homemade granola, salads. Reservations only for six or more, so bring a gang or expect to wait. Limited smoking. Open for breakfast Mon.-Fri. 7:30-11 a.m.; for lunch Mon.-Fri. 11:30 a.m.-2:30 p.m., and lite lunch Tues.-Sat. 2:30-5 p.m.; for dinner Tues.-Sat. 5:30-9 p.m. (to 9:30 Friday and Saturday); and for brunch Saturday and Sunday 9 a.m.-2:30 p.m.

And what's this? A Middle Eastern restaurant in the center of Hallowell, just down the street from Slates. The **River Café,** 119 Water St., Hallowell 04347, tel. (207) 622-2190, in a historic, brick-walled building in downtown Hallowell, draws a crowd—including lots of state government staffers at lunchtime. Best bargain is the $5.95 all-you-can-eat luncheon buffet—a chance to graze through their Mediterranean specialties. Forget dessert and concentrate on the *mazas* (appetizers). The informal atmosphere is fine for kids, but there's no children's menu. No smoking. The café is open all year (except major holidays), Mon.-Sat. 11 a.m.-2:30 p.m. and 5-9:30 p.m. It's one and a half miles south of downtown Augusta.

Hard by the Kennebec River in downtown Gardiner, adorned with flowerboxes, is the funky, first-rate **A-1 Diner,** 3 Bridge St., Gardiner 04345, tel. (207) 582-4804. The real thing, a genuine classic diner, with moderate prices and some added attractions—like air-conditioning and a yuppified menu. No smoking, no credit cards. Open all year, Mon.-Thurs. 7 a.m.-8 p.m. (to 9 p.m. Friday and Saturday), and Sunday 8 a.m.-1 p.m.

Downriver from Augusta, the **Railway Café,** 64 Main St., Richmond 04357, tel. (207) 737-2277, has been the favorite local gathering spot since 1984. Looking at the original 19th-century woodwork and tin ceiling, who'd guess it had once been a funeral parlor? If you're here on Friday (and sometimes other days), order the $7.95 lobster stew, *loaded* with lobster meat. Dinner entrées—steak, seafood, grilled chicken, pizza—run $5-12. The café is open all year, Mon.-Fri. 5:30 a.m.-8 p.m. (to 9 p.m. Friday), Saturday 7 a.m.-9 p.m., and Sunday 7 a.m.-4 p.m.

INFORMATION AND SERVICES

The information center of the **Kennebec Valley Chamber of Commerce,** 21 University Dr., P.O. Box E, Augusta 04332, tel. (207) 623-4559, fax 626-9342, is open all year, Mon.-Fri. 8:30 a.m.-4:30 p.m. (answering machine on weekends). Located in the Augusta Civic Center complex at the northern edge of the city, the office has a smallish sign that makes it a bit hard to find. Persevere; you'll get there.

A mile south of Augusta is the state headquarters of the **Maine Publicity Bureau,** 325B Water St., Hallowell 04347, tel. (207) 623-0363 or (800) 593-4072, a nonprofit organization that operates eight tourism information centers around the state. The main office is devoted primarily to administration, but helpful brochures are available. It's open weekdays 9 a.m.-5 p.m.

The Romanesque Revival **Lithgow Public Library,** Winthrop and State Sts., Augusta 04330, tel. (207) 626-2415, one of Maine's handsomest libraries, was built in 1896 of Maine granite. Do not miss the gorgeous reading room, with a Tiffany clock, stained-glass windows, and French-inspired decor. The library is open all year, Mon.-Thurs. 9 a.m.-8 p.m. and Friday and Saturday 9 a.m.-5 p.m. In July and August, Saturday hours are 9 a.m.-noon. A new **children's library** addition, built in 1978, has the same hours as the main section, except on Tuesday and Wednesday, when it closes at 5 p.m.

The **Maine State Library,** Maine State Cultural Building, Augusta 04333, tel. (207) 287-5600, in the State House complex, includes the Maine State Museum and the State Archives, tel. (207) 287-5790, within its walls. Stocked with more than 300 magazines, the reading room is a convenient place to peruse esoteric articles, rest your feet, or wait for a friend; there are also public restrooms. The library is open Mon.-Fri. 9 a.m.-5 p.m., mid-June to early September. It's also open Saturday noon-5 p.m. early September to mid-June.

Newspapers

Founded in 1825, the **Kennebec Journal,** tel. (207) 623-3811 or (800) 537-5508, began publication only five years after Maine became a state. It's published every day except Christmas. Each Friday, the paper's 20-page *What's Happening* supplement carries ads and countless calendar listings. Be sure to read through "What's for Supper," a rundown of public suppers (usually for a cause), with a guarantee of good food, low prices (under $6 pp), and local color galore. Augusta's journalistic newcomer is the Saturday *Capital Weekly,* tel. (207) 621-6000, with features and extensive calendar listings.

Emergencies

In **Augusta, Hallowell, Gardiner, and Manchester,** dial 911 for fire, police, and ambulance services. The major medical facility for the area is **Kennebec Valley Medical Center,** 6 E. Chestnut St., Augusta 04330, emergency room tel. (207) 626-1206, with round-the-clock emergency-room care.

Kennels

About seven miles west of Augusta, the **Manchester Pet Care Center,** Rt. 202, Manchester 04351, tel. (207) 623-4976, operates year round, boarding dogs for $9 a day and cats for $6 a day. The kennel is open Mon.-Fri. 8 a.m.-6 p.m., Saturday 8 a.m.-noon, and Sunday 4-6 p.m. No dropoffs or pickups on major holidays, including July Fourth and Labor Day.

GETTING THERE AND GETTING AROUND

A commuter airline with a fine track record, **Continental Connection** (formerly Colgan Air), tel. (800) 525-0280, operates 50-minute nonstop flights all year between Boston's Logan Airport and the Augusta State Airport; two or three flights on weekdays, one or two flights on weekends. It's a busy route, especially on midsummer weekends, so be sure to book well ahead.

Augusta-based **Al's & Double R's Taxi Service,** tel. (207) 622-5846 or 623-3431, has a fleet of radio-equipped taxis operating daily all year.

BELGRADE LAKES AREA

The Belgrade Lakes area is one of those Proustian memories-of-childhood places, where multigenerational family groups return year after year for idyllic summer visits full of nothing but playing, going for hikes or swims, fishing, listening for the loons, watching sunsets, and dreading the return to civilization. Today's boomer generation, recalling carefree days at one of the many Belgrade-area summer camps now send their own kids to camp here, or they rent a lakefront cottage and devote their energies to re-creating those youthful days.

Belgrade's chain of lakes comprises seven major lakes and ponds: Long Pond, North Pond, Great Pond, East Pond, Salmon Pond, McGrath Pond, and Messalonskee Lake (also known as Snow Pond). Camps and cottages are sprinkled around their shores, and each has a boat-launch ramp where you can put in a canoe, kayak, or powerboat. Incidentally, the village of Belgrade Lakes, heart of the region, has its own post office but is part of the towns of Belgrade and Rome.

Since the Belgrade Lakes area is tucked in between Waterville and Augusta, those cities serve as the easily accessible commercial and cultural hubs for Belgrade visitors.

Directly west of Belgrade Lakes village is the charming, out-of-the-way hamlet of Mount Vernon (pop. 1,480), founded in 1792 and worth a visit by car or bike.

Great Pond,
Belgrade Lakes

SIGHTS

Great Pond Mailboat

Remember the movie *On Golden Pond?* Well, author Ernest Thompson found his inspiration summering on the shore of Great Pond. (He's still here, although Hollywood's version was filmed in New Hampshire.) You can join the real-life postman on his rounds, feeding the 100-plus lakefront mailboxes—but he uses a pontoon boat instead of a Chris-Craft. Mailbox creativity is half the entertainment, and one cottager's dog dashes to the dock to pick up the mail. Bring binoculars, a camera, a jacket, and a sandwich and settle in aboard the stable, 10-passenger pontoon boat. Reservations are essential, especially in July and August; call a day or two ahead. If your kids can behave on a four-hour excursion, by all means do this, but leave them ashore if they're the restless type (and there's no restroom on board). Operated by the Great Pond Marina, the Great Pond Mailboat, tel. (207) 495-2213 or (800) 696-6329, departs Mon.-Sat. at 10 a.m., June-Sept., from the dock behind the Boat House in Belgrade Lakes village (Rt. 27). Cost is $10 adults, $8 seniors, $5 children 5-12.

D.E.W. Animal Kingdom

Allow at least an hour for a guided tour of the three-acre D.E.W. (Domestic/Exotic/Wild) Animal Kingdom, Rt. 41, Box 2820, Mount Vernon 04352, west of Belgrade Lakes village. Kids love the hands-on stuff at Julie and Bob Miner's innovative nonprofit zoo, where they raise and rehabilitate exotic and not-so-exotic animals. Among the residents are wallabies, bobcats, muntjacs, and a binturong, plus llamas, pigs, and other pettable creatures. The zoo, on Rt. 41, is in West Mount Vernon, roughly midway between Mount Vernon village and Kents Hill. It's open mid-April through October, Tues.-Sun. 10 a.m.-5 p.m. Admission is $5 adults, $3 children under 12.

RECREATION

Just north of Day's Store in Belgrade Lakes village is a cute little picnic area on Long Pond, next to an old dam. Late in the day, it's a great spot for sunset-watching. Another scenic standout, with a super photo op of Long Pond and Belgrade Lakes village, is the state-maintained overlook at **Blueberry Hill,** on the west side of Long Pond. From Rt. 27, just south of Belgrade Lakes village, take Castle Island Rd. west about three miles to Watson Pond Road. Turn right (north) and continue about one and a half miles. Voilà! (Another 2.8 miles north of Blueberry Hill is the trailhead for French's Mountain.)

If you're a golfer, inquire when you arrive about the magnificent new 18-hole **Belgrade Lakes Golf Club,** on the West Rd., south of Belgrade Lakes village. Architect for the 240-acre course is noted British designer Clive Clark.

Swimming

Rental cottages on the Belgrade Lakes have direct access to the water, but even close to shore it can be too deep for little kids. In that case, head for the beach at Sunset Camps. In the hamlet of Smithfield, northeast of Belgrade Lakes village, the owners of **Sunset Camps,** Rts. 8 and 137, P.O. Box 68, Smithfield 04978, tel. (207) 362-2611, allow public access for swimming and other activities. Cost is $1.50 pp. When it's hot, get there early. (Sunset Camps is a sporting camp, with 18 housekeeping cabins.) Pick up some lunch at the snack bar, then rent a canoe and paddle around North Pond.

Cycling

The 44-page booklet *Take a Ride . . . Road & Mountain Biking Guide,* concentrating mostly on Waterville, Skowhegan, and the Upper Kennebec Valley, also includes several mountain-biking routes in and around Belgrade's lakes.

Mountain bikes are available for rent ($15 a day) at **The Landing,** Main St., Rt. 27, Belgrade Lakes 04918, tel. (207) 495-3633, right at the outlet between Long and Great Ponds. (The Landing also rents canoes for $15 a day.) The shop is open mid-June to mid-September, from 9 a.m. on.

Hiking

Two good hikes are just north of Belgrade Lakes village, in the town of Rome. Neither is particularly high, but their summits are isolated enough to provide panoramic vistas; a fall-foliage hike is wonderful.

For lots of gain and and little pain, a good family hike, head for **French's Mountain,** on the west side of Long Pond. To reach the trailhead from Rt. 27, south of Belgrade Lakes village, take Castle Island Rd. about three miles west to Watson Pond Road. Turn right (north) and go about 4.4 miles; the trail (signposted) begins on the right. Allow about 20 minutes to reach the summit, with fantastic views of Long Pond, the village, and Great Pond. Take a picnic (and a litter bag) and stretch out on the ledges. The trail is maintained by the Belgrade Region Conservation Alliance, a dedicated land-trust organization that holds a 55-acre conservation easement on French's Mountain.

A marginally tougher, but not strenuous hike is **Mount Philip,** a 755-footer with summit views of Great Pond. Allow about 40 minutes to reach the top from the Rt. 225 trailhead. From Rt. 27, north of Belgrade Lakes village, turn right onto Rt. 225 at Rome Corner (a white wooden building is at the fork). Continue another one and a half miles. The trail (on the left) begins across from a dead-end road. Park as far off the road as possible. Climb the bank and continue on up the unmarked but well-worn trail to the summit.

Fishing

Fishing is a big deal here, particularly in May, June, and September (the season opens April 1 and closes October 1). Among the 20 species in the seven major lakes and ponds are landlocked salmon, brown trout, black bass, pickerel, white perch, and eastern brook trout. You'll have to stick to bag, weight, and length limits. Pick up tackle and nonresident fishing licenses at Day's Store, Main St., Rt. 27, P.O. Box 277, Belgrade Lakes 04918, tel. (207) 495-2205 or (800) 993-9500.

Getting Afloat

The most entertaining way to get afloat in the Belgrade Lakes is the Great Pond Mailboat, but the next best choice is to rent a canoe or kayak or take a guided paddle. To do your own thing, stop at **Red Oak Sports,** Boat House, Rt. 27, Belgrade Lakes 04918, tel. (207) 495-2199, the seasonal branch of a Farmington firm. Red Oak rents kayaks (under 14 feet) and canoes for $18 a day. The shop is open only in summer, daily 8 a.m.-8 p.m.

Belgrade Canoe & Kayak, Rt. 27, Belgrade 04917, tel. (207) 495-2005 or (888) 226-6311, rents canoes and kayaks for $25-30 a day and also does on-demand 3- to 5-hour guided trips for up to eight people. Cost is $30-50 pp; call ahead to discuss route, time, and other arrangements. From May through August, the shop is open Wed.-Mon. 10 a.m.-5 p.m. Sept.-Dec. and March-May, it's open Wed.-Sat. 10 a.m.-5 p.m. The shop and demo pond are 11 miles north of the Augusta Civic Center and about six miles south of Belgrade Lakes village.

The **Great Pond Marina,** Rt. 27, P.O. Box 405, Belgrade Lakes 04918, tel. (207) 495-2213 or (800) 696-6329, rents canoes ($18 a day), pontoon boats ($150 a day), and paddleboats ($16 a day); all require deposits of about twice the daily rental. Pickup and delivery charges are extra. The marina, a mile south of Belgrade Lakes village, is open daily in summer 8 a.m.-5 p.m. (except July Fourth).

Sunset cruises are a whole other option. The pontoon boat used for mail delivery does evening duty for two-hour sunset cruises departing from the Boat House dock daily at 6 p.m., mid-June through August, weather permitting. Reservations are advisable. Cost is $12 pp. Be sure to carry a sweater or jacket; alcohol is not allowed.

SHOPPING

You-Name-It

Cars and canoes are about the only things you can't buy at **Day's Store,** Main St., Rt. 27, P.O. Box 277, Belgrade Lakes 04918, tel. (207) 495-2205 or (800) 993-9500, a legendary institution since 1960. From firewater to fishing tackle, soups to souvenirs—and 24 kinds of homemade fudge—it's a general store par excellence. Don't expect fancy; the local flavor provides its character. Long Pond is at its back door, providing access by boat or car. The store is open daily 7 a.m.-9 p.m., Memorial Day weekend to Christmas, then 8 a.m.-7 p.m. the rest of the year. Day's is in the center of the village, across from the Boat House; you can't miss it.

Gifts and Crafts

A few doors south of the Village Inn in Belgrade Lakes is the seasonal branch of Waterville's **Maine Made Shop,** Main St., Rt. 27, Belgrade Lakes 04918, tel. (207) 495-2274, a summer landmark since 1980. Here's the place to stock up on tasteful gifts and crafts: jams and chutneys, cards and guidebooks, even unique blueberry-dyed T-shirts. The shop is open mid-June to mid-September, Mon.-Sat. 9:30 a.m.-8 p.m. and Sunday noon-5 p.m.

A few more doors to the south, and open all year, is **The Enchanted Swan,** Main St., Rt. 27, Belgrade Lakes 04918, tel. (207) 495-2264, also stocked with a good gift selection. It's open daily 10 a.m.-5 p.m. in summer, Tues.-Sun. other months. Owner Karen Swan's husband,

Bill Swan, a Master Maine Guide, operates **Swan's Guide Service,** tel. (207) 397-4152, leading all-day fishing trips, day hikes, and multiday camping trips. Figure about $150 pp for fishing excursions, all by prior arrangement.

West of Belgrade Lakes village is **Meridian Arts,** Belgrade Rd., RR 2, Box 1900, Mount Vernon 04352, tel. (207) 293-2239, a barn-based nonprofit shop featuring a world of moderately priced handicrafts—cottage-industry jewelry, carvings, clothing, musical instruments, and baskets from Third World villages in Africa, Asia, and Latin America. There's also Native American work. No credit cards. The effort is admirable, the goods are great. The shop, a mile north of downtown Mount Vernon's fire station, is open all year, daily 9 a.m.-6 p.m., but especially off season, call ahead to be sure.

Farmers' Market

The **Mount Vernon Farmers' Market** sets up shop in the middle of tiny Mount Vernon village each Saturday 9 a.m.-noon, late June to mid-September.

ACCOMMODATIONS

The Belgrade Lakes Region actually extends its reach into the Waterville area, so be sure to see details on The Pressey House Lakeside Bed and Breakfast and Alden Camps, under "Accommodations" in the "Waterville and Vicinity" section. Both are on Belgrade lakes, in Oakland.

Sporting Camps

Distant from most of Maine's sporting camps, a classic Belgrade-area operation nonetheless retains the flavor of those much farther north. And it's a heck of a lot easier to reach when driving from the south.

Established in 1910, **Bear Spring Camps,** North Bay, Great Pond, Rome, mailing address Rt. 2, Box 1900, Oakland 04963, tel. (207) 397-2341, is one of the state's largest sporting camps, with 32 rustic cottages on 400 wooded acres. All have baths and Franklin stoves and overlook nine-mile-long Great Pond; each has its own dock, and rental motorboats are available. There's daily maid service. Other facilities include a sandy beach, tennis courts, and hiking trails. Cabins are $800-1,450 a week, American Plan; meals are important here. Cabins are available only by the week from mid-June to Labor Day, and reservations are tough to come by. Some guests stay a month, and they book a year ahead. No pets. Open mid-May through September. Bear Spring Camps is on Rt. 225, four miles east of Rt. 27.

Seasonal Rentals

Seasonal rentals are the preferred lodging in the Belgrade Lakes Area. It must relate to the children's summer camps in this area—"you can't go home again," but you *can* spend a week or two trying to recapture the aura. The **Belgrade Reservation Center,** Rt. 27, P.O. Box 284, Belgrade Lakes 04918, tel. (207) 495-2525, fax 495-2527, based in the Day's Real Estate office on the southern outskirts of Belgrade Lakes village, has the best selection of rentals. Cottages with 1-5 bedrooms range $300-1,300 a week, mid-May through September.

FOOD

If you're looking for picnic fare, or a quick bite, stop in at **Day's Store** Main St., Rt. 27, P.O. Box 277, Belgrade Lakes 04918, tel. (207) 495-2205 or (800) 993-9500, and pick up pizza, sandwiches, and/or baked goodies.

Almost across the street is a restaurant that attracts patrons from all over central Maine. It's hard to imagine, from its average-looking exterior, that superb, ungreasy duckling is the menu highlight at **The Village Inn,** Main St., Rt. 27, Belgrade Lakes 04918, tel. (207) 495-3553. Even the distinctly casual interior, overlooking the inlet to Great Pond, doesn't give it away. (Don't worry—the ducks in the inlet aren't destined for your plate.) The kitchen wizards use a unique two-day roasting technique, and you can choose from a dozen interesting sauces. A half-

duckling dinner is $17.95, and you can even order it by mail. The moderately priced menu has tons of other options, including pasta dishes and "lighter side" entrées. Reservations are essential on midsummer weekends. The Village Inn is open for dinner and Sunday brunch in spring and fall (Mon.-Sat. 5-9 p.m. and Sunday 11:30 a.m.-8 p.m.), and for lunch and dinner Memorial Day weekend to Labor Day (daily 11:30 a.m.-9 p.m.). It's in the center of Belgrade Lakes village.

Just south of the village center, close to the shore of Long Pond but not endowed with a water view, is the very informal **Sunset Grille,** 4 West Rd., Belgrade Lakes 04918, tel. (207) 495-2439, where Friday and Saturday are karaoke nights. It's also a very popular hangout for lunch and a weekend breakfast buffet (8 a.m.-noon). Dinner entrées run $11-15, primarily grilled steak and seafood, Tex-Mex stuff and weekend prime ribs; no charge for the sunsets. The restaurant is open all year, Sun.-Thurs. 6 a.m.-9 p.m., and Friday and Saturday 6 a.m.-1 a.m.

INFORMATION

The **Belgrade Lakes Region Information Center,** P.O. Box 72, Belgrade 04917, tel. (207) 495-2744, is a minuscule log cabin just south of Messalonskee Stream on the east side of Rt. 27, about 10 miles north of Augusta. It's open only mid-June to mid-September, and even then the schedule is unpredictably erratic. When the office is closed, brochures are left outside, under the overhang. Safest bet is to call or write in advance for regional information.

The *Belgrade Lakes Guide,* a free tabloid with ads, features, and calendar listings, is an especially helpful local publication published weekly during the summer. Copies are available at most of the restaurants and shops in the region.

WATERVILLE AND VICINITY

Second-largest community in Kennebec County, the city of Waterville boasts a population 16,500. When you throw in its sister town of Winslow, the head count jumps to nearly 25,000. A key player in Waterville life today is prestigious Colby College, whose students and faculty provide the college-town flavor to this mill town incorporated in 1802.

As early as 1653, Europeans set up a trading entrepôt here, calling it Teconnet—the earlier version of today's Ticonic Falls, on the Kennebec—and commerce with the Indians thrived until the onset of the Indian Wars two decades later. In the late 19th century, a contingent of Lebanese immigrants arrived, finding employment in the town's mills, and many of their descendants have become respected community members. Best known of these is favorite son and former U.S. Senate Majority Leader George J. Mitchell, who still returns to spend time with his many relatives here.

Waterville has long been overshadowed by Augusta, the Kennebec County seat 20 miles to the south, but commercial turnarounds in the mid-1990s have led to rising optimism about the city's prospects for the future. A welcome addition in 1997 was the opening of a second bridge over the Kennebec River, relieving some of the Winslow-Waterville congestion on the Rt. 201 bridge. The $33.5 million Donald V. Carter Memorial Bridge is about one and a quarter miles downriver from the Rt. 201 span.

SIGHTS

Colby College

Crowning Mayflower Hill, two miles from downtown Waterville, Colby College, Mayflower Hill, Waterville 04901, tel. (207) 872-3000, is a must see. Colby's 1,700-plus students attend a huge variety of liberal-arts programs on a 714-acre campus noted for its handsome Georgian buildings. Founded by Baptists in 1813 as the all-male Maine Literary and Theological Institution, Colby received its current name in 1867 and went coed in 1871. Campus tours are available

by prior arrangement through the Admissions Office, tel. (207) 872-3168.

The **Colby College Museum of Art,** tel. (207) 872-3228, in the Bixler Art and Music Center, has earned an especially distinguished reputation for its remarkable permanent collection of 18th-, 19th-, and 20th-century American art. In 1996, the museum opened its $1.5-million Paul J. Schupf Wing to house 415 paintings and sculptures created by artist Alex Katz over a 50-year period. Other significant holdings include works by Gilbert Stuart, Winslow Homer, and John Marin; special solo and group shows are mounted throughout the year. And don't miss the tasteful gift shop. Museum hours are Mon.-Sat. 10 a.m.-4:30 p.m. and Sunday 2-4:30 p.m. Admission is free, but donations are welcomed. The museum is on the east side of the campus's main quadrangle, just north of Mayflower Hill Drive.

Also on the campus is the 128-acre **Perkins Arboretum and bird sanctuary,** with three nature trails. Bring a picnic and blanket and stretch out next to Johnson Pond. In winter, there's ice-skating on the pond. Also see "Information and Services," below, for details on Colby's Miller Library.

Fort Halifax

Left over from a fort built in 1754, the two-story Fort Halifax blockhouse, Bay St., Winslow 04901, stands sentinel where the Sebasticook River meets the Kennebec. Oldest blockhouse in the nation, it was built of doweled logs during the French and Indian Wars. In 1984, after rampaging Kennebec floodwaters swept away the building, more than three dozen of the giant timbers were retrieved downstream. Energetic fundraising allowed the blockhouse to be meticulously restored. The surrounding park is a great place for a picnic.

Two-Cent Bridge

Spanning the Kennebec from Benton Avenue in Winslow to Front Street in Waterville (walk down Temple Street in Waterville), the 700-foot-long Two-Cent Bridge (officially the Ticonic Footbridge) was built in 1903 for pedestrian commuters to the Scott Paper mill in Winslow. Until 1962, the toll literally was two cents; the bridge has been closed since 1973.

Redington House Museum

Home of the Waterville Historical Society, the Redington House Museum, 64 Silver St., Waterville 04901, tel. (207) 872-9439, has a particularly intriguing 19th-century pharmacy as well as Native American artifacts. The Federal-style Redington House was built in 1814 by early settler Asa Redington for his son, Silas. Admission is $3 adults, $2 children under 12. The museum is open Memorial Day weekend to Labor Day (closed July 4); tours are at 10 and 11 a.m. and 1 and 2 p.m.

Woolen Mill Tours

Since 1882, the five-story **Cascade Woolen Mill,** Lower Fairfield St., Rt. 23, Oakland 04963, tel. (207) 465-2511, has stood next to the falls on Messalonskee Stream in Oakland. Throughout the year, staffers conduct fascinating hour-long tours of the fabric and blanket mill. Tours occur Mon.-Fri. between 8 a.m. and 3 p.m., only by advance reservation. No children under 12, no open-toe or open-heeled shoes. Unfortunately, the company no longer has a factory-outlet store here.

PARKS AND RECREATION

Waterville can serve as a convenient base for **whitewater rafting** trips out of The Forks, on the upper Kennebec River (for details see "Whitewater Rafting" under "Recreation" in "Bingham to Jackman" later in this chapter).

Cycling

Being a college town, Waterville sees plenty of bikes during the academic year, especially in spring and fall. The handiest biking guide for Waterville and the Upper Kennebec Valley is the 44-page *Take a Ride . . . Road & Mountain Biking Guide.*

C.M. Cycle, 209 College Ave., Rt. 201/11, Waterville 04901, tel. (207) 873-5490, has bike rentals for $15 a day. Each Monday night in summer, weather permitting, there's a free off-

road group ride, departing at 6 p.m. from the shop and returning about 8 p.m. Bring your bike and helmet, or call ahead and reserve a rental bike. The shop is open Mon.-Thurs. 9 a.m.-6 p.m., Friday 9 a.m.-7 p.m., and Saturday 9 a.m.-5 p.m. in summer. Winter hours are Monday, Tuesday, Thursday 9 a.m.-6 p.m., Friday 9 a.m.-7 p.m., and Saturday 9 a.m.-5 p.m.

Golf

Public access is limited at the semiprivate 18-hole **Waterville Country Club,** Country Club Rd., Oakland 04963, tel. (207) 465-9861, so you'll need to call for a starting time—weekday mornings are reserved for members. The course, covering both sides of Country Club Road, is particularly well kept up, and facilities include a pro shop and driving range. There's a certain degree of stuffiness here, and greens fees are expensive. Open mid-April through October, the course is a mile from I-95 Exit 33. Also see "Augusta and Vicinity" for information on the tournament-level **Natanis Golf Club.**

Kids' Stuff

Across North Street from Mid-Maine Medical Center's Thayer Unit, the **North Street Playground** has very creative playground equipment plus ballfields, free tennis courts (tel. 207-877-7520), and an outdoor pool (tel. 207-873-6604).

Inside-Out Playground, Waterville Regional Arts and Community Center, 93 Main St., Waterville 04901, tel. (207) 877-8747, is just what it sounds like—a 6,000-square-foot indoor play center for children up to age 10. This energetic nonprofit enterprise is on the fourth floor

BOB RACE

of a town-owned building known for short as "The Center." The catch? A parent or babysitter has to remain with the kids; bring earplugs. Special activities include story hours, parties, craft workshops, games, and a summer-camp program. It's open all year, daily 10 a.m.-5 p.m. (to 7 p.m. Friday). Cost is $4.75 per child for the day; parents play for free.

ENTERTAINMENT

Curiously, one of Maine's premier art-film houses is in downtown Waterville. The two-screen **Railroad Square Cinema,** Railroad Sq., 4 Chaplin St., Waterville 04901, tel. (207) 873-6526, featuring esoteric and even oddball flicks more typical of big-city cinemas, attracts its clientele from all over central and mid-coast Maine, and Colby College's academic crowd beefs up the audience. After a disastrous 1994 fire, the veteran cinema (since 1978) was rebuilt close to the old location, gaining in comfort and losing none of its funkiness. Shows change weekly; there are matinees most weekends and occasional weekdays. Tickets are $6 evenings, $4.75 before 5 p.m., $3.75 children. Attached to the theater is the first-rate Third Rail Café.

FESTIVALS AND EVENTS

During the academic year, and less often in summer, Colby College is the site of exhibits, lectures, concerts, performances, and other events. Check with the school, tel. (207) 872-3192, for the schedule.

The refurbished turn-of-the-20th-century **Waterville Opera House,** City Hall, 1 Common St., P.O. Box 14, Waterville 04903, tel. (207) 873-5381, ticket hotline 873-7000, once the haunt of vaudevillians, now is the site of plays, dance performances, and concerts throughout the year. Call for a schedule.

At various locations between Waterville and Jackman the first Saturday in June, **National Trails Day** features organized noncompetitive biking, hiking, and canoeing. It's sponsored by Kennebec Valley Trails.

A gathering of New England's best fiddlers, the **East Benton Fiddlers' Convention** draws

over 2,000 enthusiasts to open-air performances at Littlefield Farm in East Benton. The convention happens the last Saturday in July, 11 a.m.-5 p.m. Call (207) 453-2017 for directions.

Downtown Waterville is the site of late July's **Taste of Greater Waterville.** The food-focused one-day festival is organized by more than two dozen restaurants. InCastonguay Square and surrounding streets, there's al fresco dining, a beer garden, plus music for kids and adults.

The **Clinton Lions Agricultural Fair** takes place the first full weekend in September. This family-oriented country fair in Clinton features agricultural and craft exhibits, live entertainment, a carnival, even apple-pie and bread-baking contests.

SHOPPING

New, Used, and Kiddie Books
Conveniently located downtown (facing Castonguay Square), **Re-Books,** 65 E. Concourse, Waterville 04901, tel. (207) 877-2484, is a basement-level shop with a fairly extensive selection of hardcovers and paperbacks. Amiable proprietor Robert Sezak's specialties include philosophy, Judaica, photography, and language titles. The shop is open all year, Monday and Friday noon-5:30 p.m., Tues.-Thurs. 10 a.m.-5:30 p.m., and Saturday 10 a.m.-5 p.m.

The **Children's Book Cellar,** 52 Main St., Waterville 04901, tel. (207) 872-4543, is *really* into kids. Not only do they have a great selection, but there are weekly multicultural art and craft workshops for children 7-12. The two- or three-hour hands-on afternoon sessions are mostly free, but occasionally there's a materials charge. The shop is open all year, Mon.-Sat. 9:30 a.m.-5:30 p.m.

Colby College's **Seaverns Bookstore,** Roberts Union, Colby College, Waterville 04901, tel. (207) 872-3609, has general books and lots of Colby-logo sweatshirts, T-shirts, and other wearables. Bookstore hours vary, depending on whether or not school is in session. Roberts Union is on the eastern side of the campus.

Crafts and Gifts
Goods from the Woods, Railroad Sq., Waterville 04901, tel. (207) 873-9334, a branch of the

original Athens shop, carries high-quality work of more than a hundred Maine artisans. Like the prototype store, this one uses an antique cash register that never fails to cause a stir. Luddites love it. The shop is open all year, Tues.-Sat. noon-8 p.m. and Sunday noon-6 p.m.

Paula and George Gordon's **Maine Made Shop**, 93 Main St., Waterville 04901, tel. (207) 872-7378, also spotlights the work of Maine individuals and companies, but you'll find far more than crafts, and everything's high quality. A new specialty is "dyed-in-the-blue" T-shirts in 20 designs—color courtesy of Maine blueberry juice. The shop is open all year, Mon.-Thurs. 9 a.m.-6 p.m., Friday 9 a.m.-8 p.m., Saturday 9 a.m.-5:30 p.m., and Sunday noon-5 p.m.

Factory Outlet
Here's the company that made the Hathaway Shirt man—he of the black eyepatch—a household symbol. Faced with extinction when its corporate parent put the company on the market in 1995, the **C.F. Hathaway Shirt Co.**, 10 Water St., Waterville 04901, tel. (207) 873-8600, rose like a phoenix thanks to industrious employees, angelic investors, and Waterville's city fathers. For genuine bargains, check out the company's factory outlet store, stocked with first- and second-quality dress shirts. Shirt-fabric bundles are $1 each; discontinued material is 50 cents to $1.80 a yard. The outlet is open all year, Mon.-Fri. 11 a.m.-6 p.m. and Saturday 10 a.m.-5 p.m.

Johnny's Selected Seeds
If you're a gardener, farmer, horticulturalist, or just plain curious, take a 15-minute drive east of Waterville to Johnny's Selected Seeds, 299 Foss Hill Rd., Albion 04910, tel. (207) 437-2979, home of the eponymous seed source with a national reputation. More than 2,000 varieties of herbs, veggies, and flowers are grown in the company's trial gardens, started in 1973. Known for high-quality seeds and service, the company makes good on anything that doesn't sprout. During the growing season, staffers give free, hour-long guided tours two or three times daily, depending on demand. Each August, there's a one-day open house featuring hayrides, food, live music, and free workshops (call for the date). Johnny's is open Mon.-Sat. 8:30 a.m.-5 p.m., all year. From March to June 1, it's also open Sunday 10 a.m.-4 p.m.

Farmers' Market
The **Waterville Farmers' Market** begins its season in late April and continues to late October. Look for it on Front and Temple Sts., on the Waterville side of the Two-Cent Bridge, Friday and Saturday 9 a.m.-5 p.m.

ACCOMMODATIONS

Most accommodations in Waterville are chain motels—**Best Western, Econo Lodge, Budget Host.** The best of these is the **Holiday Inn Waterville**, 375 Main St., Waterville 04901, tel. (207) 873-0111 or (800) 785-0111, fax (207) 872-2310, which gets high marks for convenience and a friendly staff. The 138 rooms, on three levels with a/c, cable TV, and phones, go for $85-105 d May-Oct., $65-85 d other months. Facilities include indoor pool, workout room, sauna, and Killarney's restaurant and pub. Open all year, the motel is close to I-95 Exit 34 and about a mile from downtown.

Just west of Waterville, and technically in the Belgrade Lakes region, is **The Pressey House Lakeside Bed & Breakfast**, 85 Summer St., Oakland 04963, tel. (207) 465-3500, a stunning mid-19th-century octagonal house. Four good-size suites (private baths) are $65-100 d mid-May to mid-October, $55-75 d other months. No smoking, no credit cards. Reserve well ahead; it's a popular spot, at the head of nine-mile-long Messalonskee Lake. Relax on the patio or borrow the canoe, paddleboat, or motorboat to explore the lake. The Pressey House, a five-minute drive from I-95 Exit 33, is open all year.

Most of Maine's traditional sporting camps are farther north or west, deep in the woods. **Alden Camps**, RFD 2, Box 1140, Oakland 04963, tel. (207) 465-7703, fax 465-7912, is a little more accessible—but it's worth your life to get a reservation. It's also technically in the Belgrade Lakes region. Founded in 1909, Alden Camps has an incredibly loyal following, even fourth-generation guests. The 18 rustic cottages face great sunrises across three-mile-long East Pond (also called East Lake). Daily rates, late June through August, are $160-260 d (American Plan), depending on cottage size. Children are $10-60 a day, depending on age. Most guests spend a week. Each no-frills cottage has a screened porch, electricity, bath, and a fridge, and there's daily maid service. The crew of college kids aims to please, and former staffers now show up as guests. Meals are hearty, and the Friday-night lobsterbake/clambake is a long-standing tradition. BYOL. No smoking in the dining room, which is open to the public for dinner by reservation, but space is very limited in July and August. The Friday lobsterbake is also open to the public; call for reservations. The 40-acre spread on Rt. 137 has clay tennis courts, a sandy beach, a water-skiing boat, and a kids' play area; across the road, on another 100 acres, are hiking trails. Alden Camps is seven miles off I-95 Exit 33. Open late May to mid-September.

FOOD

In a local twist on the traditional Maine public suppers—thanks to Waterville's substantial Lebanese community—**St. Joseph Maronite Church,** 3 Appleton St., Waterville 04901, tel. (207) 872-8515, puts on a Lebanese supper at least once a year (usually late April). If you enjoy Eastern Mediterranean home cooking, be there. Call the church for details.

The rest of the year, the best source of Lebanese goodies is a block away from the church. The little **Lebanese Bakery,** 34 Temple St., Waterville 04901, tel. (207) 873-7813, has homemade spinach and meat pies, hummus, tabbouleh, and kibbe. Eat at one of the four tables or get it to go. The bakery is open all year, Mon.-Fri. 9:30 a.m.-4 p.m. and Saturday 9:30 a.m.-1 p.m.

Inexpensive to Moderate

Linked like a Siamese twin to the Railroad Square Cinema, the **Third Rail Café,** Railroad Sq., 4 Chaplin St., Waterville 04901, tel. (207) 873-4632, has an eclectic menu of quasi-ethnic entrées and sandwiches, as well as burgers, homemade soups, and chilis. This cheerful operation with brightly painted tabletops is *the* place to chow down before the movies—a sliding door leads right to the cinema ticket counter. Too convenient. Run by the owners of Gardiner's A-1 Diner, it's open all year for lunch Tues.-Fri. 11:30 a.m.-2 p.m. and for dinner Mon.-Thurs. 5-9 p.m. and Fri.-Sat. 5-9:30 p.m.

A popular hangout for Colby students and faculty, **Big G's Deli,** Outer Benton Ave., Winslow 04901, tel. (207) 873-7808, has enormous "name" sandwiches such as the Miles Standish (nearly a whole turkey dinner), all on homemade bread. Price range is $3-6. Order at the counter and try to find a seat—or get it all to go for the mother of all picnics. No credit cards; no smoking. Open all year except Thanksgiving and Christmas, Sun.-Thurs. 6 a.m.-9 p.m., and Friday and Saturday 7 a.m.-9 p.m. On the east side of the Kennebec, Big G's is about a mile north of the Rt. 201 bridge to Waterville.

Tin ceilings, efficient service, good-size portions, an inventive menu, and a selective wine list make **The Last Unicorn,** 8 Silver St., Waterville 04901, tel. (207) 873-6378, downtown Waterville's best all-around restaurant. Dinner entrées, heavy on chicken and vegetarian choices, run $11-18, but you can also have Mediterranean appetizers or hefty salads and sandwiches. Order their strawberry smoothie ($3). No smoking. No reservations, so be prepared to wait. Open all year, 11 a.m.-10 p.m. in summer, to 9 p.m. in winter.

Moderate to Expensive

German food is a rare treat in Maine, and **Johann Sebastian B,** 40 Fairfield St., Rt. 23, Oakland 04963, tel. (207) 465-3223, is special. Since 1974, Colby professor Hubert Kueter and his wife, Nancy, have been serving superb sauerbraten, wiener schnitzel, bratwurst, and kassler rippchen in four rooms on the ground floor of their house. The 20-entrée menu ($9-22) also bows to the times with low-cholesterol and vegetarian choices. Linzertorte is always on the dessert menu. No smoking, no credit cards (personal checks accepted). Johann Sebastian B is open Wed.-Sat. 5-9 p.m., from mid-June to Labor Day; other months, it's only open Friday and Saturday.

INFORMATION AND SERVICES

The **Mid-Maine Chamber of Commerce,** 1 Post Office Sq., Elm and Main Sts., P.O. Box 142, Waterville 04903, tel. (207) 873-3315, has its headquarters in an elegant 1911 Greek Revival building. The office is open all year, Mon.-Fri. 9 a.m.-5 p.m.

The **Waterville Public Library,** 73 Elm St., Waterville 04901, tel. (207) 872-5433, with nearly 100,000 volumes, is open all year, Mon.-Fri. 9 a.m.-8 p.m. in summer, plus Saturday 9 a.m.-3 p.m. during the school year.

The **Miller Library,** Colby College, Waterville 04901, tel. (207) 872-3444, has state-of-the-art computer technology and 800,000 items, including a huge Irish literature collection and a room dedicated to poet Edwin Arlington Robinson.

Newspapers
The *Morning Sentinel,* tel. (207) 873-3341, published daily, is the Waterville/Winslow area's major source of information and events, although the *Bangor Daily News* also provides coverage.

Emergencies
For police, fire, and ambulance services in **Fairfield, Oakland, Waterville, and Winslow,** dial 911. The **Mid-Maine Medical Center,** 149 North St., Waterville 04901, emergency room tel. (207) 872-1300, has round-the-clock emergency-room care.

Getting Around
Brother's Cab Co., tel. (207) 872-0101 or 872-0202, provides 24-hour taxi service in the Waterville area and will also make runs to and from Bangor International Airport.

SKOWHEGAN AREA

The Abnaki named Skowhegan (skow-HE-gun), "the place to watch for fish," because that's just what the early Native Americans did at the Kennebec River's twin waterfalls here. Their spears were ready when lunch came leaping up the river. The island between the falls later formed the core for European settlement of Skowhegan (pop. 9,100), largest town and county seat in Somerset County. Named for England's Somersetshire, the county was incorporated in 1823 and covers 3,633 square miles.

Favorite daughter Margaret Chase Smith, one of Maine's pre-eminent politicians, put Skowhegan on the map, and even since her 1995 death, admirers and historians have made pilgrimages to her former home. During her years in the U.S. Congress and Senate, "The Lady from Maine" would return to her constituents—and she was never too busy to autograph placemats at her favorite local restaurant or to wave from her chair in her house's streetside solarium. Older local residents still recall the day President Dwight D. Eisenhower and his entourage visited Mrs. Smith, in 1955, when "Ike" spoke to an enthusiastic crowd at the Skowhegan Fairgrounds.

Another local institution is the nationally and internationally renowned Skowhegan School of Painting and Sculpture, founded in 1946 as a summer residency program. One of America's few art schools offering workshops in fresco painting, Skowhegan provides 65 artists with a bucolic, 300-acre lakeside setting for honing their skills and interacting with peers and prominent visiting artists. Acceptance is highly competitive for the nine-week program, and only on a one-time basis. Skowhegan's annual summer lecture series, featuring big names in the art world, is open to the public.

In the early 18th century, the town of Norridgewock (NORE-ridge-wok) was a French and Indian stronghold against the British. A century earlier, French Jesuit missionaries had moved in among the Norridgewock Indians at their settlement here and converted them to Catholicism. Best known of these was Father Sebastien Râle, beloved of his Indian parishioners. In 1724, taking revenge for Indian forays against them, a British militia detachment marched in and massacred the priest and his followers, a major milestone during what was known as Dummer's War. Today, a granite monument to Father Râle stands at the crime scene, Old Point, along the Kennebec about two miles south of downtown Madison, close to the Madison/Norridgewock town boundary.

Meaning "smooth water between rapids," Norridgewock (pop. 3,200) was the last bit of civilization for Benedict Arnold and his men before they headed into the Upper Kennebec wilderness on their March to Quebec in 1775. Stopping for almost a week, they spent most of their time caulking their leaky bateaux. Today the town has a slew of handsome 18th- and 19th-century homes.

SIGHTS

Margaret Chase Smith Library

Beautifully sited on Neil Hill, high above the Kennebec River, the Margaret Chase Smith Library, 54 Norridgewock Ave., Skowhegan 04976, tel. (207) 474-7133, fax 474-8878, bulges with fascinating memorabilia from the life and times of one of Maine's best-known politicians, who spent 36 years in the U.S. House and Senate and died in 1995. Over the entrance door is her signature red rose; inside is a 20-minute video describing her career. If a staff member is available, ask to see Sen. Smith's house, connected to the library on the 15-acre estate. (She was born at 81 North Avenue in Skowhegan.) The library is open all year, Mon.-Fri. 10 a.m.-4 p.m., except for the week between Christmas and New Year's Day. Admission is free, but donations are welcomed. The complex is half a mile west of Rt. 201 (Madison Avenue).

Skowhegan History House

When you enter the handsome red-brick Skowhegan History House, 40 Elm St., Skowhegan 04976, tel. (207) 474-6632, with only a half-dozen rooms, it's hard to believe that black-smith Aaron Spear built it in 1839 for his family of 10 children. Must have been mighty cozy sleeping. Skowhegan treasures—antique clocks, china, and other furnishings—now fill the two-story structure, with a commanding view over the Kennebec River. Open Tues.-Fri. 1-5 p.m., mid-June to mid-September. Admission is free, but donations are welcomed. The house is just west of Rt. 201, at the junction of Elm and Pleasant Streets.

The Skowhegan Indian Monument

On High Street, next to a parking lot just east of Madison Avenue (Rt. 201), stands the giant wooden **Skowhegan Indian** (irreverently dubbed the "BFI"). Rising more than 62 feet above its pedestal, the statue was carved in 1969 by Maine sculptor Bernard ("Blackie") Langlais, who died in 1977. Nationally known for his work, Langlais dedicated the monument to the Indians who first settled this area. One hand holds a spear, the other holds a stylized fishing weir. The Langlais home in Cushing, where the Indian was created, still has an open-air gallery of the artist's work. Before he died, a pond on his property held a huge, half-immersed carving of Richard Nixon in the "I am not a crook" pose.

Skowhegan Historic District

Bounded roughly by Water and Russell Streets, and Madison Avenue, the Skowhegan Historic District, close to the Kennebec River, contains 38 turn-of-the-20th-century buildings from the town's heyday as a commercial center. After trains arrived in 1856, the wireless telegraph in 1862, and telephones in 1883, Skowhegan saw incredible prosperity. It's worth a walkabout to admire the architectural details of a bygone era.

L.C. Bates Museum

Located in a Romanesque National Historic Register building on the Good Will-Hinckley School campus, The L.C. Bates Museum, Rt. 201, Hinckley 04944, tel. (207) 453-4894, fax 453-2515, has a broadly eclectic collection with a natural-history focus. Among the treasures in the dozen or so rooms are hundreds of mounted rare birds, priceless Native American artifacts, and a marlin caught by Ernest Hemingway. Maine's only similarly offbeat museums are The Wilson Museum in Castine and the Nylander Museum in Caribou.

A self-guided two-mile nature-trail network winds through the 2,400-acre campus—established in 1889 as a school for disadvantaged children. At the museum, request a trail pass and the "Forest Walking Trails" brochure. Alongside the trails are monuments to prominent conservationists; trails are open during museum hours. For a small fee, kids can attend Saturday-morning natural-history workshops May through November. The museum is open Wed.-Sat. 10 a.m.-4:30 p.m. and Sunday 1-4:30 p.m., May-Nov., plus weekends in April and the rest of the year by appointment. Admission is $2.50 adults, $1 children. The turreted brick-and-granite building is five miles north of I-95, between Fairfield and Skowhegan, visible from Rt. 201 at the southern end of the campus.

PARKS AND RECREATION

Skowhegan is the base for **Kennebec Valley Trails** (KVT), P.O. Box 144, Skowhegan 04976, tel. (207) 635-2680, an energetic membership organization working on an ambitious long-range plan for a multiuse trail between Jackman and Belgrade. KVT annually sponsors **National Trails Day** events the first Saturday in June, and trail-maintenance volunteers are needed periodically. If you'd like to volunteer, or to become a member ($10), contact KVT.

Coburn Park
Donated to the town by Abner Coburn, 15-acre Coburn Park, a wonderful riverside oasis, has a lily pond, memorial gardens (including a Hospice garden and a Margaret Chase Smith rose garden), pagodas, and more than a hundred species of trees and shrubs. Bring a picnic, grab a table, and enjoy. The park is on Water Street (Rt. 2), at the eastern edge of town.

Lake George Park
About seven miles east of Skowhegan, along Rt. 2 (Canaan Road), is 257-acre state-owned Lake George Regional Park, tel. (207) 474-1292, with facilities for swimming and picnicking, plus a boat launch, restrooms, ballfields, hiking trails, and cross-country trails.

Arnold's Way Rest Area
About three miles north of Solon, close to the Solon/Bingham town line and just north of the area known as Arnold's Landing, is the especially attractive state rest area with covered picnic tables, grills, and an outhouse. Six large interpretive panels provide a quickie summary of Benedict Arnold's doomed March to Quebec.

Traditional Skills Courses
In Canaan, east of Skowhegan, Master Maine Guide Ray Reitze, Jr., and his wife, Nancy, operate **Earthways**, RR 2, Box 2700, Canaan 04924, tel. (207) 426-8138, teaching traditional skills of plant identification and basketmaking in an eco-efficient log hogan. One-day classes are $75 pp. Six-day wilderness-survival courses are $325. Their season runs mid-May to late October, during which they also lead canoe trips

Students learn the techniques of fresco.

SKOWHEGAN SCHOOL OF PAINTING AND SCULPTURE

on the St. John River, the Allagash, and the West Branch of the Penobscot River. Ray, who learned woods lore as a youth from a Native American elder, often is tapped to teach wilderness survival skills at the annual Maine Canoe Symposium in Bridgton in early June.

Bicycling
The best biking guide to the area is **Take a Ride . . . Road & Mountain Biking Guide,** a 44-page booklet that has several good routes in and around Skowhegan. A 31.6-mile **Skowhegan-Fairfield-Norridgewock loop** is a moderate, something-for-everyone ride. Also consider the several recommended loops around **Embden Pond.**

Across from the Skowhegan Fairgrounds, **Holden Cyclery,** 317 Madison Ave., Rt. 201, Skowhegan 04976, tel. (207) 474-3732 or (800) 573-3732, rents mountain bikes, with helmet, for $20 a day; tandem mountain bikes are $30 a day, with two helmets. Contact the shop for re-

pairs, too. It's open all year, Mon.-Sat. 9 a.m.-
5:30 p.m.

Golf

The 18-hole **Lakewood Golf Course,** Rt. 201,
Madison 04950, tel. (207) 474-5955, on the
west side of Lake Wesserunsett, dates from
1925. Trickiest hole is the eighth, with a good-
size pond between you and the green. Starting
times aren't usually needed; carts are available.
Open April to early November. The course is
five miles north of Skowhegan.

Downhill Skiing

Skowhegan is an easy drive from the top-flight
skiing at Sugarloaf/USA, but you'll put a far
smaller dent in your wallet at a small, family-
operated ski area just down Rt. 2 to the east.
Eaton Mountain Ski Area, Rt. 2, HC 71, Box
128, Skowhegan 04976, tel. (207) 474-2666,
has 18 trails, novice to expert, served by a double chairlift and a T-bar. There's night skiing,
plus a snowboard park, ski school, rentals, and
a cafeteria. Thanks to top-to-bottom snowmaking, the season is roughly December to early
April, although the lodge is the site of year-round
concerts and other events. The access road is
about five miles east of Skowhegan.

ENTERTAINMENT

A blast from the past is the refurbished **Skowhegan Cinema,** 7 Court St., Skowhegan 04976,
tel. (207) 474-3451, which opened in late 1929
as the Strand Theater. Films are screened daily,
usually at 7:30 p.m. Tickets are $3 adults, $2 seniors, and there's audio equipment for the hear-
ing-impaired.

For another dose of nostalgia, plan to catch a
flick at the 350-car **Skowhegan Drive-In,** Waterville Rd., Rt. 201, Skowhegan 04976, tel.
(207) 474-9277, a landmark since 1954. Nightly double features (starting at dusk or whenever
the sun disappears) are $5 pp; kids under 12 are
free. A snack bar carries popcorn, hot dogs, ice
cream, and drinks. Your audio comes from your
car radio; they'll tell you the frequency. The
drive-in, located at the southern end of town, is
open Thurs.-Sun between late May and late

June, then daily until Labor Day. The show goes
on, rain or shine, except in fog.

Built in 1901, the **Lakewood Theater,** Rt.
201, Madison 04950, tel. (207) 474-7176, on
the shores of Lake Wesserunsett six miles north
of Skowhegan, has had a roller-coaster history,
but it's now in a decidedly "up" phase, thanks to
the Lakewood Theater Company. Maine's oldest
summer theater presents seven musicals, comedies, and light dramas each season, mid-June to
mid-September. Performances are Thurs.-Sat.
at 8 p.m., plus matinees every other Wednesday, Saturday, and Sunday at 2 p.m. Tickets
are $16 adults, $15 children 12 and under.

FESTIVALS AND EVENTS

From mid-June to early August, the evening
(usually Friday) **Barbara Fish Lee Lecture Series** draws nationally and internationally noted
artists to participate in its lecture/presentation
series at the Old Dominion Fresco Barn,
Skowhegan School of Painting and Sculpture.
Contact the school for dates and times at tel.
(207) 474-9345.

Mega-omelettes made in world's largest
omelette pan, a parade, a craft fair, live entertainment, a carnival, and fireworks are among
the features of the **Central Maine Egg Festival.**
Biggest day is Saturday. At Manson Park, Pittsfield, the third or fourth week of July.

Billed as America's oldest country fair, going
back more than 175 years, the **Skowhegan
State Fair** is a 10-day extravaganza with agricultural exhibits galore, live entertainment, harness racing, food booths, a carnival, and a demolition derby at the Skowhegan Fairgrounds,
Rt. 201, Skowhegan, early to mid-August.
Skowhegan also hosts **Skowhegan Log Days,**
with daily lumberjack-theme activities, plus live
entertainment, games for kids and adults, a craft
fair, a beanhole bean dinner, a pig roast, a road
race, a parade, and fireworks the last full week
of August.

Mid-September's low-key **New Portland
Lions Club Fair,** in North New Portland, features agricultural exhibits, a pig scramble, and a
carnival.

SHOPPING

Antiquarian Books

No old-book fan should miss **C. Seams Books,** 125 Main St., Rt. 201A, Madison 04950, tel. (207) 696-8361. Ask Colby Seams for a specific title and he'll negotiate his rabbit warren of a shop and pull it right out. Impressive. Hardcover mysteries and lots of fiction are specialties, but there's so much more in this funky shingled emporium. It's open all year, Tues.-Sat. 9 a.m.-5 p.m., Sunday and Monday by appointment.

Crafts and Gifts

Ten miles north of Skowhegan, **Goods from the Woods,** Rt. 150, Main St., Athens 04912, tel. (207) 654-3206, carries a selective array of Maine-made crafts from more than a hundred artisans: dried flowers, quilts, woodenware, baskets, honey, ironwork, walking sticks, even fishing lures. The shop's offbeat trademark is an ultra-low-tech cash register—the kind you just don't see anymore. Open June-Dec., Wed.-Sun. 10 a.m.-6 p.m.

Factory Outlet

Discounts of up to 50% are typical for athletic-shoe seconds at the **New Balance Factory Outlet,** 13 Walnut St., Skowhegan 04976, tel. (207) 474-6231. The store also carries sportswear, socks, sports bags, and such. Open all year, Mon.-Sat. 9 a.m.-6 p.m., Sunday 11 a.m.-5 p.m.; closed Sunday in winter. The outlet is just off Rt. 201 (E. Front Street), south of the Kennebec. The turn is next to Skowhegan Savings Bank.

Health Food/Farmers' Market

The Spice of Life, Madison Ave., Rt. 201, Skowhegan 04976, tel. (207) 474-8216, stocks vitamins, spices, bulk grains, and other health-food items. The shop is in the Skowhegan Village Shopping Center, a mile north of downtown (across from the Belmont Motel). In summer, it's open Mon.-Thurs. 9 a.m.-7 p.m., Friday 9 a.m.-6 p.m., and Sunday 10 a.m.-5 p.m. Winter hours are the same, except for a 3 p.m. closing on Friday.

Nearest farmers' market to Skowhegan is in Pittsfield, just east of I-95 Exit 38. The **Pittsfield Farmers' Market** sets up shop at Hathorn Park, Rt. 152, every Monday and Thursday 2-5 p.m., and Saturday 10 a.m.-2 p.m., mid-May through October. Among the goodies are goat cheeses, fresh fruits, dried herbs, and lots more.

ACCOMMODATIONS

B&Bs

A smallish sign marks the intown location of **Helen's Bed & Breakfast,** 235 Madison Ave., Rt. 201, Skowhegan 04976, tel. (207) 474-0066, a lovely 19th-century brick house with three rooms (private and shared baths; $35-55 d). Guests are allowed to use the picnic table and grill out back. Well-behaved children are welcome; no smoking. Open all year.

Motels

Also convenient to downtown Skowhegan, the **Towne Motel,** 248 Madison Ave., Rt. 201, Skowhegan 04976, tel. (207) 474-5151 or (800) 843-4405, fax (207) 474-6407, has 33 rooms with phones, a/c, cable TV, and free continental breakfast. The outdoor pool is great for kids. No pets. Rates are $57-74 July to mid-October, $43-53 other months. Open all year.

Sporting Camps

On the west side of Lower Pierce Pond, **Cobb's Pierce Pond Camps,** Pierce Pond, mailing address P.O. Box 124, North New Portland 04961, tel. (207) 628-2819, winter tel. (207) 628-3612, is far from an easy destination—but it's worth the effort once you get there. This traditional sporting camp, founded in 1902, has been a mecca for fishermen ever since, and it can be tough to get a reservation. Amazingly, the 11 rustic cabins have generator-created electricity and flush toilets. Meals are served family-style in the main lodge; it's all very chummy. BYOL and they'll supply the "pond ice"—from big blocks cut out of the frozen pond last winter. Rates are $68 pp, less for children, American Plan. Cobb's is open all year, accessible by snowmobile in winter. From Rt. 16 in North New Portland, just east of Gilman Stream, take the Long Falls Dam Rd. north about 25 mostly unpaved miles and watch carefully for signs. At the end of the road, you'll be picked up by boat for the quick run to the camps.

Campgrounds

About two and a half miles north of downtown Skowhegan, **Yonder Hill Campground,** Rt. 201, RFD 2, Box 3300, Madison 04950, tel. (207) 474-7353, has 80 mostly wooded sites on its 35 acres. Rates are $14-18 (for five), and facilities include a pool, playground, recreation hall, and laundry room. Leashed pets are allowed; no credit cards. Open mid-May through September.

Ten miles east of downtown Skowhegan, **Skowhegan/Canaan KOA Campground,** Rt. 2, Box 87, Canaan 04924, tel. (207) 474-2858, has 60 acres with more than 100 mostly open sites ($17-19 for two). As with other KOA locations, don't expect wilderness camping; there are even cable TV hookups. Other features at this well-maintained Good Sampark include a heated pool, playground, minigolf, and a laundry room. Pets are allowed; canoe and bike rentals are available. Open early May through October.

How often do you find a campground on the National Historic Register? That's the case at **The Evergreens Campground & Restaurant,** Rt. 201A, P.O. Box 114, Solon 04979, tel. (207) 643-2324, a prehistoric site used by Native Americans some 4,000 years ago. Many stone tools and weapons excavated here are now in the Maine State Museum in Augusta; a small collection is displayed at the campground. The 15-acre campground has 40 mostly wooded sites ($6 pp for tentsites, $16 d for RV sites), some right on the Kennebec River. Cottages are $25 pp. Pets are allowed; rental canoes are available for $15 a day; laundry is $2 a load. The restaurant has a bar and a riverfront deck. Directly across the river (technically in Embden) is a huge outcrop covered with ancient Indian petroglyphs. The campground, a mile south of the center of Solon, is open all year, catering to snowmobilers in winter.

FOOD

Breakfast and Miscellanea

Breakfast specials, homemade soups, great sandwiches, and super bread are the stock-in-trade at the **Fire House Bakery,** Main St., Norridgewock 04957, tel. (207) 634-2619—located, obviously, in an old fire house with lots of character. In summer, the patio is the place to be. The bakery is open all year, Mon.-Fri. 5 a.m.-5 p.m., Saturday 5 a.m.-3 p.m.

In Solon, the staff is so cordial at the **Solon Corner Market,** Main St., Solon 04979, tel. (207) 643-2458, you'll probably want to buy one of their embroidered baseball caps. Everything's here—groceries, pizza, newspapers, info, all the fixings for a picnic—and the store is open Mon.-Fri. 6 a.m.-8 p.m. (to 9 p.m. Thursday and Friday), Saturday 7 a.m.-9 p.m., and Sunday 8 a.m.-8 p.m.

Inexpensive to Moderate

Two doors from the Towne Motel, in a historic home, the **Heritage House Restaurant,** 260 Madison Ave., Skowhegan 04976, tel. (207) 474-5100, is Skowhegan's best dining choice. Dinner entrées run $8-16. Apricot-mustard chicken is a specialty. The Heritage House is open all year, Tues.-Fri. for lunch (11:30 a.m.-2 p.m.) and daily (5-10 p.m.) for dinner.

In downtown Skowhegan, **Bloomfield's Café & Bar,** 40 Water St., Skowhegan 04976, tel. (207) 474-8844, is a funky ex-drugstore presided over by a humongous copper moose and various oddball artifacts. Bar fare includes munchies, sandwiches, pizza, and exotic drinks. The decibel level gets elevated at times, but that's half the fun. Open all year, Monday noon-10 p.m., Tues.-Sat. noon-1 a.m., and Sunday noon-midnight.

Less than a block from Bloomfield's, and right on the river, the **Old Mill Pub and Restaurant,** Water St., Skowhegan 04976, tel. (207) 474-6627, gets high marks for its buffalo wings. Weather permitting, you can drink and dine on the deck. Prices are moderate, particularly for the specials. It's open all year, daily 11:30 a.m.-11 p.m.

INFORMATION AND SERVICES

The **Skowhegan Area Chamber of Commerce,** P.O. Box 326, Skowhegan 04976, tel. (207) 474-3621, operates a small brick **information center** on Russell Street (half a block east of Rt. 201), in downtown Skowhegan. It's open all year, Mon.-Fri. 9 a.m.-5 p.m. and Saturday 10 a.m.-3 p.m. in summer; Mon.-Fri. 10

a.m.-4:30 p.m. and Saturday 10 a.m.-3 p.m. in winter. Be sure to request the chamber's **Guest Guide.**

The **Skowhegan Free Public Library,** 5 Elm St., Skowhegan 04976, tel. (207) 474-9072, is open Mon.-Sat. all year: 1-5:30 p.m. in summer and 1-8:30 p.m. in winter. The library is half a block west of Madison Avenue (Rt. 201).

Newspapers
The Somerset Gazette, tel. (207) 474-0606, fax 474-0303, is a folksy, free tabloid published every Friday in Skowhegan. Each summer, it publishes a free newsprint entertainment guide with local historical features and info on events and recreational activities.

Most Skowhegan-area residents rely on Waterville's *Morning Sentinel,* Skowhegan office tel. (207) 474-9534, for daily news, although the

Bangor Daily News also provides some coverage of this area.

Emergencies
In **Skowhegan, Norridgewock, and Madison,** for fire, police, or ambulance services, dial 911. **Redington-Fairview General Hospital,** Fairview Ave., Rt. 104, Skowhegan 04976, emergency room tel. (207) 474-5085, has round-the-clock emergency care.

Money
If you're planning to head north on Rt. 201 (toward Jackman and Quebec City) and will need cash from ATM machines, better stock up in Skowhegan; ATM machines are terminally scarce north of Skowhegan. **Currency exchange** is available in Jackman.

BINGHAM TO JACKMAN

Until the arrival of whitewater rafting, in the mid-1970s, the Upper Kennebec Valley was best known to fishermen, hunters, timber truckers, and families who'd been summering here for generations. And long before that, long before dams changed the river's flow patterns, Native Americans used the Kennebec as a convenient chute from the interior's dense forests to summer encampments on the coast. In 1775, Col. Benedict Arnold led more than a thousand men up this river in a futile campaign to storm the ramparts of Quebec City.

The valley's main artery, Rt. 201, often paralleling the Kennebec River, is now the most convenient driving route from Maine to Quebec City (about a six-hour drive from the Mid-Coast region), but those motorists fly through like a horse headed for the barn. It's rafting that has awakened thousands to the attractions of the valley and spurred a tourism boomlet.

Midway between Skowhegan and The Forks, 23 miles in each direction, Bingham (pop. 1,200) is also equidistant between the North Pole and the equator (3,107 miles in each direction). It's right on the 45th parallel. This quiet valley town is a low-key commercial center with attractive, manicured homes, as well as a stopping point for many whitewater rafters en route to Caratunk and The Forks. The town was named for William

Bingham, an influential Colonial-era banker and land speculator who made a fortune in privateering. Roscoe Vernon ("Gadabout") Gaddis, TV's pioneering Flying Fisherman, built Bingham's funky grass airfield, the Gadabout Gaddis Airport, site of an annual fly-in, with plane rides and aerobatics, the last weekend in September.

Just north of Bingham is Moscow, home of the 155-foot-high Wyman Dam, harnessing the Kennebec River for hydroelectric power. Backed up behind the dam is gorgeous Wyman Lake, lined with birches, evergreens, frequent pullouts (great for shutterbugs), and a small lakeside picnic area north of Wyman Lake Cabins.

Appropriately named, The Forks stands at the junction of the Kennebec and Dead Rivers—making it obvious why rafting companies have set up shop here. The tiny year-round population of 30 supports an ever-expanding transient population for the whitewater-rafting trade from May through October.

Surrounded by mountains, Jackman (pop. 930) is the valley's frontier town, the last outpost before the Quebec provincial border, 16 miles northward on the Trans-Maine Trail. In the middle of town, the Moose River links Jackman to Moose River town (pop. 225), just to the north.

From Bingham to Jackman, Rt. 201 is better known as "Moose Alley." Even though state transportation officials have built rumble strips into the road and littered the roadsides with flashing yellow lights and cautionary Moose Crossing signs, drivers still barrel along, and every year fatalities occur. Those who drive carefully, though, have a treat in store: moose sightings are relatively frequent, especially early and late in the day. If you notice a car or two pulled off the road, it's a good bet someone has spotted a moose. Another Moose Alley in this area—a pretty sure bet for spotting one of the behemoths—is Rt. 6/15 from Jackman east to Rockwood.

SIGHTS

Moxie Falls

Here's a big reward for little effort. One of New England's highest waterfalls, Moxie Falls, with drops of as much as 100 feet, is one of the easiest to reach. From Rt. 201, just south of the Kennebec River bridge in The Forks, drive about two miles east on Lake Moxie Rd. to the signposted parking area. From here, via trail, steps, and boardwalk, it's less than a mile to the falls in Moxie Stream. Allow a relaxed hour for the roundtrip; if it's hot, cool off in the stepped pools. Avoid the falls in June, when blackflies will have you for lunch. Don't forget a camera.

Fall-Foliage Bonanza

High on everyone's list of "best roads to drive in fall" is **Route 201,** the officially designated Scenic Highway between Solon and Jackman. Every curve in the winding, two-lane road reveals a red, gold, and green palette any artist would die for.

Among the must sees along the route are the **Attean View Rest Area,** just south of Jackman (have your picnic here), and the neat little hamlet of **Caratunk** (pop. 103), a smidgen east of Rt. 201 on the way to Pleasant Pond. Include a stop at the folksy **Caratunk General Store-** cum-post office.

RECREATION

Recreational opportunities in the Upper Kennebec Valley include hiking, canoeing, bicycling, and snowmobiling, but the big business is white-

water rafting, headquartered in and around The Forks. The umbrella organization for 10 white-water rafting companies is **Raft Maine,** P.O. Box 3, Bethel 04217, tel./fax (207) 824-3694 or (800) 723-8633. The group provides info, sends out brochures, and fields reservation requests.

Whitewater Rafting

Carefully regulated by the state, the rafting companies have come a long way since the sport took off in 1976; outfitters have created sprawling base-camp complexes and diversified into such other adventure sports as mountain biking, canoeing, kayaking, camping, rock climbing, horseback riding, snowmobiling, and cross-country skiing. The state strictly monitors the number of rafts allowed on the rivers; on midsummer weekends, there's a near-capacity crowd. More than 80,000 rafters run Maine's rivers each season.

The focus of whitewater rafting in this region is the **East Branch of the Kennebec River,** a 12-mile run from Central Maine Power's Harris Station hydroelectric dam, below Indian Pond, to The Forks. The dam's water releases produce waves of up to eight feet, but the only major whitewater (Class IV and V) is at Magic Falls, near the beginning of the trip. By the end of the run, you're just floating along. More than a dozen companies operate Kennebec trips between early May and mid-October. Information about the Harris Dam water-release schedule is available round-the-clock by calling (800) 287-0999.

All of these companies also organize trips on the more challenging and oddly named **Dead River,** but Central Maine Power only releases serious water through its Long Falls Dam half a dozen times during the season, mostly on spring weekends. Competition is stiff for space on the infrequent Dead River trips, an exhilarating 16-mile run through Class III to Class V whitewater from below Grand Falls to The Forks. Biggest thrill is Poplar Hill Falls. In July and August, the Dead River lives up to its placid name, and outfitters organize moderately priced Sport-Yak and family rafting trips. Nine of the companies described below also operate rafting trips on the **West Branch of the Penobscot River,** from base or outpost camps near Millinocket.

In spring, when ice has barely left the rivers, you'll need to bring or rent a wetsuit; in fall, you'll float past brilliant riverside colors; in both these seasons, as well as on weekdays, prices are the lowest. September is a great time to be here. No matter when you come, expect to get wet; wear Polartec or wool or polypropylene, *not* cotton. Each of the outfitters sends a list of what to bring and wear.

Cost of a one-day Kennebec River trip ranges $65-114 pp, depending on whether it's a weekday, weekend, or midsummer. Prices include a hearty cookout or lunch either along the river or back at base camp. Cost of the one-day Dead River trip ranges $80-114 pp. Scads of economical package rates are available, including lodging, meals, and other activities. Be forewarned that all outfitters have **age minimums:** 10-13 on the upper Kennebec and 12-15 on the Dead. Some also impose a weight minimum, usually 90 pounds. Age minimums on the more challenging Penobscot are 14-16. Penobscot trip costs range $75-114.

If you want to make more than a day of it—definitely a good plan, since trips start early in the morning and you'll be exhilarated but dog-tired at the end of the day—spend a night or two. Most of the whitewater rafting companies have been building and refurbishing like mad, creating beds for every budget. The camaraderie is contagious when everyone around you is about to go rafting or has just done it.

Rafting Outfitters
One of the early rafting firms, **Maine Whitewater,** Rt. 201, P.O. Box 633, Bingham 04920, tel. (207) 672-4814 or (800) 345-6246, fax (207) 672-4176, based next to Gadabout Gaddis Airport, has remained relatively low-key. Solid experience, competitive rates, no frills; Kennebec, Dead, and Penobscot trips. Watch for the Llama Crossing sign on Rt. 201 near the headquarters. Maine Whitewater can arrange lodgings ranging from primitive campsites ($8 pp) to B&B ($26-36 pp).

The pioneer of Maine's rafting companies, and still the largest operation, is **Northern Outdoors,** Rt. 201, P.O. Box 100, The Forks 04985, tel. (207) 663-4466 or (800) 765-7238, fax (207) 663-2244, established in 1976 by Wayne and Suzie Hockmeyer. Northern Outdoors runs trips on the Kennebec, Dead, and Penobscot Rivers in self-bailing Maravia rafts; their trip prices are the highest. From The Forks Resort Center,

four miles south of town, buses transport rafters (about half an hour) to the Harris Station put-in. This first-rate enterprise also offers family-oriented activities, including freshwater fishing trips, rock climbing, camping overnights, Sport-Yaking, and snowmobiling. Lots of lodging possibilities—campsites, cabin tents, and log cabins —priced according to the number of occupants. Also here are tennis courts, an outdoor pool, hot tub, brewpub, and restaurant serving three meals a day. Open all year.

Five miles east of The Forks is **Moxie Outdoor Adventures,** Lake Moxie Camps, Lake Moxie Rd., HC 63, Box 60, The Forks 04985, tel. (207) 663-2231 or (800) 866-6943, fax (207) 663-4403, which runs Kennebec, Dead, and Penobscot trips from a traditional sporting-camp base on lovely Lake Moxie (also called Moxie Pond), east of Moxie Falls. Rental canoes are available, there's great hiking, and guests tend to linger here. Rustic cabins, platform tents, and primitive campsites are the lodging options; opt for American Plan. Moxie also organizes rafting trips in Massachusetts, Vermont, and Connecticut.

Professional River Runners of Maine, Rt. 201, P.O. Box 92, West Forks 04985, tel. (207) 663-2229 or (800) 325-3911, fax (207) 663-4473, does Kennebec, Dead, and Penobscot trips, as well as spring trips on New York's Hudson and Moose Rivers. Campsites are available at their base here, and they'll arrange other lodging on request.

On the banks of the Dead River, **Magic Falls Rafting Company,** P.O. Box 9, West Forks 04985, tel./fax (207) 663-2220 or (800) 207-7238, winter Rt. 4, Box 2820, Winslow 04901, tel. (207) 873-0938, does Kennebec, Dead, and Penobscot trips and also offers rock climbing with certified instructors. A unique "rock and roll" package ($119 pp) covers a day of rafting and a day of climbing. Accommodations include B&B rooms, cabin tents, and basic tentsites.

Unicorn Expeditions, Rt. 201, Lake Parlin, Jackman 04945, tel. (207) 668-7629 or (800) 864-2676, fax (207) 668-7627, another veteran rafting business (since 1979), runs Kennebec, Dead, and Penobscot trips. Its Lake Parlin Resort headquarters complex, 14 miles north of West Forks, includes two lodges, a restaurant, and nine one- and two-bedroom cabins. Unicorn also organizes mountain biking and fresh-water fishing. Its Penobscot River rafting trips are based at Big Moose Inn, west of Millinocket.

In Moose River, headquartered at the Sky Lodge Resort complex just up the hill from downtown Jackman, **Windfall Outdoor Center,** Rt. 201, Box 505, Moose River 04945, tel. (207) 668-4818 or (800) 683-2009, fax (207) 668-4055, is a newish outfitter with an experienced crew running Kennebec and Dead River rafting trips. Lodging options include B&B rooms in the main Sky Lodge building, motel rooms, modern log cabins, and tentsites. There's access to a pool and fitness facility all year, but the Bear's Den Tavern tends to be open only Thurs.-Sun. and holidays. Windfall also organizes fishing and flightseeing trips and rents mountain bikes ($25 a day) and Old Town canoes ($18 a day). In winter, there are six miles of groomed cross-country trails.

Three other Kennebec, Dead, and Penobscot rafting outfitters have their headquarters elsewhere and a variety of base camps here in the Kennebec Valley. **New England Outdoor Center,** based in Millinocket, has an impressive resort complex on Wyman Lake in Caratunk, managing its Kennebec and Dead River trips. **Wilderness Expeditions,** based at The Birches Resort in Rockwood, also has a lodge at The Forks for its Kennebec and Dead trips. **Downeast Whitewater,** headquartered in New Hampshire, Box 119, Center Conway, NH 03813, tel. (800) 677-7238, maintains attractive base facilities near The Forks. Downeast is affiliated with **Saco Bound Canoeing,** organizing canoe trips and rentals in southwestern Maine.

Canoeing

If you're a neophyte canoeist, or have never done a multiday trip, or you want to go *en famille,* your baptismal expedition probably ought to be the three-day **Moose River Bow Trip,** an easy, 45-mile loop (ergo, "bow") with mostly flatwater. Of course, you can do this yourself, and you don't even need to arrange a shuttle, but a guided trip has its advantages—not the least of which is that the guides provide the know-how for the beginners, they do the cooking and cleanup, and they're a big help during the two portages. Allow $100-110 pp a day for a guided trip.

The Moose River trip has become so popular in recent years that campsite maintenance has backslid a bit and some guides prefer to go elsewhere, but it's still a fine, fun expedition. Veteran guide services that do this trip include Mike Patterson and Edgar Eaton's **Wilds of Maine Guide Service Inc.,** 2 Abby Lane, Yarmouth 04096, tel. (207) 846-9735, and the Cochrane family's **Allagash Canoe Trips,** P.O. Box 713, Greenville 04441, tel. (207) 695-3668.

Kayaking

Experienced kayaking guides Andy and Leslie McKendry operate **Cry of the Loon Kayak Adventures,** P.O. Box 238, Jackman 04945, tel. (207) 668-7808, from Memorial Day weekend to mid-October. Their three trip options (three days and two nights each) include the Moose River Bow (with only one portage), Brassua Lake/Moosehead, and a Three-Pond Trip. The bow trip is easiest; the Moosehead trip is only for experienced paddlers. Maximum group is eight. Gourmet meals are included in the $275 pp cost. Andy and Leslie will also do one-day guided trips ($60 pp with lunch), or they'll customize a trip for you. Avoid June, when the blackflies descend; September can be cool, but the colors are fabulous. Cry of the Loon's base is on Rt. 15, six and a half miles east of Jackman.

Hiking

The **Appalachian Trail,** extending 2,158 miles from Springer Mountain, Georgia, to the summit of Maine's Katahdin, crosses the Upper Kennebec Valley near Caratunk, just south of The Forks. The *Appalachian Trail Guide to Maine* provides details for reaching several sections of the white-blazed trail accessible to short-haul hikers. Crossing the Kennebec itself would be a major obstacle were it not for the seasonal free ferry service operated for AT hikers by Steve Longley, tel. (207) 663-4441, with his Old Town canoe. Each spring, Steve prints up a notice listing his ferry-service schedule; since the mid-1980s, he's been one of the "old reliables" along the trail. Ferry hours tend to be two hours in the morning, late May through early August, and four hours a day from early August to Columbus Day.

If you're spending any time in the woods in October and November, do not go out without at least a blaze-orange cap to signal your presence to hunters; a blaze-orange vest is even better. Even though some properties are posted No Hunting, don't take a chance; one scofflaw can make a life-and-death difference. If you're skittish, or don't have the proper clothing, hike on Sunday, when hunting is banned.

The best hiking guide for this area is Susan Varney's *Take a Hike*, a 30-page booklet of easy to strenuous treks (see the Booklist). Particularly fine hikes, of varying difficulty, are **Owls Head, Pleasant Pond Mountain, Moxie Bald Mountain,** and **Enchanted Pond.**

See "Parks and Recreation" under "Skowhegan Area" earlier in this chapter for details on Kennebec Valley Trails (KVT), an energetic membership organization working on an ambitious long-range plan for a multiuse trail between Jackman and Belgrade. KVT has a solid core of active members in and around Bingham.

Mountain Biking

The major highway in the valley (Rt. 201) is winding and fairly narrow, so plan to bike primarily on the side roads—some paved, some not. The best biking guide to the area is *Take a Ride . . . Road & Mountain Biking Guide,* a 44-pager covering the Kennebec Valley as far south as Belgrade Lakes. Some of the book's routes follow or cross private paper-company roads; save these for weekends and major holidays, when you don't have to worry about barreling timber trucks, which have the right-of-way.

An easy 12-mile loop follows a disused railroad bed (no tracks) from Bingham south to Solon. Best place to pick up the trail is at the Gadabout Gaddis Airport, on the southern outskirts of Bingham. The route roughly parallels the river and Rt. 201. Endpoint is the Williams Dam public landing, alongside the Kennebec in Solon; retrace your route from here (or do the loop in reverse).

In the Jackman area, an easy-to-moderate 10-mile trip is the **Sandy Bay Loop,** beginning seven miles north of downtown Jackman. Jack-

man's chamber office has a recreational map detailing this route and others in the area.

Golf

Close to Sky Lodge Resort, the nine-hole **Moose River Golf Course,** Rt. 201, Moose River, Jackman 04945, tel. (207) 668-4841, laid out in 1935, has fabulous lake and mountain vistas. Greens fees are inexpensive, starting times aren't needed, and the course is open mid-May to mid-October.

Snowmobiling

The **Jackman/Moose River** area has more than 100 miles of groomed snowmobile trails, and the mountain setting makes it particularly appealing. In fact, the town looks a bit less raw and frontierish under a fresh coat of snow. The trail network connects east to the Moosehead Lake area and west to the Sugarloaf/USA area.

Skiing

For **cross-country skiing,** head for the 30-mile network of groomed trails at The Birches Resort, a 30-mile drive east on Rt. 6/15.

The nearest **downhill skiing** is at Sugarloaf/USA, but there's no east-west road; you'll have to go south to North Anson and take Rt. 16 northwest to Sugarloaf.

ACCOMMODATIONS

If you're planning to be in this area during snowmobiling season, especially in Jackman, be sure to book well in advance; the lodgings get chockablock full of snow-sledders.

B&Bs

The only B&B in The Forks not connected to a rafting company, **Inn by the River,** Rt. 201, The Forks, mailing address HC 63, Box 24, West Forks 04985, tel./fax (207) 663-2181, gets business from the rafting trade plus guests looking for a bit of casual elegance. Everything's new, modern, and efficient here. Guests collect in the handsome great room, and there's even a pub. Ten rooms (private baths) go for $90-120 d,

May through Labor Day; two-night minimum on weekends. Off-season rates are $60-90 d. Dinner is available nightly in summer, but you'll need to reserve ahead. Innkeepers Bill and Cori Cost's kids pitch in, and children are welcome. Open May through mid-October, Inn by the River is half a mile south of the Kennebec River bridge in The Forks.

Rocking chairs on the porch are the first clue; then there's the teddy-bear collection. **Mrs. G's Bed & Breakfast,** Meadow St., Box 389, Bingham 04920, tel. (207) 672-4034, makes you feel instantly at home, thanks to warm, grandmotherly Frances Gibson. Four second-floor rooms ($60 d) share two baths. The third-floor loft has nine single beds ($25 pp), a half-bath, a skylight, and an outside entrance. It's coed, usually filled with rafters in spring, summer, and fall, and Mrs. G admonishes everyone to behave. Children are payable by their age—how about $10 for a 10-year-old? Breakfast is a treat. If six or eight guests request it, she'll also prepare dinner (extra charge). No credit cards; smoking only in the living room. Open May through November. This popular B&B is the first house east of Main Street (Rt. 201) in downtown Bingham.

Resort Inn
The great room at **Sky Lodge Resort,** Rt. 201, Moose River 04945, tel. (207) 668-2171 or (800) 416-6181, fax (207) 668-9471, built in the 1920s, is nothing short of awesome—a two-story log room with fireplaces, bearskins, and comfortable chairs. The second-floor balcony leads to the nine guest rooms, all tastefully decorated (private and shared baths; $99 d, July through September). A fake wall in one room once served as a Prohibition hideaway. Next to the lodge building is a motel wing ($39-59 d); across the road are kitchen-equipped cabins ($100 for four) with fabulous views over Big Wood Lake and the mountains; linens are provided. The 125-acre resort has an outdoor pool, hot tub, and the Bear's Den Tavern (open weekends and holidays). See "Whitewater Rafting" under "Recreation," above, for info on the resort's Windfall Outdoor Center. Open all year, but the operation is scaled-down in winter.

Sporting Camps
Legendary on the Appalachian Trail hikers' grapevine, since the AT goes right through here, **Harrison's Pierce Pond Sporting Camps,** Pierce Pond Stream, P.O. Box 315, Bingham 04920, radiophone (207) 672-3625 or tel. (207) 279-8424 off season, serves up 12-pancake breakfasts ($4) to hungry trekkers as well as to camp guests. And the rest of the meals are just as impressive. Started in 1934, Harrison's has long catered to fishermen but encourages families in midsummer, when fishing slacks off. Special summer rates (early July to mid-August; three-night minimum) are $50 pp a day, half-price for kids 4-12, $13 for three-year-olds, and younger kids stay free. Other months, cabins are $59 pp for adults, $29 for kids 4-12. All meals are included. The huge lodge/dining hall has great views of the stream and waterfalls. Boat rentals are available; pets are allowed. Nine rustic log cabins have kerosene lamps and separate bathhouses; a few have toilet and sink (for a slightly higher rate). Vehicle access is an adventure in itself: about 20 miles (well signposted) northwest of Bingham, on paved and unpaved roads. Open May-Sept., but closed to lodging (AT breakfasts still go on) for 10 days in mid-August.

Attean Lake Lodge, Birch Island, P.O. Box 457, Jackman 04945, tel. (207) 668-3792, has certain trappings of traditional sporting camps, but it's more like upscale rustic. Owned by the Holden family since 1900, it's located on Birch Island in the center of island-sprinkled Attean Lake (also called Attean Pond). Fourteen well-maintained log cabins (2-6 beds) have bathrooms, fireplaces, kerosene lamps, and overhang porches with fantastic views of the lake and surrounding mountains. Guests tend to collect in the new main lodge, with its stone fireplace and window-walled dining room. Canoes, kayaks, and motorboats are available for rent. Rates are $225 d per day, or $1,400 d a week, American Plan (wine and beer are available); no minimum stay. Book well ahead; this is a popular getaway, open Memorial Day weekend through September. Access to the island is via the lodge launch, a five-minute run.

Campgrounds

Central Maine Power has established a campground next to its Harris Station on the East Branch of the Kennebec, where all the Upper Kennebec rafting trips begin. **Indian Pond Campground,** HC 63, Box 52, The Forks 04985, tel. (800) 371-7774, has 27 tent and RV sites (no hookups), including picnic tables and fire rings. Other facilities include showers, restrooms, laundry machines, and boat launch. Cost is $14 a site (for two); kids under 10 stay free. Leashed pets are allowed. You can hike from here to Magic Rock and watch Kennebec rafters surging through Magic Falls. If hydroelectric plants pique your interest, ask at the gatehouse about a tour of Harris Station. To reach the campground from Rt. 201 in The Forks, take Lake Moxie Rd. (also Moxie Pond Rd.) about five miles east; turn left (north) onto Harris Station Rd. and continue eight miles to the campground gatehouse. Open mid-April to mid-October.

On Heald Stream in Moose River, a mile east of downtown Jackman, the 24-acre **Moose River Campground,** P.O. Box 98, Jackman 04945, tel. (207) 668-3341, has 52 sites close to a picturesque old dam site. Now crumbling from disuse, the dam once was part of a thriving, turn-of-the-20th-century lumber mill that employed more than 700 workers to turn out 35 million board feet annually. Open and wooded campsites are $13-18 (for two); canoe rentals are $14 a day or $2 an hour. Facilities include a snack bar, heated swimming pool, trout ponds, laundry machines, and children's play area. Open mid-May through October.

FOOD

Bingham's center for down-home cooking is **Thompson's Restaurant,** Upper Main St., Rt. 201, Bingham 04920, tel. (207) 672-3245, where *everyone* eventually shows up. This friendly two-room operation (smoking in one room) is open all year, Mon.-Sat. 6 a.m.-8:30 p.m. and Sunday 7 a.m.-8:30 p.m. No credit cards.

In Jackman, on the edge of Big Wood Lake (also called Big Wood Pond), a quarter of a mile off Main Street, **Loon's Look-Out Restaurant,** Forest St., HC 64, Box 44, Jackman 04945, tel. (207) 668-3351, is a friendly, very casual place

with checked tablecloths, hunting trophies, humongous Italian meals, and real-deal prices. Wait'll you see the baseball-size meatballs. Dinner is by reservation only, Fri.-Sun. 5-9 p.m.

Jackman's most creative menu is at the **Moose Point Tavern,** Big Wood Lake, P.O. Box 807, Jackman 04945, tel. (207) 668-4012, in an 1890 lakeside lodge. Dinner entrées ($9-16) include venison and interesting variations on chicken, pork, and beef. "Tavern-fare" items include *poutine,* the artery-clogging Franco-American favorite (fries with cheese and gravy, $3.50). The wine list is small but respectable. Moose Point is open Thurs.-Mon. every month except December and April. Hours are 5-9 or 9:30 p.m.; the bar is open 4-11 p.m. From mid-June through September, Moose Point opens Thurs.-Mon. at 11 a.m. for lunches of burgers, salads, soups, and sandwiches.

If you're staying in Jackman and don't mind a 60-mile roundtrip for dinner, it's worth heading east on Rt. 6/15 for moderate-priced dinners at The Birches Resort. Be sure to call for a reservation. The pre-dinner slot is prime time for moosewatching on this route. Afterward, unless there's a moon, the road is terminally dark, so drive *very* carefully.

INFORMATION AND SERVICES

Staffers at the Bingham and Jackman information centers are especially outgoing and helpful, but their hours are limited. It's wise to request their publications in advance, then hope to find the offices open when you arrive.

The **Upper Kennebec Valley Chamber of Commerce,** Murray St., P.O. Box 491, Bingham 04920, tel. (207) 672-4100, has a well-stocked new information center in the old Scott Paper building, half a block off Main St. (Rt. 201). The office, which has public restrooms, is open Memorial Day weekend through September, daily 9 a.m.-5 p.m.

The **Jackman Moose River Chamber of Commerce,** Lakeside Town Park, Main St., Rt. 201, P.O. Box 368, Jackman 04945, tel. (207) 668-4171, has a small log-cabin information center with public restrooms out back. From Memorial Day weekend to late June, as well as Labor Day to mid-October, it's open Fri.-Sun.

11 a.m.-7 p.m.; late June through Labor Day, it's open Wed.-Sun. 11 a.m.-7 p.m. Be sure to request a copy of the *Jackman Moose River Region recreational map,* showing canoeing, biking, hiking, and snowmobile trails, plus driving routes and good moosewatching spots.

The umbrella organization for 10 whitewater rafting companies is **Raft Maine,** P.O. Box 3, Bethel 04217, tel./fax (207) 824-3694 or (800) 723-8633, which provides info, sends out brochures, and fields reservation requests. The toll-free number rotates like Russian roulette, connecting you to the next-in-line rafting outfitter. If you prefer, contact individual outfitters directly (see "Rafting Outfitters" under "Recreation," above).

Emergencies

In **Bingham,** call (207) 672-3770 for fire, (207) 672-4410 for an ambulance, and (800) 452-4664 for the state police. For police, fire, and ambulance services in **Jackman, Caratunk, and The Forks,** dial 911. The **Jackman Region Health Center,** Main St., Rt. 201, Jackman 04945, tel. (207) 268-6691, a division of Waterville's Mid-Maine Medical Center, has emergency-room care round-the-clock, but you'll need to go at least as far as Skowhegan for anything major.

Money

The **Border Trust Company,** Rt. 201 at Nichols Rd., P.O. Box 400, Jackman 04945, tel. (207) 668-2251, fax (207) 668-3361, is a convenient place to change Canadian dollars into U.S. dollars. If you're headed *into* Canada, they'll be happy to see your U.S. dollars, so don't bother changing money in that direction. Remember to carry appropriate identification if you're planning to cross the border—a driver's license will do for U.S. citizens, a passport is required for other nationals. The customs post on Rt. 201 is open round-the-clock. Border Trust is open Mon.-Thurs. 9 a.m.-3 p.m., Friday 9 a.m.-5 p.m., and Saturday 9 a.m.-noon. The drive-up window opens at 8:30 a.m. Mon.-Sat. and closes at 5 p.m. weekdays and at noon on Saturday. Jackman's only ATM is at the **Mountain Country Supermarket,** tel. (207) 668-5451, on Main St. (Rt. 201); open daily, all year.

Laundromat

At the **Jackman Landing Campground,** Big Wood Lake, P.O. Box 567, Jackman 04945, tel. (207) 668-3301, right in the center of town, the laundry facilities are open to the public round-the-clock, all year, whether or not you're renting a campsite.

BOB RACE

WESTERN LAKES AND MOUNTAINS

Whenever I tire of the summertime coastal grid-lock or I get the winter blahs, the place I'm most likely to go for refuge is Maine's western lakes and mountains—about 4,500 outstandingly scenic square miles of Franklin, Oxford, Androscoggin, and Cumberland Counties. The recreational variety is astonishing. Here are the two skiing powerhouses—Sunday River and Sugarloaf/USA—plus four smaller, family-oriented ski areas: Saddleback, Shawnee Peak, Mount Abram, and Lost Valley. While downhill may be the specialty, most of these also have miles of nordic trails.

Major "urban" destinations in the region are Bethel, Lewiston-Auburn, and Farmington. Of Maine's nine covered bridges (seven originals and two carefully built replicas), you'll find five in the western lakes and mountains—my favorite is picturesque "Artist's Covered Bridge," near Sunday River, in part because you can ski through the forest and suddenly come upon it. And one of the most rugged stretches of the 2,158-mile Appalachian Trail, which runs from Georgia to Maine, occurs in this area, right along the New Hampshire border.

Sprawling, mountainous Oxford County, with its back to New Hampshire, has fabulous trails for hiking and rivers for canoeing—and boasts the state's lowest population density. There's gold—and all kinds of other minerals—in the Oxford Hills; the official state gemstone, tourmaline (an intriguing stone that turns up in green, blue, or pink), is most prevalent in western Maine. Grab a digging tool or gold pan and have a go at amateur prospecting. You're unlikely to find more than a few flakes or some pretty specimens of sparkly pyrite ("fool's gold"), but the fun is in the adventure anyway.

East of Oxford County, Franklin County comprises Sugarloaf/USA and the lovely Rangeley Lakes recreational area. Farmington is the county seat. Mostly rural Androscoggin, fourth-smallest of the state's 16 counties, takes its commercial and political cues from Lewiston and Auburn, the state's second-largest population center.

Directly west of Portland, and partly in Cumberland County, are Sebago and Long Lakes, surrounded by towns and villages that swell with visitors throughout the summer. Also here are most of the state's youth summer camps—some many generations old. During the annual summer-camp parents' weekend, in late July, Bridgton's tiny, besieged downtown feels like Times Square at rush hour.

For tackling the many miles of trails in this region, you may find several guidebooks helpful —especially *AMC Maine Mountain Guide, 50 Hikes in the Maine Mountains, Guide to the Appalachian Trail in Maine,* and *Hikes in and around Maine's Lake Region* (details for all except *Guide to the Appalachian Trail in Maine* can be found in the Booklist). If you can afford only one, pick up the last, a handy, inexpensive booklet written by a local resident.

FARMINGTON AREA

Farmington (pop. 7,300) is a sleeper of a town— home to a respected University of Maine campus, one of Maine's best art galleries, a first-class hospital, and an unusual opera museum. What's more, mountain towns and scenery stretch out and beyond in every direction. Less than an hour's drive north of town is the stunning Carrabassett Valley, made famous by the year-round Sugarloaf/USA resort. Off to the northwest are the fabled Rangeley Lakes, and a drive southwest leads to Bethel, home of Sunday River Ski Resort, mineral quarries, and the White Mountain National Forest. Farmington itself is a bit thin on interesting lodgings, but otherwise it's an ideal base for exploring western Maine.

Farmington was incorporated in 1794 and became the county seat for Franklin County 44 years later. It remains the judicial hub but also is the commercial center for the nearby towns of Wilton, Weld, New Sharon, Temple, and Industry. To the south and west are Jay, Livermore Falls, Livermore, Dixfield, Mexico, and Rumford.

Wilton is the home of the G.H. Bass Company, makers of everyone's favorite—"Weejuns" (a nickname for Norwegian-style moccasins). In Rumford and Jay, your nose will tell you it's paper-mill territory, part of Maine's economic lifeline. Residents have become inured to the aroma, but visitors may need a chance to adjust. Livermore is the site of the Norlands Living History Center, a unique participatory museum that rewards you with a real "feel" for the past.

And, lest we forget, Farmington's leading candidate for favorite son is Chester Greenwood, who, in 1873, rigged beaver fur, velvet, and a bit of wire to create "Champion ear protectors"— earmuffs to you—when he was only 15. The clever fellow patented his invention and then went on to earn a hundred more patents for such things as doughnut hooks and shock absorbers. His early-December birthday inspires the quirky annual Chester Greenwood Day celebration in downtown Farmington.

SIGHTS

Nordica Homestead Museum
Gem-encrusted gowns, opera librettos, lavish gifts from royalty, and family treasures fill the handful of rooms in the Nordica Homestead Museum, Holley Rd., RFD 3, Box 3062, Farmington 04938, tel. (207) 778-2042, birthplace of Lillian Norton (1857-1914)—Madame Lillian Nordica, legendary turn-of-the-century Wagnerian opera diva. Her influence still pervades the house, where scratchy recordings play in the background and newspaper clips line the walls. No opera buff should miss this. A caretaker is on hand to answer questions. Admission is $2 adults, $2 children over five; even the kids get a kick out of the costumed manikins, and there's lots of space on the grounds for letting off steam. The museum is open June through Labor Day, Tues.-Sat. 10 a.m.-noon and 1-5 p.m. and Sunday 1-5 p.m. It's also open by appointment from Labor Day to mid-October. Take Rt. 4/27 north from Farmington and turn right (east) onto Holley Rd.; the farm is half a mile down the road.

University of Maine at Farmington
Founded in 1864 as Western State Normal School, with 31 teacher trainees, the University of Maine at Farmington (UMF), 86 Main St., Rt. 4, Farmington 04938, tel. (207) 778-7000, now has about 2,000 students tackling their studies in more than three dozen buildings. UMF's Education Department has always been topnotch, with a 100% placement record for its graduates.

The university's administration building, **Merrill Hall,** on Main Street, is a 19th-century Na-

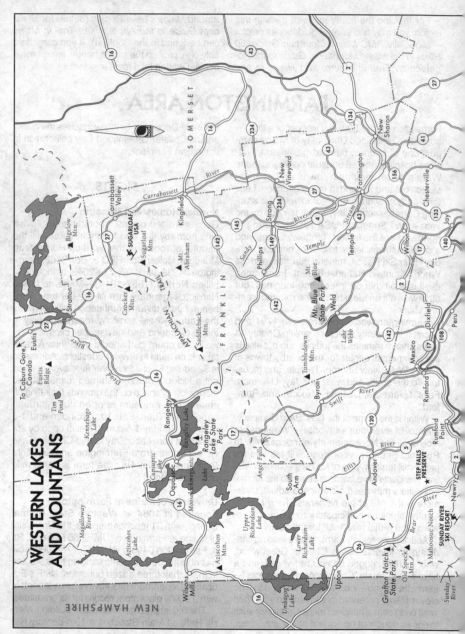

WESTERN LAKES AND MOUNTAINS

NEW HAMPSHIRE

To Coburn Gore, Canada

Eustis

Eustis Ridge ▲

Tim Pond ●

Kennebago Lake

Stratton

Magalloway River

Aziscohos Lake

Aziscohos Mtn.

Wilsons Mills

Umbagog Lake

Upton

Rangeley

Cupsuptic Lake

Oquossoc

Rangeley Lake

Rangeley Lake State Park

Mooselookmeguntic Lake

Upper Richardson Lake

Lower Richardson Lake

South Arm

Andover

Newry

Grafton Notch State Park

Old Speck Mtn.

Mahoosuc Notch

SUNDAY RIVER SKI RESORT

Sandy River

Bear River

Ellis River

Angel Falls

Swift River

Byron

Rumford

Mexico

Rumford Point

STEP FALLS PRESERVE

Bigelow Mtn.

SUGARLOAF USA

Sugarloaf Mtn.

Crocker Mtn.

Carrabassett Valley

Carrabassett

Kingfield

Mt. Abraham ▲

APPALACHIAN TRAIL

Saddleback Mtn.

Tumbledown Mtn.

F R A N K L I N

S O M E R S E T

Dead River

River

Phillips

Sandy River

Strong

New Vineyard

Temple

Temple Stream

Farmington

New Sharon

Weld

Mt. Blue ▲

Mt. Blue State Park

Lake Webb

Dixfield

Peru

Wilton

Chesterville

Joy

New Portland

16 43 2 27 134 41 156 133 140 17 108 120 5 26 16 27 142 149 145 234 43 4 142 17

Canada

Dixfield

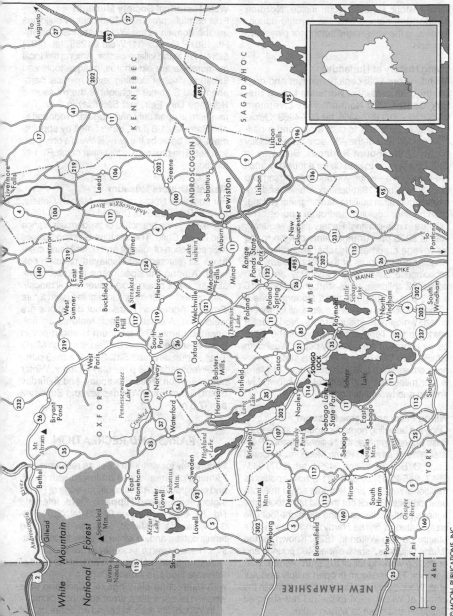

© MOON PUBLICATIONS, INC.

tional Historic Register gem. Inside, **Nordica Auditorium,** named after the favorite-daughter diva, is the year-round setting for plays and concerts.

Living History at Norlands

Abandon your 20th-century mindset and drop into the 19th century at **Norlands Living History Center,** 290 Norlands Rd., Livermore 04253, tel. (207) 897-4366, fax 897-4963. Quickest way to do this is to take a one-and-a-half-hour guided tour of the 430-acre farm officially known as **Washburn-Norlands.** Best way to do it, however, is to sign up for a four-day adult live-in program—when you don the clothing and identity of a real 19th-century Mainer and immerse yourself in quilting, farming, storytelling, churchgoing, cooking, and other chores. The ultimate in role-playing! Reservations required; cost is $225 pp. Arrangements can be made for college credit and teacher recertification. Regular guided tours of the house, barn, and schoolhouse, July through Labor Day, are $5.50 adults, $2 children; tours start on the hour, 10 a.m.-3 p.m. During the year, Norlands has a number of special weekend events, all family-oriented, which also include tours. Norlands, a name from a Tennyson poem, was the 19th-century home of the politically potent Washburn family. Two Washburns became state governors, others were U.S. congressmen. The farm is four miles east and north of downtown Livermore and two miles north of Rt. 108.

Wilton Farm and Home Museum

Once the boarding home for workers at the G.H. Bass Shoe Company, the National Historic Register Wilton Farm and Home Museum, 10 Canal St., P.O. Box 33, Wilton 04294, tel. (207) 645-2843, 645-2091, or 645-2214, now spotlights traditional rural life and features some truly offbeat exhibits. Check out the old farm tools, the antique bottle collection, and the eight-foot (life size) statue of Sylvia Hardy, an Amazon-size Mainer born in Wilton in 1823. Known as the "Maine Giantess," she weighed 400 pounds and ended up working for circus entrepreneur P.T. Barnum. The museum is open in July and August, Wednesday and Sunday 1-4 p.m. It's in the center of Wilton, next to the old red-shingled Bass Mill and close to Wilson Lake.

Weld Historical Society Museum

Four carefully preserved 19th-century buildings are the domain of the Weld Historical Society, Rt. 156, P.O. Box 31, Weld 04285, tel. (207) 585-2179, in the village center. Among the local memorabilia are old photos, antique tools and furniture, vintage clothing, even medical paraphernalia. Summer highlight is the museum's **Heritage Day Fair,** last Saturday in July. The museum is open July and August, Wednesday and Saturday 1-3 p.m., other times by appointment. Out back, by the way, is Weld's only public toilet. The museum is just east of the Rt. 142 junction.

Mainely Critters Museum

Far from your typical museum, Mainely Critters, Rt. 2, RR 1, Box 510, Dixfield 04224, tel. (207) 562-8231, is the brainchild of taxidermists Vance and Diane Child. The big blue building houses their collection of roadkill and other Maine creatures, all restored and displayed in lifelike settings. Among the specimens are raccoons, skunks, black bears, foxes, even a bull moose. Friends and motorists drift in regularly with future exhibits. Admission is free, but donations are welcomed. A small gift shop features animal-oriented items. The museum is about seven miles east of downtown Dixfield. It's open Mon.-Tues., Thursday, and Sat.-Sun. 8 a.m.-5 p.m., plus Wednesday 1-8 p.m., May-October. Winter hours are Mon.-Tues., Thursday, and Saturday 8 a.m.-5 p.m., plus Wednesday and Sunday 8 a.m.-7 p.m.

PARKS AND RECREATION

Fortunately for visitors as well as residents, the Farmington area is well endowed with parks and playgrounds. At the southern edge of Farmington, town-owned **Hippach Field,** Intervale Rd., Rt. 4/27, Farmington 04938, tel. (207) 778-3464, has playing fields, a playground, lighted tennis courts, and, in winter, a pond for ice-skating. There's even a skateboard park.

Just northeast of Hippach Field, at the head of Intervale Road, is **Abbott Park,** a lovely oasis with interesting plantings, a pond, and little wooden bridges. It's a great spot for a picnic.

In Wilton, it's easy to spend an entire day at

town-owned **Kineowatha Park,** 45 acres on the shore of Wilson Lake. Among the facilities are a beach, tennis courts, playing fields, playground, picnic tables, and even a lodge with a snack bar.

Mount Blue State Park

Mount Blue State Park, West Rd., Rt. 156, RR 1, Box 610, Weld 04285, tel. (207) 585-2347 or 585-2261 in winter, covering 5,021 acres, is one of Maine's best-kept secrets—crowded in summer, but mostly with Mainers. Yet it offers multilevel hiking, superb swimming, wooded campsites, mountain scenery, and daily interpretive natural-history programs in summer. There are movies on weekends, guided hikes, weekly guest speakers, even gold-panning expeditions—you'll never be bored. The park is split into two sections—swimming and camping are on Lake Webb's west side; the Center Hill section, including the trail to Mount Blue itself, is on the lake's east side. The main entrance, with a two-mile access road, is eight miles from Weld, on the lake's west side. Day-use admission is $2 adults, 50 cents children 5-11. Camping fees are extra (nonresidents pay $15 per site per night). Reservations for the 136 wooded campsites are handled through the state-park reservation system; call (207) 287-3824 at least two weeks ahead, and have your Visa or MasterCard handy. Reservation fee is $2 per site per night; two-night minimum. No hookups. The park season is May 15-Sept., but the Center Hill section has more than a dozen miles of groomed cross-country-ski trails.

Swimming

Five miles northeast of downtown Farmington is the hamlet of **Allens Mills** (officially the town of **Industry**), where you can swim in aptly named **Clearwater Lake.** Follow Broadway (Rt. 43) from Farmington until you reach a T-junction at the lake, where there's a little boat landing and access for swimming.

Canoeing

If you just want to paddle around, with no major energy investment, a good choice is **Clearwater Lake.** To get there from Farmington, follow Broadway (Rt. 43) until you reach a T-junction at the lake, where there's a little boat landing.

Red Oak Sports, 5 N. Main St., Farmington 04938, tel. (207) 778-5350, in addition to stocking moderately priced sportswear and camping gear, rents canoes and kayaks for $18 a day. They're also full of good advice about canoeing and kayaking hot spots; occasionally they organize guided canoe or kayak trips. The shop is open Mon.-Sat. 8 a.m.-6 p.m. (to 8 p.m. Friday) and 10 a.m.-5 p.m. Sunday. Red Oak also has a seasonal branch operation on Main Street (Rt. 27) in Belgrade Lakes village.

Hiking

You're getting into western Maine's serious mountains here, so there are plenty of great hiking opportunities, running the gamut from a cakewalk to a workout. If you're planning lots of hikes, purchase a copy of *A Native Guide to Hiking and Climbing in the Mt. Blue, Tumbledown Area.*

In Weld, a deservedly popular hiking route goes up 3,187-foot **Mount Blue,** in the eastern section of Mount Blue State Park. From Rt. 142 in Weld village, follow signs and take Maxwell Rd., then Center Hill Rd. about two and a half miles to the parking area for Center Hill itself. (There's no fee in this part of the park.) You can stop for a picnic (sweeping views even at this level, plus picnic tables and outhouses), follow the mile-long self-guided nature-trail loop (pick up a brochure here), then go on. (It's also a great spot for sunset-watching.) Continue up the unpaved road three and a half miles to the parking lot for the Mount Blue trailhead. Allow about three hours for the steepish three-mile roundtrip (easy, then moderately difficult). In midsummer, carry plenty of water. Pray for clear air on the summit; vistas of the Longfellows and beyond are awesome. Climb the stanchions of the old fire tower, now used for cellular-phone communications.

Other good hikes around Weld, on the west side of Lake Webb, are **Tumbledown Mountain** (3,068 feet via several route options; nesting peregrines can restrict access in early summer) and **Little Jackson Mountain** (3,434 feet). Tumbledown, moderately strenuous, attracts the been-there-done-that set. A much easier hike, but likely to be more crowded, is 2,386-foot **Bald Mountain,** with a scoured summit fine for picnics if it's not too blustery. Allow about two hours for the three-mile roundtrip, including lunch break. To reach the trailhead from Weld, take Rt. 156 southeast about five and a half miles. There's limited parking on the right; watch for the sign.

Mountain Biking

Thirty miles of mountain-biking trails are only part of the picture at **Troll Valley,** Red Schoolhouse Rd., RR 4, Box 5215, Farmington 04938, tel. (207) 778-3656, which also has a fitness center and snack bar. Weather permitting, group trail rides begin at 5 p.m. each Wednesday (reservations advisable). Troll Valley is about a quarter of a mile beyond the Nor'40 Campsite. Troll Valley is open for biking Memorial Day weekend through Columbus Day, Wed.-Sun. 9 a.m.-6 p.m.

Golf

Nine-hole **Wilson Lake Country Club,** Weld Rd., Rt. 156, Wilton 04294, tel. (207) 645-2016, established in 1931, is a sleeper of a course—not as well known as it should be, and no tee times are necessary. Facilities include a snack bar. The scenic, wooded course, northwest of downtown Wilton, is open May through October. There's also a fabulous (but pricey) course at Sugarloaf/USA.

Fitness Center

A rainy-day godsend is the new, $4.5-million University of Maine at Farmington **Health and Fitness Center,** 20 Lincoln St., Farmington 04938, tel. (207) 778-7495. It's open to the public for weight training, indoor jogging and tennis, and indoor swimming in a six-lane heated pool. Call ahead to reserve tennis-court time. In summer, it's open Mon.-Thurs. 5:30 a.m.-9 p.m., Friday 5:30 a.m.-7 p.m., Saturday 8 a.m.-7 p.m., and Sunday 10 a.m.-7 p.m. Winter hours are Mon.-Thurs. 5:30 a.m.-11 p.m., Friday 5:30 a.m.-9 p.m., Saturday 8 a.m.-9 p.m., and Sunday 9 a.m.-11 p.m. Cost is $8 pp, or $15 for a family, valid all day.

Kids' Stuff

Behind the W.G. Mallett School, 1 Quebec St., Farmington 04938, is a kids' paradise. **Castlemania,** centered on an intriguing wooden castle, owes its existence to a whole crew of dedicated volunteer fundraisers and builders. The Leathers-

designed creative playground is three blocks east of Main Street. The playground is off-limits during school hours.

Skiing

Most gonzo downhill skiers and snowboarders head right for the championship slopes at Sugarloaf/USA, but if you're still on the learning curve, or your budget is tight, the local alternative is family-oriented **Titcomb Mountain Ski Area,** Morrison Hill Rd., P.O. Box 138, West Farmington 04992, tel. (207) 778-9031, run by the Farmington Ski Club. This all-volunteer operation has ski lessons and rentals and only charges $12 for an all-day lift pass. For another $6, you can switch to cross-country skis and negotiate a dozen miles of groomed nordic trails. Titcomb Mountain is open Tues.-Sun., including night skiing Wednesday, Thursday, and Saturday.

Distinctly family-friendly, with cheap tickets for the T-bar and handle tow lifts, **Black Mountain,** P.O. Box 239, Rumford 04276, tel. (207) 364-8977, has nine trails, including night skiing on four trails. Snowmaking covers more than half of the slopes; vertical drop is 470 feet. Facilities include ski rentals, lessons, and a small snack bar. Off to the west of the lodge are six miles of groomed cross-country trails.

Troll Valley, Red Schoolhouse Rd., RR 4, Box 5215, Farmington 04938, tel. (207) 778-3656, has a 15-mile groomed cross-country trail network, with access to backcountry trails. Adult day passes are $6-8. Another cross-country option, and it's free, is the Center Hill section of **Mount Blue State Park,** with more than a dozen miles of groomed, underutilized cross-country trails.

ENTERTAINMENT

The multiplex at **Narrow Gauge Cinemas,** Front St., Farmington 04938, tel. (207) 778-4877, is open daily, all year, with periodic matinees Saturday and Sunday. Tickets are $4 adults, $3.50 children for evening flicks; matinee tickets are $3.50 pp.

Throughout the year, something is always happening at the **University of Maine at Farmington:** lectures, concerts, plays, you-name-it. Contact the college for schedule and details, tel. (207) 778-7000. At Meeting House Park, on Main Street in downtown Farmington, **band concerts** are held Monday evening at 7:30 p.m. in July and August; take a folding chair or a blanket. The Old Crow Indian Band holds forth in a green-and-white octagonal bandstand.

FESTIVALS AND EVENTS

Besides the events listed here, the nearby Sugarloaf area is busy with activities, too, particularly during skiing season.

Farm tours, wagon or sleigh rides, a country dinner, and maple syrup tasting all figure in **Norlands Maple Days,** at the Norlands Living History Center, Livermore, fourth weekend in March.

The family-oriented **Dixfield Summerfest** comprises a parade, games, a carnival, hot-air balloons, and food booths in Harlow Park the third weekend in June. The next weekend, **Heritage Days** is an old-fashioned summer fair with guided tours, craft booths, haywagon rides, music, and superb strawberry shortcake at the Norlands Living History Center, Livermore.

July is the month to visit Farmington. While every town has some variation on the **Independence Day celebration,** Farmington puts on a whoop-de-do affair. And the last Friday of the month, **Moonlight Madness** combines sidewalk sales, a street dance, a chicken barbecue, and an art show in downtown Farmington.

The three-day **Wilton Blueberry Festival** is a blueberry-oriented celebration (always crowded) including a parade, road races, games, craft booths, a book sale, a museum open house, live entertainment, a chicken barbecue, and a pig roast in downtown Wilton the second weekend in August.

The third week of September is given over to Farmington's **Franklin County Fair,** a weeklong country fair (one of the last of the season) with agricultural exhibits, a parade, harness racing, and live entertainment at the Farmington Fairgrounds. The last weekend of September is Norlands Living History Center's **Autumn Celebration,** with woodsmen's events, harvest demonstrations, wagon rides, guided tours, a baked-bean supper, and a barn dance.

The first Saturday in December, Farmington honors a native son on **Chester Greenwood**

Day. Festivities commemorating the inventor of earmuffs include a road race, an oddball earmuff parade, a polar-bear swim, and other activities. That same weekend, Livermore's Norlands Living History Center celebrates **Christmas at Norlands,** an old-fashioned celebration with sleigh rides, carol singing, guided tours, and a country luncheon.

SHOPPING

Art Galleries

Savvy art connoisseurs make pilgrimages to Farmington to check out one of Maine's best galleries, the **Tom Veilleux Gallery,** 30 Broadway, Farmington 04938, tel. (207) 778-0784. Tom Veilleux has been dealing in early-20th-century painters—most with a Maine connection—since 1979, selling 300-500 paintings a year. Even if your wallet's a little thin, it's worth climbing to the bright second-floor gallery for a look at his high-quality inventory. No credit cards. Summer hours are Tues.-Sat. 11 a.m.-4 p.m.; other months are less predictable. The gallery is always open by appointment, so call ahead if you're on a mission.

New and Used Books

It's hard to resist the cheerful, welcoming ambience at **Devaney Doak and Garrett Booksellers,** 29 Broadway, Farmington 04938, tel. (207) 778-3454, not to mention the upholstered chairs, classical background music, and a children's corner piled high with books, toys, and games. Cookbooks are a specialty, along with literary journals, lots of Maine books, unusual cards, and even designer coffees. The shop is open Mon.-Wed. 9 a.m.-5 p.m., Thursday 9 a.m.-6 p.m., Friday 9 a.m.-7 p.m., Saturday 9 a.m.-5 p.m., and Sunday 11 a.m.-2 p.m.

Around the corner, **Twice-Sold Tales,** 45 Main St., Farmington 04938, tel. (207) 778-4411, has a relatively small but well-chosen and well-organized selection; Maine titles are a specialty, and prices are reasonable. Ask owner Jim Logan, an avid outdoorsman, about hiking options in Farmington and beyond. Open all year, Mon.-Sat. 10 a.m.-5 p.m., but call ahead if you plan to arrive on Friday, as the schedule can be iffy.

The Falls Book Barn, 20 Main St., P.O. Box 58, Farmington Falls 04940, tel. (207) 778-3429, fax 778-5616, based in retired teacher Ethel Emerson's barn, is an eclectic, 15,000-title collection; you'll probably find yourself walking out with something. Open April to mid-October, but you'll need to call ahead to be sure. The Book Barn is .3 mile off Rt. 2/27, about five miles from downtown Farmington.

Gourmet Goodies
In downtown Farmington, Nina Gianquinto's **Up Front and Pleasant Gourmet,** 11 Front St., Farmington 04938, tel. (207) 778-5671, has all kinds of condiments, cheeses, homemade pasta, exotic coffees, plus a huge wine selection. No credit cards. Open all year, Mon.-Thurs. 10 a.m.-5 p.m., Friday 10 a.m.-6 p.m., and Saturday 10 a.m.-3 p.m.

Farmers' Market
Each Friday, 9 a.m.-1 p.m., between mid-May and early October, the **Sandy River Farmers' Market** sets up its tables in the Farmington Park & Ride lot, at the T-junction of Rts. 2/27 and 2/4, on the outskirts of town. Along with a lively, can-do spirit, you'll find herbs, homemade bread, cheeses, and organic meats and produce.

ACCOMMODATIONS

Farmington is not overrun with extraordinary places to stay, but at least the prices are reasonable, and there are several lodging options in surrounding communities.

The **Farmington Motel,** Rt. 2/27, P.O. Box 447, Farmington 04938, tel. (207) 778-4680 or (800) 654-1133 outside Maine, gets the nod for inexpensive, clean lodging in the area, but don't expect lots of amenities. All 37 rooms and two suites ($42-50 d) have phones, a/c, and cable TV. No pets. Biggest plus is behind the motel: a nature trail leading down to the Sandy River, where you can launch a canoe or just sit on the shore. The motel, one and a half miles southeast of downtown Farmington, is open all year.

In Weld village, west of Farmington and northwest of Wilton, you'll find Fred and Cheryl England's **Lake Webb House Bed & Breakfast,** Rt. 142, P.O. Box 127, Weld 04285, tel. (207)

585-2479, a cheerful sight with a wraparound porch and lovely gardens. Three second-floor rooms share a bath ($55 d in summer, lower off season). Breakfast includes goodies from the family's **Morning Glory Bake Shop,** a wholesale business open for retail in July and August, Mon.-Sat. 8 a.m.-5 p.m. and Sunday 8 a.m.-noon. In part of the garage is a gift shop, with quilts, carvings, and other handmade items. The B&B is open all year. No pets, no smoking.

About a mile south of the center of Weld, on the east shore of Lake Webb, **Kawanhee Inn,** Rt. 142, Box 119, Weld 04285, tel. (207) 585-2000, fax 585-5545, winter address 7 Broadway, Farmington 04938, tel. (207) 778-4306 or 778-3809, is a former children's summer camp retrofitted as a comfortable, rustic inn and cottage colony. Sunsets in this mountain-and-lake setting are spectacular; the loons' cries add to the magic. Nine second-floor rooms in the large, woody main lodge go for $65-95 d (shared and private baths); two-night minimum in midsummer. A dozen housekeeping cabins, available by the week, are $480-630, depending on bedroom count; all have fieldstone fireplaces and screened porches facing the lake. The lodge's lakeview dining room, open to the public by reservation, daily 5-9 p.m., mid-June to Labor Day, earns high marks for comfort food (entrées $9-16). No smoking in the lodge, no pets. Canoe and rowboat rentals are $10 a day. The sandy beach is great for kids, and superb hiking is close by. Kawanhee is open May to mid-October, but devotees keep returning here, so book well ahead for midsummer (when the dining room is open). In mid-September, nights are coolish and it's pretty quiet, but the foliage is incredible.

Twelve miles south of Weld, **Von Simm's Victorian Inn Bed & Breakfast,** 11 Main St., Rt. 2, P.O. Box 645, Dixfield 04224, tel. (207) 562-4911, has been welcoming guests since 1988. Sylvia and Bruce Simmons are the resident innkeepers—he's an antique car collector. Seven comfortable rooms (five with private bath and a/c) are $45-65 d in summer, less off season. Each room's name has a story. The parlor, with cable TV and gas fireplace, fits the Victorian label. Extensive gardens out back include a gazebo, and the back deck is great for coffee. Von Simm's is on a busy street, but double windows and air-conditioning muffle most sounds;

if you're highly noise-sensitive, request a back room. No smoking, no pets. Open all year.

Campgrounds

On the southern outskirts of Farmington, the **Nor'40 Campsite,** Red Schoolhouse Rd., RFD 4, Box 5220, Farmington 04938, tel. (207) 778-6096, a 100-acre facility, has 50 tent and RV sites ($15-17 for two). The outdoor pool, tennis court, and playground make it a great family spot. Pets are allowed. Facilities include hot showers and washing machines. The campground is open mid-May to early October. From Rt. 2/4 in West Farmington, take Red Schoolhouse Rd. (turn at the red schoolhouse, home of the information center, across from Waterfall Gardens) three-quarters of a mile to the campground.

Across Lake Webb from the Mount Blue State Park camping area, **Dummer's Beach Campground,** Rt. 142, Weld 04285, tel. (207) 585-2200 or (703) 553-9347 in winter, is a large (200 sites) family-owned campground with a half-mile-long sandy beach. Request a waterfront site for best sunset-watching. In July and August, preferred minimum stay is a week, but last-minute cancellations usually create a few vacancies. Nightly rates are $15-21 per family. Pets are allowed. The campground is open Memorial Day weekend to Labor Day.

FOOD

Miscellanea

Across from Hippach Field, there's always a line at **Gifford's Ice Cream,** Intervale Rd., Rt. 4/27, Farmington 04938, tel. (207) 778-3617, a longtime take-out spot. Besides over 40 terrific ice cream flavors, they also have foot-long hot dogs. Open mid-March to early November, 11 a.m.-10 p.m. in summer, to 9 p.m. in spring and fall.

Inexpensive to Moderate

Close to Gifford's is another local institution, the gen-u-ine classic **Farmington Diner,** Intervale Rd., Rt. 4/27, Farmington 04938, tel. (207) 778-4151. The huge portions, instantaneous service, and *really* good prices are an answer to a budgeteer's prayer. Only drawback is it can get smoky, even in the nonsmoking section. Check

it out before you settle in—or tough it out for the value. No credit cards. The diner is open all year, Mon.-Sat. 5 a.m.-8 p.m. (to 9 p.m. Friday and Saturday) and Sunday 7 a.m.-8 p.m.

The most creative menu in Farmington is at **The Homestead Bakery Restaurant,** 20 Broadway, Rt. 43, Farmington 04938, tel. (207) 778-6162, where everything's first-rate and there's plenty of ethnic variety—Mediterranean, Mexican, Thai, plus vegetarian. Industrial-strength garlic infuses the "Sorry No Kisses After Dark" pizza. Open for breakfast and lunch Mon.-Fri. 7 a.m.-3 p.m., and for brunch Sat.-Sun. 8 a.m.-3 p.m. Open for dinner Tues.-Sat. 5-9 p.m., when the operation converts to Maria's Italian Restaurant.

An attractively restored 19th-century brick building in downtown Farmington is the home of **F.L. Butler Restaurant,** 20 Front St., Farmington 04938, tel. (207) 778-5223, a reliable standby. Weather permitting, you can eat on the deck, where afternoon specials (3-5 p.m.) include cold soups, sandwiches, and appetizers. The real deal is on Wednesday—twofer night—when $15.95 will get you two entrées, even prime rib. Open Mon.-Fri. 11 a.m.-2 p.m. and 5-9 p.m., Saturday 5-9 p.m., and Sunday 11 a.m.-8 p.m. Reservations advisable Wednesday, and on summer weekends.

Brewpub

Tucked away on a side street not far from the Sandy River, **The Granary Brewpub,** 23 Pleasant St., Farmington 04938, tel. (207) 779-0710, packs 'em in, especially when the university is in session. Home of the Narrow Gauge Brewing Company, tel. (207) 778-5363, with such specialty microbrews as Iron Rail Ale and Clearwater Cream Ale. Dinner entrées range $9-20. Most weekends, there's live music; Tuesday is open-mike night. The Granary is open all year, daily 11 a.m.-11 p.m. (sometimes later on weekends).

INFORMATION AND SERVICES

The office of the **Greater Farmington Chamber of Commerce,** Rt. 2/4, P.O. Box 108, Farmington 04938, tel. (207) 778-4215, fax 778-6237, is in the historic **Red Schoolhouse** in West Farmington. Hours are Tues.-Fri. 9 a.m.-4 p.m.

The Farmington chamber works closely with
the **Wilton Chamber of Commerce,** P.O. Box
934, Wilton 04294, tel. (207) 645-3932, which
has an answering machine but no information
center. The joint Farmington/Wilton *Area Guide
and Directory* is especially useful.

The 1903 **Cutler Memorial Library,** 2 Academy St., Farmington 04938, tel. (207) 778-4312,
is worth a look just for its intriguing glass floor
and domed rotunda, but the staff is especially
helpful, too. Genealogical research is a specialty here. The National Historic Register library is open all year, Tues.-Wed. 10 a.m.-8
p.m., Thurs.-Fri. 10 a.m.-5 p.m., Saturday 10
a.m.-2 p.m. On Saturday in July and August,
the library closes at noon.

The University of Maine at Farmington's **Man-
tor Library** is on High St. in Farmington, tel.
(207) 778-7210. Summer hours are Mon.-Thurs.
8 a.m.-6 p.m., Friday 8 a.m.-4:30 p.m. UMF's
bookstore, where you can pick up typical logo-
stamped gear, is at 6 South St., tel. (207) 778-
7325.

Newspapers
The Franklin Journal, tel. (207) 778-2075, is
published every Tuesday and Friday. The "On
the Menu" section of the "What's Happening"
column lists public suppers—always a source of
hearty food, low prices, and local color. In summer, the paper produces a helpful tabloid supplement highlighting activities in Farmington
and beyond. Under the same ownership is *The
Livermore Falls Advertiser,* tel. (207) 897-
4321, published each Thursday. The preferred
daily paper here is the *Lewiston Sun-Journal,*
which maintains a Farmington office.

Emergencies
In **Farmington,** dial 911 for police, fire, and ambulance service. To reach the **Franklin County
Sheriff,** dial (800) 492-0120. **Franklin Memorial Hospital,** 1 Hospital Dr., Farmington 04938,
emergency room tel. (207) 778-2250, with a
particularly fine reputation, has round-the-clock
emergency-room care. Behind the hospital is a
fitness trail with exercise stations.

Laundromat
Across the street from the F.L. Butler Restaurant, the **Depot Laundry,** Front St., Farmington 04938, tel. (207) 778-0803, is open all year,
daily 6 a.m.-7 p.m. (to 5 p.m. Saturday and Sunday) in summer. In winter, the laundry opens
at 7 a.m.

Kennels
A 20-minute drive east of Farmington gets you to
Dew Drop Kennels, Beans Corner Rd., New
Sharon 04955, tel. (207) 778-6479, where Mary
Ann Adams runs a fine kennel with 20 long runs
on a 20-acre spread. Dogs are $7 a day, cats
are $5; no credit cards. Call well ahead or you
won't find space in summer. Usual hours are
Tues.-Sun. 9 a.m.-5 p.m., but she's flexible.
Open all year.

Public Restrooms
Across from Meeting House Park, downtown,
there's a public restroom in the basement of
the **Franklin County Courthouse,** N. Main St.,
Farmington, accessible on weekdays.

Getting Around
On call round-the-clock all year, except Thanksgiving and Christmas, **Bev's Taxi,** tel. (207)
778-1429 or 778-6852, will get you where you
want when you want.

SUGARLOAF AREA

The thread tying together the Sugarloaf area is the lovely Carrabassett River, an undammed watercourse winding its way through the smashingly scenic Carrabassett Valley from the area more or less around Sugarloaf/USA to North Anson, where it meets the mighty Kennebec. On both sides of the valley, the Longfellow and Bigelow Ranges boast six of Maine's 10 4,000-footers—a hiker's paradise.

Flanking the west side of the valley is the huge Sugarloaf/USA resort—only a germ of an idea half a century ago. In 1951, Kingfield businessman Amos Winter and some of his pals, known locally as the "Bigelow Boys," cut the first ski trail from the snowfields on Sugarloaf Mountain, dubbing it "Winter's Way." A downhill run required skiing three miles to the base of the trail, then strapping on animal skins for the uphill trek. Three runs on wooden skis was about the max in those days. By 1954, the prophetically named Winter and some foresighted investors had established the Sugarloaf Mountain Ski Club . . . and the rest, as they say, is history. In 1996, the giant American Skiing Company, owner of Sunday River Ski Resort and other properties, purchased Sugarloaf/USA, so it now operates under the ASC umbrella.

Sugarloaf/USA is the mega-taxpayer in the relatively new town of Carrabassett Valley (year-round population 350). It bills itself as a year-round resort, which is true, but winter is definitely the peak season, when the headcount is highest and so are the prices. Everything's open and humming from late October through May; in 1997, spring skiing even extended into June. More than 350,000 skiers hit the slopes here each year.

Before Amos Winter brought fame and fortune to his hometown and the valley, Kingfield was best known as a timber center and the birthplace of the Stanley twins (designers of the Stanley Steamer). Today it's an appealing slice-of-life rural town (pop. 1,185), with handsome old homes and off-mountain beds and restaurants.

Farther up the valley, old-timers reminisce over the towns of Flagstaff and Dead River—already historic two centuries before they were consigned to the history books in the 1950s. That's when the Long Falls Dam, built on the Dead River, backed up the water behind it, inundated the towns, and created 20,000-acre Flagstaff Lake. The hydroelectric dam now controls the water flow for spring whitewater rafting on the Dead River. In Stratton village, the Dead River Historical Society's museum contains fascinating memorabilia from the two submerged villages.

Flagstaff owes its name to Col. Benedict Arnold, whose troops en route to Quebec in 1775 flew their flag at the site of today's Cathedral Pines Campground. After struggling up the Kennebec River to the spot known as The Carrying Place, the disheartened soldiers turned northwest along the Dead River's North Branch at Flagstaff and then on through the Chain of Ponds to Canada.

Route 27, from Kingfield to the Canadian border at Coburn Gore, is an officially designated Scenic Highway, a 54-mile stretch that's most spectacular in mid-to-late September. Not much to Coburn Gore except a customs outpost, a convenience store (with fuel), and a few unimposing dwellings.

SIGHTS

Stanley Museum

Children of all ages love antique cars, so this museum is a must. The small but captivating Stanley Museum, School St., P.O. Box 280, Kingfield 04947, tel. (207) 265-2729, fax 265-2607, has three meticulously restored Stanley Steamers, designed at the turn of the 20th century by the Kingfield-born Stanley twins, Francis Edgar and Freelan Oscar. These versatile overachievers also gained fame with the invention of the photographic dry plate, eventually selling out to George Eastman. Freelan Stanley, the first to climb Mount Washington by car, later became a noted violinmaker. Also in the museum, based in the yellow, Georgian-style Stanley School, are hundreds of superb photographs (and glass-plate negatives) by the twins' clever sister, Chansonetta Stanley Emmons, and work by Chansonetta's artist-daughter, Dorothy. The museum gift shop contains auto-related books, pamphlets, and other specialty items. The museum is open Tues.-Sun. 1-4 p.m., May-Oct. and Dec.-March. Admission is $2 adults, $1 children.

Western Maine Children's Museum

Not open often enough, but definitely worth a look-see, The Western Maine Children's Museum, Rt. 27, RR 1, Box 2153, Carrabassett Valley 04947, tel. (207) 235-2211, practices a please-touch philosophy. Kids can try on vintage clothing, play puppeteer, make sand pictures, enter a gondola and a wigwam, climb into a cave with real crystals, and otherwise amuse themselves. Admission is $2.50 for children; adults are free. Summer hours are Monday 1-5 p.m.; winter hours are Sat.-Mon. 1-5 p.m. The museum shares a building with the Carrabassett Public Library, south of the Carrabassett Yacht Club.

The historic Wire Bridge spans the Carrabassett River in New Portland.

Nowetah's American Indian Museum

A bold, in-your-face sign announces the driveway to Nowetah's American Indian Museum, Rt. 27, Box 40, New Portland 04954, tel. (207) 628-4981, an astonishing repository of hundreds of Maine Indian baskets and bark objects —plus porcupine-quill embroidery, trade beads, musical instruments, soapstone carvings, and other Native American esoterica. Susquehanna-Cherokee owner Nowetah Timmerman loves explaining unique details about the artifacts she's displayed here since 1969. Admission is free. In the museum's gift shop are many craft items made by Nowetah and her seven children (one daughter is now a lawyer), and she runs a thriving mail-order business. Since she lives next door, the museum is open daily 10 a.m.-5 p.m., all year. It's 16 miles north of Farmington and just south of New Portland village; you can't miss the sign.

Bridge to the Past

Now here's a most unusual landmark—about seven miles south of Kingfield and not far from Nowetah's museum or the Wirebridge Diner. Twenty-five-foot-tall shingled towers announce the entrance to the **Wire Bridge** suspended over the Carrabassett River in New Portland. Built in 1841-42 at a cost of $2,000, with steel supports imported from England, the bridge is on the National Historic Register. Locals often refer to it as the "Rustproof Wire Bridge," for its stainless-steel construction, or "Floodproof Wire Bridge," for its longtime survival despite nasty spring floods. To find the bridge from Rt. 146 in New Portland, turn north onto Wire Bridge Rd. and follow signs for less than a mile.

Down on the Farms

Sugarloaf Dorsets, Freeman Ridge Rd., RR 1, Box 1709, Kingfield 04947, tel. (207) 265-4549, is one of the nation's most respected sheep farms, a high-tech facility with 300 head of Dorset sheep, some of them show champions. Pride of the flock, gene-wise, is a ram named Sugarloaf. Best time to visit is between September and March, when you can see dozens of lambs in the barn's heated nursery rooms and new ones are arriving daily. Farm managers Cliff and Debby Jo Holmquist usually are on hand to answer questions, and you can even buy sheep pelts and meat on the premises. Typical hours are daily 10 a.m.-5 p.m. The farm is 1.1 miles west of Rt. 27, at Kingfield's southern town line.

Since 1989, Scott Oliver's hobby has been raising Japanese Sika deer and European fallow and red deer, and he welcomes visitors to the creatures' 14-acre pasture at **The Deer Farm,** Millay Hill Rd., North New Portland 04961, tel. (207) 628-5361. Collect a cup of grain from the crate at the gate and watch the kids' excitement as they walk the fence lines and feed the 40 or so deer. (The $1 pp admission covers the cost of the grain.) Canada geese and turkeys also roam the farm. When Scott's available, he's happy to answer questions. The farm, open daily all year, sunrise to sunset, is 2.6 miles northeast of Rt. 27. From Rt. 146 in downtown New Portland, heading east, turn left onto Wire Bridge Road. You'll need to take three more turns from there, but the farm is well signposted.

PARKS

Picnic/Rest Areas
Several riverside and viewpoint rest areas on or near Rt. 27 make picnicking almost mandatory in the Carrabassett Valley—especially in September, when the leaf colors are fabulous. The mountains, the foliage parade, the rock-clogged river—really splendid. On Rt. 27, roughly halfway between Kingfield and the Sugarloaf access road, a lovely picnic area is sandwiched between the highway and the Carrabassett River, just north of Hammond Field Brook.

About 12 miles north of the Sugarloaf access road, turn left (west) onto Eustis Ridge Rd. and go two miles to the **Eustis Ridge Picnic Area,** a tiny park with an expansive view of the Bigelow Range.

Finally, on Rt. 27, about 23 miles north of Sugarloaf, there's another scenic picnic area, this one alongside the Dead River (east side of the highway).

Riverside Park
Carrabassett Valley's well-maintained, town-owned Riverside Park has tennis courts, a swimming pool, playing fields, playground, picnic tables, restrooms, and access to a Carrabassett

River swimming hole. It's just off Rt. 27, near Valley Crossing. The park is also a great picnic-and-swim destination after a bike ride along the old narrow-gauge railbed.

SUMMER RECREATION

The Carrabassett Valley is drop-dead gorgeous in summer, and people from away are finally beginning to recognize it. Traffic has increased dramatically in recent years, largely because of active four-season promotion of the area by Sugarloaf/USA and its golf club. The only hitch is that "four season" is a bit of a misnomer; spring (a.k.a. June, more or less) is all too short here, usually muddy and thick with blackflies. Concentrate on the other three seasons, all outstanding.

Summer activities for Sugarloaf/USA are co-ordinated primarily at the **Sugarloaf Outdoor Center,** tel. (207) 237-6830, the same handsome lodge that serves as the hub of cross-country skiing. Here you can plan hiking and mountain-biking excursions, rent a canoe or bike, and sign up for fly-fishing lessons. Each Saturday night in summer, there's a lobster and chicken bake at the center—a chance to stoke up before the weekly Moose Cruise (see "Moose-watching," below). From early June through mid-October, the Outdoor Center is open Sun.-Fri. 9 a.m.-7 p.m. and Saturday 9 a.m.-sunset. The entrance to the Outdoor Center is via Rt. 27, a mile south of the Sugarloaf access road.

Golf
Designed by Robert Trent Jones, Jr., and regularly ranked in national golf magazines as Maine's top course, the 18-hole, par-72 **Sugarloaf Golf Club,** Sugarloaf/USA, tel. (207) 237-2000, meanders through woods and alongside the Carrabassett River, in the shadow of the Longfellow Range. It's actually a town-owned course, but managed by Sugarloaf. An active bug-suppression program makes golfing pleasant even in June, when blackflies normally could dampen the fun. You get what you pay for; greens fees are steep. Sugarloaf's golf school offers multiday programs all summer, with special weeks designed for women and junior players. Club rentals and private lessons are avail-

able; carts are mandatory. A driving range, a pro shop, and a café round out the facilities. The course is open mid-May to late October, but an extended snow season can affect the season opening.

Mountain Biking

Sugarloaf/USA, with its incredible 53-mile mountain bike trail network, has cornered the market in this sport, too. A free trail map is available at the Sugarloaf Bike Shop, the Check-In Center, and other on-mountain sites, as well as at the Sugarloaf Outdoor Center. Trail passes are $10 adults, $8 teens ages 13-18, and $6 for children 12 and under.

A fun (and scenic) family or beginners' excursion is the **Narrow Gauge Trail** (number 9 on the mountain-bike map), beginning on the east side of Rt. 27 at the foot of the Sugarloaf access road and continuing seven miles, gradually downhill, to Riverside Park in Carrabassett Valley. The trail follows the abandoned narrow-gauge railway bed, along the river. Pack a picnic and wear a bathing suit under your biking duds; you'll be passing swimming holes along the way. If retracing your route doesn't appeal, just hop on the Sugarloaf Bike Shuttle (Fri.-Sun. only; see "Getting Around" under "Information and Services," below).

Besides the facilities at the Sugarloaf Outdoor Center, the on-mountain **Sugarloaf Bike Shop,** Village Center, tel. (207) 237-6986, rents mountain bikes ($25-40 a day), does repairs, and provides free trail maps and advice for trails on and off the mountain. The staff is especially helpful. Informal group rides originate from here most Wednesday nights, but contact the shop to inquire. In summer, the shop is open daily 9 a.m.-4 p.m. (It occupies the same space as the wintertime Sugarloaf Ski Shop.)

Swimming

Along the Carrabassett River between Kingfield and the Sugarloaf access road are half a dozen swimming holes used by generations of local residents. Several spots have natural water slides and room for shallow dives. They're not all easy to find, and parking is limited, but a refreshing river dip on a hot day is hard to beat. Check with the Sugarloaf Area Chamber of Commerce for exact locations.

On mountain-rimmed Flagstaff Lake in Eustis, about 11 miles north of Sugarloaf, the town-owned beach next to the Cathedral Pines Campground has a playground and changing rooms. There are no lifeguards, but there's also no admission fee. (Do not use the campground's beach unless you're staying there.)

Hiking

An easy family hike, combining a picnic and swim, goes to the twin cascades of **Poplar Stream Falls.** On Rt. 27 in Carrabassett Valley, leave your car at Valley Crossing and walk northeast one and a half miles to the falls. Pack a picnic and let the kids have a swim.

Just east of Stratton (eight miles northwest of Sugarloaf) is the dedicated hiker's dream: 35,000-acre **Bigelow Preserve**—all public land, thanks to conservationists who organized a statewide referendum and yanked it from developers' hands in 1976. Within the preserve are the multiple peaks of the **Bigelow Range**—The Horns (3,810 and 3,831 feet), West Peak (4,150 feet), Avery Peak (4,088 feet), and Little Bigelow (3,040 feet), as well as 3,213-foot Cranberry Peak. In the fall, when the hardwoods all change colors, the vistas are incomparable. In winter, snowmobilers criss-cross the preserve, and cross-country skiers often take advantage of their trails, especially along the East Flagstaff Road, where you can stop for hot chocolate at volunteer-staffed Bigelow Lodge. The trailhead for Cranberry Peak (6.6 miles roundtrip; moderate to strenuous) is next to Rt. 27 at the southern end of Stratton village.

About five miles southeast of Stratton, the **Appalachian Trail** crosses Rt. 27 and continues north and then east across the Bigelow peaks—the spine of the Bigelow Range. You can access the AT here, or drive back northwest half a mile on Rt. 27 and go .9 mile on the rugged, unpaved Stratton Brook Rd. to another AT trailhead. In any case, if you do the whole AT traverse, 16.5 miles from Rt. 27 to East Flagstaff Rd., you'll probably want to arrange a shuttle at East Flagstaff Rd. (via the Long Falls Dam Rd. from North New Portland), or opt for the Round Barn camping area on Flagstaff Lake, to save a re-traverse. The white-blazed AT route is strenuous; four free campsites with lean-tos are spotted along the way. (The most-used campsite is Horns Pond; space can be tight there.)

Depending on your enthusiasm, your stamina level, and your time frame (and maybe the weather), there are lots of options for short hikes along the AT or on a number of side trails. Preserve maps usually are available at the Sugarloaf Area Chamber of Commerce, but for planning ahead, request a copy of the Bigelow Preserve map/brochure from the **Maine Bureau of Parks and Lands,** 22 State House Station, Augusta 04333, tel. (207) 287-3821, or the regional office of the Bureau of Public Lands, tel. (207) 778-4111. Also helpful is the *Appalachian Trail Guide to Maine.*

Moosewatching

From early July to early September, Sugarloaf/USA operates a weekly **Moose Cruise,** tel. (207) 237-2000, departing from the Sugarloaf Outdoor Center around 7:30 p.m. each Saturday (following the lobsterbake at the center). Cost is $12 adults, $8 kids 12 and under. After a 10-minute moose video and a free glass of champagne or beer, the "Moose Express" van heads off to make the rounds of the well-known moose haunts. Invest in bug repellent and don't forget binoculars and a camera. Also, if you arrive close to dusk at the Sugarloaf Check-In Center, hang around the bog near the center and you may spot a moose.

For moosewatching on your own, the best bet is to head up Rt. 27 to Rt. 16 and go west. Early or late in the day, perhaps en route to dinner in Rangeley, you're almost guaranteed to see a moose in the boggy areas or near the sand-and-salt piles stored for winter use.

WINTER RECREATION

The big story in this area, of course, is **Sugarloaf/USA,** a major New England ski resort centered on 4,237-foot Sugarloaf, Maine's highest skiing mountain. Even though the resort attracts national and international ski and snowboard champions, Sugarloaf has always been especially family-friendly, with day care, reduced kids' rates, and all kinds of children's ski and entertainment programs.

The heart (and soul) of the operation is **Sugarloaf Village,** halfway up the access road (Sugarloaf Road) from Rt. 27. Here you'll find administration buildings, the Sugarloaf Mountain Hotel, the Sugarloaf Inn, the Base Lodge, a tiny chapel, and a whole commercial complex with restaurants and shops—a mini-community. Spreading out from here are side roads leading to clusters of condos.

First stop for overnight condo visitors is the **Check-In Center,** where you'll register and pick up your key. If you've decided to wing it and show up without a reservation, this is where you inquire about vacancies. Condo prices and amenities vary.

Downhill Skiing and Snowboarding

Sugarloaf covers 7,000 acres, of which 1,400 are skiable, with 95% snowmaking capability. The 119 trails and glades in the 45-mile network are served by 15 lifts, ranging from a T-bar to detachable quads. Vertical rise is 2,820 feet and the longest run is three miles. For snowboarders, the resort has the nation's largest halfpipe, courtesy of a gonzo snowboarder known as "Crazy Eddy."

If you're here just for the day, your first stop on the mountain will be the **Base Lodge,** the locale for lift tickets, trail maps, ski rentals, and ski-school signups. Snowboard rentals are handled in the Ride On Snowboard Shop, in the next building. Skiing hours are weekdays 9 a.m.-3:45 p.m. and weekends 8:30 a.m.-3:45 p.m. Be prepared for *big* crowds on weekends and holidays, but crowd control is fairly efficient, and lift lines are reasonably tolerable after the initial rush.

Full-day **lift tickets** are $46 for adults, $41 for teens, and $26 for seniors and kids 6-12; children under six ski free. Most lodging packages include lift tickets; multiday tickets are less expensive, as are tickets restricted to the lower mountain.

sugarloaf/usa®

Nordic Skiing, Snowshoeing, and Ice-Skating

On Rt. 27, about a mile south of the Sugarloaf access road, is the entrance to the **Sugarloaf Outdoor Center,** tel. (207) 237-6830, geared in winter toward cross-country skiing, snowshoeing, and ice-skating. Some sections of the 60-mile nordic trail network are on Maine Public Reserve Land and some are on Penobscot Indian Nation land. All the trails have tongue-twisting Indian names such as Bunawabskeg, Gwipdez, and Jezhawuk. All-day passes are $12 adults, $8 children 12 and under. The Outdoor Center is on the shuttle route, so you can leave your car on the mountain. Or ski to the center: an easy cross-country trail links the Snowbrook condos to the Outdoor Center; a moderately difficult trail begins higher up near the Base Lodge and hooks up with the Snowbrook route.

Also at the Outdoor Center is an Olympic-size outdoor ice-skating rink, lighted on weekend nights and holiday weeks. The huge, modern, glass-walled lodge looking out on Sugarloaf Mountain has ski, snowshoe, and skate rentals, plus the **Klister Kitchen,** a casual café serving moderately priced homemade soups, sandwiches, and baked goodies.

At the lodge, you can sign up for **group or private cross-country lessons,** but it's a good idea to call ahead and check on times. A learn-to-ski package, including skis, a group lesson, and a trail pass, is under $30.

The Outdoor Center also rents headlamps for their occasional **guided moonlight ski tours** through the woods, a really special experience. The schedule is unpredictable, so you'll need to contact the Outdoor Center or Guest Services for days and times.

Mushing

Providing a short but exciting taste of Jack London-style adventure, 8-12 enthusiastic Samoyeds —composing a team known as the White Howling Express—bound along a one-and-a-half-mile wooded route in the shadow of Sugarloaf Mountain. Musher Tim Diehl, owner of **T.A.D. Dog Sled Services,** Rt. 27, Carrabassett Valley, mailing address P.O. Box 147, Stratton 04982, tel. (207) 246-4461, stands on the sled in back, while clients sit bundled up in front of him. (Wear glasses or goggles—the dogs kick up the snow.)

Winter trips operate weather (and snow) permitting; the season begins around early December and ends in early April, and the schedule varies between weekend and midweek. Schedule information is also available from Sugarloaf/USA Guest Services, tel. (207) 237-6939; reservations are a good idea, since the sled only carries 350 pounds. Cost for the half-hour ride is $60 pp. To reach the T.A.D. warming hut, take Rt. 27 to the signposted driveway 500 feet north of the Sugarloaf Rd., then turn west for 500 feet.

In summer, weather permitting, Tim runs **cart rides** with half a dozen dogs. Capacity is two adults or three kids; cost is $40 pp.

ENTERTAINMENT

There's no night skiing at Sugarloaf, but no problem. Every night in winter, there's live music somewhere, so you can hopscotch from The Bag to Geppetto's to Theo's, and back again. The musical grand finale for the season is Reggae Ski Week in April (see "Festivals and Events," below).

If you're staying at a Sugarloaf condo and want to distract the kids with TV, **Mountain Video,** Village South, tel. (207) 237-2150, has video rentals; there's also a branch in Kingfield, tel. (207) 265-2585. Sugarloaf organizes evening **children's entertainment** Mon.-Sat. from December to early April. Separate programs—typically films, skating, or games—are geared to ages 5-12 and 13-18.

Nearest **cinema** is in Farmington, 38 miles south of Sugarloaf/USA.

FESTIVALS AND EVENTS

Sugarloaf/USA has a huge schedule of events throughout the ski season and also a sprinkling of summer activities. A few of the recurring highlights are listed below, but the resort also hosts many one-of-a-kind events, so it's best to check with the resort when you know the timing of your visit.

White White World Week is Sugarloaf's winter carnival, with discount lift tickets, reduced lodging rates, ski races, fireworks, a torchlight parade, and other special events the last week of January.

Sugarloaf hosts the **Maine Special Olympics Winter Games,** the annual skiing, showshoeing, and skating event for Maine's Special Olympians, the first weekend of February. Volunteers are welcome to lend a hand.

Sugarloaf meets the Caribbean during **Reggae Ski Week,** with West Indian cuisine, spring skiing, reggae bands day and night, and lots of boisterous fun the second week of April. Bring earplugs.

Four-day **Kingfield Festival Days** is a community celebration including a parade, a barbecue, craft exhibits, dances, and beano (bingo) in downtown Kingfield the first weekend in August.

SHOPPING

Clothing and Gifts

Limited-edition sweaters and legwarmers are the specialty at **Patricia Buck Emporium,** Main St., Kingfield 04947, tel. (207) 265-2101, but there's lots more: craft supplies, Maine books, unusual cards, tasteful souvenirs, even antiques. Quilting fabric is $2 a pound. Located in an ancient building opposite The Herbert, the shop also has a fancier but smaller seasonal branch, tel. (207) 237-2108, in the village at Sugarloaf/USA. The Kingfield shop is open daily (except major holidays) 10 a.m.-6 p.m., early July to mid-May, then weekends 10 a.m.-5 p.m., mid-May through June; the Sugarloaf shop is open late October through April, daily 10 a.m.-5 p.m.

The factory outlet at **Kingfield Wood Products,** Depot St., Kingfield 04947, tel. (207) 265-2151, the town's largest employer, has cute little wooden tchotchkes—toys and decorative woodenware—all leftovers or seconds, all inexpensive. No credit cards. The outlet is open all year, Mon.-Fri. 7 a.m.-3:30 p.m., and Saturday and Sunday 10 a.m.-5 p.m. It's two blocks off Main Street, next to Knapp Bros. Dodge at the corner of Depot Street.

In the center of Kingfield, **Keenan's,** Main St., Rt. 27, Kingfield 04947, tel. (207) 265-2011, carries reasonably priced clothing and gear for every imaginable sport, but their major business comes from the winter trade. It's hard to walk out without buying *something.* Keenan's,

which has other shops (and real auction houses) throughout Maine, is open all year, daily 9 a.m.-5 p.m. in summer, 8 a.m.-8 p.m. in winter.

On your way to the Porter House (see "Food," below), you'll pass **Dead River Gifts,** Eustis Rd., Rt. 27, P.O. Box 525, Stratton 04982, tel. (207) 246-7161, a log cabin with a beaver-chewed log hanging out front ("just the way we found it"). Besides the eclectic collection of gifts and souvenirs—gemstones, baby quilts, knitted goods—the shop has free copies of *How to Get Useless in Eustis,* an eight-page compilation of activities here and as far away as the Rangeley Lakes area. Also request a copy of their *Moos'n Map,* showing the best moosewatching spots. The shop is open daily 9 a.m.-5 p.m., May to Christmas.

ACCOMMODATIONS

When you've had a long day of skiing or snowboarding, a bed close to the slopes can be mighty tempting—plus you can be upward bound quickly in the morning. But such convenience doesn't come cheaply, so your budget may dictate where you decide to stay. Basically, the choices are on the mountain at Sugarloaf/USA (more than 7,500 beds), in Carrabassett Valley near the Sugarloaf access road, or farther afield in Kingfield, Eustis, and beyond.

Once or twice during the winter season, when international ski or snowboard races bring in big-name champions, beds are scarce to nonexistent. Beds are also hard to come by during Christmas week, February Presidents' Day week, and Sugarloaf's Reggae Ski Week in April.

Many of the lodgings in the region around Sugarloaf provide discount passes for nordic skiing out of the Sugarloaf Outdoor Center. It's a nice little perk, so if you're planning any cross-country skiing, be sure to ask when you're inquiring about a room.

Sugarloaf/USA

Accommodations are available all year at the resort; to book lodgings at Sugarloaf/USA, call (800) 843-5623.

The clusters of on-mountain **condo "villages"** each have different features (studios to multiple bedrooms), different characters, and different prices. Midwinter rates range $120-365 per condo unit in midweek, $160-450 per unit on weekend nights. Lift tickets, ski clinics, and taxes are included. Lots of special packages, even including transportation, are available. Summer rates are markedly lower, and if you're eminently flexible, you can usually even take a chance and show up at the resort in summer without a reservation.

The **Sugarloaf Inn** is the only on-mountain hotel owned by the resort itself. Conveniently located in front of the Sawduster double chairlift, it has 41 attractive rooms with rates in the same ranges as the condos.

All lodgings booked by Sugarloaf include use of the **Sugarloaf Sports and Fitness Club,** tel. (207) 237-6946, in the Sugartree condo complex on the Mountainside Road. The club has a pool, indoor and outdoor hot tubs, a fitness room, racquetball courts, evening aerobics classes (yes!), three or four massage therapists, restrooms, locker rooms, a climbing wall, and a snack bar with great pizza and the cheapest bottled beer on the mountain. You can even buy a bathing suit or get a haircut. In winter, the club opens at 8 a.m. and closes around 10 p.m.; summer hours are 11 a.m.-7 p.m. Day visitors can use club facilities for $10 pp.

Under independent management, yet right in the center of Sugarloaf Village, the imposing **Sugarloaf Mountain Hotel,** RR 1, Box 2299, Carrabassett Valley 04947, tel. (207) 237-2222 or (800) 527-9879, fax (207) 237-2874, has 120 rooms, suites, and penthouses. Amenities include microwave, refrigerator, and VCR. Guests have use of a small health club. No pets, no smoking. From Christmas to mid-March, rates are $100-180 d; from Thanksgiving to Christmas, and mid-March to early April, rates are $90-130 d; other months are $75-95 d. Suites and penthouses are pricier. Open all year.

Kingfield and Eustis
From the moose head in the lobby to the gilded-era fixtures, tradition and funkiness ooze from **The Herbert,** Main St., Rt. 27, P.O. Box 67, Kingfield 04947, tel. (207) 265-2000 or (800) 843-4372, fax (207) 265-4594, a restored three-story 1918 hostelry where you can meet kindred spirits in the lobby and bond with the canines

hanging around the front desk. "The Herb's" 33 rooms (all with private bath, some with jacuzzis) are basic, but you won't spend much time there anyway. Winter rates are $80-140 d, including continental breakfast; three-night minimum during Christmas and February vacations. Summer rates begin at $49 d, a real bargain. A variety of special packages are available throughout the year. Pets are allowed and smoking is allowed everywhere but the dining room. The hotel's top-notch dining room—**The Herbert Public Room**—is open to the public for dinner daily 5:30-9 p.m. in winter, Thurs.-Mon. in summer. The menu is imaginative (including heart-healthy options), dress is informal, and entrées are in the $12-19 range. Kids can order inexpensive pasta or chicken fingers. Sunday is twofer night (two entrées for the price of one). Reservations are a good idea, especially during holidays and on midwinter weekends. The Herbert is 18 miles south of Sugarloaf/USA.

B&Bs: Geared to skiers, hikers, and bikers, the **River Port Inn Bed & Breakfast,** N. Main St., Rt. 27, Kingfield 04947, tel. (207) 265-2552, is a comfortable 1840s farmhouse where you can bring home a takeout meal and spread it out in a huge dining room. There's cross-country skiing right from the yard, and a deepwater swimming hole adjoins the property. Five bedrooms upstairs share one bath; three downstairs rooms share a bath. Winter rates (Thanksgiving to mid-April) are $45-80; off-season rates are $40-50. Generous continental breakfast is included; a delicious grilled breakfast is $4 extra. No smoking, no credit cards, no pets. Open all year.

Next door to One Stanley Avenue (see "Food," below) and under the same ownership, **Three Stanley Avenue,** 3 Stanley Ave., P.O. Box 169, Kingfield 04947, tel. (207) 265-5541, has been a B&B since the early 1980s. The antiques-filled yellow Victorian has three first-floor rooms (private baths) and three second-floor rooms sharing two baths. It's all very welcoming, with comfortable wicker chairs on the front porch and a traditional gazebo (ex-bandstand) in the back yard. Rooms are $55-60 d with private bath in winter (Dec.-March; two-night minimum), $50-55 d with shared bath. Summer rates are $50-55 d. Open all year.

Built in 1892 by Stratton businessman Oramendal Blanchard, and now on the National Historic Register, **The Widow's Walk,** Rt. 27, P.O. Box 150, Stratton 04982, tel. (207) 246-6901 or (800) 943-6995, has been a standout on the Appalachian Trail grapevine since avid hikers and skiers Mary and Jerry Hopson opened it in 1978. The camaraderie here is contagious, inevitably focusing on the outdoors. The B&B, known for years as "The Castle" for its distinctive turret, has four no-frills rooms (sharing two baths) in one section and two basic rooms (shared bath) in another. All are on the second floor and are $46 d in winter; two-day minimum. Add $5 pp for MAP (hearty breakfast and family-style dinner). Lower rates for longer stays. Summer and fall B&B rates are a bargain $30 d. No smoking, no pets (dog and cats in residence). Open all year. The B&B is about eight miles northwest of the Sugarloaf access road.

Sporting Camps: Another of the old-time traditional sporting camps, **Tim Pond Camps,** Box 22, Eustis 04936, tel. (207) 243-2947, in winter P.O. Box 89, Jay 04239, tel. (207) 897-4056, has been operating since 1877, when guests took so long to get here that they stayed the whole summer. Harvey and Betty Calden have owned this idyllic lakeside retreat since 1980. Ten rustic log cabins nestle in the woods on either side of a modern-rustic lodge (the original lodge burned), where everyone gathers for great comfort food; the dinner bell rings promptly at 5:30 p.m. (BYOL). Daily rates are $200 d, American Plan, including use of a classic Rangeley boat and late-day moosewatching runs; half price for children under 12. Be forewarned, though, that it's worth your while to get a reservation here—about 90% of the guests are repeats, and most stay at least a week. Flyfishing for brook trout is the prime pursuit, but it's just a fine place to relax and listen to the loons. Cabins have bathrooms, electricity (until 10 p.m.), daily maid service, and fascinating guest journals. Tim Pond Camps is at the northern end of mile-long Tim Pond, on a dirt road about 10 miles west of Rt. 27 in Eustis. It's open mid-May through July, then September to early November.

Campgrounds: Located right on the 45th parallel, 40-acre **Deer Farm Campground,** Tufts Pond Rd., RR 1, Box 2405, Kingfield 04947, tel. (207) 265-4599, has 47 well-maintained, wooded tent and RV sites at $13 a night for tents, $14.50 for RVs. Facilities include laundry machines, a small store, a playground, and free hot showers. Tufts Pond is close enough for swimming, and lots of easy hiking trails fan out from the campground. Canoe rentals are $2 an hour. Pets are allowed. No credit cards. Take Rt. 27 north of Kingfield about a mile; turn left onto Tufts Pond Rd. and continue another two miles northwest to the campground. Open mid-May to mid-October.

Town-owned 300-acre **Cathedral Pines Campground,** Rt. 27, HC 72, Box 80, Eustis 04936, tel. (207) 246-3491, with 115 wooded tent and RV sites, has one of Maine's most scenic locations—amid gigantic red pines and surrounded by mountains on the shore of Flagstaff Lake. Lakeside tentsites are $15; two-night minimum. Facilities include a rec hall, laundry, swimming beach, canoe rentals ($15 a day, only for campers), and paddleboat rentals ($5 an hour). Pets are allowed. The campground is 26 miles south of the Quebec border. Historic markers at the campground entrance designate this as a temporary headquarters during Col. Benedict Arnold's March to Quebec. Open mid-May through September.

Seasonal Rentals: Both **Mountain Valley Property,** Valley Crossing, Rt. 27, Carrabassett Valley 04947, tel. (207) 235-2560 or (800) 435-7162, and **Narrow Gauge Realty,** Main St., Rt. 27, P.O. Box 9, Kingfield 04947, tel. (207) 265-4949, have plenty of experience with property management and weekly (or longer) rentals on and off Sugarloaf Mountain. Rates vary widely, mostly depending on the distance from the Sugarloaf/USA epicenter. Winter rates are the highest. There are real bargains in summer, a great time to come here, and you can even finagle a good nightly rate for a few days' stay.

FOOD

You can bounce around to different Sugarloaf-area restaurants in the winter season and catch a twofer night (two entrées for the price of one) almost every weeknight. Best day is Tuesday, when you'll have several choices. Considering the cost of lift tickets, ski rentals, and just getting here, the discount dinners are a real asset.

Sugarloaf/USA

You certainly won't starve if you stick with the food at one of the 20 eateries at Sugarloaf/USA, and the range of choices means you won't bust your budget, but do yourself a favor and explore the dining options in Carrabassett Valley, Stratton, Eustis, and Kingfield. Over holidays and winter weekends, though, be sure to make advance dinner reservations if you're heading off mountain.

Bullwinkle's Grill, a casual, trailside breakfast-and-lunch place halfway up Sugarloaf Mountain, morphs after dark each Saturday into **Bullwinkle's**, tel. (207) 237-6939, a rustically elegant gourmet restaurant. The fun starts with getting there, comfortably enough, in a 12-person cab attached to a grooming machine, then entering the restaurant over a red carpet. Not for budgeteers, the five-course candlelight dinner runs about $65. Reservations, of course, are required. After dinner, the Bombardier scoots you back down to reality—the Base Lodge. (During vacation weeks, Bullwinkle's sometimes is open other nights besides Saturday; check with Guest Services.)

At the geographic extreme, close to the bottom of Sugarloaf's access road, a bright, modern 200-seat brewpub named **Theo's**, Sugarloaf Rd., tel. (207) 237-2211, shares quarters with the glass-walled **Sugarloaf Brewing Company.** On the better-than-pub menu are generous appetizers plus burgers, sandwiches, steaks, and creative chicken—everything reliably good. Six to eight of their brews are available at any given time; best seller is Carrabassett Pale Ale. The seasonal Amos Winter Ale is super. Theo, by the way, is for Theodore Johnsen, a Portland boatbuilder (and skimaker) who wrote *The Winter Sport of Skeeing* in 1905. On-demand 15-to-30-minute brewery tours occur daily 2-4 p.m., subject to staff availability. No tours mid-April to mid-May and mid-October to mid-Nov., when lunch is not available in the restaurant.

For ample sandwiches, homemade soups, salads, and other deli fare, **D'Ellies,** Village West, tel. (207) 237-2490, is one of Sugarloaf Village's most popular eateries. It's open daily, all year, for breakfast and lunch.

The café at the Sugarloaf Golf Club is a bit pricey, but the sandwiches are hefty and you can't knock the convenience after a round of golf. **Strokes Café,** tel. (207) 237-6035, is open daily 8 a.m.-8 p.m. during the golf season (usually mid-May to mid-October).

Inexpensive to Moderate

Drive down the mountain from Sugarloaf/USA and you'll find restaurants in Carrabassett Valley, in Stratton and Eustis to the north, and in Kingfield, to the south.

Reservations are a good idea at **Hug's,** Rt. 27, Carrabassett Valley 04947, tel. (207) 237-2392, an "in" Italian restaurant camouflaged by a nondescript gray exterior. To sample one of the area's best moderately priced menus, try the artichoke-heart appetizer with eggplant, spinach, and feta, or shiitake mushroom ravioli with walnut pesto alfredo. Entrées run $10-18; kids' portions are available. Beer and wine only. Hug's, a mile south of the Sugarloaf Road, is open for dinner Tues.-Sun. 5-9 p.m., Nov.-April.

About as far as you can get from the seashore or even a lake, the whimsically named **Carrabassett Yacht Club,** Rt. 27, RR 1, Box 2161, Carrabassett Valley 04947, tel. (207) 235-2730, is five miles south of the Sugarloaf access road. It's a popular place, picking up lots of spillover traffic from Sugarloaf restaurants. Monday is pizza twofer night. No smoking in the dining area. The bar opens at 4 p.m.; dinner is served Mon.-Thurs. 5-9:30 p.m. and Friday and Saturday 5-10 p.m. Breakfast is also available Fri.-Sunday. Next to the Valley Lodge, it's open June through April.

Six miles south of the Sugarloaf access road is **Tufulio's,** Rt. 27, Carrabassett Valley 04947, tel. (207) 235-2010, producers of the valley's best pizza. The shrimp-and-artichoke pesto pizza is tops ($9 for a small one). Also on the menu are seafood, chicken, and plenty of pasta dishes ($10-16, lower prices for kids' items). In summer, you can eat on the deck. The wine list is ambitious, and there's plenty of beer on tap. Sunday is twofer night. Located at Valley Crossing, Tufulio's is open all year, daily 4 p.m. until closing (usually 9 p.m. weeknights, 9:30 p.m. weekends).

A mile north of Kingfield, **Nostalgia Tavern,** Rt. 27, Kingfield 04947, tel. (207) 265-2559, has a loyal local clientele and not one but *two* twofer nights (Tuesday and Thursday). The unfancy menu—heavy on sandwiches, burgers, and dogs—shows a sense of humor, and peanut-butter sandwiches come in five flavors (under $3). Smoking is allowed, so the air quality varies. Open all year, Tues.-Sun. 11 a.m.-9 p.m.

Popular with the Kingfield crowd, **Longfellow's Restaurant**, Main St., Rt. 27, Kingfield 04947, tel. (207) 265-4394, is a rustic, homey eatery across from The Herbert in the center of Kingfield. The daily specials are a good bet; chicken, seafood, and beef entrées run $10-14, with standard pasta dishes in the $5-10 range. Kid-size portions are available; Tuesday is twofer night. The coffee list is huge. It's open daily, all year, weekdays 11 a.m.-9 p.m., weekends 11 a.m.-9:30 p.m.

Everyone eventually shows up at **The Kingfield Woodsman**, Rt. 27, Kingfield 04947, tel. (207) 265-2561, best choice in the area for local color, especially at breakfast, which starts early. The rustic eatery has been a local landmark since the mid-1970s. Open Mon.-Fri. 5 a.m.-2 p.m., Saturday 7 a.m.-2 p.m., and Sunday 7 a.m.-1 p.m. (no lunch on Sunday, just breakfast).

Eight miles north of the Sugarloaf access road, the **White Wolf Restaurant**, Main St., Rt. 27, Stratton 04982, tel. (207) 246-2922, gets you off the mountain and into congenial, casual surroundings with an imaginative menu ($10-18 for entrées, usually including venison and buffalo). Tuesday is twofer night. Wednesday is pounder night, when $9.95 gets you a pound of steak, shrimp, or chicken—plenty for two. It's open all year, Mon.-Fri. 11 a.m.-9 p.m. and Saturday and Sunday 7 a.m.-9 p.m. Reservations are a good idea; be sure to request the nonsmoking room. During May's mud season, "The Wolf" usually shuts down Monday and Tuesday.

North of Nowetah's American Indian Museum and 22 miles south of Sugarloaf is the old-fashioned **Wirebridge Diner**, Rt. 27, New Portland 04954, tel. (207) 628-6229, great for reliable food and local color. The breakfast crowd flocks here for the pancakes. There's a nonsmoking section, but even it can get smoky. No credit cards. Open all year, Tues.-Sun. 6 a.m.-3 p.m.

Moderate to Expensive

Best restaurant in the entire area is **One Stanley Avenue**, 1 Stanley Ave., Kingfield 04947, tel. (207) 265-5541, a Kingfield magnet since 1972.

Cocktails in the Victorian lounge precede a dining experience: unobtrusive service, understated decor, and entrées ($15-26) such as roast duck with rhubarb glaze, chicken with fiddleheads, and saged rabbit. Dill-flavored Shaker dumplings come with every entrée. Reservations are essential on winter weekends; the restaurant attracts Sugarloaf's higher-end ski crowd. No smoking. Open for dinner Tues.-Sun., Dec.-April, One Stanley Avenue is 18 miles south of Sugarloaf.

Consistent, creative cuisine has drawn customers from as far as Rangeley to **The Porter House Restaurant**, Rt. 27, Eustis 04936, tel. (207) 246-7932, a back-of-beyond 1908 farmhouse along the highway to Canada. An extra touch is the choice of antiques-filled dining rooms. Specialties ($9-17) include Porter House steak, bacon-wrapped filet mignon, and roast duckling. Although it tends to be a "grownup" place, kids can order a sirloin burger or a hot dog. You'll probably be out of luck if you show up without a reservation, and it's a bit far to drive for a disappointment. No smoking. Open every day but Christmas 5-9 p.m., the Porter House is 12 miles northwest of Sugarloaf/USA and 23 miles east and north of Rangeley; allow 30-40 minutes from Rangeley, enough time for moosespotting.

INFORMATION AND SERVICES

The **Sugarloaf Area Chamber of Commerce**, Rt. 27, RR 1, Box 2151, Carrabassett Valley 04947, tel. (207) 235-2100, fax 235-2081, handles information requests for the whole valley, including Sugarloaf/USA, and publishes a helpful map/guide as well as annual dining and lodging brochures. The office, across the road from Ayotte's Country Store, also handles reservations for lodging in the valley as well as on the mountain, tel. (800) 843-2732. It's open most days, all year, 9 a.m.-4 p.m. Request copies of the chamber's two helpful free brochures, updated annually: *Sugarloaf Region Dining Guide* and *Sugarloaf Region Lodging Guide.*

For information only on **Sugarloaf/USA**, write to Sugarloaf/USA, RR 1, Box 5000, Carrabassett Valley 04947, tel. (207) 237-2000, fax 237-2718, or contact Guest Services on the main floor of the Base Lodge, tel. (207) 237-6939. There isn't much the Guest Services staff can't handle; they're real pros, knowledgeable about the resort as well as about off-mountain museums, dining, and special events. During the ski season, the free *Mountain Guide,* published weekly, carries comprehensive information about on-mountain activities.

The recorded **Snowphone** hotline, tel. (207) 237-6808, has up-to-the-minute info on snow conditions and special events at Sugarloaf/USA. If you're staying hereabouts (on the mountain or in the valley) and have cable TV, tune to channel 17 (WSKI) for weather, snow, trail, and lift updates, plus an entertainment rundown.

Emergencies

For police, fire, and ambulance services in **Kingfield, Carrabassett Valley, Sugarloaf/USA, and Eustis,** dial 911. Sugarloaf/USA has a **first-aid clinic** in the basement of the interfaith chapel at the west end of the upper parking area in Sugarloaf Village; during the ski season, a doctor or physician's assistant is on duty. The nearest major medical facility is in Farmington, 38 miles south of Sugarloaf.

Money

On the mountain at Sugarloaf/USA, the **Kingfield Bank** has an ATM in the Base Lodge.

Newspaper

The *Original Irregular,* tel. (207) 265-2773, published every Wednesday in Kingfield, carries Kingfield, Carrabassett Valley, and Sugarloaf/USA news, features, and calendar listings. The *Irregular* staff also produces the tabloid-style *Sugarloaf Area Summer Guide* and *Sugarloaf, Snowplace of the East,* both free.

Getting Around

The free **Sugarloaf Shuttle,** following scheduled routes with lots of stops on the mountain and down to Carrabassett Valley, operates Fri.-Sun. and holiday weeks throughout the ski season; other days, it's on call, tel. (207) 236-2000, 8 a.m.-midnight, and still free. Last bus on Friday and Saturday nights is usually 12:30 or 1 a.m. Pick up a schedule at the Check-In Center or at Guest Services in the Base Lodge. In summer, the **Sugarloaf Bike Shuttle,** less extensive than the winter operation, provides continuous service Fri.-Sun. 9 a.m.-4 p.m., from early July to early September. Cost per ride is $3 adults, $1 children 12 and under. The route begins on Main Street in Sugarloaf Village and ends 35 minutes later at Carrabassett Valley's Riverside Park, terminus of the seven-mile Narrow Gauge (trail 9) bike path.

RANGELEY LAKES AREA

Incorporated in 1855, the town of Rangeley (pop. 1,090) and the surrounding Rangeley Lakes region have seen ups and downs in the past century or so—grand hotels and great fires, regression and renewal. Today, the spotlight shines on inland communities such as Rangeley. The uncrowded streets, slower pace, and countless recreational opportunities are changing the face of western Maine. Centerpiece of a vast system of lakes and streams, and surrounded by mountains, Rangeley is loaded with potential for year-round activities—in summer swimming, golf, tennis, canoeing, biking, hiking, fishing, even panning for gold; in winter snowmobiling, ice fishing, snowshoeing, and downhill and nordic skiing. But there's more—Rangeley Friends of the Arts cultural events, old-fashioned annual festivals

and fairs, the unique Wilhelm Reich Museum, a flightseeing service, and shops that carry antiques, books, sportswear, and crafts.

And then there's history, even prehistory—excavations have revealed evidence of human habitation in this area as long ago as 9000 BC. More than 8,000 stone tools and other artifacts were uncovered at the Vail Site, on the edge of Aziscohos Lake. Native Americans certainly left their linguistic mark here, too, with tongue-twisting names applied to the lakes and other natural features. Mooselookmeguntic means "where hunters watch moose at night"; Umbagog means "shallow water"; Mollychunkamunk (a.k.a. Upper Richardson Lake) means "crooked water"; Oquossoc means "landing place"; and Kennebago means "land of sweet water." The more prosaic name of Rangeley comes from 19th-century landowner Squire James Rangeley.

Rangeley is a catchall name. First applied to the town (formerly known as the Lake Settlement), it now also refers to the lake and the entire region. "I'm going to Rangeley" could indicate a destination anywhere in the extensive network of interconnecting lakes, rivers, and streams backing up to New Hampshire. The Rangeley Lakes make up the headwaters of the Androscoggin River, which technically begins at Umbagog Lake and flows seaward for 167 miles to meet the Kennebec River in Merrymeeting Bay, near Brunswick and Topsham.

Southeast of Rangeley, the town of Phillips was the birthplace of fly-fishing legend Cornelia T. ("Fly Rod") Crosby (1854-1946), recipient of the first Registered Maine Guide license issued by the state—the imprimatur for outdoors professionals. Crosby, who wrote columns for the local paper, was a fanatic angler and hunter who always kept a china tea set neatly stowed in her gear.

While most visitors reach Rangeley via Rt. 4 from the Farmington area, another popular route is Rt. 17 from the Rumford/Mexico area. Designated an official Scenic Highway for 32 miles from Rumford north toward Oquossoc, the label is unquestionably deserved, and the vibrant autumn colors are unforgettable. The two-lane road winds through the rural woods of western Maine, opening up periodically to reveal stunning views of lakes, streams, forested hillsides, and the Swift River. You might even see a moose. Between Mexico and Byron, the shoulders are ample enough for biking. Highlights are two signposted viewpoints—Height of Land and the Rangeley Scenic Overlook—surveying Mooselookmeguntic and Rangeley Lakes, respectively. Height of Land, 11 miles south of Oquossoc, adjoins the Appalachian Trail. Have your camera handy.

Along Rt. 17 (about 23 miles south of Oquossoc) is Coos Canyon, in the town of Byron, where gold was found in the early 1800s on the east branch of the Swift River. Amateur prospectors still flock to the area, but don't get your hopes up—it's more play than profit.

SIGHTS

Wilhelm Reich Museum

Controversial Austrian-born psychoanalyst/natural scientist Wilhelm Reich (1897-1957), noted expert on sexual energy, chose Rangeley for his residence and research. Hour-long guided tours of The Wilhelm Reich Museum, Dodge Pond Rd., P.O. Box 687, Rangeley 04970, tel. (207) 864-3443, his handsome fieldstone mansion, include a slide presentation covering Reich's life, eccentric philosophy, experiments, and inventions such as the orgone accumulator and the cloudbuster. Reich is buried on the estate grounds. Views are spectacular from the roof of the museum, also known as **Orgonon,** so bring binoculars and a camera. A nature-trail system, including a bird blind, winds through the wooded acreage, which is open 9 a.m.-5 p.m. There are guided **nature hikes** Wednesday at 3 p.m. in July and August. From July through September, there are free natural science programs each Sunday 2-4 p.m. Museum hours are Tues.-Sun. 1-5 p.m. in July and August, plus Sunday 1-5 in September. Admission is $3 adults; children 12 and under are free. The museum is west of Rangeley, .8 mile north of Rt. 4.

Bennett Bridge

Spanning the Magalloway River beneath Aziscohos Mountain, the 92-foot-long Bennett Covered Bridge (also known as the Bennett-Bean Bridge), built in 1898-99, sees far fewer visitors than most of Maine's eight other covered bridges. The setting, in the hamlet of Wilsons Mills, makes for great photos, so it's worth detouring on the unpaved road next to the Aziscoos Valley Camping Area, .3 mile west of Rt. 16 and 28 miles west of Rangeley.

Flightseeing

Based close to Lakeside Park in downtown Rangeley, **Mountain Air Services,** Main St., Rt. 4, P.O. Box 367, Rangeley 04970, tel. (207) 864-5307, does on-demand 15-minute mini-tours via floatplane for $40 a planeload or $25 a person. Reservations aren't always needed, but call ahead to be sure. Best deal, but unpredictable, is the two-hour **fire warden's flight,** at

$30 pp (two persons maximum). Trips depend on weather, fire danger, and other factors; call for details. You may need to stand by for a phone call. The office is open daily 8:30 a.m.-5 p.m.

Rangeley Logging Museum
A work in progress, the Rangeley Logging Museum, Rt. 16, Rangeley 04970, tel. (207) 864-5595, so far has a single building with lumber-camp paintings and an eclectic assortment of lumberjack paraphernalia. Fundraising for expansion includes an annual auction, usually held July Fourth weekend, and a late-July Logging Museum Festival. In summer, the museum building typically is open noon-2 p.m., or by appointment. Donations are welcomed.

PARKS AND PRESERVES

In downtown Rangeley, overlooking both lake and mountains **Lakeside Park** has grills and picnic tables (some covered), tennis courts, a playground with plenty of swings, lots of lawn for running, and a busy boat-launching ramp. The park is open 5 a.m.-10 p.m. Access is from Main St. (Rt. 4), near the Road Kill Café and the chamber of commerce office.

Rangeley is another Maine region where foresighted conservationists have jumped in and helped set aside recreational land for everyone to enjoy. The most visible standard-bearer is the **Rangeley Lakes Heritage Trust** (RLHT), Rt. 4, P.O. Box 249, Oquossoc 04964, tel./fax (207) 864-7311, an energetic membership organization that oversees thousands of acres of protected land, including 10 islands and more than 20 miles of lake and river frontage. (Annual family membership is $25.) The RLHT office, in the Stony Batter Station building, across from The Gingerbread House in Oquossoc, is open all year, Mon.-Fri. 9 a.m.-4:30 p.m., plus Saturday 9 a.m.-noon from Memorial Day weekend to Labor Day.

Rangeley Lake State Park
With 1.2 miles of lake frontage and panoramic views toward the mountains, 690-acre Rangeley Lake State Park, South Shore Dr., HC 32, Box 5000, Rangeley 04970, tel. (207) 864-3858, gets high marks for picnicking, swimming, fishing, birding, boating, and camping. The swimming "beach" is a large patch of grass. None of the 50 campsites are on the water, but a dozen have easy shore access. For camping reservations, especially on weekends, call (207) 287-3824 at least two weeks ahead (Master-Card and Visa only). If you're doing any boating, stay close to shore until you're comfortable with the wind conditions; the wind picks up very quickly on Rangeley Lake, especially in the south and southeast coves near the park. Day-use admission is $2 adults, 50 cents children 5-11. Nonresident camping is $16 per site per night (plus $2 per site per night for a reservation); two-night minimum mid-June to Labor Day. No hookups, but there are hot showers. The park, located three miles west of Rt. 4 and three miles east of Rt. 16, is open mid-May through September, but it's also accessible for cross-country skiing and snowmobiling.

Hunter Cove Wildlife Sanctuary
Loons, ducks, and other waterfowl are the principal residents of Hunter Cove Wildlife Sanctuary, a small preserve owned by the Maine Audubon Society and managed by the Rangeley Lakes Heritage Trust. While walking the three miles of easy, color-blazed trails, best in a clockwise direction, keep an eye out for blue-flag iris, which blossoms throughout the summer. You may even spot a moose. If you launch a canoe into Hunter Cove and paddle under the Mingo Loop Road bridge early in the season, you'll come face-to-face with nesting cliff swallows. To reach the sanctuary, take Rt. 4 west of downtown Rangeley for about two and a half miles, turning left into the preserve across the road from Dodge Pond. The preserve is open daily, sunrise to sunset. Admission is free.

Smalls Falls Rest Area
One of Maine's most accessible cascades, Smalls Falls is right next to Rt. 4, at a state rest area 12 miles south of Rangeley. Pull into the parking area and walk a few steps to the overlook. Bring a picnic. For more of a challenge, ascend a bit farther to Chandler's Mill Stream Falls. The rest area is officially open mid-May through October, but it's easy to park alongside the highway early and late in the season.

RECREATION

The Rangeley Lakes area earned its vaunted reputation from world-class fishing and other summer pursuits, but it's now become a year-round destination thanks to snowmobiling and skiing. Diehard fishermen will always show up in May and early June, but most everyone else stays away then, preferring not to become lunch for hungry blackflies.

The **Rangeley Parks and Recreation Department,** 3 School St., P.O. Box 1070, Rangeley 04970, tel. (207) 864-3326, sponsors a huge number of activities for residents as well as visitors. Among the **summer programs** are canoeing, swimming, tennis, and golf lessons; hiking and canoe trips; children's workshops; a tennis tournament; and day trips for seniors. Preregistration usually is required, and most programs require at least a minimal fee. Contact the department or check with the chamber of commerce.

Moosewatching

Do-it-yourself moosespotting is a favorite pastime in this area; if you're out and about early or late in the day, the likelihood of seeing one of these big critters is very high. Route 16, between Rangeley and Stratton, is well known as "Moose Alley," especially in the boggy areas close to the road. If you're heading that way for dinner, allow time for a slow drive and plenty of gawking. Keep your camera handy. Drive slowly in any case—no one wins in a moose-car collision, and fatal accidents are not uncommon.

Professional Maine Guide **Rich Gacki,** Recreation Resources, Inc., P.O. Box 695, Rangeley 04970, tel. (207) 864-5136, leads three-and-a-half-hour guided **sunrise canoe trips** on the Kennebago River in search of moose and other wildlife. Trips go out Tuesday, Thursday, and Sunday (2-6 persons), departing at 5 a.m. from The Rangeley Inn, tel. (207) 864-3341. Cost is $38 pp, including gear, a pre-trip snack and coffee, and post-trip breakfast at the inn. To reserve a space, call the inn by 6 p.m. the evening before the trip. Between May and late October, he also does three-hour, on-demand guided **nature hikes** for a minimum of three persons ($20 pp). Rich has no answering machine, so if

Small's Falls, near Rangeley

he's not there when you call his number to arrange a nature hike, keep trying.

Hiking

Centerpiece of a 1,953-acre parcel of Maine Public Reserve Land, **Bald Mountain** is a relatively easy two-hour roundtrip hike that ascends less than 1,000 feet, yet the minimal effort leads to stunning views of Mooselookmeguntic and Upper Richardson Lakes—not to mention the surrounding mountains. Even three-year-olds can tackle this without terrorizing their parents. Pack a picnic. The trailhead is on Bald Mountain Road in Oquossoc, about a mile south of Rt. 4 and roughly across from the entrance to Bald Mountain Camps. Park well off the road.

Dropping 90 feet straight down, dramatic **Angel Falls** is one of New England's highest cascades, reached after a fairly short easy-to-moderate hike. Even in midsummer, you'll be fording running water, so wear rubberized or waterproof shoes or boots. Best time to come is autumn, when most of the rivulets have dried up and the woods are brilliantly colorful. Allow an hour to one and a half hours for the one-and-a-half-mile roundtrip. The trail is mostly red-blazed, with the addition of orange strips tied at crucial points. From Oquossoc, take Rt. 17 south 17.9 miles to the unpaved Bemis Track, on the right (look for a marker reading 6102). Follow the road along Berdeen Stream about six miles until you see a steep road descending to a gravel pit on the left. Park alongside the Bemis Track or drive down the hill and park there. This is a popular hike, so you'll see other cars. The trail leads off to the left.

A distinctive landmark on the western slope of Saddleback Mountain, **Piazza Rock** is a giant cantilevered boulder 600 feet off the Appalachian Trail. The hike up is easy to moderate, not a cakewalk but fine for families, along the white-blazed AT from Rt. 4. From downtown Rangeley, go seven miles southeast on Rt. 4 and park in the new lot on the south side of the highway. Piazza Rock is 1.2 miles northeast of the highway.

If you continue on the AT from Piazza Rock, it's another four miles to the summit of 4,116-foot **Saddleback Mountain,** but most hikers take the shorter route up the mountain from the ski area's Base Lodge. To get there from Rangeley, go south on Rt. 4 to Dallas Hill Rd., then go two and a half miles to Saddleback Mountain Road. From the lodge, hike under the Surry double chairlift to the top of the Gold Rush Trail. Connect to Haymaker Trail and continue to the top of the Stagecoach double chairlift. Then take the Cliffhanger Trail to the top of the Wells Fargo T-bar, and on up to the summit. Expect a stiff breeze and 360-degree vistas. A trail map is available at the lodge.

Other excellent hikes west and north of Rangeley are **Aziscohos Mountain** and **West Kennebago Mountain.** Both are easy to moderate, have terrific views from their summits, and require 3-4 hours roundtrip from their trailheads. West Kennebago has a fire tower.

Mountain Biking

In downtown Rangeley, **Rangeley Mountain Bike Touring Etc.,** 53 Main St., P.O. Box 126, Rangeley 04970, tel. (207) 864-5799, is the local headquarters for everything to do with mountain biking. Advice is plentiful. Eighteen-speed mountain bikes rent for $20 a day or $15 a half-day; kids' bikes are also available. See "Getting Afloat," below, for info on their canoe, kayak, and paddleboat rentals. Open daily 9 a.m.-9 p.m., May-Oct., weather permitting. In winter, call to inquire about snowshoe and cross-crountry-ski rentals.

Rangeley MBT Etc. actively supports the ongoing efforts of the **Trails for Rangeley Area Coalition** (TRAC) to build a multiuse trail network. The shop hands out the TRAC Railroad Loop Trail map for mountain biking—a 12.5-mile circuit via paved and unpaved roads and an abandoned railroad bed. (The chamber of commerce also has copies.) You can begin the loop close to the shop, but be prepared for some steep sections near the Saddleback Access Road.

Swimming

Although many lodgings have swimming facilities or access to them, not all do. If you're ready for a swim, head for downtown Rangeley's **Lakeside Park** or **Rangeley Lake State Park.** In summer, a lifeguard is on duty at Lakeside Park weekdays 11 a.m.-5 p.m. and weekends 9 a.m.-5 p.m.

Also see the Sugarloaf Area section, above, for information on swimming at Cathedral Pines in Eustis, east of Rangeley via Rt. 16.

Getting Afloat

Canoeing and motorboating are splendid throughout this region, but be forewarned that Rangeley and Mooselookmeguntic Lakes are much larger than they look, and they have wide-open expanses where flukey winds can kick up suddenly and mightily. Check on wind conditions before you head out. Do not take chances.

If you're looking for a pristine lake without the roar of motors, opt for **Saddleback Lake, Loon Lake, Little Kennebago Lake,** or **Quimby Pond,** all fairly close to Rangeley.

Good choices for **canoeing** around Rangeley are Rangeley Lake (especially around Hunter Cove), the Cupsuptic River, the lower Kennebago River, and Mooselookmeguntic Lake. For canoeing slightly farther afield, Upper and Lower Richardson Lakes are wonderfully scenic, as is Umbagog Lake (pronounced "um-BAY-gog"), straddling the Maine-New Hampshire border. The Rangeley Lakes Area Chamber of Commerce has produced a suggested canoeing itinerary for the Rangeley Lakes chain, including information about wilderness campsites en route. Some of the campsites require advance reservations and fire permits.

Besides being a fishing-gear supplier, **River's Edge Sports,** Rt. 4, P.O. Box 347, Oquossoc 04964, tel. (207) 864-5582, also rents canoes for $20 a day. For $30, including canoe rental, they'll shuttle you and the canoe up the Kennebago River to the start of an idyllic 3- to 4-hour downstream paddle to Rt. 16. The shop is open all year, daily 8 a.m.-6 p.m., except for April when hours are 9 a.m.-5 p.m.

Kayaks are $25-45 a day (depending on size), and canoes are $20 a day, from **Rangeley Mountain Bike Touring Etc.,** 53 Main St., P.O. Box 126, Rangeley 04970, tel. (207) 864-5799 For $8 an hour, you can rent a paddleboat on Haley Pond, right behind the shop. You can also rent canoes and single and double kayaks by the hour ($10-15).

Best place to rent a sturdy motorboat is **Oquossoc Marine,** Rt. 4, Oquossoc 04964, tel. (207) 864-5477, fax 864-2931, in downtown Oquossoc. Cost is about $120 a day. Oquossoc Marine's fine reputation means their boats are much in demand, so reserve well ahead. In winter, their focus turns to snowmobiles.

Golf

Noted golfers have been teeing off at **Mingo Springs Golf Course,** Country Club Rd., P.O. Box 399, tel. (207) 864-5021, since 1925, when the course started with nine holes. Today's 18-hole, par-70 course boasts panoramic vistas of lakes and mountains—and sometimes an annoying breeze. Facilities include lessons, a pro shop, and cart rentals; no tee times. Golf and-lodging packages are available at the adjacent Country Club Inn. Open Memorial Day weekend to early October. Take Rt. 4 west of Rangeley and turn left onto Mingo Loop Rd.; follow the signs.

Mingo Springs is almost as scenic as the Sugarloaf Golf Course, and a bit less expensive, but it can be hard to resist the temptation to play a round on Sugarloaf's championship course.

Winter Sports

Neighboring Sugarloaf/USA dominates the downhill world in this part of Maine, but the Rangeley area has its own first-rate, low-key, family-oriented ski resort—with prices that put less of a dent in your wallet. Seven miles southeast of Rangeley, **Saddleback,** P.O. Box 490, Rangeley 04970, tel. (207) 864-5671, snow hotline (207) 864-3380, has more than 40 novice to expert trails served by two double chairlifts and three T-bars, plus two snowboard parks. Vertical drop on the mountain is an impressive 1,830 feet. Daily lift tickets are $31 weekends and holidays, much less midweek. On-mountain facilities include the Base Lodge, ski school, rentals, a cafeteria (open daily during ski season), inexpensive day care, and two attractive condo complexes ($135-385 a night in winter, depending on size and location; Rock Pond Homes have the best views but higher prices). Ski season is late November to early April; lifts operate daily 9 a.m.-4 p.m., weather permitting.

Also based on Saddleback Mountain is **Ski Nordic at Saddleback,** P.O. Box 490, Rangeley 04970, tel. (207) 864-5671, snow hotline (207) 864-3380, with about 25 miles of groomed trails (and backcountry access). An easy-to-moderate route is the Lake Loop around Saddleback Lake, at the foot of the mountain; ski clockwise, beginning with the easier east-shore trail. Rental skis are available at the Saddleback Base Lodge. Trail passes are $8 adults, $5 children.

The town of Rangeley maintains a free, 15-mile network of three groomed cross-country trails. For details on **Rangeley Municipal Trails,** contact the chamber of commerce or call the town office at (207) 864-3326.

At **Orgonon, the Wilhelm Reich Museum,** tel. (207) 864-3443, west of downtown Rangeley, the summer nature trails are accessible for free nordic skiing weekdays 9 a.m.-4 p.m. Maine Guide **Rich Gacki** in winter leads four-hour **guided cross-country-skiing tours,** usually on Sunday. Cost is $20 pp for a minimum of three persons. Call him at (207) 864-5136; keep trying. **River's Edge Sports,** Rt. 4, P.O. Box 347, Oquossoc 04964, tel. (207) 864-5582, rents cross-country skis for $12 a day. They're open daily 8 a.m.-6 p.m.

The Rangeley area, linked to the statewide system of **snowmobile trails,** has its own 150-

mile groomed network, thanks to the diligent efforts of local snowmobile clubs. **River's Edge Sports,** Rt. 4, Oquossoc 04967, tel. (207) 864-5582, rents snowmobiles for about $150 a day. **Dockside Sports Center,** Main St., Rangeley 04970, tel. (207) 864-2424, also rents snow-mobiles.

ENTERTAINMENT

Opened in the summer of 1996 as a nonprofit community cinema, the **Lakeside Youth Theater,** Main St., Rangeley 04970, tel. (207) 864-5000, screens first-run films with surround sound and state-of-the-art equipment. Built with extra elevation, all 175 seats have unencumbered vantage points. Shows typically are 7 and 9 p.m., and adult tickets are $5 or less. In summer, Thursday is art film night. On rainy summer days, a multicolored flag announces matinees. Off season, films are only shown weekend evenings.

The Lakeside Youth Theater is also the site of performances sponsored by **Rangeley Friends of the Arts** (RFA), P.O. Box 333, Rangeley 04970, tel. (207) 863-3345, an active local cultural organization. RFA produces an annual summer musical; other events include concerts, dramas, and exhibits.

The People's Choice, Main St., Rangeley 04970, tel. (207) 864-5220, packs 'em in on Friday and Saturday nights, starting at 9 p.m., when there's live music (rock and country) and dancing.

FESTIVALS AND EVENTS

The last weekend in January, the **Snowmobile Snodeo** brings games, a snowmobile parade, and fireworks to Lakeside Park, Rangeley.

The **Rangeley Lakes Sled Dog Races** includes mushing races in various categories and makes for great spectating. In Rangeley the first or second weekend in March.

Free **guided nature hikes** happen every Wednesday July-Aug. at 3 p.m. at Rangeley's Wilhelm Reich Museum (tel. 207-864-3443). Call for specific agendas. From July through September, the museum also offers free **natural**

science programs each Sunday 2-4 p.m. Call for topics.

Rangeley goes all out with its **Independence Day** celebration fireworks display (and chicken barbecue, parade, and live music), held on the 4th or a day before or after. Be here for it if you're anywhere near the area. In Lakeside Park, Rangeley. Third Sunday in July, the **Old-Time Fiddlers' Contest** draws fiddlers galore and includes a barbecue. Bring your own chair or blanket and expect lots of foot-stomping fun. It runs 1-5 p.m. at Rangeley Inn Green, Rangeley. The last weekend in July, **Logging Museum Festival Days** includes a parade, beanhole bean supper, lumberjack events, and Little Miss Woodchip contest. On the Rangeley Logging Museum grounds, Rt. 16.

On the first Thursday in August, the **Sidewalk Art Show** is an all-day street festival featuring dozens of artists displaying a wide range of talents along Rangeley's Main Street. Second full week of August, **Phillips Old Home Days** is a down-home community-pride celebration with live music, a carnival, a parade, a barbecue, and a road race. Downtown Rangeley comes alive the third Thursday in August for the **Annual Blueberry Festival,** a day-long celebration of the blueberry harvest, with sales of blueberry-everything.

Held the first Saturday in October, the **Logging Museum Apple Festival** is a day-long, apple-centric celebration including cider pressing. On the logging museum grounds, Rt. 16, in Rangeley.

SHOPPING

Antiques Plus

Old fishing and hunting gear, antique tools, and postcards are the specialties at **Gearsyl Antiques,** Rt. 4/16, HC 32, Box 2300, Rangeley 04970, tel. (207) 864-5784, a two-story barn roughly midway between Rangeley and Oquossoc. Art and Sylvia Guerin live in the farmhouse, so the shop is open all year, daily 9 a.m.-6 p.m.

At the southern end of town, out toward Saddleback, **Blueberry Hill Farm,** Dallas Hill Rd., Box 740, Rangeley 04970, tel. (207) 864-5647, carries today's and tomorrow's antiques—crafts, quilts, baskets, used books, decoys, wildlife art, and vintage fishing gear. No credit cards. Open daily 10 a.m.-5 p.m., May through September. In August, bring a pail and pick your own wild blueberries from their 10 acres; cost is a bargain-basement 90 cents a pound. They'll even lend you a blueberry rake. The farm is three and a half miles east of Rt. 4, on the side of Saddleback Mountain.

Antiques are also part of the inventory at downtown Rangeley's Serendipity Then & Now (see below).

Books, Gifts, and Crafts

Why is the new-book selection so good at **Books, Lines, and Thinkers,** Main St. at Kennebago Rd., P.O. Box 971, Rangeley 04970, tel. (207) 864-4355? Owner Wess Connally is a high school English teacher; the small, user-friendly shop has lots of great reading. Located on the second floor over the video store, it's open daily 10 a.m.-7 p.m., mid-June to Labor Day. After that, hours can be a bit unpredictable, since Wess has school commitments, but generally it's open Monday, Wednesday, and Friday 4-7 p.m. and Saturday 10 a.m.-7 p.m.

The Rangeley area's best selection of sportswear and gifts comes from **The Alpine Shop,** 72 Main St., Rangeley 04970, tel. (207) 864-3741. Patagonia, Woolrich, and Teva are just a few of the brand names; the Icelandic sweater selection is impressive; and the Maine-theme gifts are (mostly) tasteful. The shop is open all year, daily 9 a.m.-5 p.m. in winter, 9 a.m.-8:30 p.m. in July and August.

The **Ecopelagicon Nature Store,** Pond St., Rangeley 04970, tel. (207) 864-2771, is a kind of miniaturized (and less expensive) Nature Company, emphasizing eco-oriented gifts, toys, and games. The shop, half a block off Main Street, is open daily 10 a.m.-5 p.m., Memorial Day weekend through Christmas; in July and August, it stays open to 8 p.m.

In downtown Rangeley, you can't miss the house and shop of **Rodney Richard, the Mad Whittler,** 123 Main St., Rt. 4, P.O. Box 183, Rangeley 04970, tel. (207) 864-5595, behind all the wood shavings and works-in-progress. If Rodney's working his magic with the chainsaw and jackknife, you can stand by and watch, or perhaps purchase one of his woodcarvings. His

son, Rodney Jr., a chip off the old block, has earned his own reputation as an accomplished woodcarver, specializing in loons. Rodney Sr. has achieved national and international renown as a folk artist and master carver. His work has traveled to dozens of museums and appears in collections as far afield as Archangel in Russia. He's also the prime mover behind Rangeley's fledgling Logging Museum. Look for the Open pennant outside his shop in July and August; other times, call ahead to make sure someone is home.

Ginny Spiller's **Serendipity Then & Now,** 53 Main St., P.O. Box 499, Rangeley 04970, tel. (207) 864-3959, is a terrific showcase for Maine craftspeople. Check out the "Rome Gnome," a small wooden garden creature made in Rome, Maine. Summer hours are daily 10 a.m.-6 p.m.; winter hours are less predictable.

Just up the hill west of town, **Sunrise View Farm,** Cemetery Hill, Rt. 4, HC 32, Box 1060, Rangeley 04970, tel. (207) 864-2117, has cornered one of the best views in the area. It's hard to concentrate on the herbs, flowers, jams, and herbal gifts when all of Rangeley is spread out before you. The farm shop is open late June to Labor Day, Mon.-Sat. 10 a.m.-4 p.m. From mid-May to late June, the shop also is open weekends and by appointment.

ACCOMMODATIONS

Inns/B&Bs

Entering Rangeley from the south, you can't miss the three-story **Rangeley Inn and Motor Lodge,** Main St., P.O. Box 160, Rangeley 04970, tel. (207) 864-3341 or (800) 666-3687, fax (207) 864-3634, on the edge of downtown's Haley Pond. Thirty-five rooms in the turn-of-the-century main section and 15 modern rooms in the motel annex (overlooking the pond) are $70-115 d, depending on season (highest in winter). All have private baths; some rooms have whirlpools. The large lobby has comfortable chairs, a large woodstove, and lots of woody touches. The huge, tin-ceilinged dining room (no smoking) is open to the public for dinner (6-9 p.m.) Memorial Day to Columbus Day and weekends in winter. Creative entrées run $15-22, with an interesting wine list; a children's menu is also available. Reservations are a good idea, and a must on summer weekends. A terrific breakfast, with first-rate omelettes and homefries, is served daily 7:30-10 a.m. (to 11 a.m. Sunday). Breakfast at the inn is included in the fee if you sign up for one of Rich Gacki's guided sunrise canoe trips (see "Moosewatching" under "Recreation," above). Open all year.

Next to the stunning Mingo Springs Golf Course, the **Country Club Inn,** P.O. Box 680, Rangeley 04970, tel. (207) 864-3831, claims the same knockout lake-and-mountain panorama as the golf course. Nineteen lake-view rooms (private baths) go for $99 d, including breakfast, or $144 d MAP. A room-only rate is also available, as is a two-night all-inclusive golf package. Decor is updated '60s; the inn is superbly maintained and run, and there's an outdoor pool. Children are welcome, but no pets. The dramatic windowed dining room is open to the public by reservation for breakfast and dinner (entrées $11-17) late June to Columbus Day, but tables can be scarce when the inn is fully booked. Call well ahead, especially on summer weekends. No smoking in the dining room. The inn, located 2.2 miles west of downtown Rangeley, is open mid-May to mid-October and late Dec.-March.

A genuine veteran in the B&B trade, Joanne Koob has been running **Oquossoc's Own Bed & Breakfast,** Rangeley Ave., P.O. Box 27, Oquossoc 04964, tel. (207) 864-5584, since 1980. Repeat customers are the rule at this lively, informal place. Joanne provides a cozy living room, a spare refrigerator, croquet and volleyball gear—and delicious picnics and dinners by prearrangement. (Her professional kitchen is the heart of her catering business.) Five attractively decorated second- and third-floor rooms share two baths ($60 d). Smoking only in the common room or outside. Kids under six stay free. Located a block off Rt. 4, the B&B is open all year.

Twenty-one miles southeast of Rangeley, **The Elcourt Bed and Breakfast,** Pleasant St., P.O. Box 214, Phillips 04966, tel. (207) 639-2741 or (800) 639-2741, gets high marks for its hearty country breakfast served to classical music. Cordial innkeepers Court and Elsie Dill cater to hikers, snowmobilers, and skiers at their comfortably old-fashioned village B&B; children and well-behaved pets are also welcome. Three rooms share two and a half baths ($45-55 d); no smoking. Out back are lovely formal gardens. The Dills provide pickup and dropoff service for hikers on the Appalachian Trail, 10 minutes away. Open all year.

Cabin Colony
On a quiet cove about four miles west of town, **Hunter Cove on Rangeley Lake,** Mingo Loop Rd., HC 32, Box 2800, Rangeley 04970, tel. (207) 864-3383, has eight rustically modern waterfront cabins on six acres. Each has one or two bedrooms, screened porch, woodstove, and even, alas, color TV. Weekly rates are $600-850; pets are $10 a day. Open all year, with lower rates off season. From here, it's an easy paddle to the western edge of the Hunter Cove Wildlife Sanctuary, and Mingo Springs Golf Course is nearby.

Sporting Camps
Stephen Philbrick, who manages to juggle 10 things at once, is the third-generation owner of **Bald Mountain Camps,** Bald Mountain Rd., P.O. Box 332, Oquossoc 04964, tel./fax (207) 864-3671, a family-oriented traditional sporting camp on the shore of Mooselookmeguntic Lake. Established in 1897, the superbly run operation has more than 90% repeat guests, some since the 1930s. It's tough to get a reservation, especially in July and August. Fifteen rustic, twin-bedded waterfront cabins flank the lakeview lodge, where three meals are served daily (BYOL). A highlight is the Friday-night cookout, with lobster, ribs, corn, steamed clams, and blueberry pancakes for dessert. The informal dining room is also open to the public for dinner by reservation only (about $19 pp; book well ahead). Among the activities are swimming, fishing, volleyball, tennis, motorboating, sailing, and waterskiing. Rates are $100 pp per day, AP. Three-day minimum in July, one-week minimum in August. No credit cards. Open mid-May to late September.

More rustic and remote than Bald Mountain Camps, **Grant's Kennebago Camps,** P.O. Box 786, Rangeley 04970, tel. (207) 864-3608 or (800) 633-4815 outside Maine, winter address:

Edgewater Acres, Saco 04072, tel. (207) 282-5264, is a classic sporting camp built in 1905 on remote, five-mile-long Kennebago Lake. Expect to hear lots of loons and see plenty of moose—*if* you can get a reservation. Seriously dedicated fly fishermen fill up the beds in May and September; families take their places in July and August. Daily rates for the 18 rustic cabins, with private bathrooms and hot showers, are $92 pp, AP, considerably less for children. The main lodge's lakeview dining room is open to the public for dinner by reservation (BYOL). The hearty cuisine makes it a popular place, so call well ahead. Canoe rentals are $10 a day. In July and August, Grant's arranges a daily moose run on the Kennebago River for $15 a person. (Nonguests can also go on the moose run, for a higher fee; call for details.) Credit cards are accepted only for deposits. Access is via a gated nine-mile road from Rt. 16, west of Rangeley. Open mid-May to late September.

Campgrounds and Campsites
In addition to the nonprofit and commercial campgrounds described here, the Rangeley Lakes Region Chamber of Commerce maintains a list of no-fee and low-fee **remote wilderness campsites** throughout the Rangeley Lakes.

The **Maine Forest Service**, Rt. 16, P.O. Box 267, Oquossoc 04964, tel. (207) 864-5545, responsible for more than a dozen no-fee primitive campsites, will provide a copy of its list upon request. The office also issues fire permits for campsites without fire rings or fireplaces.

The **Stephen Phillips Memorial Preserve Trust**, P.O. Box 21, Oquossoc 04964, tel. (207) 864-2003, oversees 60 primitive tentsites on the mainland and islands in Mooselookmeguntic Lake. Cost is $8 per site (for two). Best experience is to reserve one of the 18 waterfront sites on **Students Island**, accessible only by boat. Two nature trails cross and circle the island. The campsites are open May through September.

About 18 miles west of Oquossoc, **Aziscoos Valley Camping Area**, Rt. 16, HC 10, Box 302, Wilsons Mills 03579, tel. (207) 486-3271, has 31 open and wooded tent and RV sites in the shadow of two mountains and close to the Bennett

Covered Bridge. Site 5 is right next to the bridge; site 17 is a rental teepee. Swimming, canoeing, and fishing are all popular pursuits here. Rates are $8-11 per family. Leashed pets are allowed, but noise levels are strictly enforced. Facilities include a laundry room; recycling is mandatory. The campground is open mid-May through October.

At the southeast corner of Aziscohos Lake, **Black Brook Cove Campground**, Lincoln Pond Rd., P.O. Box 319, Oquossoc 04964, tel. (207) 486-3828, provides three different kinds of camping experiences. The main campground has 30 tent and RV sites with hookups; the secluded East Shore Area has 20 wooded waterfront sites; and 20-acre, boat-accessible Beaver Island, out in the lake, has 16 wilderness campsites. Rates are $14 per family per site, plus a hookup fee. Facilities include coin-operated hot showers, a private beach, a convenience store, and rental boats and canoes. The well-maintained campground, about 16 miles west of Oquossoc, is open mid-April to mid-November.

The wilderness setting on the Swift River is a big plus at **Coos Canyon Campground**, Rt. 17, HC 62, Box 408, Byron 04275, tel. (207) 364-3880, where each site includes a stone fireplace, picnic table, and a rustic swing. No hookups or electricity; RVs not allowed. Toilet facilities are outhouses only. Sites are $8 per site per night (or $10 for a lean-to) for a family. An added attraction is the chance to try your hand at gold panning. **Gold-panning lessons** (by reservation only, for campers and noncampers) are $5 pp, plus rental of a pan and trowel for $3 a day. The campground is 21 miles south of Oquossoc, 13 miles north of Mexico, across from the Byron Rest Area. The office is across Rt. 17. It's open mid-April through November.

Seasonal Rentals
The **Mountain View Agency**, 96 Main St., P.O. Box 1100, Rangeley 04970, tel. (207) 864-5648, has a wide selection of weekly and monthly rental cottages, camps, houses, and condos for winter and summer use. Costs range $400-1,000 a week; winter rates are highest.

The chamber of commerce also can assist with seasonal rentals.

FOOD

Check the local newspaper for announcements of **public suppers,** featuring chicken, beans, spaghetti, or just potluck. Most suppers benefit charitable causes, cost under $6 pp, and provide an ample supply of local color.

Miscellanea

"Meet me at the Frosty" is Rangeley's summertime one-liner, a ritual for locals and visitors. **Pine Tree Frosty,** Main St., Rangeley 04970, tel. (207) 864-5894, a tiny takeout near Haley Pond and the Rangeley Inn, serves ever-popular Gifford's ice cream, in dozens of flavors, plus good-size lobster rolls and superb onion rings. Tables outside are convenient for picnics. The Frosty is open mid-May through Labor Day, daily 11 a.m.-9:30 p.m.

Inexpensive to Moderate

Breakfast is an event at the **White Birch Café,** Richardson St., Rangeley 04970, tel. (207) 864-5844, where you learn quickly that Rangeley has no secrets. This casual spot with booths, tables, and a counter serves French toast from homemade bread and on weekends dishes up the best eggs Benedict in the county, maybe beyond. Large portions and consistently friendly service are hallmarks here. The café, tucked behind Main Street and the Historical Society, is open all year, Thurs.-Tues. 6 a.m.-2 p.m. (closing at noon on Sunday).

The People's Choice, Main St., Rangeley 04970, tel. (207) 864-5220, is a busy, locally popular restaurant—as much for the weekend entertainment as the macho menu. In winter, it's jammed to the rafters with snowmobilers. Specialties are prime ribs and steaks. Wednesday is twofer night (two entrées for the price of one). Open all year, daily 6 a.m.-9 p.m.

Meatloaf is a favorite at **The Red Onion,** Main St., Rt. 4, Rangeley 04970, tel. (207) 864-5022, a barn of a place where you can also get award-winning chili for $2.95 a bowl and a large German pizza (sauerkraut, bacon, and onions) for $9.50. Portions are large; Saturday is prime-rib night. One dining room is smoke-free. The "Onion" is open all year, daily 11 a.m.-9:30 p.m. —unless, as they say, "high winds, low humidity,

and plain laziness" inspire them to close the doors.

Bring along your sense of humor and you'll have a fine time at the **Road Kill Café,** Main St., P.O. Box 517, Rangeley 04947, tel. (207) 864-3351, one of half-a-dozen clones in a New England mini-chain. Skip it if you're cranky. The menu is appropriately outrageous, as is the waitstaff; the food is better than in the original Greenville Junction operation. Walls are hung with old license plates, insulting slogans, and road-crossing signs; beer is sold by the yard. A big asset here is the lake-view deck—even used for winter lunches by diehard snowmobilers. The Road Kill is next to the entrance to downtown Rangeley's Lakeside Park. Open all year, daily at 11:30 a.m., closing hour varies from 9 p.m. to 11 p.m.

The Gingerbread House, Rt. 4, Oquossoc 04964, tel. (207) 864-3602, underwent an incredible transformation in early 1997, going from a chummy, old-fashioned place to a casually upmarket, bright, open restaurant. Only hints of the former incarnation are the exterior gingerbread and the gussied-up antique soda fountain. On the menu are regional American items, with culinary flair (dinner entrées are $13-22). Breakfast is especially popular, as is the ice-cream takeout (Annabelle's Ice Cream). Open all year, Mon.-Sat. 6 a.m.-9 p.m. and Sunday 6 a.m.-6 p.m.

Several sporting camps in the Rangeley area open their dining rooms to the public, primarily for dinner, during the summer. Here's a chance to sample the sporting-camp ambience and the comfort food that brings guests back from one generation to the next.

INFORMATION AND SERVICES

The knowledgeable staffers at the **Rangeley Lakes Region Chamber of Commerce,** Lakeside Park, P.O. Box 317, Rangeley 04970, tel. (207) 864-5364, cope with the craziest of questions. They'll also help you find a place to sleep—call (800) 685-2537. Request copies of their annual guides to lodgings and services; their useful *Maine's Rangeley Lakes Map* costs $1.50. The office is open Mon.-Sat. 9 a.m.-5 p.m. all year, plus Sunday 10 a.m.-2 p.m. in July and August.

Newspapers

The Rangeley Highlander, tel. (207) 864-3756, published every other Friday, a folksy, community-oriented paper, carries helpful ads, features, and calendar listings. Not much escapes the staff's attention, so it provides a real flavor of small-town life.

The *Original Irregular* newspaper, based in Kingfield, tel. (207) 265-2773, each summer produces the free, tabloid-style *Rangeley Lakes Area Summertime Guide,* a very useful collection of ads, features, and events listings.

Emergencies

For police, fire, and ambulance services in **Rangeley and Oquossoc,** dial 911. The modern **Rangeley Region Health Center,** Dallas Hill Rd., P.O. Box 569, Rangeley 04970, tel.

(207) 864-3303, after hours tel. (800) 398-6031, opened in 1995, provides health care for residents and visitors and acts as the first-care provider in emergencies, but serious accident victims are transported to Franklin Memorial Hospital in Farmington, about 40 miles southeast of Rangeley. The health center is open Mon.-Fri. 8:30 a.m.-noon and 1-5 p.m., plus Thursday 5-7:30 p.m. and Saturday 9 a.m.-noon.

Photo Services

Perfect Pictures, School and Pleasant Sts., Rangeley 04970, tel. (207) 864-3336, besides being a photographic portrait studio, also has one-hour photo-lab service. The shop, a block north of Main Street, is open all year, Mon.-Sat. 10 a.m.-5 p.m. During the spring "mud season," the shop often is closed on Saturday.

BETHEL AND VICINITY

A fantastic mountain-valley locale, classic antique homes, unique boutiques, a 19th-century prep school (Gould Academy), and one of New England's hottest ski resorts give Bethel (pop. 2,360) year-round appeal, much of it outdoors-oriented. Winter—the peak season—brings alpine and nordic skiing, snowshoeing, snowboarding, dogsledding, skijoring, snowmobiling, ice-skating, ice-fishing, and ice climbing. Summer—gaining in popularity, except perhaps during early June's blackfly season—means stupendous hiking, swimming, mountain biking, rock climbing, rockhounding in local quarries, fishing, camping, picnicking, golfing, and even llama trekking.

The Sunday River Ski Resort, six miles from downtown Bethel, can take credit for many of the changes that have occurred in recent years in the Bethel area. Begun on a small scale by entrepreneur Les Otten, the mega-resort is now the flagship of the giant American Skiing Company (ASC), nearly the nation's largest ski-resort corporation. And there's no sign of a let-up; ASC has expanded well beyond New England into the Western U.S. ski market. In 1997, ASC holdings included Sugarloaf/USA in Maine; Attitash Bear Peak in New Hampshire; Killington, Mount Snow, Haystack, and Sugarbush in Vermont; Steamboat in Colorado; Heavenly in California

(on the Nevada border); and Wolf Mountain in Utah. Frequent-skier cards and all-mountain season passes encourage trying all the resorts.

But let's back up a bit. Bethel's "modern" history dates from 1774, when settlers from Sudbury, Massachusetts, called it Sudbury Canada, a name reflected in the annual August Sudbury Canada Days festival. Another present-day festival, Mollyockett Day, commemorates one of the area's most intriguing historical figures, a Pequawket Indian woman named Mollyockett, who practiced herbal medicine among turn-of-the-19th-century settlers, including a baby named Hannibal Hamlin, her remedies snatching from death in 1809 Abraham Lincoln's future vice president. (The incident actually occurred in the Hamlin home on Paris Hill, southeast of Bethel.) Mollyockett died August 2, 1816, and is buried in the Woodlawn Cemetery on Rt. 5 in Andover.

Meanwhile, the name Bethel surfaced in 1796, when the town was incorporated. Agriculture sustained the community for another half a century, until the Atlantic and St. Lawrence Railroad connected Bethel to Portland in 1851 (and later to Montreal) and access to major markets shifted the economic focus toward timber and wood products, which remain significant even today.

North of Bethel, Andover (pop. 950) has become a word-of-mouth favorite among through-hikers and section hikers on the Appalachian Trail, which snakes by about eight miles to the west. It's Maine's southernmost town near the AT, and the hikers pile in here in August and September.

East of Bethel are the communities of Locke Mills (officially in the town of Greenwood, pop. 710) and Bryant Pond (in the town of Woodstock, pop. 1,245), both with summer and winter recreational attractions. Northeast of Bethel is Rumford (pop. 6,880), a paper-manufacturing center whose favorite son was former Secretary of State Edmund Muskie.

SIGHTS

Covered Bridges
Often called the **Artist's Covered Bridge**—because so many artists have committed it to canvas—an 1872 wooden structure stands alongside a quiet country road north of the Sunday River Ski Resort. In winter, one of the Sunday River Inn's cross-country-skiing trails ends at the bridge—a great way to see it. Kids love running back and forth across the unused bridge, and in summer they can swim below in the Sunday River. The bridge is 5.7 miles northwest of Bethel; take Rt. 2 toward Newry, turn left at the Sunday River Rd., then bear right at the fork. The bridge is well signposted, just beyond a small cemetery.

About 20 miles north of Bethel, the **Lovejoy Bridge,** in South Andover, built in 1867, is one of the lesser-visited of Maine's nine covered bridges. It's also the shortest. Spanning the Ellis River, a tributary of the Androscoggin, the 70-foot-long bridge is a quarter of a mile east of Rt. 5, but not visible from the highway; it's about seven and a half miles north of Rumford Point. In summer, local kids use the swimming hole just below the bridge.

Dr. Moses Mason House
Listed on the National Historic Register, the 1813 Federal-style Dr. Moses Mason House, Bethel Common, P.O. Box 12, Bethel 04217, tel. (207) 824-2908, not only is a beautifully restored eight-room museum but also serves as the headquarters of the very active **Bethel Historical Society.** Particularly significant are the hall murals painted by noted itinerant muralist Rufus Porter or his nephew Jonathan Poor. Dr. Moses Mason, a local physician, was elected to the U.S. Congress a dozen years after Maine statehood and served two terms as a Maine congressman. The museum is open Tues.-Sun. 1-4 p.m., July to Labor Day, and by appointment other months.

Bethel Historic District
At the Dr. Moses Mason House, or at the chamber of commerce, pick up a copy of the brochure entitled, *A Walking Tour of Bethel Hill Village,* detailing information on 26 buildings and monu-

"Artist's Bridge," Newry

ments in the downtown area's Historic District. Officially, more than 60 structures are included in the district. Follow the self-guided route (allow about an hour) to appreciate the 19th- and 20th-century architecture that gives real cachet to Bethel's heart.

Flightseeing

Bethel Air Service, Northwest Bethel Rd., P.O. Box 786, Bethel 04217, tel. (207) 824-4321 or 758-0823, runs on-demand scenic flights daily, all year, but the best time is mid-September to early October, for the parade of leaf colors. A 20-minute flight along the Sunday River and over the Jordan Bowl is $20 pp or $50 per planeload (three persons maximum); an hour-long flight west toward the Mount Washington Valley is $75 a planeload. Call for reservations. Based at the airport on the outskirts of town, the air service is open daily 8 a.m.-8 p.m. in summer, 8 a.m.-5 p.m. in winter.

PARKS AND PRESERVES

Step Falls Preserve

The Nature Conservancy's first Maine acquisition (in 1962), 24-acre Step Falls Preserve, Rt. 26, Newry, mailing address The Nature Conservancy, Maine Chapter, Fort Andross, 14 Maine St., Brunswick 04011, tel. (207) 729-5181, is ideal for family hiking—an easy, one-hour roundtrip through the woods alongside an impressive series of cascades and pools. Pick up a trail map at the parking-lot box. Bring a picnic and have lunch on the rocks along the way. The waterfalls are most dramatic in late spring; the foliage is most spectacular in fall; the footing can be dicey in winter. Trailhead for the preserve is on Rt. 26, eight miles northwest of Rt. 2 and 10 miles southeast of the New Hampshire border. Watch for The Nature Conservancy oakleaf sign on the right, next to Wight Brook.

Grafton Notch State Park

Nestled in the mountains of western Maine, 3,192-acre Grafton Notch State Park, Rt. 26, Grafton Township, mailing address HC 61, Box 330, Newry 04261, tel. (207) 824-2912, boasts splendid hiking trails, spectacular geological for-

mations (some, such as **Screw Auger Falls,** almost in the drive-by category), and plenty of space for peace and quiet. It's hard to say enough about this lovely park, a must-visit. Bring a picnic.

Best hike here is the **Table Rock Loop,** a two-and-a-half-mile, moderate-to-strenuous two-hour circuit from the main trailhead (signposted Hiking Trails) at the edge of Rt. 26. The trailhead parking area is four miles inside the park's southern boundary and .8 mile beyond the Moose Cave parking area. Part of the route follows the white-blazed Appalachian Trail, otherwise the trail is orange- and blue-blazed. Some really steep sections are indeed a challenge, but it's well worth the climb for the dramatic mountain views from aptly named Table Rock.

Another favorite hike, moderate to strenuous, goes up **Old Speck Mountain** (4,180 feet), third highest of Maine's 10 4,000-footers and part of the Mahoosuc Range. The 28-foot-high viewing platform on the recently restored fire tower gets you above the wooded summit for incredible 360-degree views of the White Mountains, the Mahoosuc Range, and other mountains and lakes. Allow a solid seven hours for the eight-mile roundtrip from the trailhead on the west side of Rt. 26 in Grafton Notch. The route follows the white-blazed Appalachian Trail most of the way; the tower is about a quarter of a mile off the AT. Although there's a route map at the trailhead (same location as for the Table Rock hike), the best trail guide for this hike is in John Gibson's *50 Hikes in Southern and Coastal Maine,* 2nd edition (see the Booklist).

Park admission is $1 adults, 50 cents children 5-11; payment is on the honor system. Fee boxes are posted at Screw Auger Falls and the main hiking trailhead. The park is officially open mid-May through mid-October, but Screw Auger Falls is easily accessible off season.

If you're driving along Rt. 26 early or late in the day, keep a lookout for moose; have your camera ready and exercise extreme caution. You'll usually spot them in boggy areas, munching on aquatic plants, but when they decide to cross a highway, watch out—they don't look both ways. And their eyes don't reflect headlights, so be vigilant after dark. Moose-car collisions are often fatal—to both moose and motorists.

The Mahoosuc Range

South and east of Grafton Notch State Park is a 27,253-acre chunk of Maine Public Reserve Land known as **The Mahoosucs,** or the Mahoosuc Range, where the hiking is rugged and strenuous but the scenic rewards are inestimable. The Appalachian Trail traverses much of the reserve, and AT hikers insist that the mile-long Mahoosuc Notch section, between Old Speck and Goose Eye Mountains, is one of their biggest challenges on the 2,158-mile Georgia-to-Maine route, requiring steep ascents and descents, with insecure footing, gigantic boulders, and narrow passages. If you're an experienced hiker, go for it, and use reliable guidebooks and maps, preferably USGS maps. The best overview of the reserve is *Recreational Opportunities in the Mahoosuc Mountains,* a free foldout map/brochure available from the Bureau of Parks and Lands, 22 State House Station, Augusta 04333, tel. (207) 287-3821. The helpful brochure lists and characterizes trails, lists campsites, and provides info on wildlife, vegetation, and water supplies.

White Mountain National Forest

Just under 50,000 acres (49,800 to be exact) of the 770,000-acre White Mountain National Forest lie on the Maine side of the New Hampshire border. Route 113, roughly paralleling the border, bisects the **Caribou-Speckled Mountain Wilderness,** the designated name for this part of the national forest. It's all dramatically scenic, with terrific opportunities for hiking, camping, picnicking, swimming, and fishing. For details, see "Information and Services," below.

A drive along Rt. 113, north to south between Gilead and Stow, is worth the detour. It takes about 30 minutes nonstop, but bring a picnic and enjoy the mountain views from the tables at the Cold River Overlook, about a mile south of the Evans Notch highpoint. Route 113 is too narrow for bikes in mid-summer, when logging trucks and visitor traffic can be fairly dense. Save this bike tour for a fall weekday, and take it south

to north for a good downhill run from Evans Notch. The road is closed in winter.

RECREATION

Hiking

Much of the hiking in this area is within the various parks and preserves, but a fun family hike is the easy-to-moderate ascent of **Mt. Will** in Newry, on the outskirts of Bethel. The Bethel Conservation Commission has developed a 3.2-mile loop trail that provides mountain and river views; allow about two and a half hours to do the loop. At the chamber of commerce information center, pick up a Mt. Will trail-map brochure, which explains three different hiking options. There also may be maps at the trailhead, which is on the west side of Rt. 2/26, 1.9 miles north of the Riverside Rest Area—a terrific spot, incidentally, for a post-hike picnic next to the Androscoggin River.

Mountain Biking

The North Peak and South Ridge chairlifts whisk you up to the **Sunday River Mountain Bike Park,** tel. (207) 824-3000, where 60 miles of trails provide stellar downhill and cross-country biking. South Ridge accesses the easier trails, North Peak the more strenuous ones. In late July and early August, if you're headed for expert terrain, bring a bag or container and help yourself to wild blueberries along the ridge between Locke Mountain and White Cap.

The park opens in late May, but the lifts operate only on weekends until mid-June. From mid-June to Labor Day, they operate daily, then back to weekends-only through Columbus Day. Some years, the lift-serviced upper trails aren't usable until at least early June, so it's worth calling ahead to check. Park hours are 8 a.m.-4 p.m.; lift hours are 9 a.m.-3 p.m. All-day trail passes are $22.

Bike rentals are available at the **Great American Bike Rental Company,** Sunday River Rd., Bethel 04217, tel. (207) 824-

BOB RACE

3092, which also arranges guided bike trips. **Bethel Outdoor Adventures,** 121 Mayville Rd., Rt. 2, Bethel 04217, tel. (207) 824-4224 or (800) 533-3607, fax (207) 836-2708, also rents bikes.

Canoeing
The rivers in the Bethel area are a paddler's dream, ranging from beginner/family stretches to whitewater sections for intermediate and advanced canoeists. Fortunately, the major artery, the **Androscoggin River,** seldom has low-water problems, and you'll see lots of islands, as well as eagles, moose, and a beaver dam. West of Bethel, there's even an old cable from a one-time ferry crossing. The best source of information on the Androscoggin is Bethel Outdoor Adventures (BOA), 121 Mayville Rd., Rt. 2, Bethel 04217, tel. (207) 824-4224 or (800) 533-3607, fax (207) 836-2708, a firm founded in 1990. They'll provide canoe rentals, maps, shuttle service, and trip-planning advice. In addition, the BOA staff, especially Jeff and Pattie Parsons, can advise on canoeing the Ellis, Little Androscoggin, and Sunday Rivers.

Also see "Festivals and Events," below, for information on the annual Androscoggin River Source to the Sea Canoe Trek, a celebration of the river's revival from years of unbridled pollution caused primarily by paper-mill runoff.

Just east of Locke Mills, before the Littlefield Beaches Campground, you can put in at **Round Pond,** on the south side of Rt. 26, and continue on into North and South Ponds. Bring a picnic and before you head out, enjoy it across the road at the lovely state rest area, with grills and covered picnic tables in a wooded setting.

Veteran professional guides Polly Mahoney and Kevin Slater of **Mahoosuc Guide Service,** Box 245, Bear River Rd., Newry 04261, tel. (207) 824-2073, lead wilderness canoe trips not in the Bethel area but on the Allagash, Penobscot, and St. John Rivers, as well as in Quebec. With extensive wilderness backgrounds in such locales as Labrador and the Yukon Territory, management experience with Outward Bound, and a commitment to Native American traditions, Polly and Kevin are ideal trip leaders. Request a brochure with their schedules and rates.

Golf
Thanks to its spectacular setting, the 18-hole championship course at the **Bethel Inn & Country Club,** Bethel Common, Bethel 04217, tee times tel. (207) 824-6276, wows every golfer who plays here. Starting times are needed. In summer, luncheon ($5-6 sandwiches, $5-8 salad plates) is served on the inn's Mill Brook Terrace, overlooking the course. Special golf packages are available, including meals and several lodging options. Best bargains are mid-September through October, when the fall foliage is a bonus. The course is open early May through October.

Llama Trekking
In 1988, Steve Crone introduced llama trekking to Maine, and he's still at it, even more enthusiastically, offering one-day and multi-day trips in the White Mountain National Forest. Be forewarned, though: You'll be hiking *with* the llamas, not *on* them; they tote the gear. Schedules can vary, so call well ahead to reserve. Most popular choice is the **Scenic Day Trek,** a 4- to 6-hour hike departing about 9:30 a.m. from the Telemark Inn, 10 miles west of Bethel. Cost is $85 adults, $65 children 14 and under, including a buffet lunch en route.

Basic rooms are available at Steve's casually rustic **Telemark Inn Wilderness Lodge** ($90 d in spring, summer, and fall, including breakfast), where lots of possible lodging/ trekking packages incorporate nature hikes, mountain biking, canoeing, or llama treks. Three- to seven-day activity packages are $399-795 per adult, including meals; a six-day mountains-and-lakes llama trek is $950 per adult. In winter, cross-country skiing, and sleigh rides are on the schedule. Steve has also introduced skijoring, a fun sport best compared to mushing without a sled. Strap on your skis, strap yourself into a harness, and a couple of huskies whisk you off on the trails. For more information, contact The Telemark Inn Wilderness Lodge, King's Highway, RFD 2, Box 800, Bethel 04217, tel. (207) 836-2703.

Winter Sports
Sprawling octopus-like over eight mountains, **Sunday River Ski Resort,** Sunday River Rd., Newry, mailing address P.O. Box 450, Bethel

04217, tel. (207) 824-3000 or (800) 543-2754, fax (207) 824-2111, snow phone (207) 824-6400, defines the winter sports scene in this area, with world-class downhill skiing and snowboarding, ice-skating, access to nordic skiing, phenomenal snowmaking capability, slopeside lodging, and every possible amenity. The mega-resort has nine quads, four triples, two doubles, and two surface lifts serving 126 trails and glades, including more than 14 miles of expert terrain. Highest vertical drop is 2,340 feet, about 500 feet lower than at Sugarloaf/USA—long a competitive rival but now under the same American Skiing Company corporate umbrella.

Sunday River's trademarked Perfect Turn ski clinics, pegged as "skier development," have created hordes of enthusiastic new skiers and smoothed the style of intermediate skiers. And the resort's Learn-to-Ski in One Day Program is more than just a slogan. It works.

Sunday River has day-care facilities ($42 a

Sunday River Ski Resort is only one of Maine's superb ski venues.

MAINE OFFICE OF TOURISM

day, including lunch; reservations advised), ski school for kids, an excellent inventory of top-of-the-line rental skis and snowboards, free on-mountain trolleybus service, and plenty of places, with a wide range of prices, to grab a snack or a meal. Lift tickets for the 1997-98 season were $47 per weekend day for adults ($44 midweek), $29 per weekend day for children 6-12, $28 midweek. Kids five and under ski free. Lift tickets are included in most lodging packages.

The ski season usually runs mid-October to early May, weather permitting (average annual snowfall is 155 inches; the 1996-97 season had 177 inches). Lift hours are weekdays 9 a.m.-4 p.m., weekends and holidays 8 a.m.-4 p.m. Especially on weekends and during school vacations, make every effort to avoid the opening and closing hours for buying lift tickets, renting skis, or heading home; the congestion can be maddening. There's only one road on and off the mountain, so expect delays early and late in the day.

Mt. Abram: For anyone weak in the wallet or overawed by Sunday River, there's help about 12 miles to the east. **Ski Mt. Abram,** Howe Hill Rd., off Rt. 26, Locke Mills 04255, tel. (207) 875-5003, a low-key, well-managed, family-oriented ski area where the vertical drop is a respectable-enough 1,030 feet. Two double-chairlifts and three T-bars serve 36 trails, almost half intermediate level. Adult weekend lift tickets are a very reasonable $29. Snowmaking coverage is almost 80%, top to bottom, and 12 trails are lighted for night skiing Thurs.-Sat. and during school vacations (tickets $16). In addition to a ski school, rentals, 600-foot snow-tubing park, and ice-skating rink, Mt. Abram has such facilities as day care, cafeteria, and the new Westside Lodge. The management has also carved out a niche in Telemarking (nordic downhill on metal-edged skis). One day a month during the ski season, there's a Telemark demo clinic, and regular one-day Telemark packages (about $30, including skis, lesson, and lift ticket) are always available. Unlike other ski areas, Mt. Abram has not been distracted by rushing to build slopeside housing; see "Accommodations," below, for help finding lodging close to the mountain.

Nordic Skiing: The **Sunday River Cross Country Ski Center,** Skiway Access Rd., RFD

2, Box 1688, Bethel 04217, tel. (207) 824-2410, fax 824-3181, based at the independent Sunday River Inn, is not officially part of the Sunday River operation, but it's conveniently only half a mile away. Nearly 25 miles of lovely, well-groomed wooded trails extend out from the center. The best one leads from the lodge to the Artist's Covered Bridge. A clever innovation is the free *Kids' Trail Map*, showing locations of special surprises along the trails (totem pole, wind chimes, and more). Trail passes are $12 adults, $6 children 12 and under; ski rentals ($15 a day) are available in the small lodge, which also has a snack bar.

Right in downtown Bethel, the **Bethel Inn Touring Center**, Bethel Common, P.O. Box 49, Bethel 04217, tel. (207) 824-6276, uses its scenic golf course for nearly 25 miles of novice-to-advanced cross-country trails. In the health club are fitness machines and a sauna; outside is a heated pool. (Unless you're staying at the inn, for which special lodging packages are available, you won't have access to the health club after 4 p.m. or on Saturday or during school vacation weeks.) Ski rentals ($12 a day) are available, as are private and group lessons. Trail passes are $12 adults, $6 children.

About 33 miles of trails wind through a thousand acres at **Carter's Cross-Country Ski Center**, Middle Intervale Rd., Bethel 04217, tel. (207) 824-3880, owned and managed by Carter's Cross-Country Ski Center in Oxford, tel. (207) 539-4848. In winter, the Bethel location operates two lodges, ski and snowshoe rentals, a ski shop, and snack bar. Trail passes are $10 adults, $6 children under 18.

The Telemark Inn (see "Accommodations," below) also maintains cross-country trails.

Ice-Skating: Picture an old-fashioned Currier & Ives winter landscape, with skaters skimming a snow-circled pond, and you'll come close to the scene on Bethel Common in winter. Bring a camera. The groomed ice-skating area, in the downtown Historic District, usually is ready for skaters by Christmas vacation. Also see details above on Sunday River Ski Resort and Mt. Abram, both of which have ice-skating rinks. Skating is free at Sunday River, where the rink is open daily 8 a.m.-10 p.m.; skate rentals are available.

Mushing: When they're not off leading 2- to 5-day dogsledding trips on Richardson, Umbagog, or Chesuncook Lake ($325-725 pp), or even with the Inuit on Baffin Island ($2,500 pp), Kevin Slater and Polly Mahoney of **Mahoosuc Guide Service**, Box 245, Bear River Rd., Newry 04261, tel. (207) 824-2073, will bundle you in a deerskin blanket and take you on a one-day dogsled trip on Umbagog Lake, beyond Grafton Notch State Park. Wear goggles or sunglasses; the dogs kick up the snow. A campfire lunch and warm drinks are included in the $115 pp fee. For an extra $110, you can drive your own dog team. Trips are available late December into March; reservations are required.

ENTERTAINMENT

The **Mahoosuc Arts Council** (MAC), P.O. Box 534, Bethel 04217, tel. (207) 824-3575, sponsors more than a dozen performances throughout the year, plus about a dozen art residencies and other cultural events in local schools. An additional source of MAC schedule information is the Bethel Area Chamber of Commerce.

Part of the new Bethel Station complex, the four-screen **Casablanca Cinema**, Cross St., Bethel 04217, tel. (207) 824-8248, was the first step in an ambitious downtown Renaissance. In addition to two nightly showings in each space, there are usually two matinees on Saturday and Sunday. Monday is bargain night ($4 tickets). Open all year.

Next to the cinema, **Rick's Deli**, tel. (207) 824-4390, is a New York-style deli for eating in or takeout; sandwiches are huge. In summer, there's even an ice cream parlor. Above it is a video arcade, with pool tables. The whole operation is open daily 11 a.m.-10 p.m., all year.

At **Sunday River Ski Resort**, there's live entertainment in several locations weekends and during school vacations.

FESTIVALS AND EVENTS

During the ski season, both Sunday River Ski Resort and Carter's Cross Country Ski Center in Bethel schedule a number of ski races, festivals, and other special events. Check with the resort and the center or with the Bethel Area Chamber of Commerce. For more happenings within easy driving distance, see the events listings for the Rangeley Lakes Area, Oxford Hills, and Sebago and Long Lakes.

The annual three-mile **Carter's Last Stand Cross-Country Ski Race** begins at 1 p.m. at Carter's Cross Country Ski Center, Bethel, January 1.

On the nearest March or April Saturday to April Fools' Day, Bethel's **April Fools' Pole, Paddle, and Paw Race** pits two-person triathlon teams against one another in nordic skiing, canoeing, and snowshoeing.

The first or second weekend of June, the annual three-day **Trek Across Maine: Sunday River to the Sea** draws nearly 2,000 cyclists for the 180-mile bike expedition from Bethel to Rockport, proceeds from which benefit the Maine Lung Association. Registrations are accepted on a first-come, first-served basis, and the trek usually is fully booked by April. Pledges are required, and there's a $40 registration fee. Call (800) 458-6472 for details. Don't like cycling? Perhaps the **Androscoggin River Source to the Sea Canoe Trek** is more your style: the annual 19-day paddle (last weekend in June to mid-July) from the New Hampshire headwaters to Fort Popham, near Bath—about 170 miles—is open to all canoeists, who can participate from one to all 19 days. Requested contribution is $10 per boat, to benefit the Androscoggin Land Trust, tel. (207) 782-2302.

Bethel's **Annual Gem, Mineral, and Jewelry Show** is a long-running event with exhibits, demonstrations, and sales of almost everything imaginable in the rock-and-gem line—even guided field trips to nearby quarries. Hours are Saturday 9 a.m.-5 p.m. and Sunday 10 a.m.-4 p.m.; small admission charge. It takes place at Telstar Regional High School the second weekend in July. The third Saturday in July, on Bethel Common in downtown Bethel, **Mollyockett Day** commemorates a legendary turn-of-the-19th-century Indian healer with a parade, races, children's activities, a craft fair, food booths, and fireworks.

Andover presents a parade, live entertainment, children's games, art and flower shows, a barbecue, and a beanhole bean supper the first Friday evening and Saturday and Sunday in August as part of **Andover Old Home Days.** The second weekend that month at the Moses Mason House in Bethel, **Sudbury Canada Days** commemorates Bethel's earliest settlers with traditional crafts, an art show, parade, bean supper, and contra dance.

Maine artisans take center stage in the annual display and sale at the **Blue Mountain Arts and Crafts Festival,** the second weekend in October at the Sunday River Ski Resort, Newry.

SHOPPING

Gifts and Crafts

Hidden behind the Italianate facade of a 19th-century National Historic Register mansion is—believe it or not—an upscale mini-mall with a superb collection of boutiques. At **Philbrook Place,** 162 Main St., Bethel 04217, tel. (207) 824-2997, you can check off an entire shopping list in the specialty shops selling antiques, books, music, toys, cards, jewelry, clothing, accessories, cookware, gourmet foodstuffs, and sporting gear. The shops are open daily, all year, but hours are extended during ski season.

Check out the strikingly unusual designs and glazes at **Bonnema Potters,** 146 Main St., P.O. Box 53, Bethel 04217, tel. (207) 824-2821, located in a handsomely restored studio across the street from The Sudbury Inn. Best of all are the earth colors used on tiles, dishes, vases, and lamps. The shop is open May-March, Thurs.-Tues. 9:30 a.m.-5:30 p.m.

If something a bit more offbeat appeals, stop in for Moose-Drop earrings ($5.95 a pair), allegedly the gen-u-ine article, at **Maine Line Products,** 23 Main St., P.O. Box 356, Bethel 04217, tel. (207) 824-2522, source of whimsical souvenirs for your whimsical friends. In the same vein is the "Lobsta Parts Jewelry," but Maine Line also carries serious gifts, such as jams, syrup, buckets, and wind chimes. The shop is open all year, Mon.-Sat. 9 a.m.-5 p.m. (to 8 p.m. in summer). In 1997, owner Richard Whitney expanded his Maine Line empire to a former supermarket on Rt. 26 in Locke Mills, tel. (800) 874-0484. The "branch" shop, triple the size of the Bethel store, is open all year, Mon.-Sat. 9 a.m.-5 p.m.

Rock Shops

At **Mt. Mann,** 57 Main St. Place, P.O. Box 597, Bethel 04217, tel. (207) 824-3030, Jim Mann wears the hats of owner, miner, gemcutter, and jeweler, and he's full of information in every category. Here's the Bethel area's best place to see Maine's special gems: **tourmaline** (the official state mineral), aquamarine, amethyst, and morganite. The shop also has a basement "crystal cave," where kids can "discover" minerals and learn to identify them. For 25 cents, Jim sells maps to area mines and quarries open to the public. Inquire about guided quarry tours. The shop is open all year, 9 a.m.-5 p.m. Mon.-Fri. and 10 a.m.-5 p.m. Saturday.

Also see **Oxford Hills** for information on Perham's of West Paris, Maine's mother of all rock shops.

General Store

Even if you don't really need an end-of-the-road sub or hot dog, or a bowl of chili, it's worth driving to **The Upton Trading Post,** Rt. 26, Upton 04261, tel. (207) 533-2411, just to admire the smashing view down over Umbagog Lake. This old-fashioned general-store-cum-café is open all year, Mon.-Sat. 7 a.m.-9 p.m. and Sunday 8 a.m.-8 p.m. It's beyond Grafton Notch State Park, right on the New Hampshire border, about 27 miles from Bethel.

Health Food / Farmers' Market

The **Good Food Store,** Rt. 2, P.O. Box 467, Bethel 04217, tel. (207) 824-3754, stocks a huge array of goodies, from organic produce to healthful munchies to cookbooks to gourmet condiments. Create an instant picnic with sandwiches, beer, and wine. And if you're renting a condo, you can pick up homemade soups, stews, and casseroles to go. The barn-based shop is open all year, daily 9 a.m.-7 p.m.

Each Saturday, 9 a.m.-noon, between mid-June and mid-October, the **Bethel Farmers' Market** sells good-for-you produce and other items on Rt. 26, Railroad St., in the new Bethel Station complex at the southern edge of town.

ACCOMMODATIONS

Conveniently, the **Bethel Area Reservation Service,** tel. (800) 442-5826, provides toll-free lodging assistance for more than a thousand beds in B&Bs, motels, condos, and inns in Bethel, at Sunday River Ski Resort, and farther afield. If you're planning a winter visit, however, particularly during Thanksgiving and Christmas holidays, February school vacation, and the month of March, don't wait until the last minute. Procrastination will put you in a bed 40 miles from the slopes. The service is run by the Bethel Area Chamber of Commerce.

Sunday River Lodging

On the mountain at Sunday River Ski Resort, lodging options include more than 400 rooms and suites in two full-service condo hotels— **The Summit** and the new **Jordan Grand Hotel**—as well as more than 700 slopeside condos and townhouses. Nicest (and priciest) of the latter are the Locke Mountain Townhouses. The spiffy Jordan Grand, opened in December 1997, has two restaurants, an outdoor heated pool, video game room, and lots of extra amenities. Most of its rooms have full kitchen facilities. Least expensive lodgings are the bunk rooms at the Snow Cap Ski Dorm ($25 pp midweek, $35 pp weekend). Except for dorm rooms, lodging packages include lift tickets. For information, call (207) 824-3000; reservations: (800) 543-2754.

Country Inns

The Bethel Inn & Country Club, Bethel Common, P.O. Box 49, Bethel 04217, tel. (207) 824-2175 or (800) 654-0125, fax (207) 824-2233, centerpiece of a classic New England village scene, has 57 inn rooms and 40 modern one- and two-bedroom townhouses ($140-290 d in winter, $160-300 d in summer). Lowest rates are mid-May to mid-June ($120-260 d) and November to mid-December ($120-180 d). All rates are MAP, including dinner in the inn's elegant restaurant (candlelight and piano music; no blue jeans or T-shirts). The restaurant is open to the public daily (entrées $14-22, New England cooking, good wine list), and dinner reservations are advisable. The inn's Mill Terrace Tavern, over-looking the golf course/ski trails, serves light meals in an informal setting; a pianist usually appears around 9 p.m. Friday and Saturday. Lots of special packages are available, combining skiing or golf. All rooms include free use of the health club, with saunas, outdoor heated pool, and workout room. In winter, there's a free daily shuttle to Sunday River Ski Resort. Open all year, but the restaurant may be closed some nights in April and November.

Rustic Country Inns
Only half a mile from Sunday River Ski Resort, the **Sunday River Inn,** Skiway Access Rd., RFD 2, Box 1688, Bethel 04217, tel. (207) 824-2410, fax 824-3181, caters to families with its casual, homey atmosphere and generous buffet-style meals. Most of the 18 rooms have shared baths. A big plus is the Sunday River Cross Country Ski Center right on the premises; trail passes are included in the room rates ($130-156 d, with breakfast and dinner; BYOL). Dorm bunks (bring your own sleeping bag) are $42 pp, MAP. Open only in winter.

B&Bs
The hospitality and breakfasts are legendary at **The Chapman Inn,** Bethel Common, Broad and Main Sts., P.O. Box 206, Bethel 04217, tel./fax (207) 824-2657, an informal B&B in the heart of historic Bethel and just 10 minutes from the Sunday River ski area. In summer, you'll have access to the inn's private beach on Songo Pond, about five minutes away. Eight rooms (private and shared baths) are $45-55 d in summer, $55-65 d midweek in winter, and $75-85 d weekends in winter. One efficiency is $95 d in winter. Children under 12 are only $5 extra. The on-site sauna is a big hit after skiing, biking, or hiking. A 24-bed dormitory wing, popular with skiers, has rustic accommodations, a game room with cable TV, and reasonable rates ($30 pp, including breakfast). No pets, no smoking. Open all year.

In 1994, after 10 months of renovation, Gary and Carol Brearley opened **The Briar Lea B&B,** 150 Mayville Rd., Rt. 2/26, Bethel 04217, tel. (207) 824-4717, fax 824-7121, an outstanding B&B between downtown Bethel and the Sunday River ski area. Decor and details are topnotch in

the 1845 house; wine and cheese are served afternoons in the huge, welcoming parlor. Six attractive rooms (private baths) are $90 d January to mid-April, $59 d other months. Full breakfast is included. In summer, request a back-facing room if noise bothers you—the highway is active. In the adjoining barn is a 40-seat restaurant, open to the public for moderately priced breakfasts and dinners. Reduced-rate ski packages are available, and you can save time by buying your lift tickets from the Brearleys. No smoking. Pets are allowed. Open all year.

Established in 1982, **The Douglass Place,** 162 Mayville Rd., Rt. 2, Bethel 04217, tel. (207) 824-2229, was the first B&B in western Maine, soon followed by countless others. Barbara Douglass has a grandmotherly flair in her homey, quiet place. Four comfortable rooms (all with TVs) share two and a half baths; rates are a very reasonable $60 d. Breakfast is continental-plus; no one leaves hungry. Guests have the run of the house, including use of a pool table, a piano, and a jacuzzi. Children are welcome. No pets, limited smoking. Only credit card is American Express; checks or cash are preferable. Open all year except Christmas, two weeks in late October, and two weeks in late April.

In Bethel's Historic District, near the Bethel Common, **The Red Geranium Bed & Breakfast,** 28 Broad St., P.O. Box 598, Bethel 04217, tel. (207) 824-3771, an 1853 Greek Revival home, has three good-size, antiques-furnished rooms ($75 d, two and a half shared baths). Lower rates are available off season. Guests are welcome in the cozy living room and the backyard gardens, and in winter there's ice-skating on the Common. Breakfast is continental. No smoking, no pets, no children under 12. Open all year.

The Norseman Inn and Motel
Two buildings—a 200-year-old inn and a century-old converted barn—make up The Norseman Inn and Motel, Rt. 2, 134 Mayville Rd., HC 61, Box 50, Bethel 04217, tel. (207) 824-2002, two miles north of Bethel. Family-run and family-oriented, it's one of Bethel's most popular motel-style lodgings. The inn has nine second-floor rooms (five with private baths; four share two baths), all nonsmoking. In the barn/motel are 22 first- and second-floor rooms (private

baths), most nonsmoking; one has wheelchair access. Also in the barn are a game room and coin-operated laundry room. A complimentary expanded-continental breakfast is served in one of the inn's lovely old first-floor rooms, next to a fireplace built of stones from all over the world. Rates vary by season, $49-128 d; winter is highest. Open all year.

The Maine House and the Maine FarmHouse
In a category all their own are The Maine House and The Maine FarmHouse, Lake Rd., Bryant Pond, tel. (800) 646-8737, two attentively renovated buildings a block apart on a side road in Bryant Pond. Under a quirkily successful arrangement with no resident innkeepers or managers, the two houses cater primarily to groups but also are open to families or even individuals. Everyone shares the spacious kitchen facilities, typically with interesting dynamics. The success may be due in part to the 60-page guest handbook, which provides detailed instructions for using the facilities, emergency numbers, and extensive advice on restaurants, shops, and activities. The Maine House, right on Lake Christopher with its own small beach, has eight rooms (private and shared baths) in a variety of configurations; the Maine FarmHouse, a more modern facility closer to Rt. 26, has seven rooms. All kinds of price configurations are possible, depending on sleeping arrangements and season; minimums are imposed during school-vacation weeks. Average costs are $44-90 d, higher for suites and holidays. Kids under 14 stay free in parents' room. No smoking, no pets. Both houses have coin-operated laundry rooms; linens are provided. Open all year. The houses are just off Rt. 26 in Bryant Pond.

Campgrounds
Riverside Campground, 121 Mayville Rd., Rt. 2, Bethel 04217, tel. (207) 824-4224 or (800) 533-3607, fax (207) 836-2708, newest campground in the area and closest to downtown Bethel, has 20 RV ($18 per site) and five tent ($14) sites on the banks of the Androscoggin River north of downtown Bethel. The family-oriented campground is under the same ownership as **Bethel Outdoor Adventures** (BOA), a recreational backup operation providing gear rentals and guided tours. Canoe rentals are $25 a day, mountain bikes are $20 a day, and BOA will shuttle you upriver on the Androscoggin for a leisurely downstream paddle. Both the campground and BOA are open daily, May through October.

Well-maintained **Littlefield Beaches Campground,** Rt. 26, Locke Mills, mailing address RR 2, Box 4300, Bryant Pond 04219, tel. (207) 875-3290, catering primarily to the RV trade, has a terrific 40-acre location with a sandy beach on South Pond. Facilities include a playground, store, and coin-operated laundry room. Canoe rentals are available. Rules are enforced, including the campground's ban on water scooters (PWCs). Pets are allowed, but not on the beach; the store has pooper-scoopers you can borrow. Rate is $18 per site for two, July to Labor Day; off-season rate is $15. Open Memorial Day weekend through September.

On Rt. 113, west of Bethel, is the seven-acre **Hastings Campground,** one of several campgrounds in the White Mountain National Forest. The 24-site campground is primitive, with no hookups or showers. Route 113 is especially scenic, so this is a prime location for extensive hiking in the national forest. Trail information and maps are available from the Evans Notch Ranger District office (see "Information and Services," below). The campground is in Gilead, three miles south of Rt. 2. Fee is $10 per site, for up to eight people (for reservations call 207-824-2134). Each Saturday night (7:30 or 8 p.m.), between early July and Labor Day, the Forest Service sponsors free lectures here on natural-history or historic topics. Open mid-May to mid-October.

Seasonal Rentals
For weekly or monthly seasonal rentals, winter or summer, contact **Rentals Unlimited,** 2 Main St., Bethel 04217, tel. (207) 824-4044 or (800) 535-2220. Options include B&Bs, inns, condos, motels, and private houses. For school-vacation weeks, be sure to call well ahead, or your choices will be more limited than unlimited.

The **Bethel Area Reservation Service,** tel. (800) 442-5826, also can arrange seasonal rentals.

FOOD

On the mountain at Sunday River Ski Resort, your choices are snack bars, pubs, an Italian restaurant, a steakhouse, and casually fancy hotel restaurants.

Miscellanea

A fine addition to Bethel's food scene, **Matterhorn Wood-Fired Pizza and Fresh Pasta,** Cross St., Bethel 04217, tel. (207) 824-6836, is just down the street from the Casablanca Cinema. A half-dozen Swiss-inspired pizzas—such as the Zermatt, with chicken, spinach, feta, mozzarella, and pesto—go for $7-10. Also on the menu are fondue, homemade soup, salads, creative pasta dishes, and high-cal desserts. No smoking. Open Thanksgiving Weekend to early April, daily 4:30-10 p.m.

Part of a Maine chain founded in Orono, **Pat's Pizza,** Rt. 2, Bethel 04217, tel. (207) 824-3637, has a quasi-lumberjack theme. Choose from more than four dozen hot and cold subs ($3-6), or 14-inch pizzas in the $7-14 range; gourmet 14-inchers are $13-14. "Little Logger Portions" are for kids under 12. Smoking in the bar, but not in the dining room. Pat's is open all year, daily 11 a.m.-9 p.m. (to 10 p.m. Friday and Saturday).

Inexpensive to Moderate

A homey atmosphere, reliable food, and friendly service have made **Mother's,** Main St., P.O. Box 771, Bethel 04217, tel. (207) 824-2589, a popular destination ever since it opened. The something-for-everyone menu includes an imaginative wok pocket sandwich, a stew pot in a bread bowl, as well as traditional burgers and omelettes. On the first floor of a renovated home with small, separate dining rooms, Mother's is open daily in winter, 11:30 a.m.-2:30 p.m. and 5-9 p.m. In summer, it's open 11:30 a.m.-3 p.m. and 4:30-9:30 p.m.

Down the street from Mother's, **Café di Cocoa,** 125 Main St., Bethel 04217, tel. (207) 824-5282, is a meat-free, seafood-free, smoke-free zone, vegetarian all the way. It's Oxford County's only vegetarian restaurant, its name cleverly derived from that of co-owner Cathy diCocco. Mediterranean and other ethnic specialties (most under $10) demand your attention. Then there's the

café's trademark "gentle dining," a Saturday night (7:30 p.m.) candlelight dinner experience during ski season and midsummer. The five-course, prix-fixe dinner (BYOL), by reservation only, is $25 pp. The café is open all year, Monday and Wed.-Fri. 11 a.m.-9 p.m., Saturday 7 a.m.-9 p.m. and Sunday 8 a.m.-6 p.m.

Glass walls surround the bustling brewery at the **Sunday River Brewing Company,** 1 Sunday River Rd., P.O. Box 847, Bethel 04217, tel. (207) 824-4253, fax 824-3380, producer of Reindeer Rye, Black Bear Porter, and Brass Balls Barley Wine. To top it off, the menu is among the most creative of Maine's brewpubs—including high-quality hummus and nachos. Free half-hour brewery tours begin at 2 p.m. each Tuesday, other times by appointment. The brewpub, at the junction of Rt. 2 and Sunday River Road, is open all year, daily 11:30 a.m.-12:30 a.m. (food service ends at 10 p.m.).

Moderate to Expensive

The ambience is unbeatable at the **Iron Horse Bar & Grill,** Bethel Station, Cross St., Bethel 04217, tel. (207) 824-0961, a railroad-car restaurant parked on a siding southeast of the Casablanca Cinema. Black Angus steaks, wild game, and cheesecakes are house (oops, train) specialties (entrées $13-20). The glitzy new Good Cheer lounge car has become a popular watering hole. In summer, the Iron Horse is one of the few air-conditioned area restaurants—a good choice when the weather turns steamy. Open daily 5-9 p.m. in winter, Wed.-Sat. 5-9 p.m. in summer.

One of the area's best kitchens is at **The Sudbury Inn,** Main St., Bethel 04217, tel. (207) 824-2174 or (800) 395-7837, a warmly retrofitted 1873 hostelry with several separate dining areas. Entrée range is $12-23 (more if you order lobster), but there's no surcharge for sharing; the rack of lamb is superb. Reservations are essential at this popular spot, especially on weekends and holidays. The restaurant is open daily 5-9 p.m., all year. On the lower level is **The Suds Pub,** tel. (207) 824-6558, a very relaxing hangout with a moderately priced menu of appetizers, burgers, soups, salads, pizza, and a few entrées. Thursday night, there's live music until 1 a.m., something to remember if you're spending the night in one of the inn's 16 guest rooms and suites ($75-150 d, including breakfast; private baths).

INFORMATION AND SERVICES

Next door to the Casablanca Cinema, at the Bethel Station, is the handsome new **Bethel Area Chamber of Commerce,** Cross St., P.O. Box 439, Bethel 04217, tel. (207) 824-2282, fax 824-7123, among the state's most energetic chamber organizations. The office is open all year, weekdays 9 a.m.-5 p.m. and weekends 10 a.m.-6 p.m. During ski season (Nov.-April), it's also open Monday and Thursday to 8 p.m. The building has public restrooms.

In 1997, the **Maine Publicity Bureau,** 18 Mayville Rd., Rt. 2, P.O. Box 1084, Bethel 04217, added a new information center to its statewide network. Located just north of Bethel, the office is open all year, daily 9 a.m.-5 p.m., and has public restrooms.

In the same building as the Publicity Bureau is the visitor's center for the Evans Notch Ranger District of the **White Mountain National Forest,** 18 Mayville Rd., Rt. 2, RR 2, Box 2270, Bethel 04217, tel. (207) 824-2134. Trail maps, campsite information, bird checklists, and other helpful wildlife brochures are all available here. The office is open daily 8 a.m.-4:30 p.m. in summer, Mon.-Sat. 8 a.m.-4:30 p.m. in winter.

Newspapers
Published every Wednesday since 1895, *The Bethel Citizen,* tel. (207) 824-2444, thoroughly covers Bethel and the surrounding area, with extensive calendar listings. The *Citizen* also produces two extremely useful tabloid-style supplements, *Vacation in Bethel,* in winter and summer editions. Both are free and widely available at shops, lodgings, restaurants, and the chamber of commerce. The preferred daily newspaper is the *Lewiston Sun-Journal.*

Emergencies
For **fire and ambulance services,** and the **county sheriff,** call (800) 482-7433. **The Bethel Area Health Center,** Railroad St., P.O. Box 977, Bethel 04217, tel. (207) 824-2193 or (800) 287-2292, is a medical facility, not a hospital, but a physician or physician's assistant is always on

call for emergencies. The **Rumford Community Hospital,** 420 Franklin St., P.O. Box 619, Rumford 04224, tel. (207) 364-4581, 24 miles from downtown Bethel, has a round-the-clock emergency room. The nearest major medical center is in Lewiston, 46 miles from Bethel.

At Sunday River Ski Resort, the **Western Maine Health Clinic,** South Ridge Base Area, is staffed for medical emergencies daily 9 a.m.-6 p.m. Half a dozen **first-aid centers** are scattered throughout the resort.

Kennels
Need to stash your pooch while you're out on the slopes? **Nanny's Doggy Day Care,** West Bethel Rd., Rt. 2, P.O. Box 323, Bethel 04217, tel. (207) 824-4225, solves that problem with daytime rates of $6-9, depending on your dog's weight. Rates increase to $12-18 for 24 hours, $22-32 for a weekend. Special rates for more than one dog. This is an interesting variation on the kennel theme, with winterized doghouses for overnight and staked leads in separate yards for daytime stays. Call at least three days ahead for weekend boarding. No credit cards, no out-of-state checks. Open all year.

Special Courses
Thanks to the Bethel area's spectacular scenery and relatively rugged terrain, two excellent outdoors-oriented programs have become well established. The Rockland-based **Hurricane Island Outward Bound School,** part of the national Outward Bound network, operates mountain-oriented wilderness courses from its center in Newry, tel. (207) 824-3152, course information tel. (800) 341-1744, a few miles beyond the Sunday River access road.

Eight miles southeast of Bethel, **The Maine Conservation School,** P.O. Box 188, Bryant Pond 04219, tel. (207) 665-2068, founded in the 1960s, covers 100 acres on the shore of Lake Christopher. Environmental education is the focus for day-long and week-long hands-on programs for students and teachers, and the school does an impressive job of instilling a conservation ethic in children and adults. Activities include hiking, survival skills, wildlife studies, and conservation work projects.

In downtown Bethel, at the end of Broad Street, is the onetime Gehring estate that houses the

NTL Institute, tel. (207) 824-2693, established here in 1947 to offer courses in personal and professional development and human dynamics. The NTL bookstore is open to the public weekdays from early June through September.

GETTING THERE AND GETTING AROUND

The **Bethel Express,** 119 Main St., P.O. Box 976, Bethel 04217, tel. (207) 824-4646, with a fleet of 11-passenger vans, operates year-round on-demand and by reservation. Pickups in Portland (airport and bus station, 70 miles one way) for Bethel or Sunday River Ski Resort are about $70 pp, lower with additional passengers; special rates for families and groups. Call at least 24 hours in advance. Bethel Express also provides on-call taxi service to a variety of local destinations; one-way fare to Sunday River from Bethel is $5 pp ($3 pp for extra passengers). Another service is on-demand **Moose Tours** ($15 pp), best scheduled for early morning or late in the day; call to schedule. Convenient for those who need a designated driver, Bethel Express hours are daily sunrise to 1 a.m.

Train service from the Portland area to Bethel has been operating during ski season, primarily weekends and school vacation, since 1993, but you'll need to confirm availability, route, and schedule. Latest incarnation at press time was the **Sunday River Express,** operating Fri.-Sun. between late December and early April, with a $19 ticket price. Contact either the Sunday River Ski Resort or Bethel's chamber of commerce for an update.

OXFORD HILLS

Sandwiched between the Lewiston/Auburn area and Bethel and vicinity, with Sebago and Long Lakes off to the south, the Oxford Hills region centers on Norway and South Paris. The town of Norway (pop. 4,675) shares the banks of the Little Androscoggin River with the community of South Paris, the major commercial center for the town of Paris.

From here it gets complicated, although it's unlikely to affect a visitor. Oxford County's official seat is Paris (pop. 4,470), but all the relevant county offices are in South Paris. Next, throw into the mix the town of West Paris (pop. 1,565)—which is, in fact, mostly *north* of Paris and South Paris. Within the boundaries of West Paris is the hamlet of North Paris. Fortunately, there's no East Paris, but there is the tiny enclave of Paris Hill, a pocket paradise many people never discover.

West Paris gained its own identity when it separated from Paris in 1957, but its traditions go way back. The Pequawket Indian princess Mollyockett, celebrated hereabouts as a healer, supposedly buried a golden treasure under a suspended animal trap, hence the name of Trap Corner for the junction of Rts. 26 and 219. No such cache has been uncovered, but the corner is the site of the incredible gemstone collection at Perham's of West Paris. More recent traditions in West Paris come from Finland, home of many 19th- and early-20th-century immigrants who gravitated to a new life in this area. Finnish names are common on the town's voting registers.

Norway, fortunately, is far less complicated. The name, incidentally, comes not from Europe, or Norwegian settlers, but rather from a variation on a Native American word for waterfalls—cascades on the town's Pennesseewassee (PENN-a-see-WAH-see) Lake (called Norway Lake locally), which powered 19th-century mills. European settlement began in 1786.

Norway was the birthplace of C.A. Stephens (1844-1931), who for 55 years wrote weekly stories for a 19th-century boys' magazine, *Youth's Companion.* Colorfully reflective of rural Maine life, the entertaining tales were collected in *Stories from the Old Squire's Farm,* published in 1995.

Waterford (pop. 1,430) is a must-see, especially the National Historic District known as Waterford Flat or Flats—too pretty to believe, with classic homes and tree-lined streets alongside Keoka Lake in the shadow of Mount Tire'm —a 19th-century village frozen in time.

SIGHTS

Paris Hill/Hamlin Memorial Library

On Rt. 26, just beyond the northern edge of **South Paris,** a sign on the right marks one end of Paris Hill Road, a four-mile loop that reconnects farther along with Rt. 26. As you head uphill, past an old cemetery, you'll arrive at a Brigadoon-like enclave of elegant 18th- and 19th-century homes—a National Historic District with dramatic views off to the White Mountains and the lakes below. Centerpiece of the road is Paris Hill Common, a pristine park in front of the birthplace (not open to the public) of former Vice President Hannibal Hamlin (1809-91). South of the green stands the **Hamlin Memorial Library** (ex-Oxford County Jail), the only Paris Hill building open to the public, where you can bone up on the history of this pocket paradise.

Most children (and adults) get a kick out of entering a public library that once was a town jail. This one, built in 1822, held as many as 30 prisoners until 1896. Three prisoners somehow escaped in the 1830s, abandoning one of their pals stuck in the wall opening they had created. In 1902, the jail became the library—retaining the telltale signs of jail-bar hinges in the granite walls. Adults will appreciate Librarian/Historian Schuyler Mott's tour of the library's upper-level museum. Admission is free to the museum section, but donations are welcomed. Summer

hours at the Hamlin Memorial Library, Paris Hill, Paris 04271, tel. (207) 743-2980, fax 743-8707, are Tues.-Fri. 10 a.m.-4 p.m. (plus Wednesday 7-9 p.m.) and Saturday 10 a.m.-1 p.m. Winter hours are Tues.-Fri. 11:30 a.m.-5:30 p.m. (plus Wednesday 7-9 p.m.) and Saturday 10 a.m.-2 p.m.

If you're in the area on the first December weekend in an even-numbered year, inquire about the **Biennial Holiday House Tour,** when a dozen of these elegant homes, decorated exquisitely for Christmas, are open to the public, all to benefit the Paris Hill Community Center.

Perham's of West Paris

And now for something completely different. Welcome to rock hound heaven! **Perham's of West Paris,** 194 Bethel Rd., Rt. 26, P.O. Box 280, West Paris 04289, tel. (207) 674-2341 or (800) 371-4367, fax (207) 674-3692, is part museum, part shop, and part counseling service. You can admire shelf after shelf of spectacular rare gems, buy cut and uncut gems and minerals, and get do-it-yourself advice for a family outing in the mineral-rich quarries of the Oxford Hills. Established in 1919 at the Trap Corner crossroads, Perham's sells books, videos, rock tumblers, metal detectors, gold pans, and all the tools you'll need for treasure-hunting. Request a free map of the five quarries they own. And good luck! The shop, at the junction of Rts. 26 and 219, is open all year, daily 9 a.m.-5 p.m.

Paris Hill

Global Maine

Posted almost casually on an undistinguished corner in western Maine is a roadside landmark that inevitably appears in any travel book or slide show with a sense of the whimsical. Nine markers direct bikers, hikers, or drivers to Maine communities bearing the names of international locales: **Norway, Paris, Denmark, Naples, Sweden, Poland, Mexico, Peru,** and **China.** All are within 94 miles of the sign, which stands at the junction of Rts. 5 and 35 in the burg of Lynchville (part of Albany Township), about 14 miles west of Norway. If you approach the sign from the south on Rt. 35, you're likely to miss it; it's most noticeable when coming from the north on Rt. 35 or the west on Rt. 5. (Also see "Presidential Maine" under "Sights" in the Sebago and Long Lakes section later in this chapter for info on some brand-new competition—a directional sign for 10 Maine towns named for U.S. presidents.)

PARKS AND PRESERVES

McLaughlin Garden

In 1997, a little miracle happened in South Paris. For more than 50 years, Bernard McLaughlin had lovingly tended his three-acre perennial garden alongside the highway, eventually surrounded by commercial development, and he'd always welcomed the public into his floral oasis. In 1995, at the age of 98, McLaughlin died, stipulating in his will that the property be sold. Eager developers eyed it, but loyal flower fans dug in their heels, captured media attention, created a nonprofit foundation, and managed to purchase the property—the beginning of the little miracle. The McLaughlin Garden, 101 Main St., Rt. 26 and Western Ave., South Paris, mailing address The McLaughlin Foundation, P.O. Box 16, South Paris 04281, tel./fax (207) 743-8820, lives on, with its 98 varieties of lilacs, plus lilies and irises and so much more. Between Memorial Day weekend and late September, the gardens are open daily, dawn to dusk, for self-guided tours. Admission is free, but donations are welcomed; annual membership in the McLaughlin Foundation is $20. In the ell connecting the 19th-century house and its barn are a **tearoom/coffee bar** and a **gift shop** featuring high-end

crafts and gifts, mostly Maine-made. The shop is open daily 10 a.m.-4 p.m. in summer; off season, it's open weekends.

Snow Falls

A 300-foot gorge on the Little Androscoggin River is the eye-catching centerpiece of Snow Falls Rest Area, an easy-off-easy-on roadside park where you can commandeer a table alongside the waterfall. What better place for a relaxing picnic (no grills, some covered tables). Trucks whiz by on the highway, but the water's noise usually drowns them out. The rest area is on Rt. 26, about six miles north of the center of South Paris.

RECREATION

The most popular Oxford Hills hikes are particularly family-friendly—no killer climbs or even major ascents, no bushwhacking, just darned good exercise and some worthwhile views. From July to mid-August, don't be surprised to encounter clusters of summer campers, since camp counselors all over this region regularly gather up their kids and take 'em out on the trail or paddling the ponds.

Hiking

It's hard to resist a hike up **Mount Tire'm** (1,104 feet)—if only to disprove its name. Actually, it's supposedly a convolution of a Native American name. The only steep section is at the beginning, after the memorial marker dedicated to 19th-century Waterfordite Daniel Brown, for whom the trail (unblazed) is named. Allow an hour or so for the one-and-a-half-mile roundtrip, especially if you're carrying a picnic. From downtown Waterford (Rt. 35), take Plummer Hill Rd. about 300 feet beyond the community center; the trailhead is on the west side of the road; watch for the marker.

Straddling the Paris-Buckfield-Hebron town boundaries, **Streaked** (pronounced "STREAK-ed") **Mountain** (1,770 feet) has a moderate, then easy trail to an expansive summit with an abandoned fire tower and vistas as far as Mount Washington. Pack a picnic. If you're here in early August, take along a small pail to collect wild blueberries. In late September and early

October, it's indescribable, but remember to wear a blaze-orange hat or vest once hunting season has started—or tackle the trail on a Sunday. Allow about one and a half hours for the one-mile roundtrip, especially if you're picnicking and blueberrying. To reach the trailhead from South Paris, take Rt. 117 west to Streaked Mountain Rd., on the right (south). Turn and go about half a mile. Park well off the road. (You can also climb Streaked from the east, but it's a much longer hike that requires rubberized or waterproof footwear.)

Other good Oxford Hills hikes are **Hawk Mountain** (in Waterford; easy) and **Singlepole Ridge** (or Singepole Mountain; in Paris; easy to moderate).

Golf

At nine-hole **Paris Hill Country Club,** Paris Hill Rd., Paris 04271, tel. (207) 743-2371, founded in 1899, you'll find a low-key atmosphere, reasonable greens fees, cart rentals, and a snack bar. No tee times are needed. The rectangular course has all straight shots; the challenges come from slopes and unexpected traps. Just off Rt. 26 on the outskirts of South Paris, and part of the Paris Hill Historic District, the club is open May to mid-November.

It's not just golfers who patronize the nine-hole **Norway Country Club,** Rt. 118, P.O. Box 393, Norway 04268, tel. (207) 743-9840; this is a popular spot to have lunch or kick back on the club porch. The mountain-lake scenery, especially in the fall, is awesome. In midsummer, call for a starting time. Established in 1929, the club is a mile west of Rt. 117. It's open late April to early October.

Spectator Sports

If you're partial to guerrilla warfare on wheels, the place to be is **Oxford Plains Speedway,** Rt. 26, Oxford, tel. (207) 539-8865, mailing address P.O. Box 296, Waterbury, VT 05676, Maine's center for stock-car racing. Each weekend from late April to late September, souped-up high-performance vehicles career around the track in pursuit of substantial money prizes. Season highlight is the four-day **Oxford 250,** on a July weekend (date depends on the professional racing-circuit schedule).

Sauna

For anyone addicted to the sauna ritual, **Dave's Sauna Bath,** 96 Park St., South Paris 04281, tel. (207) 743-7409, is the best in this part of Maine—the adopted homeland of thousands of Finns. Dave Graiver has six saunas open daily 4-9 p.m., all year. He charges $5 for "as long as you can stand it."

Winter Sports

Alpine skiing isn't an Oxford Hills sport, but not far away are the slopes at Sunday River Ski Resort and Mt. Abram, and Shawnee Peak.

The best Oxford Hills locale for **cross-country skiing** is Carter's Cross-Country Ski Center, Rt. 26, Box 710, Oxford 04270, tel. (207) 539-4848, with about 15 miles of beginner and intermediate groomed trails amid lovely frozen-lake scenery in the Welchville section of Oxford. Facilities include ski and snowshoe rentals, a well-equipped ski shop, plus snack bar, solarium, and sauna. Trail pass is $10 adults, $8 seniors, $6 students. A half-day pass is $8; kids under six are free.

Ever tried **snow tubing?** The place to do it is right near Carter's at **Mountain View Sports Park,** Rt. 26, Oxford, tel. (207) 539-2454, mailing address P.O. Box 1086, Scarborough 04070, the state's pioneer snow-tube park. A single ride, lasting about 20 seconds on a thousand-foot slope, is only $2, but why not buy a three-hour pass ($8 Friday, $10 weekends)? Zip down one of the groomed tube runs, then connect to the lift (formerly a T-bar) and be whisked back up again. No dragging a tube to the top—such a deal. Mountain View has snowmaking gear and also lights the slopes at night. No children under age three; a child 4-7 years old can tube free with an adult but must wear a helmet (rental is $2). The park, half a mile south of where Rt. 121 meets Rt. 26, is open Thursday and Friday 3-9:30 p.m. and Saturday and Sunday 9 a.m.-9:30 p.m. During school vacations, arrive early; the park is incredibly popular.

ENTERTAINMENT

Marcel Marceau wannabes come to study at the nationally famed **Celebration Barn Theater,** 190 Stock Farm Rd., South Paris 04281, tel.

(207) 743-8452, fax 743-3889, established in 1972 by mime master Tony Montanaro. Mime, juggling, dance, storytelling, and improv comedy performances are open to the public in the 125-seat barn each Friday and Saturday (8 p.m.), late June through August. Reservations are advisable. Tickets are $8 adults, $5 children 12 and under. Pack a picnic and arrive early. The theater (signposted) is just off Rt. 117.

FESTIVALS AND EVENTS

For other events nearby, see the events listings for Bethel and Vicinity, Sebago and Long Lakes, and the Lewiston/Auburn Area.

Wall-to-wall paintings are for sale along Main Street in downtown Norway for the **Sidewalk Art Festival,** the second Saturday in July, in which nearly 100 artists participate. The Norway Memorial Library holds its annual book sale at the same time. **Founders' Day** brings craft and antiques exhibits, live music, storytelling, and an antique-car open house on Paris Hill Common, Paris Hill, the third Saturday in July. The **Oxford Hills Rotary Club Beanhole Bean Festival** is a community supper centered on beans baked overnight underground. It's at the Oxford County Fairgrounds the last Saturday in July. The name of North Waterford's **World's Fair** seems sort of cheeky for this three-day country medley of egg-throwing contests, talent show, live music, dancing, and more the last weekend in July. The last Sunday in July, Otisfield pays tribute to a native son of its own on **Joe Holden Day,** a whimsical homage to Joe Holden, who announced in the 1890s that the world was flat. Many attend in period costumes. The **Annual Moose Tour** is a well-organized, six-day, 265-mile bicycle trek, run by Maine Wheels Bicycle Club, from South Paris to Fryeburg, Bethel, Rangeley, Dixfield, and back from late July into August. For information call (207) 743-2577.

Offering nonstop bluegrass, Friday evening to Sunday afternoon, the **Annual Oxford County Bluegrass Festival** draws about 3,000 spectators to Record Family Farm, 486 E. Oxford Rd., South Paris, the third weekend in August.

The second week of September, the family-oriented, four-day agricultural **Oxford County Fair** features 4-H exhibits, a beauty pageant, a pig scramble, live entertainment, an apple-pie contest, and plenty of food booths at the Oxford County Fairgrounds.

SHOPPING

Art Galleries

The **Matolcsy Art Center,** 265 Main St., Norway 04268, tel. (207) 743-5411, showcase for the impressive Western Maine Art Group, sponsors exhibits, demonstrations, workshops, classes, and art auctions, as well as Norway's annual Sidewalk Art Festival. Founded in 1967 by Lajos Matolcsy (pronounced "Ma-TOLL-she"), the center occupies an old schoolhouse in downtown Norway. From early June to Labor Day, it's open Tuesday 10 a.m.-4 p.m. and Wed.-Sat. 11 a.m.-4 p.m. From Labor Day to mid-December, hours are Wed.-Sat. 11 a.m.-4 p.m.

Books, Gifts, and Crafts

Books 'n' Things of Oxford, Oxford Plaza, Rt. 26, Oxford 04270, tel. (207) 743-7197 or (800) 834-7323, is one of those full-service bookstores that inspires you to buy more than you ever planned. It's open all year, daily 9 a.m.-9 p.m. in summer, Mon.-Sat. 9 a.m.-6 p.m. off season.

Just beyond the Celebration Barn Theater, **Christian Ridge Pottery,** 210 Stock Farm Rd., South Paris 04281, tel./fax (207) 743-8419, produces functional ceramic designs and objets, including a trademarked apple baker and a bagel cutter. You can see the work in progress at the shop, open Mon.-Sat. 10 a.m.-5 p.m. and Sunday noon-5 p.m., Memorial Day weekend through December. Other months, it's open Mon.-Sat. 10 a.m.-5 p.m.

Natural Food/Farmstand

Fare Share Co-op, 18 Tannery St., Norway 04268, tel. (207) 743-9044, a membership organization, is also open to the public. Lots of bulk grains and locally grown (in season) organic produce. Open all year, Mon.-Fri. 9 a.m.-5 p.m., Saturday 10 a.m.-4 p.m.

Local produce, herbs, relishes, cheese, maple syrup, and baked goods are all part of the stock at **Carter's Farm Market,** 420 Main St., Rt. 26,

Oxford 04270, tel. (207) 539-4848. Part of an energetic family-run operation that includes the Welchville Inn Bed & Breakfast and Carter's Cross-Country Ski Center, the farmstand is just south of Rt. 121 and open spring through fall.

ACCOMMODATIONS

B&Bs

Andrea Talley spared no expense when she decided to create the **Dew Drop Inn,** 743 Paris Hill Rd., South Paris 04281, tel. (207) 743-5287 or (800) 252-3767 outside Maine, on 220 acres at the base of Paris Hill. Nine second-floor rooms ($92 d, including full breakfast and tax), furnished with antiques and reproductions, have private baths, a/c, cable TV, even good-size closets. Other amenities include a 10-person jacuzzi, indoor shuffleboard, and a treadmill. A master suite ideal for families is $135 d. In winter, cheese and wine are served in late afternoon (Dew Drop has a liquor license). If you have your own gear, you can hike, bike, and cross-country ski on the premises. No pets, no smoking. Open all year. The inn is at the corner of Rt. 26, about four miles north of South Paris.

Everything's Native American, with some touches of Mexico, at Ken Ward and Diane Lecuyer's **Inn at Little Creek,** 39 Pleasant St., Rt. 121, P.O. Box 857, Oxford 04270, tel. (207) 539-4046 or (888) 539-4046. Diane's Native American heritage inspired the decor, which continues into the guest rooms. Three comfortable rooms share a bath; rates are $75 d, in July and August, $55 d other months. Included is an exotic breakfast—Indian medicinal teas and buffalo meat used in sausage or omelettes. Also included is an evening snack in the living room, where the congeniality is contagious. Diane and Ken have masses of reference books, and exotic artifacts they're glad to identify. Don't bring your pets; you'll meet the resident caged iguana. No smoking, no children under 12. Right around the corner, Allen Hill Road has lovely old homes and a fabulous view of Thompson Lake, where you can swim with a guest pass from the Inn at Little Creek. In winter, a major snowmobile trail goes behind the house; the same trails are great in summer for hiking and mountain biking. The B&B is open all year.

For a complete change of pace, back in time and back of beyond, **Morrill Farm Bed and Breakfast,** 85 Morrill Farm Rd., Sumner 04292, tel. (207) 388-2059, is a two-century-old farm with three rustic second-floor rooms (shared bath) in the ell connecting the house and the barn. On the 217-acre spread are nature/cross-country-skiing trails, river fishing, and a menagerie of domestic farm animals. Rates are $50-60 d May-Nov., $40-50 d Dec.-April. No pets, no children under 12; smoking only on the screened porch. The farm is north and east of Norway/South Paris, a mile from Rt. 219 (West Sumner Road). Turn north on Greenwoods Rd. at Roll-In Variety and continue a mile to Morrill Farm Road. Open all year.

Waterford

Waterford—that lovely little enclave flanked by Norway/South Paris, Bridgton/Naples, and the Lovells—has a couple of fine places to put your head.

Barbara and Rosalie Vanderzanden's traditionally elegant **Waterford Inne,** Chadbourne Rd., Box 149, Waterford 04088, tel./fax (207) 583-4037, an antiques-filled 19th-century farmhouse on 25 open and wooded acres, is a prime getaway spot. Nine lovely rooms are $75-90 d (shared bath) or $90-100 d (private bath). A delicious breakfast is included. No smoking; children are welcome. Pets are allowed for $10 extra. By advance reservation, the Vanderzandens will prepare a four-course dinner for guests and the public (about $29 pp; BYOL); spring for it, they do a wonderful job. Only credit card is American Express. The inn is close to East Waterford, half a mile west of Rt. 37. Open May through March.

You have to love bears if you stay at the **Bear Mountain Inn,** Rt. 35, South Waterford 04081, tel. (207) 583-4404, a beautifully updated 1820s B&B on 40 acres overlooking Bear Pond. Enthusiastic innkeeper Lorraine Blais, a professional decorator, has created six bear-themed rooms (private and shared baths) for $85-125 d, plus a suite (sleeps four) for $125, including breakfast. Across the road are Bear Mountain and Hawk Mountain trails, and the inn has its own beach on Bear Pond. No smoking, no pets, no children under eight. Two-night minimum. Open all year.

FOOD

General-Store Restaurants

Many people flock to **The Lake Store**, Rts. 117 and 118, Norway Lake, Norway 04268, tel. (207) 743-6562, just to check out the crazy collection of Coca-Cola memorabilia, but you can also load up with picnic fixings, pizza, liquor, groceries, and videos. Summer hours are daily 5 a.m.-9 p.m.; winter hours are Mon.-Sat. 5 a.m.-7 p.m. and Sunday 6 a.m.-7 p.m. Spring and fall hours are Mon.-Sat. 5 a.m.-8 p.m. and Sunday 6 a.m.-8 p.m.

Across the road from Perham's of West Paris, **Trap Corner Store and Restaurant**, Rts. 26 and 219, West Paris 04289, tel. (207) 674-2484, serves up hearty comfort food in a casual, down-home atmosphere that sometimes gets a bit smoky. No credit cards. It's open all year, Mon.-Sat. 5 a.m.-9 p.m. and Sunday 6 a.m.-8 p.m.

What's the most intriguing short-order menu item at **Tut's General Store**, Rt. 35, P.O. Box 28, North Waterford 04267, tel. (207) 583-4447? The $3.85 buffalo burger, made from bison raised right down the road at the Jones farm. You can't miss the bison-head trophy looming over the back counter—the first to go from Richard Jones's flock. Actually, the store's most popular item, especially in summer, is Maine-made Deering ice cream for 95 cents a scoop (or five scoops for $3.60). Tut's, of course, also has all the usual general-store stuff, plus 49 seats for eating in. The store is open all year, daily 6 a.m.-9 p.m. (to 9:30 p.m. Friday and Saturday).

Inexpensive to Moderate

Located in a onetime streetcar barn, the **Trolley House Restaurant**, 110 Main St., Norway 04268, tel. (207) 743-2211, specializes in seafood and Black Angus beef; Friday and Saturday are prime-rib nights. Dinner entrées are in the $10-13 range. The two dining rooms are smoke-free and air-conditioned; smoking is allowed in the lounge. Open all year, Mon.-Sat. 11 a.m.-9 p.m. (to 11 p.m. Friday and Saturday).

Moderate to Expensive

An unassuming exterior on a busy intown thoroughfare camouflages the pleasant interior at **Maurice Restaurant Français**, 113 Main St., Rt. 26, P.O. Box 317, South Paris 04281, tel. (207) 743-2532. A veteran in this area, the popular restaurant serves creditable French cuisine in the $12-17 entrée price range. Reservations are a good idea, especially on weekends. Open all year, Mon.-Fri. 11:30 a.m.-1:30 p.m. and 4:30-8:30 p.m. (to 9 p.m. Friday), plus 4:30-8:30 Saturday. In midsummer, it's also open Sunday 11 a.m.-2 p.m. and 4:30-8:30 p.m.

INFORMATION AND SERVICES

The information center for the well-organized **Oxford Hills Chamber of Commerce**, 166 Main St., Rt. 26, South Paris 04281, tel. (207) 743-2281, fax 743-5917, is easy to find in the midst of the South Paris commercial district. The center is open Mon.-Fri. 8:30 a.m.-4:30 p.m. and Saturday 9 a.m.-1 p.m. At other times, you can pick up brochures in the kiosk out front.

Newspapers

Maine's oldest weekly, the **Advertiser Democrat,** tel. (207) 743-7011, published each Thursday in Norway since 1826, carries local features, ads, and extensive calendar listings. The daily newspaper providing best coverage of this area is the *Lewiston Sun-Journal,* Norway office tel. (207) 743-9228.

Emergencies

Dial 911 for police, fire, and ambulance in **Norway and Oxford,** and for police and fire departments in **South Paris.** For an ambulance in South Paris, call (207) 743-0700.

Stephens Memorial Hospital, 80 Main St., Norway 04268, tel. (207) 743-5933, a well-regarded community hospital, has round-the-clock emergency-room care. The nearest major medical center is in Lewiston.

Kennels

Marie's Pet Retreat, Bear Pond Rd., RFD 2, Box 2547, Buckfield 04220, tel. (207) 224-7092, is a popular boarding kennel on five rural acres, so call well ahead if you'll need one of her 15 dog pens and six cat pens. No need to bring bed or bowl. Her very reasonable fees are all-inclusive: $9 for a dog, $6 for a cat. No credit cards. About four miles east of the center of Buckfield and 15 miles from South Paris, the

kennel is open Thurs.-Tues. 8 a.m.-1 p.m. and 6-8 p.m., Wednesday 8-11 a.m.

FRYEBURG AREA

Fryeburg (pop. 3,000), a crossroads community on busy Rt. 302, is best known as the funnel to and from the factory outlets, hiking trails, and ski slopes of New Hampshire's North Conway and the White Mountains. Except during early October's annual extravaganza, the giant Fryeburg Fair, Fryeburg seldom ends up on anyone's itinerary. Too bad. The mountain-ringed community has lots of charm, historic homes, the flavor of rural life, and access to miles of Saco River canoeing waters.

Incorporated in 1763, Fryeburg is Oxford County's oldest town; even earlier, it was known as Pequawket, an Indian settlement and trading post—until skirmishes with white settlers routed the Native Americans in 1725 during Dummer's War (also known as Lovewell's War). Casualties were heavy on both sides.

In 1792, Fryeburg Academy, a private school on Main Street, was chartered; the school's Webster Hall is named after famed statesman Daniel Webster, whose undistinguished teaching career at the school began and ended in 1802. Among the students at the time was Rufus Porter, who later gained renown as a muralist, inventor, and founder of *Scientific American* magazine. Today the school is one of a handful of private academies in Maine that provide public secondary education, a uniquely successful private/public partnership.

Just north of Fryeburg is the town of Lovell, with three hamlets—known collectively as "The Lovells"—strung along Rt. 5, on the east side of gorgeous Kezar Lake. Anyone who has discovered Kezar Lake yearns to keep it a secret,

but the word is out. The mountain-rimmed lake is *too* beautiful.

Other areas convenient to Fryeburg for restaurants, recreation, and other activities are Sebago and Long Lakes, Oxford Hills, and Bethel.

SIGHTS

Covered Bridges
Two of Maine's nine covered bridges are within striking distance of Fryeburg. In the hamlet of East Fryeburg, just west of Kezar Pond, 116-foot-long **Hemlock Bridge** was built in 1857. Beneath the bridge runs the "Old Saco," or "Old Course," a former channel of the Saco River. Best time to visit is July-Oct.; mud or snow can prevent car access other months, and June is buggy. From the Rt. 5/302 junction in Fryeburg, take Rt. 302 east five and a half miles to Hemlock Bridge Road. Turn left (north) and go about three miles on a paved, then unpaved road to the bridge. Or paddle under the bridge on a detour from canoeing on the Saco River.

A bit farther south, 183-foot-long **Porter Covered Bridge,** linking Oxford and York Counties and the towns of Porter and Parsonsfield, spans the Ossipee River. Officially known as the **Parsonsfield-Porter Historical Bridge,** it was built in 1798, then rebuilt once or twice between 1858 and 1876. The bridge is just east of Rt. 160, about half a mile from the center of Porter. From Fryeburg, take Rt. 5/113 to East Brownfield, then Rt. 160 to Kezar Falls and Porter.

RECREATION

Canoeing
The **Saco River,** headwatered in Crawford Notch, New Hampshire, meanders 84 miles from the Maine border at Fryeburg to the ocean at Saco and Biddeford. Its many miles of flatwater, with intermittent sandbars and a few portages, make it wonderful for canoeing, camp-

ANNE LONG LARSEN

ing, and swimming, but there's the rub: the summer weekend scene on the 35-mile western Maine stretch looks like bumper boats at Disneyland. Aim for midweek in late September, and early October, when the foliage is spectacular, the current is slower, noise levels are lower, and the crowds are busy elsewhere. For a relaxing trip, figure about two miles an hour and you can do the Fryeburg-to-Hiram segment with two overnight stops, including a couple of interesting side-trip paddles—to Hemlock Bridge, Pleasant Pond, and Lovewell's Pond. If you put in at Swan's Falls in Fryeburg, you won't have to deal with portages between there and Hiram.

The handiest reference is the *AMC River Guide: Maine* (see the Booklist). For multiday trips, you'll need to get a **fire permit** (free), or stay at one of the commercial campgrounds. Fire permits are available at Village Variety Store in Fryeburg, open daily.

Saco River Canoe & Kayak, Rt. 5, P.O. Box 111, Fryeburg 04037, tel. (207) 935-2369, located close to the convenient put-in at Swan's Falls, rents Old Town Discovery canoes and touring kayaks ($27 a day weekends, $25 midweek) and provides delivery and pickup service along a 50-mile stretch of the Saco River. Shuttle costs range $3-10 per canoe (minimum fee $10, depending on location). Safety-conscious owners Fred and Prudy Westerberg know their turf and provide helpful advice for planning short and extended canoe trips. Open mid-May to late October.

Veteran canoeing outfitter **Saco Bound,** Rt. 302, Box 119, Center Conway, NH 03813, tel. (603) 447-2177 or 447-3801, will arrange almost everything for day-long or multiday trips—canoe or kayak rentals, shuttles, parking, private put-ins and takeouts, wilderness campsites—leaving you to concentrate on paddling and provisioning. A couple of daytime guided trips are also available, some in New Hampshire. Canoe or kayak rental is $26 a day, including parking ($2 more in July and August); shuttle fee is $11 per canoe. If you're determined to do this in summer, be sure to make reservations well in advance. (The same company also owns Downeast Whitewater, a rafting outfitter in The Forks, offering trips on the Kennebec, Dead, and Penobscot Rivers.)

Even if you're not camping at **Woodland Acres Campground,** tel. (207) 935-2529, they'll rent canoes to nonguests ($38 a day on weekends and holidays, $35 midweek, including shuttle and parking). If you have your own canoe(s), shuttle service is $18 per canoe and parking is $3 a day (extra for trailer). They make it all very convenient, even suggesting more than half a dozen day-long and multiday canoe trips for skill levels from beginner to expert. Another Brownfield campground, **River Run,** tel. (207) 452-2500, also rents canoes and provides shuttle service.

If crowds on the Saco become a bit much, head east or north with your canoe or kayak to the area's lakes and ponds, even to **Brownfield Bog.** Prime canoeing spots are **Lovewell Pond** and **Kezar Pond** in Fryeburg; **Kezar Lake** in Lovell; and **Virginia Lake** in Stoneham. (If a north wind kicks up on Kezar Lake, stay close to shore.) Most spectacular is mile-long Virginia Lake, nudged up against the White Mountain National Forest. Only one house breaks up the wooded shoreline. The access road (off Rt. 5 between North Lovell and East Stoneham) is a mechanic's delight, but persevere—tranquility lies ahead.

Hiking
Easiest (and therefore busiest) trail in the area is the 20-minute stroll up (barely up) **Jockey Cap,** named for a cantilevered ledge that's long since disappeared. At the top of the trail, with a 360-degree view of lakes and mountains, is a monument to Adm. Robert Peary, the arctic explorer who once lived in Fryeburg. The metal edge of the monument is a handy cheat sheet—profiles and names of all the mountains you're seeing, more than four dozen of them. The trail is fine for kids, but keep a close eye on the littlest ones; the dropoff is perilous on the south side. The trailhead is on Rt. 302, about a mile east of downtown Fryeburg, on the left, between the Jockey Cap Country Store and the Jockey Cap Motel.

The 60-acre **Hiram Nature Study Area,** established by Central Maine Power alongside the Hiram Dam on the Saco River, has two linked loop trails covering just over a mile. Take the Base Trail, leading down to the river. En route are signs identifying trees, shrubs, wildflowers, and other botanical specimens. Bring a picnic. From Fryeburg, take Rt. 5/113 southeast to Hiram, then continue about two miles south of Hiram village to the unpaved, signposted road into the preserve.

Allow about half an hour to reach the summit of **Sabattus Mountain** in Lovell, north of Fryeburg. This is an especially good family hike, easy and short enough for small children. Carry a picnic and enjoy the views at the top—on the ledges of the more open second summit. You'll see the White Mountains, Pleasant Mountain, and skinny Kezar Lake; in fall, it's fabulous. To reach the trailhead from Fryeburg, take Rt. 5 north to Center Lovell. About .8 mile after the junction of Rts. 5 and 5A, turn right onto Sabattus Road. Go about 1.6 miles, bearing right at the fork onto an unpaved road. Continue a very short distance to a parking area on the left; the trailhead is across the road. Roundtrip hike is about one and a half miles.

Other good hikes in this area are **Mount Tom** (easy, about two and a half hours roundtrip; just east of Fryeburg), **Burnt Meadow Mountain** (moderately difficult, about four hours roundtrip to the north peak; good views of the Presidential Range; near Brownfield); and **Mount Cutler** (moderately difficult, about two hours roundtrip; near Hiram).

FESTIVALS AND EVENTS

Anything happening in Bethel and Vicinity, Oxford Hills, or Sebago and Long Lakes is also within easy reach.

The **Ossipee Valley Fair** is an old-fashioned, four-day agricultural fair with tractor pulling, animal exhibits, live entertainment, food booths, games, and a carnival. In South Hiram the second weekend in July.

The Big Event in these parts is the **Fryeburg Fair,** the last country fair of the season (first week of October, sometimes including a few days in September), Maine's largest agricultural fair, and an annual event since 1851. A parade, a carnival, craft demonstrations and exhibits, harness racing, pig scrambles, children's activities, ox pulling, and live entertainment are all on offer, as are plenty of food booths (this is sometimes called the "fried-burg" fair). More than 400,000 turn out for eight days of festivities, so expect traffic congestion. Fair runs from Sun-

day to Sunday, and the busiest day is Saturday. No dogs allowed on the 180-acre site. Spectacular fall foliage and mountain scenery just add to the appeal. At the Fryeburg Fairgrounds (a.k.a. West Oxford Agricultural Society Fairgrounds), Rt. 5, Fryeburg.

ACCOMMODATIONS

If you're planning to be in the area during the Fryeburg Fair, you'll need to reserve beds or campsites months ahead, in some cases a year in advance. Don't procrastinate.

B&Bs
Named after the famed polar explorer who lived here in the late 19th century, the **Admiral Peary House,** 9 Elm St., Fryeburg 04037, tel. (207) 935-3365 or (800) 237-8080, has five Peary-themed rooms (private baths) that go for $98-108 d in summer, $108-118 d during foliage season (late September to mid-October), and $70-80 d in winter. Tennis enthusiasts Nancy and Ed Greenberg encourage guests to use their clay court, or wander the perennial gardens or borrow a bike. You'll have the run of several comfortable first-floor rooms, good when the weather closes in. No smoking, no small children, no pets. Open all year, but advance reservations are required in winter.

In the center of town, **The Oxford House Inn,** 105 Main St., Rt. 302, Fryeburg 04037, tel. (207) 935-3442 or (800) 261-7206, has five comfortable second-floor rooms with private baths ($75-95 d). Breakfasts, served in the mountain-view dining room, are every bit as creative as the inn's lunch and dinner menus. No smoking. Open all year.

Cottage Colony
The New York Times once headlined a story on **Quisisana,** Kezar Lake, Center Lovell 04016, tel. (207) 925-3500, winter address P.O. Box 142, Larchmont, NY 10538, tel. (914) 833-0293, as "Where Mozart Goes on Vacation." Amen. By day, the staff at this elegantly rustic 47-acre retreat masquerades as waiters and waitresses, chambermaids, boat crew, and kitchen help; each night, presto, they're the stars of musical performances worthy of Broadway and concert

hall ticket prices. Since 1947, it's been like this at "Quisi"—with a staff recruited from the nation's best conservatories. (The resort was founded in 1917.) Veteran managers attuned to guests' needs keep it all working smoothly.

The frosting on all this culture is the setting—a beautifully landscaped pine grove on the shores of Kezar Lake, looking off to the White Mountains and dramatic sunsets. No wonder that reservations for the 38 white cottages are hard to come by. The New York-heavy clientele knows to book well ahead, often for the same week, and new generations have followed their parents here. A week at Quisisana runs $1,500-2,000 d, American Plan. No credit cards; beer and wine only. Quisisana's season begins in mid-June and ends in late August. Lower rates prevail before mid-July, when a one-week minimum is imposed.

Hostel

Well off the beaten path, in a lovely rural setting, is the **Wadsworth-Blanchard Farm Hostel,** Tripp Town Rd., South Hiram, mailing address RR2, Box 5992, Hiram 04041, tel. (207) 625-7509. Ed Bradley and Sally Whitcher, longtime peace activists, have created a comfortable, modernized hostel on land once owned by cousins of Henry Wadsworth Longfellow. Affiliated with Hostelling International, the hostel draws a steady stream of American and international visitors; the camaraderie and networking have become legendary since it opened in 1994. Two dorm rooms have three or four beds each; bring a sleeping bag. Cost is $10 pp. A separate room for families, including linens, is $30. Kitchen and bath facilities are shared, and recycling is encouraged. No smoking or alcohol, no credit cards. Half a mile away is Stanley Pond, with a sandy beach. The hostel, two miles north of South Hiram village, is open May through October.

Campgrounds

Canoeing is the major focus at **Woodland Acres Campground,** Rt. 160, RFD 1, Box 445, Brownfield 04010, tel. (207) 935-2529, fax 935-3479, with a 100-canoe fleet available for rent ($35-38 a day, including shuttle service; reduced rates for additional canoes). This well-maintained campground on the Saco River has 55 wooded tent and RV sites ($19-26 a night per family; two-night weekend minimum). Riverfront sites are the best, but you'll need to stay a week in July and August unless you luck out with a cancellation. Facilities include a snack bar, beach, laundry room, and playground. Leashed pets are allowed. From Fryeburg, take Rt. 5/13 southeast to Rt. 160. Turn left (north) and go a mile to the campground. Open mid-May to mid-October.

Also in Brownfield, and also geared toward canoeists, is **River Run,** Rt. 160, P.O. Box 90, Brownfield 04010, tel. (207) 452-2500, with 21 primitive tentsites on 130 acres next to the Saco River's Brownfield Bridge; no hookups. Canoe rental is $22 a day on weekends, $18 weekdays, including parking. Saco River shuttle service is available at $8 per rental canoe, $17 for your own canoe. At the end of the season, River Run sells its rental canoes at greatly reduced rates; call to find out when the bargains begin. The campground is open mid-May through September; after Labor Day, reservations are required.

Three miles north of Fryeburg, **Canal Bridge Campground,** Rt. 5, P.O. Box 181, Fryeburg 04037, tel. (207) 935-2286, has 50 tent and RV sites, also on the Saco River ($16 a night for two). Noise rules are strictly enforced. Facilities include a canoe launch, beach, snack bar, convenience store, and playground. No credit cards. No rental canoes, but they're happy to arrange rental and shuttle service. Open mid-May to mid-October.

The Appalachian Mountain Club maintains two wilderness campgrounds on the Saco River. The **AMC Swan's Falls Campground,** Rt. 5, Fryeburg 04037, tel. (207) 935-3395, just north of Fryeburg, has 18 campsites open May through October. For reservations, call between 6 and 10 p.m. The **AMC Walker's Falls Campground,** RR 1, Box 331, East Brownfield 04010, no telephone, a five-hour paddle downriver from Swan's Falls, also is open May through October.

FOOD

The creative menu (entrées $18-20) at **The Oxford House Inn,** in downtown Fryeburg, tel. (207) 935-3442, has earned the inn a first-rate reputation. The back dining room (where B&B guests have breakfast) has wonderful mountain views. Dinner reservations are wise, especially in July and August and during the Fryeburg Fair. No smoking. Open for lunch only July to mid-October; open for dinner daily 6-9 p.m., June-Oct., and Thurs.-Sat., Nov.-May.

What do you do for an encore when you've won a country inn in an essay contest and become a cover story in *The New York Times Magazine*? You prove you deserved it, and that's what's happened at the **Center Lovell Inn & Restaurant**, Rt. 5, P.O. Box 261, Center Lovell 04016, tel. (207) 925-1575 or (800) 777-2698. Janice and Richard Cox have been here since 1993, serving an enthusiastic clientele drawn to Richard's wide-ranging continental menu, which changes weekly (entrées $17-20). Save room for one of Janice's desserts. Best tables are on the glassed-in porch, where you can watch the sun slip behind the mountains. The inn serves dinner daily 6-9 p.m. May-Oct.; reservations are advised, especially in mid-summer. From December to March, dinner is served Friday and Saturday, as well as daily

during school vacation weeks. Breakfast is served to the public daily 8:30-9 a.m., May-Oct., only by reservation. The inn has five second-floor rooms (private and shared baths) in the 1805 main building, plus five more (private and shared baths) in the adjacent Harmon House. Lodging rates are $68-98 d without meals, $128-158 d MAP (set menu), and $148-178 d (choice of menu). The inn and its restaurant are open May-Oct. and Dec.-March.

INFORMATION AND SERVICES

On the Maine side of the New Hampshire border, just west of downtown Fryeburg, the **Maine Publicity Bureau** information center, Rt. 302, Fryeburg 04037, tel. (207) 935-3639, is open mid-May to mid-October, daily 9 a.m.-5 p.m., with visitor information about the entire state. Since Fryeburg has no chamber of commerce, you'll want to pick up local information there. Or check with the **Fryeburg Town Office**, 2 Lovewell's Pond Rd., Fryeburg 04037, tel. (207) 935-2805, open weekdays only.

SEBAGO AND LONG LAKES

Maine's Lakes region, the area along the shores of Sebago and Long Lakes, includes the two major hubs of Bridgton (pop. 4,200) and Naples (pop. 3,120) as well as the smaller communities of East Sebago and Harrison and the larger communities of Raymond, Casco, and Windham.

Settled in 1768, Bridgton was incorporated in 1794; Naples was not incorporated until 1834. When the summer-vacation boom began in the mid-19th century, and then erupted after the Civil War, visitors flowed into this area—via stagecoach, the Cumberland and Oxford Canal, and later the Bridgton and Saco Railroad.

The 28-lock canal, opened in 1830 and shut down in 1870, connected the Fore River in Portland with Sebago and Long Lakes. Its only working remnant is the Songo Lock in Naples, on the Songo River between Brandy Pond and Sebago Lake.

Sebago is an apt Native American word meaning "large, open water"; it's the state's sec-

ond-largest lake (after Moosehead), and flukey winds can kick up suddenly and toss around little boats, so be prudent. Now a major water source for Greater Portland, the lake reportedly served as the crossroads for major Native American trading routes, and artifacts still occasionally surface in the Sebago Basin area.

Engage in a heart-to-heart with an adult vacationing in this area and you're likely to find someone trying to recapture the past—the carefree days at summer camp in the Sebago and Long Lakes region. The shores of Sebago, Long, and Highland Lakes shelter dozens of children's camps that have created several generations of Maine enthusiasts—"people from away" who still can't resist an annual visit. Unless your own kids are in camp, however, or you're terminally masochistic, do *not* appear in Bridgton, Naples, or surrounding communities on the third weekend in July. Parents, grandparents, and surrogate parents all show up then for the midseason summer-camp break, and there isn't a bed or restaurant seat in the entire county, maybe beyond. Gridlock is the rule.

The rest of the time, congestion can occur on a regular basis in the center of Naples, where traffic backs up half a mile when the drawbridge on the causeway opens for boat traffic passing between Brandy Pond and Long Lake. Openings are on the hour—every hour on weekends, every other hour on weekdays. Plan accordingly.

Aside from those minor glitches, this mountain-lake setting has incredible locales for canoeing, swimming, hiking, fishing, golfing, camping, biking, ice-skating, snowshoeing, and skiing. (Maine's first ski lift opened in 1938 on Pleasant Mountain, now the Shawnee Peak ski area.) If rain descends, head for Bridgton's historic Magic Lantern movie theater, or the unique Jones Museum in East Sebago. And be sure to check the schedule for Harrison's Deertrees Theatre—a fascinating National Historic Register building recently restored for summertime plays and concerts.

The lakes are terribly convenient to Portland—Sebago is the large body of water on the west as you descend into the Portland Jetport.

SIGHTS

The Jones Museum
Each year, amateurs, experts, and the curious from more than two dozen countries arrive at **The Jones Museum of Glass and Ceramics,** Douglas Mountain Rd., Sebago 04029, tel.

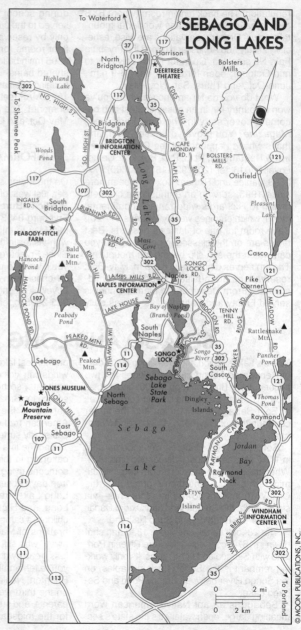

SEBAGO AND LONG LAKES

© MOON PUBLICATIONS, INC.

(207) 787-3370, fax 787-2800, to view the 8,000-piece collection assembled by glass and ceramics specialist Dorothy-Lee Jones, who founded the museum in 1978. There's nothing in New England quite like this astonishing collection of antique and ancient artifacts. Special exhibits—on Wedgwood or paperweights or tiles—add to the phenomenon; related summertime seminars are held at the museum's Douglas Mountain Conference Center. The user-friendly library has thousands of specialized reference books, so you can research your own treasures. The only minor drawback is too-brief labeling for nonaficionados. The **Gallery Shop** stocks reasonably priced antique glass and china, plus contemporary replicas. Youngsters enjoy some of the offbeat items in the museum collection, but this is no place for hyperactive ones—leave them outside to run on the spacious lawn. Bring along a picnic, grab a table, and absorb the dramatic view of the White Mountains. Afterward, you can head farther up the road to the Douglas Mountain Preserve. Located 28 miles northwest of Portland, the museum is a mile west of Rt. 107 (Douglas Mountain Road is also called Douglas Hill Road). It's open May to mid-November, Mon.-Sat. 10 a.m.-5 p.m. and Sunday 1-5 p.m. Admission is $5 adults, $3.50 seniors, $3 students; children under 12 are free.

Narramissic, the Peabody-Fitch Farm

Built in 1797 and converted to Federal style in 1828, the Peabody-Fitch Farm is the crown jewel of the Bridgton Historical Society. Still undergoing restoration—now to the pre-Civil War era—the homestead includes a carriage house, ell, barn, blacksmith shop, and historic gardens. The barn has its own story: it's known as the "Temperance Barn" because the landowners were avowed teetotalers, so the volunteer barn-raisers earned only water for their efforts. Narramissic is a relatively recent name, given to it by the 20th-century owner who donated it to the historical society in 1986. The name is a Native American word meaning "hard to find," reflecting her lengthy search for a family summer home. But it also suits the circuitous route, fortunately signposted, to the South Bridgton farm from downtown Bridgton (Main St. to Rt. 117 to Rt. 107 to Ingalls Road). Season highlights are the annual antiques show and the Western Maine Heritage Festival. The farm is open for guided tours in July and August, Wed.-Sun. 11 a.m.-3 p.m. Tickets are $3 adults, $2 seniors and children. A gift shop in the farmhouse ell stocks interesting crafts and relevant books. Contact the **Bridgton Historical Society,** P.O. Box 44, Bridgton 04009, tel. (207) 647-3699 or 647-2765, for more information.

Shades of Mississippi

Berthed in downtown Naples, Maine, is a 90-foot Mississippi sternwheeler replica that operates narrated cruises throughout the summer: the *Songo River Queen II,* Bay of Naples Causeway, Rt. 302, P.O. Box 917, Naples 04055, tel. (207) 693-6861. Opt for the two-and-a-half-hour Songo River trip: you'll cross Brandy Pond and head downriver, transiting the 19th-century **Songo River Lock** via a hand-turned swing bridge that raises and lowers the river level by five feet. Kids love it, and the lockkeeper plays to his audience. Cost is $10 adults, $6 children. The other option is a one-hour Long Lake cruise ($7 adults, $4 kids). Cruises operate daily, rain or shine, July to Labor Day (two Songo cruises, three Long Lake trips). In June and September, the boat only operates weekends, making one Songo Lock cruise daily at 9:45 a.m. On a clear day, you can even spot Mount Washington, centerpiece of the White Mountains; bring binoculars and a camera. On board are restrooms and a snack bar.

Also berthed at the causeway is the *U.S. Mailboat* (same address and telephone as *Songo River Queen II*), a pontoon boat that departs Mon.-Sat. at 10:30 a.m. to deliver mail to lakefront homeowners. Mailboat season is the last Saturday in June to the Saturday before Labor Day. Cost is $5.50 adults, $3.50 children.

Presidential Maine

Inspired by a famous western Maine signpost giving directions to nine Maine towns named for foreign cities and countries, Boy Scouts in Casco decided to create some competition—a directional sign for 10 Maine towns named for U.S. presidents. The marker stands next to the Village Green in **Casco,** at the corner of Rt. 121 and Leach Hill Road, pointing to towns such as Washington (76 miles), Lincoln (175 miles), Madison, and Monroe. There's even a Clinton (84 miles).

If you're here in the fall, take time to detour briefly to Casco's "million-dollar view." Continue south from the signpost less than two miles on Rt. 121 to Rt. 11 (Pike Corner), turn right (west) and go about half a mile to Quaker Ridge Rd. and turn left (south). Views are spectacular along here, especially from the Quaker Hill area —worth bringing a panorama camera.

PARKS AND PRESERVES

Sebago Lake State Park
Fourth largest of Maine's state parks, 1,300-acre Sebago Lake State Park, State Park Rd., RR 1, Box 101, Naples 04055, tel. (207) 693-6613 late June to Labor Day, (207) 693-6231 off season, is one of the most popular—so don't look for peace and quiet here during July and August. Swimming and picnicking are superb, fishing is so-so, personal watercraft are an increasing hazard. During the summer, park officials organize lectures, hikes, and other activities; the schedule is posted at the gate. Day-use admission is $2.50 adults, 50 cents children 5-11; children under five are free. More than 70,000 campers sleep at the 250 sites each year, so far-ahead reservations are essential for midsummer, tel. (207) 287-3824 with Visa or MasterCard; two-night minimum, no hookups. Nonresident rate is $16 per site per night, plus a $2-per-night reservation fee. No pets. The park is open May to mid-October, but there's winter access for four and a half miles of groomed cross-country-skiing trails, mostly beginner terrain. It's ideal, too, for snowshoeing.

You can access the park's separate picnicking and camping areas from Rt. 302 in Casco. Take State Park Rd. to the fork, where you go left to the picnic area or right to Songo Lock and the camping area. (Both sections have sandy beaches, now slightly diminished after major storms in 1996.) Or, from downtown Naples, take Rt. 11/114 to Thompson Point Rd. and follow the signs.

Douglas Mountain Preserve
Just up the hill from the Jones Museum is the trailhead for the Douglas Mountain Preserve. Formerly owned by The Nature Conservancy, it was deeded to the town of Sebago in 1997. Fortunately or unfortunately, Douglas Mountain

(also called Douglas Hill) is one of southern Maine's most popular hikes, so you probably won't be alone. Park in the lot (on the left, above the museum), a welcome new addition ($3 per vehicle); a parking attendant is on duty 9 a.m.-6 p.m. Walk farther up, take a brochure from the registration box, and follow the easy Woods Trail to the 1,415-foot summit—30 minutes maximum. At the top is a .75-mile nature-trail loop, plus a 16-foot stone tower with a head-spinning view. In the fall, the vistas are incomparable. Be ecosensitive and stick to the trails in this 169-acre preserve. No pets. The trails are accessible dawn to dusk.

RECREATION

Hiking
Six interconnecting trails provide access to the main summit (2,000 feet) of **Pleasant Mountain,** but one of the most popular—and relatively easiest for kids—is the Ledges (or Moose) Trail. In late July, allow four hours for the three-and-a-half-mile roundtrip, so you can pick blueberries on the open ledges midway up. At the top is a disused fire tower—and plenty of space for spreading out a picnic overlooking panoramic vistas of woods, lakes, and mountains. The mountain straddles the Denmark/Bridgton town line, as well as the Cumberland/Oxford county line. From Bridgton, drive five and three quarter miles west on Rt. 302 to Mountain Rd. (just after the causeway over Moose Pond). Turn left (south) at signs for Shawnee Peak ski area and go 3.3 miles to the trailhead for the Ledges (or Moose) Trail; parking is limited. An alternative access route, from the west side of the mountain, is via the Wilton Warren Road, also south of Rt. 302.

Swimming
Besides two sandy beaches at Sebago Lake State Park, other swimming locations are the **Naples Town Beach, Crystal Lake Beach** in Harrison, **Salmon Point** and **Highland Lake** in Bridgton, and **Tassel Top Beach** in Raymond.

Golf
Bridgton Highlands Country Club, Highland Ridge Rd., RR 3, Box 1065, Bridgton 04009, tel. (207) 647-3491, recently expanded to 18 holes,

is outstandingly scenic and very popular, especially at the height of summer. Call for a starting time. Greens and cart fees are not cheap, but no one seems to object. Also at the club are four tennis courts, a pro shop, and a snack bar. The course, about two miles from downtown Bridgton, is open May through October.

Less expensive but also scenic is the nine-hole **Naples Golf and Country Club**, Rt. 114, Naples 04055, tel. (207) 693-6424, established in 1922. Light meals are available at the clubhouse, and there's a pro shop. On midsummer weekends, call for a starting time. The course, across from the Naples Golf Driving Range, adjoins Bay of Naples Family Camping. It's open mid-April through October.

One of the newest courses in the area is the championship-level **Point Sebago Golf Club**, Rt. 302, RR 1, Box 712, Casco 04015, tel. (207) 655-2747, part of a once-low-key campground transformed into the 800-acre Club-Med-style Point Sebago Golf and Beach Resort. Call for starting times at the 18-hole course, which is open to the public. Golf-and-lodging packages are available. Open May to mid-October.

Getting Afloat

In addition to cruises on the *Songo River Queen II,* and the mailboat rides, you can rent your own pontoon boat, powerboat, or, if you must, a water scooter (officially, a personal watercraft, PWC, often referred to by the trademark-name Jetski). Water scooters have become a major itch on huge Sebago Lake, as well as many other Maine lakes, and there's no gray area in the opinion department. Biggest objections are noise pollution and excessive speed. The state requires PWCs to be licensed as powerboats, but regulations are weak, the state legislature has taken little action, and inadequate funding has led to inadequate enforcement. Each year, fatalities occur, spurring towns to try (usually unsuccessfully) to ban or limit PWCs. If you *do* rent one, play by the rules, exercise caution, and operate at sensible speeds.

Naples Marina, Rts. 302 and 114, Naples 04055, tel. (207) 693-6254, behind Rick's Café, rents pontoon boats, runabouts, and fishing boats. **Causeway Marina,** Rt. 302, Naples 04055, tel. (207) 693-6832, rents canoes, powerboats, pontoon boats, water-skiing boats and gear, and PWCs. Both marinas are open daily during the summer.

If you've brought a **canoe or kayak,** don't launch it into Sebago Lake; save it for the smaller lakes and ponds, where the winds are less flukey and the boat traffic is less congested. Long Lake is also a possibility, if you put in at Harrison, on the east side.

Winter Sports

Judicious marketing, reasonable rates, top-to-bottom snowmaking, and 16 trails lighted for night skiing have made **Shawnee Peak,** Rt. 302, Bridgton 04009, tel. (207) 647-8444, an increasingly popular destination. Its proximity to Portland (45 miles) boosts the appeal for day-trip skiing. Vertical drop is 1,300 feet; one quad, two triples, a double, and a surface lift serve 34 trails, more than half intermediate. Weekend and holiday lift tickets for adults are $38 for day skiing, $24 for night skiing, and $42 for all day and all night. Midweek rates are lower, except for night skiing. Children six and under (with an adult) ski free. Lots of special rates depend on the day and season. There's even a lighted tubing park. Rental skis are $17 a day, $13 at night, less for children. Snowboards are $21 a day ($5 extra for boots). When you've had your fill of night skiing, the **Blizzards Pub,** in the base lodge, is a lively spot to kick back. Friday and Saturday nights, there's usually live entertainment. Lodging information is available through Shawnee Peak's main phone line, or see "Seasonal Rentals," below, under "Accommodations." The ski area is six miles west of downtown Bridgton.

In 1997, Shawnee Peak introduced mountain biking trails, primarily intermediate and expert, served by the triple chairlift. Call (207) 647-8444 for information on hours and cost.

ENTERTAINMENT

Tucked away on a back road in Harrison, east of Long Lake, dramatic-looking, 278-seat **Deertrees Theatre,** Deertrees Rd., P.O. Box 577, Harrison 04040, tel. (207) 583-6747, is a must-see even if you don't attend a performance. The acoustically superior National Historic Register building, constructed of rose hemlock in 1936, has seen the likes of Rudy Vallee, Ethel Barrymore, Tallulah Bankhead, and Henry Winkler; recent restoration of the rustic building has given it an exciting new life. Each summer season (early July to early September) includes five concerts in the acclaimed annual Sebago-Long Lake Chamber Music Festival, plus jazz, ragtime, pops, and classical programs. The theater is off Rt. 117 (signposted) in the Harrison woods.

In the center of Bridgton, the **Magic Lantern,** 69 Main St., Bridgton 04009, tel. (207) 647-5065 recorded message, is a 1929 movie house showing first-run films. Tickets are $5.50 adults, $4 seniors and kids (under 12); matinees (Sat.-Thurs. at 3:30 p.m.) are $3.50 for all. Open all year.

One of a dying species, **Bridgton Drive-In,** Rt. 302, Bridgton 04009, tel. (207) 647-8666, screens a double feature each night in summer, beginning at dusk. Tickets are $5 adults, $3 children 11 and under. The drive-in is two and a half miles south of downtown Bridgton.

Nearest first-run multiplex is in North Windham. The seven-screen **Cinema Center,** tel. (207) 892-7000, is at the Windham Mall on Rt. 302. Depending on the films, the earliest show begins around noon, last show begins around 9:45 p.m.

FESTIVALS AND EVENTS

The **Shawnee Peak** ski area, tel. (207) 647-8444, has a full schedule of family-oriented special events, including races, throughout the winter; call for information.

Nearly a hundred teams compete in the **Mushers Bowl,** two days of dogsled and ski-joring races on Highland Lake, a great spectator event in West Bridgton the first full weekend in February. Be sure to leave your own pets at home.

Naples celebrates **Naples Days** with a carnival, a parade, bike and road races, and plenty of food the third weekend in June.

Bridgton's **Pondicherry Days** take place over three or four days of festivities around July Fourth and include an art show, a parade, a concert, a book sale, a road race, food, and fireworks. The name comes from the former Pondicherry Mills factory, which once operated here. Bridgton's annual **Chickadee Quilters Quilt Show** features exhibits and sales of magnificent quilts and wall hangings at the Bridgton Town Hall the second Saturday in July. From mid-July to mid-August, the **Sebago-Long Lake Chamber Music Festival** brings Tuesday-night (8 p.m.) chamber-music concerts to Harrison's Deertrees Theatre, Harrison. Advance booking is essential for this popular series, founded in 1975, tel. (207) 583-6747. Single tickets cost $15. Also mid-July to mid-August, Sunday-evening **band concerts** around the gazebo behind the Naples Information Center are free. Bring a chair or blanket to the Village Green, Rt. 302, Naples. The third Saturday in July, the Bridgton Historical Society's long-running and respected **Annual Antiques Show** takes place at Peabody-Fitch Farm, South Bridgton.

The **Great State of Maine Sailboat Regatta,** the first Saturday in August on Long Lake, is open to everyone and offers lots of prizes. Registration is at 11 a.m., race at noon. The same day sees the **Western Maine Heritage Festival,** a day-long (10 a.m.-4 p.m.) rural-heritage celebration at South Bridgton's 18th-century Peabody-Fitch Farm. You'll see period clothing and demos of traditional handcrafts, plus live music and food.

SHOPPING

Interesting shops fill historic buildings along the main drag in downtown Bridgton, best source in this region for crafts, gifts, and more—especially the work of Maine artisans.

Antiques

Nearly 40 dealers sell their wares at **Wales & Hamblen Antique & Gift Center,** 134 Main St., Bridgton 04009, tel. (207) 647-3840. Inventory includes antiques as well as "tomorrow's antiques." The quirky old National Historic Register building in downtown Bridgton is open Memorial Day weekend to late October, Wed.-Mon. 9 a.m.-5 p.m. (opening at noon on Sunday).

Carol Honaberger's **Lamp and Shade Shop,** 95 Main St. Bridgton 04009, tel. (207) 647-5576, has cornered the market in antique lighting fixtures and custom-made new lampshades. They'll also repair damaged fixtures or convert any kind of treasured objet into a serviceable lamp. The shop is open daily, Memorial Day to

Columbus Day; in winter, the schedule can be erratic, so call ahead to be sure.

Art Gallery

The **Lakes Gallery and Sculpture Garden,** Rt. 302, P.O. Box 40, South Casco 04077, tel. (207) 655-5066, features paintings and prints, primarily Maine artists, with changing shows each month. Outside is the state's largest sculpture garden, displaying work in bronze, steel, stone, and wood. The respected gallery is open April to late December, daily 10 a.m.-5 p.m. (Also see Cry of the Loon Gift Shop, below.)

Books

Bridgton Books, 74 Main St., Bridgton 04009, tel. (207) 647-2122, carries an excellent selection of books, cards, and classical CDs—a browser's (and buyer's) delight, with user-friendly hours. It's open all year, daily 9:30 a.m.-5:30 p.m. In July and August, the store is open Tues.-Sat. to 8 p.m.

Crafts and Gifts

A onetime Unitarian church and its church hall make terrific settings for the carefully chosen inventory at **Craftworks,** 53 Main St., Bridgton 04009, tel. (207) 647-5436, a Bridgton landmark since the early 1970s. Owner Judith Evergreen combs studios, fairs, and national gift shows for her superbly eclectic stock. In the church building are clothing, jewelry, and pottery; in the church hall are garden and kitchen specialty items, plus wine and gourmet goodies. Both buildings are open April to mid-October (daily 9 a.m.-6 p.m., to 9 p.m. in midsummer); the smaller building then stays open until late December.

Hezekiah's Cupboard, 93 Main St., Bridgton 04009, tel. (207) 647-5649, concentrates on Maine-made crafts, with high-end pottery, unique jewelry and crocheted items, baskets, and dolls. No credit cards. The shop is open daily 11 a.m.-6 p.m., July through Labor Day. From September to December, it's open Thurs.-Tues. 11 a.m.-5 p.m.; Jan.-June, Fri.-Sun. 10 a.m.-4 p.m., or by appointment.

On the east side of Long Lake, **The Sheep Shop,** 1533 Maple Ridge Rd., Harrison 04040, tel. (207) 583-2996, is the ultimate source for sheepskins in six colors ($65), washable wool blankets, sheepskin vests and jackets, sheepskin toys, Christmas ornaments, and wool and wool/mohair yarns. The Berry family produces a mail-order catalog, but it's more fun to visit the shop, open daily 9:30 a.m.-4:30 p.m., March-January. From Rt. 117 in Harrison, at the northeast corner of Crystal Lake, pick up Maple Ridge Rd. south to the farm.

The **Cry of the Loon Gift Shop,** Rt. 302, P.O. Box 40, South Casco 04077, tel. (207) 655-5060, at the same location as the Lakes Gallery and Sculpture Garden, has three floors of gifts, a tasteful, eclectic mix of gourmet condiments, Maine crafts, and much more. The shop is open daily 9 a.m.-7 p.m. in summer, daily 10 a.m.-6 p.m. off season, and 10 a.m.-5 p.m. in midwinter.

Sportswear and Sporting-Gear Rentals

No matter what the season, there isn't much you can't rent, sports-wise, at the **Sportshaus,** 61 Main St., Bridgton 04009, tel. (207) 647-5100, which also stocks a selection of sportswear. In summer, the shop rents mountain bikes ($25 a day), canoes and kayaks ($20 a day), Sunfish ($35 a day), and in-line skates ($15 a day). For an extra fee, they'll deliver. If you want to try waterskiing, a demo is $15 pp. In winter, you can rent downhill skis ($14 a day on weekends), snowboards ($16 a day, plus $4 for boots), and cross-country skis and snowshoes ($15 a day). Rates are lower for additional days and weekdays, as well as for kids. The shop is open daily 9 a.m.-5:30 p.m., summer and winter; it's closed Sunday and Monday in spring and fall.

Sportshaus also has a seasonal branch, tel. (207) 647-3000, on Rt. 302 near the Shawnee Peak ski area. It's open daily, Dec.-Feb. 8 a.m.-8 p.m., and Oct.-Nov. and March 9 a.m.-5 p.m.

Farmers' Markets

Bridgton and Naples are relatively new to the farmers' market scene, so their selections are not quite as broad as some of the longer-running operations. Still, you're bound to find something that tempts you to open your wallet. The **Bridgton/Naples Farmers' Market** is open Thursday 8 a.m.-1 p.m. in Naples, in the American Legion parking lot, Rt. 11 (just off Rt. 302). In Bridgton, it's open Saturday 8 a.m.-1 p.m., in the

Crafters Outlet parking lot on Main St. (Rt. 302). The markets run early May to early October.

ACCOMMODATIONS

B&Bs

Our Home Bed & Breakfast, 79 S. High St., Bridgton 04009, tel. (207) 647-2381, is just what it sounds like—Tricia and Chris Dillman's well-maintained 1870s home where guests get special treatment. Three second-floor rooms share two baths; a first-floor room has a private bath ($75 d with private bath, $65 d shared). A high point is ex-caterer Tricia's gourmet breakfast, with eggs Benedict a daily menu option. Two common rooms have cable TV and lots of games; light afternoon tea always includes a homebaked treat. In winter, Chris hitches up the huskies and takes guests on dogsled rides. Children are welcome, but no pets. No smoking, no credit cards. Open all year.

On a busy corner in downtown Bridgton, convenient to all the shops, **The Bridgton House Bed & Breakfast,** 2 Main St., Bridgton 04009, tel. (207) 647-0979, was opened by genial innkeepers Joan Opper and Lois Patterson in 1995. Built in 1815, the house has been tastefully updated. Three rooms have private baths ($90 d), two share a bath ($85 d). If you're highly noise-sensitive, request a back-facing room. No pets, no small children, no smoking, no credit cards. Open May through October.

Book a room at the **Songo Locks Bed & Breakfast,** 120 Songo Locks Rd., Naples 04055, tel. (207) 693-6955, then pull up a riverside lawn chair and watch the water go by—to and from the historic, hand-cranked Songo Lock close by the B&B. (The lock operates May 1-Oct. 15, 8 a.m.-8 p.m.) The pine-paneled, carpeted guest rooms overlook the Songo River, too—as does the windowed dining area, where the blueberry pancakes are legendary. Five rooms share three baths ($75 d). An entrance to Sebago Lake State Park is just across the road—for swimming and cross-country skiing. Extras for guests include canoes, a park pass, and ski and restaurant discounts. No pets, no smoking; children are welcome. The B&B, open all year, is four miles from downtown Naples. It's just behind the Songo Locks Snack Bar, a fa-

vorite munchie stop for boaters and bikers (open 11 a.m.-9 p.m. June-Sept. and weekends in October).

Cottage-Colony Resort

On the east side of Sebago Lake is a cottage-colony resort so popular that reservations are truly scarce. Persevere. July and August are the sticking points; other months are not as booked up.

At **Migis Lodge,** Migis Lodge Rd., P.O. Box 40, South Casco 04077, tel. (207) 655-4524, fax 655-2054, guests often confirm their next-year's July or August booking before they depart for home. The rustic elegance of 100-acre Migis, along with attentive service and a fabulous lakeside setting have drawn big-name guests over the years—ever since the resort was established in the early 20th century as lodging for the parents of summer campers. Men wear jackets for dinner, and special arrangements are made for kids' suppers. All this comes at a price, which includes almost everything but tax and tips: sailboats, island cookouts, waterskiing, tennis courts, even a cinema. Daily rates in July and August for the 29 lake-view cottages (1-3 bedrooms) are $230-360 d, American Plan; one-week minimum. In the main lodge, seven rooms (private and shared baths) are $160-230 d per day, also AP. Shorter stays, and slightly lower rates, are available early and late in the season. No credit cards, no pets. Open mid-June to mid-October. Migis is down an unpaved road off Rt. 302.

Campgrounds

Camping is especially popular in this part of Maine, and many campgrounds have long-term RV or "immobile" home rentals, so you'll need to plan well ahead and reserve sites in advance. Be forewarned, though, that if you're looking for a wilderness camping experience, especially in midsummer, you probably ought to head for the hills. Many of the campgrounds in this area feature nonstop organized fun, which is fine for enthusiastic families, but the intense activity can be overwhelming. Most campground managers do a creditable job of maintaining order and quiet, but even the best ones are chockablock in July and August.

Bay of Naples Family Camping, Rt. 11/114, Box 240, Naples 04055, tel. (207) 693-6429 or (800) 348-9750 outside Maine, fax (207) 693-6052, has a fine track record for noise-level control. It also has such nice touches as a private sand beach, two playgrounds, and an outside slate sink at the showerhouse for dishwashing. The 23-acre campground on the Bay of Naples (a.k.a. Brandy Pond, between Long and Sebago Lakes) has 150 good-size wooded sites at $20-26 for four; the tenting area is separate. No pets. Open late May to mid-October, the campground is a mile off Rt. 302, next to the Naples Golf and Country Club.

Seasonal Rentals
The Bridgton Group, 1 Mountain Rd., Bridgton 04009, tel. (207) 647-2591, coordinates a huge list of summer rentals—cottages to condos, most with access to a lake or pond—and winter homes and condos at or near the Shawnee Peak ski area. Most summer rentals are weekly; winter bookings are for a week or a weekend.

Krainin Real Estate, Rt. 302, P.O. Box 464, South Casco 04077, tel. (207) 655-3811, handles weekly (Saturday to Saturday) and monthly rentals for cottages on Sebago and Long Lakes as well as many of the surrounding smaller lakes and ponds. Krainin also arranges rentals on **Frye Island,** a thousand-acre summer community in the middle of Sebago Lake. It's accessible only by car ferry. Office hours are Mon.-Fri. 10 a.m.-4 p.m.

FOOD

See the "Public Suppers" listings in *The Bridgton News,* for details on chicken barbecues, potluck buffets, baked-bean suppers, and public breakfasts—all to benefit good local causes and all in the $5-7 range (less for kids).

Inexpensive to Moderate
Sharing space with Bridgton Books, the **Bountiful Berry Café,** 72 Main St., Bridgton 04009, tel. (207) 647-4100, starts you out with breakfast burritos and organic coffee, moves on to chili and delicious wrap sandwiches for lunch, then does gourmet pizzas and daily specials for dinner. You almost can't go wrong here. The porch

seats six; there are 15 inside seats. Or order it all to go. No credit cards. The café is open all year: daily 7 a.m.-9 p.m. in summer, 7 a.m.-2 p.m. (no dinner) off season.

If you get an outdoor table at **Rick's Café,** Rt. 302, on the Causeway, Naples 04055, tel. (207) 693-3759, you'll be right in the middle of all the action in downtown Naples. The café, with a reasonably priced menu and evidence of creativity, is open daily 11 a.m.-1 a.m., May to late September. Dinner service ends about 9 p.m., and there's light fare until 11 p.m. Most nights in summer, there's live entertainment, occasionally with a small cover charge.

Almost across the street from Rick's, **Sandy's at the Flight Deck,** Rt. 302, on the Causeway, Naples 04055, tel. (207) 693-3508, is practically *in* Long Lake, so you can watch floatplane takeoffs and all the boating traffic. An especially kid-friendly spot, the Flight Deck is open daily 7 a.m.-9 p.m., mid-May to Labor Day.

A popular landmark since the 1970s, the **Naples Lobster Pound,** Rt. 302, Naples 04055, tel. (207) 693-6580, satisfies lobster cravings but also serves up steak and pizza. The gray building, with outdoor tables, is a mile south of the Naples Causeway. Open July to Labor Day, Mon.-Fri. 4-11 p.m., Saturday and Sunday noon-11 p.m.

Located in a Victorian farmhouse previously known as the Epicurean Inn, **Bray's Brewpub and Eatery,** Rts. 302 and 35, Naples 04055, tel. (207) 693-6806, is the pioneer brewpub in this part of Maine. Dinner specialties are steaks, seafood, and ribs—$11-18. Most popular brew is Old Church Pale Ale, drawing raves from reviewers; four other "styles" are always available. If the brewmaster can spring free, he'll give a brewery tour on request—a 15-minute "quickie" or a 30-minute in-depth explanation of the process. Bray's is open all year, daily 11:30 a.m.-10 p.m. (to midnight Fri.-Sunday).

Around the other side of Long Lake, in a restored grist mill, the **Olde Mill Tavern,** Main St., Rt. 35, Harrison 04040, tel. (207) 583-4992, serves comfort food with flair, for mostly moderate prices (entrée range is $6-21). Every day has a special feature, and lobster is available year-round. The Thursday buffet (5-9 p.m.) is a bargain at $8.95; Sunday brunch is a breakfast-plus buffet for $7.95. Ethnic nights feature

Italian or Cajun cuisine. Most Saturdays, there's live entertainment. The Olde Mill is open all year, Mon.-Sat. 11:30 a.m.-9:30 p.m. (to 10 p.m. Friday and Saturday), and Sunday 10 a.m.-9:30 p.m. In winter, it's closed Tuesday.

INFORMATION AND SERVICES

The **Bridgton-Lakes Region Chamber of Commerce,** Rt. 302, P.O. Box 236, Bridgton 04009, tel. (207) 647-3472, has an attractive information center (with public restrooms) half a mile south of downtown Bridgton. In July and August, it's open daily 9 a.m.-5 p.m. Other months, it's open weekdays, but the hours are hard to predict.

In Naples, the **Naples Business Association,** Rt. 302, P.O. Box 412, Naples 04055, tel. (207) 693-3285 or (888) 623-5379, fax (207) 693-4557, operates a small brick information center on the Village Green, next to the 1831 Naples Town Hall on Rt. 302. It's open weekends 10 a.m.-4 p.m. in June, then daily 10 a.m.-4 p.m. July through Labor Day. If you're arriving off season, plan to write or phone for info in advance.

The **Windham Chamber of Commerce,** 835 Roosevelt Trail, Rt. 302, P.O. Box 1015, Windham 04062, tel. (207) 892-8265, has a small seasonal information booth along the Rt. 302 commercial strip. It's open Memorial Day weekend to Labor Day, 9 a.m.-5 p.m.

The **Bridgton Public Library,** Main St., Bridgton 04009, tel. (207) 647-2472, has extensive summer programs for children, including discussion groups for older kids, several levels of story hours, and a special Monday-morning "finger fun" event for babies and toddlers. The library is open Monday and Thursday 10 a.m.-5 p.m., Tuesday 1-8 p.m., Wednesday 1-5 p.m., and Friday and Saturday 10 a.m.-2 p.m.

Technologically in the forefront of small-town libraries, the **Naples Public Library,** Rt. 302, Naples 04055, tel. (207) 693-6841, was the first public library in the state to be hooked into the Internet. Located in a Victorian farmhouse, the library is open Tuesday and Thursday 10 a.m.-6 p.m., Saturday 10 a.m.-2 p.m., and Sunday noon-4 p.m.

Newspapers
The Bridgton News, tel. (207) 647-2851, published each Thursday, covers the Bridgton/Naples area as well as communities on the east shores of Sebago and Long Lakes. Calendar listings are extensive; the special "Summer Scene" section focuses on area happenings and recreational activities. The daily newspaper of choice is the *Portland Press Herald.*

The Lakes Guide, a free tabloid published weekly throughout the summer, contains calendar listings, ads, and feature articles. It's widely available throughout the area at shops, restaurants, and lodgings.

Emergencies
The **Northern Cumberland Memorial Hospital,** S. High St., Bridgton 04009, tel. (207) 647-8841, a small acute-care facility, has round-the-clock emergency-room service. For fire, police, and ambulance services in **Bridgton,** dial 911. For ambulance and fire departments in **Naples, Sebago, and Casco,** dial 911; for the county **sheriff (police),** call (800) 501-1111. The sheriff also has a Naples office, tel. (207) 693-3369.

LEWISTON/AUBURN AREA

A river runs through the heart of Lewiston and Auburn—the Androscoggin River, headwatered in the Rangeley Lakes and coursing southeastward until it joins the Kennebec in Merrymeeting Bay, near Brunswick. Surging over Great Falls, the mighty Androscoggin spurred 19th-century industrial development of the Twin Cities, where giant textile mills drew their power from the river

and their hardworking employees from the local community of Yankees, then Irish, French-Canadian, and other immigrants. The Quebecois and Acadian French, who flocked to mills in Lewiston, Biddeford, Sanford, Augusta, and Brunswick, today comprise Maine's largest ethnic minority. In Lewiston and Auburn, the French-accented voting registers reveal long lists of Plour-

des and Pomerleaus, Carons and Cloutiers, and the spires of Catholic churches still dominate the skyline.

Long before white men harnessed the falls of the Androscoggin, Native Americans recognized the area for its prime salmon fishing and set up seasonal campsites and year-round settlements. Nowadays, their artifacts occasionally turn up along the riverbanks.

European settlers began putting down roots around 1770, earning their keep from small water-powered mills. Quakers established a community as early as 1773. By 1852, the giant Bates Mill (of bedspread fame) began manufacturing cotton, expanding by century's end to an annual output of more than 10 million yards. During the Civil War, Bates was a prime supplier of fabric for soldiers' tents. In 1861, Lewiston was incorporated as a city; Auburn was incorporated in 1869.

By the early 20th century, with a dozen more mills on line, taking advantage of the conve-

nient hydropower, the lower reaches of the Androscoggin became quite polluted, a stinky eyesore until the 1980s, when environmental activists took up the cause. The river isn't 100% pristine, but it's getting there. You can stroll the banks, fish the waters, paddle a canoe, and get up close without holding your nose.

Lewiston (pop. 37,300) and Auburn (pop. 23,700)—quaintly called "the *other* LA"—still are not usual vacation destinations, but they deserve more than a drive-through glance. Lewiston is the state's second-largest city and the home of Bates College, a highly selective private liberal-arts school and a magnet for visiting performers, artists, and lecturers.

Auburn, the Androscoggin County seat, began its industrial career with a single shoe factory in 1836, expanding swiftly in those heady days. By the turn of the 20th century, Auburn's shoe factories were turning out six million pairs a year.

Lewiston and Auburn occupy a pivotal location in southern Maine, with easy access to Portland (35 miles away) and Freeport (28 miles), the western mountains, and the state capital (30 miles).

SIGHTS

Bates College

Founded in 1855 on foresighted egalitarian principles, Bates College received its current name after major financial input from Benjamin Bates of the Bates Mill. Located on a lovely wooded, 109-acre campus in the heart of Lewiston, the college earns high marks for small classes, a stellar faculty, a rigorous academic program, and a low faculty-to-student ratio. The student body of 1,600 comes from almost every state and more than two dozen foreign countries; diversity has always been evident. Oldest campus building is red-brick **Hathorn Hall,** built in 1856 and listed on the National Historic Register; one of the newest buildings, the Olin Arts Center, built in 1986, is an award-winning complex overlooking manmade Lake Andrews.

Within the **Olin Arts Center,** Russell and Bardwell Sts., tel. (207) 786-6135, are the **Bates College Museum of Art,** tel. (207) 786-6158, and the 300-seat **Olin Concert Hall.** Most college-sponsored exhibits, lectures, and concerts

Bates Chapel, at Bates College, Lewiston

MAINE OFFICE OF TOURISM

at the Arts Center are free and open to the public (other organizations also use the concert hall). Monthly events calendars are published in the Lewiston papers. Each Thursday (6 p.m.) from mid-July to mid-August, free **lakeside concerts** are presented outside the Arts Center; bring a picnic and a blanket or chair. The Museum of Art, with rotating exhibits, is open all year, Tues.-Sat. 10 a.m.-5 p.m. (free admission).

Also open to the public are sporting events in Merrill Gym, Alumni Gym, and Underhill Ice Arena; except for the outdoor track (for walking or jogging) and Lake Andrews (for ice-skating), none of the athletic facilities are open to the public.

The college has won national and international acclaim for the summertime (mid-July to mid-August) **Bates Dance Festival,** featuring modern-dance workshops, lectures, and performances. Sell-out student and faculty programs, most presented in 300-seat Schaeffer Theater, are open to the public. Call well ahead for tickets ($4-14), tel. (207) 786-6161.

At the western edge of the campus, between Main and College Sts., walk up **Mount David,** a grandly named hill, for a surprisingly good view of the Lewiston/Auburn skyline.

Bates Mill

Thanks to a progressive public/private partnership, the 19th-century Bates Mill, on Canal Street in downtown Lewiston, is being revitalized for a variety of new uses. Occupying 1.2 million square feet in nine buildings spread over five acres, the mill once produced nearly a third of the nation's textiles. Bates still turns out its popular bedspreads and other items, but on a greatly reduced scale. Since 1992, much of the hulking brick complex has been undergoing a long-term makeover—offices, studios, shops, and restaurants have moved in, helping the mill to reinvent itself.

One of the mill's most intriguing tenants is **The Creative Photographic Art Center of Maine,** Bates Mill, 59 Canal St., Lewiston 04240, tel. (207) 782-1369. Established by J. Michel Patry in 1994, it occupies more than 40,000 square feet of gallery and studio space on the fourth floor. Rotating exhibits and high-school and college photography classes keep the center busy all year. Summer gallery hours are

Mon.-Fri. 9 a.m.-5:30 p.m. and Saturday 10 a.m.-2 p.m. Winter hours are Mon.-Fri. 9 a.m.-9 p.m. and Saturday 10 a.m.-5 p.m.

Saints Peter and Paul Church

Most distinctive of Lewiston/Auburn's churches is the Gothic Revival Saints Peter and Paul Roman Catholic Church, Bartlett and Ash Sts., Lewiston 04240, tel. (207) 777-1200, where separate services are held in English and French. Dedicated in 1938, the church can seat more than 2,000.

Shaker Museum

Twelve miles southwest of Lewiston/Auburn, only a handful of Shakers remain in America's last inhabited Shaker community. Nonetheless, the members of the United Society of Shakers, an 18th-century religious sect, keep a relatively high profile with a living-history museum, craft workshops, publications, mail-order herb and gift business, and even a music CD released in 1995. Each year, some 8,000 visitors arrive at the 1,800-acre **Sabbathday Lake Shaker Community,** 707 Shaker Rd., Rt. 26, New Gloucester 04260, tel. (207) 926-4597, to glimpse an endangered lifestyle, and the Shakers welcome the public to their Sunday (10 a.m.) service (men and women sit separately). The hour-long basic guided tour costs $5 adults, $2 children under 12. During July and August, a longer tour, including more buildings, costs $6.50 adults and $2.75 children under 12. Children under six are free. The village is open Mon.-Sat. 10 a.m.-4:30 p.m., Memorial Day weekend to Columbus Day.

PARKS AND PRESERVES

Thorncrag Bird Sanctuary

Imagine being able to birdwatch, hike, cross-country ski, and snowshoe on 228 acres within the city limits of Lewiston. At the Thorncrag Bird Sanctuary, Montello St., Lewiston, mailing address Stanton Bird Club, P.O. Box 3172, Lewiston 04243, tel. (207) 782-5238, pick up a trail map at the gate and head out on the three miles of well-maintained, color-coded, easy-to-moderate trails—past ponds, an old cellar hole, stone memorials and benches, and through stands of beech, hemlock, white pine, and mixed hardwoods. Bicycles are banned in the preserve, which is open dawn to dusk daily, year-round. Bring a picnic. Admission is free. Throughout the year, the **Stanton Bird Club** sponsors more than three dozen lectures and field trips; call for schedule. From downtown Lewiston, take Sabattus St. (Rt. 126) east about three miles to Highland Springs Road. Turn left (north) and continue to the end (Montello Street). You'll be facing the entrance to the sanctuary.

Range Ponds State Park
Brimming with swimmers when the temperature skyrockets, 750-acre Range (RANG) Ponds State Park, Empire Rd., Poland, mailing address P.O. Box 475, Poland Spring 04274, tel. (207) 998-4104, has facilities for swimming (including lifeguard and bathhouse) and picnicking, plus 1.2 miles of nature trails. (Part of the trail verges on a marsh; be prepared with bug repellent.) Most of the park's acreage once was the estate of Hiram Ricker, owner of Poland Spring Water (now owned by Perrier). Bring a canoe or kayak and launch it into Lower Range Pond. Admission is $2.50 adults, 50 cents children 5-11; the park is open mid-May to mid-October. From Lewiston/Auburn, take Rt. 202/11/100 south to Rt. 122. Turn right (east) and continue to the Empire Rd. in Poland Spring; the turnoff to the park is well signposted.

RECREATION

Golf
Prospect Hill Golf Course, 694 S. Main St., Auburn 04210, tel. (207) 782-9220, an 18-hole par-72 course, is open mid-April through October. Nine-hole **Apple Valley Golf Course,** 316 Pinewoods Rd., Lewiston 04240, tel. (207) 784-9773, is open mid-April to mid-November. Tee times aren't needed, but call ahead to reserve a cart.

North of Auburn, the nine-hole **Turner Highlands Country Club,** Rt. 117, Turner 04282, tel. (207) 224-7060, has a pastoral feel, with broad vistas. The club's restaurant, Eli's at the Highlands, draws an enthusiastic crowd. The course is open May through October.

Cycling
From early May through November, 300 acres at

Lost Valley, Lost Valley Rd., off Young's Corner Rd., P.O. Box 260, Auburn 04210, tel. (207) 784-1561, become the local destination for avid mountain bikers. Hours are 9 a.m.-6 p.m.; an all-day pass is $5. Offroad races occur most Mondays ($10 registration fee) from early June to late September. In summer, Lost Valley also organizes "Skirmish" events, dubious militaristic "games" involving paintballs as the weapon of choice. Minimum age is 14, in organized groups. Call for details if you can't resist.

The countryside in this area is mostly gentle, not much of a challenge for gonzo bikers but a decent workout for anyone looking for an average challenge. Although Rt. 202 between Lewiston and Augusta is a well-traveled highway, it has good, broad shoulders for biking—a rarity in Maine. Distance is about 30 miles one-way; a shorter pedal, as far as Greene or Monmouth and return, makes a good day-trip. One of the best vistas along Rt. 202 is from the hilltop near Highmoor Farm, just north of Rt. 106 near the Androscoggin/Kennebec county line.

Winter Sports
The championship alpine slopes of Sunday River Ski Resort are only 45 miles northwest of Lewiston/Auburn, but even closer is family-oriented **Lost Valley,** Lost Valley Rd., off Young's Corner Rd., P.O. Box 260, Auburn 04210, tel. (207) 784-1561, two miles from downtown Auburn. Vertical drop is 240 feet. An unexpected thaw or winter rain sometimes sabotages business here, but top-to-bottom snowmaking lends a big assist. The crowds swarm in when the weather's right—especially for night skiing (to 10 or 11 p.m.) on the lighted slopes. Lost Valley has 15 trails, a snowboard park, two double chairlifts, and a T-bar. Ski and snowboard rentals are available, the ski school is especially active, and the cafeteria usually teems with families. And where else can you get lift tickets for $6 an hour? One-day tickets are $30 weekends and $18 midweek for adults. Lost Valley's season typically is mid-December to mid-March. The ski area is just west of Lake Auburn.

Also part of the Lost Valley operation is the **Lost Valley Touring Center,** with seven miles of groomed trails. An adult day pass is $7; rentals are available in the lodge, used by both alpine and nordic skiers.

ENTERTAINMENT

Established in 1991, **The Public Theatre,** Lisbon and Maple Sts., Lewiston 04240, mailing address 2 Great Falls Plaza, Box 7, Auburn 04210, box office tel. (207) 782-3200 or (800) 639-9575, has been mounting professional theatrical performances, leading the way in the Twin Cities cultural scene. Comedies and dramas predominate, with Equity actors onstage. Adult ticket prices are under $13, less for students and seniors.

Since 1973, **L/A Arts,** 49 Lisbon St., Lewiston 04240, tel. (207) 782-7228 or (800) 639-2919, a respected nonprofit arts-sponsorship organization, has been bringing eight or so nationally noted cultural events to the area between early October and mid-April. Adult tickets are in the $10-20 range, students $10-14. In early May (usually the first Saturday), L/A Arts holds its annual **art auction,** a fundraiser that draws bidders from around the state. Activities of both The Public Theatre and L/A Arts are listed in the *Lewiston Auburn Arts Calendar* (see "Festivals and Events," below).

The 10-screen **Hoyts Cinemas,** Auburn Plaza, 746 Center St., Auburn 04210, tel. (207) 786-8605, has bargain matinees before 6 p.m. Open all year.

FESTIVALS AND EVENTS

Throughout the year, **Bates College,** tel. (207) 786-2330 weekdays, presents a full schedule of concerts, lectures, exhibits, sporting events, and other activities. Call for details.

Each year, a community committee produces the *Lewiston Auburn Arts Calendar,* a free brochure listing concerts, plays, dances, and even lectures scheduled for the academic year in and around the Twin Cities, including some Bates events. Copies of the brochure are available at many locations or from the chamber of commerce.

The **Maine State Parade** is, not surprisingly, the state's biggest parade, an annual theme event drawing more than 30,000 spectators to downtown Lewiston the first Saturday in May. The *third* Saturday that month brings the **An-**nual **Thorncrag Community Day,** replete with flower and bird walks, kids' games, and other activities. At the Thorncrag Bird Sanctuary, Lewiston.

Auburn's Great Falls Plaza is the venue for **Auburn Community Band Concerts,** Wednesdays at 7 p.m. mid-June to mid-August.

Lewiston and Auburn celebrate the Fourth of July with the all-day **Liberty Festival** of nonstop music, children's games, and evening fireworks at Heritage Park in Lewiston and Great Falls Plaza in Auburn. The second Saturday in July brings the **Lewiston-Auburn Garden Tour,** putting half a dozen gardens (including the Bates College campus) on display and benefiting the Maine Music Society, tel. (207) 782-1403. Hours are 10 a.m.-4 p.m.; tickets are $12. The **Moxie Festival** is a certifiably funky annual celebration of the obscure soft drink Moxie, invented in 1884 and still not consigned to the dustbin of history. There's a huge offbeat parade, food booths, a Moxie recipe contest, a pancake breakfast, games, a carnival, live entertainment, a Slovak public supper, a chicken barbecue, and collectibles exhibits and sales. It all happens the second weekend of July in downtown Lisbon. The acclaimed annual **Bates Dance Festival,** at Bates College, Lewiston, mid-July to mid-August, features behind-the-scenes classes and workshops, as well as performances, which are open to the public.

Lewiston hosts the **Festival de Joie,** a three-day multicultural heritage celebration, the first weekend in August. The festival, at the Central Maine Civic Center and Drouin Field in Lewiston, features live entertainment, dancing, cultural displays, a road race, art and craft exhibits, children's games and rides, and a dozen kinds of ethnic food. Originally a Franco-American event, it now encompasses all the ethnic groups that have settled in the area—Greek, Russian, French, African-American. Even Native Americans and Shakers are represented. Adult tickets are $5 per day. The **Great Falls Balloon Festival,** the third or fourth weekend in August, entails live music, a carnival, food booths, a craft show, games, and morning (5:30 a.m.) and evening (5:30 p.m.) hot-air-balloon launches (balloon rides available by advance reservation, tel. 207-786-6674).

SHOPPING

Lewiston and Auburn have several shopping malls and mini-malls; largest is the 50-store **Auburn Mall,** at 550 Center St (Rt. 4), open Mon.-Sat. 10 a.m.-9 p.m. and Sunday noon-5 p.m.

Collectibles

Vintage clothing, antique and collectible glass and housewares, and antique jewelry are only a few of the possibilities in Danny Poulin's 3,000-square-foot space at **Orphan Annie's,** 96 Court St., Auburn 04210, tel. (207) 782-0638. Want more? The overflow warehouse, a block away at 10 Pleasant St., is open every Monday 11 a.m.-1 p.m., with deals galore. Orphan Annie's is open all year, Mon.-Sat. 10 a.m.-5 p.m. and Sunday noon-5 p.m.

Gifts and Crafts

Patronize Maine's topflight artists and crafts-people at **Stone Soup Artisans,** Vernon and Center Sts., Auburn 04210, tel. (207) 783-4281, a high-end cooperative that's open all year, Tues.-Sat. 10 a.m.-5 p.m.

Discount Shopping

Alongside the canal just off Lisbon Street in downtown Lewiston, the **Bates Mill Store,** 49 Canal St., P.O. Box 591, Lewiston 04240, tel. (207) 784-7626 or (800) 552-2837 outside Maine, fax (207) 784-2598, is loaded with irregulars and closeouts of Bates spreads, blankets, towels, sheets, and more. The shop also does a big mail-order business in cotton bedspreads; send for brochure. Open all year, Mon.-Fri. 9 a.m.-4 p.m., Saturday 9 a.m.-1 p.m.

Marden's, Northwood Park Shopping Center, 750 Main St., Rt. 202, Lewiston 04240, tel. (207) 786-0313, almost belongs in a category by itself. The original store of a statewide chain, it's a huge collection of leftovers—maternity clothes, tools, lemonade mix, shoes, what-have-you. Each visit is an adventure, and the stock keeps changing. Prices are rock-bottom, great for bargain-hunters, but examine goods carefully before purchasing. Open all year, Mon.-Fri. 9 a.m.-8 p.m., Saturday 9 a.m.-5 p.m., and Sunday 11 a.m.-5 p.m.

Farmers' Market and Farm Shops

Look for the **Auburn Mall Farmers' Market** in the Porteous back lot, near Turner Street, at the Auburn Mall, 550 Center St., Rt. 4, each Thursday 3-7 p.m. and Saturday 9 a.m.-1 p.m. The market operates from mid-May to mid-October.

The Red Radish, 996 Sabattus St., Rt. 126, Lewiston 04240, tel. (207) 783-7374, carries a terrific selection of fresh seasonal produce. Watch for the farmstand just east of the Shop 'n Save supermarket. Open 9 a.m.-6 p.m. Memorial Day weekend to early October.

Named for the river running through town, **Nezinscot Farm Natural Food Store and Wool Shop,** N. Parish Rd., Rt. 117, Turner 04282, tel. (207) 225-3231, is worth the detour. Besides organically grown produce, the cookies and breads are fabulous; a small café serves good-for-you breakfasts, lunches, and Sunday brunches. No credit cards. Shop and café hours are Mon.-Fri. 6 a.m.-6 p.m. and Saturday and Sunday 8 a.m.-5 p.m. Open all year. The farm is five miles east and north of the junction of Rts. 4 and 117 (about 16 miles north of downtown Auburn).

ACCOMMODATIONS

Motels are the primary lodging type in the Lewiston/Auburn area, running the gamut from respectable national chains to no-tell motels. Best of the nationals are the **Ramada,** 490 Pleasant St., Lewiston 04240, tel. (207) 784-2331 or (800) 228-2828, and the **Coastline Inn,** 170 Center St., Rt. 4, Auburn 04210, tel. (207) 784-1331 or (800) 470-9494.

Only a block from Bates College, **Farnham House Bed & Breakfast,** 520 Main St., Rt. 202/11/100, Lewiston 04240, tel. (207) 782-9495, fax 782-7448, caters to college visitors—parents, guest artists, prospective profs—so gather 'round for the breakfast discussions. Among noted guests have been Jesse Jackson and Mstislav Rostropovich. Barbara Laprise has five lovely rooms in her elegant Victorian home; two have fireplaces, three have private baths. If you're highly noise-sensitive, request a back room; four rooms have a/c. Children are welcome, but no pets. Private-bath rooms are $75-90 d; shared-bath rooms are $50-65 d. Bates graduation weekend (late May) is fully booked four years ahead; summer reservations are easier to arrange. Open all year.

Campgrounds

On the shore of Lower Range Pond, 40-acre **Poland Spring Campground,** Rt. 26, P.O. Box 409, Poland Spring 04274, tel. (207) 998-2151, is a family-run Good Sampark with 100 wooded tent and RV sites ($16-21 for four). Facilities include an outdoor pool, coin-operated showers, a general store, laundry, play areas, and rental canoes. There's lots of organized fun; be prepared for theme weekends, barbecues, and other activities. The campground, open May through October, is about 10 miles west of Auburn.

FOOD

Lunch and Miscellanea

Get your picnic fixings at **Austin's Fine Wines & Foods,** 78 Main St., Auburn 04210, tel. (207) 783-6312; you can't beat the sandwiches, and they also have salads, cheeses, and a super wine selection. Eat at the counter or one of the nine tables, or order it all to go. Austin's is open all year, Mon.-Fri. 7:30 a.m.-7 p.m. and Saturday 9 a.m.-6 p.m.

In the retrofitted Bates Mill, **DaVinci's Eatery,** Bates Mill, 32 Canal St., Lewiston 04240, tel. (207) 782-2088, specializes in brick-oven pizza but has a variety of other regional American entrées in the $9-13 range. The choice luncheon buffet is $6. The 150-seat restaurant, with liquor license, is open all year, Mon.-Thurs. 11 a.m.-9 p.m., Friday and Saturday 11 a.m.-10 p.m., and Sunday 11 a.m.-8 p.m.

Inexpensive to Moderate

The college crowd beats a path to **Nothing But the Blues Café,** 81 College St., Lewiston 04240, tel. (207) 784-6493, a casual, 32-seat restaurant not far from Bates. Entrées on the eclectic menu, emphasizing vegetarian and changing daily, are all under $10. Lunch portions are smaller, designed for speedy service. No smoking, no credit cards, no liquor license. Open all year, Mon.-Fri. 11:30 a.m.-3 p.m. and 5-9 p.m.

Greek and Cajun specialties join French and regional American dishes on the menu at **Marois Restaurant,** 249 Lisbon St., Lewiston 04240, tel. (207) 782-9055, in the heart of downtown. Its decor a bit overglitzed, Marois has been a Lewiston landmark since 1919. Entrées run $4-8 for lunch, $10-19 for dinner, and the restaurant's long hours solve the problem of late night hunger pangs—it's open daily 11 a.m.-11 p.m., all year.

The sign outside **Ristorante Bella Italia,** 700 Lisbon St., Rt. 196, Lewiston 04240, tel. (207) 783-1202, promises "real authentic Italian cuisine"—and comes through. The family-run kitchen produces Neapolitan comfort food at its freshest ($10-14 for entrées). Ambience is so-so, but who cares? Don't leave without ordering the world-class tiramisu. Reservations are necessary on weekends. No smoking. Open all year, Tues.-Thurs. 4:30-9 p.m., Friday and Saturday to 10 p.m. Bella Italia is easy to miss; keep an eye out for it at the corner of Androscoggin Avenue, about a block west of the turnoff for Lewiston High School.

A few miles southeast of Lewiston is **Graziano's Casa Mia Restaurant,** Lisbon Rd., Rt. 196, Lisbon 04250, tel. (207) 353-4335, a locally colorful eatery lined floor-to-ceiling with classic autographed boxing portraits and a few ringers: Edmund Muskie, Frank Sinatra, Jimmy Carter, and the pope. Even if boxing is your least-favorite sport, you'll get a kick out of this traditional "tomato Italian" spot owned by Joe Graziano since 1968. The atmosphere in the sprawling, six-room restaurant is funky and friendly, entrées range $8-17, and the pasta and sauces are homemade, with some upscale touches. If you're into veal, eat it here. Children are welcome (the booths are convenient); the menu even has a "bambino corner." Open all year, Tues.-Fri. 11 a.m.-9:30 p.m. (to 10 p.m. Friday), Saturday 4-10 p.m., Sunday 11 a.m.-9 p.m. In July and August, only dinner is served on Sunday 4-9 p.m.

Eli's at The Highlands, Turner Highlands Country Club, N. Parish Rd., Rt. 117, Turner 04282, tel. (207) 224-7090, on the second floor of the bright, modernized clubhouse, has earned a fine reputation for creative regional cuisine with flair. Entrées are $5-8 for lunch, $10-15 for dinner. Reservations are a good idea, especially for Sunday brunch. No smoking except in the lounge. The restaurant is open mid-May through October, Tues.-Sat. 11 a.m.-9 p.m., Sunday 10 a.m.-2 p.m., and Monday 5-9 p.m. Turner is about 11 miles north of Auburn.

Moderate to Expensive
Reservations are a must at **The Seasons Café,** 199 Main St., Lewiston 04240, tel. (207) 782-5054, a newish bistro that prides itself on its regional American menu. It's open all year, Tues.-Sat. 5:30-10 p.m.
The Sedgley Place, Sedgley Rd., P.O. Box 28, Greene 04236, tel. (207) 946-5990, menu line (207) 946-5989, has a rather unusual dinner-by-reservation arrangement: first call the menu line to hear the current choices, then call back to reserve a table and order your preferences. The menu changes each week, usually featuring reliable beef, fish, and poultry options. Five-course dinners are $19.95 pp, but there's always a $12.95 special. Located in a lovely Federal-style homestead a mile southwest of Rt. 202 (north of Lewiston), the restaurant is open all year, Tues.-Sun.; seatings are at 5, 6, 7, and 8 p.m.

INFORMATION AND SERVICES

The **Androscoggin County Chamber of Commerce,** 179 Lisbon St., Lewiston 04240, tel. (207) 783-2249, serves as the tourism information center for the entire county. The office is open Mon.-Thurs. 8 a.m.-5 p.m. and Friday 8 a.m.-3 p.m. Parking can be a problem in this part of Lewiston, so use the Canal Street parking garage and take the fourth-floor walkway; you'll be right on the chamber's level. (Parking is only 25 cents an hour; the chamber office will validate your ticket so you can park free.)

The handsome granite Romanesque Revival (1903) **Lewiston Public Library,** 105 Park St., Lewiston 04240, tel. (207) 784-0135, is open Mon.-Thurs. 9 a.m.-8 p.m., Friday 9 a.m.-5 p.m., and Saturday 9 a.m.-2 p.m.

Newspapers
The daily newspaper of choice is the *Lewiston Sun-Journal,* tel. (207) 784-5411, plus the weekend *Sunday.* Many residents also read the *Portland Press Herald,* published daily. Its Thursday "Go" section contains features and calendar listings that include the Lewiston/Auburn area.

Emergencies
For **police, fire, and ambulance services,** dial 911. The major medical facility is **Central Maine Medical Center,** 300 Main St., Lewiston 04240, emergency room tel. (207) 795-2200. Also here is **St. Mary's Regional Medical Center,** Campus Ave., Lewiston 04240, emergency room tel. (207) 777-8120. Both hospitals have round-the-clock emergency rooms.

Getting Around
City Cab Co., tel. (207) 784-4521 or (800) 784-4521, and **Wes Taxi,** tel. (207) 786-3433, both provide 24-hour service in the Lewiston/Auburn area.

BOOKLIST

Prices listed are for the least-expensive edition available—usually paperback. For anyone consummately interested in books about Maine, the ultimate source is **Maine Writers and Publishers Alliance,** 12 Pleasant St., Brunswick, ME 04011, tel. (207) 725-0690, fax 725-1014, which serves as a distribution center for hundreds of titles. The bookshop is open to the public. The $30 annual membership fee includes discounts on books, workshops, and other events; a monthly newsletter; and opportunities to meet Maine authors.

DESCRIPTION AND TRAVEL

Guidebooks

Ackerman, R., and K. Buxton. *The Coast of Maine Book.* 2d ed. Lee, MA: Berkshire House Publishers, Great Destinations Series, 1996; 304 pages, $17.95. Lively writing style and useful information arranged by regions within topics.

Arlen, A. *In the Maine Woods.* Originally self-published, a fully revised edition of this survey of more than four dozen Maine sporting camps and their owners is due to be published in the fall of 1998 by Countryman Press (Woodstock, VT). In addition to being highly entertaining, it's also the only book on the subject.

Bumsted, L. *Hot Showers! Maine Coast Lodgings for Kayakers and Sailors.* Brunswick, ME: Audenreed Press (P.O. Box 1305, Brunswick, ME 04011), 1997; 256 pages, $17.95. Excellent, well-researched resource for anyone cruising the shoreline and yearning for alternatives to a sleeping bag.

Calhoun, C.C. *Maine.* 2d ed. New York: Fodor's Travel Publications, Compass American Guides, 1997; 320 pages, $18.95. Entertaining prose, outstanding photography.

Clark, S. *Katahdin: A Guide to Baxter State Park & Katahdin.* 3d ed. Unity, ME: North Country Press, 1996; 213 pages, $16.95. Although flawed with typographical errors, this is the only comprehensive guidebook to Baxter and Katahdin.

A Collector's Guide to Maine Mineral Localities. Augusta, ME: Maine Geological Survey (at our press time, the 3rd ed. was due out in early 1998; approx. 100 pages, $8-10). For amateur rock hounds, details on and directions to abandoned quarries and other sites.

Cone, K. *What's Brewing In New England.* Camden, ME: Down East Books, 1997; 224 pages, $12.95. Maine is well represented in this guide to New England's microbreweries and brew-pubs.

Curtis, W. *Maine: Off the Beaten Path.* 2d ed. Old Saybrook, CT: Globe Pequot Press, 1995; 176 pages, $10.95. Introduction to off-beat and unexpected locales; a good supplementary guide for would-be explorers.

Silliker, B., Jr. *Maine Moose Watcher's Guide.* South Berwick, ME: R.L. Lemke Corp., 1993; 50 pages, $9.95.

Taft, H., J. Taft, and C. Rindlaub. *A Cruising Guide to the Maine Coast.* 3d ed. Peaks Island: Diamond Pass Publishing (19 Brook Ln., Peaks Island, ME 04108), 1996; 480 pages, $39.95. Don't even consider cruising the coast without this volume.

Tree, C., and E. Roundy. *Maine: An Explorer's Guide.* 8th ed. Woodstock, VT: Countryman Press, 1997; 520 pages, $18. Long recognized as a bible for Maine exploration; emphasizes lodging and food.

Literature, Art, and Photography

Bennett, D. *Allagash: Maine's Wild and Scenic River.* Camden, ME: Down East Books, 1994;

112 pages, $35. Elegant portrait of the Allagash Wilderness Waterway, by a veteran Maine naturalist.

Curtis, J. and W., and F. Lieberman. *Monhegan: The Artists' Island*. Camden, ME: Down East Books, 1995; 192 pages, $50.

Maine Speaks: An Anthology of Maine Literature. Brunswick, ME: Maine Writers and Publishers Alliance, 1989; 466 pages, $19.95.

Spectre, P.H. *Passage in Time*. New York: W.W. Norton, 1991; 222 pages, O.P. A noted marine writer cruises the coast aboard traditional windjammers; gorgeous photos complement the colorful text.

Thompson, C. *Maine Lighthouses: A Pictorial Guide*. Stowe, VT: CatNap Publications, 1996; 128 pages, $19.95. What they look like, where to find them, and a bit of background detail.

Thoreau, H.D. *The Maine Woods*. New York: Penguin Books, 1988 ed. [orig. pub. 1864]; 480 pages, $12.95. A Maine classic, first published two years after the author's death; mid-19th-century exploration of Maine's wilderness around Greenville, Chesuncook, Katahdin, and more.

Villani, R. *Forever Wild: Maine's Magnificent Baxter State Park*. Camden, ME: Down East Books, 1991; 112 pages, $35. Spectacular photos of Baxter in every season, taken by an accomplished professional.

REFERENCE

Maine Alternative Yellow and Green Pages. Monroe: Invert Publishing (P.O. Box 776, Monroe, ME 04951), 1997; 248 pages, $9. Revised and updated version of the original *Maine Alternative Yellow Pages,* now including 25 in green. A valuable resource for contacting alternative and even mainstream social and socially conscious organizations, institutions, and individual practitioners.

The Maine Atlas and Gazetteer. Yarmouth, ME: DeLorme, updated annually; 96 pages, $16.95. You'll be hard put to get lost if you're carrying this essential volume; 70 full-page (oversize format) topographical maps with GPS grids.

HISTORY

Acadian Culture in Maine. Washington, DC: National Park Service, North Atlantic Region, 1994; 104 pages, $10. A project report on Acadians and their traditions in the Upper St. John Valley.

Cook, D.S. *Above the Gravel Bar: The Indian Canoe Routes of Maine*. 2d ed. Self-published (Rt. 2, Box 1300, Winthrop, ME 04364), 1985; 138 pages, $10.

Duncan, R.F. *Coastal Maine*. New York: W.W. Norton, 1992; 574 pages, $35. Accessible maritime history from a distinguished historian and sailor.

Isaacson, D., ed. *Maine: A Guide "Down East."* 2d ed. n.p.: Maine League of Historical Societies and Museums, 1970; 554 pages, O.P. Revised version of the Depression-era WPA guidebook. Still interesting for background reading.

Judd, R.W., E.A. Churchill, J.W. Eastman, eds. *Maine: The Pine Tree State from Prehistory to the Present*. Orono: University of Maine Press, 1995; 630 pages, $30. The best available Maine history, with excellent historical maps.

Memoirs

Dawson, L.B. *Saltwater Farm*. Westford: Impatiens Press (50 North St., Westford, MA 01886), 1993; 110 pages, $7.95. Witty, charming stories of growing up on the Cushing peninsula.

Wass, P.B. *Lighthouse in My Life: The Story of a Maine Lightkeeper's Family*. Camden, ME: Down East Books, 1987; 272 pages, $9.95. Offshore adventures, growing up on Libby Island, near Machias.

Natural History

Bennett, D. *Maine's Natural Heritage: Rare Species and Unique Natural Features.* Camden, ME: Down East Books, 1988; 302 pages, $39.95.

Kendall, D.L. *Glaciers & Granite: A Guide to Maine's Landscape and Geology.* Unity, ME: North Country Press, 1993; 240 pages, $12.95. Shows you why Maine looks the way it does.

RECREATION

AMC Maine Mountain Guide. 7th ed. Boston: Appalachian Mountain Club Books, 1993; 352 pages, $15.95. The definitive statewide resource for going vertical. In a handy small format.

AMC River Guide: Maine. 2d ed. Boston: Appalachian Mountain Club Books, 1991; 360 pages, $11.95. Detailed guide to canoeing or kayaking Maine's large and small rivers. In a convenient small format.

Chunn, C. *50 Hikes in the Maine Mountains: Day Hikes and Backpacks in the Fabled Northern Peaks and Lake Country.* 2d ed. Woodstock, VT: Backcountry Publications, 1997; 240 pages, $14.95. Well-researched and well-written guide (complements the Gibson guide, below).

Cobscook Trails: A Guide to Hiking Opportunities Around Cobscook Bay and the Bold Coast. Whiting: Quoddy Regional Land Trust (Box 49, Whiting, ME 04691), 1997; 44 pages, $2. Essential handbook for exploring this part of the Sunrise Coast. Excellent maps.

Collins, J., and J.E. McCarthy. *Nature Walks in Southern Maine.* Boston: Appalachian Mountain Club Books, 1996; 336 pages, $12.95. Easy walks, mostly horizontal, and good natural-history commentary. Maps are primitive but do the job.

Cooking with the Maine Sporting Camp Association. Olathe, KS: Cookbook Publishers, 1993; 124 pages, $8. Entertaining, occasionally offbeat recipes from traditional Maine fishing and hunting camps.

Gibson, J. *50 Hikes in Southern and Coastal Maine.* 2d ed. Woodstock, VT: Backcountry Publications, 1996; 208 pages, $15. Well-researched, detailed resource by a veteran hiker (complements the Chunn guide, above).

Seymour, T. *Hiking Maine.* Helena, MT: Falcon Press, 1995; 206 pages, $12.95. Helpful—especially for less-well-known hikes in the Mid-Coast Region. Not as comprehensive, statewide, as the Gibson and Chunn hiking guides or the AMC Maine Mountain Guide.

Varney, S. *Take A Hike.* Waterville: Bread & Water Books (10 Glidden St., Waterville, ME 04901), 1990; 28 pages, $5. Small but useful booklet covering hikes in the Kennebec River Valley; written by a knowledgeable local resident.

Wilson, A., and J. Hayes. *Quiet Water Canoe Guide, Maine: Best Paddling Lakes and Ponds for All Ages.* Boston: Appalachian Mountain Club Books, 1995; 336 pages, $14.95. Comprehensive handbook, with helpful maps, for inland paddling.

Wiser, M. *Hikes in and around Maine's Lake Region.* 2d ed. Self-published (RR 1, Box 707, Bridgton, ME 04009), 1994; 44 pages, $5.95. More than 20 hikes in the Sebago Lake/Oxford Hills area. Chapters originally appeared in a local newspaper.

ACADIA NATIONAL PARK/ MOUNT DESERT ISLAND

Abrell, D. *A Pocket Guide to the Carriage Roads of Acadia National Park.* 2d ed. Camden, ME: Down East Books, 1995; 40 pages, $4.50.

Brechlin, E.D. *A Pocket Guide to Paddling the Waters of Mount Desert Island.* Camden, ME: Down East Books, 1996; 64 pages, $7.95.

Gillmore, R. *Great Walks of Acadia National Park & Mount Desert Island.* rev. ed. Goffstown, NH: Great Walks (P.O. Box 410, Goffstown, NH 03045), 1994; 176 pages, $8.95.

Helfrich, G.W., and G. O'Neil. *Lost Bar Harbor.* Camden, ME: Down East Books, 1982; 125 pages, $9.95. Fascinating collection of historic photographs of classic, turn-of-the-century "cottages," many obliterated by Bar Harbor's Great Fire of 1947.

Minutolo, A. *A Pocket Guide to Biking on Mount Desert Island.* Camden, ME: Down East Books, 1996; 64 pages, $7.95.

Morison, S.E. *The Story of Mount Desert Island.* Boston: Little, Brown, 1960; 94 pages, $15.

Newlin, W.V.P. *The Lakes and Ponds of Mt. Desert.* Camden, ME: Down East Books, 1989; 208 pages, $12.95. Mount Desert's waterholes, secret and not-so-secret, entertainingly described by a longtime summer-cator.

Roberts, A.R. *Mr. Rockefeller's Roads.* Camden, ME: Down East Books, 1990; 184 pages, $14.95. The story behind Acadia's scenic carriage roads, written by the granddaughter of John D. Rockefeller (who created them).

Gold, D. *Country Roads of Maine.* Castine, ME: Country Roads Press, 1995; 240 pages, $9.95.

Gould, J. *Maine Lingo: Boiled Owls, Billdads, and Wazzats.* Camden, ME: Down East Books, 1975; 364 pages, $14.95. A seasoned student of local jargon—*Christian Science Monitor* columnist John Gould—provides advice on "speaking Maine."

The Maine Island Trail: Stewardship Handbook and Guidebook. Rockland, ME: Maine Island Trail Association, updated annually; approximately 224 pages. Available only with MITA membership (annual dues $40), providing access to dozens of islands along the watery trail.

Pierson, E.C., J.E. Pierson, and P.D. Vickery. *A Birder's Guide to Maine.* Camden, ME: Down East Books, 1996; 400 pages, $23.95. An expanded version of *A Birder's Guide to the Coast of Maine.* No ornithologist, novice or expert, should explore Maine without this valuable guide.

St. Germain, T.A., Jr. *A Walk in the Park: Acadia's Hiking Guide.* 3d ed. Bar Harbor: Parkman Publications (P.O. Box 826, Bar Harbor, ME 04609), 1994; 244 pages, $10.95. The most comprehensive and useful Acadia National Park hiking guide.

GLOSSARY
A DOWN EAST DICTIONARY

To help you translate some of the lingo in off-the-beaten-track Maine (e.g., country stores and county fairs, farmers' markets and flea markets), here's a sampling of local terms and expressions, followed by a list of place names that have difficult or unusual pronunciations.

Airline, The—the 98-mile stretch of Route 9 between Bangor and Calais

alewives—herring

ayuh—yes

barrens—as in "blueberry barrens"; fields where wild blueberries grow

beamy—wide (as in a boat or a person)

beans—shorthand for the traditional Saturday-night meal, which always includes baked beans

blowdown—a forest area leveled by wind

blowing a gale—very windy

camp—a vacation house (small or large), usually on fresh water and/or in the woods

chance—serendipity or luck (as in "open by appointment or by chance")

chicken dressing—chicken manure

chowder (pronounced "chowdah")—soup made with lobster, clams, or fish, or a combination thereof; lobster version sometimes called lobster stew

coneheads—tourists (because of their presumed penchant for ice cream)

cottage—a vacation house (anything from a bungalow to a mansion), usually on salt water

County, The—Aroostook County, northernmost in Maine

culch—"stuff"; the contents of attics, basements, and some flea markets

cull—a discount lobster, usually minus a claw

cunnin'—cute (usually describing a baby or small child)

dinner (pronounced "dinnah")—the noon meal

dinner pail—lunchbox

dite—a very small amount

dooryard—the yard near a house's main entrance

Down East—with the prevailing wind; the old coastal sailing route from Boston to Nova Scotia

downcellar—in the basement

downstate—the rest of Maine, according to residents of The County

dry-ki—driftwood, usually remnants from the logging industry

ell—a residential structural section that links a house and a barn; formerly a popular location for the "summer kitchen," to spare the house from woodstove heat

exercised—upset; angry

fiddleheads—unopened ostrich-fern fronds, a spring delicacy

finest kind—top quality; good news; an expression of general approval; also, a term of appreciation

Flatlander—a person not from Maine, often but not exclusively someone from the Midwest

floatplane—a small plane equipped with pontoons for landing on water; the same aircraft often becomes a skiplane in winter

flowage—a water body created by damming, usually beaver handiwork (also called "beaver flowage")

frappe—a thick drink containing milk, ice cream, and flavored syrup—as opposed to a milkshake, which does not include ice cream (but beware: a frappe offered in other parts of the United States is an ice-cream sundae topped with whipped cream!)

from away—not native to Maine

galamander—a wheeled contraption formerly used to transport quarry granite to building sites or to boats for onward shipment

gore—a sliver of land left over from inaccurate boundary surveys; Maine has Misery Gore, Coburn Gore, Moxie Gore, Hibberts Gore, and more

got done—quit a job; was let go

harbormaster—local official who monitors water traffic and assigns moorings

hardshell—lobster that hasn't molted yet (more scarce, thus more pricey in summer)

hod—wooden "basket" used for carrying clams

ice-out—the departure of winter ice from ponds, lakes, rivers, and streams; many communities have ice-out contests, awarding prizes for guessing the exact time of ice-out, in April or May

Italian—long bread roll sliced and filled with peppers, onions, tomatoes, sliced meat, shredded lettuce, olive oil, seasonings, and more, according to taste; veggie versions available; elsewhere known as a hoagie, submarine, poor boy, hero, or grinder

lobster car—a large floating crate for storing lobsters

Maine Guide—a member of the Maine Professional Guides Association, trained and tested for outdoor and survival skills; also Registered Maine Guide

molt—what a lobster does when it sheds its shell for a larger one; the act of molting is called ecdysis (as a stripper is an ecdysiast)

money tree—a collection device for a monetary gift

mud season—mid-March-mid-April, when back roads and unpaved driveways become virtual tank traps

nasty neat—extremely meticulous

Near—stingy

notional—stubborn, determined

off island—the mainland, to an islander

place—another word for house (as in "Herb Pendleton's place")

pot—trap, as in "lobster pot"

public landing. See "town landing"

rake—handtool used for harvesting blueberries

rusticator—a summer visitor, particularly in bygone days

scooch (or scootch)—to squat; to move sideways

sea smoke—heavy mist rising off the water when the air temperature suddenly becomes much colder than the ocean temperature

select—a lobster with claws intact

Selectmen—the elected men and women who handle local affairs in small communities; the First Selectman chairs meetings

shedder—a lobster with a new (soft) shell; generally occurs in July and August (more common then, thus less expensive than hardshells)

shire town—county seat

shore dinner—the works: chowder, clams, lobster, and sometimes corn-on-the-cob, too

short—a small, illegal-size lobster

slumgullion—tasteless food; a mess

slut—a poor housekeeper

slut's wool—dust balls found under beds, couches, etc.

snapper—an undersize, illegal lobster

softshell—(see "Shedder")

some—very (as in "some hot")

spleeny—overly sensitive

steamers—clams (before or after they are steamed)

sternman—a lobsterman's helper (male or female)

summer complaint—a tourist

supper (pronounced "suppah")—evening meal, eaten by Mainers around 5 or 6 p.m. (as opposed to flatlanders and summer people, who eat dinner between 7 and 9 p.m.)

tad—slightly; a little bit

thick-o'-fog—zero-visibility fog

to home—at home

tomalley—a lobster's green insides; considered a delicacy by some

town landing—shore access; often a park or a parking lot, next to a wharf or boat-launch ramp

upattic—in the attic

Whoopie! Pie—the trademarked name for a high-fat, calorie-laden, cake-like snack that only kids and dentists could love

wicked cold!—frigid

wicked good!—excellent

williwaws—uncomfortable feeling

CAN YOU GET THERE FROM HERE?

Countless names for Maine cities, towns, villages, rivers, lakes, and streams have Native American origins; some are variations on French; and a few have German derivations. Below are some pronunciations to give you a leg up when requesting directions.

Arundel—Uh-RUN-d'l

Bangor—BANG-gore

Bethel—BETH-l

Bremen—BREE-m'n

Calais—CAL-us

Carmel—CAR-m'l

Damariscotta—dam-uh-riss-COTT-uh

Harraseeket—Hare-uh-SEEK-it

Hebron—HE-brun

Isle au Haut—i'll-a-HO, I'LL-a-ho (subject to plenty of dispute, depending on whether or not you live in the vicinity)

Katahdin—Kuh-TA-din

Kokadjo—Ko-KAD-joe

Lubec—Loo-BECK

Machias—Muh-CHIGH-us

Maranacook—Muh-RAN-uh-cook

Matinicus—Muh-TIN-i-cuss

Medomak—Muh-DOM-ick

Megunticook—Muh-GUN-tuh-cook

Monhegan—Mun-HE-gun

Mount Desert—Mount Duh-ZERT (subject to dispute; some say Mount DEZ-ert)

Narraguagus—Nare-uh-GWAY-gus

Passagassawaukeag—Puh-sag-gus-uh-WAH-keg

Passamaquoddy—Pass-uh-muh-QUAD-dee

Piscataquis—Piss-CAT-uh-kwiss

Saco—SOCK-oh

Schoodic—SKOO-dick

Skowhegan—Skow-HE-gun

Steuben—Stew-BEN

Topsham—TOPS-'m

Umbagog—Um-BAY-gog

Wiscasset—Wiss-CASS-it

Woolwich—WOOL-itch

Wytopitlock—Wit-a-PIT-luck

INDEX

BEACHES

FLIGHTSEEING

LOBSTER POUNDS

Mount Tom: 605
Moxie Falls: 543
Moxie Festival: 621
Mt. Mann: 591
Mt. Will: 586
mudflats: 15
Mulholland Point Lighthouse: 430
Mulholland Point Picnic Area: 433
Munjoy Hill (Portland): 132-133
Museum at Portland Head Light, The: 138
museums: 43; Abbe Museum 381; Acadian
Village 507; Aroostook Agricultural
Museum 499-500; Aroostook County
Historical and Art Museum 493; Ashland
Logging Museum 514; Benjamin C. Wilder
Homestead museum 499-500; Boothbay
Railway Village 208; Bowdoin College
Museum of Art 175; Brick Store Museum,
The 110; Bryant Stove and Music Museum
296; Bucksport Historical Society Museum
314; Burnham Tavern 423; Castine
Historical Society museum (Abbott School)
353; Children's Discovery Museum 520;
Children's Museum of Maine 142; Colby
College Museum of Art 531; Cole Land
Transportation Museum 324; Colonel Black
Mansion 315; Colonial Pemaquid Museum
220; Dr. Moses Mason House 584;
Farnsworth Art Museum, The 253;
Fishermen's Museum 220; Gates House
423; Great Harbor Maritime Museum 390-
391; Hamilton House 86; Hendricks Hill
Museum 208; Historic Meetinghouse
Museum 99; Hudson Museum 332-333;
Islesboro Historical Society museum 292;
Islesford Historical Museum 400; John E.
and Walter D. Webb Museum of Vintage
Fashion 494; Jones Museum of Glass and
Ceramics 608-609; Joshua L. Chamberlain
Museum 176; Kittery Historical and Naval
Museum 81; L.C. Bates Museum 537;
Leonard's Mills 333-334; Lincoln County
Jail and Museum 199; Mainely Critters
Museum 554; Maine Maritime Museum
188; Maine Narrow Gauge Railroad
Company and Museum 134; Maine State
Museum 517-518; Maine Watercraft
Museum 238-239; Marshall Point
Lighthouse Museum 242-243; Mary
Meeker Cramer Museum 273; Milbridge
Historical Society Museum 414; Monhegan

Museum 250; The Museum at Portland
Head Light 138; Musical Wonder House
199; Natural History Museum 381; New
Sweden Historical Museum 506; Nordica
Homestead Museum 551; The Nott House
110; Nowetah's American Indian Museum
562; Nylander Museum 500; Oakfield
Railroad Museum 494; Ogunquit Museum
of American Art 99; Old Conway
Homestead and Museum 272-273; Old Fort
Western 519; Old Town Museum 333;
Olson House 241; Orland Historical Society
Museum 314; Owls Head Transportation
Museum 255; Patten Lumberman's
Museum 455; Peary-MacMillan Museum
175; Pejepscot Museum 175-176;
Penobscot Marine Museum 305;
Penobscot Nation Museum 333; Petite
Plaisance 390; Portland Museum of Art
133; Portsmouth Naval Shipyard Museum
and Visitor Center 81; Rangeley Logging
Museum 574; Raye's Mustard Mill Museum
436-437; Redington House Museum 532;
Rev. Daniel Merrill House 345; Ruggles
House 417-418; Sailors' Memorial Museum
292; Salome Sellers House 358; Sarah
Orne Jewett House 86; Seal Cove Auto
Museum 394; Seashore Trolley Museum
110-112; Seguin Museum 192; Shaker
Museum 619; Shore Village Museum 255;
Skowhegan History House 537; Spring
Point Museum 134-135; Stanley Museum
561; Stanwood Homestead Museum 315;
Tante Blanche Museum 508; Thomas A.
Hill House 323; Victoria Mansion 133-134;
Vinalhaven Historical Society museum 266;
Wadsworth-Longfellow House 133;
Waponahki Museum 437; Weld Historical
Society Museum 554; Wells Auto Museum
100; Wendell Gilley Museum 393; Western
Maine Children's Museum 562; Wilhelm
Reich Museum 573; Willowbrook at
Newfield 89; Wilson Museum 352; Wilton
Farm and Home Museum 554; Woolwich
Historical Society Museum 189; York
Institute Museum 124
Mushers Bowl: 612
mushing: 566, 589
music: 44
Musical Wonder House: 199

SKIING/SNOWBOARDING

ABOUT THE AUTHOR

Born in New York and raised near Chicago, Kathleen Brandes managed to squeeze in stints as a UN proofreader, a West African Peace Corps volunteer, and a Time-Life Books editor before abandoning the Big Apple for a coastal Maine fishing village in the early 1970s. Since then, she has been the proprietor of Wordsworth Editorial Services and a contributing editor to *Down East,* the Maine lifestyle magazine. Her travels or extended stays in more than 40 countries and 39 states have convinced her, and husband Michael Drons, that adopting Maine was a brilliant decision (reinforced over and over during the thousands of miles of driving, hiking, and otherwise exploring the state's 33,215 square miles for the *Maine Handbook*). She has slept in mud huts, caves, a nomad tent, and a Cameroonian brothel—not to mention the island she rented in Finland—and she still thinks there's no place like home.

MOON
TRAVEL
HANDBOOKS

LOSE YOURSELF
IN THE EXPERIENCE,
NOT THE CROWD

For 25 years, Moon Travel Handbooks have been the guidebooks of choice for adventurous travelers. Our award-winning Handbook series provides focused, comprehensive coverage of distinct destinations all over the world. Each Handbook is like an entire bookcase of cultural insight and introductory information in one portable volume. Our goal at Moon is to give travelers all the background and practical information they'll need for an extraordinary travel experience.

The following pages include a complete list of Handbooks, covering North America and Hawaii, Mexico, Latin America and the Caribbean, and Asia and the Pacific. To purchase Moon Travel Handbooks, check your local bookstore or order by phone: (800) 345-5473 M-F 8 am.-5 p.m. PST or outside the U.S. phone: (530) 345-5473.

"An in-depth dunk into the land, the people and their history, arts, and politics."
—*Student Travels*

"I consider these books to be superior to Lonely Planet. When Moon produces a book it is more humorous, incisive, and off-beat."
—*Toronto Sun*

"Outdoor enthusiasts gravitate to the well-written Moon Travel Handbooks. In addition to politically correct historic and cultural features, the series focuses on flora, fauna and outdoor recreation. Maps and meticulous directions also are a trademark of Moon guides."
—*Houston Chronicle*

"Moon [Travel Handbooks] . . . bring a healthy respect to the places they investigate. Best of all, they provide a host of odd nuggets that give a place texture and prod the wary traveler from the beaten path. The finest are written with such care and insight they deserve listing as literature."
—*American Geographical Society*

"Moon Travel Handbooks offer in-depth historical essays and useful maps, enhanced by a sense of humor and a neat, compact format."
—*Swing*

"Perfect for the more adventurous, these are long on history, sightseeing and nitty-gritty information and very price-specific."
—*Columbus Dispatch*

"Moon guides manage to be comprehensive and countercultural at the same time . . . Handbooks are packed with maps, photographs, drawings, and sidebars that constitute a college-level introduction to each country's history, culture, people, and crafts."
—*National Geographic Traveler*

"Few travel guides do a better job helping travelers create their own itineraries than the Moon Travel Handbook series. The authors have a knack for homing in on the essentials."
—**Colorado Springs** *Gazette Telegraph*

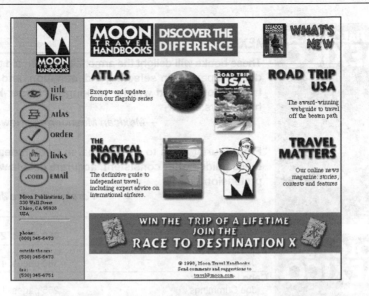

www.moon.com

Enjoy our travel information center on the World Wide Web (WWW), loaded with interactive exhibits designed especially for the Internet.

ATTRACTIONS ON MOON'S WEB SITE INCLUDE:

ATLAS
Our award-winning, comprehensive travel guides cover destinations throughout North America and Hawaii, Latin America and the Caribbean, and Asia and the Pacific.

PRACTICAL NOMAD
Extensive excerpts, a unique set of travel links coordinated with the book, and a regular Q & A column by author and Internet travel consultant Edward Hasbrouck.

TRAVEL MATTERS
Our on-line travel zine, featuring articles; author correspondence; a travel library including health information, reading lists, and cultural cues; and our new contest, **Destination X,** offering a chance to win a trip to the mystery destination of your choice.

ROAD TRIP USA
Our best-selling book, ever; don't miss this award-winning Web guide to off-the-interstate itineraries.

Come visit us at: **www.moon.com**

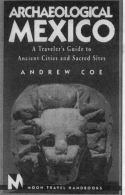

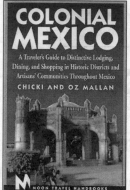

MEXICO

"These books will delight the armchair traveler, aid the undecided person in selecting a destination, and guide the seasoned road warrior looking for lesser-known hideaways."

—*Mexican Meanderings* Newsletter

"From tourist traps to off-the-beaten track hideaways, these guides offer consistent, accurate details without pretension."

—*Foreign Service Journal*

Archaeological Mexico	**$19.95**
Andrew Coe	450 pages, 25 maps
Baja Handbook	**$15.95**
Joe Cummings	380 pages, 44 maps
Cabo Handbook	**$14.95**
Joe Cummings	265 pages, 18 maps
Cancun Handbooks	**$13.95**
Chicki Mallan	270 pages, 25 maps
Colonial Mexico	**$16.95**
Chicki Mallan	300 pages, 38 maps
Mexico Handbook	**$21.95**
Joe Cummings and Chicki Mallan	1,200 pages, 232 maps
Northern Mexico Handbook	**$16.95**
Joe Cummings	590 pages, 68 maps
Pacific Mexico Handbook	**$17.95**
Bruce Whipperman	580 pages, 69 maps
Puerto Vallarta Handbook	**$14.95**
Bruce Whipperman	330 pages, 36 maps
Yucatan Handbook	**$15.95**
Chicki Mallan	470 pages, 62 maps

LATIN AMERICA AND THE CARIBBEAN

"Solidly packed with practical information and full of significant cultural asides that will enlighten you on the whys and wherefores of things you might easily see but not easily grasp."

—Boston Globe

Belize Handbook	**$15.95**
Chicki Mallan	390 pages, 45 maps
Caribbean Handbook	**$16.95**
Karl Luntta	400 pages, 56 maps
Costa Rica Handbook	**$19.95**
Christopher P. Baker	780 pages, 74 maps
Cuba Handbook	**$19.95**
Christopher P. Baker	740 pages, 70 maps
Dominican Republic Handbook	**$15.95**
Gaylord Dold	420 pages, 24 maps
Ecuador Handbook	**$16.95**
Julian Smith	450 pages, 43 maps
Honduras Handbook	**$15.95**
Chris Humphrey	330 pages, 40 maps
Jamaica Handbook	**$15.95**
Karl Luntta	330 pages, 17 maps
Virgin Islands Handbook	**$13.95**
Karl Luntta	220 pages, 19 maps

NORTH AMERICA AND HAWAII

"These domestic guides convey the same sense of exoticism that their foreign counterparts do, making home-country travel seem like far-flung adventure."

—Sierra Magazine

Alaska-Yukon Handbook	**$17.95**
Deke Castleman and Don Pitcher	530 pages, 92 maps
Alberta and the Northwest Territories Handbook	**$17.95**
Andrew Hempstead and Nadina Purdon	530 pages, 72 maps,
Arizona Traveler's Handbook	**$17.95**
Bill Weir and Robert Blake	512 pages,54 maps
Atlantic Canada Handbook	**$17.95**
Nan Drosdick and Mark Morris	460 pages, 61 maps
Big Island of Hawaii Handbook	**$15.95**
J.D. Bisignani	370 pages, 23 maps
British Columbia Handbook	**$16.95**
Jane King and Andrew Hempstead	430 pages, 69 maps

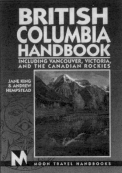

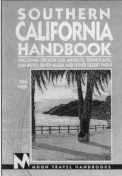

Colorado Handbook	**$18.95**
Stephen Metzger	480 pages, 59 maps
Georgia Handbook	**$17.95**
Kap Stann	370 pages, 50 maps
Hawaii Handbook	**$19.95**
J.D. Bisignani	1,030 pages, 90 maps
Honolulu-Waikiki Handbook	**$14.95**
J.D. Bisignani	380 pages, 20 maps
Idaho Handbook	**$18.95**
Don Root	610 pages, 42 maps
Kauai Handbook	**$15.95**
J.D. Bisignani	320 pages, 23 maps
Maine Handbook	**$18.95**
Kathleen M. Brandes	660 pages, 27 maps
Massachusetts Handbook	**$18.95**
Jeff Perk	600 pages, 23 maps
Maui Handbook	**$14.95**
J.D. Bisignani	410 pages, 35 maps
Montana Handbook	**$17.95**
Judy Jewell and W.C. McRae	480 pages, 52 maps
Nevada Handbook	**$18.95**
Deke Castleman	530 pages, 40 maps
New Hampshire Handbook	**$17.95**
Steve Lantos	500 pages, 18 maps
New Mexico Handbook	**$15.95**
Stephen Metzger	360 pages, 47 maps
New York City Handbook	**$13.95**
Christiane Bird	300 pages, 20 maps
New York Handbook	**$19.95**
Christiane Bird	780 pages, 95 maps
Northern California Handbook	**$19.95**
Kim Weir	800 pages, 50 maps
Oregon Handbook	**$17.95**
Stuart Warren and Ted Long Ishikawa	588 pages, 34 maps
Pennsylvania Handbook	**$18.95**
Joanne Miller	448 pages, 40 maps
Road Trip USA	**$22.50**
Jamie Jensen	800 pages, 165 maps
Southern California Handbook	**$19.95**
Kim Weir	750 pages, 30 maps
Tennessee Handbook	**$17.95**
Jeff Bradley	530 pages, 44 maps
Texas Handbook	**$18.95**
Joe Cummings	692 pages, 70 maps
Utah Handbook	**$17.95**
Bill Weir and W.C. McRae	490 pages, 40 maps

Washington Handbook	**$19.95**
Don Pitcher	870 pages, 113 maps
Wisconsin Handbook	**$18.95**
Thomas Huhti	590 pages, 69 maps
Wyoming Handbook	**$17.95**
Don Pitcher	610 pages, 80 maps

ASIA AND THE PACIFIC

"Scores of maps, detailed practical info down to
business hours of small-town libraries. You can't beat
the Asian titles for sheer heft. (The) series is sort of
an American Lonely Planet, with better writing but
fewer titles. (The) individual voice of researchers
comes through."

—*Travel & Leisure*

Australia Handbook	**$21.95**
Marael Johnson, Andrew Hempstead,	
and Nadina Purdon	940 pages, 141 maps
Bali Handbook	**$19.95**
Bill Dalton	750 pages, 54 maps
Bangkok Handbook	**$13.95**
Michael Buckley	244 pages, 30 maps
Fiji Islands Handbook	**$13.95**
David Stanley	280 pages, 38 maps
Hong Kong Handbook	**$16.95**
Kerry Moran	378 pages, 49 maps
Indonesia Handbook	**$25.00**
Bill Dalton	1,380 pages, 249 maps
Japan Handbook	**$22.50**
J.D. Bisignani	970 pages, 213 maps
Micronesia Handbook	**$14.95**
Neil M. Levy	340 pages, 70 maps
Nepal Handbook	**$18.95**
Kerry Moran	490 pages, 51 maps
New Zealand Handbook	**$19.95**
Jane King	620 pages, 81 maps
Outback Australia Handbook	**$18.95**
Marael Johnson	450 pages, 57 maps
Philippines Handbook	**$17.95**
Peter Harper and Laurie Fullerton	670 pages, 116 maps
Singapore Handbook	**$15.95**
Carl Parkes	350 pages, 29 maps
Southeast Asia Handbook	**$21.95**
Carl Parkes	1,000 pages, 196 maps

South Korea Handbook	$19.95
Robert Nilsen	820 pages, 141 maps
South Pacific Handbook	**$22.95**
David Stanley	920 pages, 147 maps
Tahiti-Polynesia Handbook	**$13.95**
David Stanley	270 pages, 35 maps
Thailand Handbook	**$19.95**
Carl Parkes	860 pages, 142 maps
Vietnam, Cambodia & Laos Handbook	**$18.95**
Michael Buckley	720 pages, 112 maps

OTHER GREAT TITLES FROM MOON

"For hardy wanderers, few guides come more highly recommended than the Handbooks. They include good maps, steer clear of fluff and flackery, and offer plenty of money-saving tips. They also give you the kind of information that visitors to strange lands—on any budget—need to survive."

—*US News & World Report*

Moon Handbook	**$10.00**
Carl Koppeschaar	141 pages, 8 maps
Moscow-St. Petersburg Handbook	**$13.95**
Masha Nordbye	259 pages, 16 maps
The Practical Nomad: How to Travel Around the World	**$17.95**
Edward Hasbrouck	575 pages
Staying Healthy in Asia, Africa, and Latin America	**$11.95**
Dirk Schroeder	197 pages, 4 maps

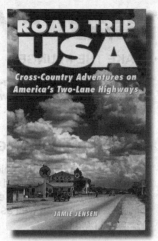

ORDER FORM

Prices are subject to change without notice. Be sure to call (800) 345-5473,
or (530) 345-5473 from outside the U.S. 8 a.m.–5 p.m. PST for current prices and editions,
or for the name of the bookstore nearest you that carries Moon Travel Handbooks.
(See important ordering information on preceding page.)

Name: _____ Date: _____

Street: _____

City: _____ Daytime Phone: _____

State or Country: _____ Zip Code: _____

QUANTITY	TITLE	PRICE

Taxable Total _____

Sales Tax (7.25%) for California Residents _____

Shipping & Handling _____

TOTAL _____

Ship: ☐ UPS (no P.O. Boxes)   ☐ 1st class   ☐ International surface mail

Ship to: ☐ address above   ☐ other _____

_____

Make checks payable to: **MOON TRAVEL HANDBOOKS**, P.O. Box 3040, Chico, CA 95927-3040
U.S.A. We accept Visa, MasterCard, or Discover. **To Order**: Call in your Visa, MasterCard, or Discover number,
or send a written order with your Visa, MasterCard, or Discover number and expiration date clearly written.

Card Number: ☐ **Visa**   ☐ **MasterCard**   ☐ **Discover**

☐ ☐ ☐ ☐ ☐ ☐ ☐ ☐ ☐ ☐ ☐ ☐ ☐ ☐ ☐ ☐

Exact Name on Card: _____

Expiration date: _____

Signature: _____

WHERE TO BUY MOON TRAVEL HANDBOOKS

BOOKSTORES AND LIBRARIES: Moon Travel Handbooks are distributed worldwide. Please contact our sales manager for a list of wholesalers and distributors in your area.

TRAVELERS: We would like to have Moon Travel Handbooks available throughout the world. Please ask your bookstore to write or call us for ordering information. If your bookstore will not order our guides for you, please contact us for a free catalog.

> **Moon Travel Handbooks**
> **P.O. Box 3040**
> **Chico, CA 95927-3040 U.S.A.**
> **tel.: (800) 345-5473, outside the U.S. (530) 345-5473**
> **fax: (530) 345-6751**
> **e-mail: travel@moon.com**

IMPORTANT ORDERING INFORMATION

PRICES: All prices are subject to change. We always ship the most current edition. We will let you know if there is a price increase on the book you order.

SHIPPING AND HANDLING OPTIONS: Domestic UPS or USPS first class (allow 10 working days for delivery): $4.50 for the first item, $1.00 for each additional item.

Moonbelt shipping is $1.50 for one, 50 cents for each additional belt.

UPS 2nd Day Air or Printed Airmail requires a special quote.

International Surface Bookrate 8-12 weeks delivery: $3.00 for the first item, $1.00 for each additional item. Note: We cannot guarantee international surface bookrate shipping. We recommends sending international orders via air mail, which requires a special quote.

FOREIGN ORDERS: Orders that originate outside the U.S.A. must be paid for with an international money order, a check in U.S. currency drawn on a major U.S. bank based in the U.S.A., or Visa, MasterCard, or Discover.

TELEPHONE ORDERS: We accept Visa, MasterCard, or Discover payments. Call in your order: (800) 345-5473, 8 a.m.-5 p.m. Pacific standard time. Outside the U.S. the number is (530) 345-5473.

INTERNET ORDERS: Visit our site at: www.moon.com

U.S.~METRIC CONVERSION

1 inch	=	2.54 centimeters (cm)
1 foot	=	.304 meters (m)
1 mile	=	1.6093 kilometers (km)
1 km	=	.6214 miles
1 fathom	=	1.8288 m
1 chain	=	20.1168 m
1 furlong	=	201.168 m
1 acre	=	.4047 hectares
1 sq km	=	100 hectares
1 sq mile	=	2.59 square km
1 ounce	=	28.35 grams
1 pound	=	.4536 kilograms
1 short ton	=	.90718 metric ton
1 short ton	=	2000 pounds
1 long ton	=	1.016 metric tons
1 long ton	=	2240 pounds
1 metric ton	=	1000 kilograms
1 quart	=	.94635 liters
1 US gallon	=	3.7854 liters
1 Imperial gallon	=	4.5459 liters
1 nautical mile	=	1.852 km

To compute celsius temperatures, subtract 32 from Fahrenheit and divide by 1.8. To go the other way, multiply celsius by 1.8 and add 32.

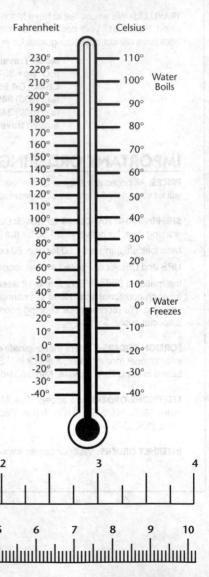

inch 0   1   2   3   4

cm 0 1 2 3 4 5 6 7 8 9 10